T0189064

Lecture Notes in Computer Science 11420

Commenced Publication in 1973
Founding and Former Series Editors:
Gerhard Goos, Juris Hartmanis, and Jan van Leeuwen

More information about this series at http://www.springer.com/series/7409

Natalie Greene Taylor ·
Caitlin Christian-Lamb ·
Michelle H. Martin ·
Bonnie Nardi (Eds.)

Information in Contemporary Society

14th International Conference, iConference 2019
Washington, DC, USA, March 31 – April 3, 2019
Proceedings

Springer

Editors
Natalie Greene Taylor
University of South Florida
Tampa, FL, USA

Caitlin Christian-Lamb
University of Maryland
College Park, MD, USA

Michelle H. Martin
University of Washington
Seattle, WA, USA

Bonnie Nardi
University of California, Irvine
Irvine, CA, USA

ISSN 0302-9743   ISSN 1611-3349   (electronic)
Lecture Notes in Computer Science
ISBN 978-3-030-15741-8   ISBN 978-3-030-15742-5   (eBook)
https://doi.org/10.1007/978-3-030-15742-5

Library of Congress Control Number: 2019934340

LNCS Sublibrary: SL3 – Information Systems and Applications, incl. Internet/Web, and HCI

This Springer imprint is published by the registered company Springer Nature Switzerland AG
The registered company address is: Gewerbestrasse 11, 6330 Cham, Switzerland

Preface

Now in its 14th year, the iConference is an annual meeting devoted to research on critical information issues in contemporary society. Each year, an international and interdisciplinary community of scholars, researchers, and practitioners gathers to explore core concepts and ideas in information scholarship and to develop new avenues of research. iConference 2019 was hosted by the University of Maryland, College Park, in collaboration with Syracuse University and the University of Maryland, Baltimore County. The conference was held in Washington, DC from March 31 to April 3 with the theme of "inform. include. inspire." The aim of this year's conference was to discuss what it means to inform in the 21st century, to consider who is included in and excluded from the information revolution, and to question how scholars can best inspire individuals and organizations to use information for good in the rapidly changing knowledge society. The conference's geographic location in the U.S. capital emphasized the role that national and international policies play in technological advances and access.

The scholarship presented at the conference included two subcategories of research papers: short papers, which present new, provocative, and cross-cutting themes in a focused and succinct manner, and full papers, which present new and original research results from empirical investigations and experiments, or from theory and model development. Of the 88 short papers submitted, 33 were accepted (37.5% acceptance rate). Of the 133 full papers submitted, 44 were accepted (33% acceptance rate). Both subcategories underwent a rigorous double-blind review process managed by the paper chairs and a Program Committee of associate chairs. Each paper was reviewed by three external reviewers. The high level of scholarship of the papers is a result of the efforts of our hard-working reviewers and the Program Committee who oversaw the full process.

This is the second year that the proceedings of the iConference are published by Springer in their *Lecture Notes in Computer Science* (LNCS) series. These proceedings comprise the complete version of short and full papers presented at the conference. To organize the papers, the paper chairs developed 24 thematic categories that represent the broad range of scholarship shared at the conference. Additional research presented at the conference in the form of posters and "Blue Sky" papers, which feature ideas and visions for the iSchool research community, can be found through the IDEALS open access repository (https://www.ideals.illinois.edu/handle/2142/102118).

The goal of the iConference series and these proceedings is to inspire conversation, encourage further research, and inform diverse audiences about today's critical information needs.

March 2019

Natalie Greene Taylor
Caitlin Christian-Lamb
Michelle H. Martin
Bonnie Nardi

Organization

Organizers

University of Maryland, College Park, USA

Institutional Collaborators

Syracuse University, USA
University of Maryland, Baltimore County, USA

Conference Chairs

Mega Subramaniam   University of Maryland, College Park, USA
Kevin Crowston   Syracuse University, USA
Wayne Lutters   University of Maryland, College Park, USA

Program Committee Chairs

Michelle H. Martin   University of Washington, USA
Bonnie Nardi   University of California, Irvine, USA

Papers Chairs

Aleksandra Sarcevic   Drexel University, USA
Nick Weber   University of Washington, USA

Posters Chairs

Yong Ming Kow   University of Hong Kong, SAR China
Eric Meyers   University of British Columbia, Canada

Workshops Chairs

Marianne Martens   Kent State University, USA
Gitte Balling   Københavns Universitet, Denmark

Sessions for Interaction and Engagement (SIE) Chairs

James Howison   University of Texas, Austin, USA
Kate Marek   Dominican University, USA

Doctoral Colloquium Chairs

Sun Young Park   University of Michigan, USA
Anita Komlodi   University of Maryland, Baltimore County, USA

Early Career Colloquium Chairs

Dick Kawooya   University of South Carolina, USA
Hamid Ekbia   Indiana University, USA

Blue Sky Chairs

Kevin Crowston   Syracuse University, USA
John King   University of Michigan, USA

Undergraduate Symposium Chairs

Matthew Bietz   University of California, Irvine, USA
Yubo Kou   Florida State University, USA

Social Media Chairs

Amelia Gibson   University of North Carolina, Chapel Hill, USA
Jessica Vitak   University of Maryland, College Park, USA

Proceedings Chairs

Natalie Greene Taylor   University of South Florida, USA
Caitlin Christian-Lamb   University of Maryland, College Park, USA

iSchools Partnerships and Practices Chairs

Timothy Summers   University of Maryland, College Park, USA
Sean McGann   University of Washington, USA
Elke Greifeneder   Humboldt-Universität, Germany

Keynotes Chair

Dan Russell   Google

Student Volunteers Chairs

Samantha McDonald   University of California, Irvine, USA
J. Elizabeth Mills   University of Washington, USA
Katy Lawley   University of Maryland, College Park, USA

Diversity and Accessibility Chair

Renee Hill   University of Maryland, College Park, USA

Conference Management

Clark Heideger   iSchools
Mary Kendig   University of Maryland, College Park, USA

Doctoral Dissertation Award Chairs

Tawanna Dillahunt   University of Michigan, USA
Volker Wulf   Universität Siegen, Germany

Best Paper Award Committee

Katrina Fenlon   University of Maryland, College Park, USA
Mohammad Hossein Jarrahi   University of North Carolina at Chapel Hill, USA
Irene Lopatovska   Pratt Institute, USA
Craig M. MacDonald   Pratt Institute, USA
Yong Ming Kow   University of Hong Kong
Peter Organisciak   Denver University, USA
Patrick Shih   Indiana University, Bloomington, USA

Blue Sky Program Committee

Diane Bailey   University of Texas, Austin, USA
Christine Borgman   University of California Los Angeles, USA
Jonathan Grudin   Microsoft Corp.
Jens-Erik Mai   University of Copenhagen, Denmark
Leysia Palen   University of Colorado, USA

Associate Papers Chairs

Amelia Acker   University of Texas, Austin, USA
Jack Andersen   University of Copenhagen, Denmark
Christoph Becker   University of Toronto, Canada
Catherine Blake   University of Illinois at Urbana Champaign, USA
Rachel Ivy Clarke   Syracuse University, USA
Kaitlin Costello   Rutgers University, USA
Andrew M. Cox   University of Sheffield, UK
Dharma Dailey   University of Washington, USA
Peter Darch   University of Illinois at Urbana-Champaign, USA
Rosta Farzan   University of Pittsburgh, USA
Katrina Fenlon   University of Maryland, College Park, USA
Koraljka Golub   Linnaeus University, Sweden

Roberto González-Ibáñez	University of Santiago, Chile
Frank Hopfgartner	University of Sheffield, UK
Yun Huang	Syracuse University, USA
Isa Jahnke	University of Missouri, USA
Mohammad Hossein Jarrahi	University of North Carolina at Chapel Hill, USA
Jaap Kamps	University of Amsterdam, The Netherlands
Yubo Kou	Florida State University, USA
Irene Lopatovska	Pratt Institute, USA
Jorge Martins	University of Sheffield, UK
Yong Ming Know	City University of Hong Kong, SAR China
Hanna Maurin Söderholm	University of Boras, Sweden
Craig M. MacDonald	Pratt Institute, USA
Rachel M. Magee	University of Illinois at Urbana-Champaign, USA
Atsuyuki Morishima	University of Tsukuba, Japan
Peter Organisciak	Denver University, USA
Tamara Peyton	Harrisburg University of Science and Technology, USA
Alex Poole	Drexel University, USA
Miriam Posner	University of California, Los Angeles, USA
Matt Ratto	University of Toronto, Canada
Rebecca Reynolds	Rutgers University, USA
Colin Rhinesmith	Simmons University, USA
Dan Sholler	University of California, Berkeley, USA
Patrick Shih	Indiana University, Bloomington, USA
Vivek Singh	Rutgers University, USA
António Lucas Soares	University of Porto, Portugal
Olivier St-Cyr	University of Toronto, Canada
Joseph T. Tennis	University of Washington, USA
Andrea Thomer	University of Michigan, USA
Aaron Trammell	University of California, Irvine, USA
Karen Wickett	University of Illinois at Urbana-Champaign, USA
Dan Wu	Wuhan University, China
Erja Yan	Drexel University, USA
Hideo Yoho	University of Tsukuba, Japan
Zhan Zhang	Pace University, USA

Additional Reviewers

Pamela Abbott
Jacob Abbott
Dhary Abuhimed
Waseem Afzal
Noa Aharony
Shameem Ahmed
Isola Ajiferuke
Bader Albahlal
Kendra S. Albright
Daniel Gelaw Alemneh
Hamed Alhoori
Suzie Allard
Robert B. Allen
Wafaa Ahmed Almotawah
Anas Hamad Alsuhaibani
Sharon Amir
Lu An
Jack Andersen
Muhammad Naveed
    Anwar
Ahmer Arif
Marilyn Arnone
Diane Bailey
Alex Ball
Judit Bar-Ilan
Syeda Hina Batool
Edith Beckett
Andrew Berry
Nanyi Bi
Matthew Bietz
Dania Bilal
Bradley Wade Bishop
Phuritsabam Bobby
Toine Bogers
Marc Bonne
Christine L. Borgman
Bernie Boscoe
Kelly Boudreau
Ceilyn Boyd
Sarah Bratt
Jo Ann M. Brooks
Sarah A. Buchanan
Steven Buchanan

John M. Budd
Jhon Bueno
Christopher Sean Burns
Yao Cai
Aldrin Joseph Parilla
    Campos
Daniel Carter
Vittore Casarosa
Biddy Casselden
Niel Chah
Yung-Sheng Chang
Tiffany Chao
Hsin-liang Chen
Jiangping Chen
Hsuanwei Chen
Yi-Yun Cheng
Chola Chhetri
Shih-Yi Chien
Yunseon Choi
Steven Siu Fung Chong
Heting Chu
Josep Cobarsi-Morales
Johanna Cohoon
Monica Colon-Aguirre
Anthony Joseph Corso
Jose Curto Diaz
Mats Dahlstrom
Marija Dalbello
Gabriel David
Rebecca Davis
Miguel de Castro Neto
Ernesto William De Luca
Shengli Deng
Edward Claudell Dillon
Bridget Disney
Brian Dobreski
Philip Doty
Jennifer Douglas
Kedma Duarte
Patrick Michael Dudas
Catherine Dumas
Quinn DuPont
Emory James Edwards

Elizabeth V. Eikey
Heidi Enwald
Kristin R. Eschenfelder
Ali Eshraghi
Nina Exner
Travis Faas
Jannatul Fardous
Yuanyuan Feng
Bruce Ferwerda
Kristin Fontichiaro
Helena Francke
Guo Freeman
Henry A. Gabb
Maria Gaede
Chunmei Gan
Daniel L. Gardner
Radhika Garg
Emmanouel Garoufallou
John Gathegi
Rich Gazan
Tali Gazit
Yegin Genc
Ruili Geng
Lynette Gerido
Susan German
Patrick Golden
Timothy Gorichanaz
Michael Gowanlock
Elke Greifeneder
Melissa Gross
Jonathan Thomas Grudin
Michael Robert Gryk
Ayse Gursoy
Oliver Haimson
Lala Hajibayova
Shefali Haldar
Carina Hallqvist
Björn Hammarfelt
Shuguang Han
Xi Han
Susannah Hanlon
Preben Hansen
Jenna Hartel

Helmut Hauptmeier
Caroline Haythornthwaite
Daqing He
Hao He
Yurong He
Zhe He
Jiangen He
Niels-Peder Osmundsen
  Hjøllund
Shuyuan Mary Ho
Chris Holstrom
Liang Hong
James Howison
Jiming Hu
Ruhua Huang
Kun Huang
Jette Seiden Hyldegaard
Raj Inamdar
Sharon Ince
Charles Inskip
Joshua Introne
Corey Jackson
Swathi Jagannath
Hamid R. Jamali
David Andrew Jank
Tingting Jiang
Veronica Johansson
Soohyung Joo
Nicolas Jullien
Beth Juncker
Jenna Kammer
Amir Karami
Mary Anne Kennan
Halil Kilicoglu
Meen Chul Kim
Jeonghyun Kim
Youngseek Kim
Kyung Sun Kim
Vanessa Kitzie
Emily Knox
Kyungwon Koh
Kolina Sun Koltai
Anita Komlodi
Rebecca Koskela
Peter Krafft
Adam Kriesberg

Ravi Kuber
Priya Kumar
Pei-Yi (Patricia) Kuo
Myeong Lee
Jin Ha Lee
Keeheon Lee
Kijung Lee
Lo Lee
Noah Lenstra
Kai Li
Meng-Hao Li
Daifeng Li
Xiaoge Li
Shijuan Li
Honglei Li
Yuting Liao
Chi-Shiou Lin
Zack Lischer-Katz
Elizabeth Lomas
James Lowry
Kun Lu
Quan Lu
Bertram Ludaescher
Christopher Lueg
Marc Lundstrom
Jessie Lymn
Clifford Lynch
Long Ma
Monica Grace Maceli
Jens-Erik Mai
Agnes Mainka
Krista-Lee Malone
Rita Marcella
Kate Marek
Marianne Martens
Paul Martin
Aqueasha
  Martin-Hammond
Kathryn Masten
Matthew S. Mayernik
Sean McGann
Claire McGuinness
Julie McLeod
David McMenemy
Itzelle Aurora Medina
  Perea

Eric Meyers
Shawne D. Miksa
Stasa Milojevic
Nancy Mimm
Chao Min
Alex Mitchell
Lorri Mon
Robert Montoya
Camilla Moring
Michael Moss
Adrienne Muir
Sarah Beth Nelson
David Nemer
Valerie Nesset
David M. Nichols
Michael Nitsche
Jan Nolin
Rebecca Noone
Ragnar Nordlie
Karen Nowé Hedvall
Brian Clark O'Connor
Felipe Ortega
Virginia Ortiz-Repiso
Yohanan Ouaknine
Kathleen Padova
Drew Paine
Galen Panger
Britt Paris
Sun Young Park
Min Park
Albert Park
Laura Pasquini
Daniel A. Pauw
Diane Pennington
Olivia Pestana
Ei Pa Pa Pe-Than
Vivien Petras
Ola Pilerot
Anthony T. Pinter
Jennifer Proctor
Ricky Punzalan
Jian Qin
Marie L. Radford
Angela U.
  Ramnarine-Rieks
Susan Rathbun-Grubb

Cristina Ribeiro
Nathan Riedel
Kathryn E. Ringland
John Robinson
Joan Rodriguez-Amat
Corinne Rogers
Abebe Rorissa
Vassilis Routsis
Bonnie (Bo) Ruberg
Spencer Ruelos
Chen Sabag Ben Porat
Ehsan Sabaghian
Simone Sacchi
Gayathri Sadanala
Ashley Sands
Madelyn Rose Sanfilippo
Yisi Sang
Sally Sanger
Vitor Santos
Maria Janina Sarol
Laura Saunders
Laura Sbaffi
Kirsten Schlebbe
Sarita Schoenebeck
Barbara Schultz-Jones
Kristen Schuster
Rainforest Scully-Blaker
Melinda Sebastian
John S. Seberger
Ryan Shaw
Elizabeth Jane Shepherd
Noa Sher
Mette Skov
Shijie Song
Darshan Songara
Daniel Southwick

Laura I. Spears
Clay Spinuzzi
Emma Spiro
Beth St. Jean
Amanda Stafford
Hrvoje Stancic
Karen Stepanyan
Juliane Stiller
Besiki Stvilia
Yalin Sun
Sebastian Sünkler
Will Sutherland
Miriam Sweeney
Sue Yeon Syn
Ella Tallyn
Anna Maria Tammaro
Rong Tang
Jian Tang
Cheryl Annette Thompson
Megan Threats
Tien-I Tsai
Chunhua Tsai
Yuen-Hsien Tseng
Michael Twidale
Alex Urban
Merce Væzquez
Pertti Vakkari
Jieyu Wang
Xiao Wang
Ping Wang
Rosina Weber
Yanlong Wen
Brian Wentz
Michael Majewski
    Widdersheim
Rachel Williams

R. Jason Winning
Hanna Elina Wirman
Dietmar Wolfram
Adam Worrall
MeiMei Wu
Peng Wu
Qunfang Wu
Lin Wu
Lu Xiao
Qiuhui Xiao
Iris Xie
Tan Xu
Lifang Xu
Hui Yan
Seungwon Yang
Hui Yang
Ayoung Yoon
Himanshu Zade
Oksana L. Zavalina
Marcia L. Zeng
Ziming Zhang
Chengzhi Zhang
Chenwei Zhang
Jane Zhang
Bin Zhang
Yuxiang Zhao
Enguo Zhou
Lihong Zhou
Grace Zhou
Xiaoying Zhou
Qinghua Zhu
Michael Zimmer
Annuska Zolyomi
Zhiya Zuo

Contents

Identity Questions in Online Communities

Measuring and Tracking Scientific Literature

Limits and Affordances of Automation

Data-Driven Storytelling and Modeling

Online Activism

Digital Libraries, Curation and Preservation

Social-Media Text Mining and Sentiment Analysis

Data and Information in the Public Sphere

Engaging with Multi-media Content

Information Behaviors on Twitter

Data Mining and NLP

Informing Technology Design Through Offline Experiences

Digital Tools for Health Management

Environmental and Visual Literacy

Addressing Social Problems in iSchools Research

Scientific Work and Data Practices

A Comparative Study of Biological Scientists' Data Sharing Between Genome Sequence Data and Lab Experiment Data

Youngseek Kim[(✉)] (iD)

University of Kentucky, Lexington, KY 40506, USA
youngseek.kim@uky.edu

Abstract. This research aims to explore how the institutional pressure, resource, and individual motivation factors all affect biological scientists' data sharing behaviors in different data types. This research utilized a combined theoretical framework including institutional theory and theory of planned behavior to examine institutional pressure, resource, and individual motivation factors influencing biological scientists' data sharing intentions between different data types including genome sequence data and lab experiment data. A total of 342 survey responses from biological sciences were employed for a series of statistical analyses including Cronbach's alpha, factor analysis, hierarchical regression, and t-test. This research shows that biological scientists' data sharing intentions are led by institutional pressure, resource, and individual motivation factors, and the levels of those factors are significantly different between genome sequence data and lab experiment data. This research shows that biological scientists' data sharing differs depending on the data they share, and different policies and support needs to be applied to encourage biological scientists' data sharing of different data types.

Keywords: Data sharing · Biological science · Genome sequence data ·
Lab experiment data · Hierarchical regression

1 Introduction

Data sharing behaviors within the same scientific communities may vary depending on the types of data generated. For example, biological sciences generate two distinctive types of data, including genome sequence data and lab experiment data, and they each have different institutional contexts, disciplinary resources, and individual motivations with regards to each type of data they generate. To better understand biological scientists' data sharing behaviors more clearly, it is important to investigate how institutional context, disciplinary resources, and individual motivations differ between two different data types, and how they influence biological scientists' data sharing behaviors.

This research focuses on data sharing behavior, which refers to scientists' providing raw data of their published articles to other scientists by making it accessible through data repositories, or by sending data via personal communication methods upon request. This research looks into how the effects of institutional, resource, and

© Springer Nature Switzerland AG 2019
N. G. Taylor et al. (Eds.): iConference 2019, LNCS 11420, pp. 3–14, 2019.
https://doi.org/10.1007/978-3-030-15742-5_1

individual factors vary across different data types with which biological scientists may share (i.e., genome sequence data and lab experiment data), and how biological scientists are imposed on by different levels of institutional, resource, and individual factors. I consider institutional pressure, especially, such as pressure from funding agencies and journals, institutional resources such as the availability of a data repository and/or metadata standard, and finally individual motivations such as perceived career benefit and risk, and perceived effort involved in data sharing.

2 Literature Review

Even though data sharing is an important practice in scientific research [1, 2], data sharing is not well established in biological sciences. Prior studies in data sharing have examined the prevalence of data withholding in biological sciences. Blumenthal et al. [3] and Campbell et al. [4] reported that 8.9% of the life scientists and 12% of geneticists in the U.S. academic institutions respectively had declined the requests for the data or other relevant information of their published articles. However, the rate of denial for publication related data and information was even worse in actual behavioral studies. Louis and colleagues [5] found that 30% of geneticists reported that they withheld data at least once, pre-publication, within the past three years. In a later study, Blumenthal et al. [6] conducted a behavioral study, and they found that 44% of geneticists and 32% of life scientists withhold the data of their published articles.

Studies related to data sharing often use bibliometric analyses to explain the prevalence of biological scientists' data sharing behaviors. One such study by Piwowar and Chapman [7] investigated the prevalence of data sharing regarding gene expression microarray data by counting the papers that linked to the NCBI (National Center for Biotechnology Information)'s Gene Expression Omnibus (GEO) database. Later, Piwowar [8] conducted another study to identify how frequently raw gene expression microarray datasets were shared after publication. She found that 25% of the 11,603 articles about gene expression microarray published between 2000 and 2009 provided their raw datasets in major data repositories.

A good number of prior studies in data sharing have investigated diverse factors affecting scientists' data sharing behaviors, and those data sharing factors can be categorized into institutional pressure, individual motivation, and resource factors. First of all, previous studies examined the regulative pressure from funding agencies (e.g., NSF and NIH) [8, 9] and journal publishers [10–12] as important factors influencing scientists' data sharing behaviors. Second, prior studies reported that scientists' data sharing behaviors were either facilitated or hindered by diverse individual motivations. Prior studies reported that scientists who expect potential benefits such as academic recognition and credit (i.e., citations) are likely to share their data [11, 13, 14]. However, scholars found that scientists would be unlikely to share their data due to the potential risks in data sharing including getting scooped by other scientists [15, 16], missing commercialization chances [6, 17], and being criticized by others [18]. Additionally, prior studies found that scientists' effort expectancy involved in data sharing (e.g., organizing data for sharing) significantly decreases scientists' data sharing behaviors [2, 17, 19]. Lastly, prior studies also found that institutional resources (such as availabilities of metadata standard and repository) significantly increased scientists' data sharing. Bowker and Star [20] and Michener [21] reported that the availability of metadata standards also assists scientists' data sharing especially among those outside their research teams. Kim and Burns [22] found that even though a metadata standard does not have a direct effect on scientists' data sharing behaviors, it does have an indirect effect on scientists' data sharing behaviors mediated by their norms of data sharing. Cragin et al. [23] and Marcial and Hemminger [24] found that the availability of data repositories assists scientists' data sharing significantly; however, Kim and Stanton [11] did not find any significant relationship between the availability of data repositories and data sharing among STEM researchers.

Prior studies have investigated scientists' data sharing behaviors without considering different data types, limiting our comprehension of the differences of this behavior in diverse data types. As biological scientists' data sharing differs by the type of data being shared, their data sharing motivations need to be investigated. Therefore, this research plans to examine how biological scientists' data sharing varies depending on different data types, including genome sequence data and lab experiment data.

3 Theoretical Framework

Biological scientists' data sharing can be understood through the perspective of institutional pressure, availability of resources, and individual motivations. This research explored how different institutional pressure, resource, and individual motivation factors influence biological scientists' data sharing by using a theoretical model developed from institutional theory [25] and the Theory of Planned Behavior (TPB) [26]. The integrated theoretical framework can show how institutional pressure, availability of resources, and individual motivations all influence biological scientists' data sharing behaviors between different data types.

First, this research employed institutional theory to understand how institutional pressure by funding agencies and journal publishers affect biological scientists' data sharing. According to Bjorck [27], institutional influences can be defined as social structures which include formal or informal rules that restrict social behaviors. Previous institutional theory based studies have focused on how institutional pressure influences organizations and their structures, but neo-institutional theory has primarily focused on how institutional pressure influences individuals in an institutional environment [28–30]. Therefore, this research employed neo-institutional theory to examine how institutional pressure from funding agencies and journals affect biological scientists' data sharing between different data types.

Second, this research also employed the TPB to explain how individual motivations as well as resources affect biological scientists' data sharing. The TPB explains and predicts how an individual's belief structure for a particular behavior affects his/her behavioral intention, which also predicts their actual behavior [31, 32]. Based on the TPB, this research explains how the availability of resources (e.g. a metadata standard and a data repository) and individual motivations (e.g. perceived career benefit, perceived career risk, and perceived effort), all affect biological scientists' data sharing between data types. The integrated theoretical framework combining institutional theory and TPB can help better articulate how different institutional pressure, availability of resources, and individual motivations influence biological scientists' data sharing between the two data types (i.e., genome sequence data and lab experiment data).

4   Research Model and Hypothesis Development

Based on the combination of institutional theory and TPB, the biological scientists' data sharing model examines how institutional pressure factors including funding agency's pressure (H1) and journal's pressure (H2), institutional resource factors including metadata standard (H3) and data repository (H4), and individual motivation factors including perceived career benefit (H5), perceived career risk (H6), and perceived effort (H7) all affect biological scientists' data sharing intentions. The research model of biological scientists' data sharing is presented in Fig. 1 below.

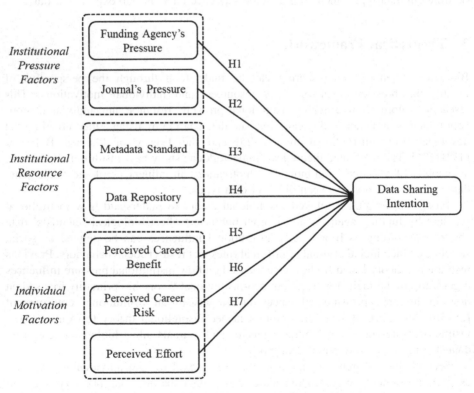

Fig. 1.   Research model of biological scientists' data sharing.

The main objective of this research is to compare how the influence of data sharing factors differ between different data types – this research compares and contrasts the effects of these factors between two different data types: genome sequence data and lab experiment data. For genome sequence data, scientists have data sharing regulations set forth by funding agencies and journals, more resources (i.e., metadata standard and data repository) available, more career benefits, and less career risks and expected effort. On the other hand, for lab experiment data, scientists do not have data sharing regulations set forth by funding agencies and journals, they have less resources available to them, less perceived career benefit, and more perceived career risk and expected effort. Therefore, this research hypothesizes that data sharing with genome sequence data is driven by strong institutional forces, supportive resources, and positive individual motivations when compared to data sharing with lab experiment data.

5   Research Methods

This research identified biological scientists in the United States (U.S.) as its target population and used the Community of Scientists' (CoS) Scholar Database for its sampling frame. In the U.S., there were 91,923 registered biological scientists in 15 specific biological science disciplines categorized by the CoS Scholar Database (as of November 1st, 2016). By using query, I identified a total of 8,000 biological scientists in 15 biological science disciplines as the research sample.

The research constructs were primarily adapted from Kim and Stanton's [11] study on scientists' data sharing behaviors. The initial survey items were refined through pilot-test with 31 potential survey participants to ensure the understandability of the survey items and for the flow of the survey. The survey measured scientists' perceptions of the institutional pressures of data sharing, availability of institutional resources, scientists' perceptions toward data sharing, and their data sharing intentions. The majority of questions used a 5-point Likert scale. In addition, the survey asked the type of data they generate and their demographic information.

The online survey included structured questions about biological scientists' perceptions toward data sharing behaviors, their institutional setting and institutional resources, and their intentions to share their data with others. The online survey was set up on the Qualtrics website, and the online survey questionnaires were available from November 7th, 2016 to February 15th, 2017. From the online survey distribution, a total of 675 valid responses were received (response rate: 675/5,986 = 11.28%). Since this research only focuses two data types including genome sequence data and lab experiment data, any responses other than those two data types were removed; therefore, a total of 342 valid responses were used for the final data analysis.

The survey asked respondents about brief demographic information including their gender, age, and position. Among the 342 survey responses, there were 221 males (64.6%) and 114 females (33.3%), while 7 respondents (2.1%) did not answer the gender question. With regards to age, the survey participants were spread out across diverse age ranges including 25–34 (25, 7.3%), 35-44 (76, 22.2%), 45–54 (94, 27.5%), 55–64 (84, 24.6%), more than 65 (51, 14.9%), while 12 participants did not provide their age. The survey participants have diverse academic positions and career levels, and they are from diverse biological science fields of study.

6 Data Analysis and Results

6.1 Assessment of Measures

First, the measurement items for the research constructs were evaluated for reliability and validity by employing Cronbach's alpha and factor analysis. The Cronbach's alpha values ranged from 0.781 (perceived effort) to 0.948 (data sharing intention), which are greater than the recommended value of 0.70 [33, 34]. The construct validity including convergent and discriminant validity was ensured by conducting a principal component factor analysis with Varimax rotation. A total of eight factors were identified, and those eight factors account for 85.36% of the total variance. Each measurement item was loaded to its designated construct with a loading value of 0.586 or greater, and the other measurement items were loaded to its non-designated construct with loading values of 0.377 or less. This result shows sufficient convergent and discriminant validity [35, 36].

6.2 Hierarchical Regression Analysis

A hierarchical regression analysis was conducted with the entire data set including the genome sequence data and the lab experiment data groups. As the first step, institutional pressure factors were included in the regression analysis. The two institutional factors including regulative pressure by funding agencies ($\beta = 0.216$, $p < 0.001$) and regulative pressure by journals ($\beta = 0.326$, $p < 0.001$) were found to have significant positive relationships to scientists' data sharing intentions. Those two institutional factors account for 23.2% of the total variance in scientists' data sharing intentions ($R^2 = 0.232$).

As the second step, resource factors including the availability of a metadata standard and a data repository were included in the regression analysis along with the institutional pressure factors. The two resource factors including availability of metadata standard ($\beta = 0.157$, $p < 0.01$) and availability of data repository ($\beta = 0.211$, $p < 0.001$) were found to have significant positive relationships with scientists' data sharing intentions. Those two resource factors explained an additional 8.3% of the total variance in scientists' data sharing intentions (R^2 change $= 0.083$). Also, the two institutional factors including regulative pressure by funding agencies ($\beta = 0.173$, $p < 0.01$) and regulative pressure by journals ($\beta = 0.206$, $p < 0.001$) still remained statistically significant. All the institutional pressure factors and resource factors account for 31.5% of the total variance towards scientists' data sharing intentions ($R^2 = 0.315$).

As the last step, individual motivation factors including perceived career benefit, perceived career risk, and perceived effort involved in data sharing were included in the regression analysis along with the institutional pressure and resource factors. Perceived career benefit ($\beta = 0.344$, $p < 0.001$) and perceived career risk ($\beta = -0.193$, $p < 0.001$) were found to have significant positive and negative relationships with scientists' data sharing intentions, respectively. However, perceived effort ($\beta = -0.070$, $p > 0.05$) was found to have no significant relationship with scientists' data sharing intentions. Both perceived career benefit and perceived career risk explain an additional 16.0% of the total variance in scientists' data sharing intentions (R^2 change $= 0.160$). Also, the two institutional factors including regulative pressure by funding agencies ($\beta = 0.118$, $p < 0.05$) and regulative pressure by journals ($\beta = 0.121$, $p < 0.05$), and the two resource factors including the availability of a metadata standard ($\beta = 0.120$, $p < 0.05$) and the availability of a data repository ($\beta = 0.140$, $p < 0.01$) still remained as statistically significant. All the institutional pressure, resource factors, and individual motivation factors accounted for 47.5% of the total variance of scientists' data sharing intentions ($R^2 = 0.475$). Table 1 shows the results of the hierarchical regression analysis.

Table 1. Results of the hierarchical regression analysis.

H	Predictor variables	Stage 1		Stage 2		Stage 3	
		Beta	p-value	Beta	p-value	Beta	p-value
1	Funding's pressure	0.216	0.000	0.173	0.003	0.118	0.020
2	Journal's pressure	0.326	0.000	0.206	0.001	0.121	0.024
3	Metadata standard			0.157	0.006	0.120	0.019
4	Data repository			0.211	0.000	0.140	0.007
5	Perceived career benefit					0.344	0.000
6	Perceived career risk					−0.193	0.000
7	Perceived effort					−0.070	0.131
R^2		0.232		0.315		0.475	
R^2 Change		0.232		0.083		0.160	

6.3 Independent Sample t-test

Finally, an independent sample t-test was conducted to compare the differences of the data sharing factors and data sharing intentions between the genome sequence data and lab experiment data groups. In terms of institutional pressure factors, the genome sequence data group had higher regulative pressure by funding agencies (3.87 vs. 3.40, $p < 0.001$) and journals (3.68 vs. 3.10, $p < 0.001$) than the lab experiment data group. In terms of resource factors, the genome sequence data group also had more resources available in the form of metadata standard (3.26 vs. 2.80, $p < 0.001$) and access to a data repository (4.01 vs. 2.96, $p < 0.001$) than the lab experiment data group. In terms of individual motivation factors, the genome sequence data group had higher perceived career benefits than the lab experiment data group (3.44 vs. 3.11, $p < 0.01$), and the genome sequence data group also had lower perceived career risks than the lab experiment data group (2.51 vs. 2.77, $p < 0.05$). However, there was no significant difference in perceived effort between the genome sequence and lab experiment data groups (3.02 vs. 3.05, $p > 0.05$). Finally, in terms of data sharing intentions, the genome sequence data group had a higher data sharing intention than the lab experiment data group (4.29 vs. 3.59, $p < 0.001$). Table 2 shows the results of the independent sample t-test.

Table 2. Results of independent sample t-test.

Variables	Genome sequence		Lab experiment		Difference	t-value	Sig.
	Mean	SD	Mean	SD			
Funding's pressure	3.87	0.82	3.40	1.03	0.47	4.51	0.000
Journal's pressure	3.68	0.96	3.10	1.09	0.58	4.97	0.000
Metadata standard	3.26	1.02	2.80	0.99	0.46	3.81	0.000
Data repository	4.01	1.06	2.96	1.20	1.05	8.13	0.000
Perceived career benefit	3.44	0.86	3.11	1.04	0.33	3.06	0.002
Perceived career risk	2.51	0.80	2.77	1.06	−0.27	−2.57	0.011
Perceived effort	3.02	0.86	3.05	0.81	−0.03	−0.34	0.733
Data sharing intention	4.29	0.79	3.59	1.02	0.70	6.98	0.000

7 Discussion

The results show that biological scientists' data sharing intentions are significantly affected by institutional pressure (i.e., pressures by funding agency and journal), institutional resources (i.e., metadata standard and data repository), and individual motivations (i.e., perceived career benefit and risk). This research also confirms that there are significant differences in those data sharing factors and data sharing intentions between genome sequence data and lab experiment data.

In terms of institutional pressure factors, this research found that both regulative pressures by funding agencies and journals significantly increase biological scientists' data sharing intentions, and those findings also confirmed the findings of prior studies [11, 37]. This research especially found that the scientists who collect genome sequence data have more pressure from funding agencies and journals than those who deal with lab experiment data. The results suggest that biological scientists who collect genome sequence data are more willing to share their data because they perceive more pressure from their funding agencies and journals than those who collect lab experiment data. In contrast, the biological scientists who collect lab experiment data are less likely to share their data because they perceive less pressure from their funding agencies and journals. This is because the major funding agencies (e.g. NIH and NSF) and academic journals in the biological sciences have regulated researchers to share their genome sequence data but not their lab experiment data [38, 39]; therefore, biological scientists recognize more regulative pressure from funding agencies and journals, especially when they generate genome sequence data. In contrast, funding agencies and journals do not require their scientists to share regular lab experiment data [38, 39], so biological scientists who produce lab experiment data perceive less regulative pressure from funding agencies and journals about sharing the lab experiment data.

With regards to institutional resource factors, the availability of both metadata standard and data repository were found to have significant and positive influences on biological scientists' data sharing intentions. This research newly discovered the significant relationship between availability of metadata standard and data sharing intention, which was not found in prior studies [22, 40]. Also, this research found that the biological scientists who collect genome sequence data recognize more relevant metadata standards and data repositories for sharing the genome sequence data than those who produce lab experiment data. The findings suggest that biological scientists who produce genome sequence data are more likely to share their data because they have more relevant metadata standards and data repositories that can facilitate their data sharing; those who collect lab experiment data are less likely to share their data because they do not have relevant metadata standards and data repositories which can support sharing their lab experiment data. The research community of biological sciences has developed a system of data sharing for the genome sequence data through standardized languages and data repositories for genome sequence data [41], but they do not have any relevant metadata standards and data repositories which are specialized for sharing lab experiment data.

Lastly, with regards to individual motivation factors, this research found that both perceived career benefit and perceived career risk have strong positive and negative influences on biological scientists' data sharing intentions, respectively. This research also found that scientists who collect genome sequence data have more expectation about career benefits and less concerns about career risks than those who collect lab experiment data. The results suggest that the biological scientists who collect genome sequence data are more willing to share their data because they perceive more career benefits and less career risks with data sharing than those who collect lab experiment data. In contrast, the biological scientists who collect lab experiment data are less likely to share their data because they perceive less career benefits and more career risks with sharing their lab experiment data. This is because the data sharing of genome sequence data is a well-established research practice compared to sharing lab experiment data, so biological scientists can receive more citations and recognition by sharing their genome sequence data; in the same vein, since the data sharing of genome sequence data is a well-received research practice, scientists who collect genome sequence data also have less career concerns associated with data sharing, which eventually promotes their data sharing decision making with the genome sequence data.

8 Conclusion

This research identified diverse data sharing factors including institutional pressure (i.e., funding agency's pressure and journal's pressure), institutional resources (i.e., availability of metadata standard and data repository), and individual motivations (i.e., perceived career benefit and perceived career risk), and how those data sharing factors in addition to data sharing intentions significantly differs between genome sequence data and lab experiment data types. The biological scientists who collect genome sequence data have more institutional pressure to engage in data sharing from funding agencies and journals and more institutional resources such as metadata standards and data repositories to facilitate data sharing. Researchers working with genome sequence data also perceive more career benefits and less career risks associated with data sharing. As a result, researchers who collect genome sequence data are more willing to share data than those who collect lab experiment data.

Although biological sciences have a long history of data sharing facilitated by funding agencies, journal requirements, and the availability of relevant resources such as metadata standards and data repositories [10, 42, 43], their data sharing intentions and key data sharing factors are significantly different in between types of data (i.e., genome sequence data vs. lab experiment data). This is because the funding agency's rules and the journal's requirements primarily focus on genome sequence data rather than lab experiment data [39, 41], and the metadata standards and data repositories are primarily designed and developed to support data sharing of genome sequence data [41, 44]. Those differences naturally influence scientists' perceptions about their career benefits and risks involved in data sharing; scientists who collect genome sequence data assume more career benefits, such as citations and recognition, and less career risks, such as losing publication opportunities, being scooped, and misuse of data.

Therefore, to better facilitate biological scientists' data sharing, especially with lab experiment data, it is necessary to carefully examine the current institutional settings, availability of resources, and their underlying motivations regarding data sharing. First, the community of biological sciences should develop more regulative data sharing policies and practices and implement them by funding agencies and journals within the field. Even though data sharing policies for lab experiment data are only recently required by funding agencies and a good number of journals, those regulations are not well-received by many biological scientists yet. To remedy this, stronger regulative mechanisms by funding agencies and journals should be implemented to increase biological scientists' perceived pressure from funding agencies and journals, which will eventually increase researchers' data sharing intentions. Second, the results of this research also suggest that the community of biological sciences need to design and develop more relevant resources, such as metadata standards and data repositories, to promote the sharing of lab experiment data. The results indicated the lack of metadata standards and data repositories for lab experiment data, so it is necessary to have more relevant technical resources for those who share their lab experiment data. Finally, this research also indicates that the community of biological sciences needs to increase the career benefits and decrease the perceived career risks associated with sharing lab experiment data. It is necessary to provide an appropriate reputation mechanism for sharing lab experiment data through data citations and recognition, and reduce researchers' concerns about any potential risks in sharing lab experiment data. Those endeavors can positively affect biological scientists' perceptions in institutional pressure, institutional resources, and their own motivations in sharing lab experiment data, and will eventually increase their decision to share both lab experiment data and genome sequence data.

Note: All data have been made publically available via Open ICPSR (Inter-university Consortium for Political and Social Research) and can be accessed at http://doi.org/10.3886/E105060V1.

References

1. Borgman, C.L.: Scholarship in the Digital Age: Information, Infrastructure, and the Internet. MIT Press, Cambridge (2007)
2. Tenopir, C., et al.: Changes in data sharing and data reuse practices and perceptions among scientists worldwide. Plos One 10(8) (2015)
3. Blumenthal, D., Campbell, E.G., Anderson, M.S., Causino, N., Louis, K.S.: Withholding research results in academic life science - evidence from a national survey of faculty. J. Am. Med. Assoc. 277(15), 1224–1228 (1997)
4. Campbell, E.G., et al.: Data withholding in academic genetics - evidence from a national survey. J. Am. Med. Assoc. 287(4), 473–480 (2002)
5. Louis, K.S., Jones, L.M., Campbell, E.G.: Sharing in science. Am. Sci. 90(4), 304–307 (2002)
6. Blumenthal, D., et al.: Data withholding in genetics and the other life sciences: prevalences and predictors. Acad. Med. 81(2), 137–145 (2006)
7. Piwowar, H.A., Becich, M.J., Bilofsky, H., Crowley, R.S.: Towards a data sharing culture: recommendations for leadership from academic health centers. Plos Medicine. 5(9), 1315–1319 (2008)
8. Piwowar, H.A.: Who shares? Who doesn't? Factors associated with openly archiving raw research data. Plos One 6(7) (2011)
9. Piwowar, H.A.: Foundational studies for measuring the impact, prevalence, and patterns of publicly sharing biomedical research data, University of Pittsburgh (2010)
10. Noor, M.A.F., Zimmerman, K.J., Teeter, K.C.: Data sharing: how much doesn't get submitted to GenBank? PLoS Biol. 4(7), 1113–1114 (2006)
11. Kim, Y., Stanton, J.M.: Institutional and individual factors affecting scientists' data-sharing behaviors: a multilevel analysis. J. Assoc. Inf. Sci. Technol., 1–24 (2016)
12. Weber, N.M., Piwowar, H.A., Vision, T.J.: Evaluating data citation and sharing policies in the environmental sciences. Proc. Am. Soc. Inf. Sci. Technol. 47(1), 1–2 (2010)
13. Piwowar, H.A., Day, R.S., Fridsma, D.B.: Sharing detailed research data is associated with increased citation rate. Plos One 2(3) (2007)
14. Kling, R., Spector, L.: Rewards for scholarly communication. In: Andersen, D.L. (ed.) Digital Scholarship in the Tenure, Promotion, and Review Process. M.E. Sharpe, Inc., Armonk (2003)
15. Reidpath, D.D., Allotey, P.A.: Data sharing in medical research: an empirical investigation. Bioethics 15(2), 125–134 (2001)
16. Savage, C.J., Vickers, A.J.: Empirical study of data sharing by authors publishing in PLoS journals. Plos One 4(9) (2009)
17. Tenopir, C., et al.: Data sharing by scientists: practices and perceptions. Plos One 6(6) (2011)
18. Liotta, L.A., et al.: Importance of communication between producers and consumers of publicly available experimental data. J. Natl Cancer Inst. 97(4), 310–314 (2005)
19. Kim, Y., Stanton, J.M.: Institutional and individual influences on scientists' data sharing practices. J. Comput. Sci. Educ. 3(1), 47–56 (2012)
20. Bowker, G.C., Star, S.L.: Sorting Things Out: Classification and Its Consequences. MIT Press, Cambridge (1999)
21. Michener, W.K.: Meta-information concepts for ecological data management. Ecol. Inform. 1(1), 3–7 (2006)
22. Kim, Y., Burns, C.S.: Norms of data sharing in biological sciences: the roles of metadata, data repository, and journal and funding requirements. J. Inf. Sci. 42(2), 230–245 (2016)

23. Cragin, M.H., Palmer, C.L., Carlson, J.R., Witt, M.: Data sharing, small science and institutional repositories. Philos. Trans. R. Soc. A-Math. Phys. Eng. Sci. **2010**(368), 4023–4038 (1926)
24. Marcial, L.H., Hemminger, B.M.: Scientific data repositories on the web: an initial survey. J. Am. Soc. Inform. Sci. Technol. **61**(10), 2029–2048 (2010)
25. Scott, W.R.: Institutions and Organizations: Ideas and Interests. Sage Publications, Thousand Oaks (2007)
26. Ajzen, I., Fishbein, M.: The influence of attitudes on behavior. In: Albarracin, D., Johnson, B.T., Zanna, M.P. (eds.) Handbook of Attitudes and Attitude Change, pp. 173–221. Lawrence Erlbaum Associates, Mahwah (2005)
27. Bjorck, F. (ed.): Institutional theory: a new perspective for research into IS/IT security in organisations. In: Proceedings of the 37th Hawaii International Conference on System Sciences. Citeseer (2004)
28. Battilana, J.: Agency and institutions: the enabling role of individuals' social position. Organization **13**(5), 653–676 (2006)
29. Vandenabeele, W.: Toward a public administration theory of public service motivation - an institutional approach. Public Manag. Rev. **9**(4), 545–556 (2007)
30. Zucker, L.G.: The role of institutionalization in cultural persistence. In: Powell, W.W., DiMaggio, P.J. (eds.) The New Institutionalism in Organizational Analysis, pp. 83–107. University of Chicago Press, Chicago (1991)
31. Ajzen, I.: The theory of planned behavior. Organ. Behav. Hum. Decis. Process. **52**(2), 179–211 (1991)
32. Ajzen, I.: Perceived behavioral control, self-efficacy, locus of control, and the theory of planned behavior. J. Appl. Soc. Psychol. **32**(4), 665–683 (2002)
33. Nunnally, J.C., Bernstein, I.H.: Psychometric Theory, 3rd edn. McGraw-Hill, New York (1994)
34. Field, A.: Discovering Statistics Using SPSS, 3rd edn. Sage Publications, Thousand Oaks (2009)
35. Gefen, D., Straub, D.W., Boudreau, M.-C.: Structural equation modeling and regression: guidelines for research practice. Commun. AIS **4**(7), 1–77 (2000)
36. Hair, J.F., Black, W.C., Babin, B.J., Anderson, R.E., Tatham, R.L.: Multivariate Data Analysis, 6th edn. Prentice Hall, Upper Saddle River (2006)
37. Kim, Y.: Fostering scientists' data sharing behaviors via data repositories, journal supplements, and personal communication methods. Inf. Process. Manage. **53**(4), 871–885 (2017)
38. McGuire, A.L., et al.: To share or not to share: a randomized trial of consent for data sharing in genome research. Genet. Med. **13**(11), 948–955 (2011)
39. Paltoo, D.N., et al.: Data use under the NIH GWAS data sharing policy and future directions. Nat. Genet. **46**(9), 934–938 (2014)
40. Kim, Y., Zhang, P.: Understanding data sharing behaviors of STEM researchers: the roles of attitudes, norms, and data repositories. Libr. Inf. Sci. Res. **37**(3), 189–200 (2015)
41. Rung, J., Brazma, A.: Reuse of public genome-wide gene expression data. Nat. Rev. Genet. **14**(2), 89–99 (2013)
42. Fennema-Notestine, C.: Enabling public data sharing: encouraging scientific discovery and education. Methods Mol. Biol. **569**, 25–32 (2009)
43. Duke, C.S., Porter, J.H.: The ethics of data sharing and reuse in biology. Bioscience **63**(6), 483–489 (2013)
44. Manolio, T.A., et al.: New models of collaboration in genome-wide association studies: the genetic association information network. Nat. Genet. **39**(9), 1045–1051 (2007)

Surfacing Data Change in Scientific Work

Drew Paine$^{(\boxtimes)}$ (iD) and Lavanya Ramakrishnan (iD)

Data Science and Technology Department, Lawrence Berkeley National Laboratory,
Berkeley, CA 94720, USA
{pained,lramakrishnan}@lbl.gov

Abstract. Data are essential products of scientific work that move among and through research infrastructures over time. Data constantly changes due to evolving practices and knowledge, requiring improvisational work by scientists to determine the effects on analyses. Today for end users of datasets much of the information about changes, and the processes leading to them, is invisible—embedded elsewhere in the work of a collaboration. Simultaneously scientists use increasing quantities of data, making ad hoc approaches to identifying change difficult to scale effectively. Our research investigates data change by examining how scientists make sense of change in datasets being created and sustained by the collaborative infrastructures they engage with. We examine two forms of change, before examining how trust and project rhythms influence a scientist's notion that the newest available data are the best. We explore the opportunity to design tools and practices to support user examinations of data change and surface key provenance information embedded in research infrastructures.

Keywords: Data change · Invisible work · Research infrastructures

1 Introduction

Research infrastructures are long-lasting networks of people, institutions, and artifacts that produce, share, and sustain information about the world [4]. Those enacted for collaborative science are rooted in the data they produce and sustain over time [2,5,10,15]. Data are an essential element of scientific practices that depend on context and individual's interpretations, providing 'monopoly rents' [1] and serving as the 'lifeblood' [10] of this enterprise. Studies of data and research infrastructures highlight the contextually dependent work to produce, process, share, support, and facilitate use and reuse of data over time [1,2,19,25]. This process comes with some amount of friction [4,6] as data moves among different sets of stakeholders, systems, and practices such that the narratives shaping it shift and evolve, making data change a fundamental element of scientific work. Frustratingly these narratives are often invisible when the work and decisions leading to data changes are embedded inside infrastructural processes that end users do not or cannot see.

© Springer Nature Switzerland AG 2019
N. G. Taylor et al. (Eds.): iConference 2019, LNCS 11420, pp. 15–26, 2019.
https://doi.org/10.1007/978-3-030-15742-5_2

Star and Strauss [21] stress that work is not inherently visible or invisible, it depends on the perspective of the person. Consequently, the practices of researchers producing and analyzing data in research infrastructures make (in)visible the change in the products being produced, in part because there are not clearly established guidelines within or across communities for surfacing and sharing this information. Each discipline or infrastructure "has its own norms and standards for the imagination of data, just as every field has its accepted methodologies and its evolved structures of practice" [9]. Some scientific collaborations provide high-level information about changes between versions of datasets while others provide none or minimal. As a result, the work of researchers calculating and sharing data change information is currently often ad-hoc, with inconsistent tools and practices that are often invisible to collaborators and inefficient at large scales. Our study's contribution is to address this gap by examining conceptualizations of data change in research infrastructures so that we might move towards a more systematic set of practices and tools for use within and among infrastructures. This is a formidable design opportunity as the quantities of data scale up and ad-hoc approaches no longer suffice, leading us to ask: *How do scientists make sense of data change in their research work?*

In the remainder of this paper, we discuss work on research infrastructures and scientific data that ground our study, including research on data cleaning as well as invisible work, before describing our research site and methods. Our findings examine some ways participants think about data change and how it shapes their work within infrastructures today. We conclude by discussing opportunities to make this invisible work more visible.

2 Literature Review

Investigations of scientific collaboration and the development and emergence of research infrastructures are commonly theorized using Star and Ruhleder's [20] relational infrastructure lens. This theoretical lens articulates eight facets, from having reach across sites and being learned as part of membership in groups and transparent in use, to existing within other structures through inherent embeddedness. Embeddedness is of particular concern here as we work to surface data change as an invisible, sunk in aspect of everyday scientific work for end users of datasets. To conceptualize data change we need to first articulate what data means in scientific work then explore ways of investigating infrastructure so that we can connect this notion to work on data processing and cleaning.

Data do not arise from nothing. Gitelman [9] emphasizes that "data need to be imagined *as* data to exist and function as such" while Kitchin [12] posits that data are the "material produced by abstracting the world into categories, measures and other representational forms that constitute the building blocks from which information and knowledge are created." In collaborative science, data help define boundaries among stakeholders with different communities of practice, can act as a gateway into different communities, and often indicate status [1]. Scientists must iteratively seek information and narrate their evolving products to successfully work with data [3,25], and essential to the use and reuse of data is scientist's trust in those who created it and their ability to find relevant information to answer questions about its production [7,19].

Studying infrastructures as a relational process requires a researcher constantly make decisions about what to include and exclude from an inquiry. The researcher, their subjects, and the research context co-construct what is visible and invisible in the study. Karasti and Blomberg [11] emphasize the need to 'construct the field' when undertaking ethnographic inquiries of infrastructures. A key part of constructing a field can be examining what work is visible and invisible. Star and Strauss [21] state that "what exactly counts as work varies a lot" depending on the context and who is viewing the activity at hand. Traditional 'women's work' of taking care of a household was invisible to many classifications, marginalizing this important effort and leaving it out of potential conversations in the design of systems and policies. Star and Strauss emphasize disembedding background work, examining that which is right in front of the observer but not always focused on, to make invisible work visible.

In our study we constructed our field to start surfacing the invisible work behind data change in some infrastructures of scientific research by drawing upon data processing or cleaning studies. Previous work stresses the labor intensive work of data processing or cleaning [14,16–18]. Rawson and Muñoz [18] note that specifics of data cleaning often "reside in the general professional practices, materials, personal histories, and tools of the researchers" rather than explicitly captured and included with a data release. Plantin [16] similarly highlights that cleaning is often invisible work. Earlier, Paine et al. [14] foreground and unpack the intricate, challenging data processing work scientists undertake to clean data by removing or fixing spurious values, selecting subsets of data for particular analyses, and transforming between formats to produce a product that meets their needs. From this body of work we see a gap where information underlying changes to datasets during cleaning and processing may be embedded and invisible to end users, something our work aims to tackle.

3   Research Sites and Methods

Our study[1] is investigating data change in different disciplines at Lawrence Berkeley National Laboratory, a US Department of Energy national lab. A long-standing defining feature of US national labs is a collaborative, often multidisciplinary, approach to research such that all of our subjects participate in projects with members distributed around the US and world. This paper's findings emerge from interviews with subjects in astronomy and earth sciences.

We conducted semi-structured interviews with five astronomers and five earth scientists between October 2017 and February 2018. Interviewees fulfill two general roles (sometimes both): Data Producers, individuals working on producing

---

[1] This work is part of the Deduce project (http://deduce.lbl.gov). The goal of the Deduce project is to develop methods and tools that support data change exploration and management in the context of data analysis pipelines.

data releases; and, Data Users utilizing data releases for analyses. Astronomy interviews included members of the Sloan Digital Sky Survey (SDSS) and/or the Dark Energy Spectroscopic Instrument (DESI) projects[2] collecting observational data. The earth science projects[3] produce sensor-based observation data at field sites. Some users augment field data with additional satellite data. Our interviewees included four astronomy data producers, one astronomy data user, two earth science data producers/users, and three earth science data users. The SDSS and Ameriflux projects provide high-level information about changes between data releases, but low-level details that would help end users assess potential effects to their analyses are not available with the data at this time.

Interviews were recorded, transcribed, and cleaned by the first author for analysis. They ranged from 58 to 80 min (avg 63 min). Our interview protocol was designed to learn about various aspects of an individual's research projects, focusing on data they work with and how it is obtained. We asked how subjects determine which version of data products to use for an analysis, and effects (both expected and unexpected) from changes in data products. We analyzed our data using a modified grounded theory process, open coding transcripts for responses to our questions and emergent ideas [26] and assessing these codes in relation to the literature identified earlier. Coding enabled us to distinguish sources of data change among our interviewees. We identified common themes such as the general categories of data change for our subjects as well as thoughts on the process of selecting data for use that inform our findings.

4   Findings

Our findings explore multiple facets to data change in scientific infrastructures. We examine interviewee concerns and characterize two types of data change in their work. We then unpack their expectations that newer datasets are better than older by considering our subject's trust in their collaborators and project data release processes. Finally, we examine how a project's rhythms and organizational structures for data release are part of scientist's trust in processes.

4.1   Why Scientists Are Concerned About Data Change

Change in datasets is an expected facet of work for our scientific subjects. The processes leading to different data releases are not always visible to different stakeholders, making it hard to evaluate the effects of nuanced changes. A lack of actionable information makes it hard for these producers and users to assess when they need to re-run a past analysis or adapt a new one as a result of changes to some part of dataset.

Our subjects work with datasets that are continuously expanding, adding new data, even as ongoing data processing work employs different cleaning practices to refine existing data. Data producers putting out new releases need to

---

[2] http://www.sdss.org/, http://www.desi.lbl.gov/.
[3] http://watershed.lbl.gov/, http://ameriflux.lbl.gov.

be able to check copies mirrored across archives for unexpected changes and evaluate the impact of processing on data values. Science users need to be able to assess whether changed data values will impact their current or past analyses in a significant way. Information about data change also provides necessary provenance information about the data. The lineage or history of the data is critical to allow scientists to make important decisions when processing data. One example comes from an astronomer who leads their project's data release team. They emphasized that while developing a new yearly release the collaboration will reprocess all of the data from the start for big and small changes.

"So every year they release an updated set. ... We reprocess all of the data from the start. ... Some years it's just sort of a slight incremental change. You know, fixing one thing here or there and it's just like, for completeness, you rerun it on everything. Other times, it's a fairly major update." (Astronomy data release manager)

These changes can be due to an incremental or major revision to their scientific approach expressed through various software pipelines. In other cases the collaboration, or a sub-group, shifts their scientific focus. At one point these astronomers began to try to image faint objects rather than bright objects, altering the characteristics of the signals sought and the scientific approach to processing data. This type of shift upends the assumptions they have embedded into their practices and artifacts. The data produced is different as a result of foregrounding issues with their software pipeline that were previously invisible to, or intentionally ignored by, these data producers (and as a result the end users of data) in the course of their work.

"There was a transition of the kind of object that we were looking at. Going from brighter objects to fainter objects so we could see further out. ... And when we went to the fainter objects, at lower signal-to-noise. It revealed problems in the pipeline that there were biases that you don't have at high signal-to-noise, but you do have at low signal-to-noise and it was just trashing everything." (Astronomy data release manager)

Here this astronomer's explanation intentionally doesn't delve into the complex work undertaken by these collaborations, instead conveying that many of the nuances are fairly invisible to data users. Our subjects know changes are present between releases of their data but they tended to not have enough information to effectively evaluate how they impacted their work, at least until some part of their analysis infrastructure broke down. Documenting and surfacing the provenance behind these data changes is an aspect of this infrastructural work that is underdeveloped. Surfacing these changes through better tools and practices will become even more crucial to the longevity and utility of this essential scientific resource. Understanding types of change is a first step to doing so.

4.2   Two Broad Types of Data Change

While we find that data change is an issue for scientific work, investigating and designing for the issue in different scientific contexts requires first developing a characterization of the notion. Our interviews foreground two general types of change for our subjects (1) change in the context and (2) a change in the data values themselves. These are not meant to be comprehensive or detailed, rather they're a first step at disambiguating what may be a highly variable concern among different disciplinary infrastructures.

Change in Context. Interest in changes to the context of datasets was consistently noted by subjects involved in managing data releases and archives, and sometimes by scientists using the files for their analyses. Such changes include: the organization of a data release's structure on the file system; the file naming scheme; the internal structure of files; and the metadata associated with the dataset, often encapsulated at least in part in file names and folder structures.

Data producers were particularly interested in unexpected changes to the context. These individuals are responsible for mirroring datasets across multiple computing systems for long-term storage and sharing. Verifying the consistency of the context, along with the data itself, is essential in this process. This work is difficult to easily do at scale with millions of files where thousands of changes may need to be assessed. It is also often invisible to most science end users of the datasets even though the results can impact their own work. Scientists were interested in context changes since they easily disrupt the operation of their software pipelines. They rely upon such pipelines to process and analyze their data. If changes to some structural aspect are not made visible they may encounter unexpected computational errors that waste valuable research time.

Change in Data Values. Scientists using data for analyses, as well as data producers managing releases, were concerned about changes to the data values stored within files. These end users indicate that they need to know not just that values have changed but importantly the amount of change. The magnitude of the changes influences how these users expect their analyses to be affected. This influences their decision process for further investigating the changes and potentially re-doing an analysis or resetting the starting conditions of a computational model they're building.

For example, earth scientists in our study use many streams of observational data collected at different sites, along with some satellite data, as input to computational models they're developing. Whether particular changes to data values matter significantly in this work varies, depending both on the amount of change and the specific type of data. One earth scientist explained such a case happening when the coordinates of a dataset were shifted by more than a meter. The project's cleaning process uncovered this mistake and disrupted the basis for gridding all of the data in their model. A data producer colleague adjusted the data being released, but their action was not readily visible to them or other end users. Our interviewee was informed about the change through their regular communication with this data producer and they had to go back and re-examine certain assumptions in the model, then re-execute it with the revised data. This scientist was effectively resetting their software instrument as a result of the change to the underlying data. Their work was influenced by the flow of the project's releases, but they still expressed a belief that newer data releases were better due to the ongoing collection and cleaning work.

4.3   Trusting Collaborators and Processes to Make Datasets 'Better'

Collaborative projects release datasets with differing degrees of quality on varying timelines based on different factors, and with varying purposes. Our subject's work unfolds in concert with a changing web of relationships that interweave different artifacts, people, and practices. A science end user of a dataset may only be loosely connected to the infrastructural processes that created it. The details of the work can be a murky and invisible feature requiring trust in collaborators and their practices.

The work embedded within science infrastructures has effects which can shape decisions about which versions of data to use for analysis work. Exploring this, we wanted to know how our interviewees determine which version(s) of datasets to use for particular analyses given the fluctuating, evolving infrastructures and data releases. Our subjects reflexively stated that they use the latest data release available because it is the 'best' or 'better' than earlier versions. An exception was when the scientist knew that some data is no longer present in newer data releases, requiring they use an older version. Interviewees explained that they believe their data producer collaborators are always expanding their knowledge about the work and refining their practices. Astronomers continue to better understand their software pipelines, improving signal-to-noise ratios, creating cleaner and clearer images, and so on. Earth scientists remove bad data, fix sensors and instruments, and develop a longer record to base findings on. They trust that their colleagues are producing better products overall.

Our subject's trust in collaborators is closely connected to the organization of projects and their processes for producing data. Data production and cleaning is complex enough that no single person can fully follow every nuance of the work. For these astronomers the telescope and software pipelines build upon the long-term work of many researchers who develop deep knowledge of particular elements of the infrastructure's components. These earth scientists have little choice but to trust their colleagues who are directly connected to particular field sites and instruments, the individuals who can develop the strong tacit knowledge about this ongoing, remote work.

For example, an astronomy postdoc interviewed uses a numeric subset (rather than processed images) of the SDSS project's primary data release to develop statistical calculations of galaxy distribution. The postdoc has to trust colleagues who produce the overall release, as well as those creating the subset. This scientist won't know all of the subtle decisions that resulted in changes. Asked how they determine which version of data to use the postdoc replied "the latest" before explaining how they rely upon a chain of colleagues who are more hands on producing the numeric data subset. This individual is well aware of the complexity of the telescope and the software processing pipeline for removing bugs or systematics [13] and knows they can't reanalyze all of it themselves. Instead they will call upon trusted collaborators when a bug arises and they lack the information needed to make an appropriate choice. A change may have little impact on their scientific analysis, or it may undermine the approach they're taking. At a glance the required knowledge is invisible and buried in the background.

> *So you need to have a close hand on the data to understand all of these potential systematics which could come in. So the people who create the datasets, which is not me. They know about this and I make sure that I'm using the latest datasets so that, I know that, that I have the, the best kind of dataset. ... And I don't do a re-analysis of the dataset. I, I trust the people who produce these datasets.* (Astronomy Postdoc)

This trust in data producer colleagues depends upon work embedded elsewhere in the project infrastructure. Change is expected in this iterative work, but the effects and particulars of changes are not readily visible to the end users of this infrastructure's key resource, even those who are members. Trust is essential to collaborative work [1,6,7,19], but the ability for an end user to verify and help identify issues if they have more information about changes to their data in between versions is important to further sharing of data widely outside the collaboration. Doing so may even take place outside of a project's established rhythms of data production and release.

4.4   Rhythms and Organizational Structures of Projects

Beyond trust, our subjects expect newer data releases to be better due to the organizational structure and community practices embedded in their research infrastructure shaping the rhythms of data production and release. The collaborative, multinational projects our subjects contribute to each gather, process, and release data with different timelines. This affects when versions of data are available to use in different forms of analysis work.

Astronomers in our study work on a yearly cycle that coincides with an annual weather pattern when observing is not possible. This data release team uses the time to wrap-up a year's data collection and get a release together. Some members of the project's different experiments (the way they organize different observing campaigns) have ongoing access to new data as it is collected since they are developing and refining software used to produce the final release. The eventual release, with re-processed data, is made available for members of the collaboration, then in time the public at large. For collaborators with some, or a lot of, visibility into this process they can influence the data by using them in preliminary analyses and reporting unexpected or incorrect effects. Their feedback can be folded back in to the data release team's work. End users not contributing to this process may eventually find changes in a new release and they may not have insight into the origin of these changes.

The earth scientists face a more fluid rhythm of data production, depending on the type of instruments and person(s) managing the flow of data from a field site to repository. Some PIs and groups may take many months or years to gather and process data from one site before sharing with their larger collaboration. They develop and rely upon nuanced understandings of the physical context underlying their data and use this to process data to distribute within their collaboration. In other situations, the collaboration itself may directly manage instruments and the release of their data, applying standardized processing techniques and turning around new data within days, weeks, or months. Circumventing these rhythms, earth science subjects explained how at times they may have to go directly to a particular PI or instrument manager to get early access to data that has not fully been cleaned. This can be necessary when attempting to develop a baseline model of some system under study. In other scenarios, it is simply that a phenomena is so new that studying it requires rapid access to data that might not otherwise be available for years.

5   Discussion and Conclusion

We see that data change is an expected facet in scientist's work with inconsistent support for helping identify and address sources of change. Across our interviews and literature review we see that a focus of research infrastructures is producing and processing data for eventual use by scientists, typically project members but also in time a larger community too. Regardless of the timeline or rhythm to this work, important contextual information about changes to datasets is generated (whether explicitly or implicitly) and embedded within the enacted infrastructures. This information may not be readily conveyed in a visible manner to people beyond data production teams and a project's work practices may allow information underlying changes to fall by the wayside.

Surfacing concerns of data producers and science users trying to make sense of data change, one contribution of our study is to convey a general split between interest in types of changes in the contexts and in the data values, even as our subjects believe the latest data releases of a project are the 'best' available. Part of the challenge we as a community can address is determining what information it is possible to systematically produce to help end users of data products answer questions of relevance, trust, etc. Previous work that has explored trust and information seeking considerations [1,2,7,19,25] can be built upon to help scientists be able to more clearly understand and articulate why they find the latest data releases 'better' as their products evolve. At the same time, investigating non-computational provenance, as Thomer et al. [24] emphasize, along with provenance from particular computational workflows [22] is necessary.

Our findings offer a starting point for inquiries, even as there is more work to be done. Instead of treating data change as just a given facet of science we should continue to explore this realm as an opportunity for designing tools and practices to support scientists and help them grow and sustain their research infrastructures. We should design to support the capture and articulation of data changes that provide critical provenance, including quantitative information about its impact on downstream data analyses as well as qualitative insights. Our participant's projects (SDSS and Ameriflux in particular) currently do include some information about changes between releases that is very general (e.g., new sites or observations added, major format changes, etc.). However, they do not provide much in-depth information that an end user scientist would need to assess whether they need to re-run analyses as they use the latest, 'best' data release. For example, changes in the filesystem may be encapsulated as part of the relevant contexts since many scientists in our study rely on folder structures or file names for at least some metadata in their work. In the moment, ephemeral information seeking leaves much of the labor less visible, if not invisible, to a variety of colleagues who take practices of the research infrastructure for granted. This iterative, ad hoc labor to identify and work with changes is another aspect to cleaning and processing data [14,16]. The resulting information produced about changes is really additional metadata about the scientific process itself that must be aligned to different contexts in spite of friction [6].

We see opportunities to design new tools and practices to help both end users of data and the collaborations producing releases since the process of working out and communicating changes between data releases is not well defined within the rhythms and organizational structures of our subject's projects. Currently, to effectively and appropriately use datasets scientists must undertake ad hoc, time consuming, iterative work to understand the product's structure and content, and differences from any past versions, among other concerns. Systematically designing tools and practices to surface data change should begin by supporting the work of users relying upon the data of research infrastructures. We can design tools to help calculate context changes so that data release teams—who are essential members of research infrastructures—can better communicate change information as a key element in their releases. Making visible their effort will furthermore help convey the care and craft that goes into change analyses.

In essence, designing to help construct information about data change means we are undertaking articulation work or metawork [8,23], ensuring that other researcher's (in this case science users) work can go well. Longer-term we should help communities develop common practices for explaining change in datasets, contributing to the sustainability of their research infrastructures. We can facilitate such efforts by building flexible software tools to integrate into different components of infrastructures and their shifting contexts. Infrastructure projects themselves should support and sustain these elements and produce change information as part of their data releases to aid their communities. There is a rich area of inquiry for design when investigating data change that has the potential to impact and shape a variety of research practices and facets of infrastructures at different scales. Shedding light on this work that is often invisible to end users is a first step in making such an impact.

Acknowledgements. The authors thank the members of the Deduce project, the study participants, and the anonymous reviewers of this work. This work is supported by the U.S. Department of Energy, Office of Science and Office of Advanced Scientific Computing Research (ASCR) under Contract No. DE-AC02-05CH11231.

References

1. Birnholtz, J.P., Bietz, M.J.: Data at work: supporting sharing in science and engineering. In: Proceedings of the 2003 International ACM SIGGROUP Conference on Supporting Group Work, GROUP 2003, pp. 339–348. ACM, New York (2003). https://doi.org/10.1145/958160.958215
2. Borgman, C.L.: Big Data, Little Data, No Data: Scholarship in the Networked World. MIT Press, Cambridge (2015)
3. Dourish, P., Gómez Cruz, E.: Datafication and data fiction: narrating data and narrating with data. Big Data Soc. **5**(2) (2018). https://doi.org/10.1177/2053951718784083
4. Edwards, P.N.: A Vast Machine: Computer Models, Climate Data, and the Politics of Global. MIT Press, Cambridge (2010)
5. Edwards, P.N., Jackson, S.J., Bowker, G.C., Knobel, C.P.: Understanding infrastructure: dynamics, tensions, and design. Workshop report, University of Mighican (2007). http://hdl.handle.net/2027.42/49353
6. Edwards, P.N., Mayernik, M.S., Batcheller, A.L., Bowker, G.C., Borgman, C.L.: Science friction: data, metadata, and collaboration. Soc. Stud. Sci. **41**(5), 667–690 (2011). https://doi.org/10.1177/0306312711413314
7. Faniel, I., Jacobsen, T.: Reusing scientific data: How earthquake engineering researchers assess the reusability of colleagues' data. Comput. Support. Coop. Work (CSCW) **19**(3), 355–375 (2010). https://doi.org/10.1007/s10606-010-9117-8
8. Gerson, E.M.: Reach, Bracket, and the Limits of Rationalized Coordination: Some Challenges for CSCW Resources, Co-Evolution and Artifacts, Computer Supported Cooperative Work, pp. 193–220. Springer, London (2008). https://doi.org/10.1007/978-1-84628-901-9
9. Gitelman, L., Jackson, V.: Introduction. In: Gitelman, L. (ed.) "Raw Data" is an Oxymoron. Infrastructure Series, pp. 1–14. MIT Press, Cambridge (2013)
10. Jirotka, M., Lee, C.P., Olson, G.M.: Supporting scientific collaboration: methods, tools and concepts. Comput. Support. Coop. Work (CSCW) **22**(4–6), 667–715 (2013). https://doi.org/10.1007/s10606-012-9184-0
11. Karasti, H., Blomberg, J.: Studying infrastructuring ethnographically. Comput. Support. Coop. Work **27**(2), 233–265 (2018). https://doi.org/10.1007/s10606-017-9296-7
12. Kitchin, R.: The Data Revolution: Big Data, Open Data, Data Infrastructures and their Consequences. Sage, London (2014)
13. Paine, D., Lee, C.P.: Who has plots? contextualizing scientific software, practice, and visualizations. In: Proceedings of the ACM on Human-Computer Interaction 1(CSCW) (2017). https://doi.org/10.1145/3134720
14. Paine, D., Sy, E., Piell, R., Lee, C.P.: Examining data processing work as part of the scientific data lifecycle: Comparing practices across four scientific research groups. In: iConference 2015 (2015). http://hdl.handle.net/2142/73644
15. Pipek, V., Karasti, H., Bowker, G.C.: A preface to 'infrastructuring and collaborative design'. Comput. Support. Coop. Work (CSCW) **26**(1), 1–5 (2017). https://doi.org/10.1007/s10606-017-9271-3
16. Plantin, J.C.: Data cleaners for pristine datasets: visibility and invisibility of data processors in social science. Sci. Technol. Hum. Values **44**(1), 52–73 (2019). https://doi.org/10.1177/0162243918781268
17. Rahm, E., Do, H.H.: Data cleaning: problems and current approaches. IEEE Data Eng. Bull. **23**(4), 3–13 (2000)

18. Rawson, K., Munoz, T.: Against cleaning. Curating Menus **6** (2016). http:// curatingmenus.org/articles/against-cleaning/
19. Rolland, B., Lee, C.P.: Beyond trust and reliability: reusing data in collaborative cancer epidemiology research. In: Proceedings of the 2013 Conference on Computer Supported Cooperative Work, CSCW 2013, pp. 435–444. ACM, New York (2013). https://doi.org/10.1145/2441776.2441826
20. Star, S.L., Ruhleder, K.: Steps toward an ecology of infrastructure: design and access for large information spaces. Inf. Syst. Res. **7**(1), 24 (1996)
21. Star, S.L., Strauss, A.: Layers of silence, arenas of voice: the ecology of visible and invisible work. Comput. Support. Coop. Work (CSCW) **8**, 9–30 (1999)
22. Stodden, V., et al.: Enhancing reproducibility for computational methods. Science **354**(6317), 1240–1241 (2016). https://doi.org/10.1126/science.aah6168
23. Strauss, A.: The articulation of project work: an organizational process. Sociol. Q. **29**(2), 163–178 (1988)
24. Thomer, A.K., Wickett, K.M., Baker, K.S., Fouke, B.W., Palmer, C.L.: Documenting provenance in noncomputational workflows: research process models based on geobiology fieldwork in yellowstone national park. J. Assoc. Inform. Sci. Technol. **69**(10), 1234–1245 (2018). https://doi.org/10.1002/asi.24039
25. Vertesi, J., Dourish, P.: The value of data: considering the context of production in data economies. In: Proceedings of the ACM 2011 Conference on Computer Supported Cooperative Work, CSCW 2011, pp. 533–542. ACM, New York (2011). https://doi.org/10.1145/1958824.1958906
26. Weiss, R.S.: Learning From Strangers: The Art and Method of Qualitative Interview Studies. The Free Press, New York (1995)

Understanding Hackathons for Science: Collaboration, Affordances, and Outcomes

Ei Pa Pa Pe-Than$^{(\boxtimes)}$ and James D. Herbsleb

Carnegie Mellon University, Pittsburgh, PA 15213, USA
{eipapapt, jdh}@cs.cmu.edu

Abstract. Nowadays, hackathons have become a popular way of bringing people together to engage in brief, intensive collaborative work. Despite being a brief activity, being collocated with team members and focused on a task—*radical collocation*—could improve collaboration of scientific software teams. Using a mixed-methods study of participants who attended two hackathons at Space Telescope Science Institute, we examined how hackathons can facilitate collaboration in scientific software teams which typically involve members from two different disciplines: science and software engineering. We found that hackathons created a focused interruption-free working environment in which team members were able to assess each other's skills, focus together on a single project and leverage opportunities to exchange knowledge with other collocated participants, thereby allowing technical work to advance more efficiently. This study suggests "hacking" as a new and productive form of collaborative work in scientific software production.

Keywords: Hackathons · Time-bounded events · Collaboration · Coordination · Collocation · Scientific software development

1 Introduction

Time-bounded intensive events such as hackathons have rapidly gained traction among both researchers and practitioners in various disciplines due to their potential to leverage collective intelligence, foster innovation, advance technical work, and serve as a ground for future work outside the usual constraints and processes of the workplace [11]. The popularity of hackathons and similar collaborative events has increased dramatically in recent years. For example, collegiate hackathons, just one of the many types of hackathons, in 2017, attracted more than 65,000 participants from 16 different countries[1].

In collocated hackathons, people gather together in the same physical space and form small teams to solve problems within a specified timeframe, typically 2–5 days, leveraging members' diverse backgrounds, familiarity, experience, and expertise. Such events originated in the tech industry where teams consisting of members with a relatively homogeneous background (i.e., software engineers) produced software

---

[1] Major League Hacking, MLH. https://mlh.io.

© Springer Nature Switzerland AG 2019
N. G. Taylor et al. (Eds.): iConference 2019, LNCS 11420, pp. 27–37, 2019.
https://doi.org/10.1007/978-3-030-15742-5_3

prototypes [7]. Hackathons were subsequently used in other disciplines, such as astronomy[2], biology [13, 17, 19], and polar science [20].

Team collaboration for scientific software production introduces additional coordination and communication challenges due to the involvement of members who are generally trained in two different disciplines: science and computer science or software engineering [1, 6, 16, 19, 20]. However, effective interaction between these two communities is essential not only to foster the correctness and long-term maintainability of scientific software produced [9, 19], but also to cultivate collaboration and the exchange of knowledge between scientists and software engineers.

Previous work on radical collocation [8, 14, 18], which is a situation where team members are together in a room for an extended period of time, suggests that teams collocated in this setting were able to communicate and coordinate their work better, which, in turn, increased productivity and team performance. These studies further noted that radical collocation enabled team members to overhear and participate in conversations, learn from each other, and provide useful inputs, and seek help when needed, resulting in an increase in familiarity among members. Further, face-to-face interaction in teams is known to have a positive influence on participation in follow-up work and facilitate socialization among new members [3].

However, in prior work on radical collocation, teams were either radically collocated for four months [18] or placed in their distant co-workers' workplace for an extended period [8]. These time scales were sufficient for participants to develop familiarity and shared norms that would allow teams to effectively utilize the affordances of radical collocation. This extended radical collocation is quite different from a typical hackathon's 2–5 days. Here, affordances in this study, drawing upon Gibson's concept [4], refer to everything about the hackathon environment that contributes to any kinds of interactions occurred. We examine whether and how hackathons offer the advantages of radical collocation to a team with members of different areas of expertise collaborating on scientific software production. Accordingly, we ask the following two research questions. In the context of scientific software production,

1. How did teams use the affordances of hackathons to collaborate?
2. What were the enduring effects of the hackathons?

To address these questions, using a mixed-methods approach – a combination of interviews and a questionnaire, we studied eight scientific software teams participating in two daylong hackathons held at the Space Telescope Science Institute (STScI)[3] in Baltimore, Maryland. We found that the hackathons offered participants a focused interruption-free workspace, and opportunities for collocated knowledge exchange through which teams were able to concentrate on their work while exchanging technical and/or scientific information, leading the teams to quickly advance their projects. Despite being brief, team members were able to identify others' specific skills and knowledge, thereby possibly enhancing the team overall knowledge about who knows

---

[2] Astro Hack Week. http://astrohackweek.org/2018/.

[3] The Space Telescope Science Institute (STScI) is operated by the Association of Universities for Research in Astronomy. http://www.stsci.edu/institute/.

what. As participants self-reported that they were willing to adopt hacking practices in their day-to-day work, hackathons could be seen as a new mode of work in scientific software production. In the following sections, we present the background of our study, describe research methods and setting, present our findings, and finally discuss implications of our findings.

2 Background

"Radical collocation" refers to a situation where team members are together in a room for the duration of the project [18]. This strategy was developed in response to communication delays and breakdowns that occurred in distributed software development. Prior studies on software teams have documented the affordances of radical collocation, which – as earlier noted – include: overhearing, spontaneous feedback, learning, ad-hoc collaboration, shared visual space, and increased members' familiarity [8, 18]. These affordances support easier coordination and communication among software team members, resulting in increased productivity and outcome quality.

Coordination is difficult, yet important, for an effective team process [12], and it is even harder when teams consist of members with diverse expertise. Prior studies concerning software work in science have shown that software engineers and scientists tend to approach a task very differently [10, 15, 16]. Software engineers focus on the idea that software engineering methodologies can help assess, test, and improve software correctness [5, 9]. However, scientists are usually not trained or well versed in software engineering practices, and this line of research often concludes with the recommendation that scientists learn and adopt those practices [9]. Scientists, on the other hand, generally just want to "get the plots out," [9, 16], i.e., produce publishable results as quickly and efficiently as possible.

Hackathons are often used as a means to fill the gap between science and software engineering [13, 17, 19, 20]. Prior work on this line of research suggests that hackathons are partially effective in, for example, educating polar scientists how to use high-performance and distributed computing resources, methods, and tools [20], and bringing together software engineers and scientists for skill and knowledge exchange [13]. Since the development of scientific software is a collaborative process of knowledge discovery [15], bringing people from these two different disciplines into the same physical space through hackathons might not only help advance the technical work more quickly but also identify specific practices that work best for scientific software production. However, we do not yet fully understand what kinds of hackathon interactions most effectively encourage collaboration between scientists and software engineers. Therefore, drawing on the theory of radical collocation, this study aims to understand how participants use affordances of hackathons in the production of scientific software, and what are the enduring effects of hackathons in this context.

3 Methods

3.1 The Setting: Two Hackathons at STScI

We studied two hackathons that were held by the STScI in March and May of 2018. The STScI's motivation for running these events was twofold. First, these hackathons were part of the STScI's program of transitioning their tool written in IRAF (Image Reduction and Analysis Facility) scripting language to a Python-based tool due to the discontinued support of IRAF, with the particular aim of assisting this transitioning process. This was also a priority task for the STScI because many instrument scientists and astronomers relied heavily on IRAF for their day-to-day research. Further, scientists were very familiar with the functionality of IRAF, but they were not well versed in Python. Conversely, software engineers were experts in Python but lacked the required domain knowledge. Although both scientists and software engineers were part of the same instrument team in STScI, they all spent most of their day working in silos and their days were fragmented by focusing on various tasks and responsibilities. Accordingly, the second motivation was to bridge the gap between these two groups of people who have different backgrounds (i.e., science and software engineering) by bringing them together in the same physical space for a short period of time to work together on specific projects.

Participants of both hackathons were STScI's employees who were either software engineers or scientists who used IRAF-based tools to perform data calibrations and analyze scientific data, and to provide scientific support to other astronomers dealing with data coming from the instruments installed on the Hubble Space Telescope (HST). The majority of participants knew each other, had worked together before, and had varying levels of Python skills (see Table 1).

Each event was organized by a scientist and held at the STScI's office at the Rotunda in Baltimore, Maryland. Prior to the event, the organizer administered a pre-survey to elicit participants' skills and their project preferences. Based on information it yielded, the organizers assigned participants to specific projects/teams. The organizers then created a shared folder for each team and advised teams to perform preparatory activities such as pre-meetings to identify project goals and tasks, to assign tasks to team members, and to familiarize themselves with the development environment such as GitHub and legacy IRAF code. Prior to the event, the organizers had also sent out tutorial materials related to GitHub, basic Python and Python for astronomy to the teams. On each hackathon day, the participants gathered in the single room, and worked together with team members on a pre-assigned project. Both events, which ran from 9:00 am to 4:00 pm, started with a session during which each team presented the project goals to all participants and ended with a session during which each team reported back to the entire group about what they had accomplished during the event. The two hackathons we studied are described in detail in the following section.

Event A (STIS Hackathon). Event A took place on March 28, 2018. Participants were software engineers and scientists from a team in the STScI that handles data calibration and scientific support activities related to an HST's instrument called the Space Telescope Imaging Spectrograph (STIS). Prior to the hackathon, the event organizer worked closely with STIS team to identify three projects (A1-3) associated with three highest priority IRAF software packages that needed to be converted to Python. A total of 12 participants took part in this event. They were divided into three teams of four members that worked on one of the three projects mentioned above. Each team contained a mix of software engineers and scientists. All teams met once prior to the event and briefly discussed their projects.

During the event, team A1 which consisted of a software engineer (A14), one scientist with advanced Python skills (A13), and two scientists with basic Python skills (A11 and A12), decided to work in a different room. The group started with a hands-on session about GitHub development workflow led by the software engineer (A14). After this, A13 wrote all the tasks that needed to be implemented in Python on a whiteboard, and divided the labor. A13 performed line-by-line conversion of IRAF to Python while A11 implemented the science-oriented aspect of the module in Python which was then integrated with A13's code. A12 prepared the test data/files for their project. The group worked very closely throughout the day, and A13 and A14 assisted with Python and development-related help when needed.

Team A2 consisted of one software engineer (A24), one software engineer with a science background (A22), and two scientists with basic Python skills (A21 and A23). A21 and A22 started off by identifying the functionality of the existing legacy IRAF code through flowcharts included in their project documentation, and their project consisted of four scripts to be converted to Python. At first, A21 and A22 worked on different chunks of the same script while A22 was occasionally teaching A21 how to write code in object oriented style. The more experienced scientist with basic Python skill (A23) assumed the role of tester and consultant by preparing data/test files and providing science-oriented information when required.

The group process of team A3 was slightly different from those of A1 and A2. A software engineer (A34) introduced the rest of the team to a generalized software package to be used for their project. A software engineer with science background (A32) and a scientist with basic Python skills (A33) tested this package to implement the science-oriented part of their project. A more experienced scientist with basic Python skills (A31) not only provided science knowledge to the team but also helped validate the correctness of the new Python-based program by comparing its results to those produced by his/her own program written in Fortran.

Although teams A2 and A3 were working on different projects, they helped each other by sharing information, especially when they overheard the other group's conversation. Examples of this include referring members of the other team to a specific section in the documentation, and sharing information about specific implementations or calculations that did not work.

Event B (ACS Hackathon). This event took place on May 31, 2018. Participants, again, were both software engineers and scientists who carried out activities related to another HST's instruments called Advanced Camera for Surveys (ACS). One day before the event, the ACS team got together and discussed their hackathon projects. There were six projects/teams in total, of which we managed to interview members from five projects/teams (B1-5). All projects were "timeboxed", i.e., they were to be completed within a day by the team. A total of 12 participants took part in this event, and each team consisted of three or four members. Each participant in Event B was assigned to at least two projects. In particular, each scientist was appointed as a leader in one project and a consultant in another project. Scientists led all projects except one (B3). All teams worked in the same room most of the day. Each team included members with varying levels of expertise in science and software engineering.

Team B1 was led by a scientist (B11) who brought to the event a pre-written data analysis script in a Jupyter Notebook. He/she advised an experienced scientist who had basic Python skills (B13) to perform end-to-end testing, i.e., including all activities: setting up the environment, running the scripts, and reviewing the explanations and instructions for these scripts. Similarly, a software engineer (B12) also tested the notebook. B11 and B12 troubleshot the errors reported by B13 and opened issues on GitHub, and also provided B13 with help related to both Python and Jupyter Notebook.

The leader of team B2, who was a scientist (B21), worked closely with a software engineer (B22), who also had a science background but little knowledge of Python, but they had not worked together before. B22 worked on optimizing the existing data calibration scripts needed by B21. B21 wrote data analysis scripts and also provided B22 with needed test data/files. Next, B31, a software engineer who had worked with the ACS team before, worked on the project B2 alone while other senior scientists provided him/her with domain expertise. B31 often helped other teams with Python when he/she overheard conversations of other participants. Team B4 was led by a scientist with advanced Python skills, but he/she was not familiar with GitHub (B41). Throughout the day, B41 and B42, a software engineer, adopted a pair programming style in which both worked together to set up a GitHub repository for their project and to convert legacy scripts to Python. The group received Python-related help from B31 and the event organizer (BO1). Another scientist (B51) worked alone on the project B5.

The hackathon model used in event B seemed to encourage both intra- as well as inter-team interaction, observed when participants received help from the other teams' members. Most participants focused only on the projects that they were leading and other projects where they had a consulting role did not reach a state that required their inputs.

3.2 Data Collection and Analysis

The data collection procedure consisted of two phases. In the first phase, we conducted observations during the events where the researcher took detailed notes regarding coordination activities performed by team members throughout the event. In the second phase, immediately after the event, we conducted semi-structured post-event interviews and administered a questionnaire. In post-event interviews, a total of 20 participants (11 from A and nine from B) participated. The topics covered in our interviews include participant's motivations (*"Why did you decide to participate in the hackathon?"*), group dynamics (*"How did your group work together?"*), outcomes (*"How did you perceive the outcome of your project? Did you learn anything at the hackathon that you expect to apply in your daily work?"*), and relationship of hackathon to their day-to-day work (*"How was the hackathon different from how you usually work?"*).

Ten participants completed the questionnaire (four from A and six from B), which elicited participants' satisfaction with the group processes and outcomes on multi-item scales. Participants rated their experience of satisfaction with group processes on five-points scales as inefficient/efficient, uncoordinated/coordinated, unfair/fair, and confusing/easy to understand. Participant's satisfaction with outcomes was evaluated on a five-point Likert scale ranging from 1 (strongly disagree) to 5 (strongly agree). Example question items include *"I am satisfied with the work competed in my project."* and *"I am satisfied with the quality of my project's outcome."* Two months after the event, we conducted follow-up interviews (post-post-interviews) with one participant from each team. We also interviewed the event organizers to understand the objectives and their expectations of the event. Interviews lasted from 18 to 56 min. Table 1 summarizes the backgrounds of the 22 participants in our sample.

We performed open coding on the interview transcripts and observation notes [2] using Dedoose, a Web-based qualitative data analysis tool. This process resulted in eight codes: *focused environment*, *goal-directed workflow*, *information exchange*, *team building*, *meet new people*, *identify future contact*, *group process and outcome*, and *intention to adopt hacking practices in regular workplace*. These codes were the result of a process in which we wrote and shared descriptive memos by interpreting our initial open codes and then repeatedly analyzing them collaboratively to find similarities among the codes in order to develop higher-order codes or categories. We continued this process until no new codes were revealed in our interview data. This process revealed categories related to collaboration practices and the perceived impact of the hackathon on participants and their regular work style.

Table 1. Summary of interview participants (N = 22).

Projects/Teams	Software engineer	Software engineer with science background	Scientist with basic python skills	Scientists with advanced python skills
Event A			AO1	
A1	A14		A11, A12	A13
A2	A24	A22	A21, A23	
A3		A32	A31, A33	
Event B				
B1	B12		B13	B11
B2		B22		B21
B3	B31			
B4	B42			B41, BO1
B5				B51

Note. B1-5 were timeboxed projects. AO1 and BO1 were organizers of Event A and B respectively.

4 Results

Our results revealed how participants made use of affordances offered by hackathons to get their work done, exchange knowledge, extend their social networks and cultivate skills and practices that they could apply in their day-to-day work.

First, participants perceived hackathons as a **focused interruption-free workspace** which enabled them to concentrate on a single project (A32, B20, B11, B21, B41) in contrast to their usual typically fragmented days. Participants also used the hackathon to assess the feasibility of their ideas by attempting to develop them. B20 described how they perceived the hackathon: *"Okay, I'm going to work on this for the entire day, not be interrupted and I'm going to see whether or not this is actually feasible."* (B20). Many participants **felt more directed** in the hackathon as it encouraged them to set and focus on specific goals for the day (A13, A32, B11, B20, B21, B41). A13 noted: *"... it's hard sometimes to find a goal at the end of the day when I come into work that's I need to get to that point. But the hack day is based on that, and at the end of the day you should be at this point, or you should at least try to be at this point."*

Second, hackathons enabled **collocated knowledge exchange** among participants who viewed hackathons as a shortcut to seeking feedback on technical or science-related issues (A12, A14, A21, A32, A33, B20, B31, B41, B42). Otherwise, they would have to formally request assistance from people with relevant skills, who, however, had their own priorities to address and might not be immediately available, causing the progress on work to slow. For example, B42 described how the participants received technical help from others: *"There were a couple times that I had a question about a Python-specific coding thing. One of them was, 'How do I open this file and read the lines out, but I need to read every three lines at a time? How do I effectively do that in a loop?' And [B31], one of the other members of the Hack Day, helped"* (A31). Similarly, A21 noted: *"... being in the same room made the interaction much faster in that someone could ask a question right away. Or – and as soon [A23] had some code written, I could test it. So in that sense, it was certainly much faster turnaround and more efficient in that sense because everyone's mind is fresh."* (A21). Similarly, one scientist (B41) noted how working side-by-side with a subject matter expert was exceedingly helpful and productive: *"I think that I normally wouldn't have had that many hours of [B42]'s attention on any given day and [even though] I could've done that coding myself, ... it would've taken a lot longer."* (B41).

Third, several participants noted how hackathons enhanced **a sense of team identity** and described their experience as "some good synergy that develops it as a team." (A22). Other members commented that it is typical to *"feel united when you're all working together on one issue in a little bit more of a relaxed environment"* (B21), and noted *"the sense of community and a sense of we're all working towards this common goal of getting stuff done for the ACS team"* (B42). Despite being a brief collaboration, participants seemed to be able to **identify go-to persons for future**—persons with required skills who they could ask to help them with certain issues and problems. This was especially the case when the hackathon teams involved members who were outside of their regular workgroup (A30, A40). For example, A40 noted: *"I think it [the hack day] just sort of gave me a little bit more confidence to go talk to – who to approach"* (A40).

Further, brief interaction with active contributors of open communication channels (e.g., institution-wise python channel) during the hackathon seemed to have reduced a perceived barrier for scientists to take part in those channels (B41).

Fourth, many participants commented on having encountered several **learning opportunities** by working side-by-side with subject matter experts during the hackathon (A13, A14, A31, B21, B22, B41). The team members also overheard conversations with other teams and provided **useful technical and/or scientific information**. A31 recalled the participant's experience as follows: *"We were talking about a particular issue. One of the things that goes on in this code, and somebody from the other group kind of chimed in from his experience, giving some additional perspective on that particular issue."* (A31). Likewise, scientists who knew Python but were not familiar with software engineering learned **best practices and development workflow** (e.g., object oriented style coding and GitHub (A11, A23, B13)), as well as **tool-specific nuances** (e.g., using multiple languages in a Jupyter Notebook (B41)). In some cases, the actual learning process did not take place during the event, but subsequently. For example, participants (B11, B12) reported that they aimed, in the future, to explore more about tools that they learned about from other participants (e.g., Ginga – a Python toolkit for building viewers for scientific image data).

Finally, several participants indicated that participating in the hackathon made them realize how they could be more productive during their regular workday, and that they **intended to use hacking practices in their regular work** (A13, A22, A23). Participants of both events appreciated the value of the hackathon and suggested having more hackathons with the entire team at least twice a year. Some participants reported that they had discussed the possibility of using common free time to work side-by-side like a mini-hackathon (A22, A23). Further, the post-post interview conducted with A11 (the team lead of STIS) revealed that the team had organized another hackathon and planned to organize one every two months. A participant of Event B (B11) had been organizing "lunch hacks" every Thursday, where attendees brought in issues to solve together with other attendees. One participant (A22) expressed how he imagined hackathons as the future of work: *"I think that it was very useful in helping us see how productive it can be. And I think, that's only going to make us feel like it's a way we could – it's something we could bring to the way we work in the future"* (A22).

Questionnaire Results. While the small number of participants does not support meaningful statistical analysis, we present our questionnaire results to enrich our qualitative descriptions. The analysis of questionnaire data revealed differences in satisfaction between participants of these events. Participants of Event A ($M = 3.88$; $SD = 0.66$) were slightly more satisfied with their team process than those of Event B ($M = 3.67$; $SD = 0.58$). In contrast, participants of Event B reported having higher levels of satisfaction ($M = 4.47$; $SD = 0.45$) with the outcome than those of Event A did ($M = 3.67$, $SD = 0.58$). This finding corroborated our interview data in which several participants of Event B (B21, B42, B51) expressed the view that being able to get the work done felt fulfilling and rewarding, whereas a participant of Event A expressed a little disappointment noting that the *"project was not the one that could be completed within a day"* (A21).

5 Discussion and Conclusion

We found that brief intensive collocated collaboration or hackathons can effectively bring two communities with different expertise for productive interactions on specific issues and problems, resulting in quick progress on technical work or projects. Participants perceived an increase in productivity that they attributed to being able to work in a focused interruption-free space that enabled them to concentrate on one thing at a time, and then discuss technical and/or science-related matters with other participants. This finding is consistent with prior work on radically collocated teams for extended periods of time, which demonstrated that affordances of radical collocation enabled easier coordination, and reinforced relationships among members which, in turn, increased team performance [8, 14, 18].

In addition to being a space for "getting the work done", hackathons facilitated opportunities for knowledge exchange and serendipitous learning, which often happened by overhearing conversations among other participants. Learning also was seen to happen when a scientist with little software engineering experience was paired up with a software engineer or a scientist with advanced Python skills. In other words, our findings suggest that hackathons could be used as an integral element in the process of producing a consistent set of scientific tools for long-term maintainability. This process requires an intensive collaboration between scientists and software engineers [9, 19]. Here, hackathons have an ability to bring in scientists, who typically work in silos either focusing on their own scientific research agenda or having insufficient time to work on needed tasks due to various responsibilities, to the same space with software engineers in order to collaboratively discover scientific knowledge while following and adjusting best software engineering practices for their scientific needs.

Despite their being brief, hackathons enabled participants to explore each other's skills and expertise and identify future useful contacts, perhaps suggesting that hackathons can enhance the team's transactive memory [21]. Taken together, our results suggest that in order to advance technical work more quickly and effectively for scientific software teams embedded in an organization, it is helpful to give them common free time, and that doing so is beneficial not only for getting the work done but also for enabling knowledge exchange and learning among members.

As a general rule, we found that it is important for participant satisfaction to have the scope of the project aligned with the event time frame and team size (i.e., time-boxed project). As reflected in the questionnaire results, teams that performed time-boxed projects were more likely to be satisfied with their project outcomes. On the other hand, participants might be motivated to return to, and finish the projects that they were not able to complete during the event. This calls for future research as we were not able to draw any conclusions based on our current data. We found that the teams we studied have continued running weekly mini-hackathons, and that participants appreciated a way of solving problem on the fly. The experience as a whole seemed to have added "hacking" as a new way of working, a new element in the team "toolbox" they could use as the need was perceived. Nonetheless, future research is needed to investigate whether hackathons introduce other changes in the way that people work.

References

1. Bos, N., et al.: From shared databases to communities of practice: a taxonomy of collaboratories. J. Comput.-Mediat. Commun. **12**, 652–672 (2007)
2. Corbin, J., Strauss, A.: Basics of Qualitative Research: Techniques and Procedures for Developing Grounded Theory, 4th edn. SAGE Publications Inc., Thousand Oaks (2014)
3. Crowston, K., Howison, J., Masango, C., Eseryel, Y.: Face-to-face interactions in self-organizing distributed teams. In: Presentation at the OCIS Division, Academy of Management Conference (2005). http://floss.syr.edu/StudyP/ftf2005.pdf
4. Greeno, J.G.: Gibson's affordances. Psychol. Rev. **101**(2), 336–342 (1994)
5. Hatton, L., Roberts, A.: How accurate is scientific software? IEEE Trans. Software Eng. **20**, 785–797 (1994)
6. Heaton, D., Carver, J.C.: Claims about the use of software engineering practices in science: a systematic literature review. Inf. Softw. Technol. **67**, 207–219 (2015). Carver
7. Henderson, S.: Getting the most out of hackathons for social good. In: Rosenthal, R.J. (ed.) Volunteer Engagement 2.0: Ideas and Insights Changing the World, pp. 182–194 (2015)
8. Hinds, P.J., Cramton, C.D.: Situated coworker familiarity: how site visits transform relationships among distributed workers. Organ. Sci. **25**, 794–814 (2013)
9. Howison, J., Herbsleb, J.D.: Scientific software production: incentives and collaboration. In: The ACM 2011 Conference on Computer Supported Cooperative Work, pp. 513–522. ACM, New York (2011)
10. Kelly, D.: Scientific software development viewed as knowledge acquisition: towards understanding the development of risk-averse scientific software. J. Syst. Softw. **109**, 50–61 (2015)
11. Komssi, M., Pichlis, D., Raatikainen, M., Kindström, K., Järvinen, J.: What are hackathons for? IEEE Softw. **32**, 60–67 (2015)
12. Kraut, R.E., Streeter, L.A.: Coordination in large scale software development. Commun. ACM **38**, 69–81 (1995)
13. Möller, S., et al.: Community-driven development for computational biology at sprints, hackathons and codefests. BMC Bioinf. **15**, S7 (2014)
14. Olson, G.M., Olson, J.S.: Distance matters. Hum.-Comput. Interact. **15**, 139–178 (2000)
15. Paine, D., Lee, C.P.: Who has plots? Contextualizing scientific software, practice, and visualizations. ACM Hum. Comput. Interact. **1**, 21 (2017). Article 85
16. Segal, J.: Scientists and software engineers: a tale of two cultures. In: The 20th Annual Meeting of the Psychology of Programming Interest Group, PPIG 2008, University of Lancaster, UK (2008)
17. Stoltzfus, A., et al.: Community and code: nine lessons from nine NESCent Hackathons. F1000Research **6** (2017)
18. Teasley, S., Covi, L., Krishnan, M.S., Olson, J.S.: How does radical collocation help a team succeed? In: The 2000 ACM Conference on Computer Supported Cooperative Work, pp. 339–346, ACM, New York (2000)
19. Trainer, E.H., Kalyanasundaram, A., Chaihirunkarn, C., Herbsleb, J.D.: How to hackathon: socio-technical tradeoffs in brief, intensive collocation. In: The 19th ACM Conference on Computer-Supported Cooperative Work & Social Computing, pp. 1118–1130. ACM, New York (2016)
20. Wyngaard, J., Lynch, H., Nabrzyski, J., Pope, A., Jha, S.: Hacking at the divide between polar science and HPC: using hackathons as training tools. In: 2017 IEEE International Parallel and Distributed Processing Symposium Workshops (IPDPSW), pp. 352–359. IEEE (2017)
21. Zhang, Z.-X., Hempel, P.S., Han, Y.-L., Tjosvold, D.: Transactive memory system links work team characteristics and performance. J. Appl. Psychol. **92**, 1722 (2017)

Methodological Concerns in (Big) Data Research

Modeling the Process of Information Encountering Based on the Analysis of Secondary Data

Tingting Jiang[1,2](✉) , Shiting Fu[1] , Qian Guo[1] ,
and Enmei Song[1]

[1] School of Information Management, Wuhan University, Wuhan, Hubei, China
tij@whu.edu.cn
[2] Center for Studies of Information Resources, Wuhan University,
Wuhan, Hubei, China

Abstract. The critical incident technique (CIT) has been applied extensively in the research on information encountering (IE), and abundant IE incident descriptions have been accumulated in the literature. This study used these descriptions as secondary data for the purpose of creating a general model of IE process. The grounded theory approach was employed to systematically analyze the 279 IE incident descriptions extracted from 14 IE studies published since 1995. 230 conceptual labels, 33 subcategories, and 9 categories were created during the data analysis process, which led to one core category, i.e. "IE process". A general IE process model was established as a result to demonstrate the relationships among the major components, including environments, foreground activities, stimuli, reactions, examination of information content, interaction with encountered information, valuable outcomes, and emotional states before/after encountering. This study not only enriches the understanding of IE as a universal information phenomenon, but also shows methodological significance by making use of secondary data to lower cost, enlarge sample size, and diversify data sources.

Keywords: Information encountering · Process model ·
Secondary data analysis · Grounded theory approach

1 Introduction

In contrast to active and purposive information seeking, information encountering is finding unexpected information passively [1, 2]. Despite the variety of terminologies for describing such phenomenon, "information encountering (IE)" is used consistently throughout this paper to avoid possible confusion. How IE occurs has been one of the most important themes of existing related studies, and a number of empirical models have been established to demonstrate the process of IE [2–7]. These models, however, are mostly constrained to specific contexts (e.g. information retrieval, social media, and work-related) or specific user groups (e.g. professionals, students, and researchers). They were built upon the qualitative data provided by individuals who had experienced IE. The absence of a general model that reveals the process of IE as a universal

© Springer Nature Switzerland AG 2019
N. G. Taylor et al. (Eds.): iConference 2019, LNCS 11420, pp. 41–49, 2019.
https://doi.org/10.1007/978-3-030-15742-5_4

information phenomenon, to a great extent, can be attributed to the shortage of time and budget, which would inhibit any single study from achieving larger data size or greater variety of data sources.

As a result, this study introduced secondary data analysis to the investigation of IE process. Secondary data analysis is a cost-efficient way to make full use of data that are already collected by previous studies to address potentially important new research questions [8]. A total of 279 IE incident descriptions were extracted as secondary data from 14 IE studies published since 1995. These studies were chosen because they relied on the combination of self-report methods and the critical incident technique (CIT) for data collection. The grounded theory approach was employed to systematically analyze the descriptions in QSR Nvivo 11, which gave birth to a general IE process model.

2 Literature Review

2.1 Existing IE Process Models

According to the earliest model by Erdelez [9], IE is embedded within a high-level process of information seeking. A typical IE episode contains five functional steps, i.e. noticing, stopping, examining, capturing, and returning. A further development is the integrated model of online IE which provides a global view of the three phases respectively accommodating, the pre-, mid-, and post-activities of IE. Specifically, IE may happen during online browsing, searching, or social interaction; noticing an information stimulus and examining the information content are both indispensable to acquiring interesting or useful information; and the encountered information may be explored further, used immediately, saved, and/or shared [6].

There are four components in Cunha [7] model of serendipity process: searching for a solution for problem A, precipitating conditions, a bisociation between previously unconnected pieces of information, and an unexpected solution to problem B. Mccay-Peet and Toms [4] modified this model by adding trigger as a necessary element for activating the bisociation as well as an unexpected solution to Task A. More recently, they consolidated several previous models into a new one that consists of trigger, connection, follow-up, valuable outcome, unexpected thread, and perception of serendipity [5].

In the perceptual model of serendipity, Lawley and Tompkins [10] indicated that the happening of an unplanned and unexpected event is preceded by a prepared mind and followed in sequence by recognizing the potential of the event, seizing the moment, amplifying the benefit of the event, and evaluating the effects. This model provided a basis for a later study that established an empirically-grounded model: the serendipity process begins with a mental connection; then there is a cyclic sub-process including forward-facing projections, connection exploiting, and backward-facing reflections; and finally, the whole experience is considered as serendipity given both the value of the outcome and the involvement of insight [3].

2.2   CIT-Based IE Research

According to Flanagan [11] definition, the critical incident technique (CIT) is "a set of procedures for collecting direct observations of human behavior in such a way as to facilitate their potential usefulness in solving practical problems and developing broad psychological principles". An incident refers to any observable human activity that allows for inferences and predictions to be made about the subject of the activity. The critical incident data can be collected through interviews, questionnaires, and written records, which engenders functional descriptions of people's experiences as reflected in the integration of time, places, persons, conditions, and activities [12]. Such qualitative data then enters an inductive analysis process in which incidents are sorted and grouped into categories for important themes and patterns to surface.

The CIT aims to elicit an accurate and in-depth description of the event from the participants and ensures that the incidents are meaningful to participants instead of researchers, which particularly attends to occasional or rare incidents such as IE. IE researchers tended to apply the CIT in interviews or diaries. It should be mentioned that some studies did not indicate explicitly that the CIT was applied, but their data collection processes did reflect the procedure of the CIT.

CIT-based interviews focus on individual events and attach great importance to the details of the interviewees' behavior and mind. Proper guide from the researcher side is often indispensable to effective face-to-face communication [3, 5]. For example, Makri and Blandford [3] invited 28 interdisciplinary researchers to participate in their semi-structured CIT-based interview. The participants firstly needed to talk about their understanding of IE; then an interview guide with several questions was used loosely to help them recall and recount in detail the events in their work and life that they deemed IE incidents; and lastly they were asked about their attitudes towards and opinions on IE. Each interview took about 50 min on average. The 28 participants contributed 46 IE incidents in total.

CIT-based diaries ask participants to record the events as soon as they happen. It is necessary to provide the participants with a recording tool, such as electronic questionnaires and mobile applications, to create diaries by themselves, sometimes following specific instructions or requirements [13, 14]. For example, Rahman and Wilson [15] recruited 14 active Facebook users to fill in a diary entry daily to report their interactions with a search engine. The participants needed to provide an open-ended description of any IE experience. Illustrated examples of their queries were presented to assist recollection. Then they were asked to explain why they clicked on or did not click on highlighted serendipitous results. The diary study lasted 11 days and collected 57 IE incidents.

3   Data Collection

Thanks to the extensive application of the CIT in IE research, abundant descriptions of IE incidents have been accumulated in the literature. Such qualitative data was collected and analyzed in the original studies as primary data to address various research questions. This study, instead, used these descriptions as secondary data for the purpose of creating a general model of IE process. The foremost advantage of reusing the data in published studies is the decreased investment in time, money, and manpower for data collection. Second, the validity and reliability of secondary data have been ensured during the publication of original studies. Last but not least, resorting to multiple data sources enabled this study to base the investigation on much larger and more widely distributed samples.

This study conducted several rounds of searches on Google Scholar which provides more complete coverage of IE studies, with a series of queries consisting of "critical incident technique" and "serendipity", "information encountering", "opportunistic/ incidental acquisition of information", "incidental information acquisition", or "accidental/opportunistic discovery of information", between July 8th and July 12th, 2018. The time span of the searches was set to "1995 ~ now". The returned publications were further screened according to three criteria: (1) IE-related research papers written in English; (2) the CIT adopted for data collection; and (3) original data provided. As a result, 14 papers were selected as data sources, including Erdelez [2], Makri and Blandford [3], Mccay-Peet and Toms [5], Jiang et al. [6], Sun et al. [13], Pontis et al. [14], Rahman and Wilson [15], Foster and Ford [16], Makri and Warwick [17], Dantonio [18], Yadamsuren and Erdelez [19], Miwa et al. [20], Yadamsuren and Heinström [21], Makri, Ravem, and Mckay [22]. They contained 279 IE incident descriptions collected for exploring the characteristics, process, factors, and value of IE. These descriptions were found in different sections of the above papers, such as data analysis, results, and appendix. A number of example descriptions are provided in the Appendix. Although the 14 studies were conducted at different times and/or in different contexts, the participants provided their IE experiences in similar ways, which made it possible to analyze the descriptions in a uniform framework.

4   Data Analysis and Results

The 279 IE incident descriptions were transcribed without any changes into text files, which were then imported into QSR Nvivo 11 for data analysis. Since this study intended to derive a new theoretical model from a large amount of qualitative data, the grounded theory approach was the most appropriate method. The idea was to extract important concepts from original data and integrate them into categories in a bottom-up fashion [23]. Specifically, the data analysis followed a three-step process: open coding for identifying categories and subcategories, axial coding for relating the categories to one another, and selective coding for determining a core category that represents the central phenomenon.

In the open coding step, the researchers read each IE incident description carefully and annotated the critical statements. Take the four statements in Table 1 for examples. Conceptual labels were created for them in the first place. Upon the completion of the annotating for all the descriptions, similar labels were merged into subcategories. The open coding of the 279 descriptions engendered 230 conceptual labels and 33 subcategories in total. The top 10 subcategories were "textual stimuli" (N = 79), "useful" (N = 69), "positive emotions after encountering" (N = 54), "information content" (N = 45), "online environments" (N = 32), "purposeful searching" (N = 32), "interesting" (N = 31), "negative emotions before encountering" (N = 30), "verbal stimuli" (N = 25), and "negative emotions after encountering" (N = 24).

Table 1. Open coding examples

Original statements	Conceptual labels	Subcategories
"…searching for the library catalogue for a specific book…"	Searching for specific books	Purposeful searching
"…an eBook with a similar title caught her eye…"	eBook-triggered	Textual stimuli
"…decided it was a better match for her information need than original target…"	Satisfying one's need	Useful
"…helping her to write her literature…"	Helpful to one's research	Satisfy their own needs

The axial coding involved the constant comparisons of the 33 subcategories deriving from the open coding. The researchers focused on discerning the particular aspect of the IE phenomenon reflected by each subcategory. If two subcategories reflected the same aspect, they belonged to the same category. For example, both "positive emotions after encountering" and "negative emotions after encountering" are pertinent to the emotional state one might have after IE occurred. It is therefore reasonable to relate them to each other and incorporate them into a higher-level category "emotional state after encountering". The 33 subcategories were incorporated into 9 main categories, including "stimuli" (N = 131), "foreground activities" (N = 102), "examination of information content" (N = 97), "emotional state after encountering" (N = 78), "valuable outcomes" (N = 56), "environments" (N = 55), "interaction with encountered information" (N = 55), "emotional state before encountering" (N = 53), and "reactions" (N = 22).

The final step of data analysis, i.e. selective coding, was devoted to detecting the connections among the 9 main categories. The researchers traced these categories back to the original statements and found that they were mentioned in specific sequence in the descriptions. For instances, "foreground activities" was often mentioned in the beginning, and "stimuli" preceding "examination of information content". Therefore, the 9 main categories were unified around a core category, i.e. "IE process". The resulting theory is shown in the general model of IE process (Fig. 1). It comprises the 9 components (categories) that each is enriched with all the possible situations (subcategories). The overall process can be further divided into three phases, i.e. pre-encountering, encountering, and post-encountering.

There are two major types of environments in which IE occurs, i.e. offline and online. The former refers to physical places such as homes, schools, libraries, stores, cafes, and movie theaters, etc., while the latter virtual places on the Internet such as social media, digital libraries, search engines, E-commerce platforms, Internet forums, and so on. These environments are built for different purposes which support users' foreground activities, including typical online information behavior like purposeful searching, purposeless scanning, exploratory searching, and browsing, as well as everyday routines (e.g. listening to music and shopping), social networking (e.g. chatting), and work and study (e.g. doing research and attending conferences). When engaged in the foreground activities, users may feel positive (e.g. happy and excited) or negative emotions (e.g. bored and frustrated).

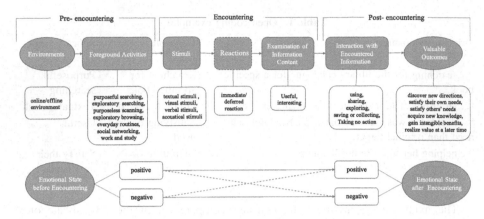

Fig. 1. The general IE process model

IE occurs when a stimulus in the environment that is irrelevant to the foreground activity attracts one's attention. Although written text is the most common type of stimuli, IE can be also triggered by visual (e.g. images, videos, and TV programs), verbal (e.g. conversation), or acoustical (e.g. music and radio) stimuli. After noticing the stimuli, users may make an immediate or a deferred reaction, depending on the urgency of their foreground activities, and examine the information content represented by the stimuli. The content may be determined as useful (i.e. solving an existing problem) or interesting (i.e. matching one's interests or leading one to new domains).

After encountering, users may interact with the encountered information in various ways, including saving or collecting, using, sharing, and exploring etc., or take no further action. It is common for users to adopt multiple ways for their interaction. The value of IE takes different forms to different users. The encountered information may help them discover new directions, satisfy their own needs, satisfy others' needs, acquire new knowledge, and gain intangible benefits (e.g. opportunities), or has its value realized at a later time. The IE experience may maintain or reverse users' emotional states or strengthen or weaken their initial emotions.

5 Discussion and Conclusions

A comprehensive understanding of how IE occurs is indispensable to taking advantage of encountering for more effective information acquisition. Despite the variety of existing IE process models, this study made a special effort to enrich this stream of research by contributing a general model that provides a panoramic view of this universal information phenomenon and combines the behavioral and affective components of IE processes. The significance of this study not only consists in the identification or clarification of some essential components of an IE process which have been ignored in previous models, but also the introduction of secondary data analysis to IE research.

5.1   The Value of the General IE Process Model

The model established in this study is characteristic of a multi-dimension (i.e. behavior and emotions) and multi-phase (i.e. pre-encountering, encountering, and post-encountering) demonstration of the process of IE. It provides important improvement for or addition to the previous understanding.

First and foremost, the general IE process model recognizes the roles of emotions. Previous models either failed to take the affective aspect into consideration [5, 9] or just deemed positive emotions after encountering a kind of valuable outcome [3, 25]. In contrast, the new model reflects the transition of emotional states as aroused by encountering. It is widely believed that emotions have an impact on humans' information seeking behavior [24]. As IE behavior is almost effortless, it is more likely to be emotionally charged [21]. Therefore, it is possible to facilitate or hinder IE by affecting users' emotions. The interaction between the behavioral and emotional dimensions during an IE process is a promising direction for future research.

Second, environments are treated as an independent component. They were usually mixed with foreground activities as the contexts of IE [5, 14]. It has been found that certain environmental characteristics are conducive to IE [26, 27]. Focused research on this component will generate more practical implications for designing IE-friendly environments.

Third, an inclusive categorization has been engendered for the stimuli that trigger IE. Although researchers have noticed the importance of stimuli [5, 6], there still lacks an in-depth understanding of the triggering mechanisms, let alone taking different types of stimuli into consideration. Besides, this model adds the possible reactions to the stimuli, suggesting the underlying selection between processing stimuli and proceeding with foreground activities.

Last but not least, the post-encountering phase is critical to realizing the value of IE. The phase was originally referred to as "capturing" [28]. The rise of online IE has greatly enriched the modes of dealing with encountered information. It is desirable that more powerful support is provided to encourage the immediate using of encountered information that can be easily forgotten.

5.2   Limitations

This study relied on secondary data analysis, which involves the reuse of the existing qualitative data from published studies, to explore the process of IE. The benefits of secondary data mainly consisted in the lower cost, larger samples, and diversified sources. However, this study was also limited to some extent by the data collection method. Since the 14 studies collected the IE incidents for their own research objectives, some of them failed to provide complete and detailed descriptions as desired in this study. There might lack certain important components in some descriptions, such as "environments" and "interaction with encountered information". The absent components might have not been collected or have been omitted in the papers. In addition, not every CIT-based IE study disclosed their original data. Therefore, research data sharing should be encouraged to facilitate reuse as long as it does not invade the participants' privacy. In addition, the researchers plan to test the validity of the general IE process model which was generated in an inductive process, with real users in case studies.

Acknowledgement. This research has been made possible through the financial support of the National Natural Science Foundation of China under Grants No. 71774125 and No. 71420107026.

Appendix

The 3 representative types of IE incident descriptions are provided as follows:

Complete Incident: "While booking train tickets from Brussels to London on the Eurostar website, P5 noticed a carousel advertising free entry to London museums with the purchase of a train ticket. As she likes to visit museums, P5 clicked for more information and discovered 'you can go to galleries that I didn't even know existed in London. So it was pretty interesting to know.' The page mentioned a few attractions she would like to visit, but she was not sure if she would have time; she made a mental note of these attractions and booked her train tickets. The information she had encountered had the potential to be useful but this potential had not yet been realized" [22, p. 283].

Partial Incident: "R14 stated that she visits the Yahoo! Site because 'they have just a ton of random links'. She said she likes just 'clicking on something' and finding 'interesting things' that she 'wasn't intending to read about'" [19, p. 5].

Psychological Activities: "R20 explains that her negative feelings about incidental exposure to online news often were triggered by her thinking that she mostly finds unpleasant or doubtful information on the Internet" [21, p. 486].

References

1. Case, D.O.: Looking for Information: A Survey of Research on Information Seeking, Needs, and Behavior. Emerald Group Publishing, Bingley (2012)
2. Erdelez, S.: Information Encountering: An Exploration Beyond Information Seeking. Syracuse University, New York (1995)
3. Makri, S., Blandford, A.: Coming across information serendipitously – Part 1. J. Doc. **68**(5), 684–705 (2012)
4. McCay-Peet, L., Toms, E.G.: The process of serendipity in knowledge work, pp. 377–382 (2010)
5. McCay-Peet, L., Toms, E.G.: Investigating serendipity: how it unfolds and what may influence it. J. Assoc. Inf. Sci. Technol. **66**(7), 1463–1476 (2015)
6. Jiang, T., Liu, F., Chi, Y.: Online information encountering: modeling the process and influencing factors. J. Doc. **71**(6), 1135–1157 (2015)

7. Cunha, M.P.E.: Serendipity: Why Some Organizations are Luckier than Others Universidade Nova de Lisboa, Lisbon (2005)
8. Heaton, J.: Secondary analysis of qualitative data: an overview. ANS Adv. Nurs. Sci. **33**(3), 33–45 (2008)
9. Erdelez, S.: Towards understanding information encountering on the web. In: Proceedings of the ASIS Annual Meeting, pp. 363–371 (2000)
10. Lawley, J., Tompkins, P.: Maximising serendipity: the art of recognising and fostering unexpected potential - a systemic approach to change. In: The Developing Group 2008 (2008)
11. Flanagan, J.C.: The critical incident technique. Psychol. Bull. **51**(4), 327–358 (1954)
12. Gremler, D.D.: The critical incident technique in service research. J. Serv. Res. **51**(1), 65–89 (2004)
13. Sun, X., Sharples, S., Makri, S.: A user-centred mobile diary study approach to understanding serendipity in information research. Inf. Res. **16**(3), 492 (2011)
14. Pontis, S., et al.: Academics' responses to encountered information: context matters. J. Assoc. Inf. Sci. Technol. **67**(8), 1883–1903 (2015)
15. Rahman, A., Wilson, M.L.: Exploring opportunities to facilitate serendipity in search. In: Proceedings of the 38th International ACM SIGIR Conference on Research and Development in Information Retrieval 2015, pp. 939–942. ACM, New York (2015)
16. Foster, A., Ford, N.: Serendipity and information seeking: an empirical study. J. Doc. **59**(3), 321–340 (2003)
17. Makri, S., Warwick, C.: Information for inspiration: understanding architects' information seeking and use behaviors to inform design. J. Assoc. Inf. Sci. Technol. **61**(9), 1745–1770 (2010)
18. Dantonio, L.: Reciprocity and investment: the role of social media in fostering serendipity University College London, London (2010)
19. Yadamsuren, B., Erdelez, S.: Incidental exposure to online news. Proc. Am. Soc. Inf. Sci. Technol. **47**(1), 1–8 (2010)
20. Miwa, M., Egusa, Y., Saito, H., Takaku, M., Terai, H., Kando, N.: A method to capture information encountering embedded in exploratory web searches. Inf. Res. **16**(3), 487 (2011)
21. Yadamsuren, B., Heinström, J.: Emotional reactions to incidental exposure to online news. Inf. Res. **16**(3), 486 (2011)
22. Makri, S., Ravem, M., Mckay, D.: After serendipity strikes: creating value from encountered information. Proc. Assoc. Inf. Sci. Technol. **54**(1), 279–288 (2017)
23. Corbin, J.M., Strauss, A.: Grounded theory research: procedures, canons, and evaluative criteria. Zeitschrift Für Soziologie **19**(6), 418–427 (1990)
24. Case, D.O., Andrews, J.E., Johnson, J.D., Allard, S.L.: Avoiding versus seeking: the relationship of information seeking to avoidance, blunting, coping, dissonance, and related concepts. J. Med. Libr. Assoc. **93**(3), 353–362 (2005)
25. Rubin, V.L., Burkell, J., Quan-Haase, A.: Facets of serendipity in everyday chance encounters: a grounded theory approach to blog analysis. Inf. Res. **16**(3), 488 (2011)
26. Martin, K., Quan-Haase, A.: "A process of controlled serendipity": an exploratory study of historians' and digital historians' experiences of serendipity in digital environments. Proc. Assoc. Inf. Sci. Technol. **54**(1), 289–297 (2017)
27. McCay-Peet, L., Toms, E.G., Kelloway, E.K.: Examination of relationships among serendipity, the environment, and individual differences. Inf. Process. Manage. **51**(4), 391–412 (2015)
28. Erdelez, S.: Investigation of information encountering in the controlled research environment. Inf. Process. Manage. **40**(6), 1013–1025 (2004)

Methodological Transparency and Big Data: A Critical Comparative Analysis of Institutionalization

Madelyn Rose Sanfilippo[1]([⊠]) (iD) and Chase McCoy[2] (iD)

[1] Center for Information Technology, Princeton University,
Princeton, NJ 08544, USA
madelyns@princeton.edu
[2] Department of Information and Library Science, Indiana University,
Bloomington, IN 47408, USA
chamccoy@indiana.edu

Abstract. Big data is increasingly employed in predictive social analyses, yet there are many visible instances of unreliable models or failure, raising questions about methodological validity in data driven approaches. From meta-analysis of methodological institutionalization across three scholarly disciplines, there is evidence that traditional statistical quantitative methods, which are more institutionalized and consistent, are important to develop, structure, and institutionalize data scientific approaches for new and large n quantitative methods, indicating that data driven research approaches may be limited in reliability, validity, generalizability, and interpretability. Results also indicate that inter-disciplinary collaborations describe methods in significantly greater detail on projects employing big data, with the effect that institutionalization makes data science approaches more transparent.

Keywords: Meta-analysis · Critical data studies · Ethics · Big data · Research design

1 Introduction

Data generation in the contemporary information society drives optimism about potential data analytic applications in business, consumer, and government decision-making [e.g. 1, 2], as well as for academic research [e.g. 3]. Increasingly, data is aggregated, shared, and processed in non-transparent ways [4]. Trends in big data emphasize prediction [2], which has long been a complex quantitative research ideal [e.g. 5–7].

Complexity is particularly apparent when examining predictions in elections and sports. Election outcome predictions based on data from the 2010 Senate races [e.g. 8] illustrate how models often depend on correlated but not causal traits, explaining why predictions are wrong. Predictions and reality diverge, as do approaches to prediction. For example, Google Flu Trends predicted more flu cases in 2013 than the CDC even though it was designed to predict CDC models [9]. Furthermore, some predictive analytics, as for the Philadelphia 76ers and the Houston Astros, is entirely unproductive,

© Springer Nature Switzerland AG 2019
N. G. Taylor et al. (Eds.): iConference 2019, LNCS 11420, pp. 50–62, 2019.
https://doi.org/10.1007/978-3-030-15742-5_5

despite significant investments [e.g. [10]. Predictions often vary due to interpretation strategies, as with diverse models with identical data for the 2016 presidential race [e.g. 11], and it is difficult to trust individual predictions. Furthermore, analysis of why a vast majority of predictive models projected that Hillary Clinton would win the 2016 presidential election with 99% confidence intervals, in contrast to actual outcomes, illustrates why big data cannot overcome the challenges of predicting low frequency events that are dependent on predictive variables with a high rate of change [12].

Examining these differences raises a number of questions about data and methods, including: Why do predictions differ if methods are equally valid; What values shape these methods; What structures distinct methods; How does institutionalization differentiate between data driven and statistical approaches; and What structures, values, and institutionalisms contribute to better predictions (reliability, validity)? We address these questions through a meta-analysis of data-driven and conventional statistical empirical studies from education, ILS, and political science, following an overview of critical data studies and background discussion of institutions in good research design.

2 Background

Quantitative social science has long provided tools to analyze macro-level problems, causation, and predictive models [6, 7]. These approaches are employed to test hypotheses and understandings, drawn from detailed qualitative analysis, at a larger scale [13]. Quantitative social science is most useful when it is reproducible; standards and transparent research methodologies allow for verification of scholarly work [14].

Statistical modeling requires: large, representative samples; iteration; known population boundaries; and null hypothesis testing [15, 16]. These traits historically supported methodological innovation [17], as with data analytics in drawing on large samples [18]. However, in magnifying particular useful qualities of statistical methods, many new approaches fail initially to recognize what design aspects are critical [17].

One of the greatest criticisms of quantitative social science is its strict dependence on established statistical methods, without innovation or development of new approaches [19]. While slow introduction of and resistance to alternative methods or change [20] is limiting, consensus is also advantageous, in that there is common understanding, consistency, and compatibility within research domains [19]. In contrast, data science, as a specific emerging quantitative social science, is extremely innovative [21].

Data driven approaches are increasingly attractive due to the volume, variety, and velocity of data capture and analysis [22–26]. Kitchin [25] identifies additional assumed characteristics: exhaustive, fine-grained resolution, relational, and flexible in use. Given these seven characteristics, Big Data is attractive based on its predictive potential [27], and its ability to "track human behavior with unprecedented fidelity and precision…than imperfect models of people behavior" [28], pp. 147–148]. Big Data utilize multiple analytical approaches (e.g. text, audio, video, and social media) and various techniques and methods (e.g. sentiment analysis, community detection, machine learning) to manage, model, analyze, and interpret the data [22].

Given the scope and breadth of Big Data, data science research often hybridizes techniques [24]. For example, content analysis of social media often makes use of text, audio, and video analytic methods [22]; furthermore, hybridization often produces complexity and limits shared institutions [25]. The lack of rules and norms undergirding Big Data research methods raises concerns related to methodological transparency [4, 29], analytical rigor [30], and inductive reasoning [3, 25, 26, 29].

Conventional experimental social science research generally provides detailed steps involved in formulating a hypothesis, identifying a population frame, designing a sampling technique [23], and controlling confounding factors [29]. However, precise methodologies are "black-boxed" in most data science manuscripts [4]. Data science is often inductive [25, 26, 29] and approaches often allow the data to speak for themselves [31], which is a contentious notion [29]. There is also debate over whether Big Data research is a new epistemological approach, rather than a new scientific methodology [26]. Critics of inductive Big Data research argue that domain knowledge is often absent from the theoretical and methodological choices grounding the research [3, 31–33], which can cause sampling bias, provenance conflicts, and increased errors [34].

Data science research departs from the traditional scientific method in eschewing hypothesis testing and dismissing population-based statistics. Arguments that data volume can overcome representation issues are unproven. The convention of allowing data to speak for itself clear delineates between inductive data science approaches and deductive or abductive approaches. Furthermore, data scientists often lack domain knowledge, whereas statistical approaches are applied in disciplinary contexts. The results have implications for research reliability and validity, given that conceptual knowledge improves accuracy, utility, and fit of measures and variables [35–37].

These differences and concerns over (lack of) conventions in data science can be explained relatively in terms of institutionalization. Institutions can be understood as the strategies, rules, and norms structuring actions through a syntax of attributes, deontics, aims, conditions, and consequences [38]. In the context of institutions, deontics refer to words signaling deontic modality, as linguistic expression of how a particular aim ought to be done according to norms; these words indicate social pressures or expectations like "must," "should," or "cannot." While strategies consist of attributes, aims, and conditions, norms and rules also include deontics, and rules additionally have consequences [38]. Increasing institutionalization includes modal operators and speaks to consequences to clarify consensus and why conventions are in place. Institutions are created and enforced to ensure all play by the same rules and safeguard community interests. Institutionalization often occurs over time, evolving with social change, yet reflecting cultural origins. In academia, institutions ensure that shared language, theory, and methods unify disciplines and assure validity and reliability of scholarship.

Validity and reliability, in keeping with the concerns of Borgman [3] and Boyd and Crawford [31], as discussed with respect to research design and critical data studies, are supported by sound research design and consistent structure. These concepts intrinsically have mutually shared definitions and can be assessed. Validity is most simply understood as the extent to which research assesses what it is supposed to [36]. Reliability, in contrast, is the extent to which results are consistent within a context [35].

As a result of the differences between statistical and Big Data approaches to research design, it is logical that there is criticism about the validity, reliability, etc. of new data analytic approaches. It is also likely that institutionalization is the differentiating factor. This paper will present a meta-analysis to explore whether: (1) statistical approaches are more institutionalized and (2) academic disciplines that are traditionally more quantitative provide more detail about methodological institutions. It is logical to assume that approaches that are more established will be supported by greater structure and that those who are more familiar with an approach will provide more insight into how and why it is appropriate, as well as when to apply it, within the confines of accepted institutions.

3 Methods

Meta-analysis was employed to comparatively assess differences between data driven approaches and statistical analysis. Data, including the 50 most cited papers from 2010 to 2018 by discipline for both research designs, was collected from Web of Science. This sample was also limited to empirical papers and those that specifically outlined methodological design. The sample included data driven and statistical approaches within the domains of "government and law", "education educational assessment", and "information science library science". These domains were selected both for author expertise and because they provided definable differences, beyond those associated with culture. While political science has a strong quantitative tradition, education has historically been dominated by qualitative scholarship. ILS has historically been interdisciplinary, in part, because it is a smaller academic community and has incorporated robust theories from many other domains. Most cited papers, as opposed to a random sample or papers from top journals, allows for consideration of socially validated works [39].

Specific keyword sets, drawn from exemplar papers, were employed to derive this sample from Web of Science. For data driven approaches, keywords included: Big data, Data Science, and Analytics. While these keywords imply different data driven approaches, current research literature does not often clearly differentiate between big data and data science in empirical applications, making it necessary to explore data driven approaches as a whole. For statistical approaches, keywords included: Bayesian, Statistic, and Factor Analysis. Results were also limited to domain specific journals, including applied titles but excluding titles from other related domains. For example, medical informatics titles were excluded, but information science special issues on health information seeking and human computer interaction with respect to electronic medical records were included. It is of note that there were significantly more papers matching these keys in political science, for data-driven approaches, though the ILS results were still larger than education, while for conventional statistical designs, political science and education had many more results than ILS. Delimiting samples to the 50 most cited works was thus also a useful frame to ensure consistent sample size.

Methods and research design were identified in each paper, including all institutionalisms structuring design and analysis. Specific attention was paid to reliability, validity, and reproducibility of results. Codes were developed from institutional theory [38], literature on research design [e.g. 36], and a grounded approach differentiating specific interests and values within approaches considered. Codes were applied to both papers as entities and sections of text, based on the institutional grammar codebook presented in Table 1. Values were coded using a grounded approach and aspects of research design were coded with respect to all relevant aims, conditions, and consequence statements.

Table 1. Codebook applied from Crawford and Ostrom [38]

Institution			Component	Definition
Rules	Norms	Strategies	Attributes	To whom does this apply?
				Individual, organizational variables
				Stage or role in research
			Aims	Specific action
			Conditions	When, where, how aims apply
			Deontics	Modal operators
				Examples: permitted, obliged, forbidden
			Consequences	Sanction for non-compliance

Furthermore, co-coding of "information science library science" (ILS) allowed for the calculation of inter-rater reliability, while literature on political development and educational and institutional assessment were coded independently by domain expertise. Inter-rater agreement regarding attributes, aims, conditions, deontics, and consequences, defined in Table 1, ranged from 91.4% to 98.6% across categories with Cohen's Kappa coefficients from 0.826 to 0.948, reflecting excellent agreement.

Examples based on the research design and methods structuring this paper can illustrate how to apply the coding scheme. Scholarly domain selection was structured by a strategy: researchers select domains with different attributes and in which they have expertise when developing the sampling frame. There is no modal pressure to do this or consequence, however, it was based on implicit logic that manual coding requires familiarity with the literature. An example of a norm lies in selecting highly cited articles to connote consensus of value in the sample, as scholarly communication literature supports citations as a measure of research value [e.g. 39]. This is what *should* be done. Finally, an example of a rule followed, related to reliability, can be identified within calculation of inter-rater reliability; it is necessary to co-code a section of the sample in order to assess agreement or else it will be impossible to interpret across the entire sample given the possibility of inconsistent application.

4   Discussion of Results

4.1   What Structures Distinct Bodies of Methods?

Rules, norms, and strategies were present across both Big Data and statistical approaches. Examples of each institutional type from the co-coded ILS literature can be provided. For example, in Feng et al.'s [40] "A Bayesian Feature Selection Paradigm for Text Classification", strategies are clearly evident within "The first term on the right-hand side can be estimated using the document ratio of the corresponding category in the training set, while the second term is similar to, but contains only the relevant feature part." With "researchers" as attributes and "using the document ratio category" as conditions, aims can be found in estimating both precision and recall.

An example of a norm can be seen in Vakkari and Serola's [41] "Perceived Outcomes of Public Libraries":

> By implication, the sample was biased toward more active library users. The greater response rate of those interested in the phenomenon observed is a common feature in surveys. The bias in the sample implied that the effect of both gender and educational level would need to be controlled in the results.

The implied norm is that researchers *should* control for sample bias when intervening variables are present. Modal language indicates that the community expects this action.

A common rule, across domains, related to IRB approval of research. This rule was more prevalent within statistical approaches, but some data science research designs that acknowledged this constraint, such as in Herrera's [42] "Google Scholar Users and User Behaviors". Within "These research methods were reviewed and approved by the university's Institutional Review Board", it is implicit that human subjects research designs much be reviewed by the IRB, including studies employing user data. Some papers clearly articulated consequences, while others merely implied consequences of non-compliance. Rules addressing validity, reliability, and statistical significance will be discussed with respect to other research questions.

4.2   How Does Institutionalization Differentiate Between Data Driven and Statistical Approaches?

Table 2 specifically illustrates that while there are on average more than twice as many strategies in data science as in statistical approaches, the reverse is true of norms. Furthermore, there are more than four times the number of rules in statistical papers than in data science papers. Overall, while statistically driven research is more institutionalized, data science strategies are more diverse, indicating more experimentation in design and methodology. This is promising for innovation, but concerning for reproducibility, as the level of detail and underlying logic for design and methods are unclear.

Among statistical analyses, regardless of domain, norms were most prevalent, followed by rules, then strategies. This implies social consensus, thereby increasing structure from strategies to norms and in some cases to rules, as consequences are imposed when there is non-compliance with norms. Deontic language and potential

Table 2. Mean institutional distributions by domain

Type	Domain	Strategies	Norms	Rules	Average institutions
Data science		7.49	3.09	0.93	11.50
	Education (n = 50)	7.60	3.40	1.02	12.02
	ILS (n = 50)	7.44	2.88	0.62	10.94
	Political science (n = 50)	7.42	2.98	1.14	11.54
Statistics		3.06	7.73	4.52	15.31
	Education (n = 50)	2.26	6.78	3.76	12.80
	ILS (n = 50)	3.20	6.32	3.72	13.24
	Political science (n = 50)	3.72	10.08	6.08	19.88

consequences were often similar across articles and domains. Rules ensured research concerns, such as protecting validity and reliability, and ethical concerns, including about guaranteeing participant privacy. Discussion of consequences often addressed community standards, as well as IRB expectations, more so than individual preferences or understanding of the consequences. It is notable that political science was more heavily institutionalized than either ILS or education, with greater magnitude in each institutional category.

Institutionalization of data science methods across domains is relatively similar on average, though was much less structured than for traditional statistical approaches. Strategies were the most common, followed by norms, and then rules. As is shown in Table 2, each domain displays a relatively similar number of strategies, with an average of 7.60 for education, 7.44 for ILS, and 7.42 for political science. Strategies often detailed data capture methods and construction of analytic technologies. There are fewer norms on average as compared to strategies. Although strategies and norms can be differentiated by deontic language, modal operators were often implicit. Norms can still be identified by references to established domain specific literature. However, methodological references predominately cited authors' previous works or specific systems or algorithms modified or adopted for the paper. ILS literature has the fewest rules; 26 of 50 articles do not contain a single rule, compared with 22 articles from the education literature and 14 political science articles. It is also notable that many of these rules were mentioned as not being applicable, given the conditions of their research.

Results indicate that there is relative consensus about appropriate ways to conduct statistical research, with acceptable alternate strategies, and transparency in research design. There is common understanding of potential consequences. Many rules read so similarly they could be exchanged between papers, though little context was given about rules, raising questions about scholarly concerns versus mere compliance. In contrast, there is less consensus surrounding data science approaches. Strategies were numerous, yet across domains, methods sections contained many functions that were left un-coded by this analysis. Functions contained an attribute and an aim, but did not contain a condition for when, where, and how to apply. These data science functions are ambiguous and without structure; they could be interpreted in myriad of ways, thus not supporting reproducibility. Moreover, functions were most prevalent in those papers that designed and developed new technologies or algorithms.

4.3   Why Do Predictions Differ if Methods Are Equally Valid? What Values Shape These Methods?

Disciplinary differences, applying both approaches, appear to differentiate between types of methods and institutionalization around them. Deontic modality is most explicit in statistical political science. This likely reflects that scholars are better trained in statistical methods and expect colleagues to be more knowledgeable about quantitative methods than in fields like ILS, which is more often qualitative [e.g. 43, 44]. The quantitative tradition of political science was also evident in the data driven sample, where there were more rules and fewer articles without rules on average as compared to the other domains. Much of the educational literature detailed the development of novel technologies for capturing and analyzing data generated from the learning environment, thus methods described many un-codable functions. This is unsurprising given our educational sample comes from the relatively new field of learning analytics.

Results suggest why predictions vary so widely: methods are inconsistent. This is a consequence of a lack of consensus on strategies and non-conditional functions. The latter is more problematic, because functions do not detail the conditions of application to support reproducibility. While disclosing functions, rather than strategies, may make sense in a competitive corporate environment [45], it is problematic for reliability and trustworthiness of results, as well as reproducibility [3, 31]. Results also indicate why this is a challenging question to address in this or any individual study. While it is perfectly valid to approach the same research question using different methods, not all methods are equally valid and differences in predictions are more likely to result from research designs, more prevalent among data-driven papers sampled in this study, that ignore or do not adequately institutionalize research design conventions.

Different implicit values underlie disciplinary training, methods, and experiences that may differentiate patterns of institutionalization. While it is difficult to specify what values shape methods, examples provide some insight. Clear consequences for non-compliance stem from the logical, predictable nature of these methods and their communities of origin. Sjoberg and Nett wrote "that science is a social enterprise and that research procedures are social norms" [46, pp. 213–214], implying social production of research practices. Yet discussion of consequences often emphasized meeting exogenous standards, rather than personal values (e.g. precision or accuracy), and was often brief. For example, Seba, Rowley, and Lambert [47, p. 376] explained:

> SEM was used to generate both the measurement model and the structural model. The measurement model is estimated using confirmatory factor analysis (CFA) to test whether the constructs possess sufficient validation and reliability. The structural model is used to investigate the strength and direction of the relationship between the theoretical constructs.

This example from the ILS sample illustrates that values of validity and reliability underlie institutionalization, but reflect concerns about compliance rather than explaining why those are important concerns. Since big data is relatively new to empirical social science, it is unsurprising that there are uncertain values and fewer methodological institutions as compared with statistical approaches. The dearth of norms and rules on research design, along with the prevalence of hybrid techniques and a focus on the design of "novel" algorithmic approaches and computational methods, significantly shape methodological decisions and transparency in reporting methods [e.g. 29].

In an example from the education sample, student achievement was predicted by monitoring and capturing student learning activities in a virtual learning environment [48]. This study blended new technological development—a student monitoring tool—with statistical analysis of learning outcomes. There were more strategies and fewer norms than average for education studies. Due to the study's foregrounding of the technical, absent are guiding theories on student learning in virtual spaces. This study was representative of our data science sample; it lacked theoretical guidance, methodological hybridity, and focused on the technical.

Differences in approaches were evident with respect to publication domain and authors' departmental affiliations. Table 3 illustrates that papers with interdisciplinary authorship for data science describe more total methodological institutions and combinations with more human subject research experience discuss more rules, on average.

Table 3. Mean institutional distributions by author affiliation discipline

Type	Journal domain/author discipline	Strategies	Norms	Rules	Average Institutions
Data science		7.49	3.09	0.93	11.5
	Education/Education (n = 19)	7.37	2.84	0.84	11.05
	Education/Interdisciplinary (n = 31)	7.74	3.74	1.13	12.61
	Political Science/Political Science (n = 29)	6.83	2.9	1.07	10.79
	Political Science/Interdisciplinary (n = 21)	8.24	3.1	1.24	12.57
	ILS/ILS (n = 22)	6.18	2.14	0.23	8.55
	ILS/Interdisciplinary (n = 28)	8.43	3.46	0.93	12.82
Statistics		3.06	7.73	4.52	15.31
	Education/Education (n = 27)	2.52	6.56	3.7	12.78
	Education/Interdisciplinary (n = 23)	1.96	7.04	3.83	12.78
	Political Science/Political Science (n = 26)	3.92	10.04	6	19.96
	Political Science/Interdisciplinary (n = 24)	3.5	10.13	6.17	19.79
	ILS/ILS (n = 16)	2.81	5.5	3.81	12.13
	ILS/Interdisciplinary (n = 34)	3.38	6.71	3.68	13.76

4.4   What Structures, Values, and Institutionalisms Contribute to Better Predictions (Reliability, Validity)?

Better predictions, in terms of accuracy, validity, reliability, and reproducibility, likely result from more structure, given that rules most often address these concerns. Rules common to the statistics literature address validity, reliability, and the statistical significance of the research results. Inanc and Tuncer provide a significance rule:

> caution must be practiced before reaching to any conclusions when comparing subsets (i.e., inbred vs. noninbred) to one another, especially should one of these not contain enough number of observations to yield a statistically meaningful average" [49, p. 892].

The consequence component refers to insignificance given few observations. Specific to reliability, employment of inter-rater reliability tests is common to satisfy rules, yet few norms addressed reliability. Manatschal and Stadlemann-Stefan [50, p. 682] provide a convention for approximating reliability:

> For an easy interpretation of the Bayesian estimation results, the mean and the standard deviation of the posterior distribution are presented, which can be interpreted like in a standard regression situation: the mean is the average effect of an independent variable on the outcome variable and the standard deviation gives a sense of the statistical reliability of this estimate.

Formal concept analysis often assessed operationalized conceptual validity, embedded in rules about predictive interpretations.

However, rules and norms about validity and reliability were largely absent in data science articles. Given that more computer scientists than social scientists conduct applied data research, limiting domain appropriate interpretation [3, 33], interdisciplinary collaboration is a possible means to further develop data rules and norms [e.g. 31, 32].

5   Conclusion

Given the importance of reproducibility, which requires transparency and consistent application of methods, it is easy to understand why data driven social science and prediction have erratic outcomes. Designs with low institutionalization produce unexpected outcomes. With only superficial description of methods, it is dangerous to develop predictions, because science depends on reproducibility; the scientific method requires replication and clear methods. Data science will likely institutionalize further with time, yet at present, concerns are legitimate. Data driven methods also may yield conclusions that are spurious, tautological, or random, due to correlation rather than causation, as has been illustrated in other critical treatments [22]. While misinterpretation of correlation as causation is not unique to data science or big data, it has long been dealt with by robust methodological training and institutionalization. This is not to say that innovative strategies cannot be reproducible; they simply must be clearly defined. Norms and rules are not required, but reproducible strategies may become norms.

Furthermore, there are two major implications from this work: (1) context specificity shapes information practices and (2) institutionalization strengthens research quality. Specific disciplinary contexts have unique expectations about methodology, research design, data, and norms of research; while this research does not address how these are shaped in context, it shows that institutional distributions differ by publication discipline and discipline impacts institutions and details. Results also indicate that more structured institutions and increased overall structure better address validity, reliability, and reproducibility, consistent with past research addressing what produces and mitigates unexpected consequences associated with technology, including data analytics.

Future research ought to explore how specific institutions relate to particular research values and ethical issues, such as transparency. Privacy institutionalization around the use of personal data in research will be scrutinized in forthcoming work. It is also important to address specific institutions and institutional arrangements unique to disciplines and what shapes values and institutions within communities. Comparison of data driven approaches, contrasting Big Data and Data Science, may also be fruitful.

References

1. Chen, H., Chiang, R.H., Storey, V.C.: Business intelligence and analytics: from big data to big impact. MIS Q. **36**(4), 1165–1188 (2012)
2. Mayer-Schönberger, V., Cukier, K.: Big Data: A Revolution that will Transform How We Live, Work, and Think. Houghton Mifflin Harcourt, Boston (2013)
3. Borgman, C.L.: Big Data, Little Data, no Data: Scholarship in the Networked World. MIT Press, Cambridge (2015)
4. Driscoll, K., Walker, S.: Big data, big questions| working within a black box: transparency in the collection and production of big Twitter data. Int. J. Commun. **8**, 20 (2014)
5. Jick, T.D.: Mixing qualitative and quantitative methods: triangulation in action. Adm. Sci. Q. **24**(4), 602–611 (1979)
6. Thompson, B.: What future quantitative social science research could look like: confidence intervals for effect sizes. Educ. Res. **31**(3), 25–32 (2002)
7. Weidlich, W.: Quantitative social science. Phys. Scr. **35**(3), 380 (1987)
8. Livne, A., Simmons, M.P., Adar, E., Adamic, L.A.: The party is over here: structure and content in the 2010 election. In: ICWSM 2011, pp. 17–21 (2011)
9. Lazer, D., Kennedy, R., King, G., Vespignani, A.: The parable of Google flu: traps in big data analysis. Science **343**(6176), 1203–1205 (2014)
10. Wagner, K.: "Sports Analytics" is bullshit now. Deadspin (2015). http://deadspin.com/sports-analytics-is-bullshit-now-1688293396
11. Enten, H.: Live polls and online polls tell different stories about the election. FiveThirtyEight (2016). http://fivethirtyeight.com/features/live-polls-and-online-polls-tell-different-stories-about-the-election/
12. Bruer, T.: US elections: How could predictions be so wrong? J. Mark. Anal. **4**(4), 125–134 (2016)
13. Stevens, J.P.: Applied Multivariate Statistics for the Social Sciences. Routledge, New York (2012)
14. Goodman, S.N., Fanelli, D., Ioannidis, J.P.: What does research reproducibility mean? Sci. Transl. Med. **8**(341), 1–6 (2016)
15. Agresti, A., Finlay, B.: Statistical Methods for the Social Sciences. Dellen Publishers, CA (2009)
16. Runyon, R.P., Coleman, K.A., Pittenger, D.J.: Fundamentals of Behavioral Statistics. McGraw-Hill, New York (2000)

17. Miles, M.B., Huberman, A.M.: Qualitative Data Analysis: A Sourcebook of New Methods. Sage, California (1984)
18. Aggarwal, C.C., Philip, S.Y.: A survey of uncertain data algorithms and applications. IEEE Trans. Knowl. Data Eng. **21**(5), 609–623 (2009)
19. Sayer, A.: Method in Social Science: Revised 2nd edn. Routledge, London (2010)
20. Watson, G.: Resistance to change. In: Bennis, W., Benne, K., Chin, R., (eds.) Washington (1967)
21. LaValle, S., Lesser, E., Shockley, R., Hopkins, M.S., Kruschwitz, N.: Big data, analytics and the path from insights to value. MIT Sloan Manage. Rev. **52**(2), 21 (2011)
22. Gandomi, A., Haider, M.: Beyond the hype: Big data concepts, methods, and analytics. Int. J. Inf. Manage. **35**(2), 137–144 (2015)
23. Japec, L., et al.: Big data in survey research AAPOR task force report. Public Opin. Q. **79**(4), 839–880 (2015)
24. Kaisler, S., Armour, F., Espinosa, J.A., Money, W.: Big data: issues and challenges moving forward. In: 2013 46th Hawaii International Conference on System Sciences (HICSS), pp. 995–1004. IEEE (2013)
25. Kitchin, R.: The Data Revolution: Big Data, Open Data, Data Infrastructures and their Consequences. Sage Publications, London (2014)
26. Kitchin, R.: Big Data, new epistemologies and paradigm shifts. Big Data Soc. **1**(1), 1–12 (2014)
27. Ekbia, H., et al.: Big data, bigger dilemmas: a critical review. J. Assoc. Inform. Sci. Technol. **66**(8), 1523–1545 (2015)
28. González-Bailón, S.: Social science in the era of big data. Policy Internet **5**(2), 147–160 (2013)
29. Frické, M.: Big data and its epistemology. J. Assoc. Inform. Sci. Technol. **66**(4), 651–661 (2015)
30. Sivarajah, U., Kamal, M.M., Irani, Z., Weerakkody, V.: Critical analysis of Big Data challenges and analytical methods. J. Bus. Res. **70**, 263–286 (2017)
31. Boyd, D., Crawford, K.: Critical questions for big data: Provocations for a cultural, technological, and scholarly phenomenon. Inform. Commun. Soc. **15**(5), 662–679 (2012)
32. Manovich, L.: Trending: the promises and the challenges of big social data. Debates Digital Humanit. **2**, 460–475 (2011)
33. Ruppert, E.: Doing the Transparent State: open government data as performance indicators. In: Mugler, J., Park, S.-J. (eds.) A World of Indicators: The Production of Knowledge and Justice in an Interconnected World, pp. 51–78. Cambridge University Press, Cambridge (2013)
34. McNeely, C.L., Hahm, J.O.: The big (data) bang: policy, prospects, and challenges. Rev. Policy Res. **31**(4), 304–310 (2014)
35. Carmines, E.G., Zeller, R.A.: Reliability and Validity Assessment, vol. 17. Sage Publications, Thousand Oaks (1979)
36. Furr, R.M., Bacharach, V.R.: Psychometrics: An Introduction. Sage, Thousand Oaks (2013)
37. Johnson, J.B., Reynolds, H.T., Mycoff, J.D.: Political Science Research Methods. CQ Press, Washington, D.C (2015)
38. Crawford, S.E., Ostrom, E.: A grammar of institutions. Am. Polit. Sci. Rev. **89**(03), 582–600 (1995)
39. Borgman, C.L.: Scholarly communication and bibliometrics (1990)
40. Feng, G., Guo, J., Jing, B.Y., Hao, L.: A Bayesian feature selection paradigm for text classification. Inf. Process. Manage. **48**(2), 283–302 (2012)
41. Vakkari, P., Serola, S.: Perceived outcomes of public libraries. Libr. Inform. Sci. Res. **34**(1), 37–44 (2012)

42. Herrera, G.: Google Scholar users and user behaviors: An exploratory study. College & Research Libraries **72**(4), 316–330 (2011)
43. Egghe, L., Rousseau, R.: Introduction to informetrics: Quantitative methods in library, documentation and information science (1990)
44. Fidel, R.: Are we there yet?: Mixed methods research in library and information science. Libr. Inform. Sci. Res. **30**(4), 265–272 (2008)
45. Richards, N.M., King, J.H.: Three paradoxes of big data. Stanford Law Review, September 2013
46. Sjoberg, G., Nett, R.: A methodology for social research, pp. 213–214. Harper & Row, New York (1968)
47. Seba, I., Rowley, J., Lambert, S.: Factors affecting attitudes and intentions towards knowledge sharing in the Dubai Police Force. Int. J. Inf. Manage. **32**(4), 372–380 (2012)
48. Romero-Zaldivar, V.A., Pardo, A., Burgos, D., Kloos, C.D.: Monitoring student progress using virtual appliances: a case study. Comput. Educ. **58**(4), 1058–1067 (2012)
49. Inanc, O., Tuncer, O.: The effect of academic inbreeding on scientific effectiveness. Scientometrics **88**(3), 885–898 (2011)
50. Manatschal, A., Stadelmann-Steffen, I.: Cantonal variations of integration policy and their impact on immigrant educational inequality. Comp. Eur. Politics **11**(5), 671–695 (2013)

Spanning the Boundaries of Data Visualization Work: An Exploration of Functional Affordances and Disciplinary Values

Jaime Snyder[1]([envelope]) and Katie Shilton[2]

[1] University of Washington, Seattle, WA 98195, USA
jas1208@uw.edu
[2] University of Maryland, College Park, MD 20742, USA
kshilton@umd.edu

Abstract. Creating data visualizations requires diverse skills including computer programming, statistics, and graphic design. Visualization practitioners, often formally trained in one but not all of these areas, increasingly face the challenge of reconciling, integrating and prioritizing competing disciplinary values, norms and priorities. To inform multidisciplinary visualization pedagogy, we analyze the negotiation of values in the rhetoric and affordances of two common tools for creating visual representations of data: R and Adobe Illustrator. Features of, and discourse around, these standard visualization tools illustrate both a convergence of values and priorities (clear, attractive, and communicative data-driven graphics) side-by-side with a retention of rhetorical divisions between disciplinary communities (statistical analysis in contrast to creative expression). We discuss implications for data-driven work and data science curricula within the current environment where data visualization *practice* is converging while values in *rhetoric* remain divided.

Keywords: Data visualization · Data science practice · Digital tool analysis · Materiality · Values

1 Introduction

Creating visualizations to help humans understand complex data requires skills ranging from coding to statistics to graphic design. However, data visualization has traditionally drawn sharp disciplinary and professional boundaries between graphic and information *design* practitioners, typically trained in the arts and visual communication, and information *visualization* researchers, typically trained in computer and data science [1]. As Kosara points out,

> "Two cultures exist in visualization: very technical, analysis-oriented work in one, and artistic pieces on the other hand. ... pragmatic visualization is mostly practiced by people in computer science with no background in art or design. A student once put it aptly: 'Computer graphics is mostly computers, but little graphics.' At the same time, artists and designers often work on visualizations without much knowledge of the technical work being done in computer science" [2, p. 631].

© Springer Nature Switzerland AG 2019
N. G. Taylor et al. (Eds.): iConference 2019, LNCS 11420, pp. 63–75, 2019.
https://doi.org/10.1007/978-3-030-15742-5_6

However, online tutorials and commentaries focused on data visualization suggest that, in practice, the boundaries of what are considered "core" visualization skills and tools are blurry [e.g., 3–6]. Further, industry and academic conferences such as OpenVis [7] and IEEE Vis [8] attract graphic artists and designers as well as computer scientists.

Attempts to delineate the skills, and practices of data visualization are especially complicated in the classroom. University curricula often echo siloed disciplinary boundaries, with departmental prerequisites, class size limits, and advising resources conspiring to keep graphics students in Departments of Art and Design and programming students in Departments of Computer Science. Because iSchools attract students with interests in both technical and design areas, our programs are in a position to lead more comprehensive data visualization training programs [9].

In order to probe implications for boundary-spanning visualization education, we performed an initial high-level analysis of two data visualization tools with strong connections to different communities of practice: R and Adobe Illustrator. We intentionally chose to begin with an analysis of tools for two reasons. First, we will be engaging directly with visualization designers in future work; there is such diversity among this community of practitioners that we felt it was advantageous to begin with a relatively straightforward analysis of functionality and technical specifications of common tools in order to inform decisions about how best to pursue more user-focused observations and interviews. Second, decisions regarding which software applications will be used in a course are often a strong influence on how the practice of data visualization will be taught. We wanted to understand these impacts at a high level before delving into other pedagogical influences in future work.

There are a host of tools currently available to generate data visualizations. Platforms focused on intelligence and other forms of business analytics, such as Power BI and Tableau, provide sophisticated dashboards for users to explore and annotate large datasets. These enterprise-level tools are typically web-based, carry expensive licensing agreements, and are often integrated in established work flows in large organizations. On the other end of the spectrum are open source tools, such as the very popular D3.js web-based platform, with ever-expanding sets of libraries, very active online user groups, and steep learning curves.

According to a series of recent surveys, both R and Adobe Illustrator are among the top five data visualization software applications used by professionals [10, 11]. R is an open source programming language and software environment designed to support complex computational statistics [12]. Adobe Illustrator was created as a tool for designers and artists to harness emerging digital frameworks to make precise graphic assets. These tools were originally designed to serve different communities, but our analysis shows that their functionality is moving towards becoming more similar, adapting to support a broadening range of practices associated with data visualization. Our analysis provides (1) examples of what it looks like when data practices *converge* from multiple work traditions and community values, and (2) implications for the boundary spanning curricular work and research that characterizes many data science programs fostered by iSchools.

2 Background: The Data Visualization Process

Phrases like "data visualization," "information visualization," and "information design" are often used interchangeably. In this paper, we use *data visualization* to refer to the process of conceptualizing, designing, and building visual representations of data. Data visualization is practiced by a wide range of people, from data scientists to graphic designers, and generates artifacts as diverse as information graphics, interactive maps, and dynamic charts. In this sense, data visualization provides an umbrella term for more specialized disciplines. For example, *information visualization*, in its most precise definition, refers to the creation of interactive systems for representing abstract data (i.e., data that has no inherent spatial relations, unlike GIS or data derived from observations of physical phenomena) [13]. Information visualization systems are often built by computer scientists, data scientists and statisticians striving for objective and comprehensive representations of data for the purpose of analysis [14]. Information visualization training is often focused on quantitative methods and algorithms. The field's orientation to visual perception is typically cognitive rather than aesthetic. *Information design*, on the other hand, is frequently used to describe the work of graphic designers, information architects, and user experience specialists who create information-driven visual artifacts that help people communicate and explain things [15]. Information design artifacts include wayfinding signs, user interfaces for web and mobile applications, and information graphics. Practitioners often have formal training in visual communication and graphic design, and they tend to prioritize clarity of presentation and aesthetics. Technology skills in this community are more frequently self-taught [16]. In spite of similar sounding names, the differences between these approaches to data visualization are important. These groupings are the basis for professional and philosophical identities, and they reflect values differences that we discuss in more depth below.

Despite these distinctions, a generalized data visualization design process is shared by those who create visual representations of data. Ben Fry [17], one of the creators of Processing, a computer programming environment created for artists and designers which has become a popular tool for data art projects, outlines seven stages of the data visualization process [17, p. 5]:

- *Acquire*: Obtain data
- *Parse*: Structure data's meaning
- *Filter*: Remove all but core data
- *Mine*: Find patterns

- *Represent*: Choose a visual model
- *Refine*: Improve representation
- *Interact*: Add methods for manipulating or interacting with data

These steps echo other descriptions of the visualization process [cf.: 13, 14, 18] and provide a vocabulary to analyze R and Illustrator: tools designed to serve information visualization and information design communities, respectively. The values associated with these tools, and functionality built to support those values, reflect the concerns and practices of the people who design and use them. The following section describes how we decomposed these tools to interpret their supported values and practices.

3 Method

In order to better understand connections among technology, practices, and values, software applications and tools can be decomposed to identify functional elements and affordances, followed by consideration of what practices those affordances support [19–21]. We first performed a comparison of R and Adobe Illustrator as products by juxtaposing their respective audiences, support structures, licensing, purpose, and extensibility. Next, we unpacked the data visualization tools in each package, comparing graphic functionality, how data is entered or imported, the graphic outputs available, design patterns, features for manipulation of aesthetics and layout, and features for optimization. To trace change over time, we created a timeline of features and functionality for each of the tools. The timeline drew from current and historical documents, including archived web pages, that provided detailed descriptions of software features and functionality. These included software documentation (e.g., release notes, user guides), training materials (online tutorials, videos, demos), and marketing and media materials (e.g., new feature announcements, advertisements, reviews, blog posts). Finally, we examined public discourse around each product's visualization features, as well as the current state of both tools as evidenced by materials on their websites. To present our analysis, we begin with descriptions of R and Illustrator as products (Appendix: Table 1[1]), then describe the chronology of feature updates most relevant to their capacity to support data visualization (Appendix: Table 2). We close with a discussion of public discourse and rhetoric surrounding each product.

4 Findings

4.1 Adobe Illustrator

Adobe Illustrator, a core component of the Adobe Creative Suite, is a vector-based graphics tool. Adobe, Inc. was founded in 1982, and Adobe Illustrator was introduced in 1986 as a digital tool for graphic and typographic design. According to an early marketing video for Adobe Illustrator 88:

> "Now anyone can create high quality graphics and illustrations quickly and easily because today there's a revolution taking place in graphic design and production, a revolution born of computers and laser technology but with its roots in the tradition of quality and creativity, a revolution based on new tools, tools which free the imagination and eliminate drudgery" [22].

As a vector-based system, Illustrator renders line art using mathematical calculations called Bezier curves, generating smoothly arcing lines that can be scaled to any size without degradation or loss of sharpness. The scalability offered by Illustrator's underlying mathematics catalyzed the accessibility of digitized font and the evolution

---

[1] See appendix at https://evidlab.umd.edu/2019/02/iconference-2019-appendix/.

of typography in the digital age [23]. For decades, Adobe products have remained industry standard despite expensive annual licensing fees. Currently, the Adobe collection of software applications is bundled as a cloud-based suite of tools with updates delivered automatically to users in return for a monthly subscription fee.

4.2 Adobe Illustrator's Data Visualization Arc

When Adobe Illustrator launched in 1986, its primary purpose was to give users creative and artistic control of vector-based graphic output. Illustrator's ability to scale an image without quality loss provided significant benefits over raster-based images built from pixels (such as the jpeg file format) that pixelated and degraded when enlarged.

Illustrator has gradually adapted to support elements of Fry's data visualization process, particularly *represent* and *refine*. The earliest functionality directly related to data-driven graph creation was a chart-building tool incorporated into Illustrator 3.0 in 1990 [24]. Originally this tool included a spreadsheet-like interface for adding a dataset and a set of six chart templates to represent that data (grouped column, stacked column, line chart, pie chart, area graph and scatter plot). Three additional chart templates were added around 1997 (bar graph, stacked bar graph, and radar graph) [25]. To create a visualization, users entered their data, made adjustments as needed through the spreadsheet interface, and selected a chart template using a graphical user interface (GUI) tool window. Illustrator then generated a vector image. That image could be refined using Illustrator's extensive graphic design tools, including changing color, typography, replacing the shapes of plot points, or altering scale or orientation.

Today, users can use data to create and customize nine different types of graphs [26]. Using the Graph Data window, users can enter data into a spreadsheet-like interface by hand, copy and paste data from a spreadsheet application such as Microsoft Excel, or import data in a tab delineated file format. The resulting editable, vector-based graph is generated within the document art board and can be manipulated using the full suite of editing tools native to Illustrator.

Historically, one of the primary limitations of using the Illustrator chart-building tool was that once a chart is generated, connections with underlying data are lost. In exchange for the ability to manually make creative and artistic refinements to a chart, designers had to give up a degree of automaticity. However, with Illustrator 8.0, launched in 1998, the introduction of action scripting enabled users to routinize specific tasks using a set of common scripting languages. This change automated at least some parts of the tedious process of updating charts when data changed. The motivation for adding this functionality came from Adobe's primary audience of digital publishing designers [23]. However, Illustrator was still marketed primarily as a generalized graphics application as indicated by the Adobe Creative Suite reference book:

"...the purpose of a chart or graph is clear communication of numeric information as a visual aid. A properly selected chart design will accomplish this. If you create a lot of charts or graphs, look into a specialty graphics application" [27].

In 2015, Adobe made further steps to support dynamic data—steps towards Fry's *interact* stage of visualization—with Creative Cloud Charts [28]. Creative Cloud Charts enabled a constant connection between streaming data and Illustrator visualizations. Adobe introduced this feature as a "Technology Preview": experimental, non-permanent beta functionality enabled by cloud-based software updates. Just a few months after making the Creative Cloud Charts preview available, Adobe announced that it would "pause" development based on user feedback [29]. However, its temporary inclusion reflected growing interest in data-driven graphic design tools and hinted at the challenges of integrating robust graphics and dynamic data functionality into a single tool. Most recently, Adobe researchers, arguing that "graphic designers approach visualization authoring differently from computer scientists," have prototyped the new (not yet available) Data Illustrator, tailored specifically for data visualization [30].

4.3   R

The open source statistical software R, a GNU project, first appeared in 1993 [12]. R was developed to support both statistical computing and graphics. In addition to a command line interface, freely available development environments such as RStudio enable users to interact with the R environment through a GUI. Data visualizations such as scatterplots and bar charts can be exported as PDFs and viewed on the web or printed at any scale. By making adjustments to default parameters included in the R library, users can customize graphic elements including labels, colors, size, transparency and orientation. Users can also add legends and other explanatory text directly through commands in the R code, rather than adding these details using editing software after the plot has been generated. R software is currently supported by the R Foundation for Statistical Computing and is freely available for download and development by users, primarily through the creation of libraries or packages. Because of its open licensing, its extensibility, and the ability for users to control and generate print-quality graphic output, R has become an increasingly popular choice with statisticians, data scientists and others for performing quantitative analysis, data mining and visualization [12].

4.4   R's Data Visualization Arc

Early in its development, data visualization in R benefitted from the introduction of the grid package, created in 2001 to aid in the creation of graphical output. The grid package marked a transition from the original lattice package that provided users with an array of options for displaying multivariate data [31]. Grid built on lattice by providing an expanded set of low-level commands to control the appearance and arrangement of vector-based graphic output [32]. For example, grid added the functionality to open a view window and to position elements within that space. The base graphics in R rely on the templates included with the grid package, enabling users to generate approximately seven different types of standardized charts including density plots, dot plots, bar charts, line charts, pie charts, boxplots and scatter plots [33].

Grid also provided the framework necessary for ggplot2, launched in 2005 and currently the second most popular R package [34]. ggpplot2 retains many of the same features and functionality as R's base graphics [35], and also extends R's capabilities for *representing* and *refining* visualizations through approximately 20 additional functions for generating data visualizations (or plots, as they are called in R) [36]. One of the key advantages to using ggplot2 is the method by which vector-based graphics are layered when exported. Rather than grouping graphic elements (such as plot points, axes, fit lines, labels, titles, legends, etc.) arbitrarily or in an order determined by the sequence in which code is compiled, ggplot2 writes visual elements into semantic components based on Leland Wilkinson's *Grammar of Graphics*, a structural framework for identifying the meaning-making components of a graphic [32]. When ggplot2 writes the graphic output file (typically a PDF), related elements are on the same or adjacent layers (i.e., axis labels and tick marks are grouped together, grid lines are separate from plot points). Because adjustments to the aesthetics and layout of a graphic are conducted by changing parameters of specific elements in the code, the grouping of elements according to semantic (rather than algorithmic) proximity makes it easier to refine graphics in ggplot2 with minimal additional code. This enables users to add, remove or change visual components of a graphic more easily [37].

While ggplot2 remains a highly popular package for R users, a series of new web-based data visualization tools have been introduced in recent years, such as D3.js and Tableau. The value of these newer tools lies in their ability to create and display visual representations of streaming data through a web browser. D3.js, in particular, supports streaming data through its JavaScript-based open source framework, making it highly accessible and flexible. However, much like the tradeoffs made by users of Illustrator, these tools do not do everything. While D3.js allows for highly nuanced refinement of graphic output, it does not have the analytic power of R.

In response to tools like D3.js, the Shiny package was introduced to the R suite of resources in 2012. Shiny provides a two-way interface between a web-based database and a dynamic webpage [38]. Using Shiny, a data visualization can be updated as its database changes, and, conversely, changes made to a visualization can be reflected in the database in real time. As a result, R can now interact with D3.js and visualization designers benefit from features of each to present a more fluid, refined and responsive representation of data.

R, combined with its extensions through ggplot and Shiny, emphasizes Fry's *parse* and *mine* stages of visualization, while also supporting *represent*, *refine*, and *interact*. Its built-in templates and structural frameworks illustrate how it relies on systematic rules for the structured representation and standardized output of data.

4.5   Converging Material Practices, Distinct Rhetoric

As noted above, R and Illustrator have evolved from different origins; however, growing connectivity, cloud-based computing, and data-driven work practices have influenced both applications. Both tools enable users to import or create a dataset within the application, then use that dataset to represent and refine a visualization. Each application facilitates parsing and representing data by providing users with a set of standardized design patterns to generate data visualizations. Both tools have also introduced recent functionality for interaction, enabling visualizations to respond dynamically to changes in the underlying dataset. And documentation for each tool boasts of high quality, professional graphic output. As a blogger writes of Illustrator:

"Illustrator is pretty much the only [graphic design] application I know that can build live graphs so the numbers actually are well represented in proportion in your graph and can make them press ready and ... really beautiful" [39].

R's website claims:

"One of R's strengths is the ease with which well-designed publication-quality plots can be produced ... Great care has been taken over the defaults for the minor design choices in graphics, but the user retains full control" [12].

4.6 Language, Values, and Communities of Practice

Closer inspection of the iterative development of data visualization features over time in both R and Illustrator shows a steady convergence of the practices supported by each application, as the tools' affordances have expanded to address a majority of the data visualization process outlined by Fry and others [13, 14, 17] (Appendix: Table 3). Although the functionality of these tools has converged over time, each has retained a strong identity within distinct communities of practice. The iterative alignment of each tool's material practices around the data visualization process (shown in Appendix: Table 3) contrasts with the distinct language used to talk about these tools in documentation, marketing materials, and popular media. As a tutorial for working with data in Illustrator asks:

"What if you want to make a graphic for a publication or a presentation that's polished and fully customized? Adobe Illustrator gives you the control you need to do this...It's not graphing software. It's illustration software, but once you get the hang of things, Adobe Illustrator can be a valuable tool in your visualization arsenal" [6].

In contrast, as an R-Bloggers tutorial explains, R's output has been optimized for analytic tasks rather than communication:

"Even for beginners, it's pretty easy to get out a basic plot to learn something about a data set. The trouble starts, however, when you want to show the plot to someone else. And, that is not the documentation's "fault". The documentation is all there. Typing help(package="graphics") at the command line will put most everything you need to know about base graphics at your reach. However, I think that until a person gets used to thinking of R as a system of interacting functions it takes a bit of ingenuity for a beginner to figure out how to accomplish a basic "functional" task like produce a plot that you can show around" [40].

The rhetoric used to describe these tools on their respective support websites also reflects their intended target audiences. R is described as primarily statistical, extensible, and having formulaic defaults:

"R provides a wide variety of statistical (linear and nonlinear modeling, classical statistical tests, time-series analysis, classification, clustering, ...) and graphical techniques, and is highly extensible...One of R's strengths is the ease with which well-designed publication-quality plots can be produced, including mathematical symbols and formulae where needed. Great care has been taken over the defaults for the minor design choices in graphics, but the user retains full control" [12].

Illustrator evokes aesthetics and creative expression:

"Artists use Illustrator for creating clean visual compositions that can be scaled infinitely without losing quality, creating free hand drawings in illustrations, tracing and recoloring scanned in artwork and also creating wireframes from which to create digital paintings" [41].

Illustrator's tools for customization are described in terms of values associated with creativity, such as flexibility and self-expression. For example, Illustrator's help documents reiterate the many ways you can change the template options:

"For example, you can change the appearance and position of the graph's axes, add drop shadows, move the legend, and combine different graph types... You can also manually customize your graph in numerous ways. You can change the colors of shading; change the typeface and type style; move, reflect, shear, rotate, or scale any or all parts of the graph; and customize column and marker designs. You can apply transparency, gradients, blends, brush strokes, graphic styles, and other effects to graphs" [42].

The rhetoric around customization in statements like this is much more strongly associated with subjective expression than with rule-based objectivity. Attention to appearance and position, shading, typeface, and substantial customization features all support values of flexibility and the pursuit of craft. Illustrator's long history of supporting customization through its vector-based framework and explicit marketing to artists has led to strong associations with values of creativity, flexibility, and aesthetics.

Even as R packages have been introduced that enable increasingly refined representation and refinement of data visualizations (such as ggplot2), the grid framework at the heart of the platform anchors these packages in standardized (rather than customized) methods for image construction. As the *R for Data Science* online tutorial describes: "ggplot2 implements the grammar of graphics, a coherent system for describing and building graphs" [43]. While it is possible to make adjustments to individual graphic elements, defaults built into the package are emphasized in practice: "Once you set an aesthetic, ggplot2 takes care of the rest. It selects a pleasing set of levels to use for the aesthetic, and it constructs a legend that explains the mapping" [43]. Although R does allow for customization, it assumes that users will value the systematic application of rules over the need to make creative decisions themselves: "In practice, you rarely need to supply all seven parameters because ggplot2 will provide useful defaults for everything except the data, the mappings, and the geom function" [43]. Discourse around R strongly evokes values of standardization, automation and quantification, contributing to an analytic identity for the data visualization features of the R software.

5 Discussion

Comparing values evident in both the functionality of and the discourse surrounding R and Illustrator reveals a gap between converging material practices and divergent rhetoric. In previous work, we have explored the many ways researchers can observe values in practices, design, and language [44], and this study illustrates the importance of examining all three. While R and Illustrator currently lack *rhetorical values convergence*, we have seen a *convergence of values in design and practice*. Major recent developments in the visualization trajectories of each tool (Creative Cloud Charts for Illustrator and Shiny for R) are observable indicators of values convergence in practice among traditionally disconnected communities. Data-driven work combined with increasing emphasis on sharing and publication act as a catalyst for this convergence, spurred by the expansion of data-driven work practices.

We argue that this indicates that data visualization is increasingly *both* information visualization and information design. Practitioners are blending traditionally separate values as they balance standardized visual representation techniques for analysis with the creativity expected of graphical communication. In response, developers are adapting their tools to support this convergence. R has added features that enable users to consider aesthetics when making data visually clear and compelling. At the same time, Illustrator has added support for designing with data, acknowledging that an increasing number of artists and graphic designers work with quantitative source materials. As data-driven work expands beyond practices associated primarily with statistics or computer science, values associated with quantification will be brought to creative practice, and creativity and expression become values in data science.

6 Conclusion

Research has demonstrated that values convergence facilitates group work and collaboration [45, 46]. Shared values encourage trust between parties and smooth technology acceptance [45, 47]. Convergence of values within the domain of data visualization signals an opportunity for iSchools to play an important role in facilitating the productive and constructive merging of disciplinary expertise. Our analysis of two tools from previously distinct communities of practice indicates that data-driven work may encourage new kinds of collaborations, as artists and analysts find themselves sharing interests, tools, and practices, if not yet language to describe this work.

However, boundary spanning of this nature requires scaffolding. To date, little research has examined situations where values in *practice* are converging while values in *rhetoric* remain divided. Within the domain of data visualization, a convergence of values across practitioner groups has the potential to create opportunities for knowledge sharing, but also carries the threat of backlash, provoking divisive discourse among disciplines as stakeholders perceive a need to protect their positions of expertise. Gatherings such as OpenVis and recent workshops being offered through the IEEE Vis conference [i.e., 48] encourage convergence by providing opportunities for cross-pollination and the creation of new professional identities for those embracing the converged values of quantification and creative expression. However, higher education institutional structures (e.g., departments, curricular requirements, and hiring practices) more typically reflect the siloed values of design and computer science. It remains to be seen, however, how data-driven workers who must navigate values in both practice and rhetoric will balance these tensions to engage in productive collaboration.

This research prompts us to turn attention to the educational implications of values and practice convergence paired with rhetorical divergence. As we develop data science curricula, we have a unique opportunity to introduce new pedagogical approaches to bridging technical and communicative facets of many of the professions for which we are training our students. We believe that further work in this area can expand our understanding of other emerging and converging multidisciplinary data practices.

References

1. Ziemkiewicz, C., Kosara, R.: Embedding information visualization within visual representation. In: Ras, Z.W., Ribarsky, W. (eds.) Advances in Information and Intelligent Systems. SCI, vol. 251, pp. 307–326. Springer, Heidelberg (2009). https://doi.org/10.1007/978-3-642-04141-9_15
2. Kosara, R.: Visualization criticism: the missing link between information visualization and art. In: Proceedings of the IEEE Information Visualization, pp. 631–636. IEEE (2007)
3. Garrett, J.: How to Use Adobe Illustrator Variable Data with XML. Hypertransitory.com (2014). http://hypertransitory.com/blog/2014/05/27/use-adobe-illustrator-variable-data-xml/. Accessed 12 Dec 2018
4. Gordon, M.: Exporting nice plots in R. R-Bloggers (2013). http://www.r-bloggers.com/exporting-nice-plots-in-r/. Accessed 12 Dec 2018
5. Smith, D.: 10 tips for making your R graphics look their best. Revolutions (2009). http://blog.revolutionanalytics.com/2009/01/10-tips-for-making-your-r-graphics-look-their-best.html. Accessed 12 Dec 2018
6. Yau, N.: How to make a graph in adobe illustrator. FlowingData (2008). https://flowingdata.com/2008/12/16/how-to-make-a-graph-in-adobe-illustrator/. Accessed 12 Dec 2018
7. OpenVisConf OpenVisConf. http://openvisconf.com. Accessed 12 Dec 2018
8. IEEE VIS Conference. http://ieeevis.org/year/2018/welcome. Accessed 24 Aug 2018
9. Hemsley, J., et al.: Visualization Pedagogy in iSchools. In: Proceedings of the iConference 2015 (2015)
10. Meeks, E.: 2018 data visualization survey results. Elijah Meeks (2018). https://medium.com/@Elijah_Meeks/2018-data-visualization-survey-results-26a90856476b. Accessed 24 Aug 2018
11. Meeks, E.: 2017 data visualization survey results. Elijah Meeks (2017). https://medium.com/@Elijah_Meeks/2017-data-visualization-survey-results-40688830b9f2. Accessed 24 Aug 2018
12. R: What is R? https://www.r-project.org/about.html. Accessed 12 Dec 2018
13. Card, S.K., Mackinlay, J.D., Shneiderman, B.: Readings in Information Visualization: Using Vision to Think. Morgan Kaufmann, San Francisco (1999)
14. Few, S.: Now You See It: Simple Visualization Techniques for Quantitative Analysis, 1st edn. Analytics Press, USA (2009)
15. Jacobson, R.: Information Design. MIT Press, Cambridge
16. Yau, N.: Visualize This!. Wiley, New York (2012)
17. Fry, B.: Visualizing Data: Exploring and Explaining Data with the Processing Environment. O'Reilly Media, Sebastopol (2008)
18. Tufte, E.R.: Envisioning Information. Graphics Press, Cheshire (1990)
19. Brey, P.: Disclosive computer ethics. SIGCAS Comput. Soc. 30, 10–16 (2000). https://doi.org/10.1145/572260.572264

20. Flanagan, M., Howe, D.C., Nissenbaum, H.: Values at play: design tradeoffs in socially-oriented game design. In: Proceedings of the CHI, NY, USA, New York, pp. 751–760 (2005)
21. Friedman, B., Kahn Jr., P.H., Borning, A.: Value sensitive design and information systems. In: Himma, K.E., Tavani, H.T. (eds.) The Handbook of Information and Computer Ethics, pp. 69–102. Wiley, Hoboken (2008)
22. Slomacuser Adobe Illustrator 88. https://www.youtube.com/watch?v=eNLFXKyCy0A. Accessed 12 Dec 2018
23. Dill, E.: The History of Adobe Illustrator. Vecteezy. http://www.vecteezy.com/blog/2010/5/24/the-history-of-adobe-illustrator. Accessed 12 Dec 2018
24. Inc IMG (1990) InfoWorld. InfoWorld Media Group, Inc
25. Adobe (1997) Adobe Illustrator 7.0 for the Macintosh New Features (web archive). https://web.archive.org/web/19970726030201/http://www3.adobe.com/prodindex/illustrator/PDFS/ai7newfeatures.pdf
26. Adobe Illustrator website. http://www.adobe.com/products/illustrator.html?sdid=KKQML&mv=search&s_kwcid=AL!3085!3!81143514756!e!!g!!adobe%20illustrator&ef_id=VOOJXgAABfd1VP64:20160523174240:s. Accessed 12 Dec 2018
27. Steuer, S.: The Adobe Illustrator CS Wow! Book. Peachpit Press, Berkeley (2004)
28. Creative Cloud Charts (Technology Preview). https://helpx.adobe.com/illustrator/using/creative-cloud-charts-graphs-infographics.html. Accessed 12 Dec 2018
29. RoyCreative.com Pausing Creative Cloud Charts (Preview). Adobe Illus. Blog. http://blogs.adobe.com/adobeillustrator/2015/11/pausing-creative-cloud-charts-preview.html. Accessed 12 Dec 2018
30. Liu, Z., et al.: Data illustrator: augmenting vector design tools with lazy data binding for expressive visualization authoring. In: Proceedings of the 2018 CHI Conference on Human Factors in Computing Systems, pp 123:1–123:13. ACM, New York (2018)
31. Sarkar, D.: Package "lattice." (2015). https://cran.r-project.org/web/packages/lattice/lattice.pdf. Accessed 12 Dec 2018
32. Murrell, P.: R Graphics, 2nd edn. CRC Press, Boca Raton (2011)
33. Quick-R: Basic Graphs. http://www.statmethods.net/graphs/. Accessed 12 Dec 2018
34. Top 20 R packages by popularity. http://www.kdnuggets.com/2015/06/top-20-r-packages.html. Accessed 12 Dec 2018
35. Yau, N.: Comparing ggplot2 and R Base Graphics. FlowingData (2016). http://flowingdata.com/2016/03/22/comparing-ggplot2-and-r-base-graphics/. Accessed 12 Dec 2018
36. https://plot.ly/ggplot2/. Accessed 12 Dec 2018
37. Introduction to R Graphics with <code>ggplot2</code>. http://tutorials.iq.harvard.edu/R/Rgraphics/Rgraphics.html#orgheadline19. Accessed 12 Dec 2018
38. Shiny. http://shiny.rstudio.com/. Accessed 12 Dec 2018
39. Paradis, A.: Illustrator: Graphs. https://www.youtube.com/watch?v=K_vENVmUluM. Accessed 12 Dec 2018
40. Rickert, J.: R-bloggers: Some basics for base graphics. R-Bloggers (2015). http://www.r-bloggers.com. Accessed 12 Dec 2018
41. What is Adobe Illustrator? Adobe Illustrator CC tutorials. https://helpx.adobe.com/illustrator/how-to/what-is-illustrator.html. Accessed 12 Dec 2018
42. How to create graphs in Illustrator. https://helpx.adobe.com/illustrator/using/graphs.html. Accessed 12 Dec 2018
43. Grolemund, G., Wickham, H.: R for data science: data visualization (2017). https://r4ds.had.co.nz/data-visualisation.html. Accessed 12 Dec 2018
44. Snyder, J., Shilton, K., Anderson, S.: Observing the materiality of values in information systems research. In: Proceedings of the HICSS (2016)

45. Fleischmann, K.R.: Information and human values. Synth. Lect. Inf. Concepts Retr. Serv. **5**, 1–99 (2013)
46. Miller, J.K., Friedman, B., Jancke, G., Gill, B.: Value tensions in design: the value sensitive design, development, and appropriation of a corporation's groupware system. In: Proceedings of the GROUP, NY, USA, New York, pp. 281–290 (2007)
47. Siegrist, M., Cvetkovich, G., Roth, C.: Salient value similarity, social trust, and risk/benefit perception. Risk Anal. **20**, 353–362 (2000). https://doi.org/10.1111/0272-4332.203034
48. Kosara, R.: Visualization for communication. In: IEEE VIS 2018 Workshop Visualization for Communication VisComm (2018). https://viscomm.io/. Accessed 24 Aug 2018

Concerns About "Smart" Interactions and Privacy

A Study of Usage and Usability of Intelligent Personal Assistants in Denmark

Toine Bogers[✉], Ammar Ali Abdelrahim Al-Basri, Claes Ostermann Rytlig,
Mads Emil Bak Møller, Mette Juhl Rasmussen,
Nikita Katrine Bates Michelsen, and Sara Gerling Jørgensen

Science, Policy and Information Studies, Department of Communication
and Psychology, Aalborg University Copenhagen, Copenhagen, Denmark
toine@hum.aau.dk

Abstract. Intelligent personal assistants (IPA), such as Siri, Google Assistant, Alexa, and Cortana, are rapidly becoming a popular way of interacting with our smart devices. As a result, there has been a wealth of research on all aspects of IPAs in recent years, such as studies of usage of and user satisfaction with IPAs. However, the overwhelming majority of these studies have focused on English as the interaction language. In this paper, we investigate the usage and perceived usability of IPAs in Denmark. We conduct a questionnaire with 357 Danish-speaking respondents that sheds light on how IPAs are used in Denmark. We find they are only used regularly by 19.9% of respondents and that most people do not find IPAs to be reliable. We also conduct a usability study of Siri and find that Siri suffers from several issues when used in Danish: poor voice recognition, unnatural dialogue responses, and an inability to support mixed-language speech recognition. Our findings shed light on both the current state of usage and adoption of IPAs in Denmark as well as the usability of its most popular IPA in a foreign-language setting.

Keywords: IPA · Siri · Usability · Intelligent Personal Assistants · Information behavior

1 Introduction

Intelligent Personal Assistants (IPA), such as Siri, Google Assistant, Alexa, and Cortana, are becoming an increasingly popular way of interacting with our smartphones and typically the only way of interacting with smart speakers. In April 2018, 41.4% of US adults surveyed reported using IPAs on their smartphone and 19.7% using smart speaker IPAs [13]. IPAs are a type of software agents that support task-oriented sequences of exchanges between the user and the IPA, such as assisting in booking a table at a restaurant, route planning, searching the Web, dictating and sending text messages, and so on. The design of an effective and satisfactory IPA requires the integration of many different

© Springer Nature Switzerland AG 2019
N. G. Taylor et al. (Eds.): iConference 2019, LNCS 11420, pp. 79–90, 2019.
https://doi.org/10.1007/978-3-030-15742-5_7

fields, such as user modeling and multi-turn user-machine dialogue systems for information access and retrieval. When executed well, however, IPAs have the potential to change our information (seeking) behavior. The hands-free, conversational interaction style of IPAs could be beneficial in many scenarios, such as interacting with a handheld device while driving a car [21] or assisting visually impaired people [11].

For IPAs to be adopted successfully, they must be seen as both useful to and usable by people. As a result, some of the recent work on IPAs has focused on usability testing voice-controlled IPAs when performing everyday tasks in English. Both Kiseleva et al. [15] and López et al. [17] conducted user studies to measure the usability of and user satisfaction with different IPAs for a variety of different tasks. Strayer et al. [21] specifically tested the usability of Siri, Google Assistant, and Cortana in the hands-free setting of driving a car.

All of this work has focused on the English-language version of IPAs which has been at the forefront of IPA developments and research. Little is known, however, about the use and usability of Siri and other IPAs in non-Anglo-Saxon countries where they do support the local language, but not to the same degree as English. We know little about people's usage and preferences in these scenarios. Do people interact with IPAs in their native language or do they prefer to interact with them in English instead? Are there any difference in their usage patterns and preferences? Does the user's experience with IPAs influence their satisfaction and usage? And (how) is the usability of the IPA affected by using a language other than English?

In this paper, we provide some first insights into some of these questions by investigating the usage and perceived usability of IPAs in Denmark. More specifically, we make the following two contributions:

1. We present the results of a questionnaire with 357 respondents that sheds light on how IPAs are used in Denmark. We find that only 19.9% of respondents self-report themselves as being regular users of IPAs and that, in general, attitudes towards technology adoption appears to influence people's usage of and satisfaction with IPAs, while local language variation does not.
2. We discuss the results of usability testing the most popular IPA in Denmark, Siri, with 20 participants. A lack of knowledge of the limitations of IPAs in general influenced the satisfaction with Siri. Our research also suggests that barriers to Siri adoption are poor voice recognition, unnatural dialogue responses, and an inability to support mixed-language speech recognition.

Our findings shed light on both the current state of usage and adoption of IPAs in Denmark as well as the usability of its most popular IPA in a foreign-language setting. The rest of this paper is organized as follows. We discuss relevant related work in the next section, followed by our investigations into the usage and usability of IPAs in Danish in Sects. 3 and 4 respectively. We conclude in Sect. 5.

2   Related Work

The increased popularity of IPAs has cause a commensurate increase in the amount of research dedicated to all aspects of conversational interaction with IPAs. Several studies have attempted to measure the usability of and user satisfaction of different IPAs for a variety of different tasks. Kiseleva et al. [15] focused on a range of different scenarios, such as device control, Web search and structured search. They found that what makes an interaction satisfying depends strongly on the task: in some cases the amount of effort spent is important, while in other cases task completion is key. In follow-up work, Kiseleva et al. [14] attempted to predict user satisfaction from a variety of different user interactions, such as physical touch gestures on the device and voice commands. Other work on measuring usability and user satisfaction of IPAs includes the work by López et al. [17] and Luger and Sellen [18]. Strayer et al. [21] attempted to measure usability while driving a car, a scenario that focuses on the potential hands-free advantages of IPAs.

Other researchers have used questionnaires to study how IPAs are used in everyday life. Garcia et al. [8] conducted their questionnaire about IPA usage in Argentina, Brazil, Chile, Germany, Spain, the UK and the US. They found that IPA usage in most countries is lagging behind the US, but that around 50–60% of those who do use it, do so at least several times a week. Brill [3] modeled the responses of his questionnaire about IPA use to determine the factors that predict customer satisfaction with IPAs and found that user perceptions of trust as well as information privacy issues has a strong influence on satisfaction,

Other related work on IPAs includes attempts at automatic evaluation of IPAs [12], the quality of its speech recognition [1], and the role that personality preferences play in our interaction with IPAs Ehrenbrink et al. [6]. Guy [10] and Mehrotra et al. [19] have analyzed IPAs from an information retrieval perspective, analyzing voice query logs and automatically detecting voice interaction sessions. All of the research described above has one thing in common: a focus on English as the language of interaction. In this paper, we therefore examine usage and usability in Danish to compare and contrast with earlier work.

3   Usage

3.1   Methodology

In order to answer our research questions about IPA usage and usability in non-English speaking countries and Denmark in particular, we used a combination of a questionnaire and usability testing. The goal of the questionnaire was two-fold: (1) to get an overview of how (often) IPAs are being used, and (2) to serve as input for the usability test described in Sect. 4 to target the most popular IPA and to include realistic tasks for participants to complete based on actual usage.

Development. Our questionnaire consisted of 23 questions (in Danish) divided over six main parts to ensure a possible analysis of how language affects usage and behavior[1]. The first part focused on participants' awareness of IPAs and their functionality, whereas the second part focused on frequency of use. We included six IPAs—Siri, Cortana, Google Assistant, Bixby, S Voice, Alexa—and asked participants how often they used them and their preferred IPA. In addition, we asked about the language(s) they interact with their IPA(s) in. The third part focused on where participants used their IPA(s) and how often the IPA(s) were used to perform different tasks, ranging from controlling the device, checking the weather, and sending messages or e-mails, to searching the Web or the device itself, and requesting navigation assistance. In the fourth part, we asked participants to rate how satisfied they were with the performance of their preferred IPA on these tasks. The fifth part included questions about general attitudes towards technology, such as interest, expertise and adoption behavior. The sixth and final part of the questionnaire focused on demographics (e.g., gender, age, occupation, education, native language(s), and city they grew up in). The last two questions were used to uncover the influence of language proficiency and dialect on interaction with IPAs.

Deployment. In this paper, we focus specifically on Denmark because of the authors' personal and academic ties to Denmark, so we recruited only participants proficient in Danish. We distributed out questionnaire through Facebook, because it is the most popular social media service in Denmark, with approximately 3.84 million users [22, p. 25]. To maximize our sample size and reduce potential biases [2], we posted the questionnaire in 15 different Facebook groups with a total of 116,321 (overlapping) members. The questionnaire was active during a two-week period from October 20 to November 3, 2017. We are aware that using Facebook as a sampling frame generates a convenience sample with the associated risks and biases. We attempted to remedy some of these by performing purposive sampling and selecting a diverse set of Facebook groups.

3.2 Results and Analysis

Demographics. Fig. 1 shows the demographic composition of our sample of 357 participants. It shows a sample made up predominantly of younger participants, with 59.1% ($n = 211$) of them falling in the 20–29 year-old age range and only 10.4% of our participants were age 50 and up. Our sample is clearly skewed towards a younger demographic, but these are also more likely to use new technological features. Furthermore, our goal is not to make any generalizations about IPA usage by different age groups in Denmark, but instead provided a reasonable overview of how IPAs are used. In terms of gender, 64.1% ($n = 229$) of our participants were female and 35.6% ($n = 127$) self-identified as male. Finally, 95.2% ($n = 240$) of our participants were native Danish speakers, which eliminates some potential bias in their self-reported task satisfaction due to mispronunciation and grammatical errors.

---

[1] The full questionnaire is available at http://toinebogers.com/?page_id=796.

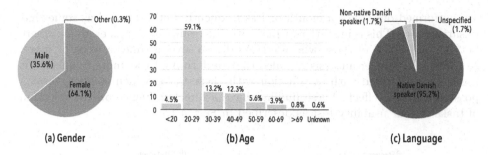

Fig. 1. Demographic composition of our survey participants ($N = 357$) by (a) gender, (b) age, and (c) mastery of the Danish language.

Usage and Familiarity. An overwhelming majority of our participants (94.4%, $n = 337$) were familiar with the concept of IPAs, with Siri commanding a 99.5% name recognition and a share of 68.6% ($n = 246$) of our participants actively used Siri and were most comfortable with this IPA. This is followed by Google Assistant with a 69.9% name recognition share, but it was only used by 10.4% ($n = 37$) of our participants. The considerably higher market share of Siri is echoed by Konrad and Jørgensen [16], who found that 83.2% of all mobile traffic comes from devices running iOS. None of the other IPAs that we included in our questionnaire—Alexa, Bixby, Cortana, and S Voice—were used by more than 2%, so we exclude them from our analysis. At the time of questionnaire deployment, Google Assistant did not yet support Danish, so in the remainder of this analysis we will only focus on the usage of Siri.

Language. Siri's native support for Danish is mirrored in the share of the 246 Siri users: 75.5% ($n = 185$) of them only use Danish, 22.9% ($n = 56$) only use English. The remainder used another language or a mix of both Danish and English. One possible reason for the large share of Danish could be the simple convenience of having your smartphone set to your native language, which would include Siri's interaction language. Another possibility is that participants used Siri relatively infrequently, making the change to a different language a low priority.

Tasks. Figure 2 shows an overview of the most frequently performed tasks using Siri and how satisfied our participants were with Siri's performance. Of the 16 tasks we asked about in our questionnaire, five had a median frequency rating 0 as most people never performed them. Reporting satisfaction for these tasks is meaningless, so we only report on the frequency and satisfaction for the 11 tasks that at least 10% ($n = 24$) of our participants reported performing at least once. The results show that despite being available in Danish, even participants who identify Siri as their preferred IPA only rarely use it. Only 19.9% ($n = 71$) of the participants reported using Siri monthly or more frequently. Setting alarms and countdown timers was the only task with median of 3, signifying weekly use. Even this task was rated only slightly above neutral satisfaction. Most other tasks are performed only once a month or less frequently and are rated as somewhat unsatisfactory. This is in stark contrast with the results of Garcia et al. [8], where between 50%–60% of those who use IPAs did so several times a week or more. Nevertheless, further analysis revealed that performing tasks more frequently is positively correlated with satisfaction with these tasks, which could suggest a possible learning effect. These findings have a direct influence on the selection of tasks for our usability test as described in Sect. 4.1.

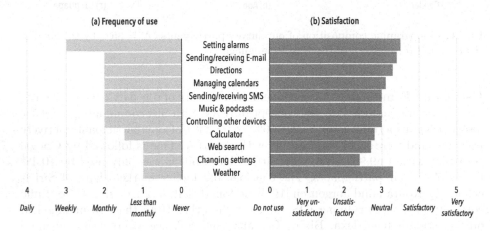

Fig. 2. Frequency (median value) of and satisfaction (average value) with the most commonly performed tasks using Siri ($N = 246$).

We did not find any relationship between demographic variables and satisfaction with or usage of Siri-supported tasks. We hypothesized a potential influence of dialects and accents on comprehension by Siri, but did not find such an effect. This is perhaps due to the smaller-than-expected influence of city of origin on their Danish dialect and/or accent. Another reason could be that users know they have to accommodate their speech to be understood by Siri, leading them to drop their accent or dialect. This type of accommodation is common between humans to promote closeness [9] and could possibly also play a role in communication with IPAs.

Attitudes towards technology adoption [20, p. 246] appeared to influence usage and user satisfaction: early adopters were more likely to use Siri in our sample and also reported considerably greater satisfaction with Siri than late adopters, although more work is needed to assess this influence conclusively. Finally, content analysis of comments about satisfaction—using emergent coding by two of the authors—showed that while participants liked the idea of Siri and other IPAs, their biggest problem with them was that they were seen as unreliable. Over a fifth of our participants (22.4%, $n = 55$) explicitly mentioned not trusting Siri to perform the tasks correctly, something also shown by Cowan et al. [5].

4   Usability

4.1   Methodology

When investigating the usability of IPAs in a non-Anglo-Saxon country such as Denmark, we wanted to focus only on the most popular IPA(s) in Denmark. Usability testing an IPA used by only a fraction of Danish smartphone owners is unlikely to paint a representative picture of how usable that IPA is for the average Dane. Because over two-thirds of our questionnaire participants listed Siri as their preferred IPA, with Google Assistant a distant second, we only focused on usability testing Siri.

Participants. We used convenience sampling to recruit 20 participants, which is an appropriate number of participants for usability testing with relatively simple tasks according to Faulkner [7]. Of our 20 participants, 18 studied at the same university, but not the same degree. They ranged in age from 20 to 34 with 7 women and 13 men. Our sampling process had an element of purposive sampling in that we attempted to recruit an equal number of participants with and without experience with IPAs (in general). This was only partially successful with 7 experienced and 13 inexperienced users. All participants spoke Danish and 19 as their native language.

Procedure and Tasks. We performed a user-based summative usability testing with each of our participants. The usability test was conducted in Danish and was scheduled to take around 25 min². All usability tests were both audio and video recorded for later analysis. The protocol for the usability test was pilot-tested on two potential participants, one experienced with Siri and the other inexperienced. Each participant was asked to use the same iPhone 5 provided by the experimenters to reduce any biases due to familiarity and/or personalization. Any data created in the previous test was erased from the device.

After greeting the participants, we introduced them to the purpose and procedure of the study and obtained their informed consent. Next, we asked participants some questions about their smartphone and IPA usage as well as some demographic questions in the pre-test interview. The usability test consisted of seven different tasks, shown in Table 1. They were inspired both by the most frequently performed tasks in our questionnaire and as well as those tested by Kiseleva et al. [15]. Before participants started the test, they were asked to complete a training task, which had them ask Siri to tell a joke. Participants were given 10 min in total to complete these seven tasks.

After completing the seven tasks, participants were asked to fill out a short post-test questionnaire, which included the System Usability Scale [4] as well as questions about how satisfied the participants were with Siri's performance as well as how much effort they felt they had to put in during the test. Finally, participants were asked whether their impression of Siri had changed after participating in the usability test, followed by the final debriefing.

---

² Our usability test protocol is available at http://toinebogers.com/?page_id=796.

Analysis. We performed content analysis on the qualitative data collected from the pre-test interview and their feedback during the usability test. Two of the authors developed individual coding schemes using emergent coding focused on subjects as well as on the sentiment towards these subjects, after which differences were merged and codes were consolidated and merged where relevant.

Table 1. Overview of the seven different tasks in our usability test and the IPA feature they test. The descriptions below are condensed, translated versions of the original Danish descriptions.

Task	Feature tested	Task description
1	Weather	Check what the weather will be like in the weekend
2	Alarm	Set an alarm for the next morning
3	Texting	Send a text message to a friend about arriving late to your meeting
4	Currency	Convert 100 USD into Danish Crowns
5	Calendar	Check your calendar whether you're free on a specific date/time. If so, add an event to your calendar for that date/time
6	Directions	Find the address of a Copenhagen restaurant named 'Gorilla'
7	Web search	Find the age and some photos of your favorite actor/actress

4.2   Results and Analysis

Figure 3 shows an overview of task performance on five different metrics as collected from the usability test and the post-test questionnaire. Figure 3a shows that, in terms of the average number of performed steps, some tasks could be completed more efficiently than others, but not all of this is due to task complexity. The calendar and Web search tasks both required a minimum of two steps to complete, but speech recognition errors in the Web search tasks increased the average number of steps considerably, as also reflected in average task times in Fig. 3b. This is because the task required users to mix Danish and English in their interaction with Siri, which is problematic for Siri's mono-lingual speech recognition model. Task 6, where participants had to locate the restaurant 'Gorilla' also showcased these problems as the word is spelled the same in Danish, but pronounced differently. Participants pronouncing the word in English were often forced to reformulate their request. As a result of the speech recognition problems, seven participants failed to complete the Web search task, as shown in Fig. 3c.

A good example of the typical speech recognition errors made by Siri is when participant T1 asked (in Danish) *"Can you show me some pictures of*

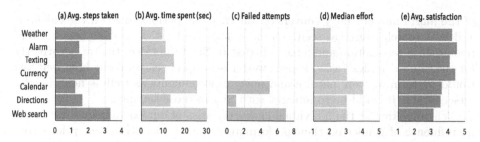

Fig. 3. Overview of the (a) average steps taken to complete a task; (b) average time spent (in seconds); (c) total number of failed attempts over all participants; (d) median self-assessed perceived effort; and (e) average satisfaction over the seven different tasks ($N = 20$).

Scarlett Johansson?", and Siri replied with *"Let me see. Here are some pictures of skør Johansson (= 'crazy Johansson'), that I found on the Internet."*. Another example is the failed recognition of *"Arnold Schwarzenegger"* as the Danish name *"Anders"* and there are several more examples of English celebrity names being recognized incorrectly as Danish words. Surprisingly, the weather task also required a relatively high number of steps. This was not due to speech recognition problems though; instead, Siri can be quite particular when it comes to how requests for the weekend weather should be phrased. However, all participants eventually figured out which specific formulations Siri understands, regardless of their initial experience with IPAs. Related to this is another observation about what could be called politeness: 75% of participants started each interaction with *"Hey Siri"* during their first task, but this number dropped to 15% for the last task. This suggests a learning effect in terms of how to most efficiently use Siri over the course of the usability test.

Another issue, especially in the Web search task, was Siri's poor support for anaphoric resolution: after participants managed to find the age of their preferred celebrity and had to locate photos of them, some of them would refer to the celebrity using anaphoric expressions like 'him' or 'her'. Siri was incapable of resolving these expressions back to the celebrity in question, necessitating an additional formulation step to complete the task. This suggests that turn-taking and anaphoric resolution could be improved.

These speech recognition and formulation errors do not seem to have had a major influence on the effort participants felt they had to put in to complete the weather and Web search tasks, as seen in Fig. 3d. In general, participants' satisfaction with Siri was positive for nearly all tasks (Fig. 3e), except for Web search where it was neutral, which we believe to be due to the aforementioned difficulties and the recency effect as it was always performed as the last task.

Our post-test interviews revealed that while some users were convinced that manually completing theses tasks would be faster than using Siri, others believed the opposite, although this did not seem to be influenced by prior experience. The interviews also showed that people were most positive about Siri's handling of the alarm and currency conversion tasks, while performance on the calendar and Web search tasks was seen in a more negative light. Recurring themes were poor speech recognition and a lack of trust in Siri to perform the tasks correctly for the more complex tasks. People were also apprehensive about how well Siri would perform in more natural and noisy environments as well as how socially unacceptable it could be to interact with Siri in those settings.

When looking at the individual characteristics of our participants, we found no influence of gender on their performance or attitudes. However, prior experience with IPAs did influence performance. Perhaps unsurprisingly, more experienced participants needed fewer steps and less time to complete their tasks, especially on the multi-stage tasks such as calendar management and Web search, and were also more patient and accommodating in their interaction with Siri. Interestingly, inexperienced participants reported higher satisfaction scores for the majority of tasks than experienced participants, which is perhaps due to the lower expectations they have as they are simply less familiar with Siri's capabilities.

5   Discussion and Conclusions

Despite the growing popularity of IPAs and the resulting research interest, most of our knowledge about their usage and usability pertains exclusively to the English-language version. In this paper, we have presented the results of two studies focused on the use of IPAs in a non-Anglo-Saxon country.

Our first study, a questionnaire of IPA usage in Denmark, showed that Siri is the most popular IPA in Denmark, but only one-fifth of the respondents considered themselves as regular users. The overwhelming majority interact with IPAs in their native language and use them for only a small set of tasks that are typically performed once a month or less. While not dissatisfied with the performance of their IPA, our respondents do see IPAs as unreliable and do not trust them to complete anything but the simplest tasks correctly.

A usability test of the Danish version of Siri with seven different tasks revealed that speech recognition and comprehension errors had a negative influence on effectiveness, efficiency, and user satisfaction. This was even more problematic for mixed-language interactions where participants combined Danish requests with English terms. As a result, participants had to spend more time and effort correcting Siri. A possible suggestion for improving the speech recognition in non-English languages could be to train their models in mixed-language settings, perhaps by modeling the pronunciation of popular expressions (e.g., celebrities, movies, TV shows, sports teams) to ensure these can be captured accurately. Similar to Kiseleva et al. [15], we also found that the task type influenced whether perceived effort or the required number of steps affected user satisfaction. A lack of contextual understanding and memory—remembering information from previous steps and/or tasks or resolving anaphoric expressions—was another issue raised by participants. In general, the more interaction was required, such as in dictation or multi-stage tasks, the lower the user satisfaction.

Participants again were hesitant to trust Siri's correct completion of a task, preferring to perform several of the tasks manually instead. Perhaps surprisingly, we also found that experienced IPA users were more effective and efficient in their interaction with Siri and were also more patient, yet they were less satisfied than the inexperienced users. This could possibly be the result of the higher expectations that come with increased experience.

In the future, we would like to perform a more controlled study of how mixing multiple languages influences speech recognition quality and how this affects the IPAs perceived usability. Evaluation in other non-English languages, such as German, Dutch and other non-Germanic languages could also be a promising avenue of future research. Another interesting possibility could be to performed a controlled test how robust IPAs are with regards to dialects and accents.

References

[1] Assefi, M., Liu, G., Wittie, M.P., Izurieta, C.: An experimental evaluation of apple siri and google speech recognition. In: Proceedings of the 2015 ISCA SEDE (2015)

[2] Bhutta, C.B.: Not by the book: Facebook as a sampling frame. Sociological Methods Res. 41(1), 57–88 (2012)

[3] Brill, T.M.: Siri, Alexa, and Other Digital Assistants: A Study of Customer Satisfaction With Artificial Intelligence. Ph.D. thesis, University of Dallas, February 2018

[4] Brooke, J.: SUS: a 'quick and dirty' usability scale. Usability Eval. Ind. 189(194), 4–7 (1996)

[5] Cowan, B.R., et al.: "What can I help you with?" – infrequent users' experiences of intelligent personal assistants. In: Proceedings of MobileHCI 2017, pp. 1–12. ACM Press, New York (2017)

[6] Ehrenbrink, P., Osman, S., Möller, S.: Google now is for the extraverted, Cortana for the introverted: investigating the influence of personality on IPA preference. In: Proceedings of OZCHI 2017, pp. 257–265 (2017)

[7] Faulkner, L.: Beyond the five-user assumption: benefits of increased sample sizes in usability testing. Behav. Res. Methods Instrum. Comput. 35(3), 379–383 (2003)

[8] Garcia, M.P., Lopez, S.S., Donis, H.: Everybody is talking about voice activated virtual assistants, but how are people really adopting and using them? lessons from a multi-country study. In: Proceedings of the 32nd Human Computer Interaction Conference. BCS (2018)

[9] Giles, H., Powesland, P.: Accommodation theory. In: Coupland, N., Jaworski, A. (eds.) Sociolinguistics. MLS, pp. 232–239. Macmillan Education UK, London (1997). https://doi.org/10.1007/978-1-349-25582-5_19

[10] Guy, I.: Searching by talking: analysis of voice queries on mobile web search. In: Proceedings of SIGIR 2016, pp. 35–44. ACM, New York (2016)

[11] Ho, D.K.-H.: Voice-controlled virtual assistants for the older people with visual impairment. Eye 32(1), 53 (2017)

[12] Jiang, J., et al.: Automatic online evaluation of intelligent assistants. In: Proceedings of WWW 2015, pp. 506–516 (2015)

[13] Kinsella, B.: Over half of smartphone owners use voice assistants, Siri leads the pack. https://voicebot.ai/2018/04/03/over-half-of-smartphone-owners-use-voice-assistants-siri-leads-the-pack/. Accessed 10 Sep 2018

[14] Kiseleva, J., Williams, K., Hassan Awadallah, A., Crook, A.C., Zitouni, I., Anastasakos, I.: Predicting User satisfaction with intelligent assistants. In Proceedings of SIGIR 2016, pp. 45–54. ACM, New York (2016)

[15] Kiseleva, J., et al.: Understanding user satisfaction with intelligent assistants. In: Proceedings of CHIIR 2016, pp. 121–130. ACM, New York (2016)

[16] Konrad, P., Jørgensen, S.: Ny rekord: Vi bruger Appleprodukter som aldrig før. Via Ritzau, July 2017. https://via.ritzau.dk/pressemeddelelse/ny-rekord-vi-bruger-appleprodukter-som-aldrig-for?publisherId=10330283&releaseId=11205808

[17] López, G., Quesada, L., Guerrero, L.A.: Alexa vs. Siri vs. Cortana vs. Google assistant: a comparison of speech-based natural user interfaces. In: Nunes, I. (ed.) AHFE 2017. AISC, vol. 592, pp. 241–250. Springer, Cham (2018). https://doi.org/10.1007/978-3-319-60366-7_23

[18] Luger, E., Sellen, A.: "Like having a really bad PA": the gulf between user expectation and experience of conversational agents. In: Proceedings of CHI 2016, pp. 5286–5297. ACM, New York (2016)

[19] Mehrotra, R., Kholy, A.E., Zitouni, I., Shokouhi, M., Hassan, A.: Identifying user sessions in interactions with intelligent digital assistants. In: Proceedings of WWW 2017, pp. 821–822 (2017)

[20] Rogers, E.M.: Diffusion of Innovations, chap. 7. Simon & Schuster (1983)

[21] Strayer, D.L., Cooper, J.M., Turrill, J., Coleman, J.R., Hopman, R.J.: The smartphone and the driver's cognitive workload: a comparison of Apple, Google, and Microsoft's Intelligent Personal Assistants. Can. J. Exp. Psychol. 71(2), 93 (2017)

[22] Tassy, A.: It-anvendelse i befolkningen - 2017. Technical report, Danmarks Statistik (2017). https://www.dst.dk/da/Statistik/Publikationer/VisPub?cid=20739

Eliciting Privacy Concerns for Smart Home Devices from a User Centered Perspective

Chola Chhetri$^{(\boxtimes)}$ and Vivian Genaro Motti

George Mason University, Fairfax, VA 22030, USA
{cchhetri, vmotti}@gmu.edu

Abstract. Smart homes are equipped with an ecosystem of devices that support humans in their everyday activities, ranging from entertainment, lighting and security systems. Although smart devices provide home automation features that are convenient, comfortable, and easy to control, they also pose critical privacy risks for users, especially considering their continuous ability to sense users' information and connect to web services. To elicit privacy concerns from a user-centric perspective, the authors performed a thorough analysis of 128 online reviews of consumers of smart home hubs – including Amazon Echo, Google Home, Wink and Insteon. The reviews expressed users' concerns about privacy. The reviews were coded and classified according to four information security principles and temporal dimensions ranging from data collection to information sharing. A discussion on how to improve the design of smart home devices with privacy-enhanced solutions is provided.

Keywords: User-centered design · Security and privacy protection · Privacy · Privacy concerns · Smart home devices

1 Introduction

The Internet of Things (IoT) includes smart home devices that automate user tasks at home. According to a report from 2017, there exist 8.4 billion connected gadgets [1] and IoT field is expected to continue growing in the near future. Smart home technologies, a subset of IoT devices, are also expected to face significant growths. Business Insider Intelligence estimates that 1.8 billion smart home devices are expected to be sold by 2019, generating an estimated annual revenue of $490 billion [2]. In 2017, the estimated sale of smart home technologies in the United States (US) was 39 million units (35.9 million devices and 3.1 million hubs). Based on this data, one in every ten US households has at least one smart home device [3].

The primary motivator for users of smart home devices is the convenience that such devices offer. These technologies also promise comfort, control, safety and security [3]. However, the rise in adoption of smart home technologies presents new challenges to security and privacy [4, 5]. In 2016, the Mirai botnet affected hundreds of thousands of IoT devices—including Internet Protocol (IP) cameras, Digital Video Recorders (DVRs), routers, printers and Voice over Internet Protocol (VoIP) phones. In this attack a large scale distributed denial of service (DDOS) against multiple targets was executed. Targets of this attack included Krebs on Security, Lonestar Cell and Dyn, a

© Springer Nature Switzerland AG 2019
N. G. Taylor et al. (Eds.): iConference 2019, LNCS 11420, pp. 91–101, 2019.
https://doi.org/10.1007/978-3-030-15742-5_8

popular Domain Name System (DNS) provider. The DDoS on Dyn affected popular services such as Amazon, Github, Netflix, Paypal, Twitter and Reddit [6].

As the number of smart home devices grows, attacks of such nature are also likely to grow, not only in scale but also in sophistication [7]. Do users know about it? Are users concerned? What are they primarily concerned about? To address such questions, further investigation focusing on users concerns about smart home privacy is needed.

Previous studies about user adoption of smart speakers found privacy as the primary reason for non-adoption of these devices and adopters placed value on their privacy [8]. Privacy concerns of users are positively correlated to privacy importance [9]. In a study of fitness trackers, privacy concerns of users were found to be directly related to their valuation of data collected by the tracking devices [10]. Privacy behaviors also depend on context and evolve over time [11]. However, little work has been done to understand privacy concerns of smart home users [12, 13]. Understanding the privacy concerns of users of smart home devices helps stakeholders, investigators, and vendors to develop hardware and software solutions that are better suited to address privacy concerns of users. Improving smart home technologies with privacy-enhanced solutions has potential to boost user confidence and trust in such technologies [13, 14].

To elicit privacy concerns from a user-centric perspective, we analyzed thoroughly privacy-related online reviews of users of smart home hubs – including Amazon Echo [15], Google Home [16], Wink Hub 2 [17] and Insteon Hub [18]. One hundred twenty eight reviews expressing privacy concerns were retrieved and classified according to their contents, security principles involved and temporal dimensions regarding the automation process and information lifecycle, from data collection to sharing. A discussion on how to improve the design of smart home devices with privacy-enhanced solutions is provided.

The rest of the paper is organized as follows: Sect. 2 describes the research methodology; Sect. 3 presents research results; and Sect. 4 includes conclusions, recommendations, limitations and next steps.

2 Methodology

To analyze privacy concerns of users, five common smart hubs were selected, namely Amazon Echo Dot 2, Samsung SmartThings Hub, Google Home, Wink Hub 2 and Insteon Hub [19, 20]. There was no single portal containing customer reviews of smart home devices. We selected amazon.com and bestbuy.com as our sources as they contained the largest number of user reviews on these selected products (n = 66656). Table 1 shows the number of reviews and the source for the selected devices.

We filtered out the reviews that did not include the keyword 'privacy'. Our resulting dataset included 128 reviews: 120 for Amazon Echo, six for Google Home, one for Wink Hub 2, and one for Insteon Hub. No privacy-related reviews were found for Samsung SmartThings hub [21]. The reviews in our data set dated from October 2016 to October 2017 and included reviews that were classified as verified purchases by amazon.com and bestbuy.com.

We extracted and coded the reviews manually, and analyzed the qualitative data. For sentiment analysis, the reviews were manually read and then coded as positive,

Table 1. Number of reviews for five smart hubs. The source of reviews for all devices, except Google Home (*), was amazon.com. Google Home reviews were obtained from bestbuy.com

Device	Number of reviews (n = 66656)
Amazon Echo Dot 2	57079
Google Home *	6902
Samsung SmartThings Hub	1856
Wink Hub 2	558
Insteon Hub	261

neutral or negative. For temporal analysis, the reviews were coded based on the life cycle of data in the smart home architecture, namely collection, transmission, storage and sharing. For security principle analysis, the reviews were coded based on the security principles confidentiality, integrity, availability and authentication. Table 2 illustrates the codebook showing the main themes of coding. All authors were in consensus with the codes.

Table 2. Codebook showing codes/themes for analyses performed in the study.

Concern	Sentiment	Temporal	Principle
Specific	Positive	Collection	Confidentiality
Non-specific	Neutral	Transmission	Integrity
	Negative	Storage	Availability
		Sharing	Authentication

Our methodology was inspired by [22], an analysis of privacy concerns in user comments on wearable devices involving exploratory and empirical methods.

3 Results

3.1 Specific Concerns

While 33% of the reviews were general, in which the users mentioned privacy concern but did not specify their privacy concern in detail, 67% of the users specified precisely what their privacy concern was. The top user concern was that these devices were always listening to their conversations. Other five user concerns sorted per order of popularity were: (1) tracking of users, their actions and preferences, (2) storage of conversations and their transcripts (for audio conversations) in the cloud, (3) the lack of security of such content in the cloud, (4) the potential of private conversations to be hacked, and (5) the likelihood of such information to be subject to legal discovery by law enforcement and eventually disclosed publicly. Figure 1 depicts these concerns and their frequencies of occurrence.

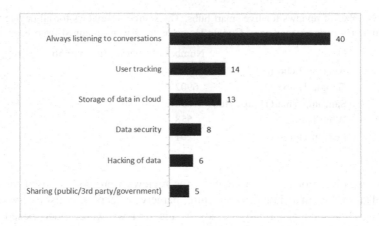

Fig. 1. Top six themes in users' privacy concerns and their frequencies

The identified concerns resonate with recent studies that discuss and demonstrate various smart home vulnerabilities, such as network observing, tracking, eavesdropping, user behavior prediction, data leakage, data theft, identity theft, social engineering, disruption or denial of service and software exploitation [7, 23, 24].

Users in our analysis were concerned that microphone-enabled smart home devices were recording private conversations, background conversations and noise. Such content included personal conversations, such as family members speaking to one another, and conversations not directed to the device. For example, Amazon Echo is expected to record only conversations following the wake-up word 'Alexa'; however, users reported to find recordings of private conversations not including such wake-up word.

According to one user, "Echo thinks my TV is talking to it. Very often, without the word Alexa being said the Echo will start jabbering or playing a song while watching TV." Another user reported that when he/she checked the history of the requests made to Alexa, he/she found many recordings of strange people talking that did not live in the house. He/she mentioned that "It even randomly records things in my house like my dog barking, the TV audio and a regular conversation without requesting 'Alexa'… I'm either going to send it back or keep it turned off unless I want to use it. I don't want the world to know what's being said in the privacy of my home and I don't want to hear what's going on in their homes. Very scary."

Users expressed that they believed the features and convenience offered by smart home technologies outweighed their privacy concerns, which led them to utilize smart home technologies despite their privacy concerns.

3.2   User Sentiments

We analyzed the sentiments expressed by users in their privacy concerns, by coding them as negative, neutral or positive. We found that user sentiments associated with privacy concerns are mostly negative (74%). Among the remaining 26% reviews, three quarters (75%) expressed positive sentiments and the rest of them were neutral. Examples of reviews are shown in Table 3.

Table 3. Three examples of reviews with negative, positive and neutral sentiments.

Sentiment	Sample reviews
Negative	"I am a bit paranoid that such a device will support furthering the evolution in the loss of privacy"
	"There's no privacy because every question that is asked is seen on the Alexa app which it should be private. I am disappointed with it"
Positive	"We love it even though we were initially concerned about it eavesdropping and related privacy issues"
Neutral	"For those concerned about privacy (like a few of my friends) just unplug when you don't want the device to listen in on your conversations or activities"

3.3 Temporal Analysis

Smart home devices collect information from users, transmit to a remote server on the cloud for storage, processing, and sharing. In a smart home, the life cycle of data ranges from collection and transmission to storage and sharing.

Based on our investigation, data collection stands out as the stage that concerns users the most. As Table 4 illustrates, about half (49%) of the 128 reviews analyzed mentioned the user concern was related to data collection, followed by storage (23%), sharing (9%), and transmission (2%).

3.4 Security and Privacy Principles

The breach of the four main security principles—Confidentiality, Integrity, Availability [25], and Authentication [26]—results in critical consequences for users. Confidentiality deals with keeping data secret from unauthorized parties using techniques like encryption. Integrity deals with prevention of tampering of data. Availability ensures data is available to authorized parties when necessary and authentication checks credentials of parties trying to access data [27]. An insight into the principles that concern users the most can direct research and development focus towards those areas.

As expected, users did not clearly utilize these terms in their reviews. Hence, we coded and mapped the reviews to these principles. Content of some reviews did not fall into any of the four principles. Such reviews could not be coded for this analysis but were still used for other analyses. Among the 73 reviews that were successfully mapped to a principle, 90% were related to confidentiality and 10% were related to authentication. None were directly related to integrity and availability. Thus, confidentiality of data was a leading privacy concern of users of smart home devices.

3.5 Privacy Protection Strategies

Users of smart home devices who expressed concern about privacy seemed to adopt individual controls to address their concerns. Our analysis revealed that users concerned about privacy adopt three major approaches. The first approach consists in deleting the

Table 4. Four examples of privacy concerns quoted from end users' reviews considering the lifecycle of data from collection and transmission to storage and sharing.

Stage	Examples/tasks	Sample reviews	Percentage of reviews (n = 128)
Collection	Devices with microphones and sensors collect data	"It is connected to the internet and listens and records all of the time, not just when you talk to it"	49%
		"Everything you say to it is recorded… even things you don't say to it"	
Transmission	Collected data is usually transmitted to a remote server or cloud for storage	"Records and uploads your conversations automatically"	2%
		"I would prefer to remove the cloud or any data sent which is collected, retained and resold as I have no need to control outside my network and have ways I can connect to my local network remotely without their spying servers being involved"	
Storage	Data is stored in a remote server or cloud	"This device records and stores everything it hears offsite forever"	23%
		"RECORDS everything you ask it. It keeps the text of what you ask, but it also actually keeps the audio recording of what you asked it"	
Sharing	Vendors may share this retained data to third parties or collected data may be requested by law enforcement	"I attempted to read all of the terms and conditions but soon found out that agreeing to them means that third parties can end up with my voice print!"	9%
		"It is another window into your privacy so that they can build a more precise profile on you for marketing purposes"	

history of audio and text data when possible. According to users, a common drawback of such products is the inability to delete collected and stored data in bulk. Having to delete large collection of data one-by-one is a major annoyance for users.

The second approach consists in turning off the device when it is not in use. Devices with the ability to turn off the microphone seemed to be the favorite for concerned users. Switching the microphone off or even the entire device when not in use is a user practice to prevent disclosure and misuse of private information mainly by ensuring that the device is not listening and recording private conversations that are not directed to it.

The third approach was deciding to use a product from a vendor who has demonstrated to advocate for data privacy. Users expressed confidence with companies that stood up against providing data to law enforcement. For instance, one user expressed confidence in trusting the vendor to fight for the privacy of user data: "I also trust this vendor and they have shown to fight for users' data privacy so far."

4 Conclusions

4.1 Recommendations for Privacy Enhancing Solutions

Online reviews in the data set analyzed included six suggestions for enhancing privacy in smart home technologies. We discuss those suggestions and also add our own recommendations for privacy-enhanced smart home technology solutions. Author recommendations are based on team discussion and experience. Recommendations in both categories are in alphabetical order.

4.2 User-Suggested Recommendations

Advocacy. Users Asked Vendors to Advocate More for Data Protection. Such protection can be ensured by utilizing and informing users of techniques used to safeguard data from insider and outsider attackers. Users mentioned they trust vendors that stand up against the release of data collected to third parties.

Interface. Another user suggestion is that vendors provide a user-friendly interface with the ability to view, manage and delete data collected by the devices.

Local Control. Users suggested that vendors develop locally controlled hubs for smart home automation instead of using the cloud. A local storage hub will eliminate the need to store data in the cloud and elevate user trust by eliminating privacy concerns related to data stored in the cloud.

Policy. Users showed interest to understand what data is collected, how the data collected is or will be used, and who has access to it. Users suggested vendors clearly state the policies regarding collection, storage, sharing and protection of data.

Safeguarding. Users were concerned about protection of data in the cloud by the vendors. They suggested that vendors take steps, such as encryption, to protect their data from being hacked.

Trust. Users mentioned that they prefer the ability to control the collection of smart home data. Users expressed frustration over the inability to control the data collection and recordings. They suggested that vendors provide a way to manage and especially to delete the collected data.

4.3   Recommendations

Accuracy. Manufacturers of smart home technologies must address programming flaws and lack of accuracy, for example, accuracy in recognizing wake-up words (words that activate a voice enabled smart home device) and eliminating false positives.

Authentication. Smart home devices should provide mechanisms to authenticate the user to avoid unwanted users from using the devices or accessing their services in an unauthorized manner.

Data Protection. Vendors should employ data protection techniques, such as encryption, to safeguard data in all stages of its lifecycle—collection, transmission, storage, and sharing.

Opt In. Data collection is necessary for vendors to improve the services offered to users. However, users are concerned about excessive data collection and have questioned it. Vendors can address such concern by providing users with the option to opt-in for such data collection. Making data collection an opt-in rather than mandatory can bring in more users who would otherwise not utilize such devices due to privacy concerns.

Policy. Providers of smart home technologies can gain higher consumer confidence by clearly stating what data they collect from the smart home device, how they transmit the data collected, how they handle smart home data and what measures they take to safeguard the data for ensuring its confidentiality and privacy.

Regulatory Framework. The data collected from smart homes should be subject to data protection law or regulation. A legal framework for the protection of data collected by smart home devices is necessary. Industry-level guidelines and best practices in smart home data protection are needed to make the smart home domain more secure and more private. The user-vendor-government trio needs to work collectively to preserve privacy in the age of smart homes. Past research [28] has also shown that users expect strong legal protection of their data.

Stop Technique. When a device is recording conversations, it is essential for the device to know when to stop recording. If a device does not know when to stop recording the conversation, it can record private conversations not directed to it. We recommend introducing a stop word (for example, 'thank you', 'bye bye', bye [name of device], etc.) or a stop technique. Such a method can be beneficial in informing the device of the end of the conversation, indicating it to stop recording or collecting data. An indicator light is recommended as a method of informing users of the recording action.

Visibility. Placing the on/off switch in a visible location and an indicator light depicting the recording action can elevate the comfort level of concerned users. Live status may also be helpful concerning collection of data.

4.4 Limitations

The extraction, reading and coding of reviews was performed manually. The resulting data set contained more reviews provided by Echo consumers than other devices. Thus, there may be a bias towards Echo. The study focuses on analyzing privacy concerns of only consumers that chose to write an online review for the product. Demographic analysis was not feasible as the online reviews lacked such information.

Privacy may be addressed without explicitly mentioning it. This study was limited to the content analysis of reviews that explicitly mentioned the word 'privacy'. Another limitation is that users who post comments tend to have more extreme opinions about those devices and belong to a subset of users who are tech savvy, young, and literate.

4.5 Next Steps

In this paper, we analyzed privacy concerns of smart home device users to shed light into privacy concerns of actual consumers and we discuss recommendations for making the devices more privacy preserving. We expect this paper to motivate researchers, developers and manufacturers to develop privacy-enhanced smart home solutions.

We will further explore smart home privacy concerns through complementary research methods including responses from an online survey, and we will extend the data set analyzing comments of additional smart home devices. It is likely that people who are concerned about privacy are choosing not to use such technologies [29]. We will also analyze concerns of such non-users of smart home devices to address their privacy concerns and smart home technology adoption. Future work will include research into educational tools and training to promote awareness on smart home privacy. The smart home domain can benefit from an investigation into the legal framework for smart home data protection.

References

1. Gartner, Inc. https://www.gartner.com/technology/research.jsp
2. BI Intelligence. http://www.businessinsider.com/research
3. Smart Home Ecosystem: IoT and Consumers. Park Associates and Consumer Electronics Association, USA (2014)
4. Ye, M., Jiang, N., Yang, H., Yan, Q.: Security analysis of internet-of-things: a case study of August smart lock. In: MobiSec 2017: Security, Privacy, and Digital Forensics of Mobile Systems and Networks, Georgia, pp. 499–504 (2017)
5. Fernandes, E., Jung, J., Prakash, A.: Security analysis of emerging smart home applications. In: 2016 IEEE Symposium on Security and Privacy (SP), pp. 636–654. IEEE California (2016)

6. Antonakakis, M., et al.: Understanding the Mirai Botnet. In: Proceedings of the 26th USENIX Security Symposium, Vancouver, Canada, pp. 1093–1110 (2017)
7. Arabo, A., Brown, I., El-Moussa, F.: Privacy in the age of mobility and smart devices in smart homes. In: ASE/IEEE International Conference on Privacy, Security, Risk and Trust, and ASE/IEEE International Conference on Social Computing, SocialCom/PASSAT, pp. 819–826. IEEE (2012)
8. Lau, J., Zimmerman, B., Schaub, F.: Alexa, are you listening ? privacy perceptions, concerns and privacy-seeking behaviors with smart speakers. In: Proceedings of ACM Human-Computer Interaction, pp. 102:1–120:31 (2018)
9. Acquisti, A., Grossklags, J.: Privacy and rationality in individual decision making. IEEE Secur. Priv. **3**, 26–33 (2005)
10. Vitak, J., Liao, Y., Kumar, P., Zimmer, M., Kritikos, K.: Privacy attitudes and data valuation among fitness tracker users. In: Chowdhury, G., McLeod, J., Gillet, V., Willett, P. (eds.) iConference 2018. LNCS, vol. 10766, pp. 229–239. Springer, Cham (2018). https://doi.org/10.1007/978-3-319-78105-1_27
11. Nissenbaum, H.: A contextual approach to privacy online. Digit. Enlight. Yearb. **2012**, 219–234 (2012)
12. Fruchter, N., Liccardi, I.: Consumer attitudes towards privacy and security in home assistants. In: CHI 2018 Extended Abstracts. ACM, Canada (2018)
13. Zeng, E., Mare, S., Roesner, F.: End user security & privacy concerns with smart homes. In: Symposium on Usable Privacy and Security (SOUPS) (2017)
14. Kugler, L.: The war over the value of personal data. Commun. ACM **61**, 17–19 (2018)
15. Echo Dot (2nd Generation). https://www.amazon.com/dp/B01DFKC2SO
16. Google Home. https://store.google.com/us/product/google_home
17. Wink Hub 2. https://www.wink.com/products/wink-hub-2/
18. Insteon Hub. https://www.insteon.com/insteon-hub/
19. The Best Smart Home Devices of 2017. https://www.pcmag.com/article2/0,2817,2410 889,00.asp
20. Best Smart Home Devices of 2017. https://www.cnet.com/topics/smart-home/best-smart-home-devices/
21. SmartThings Hub. https://www.smartthings.com/products/smartthings-hub
22. Motti, V.G., Caine, K.: Users' privacy concerns about wearables: impact of form factor, sensors and type of data collected. In: Brenner, M., Christin, N., Johnson, B., Rohloff, K. (eds.) FC 2015. LNCS, vol. 8976, pp. 231–244. Springer, Heidelberg (2015). https://doi.org/10.1007/978-3-662-48051-9_17
23. Geneiatakis, D., Kounelis, I., Neisse, R., Nai-Fovino, I., Steri, G., Baldini, G.: Security and Privacy Issues for an IoT based Smart Home. Information and Communication Technology. Electronics and Microelectronics (MIPRO), pp. 1292–1297. Opatija, Croatia (2017)
24. Apthorpe, N., Reisman, D., Feamster, N.: A smart home is no castle: privacy vulnerabilities of encrypted IoT traffic. In: Data and Algorithmic Transparency Workshop (DAT), New York (2016)
25. Jacobsson, A., Davidsson, P.: Towards a model of privacy and security for smart homes. In: IEEE World Forum Internet Things, WF-IoT 2015 - Proceedings, pp. 727–732. IEEE (2016)
26. Fisher, B.: Identity and Access Management for Smart Home Devices. National Institute of Standards and Technology (2016)
27. Gibson, D.: Managing Risk in Information Systems. Jones and Bartlett Learning, Burlington (2011)

28. Malkin, N., Bernd, J., Johnson, M., Egelman, S.: "What Can't Data Be Used For?" privacy expectations about smart TVs in the U.S. In: Proceedings of the European Workshop on Usable Security (EuroUSEC). IEEE, London (2018)
29. Zheng, S., Apthorpe, N., Chetty, M., Feamster, N.: User perceptions of smart home IoT privacy. In: Proceedings of ACM Human-Computer Interaction, pp. 200:1–200:20. ACM (2018)

Understanding the Role of Privacy and Trust in Intelligent Personal Assistant Adoption

Yuting Liao[1(✉)], Jessica Vitak[1], Priya Kumar[1], Michael Zimmer[2], and Katherine Kritikos[2]

[1] University of Maryland, College Park, MD 20742, USA
{yliao598, jvitak, pkumar12}@umd.edu
[2] University of Wisconsin—Milwaukee, Milwaukee, WI 53211, USA
{zimmerm, kritikos}@uwm.edu

Abstract. Voice-controlled intelligent personal assistants (IPAs) have seen tremendous growth in recent years on smartphones and as standalone devices in people's homes. While research has examined the potential benefits and drawbacks of these devices for IPA users, few studies have empirically evaluated the role of privacy and trust in individual decision to adopt IPAs. In this study, we present findings from a survey of IPA users and non-users (N = 1160) to understand (1) the motivations and barriers to adopting IPAs and (2) how concerns about data privacy and trust in company compliance with social contract related to IPA data affect acceptance and use of IPAs. We discuss our findings in light of social contract theory and frameworks of technology acceptance.

Keywords: Intelligent personal assistant · Internet of Things · Privacy · Technology adoption · Amazon Alexa · Google Home · Social contract theory

1 Introduction

As a component of the Internet of Things (IoT) ecosystem, voice-controlled intelligent personal assistants (IPAs) have seen tremendous growth in recent years, with nearly half (47%) of Americans saying they now use an IPA on their smartphone or in their home [24]. IPAs—including Apple's Siri, Amazon's Alexa, and Google's Assistant—are increasingly being integrated into many consumer mobile devices, vehicles, and homes, as well as university dorms and hotels [28, 33].

Utilizing artificial intelligence, machine learning, and natural language processing techniques, IPAs facilitate information retrieval by providing information based on user input (e.g., offering weather updates) and acting on behalf of users to complete tasks (e.g., turning on/off lights at home). Despite these potential benefits, IPAs raise several security and privacy challenges for consumers. IPAs rely on cloud computing, with devices transmitting a large amount of users' behavioral data—including real-time voice data—through the internet to remote cloud servers. In the event of a data breach, an adversary could access users' detailed IPA usage history and potentially infer additional information about users' lifestyles and behavioral patterns through data mining techniques [4, 8]. Researchers have also identified privacy concerns among

© Springer Nature Switzerland AG 2019
N. G. Taylor et al. (Eds.): iConference 2019, LNCS 11420, pp. 102–113, 2019.
https://doi.org/10.1007/978-3-030-15742-5_9

users who control their smart home appliances via IPA devices, including continuous audio/video recording, data collection and mining, adversarial remote control, and network attacks on local devices [35].

In general, previous IPA studies have been conducted in a particular socio-technical context using qualitative methods with a small number of users and ignoring the non-user population. Thus, their findings limit our ability to understand broader attitudes toward IPAs among users and non-users alike, as well as why some people may adopt these technologies while others do not. To begin to address these gaps, we conducted a survey with 1178 users and non-users of IPAs in the United States to investigate factors that affect adoption of IPAs, with a special focus on the role privacy and trust play in decision-making processes. Specifically, we ask the following research questions:

RQ1:   *What are the motivations and barriers for people to adopt IPA devices?*

RQ2:   *What differences—if any—exist between people who use IPAs and those who do not?*

RQ3:   *How are individual characteristics and privacy attitudes associated with non-users' behavioral intention to adopt a Home IPA?[1]*

In the following sections, we synthesize the existing research on IPAs, as well as present our theoretical frameworks—privacy as social contract and technology acceptance model—for interpreting the data. After describing our findings, we discuss them through the lens of these frameworks. We argue that a deeper and more robust understanding of the privacy and trust implications of IPA adoption and use will provide critical insights into the design of future voice-controlled IPAs—as well as IoT devices in general, which will see significant growth over the next decade.

2 Related Work

2.1 Research on IPAs, Privacy, and Trust

Research in information science and human-computer interaction has explored various social dimensions of the current generation of IPAs, including how people use these devices at home [3] and in group conversation [25], whether users personify their devices [14, 27], how children interact with the devices [9], and how IPAs can support people with disabilities [26]. One diary study with 19 users found they were largely satisfied with their Alexa interactions [13], while an interview study with 14 users found that IPAs did not behave as users expected them to; the lack of system feedback made it difficult for these users to refine their mental models of how IPAs worked [15].

This uncertainty about how IPAs function raises clear implications for privacy and security, since these devices rely on collecting and processing potentially sensitive data from users (i.e., their home). Dorai et al. [8] conducted a forensic

---

[1] In this paper, we refer to interactions with IPAs embedded within a smartphone (e.g., Siri) as Phone IPA use and interactions with a standalone smart home device (e.g., Amazon Echo) as Home IPA use.

analysis to extract data and infer user information from a smart home system involving IPAs. Likewise, Chung and Lee [4] analyzed four months of data from an Alexa user and inferred patterns about the person's schedule, interests, and location. In a separate analysis, Chung et al. [3] identified four ways malicious actors could put IPA users' privacy and security at risk, including wiretapping, exploiting security vulnerabilities, impersonating a user, or eavesdropping on unintentional recordings.

Researchers are beginning to explore how IPA users evaluate privacy and security threats. One study found that only 2% of online product reviews for IPAs referenced privacy and security [12]. Those that did focused on the amount and type of data IPAs collect as well as its "creepiness" [12]. Zeng et al. [35] interviewed 15 smart home users, many of whom also used IPAs, and found that those with less sophisticated mental models of their smart home systems did not perceive many security threats. In addition, most respondents did not express privacy concerns; their reasons included not feeling personally targeted, trusting companies or governments who may access IPA data, or feeling satisfied their existing strategies to mitigate threats [35].

Only four of Pradhan et al.'s [26] 16 respondents discussed IPA security concerns, but half expressed privacy concerns about the "always on" nature of IPAs and their collection of personal data. Nearly one-third avoided certain IPA tasks or turned off the device at certain times. Social contexts also influence IPA use; for example, Moorthy and Vu [21] found that smartphone users were hesitant to use a mobile IPA for a task that involved private information—even more so if they were in a public location. This work highlights that privacy and security considerations draw on a complex interplay of technical operations, users' experiences and mental models, and contextual cues. However, most research only considers experiences of people who already use IPAs. In this study, we provide perspectives of non-users as well as users.

2.2 Applying Social Contract Approach to IPA Privacy

A growing body of scholarship argues that privacy is contextual in nature, and that protecting privacy depends on maintaining appropriate information flows between actors within a given context [16, 22, 23, 29]. Martin [16] notes that contextually dependent approaches to privacy mirror a contractual approach to norms, where privacy evolves as a social contract—a mutually beneficial agreement within a contracting community about how information is used and shared. Privacy as social contract implies that (1) online privacy expectations should depend on the context of the exchange, (2) users do not relinquish information without an expectation about how that information will be used within that context, and (3) companies that derive benefits from users, consumers, and employees disclosing information have an obligation to respect the privacy norms within their community [17].

The social contract framework suggests that information is governed by the norms of a contracting community, a self-described group of people with shared tasks, values, or goals and who are capable of establishing norms of ethical behavior for themselves [7]. Although contractors have the moral free space to develop authentic and legitimate privacy norms and expectations, privacy violations occur when "information is tracked, disseminated, or used against the agreement of the actors within the community through a breach of microsocial contracts" (p. 558) [17]. Through the lens of social contract theory, IPA users and IPA service providers form a contracting community. Both acting as the recipient and disseminator of information, they have a right and an obligation to abide by the privacy norms associated with IPA use. Empirically, respondents within a particular contracting community have a better understanding of the privacy norms than outsiders [16]. From this perspective, existing IPA users might hold different privacy attitudes compared to non-users. Similarly, we might expect one's level of trust in company compliance with social norms regarding data privacy and security to vary.

2.3   Technology Adoption and the Role of Privacy

Frameworks for understanding technology acceptance explain how users come to adopt and use a specific technology [19]. The Technology Acceptance Model (TAM) and its extensions inform the current study's exploration of the factors that affect IPA use. According to the original model [5], users' attitudes toward technology use determine their behavioral intentions, which directly influence the individuals' final use or rejection of the technology. In TAM, attitudes toward technology use are influenced by two personal beliefs: perceived ease of use and perceived usefulness. However, TAM falls short in recognizing how external contextual factors inform technology acceptance [1]. In response, the Unified Theory of Acceptance and Use of Technology (UTAUT) [31] suggests that three key constructs drive behavioral intentions to use the technology: *performance expectancy* (the perceived usefulness of the system), *effort expectancy* (the perceived ease of use), and *social influence* (to what degree an individual perceives that important others believe he or she should use the system). Additionally, *facilitating condition*, influences only the final decision to use or reject the technology [30]. Researchers have further extended the model by incorporating the constructs of *hedonic motivation* (i.e., fun or pleasure derived from the technology use), *price value* (consumers' cognitive tradeoff between the perceived benefits and the monetary cost), and *experience* and *habit* [30] to examine use of various technologies, including mobile health services [10] and social media [6].

In recent years, researchers have increasingly considered how privacy and security affects technology acceptance and use. For instance, Miltgen et al. [19] examined end-user acceptance of biometric-based identification systems and found that users who expressed higher data privacy concerns were more likely to perceive the technology as risky—and consequently, they were less likely to use the technology. However, as the current generation of IPAs is a relatively new technology for most consumers, research is just beginning to explore consumer attitudes toward IPAs. This study provides an opportunity to apply and extend technology acceptance frameworks by investigating privacy and trust as determinants of IPA acceptance and use.

3   Method

In January 2018, authors at two universities each invited a random sample of 3000 university staff to participate in a 10–15 min online survey on technology use, with an opportunity to win one of five US$50 Amazon gift cards from a random drawing. The study was part of a larger project examining privacy attitudes and behaviors among adult smartphone users; therefore, participation was limited to smartphone owners 18 or older. At the close of the survey, 1178 people had completed the survey. The research team removed 18 cases for not meeting participation criteria or significant missing data, for a final sample size of 1160. Across the full sample, 59% of respondents were women, and 92% had obtained at least a bachelor's degree; respondents were generally young ($M = 38.17$, $SD = 12.72$, range: 20–82), with most (61.5%) owning an iPhone, compared with 37.8% owning an Android.

3.1 Measures and Variables

IPA Data Concerns and Data Confidence. We used an original, 7-item scale to measure privacy and security concerns associated with IPA device use (IPA Data Concerns; $M = 3.12$, $SD = 1.14$, $\alpha = .91$). Responses were recorded on a five-point Likert scale from 1 (Not at All Concerned) to 5 (Extremely Concerned). Example statements include: "I am concerned that the device is always listening" and "I am concerned that other people might activate/access the device and trigger unauthorized purchases."

To measure respondents' trust of companies' compliance with the IPA social contract (i.e., that their use of IPAs are private, safe, and secure), we included an original, 4-item scale (IPA Data Confidence; $M = 1.94$, $SD = .86$, $\alpha = .84$). Responses were recorded on a five-point Likert scale from 1 (Not at All Confident) to 5 (Very Confident). Example statements are: "I'm confident information communicated between the device and the service provider is always encrypted" and "I'm confident that microphones on these devices are not activated without a user's direct action."

General Privacy and Mobile Data Concerns. General privacy concerns were measured by an 11-item scale [32] evaluating the level of concern respondents have in association with their use of communication technologies. Sample prompts include: "Private messages becoming public available" and "Your picture being used in a social media app." Respondents selected from a five-point Likert scale from 1 (Not at all concerned) to 5 (Very concerned) ($M = 3.27$, $SD = .97$, $\alpha = .93$).

Respondents' mobile data concerns were measured through an 8-item scale [34] asking, "How much do you agree or disagree with the following statements about your use of mobile phone apps." Sample statements include: "I believe that the location of my mobile device is monitored at least part of the time" and "I am concerned that mobile apps are collecting too much information about me." Respondents chose along a five-point Likert scale from 1 (Strongly Disagree) to 5 (Strongly Agree) ($M = 3.93$, $SD = .77$, $\alpha = .93$).

Digital Literacy Related to Smartphone Use. To measure users' digital literacy related to their smartphone use ($M = 4.16$, $SD = .83$, $\alpha = .89$), we asked respondents to indicate how confident they felt performing eight tasks on a smartphone. Example tasks include: "Adjusting which apps have permission to access my microphone," and "Creating a personal hotspot with my phone." Respondents responded along a five-point Likert scale from 1 (Not at All Confident) to 5 (Very Confident).

Experience Related to Phone IPA Use and Non-use. We asked respondents if they had Siri, Google Assistant, or another IPA activated on their smartphones: 524 (45%) were current Phone IPA users, while 332 (28%) never used IPAs on their phones. An additional 128 (11%) reported they had used it in the past, but no longer used it, and 127 (11%) had disabled the feature. We also asked follow-up questions on use or non-use based on their response to this question.

Experience Related to Home IPA Use and Non-use. We also asked respondents whether they owned a Home IPA device. Twenty-nine percent (n = 319) reported that they owned at least one Home IPA device. Among this subgroup of Home IPA users, 227 (71%) owned an Amazon Echo or Echo Dot, while 92 (29%) reported owning a Google Home or Home Mini, and 39 (12%) owned both Home IPAs. We asked users to provide more information on their motivations for getting a device, and we asked non-users follow-up questions on whether they intended to purchase one in the future.

Control Variables. Our respondents provided basic demographic information, including their sex, current age, annual income, and education. We also asked questions about their knowledge of smartphone data sharing and, when applicable, tasks they performed with a Phone IPA. For the analyses presented below, we exclude education because the dataset is heavily skewed toward those with college degrees.

4 Findings

4.1 RQ1: Exploring Reasons for IPAs Use and Non-use

Motivations for IPA Adoption. For the 652 respondents who had ever used a Phone IPA—including those who currently used it and those who had used it in the past—we asked them to identify why they used it. The survey included a list of 11 possible reasons, (plus an open-ended option), and respondents could select multiple responses. The most popular reasons for using a Phone IPA were: (1) asking factual questions (82%); (2) getting directions/location of a place (65%); (3) asking silly/funny questions just for laughs (60%); (4) dictating a text message or email (51%); (5) setting a timer (47%). Additional responses that garnered fewer votes included asking advice, asking health-specific questions, and home automation.

For the 380 respondents who reported owning a Google Home or Amazon Alexa, we asked them to list their motivations for purchasing the device. Nearly half (47%) said they had received the IPA as a gift; others said they had purchased the device primarily to control smart home devices (13%), out of curiosity or for fun (12%), to stream music (10%), and to have hands-free access to online information (8%).

Barriers to IPA Adoption. For the 457 respondents who said they did not currently use a Phone IPA—including those who had never used it and those who had deactivated IPA features on their phone—we asked them to rate factors that may have played a role in their decision. They responded on a five-point Likert scale (1 = Not at All Important to 5 = Very Important). The factors most often cited by these respondents reflected concerns about utility, design, and privacy. They included: I don't see any benefits from this feature ($M = 3.48$, $SD = 1.23$); I don't like talking aloud to my phone (M = 3.38, SD = 1.36); the user interface is frustrating (M = 3.18, SD = 1.03); it's awkward to use (M = 3.14, SD = 1.03); it doesn't understand my voice most of the time (M = 2.96, SD = 1.34); and I have privacy/security concerns about these features (M = 2.88, SD = 1.37).

In addition, 425 Phone IPA non-users provided open-ended responses to the question, "What is the main reason you don't use or stopped using your phone's IPA?" The vast majority of responses reflected classical constructs in TAM and UTAUT, with many revealing low performance expectancy (i.e., low perceived usefulness) associated with IPA use. A second cluster of responses suggested a high effort expectancy (i.e., low perceived ease of use) associated with IPA use. For example, one respondent said, "*I find it more time consuming compared to just doing the task myself.*" Finally, social influence played a role in respondents' decision not to use IPA, with one respondent noting, "*I use my phone in places where silence is of utmost importance and I, therefore, do not talk directly to personal assistants.*"

Only 28 respondents (7%) identified privacy concerns and trust issues as their primary reason for not using Phone IPAs. For instance, one respondent said, "*I do not want my phone listening to every word I have to say during the day. I do not trust Siri or Google not to store information it hears while in listening mode.*" Another respondent expressed heightened concerns about the privacy of voice data: "*How do I know my voice patterns being stored for future use? Inflections are just as identifiable as other human characteristics.*" Other respondents feared "*the app listening all the time*" and felt their privacy would be "*compromised*" or "*invaded.*"

4.2   RQ2: Predicting Adoption and Use of IPAs

To explore differences among people who use and do not use IPAs, we built binary logistic regression models to predict IPA adoption. Table 1 summarizes the statistics for the final models predicting use of Phone and Home IPA devices, respectively. Predictors included background/demographic variables, privacy and security concerns, and experience with other types of IPAs.

Results from Model 1 (predicting Phone IPA adoption) indicated a significant correlation between Phone IPA use and age, smartphone digital literacy, the type of smartphone used, general privacy concerns, IPA data confidence, and using a Home IPA ($\chi^2(11)$ = 141.0, $p < .001$). Specifically, respondents who used their phone's IPA were more likely to be older but have a higher level of digital literacy related to smartphone use. They were also more likely to use an iPhone compared to an Android device. Phone IPA users reported a lower level of general privacy concerns and greater confidence in how data from their IPA was used. Finally, they were likely to also use a Home IPA device. Model 2 (predicting Home IPA adoption) revealed a significant association between Home IPA use and income, smartphone digital literacy, mobile privacy concerns, IPA data concerns, IPA data confidence, and having used Phone IPA ($\chi^2(11)$ = 117.98, $p < .001$). Compared with those who did not own a Home IPA, respondents who used Home IPAs reported higher income, grater smartphone skills, and more mobile privacy concerns. Home IPA users were also more likely to have a higher IPA data confidence, paired with a lower level of IPA data concerns. They were more likely to have used their phone's IPA as well.

Table 1. Predicting adoption and use of Phone and Home IPAs

	Model 1 Use of Phone IPA	Model 2 Use of Home IPA
	Parameter Estimates: Beta (Odds Ratio)	
Background		
Sex (Male)	−.23 (.79)	.00 (1.00)
Age	.02 (1.02)***	−.00 (.99)
Income	−.00 (1.00)	.11 (1.12)**
Smartphone digital literacy	.59 (1.77)***	.24 (1.24)*
Smartphone type (iPhone)	.45 (1.58)***	−.03 (.98)
Privacy and Security		
General privacy concerns	−.18 (.83)*	.01 (1.02)
Mobile privacy concerns	.02 (1.02)	.35 (1.41)**
IPA data concerns	−.07 (.93)	−.49 (.61)***
IPA data confidence	.31 (1.36)***	.27 (1.31)*
Experience with IPA		
Home IPA use (Yes)	.54 (1.58)***	–
Phone IPA use (Yes)	–	.54 (1.72)***
Model fit|	**χ^2 = 141.0, df = 11*****	**χ^2 = 117.98, df = 11*****
Nagelkerke Pseudo R^2	**.16**	**.14**

*$p < .05$, **$p < .01$, ***$p < .001$

4.3   RQ3: Explaining Behavioral Intention to Adopt Home IPA Devices

To answer RQ3, we built a multinomial logistic regression model to explore individual differences across non-users' (N = 816) behavioral intentions to adopt Home IPAs in the future. The dependent variable was measured through respondents' response to the question, "How likely are you to buy a Home IPA device in the future?" Respondents had three options: "I'm confident I won't be purchasing one" (Adamant; 52.1%); "I might or might not buy one" (Ambivalent; 41.4%); and "I'll probably purchase one in the next year" (Likely-converted; 6.5%). In the final model, the reference category is "Adamant non-adopters" who stated they had no intention of purchasing a Home IPA. Table 2 summarizes the multinomial regression results.

In evaluating Home IPA non-users' likelihood of purchasing a device in the future, we found a number of factors predicted their intentions. Compared to those who were adamant they will not purchase a Home IPA, those who were more ambivalent or leaning toward purchasing a device had significantly higher smartphone digital literacy and higher general privacy concerns. These respondents were also more likely to currently use a Phone IPA than those who said they had no intention of buying a Home IPA. When compared to the ambivalent and likely-converted, those who had no plans to purchase a Home IPA had significantly higher concerns about how IPA-generated data might be used and significantly less confidence that data generated by IPAs is sufficiently secure and protected.

Table 2. Explaining behavioral intention to adopt Home IPA devices

Reference category: Adamant (I'm confident I won't be purchasing one)	Intention to Adopt Home IPA Devices	
	Ambivalent (I might or might not buy one)	Likely-converted (I'll probably purchase one in the next year)
	Parameter Estimates: Beta (Odds Ratio)	
Background factors		
Sex: Male	−.05 (.95)	.81 (2.24)*
Age	.01 (1.01)	.00 (1.00)
Smartphone digital literacy	.22 (1.24)*	.49 (1.64)*
Privacy attitudes		
General privacy concerns	.37 (1.45)***	.53 (1.69)*
Mobile data concerns	−.26 (.77)	−.03 (.98)
IPA-specific factors		
Don't use Phone IPA	−.68 (.51)***	−2.06 (.13)***
IPA data concerns	−.24 (.79)**	−.22 (.81)
IPA data confidence	.52 (1.67)***	.76 (2.14)***
Model fit: χ^2 = 147.75, df = 14, p < 0.001 | Nagelkerke Pseudo R^2 = .20		

*p < .05, **p < .01, ***p < .001

5 Discussion

In this paper, we considered users' perceived motivations and barriers to adopting IPA devices, which are popular both on smartphones and as standalone home devices. IPAs can be integrated into existing smart home ecosystems, which can include smart speakers, thermostats, lighting, home security, and more. As IPAs are a relatively new technology, this study sought to understand how consumers make decisions to use these devices (or not), and to consider how concerns about privacy and trust influence their decisions. For Phone IPAs users, the convenience these tools provide—especially in allowing for personalized, hands-free information-seeking and task completion—was very appealing. Users of Phone IPAs like Siri or Google Assistant were more likely to be older and have a higher level of smartphone digital literacy. They also reported both a lower level of general privacy concerns and greater confidence in how data from their IPA was used. These findings paint a picture of a Phone IPA user who is technologically literate and confident in how IPA providers manage their data.

For Home IPA users, nearly half of respondents reported receiving the device as a gift. This suggests that some users might not have considered issues of privacy and trust before deciding to allow an IPA into their home. Home IPA users tended to use their devices for tasks other than personalized services or information seeking, such as streaming music or controlling other smart devices. This data suggests that users of Home IPAs relate to these devices as novel additions—often via gifts—to their home, and rely on them for more basic functions compared to Phone IPA users. The increased mobile privacy concerns among Home IPA users might contribute to the lack of more personalized usage within the home, such as linking the device to their Amazon account to enable voice-activated purchasing.

Overall, IPA users tended to report lower levels of general privacy concerns, while also reporting high confidence that IPA providers ensured their use of such devices was private, safe, and secure. From a social contract theory perspective, this suggests users trust IPA service providers (Google, Amazon, and Apple) to abide by the anticipated norms of information flow and assure consumer data privacy and security.

The social contract framework also informs our findings for non-users. While reasons for not using IPAs ranged across many factors (e.g., lack of need, minimal perceived usefulness, and price), we highlight the role of privacy in non-adoption of IPAs. While only 7% of respondents articulated privacy concerns as the primary reason for not using IPAs, our analysis of intentions to adopt them in the future reveals a more complex story. Respondents who were adamant in their refusal to consider purchasing a Home IPA, for example, had significantly higher concerns about how IPA data might be used and significantly less confidence that data generated by IPAs is sufficiently secure. Those who were ambivalent or considering a purchase within the next year exhibited greater trust, mirroring existing users. This suggests that perceptions of whether IPA providers abide by the social contract around data privacy and security influence one's likelihood to adopt Home IPAs.

Overall, we see various aspects of the TAM and UTAUT adoption frameworks in respondents' decisions to adopt—or reject—IPAs. Issues of perceived usefulness, expected performance, and the effort to make such devices perform as expected influenced adoption decisions. More notably, respondents' attitudes towards IPAs were rooted in their trust—or lack thereof—that the IPA provider adhered to the implicit social contract about maintaining private and secure information flows appropriate to the use of such devices.

6 Limitations, Future Work, and Conclusion

Some limitations to this research must be noted. While we took steps to reach a diverse set of respondents through our sampling method, we were constrained to university employees, leading to a highly educated sample. Therefore, results may not generalize to the wider population of American adults. Furthermore, results were based on a one-time survey and therefore provide a snapshot of a particular moment in time. Because of this, we can only identify correlations between variables and not establish causation.

The results from this study reveal a complex picture of IPA users and non-users. Users of IPAs tend to trust that providers adhere to a social contract about the flow and usage of their information, yet privacy concerns differ between Phone and Home IPA users. Additional research can further examine these differences and potentially highlight whether users approach these different contexts of IPA usage with different sets of privacy expectations.

Our analysis of non-users' behavioral intentions to purchase an IPA in the future reveals the importance of trust within the social contract between users and IPA providers. Thus, IPA providers should note that not only does meeting consumer privacy expectations increase consumers' likelihood to adopt such devices [2, 11], but meeting consumer privacy expectations also increases overall trust in the company [18].

Conversely, violating privacy expectations inevitably leads to adverse consumer reactions, including non-adoption or rejection of a tool or service [20].

Future researchers should take a more inductive approach to identify consumers' privacy expectations. Understanding the factors that drive mutually beneficial and sustainable privacy norms is also important for IPA service providers to best meet the privacy expectations of consumers and maintain the social contract proven essential for continued adoption of such devices. Providing a fuller understanding of the contextual expectations of privacy and security within the IPA ecosystem can enhance the future design of these smart devices and related IoT technologies.

Acknowledgements. This publication is based upon work supported by the National Science Foundation under grants No. 1640640 and 1640697.

References

1. Bagozzi, R.P.: The legacy of the technology acceptance model and a proposal for a paradigm shift. J. Assoc. Inf. Syst. **8**(4), 3 (2007)
2. Cases, A.-S., et al.: Web site spill over to email campaigns: the role of privacy, trust and shoppers' attitudes. J. Bus. Res. **63**(9–10), 993–999 (2010)
3. Chung, H., et al.: Digital forensic approaches for Amazon Alexa ecosystem. Digit. Investig. **22**, S15–S25 (2017)
4. Chung, H., Lee, S.: Intelligent virtual assistant knows your life. CoRRabs/1803.00466 (2018)
5. Davis, F.D.: Perceived usefulness, perceived ease of use, and user acceptance of information technology. MIS Q. **13**, 319–340 (1989)
6. Doleck, T., et al.: Examining the antecedents of social networking sites use among CEGEP students. Educ. Inf. Technol. **22**(5), 2103–2123 (2017)
7. Donaldson, T., Dunfee, T.W.: Ties That Bind: A Social Contracts Approach to Business Ethics. Harvard Business School Press, Boston (1999)
8. Dorai, G., et al.: I know what you did last summer: your smart home Internet of Things and your iPhone forensically ratting you out. In: Proceedings of the 13th International Conference on Availability, Reliability and Security, pp. 49:1–49:10. ACM, New York (2018)
9. Druga, S., et al.: "Hey Google is it OK if I eat you?": initial explorations in child-agent interaction. In: Proceedings of the 2017 Conference on Interaction Design and Children, pp. 595–600. ACM, New York (2017)
10. Dwivedi, Y.K., et al.: A generalised adoption model for services: a cross-country comparison of mobile health (m-health). Gov. Inf. Q. **33**(1), 174–187 (2016)
11. Eastlick, M.A., et al.: Understanding online B-to-C relationships: an integrated model of privacy concerns, trust, and commitment. J. Bus. Res. **59**(8), 877–886 (2006)
12. Fruchter, N., Liccardi, I.: Consumer attitudes towards privacy and security in home assistants. In: Extended Abstracts of the 2018 CHI Conference on Human Factors in Computing Systems, pp. LBW0501–LBW0506. ACM, New York (2018)
13. Lopatovska, I., et al.: Talk to me: exploring user interactions with the Amazon Alexa. J. Librariansh. Inf. Sci., 1–14 (2018)
14. Lopatovska, I., Williams, H.: Personification of the Amazon Alexa: BFF or a mindless companion. In: Proceedings of the 2018 Conference on Human Information Interaction & Retrieval, pp. 265–268. ACM Press, New Brunswick (2018)

15. Luger, E., Sellen, A.: "Like Having a Really Bad PA": the Gulf between user expectation and experience of conversational agents. In: Proceedings of the 2016 CHI Conference on Human Factors in Computing Systems, pp. 5286–5297. ACM, New York (2016)
16. Martin, K.E.: Diminished or just different?: A factorial vignette study of privacy as a social contract. J. Bus. Ethics **111**(4), 519–539 (2012)
17. Martin, K.E.: Understanding privacy online: development of a social contract approach to privacy. J. Bus. Ethics **137**(3), 551–569 (2015)
18. McCole, P., et al.: Trust considerations on attitudes towards online purchasing: the moderating effect of privacy and security concerns. J. Bus. Res. **63**(9), 1018–1024 (2010)
19. Miltgen, C., et al.: Determinants of end-user acceptance of biometrics: Integrating the "Big 3" of technology acceptance with privacy context. Decis. Support Syst. **56**, 103–114 (2013)
20. Miyazaki, A.D.: Perceived ethicality of insurance claim fraud: do higher deductibles lead to lower ethical standards? J. Bus. Ethics **87**(4), 589–598 (2008)
21. Moorthy, A.E., Vu, K.-P.L.: Privacy concerns for use of voice activated personal assistant in the public space. Int. J. Hum. Comput. Interact. **31**(4), 307–335 (2015)
22. Nissenbaum, H.: Privacy as contextual integrity. Wash. Law Rev. **79**, 119–157 (2004)
23. Nissenbaum, H.: Privacy in Context: Technology, Policy, and the Integrity of Social Life. Stanford Law Books, Stanford (2010)
24. Olmstead, K.: Nearly half of Americans use digital voice assistants, mostly on their smartphones (2017). http://www.pewresearch.org/fact-tank/2017/12/12/nearly-half-of-americans-use-digital-voice-assistants-mostly-on-their-smartphones/
25. Porcheron, M., et al.: "Do Animals Have Accents?": talking with agents in multi-party conversation. In: Proceedings of the 2017 ACM Conference on Computer Supported Cooperative Work and Social Computing, pp. 207–219. ACM, New York (2017)
26. Pradhan, A., et al.: "Accessibility came by accident": use of voice-controlled intelligent personal assistants by people with disabilities. In: Proceedings of the 2018 CHI Conference on Human Factors in Computing Systems, pp. 459:1–459:13. ACM, New York (2018)
27. Purington, A., et al.: "Alexa is my new BFF": social roles, user satisfaction, and personification of the Amazon echo. In: Proceedings of the 2017 CHI Conference Extended Abstracts on Human Factors in Computing Systems, pp. 2853–2859. ACM, New York (2017)
28. Shoot, B.: St. Louis University Installs Amazon Echo Dots Campus-Wide (2018). http://fortune.com/2018/08/15/amazon-alexa-echo-back-to-school-dorm-room/
29. Stutzman, F., Hartzog, W.: Obscurity by design: an approach to building privacy into social media. In: Workshop on Reconciling Privacy with Social Media. ACM (2012)
30. Venkatesh, V., et al.: Consumer acceptance and use of information technology: extending the unified theory of acceptance and use of technology. MIS Q. **36**(1), 157–178 (2012)
31. Venkatesh, V., et al.: User acceptance of information technology: toward a unified view. MIS Q. **27**, 425–478 (2003)
32. Vitak, J.: A digital path to happiness? In: Reinecke, L., Oliver, M.B. (eds.) Handbook of Media Use and Well-Being. Routledge, New York (2016)
33. Welch, C.: Amazon made a special version of Alexa for hotels that put Echo speakers in their rooms (2018). https://www.theverge.com/2018/6/19/17476688/amazon-alexa-for-hospitality-announced-hotels-echo
34. Xu, H., et al.: Measuring mobile users' concerns for information privacy. In: Proceedings of the International Conference on Information Systems 2012 on Digital Innovation in the Service Economy, pp. 1–16 (2012)
35. Zeng, E., et al.: End user security and privacy concerns with smart homes. In: Symposium on Usable Privacy and Security (SOUPS 2017), pp. 65–80 (2017)

Identity Questions in Online Communities

Looking for Group: Live Streaming Programming for Small Audiences

Travis Faas[✉], Lynn Dombrowski, Erin Brady, and Andrew Miller

Indiana University – Purdue University Indianapolis,
Indianapolis, IN 46202, USA
{tfaas,lsdombro,brady,andrewm}@iupui.edu

Abstract. Live streams are used by some people to broadcast themselves doing creative work such as programming. To understand why individuals choose to stream themselves writing code, we interviewed eight streamers with small audiences of ten or fewer viewers. Several of these individuals were in a transitionary stage that supported a streaming lifestyle, and were seeking feedback and live companionship. These findings guide a discussion of the implications of creative live streams for people undergoing life transitions, and how learners might use streams to support their learning objectives.

Keywords: Personal learning environments · Live streaming · Twitch

1 Introduction

Live streaming, a practice of broadcasting real-time video of oneself, has become a popular medium for showing video game-play for the entertainment of viewers. However, people also use the medium for broadcasting skilled crafts as seen in the "creative" stream genre. In creative streams, people stream themselves engaged in skilled work such as knitting, music creation, or programming. Developers who host programming-focused streams broadcast their computer's screen as they design, build, and debug software, typically augmented by a web camera featuring their face and voice.

Previous research has studied consistently popular streamers and their associated communities, but little is known about the experiences and motivations of streamers with smaller audiences who make up the majority of streamers on live streaming platforms. Streaming to small audiences can be demotivating to many individuals [8], but appears to be a standard mode of operation for these creative streamers. To understand what motivates these streamers to continue to broadcast, we interviewed eight streamers who broadcast their work in the programming directory on Twitch. We found that many of these individuals were in a transitionary life period that supported streaming, and that they streamed to get feedback on their programming and for companionship.

© Springer Nature Switzerland AG 2019
N. G. Taylor et al. (Eds.): iConference 2019, LNCS 11420, pp. 117–123, 2019.
https://doi.org/10.1007/978-3-030-15742-5_10

2 Background and Related Literature

Live streaming is broadcasting online video ('streams'), typically of a person (the 'streamer') engaged in a task for others to watch. Often an audience interacts with the streamer and other audience members via text chat. While the predominant media featured on streaming sites like Twitch has been video games, non-game related content is also streamed for others' entertainment and has been endorsed on the Twitch since 2015 with the addition of the Twitch 'creative' section [10].

As live streaming has gained popularity, researchers across the information disciplines have begun to study live streaming in earnest. One key theme in these early studies is that a strong motivating drive to host or view a stream on a live streaming platform is the opportunity for socialization [5, 8]. Additionally, viewers use Twitch to learn from observing the broadcasts [9]. Due to this learning need, streams appear to be an early part of some users personal learning environments (PLE), helping them to find and answer questions [4]. These PLEs are constructed of resources found across the internet, making them an example of networked individualism where individuals connect to different communities on the web for different needs [11].

Creative live streams found on Twitch have other educational uses. The programming and game development communities on Twitch share the social orientation of other streams and also feature a focus on skills desired by employers, such as web development or database programming. Additionally, researchers have found that many viewers return to future broadcasts in the programming directory of Twitch, and eventual form learning communities that support both the community members and stream host in growing to master the practice of programming [3].

In this paper, we extend this prior work to provide insight into the contexts of use that allow individuals to become streamers, before mentorship communities form.

3 Methods

In this study, we sought to understand how and why Twitch hosts start to stream themselves writing code, and their perceived benefits and continued motivators for streaming. We focused on programming-focused Twitch streamers who had small audiences (*i.e.*, defined as less than 10 average audience members). This number was selected as it would place the selected streamers beneath the most popular channels in the programming directory, who averaged twelve or more viewers per broadcast.

Twitch's listing of streamers in a given directory is limited to only those who are currently broadcasting. Thus, it is hard to get a sense of all of the streamers who have been broadcasting in a directory even from visiting the listing over the course of a few different hours every day. To get a broader picture of the individuals who were broadcasting and to identify small audience streamers, we used Twitch's public API to gather an hourly listing of all the streamers who were actively streaming in the programming directory over the course of four weeks. We filtered the data to select streamers who had at least three unique broadcasts throughout each week and an average of ten viewers or less during those broadcasts.

We used the direct message feature of Twitch to invite eleven streamers who met these criteria to participate in a semi-structured interview. Eight individuals were interviewed via either text chat (3) or audio (5) based on their preference. Interviews conducted via text ranged from paragraph-length responses to one line responses, favoring single lines. Interviews done via voice lasted for thirty minutes. Demographics were not collected, though six of the eight appeared to be male-presenting based on their face cameras. Interview themes focused on motivations to stream, and how they or their streamers learned through engagement with the stream. Interviews were analyzed via thematic analysis, starting with an open coding pass. A subsequent axial coding pass was conducted with codes focused on personal learning environments.

4   Results

Half of the streamers interviewed were in a transitional life stage that supported a streaming-oriented lifestyle. The streamers reported two main motivations for streaming: for help on their work, and for companionship they were not able to get elsewhere.

4.1   Streaming During a Transitionary Life Stage

While all of the streamers used streams to enhance their working experience, half of the streamers were in a transitionary period between jobs, cities, or lifestyles. For these individuals, streams were a way to address deficiencies they encountered while they explored new interests and developed skills. Due to Twitch's gaming focus, three of these individuals in transition between jobs or spaces were learning how to program games. After leaving a job, S5 chose to develop a game and stream in his newfound free time: *"I had time. I decided to try something I've always wanted to do."*

While streaming could be used to hone job-related skills, most of these streamers were not seeking to enter the games industry. S6, when discussing the ability for his project in helping him to get a job, assumed he would be working in an area not related to games: *"I'm probably not going to go to a AAA studio."* Managing the difference between developing the skills to get a job and becoming an effective streamer proved difficult for some. S1, for instance, had seen others struggle with this split in skills: *"They introspect themselves and there's a turning point – am I streamer or am I going to make a game?"*

These four streamers were working to find new or steady employment, which had an effect of placing a deadline on their ability to be able to keep their demanding streaming schedules. Two of these 'transitionary' streamers had accepted full-time work by the time interviews were conducted. These streamers were unable to maintain their normal schedule as streamers when they started at their new jobs. S8 gave up streaming entirely, running one final "goodbye" stream for his audience before letting his channel become inactive. S6, who had also accepted a job, intended to continue streaming when he had free time. He felt an obligation to continue streaming for his regular viewers, but also noted that he would not be able to stream has much as he had in the past.

4.2   Motivations to Stream

While all the streamers were driven by some amount of curiosity about streaming, several also expressed a desire for assistance on their work or to find companionship they could not get in their current circumstances.

Help and Feedback. Five streamers ran broadcasts with the goal of gathering help from viewers as they worked. S1, for example, began streaming for this reason, sharing that *"the initial goal of streaming was to get feedback."* Three of these five were novice programmers or new to the development context that they had chosen to practice on stream. S7 had made a habit of using streams to seek assistance when learning something new. He perceived Twitch as a place where there was a lot of ambient expertise among the potential viewers that could help him when he was starting a new project: *"I venture into new languages a lot, and at some point I'll be a newbie at something."*

The streamers had success in obtaining viewers who were willing to provide help and who would return to assist during future streams. S5 was surprised by the dedication of some of the people who offered help: *"There was one person who was there for every stream, and checking in on my progress."* This degree of investment from his viewers changed S5's outlook on learning as a whole: *"I didn't feel bad learning programming. It was entertaining."*

Though many of the streamers used their streams to find help, three of the five help-seeking streamers found their viewers sometimes unable to offer quality assistance. S1 found the initial feedback useful, but as his skill developed the advice became counterproductive: *"...you get a bit better, and then the average feedback is nice to have, but it's not as useful."* S6 found himself often having to providing assistance in lieu of receiving help or advice: *"There's definitely an epidemic of young computer science students who stay up way too late and go to Twitch for help."*

Companionship. Six streamers noted that they began streaming to address their solitary working conditions. S3 was looking to fill a social gap in his life: *"I never really looked into doing anything with it other than attract like-minded people to communicate with while I did whatever I was streaming at the moment."* The streamers commented on the difficulties of working from home or being in situations where they could not form a social group. S1 and S3 were working from home and used streams to simulate the experience of being among coworkers in a shared workspace. For S1, streaming filled this gap by providing social interaction, or *"some way to have some social time while you're alone and in front of the computer."*

While some were looking only for companionship, others were interested in gathering viewers that were part of a specific community they did not have access to in their current location. S5 and S6 sought to create a community of viewers who were specifically interested in game development. For them, streaming was a method of advertising themselves and finding other people who could come and chat with them about a shared passion. S5 talked about how streaming had brought him a set of friends he was unable to find elsewhere: *"I've met good friends through doing this. In my personal life, a lot of them don't have the same core interests."*

5 Discussion

In this paper, we describe motivations and practices of less established programming streamers on the streaming site Twitch. In the following section, we discuss challenges that streaming sites need to consider should they choose to support creative streamers. Additionally, we touch upon the emerging use of these streaming sites to gather help and discuss how streaming could play a part in a learner's attempts to create a personal learning environment for themselves.

5.1 Design for Individuals Experiencing Transition

Half of our participants took up streaming during life transitions, though streaming sites are not necessarily designed to support individuals during these changes. Streaming sites could support streamers during their times of difficult transitions, including times when streamers' lives become busier again and they are less able to stream. Streamers actively working to find a balance for their life may move past their streaming stage entirely as they get jobs or their life situations change. This creates several design implications for such transitionary use and communities.

First, the streamer's needs during their transition should be considered. For the streamers, it appears that streaming supports a life transition by providing a daily ritual that helps to establish a "new normal" for the streamer [7]. This ritual actively encourages the streamer to engage with people and tasks that will help ground themselves and give them access to social capital to reconnect and reskill. The practice of streaming could be positioned as a way for individuals who are in a transitionary state to get started on reskilling by guiding viewers to find and assist these streamers.

Not all transition tools are equally as useful for bringing an individual to a better life state. The life course approach notes that some experiences or circumstances will impact the quality of those circumstances that follow [2]. Though streaming may be an effective tool for an individual to use to reskill, once they complete their transition the streamer will be forced to decide on the future of their channel. The streamer can either continue to stream to support the companionship needs of their viewers, or choose to disband their stream and lose the support of their community. Choosing to continue to stream after the transition has led to new circumstances like a job could be a large burden on the streamer as they will need to stream after work hours, potentially resulting in less access to future developmental opportunities.

5.2 Streams as Personal Learning Environments

Streaming was not designed to be a personal learning environment (PLE) for its users, but it is nonetheless used as such. As streamers broadcast they passively piece together the people, resources, and technology that make up PLE [1]. PLEs often rely on the employment of interpersonal literacies that can grant access to individuals who can share their own knowledge [6]. Streaming, with its focus on social interaction, appears to be an emerging literacy that can be used by learners to grow a learning environment centered on themselves, a process well-suited for the age of networked individualism where people use the internet to find disparate communities to fill different needs [11].

The viewers of a stream appear to work together to fill several needs of the streamer simultaneously, such as those in this study receiving both learning and social input from their communities. Unlike other literacies that are proactive such as posting on a message board, streaming is initially passive for the streamer. Teachers or online learning platforms could encourage individuals to learn the basics of streaming and to run a series of broadcasts early on in their learning process, growing the student's capability for interpersonal literacies along with giving them access to a set of tutors in their viewers.

5.3   Employing Amicable Liveness

Presence on live streams focuses on being welcoming and warm, which has implications for how the media could be used in both educational contexts. Many learners, such as the ones who came to broadcasts looking for help on projects, were seeking individuals who would be willing to assist on a project immediately. It appears as if streams were chosen by these students due to their combination of having someone who is currently on (or 'live') and had a helpful affect, something we have termed "amicable liveness". While this type of presence is currently found in live streams and other, assistance-oriented contexts like paid peer tutoring, it could also be transferred to learning contexts. For instance, in a distance education context we imagine a user to be able to mark themselves "looking to help", indicating that they would be happy to interact with others who are looking to work through a problem.

5.4   Limitations and Future Work

This study had several limitations that could be addressed in future work. The sample we gathered was limited to the four weeks that we mined the programming directory of streamers and may have changed in the next months. Most of the streamers we interviewed were male-presenting, as we did not strategically sample for gender. Our selection criteria of at least three broadcasts per week could have inadvertently lost early stage streamers who chose not to continue their streaming practice. Thus, this limited sample is likely not representative of all creative streamers, and future work could focus on strategically sampling populations that are likely to refrain from continued streaming. Finally, future work could focus on the types and outcomes of transitions that are best supported or most prevalent on live streaming platforms.

6   Conclusion

In this paper, we presented study of less popular programming streamers on the live streaming site Twitch. We found that these streamers were sometimes in a transitionary state, and used streaming as a way to seek help and companionship. Drawing from these findings, we identified ways in which streaming sites could explicitly design for people who take up streaming during a life transition, and potential applications of streams in supporting the learning needs for both streamers and viewers.

References

1. Attwell, G.: Personal learning environments-the future of eLearning? eLearn. Pap. **2**(1), 1–8 (2007)
2. Elder, G.H., et al.: The emergence and development of life course theory. In: Mortimer, J.T., Shanahan, M.J. (eds.) Handbook of the Life Course, pp. 3–19. Springer, Boston (2003). https://doi.org/10.1007/978-0-306-48247-2_1
3. Faas, T., et al.: Watch me code: programming mentorship communities on Twitch.tv. In: Proceedings of the ACM on Human-Computer Interaction. CSCW, vol. 2, pp. 50:1–50:18 (2018)
4. Haaranen, L.: Programming as a performance: live-streaming and its implications for computer science education. In: Proceedings of the 2017 ACM Conference on Innovation and Technology in Computer Science Education, pp. 353–358. ACM, New York (2017)
5. Hamilton, W.A., et al.: Streaming on twitch: fostering participatory communities of play within live mixed media. In: Proceedings of the 32nd Annual ACM Conference on Human Factors in Computing Systems, pp. 1315–1324. ACM, New York (2014)
6. Kop, R.: The challenges to connectivist learning on open online networks: learning experiences during a massive open online course. Int. Rev. Res. Open Distrib. Learn. **12**(3), 19–38 (2011)
7. Massimi, M., et al.: Finding a new normal: the role of technology in life disruptions. In: Proceedings of the ACM 2012 Conference on Computer Supported Cooperative Work, pp. 719–728. ACM, New York (2012)
8. Pellicone, A.J., Ahn, J.: The game of performing play: understanding streaming as cultural production. In: Proceedings of the 2017 CHI Conference on Human Factors in Computing Systems, pp. 4863–4874 ACM, New York (2017)
9. Sjöblom, M., Hamari, J.: Why do people watch others play video games? An Empirical Study on the Motivations of Twitch Users. Social Science Research Network, Rochester, NY (2016)
10. Twitch: Introducing Twitch Creative. https://blog.twitch.tv/introducing-twitch-creative-fbfe23b4a114
11. Wellman, B.: Little boxes, glocalization, and networked individualism. In: Tanabe, M., et al. (eds.) Digital Cities II: Computational and Sociological Approaches, pp. 10–25. Springer, Heidelberg (2002). https://doi.org/10.1007/3-540-45636-8_2

Skins for Sale: Linking Player Identity, Representation, and Purchasing Practices

Alia Reza[5], Sabrina Chu[6], Zuaira Khan[1], Adanna Nedd[2],
Amy Castillo[3], and Daniel Gardner[4(✉)]

[1] Stony Brook University, Stony Brook, NY, USA
zuaira.khan@stonybrook.edu
[2] Penn State University, State College, PA, USA
adanna.nedd@gmail.com
[3] College of Westchester, White Plains, NY, USA
acastillo19.arc@gmail.com
[4] University of California Irvine, Irvine, CA, USA
dlgardne@uci.edu
[5] Denver, CO, USA
[6] San Gabriel, CA, USA

Abstract. Although understudied, microtransactions are becoming widespread in games, especially for the purchase of aesthetic variation in-game. In this paper, we review literature around representation in games and purchasing practices tied to player racial identity to provide insight on how in-game racial representational options and microtransactions may impact purchasing practices of players of diverse racial backgrounds. We selected articles which articulate racial identity, representation in games, and purchasing practices in ways that could be applied to the in-game purchases of non-white character representation in the form of "skins." The diversity of both players and game characters is steadily increasing in the US. Several of the sources we review here examine this theme and how it is *felt* by players of color. In this review we thread together research that has focused on the state and effect of representation in games, with research considering the role of racial identity in consumer practice to better examine how players of color feel about purchasing self-representation in games.

Keywords: Microtransactions · Representation in games · Diversity in gaming

1 Introduction

According to the Electronic Software Association, the United States video game industry generated 36 billion dollars in revenue in 2017 [5]. Although exact numbers are difficult to come by, a growing percentage of the industry's revenue is driven by microtransactions, a term simply referring to "the processing of transactions involving small monetary amounts" [23], often "a one-time transaction that in some cases can be repeated" [24]. Microtransactions are increasingly common in games, especially so-called "Free to Play" games [1]. Microtransactions in games generally fall into two high-level categories. The first allows the acquisition of in-game practical items, such as weapons and power-ups, which directly affect game-play. The second allows the acquisition of cosmetic items, which may change the appearance of game items and/or characters. In this review, we are concerned with the second category, specifically the purchase and use of cosmetic "skins." In the context of video games, the term "skins" derives from the application of visual surface detail to otherwise featureless 3D character models (a literal, virtual, epidermis). Skins are cosmetic, offering no in-game mechanical advantage or player-performance enhancement. It may take hundreds of transactions and cost upwards of thousands of dollars to acquire all skins even in a single game [2, 11, 15, 25, 26]. Additional research is required to understand the amount players are willing to spend, and their motivations for doing so.

As an example of how these microtransactions may function consider the game *Overwatch,* which allows players to purchase "loot boxes" containing five randomly generated in-game items. Although not always literally called "loot boxes," as in *Overwatch,* this practice of selling virtual containers that randomly award a selection of in-game items and rewards is widely used. Skins are often highly sought after items from a larger pool of possible selections [26]. Other forms of micro-transactions are more direct. *Fortnite: Battle Royal,* for instance, allows players to buy skins directly, either with in-game currency acquired through gameplay or with actual money. While they can be purchased directly, skins in *Fortnite Battle Royal* are not always available to players, as the shop rotates daily or weekly. While both games are notable for their relatively diverse casts, diverse "skins" in games *like* these may only be available through microtransactions—meaning that players from underrepresented communities may have to either play more or pay more just to obtain a "skin" like their own in-game.

In her article "Race in/for Cyberspace," Lisa Nakamura found many white Multi-User Dungeon (MUD) players donning Asian "performances" to *play* at identities other than their own [16]. While the popularity of MUDs has mostly declined, in the current microtransaction scenario, white players may be able to more literally acquire "other" skins or simulations, whereas players of color may be required to pay extra just to play a character that looks like them—an evolution of the situation that Nakamura describes.

Though the industry has grown immensely in recent decades, and its customer base has diversified along axes of race, gender, and socio-economic background [3, 18, 21], the playable characters in these video games have not achieved the same diversity [7, 8, 12, 17, 27]. Census data shows that African American and Hispanic youth play video games at higher rates than players of any other race [19], but are grossly underrepresented as main characters in games [7], and in games more broadly [27]. Default player characters commonly conform to outdated assumptions of audience demographics (i.e. white, male). Characters of different races or genders are increasingly available, but may only be accessible through microtransactions.

With the growth of micro-transactions and in-game purchases as a central revenue stream for the games industry, research is required to understand their impact on players of color, especially when these microtransactions may be the only way to acquire "skins" like theirs. In this paper, we review literature around representation in games as well as purchasing practices tied to racial identity to investigate how in-game representational options tied to microtransactions may impact purchasing practices of players of diverse racial backgrounds.

2 Methods

Our primary goal in this review is to thread together research that has charted the domain of representation in games [7, 8, 12, 17, 22, 27] and those who have described the broader stakes of representation in media and games [10, 14, 16, 18, 21], with those who have considered the role of racial identities in consumer practices [6, 13, 20]. It should be noted that our focus is on commonly and academically defined discursive racial categories and identities that may signify cultural, ethnic, regional, or cultural heritage. While no publications, case studies, or other research could be found that have dis-

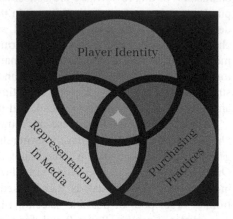

Fig. 1. Illustration of our literature categories.

cussed the intersection between all three of our areas of interest, to provide a basis for our future work we needed to identify scholars and research that helps frame a discussion at the intersection of these themes (Fig. 1).

We conducted keyword searches through the Association for Computing Machinery (ACM), Illinois Digital Environment for Access to Learning and Scholarship (IDEALS), the Digital Games Research Association (DiGRA) digital libraries, and Google Scholar when very little was found in the first three. Our keyword search comprised different single-word uses and combinations of the following words (at times with additional prepositions such as "in" and "of," or conjunctions such as "and" or "&"): color, consumerism, consumption, digital, games, identity, media, play, players, purchasing, race, racial, representation, video, and video games. We did not include search terms for broader cultural or national identities, as these often exist apart from racial identity, and outside the scope of our research question.

Although we initially sought recent work, our search needed to be expanded, eventually resulting in only twenty-three sources, some of which we ended up leaving out of the final review because they proved to be less relevant and eight we highlight here in the paper to varying extents. Sources published in non-peer reviewed venues, master's theses, or sources whose analysis didn't appear to address the intersection of our broader categories of interest based on title and abstract were ignored.

All articles or books found to be relevant to the subject were uploaded to a shared Zotero library and divided amongst authors for closer screening. We focused on literature that addresses intersections of our three categories: player identity, representation in media, and purchasing practices. Each author identified the primary arguments and concepts related to our broader research question. Scholars such as Passmore et al., Shaw, Nakamura, Hart, and Higgin, address the intersection of players' identities and representation in media and games. Lamont and Molnar, Gandy, and Shankar et al. address the intersection of racial identity and consumption. We found a lack of literature addressing the intersection of representation in media and purchasing practices.

3 Findings

While the scope of this paper makes detailing every article we reviewed difficult, in this section we outline the arguments of some of the sources we consider significant for our topic and future work. These include Passmore et al. [18] and Hart [9] —whose work suggests the *kinds* of data we are likely to collect in future research—and Nakamura [16], Higgin [10], Shanker et al. [20], and Gandy [6], who provide possible lenses for analyzing that data.

Passmore et al. stress the fast growing buying power of players of color. Although, they also find a general agreement between white and non-white developers and players that more diversity in games is needed [18]. Passmore et al. observe a discrepancy between this desire and the incorporation of diversity in games. They argue racial and ethnic representation in games has become "a social and moral demand" [18].

In his article, "Getting into the Game," Casey Hart researches the way that players design and present their avatars in the gaming world, bringing to light a core relationship between player and character. Hart argues that players use avatars to "explore alternate versions of themselves" or what he calls "anti-projections" of themselves, as opposed to reflections of themselves" [9]. Though he is chiefly concerned with correlations of personality and performance, Hart's analysis raises questions around the relationship between players and diversity.

Nakamura describes the "the cybernetic world" as a unique social space where people may easily perform identities other than their own [16]. Nakamura is an early scholar to highlight that performativity—especially how people use speech and mannerisms to present their identities—is as important in cyberspace as it is in "real life." She evaluates textual performances in online communities and develops the concept "virtual tourism," to describe (white) participants in her observations performing "personae" other than their own, especially "asianness" [16]. Nakamura states, "programming language and internet connectivity have made it possible for people to interact without putting into play any bodies but the ones they write for themselves" [16]. That is, regardless of their real-world identities, players may choose to rewrite their virtual identities through the ways they choose to represent themselves online.

While Nakamura expands our understanding of the complexities of race in virtual spaces by examining performances of participants, Tanner Higgin's "Blackless Fantasy" highlights the exclusion of non-European narratives in many fantasy games [10]. Higgin critiques the erasure of black characters from many games which seems to also apply to the difficulty of obtaining diverse skins in other games; by putting diversity behind a paywall, developers are hindering potential diversity within their games, and forcing many players of color to settle for white male avatars.

Although there is a lack of literature directly addressing the intersection of racial identity and consumption in video games, there is literature that discusses how players often seek to "reproduce their identit[ies]" in economic terms [20]. Shankar et al. argue that purchasing material possessions, such as music albums is a practice that aligns with consumer identity and a sense of belonging to their social groups [20]. Lamont and Molnar argue the black community utilizes consumption as a means to create a collective identity that pushes against negative stereotypes about black purchasing power [13]. Oscar Gandy presents a contrasting argument that troubles attempts to identify the influence of racial and ethnic identities on media consumption because of obvious variation within ethnic groups [6]. These scholars help us consider the various ways players may use microtransactions to express their identities.

4 Discussion

It is clear that there is more to the purchase of in-game skins than it would seem on the surface. How players of color engage with these skins is a critical consideration as these players are an ever growing portion of the game industry's customer base [3, 4, 18, 21]. We expect that players of color will choose skins similar to their own at a higher rate than those that do not, as these characters may be more appealing to them.

In line with Passmore et al., if players and developers alike want more diversity in games, then players—especially players of color—are more likely to pursue or purchase more diverse skins. By Hart's analysis however, players may choose skins based on how they want their "anti-projection" to appear, rather than how it relates to their demographic category. This would suggest, somewhat counter to Passmore et al., that there may not be a significant difference between the quantities or qualities of skins purchased by players of color and skins purchased by white players, as their goals may not be to simply create or acquire avatars similar to themselves.

Regardless of our hypothetical outcome, scholars like Nakamura and Higgin suggest ways the data may provide insight. While Nakamura studied a community where players performed with only "keystrokes and mouse-clicks," visual representation adds complexity to her phenomenon of "identity tourism" [16]. With the presence of "skins" players may virtually change their appearance to reflect a racial or ethnic performance they choose to adopt. Regardless of whether our future results contain participants who are "trying" a visual representation other than their own, claiming one similar to their own, or something else, however players portray themselves in-game, examining the details and privileges of how or why they choose to purchase skins or play games that allow them to portray the identities that they desire is clearly an important topic.

The relationship between racial identity and purchasing practices is another intersection that has been studied more generally, or in other contexts [6, 7, 13]. However, the relationship between representation in games and purchasing practices has not been studied, especially tied further to racial identity. Gandy writes that, although Black players' often criticize representations of black characters in media, they are still some of the highest consumers of them [6]. Despite this, black players are often left with the a choice to either spend more time or money attempting to obtain an avatar that looks like them, or simply accept that their character will never be representative of their racial identity. The 'loot box' system becomes a prime example of one way players interact with skins in the games they buy. That these players pay for the *chance* of obtaining desired items, with the probability of receiving their desired "skin" often being low further indicates the importance of our topic and future work.

The intersection between representation in games and the purchasing practices of players is an important aspect of the relationship between games and players, and their wallets. Studying this intersection may illustrate the extent to which players are willing to go in order to represent themselves in the games they play, especially when they may require extensive play or payment to obtain more diverse cosmetics. Skins may not affect gameplay but, as Adrienne Shaw argues in her book *Gaming at the Edge,* views, behavior, and experience can be highly influenced by many elements of games, such as the diversity of characters [21]. Since players and developers widely agree that playable characters are lacking in diversity [18, 21], it is important that we take steps to understand how that lack of diversity may influence players of color beyond the games they play, to include the cosmetic purchases they make in those games.

5   Conclusion

There has been limited research on how players of diverse backgrounds interact financially with character diversity in games. The purchase of skins through micro-transactions is one clear, observable example of this interaction, which we have chosen to focus on here. It is already clear that these microtransactions have a substantial, yet growing impact on players, developers, and the digital games industry itself more broadly, and we want to highlight their potential effect in this specific context.

Purchasing skins through microtransactions may give players the benefit of choosing a character appearance that is more diverse than the default. This allows for a greater possibility of self-expression and social belonging for players. However, it also creates a space where the commodification of character appearance may contribute to psychological burdens on players of color. Passmore et al. discovered in their work that racism and discrimination present in video games left negative psychosocial effects on players of color [18]; this additional financial component stands to increase those effects. Gandy notes that although marginalized groups are the most critical of their own por-trayals in media and they are still the most common consumers of such media [6]. Should microtransactional purchases of "skins" become a primary method for players of color to self-represent, it literally becomes more expensive to be a player of color.

In our future work, we will conduct surveys directed at physical and online gaming communities in order to examine trends in player purchases of cosmetic skins and features in various games. As earlier stated, underrepresented players whose own skins are not the 'default' may be given the option to acquire skins that represent themselves, but only through additional costs in time or money. When players of color *must* pay more or play more to be represented in their games, it begs questions of an industry willing to put a premium on diversity.. Our future work will include U.S.-based players from a variety of racial identities in order to identify trends and opinions regarding the acquisition of cosmetic skins. With the pervasiveness of gaming in our present culture, the phenomenon we describe in this paper is one that warrants attention, and numerous future projects, especially concerning other types of diversity such as gender, sexuality, and class.

Acknowledgements. Kayla Booth, Mike Depew, iSchool Inclusion Institute, and more!

References

1. Alha, K., Koskinen, E., Paavilainen, J., Hamari, J., Kinnunen, J.: Free-to-play games: professionals' perspectives. In: Proceedings of Nordic DiGRA (2014)
2. Busby, M.: "Easy Trap to Fall Into": why video game loot boxes need regulation. The Guardian, May 2018
3. Chess, S., Evans, N.J., Baines, J.J.: What does a gamer look like? Video games, advertising, and diversity. Telev. New Media 18(1), 37–57 (2017)
4. Duggan, M.: Gaming and Gamers. PEW Internet Research, December 2015
5. Electronic Software Association (ESA). US Video Game Industry Revenue Reaches $36 Billion in 2017. In Press Releases, ESA (2018)
6. Gandy, O.H.: Racial identity, media use, and the social construction of risk among African Americans. J. Black Stud. 31(5), 600–618 (2001)
7. Gardner, D.L., Tanenbaum, J.: Dynamic demographics: lessons from a large-scale census of performative possibilities in games. In: Proceedings of the 2018 CHI Conference on Human Factors in Computing Systems, New York, NY, USA, pp. 93:1–93:12 (2018)
8. Glaubke, C.R., Miller, P., Parker, M.A., Espejo, E.: Fair play? Violence, gender and race in video games. Child. Now 143, 38 (2001)
9. Hart, C.: Getting into the game: an examination of player personality projection in videogame avatars. Game Stud. 17, 2 (2017)
10. Higgin, T.: Blackless fantasy the disappearance of race in massively multiplayer online role-playing games. Games Cult. 4(1), 3–26 (2009)
11. Jacobs, H.: Gamers are Spending Thousands of Dollars a Year on This "Free" Video Game. Business Insider, March 2015
12. Jeroen, J., Martis, R.G.: The representation of gender and ethnicity in digital interactive games. In: Proceedings of the 2003 DiGRA International Conference: Level Up (2003)
13. Lamont, M., Molnár, V.: How blacks use consumption to shape their collective identity: evidence from marketing specialists. J. Consum. Cult. 1(1), 31–45 (2001)
14. Leonard, D.: High tech blackface: race, sports, video games and becoming the other. Intell. Agent 4(4.2), 1 (2004)
15. Molloy, M., Dias, D., Lyons, I.: Meet the gamers willing to spend hundreds of thousands living their video game fantasy. Telegraph, July 2018
16. Nakamura, L.: Race in/for cyberspace: identity tourism and racial passing on the internet. Works and Days 13(1–2), 181–193 (1995)
17. Passmore, C.J., et al.: Racial diversity in indie games: patterns, challenges, and opportunities. In: Extended Abstracts Publication of the Annual Symposium on Computer-Human Interaction in Play, New York, NY, USA, pp. 137–151 (2017)
18. Passmore, C.J., et al.: The privilege of immersion: racial and ethnic experiences, perceptions, and beliefs in digital gaming. In: Proceedings of the 2018 CHI Conference on Human Factors in Computing Systems, New York, NY, USA, pp. 383:1–383:19 (2018)
19. Rideout, V., Roberts, D., Foehr, U.: Generation M: Media in the Lives of 8–18 Year-olds. Kaiser Family Foundation, Washington, D.C. (2005)
20. Shankar, A., et al.: Identity, consumption and narratives of socialization, identity, consumption and narratives of socialization. Mark. Theory 9(1), 75–94 (2009)
21. Shaw, A.: Gaming at the Edge: Sexuality and Gender at the Margins of Gamer Culture. University of Minnesota Press, Minneapolis (2014)
22. Shaw, A., Friesem, E.: Where is the queerness in games?: Types of lesbian, gay, bisexual, transgender, and queer content in digital games. Int. J. Commun. 10, 13 (2016)

23. Sheehan, M., Wallace, W., Knackstedt, L.: JP Morgan Chase Bank. System and method for processing microtransactions. U.S. Patent 8,065,228 (2011)
24. Shokrizade, R.: The Language of Monetization Design. Gamasutra (2013)
25. Tassi, P.: It Costs over $450 to Buy Every 'Fortnite: Season 5' Skin. Forbes, September 2018
26. Tassi, P.: The Cost of a Complete 'Overwatch' Item Collection is between $1,000 and $3,000. Forbes, April 2017
27. Williams, D., Martins, N., Consalvo, M., Ivory, J.D.: The virtual census: representations of gender, race and age in video games. New Media Soc. **11**(5), 815–834 (2009)

"Autsome": Fostering an Autistic Identity in an Online Minecraft Community for Youth with Autism

Kathryn E. Ringland[(✉)] ⓘ

Northwestern University, Chicago, IL 60611, USA
kathrynringland@northwestern.edu

Abstract. Autism is a medical diagnosis that has attracted much attention in recent decades, particularly due to an increase in the numbers of children being diagnosed and the changing requirements for getting the diagnosis. In parallel online communities around autism—both those supporting individuals, families seeking treatment and those supporting embracing the autism identity—have grown. Previous literature has shown the positive impact support groups can have for those encountering hardship in their lives, such as depression. In this qualitative study of an online community for autistic children centered around a virtual world, I explore how the label "autism" can be not only a source of disenfranchisement, leading to harassment and violence—in both the virtual and physical world—but also a source of empowerment and identity. I illuminate the tension in claiming the autistic identity within this community—having a sense of identity in the community, but, in doing so, also "othering" those with autism further. The walls of the community work to keep community members safe, but also set them apart from others on the internet. I see that the Autcraft community goes beyond being a support group for victims of targeted violence, to one that redefines and helps community members embrace their own autistic identities.

Keywords: Online community · Autism · Youth · Disability · Minecraft · Virtual worlds · Identity

1 Introduction

Autism has been the topic of much public concern in recent decades, especially since the sensationalized "autism epidemic" swept through the media [36]. As a medical diagnosis, autism focuses on challenges for individuals; such as whether they are verbal, make eye-contact, or are sensitive to change [1]. Often, as a label, autism is given to youth in order to gain accommodations in school, or for medical treatment. Therefore, autistic youth often experience various ways in which this label is used to disempower and disenfranchise them.

This is the case for many youth that are a part of an online community, "Autcraft," a community centered on a Minecraft virtual world for autistic youth. While those with autism are often the target of harassment and violence in online spaces, the Autcraft community has been actively engaged in making themselves a safe space for youth

© Springer Nature Switzerland AG 2019
N. G. Taylor et al. (Eds.): iConference 2019, LNCS 11420, pp. 132–143, 2019.
https://doi.org/10.1007/978-3-030-15742-5_12

with autism. Beyond simply keeping bullies out, however, the community has taken the label of "autism" and turned it into something positive—a label worth identifying with.

The rest of this paper is as follows: First, I discuss autism as a socially constructed identity. Next, I review related literature and the methods used in this work. Then, I describe the findings of this study, including examination of the autism label as a target and as a source of identity for community members. Finally, I conclude with a discussion of some of the implications for the use of the autism label in the Autcraft community, including how the Autcraft community moves beyond being a support group for victims of the autism label to one that reclaims and redefines the autism label, allowing members to embrace their own autistic identities.

2 The Social Construction of Autism

The analytical lens of this work primarily uses the social model of disability, which focuses on disability as a social construction. Society creates the barriers that make individuals, who may be differently abled, into "disabled" [12]. The medical model of disability is the clinical perspective of disability, wherein diagnosis (labeling), treatment, and cure of the individual is the directed course of action [11, 38]. The medical model portrays disability as a flaw of the body that is "inherently abnormal and pathological" [12]. Historically, for cases such as mental illness, the diagnosis was created by the medical community to help categorize groups of symptoms.

For many who have been labeled with an autism diagnosis, from a medical perspective, their label will follow them for the rest of their lives. It is quite possible a person could have the label of autism from a very early age, whether they are aware or told about it or not, but only really begin to grapple with it as an identity later (*e.g.*, when they are preteens). However, whether an individual then decides to join a particular autistic community is their choice.

In concert with the social model of disability, I use intersectionality as a lens to understand the different facets of the Autcraft community members' identities. Intersectionality is the understanding that race, class, gender, sexuality, ethnicity, ability, and age are not mutually exclusive parts of one's identity [8, 9]. The concept of intersectionality helps avoid reducing a person's identity to a single trait [9, 13]. Intersectionality supports the understanding that individuals will often identify with multiple groups (*e.g.*, gender, race, class, dis/ability) [13, 24, 37]. These identities may or may not be distinct categories, but they flow between and influence one another. Intersectionality occurs across all ages, but preteens and teenagers may be especially impacted as they are working to solidify their identities [26]. This is especially salient as many of the Autcraft community members are youth looking to assert their own identities and understanding of the world.

3 Related Work

Research of social media and online communities has covered a wide range of issues that people face including eating disorders [23] or pregnancy loss [3]. Many of these studies look at the effect of a specific social media platform, such as Facebook's impact on depression [25]. Research has found that these online support groups can have a positive impact on people [2, 6, 20].

When looking at autism specifically, researchers have found that autistic individuals have mixed experiences online. One study found that Facebook support groups fostered expression of positive emotions among users [39]. Autistic individuals may appreciate the mediation provided by social media platforms (*e.g.,* mitigating the need for eye-contact), but also struggle with navigating trust and privacy issues on various platforms [6]. However, despite these problems, finding socialization and support online is particularly salient for autistic individuals because of their discomfort in face-to-face interactions [33]. Scholars have proposed that this type of sociality mediated by online platforms is a space where autistic individuals are no longer disabled [28].

For any vulnerable population, navigating online spaces is fraught with challenges. Online harassment, bullying, and threats of violence are commonplace and often target marginalized groups (*e.g.,* people of color, LGBTQIA [18], women [35] and autism [32]). A solution to this has been to create private, policed spaces online that keep specific groups of marginalized people safe [21, 32]. Previous research has found how these online spaces have been a source of social support for marginalized individuals as well [2, 6, 20]. In this paper, I build on this previous research by examining the tension that occurs because of these "safe spaces"—allowing for this safety but also increasing the likelihood of being targeted by those outside the community.

4 Methods

This paper reports on results from a qualitative digital study of an online community that has grown around a Minecraft server known as Autcraft[1]. I collected data through interviews with children and parents; participant observations; directed and non-directed forum discussions; chat logs; and digital artifacts.

4.1 Setting

The multiplayer virtual world in our study, Autcraft, is a semi-private server on Minecraft created for children with autism, their families, and allies. Anyone wishing to join must first complete an application. Only those on the "white list" of approved players can access the server. Autcraft currently has more than 7,000 white-listed members with a daily average of approximately 50 players in-world at peak hours of the day and approximately 1,200 individual players logging in each month. While there are no age-restrictions in the community, the content is aimed at members aged 8–12 years old.

---

[1] http://Autcraft.com.

Minecraft is an open-ended virtual world with no particular goals or play requirements [10, 27]. Players can build and create new objects by manipulating blocks in the game. Autcraft is a version of Minecraft that includes modifications and add-ons to the software to allow for the safety of community members [32] and to enhance their socialization [31, 33]. In addition to the Minecraft virtual world, the community uses in tandem including YouTube, Twitch, Twitter, Facebook, and a community-maintained website (including an administrator's blog, community forums, member profiles, and an in-browser web messenger).

4.2 Data Collection and Analysis

This work employs virtual ethnographic methods and techniques that have been developed in other studies of virtual world communities [4]. After receiving ethical approval, I gained access to Autcraft via permission of the server's creator for this study and used an avatar labeled as a researcher in-world. Both my presence and purpose were made clear to the community through the Autcraft web-based forum and the in-world chat. Parents were informed of my presence via a parent message board and the Facebook page of the community. Parents and children were encouraged to voice their concerns and ask questions about the research through all communication platforms used by the community.

From May 2014 to May 2017, I collected approximately 200 h of immersive in-world observations, including participating in activities on the server, recording chat-based dialogue, and taking extensive field notes on everyday practices of community members and events as they occurred in the virtual world. I also participated in community activities outside the Minecraft world, including observing discussions in the forums and on the social networking sites. Digital artifacts from the various platforms used by the community were also included in the analysis. These data include approximately 5,000 forum threads and 150 blog posts created by players, parents, and administrators.

I used an iterative, inductive approach where emergent phenomena were identified, named, and categorized following techniques similar to those employed in grounded theory [7]. I used an inductive method of analysis to understand how participants engaged in social play through practice, rather than testing theoretical definitions found in the literature, because I was explicitly interested in understanding how the community views and experiences their autistic identity within the Autcraft community. This approach was iterative as is an established best practice for qualitative data analysis [7].

5   Results: Finding Autism in the Autcraft Community

As discussed above, the label of "autism" is one that is socially constructed—first being used as a medical label for those displaying specific symptoms that can be diagnosed as "autism." Below I describe how the label "autism" has morphed from a medical diagnosis to have different meanings for those interacting in online communities. Autism has become a point of harassment, a means of *targeting those with autism*. However, the Autcraft community has reclaimed the label of autism as their own, *redefining autism*.

5.1 Targeting Autism

Concerns over safety of children is an ongoing concern for parents and other care-givers. This is particularly true of those with autistic children, as those with autism tend to be targeted both by their peers and by strangers [32]. Much like other marginalized groups, "autism" is used as a derogatory term. Further, threats of violence can be found across the internet, including in the comments section of YouTube videos, a site used by Autcraft community members. This is especially meaningful as other related work has shown the embodied experience in these online spaces can be as impactful as in physical spaces [29]. Unfortunately, these threats of violence can also result in actual physical harm.

Verbal harassment and attacks on autistic individuals can be found in many corners of the internet. One prime example is in the comments on YouTube videos. This bullying and harassment of autistic players is troubling for parents who allow their children to participate in the Autcraft community, but then must make decisions about what other websites and applications their children are permitted to use.

YouTube comments reveal some of this bias as commenters refer to Minecraft as a game solely for autistic people. In one YouTube comment, a non-Autcraft member wrote, *"i feel like the game itself is dedicated to autistic people."* The implication is that Minecraft only attracts players that have autism—or at least exhibit behavior that others might construe as autistic. Having the Autcraft space labeled for autistic members also means that they can potentially be targeted more easily, as one YouTube commenter put it, *"All the autistics in one place. Sounds like a trolling paradise XD."* Among a subset of internet users, autism is a reason to troll, or harass or bully, an individual.

In his TEDx talk, the founder of Autcraft describes how autistic children have been told by strangers on the internet that they should kill themselves. In the comments of that video, one respondent wrote:

> *Probably the wrong place to say it, but autist people should not live. What people call love and humanity are just really intricate instincts and neuro-connections, but still, they are sentient and for some reason i am happy that they can get help like this...*

Comments such as the above are common enough to not be surprising, but, for-tunately, are outnumbered by positive comments (in the above post, for example, there were five negative comments out of 80 overall). This is not the only Autcraft video on YouTube. Many of Autcraft's younger members create YouTube content as well—sharing their own experiences with autism and anti-bullying messages [30]. By creating the Autcraft community and having a social divide between community members and others, there runs the risk of affirming the otherness of community members.

Harassment, threats of violence, and comments about autistic people killing themselves can have a large impact on those targeted, such as additional stress and other psychological harm [22]. The harm, however, does not stop with verbal and written threats. Like other marginalized communities, those with autism face the very real threat of violence against them [14, 15].

Fig. 1. Colorful sheep wander through the rows of names in a memorial to those with disabilities as victims of filicide. (Color figure online)

To exemplify and remind us of this violence, an adult Autcraft community member built a secret chamber to memorialize victims of filicide. The builder has recorded the names of approximately 420 victims from 1980 to May 2016 (the date of the interview). When asked about where he obtained the list of names from he answered, *"I was a chapter [coordinator] for the autistic self advocacy network and they sent it to me."* The Autism Self Advocacy Network (ASAN) provides an Anti-Filicide Toolkit[2] on their website that coordinates with the Disability Day of Mourning[3].

The memorial contains light glass walls and signs with names, ages, and dates of victims. The chamber itself has cathedral ceilings and colorful sheep wander through the rows of names, giving the place a light, open feeling despite the sad nature of the motivation for the space (See Fig. 1). The father explained to me in the interview that he does not allow the children to enter this space, because of the content, saying, *"I don't really talk [to] any of the [players] about this because there are young kids who might get upset. I try to keep it age appropriate. If anyone asks me I just tell them it's a memorial for disabled people and leave it at that."* But despite the fact he does not invite young children to see the space and that building the memorial *"took a lot out of [him] to do this,"* he still felt the need to create it. Because Disability Day of Mourning is a day set aside by many advocacy groups (*e.g.,* ASAN), this seems to have translated into sites of mourning not only in the physical world, but also in the virtual.

While this site can be seen as a place of sadness and mourning, there is also a sense of pride. Pride in the beauty of the architecture, which this parent designed and built single-handedly. But also pride in the sense of belonging to the Autcraft community. Much of the Autcraft community strives for members to accept and be accepted as someone with autism, but this memorial chamber invokes a sense that while others may hurt them (be it physically or emotionally), they are not forgotten, and they have a safe place to belong—albeit virtually.

The label of "autism" has become a widespread target for harassment, bullying, and even physical violence. The example above from anonymous, harassing comments on YouTube to reminders of physical-world violence are just part of the larger cultural

---

[2] http://autisticadvocacy.org/projects/community/disability-community-day-of-mourning/anti-filicide/.

[3] http://disability-memorial.org/.

story about violence against autistic people. The toxic culture, as found in some online game cultures [15, 35], goes beyond targeting those in the Autcraft community. In some ways, Autcraft is this community's answer to how to deal with this wider culture of hate against those who are different.

5.2 Redefining Autism

Where the terms of disability may be used to flatten and marginalize individuals, they can also be a source of empowerment and strength [19]. Those who join the Autcraft community are connected to autism in some way—they may or may not have a formal diagnosis or they may have a close loved one who is autistic. There is evidence throughout the Autcraft community of those who are expressing this facet of their identity. As many members are still coming to understand their autism, there is also teaching and learning that occurs in this space. Autcraft community members may be learning to understand and accept themselves or their child as an autistic individual, but they are also learning to deal with challenges found outside the Autcraft community where they may not find themselves accepted and face opposition.

Adopting "autism" and various forms of the word—as seen in the name of the community "*Aut*craft"—lends to a sense of identity with others who have the same or similar medical diagnosis. Aside from using "aut" or "autistic" in their user names (*i.e.,* the names that are displayed with their avatars and forum posts, rather than a real-world name), the Autcraft community displays this acceptance through the creation of autism-centric words, such as "autsome." According to a community post, "autsome" means, *"Having autism and being extremely impressive or daunting"* and *"extremely good; excellent."* Disability Studies scholars have described how those with disability are often held to a higher standard and those who are "extreme" tend to be held up as inspirational [17, 34]. This type of "inspiration" frames disability as something to be overcome, while achieving difficult objectives [17]. However, I argue that having language such as "autsome" is meant to be inspirational not for others looking in to the Autcraft community, but for the autistic children who are otherwise dealing with a barrage of negative language about autism. This is a reframing of the autism label as an identity that is worth *embracing*, rather than *overcoming*.

Autcraft community members also engage in learning and educating about autism. They write educational pieces and essays and post them in the Autcraft community forums. Their research projects and essays about autism are also often presented to their classes at school, with the student reporting back to the Autcraft forums with the results. These acts of learning and educating about autism help solidify what it means to be autistic as part of the Autcraft community. This identity may be different from how an autistic identity is performed in school or at the doctor's office—given the varying expectations of others in these spaces. In Autcraft, community members engage in an education process that ultimately defines what it means in be autistic in the space of the Autcraft community. And this form of education process spills out into other spaces when community members work to educate those outside of the Autcraft community, such as when they create YouTube videos.

Parents also educate each other on their children's autism through a forum dedicated specifically to parents, as well as through other social media. Here they swap

Fig. 2. A statue at the head of a classroom labeled with a sign "Professor Enderman."

information on how to deal with "meltdowns" or how to get their children's needs met at school. There is a mix among the parents of those who have their own diagnosis of autism and those who are considered neurotypical. The parenting board on the forum also includes autistic adults who often give advice to neurotypical parents about why their children may be acting in specific ways. These parents end up, through the Autcraft community, aligning themselves in some ways with the autism community while looking for ways to support their children.

For example, in the Autcraft virtual world, one father built an entire school campus where other Autcraft community members could visit and learn about autism. Some of the classrooms even have golems walking through them and statues set up to be professors at the head of the class (See Fig. 2). The building has many classrooms, with informational and inspirational signs posted throughout. In one, the material reads as follows:

> *What's the problem with body listening? Eye contact can be physically painful for some. You don't have to look to be good at listening. Your ears can do their job all by themselves. Sometimes verbal stims help to process. And that's ok if making sounds helps you listen and learn. Flappy hands happy hands. ... Your boundaries are just as important as anyone elses. Your brain is always thinking even when others don't understand. You are 'aut'some just the way you are. Your heart is caring about others & you deserve the same.*

This posting educates autistic members about some of the ways they may process information differently. This gives the members a way to speak about their own needs and communicate these needs to others. The end of the post reinforces that being different and being autistic is okay, showing again the inclusive nature of the autism community as found within the Autcraft community. Beyond inclusion, the naming and describing of symptoms in a positive light reshapes the discourse about autism as an identity. While symptoms are typically seen as a deficit they are reframed by the Autcraft community into positive identity markers.

Learning and educating others about autism is a way for Autcraft community members to align themselves with the autism community and to empower themselves as informed autistic individuals. These practices also allow for the Autcraft community members to shape their own version of autism community, one that is inclusive and understanding of children and their neurotypical (*i.e.,* those who do not have autism or are "typical") family members.

6 Discussion and Conclusion

Being able to explore and express their identities is important for all youth [16], but it is especially salient for the autistic youth of Autcraft. The Autcraft community has a variety of social media that support expression of these identities. As Autcraft is a community that supports autistic children as part of their mission statement, having the freedom to be able to play with and perform autistic identities is important to members. Engaging in activities such as self-labeling and education helps to both assert membership into the autism community as well as reshape the autism identity of the Autcraft community to meet the overall goals of inclusion.

Members of Autcraft do not necessarily have a medical diagnosis of autism—membership requires only that they *identify* as autistic or with autism—but they have still opted into the Autcraft community, which is first and foremost a community for children with autism. Many community members in the Autcraft are grappling with a variety of social and medical autistic identities at once or, at the very least, dealing with each in the various contexts of their lives. Members may have other therapies, school, or a home life that entertains a more medical model approach to autism in addition to the more accepting, social model of the Autcraft community. As with other disability identities, individuals need to find a balance, dependent on the current context, that allows them to get the services they need as well as the desired social outcomes.

Autcraft community members actively work to reshape the mainstream dialog about autism. Primarily, members try to lead by example, following a set of tenets set out by community founders that encourage and promote pro-social behavior. Community members also engage in outreach to both educate others and to make their own expressions of their autistic identities more visible to others. Members of the Autcraft community engage in activities—much like creating memorials for victims of violence—that purposefully shed light on the hardships they have faced. These efforts are examples of how those with marginalized identities fight back against oppression. As scholars, by listening to these community members and understanding their activities, we can begin to elevate the voices of those who have long been silenced.

The Autcraft community engages in gatekeeping practices to maintain exclusive membership. Community members must have a connection to autism, if they do not themselves have autism. These gatekeeping practices are meant to keep people out who mean to do community members harm (*i.e.,* the bullies and trolls). However, this works both ways. This gatekeeping also works to keep community members *in*. Choosing to be a part of this separate non-normative identity and space has the effect of "othering" community members. Othering is when a group of people are classified as "other," which becomes a way to reify the self (*e.g.,* in-group or the self and the out-group or the other) [5]. For members of the Autcraft community, their othering began long before joining Autcraft (in fact, for many, this ostracization is the reason for joining).

The consequences of othering in the case of children with autism are alienation and bullying. The Autcraft community creates a space that feels safe for the members, but there is a balance that must be struck between keeping members safe and alienating them from larger society. Especially as children grow up and age out of the community, there is currently little support in place for community members who feel they are too old for Autcraft. Some of these members may "age out" of Minecraft altogether, but more are simply looking for a less restrictive server. More work needs to be done to understand how the transition for autistic youth can be supported as they spend more time in other communities, beyond Autcraft—especially as these children become young adults.

The data in this paper is largely from the perspective of older caregivers in the Autcraft community, many of whom identify as autistic (See related work for more from the children's perspective [29–33]). These caregivers are in the difficult position of creating a safe space that allows younger children to play with fear, but simultaneously needing to prepare them to be in the (sometimes harsh) outside world. At the same time, these parents and caregivers also need the social support found within the Autcraft community, as they (and their families) are also targets as part of this community.

The Autcraft community acts as a support group for its members—creating a sense of community for those who have faced similar hardship. The group is critical for its members to come to as a community and a place to learn about a facet of their autistic identity. The emphasis, for Autcraft community members, is rather than *overcoming* autism as a medical problem, they *embrace* autism as their identity. And despite the label "autism" being a target for harassment and violence, the Autcraft community is about identity support, rather than victim support. Threats of violence permeate through many spaces and contexts in the lives of autistic individuals. These children face these threats in the physical and virtual world. As the memorial to victims of filicide reminds us, these threats have very real consequences. The Autcraft community strives to create a haven for those who need respite from bullying and harassment in other online communities. In creating a safe haven, however, they have moved beyond being a support group for victims to reclaim and embrace their own autistic identities.

Acknowledgements. I thank the members of Autcraft for the warm welcome to their community. Thank you to members of LUCI for their feedback and special thanks to Severn Ringland for his diligent editing. I would also like to thank Robert and Barbara Kleist for their support, as well as the ARCS Foundation. This work is covered by human subjects protocol #2014-1079 at the University of California, Irvine.

References

1. American Psychiatric Association. Diagnostic and Statistical Manual of Mental Disorders (2013)
2. Andalibi, N.: Social media for sensitive disclosures and social support: the case of miscarriage. In: Proceedings of the 19th International Conference on Supporting Group Work - GROUP 2016, pp. 461–465 (2016). https://doi.org/10.1145/2957276.2997019
3. Andalibi, N., Forte, A.: Announcing pregnancy loss on Facebook: a decision-making framework for stigmatized disclosures on identified social network sites. In: Proceedings of the 2018 CHI Conference on Human Factors in Computing Systems - CHI 2018, pp. 1–14 (2018). https://doi.org/10.1145/3173574.3173732
4. Boellstorff, T., Nardi, B., Pearce, C., Taylor, T.L.: Ethnography and Virtual Worlds: A Handbook of Method. Princeton University Press, Princeton (2012)

5. Brons, L.L.: Othering, an analysis. Transcience **6**(1), 69–90 (2015)
6. Burke, M., Kraut, R., Williams, D.: Social use of computer-mediated communication by adults on the autism spectrum. In: Proceedings of the 2010 ACM Conference on Computer Supported Cooperative Work, pp. 425–434 (2010). http://dl.acm.org/citation.cfm?id=1718991. Accessed 12 Jan 2014
7. Charmaz, K.: Constructing Grounded Theory: A Practical Guide to Qualitative Analysis. Sage Publications Ltd., Thousand Oaks (2006)
8. Collins, P.H.: Intersectionality's definitional dilemmas. Annu. Rev. Sociol. **41**(1), 1–20 (2015). https://doi.org/10.1146/annurev-soc-073014-112142
9. Crenshaw, K.: Mapping the margins: intersectionality, identity politics, and violence against women of color. Stanf. Law Rev. **43**(6), 1241 (1991). https://doi.org/10.2307/1229039
10. Duncan, S.C.: Minecraft, beyond construction and survival. Well Play. J. Video Games Value Mean. **1**(1), 1–22 (2011)
11. Garland-Thomson, R.: Extraordinary Bodies: Figuring Physical Disability in American Culture and Literature. Columbia University Press, New York (1997)
12. Goodley, D.: Introduction: global disability studies. In: Disability Studies: An Interdisciplinary Introduction, pp. 1–21. Sage Publications Ltd., Thousand Oaks (2011)
13. Goodley, D.: Intersections: diverse disability studies. In: Disability Studies: An Interdisciplinary Approach, pp. 33–47. Sage Publications Ltd., Thousand Oaks (2011)
14. Goodley, D., Runswick-Cole, K.: The violence of disablism: the violence of disablism. Sociol. Health Illn. **33**(4), 602–617 (2011). https://doi.org/10.1111/j.1467-9566.2010.01302.x
15. Gray, K.L., Buyukozturk, B., Hill, Z.G.: Blurring the boundaries: using Gamergate to examine "real" and symbolic violence against women in contemporary gaming culture. Sociol. Compass **11**(3), e12458 (2017). https://doi.org/10.1111/soc4.12458
16. Grotevant, H.D., Cooper, C.R.: Patterns of interaction in family relationships and the development of identity exploration in adolescence. Child Dev. **56**(2), 415 (1985). https://doi.org/10.2307/1129730
17. Grue, J.: The problem with inspiration porn: a tentative definition and a provisional critique. Disabil. Soc. **31**(6), 838–849 (2016). https://doi.org/10.1080/09687599.2016.1205473
18. Haimson, O.L., Brubaker, J.R., Dombrowski, L., Hayes, G.R.: Disclosure, stress, and support during gender transition on Facebook, 1176–1190 (2015). https://doi.org/10.1145/2675133.2675152
19. Haller, B.A.: Representing Disability in an Ableist World. The Avacado Press, Louisville (2010)
20. Hernandez, H.A., et al.: Design and evaluation of a networked game to support social connection of youth with cerebral palsy, 161–168 (2014). https://doi.org/10.1145/2661334.2661370
21. Irani, L.C., Hayes, G.R., Dourish, P.: Situated practices of looking: visual practice in an online world. In: Proceedings of the 2008 ACM Conference on Computer Supported Cooperative Work, pp. 187–196 (2008). http://dl.acm.org/citation.cfm?id=1460592. Accessed 31 Jan 2014
22. Jones, L., et al.: Prevalence and risk of violence against children with disabilities: a systematic review and meta-analysis of observational studies. Lancet **380**(9845), 899–907 (2012). https://doi.org/10.1016/S0140-6736(12)60692-8
23. Li, V., et al.: Losing it online: characterizing participation in an online weight loss community, 35–45 (2014). https://doi.org/10.1145/2660398.2660416
24. McCall, L.: The complexity of intersectionality. Signs J. Women Cult. Soc. **30**(3), 1771–1800 (2005). https://doi.org/10.1086/426800

25. Park, S., Kim, J., Lee, S.W., Yoo, J., Jeong, B., Cha, M.: Manifestation of depression and loneliness on social networks: a case study of young adults on Facebook. In: Proceedings of the 18th ACM Conference on Computer Supported Cooperative Work & Social Computing - CSCW 2015, pp. 557–570 (2015). https://doi.org/10.1145/2675133.2675139
26. Penuel, W.R., Wertsch, J.V.: Vygotsky and identity formation: a sociocultural approach. Educ. Psychol. **30**(2), 83–92 (1995). https://doi.org/10.1207/s15326985ep3002_5
27. Markus "Notch" Persson. Minecraft. Mojang, Stockholm, Sweden (2011)
28. Pinchevski, A., Peters, J.D.: Autism and new media: disability between technology and society. New Media Soc. **18**, 2507–2523 (2015). https://doi.org/10.1177/1461444815594441
29. Ringland, K.E.: A place to play: the (dis)abled embodied experience for autistic children in online spaces. In: CHI 2019 (2019)
30. Ringland, K.E., Boyd, L.E., Faucett, H., Cullen, A.L.L., Hayes, G.R.: Making in minecraft: a means of self-expression for youth with autism. In: Interaction and Design for Children (2017)
31. Ringland, K.E., Wolf, C.T., Boyd, L.E., Baldwin, M., Hayes, G.R.: Would You Be Mine: appropriating minecraft as an assistive technology for youth with autism. In: ASSETS 2016 (2016)
32. Ringland, K.E., Wolf, C.T., Dombrowski, L., Hayes, G.R.: Making "Safe": community-centered practices in a virtual world dedicated to children with autism. In: CSCW 2015 (2015)
33. Ringland, K.E., Wolf, C.T., Faucett, H., Dombrowski, L., Hayes, G.R.: "Will I always be not social?": re-conceptualizing sociality in the context of a minecraft community for autism. In: CHI 2016 (2016)
34. Rousso, H.: Don't Call Me Inspirational. Temple University Press, Philadelphia (2013)
35. Salter, A., Blodgett, B.: Toxic Geek Masculinity in Media: Sexism, Trolling, and Identity Policing. Palgrave Macmillan, Cham (2017)
36. Silberman, S.: NeuroTribes: The Legacy of Autism and the Future of Neurodiversity. Avery (2015)
37. Söder, M.: Tensions, perspectives and themes in disability studies. Scand. J. Disabil. Res. **11**(2), 67–81 (2009). https://doi.org/10.1080/15017410902830496
38. Straus, J.N.: Autism as culture. In: Davis, L.J. (ed.) The Disability Studies Reader, 3rd edn., pp. 535–559. Routledge, London (2010)
39. Zhao, Y., Zhang, J., Wang, Y.: Social media and autism support: investigation on autism support groups on Facebook. In: iConference 2017 Proceedings (2017)

Measuring and Tracking Scientific Literature

Exploring Scholarly Impact Metrics in Receipt of Highly Prestigious Awards

Dong Joon Lee[1]([✉]) [iD], Kartik Mutya[2] [iD], Bruce E. Herbert[1] [iD],
and Ethelyn V. Mejia[1] [iD]

[1] University Libraries, Texas A&M University, College Station,
TX 77843, USA
djlee@tamu.edu
[2] Industrial and Systems Engineering Department, Texas A&M University,
College Station, TX 77843, USA

Abstract. The authoritative data that underlies research information management (RIM) systems supports fine-grained analyses of faculty members' research
practices and output, data-driven decision making, and organizational research
management. Administrators at Texas A&M University (TAMU) asked the
University Libraries to develop institutional reports that describe faculty research
practices and identify their research strengths. The library runs Scholars@TAMU
(https://scholars.library.tamu.edu/) based on VIVO, a member-supported, open
source, semantic-web software program, as the university's RIM system. This
paper explores the scholarly impact and collaboration practices of senior faculty
members in the College of Engineering at TAMU and identifies relationships
between their impact metrics and collaboration practices. Full professors were
divided into three groups: (1) those who received highly prestigious (HP) awards,
(2) those who received prestigious (P) awards, and (3) those who did not receive
any awards categorized as either HP or P by the National Research Council. The
study's results showed that the faculty members with HP awards had significantly
higher mean ranks for their total citation count, the citation count of their top
cited article, their h-index, and their total number of publications than did the
faculty members without any HP or P awards. The findings from this study can
inform researchers, university administrators, and bibliometric communities
about the use of awards as an indicator that corresponds to other research performance indicators. Furthermore, researchers could also use the study's results
to develop a machine-learning model that could identify those faculty who are on
track to win HP awards in the future.

Keywords: Impact metrics · Research information management system ·
Highly prestigious awards

1 Introduction

As technologies that support sharing, reusing, and aggregating scholarly information
continue to advance, research information management (RIM) systems become more
comprehensive and heterogeneous databases, and constitute academic institutions'
authoritative records for their scholarly output [1, 2]. RIM systems can generally be

© Springer Nature Switzerland AG 2019
N. G. Taylor et al. (Eds.): iConference 2019, LNCS 11420, pp. 147–153, 2019.
https://doi.org/10.1007/978-3-030-15742-5_13

defined as systems that aggregate, curate, analyze, and use research activities' metadata, including research output, grants, equipment, statements of impact, media, service, awards, instructional history, and collaborators [1]. Large academic institutions with RIM systems encounter challenges in the systematic use and consumption of the data. The heterogeneous data available in RIM systems expands the scope of bibliometric study and information science. Unlike traditional bibliometric studies that only used citation data, researchers now work on research graphs that use person (e.g., researcher, investigator), work (e.g., publication, dataset), and grant (project, contract) data [3, 4]. These large volumes of data enable researchers to develop machine-learning models that can identify future research collaborators or deliver individually customized information to researchers [5, 6]. The research literature shows that tailoring system design and communication messages for users' needs has proven to be successful in supporting users' information-seeking behaviors [7].

The Texas A&M University (TAMU) Libraries developed and maintains Scholars@TAMU, a RIM System that includes the identities and scholarly records of TAMU's faculty. Scholars@TAMU is based on VIVO, a member-supported, opensource, semantic-web software program. Since the system's launch in January 2018, the library has received multiple service requests from a variety of academic groups (e.g., departments, colleges, centers, institutes) to generate local institutional reports describing faculty research practices, strengths, and impact. In addition, the library is being recognized as a potential partner for data science research groups within the university. The library's research team conducts multiple pilot-tests to identify new use cases for the data stored in the RIM system. This study explores the bibliographic impact indicators of researchers who won awards categorized as either Highly Prestigious (HP) or Prestigious (P) by the National Research Council (NRC).[1] The findings from this study can inform researchers, university administrators, and bibliometric communities about the use of awards as an indicator that corresponds to other research performance indicators (e.g., h-index, number of publications, citation count). Furthermore, researchers could also use the study's results to develop a machine-learning model that could identify those faculty who are on track to win highly prestigious awards in the future.

The study specifically explores and examines the following research questions:

- Are there any differences in research performance indicators for researchers who won highly prestigious awards and those that have not?
- Are there any differences in research collaboration practices for researchers who won highly prestigious awards and those that have not?

---

[1] The National Academies of Sciences, Engineering, and Medicine, Retrieved from: http://sites.nationalacademies.org/pga/resdoc/pga_044718.

2 Study Design

This preliminary study reports the analysis of statistical differences in research performance indicators and collaboration practices among faculty members in the College of Engineering at TAMU who have achieved the rank of full professor. Data are from both Scholars@TAMU, which aggregates information on TAMU faculty from multiple internal and external data sources (e.g., TAMU human resources database, grants/awards databases, institutional repositories, faculty CVs) and the Scopus database. Scholars@TAMU provides an authoritative record of TAMU faculty's scholarly output [2]. The faculty included in this study were divided into three groups: (1) those who received HP awards, (2) those who received P awards, and (3) those who did not receive awards (N) categorized as HP or P by the NRC. Table 1 presents sampled faculty members' frequency in each group, and some examples of the awards received by faculty in the first two groups. The researchers identified 13 and 65 professors from the College of Engineering in the HP and P groups, respectively. For the last group, 78 professors were randomly selected from the list of full professors who have not received an award.

Table 1. Number of sampled faculty members who received HP, P, N awards and some examples of awards.

Category: Examples of each category's award societies/award names	Freq

Highly Prestigious (HP):
  National Academy of Engineering/Membership
  National Academy of Science/Members
  John Simon Guggenheim Memorial Foundation/Fellowship
	13

Prestigious (P):
  American Association for the Advancement of Science/AAAS Fellow
  American Society of Civil Engineers/Norman Medal
  American Institute of Aeronautics and Astronautics/AIAA Fellow
	65

None (N)	78

3 Findings

In order to explore the relationship between research performance indicators and research collaboration practices with receiving a highly prestigious award, a statistical analysis was completed using the Kruskal-Wallis test (i.e., a non-parametric statistical method). The data in this study (see Table 2 and Fig. 1) is better represented by the median and interquartile range, which indicates a non-normal distribution of the residuals [8, 9].

The analysis revealed significant differences between faculty in the HP, P, and N groups in terms of their number of total citations, the citation count of their top cited article, their h-index, and their total number of publications (see Table 3). However there were no significant relationships on their collaboration practices.

Table 2. Characteristics of sampled TAMU College of Engineering professors' scholarly impact metrics and collaboration practices.

	Total		HP		P		N	
	N = 156		N = 13		N = 65		N = 78	
	Median	IQR	Median	IQR	Median	IQR	Median	IQR
Total citations	2092	2921	3685	10551	2272	3308	1752	2442
Citation count of top cited article	189.5	221	363	1520	185	237	185.5	203
h-Index	23	18	34	25	23	19	22	15
Total publications	139.5	133	216	201	147	167	128	86
Locally coauthored paper	23	35	53	49	24	35	18.5	33
Globally coauthored paper	16.5	32	23	54	18	29	15	33

Note. IQR: interquartile range.

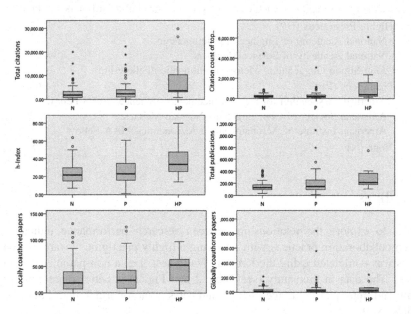

Fig. 1. Boxplots of sampled TAMU College of Engineering professors' scholarly impact metrics and collaboration practices.

Table 3. Kruskal-Wallis analysis of TAMU College of Engineering professors' scholarly impact metrics and collaboration practices.

	Receipts of awards		
	χ^2	df	Asymp. Sig.
Total citations	*9.829*	2	*0.007*
Citation count of top cited article	*6.822*	2	*0.033*
h-Index	*9.352*	2	*0.009*
Total publications	*13.711*	2	*0.001*
Locally coauthored paper	4.561	2	0.102
Globally coauthored paper	1.571	2	0.456

Note. Significant relationships are in italics

In addition, to identify the pairwise relative importance of the performance indicators among the researcher categories, the study analyzed the variables that exhibited significant differences by using the Bonferroni tests of *post hoc* pairwise comparisons. The test showed statistically significant differences among the three categories for all of the significant variables from the Kruskal-Wallis test (see Table 4).

Table 4. Bonferroni multiple comparison tests between N, P, and HP.

	Mean ranks 0/1/2	Sample 1 – Sample 2	SE	Adj. Sig.
Total citations	71.15/80.39/113.15	0–1	7.587	0.669
		0–2	13.534	*0.006*
		1–2	13.726	0.051
Citation count of top cited article	75.30/76.08/109.81	0–1	7.587	1.000
		0–2	13.533	*0.032*
		1–2	13.725	*0.042*
h-Index	71.13/80.66/111.92	0–1	7.583	0.626
		0–2	13.526	*0.008*
		1–2	13.718	0.068
Total publications	68.96/82.09/117.77	0–1	7.587	0.251
		0–2	13.533	*0.001*
		1–2	13.725	*0.028*

Note. Indicators 0, 1, and 2 specify N, P, and HP respectively. Significant relationships are in italics

Based on the pairwise comparisons, the professors with HP had significantly higher mean ranks for their number of total citations, the citation count of their top cited article, h-index, and total number of publications than did the professors with N, and the professors with HP had significantly higher mean ranks for their citation count of top cited article and total number of publications than did the professors with P. However there were no significant differences between the professors with P and N. Figure 2 summarizes the relationships between the research performance indicators and the three categories.

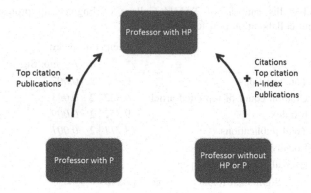

Fig. 2. Relationships between the three categories and the research performance indicators. Only statistically significant variables are included. The arrows point toward greater mean ranks of the variables.

4   Conclusion

Recent studies on RIM systems and their metadata demonstrate not only the complexity of the metadata used to identify research and researchers, but also the diversity of the data sources used to build scholarly identity [1, 10–13]. Researchers explore factors that influence scholars' research productivity and excellence. The literature has found many different internal and external factors, including academic rank, time management skill, the value placed on research, the time available to conduct research, as well as institutional support in the form of graduate assistants, summer research support, course load, and department culture [14]. Researchers have also explored the relationships between research productivity and receipt of grant funding or research awards [5, 9, 15]. This study compared research performance indicators of professors in TAMU's College of Engineering to examine any differences based on their receipt of prestigious or highly prestigious research awards. Based on the results, a list of award recipients could be used as a factor for evaluating researchers, since receipt of an award was correlated with higher performance indicators. This study also offers bibliometric researchers some initial data that could be used to develop machine-learning models that could anticipate the next recipients of highly prestigious awards. In addition, university libraries with a RIM system could conduct a similar analysis and partner with university administrators to build strategies that would enhance the university's scholarly reputation.

References

1. Bryant, R., et al.: Research information management: defining RIM and the library's role. OCLC Research Position Paper. OCLC Research, Dublin (2017)
2. Graham, S., Lee, D.J., Radio, E., Tarver, H.: "Who is this?" Moving from authority control to identity management. AALL Spectr. **22**(5), 24–27 (2018). http://hdl.handle.net/1969.1/166339

3. Conlon, M., Aryani, A.: Creating an open linked data model for research graph using VIVO ontology. In: Open Repositories Conference. Figshare, Brisbane (2017). http://doi.org/10. 4225/03/58ca600d726bd

4. Aryani, A., et al.: A research graph dataset for connecting research data repositories using RD-Switchboard. Sci. Data **5**, 180099 (2018). https://doi.org/10.1038/sdata.2018.99

5. Rokach, L., Kalech, M., Blank, I., Stern, R.: Who is going to win the next Association for the Advancement of Artificial Intelligence Fellowship Award? Evaluating researchers by mining bibliographic data. J. Am. Soc. Inf. Sci. Technol. **62**(12), 2456–2470 (2011). https:// doi.org/10.1002/asi.21638

6. Simović, A.: A big data smart library recommender system for an educational institution. Libr. Hi Tech **36**(3), 498–523 (2018). https://doi.org/10.1108/LHT-06-2017-0131

7. Kreuter, M.W., Farrell, D.W., Olevitch, L.R., Brennan, L.K.: Tailoring Health Messages: Customizing Communication With Computer Technology, 1st edn. Routledge, Mahwah (1999)

8. Nonparametric tests. http://sphweb.bumc.bu.edu/otlt/MPH-Modules/BS/BS704_Nonpara metric/BS704_Nonparametric_print.html. Accessed 8 Aug 2018

9. Warner, E.T., Carapinha, R., Weber, G.M., Hill, E.V., Reede, J.Y.: Gender differences in receipt of National Institutes of Health R01 Grants among junior faculty at an Academic Medical Center: the role of connectivity, rank, and research productivity. J. Women's Health **26**(10), 1086–1093 (2017). https://doi.org/10.1089/jwh.2016.6102

10. Lee, D.J., Stvilia, B., Wu, S.: Towards a metadata model for research information management systems. Libr. Hi Tech (2018). https://doi.org/10.1108/lht-01-2018-0013

11. Main features of CERIF. https://www.eurocris.org/cerif/main-features-cerif. Accessed 8 Aug 2018

12. Ilik, V., et al.: OpenVIVO: transparency in scholarship. Front. Res. Metrics Anal. **2**, 12 (2018). https://doi.org/10.3389/frma.2017.00012

13. Stvilia, B., Wu, S., Lee, D.J.: Researchers' participation in and motivations for engaging with research information management systems. PLoS ONE **13**(2), e0193459 (2018). https:// doi.org/10.1371/journal.pone.0193459

14. White, C.S., James, K., Burke, L.A., Allen, R.S.: What makes a "research star"? Factors influencing the research productivity of business faculty. Int. J. Prod. Perform. Manage. **61**(6), 584–602 (2012). https://doi.org/10.1108/17410401211249175

15. Ali, M., Bhattacharyya, P., Olejniczak, A.J.: The effects of scholarly productivity and institutional characteristics on the distribution of federal research grants. J. High. Educ. **81**(2), 164–178 (2010). http://www.jstor.org/stable/40606849

Are Papers with Open Data More Credible?
An Analysis of Open Data Availability
in Retracted *PLoS* Articles

Michael Lesk[1] , Janice Bially Mattern[2] ,
and Heather Moulaison Sandy[3]([✉])

[1] Rutgers University, New Brunswick, NJ 08901, USA
lesk@acm.org
[2] Villanova University, Villanova, PA 19085, USA
[3] University of Missouri, Columbia, MO 65211, USA
moulaisonhe@missouri.edu

Abstract. Open data has been hailed as an important corrective for the credibility crisis in science. This paper makes an initial attempt to measure the relationship between open data and credible research by analyzing the number of retracted articles with attached or open data in an open access science journal. Using Retraction Watch, retracted papers published in *PLoS* between 2014 and 2018 are identified. Of the 152 total retracted papers, fewer than 15% attached their data. Since about half of the published articles have open data, and so few of the retracted ones do, we put forth the preliminary notion that open data, especially high quality and well-curated data, might imply scientific credibility.

Keywords: Retractions · Open data · Credibility

1 Science's Credibility Crisis

By many accounts, the credibility of scientific research is in crisis (Saltelli and Funtowicz 2017). Mounting evidence suggests that surprisingly few scientific studies are reproducible and/or replicable (Sayre and Riegelman 2018). In medical research, for instance, Prinz et al. (2011) found that Bayer could only replicate some 20–25% of 67 studies in the fields of cancer biology, women's health, and cardiovascular diseases. Similar replication challenges are found in psychology (Bohannon 2015) and social science (Camerer et al. 2018).

In some cases, dubious results can be traced to sloppy analysis—for instance, computational errors, corner cutting, or statistical misinterpretation like 'p-hacking' (Benjamin et al. 2017). In others cases, the problem arises from data manipulation, plagiarism or outright research fraud. Marcus and Oransky (2015), from the Retraction Watch database (http://retractiondatabase.org/) and blog (https://retractionwatch.com/) report that "every day on average, a scientific paper is retracted because of misconduct" (p. A19). Some instances are high profile, including contrived data linking vaccinations to autism; tampered and falsified data on predictors of cancer; and fully fabricated data

© Springer Nature Switzerland AG 2019
N. G. Taylor et al. (Eds.): iConference 2019, LNCS 11420, pp. 154–161, 2019.
https://doi.org/10.1007/978-3-030-15742-5_14

on political opinions about same-sex marriage. When taken in combination with unwitting research errors, the credibility of scientific research is eroding.

The result is a crisis at multiple levels of society. First, at the level of research, it raises questions about how much undetected faulty research is out there. Research from a range of disciplines confirms that doubtful findings or even myths can and do become foundational knowledge, taken for granted through repeated citations (cf. Begley and Ellis 2012; Rekdal 2014). These mistakes waste effort and contribute to a skepticism of research in general.

Second, the eroding credibility of scientific research suggests a crisis for the role of science in policy. Although reverence for evidence-based decision and action has long meant that scientific research is an authoritative basis for social and political policy (Saltelli and Giampietro 2017), faulty science related to issues such as public safety, education, and economic development have begun to take a toll. Consider austerity policies that aim to reduce budget deficits through deep cuts to government spending; they ultimately impose great social costs, especially for society's most needy members. Yet, the science justifying these punishing policies is largely rooted in an analysis that has been exposed as sloppy and unjustified (Cassidy 2013). Anti-vaccine sentiment is also based on work which has been found faulty. This supports the idea that we have entered a post-factual world in which science is no longer trusted as the basis for policy.

The social legitimacy of scientific knowledge depends upon solving the problem of undetected faulty research. An ethos of open data can help by improving research transparency. Scientists can identify irreproducible results, catch sloppy computations, highlight and correct each other's errors, and ensure that they are building upon only the most reliable and verified findings (Molloy 2011; Gewin 2016; Leeming 2017).

2 Open Data in Science

Despite the potential to restore credibility to the scientific endeavor, open data sharing has not caught on the way its advocates might hope. Academics are notoriously reticent about openly sharing their data. As Fecher et al. (2015) point out, this reticence generally arises from a mismatch between taking an action (sharing) that benefits the greater good, and disincentives to sharing. For instance, where raw data discloses sensitive or confidential personal information about subjects, researchers' unwillingness to share data can be an ethical matter. Other resistance to sharing could be due to the commercial value of raw data, or because it is licensed.

Most of the reasons that researchers resist openly sharing data, however, are less simple. As the literature documents, many researchers are concerned about their results being called into question. After all, if their data are not available, nobody can attack their findings. To make data shareable is time consuming, requiring proper curation. Researchers are hesitant about the preparation required to make data intelligible to others (c.f. Tenopir et al. 2011). Some researchers are also concerned about data theft (Teixeira da Silva and Dobránszki 2015), and providing the proper metadata can be challenging (Fecher et al. 2015; Sadiq and Indulska 2017). In short, researchers are more disposed toward activities that directly facilitate their research than to the data curation activities required for open data. Most universities are insufficiently incentivizing data sharing (Bolukbasi et al. 2013), and in the time it takes to curate data, another research team could publish the idea, "scooping" the work (Van Noorden 2014). In sum, there are a number of reasons data sharing is limited and remains limited.

Going forward, some improvements can be expected. First, new mandates require that U.S. federally funded research results must be made available with open access to the relevant data, although compliance has been limited (Nelson 2009). As well, some journal publishers have increasingly required that authors share the data that supports their research articles. For instance, in 2013, *PLoS* (Public Library of Science: https://www.plos.org/) established a policy that authors must provide open access to their research data unless they receive permission from the editor ("Editorial and Publishing Policies" 2018; Teixeira da Silva and Dobránszki 2015). Not all journals have such requirements. The social sciences, for example, have been slower. Few journals have policies that encourage open data (cf. *International Studies Quarterly*) with even fewer requiring it (cf. *The Journal of Politics*). Advocates are pressuring for change but scholars remain ambivalent. An ethos of open data remains nascent, at best.

Reticence to publish datasets does not mean that faulty research is going unattended. Retractions are nonetheless rare, and can be due to a number of possible problems (Marcus and Oransky 2015) and many are not due to data problems. Articles can be retracted because they have been previously published, because ethical principles of human subjects research were not followed, or because of complaints about the soundness of the methodology. Plagiarism, self-plagiarism, and "salami slicing" are other reasons that articles might be retracted. Sloppy computation, corner cutting, and more flagrant research misconduct can also lead to retractions or sanctions of some kind. Although misconduct is possible to detect without open data, it is easier if the data can be inspected.

Such verification, however, can be experienced as a threat, which creates an obstacle to an open data ethos in science. Researchers may worry that by opening their open data, their work is more likely to be retracted simply because it is easier to verify than that for which the data is not provided. But the reverse might also be true: articles with open data may be less likely to be retracted, precisely because in the onerous process of curating the data, authors are more likely to discover and address mistakes before publication. Peer's (2018) process for validating work in her organization and avoiding common statistical mistakes exemplifies this suggestion.

2.1 Guiding Questions

The current research considers the relationship between open data and retraction by asking: Does open data put researchers at greater risk or does it help establish their contributions as real and meaningful, beyond reproach? Put differently, is open data a hindrance or help to the cultivation of more credible science?

3   Method

We focused on articles in *PLoS* because it (1) is entirely open access for the text of articles and (2) has a standard way of indicating when an article has attached data files. In addition, *PLoS* is a prolific publisher of scientific papers, with many articles that have been retracted[1] and subsequently tracked on Retraction Watch. "Retraction Watch is a Web site set up by two science journalists, Adam Marcus and Ivan Oransky, who have received international attention for tracking high-profile retractions of papers" (Bonnell et al. 2012, p. 2). Our study looks at 2014 to the present for a number of reasons. First, as mentioned, *PLoS* began requiring data in 2013. In addition, the U.S. National Science Foundation began requiring open data be made available on funded projects starting in 2011 (National Science Foundation 2016), which resulted in many projects of 3-year duration being published starting in 2014. Such projects required a "data management plan" explaining how the data collected would be made available to other researchers, often through deposit in an archive but sometimes by arrangement with the authors, and not necessarily publication in a journal. Another reason for focusing on 2014 onwards is to exclude the thousands of retractions resulting from the detection of published research papers discovered to have been generated by the Sci-Gen chatterbot (Labbé et al. 2015), a chatterbot that produces documents resembling scientific research papers, and that some journals and conferences published only to retract later.

PLoS articles were obtained from PubMed Central where they are available for download; Retraction Watch data was obtained through its website. Articles were matched via DOIs (digital object identifiers) and analyzed using Python.

4   Results[2]

Ultimately, very few papers are retracted from *PLoS* per year, as shown in Table 1.

Overall, about half the papers in *PLoS* have some kind of attached data. Table 2 shows the fraction of *PLoS* papers with data availability.

Of the retracted papers identified, fewer than average had accompanying data. Figure 1 show the counts of retracted articles by year, providing a red bar for all retracted papers and a green bar for those with open data. What is striking about this, is that in total about 27% of the retracted papers had open data. We did not examine the detailed reasons for retraction – as noted before, some retractions have nothing to do with data (e.g., plagiarism or publisher error) and many may have multiple causes.

---

[1] The *PLoS* retraction policy is at https://journals.plos.org/plosone/s/corrections-and-retractions, referencing and including the ICMJE (International Committee of Medical Journal Editors) rules given at http://www.icmje.org/recommendations/browse/publishing-and-editorial-issues/scientific-miscon duct-expressions-of-concern-and-retraction.html. Note that a retraction does not necessarily imply either malfeasance or a significant error; articles can be retracted for a missing author, for example.

[2] Data for this project is available through the RUcore repository: https://rucore.libraries.rutgers.edu/.

Table 1. Number of articles and retracted articles in *PLoS*, by year (2014–2018).

Year	Total articles	Retracted articles	% Retracted
2014	35393	33	0.09%
2015	33449	37	0.1%
2016	26981	23	0.09%
2017	24670	30	0.1%
2018 (part year)	12693	29	0.2%
Total	133186	152	0.1%

Table 2. Percentage of articles published in *PLoS* that include accompanying data, by year (2014–2018).

Year	Total articles	Articles with data	% With data
2014	35393	6573	19%
2015	33449	17075	51%
2016	26981	13631	50%
2017	24670	11516	47%
2018 (part year)	12693	5696	45%

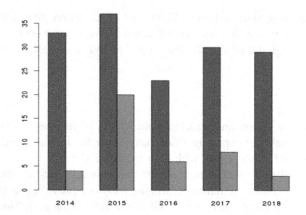

Fig. 1. Count of retracted articles in *PLoS*, by year (2014–2018). Red bars indicate retractions, green bars indicate retracted papers accompanied by open data. (Color figure online)

5   Discussion

From 2015 onward, roughly half the articles published in *PLoS* were accompanied by data, but the percentage did not increase. The steady level of open data–despite the expectations of data sharing—suggests that concerns over costs or misuse persist.

Yet, the risk to authors of re-examination appears to be overimagined: The articles with open data are not routinely being retracted because their data has been examined and found faulty. As demonstrated in Table 1, the risk of being accused of fraudulence or sloppiness is very low (for example, for 2017 in all of *PLoS* there were more than 24,000 articles with data and only 30 were retracted).

The more onerous aspects of data curation may have inhibited some authors from preparing to distribute their data, but increasingly there is support for this activity. Many university libraries are able to assist with both organizing data and promising long-term storage (Heidorn 2011). Over time, making data available will become more expected, especially as funding organizations insist on it, and researchers should understand the benefits to them and to their field if they will be expected to take part.

As the findings of this paper suggest, (however preliminarily) it makes little sense to invoke fear of being criticized as a justification for withholding data.

6 Conclusion and Next Steps

In this short paper, we have examined the retraction rates for published articles in *PLoS* that include and do not include open data. More systematic research is needed to confirm our preliminary findings and we will continue to pursue it. We intend to keep using Retraction Watch as a source of information on rejected papers, and attempt to classify a larger variety of papers as with or without open data. Areas with a tradition of open data (astronomy, as an example) will be particularly interesting to observe, although these do not necessarily overlap with the areas that are readily available from archives such as PubMed. We believe that papers with high quality, well-curated open data will turn out to be more reliable and should deserve greater credibility, and be entitled to both more prestige in the university community and higher rankings in search engines, but acknowledge that much more study is needed to investigate these preliminary conclusions.

A number of good reasons for publishing data exist. Scientific results, whether they be about vaccine risks or climate change, are in doubt. If the credibility of our literature can be improved by including more of the data, everyone will be better off. Researchers might be incentivized to publish data since papers with open data get more citations (Piwowar and Vision 2013). Borgman (2012) discusses other advantages of open data, such as accelerating research if people can see each other's work.

This study's findings should encourage further research into the role of data sharing in promoting an ethos of transparency in science as a way of potentially ameliorating the credibility crisis. In the effort to establish with greater certainty the inverse relationship between open data and having one's findings impugned, clearer notations in articles about whether they make their data available would be helpful. For instance, the ACM (Association for Computing Machinery) does a good job of this e.g., with the badge. The preliminary results of this research therefore support further inquiry into the standardized recognition across publishers and publishing platforms for papers that attach or otherwise make their data open and available, and the quality and process of making that data available.

References

Begley, C.G., Ellis, L.M.: Raise standards for preclinical cancer research. Nature **483**, 531–533 (2012)

Benjamin, D.J., et al.: Redefine statistical significance, 22 July 2017. https://doi.org/10.31234/osf.io/mky9j

Bohannon, J.: Many psychology papers fail replication test. Science **349**(6251), 910–911 (2015)

Bolukbasi, B., et al.: Open data: crediting a culture of cooperation. Science **342**(6162), 1041–1042 (2013)

Bonnell, D.A., et al.: Recycling is not always good: the dangers of self-plagiarism. ACS Nano **6**(1), 1–4 (2012). https://doi.org/10.1021/nn3000912

Borgman, C.L.: The conundrum of sharing research data. J. Am. Soc. Inf. Sci. Technol. **63**(6), 1059–1078 (2012)

Camerer, C.F., et al.: Evaluating the replicability of social science experiments in *Nature* and *Science* between 2010 and 2015. Nat. Hum. Behav. **2**, 637–644 (2018)

Cassidy, J.: The Reinhart and Rogoff Controversy: A Summing Up. The New Yorker, New York (2013)

Editorial and Publishing Policies. PLoS (2018). https://www.plos.org/editorial-publishing-policies

Fecher, B., Friesike, S., Hebing, M.: What drives academic data sharing? PLoS ONE **10**(2), e0118053 (2015). https://doi.org/10.1371/journal.pone.0118053

Gewin, V.: Data sharing: an open mind on open data. Nature **529**(7584), 117–119 (2016). https://doi.org/10.1038/nj7584-117a

Heidorn, P.B.: The emerging role of libraries in data curation and e-science. J. Libr. Adm. **51**, 662–672 (2011)

Kønig, N., Børsen, T., Emmeche, C.: The ethos of post-normal science. Futures **91**, 12–24 (2017). https://doi.org/10.1016/j.futures.2016.12.004

Labbé, C., Labbé, D., Portet, F.: Detection of computer generated papers in scientific literature <hal-01134598> (2015). https://hal.archives-ouvertes.fr/hal-01134598

Leeming, J.: How will open data advance scientific discovery? Naturejobs Blog (2017). http://blogs.nature.com/naturejobs/2017/10/25/how-will-open-data-advance-scientific-discovery/. Accessed 9 May 2018

Marcus, A., Oransky, I.: What's Behind Big Science Frauds?. The New York Times, New York (2015). https://www.nytimes.com/2015/05/23/opinion/whats-behind-big-science-frauds.html

Molloy, J.C.: The Open Knowledge Foundation: open data means better science. PLoS Biol. **9**(12), e1001195 (2011). https://doi.org/10.1371/journal.pbio.1001195

The National Science Foundation Open government plan: 4.0, September 2016. https://www.nsf.gov/pubs/2016/nsf16131/nsf16131.pdf

Nelson, B.: Data sharing: empty archives. Nature **461**, 160–163 (2009). https://doi.org/10.1038/461160a

Peer, L.: Reproducible research practices at ISPS, 30 April 2018. https://isps.yale.edu/news/blog/2018/05/reproducible-research-practices-at-isps

Piwowar, H.A., Vision, T.J.: Data reuse and the open data citation advantage. PeerJ: Bioinformatics and Genomics section, 1 October 2013

Prinz, F., Schlange, T., Asadullah, K.: Believe it or not: how much can we rely on published data on potential drug targets? Nat. Rev. Drug Discov. **10**, 712 (2011)

Rekdal, O.B.: Academic urban legends. Soc. Stud. Sci. **44**(4), 638–654 (2014). https://doi.org/10.1177/0306312714535679

Sadiq, S., Marta Indulska, M.: Open data: quality over quantity. Int. J. Inf. Manage. **37**, 150–154 (2017). https://doi.org/10.1016/j.ijinfomgt.2017.01.003

Saltelli, A., Funtowicz, S.: What is science's crisis really about? Futures **91**, 5–11 (2017). https://doi.org/10.1016/j.futures.2017.05.010

Saltelli, A., Giampietro, M.: What is wrong with evidence based policy, and how can it be improved? Futures **91**, 62–71 (2017). https://doi.org/10.1016/j.futures.2016.11.012

Sayre, F., Riegelman, A.: The reproducibility crisis and academic libraries. Coll. Res. Libr. **79**(1), 2 (2018). https://crl.acrl.org/index.php/crl/article/view/16846/18452

Tenopir, C., et al.: Data sharing by scientists: practices and perceptions. PLoS One, 29 June 2011. https://doi.org/10.1371/journal.pone.0021101

Teixeira da Silva, J.A., Dobránszki, J.: Potential dangers with open access data files in the expanding open data movement. Publ. Res. Q. **31**, 298–305 (2015). https://doi.org/10.1007/s12109-015-9420-9

Van Noorden, R.: Publishers withdraw more than 120 gibberish papers: conference proceedings removed from subscription databases after scientist reveals that they were computer-generated. Nature News (February 24, 2014; Updated February 25, 2014)

The Spread and Mutation of Science Misinformation

Ania Korsunska(✉) ⓘ

Syracuse University, Syracuse, USA
akorsuns@syr.edu

Abstract. As the media environment has shifted towards digitization, we have seen the roles of creating, curating and correcting information shift from professional "gatekeeper" journalists to a broader media industry and the general public. This shift has led to the spread of misinformation. Though political "fake news" is currently a popular area of study, this study investigates another related phenomenon: science misinformation. Consistent exposure to science misinformation has been shown to cultivate false beliefs about risks, causes and prevalence of illnesses and disincentivize the public from implementing healthy lifestyle changes. Despite the need for more research, science misinformation dissemination studies are scarce. Through a case study that traces the spread of information about one specific article through hyperlink citations, this study adds valuable insights into the inner workings of media networks, conceptualizations of misinformation spread and methodological approaches to multi-platform misinformation tracing. The case study illustrates the over-reliance of media sources on secondary information and the novel phenomenon of constantly mutating online content. The original misinformant is able to remove misleading information, and as a result, all of the subsequent articles end up referencing misinformation to a source that no longer exists. This ability to update content online breaks the information flow process: news stories no longer represent a snapshot in time but instead living, mutating organisms, making any study of media networks increasingly complex.

Keywords: Science misinformation · Network analysis · Network gatekeeping

1 Introduction

Traditionally, journalists in the U.S. have been called upon to inform the public of the new and important issues of the day. They are content producers, as well as gatekeepers of information, deciding what is worthy of coverage (Lewin 1947; Shoemaker and Vos 2009). As the media environment has shifted towards digitization, we have seen the roles of creating and curating information, and correcting misinformation spread throughout a broader media industry as well as the public (Barzilai-Nahon 2008; Lazer et al. 2018). This shift in the media environment has helped give rise to the creation and dissemination of misinformation through oversimplification and exaggeration (Woloshin and Schwartz 2002; Lewandowsky et al. 2012; Howell 2013). Though political "fake news" is currently a popular area of study (Allcott and Gentzkow 2017;

© Springer Nature Switzerland AG 2019
N. G. Taylor et al. (Eds.): iConference 2019, LNCS 11420, pp. 162–169, 2019.
https://doi.org/10.1007/978-3-030-15742-5_15

Flynn et al. 2017; Vosoughi et al. 2018), this study aims to draw attention to another related phenomenon: science misinformation.

2 The Impact of Misinformation

Misinformation, defined as the unintentional spread of false, inaccurate or misleading information (Kumar and Geethakumari 2013; Lazer et al. 2018) about scientific studies is abundant. It is false, because it is contradicted by the best available evidence in the public domain - the scientific consensus. Misinformation is virtually unavoidable in our current media environment (Moynihan et al. 2000; Schwitzer 2008, 2017) and can have lasting, negative effect on people's lives. Consistent exposure to misinformation related to science and health has been shown to cultivate false beliefs about risks, causes and prevalence of illnesses and disincentivize the public from implementing healthy life-style changes and getting routine checkups (Niederdeppe and Levy 2007). Misinformation has also been shown to spread much faster and wider than the truth (Vosoughi et al. 2018), and be very difficult to eliminate from people's minds, even after being debunked (Hochschild and Einstein 2015; Nyhan and Reifler 2015). Despite the dire need, multi-platform approaches to the study of science misinformation dissemination are few and far between. Though current research has looked at the spread of misinformation within platforms where the flow can be easily traced, such as sharing/retweets on Twitter or Facebook (Vosoughi et al. 2018; Allcott and Gentzkow 2017; Wu and Liu 2018; Vraga and Bode 2018), to my knowledge there has not been an attempt to develop a method of tracing information in relation to specific topics across the Internet.

This case study proposes the idea of hyperlink citation tracing, which enables us to see the flow of information in between various media sources: peer-review journals, press release websites, traditional media and "new" media (blogs, social media, etc.). With this method we will be able to understand the information's life cycle: creation, spread, mutation, and possibly death. In this study, I ask the following questions: (1) How does misinformation flow in between different media sources? (2) Which media outlets rely on primary sources and which on secondary sources? (3) Which media outlet is the source of the misinformation? Answering these questions in the context of this case study will helps us understand the complexity of the misinformation spread and is the first step to developing methodological approaches to multi-platform misinformation tracing, as well as future misinformation prevention algorithm development.

3 Scientists Say Smelling Farts Might Prevent Cancer

Published in the *MedChemComm Journal* on April 7, 2014, the article at the heart of this case study is titled "The synthesis and functional evaluation of a mitochondria-targeted hydrogen sulfide donor(10-oxo-10-(4-(3-thioxo-3H-1,2-dithiol-5-yl) phenoxy) decyl) triphenylphosphonium bromide (AP39)" (Le Trionnaire et al. 2014). On July 9, 2014 the press release was published by the University of Exeter, with which 6 out of 8 authors are affiliated. It is titled "Rotten egg gas holds key to healthcare therapies" (University of Exeter 2014). In its introduction the authors state that even though "it may smell of flatulence" hydrogen sulfide "is now being found to offer potential health benefits in a range of issues, from diabetes, to stroke, hearts attacks and dementia" (University of Exeter 2014). Though *the Daily Mail* was the first popular media publication to report on this study, it did not spread the information very far. *Time* published an article on July 11, 2014 with the unfortunate title "Scientists Say Smelling Farts Might Prevent Cancer" (Stampler 2014a). Three days later on July 14, the title was amended, removing the scientists: "Ridiculous study of the day says smelling farts might prevent cancer" (Stampler 2014b). On July 18 the was fully rewritten and retitled "A stinky compound may protect against cell damage, study finds" (Stampler 2014c). The author included a correction notice: "An earlier version of this article incorrectly summarized the findings and implications of this study" (Stampler 2014c). Once *Time* introduced specific elements to the story, such as cancer and farts, neither of which is mentioned in the original paper or the press release, the story spread rapidly.

4   Methods: Building the Citation Network

This case study analyzed the flow of information by utilizing hyperlink citations of popular media publications. The Google search engine was used as a data source, with keywords "farts," "cancer" and "study" and date range July 1–31, 2014. Though the study was published in April, there was no media coverage until the press release in July. The first six pages of Google results were scraped, excluding duplicates and stories not directly related to the topic (n = 48). Including the peer-review publication and the press release, total sample size was 50 articles. From each popular media article all external, working hyperlinks, article titles, URLs and dates of publication were extracted. Titles were coded as to whether they were proliferating the misinformation or taking an opposing, fact-checker role. The hyperlinks were converted into numerical values and coded as edges, with the transfer of information from source to target. The network was visualized with Gephi, an open-source network analysis software (Bastian et al. 2009). Once it became clear that *Time* produced multiple versions of the same article, additional analysis was conducted by utilizing Archive.org, the digital library of Internet content.

The resulting network contained 71 nodes (total sources cited) and 123 edges (total hyperlink citations). The most important nodes were the peer review publication *MedChemComm Journal* (cited by 13 sources), the University of Exeter press release (cited by 24 sources) and *Time* (cited by 22 sources). Out of the 49 articles (excluding the peer-review publication), 37 (76%) were proliferating the misinformation in their titles (Fig. 1).

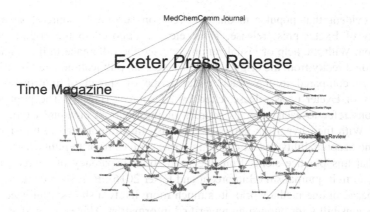

Fig. 1. Information spread network. Nodes represent article sources, edges – hyperlink citations, and arrows - the directionality of information transfer (from source to target)

5   Analysis: Tracing Misinformation Flow

First, to broadly look at the flow of misinformation in between the different media sources. Out of the sample, 12 articles were published on the same day as the *Time* article, all with titles regurgitating the misinformation; 10 were published the next day (with 7 misleading titles). From there, coverage dwindles to just 8, 8, 3 and 1 throughout the next four days. Curiously, 7 articles were published after *Time* rewrote their article on 7/18/2014, with 5 continuing to spread misinformation. Those 5 listed either no sources, no reliable sources (small, unknown blogs) nor did they reference *Time*. The 2 skeptical articles listed the *MedChemComm Journal,* among others, in their hyperlink citations. This is consistent with literature that shows that misinformation spreads much faster and wider than the truth (Vosoughi et al. 2018), making the job increasingly more difficult for both official fact-checking organizations such as FactCheck.org and Snopes, and for popular media publications that are trying to correct the story, to correct misinformation once it spreads throughout media networks.

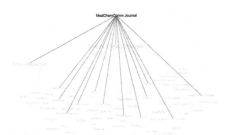

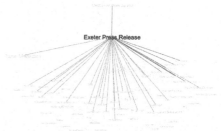

Fig. 2. *MedChemComm Journal* article spread

Fig. 3. University of Exeter press release spread

It is evident that popular media over-rely on secondary sources, such as The University of Exeter press release, *Time*, etc., as opposed to the original scientific publication. With the help of visualizations, we see the difference in the spread of the information directly from the original *MedChemComm* publication, cited by 13 sources (Fig. 2), as compared to the much wider scope of spread of information of the University of Exeter press release, cited by 24 sources (Fig. 3). The popular media publications refer to each other as sources of information, creating a type of echo-chamber. With their hyperlink language they also illustrate a need to transfer responsibility and accountability of fact checking one's sources prior to publication. It can be argued that this practice stems from the need for transparency of sources as a professional norm in journalism (Humprecht and Esser 2016). But when contextualized in the fast-paced online media world, it is much more likely a short-cut utilized to avoid taking responsibility for publishing unverified information. This is likely due to the de-professionalization of science journalism and overuse of amateur, freelance writers (Schwitzer 2008) coupled with the need to publish high quantity with high speed, little emphasis on quality or depth (Usher 2014).

Another interesting and novel theme that comes to light through this case study is the live mutation of information. The culprit in this study, *Time*, is a trusted, traditional media gatekeeper. By looking at just *Time* citations data (Fig. 4), we see that half of the other publications referenced it as a source of information (49%). It can be inferred that the authors of publications were influenced by *Time*'s reputation and attributed credibility to them as a source. Individuals' evaluations of the strength of an argument largely rely on heuristics and their perception of source credibility (Hovland and Weiss 1951; Kahan et al. 2010). If traditional gatekeepers do not live up to their reputation, they stand to lose the public's perception of credibility.

Unfortunately, in this case, *Time* was the source of misinformation. By looking at Archive.org, we can see that *Time* published misinformation and then was able to remove it completely. This is a novel complication to the media spread network structure, as all of the references to the *Time* were made prior to the article being completely rewritten on 7/18/2014. The hyperlink citations as they stand now in all the blog posts are actually referencing information that no longer exists.

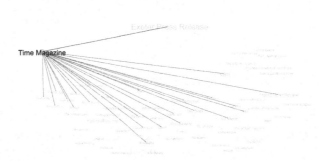

Fig. 4. *Time Magazine* article spread

This is a finding with significant implications for any further research in this subfield: the ability to update content online breaks the information flow process. News stories no longer represent a snapshot in time but instead living, mutating organisms (Fass and Main 2014).

6 Conclusion

The recent rise of media technology has meant an unprecedented increase in the speed and scope of the public's access of information, impacting how information flows in the media, as well as who creates and curates it (Hesse et al. 2005; Cline and Haynes 2001; Panth and Acharya 2015). There is more information available than ever before, with varying degrees of accuracy. Articles published online have a special opportunity: to not only reference their sources, but to directly hyperlink the sources to the original content. This is a style of citing and referencing that not only accomplishes the traditional goals of academic citations, but also allows us to see the flow of information in this unique, fast-paced media environment. This becomes especially important in the current age of "fake news" as we move towards what some have referred to as a "post-truth" world (Gewin 2017).

The aim of this case study was to present a sample approach to studying misinformation: the idea of investigatory hyperlink tracing, which enables us to see the entire flow of information through various media sources, and to draw attention to the issue of science misinformation and the real-time mutation of information online. By its nature as a case study with a limited sample, I make no claims as to generalizability of these themes. Utilizing the Google search was not ideal, as the "top" search results may be adjusted to the user and change according to the popularity of the websites at the time of search. Despite these limitations, the Google sample offered the closest available snapshot of what search results were available to general public at the time. Furthermore, coding was done without utilizing any computational software, so the sample size and analysis was limited. This case study, though, provides a myriad of future research ideas. Understanding the complexities of the misinformation spread process and various influencing factors involved can greatly aid in any larger-scale analysis utilizing machine learning algorithms, which is very timely in our current media environment. Additional research is needed to compare hyperlink tracing to other network analysis methods in order to see how useful this approach will be in a large-sale study. Further research should also focus on the evaluation of general trends of information spread throughout the media and continue to trace the life cycle of science misinformation back to its sources. This is the first step in developing methods for the detection or prevention of science misinformation spread, one of the most salient problems of our time.

References

Allcott, H., Gentzkow, M.: Social media and fake news in the 2016 election. J. Econ. Perspect. **31**(2), 211–236 (2017)

Barzilai-Nahon, K.: Toward a theory of network gatekeeping: a framework for exploring information control. J. Assoc. Inf. Sci. Technol. **59**(9), 1493–1512 (2008)

Bastian, M., Heymann, S., Jacomy, M.: Gephi: an open source software for exploring and manipulating networks. In: ICWSM, vol. 8, pp. 361–362 (2009)

Cline, R.J., Haynes, K.M.: Consumer health information seeking on the Internet: the state of the art. Health Educ. Res. **16**(6), 671–692 (2001)

Fass, J., Main, A.: Revealing the news: how online news changes without you noticing. Digit. Journal. **2**(3), 366–382 (2014)

Flynn, D.J., Nyhan, B., Reifler, J.: The nature and origins of misperceptions: understanding false and unsupported beliefs about politics. Polit. Psychol. **38**(S1), 127–150 (2017)

Gewin, V.: Communication: post-truth predicaments. Nature **541**(7637), 425–427 (2017)

Hesse, B.W., et al.: The impact of the internet and its implications for health care providers: findings from the first health information national trends survey. Arch. Intern. Med. **165**, 2618–2624 (2005)

Hochschild, J.L., Einstein, K.L.: Do Facts matter? Information and misinformation in American politics. Polit. Sci. Q. **130**(4), 585–624 (2015)

Hovland, C.I., Weiss, W.: The influence of source credibility on communication effectiveness. Public Opin. Q. **15**(4), 635–650 (1951)

Howell, L.: Digital wildfires in a hyperconnected world. WEF Report (2013). http://reports. weforum.org/global-risks-2013/risk-case-1/digital-wildfires-in-a-hyperconnected-world/. Accessed 14 Aug 2018

Humprecht, E., Esser, F.: Mapping digital journalism: comparing 48 news websites from six countries. Journalism **19**(4), 500–518 (2016)

Kahan, D.M., Braman, D., Cohen, G.L., Gastil, J., Slovic, P.: Who fears the HPV vaccine, who doesn't, and why? an experimental study of the mechanisms of cultural cognition. Law Hum. Behav. **34**(6), 501–516 (2010)

Kumar, K.K., Geethakumari, G.: Information diffusion model for spread of misinformation in online social networks. In: 2013 International Conference on Advances in Computing, Communications and Informatics (ICACCI), pp. 1172–1177. IEEE, August 2013

Lazer, D.M.J., et al.: The science of fake news. Science **359**(6380), 1094–1096 (2018)

Le Trionnaire, S., et al.: The synthesis and functional evaluation of a mitochondria-targeted hydrogen sulfide donor, (10-oxo-10-(4-(3-thioxo-3 H-1, 2-dithiol-5-yl)phenoxy)decyl) triphenylphosphonium bromide (AP39). MedChemComm **5**(6), 728–736 (2014)

Lewandowsky, S., Ecker, U.K., Seifert, C.M., Schwarz, N., Cook, J.: Misinformation and its correction: continued influence and successful debiasing. Psychol. Sci. Public Interest **13**(3), 106–131 (2012)

Lewin, K.: Frontiers in group dynamics: II. Channels of group life, social planning, and action research. Hum. Relat. **1**(2), 143–153 (1947)

Moynihan, R., et al.: Coverage by the news media of the benefits and risks of medications. N. Engl. J. Med. **342**(22), 1645–1650 (2000)

Niederdeppe, J., Levy, A.G.: Fatalistic beliefs about cancer prevention and three prevention behaviors. Cancer Epidemiol. Prev. Biomark. **16**(5), 998–1003 (2007)

Nyhan, B., Reifler, J.: Displacing misinformation about events: an experimental test of causal corrections. J. Exp. Polit. Sci. **2**(1), 81–93 (2015)

Panth, M., Acharya, A.S.: The unprecedented role of computers in improvement and transformation of public health: an emerging priority. Indian J. Commun. Med. Official Publ. Indian Assoc. Prev. Soc. Med. **40**(1), 8 (2015)

Schwitzer, G.: How do US journalists cover treatments, tests, products, and procedures? an evaluation of 500 stories. PLoS Med. **5**(5), e95 (2008). 0700–0704

Schwitzer, G.: Pollution of health news. BMJ **1262**, j1262 (2017)

Shoemaker, P.J., Vos, T.P.: Gatekeeping Theory. Routledge, New York (2009)

Stampler, L.: Scientists Say Smelling Farts Might Prevent Cancer. Time Magazine. Internet Archive, WayBackMachine, 11 July 2014a. https://web.archive.org/web/20140711162609/http://time.com/2976464/scientists-say-smelling-farts-might-prevent-cancer/. Accessed 5 Aug 2018

Stampler, L.: Ridiculous Study of the Day Says Smelling Farts Might Prevent Cancer. Time Magazine. (2014b, July 14) Internet Archive, WayBackMachine. https://web.archive.org/web/20140714011647/http://time.com/2976464/scientists-say-smelling-farts-might-prevent-cancer/. Accessed 5 Aug 2018

Stampler, L.: A Stinky Compound May Protect Against Cell Damage, Study Finds. Time Magazine. Internet Archive, WayBackMachine, 18 July 2014c. https://web.archive.org/web/20140718153720/http://time.com/2976464/rotten-eggs-hydrogen-sulfide-mitochondria/. Accessed 5 Aug 2018

University of Exeter Research News: Rotten egg gas holds key to healthcare therapies, 9 July 2014. http://www.exeter.ac.uk/news/research/title_393168_en.html. Accessed 5 Aug 2018

Usher, N.: Making News at The New York Times. University of Michigan Press, Ann Arbor (2014)

Vosoughi, S., Roy, D., Aral, S.: The spread of true and false news online. Science **359**(6380), 1146–1151 (2018)

Vraga, E.K., Bode, L.: I do not believe you: how providing a source corrects health misperceptions across social media platforms. Inf. Commun. Soc. **21**(10), 1337–1353 (2018)

Woloshin, S., Schwartz, L.: Translating research into news. JAMA **287**(21), 2856–2858 (2002)

Wu, L., Liu, H.: Tracing fake-news footprints: characterizing social media messages by how they propagate. In: Proceedings of the Eleventh ACM International Conference on Web Search and Data Mining, pp. 637–645. ACM (2018)

Dead Science: Most Resources Linked in Biomedical Articles Disappear in Eight Years

Tong Zeng[1,2], Alain Shema[1], and Daniel E. Acuna[1(✉)]

[1] School of Information Studies, Syracuse University, Syracuse, USA
deacuna@syr.edu
[2] School of Information Management, Nanjing University, Nanjing, China

Abstract. Scientific progress critically depends on disseminating analytic pipelines and datasets that make results reproducible and replicable. Increasingly, researchers make resources available for wider reuse and embed links to them in their published manuscripts. Previous research has shown that these resources become unavailable over time but the extent and causes of this problem in open access publications has not been explored well. By using 1.9 million articles from PubMed Open Access, we estimate that half of all resources become unavailable after 8 years. We find that the number of times a resource has been used, the international (int) and organization (org) domain suffixes, and the number of affiliations are positively related to resources being available. In contrast, we found that the length of the URL, Indian (in), European Union (eu), and Chinese (cn) domain suffixes, and abstract length are negatively related to resources being available. Our results contribute to our understanding of resource sharing in science and provide some guidance to solve resource decay.

1 Introduction

Reproducibility and replicability are key components of science. Increasingly, this depends on the ability of scientists to use the resources shared in scientific articles. Many studies have found that resources embedded in scientific publications suffer from decay over time [1–6] directly affecting the incremental nature of science. In particular, biomedical sciences is a discipline that reuses resources regularly (e.g., software [7], protocols [8], and datasets [9]). However, a systematic study of the decay of such resources in biomedical publications is lacking.

The mechanisms governing sharing of data and resources are important for science. As early as 2003, the National Institutes of Health published a policy requiring applications for grants greater than $500,000 to include data sharing plans [10]. The National Science Foundation also has policies encouraging data sharing [11]. There are other institutions that recognize the importance of this practice (e.g., [12,13]) and its actual impact on the acceleration of science

© Springer Nature Switzerland AG 2019
N. G. Taylor et al. (Eds.): iConference 2019, LNCS 11420, pp. 170–176, 2019.
https://doi.org/10.1007/978-3-030-15742-5_16

(e.g., [9]). Sharing of resources is important and how they decay is still poorly understood.

One way of understanding how long and why resources are available is to analyze how resources decay over time. Several studies have tried to understand this phenomenon in several disciplines. In [14], the authors extracted 4,387 unique URLs published from 1995 to 2004 in D-Lib Magazine, revealing that 30% of the URLs failed to resolve, leading to a half-life of approximately 10 years. A similar quantity of 9.3 years was found by [15] using median survival lifespan analysis. There are similar studies in Law [16], Ecology [3] and Library and Information Science [4,14]. [2] analyzed 2,822 medical articles in a small sample of journals, finding half-lives between and 2.2 and 5.3 years. All this previous work has focused mostly on closed access publications and, to the best of our knowledge, the biggest dataset has around 1 million URLs [5,6]. In our work, we examine resource decay at a significantly larger volume in open access biomedical articles.

2 Materials and Methods

We obtained a copy of Pubmed Open Access Subset in June 2018 which consists of 1,904,971 articles. Not all URLs in these files are interesting or represent a resource being shared. We apply the following filters to discard URLs. First, we remove links to local file systems, URLs without any paths, and we canonicalize the URLs. The URL availability checker followed standard detection methods [17]. This checker, however, does not consider resources that are available but moved from the original URL. The final dataset contains 2,642,694 URLs of which 1,883,622 are unique.

3 Results

Exponential Growth in Link Sharing. We wanted to examine how resource sharing in the form of URLs has evolved over time. For each year of publication, we computed the number of links per article. This trend is exponential (Fig. 1a). We also analyze the percentage of articles with at least one URL. We found that this trend is exponential and that articles published today are more likely than not to have a link to a resource (Fig. 1b). These findings suggest that a URL has become a primary mechanism for sharing resources and that keeping track of decay of these resources will therefore become more important.

Most Resources Shared in Publications Disappear After Eight Years. The point at which half of the resources become obsolete is important. Here we simply examined the average availability of a resources as a function of age (Fig. 2) and found that this point happens after eight years. Surprisingly, we notice that new resources (age = 0) have a 20% chance of being unavailable, similar to previous findings [18]. Resources tend to follow a steady decline from ages 1 to 10 years. Then, it seems that resources 10 years and older stabilize around 42% availability. The data in our research showed that half of links

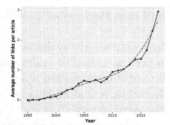 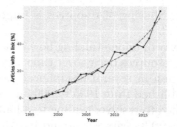

(a) Average links per paper as a function publication year. A locally weighted regression (loess, red line) is shown as well..

(b) Percent of articles with a link as a function of publication year. A locally weighted regression ("loess", red line) is shown as well.

Fig. 1. Some trends about the resource sharing. There is a clear exponential growth in these trends. (Color figure online)

become unavailable after 8 years, but this trend does not continue on the second 8-year period, as the available percentage fluctuates around 42%. Thus, the decay trend does not follow the typical half-life analysis found in Physics research [19].

Factors Related to Link Availability. The availability of resources might be associated with several characteristics. We computed several features to get at these characteristics (Table 1). Some of these features are related to the article (e.g., h-index of the journal, number of authors and affiliations, title), and the link itself (e.g., number of occurrences, link length). Also, we analyzed the suffixes of the domains to get at country or organizational effects. These features allowed us to tell apart several factors influencing link presence.

We used a logistic regression model with elastic net regularization [20] on standardized features to understand the relative importance of all the previously described factors. The cross validated performance of our model has an $F_1 = 0.67$. The most positive weights were the number of times a link has been used and the domain suffix "int". Interestingly, the "org" domain suffix, the size of the resource being shared, and the number of affiliations in the paper had all large positive associations. These positive associations intuitively suggest that links that have been shared in many articles, articles in government or non-profit organizations, and articles with many authors are all factors that contribute to a link being available.

There are other features that are negatively associated with availability. Expectedly, the most important negative feature is the link's age. In absolute terms, it is also the biggest contributor to the prediction. The length of the path (related to the length of the URL) is also an important predictor. Domain suffixes related to India (in), the European Union (eu), China (cn), and Korea (kr) are all also negatively related to availability (Table 1). These features could help to identify which links are in danger of becoming lost.

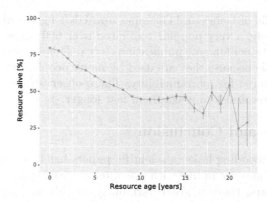

Fig. 2. Probability of resources being available as a function of age in years.

Table 1. List of top features and their standardized weights for predicting availability in a regularized logistic regression model

Features	Feature type	Weight
The frequency of a URL across articles	Link	0.26
int (domain suffix)	Link	0.20
org (domain suffix)	Link	0.12
gov (domain suffix)	Link	0.07
Size in bytes of the resource referred by the URL	Link	0.07
Number of affiliations of the article which cites the URL	Article	0.07
The h-index of a journal	Article	0.02
Years back from 2018	Article	−0.37
The length of the path in the URL	Link	−0.18
in (domain suffix)	Link	−0.06
eu (domain suffix)	Link	−0.05
cn (domain suffix)	Link	−0.05
The number of query string parameters in the URL	Link	−0.05
Length of abstract of the article	Article	−0.05
Number of references of the article	Article	−0.03
The length of the query string in the URL	Link	−0.02
Number of authors of the article which cites the URL	Article	−0.01
Length of article's title	Article	−0.01

Top Cited Links Are Mostly Tools. We performed a qualitative analysis of the most shared links and their availability. Interestingly, most of these highly cited links were tools related to gene expression and sequence search. The most cited of them is the Gene Expression Omnibus (GEO) from NIH. Several URL aliases related to the image processing tool ImageJ were at the top. Japan's

Kyoto Encyclopedia of Genes and Genomes and UK's figtree were two top non-US tools. Conversely, a very popular tool cited over 600 times was unavailable at https://tcga-data.nci.nih.gov/publications/tcga. This suggests that tools tend to be more available because they are used by many people, are maintained by a team, and are required for reproducibility. These observations could be applied to other non-tool resources to make them last longer.

4   Discussion and Conclusion

The practice of embedding links in scientific papers has been growing exponentially, and our findings are in line with previous research [3,15]. While we found a half-life of 8 years, there is great variability in this number—2.2 years [2], 5 years [4], 5.3 years [2], 9.3 years [15], 10 years [14]. However, all this previous work has analyzed a smaller volume of links and shorter time spans compared to our analysis, which may explain this variability.

There could be other more detailed analysis of how links become unavailable. Unavailability is mainly due to two types of problems: (1) the URL becomes inaccessible or (2) the content of the resource changes since the publication—a phenomenon known as content drift [21]. The first type of problem is usually related to change of domain, movement of resource, or cessation of operation. The second type of problem can be detected by manual checking [16] or using third-party web archiving services [6]. Due to the dynamic nature of the web, tackling content drift at scale is a challenging.

There are few research projects aimed at modeling link decay in science. [21] builds several SVM models to predict the availability of a link, achieving a performance of 0.72 in AUC. SVM classification analysis are however hard to interpret. [15] uses survival regression modeling to predict the median survival lifetime of a link and provide interpretable results. However, survival analysis does not predict probability of availability. Our long term-goal is to predict availability and understand the factors affecting it, and our logistic regression achieves these two goals simultaneously. If only performance is a concern, we will in the future explore more advanced techniques, such as deep learning, that sacrifice interpretability for better predictions.

While our findings are only correlations, they offer some intuitive suggestions. We would propose that authors use shorter, easier to remember URLs, hosted in non-profit domains. For links that are available, we should consider archiving those that are old, have complex URLs, are published in low h-index journals, and are hosted in country-based domains. In none of this is possible, we can explicitly archive links with services such as Perma [16], the Internet Archive [22], and WebCite [23,24].

In spite of the shortcomings of the present research, it offers previously unknown factors affecting link decay in open access biomedical journals at a much larger scale than before. Future research will investigate how to develop more precise predictions by expanding the data sources beyond open access biomedical articles, by improving the URL checking process, and by increasing the complexity of prediction model.

Acknowledgements. Tong Zeng was funded by the China Scholarship Council #201706190067. Daniel E. Acuna was funded by the National Science Foundation awards #1646763 and #1800956.

References

1. Koehler, W., et al.: A longitudinal study of web pages continued: a consideration of document persistence. Inf. Res. **9**(2) (2004)
2. Habibzadeh, P.: Decay of references to web sites in articles published in general medical journals: mainstream vs small journals. Appl. Clin. Inf. **04**(4), 455–464 (2013)
3. Duda, J.J., Camp, R.J.: Ecology in the information age: patterns of use and attrition rates of internet-based citations in ESA journals, 1997–2005. Front. Ecol. Environ. **6**(3), 145–151 (2008)
4. Goh, D.H.-L., Ng, P.K.: Link decay in leading information science journals. J. Am. Soc. Inf. Sci. Technol. **58**(1), 15–24 (2007)
5. Klein, M., et al.: Scholarly context not found: one in five articles suffers from reference rot. PloS ONE **9**(12), e115253 (2014)
6. Jones, S.M., Van de Sompel, H., Shankar, H., Klein, M., Tobin, R., Grover, C.: Scholarly context adrift: three out of four URI references lead to changed content. PLoS ONE **11**(12), e0167475 (2016)
7. Mangul, S., et al.: A comprehensive analysis of the usability and archival stability of omics computational tools and resources. bioRxiv, p. 452532 (2018)
8. Collaboration, O.S., et al.: Estimating the reproducibility of psychological science. Science **349**(6251), aac4716 (2015)
9. Bonàs-Guarch, S., et al.: Re-analysis of public genetic data reveals a rare x-chromosomal variant associated with type 2 diabetes. Nature Commun. **9** (2018)
10. National Institutes of Health: Final NIH statement on sharing research data (2003). https://grants.nih.gov/grants/guide/notice-files/NOT-OD-03-032.html. Accessed 5 Dec 2018
11. National Science Foundation: NSF data sharing policy (2017). https://www.nsf.gov/pubs/policydocs/pappguide/nsf13001/aag_6.jsp#VID4. Accessed 5 Dec 2018
12. Van Horn, J.D., Gazzaniga, M.S.: Why share data? Lessons learned from the fMRIDC. NeuroImage **82**, 677–682 (2013)
13. Milham, M.P., et al.: Assessment of the impact of shared brain imaging data on the scientific literature. Nature commun. **9** (2018)
14. McCown, F., Chan, S., Nelson, M.L., Bollen, J.: The availability and persistence of web references in d-lib magazine. arXiv preprint cs/0511077 (2005)
15. Hennessey, J., Ge, S.X.: A cross disciplinary study of link decay and the effectiveness of mitigation techniques. BMC Bioinf. **14**, S5 (2013)
16. Zittrain, J., Albert, K., Lessig, L.: Perma: scoping and addressing the problem of link and reference rot in legal citations. Legal Inf. Manag. **14**(2), 88–99 (2014)
17. Gourley, D., Totty, B., Sayer, M., Aggarwal, A., Reddy, S.: HTTP: The Definitive Guide. O'Reilly Media Inc. (2002)
18. Aronsky, D., Madani, S., Carnevale, R.J., Duda, S., Feyder, M.T.: The prevalence and inaccessibility of internet references in the biomedical literature at the time of publication. J. Am. Med. Inf. Assoc. **14**(2), 232–234 (2007)
19. Burton, R.E., Kebler, R.: The 'half-life' of some scientific and technical literatures. Am. Documentation **11**(1), 18–22 (1960)

20. Hastie, T., Tibshirani, R., Friedman, J.: The Elements of Statistical Learning. SSS. Springer, New York (2009). https://doi.org/10.1007/978-0-387-84858-7
21. Zhou, K., Grover, C., Klein, M., Tobin, R.: No more 404s: predicting referenced link rot in scholarly articles for pro-active archiving. In: Proceedings of the 15th ACM/IEEE-CE on Joint Conference on Digital Libraries - JCDL 2015, pp. 233–236. ACM Press (2015)
22. Internet Archive: Wayback machine. https://archive.org/web/. Accessed 5 Dec 2018
23. Eysenbach, G., Trudel, M.: Going, going, still there: using the webcite service to permanently archive cited web pages. J. Med. Internet Res. **7**(5), e60 (2005)
24. Eysenbach, G.: Preserving the scholarly record with webcite(r): an archiving system for long-term digital preservation of cited webpages. In: Proceedings ELPUB 2008 Conference on Electronic Publishing, pp. 378–389, Toronto, Canada (2008). www.webcitation.org

Limits and Affordances of Automation

Illegal Aliens or Undocumented Immigrants? Towards the Automated Identification of Bias by Word Choice and Labeling

Felix Hamborg[✉], Anastasia Zhukova, and Bela Gipp

University of Konstanz, Constance, Germany
{felix.hamborg,anastasia.zhukova,
bela.gipp}@uni-konstanz.de

Abstract. Media bias, i.e., slanted news coverage, can strongly impact the public perception of topics reported in the news. While the analysis of media bias has recently gained attention in computer science, the automated methods and results tend to be simple when compared to approaches and results in the social sciences, where researchers have studied media bias for decades. We propose Newsalyze, a work-in-progress prototype that imitates a manual analysis concept for media bias established in the social sciences. Newsalyze aims to find instances of bias by word choice and labeling in a set of news articles reporting on the same event. Bias by word choice and labeling (WCL) occurs when journalists use different phrases to refer to the same semantic concept, e.g., actors or actions. This way, instances of bias by WCL can induce strongly divergent emotional responses from readers, such as the terms "illegal aliens" vs. "undocumented immigrants." We describe two critical tasks of the analysis workflow, finding and mapping such phrases, and estimating their effects on readers. For both tasks, we also present first results, which indicate the effectiveness of exploiting methods and models from the social sciences in an automated approach.

Keywords: Media bias · News slant · News bias · Content analysis · Frame analysis

1 Introduction

Media bias describes differences in the content or presentation of news [22]. It is an ubiquitous phenomenon in news coverage that can have severely negative effects on individuals and society [22], for example when slanted news coverage influences voters and, in turn, also election outcomes [1, 11]. Potential issues of one-sided coverage, whether through selection of topics or how they are covered, are compounded by the fact that in many countries only a few corporations control large parts of the media landscape – in the US, for example, only six corporations control 90% of the media [6].

Subtle changes in the words used in a news text can significantly impact opinions [42, 46, 48, 49]. When referring to a semantic concept, such as a politician or generally named entities, authors can *label* the concept, e.g., "illegal aliens," and *choose from various words* to refer to it, e.g., "immigrants" or "aliens." Instances of bias by *word*

© Springer Nature Switzerland AG 2019
N. G. Taylor et al. (Eds.): iConference 2019, LNCS 11420, pp. 179–187, 2019.
https://doi.org/10.1007/978-3-030-15742-5_17

choice and labeling (WCL) *frame* the referred concept differently [13, 14, 38], whereby a broad spectrum of effects occurs [21], e.g., the frame may change the polarity of the concept, i.e., positively or negatively, or the frame may emphasize specific parts of an issue, such as the economical or cultural effects of immigration [13].

In the social sciences, research over the past decades has developed comprehensive models to describe media bias as well as effective methods for the analysis of media bias, such as the *content analysis* [31] and the *frame analysis* [13]. Because researchers need to conduct these analyses mostly manually, the analyses do not scale with the vast amount of news that is published nowadays. In turn, such studies are always conducted for topics in the past, and do not deliver insights for the current day (cf. [31, 41]), which would, however, be of primary interest to regular news consumers. Revealing media bias to news consumer would also help to mitigate bias effects, and, for example, support news consumer in making more informed choices [21].

In contrast, in computer science, few approaches systematically analyze media bias. The models used to analyze media bias in computer science tend to be simplistic (cf. [22, 25, 35, 36, 43, 50]) compared to models established in the social sciences; most approaches analyze media bias from the perspective of every-day news readers while neglecting both the established approaches and the comprehensive models that have already been developed in the social sciences (cf. [15, 32, 35, 36, 40, 43, 50]). Correspondingly, their results are often inconclusive or superficial, despite the approaches being technically promising. To address these issues, we define the research question:

> *How can an automated approach identify instances of bias by word choice and labeling in a set of English news articles reporting on the same event, and enable every-day news consumers to explore these instances?*

We propose a cross-disciplinary approach that exploits the established models from the social sciences to describe and methods to analyze media bias, while taking advantage of the fast, scalable methods for text analysis developed and used in computer science (Sect. 3). Our approach imitates the process of an inductive frame analysis, and uses state-of-the-art natural language processing (NLP) methods to identify and map bias inducing coreferences (currently only noun phrases (NPs), i.e., phrases referring to the same semantic concept. To estimate the effects of such coreferences on readers, we use psychometric dictionaries devised in psychology and linguistics. Further contributions are a brief overview of techniques for the analysis of bias by WCL and exemplary results from the social sciences and related approaches from computer science (Sect. 2), and first results demonstrating the effectiveness of our cross-disciplinary approach (Sect. 3). We conclude our paper with future work for the prototype (Sect. 4).

2   Related Work

In the social sciences, the *news production and consumption process* is an established model that defines nine forms of media bias, and describes where these forms originate from [3, 22, 43]. For example, first journalists *select events, sources*, and from these sources the *information* they want to publish in a news article. These initial selection processes introduce a bias into the resulting news story. While writing an article, journalists can affect the reader's perception of a topic through *word choice and labeling* as described in Sect. 1 [3, 19, 40]. Lastly, the *placement* and *size* of an article within a newspaper or on a website determine how much attention the article will receive.

Researchers in the social sciences primarily conduct *frame analyses* or more generally *content analyses* to identify instances of bias by WCL, and investigate their effects on individuals or societies [31, 41][1]. In a content analysis, researchers first define analysis questions or hypotheses. Then, they gather the relevant news texts, and coders read the texts, annotating parts of the texts that indicate instances of media bias relevant to the analysis questions, e.g., phrases that change the readers' perception of a specific person or topic. In an *inductive* content analysis, coders read and annotate the texts without prior knowledge other than the analysis question. In a *deductive* content analysis, coders adhere to a set of coding rules defined in a code book, which researchers usually create using the findings from an inductive content analysis conducted prior to the deductive analysis. After the coding, researchers use the annotated findings, for example, to accept or reject their hypotheses.

The content analyses conducted for bias by WCL are typically either *topic-oriented* or *person-oriented*. For example, Papacharissi and Oliveira investigated WCL in the coverage of different news outlets on topics related to terrorism [42]. One high-level finding was that the New York Times used more dramatic tones than the Washington Post, e.g., news articles dehumanized terrorists by not ascribing any motive to terrorist attacks or usage of metaphors, such as "David and Goliath" [42]. Both the Financial Times and the Guardian focused their news articles on factual reporting. Another study analyzed whether articles portrayed Bill Clinton, the U.S. president at that time, positively, neutrally, or negatively [39].

Most automated approaches treat media bias vaguely, and view it only as "differences of [news] coverage" [45], "diverse opinions" [37], or "topic diversity" [36], resulting in inconclusive or superficial findings [21]. Few approaches use the bias models from the social sciences and focus on a specific form of media bias. Likewise, few approaches specifically aim to identify instances of bias by WCL. Lim et al. propose to investigate words with a low document frequency in a set of news articles reporting on the same event, to find potentially biasing words that are characteristic for a single article [29]. NewsCube 2.0 employs *crowdsourcing* to estimate the bias of articles reporting on a topic. The system allows users to annotate WCL in news articles collaboratively [44]. A closely related, fully automated field of methods is *sentiment analysis*, which aims to find the connotation of a phrase. On news texts, however, sentiment analysis performs poorly for three reasons. First, news texts have rather subtle connotations due to the journalistic objectivity [18, 22]. Second, no sentiment dictionary exists that is specifically designed for news texts, and generic dictionaries tend to perform poorly on news texts (cf. [4, 27, 40]). Third, the one-dimensional positive-negative scale used by all mature sentiment analyzers likely falls short of representing the complexity of news articles [40]. To avoid the difficulties of highly context-dependent sentiment connotations in news articles, researchers have proposed

---

[1] The paragraphs about manual and automated approaches have been adapted partially from [21].

approaches to perform sentiment analysis specifically on quotes [4] or on the comments of readers [45], which more likely contain an explicit statement of sentiment. First research projects suggested to investigate *emotions* induced by headlines but they achieved mixed results [53]. Other approaches use dictionaries to find bias words in Wikipedia articles [47] and news articles [5]. Both approaches achieve an accuracy close to human coders, but do not estimate the effects of the found words on readers.

In conclusion, there is currently no automated approach that enables users to view instances of bias by WCL in news coverage of the current day, despite the reliable analysis concepts developed and used in the social sciences, and fast, scalable text analysis methods developed in computer science and computational linguistics.

3   Identification of Bias by Word Choice and Labeling

Newsalyze is a research prototype that aims to find groups of articles that *frame* an event similarly, i.e., report similarly on the named entities (NEs) and other semantic concepts involved in the event. Therefore, Newsalyze implements a three-tasks analysis pipeline as depicted in Fig. 1. From a set of articles reporting on the same event, Newsalyze first performs state-of-the-art NLP *preprocessing*. The second task, *frame device analysis*, finds so called *frame devices* [8], i.e., in our project phrases referring to any concept (candidate extraction), and then aligns all phrases referring to the same concept from all articles (candidate alignment). Our prototype currently analyzes noun phrases (NPs). The third task, *frame identification*, estimates the effect of such phrases on readers (Effect on Readers (EoR) estimation), and finally clusters articles that have a similar EoR of aligned phrases (frame clustering). The output of the system are groups of articles framing the event similarly, which the system *visualizes* to users finally.

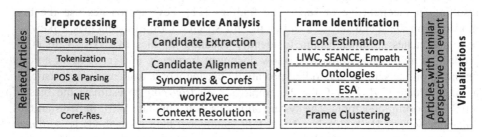

Fig. 1. The three-tasks analysis pipeline preprocesses news articles, extracts and aligns phrases referring to the same semantic concepts, and groups articles reporting similarly on these concepts.

The two main challenges in automatically identifying instances of bias by WCL are the candidate alignment and the EoR estimation, which we describe in more detail.

3.1   Candidate Alignment

The first task is to align coreferences across multiple articles, commonly called *cross-document coreference resolution*, a task that current NLP methods cannot reliably perform for coreferences as they occur in bias by WCL in news articles. Current NLP methods, such as named entity linking (NEL), NE recognition (NER) and disambiguation (NERD), and coreference resolution capably identify synonyms of the same NE, such as 'Mr. Trump' and 'US President' (precision $p \approx 0.8$ [7]), and pronominal and nominal coreferences, such as 'he' and 'Donald J. Trump' ($p \approx 0.8$ [9]).

The automated alignment of WCL candidates, however, is more challenging because often journalists refer to the same concept in a broader sense than currently addressed by the previously mentioned coreference resolution methods. Instead, such coreferences are highly dependent on the context, may only be valid in a single article or across related articles, or are only meaningful in conjunction with an attribute, e.g., in articles reporting on the end of DACA in 2018 the terms 'illegal aliens' and 'undocumented immigrants' referred to the people that were protected by DACA [28].

To align WCL candidates, we currently use word embeddings produced by word2vec with the generic Google News model (300 M words) [33]. Specifically, in the candidate extraction we extract all NPs, such as "undocumented immigrants," and mentions of coreference chains. Then, we use affinity propagation [17] on the Euclidean distance in the word2vec space to align coreferential NPs. First results depicted in Table 1 indicate the suitability of the approach to align such coreferences, e.g., our approach was able to align the bias by WCL instances "undocumented worker" and "illegal immigrant" across multiple articles of the DACA topic. For each topic, we collected articles published in the year shown in Table 1 from major news outlets representing the whole political spectrum from the US (DACA and Denuclearization) and UK (Brexit). Such coreferences cannot be resolved by neither coreference resolution nor NER.

Table 1. Automatically aligned coreferences for exemplary topics.

Topic	# articles	Aligned coreferences
DACA US, 2017	25	immigrant(s), migrant(s), illegal immigrant(s), undocumented immigrants, Latino immigrants, illegals, undocumented workers, sympathetic group of immigrants, ...
Denuclearization PRK, 2018	25	American military presence, unilateral US military operation, US mere presence, US military action, US military installations, US military presence, US military threat, ...
Brexit EU, 2016	35	Brexit negotiations, EU divorce negotiations, exit negotiations, discussions, negotiations between UK and EU, negotiations over terms of divorce, ...

3.2 Estimation of the Effects on Readers

To estimate the EoR of coreferences, only considering their sentiment would not be sufficient, mainly due to the complexity of news topics, and also due to the subtlety of connotations motivated by the journalistic objectivity (see Sect. 2). Thus, we analyze *frame properties*, which we define as properties that make up a frame induced by a phrase, including emotions [30], polarity (cf. [2]), and topic-specific properties common in frame analyses (see Sect. 2), such as in person-oriented news competence, honesty, wisdom, and empathy (cf. [42]); and on a broader scale also topical categories, such as finance, economic, and culture (cf. [16]).

The current prototype estimates the EoR by comparing terms in documents to a set of seed words representing frame properties. We derived the following frame properties from an inductive content analysis, which we conducted on the topics shown in Table 1: aggression, honesty, competence, authority, confidence, sympathy, and their antonyms. We also add seed words representing six basic emotions [12] to the set: anger, disgust, fear, happiness, sadness, and surprise. Our initial findings on the topics from Table 1 indicate the effectiveness of our approach, e.g., in the DACA topic the most frequent frame properties ascribed by the right news website Fox News to US President Trump are mostly positive, such as honesty, sympathy, happiness, whereas the left New York Times used mainly negative properties, such as anger, fear, and sadness. Our findings are conformal with manually conducted studies on the ideological placement of the news outlets (cf. [20, 34]).

4   Conclusion and Future Work

Newsalyze is a work-in-progress prototype that aims to automatically identify instances of bias by word choice and labeling in a set of news articles reporting on the same event. In this paper, we describe the key concepts of the two fundamental tasks of the analysis workflow, i.e., the (1) alignment of context-dependent coreferences and the (2) estimation of the effects of the aligned coreferences on readers (EoR). In the first task, we currently use parsing and word2vec to find phrases referring to the same semantic concept. This way, Newsalyze finds and aligns context-specific coreferences, such as "undocumented worker" and "illegal immigrant" in the context of an immigration topic, that cannot be found by generic methods such as coreference resolution or synonym resolution. In the second task, we use a predefined set of frame properties, such as aggression and competence, represented in ConceptNet to analyze the EoR of phrases.

While the first results generally indicate the usefulness of the approach, we propose the following improvements. For candidate alignment, we want to improve the results by training a custom word2vec model on a current news dataset, for instance from the commoncrawl archive using a news crawler [26]. Besides the word2vec-based alignment approach, we plan to devise a second, syntax-based approach, which analyzes the relations between extracted candidates, such as the constituents of a sentence, particularly subject-predicate-object triples, e.g., using OpenIE [2], and event descriptors, such as the journalistic 5 W phrases [23, 24], which describe the main event of news articles. The conceptual idea is that if, for example, supposedly different subjects perform the same action in related news articles, the subjects will likely refer to the same actor. We also want to investigate the extraction and alignment of non-NP coreferences, e.g., when activities are described differently, e.g., "invade" or "cross border".

To estimate the EoR, we also want to investigate the use of dictionaries, such as LIWC [54], SEANCE [10], Empath [16], categories from the General Inquirer [51], and dictionaries of bias-inducing phrases (cf. [5, 47]). We think, however, that our current approach is better at estimating the effects of new terms, since ConceptNet is updated regularly from Wikipedia and other sources [52]. Finally, we need to cluster articles similarly framing an event, e.g., articles with similarly framed coreferences.

Lastly, we need to visualize the results of the automated analysis to every-day news consumers. A news topic view used in the bias-aware news analysis could show phrases containing the most contrastive cases of bias by word choice and labeling [22].

Acknowledgements. This work was partially supported by the Carl Zeiss Foundation and the Zukunftskolleg program of the University of Konstanz. We thank the anonymous reviewers for their valuable comments.

References

1. Alsem, K.J., et al.: The impact of newspapers on consumer confidence: does spin bias exist? Appl. Econ. **40**(5), 531–539 (2008). https://doi.org/10.1080/00036840600707100
2. Angeli, G., et al.: Leveraging linguistic structure for open domain information extraction. In: Proceedings of the 53rd Annual Meeting of the Association for Computational Linguistics and the 7th International Joint Conference on Natural Language Processing (vol. 1: Long Papers), pp. 344–354 (2015)
3. Baker, B.H., et al.: How to Identify, Expose & Correct Liberal Media Bias. Media Research Center, Alexandria (1994)
4. Balahur, A., et al.: Sentiment analysis in the news. arXiv preprint arXiv:1309.6202 (2013)
5. Baumer, E.P.S., et al.: Testing and comparing computational approaches for identifying the language of framing in political news. In: Human Language Technologies: The 2015 Annual Conference of the North American Chapter of the ACL, Denver, Colorado, USA, pp. 1472–1482 (2015)
6. Business Insider: These 6 Corporations Control 90% of the Media in America. Lutz, Ashley (2014)
7. Chang, A.X., et al.: A comparison of named-entity disambiguation and word sense disambiguation. In: LREC, pp. 860–867 (2016)
8. Chong, D., Druckman, J.N.: Framing theory. Ann. Rev. Polit. Sci. **10**(1), 103–126 (2007). https://doi.org/10.1146/annurev.polisci.10.072805.103054
9. Clark, K., Manning, C.D.: Deep reinforcement learning for mention-ranking coreference models. In: Empirical Methods on Natural Language Processing (2016)
10. Crossley, S.A., et al.: Sentiment analysis and social cognition engine (SEANCE): an automatic tool for sentiment, social cognition, and social-order analysis. Behav. Res. Method. **49**(3), 803–821 (2017). https://doi.org/10.3758/s13428-016-0743-z
11. DellaVigna, S., Kaplan, E.: The fox news effect: media bias and voting. Q. J. Econ. **122**(3), 1187–1234 (2007). https://doi.org/10.3386/w12169
12. Ekman, P.: An argument for basic emotions. Cogn. Emot. **6**, 169–200 (1992). https://doi.org/10.1080/02699939208411068
13. Entman, R.M.: Framing: toward clarification of a fractured paradigm. J. Commun. **43**(4), 51–58 (1993)

14. Entman, R.M.: Framing bias: media in the distribution of power. J. Commun. **57**(1), 163–173 (2007)
15. Evans, D.K., et al.: Columbia newsblaster: multilingual news summarization on the web. In: Demonstration Papers at HLT-NAACL, pp. 1–4 (2004)
16. Fast, E., et al.: Empath: understanding topic signals in large-scale text. In: Proceedings of the 2016 CHI Conference on Human Factors in Computing Systems, CHI 2016, San Jose, California, USA, pp. 4647–4657 (2016)
17. Frey, B.J., Dueck, D.: Clustering by passing messages between data points. Science **315**(5814), 972–976 (2007). https://doi.org/10.1126/science.1136800
18. Gauthier, G.: In defence of a supposedly outdated notion: the range of application of journalistic objectivity. Can. J. Commun. **18**(4), 497 (1993)
19. Gentzkow, M., Shapiro, J.: Media bias and reputation. J. Polit. Econ. **114**(2), 280–316 (2006). https://doi.org/10.1086/499414
20. Groseclose, T., Milyo, J.: A measure of media bias. Q. J. Econ. **120**(4), 1191–1237 (2005). https://doi.org/10.1162/003355305775097542
21. Hamborg, F., et al. Automated identification of media bias in news articles: an interdisciplinary literature review. Int. J. Digit. Libr. (2018). https://doi.org/10.1007/s00799-018-0261-y
22. Hamborg, F., et al.: Bias-aware news analysis using matrix-based news aggregation. Int. J. Digit. Libr. (2018). https://doi.org/10.1007/s00799-018-0239-9
23. Hamborg, F., et al.: Extraction of main event descriptors from news articles by answering the journalistic Five W and One H questions. In: Proceedings of the ACM/IEEE-CS Joint Conference on Digital Libraries (JCDL), Fort Worth, Texas, USA, pp. 339–340 (2018)
24. Hamborg, F., Lachnit, S., Schubotz, M., Hepp, T., Gipp, B.: Giveme5 W: main event retrieval from news articles by extraction of the five journalistic W questions. In: Chowdhury, G., McLeod, J., Gillet, V., Willett, P. (eds.) iConference 2018. LNCS, vol. 10766, pp. 356–366. Springer, Cham (2018). https://doi.org/10.1007/978-3-319-78105-1_39
25. Hamborg, F., et al.: Identification and analysis of media bias in news articles. In: Proceedings of the 15th International Symposium of Information Science, pp. 224–236 (2017)
26. Hamborg, F., et al.: News-please: a generic news crawler and extractor. In: Proceedings of the 15th International Symposium of Information Science, pp. 218–223(2017)
27. Kaya, M., et al.: Sentiment analysis of Turkish political news. In: Proceedings of the 2012 IEEE/WIC/ACM International Joint Conferences on Web Intelligence and Intelligent Agent Technology, vol. 01, pp. 174–180 (2012)
28. Lee, Y.: To dream or not to dream: a cost-benefit analysis of the development, relief, and education for alien minors (DREAM) act. Cornell J. Law Public Policy **16**(1), 231 (2006)
29. Lim, S., et al.: Towards bias inducing word detection by linguistic cue analysis in news articles (2018)
30. Lin, K.H.-Y., et al.: What emotions do news articles trigger in their readers? In: Proceedings of the 30th Annual International ACM SIGIR Conference on Research and Development in Information Retrieval - SIGIR 2007, p. 733 (2007)
31. McCarthy, J., et al.: Assessing stability in the patterns of selection bias in newspaper coverage of protest during the transition from communism in Belarus. Mobil.: Int. Q. **13**(2), 127–146 (2008)
32. Mehler, A., et al.: Spatial analysis of news sources. IEEE Trans. Vis. Comput. Graph. **13**, 127–146 (2006)
33. Mikolov, T., et al.: Efficient estimation of word representations in vector space. In: Proceedings of the International Conference on Learning Representations (ICLR 2013) (2013). https://doi.org/10.1162/153244303322533223

34. Mitchell, A., et al.: Political polarization and media habits. Pew Research Center (2014)
35. Munson, S.A., et al.: Encouraging reading of diverse political viewpoints with a browser widget. In: ICWSM (2013)
36. Munson, S.A., et al.: Sidelines: an algorithm for increasing diversity in news and opinion aggregators. In: ICWSM (2009)
37. Munson, S.A., Resnick, P.: Presenting diverse political opinions: how and how much. In: Proceedings of the SIGCHI Conference on Human Factors in Computing Systems, pp. 1457–1466 (2010)
38. News Bias Explored - The art of reading the news (2014). http://umich.edu/~newsbias/. Accessed 01 Aug 2018
39. Niven, D.: Tilt?: The Search for Media Bias. Greenwood Publishing Group, Westport (2002)
40. Oelke, D., et al.: Visual analysis of explicit opinion and news bias in German soccer articles. In: EuroVis Workshop on Visual Analytics, Vienna, Austria (2012)
41. Oliver, P.E., Maney, G.M.: Political processes and local newspaper coverage of protest events: from selection bias to triadic interactions. Am. J. Sociol. **106**(2), 463–505 (2000)
42. Papacharissi, Z., de Fatima Oliveira, M.: News frames terrorism: a comparative analysis of frames employed in terrorism coverage in U.S. and U.K. newspapers. Int. J. Press/Polit. **13**(1), 52–74 (2008). https://doi.org/10.1177/1940161207312676
43. Park, S., et al.: NewsCube: delivering multiple aspects of news to mitigate media bias. In: Proceedings of CHI 2009, The SIGCHI Conference on Human Factors in Computing Systems, pp. 443–453 (2009). https://doi.org/10.1145/1518701.1518772
44. Park, S., et al.: NewsCube 2.0: an exploratory design of a social news website for media bias mitigation. In: Workshop on Social Recommender Systems (2011)
45. Park, S., et al.: The politics of comments: predicting political orientation of news stories with commenters' sentiment patterns. In: Proceedings of the ACM 2011 Conference on Computer Supported Cooperative Work, pp. 113–122 (2011)
46. Price, V., et al.: Framing public discussion of gay civil unions. Public Opin. Q. **69**, 179–212 (2005)
47. Recasens, M., et al.: Linguistic models for analyzing and detecting biased language. In: Proceedings of the 51st Annual Meeting on Association for Computational Linguistics, pp. 1650–1659 (2013)
48. Rugg, D.: Experiments in wording questions: II. Public Opin. Q. **5**, 91 (1941). https://doi.org/10.1086/265467
49. Schuldt, J.P., et al.: "Global warming" or "climate change"? Whether the planet is warming depends on question wording. Public Opin. Q. **75**, 115–124 (2011). https://doi.org/10.1093/poq/nfq073
50. Smith, A., et al.: Hiérarchie: interactive visualization for hierarchical topic models. In: Proceedings of the Workshop on Interactive Language Learning, Visualization, and Interfaces, pp. 71–78 (2014)
51. Smith, M.S., et al.: The General Inquirer: A Computer Approach to Content Analysis. American Sociological Review (1967)
52. Speer, R., Havasi, C.: Representing general relational knowledge in ConceptNet 5. In: Proceedings of the Eight International Conference on Language Resources and Evaluation, LREC 2012 (2012)
53. Strapparava, C., Mihalcea, R.: Semeval-2007 task 14: affective text. In: Proceedings of the 4th International Workshop on Semantic Evaluations, pp. 70–74 (2007)
54. Tauszcik, Y.R., Pennebaker, J.W.: The psychological meaning of words: LIWC and computerized text analysis methods. J. Lang. Soc. Psychol. **29**(1), 24–54 (2010). https://doi.org/10.1177/0261927X09351676

Toward Three-Stage Automation of Annotation for Human Values

Emi Ishita[1]([✉]), Satoshi Fukuda[1], Toru Oga[1], Douglas W. Oard[2],
Kenneth R. Fleischmann[3], Yoichi Tomiura[1], and An-Shou Cheng[4]

[1] Kyushu University, Fukuoka 819-0395, Japan
ishita.emi.982@m.kyushu-u.ac.jp
[2] University of Maryland, College Park, MD 20742, USA
[3] University of Texas at Austin, Austin, TX 78705, USA
[4] National Sun Yat-sen University, Kaohsiung 804, Taiwan

Abstract. Prior work on automated annotation of human values has sought to train text classification techniques to label text spans with labels that reflect specific human values such as freedom, justice, or safety. This confounds three tasks: (1) selecting the documents to be labeled, (2) selecting the text spans that express or reflect human values, and (3) assigning labels to those spans. This paper proposes a three-stage model in which separate systems can be optimally trained for each of the three stages. Experiments from the first stage, document selection, indicate that annotation diversity trumps annotation quality, suggesting that when multiple annotators are available, the traditional practice of adjudicating conflicting annotations of the same documents is not as cost effective as an alternative in which each annotator labels different documents. Preliminary results for the second stage, selecting value sentences, indicate that high recall (94%) can be achieved on that task with levels of precision (above 80%) that seem suitable for use as part of a multi-stage annotation pipeline. The annotations created for these experiments are being made freely available, and the content that was annotated is available from commercial sources at modest cost.

Keywords: Content analysis · Human values · Text classification ·
Annotation cost · Nuclear power debate

1 Introduction

Sentiment analysis has provided an effective and efficient way to measure popular sentiment at Web scale, allowing us to detect trends such as positive sentiment toward a particular politician or negative sentiment toward a specific policy position [12]. However, a much deeper and more interesting question is why people hold the sentiment that they hold. Human values, or what people consider important in life [4], can be used to predict individuals' attitudes [15] and behaviors [13]. Thus, this study adopts the approach of attempting to automate the annotation of human values in documents about contentious public policy issues to provide a richer and more nuanced understanding of popular views toward specific policy issues [3].

© Springer Nature Switzerland AG 2019
N. G. Taylor et al. (Eds.): iConference 2019, LNCS 11420, pp. 188–199, 2019.
https://doi.org/10.1007/978-3-030-15742-5_18

Earlier studies of values in public policy debates include Cheng et al.'s analysis of the relationship between values and sentiment in net neutrality public hearings [2] and Verma et al.'s examination of the relationship between trust and human values for online information [17]. These studies were based upon relatively modest corpora, which could be annotated by hand by experts or crowd workers. However, today, millions of people's opinions can be found in social networking services such as Facebook and Twitter, on discussion forums, through reports in the mass media, and in many other places. Making productive use of this wealth of human expression demands, however, that we analyze huge amounts of content efficiently and effectively, at a scale that would be impossible to do by hand. There has been some work on automated content analysis (e.g., [5, 10, 11, 18]), but much remains to be done if we are to make it possible for social scientists to extend their analysis to this scale.

Prior work on automating values classification by Takayama et al. makes two implicit assumptions [14]. First, they assume that the documents to be labeled have already been assembled. While this can be a reasonable assumption for small-scale studies in which content analysis is performed by people, scaling that process up to larger collections requires some level of automation in the determination of which documents should be labeled. Second, they assume that the process of determining which spans of text should be labeled can be conflated with the process of determining which human values label(s) should be assigned to each span. This conflation is reasonable when most sentences should express or reflect some human value(s), as was the case in the collection with which Takayama et al. worked, but there are other settings in which the expression of human values is less frequent.

The approach to automating parts of the content analysis process that we propose in this paper thus consists of three stages; (1) identification of the documents to be labeled, (2) determination of which text spans should be labeled in each document, and (3) annotating of human values for those selected text spans. For the second and third stages, we adopt Takayama's approach of using sentences as text spans, which limits the complexity of the text span selection without a serious adverse effect on the utility of the labeling process as a basis for content analysis, as shown by Cheng et al. [6]. As a result, our first stage is binary (on-/off-topic) topic classification at document scale, our second stage is non-topical binary classification (values present/values absent) at sentence scale, and our third stage, as in Takayama et al., is non-topical multi-label classification for each possible values label, again at sentence scale.

In this paper, we report findings from automatic on/off topic identification using classifiers, as well as determining whether value invocations would be interpreted by an annotator as present or absent within sentences from on-topic articles. Classifiers require significant amounts of annotation content for training, annotations that can be expensive to obtain. We are therefore interested in techniques that make the best use of limited amounts of human annotation effort. We consider two ways of creating training annotations, one in which annotators work together to create the best possible annotations for each document, and the other in which they work along to annotate the largest possible number of different documents for a given level of annotation effort. We then compare classifiers trained with each approach to annotation by plotting learning curves that show how well we can do as the number of annotations increases. We find that in cases where we have limited training data, training a classifier with lower quality, but lower cost, annotations can be a cost-effective choice. We also show, using a more limited set of experiments, that promising levels of precision and recall can be achieved for the value sentence identification task. First, however, we begin by introducing the new corpus of newspaper editorials that we have assembled for these experiments.

2 Nuclear Power Debate Editorial News Corpus

Our focus in this work is on automation of content analysis to identify the role of human values in the nuclear power debate in Japan. The Great East Japan Earthquake occurred on March 11, 2011, damaging the Fukushima Daiichi nuclear power plant. After this disaster, the safety of other nuclear power plants received extensive discussion in the Japanese mass media. This event also reignited the global debate over the safety of nuclear power that dates back to the early days of nuclear power, implicating a broad range of human values, and playing out differently in different countries. We have chosen newspaper editorials as our focus for this study, but other work is also looking at the ways in which human values are expressed in newspaper articles. Most newspaper articles adopt a third-person perspective to report on events and the statements of others, but we have chosen to focus here on newspaper articles because we might expect to find a first-person perspective in editorials.

We performed focused collection to obtain a Japanese Editorial corpus. To create the corpus, we searched for editorials (as labeled by metadata) in the commercially available Mainichi Shimbun CD-ROM [1] from 2011 to 2016 using the query "原発 (abbreviation of nuclear power plant) OR 原子力 (nuclear power)". This query retrieved 750 documents. There are 242 articles from 2011, 166 from 2012, 124 from 2013, 93 from 2014, 62 from 2015, and 63 from 2016. The number of editorials decreased with the passing of years. However, nuclear power has become somewhat of a meme in Japanese society, often invoked tangentially or as a point of comparison, rather than being the focus of the editorial. It is therefore necessary to separate those documents that we wish to analyze from those that simply happen to use the term. This on-topic/off-topic classification task is our first stage.

To support text classification experiments for this first stage, we performed 10 rounds of annotation. In Round 1 we randomly selected 7 editorials from the first year of the corpus. Two annotators, the first and third authors of this paper, both native speakers of Japanese, then independently annotated each editorial as on topic or off topic. The two annotators then met and created adjudicated on/off topic labels by consensus, formalizing the basis for their decisions as written annotation guidelines. As Table 2 shows, Annotator A, a social science researcher, exhibited perfect agreement with the consensus; Annotator B, an information science researcher who was new to the task, achieved considerably lower agreement with the consensus adjudicated judgments. As shown in Table 1, this process of independently annotating, reaching consensus, and updating the annotation guidelines was then repeated for a total of 10 rounds of progressively increasing size,[1] in each subsequent case using documents

---

[1] Two documents in Round 9 were discovered to be duplicates and removed.

selected from across the time span of the corpus. As can be seen in Table 2, Annotator B's decisions came to more closely agree with the consensus as iterations proceeded, ultimately achieving noticeably closer agreement with the consensus than Annotator A in two of the last three rounds.

Table 1. Stratified document samples for the ten-round annotation process.

	2011	2012	2013	2014	2015	2016	Total
Round 1	7						7
Round 2		5	3	2	1	2	13
Round 3	8	4	2	2	2	2	20
Round 4	8	4	2	2	2	2	20
Round 5	7	7	5	5	3	3	30
Round 6	7	7	5	5	3	3	30
Round 7	7	7	5	5	3	3	30
Round 8	33	22	17	12	8	8	100
Round 9	33	22	17	10	8	8	98
Round 10	33	22	17	12	8	8	100
Total	143	100	73	55	38	39	448

Table 2. Cohen's Kappa for each round.

Round	#docs	A vs. B	Adjudicated vs. A	Adjudicated vs. B
1	7	0.588	1.000	0.588
2	13	0.806	0.806	1.000
3	20	0.875	1.000	0.875
4	20	0.494	0.886	0.583
5	30	0.430	0.796	0.605
6	30	0.474	0.735	0.730
7	30	0.437	0.769	0.651
8	100	0.535	0.705	0.816
9	98	0.464	0.730	0.741
10	100	0.477	0.635	0.821

3 On/Off Topic Identification

3.1 Annotation Guidelines

The central principle of our annotation guidelines is that a circumstance, a current status, or government policy related to the Fukushima Daiichi nuclear power disaster are on topic content. For examples, editorials describing discussions caused by the disaster, or that expressed value judgments regarding one or more events relating the disaster, would be classified as on topic. On the other hand, an editorial about a government or local election would be classified as off topic if it mentioned that issues related to the disaster were important in a campaign, but those issues were not the focus of the editorial. Editorials about restarting some other nuclear power plant, without mentioning the Fukushima Daiichi disaster, would also be off topic.

Figure 1 illustrates some of the challenges of topic classification. The editorial on the left is about the contentious issue of storage of nuclear waste that results from the operation of nuclear power plants. The editorial on the right, by contrast, is about commercial overseas sales of nuclear power technology. Unquestionably, both address topics related to the commercial production of nuclear power, but according to our annotation guidelines, only the editorial on the left is on topic. The focus of the editorial on the right is on limiting the proliferation of nuclear weapons by imposing limitations on how the spent fuel for nuclear power plants can be reprocessed.

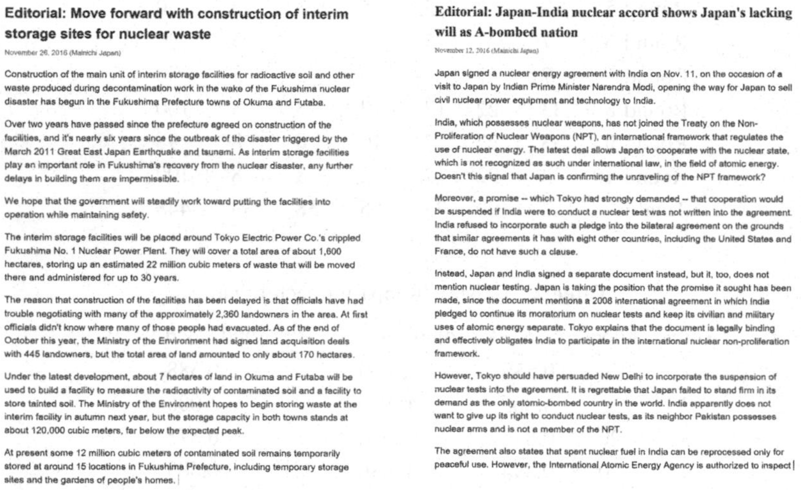

Editorial: Move forward with construction of interim storage sites for nuclear waste

November 26, 2016 (Mainichi Japan)

Construction of the main unit of interim storage facilities for radioactive soil and other waste produced during decontamination work in the wake of the Fukushima nuclear disaster has begun in the Fukushima Prefecture towns of Okuma and Futaba.

Over two years have passed since the prefecture agreed on construction of the facilities, and it's nearly six years since the outbreak of the disaster triggered by the March 2011 Great East Japan Earthquake and tsunami. As interim storage facilities play an important role in Fukushima's recovery from the nuclear disaster, any further delays in building them are impermissible.

We hope that the government will steadily work toward putting the facilities into operation while maintaining safety.

The interim storage facilities will be placed around Tokyo Electric Power Co.'s crippled Fukushima No. 1 Nuclear Power Plant. They will cover a total area of about 1,600 hectares, storing up an estimated 22 million cubic meters of waste that will be moved there and administered for up to 30 years.

The reason that construction of the facilities has been delayed is that officials have had trouble negotiating with many of the approximately 2,360 landowners in the area. At first officials didn't know where many of those people had evacuated. As of the end of October this year, the Ministry of the Environment had signed land acquisition deals with 445 landowners, but the total area of land amounted to only about 170 hectares.

Under the latest development, about 7 hectares of land in Okuma and Futaba will be used to build a facility to measure the radioactivity of contaminated soil and a facility to store tainted soil. The Ministry of the Environment hopes to begin storing waste at the interim facility in autumn next year, but the storage capacity in both towns stands at about 120,000 cubic meters, far below the expected peak.

At present some 12 million cubic meters of contaminated soil remains temporarily stored at around 15 locations in Fukushima Prefecture, including temporary storage sites and the gardens of people's homes.

Editorial: Japan-India nuclear accord shows Japan's lacking will as A-bombed nation

November 12, 2016 (Mainichi Japan)

Japan signed a nuclear energy agreement with India on Nov. 11, on the occasion of a visit to Japan by Indian Prime Minister Narendra Modi, opening the way for Japan to sell civil nuclear power equipment and technology to India.

India, which possesses nuclear weapons, has not joined the Treaty on the Non-Proliferation of Nuclear Weapons (NPT), an international framework that regulates the use of nuclear energy. The latest deal allows Japan to cooperate with the nuclear state, which is not recognized as such under international law, in the field of atomic energy. Doesn't this signal that Japan is confirming the unraveling of the NPT framework?

Moreover, a promise -- which Tokyo had strongly demanded -- that cooperation would be suspended if India were to conduct a nuclear test was not written into the agreement. India refused to incorporate such a pledge into the bilateral agreement on the grounds that similar agreements it has with eight other countries, including the United States and France, do not have such a clause.

Instead, Japan and India signed a separate document instead, but it, too, does not mention nuclear testing. Japan is taking the position that the promise it sought has been made, since the document mentions a 2008 international agreement in which India pledged to continue its moratorium on nuclear tests and keep its civilian and military uses of atomic energy separate. Tokyo explains that the document is legally binding and effectively obligates India to participate in the international nuclear non-proliferation framework.

However, Tokyo should have persuaded New Delhi to incorporate the suspension of nuclear tests into the agreement. It is regrettable that Japan failed to stand firm in its demand as the only atomic-bombed country in the world. India apparently does not want to give up its right to conduct nuclear tests, as its neighbor Pakistan possesses nuclear arms and is not a member of the NPT.

The agreement also states that spent nuclear fuel in India can be reprocessed only for peaceful use. However, the International Atomic Energy Agency is authorized to inspect

Fig. 1. English examples of on-topic (left) and off-topic (right) editorials (trimmed for display). The actual articles used in the study are in Japanese.

3.2   Experimental Design

The second author of this paper used the resulting annotations to train and evaluate automated text classifiers for the on-off topic identification task. We first used the standard Juman package 7.01 [8] to perform tokenization and morphological analysis for Japanese. We performed feature selection by using only nouns, verbs and adjectives that occur two or more times in the corpus as the term space for each classifier. We used all such terms found in the body of each editorial. The bodies of the editorial contained, on average, 668.2 terms before feature selection, and 323.0 terms after feature selection. We conducted experiments with two types of classifiers. The first was a Support Vector Machine (SVM), a commonly used binary classifier that we implemented using TinySVM [16], for which we tried either a linear or a quadratic kernel (second-order polynomial kernel) function. The second was fastText, a neural network "deep learning" classifier developed by Facebook's AI Research lab [7][2].

Figure 2 illustrates the evaluation design. To create learning curves, we first randomly shuffle the documents within each of the first 9 annotation rounds. Specifically, we shuffle the 7 documents in Round 1 into a random order, we then shuffle the 13 documents in Round 2 into another random order, and we continue that process through Round 9. We then iteratively train a classifier by incrementally adding training data. Specifically, we train a classifier with just the first document, evaluate that classifier using F_1 (the harmonic mean of precision and recall) using the 100 annotated documents from Round 10 as a held-out evaluation set, then retrain the classifier on the first two documents from Round 1, then evaluate that classifier in the same way, and so on until all 348 documents from Round 1 through Round 9 have been used for training. We repeat that entire process 100 times, with 100 random shuffles of each Round, and then we plot the average F_1 (or accuracy) over those 100 rounds as a learning curve. The evaluation set, which by construction was randomly sampled from the entire collection, is nearly balanced, with 48 on-topic and 52 off-topic editorials. The learning curves for F_1 and accuracy are therefore similar, so for space reasons we show learning curves only for F_1 in this paper.

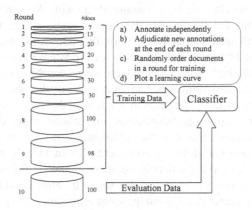

Fig. 2. Experiment design.

We plot learning curves by placing the number of annotations on the horizontal axis and the F_1 value for that number of annotations on the vertical axis. We plot four types of learning curves:

- A: we use Annotator A's annotations for training.
- B: we use Annotator B's annotations for training.

---

[2] As fastText parameters we selected: -dim 50; -loss negative sampling (ns); -epoch 1000; -wordNgrams 5; -minCount 2.

- Hybrid: we alternate between using Annotator A's or Annotator B's annotations for training.
- Adjudicated: we use the adjudicated annotations for training.

Note that creating one adjudicated annotation requires that Annotator A and Annotator B each first independently annotate the same document. In order to plot all four learning curves consistently, we randomly select half of the documents from each round when training using Adjudicated annotations, and we plot the resulting values based on the original number of independent annotations. For this reason, the learning curve for Adjudicated annotations are plotted only at even numbers of annotations.[3] Note also that it is not possible to meaningfully train a classifier until at least one on-topic and at least one off-topic editorial are available for training, and with some annotators and some random shuffles that does not happen until several annotated documents have been seen. We therefore suppress the plotting of the learning curve until meaningful F_1 values are available for all 100 random shuffles.

3.3 Results

Figure 3 shows four learning curves, all of which are evaluated using adjudicated annotations from Round 10. These are for a quadratic kernel SVM, which was the better of the two SVM kernel functions that we tried. As can be seen, Annotator A's annotations initially provide the best training data, with Annotator B's annotations becoming more useful for training in the later rounds, where they more closely approximate the adjudicated annotations. Alternating annotation between Annotator A and Annotator B (the Hybrid learning curve) unsurprisingly comes out between the two. Using the Adjudicated annotations, which we reasonably presume are of higher quality than the annotations from either annotator, is not the best choice, at least not until rather late in the process. The reason for this is that the x axis here shows the number of annotations, and to get adjudicated annotations, every document has to be annotated twice. It seems clear that the additional diversity introduced by having different annotators annotate different documents (as in the Hybrid learning curve) yields better results than having different annotators annotate the same documents.

Figure 4 shows learning curves for the same training conditions, in this case evaluated using either Annotator A's independent annotations from Round 10 (left) or Annotator B's (right) independent annotations from Round 10. Unsurprisingly, each annotator's training data is better matched to their own evaluation data, but note that the Hybrid training learning curve still dominates the Adjudicated training learning curve until quite a substantial number of annotations have been obtained. From Figs. 3 and 4 we can therefore conclude that the central message of Fig. 3, that the Hybrid training strategy works well early in the training process, does not depend on an assumption that our adjudicated annotations are perfect (which they are not).

---

[3] We have also generated learning curves using all of the adjudicated annotations, again plotting only at even values for the number of original annotations. This yields similar results.

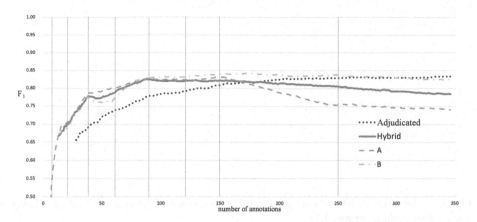

Fig. 3. F_1 for quadratic kernel SVM, 100 held out adjudicated annotations used for evaluation, average of 100 random shuffles within each round (best viewed in color). (Color figure online)

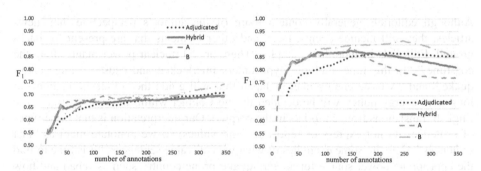

Fig. 4. F_1 for quadratic kernel SVM, 100 held out annotations by Annotator A (left) or Annotator B (right) used for evaluation; average of 100 random shuffles per round.

Figure 5 shows the same four learning curves when using the fastText classifier. As in Fig. 3, these are evaluated using the adjudicated judgments from Round 10. The fastText results exhibit a similar pattern to what we observe with the SVM, although the initial learning rate for fastText is somewhat lower. We do see that fastText ultimately does outperform the SVM with Hybrid annotations, but that only happens rather late in the learning process. This is consistent with what we would expect from neural methods, which can achieve good results in data-rich settings. Although not shown, learning curves using Annotator A's or Annotator B's annotations for evaluation show similar patterns.

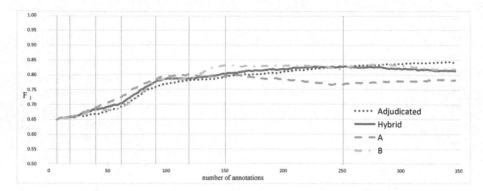

Fig. 5. F_1 for fastText, 100 held out adjudicated annotations used for evaluation, averaged over 100 random shuffles per round.

4   Identifying Value Sentences

Although editorials generally contain more of the author's perspective than news articles, they still include events, facts, and other elements that are present for background. Editorials include, for example, "There are 54 nuclear power plants along the coastline," "In this time, multiple hypocenters interlocked and caused a huge earthquake," and "A basic energy plan in Japan that will guide the country's medium- to long-term energy policy will be decided by the Cabinet within the month" (these are English translations from editorials in the corpus). Our interpretation is that these types of sentences do not express or reflect specific values, so we annotate them as "fact sentences." Here are some examples of what we call value sentences: "It is time to find the appropriate power source for an earthquake-prone country such as Japan and how to live based on it," "It could be said that securing transparency is the most important issue in selecting new policies," and "The government and electric power companies need to deepen their political discussion by accepting citizens' anxiety." For our initial experiments with automatically determining which sentences an annotator would interpret as value sentences, we have built a small training set and conducted a pilot study to characterize classification effectiveness. The same two annotators as above independently reviewed each sentence in a total of 28 on-topic editorials to distinguish between value and fact sentences. Three rounds of independent annotation were used, with adjudication by consensus between the two annotators performed at the end of each round. Table 3 shows the number of documents and sentences in each round, along with agreement statistics before adjudication. A total of 578 of the 762 sentences were annotated as value sentences in the adjudicated annotations.

Table 3. Cohen's Kappa for each round.

Round	#docs	#sentences	A:B
1	2	91	0.505
2	12	317	0.639
3	14	354	0.640

We then trained a quadratic-kernel SVM classifier on the adjudicated judgments, evaluating it using 10-fold cross-validation at sentence scale. For the first fold we selected the first 686 sentences for training and the remaining 76 for evaluation, repeating a similar process for ten different sets of 76 (or 77) evaluation sentences. As Table 4 shows, this yielded F_1 values near 0.87, regardless of whether we performed feature selecting as above of simply used all of the terms in each sentence as features. Because we plan to perform value labeling only on sentences that have been automatically classified as values sentences, a high level of recall from the stage that finds value sentences is needed. As Table 3 shows, recall values near 0.94 are possible (with feature selection) on this collection.

Table 4. Precision, recall, and F_1 by SVM with quadratic kernel for finding value sentences.

Features	Precision	Recall	F_1
Noun, verb, adjective	0.805	0.938	0.867
All	0.818	0.924	0.868

5 Conclusion and Future Work

We have introduced a three-stage model for automating the association of human values with specific passages of text on large-scale collections, and we have shown results for the first two stages: on/off topic detection, and automating the determining of which sentences an annotator would interpret as reflecting values. Prior work has shown that the third stage, automatically assigning values labels to sentences, is possible [6, 14]. Moreover, we have shown that when annotation budgets are limited, it can be useful to focus on single-labeled training examples rather than adjudicated training examples that are created by assigning multiple annotators to the same document, and that an SVM classifier can be a better choice than a state of the art neural deep learning classifier. Both of these results are consistent with results that have been reported in other settings (e.g., [9]); our contribution has been to bring these insights to bear in the context of a multi-stage annotation process for human values.

The annotations created for these experiments are being made freely available, and the content that was annotated is available from the publisher at modest cost. Much remains to be done, however. First, our motivation for introducing a stage to predict whether an annotator would interpret a sentence as a value sentence is that we need systems that can operate effectively and efficiently in settings in which values sentences are relatively uncommon. As our sentence counts in Sect. 4 indicate, however, that is not the case for editorials. We therefore plan to next automate value sentence annotation for news articles, where we expect values sentences to be considerably less common. Second, we of course next need to build classifiers to automatically assign human values labels to the resulting sentences. Preliminary results for that task have already been reported on a collection of 2,100 Japanese news articles on the nuclear power debate for a set of ten human values (effectiveness, human welfare, importance, independence, innovation, law and order, nature, personal welfare, power, wealth) with fairly good recall (between 0.55 and 0.73), but with relatively poor precision (0.05 to .38) [6]. Indeed, it is in part those relatively poor levels of precision when labeling values in news articles that motivates our interest in a multi-stage process. Automating the interpretation of value sentences on that collection of 2,100 news stories will thus be a natural next step in our research.

Acknowledgements. This work has been supported in part by JSPS KAKENHI Grant Number JP18H03495.

References

1. CD-Mainichi Shimbun Data Collection 2011 version; 2012 version; 2013 version; 2014 version; 2015 version; and 2016 version
2. Cheng, A.-S., Fleischmann, K.R., Wang, P., Ishita, E., Oard, D.W.: The role of innovation and wealth in the net neutrality debate: a content analysis of human values in congressional and FCC hearings. J. Am. Soc. Inf. Sci. Technol. **63**, 1360–1373 (2012)
3. Fleischmann, K.R.: Information and Human Values. Morgan & Claypool, San Rafael (2014)
4. Friedman, B., Kahn Jr., P.H., Borning, A.: Value sensitive design and information systems. In: Zhang, P., Galletta, D. (eds.) Human-Computer Interaction and Management Information Systems: Foundations, pp. 348–372. M.E. Sharpe, Armonk (2006). https://doi.org/10.1002/9780470281819.ch4
5. Grimmer, J., Stewart, B.M.: Text as data: the promise and pitfalls of automatic content analysis methods for political texts. Polit. Anal. **21**, 267–297 (2013)
6. Ishita, E., et al.: Toward automating detection of human values in the nuclear power debate. In: Proceedings of 80th Annual Meeting of the Association for Information Science and Technology, vol. 54, no. 1, pp. 714–715 (2017). https://doi.org/10.1002/pra2.2017.14505401127
7. Joulin, A., Grave, E., Bojanowski, P., Mikolov, T.: Bag of tricks for efficient text classification. https://arxiv.org/abs/1607.01759. Accessed 10 Sept 2018
8. JUMAN (a user-extensible morphological analyze for Japanese). http://nlp.ist.i.kyoto-u.ac.jp/EN/index.php?JUMAN. Accessed 10 Sept 2018
9. Khetan, A., Lipton, Z.C., Anandkumar, A.: Learning from noisy singly-labeled data. In: Proceedings of ICLR 2018, 15 p. (2018). https://arxiv.org/abs/1712.04577. Accessed 10 Sept 2018
10. Nelson, L.K.: Computational grounded theory: a methodological framework. Sociol. Methods Res. (2017). https://doi.org/10.1177/0049124117729703
11. Nelson, L.K., Burk, D., Knudsen, M., McCall, L.: The future of coding: a comparison of hand-coding and three types of computer-assisted text analysis methods. Sociol. Methods Res. (2018). https://doi.org/10.1177/0049124118769114
12. Pang, B., Lee, L.: Opinion mining and sentiment analysis. J. Found. Trends Inf. Retr. **2**(1–2), 1–135 (2008). https://doi.org/10.1561/1500000011
13. Schwartz, S.H.: Value orientations: measurement, antecedents and consequences across nations. In: Jowell, R., Roberts, C., Fitzgerald, R., Eva, G. (eds.) Measuring Attitudes Cross-Nationally: Lessons from the European Social Survey, pp. 169–203. Sage, London (2007). https://doi.org/10.4135/9781849209458.n9

14. Takayama, Y., Tomiura, Y., Ishita, E., Oard, D.W., Fleischmann, K.R., Cheng, A.-S.: A word-scale probabilistic latent variable model for detecting human values. In: Proceedings on ACM International Conference on Information and Knowledge Management (CIKM 2014), pp. 1489–1498 (2014). https://doi.org/10.1145/2661829.2661966
15. Clay, T., Fleischmann, K.R.: The relationship between human values and attitudes toward the Park51 and nuclear power controversies. In: Proceedings of the 74th Annual Meeting of the American Society for Information Science and Technology, New Orleans, LA (2011). https://doi.org/10.1002/meet.2011.14504801172
16. TinySVM: Support Vector Machines. http://chasen.org/~taku/software/TinySVM/. Accessed 10 Sept 2018
17. Verma, N., Fleischmann, K.R., Koltai, K.S.: Human values and trust in scientific journals, the mainstream media and fake news. In: Proceedings of 80th Annual Meeting of the Association for Information Science and Technology, vol. 54, no. 1, pp. 426–435 (2017)
18. Yan, J.L.S., McCracken, N., Crowston, K.: Semi-automatic content analysis of qualitative data. In: Proceedings of the iConference, pp. 1128–1132 (2014)

Automating Documentation: A Critical Perspective into the Role of Artificial Intelligence in Clinical Documentation

Matt Willis[1](✉) ⓘ and Mohammad Hossein Jarrahi[2] ⓘ

[1] Oxford Internet Institute, University of Oxford, Oxford OX1 3JS, UK
matthew.willis@oii.ox.ac.uk
[2] University of North Carolina, Chapel Hill, NC 27599, USA

Abstract. The current conversation around automation and artificial intelligence technologies creates a future vision where humans may not possibly compete against intelligent machines, and that everything that can be automated through deep learning, machine learning, and other AI technologies will be automated. In this article, we focus on general practitioner documentation of the patients' clinical encounters, and explore how these work practices lend themselves to automation by AI. While these work practices may appear perfect to automate, we reveal potential negative consequences to automating these tasks, and illustrate how AI may render important aspect of this work invisible and remove critical thinking. We conclude by highlighting the specific features of clinical documentation work that could leverage the benefits of human-AI symbiosis.

Keywords: Automation · Artificial Intelligence · Healthcare · Clinical documentation

1 Introduction

Artificial Intelligence (AI) is lauded for its promising potentials to transform work, from robots performing a variety of services to algorithms performing knowledge-intensive work practices in healthcare [1]. In this paper, we take a measured approach grounded in extensive ethnographic fieldwork in healthcare to examine the complex and contextual documentation practices of general doctors that requires the ability to overcome not only technical challenges, but also social ones. This paper builds on an empirical investigation of the Primary Care service sector of the National Health Service (NHS) in England, and presents a detailed account of clinical documentation work, critical work that happens after a provider sees a patient. As Bansler et al. [2] note: "clinical notes form the core of the medical record" (p. 503). While some argue this work can be largely automated [3, 4], in this paper we ask the key question: just because something can technically be automated, should it necessarily be?

N. G. Taylor et al. (Eds.): iConference 2019, LNCS 11420, pp. 200–209, 2019.
https://doi.org/10.1007/978-3-030-15742-5_19

1.1   The Need for Automation in Healthcare

The NHS in England is under remarkable pressure to improve services, cut costs, and address low staff morale [5]. These challenges must be met under the backdrop of the longest financial crunch in the history of the NHS with a dramatic increase in service demand and use, lagging performance in mental health services, staff shortages, ageing population, and increased wait times [6].

The British Medical Association (BMA) also designed a survey that was conducted by ICM Research to survey General Practitioners (GPs) in England. Of the over 5,000 GP respondents, 84% describe their workload as excessive and prevents the safe delivery of care; only one in ten said their workload is manageable and allows for quality and safe care. This has caused 38% of primary care partners to consider closing their lists to better manage workload [7].

A similar survey on GP worklife from the Policy Research Unit in Commissioning and the Healthcare System has measures on stressors and job satisfaction that are relevant to this discussion on workload and care. Of the 14 stressors the survey measures, the most stressful are workload and meeting requirements of external bodies. The least stressful are finding a locum and emergency call interruptions. However, every single stressor was at its highest point (on a 5-point scale) since the beginning of the National GP Worklife Survey in 1998. Job satisfaction declined from 4.5 points in 2012 to 4.1 points in 2015, with the most significant areas for dissatisfaction being hours worked and remuneration [8].

This review of multiple reports suggests a crucial sector of the NHS is burnt-out, over-worked, dissatisfied, and at a disadvantage for resources, staff, and time. It is easy to see how automation and other appropriate and strategic implementations of intelligent systems could play a role in reducing stress and increase effectiveness by providing more time to primary care staff and doctors.

In this paper, we focus on one specific area of work in primary care that can benefit from the application of AI to address many of the previously noted ailments: clinical documentation. Little research has been done on documentation work and how it may benefit from AI.

1.2   Documentation and Automation

Automation of work using intelligent systems has long been an object of academic research and practical concerns [9]. Automation technologies are expensive investments and take time to develop and implement into an organization. It is not the best economical decision to automate a task that is performed once a month for an hour. Automation provides the greatest advantages when it is applied to a task that is frequent or time consuming, is important, and requires a degree of repetitiveness. Many may see clinical documentation as a fertile ground for automation because it fits three hallmarks of tasks that benefit most from automation in healthcare [10].

First, it is a task that every clinician must complete, and with a sense of urgency. It is routinely described as a sensible medical practice to document the patient consultation as near the end of the appointment as possible. However, documentation of all patient encounters at the end of the day is an unwanted situation and, in many cases, it is impossible with the number of patients seen over the duration of a clinic. Second, documentation takes attention and time [3]. Although the amount of necessary attention depends on the patient's unique condition and the relationship between the patient and the provider, even brief notes require the clinician to accurately describe brief encounters [11]. Third, clinicians are typically given no time to document. As important as proper documentation is to the practice of medicine, a clinician typically documents during the amount of time it takes a patient to leave the examination room and the next patient to walk into the examination room with no time buffer. During a full clinic, the tempo of documentation and patient examination can be challenging and exhausting.

Clinical documentation constitutes a large portion of doctors' administrative tasks; doctors may need to spend up to 55% of their workday to generate notes and to review patient's records [3]. Studies suggest workload caused by clinical documentation is an important barrier to effective patient care [12]. Using existing technologies, vendors of electronic health record systems and researchers have long looked for ways to facilitate the process by pulling in structured data/format into doctor's note to reduce duplicate work [13]. Recently some researchers have advocated for the application of AI systems to streamline and automate documentation tasks in healthcare [3, 4], for example, by using natural language processing to dissect patient-doctor conversation and create notes [14]. However, incorporation of smart technologies into clinical documentation practices has been a controversial topic since research presents them as a web of complex work practices with institutional, social and situated dimensions [2].

Given the centrality of documentation work in healthcare and the new wave of computerization and AI that provide promising opportunities for automating work, we ask the research question: *What are the general challenges of integrating AI to automate general practitioners' clinical documentation practices?*

2 Method

To understand detailed work in a complex and fast paced clinical environment we employ observational fieldwork to gather empirical data. The first author observed six primary care practices across England spending on average a week at each practice (located in the areas of: Oxfordshire, Yorkshire, Berkshire, Surrey, and West-Midlands). The patient registry of observed practices ranges from the smallest of 5,000 to the largest of 24,000, with an average of about 11,500 patients per surgery.

The focus of the fieldwork was to understand the situated work practices of each occupational type at each primary care practice for a larger research project. The observation of each occupation does not focus on every staff member in the practice, but the occupations at that practice. For example, if there are 12 receptionists working at the practice the field researcher does not observe and interview all 12, but a sample of them, depending on availability and consent, till the work of a receptionist is clearly understood and can be accurately represented in the data. In total this resulted in 65 sessions of observation ranging from 45 min to an hour and 20 min in length. The observed occupations across all field sites are: Administrator, Deputy Practice Manager, General Practitioner, Healthcare Assistant, Nurse Practitioner, Pharmacy

Technician, Phlebotomist, Practice Manager, Practice Nurse, Practice Pharmacist, Prescription Clerk, Receptionist, Secretary, and Summarizer. Because this article concerns the documentation work of GPs specifically, the field researcher observed and attended clinics of 12 GPs. However, other occupations such as practice nurses, physician's assistants, nurse practitioners, and to some extent healthcare assistants also document clinical encounters with the patient.

Interviews were semi-structured, and questioning took place while the participants were observed working on their daily routine or showing the field researcher different tasks. At some points the field researcher would hold on asking questions or interacting with participants if critical events occurred that required immediate focus and attention of the participant. At the end of fieldwork at each site the field researcher would conduct a focus group open to all practice staff. The conversation of the focus group was on verifying and member checking the accuracy of data gathered about tasks observed, and to have a discussion on the use of automation and AI at that practice.

The field researcher was present during clinical appointments to observe the clinician when patients consented to the presence of the researcher. During clinical appointments the field researcher sat in the corner of the room watching the general practitioner or other clinicians, taking notes on how they work and what tools they use during patient appointments. Follow up questions during the clinical encounter were written down and asked to the provider after the patient left the examination room. Additionally, at each field site GPs have a coffee break, or case study, where all GPs available would gather in the break room or similar meeting room to discuss difficult patient cases, advice on documentation, or mentor other GPs in training. The field researcher was invited to, and attended, these coffee break case study meetings where often additional documentation, writing, and conversation occurred.

While in the field, documents that describe occupational responsibilities or work tasks were gathered, along with photos or sample of any other documents, tools, or software that clarify or represent the work a staff member engages. The field researcher wrote detailed field notes of observations. Then, the researcher developed a spreadsheet of each occupation and a list of the tasks they perform. These data were used at subsequent field observations and shown to the same occupational type at different primary care centers to help confirm each tasks representativeness and accuracy.

In addition to member checking and focus groups for establishing trustworthiness in this study, findings and fieldwork experiences were regularly reported and discussed with the project advisory board. The project advisory board membership includes two general practitioners and two policy stakeholders with experience in NHS and in primary care. The field researcher also produced an audit trail through memo writing and keeping a detailed research log data file.

Task data were coded in the spreadsheet and further enriched through a series of categories that include the frequency of task, any tools used, type of software required, and other features of the task including conceptual inductive categories. Analysis for this paper focused on the documentation practices of GPs. Important themes discussed in the finding's sections were elicited and refined after a continuous process of conversation and collaborative sensemaking between the two authors.

3 Findings

The series of tasks that form a critical part a general practitioners (GP) work concern the medical documentation of the clinical encounter. Writing notes in the patient's electronic medical record ranges from simple and quick to complex and time consuming. The complexity and length of time it takes a GP to document the patient encounter depends on what the patient is being seen for, the prior relationship between the patient and provider, when they were last seen, and even the experience of the provider. This can amount to writing a few codes – a standardized medical taxonomy for diagnosis – and a sentence or two that captures the patient's current appointment, progress, change in therapy, or anything else clinically relevant about the appointment. Or, the documentation work can involve multiple codes, referencing information in the British National Formulary, looking up information online, studying lab work, revising previously written text, calling a specialist for advice, and writing a detailed multi paragraph account of the consultation.

Our fieldwork suggests this important work must be done promptly. The time GPs have to document is from when the patient exits the examination room, to when the next patient is called to see the provider (several minutes at most). It is considered by many GPs involved in this study a best practice to finish documentation work right after the patient's appointment, not letting it wait till the end of the day.

The interpersonal style with which GPs write ranges from not looking directly at the patient while loudly banging away on the keyboard typing rapidly as patients discuss their concerns; to the GP directly facing the patient, hands on lap, listening and discussing them and only writing on the computer when they leave or near the end of the appointment. We observed GPs incorporate the computer into the clinical appointment in different ways, some minimize its presence and others bring the computer in as a third member to reference information and write notes. This use, too, is influenced by the context for the patient's appointment, how friendly the patient and provider are with each other, and the clinicians experience.

Every primary care practice in this study but one uses an electronic medical record called EMIS. Although its functionality is too large to detail here, the section of the record most pertinent are the patient notes. The record has preformatted sections for notes that are typically organized in the following structure: problem, history, examination, family history, social, comment, medication, follow up, procedure, test request, referral, document, and allergy. Not all these sections are used, and GPs exercise their own authorial voice and style when documenting their patients. In fact, several experienced GPs were able to discern what notes from a new patient were written by locums or other staff such as a nurse or physicists assistant.

We observed that during a chronic disease clinic one GP kept two patient notes open, thinking about one complex situation while they worked on the most recent patient's documentation notes. This allowed them to mull over the patient's case and ask some advice from their colleague as they considered the pros and cons of treatment options. The GP had captured the core of what the appointment was about. The remaining documentation work was the careful and considerate work that comes with the practicing of medicine. The decisions to continue or change this patients therapy was a decision that needed to be personalized to that patient's context, not only the patients' specific health situation but also their families concern, the patient's own considerations, and the informed decision that comes with medical treatment. It was through this event that the personal preferences in documentation work become apparent. The need to carefully consider a case is shown through its persistence on the clinician's screen, not to have notes quickly typed and closed.

Another important observation the field researcher made is the use of templates that come with the medical record. The GP attending to their clinical hours receives suggestions for what templates to use when seeing a patient. The suggested template is based on what the patient is being seen for and is a nationally standardized template. These templates automatically pop up through a notification and offer a suggestion that will pre-populate some of the documentation fields, like auto-complete word suggestions when texting on a mobile phone. These popups and suggestions were ignored every time by this clinician. In favor of their own personal style to document by creating a notes section in the patients record and writing the following sections: problem, history, and open comment. The GP will use discretion to write a few notes in the record during the clinical appointment but complete the rest of their documentation work when the patient leaves.

The work of documenting clinical encounters is complicated and highly situated, constantly negotiated by the patient and provider we studied. As noted, researchers have presented this experience to be automated. There are smart technologies that currently capture a natural language discussion between two people. Most all consumer smart phones, the current flood of smart speakers and other smart devices have speech recognition functionality. High quality speech recognition and transcription has been available on consumer smart phones for years.

It is reasonable to consider the use of a speech recognition device that can turn the patient and provider discussion into a text transcript. Using natural language processing this text could be further reduced and annotated to provide clinically relevant information that matches the way the provider writes or is categorized by the previously mentioned sections of the medical record.

Connected to the electronic medical record, this device could utilize data already in the patients' record as well as similar patients at this practice, providing the technology with data to learn from and support the providers' decision making and documentation responsibilities. After the clinical encounter the clinician reviews a summary they can edit and save to the patients file. Almost the entire process would be automated, invisible, and would allow the provider to interact directly with the patient, not having to consider documenting the encounter.

This scenario was presented at each focus group and provided lengthy discussion during several interviews with clinicians. This potential solution to automate the documentation of the clinical encounter was seen by many providers as useful, including many "when can we have that" comments. While technically possible and able to reduce cumbersome documentation work, this is a set of tasks that if made invisible through automation would have negative consequences on the clinical encounter and even undermine the skills and problem-solving ability of the clinician.

One GP critiqued an AI generating an entire transcript of the patient and providers conversation with "*I don't need the entire transcript, it's not useful or clinically relevant to me.*" It was a flood of information. Not everything being relevant to the diagnosis, treatment, or continuing therapy for the patient.

It was observed that it was not uncommon for GPs to rewrite, backspace, or edit the notes they wrote, particularly notes for new cases or complex circumstances, particularly mental health encounters, as well as newer or training GPs. What looks like GPs writing down notes on a computer is a medically trained clinician dealing with qualitative data (clinical narrative) through the process of writing to themselves and to other medical professionals: an act they spent years at school and training for to think in a critical way about medicine and treatment.

If the practice of writing and thinking through writing is wholly removed from the clinicians' workflow then it removes an opportunity for the clinician to apply the skills that they have trained over years of a medical education, and it removes an opportunity for the clinician to think and reflect critically, in the way they practice medicine. Research shows that writing engages the brain, allows GPs to be better observers, supports empathy, and engages critical thinking [15].

4 Discussion

Findings presented here offer a deeper and situated perspective into the documentation activities of GPs. These activities can be understood as information practices, which are defined as socially and culturally established ways of identifying, seeing, using and sharing information [16]. Information practices reflect not only individual choices that each GP makes but also his or her encounter with the social context within which the documentation is done, particularly the social interactions with the patient and other medical professionals. Bansler et al. [2] similarly highlight differences between personal and social context of clinical documentation practices; they suggest that documentation can serve as "tool of thinking" for doctors and as an artifact of coordination and communication with other involved parties.

In addition, documentation as an information practice involves both manipulation of explicit information artifacts (e.g., the patient digital record) and tacit and embodied interactions with the information environment (e.g., subjective ways to make sense of patients' data and communicate it to the patient) [17]. Intelligent technological systems are likely to capture and automate the process of manipulating and analyzing the information artifacts; new AI systems will provide decision support to medical professionals based on their superior capabilities in searching and analyzing big data and comparing patients' data with previous cases. However, the tacit and more contextual dimension of the information practice of documentation such as reading social cues and combining them with decisions suggested by AI to communicate with patients continues to lie outside of the capabilities of intelligent systems and are best handled by humans. Automating the whole documentation process by implementing AI systems as advocated by many technologists and some academic researchers is shortsighted and tends to gloss over the intricacies of situated practices that we outlined in this paper. In fact health informatics researchers and electronic health record vendors for years have sought to invoke smart technologies to transform doctor's note into structured content;

however, these notes include clinical narratives, which serve different purposes such as collective sensemaking by medical professionals [2].

Below (Fig. 1), we present a bisection of our empirical investigation of clinical documentation work, with suggestions on the most advantageous configurations that leverages the strengths of healthcare providers and artificial technologies. This builds on the concept of human-AI symbiosis; suggesting human and AI serve complementary roles based on their unique and irreplaceable capabilities [18].

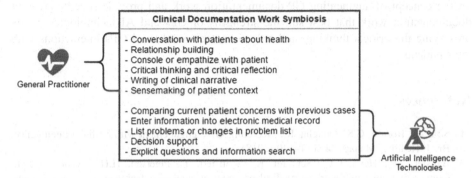

Fig. 1. List of documentation tasks best performed by clinicians and AI technologies.

New machine and deep learning algorithms provide avenues for automating tasks that were done exclusively by humans. However, the vision of human-AI symbiosis involves a normative stance: the fact that many tasks can be automated does not necessarily mean they should [9]. This runs against the old trope of automation, which implicitly espouses automating whatever that can be automated. Such technological imperatives grossly overlook the complexity of healthcare sociotechnical systems including people roles, sensemaking practices and the nature of human interaction and care. Human-AI symbiosis implies that more effective (not necessarily more efficient) practices in healthcare will likely exhibit a synergetic partnership between medical professionals and AI systems.

The symbiosis also means as more advanced AI algorithms are developed and introduced into healthcare, health professionals must adapt and develop new skills and competencies. To keep a balanced division of work between AI and humans, doctors and other medical professionals must continuously upgrade skills that are considered competitive edge of humans (such as those listed in Fig. 1). In addition, medical professionals need to acquire literacies on how to harness the capabilities of intelligence systems in their work practices, what Jarrahi [18] calls "AI literacies".

5 Conclusions

In this paper we explore the practice of documentation work in primary care as performed by general practitioners. We posit that, while important work that should be automated to avoid GP burnout and stress, this is a task that should not be wholesale automated. Integration of AI without an understanding of situated practices of GPs will likely yield several challenges around individual clinician style, tradition, patient context, tacit information, and the practice of writing enabling critical thought and critical reflection. While AI technologies are capable to automate most of the tasks involved in the workflow of clinical documentation, we raise the concern that this new configuration of deep learning and AI technologies, while impressive in their ability to mimic and augment thinking, decision making, and knowledge work, will change the clinician's ability to think critically, reflect, and practice medicine effectively. We side on the concept of augmenting GP documentation work and provide specific areas of documentation work that best suit the strengths of GPs and AI technologies, while preserving the critical thinking, and reflection, tacit work, and GPs interactions with their patients.

References

1. Sola, D., Borioli, G.S., Quaglia, R.: Predicting GPs' engagement with artificial intelligence. Br. J. Healthc. Manag. **24**, 134–140 (2018)
2. Bansler, J.P., Havn, E.C., Schmidt, K., Mønsted, T., Petersen, H.H., Svendsen, J.H.: Cooperative epistemic work in medical practice: an analysis of physicians' clinical notes. Comput. Support. Coop. Work **25**, 503–546 (2016)
3. Lin, S.Y., Shanafelt, T.D., Asch, S.M.: Reimagining clinical documentation with artificial intelligence. Mayo Clin. Proc. **93**, 563–565 (2018)
4. Verghese, A., Shah, N.H., Harrington, R.A.: What this computer needs is a physician: humanism and artificial intelligence. JAMA **319**, 19 (2018)
5. Baird, B., Charles, A., Honeyman, M., Maguire, D., Das, P.: Understanding Pressures in General Practice, London, UK (2016)
6. Hopson, C.: The sate of the NHS provider sector (2016)
7. Byrne, L., Bottomley, J., Turk, A.: British Medical Association Survey of GPs in England, London (2016)
8. Gibson, J., et al.: Eighth National GP Worklife Survey. Manchester (2016)
9. Zuboff, S.: In the Age of the Smart Machine: The Future of Work and Power. Basic Books, New York (1988)
10. Smith, K., Smith, V., Krugman, M., Oman, K.: Evaluating the impact of computerized clinical documentation. Comput. Inform. Nurs. **23**, 132–138 (2005)
11. Ammenwerth, E., Spötl, H.-P.: The time needed for clinical documentation versus direct patient care. A work-sampling analysis of physicians' activities. Methods Inf. Med. **48**, 84–91 (2009)
12. Erickson, S.M., Rockwern, B., Koltov, M., McLean, R.M.: Medical practice and quality committee of the American College of Physicians: putting patients first by reducing administrative tasks in health care: a position paper of the American College of Physicians. Ann. Intern. Med. **166**, 659 (2017)
13. Rule, A., et al.: Validating free-text order entry for a note-centric EHR. In: AMIA Annual Symposium Proceedings, vol. 2015, pp. 1103–1110 (2015)
14. Klann, J.G., Szolovits, P.: An intelligent listening framework for capturing encounter notes from a doctor-patient dialog. BMC Med. Inform. Decis. Mak. **9**(Suppl 1), S3 (2009)

15. Wald, H.S., Borkan, J.M., Taylor, J.S., Anthony, D., Reis, S.P.: Fostering and evaluating reflective capacity in medical education: developing the REFLECT rubric for assessing reflective writing. Acad. Med. **87**, 41–50 (2012)
16. Savolainen, R.: Everyday Information Practices: A Social Phenomenological Perspective. Scarecrow Press (2008)
17. Jarrahi, M.H., Thomson, L.: The interplay between information practices and information context: the case of mobile knowledge workers. J. Assoc. Inf. Sci. Technol. **68**, 1073–1089 (2017)
18. Jarrahi, M.: Artificial intelligence and the future of work: human-AI symbiosis in organizational decision making. Bus. Horiz. **61**, 577–586 (2018)

Collecting Data about Vulnerable Populations

Investigating Health Self-management Among Different Generation Immigrant College Students with Depression

Jordan Dodson[1]([⊠]), Jenni Thang[2], Naika Saint Preux[3],
Christopher Frye[4], Linh Ly[5], Julissa Murrieta[6], Linda Sun[4],
and Elizabeth V. Eikey[7]

[1] The University of North Carolina at Chapel Hill, Chapel Hill, NC, USA
jordodson@gmail.com
[2] Indiana University Bloomington, Bloomington, IN, USA
jennysui22@gmail.com
[3] The College of Westchester, White Plains, NY, USA
naikasp4@gmail.com
[4] University of Pittsburgh, Pittsburgh, PA, USA
ccfl5@pitt.edu, lindaxsun@gmail.com
[5] University of Washington, Seattle, WA, USA
linhly8015@gmail.com
[6] University of Maryland, College Park, MD, USA
jmurriet@umd.edu
[7] University of California, Irvine, Irvine, CA, USA
eikeye@uci.edu

Abstract. Digital tools for health hold a lot of promise in terms of empowering individuals to take control over their health and improving access to care. This may be especially critical for marginalized individuals, such as immigrant college students, and those who face stigmatizing conditions, such as depression. However, research is limited on how these tools fit into users' existing practices around health management. In order to address this gap, we first investigate existing practices by focusing on a specific population: college students with depression ranging from immigrant generation 1 to 2.5. This group is important to study as they are at an increased risk for depression but may be less likely to access traditional treatment. We present results about their practices around health self-tracking and digital tools specific to depression management. Based on a survey of 83 participants, we found that although students with depression across these various immigrant generations engage in health self-tracking (94%), few track mental health indicators and most do not use mobile apps (81.9%) or other online resources (86.7%) to help with their depression. Those that do use apps and online resources offer insights into their depression management needs.

Keywords: Mental health · Depression · mHealth · Mobile app · Self-tracking · Self-management · Digital tools · College student · Immigrants

© Springer Nature Switzerland AG 2019
N. G. Taylor et al. (Eds.): iConference 2019, LNCS 11420, pp. 213–221, 2019.
https://doi.org/10.1007/978-3-030-15742-5_20

1 Introduction

Increasingly, people are turning to technology to track their health and get access to health information [1]. With the prevalence of smartphones, it is becoming easier to not only look up health information online, but also utilize digital tools to track and monitor a number of health indicators, such as sleep, mood, exercise, and even illness symptoms. Younger individuals, in particular, are showing an increased interest in using digital technology for health [2, 3]. According to Pew Research Center, 72% of all adults ages 18–29 look online for health information [2]. In a study of 1,604 mobile phone users in the U.S., researchers found over half use mobile health apps [3]. Digital tools for health hold a lot of promise in terms of empowering individuals to take control over their health and increasing access to resources and care. This may be especially critical for marginalized individuals, such as immigrant college students, and those who face stigmatizing conditions, such as depression, because they may be less likely to access traditional healthcare services [4–6].

However, what is not yet fully understood is how these digital tools fit into individuals' lives, particularly those who marginalized and stigmatized. In order to investigate this, we first must understand what tools users are currently using. We look at one example: college students with depression symptoms from varying immigrant generations. We focus on students who were born in a country other than the U.S. and moved to the U.S. (sometimes referred to as generation 1 to 1.75) as well as those born in the U.S. but whose parent(s) were born in a country other than the U.S. (sometimes referred to as generation 2 and 2.5) [7–9]. Although there are differences across immigrant generations, some research has shown similar rates of depression. For example, Peña et al. [10] found no statistically significant differences in depression symptoms across first, second, or later generations of Latino immigrant adolescents. Additionally, because we found no statistically significant differences across our sample's generation groups on depression scores, acculturation scores, or digital tools used to manage depression, we combine them and refer to them as immigrants.

This population is important to study because they are at an increased risk for depression as both college students and immigrants [11–13], and they are a rapidly growing population [14, 15]. In addition to dealing with stressors as a college student, immigrant college students face additional challenges, such as navigating the college process and balancing personal goals with those of their family [16]. A shared experience of acculturation, which occurs when people try to adapt to new and diverse cultures, often exists across different immigrant generations [17]. Immigrants often face acculturation stress, and many face pressures in balancing more than one culture, which may lead to feelings of distress and poor health [18]. Additionally, they are more likely to go undiagnosed [19] and less likely to access professional mental health services due to financial barriers [19], stigma within their communities [6], language barriers [20] and lack of providers from similar ethnic and cultural backgrounds [21, 22].

In order to understand if digital tools are appropriate or effective for this population, we need to first understand their existing practices around health and depression management. Using college students with depression from different immigrant generations 1 to 2.5[1] as a case study, we conducted a survey focusing on what health indicators are already being tracked (using analog and digital tools) and then aimed to understand what digital tools (apps and online resources) they use to aid specifically in their depression management. We identified 2 main research questions:

RQ1: What health indicators are college students with depression from different immigrant generations already tracking?
RQ2a: Are college students with depression from different immigrant generations using digital tools (apps, online resources) to help with depression?

- *RQ2b: If so, then what tools are they using?*

2 Methodology

2.1 Questions, Measures, and Analysis

In order to characterize our sample, we used a Qualtrics questionnaire to obtain information about demographics, acculturation, and depression. To assess symptoms, we included the 21-item Beck's Depression Inventory II (BDI-II) [23], which is a reliable tool [24]. Questions cover a range of depressive symptoms, including feelings of worthlessness, loss of focus, difficulty sleep, appetite levels, and loss of energy. Each item is scored on a 0–3 range and then added together to get the overall score symptoms (higher scores indicate greater severity) [23]. These scores can also be grouped into categories to convey the severity of depression symptoms: minimum = 0–13, mild = 14–19, moderate = 20–28, and severe = 29–63.

To answer our research questions, we asked 3 main survey questions: "What aspects (if any) of your health do you track?" [RQ1]; "Do you use any mobile applications or apps to help with your depression?" [RQ2a]; and "Do you use any other online resources or websites to manage your depression or get information about depression?" [RQ2a]. If participants answered yes to either of the questions for RQ2a, then they were asked an additional question about what apps or online resources they use [RQ2b]. We used Excel and JASP to organize and analyze our data. Qualitative data was inductively coded and grouped into broader categories.

---

[1] *Immigrant generation status:*
1 = moved to U.S. after age 17
1.25 = moved to U.S. between ages 13–17
1.5 = moved to U.S. between ages 6–12
1.75 = moved to U.S. before age 6
2 = born in U.S. and both parents born outside of U.S.
2.5 = born in U.S. and one parent born outside of U.S. [33].

2.2   Recruitment, Eligibility, and Participants

We recruited participants through Amazon Mechanical Turk (mTurk). Investigating health self-tracking and information seeking was part of a larger survey examining immigrant students' perceptions of digital tools, including social media and apps. We limited participation to only within the U.S. Our participants were compensated $2 for approximately 20 min of their time. Eligibility criteria included: currently reside in the U.S.; identify as an immigrant (either they were born in another country and moved to the U.S. or one or both of their parents were born in another country but they were born in the U.S.) [7]; 18 to 24 years old; currently an undergraduate; use at least one social media platform; speak English; and have experienced depression symptoms within the last 12 months. Participants were excluded if they have a history of a manic episode, schizophrenia, or bipolar disorder.

In our final analysis, we had 83 participants (139 responses; 28 removed for being incomplete, and 28 excluded based on quality checks). In our sample, 33 participants identified as female and 50 as male. Their age ranged from 18 to 24 (mean = 21.5; SD = 12.54). Based on reported birth country, parents' birth countries, and age moved to the U.S., we categorized participants into 6 generation groups: 1 (n = 6, 7.2%), 1.25 (n = 8, 9.6%), 1.5 (n = 13, 15.7%), 1.75 (n = 15, 18.1%), 2 (n = 26, 31.3%), 2.5 (n = 15, 18.1%). In terms of diagnosis and treatment, the majority (n = 64) had not received a clinical diagnosis or sought professional treatment. Based on the BDI-II, the mean depression score among our participants was 21.25 (SD = 12.54), which is significantly higher than norms of undergraduates in the U.S. (norms: mean = 9.14, SD = 8.45; our participants: mean = 21.25, SD = 12.54) [25] Although there are no clinical cut-off points, Dozois et al. [26] suggest 13 or higher may be considered depressed, and 74.7% (n = 62) of our participants reached this threshold. However, scores less than 13 may not necessarily mean not depressed but rather lower symptom severity, especially given that all participants identified as experiencing depression.

3   Findings

3.1   RQ1: General Health Self-tracking

Our findings indicate that health self-tracking is very common among immigrant college students. In fact, out of our 83 participants, only 5 did not track any health indicators. Most commonly, participants reported tracking exercise (n = 42) and food, calories, and nutrition (n = 40), as shown in Fig. 1[2]. Despite all participants identifying as having depression, few participants reported tracking indicators specific to mental and emotional health, such as their mood (n = 11) and stress (n = 16).

---

[2] Many participants reported tracking more than one health indicator.

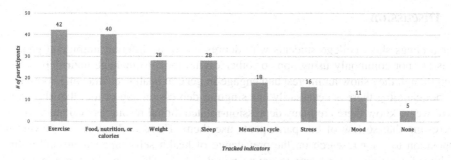

Fig. 1. General health self-tracking

3.2 RQ2: Digital Tools for Depression Management

We asked participants about digital tools, specifically mobile apps and online resources, they use for depression management, including non-depression specific tools. Out of 83 participants, the majority did not report using any apps ($n = 68$) or online resources ($n = 72$) to help them with their depression symptoms, as shown in Fig. 2.

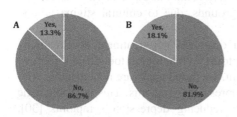

Fig. 2. (A) Online resources or websites; (B) Apps

Table 1 shows the types of apps and online resources participants used. Only 15 participants used apps to aid in the management of their depression. These apps included apps specific and not specific to mental health, such as MoodTools ($n = 1$), Positive Thinking ($n = 1$), Uplift ($n = 2$), Mindfulness Meditation ($n = 1$), Calm ($n = 1$), Headspace ($n = 1$), Spotify ($n = 1$), Daylio ($n = 1$), Notes ($n = 1$), Google Fit ($n = 1$), and Lose It ($n = 1$). Only 11 participants reported using other online resources and websites, which included general healthcare resources and those specific to depression, such as Rethink Depression ($n = 1$), Students Against Depression ($n = 2$), WebMD ($n = 1$), Mayo Clinic ($n = 1$), Beyondblue Healthcare ($n = 1$), Google Search ($n = 1$), DepressionForums.org ($n = 1$), and Depressed Help ($n = 1$).

Table 1. Types of apps and online resources

App type	Depression and anxiety–specific apps ($n = 1$)	Positivity apps ($n = 3$)	Meditation/mindfulness apps ($n = 3$)	Music apps ($n = 2$)	Diet and fitness apps ($n = 3$)
Online resource type	Depression/mental health websites ($n = 4$)	General online medical resources ($n = 4$)	Depression forums ($n = 2$)	Online counseling ($n = 1$)	Self-help websites ($n = 1$)

4 Discussion

Our findings show college students with depression from different immigrant generations are not commonly using apps or other digital tools to manage their depression,
even though they show an interest and engage in general health self-tracking. While we
are not claiming there is necessarily one singular depression app or tool that should be
used, we do know there are many depression-related digital resources available, so it is
interesting that so few of our participants use them. These findings are somewhat in
opposition to prior research on the prevalence of health self-management and online
health information seeking among young people [2, 3]. This suggests that a potential
distinction needs to be made between health management and information seeking and
mental health management and information seeking. Our findings are consistent with
prior work on mental health tracking among college students, which shows tracking
indicators like exercise and weight are more common than tracking mental health [27].
For example, Kelley et al. [27] found many college students whose self-tracking is
related to mental illness monitor behavioral proxies related to mental health rather than
mental health indicators directly. It is possible that using digital tools for general
health-management is common among college students, but using apps and online
resources specific to depression may be much less common, especially for those who
are of minority and ethnically diverse backgrounds, due to cultural stigma around
mental health issues [6, 28, 29].

Most of our participants never sought a diagnosis nor treatment despite many
reporting moderate to severe depression symptoms. While digital tools could improve
access to resources and alternatives to treatment, we found many are not engaging with
apps or online resources to help with their depression symptoms. This is problematic
given that these tools may be effective in reducing depression symptoms [30],
increasing social support [31], and improving mental health literacy [32]. Because
many of them are not utilizing digital tools for depression management or care and not
seeking professional mental health services, they may be utilizing very little if any
depression resources and treatment.

Because this was part of a larger study, we know that this sample regularly uses
digital tools; thus, access to technology is likely not an issue. For instance, all participants are social media users, and at least 77% (n = 64) access social media on their
own smartphones. Therefore, more research is needed to understand why they are not
utilizing tools to manage their depression. Is it lack of awareness, stigma, language
barriers, or misconceptions about depression? Are they simply uninterested in
managing their depression in this way? Answers to these questions can help us improve
access to alternative depression treatment and support for immigrant students.

Those that did use technology for depression can offer us insights into the types of
tools immigrant students want. The way in which we framed the question offers a
unique advantage and served as a mechanism to understand how they envision digital
tools serving them. For example, even among those who used apps to help with
depression, the majority did not use depression-specific apps but rather more general
apps that may have some impact on depression symptoms, such as mood tracking,
meditation/mindfulness, and positivity apps. This suggests their idea of what an app

should focus on to help with depression may be broader than simply translating traditional mental health services to the digital world. For online resources, on the other hand, immigrant students often sought and used depression-specific websites and online services as well as general health and medical websites to get information about depression. These sources tend to focus more on depression as a condition, and therefore, those using these resources may have a different level of depression literacy or conceptualization than those that reported using apps.

5   Limitations and Future Work

This paper focuses on health management of different immigrant generations; however, we found few differences across these generations or by symptom severity. It is possible that differences in use of apps and resources exist but were not uncovered as part of this study. Our findings shed light on *what* individuals are currently doing around depression management but do not explore *why* and *how* they use or do not use these tools. At this stage, we are not trying to create one-size-fits-all tool. To address these limitations, we are conducting a larger study assess college students' current practices around depression management, which will inform the design of digital tools.

6   Conclusion

In this paper, we examined health self-management among college students with depression from immigrant generations 1 to 2.5. We focused on health self-tracking and digital tools for depression. We found that while many students track some aspect of their health, the majority do not use apps or online resources to manage depression. This research acts as a foundation to understanding existing practices around mental health self-management among this group. This research leads to additional questions regarding why these tools are not used and how they could be used in the future.

Acknowledgements. We would like to thank iSchool Inclusion Institute (i3) Director Dr. Kayla Booth, Michael Depew, the 2017 cohort, our research advisor and i3 Assistant Director Dr. Elizabeth Eikey, and Team Dopamine. This work was supported by the National Center for Research Resources, the National Center for Advancing Translational Sciences, and the NIH (UL1 TR001414). It is solely the responsibility of the authors and does not necessarily represent the official views of the NIH.

References

1. Fox, S., Duggan, M: Tracking for health. Pew Internet, pp. 1–40 (2013). https://doi.org/10.1001/jamainternmed.2013.1221.2
2. Fox, S.: The social life of health information. Pew Research Center, Pew Internet Research (2014). http://www.pewresearch.org/fact-tank/2014/01/15/the-social-life-of-health-information/

3. Krebs, P., Duncan, D.T.: Health app use among us mobile phone owners: a national survey. JMIR mHealth uHealth **3**, e101 (2015). https://doi.org/10.2196/mhealth.4924
4. Abe-Kim, J., et al.: Use of mental health-related services among immigrant and US-born Asian Americans: results from the national Latino and Asian American Study. Am. J. Public Health **97**, 91–98 (2007). https://doi.org/10.2105/AJPH.2006.098541
5. Corrigan, P.: How stigma interferes with mental health care. Am. Psychol. **59**, 614–625 (2004). https://doi.org/10.1037/0003-066X.59.7.614
6. Nadeem, E., Lange, J.M., Edge, D., Fongwa, M., Belin, T., Miranda, J.: Does stigma keep poor young immigrant and U.S.-born black and Latina women from seeking mental health care? Psychiatr. Serv. **58**, 1547–1554 (2007). https://doi.org/10.1176/ps.2007.58.12.1547
7. Trevelyan, E., et al.: Characteristics of the U.S. Population by Generational Status: 2013 Current Population Survey Reports (2016)
8. Ramakrishnan, S.K.: Second-generation immigrants? The "2.5 generation" in the United States. Soc. Sci. Q. **85**, 380–399 (2004)
9. Rumbaut, R.G.: Ages, life stages, and generational cohorts: decomposing the immigrant first and second generations in the United States1. Int. Migr. Rev. **38**, 1160–1205 (2006). https://doi.org/10.1111/j.1747-7379.2004.tb00232.x
10. Peña, J.B., et al.: Immigration generation status and its association with suicide attempts, substance use, and depressive symptoms among Latino adolescents in the USA. Prev. Sci. **9**, 299–310 (2009). https://doi.org/10.1007/s11121-008-0105-x.Immigration
11. Cho, Y.B., Haslam, N.: Suicidal ideation and distress among immigrant adolescents: the role of acculturation, life stress, and social support. J. Youth Adolesc. **39**, 370–379 (2010). https://doi.org/10.1007/s10964-009-9415-y
12. Lyubomirsky, S., Kasri, F., Zehm, K.: Dysphoric rumination impairs concentration on academic tasks. Cogn. Ther. Res. **27**, 309–330 (2003). https://doi.org/10.1023/A:1023918517378
13. Mejía, O.L., McCarthy, C.J.: Acculturative stress, depression, and anxiety in migrant farmwork college students of mexican heritage. Int. J. Stress Manag. **17**, 1–20 (2010). https://doi.org/10.1037/a0018119
14. Keller, G.: The new demographics of higher education. Rev. High. Educ. **24**, 219–235 (2001). https://doi.org/10.1353/rhe.2001.0004
15. Schwartz, S.J., et al.: Converging identities: dimensions of acculturation and personal identity status among immigrant college students. Cult. Divers. Ethn. Minor. Psychol. **19**, 155–165 (2013). https://doi.org/10.1037/a0030753
16. Deenanath, V.: First-generation immigrant college students: an exploration of family support and career aspirations. Thesis Submitted to the Faculty of the Graduate School of University of Minnesota by Veronica Deenanath in Partial Fulfillment of the Requirements for T. University of Minnesota (2014)
17. Berry, J.W.: Acculturation: living successfully in two cultures. Int. J. Intercult. Relat. **29**, 697–712 (2005). https://doi.org/10.1016/j.ijintrel.2005.07.013
18. Schwartz, S.J., et al.: Acculturation and well-being among college students from immigrant families. J. Clin. Psychol. **69**, 298–318 (2013). https://doi.org/10.1002/jclp.21847
19. Pitkin Derose, K., Bahney, B.W., Lurie, N., Escarce, J.J.: Immigrants and health care access, quality, and cost (2009)
20. Sentell, T., Shumway, M., Snowden, L.: Access to mental health treatment by English language proficiency and race/ethnicity. J. Gen. Intern. Med. **22**, 289–293 (2007). https://doi.org/10.1007/s11606-007-0345-7
21. Kirmayer, L.J., et al.: Common mental health problems in immigrants and refugees: general approach in primary care. CMAJ **183**, 1–9 (2011). https://doi.org/10.1503/cmaj.090292

22. Kirmayer, L.J., Rousseau, C., Jarvis, G.E.: Assessment Introduction: The Cultural Matrix. Assessment (2008)
23. Beck, A.T., Steer, R.A., Brown, G.K.: Beck Depression Inventory–II (1996)
24. Wang, Y.P., Gorenstein, C.: Psychometric properties of the beck depression inventory-II: a comprehensive review. Rev. Bras. Psiquiatr. **35**, 416–431 (2013). https://doi.org/10.1590/1516-4446-2012-1048
25. Whisman, M.A., Richardson, E.D.: Normative data on the beck depression inventory - second edition (BDI-II) in college students. J. Clin. Psychol. **71** 898–907 (2015). https://doi.org/10.1002/jclp.22188
26. Dozois, D.J.A., Dobson, K.S., Ahnberg, J.L.: A psychometric evaluation of the beck depression inventory–II. Psychol. Assess. **10**, 83–89 (1998)
27. Kelley, C., Lee, B., Wilcox, L.: Self-tracking for mental wellness. In: Proceedings of the 2017 CHI Conference on Human Factors in Computing Systems - CHI 2017, pp. 629–641 (2017)
28. Chen, J.A., et al.: Association between stigma and depression outcomes among Chinese immigrants in a primary care setting. J. Clin. Psychiatry **77**, e1287–e1292 (2016). https://doi.org/10.4088/JCP.15m10225
29. Nadeem, E., Lange, J.M., Miranda, J.: Perceived need for care among low-income immigrant and U.S.-born black and Latina women with depression. J. Women's Heal **18**, 369–375 (2009). https://doi.org/10.1089/jwh.2008.0898
30. Arean, P.A., et al.: The use and effectiveness of mobile apps for depression: results from a fully remote clinical trial. J. Med. Internet Res. **18** (2016). https://doi.org/10.2196/jmir.6482
31. Griffiths, K.M., Mackinnon, A.J., Crisp, D.A., Christensen, H., Bennett, K., Farrer, L.: The Effectiveness of an online support group for members of the community with depression: a randomised controlled trial. PLoS One **7** (2012). https://doi.org/10.1371/journal.pone.0053244
32. Brijnath, B., Protheroe, J., Mahtani, K.R., Antoniades, J.: Do web-based mental health literacy interventions improve the mental health literacy of adult consumers? Results from a systematic review. J. Med. Internet Res. **18**, e165 (2016). https://doi.org/10.2196/jmir.5463
33. Moffett, D.: Is an immigrant considered first or second generation (2018)? https://www.thoughtco.com/first-generation-immigrant-defined-1951570. Accessed 12 Dec 2018

Applying Photovoice to the Study of Asian Immigrants' Information Needs

Safirotu Khoir[1]([⊠]) [iD], Jia Tina Du[2] [iD], and Robert M. Davison[3] [iD]

[1] Universitas Gadjah Mada, Yogyakarta, Indonesia
safirotu@ugm.ac.id
[2] University of South Australia, Adelaide, Australia
tina.du@unisa.edu.au
[3] City University of Hong Kong, Kowloon Tong, Hong Kong
isrobert@cityu.edu.hk

Abstract. Immigrants in their new country may have diverse and complex information needs. Appropriate methods are part of scientific discourse on how to effectively engage with immigrants to reflect their information needs and life experiences. This paper discusses the application of the photovoice method to study Asian immigrants' information needs as they settled in South Australia. As a participatory approach, photovoice allowed immigrants to take photos to actively record their own information needs and concerns. We reflected how photovoice can contribute to a comprehensive understanding of immigrants' information needs by overcoming language barriers and expressing personal feelings and emotions. Photovoice is considered to be a useful method for studying vulnerable or underrepresented populations.

Keywords: Asian immigrants · Immigrants · Information need · Photovoice · Visual method

1 Introduction

Photovoice is a method using photographs to give people a voice within their community (Wang and Burris 1997). Wang and Burris (1994) used the idea of a "novella" composed of images representing someone's "story". Some years later, they used the term "photovoice" to describe "a process by which people can identify, represent, and enhance their community through a specific photographic technique" (Wang and Burris 1997, p. 369). As the focus of the photovoice is the photographs, the participants may feel part of the research team rather than the research subject (Julien et al. 2013). Photovoice was explicitly devised to give a voice to people who have little or no access to policy makers to record, document, and discuss their life as they see and capture it through images (Wang and Burris 1997).

Besides written and spoken resources, visual information is also an important component in the process of information sharing between the researcher and the participant (Given et al. 2011). Photos taken by research participants provide visual information from the participants' perspectives, facilitate their self-expression, and offer a basis for discussion (Wang and Burris 1997). Importantly, photos may provide a

© Springer Nature Switzerland AG 2019
N. G. Taylor et al. (Eds.): iConference 2019, LNCS 11420, pp. 222–227, 2019.
https://doi.org/10.1007/978-3-030-15742-5_21

bridge linking researchers and participants, where communication, especially involving emotions, may be inhibited by cultural norms or language inadequacies. Visual methods including participatory photography have been recently utilized in studying human information behavior but such studies are still scarce.

Previous research in the information behavior field has employed photovoice as a data gathering method that can capture rich details of participant expression (Julien et al. 2013). However, there is limited research concerning immigrants' information behavior using visual methods (Hicks and Lloyd (2018); Pollak (2017)), particularly in the Australian context (Khoir et al. 2015). Corresponding with Prosser and Loxley's (2008) and Hartel and Thomson (2011) epistemological approach as "positivist-interpretivist continuum", the paper presents a methodological discussion drawing upon the study of Asian immigrants in South Australia, reflecting of photovoice use within the context of immigrants' settlement. It explores how a photo can provide a voice to a participant's experience and open a dialogue between researchers and participants, providing a rich contextual narrative by overcoming barriers of verbal expression. The paper seeks to answer the research question: How can photos capture immigrants' information needs? The study contributes to the value enrichment and more nuanced understanding of using photos as data within an information behavior study, particularly when dealing with people from non-English speaking backgrounds. The deepening and enhancing of perspective that comes from the use of photos taken by participants, which are then discussed in depth with the researcher, allows the complexities of information needs to be revealed.

2 Study Context and Procedure

The study was conducted in Adelaide, the capital city of South Australia. The South Australia population is 1,716,966, with one-third of these being immigrants (Australian Bureau of Statistics 2016). Despite the fact that the number of immigrants continues to grow, more research is needed concerning immigrants' information behavior in the Australian context (Khoir et al. 2015). The 2016 census shows that India, China, Vietnam, Philippines, and Malaysia have become the top five Asian countries contributing to immigration in Australia. A total of 35 participants living in Adelaide, the capital city of South Australia (average length of stay was 7 months), were recruited to participate in the study. They comprised: eight Indians, 15 Chinese, five Vietnamese, four Filipinos, and three Malaysians, reflecting the distribution (Creswell 2009) of the total immigrant population of each country of origin.

The original use of photovoice by Wang and Burris (1994) employed a camera provided by the researcher. From the research viewpoint, "cameras are powerful data-gathering tools for complex or busy research environments in which the fieldworker is not able to observe everything of relevance in a limited timeframe" (Hartel and Thomson 2011, p. 2221). In this study, all participants chose to use their own mobile phones with camera features, smartphones now being an everyday aspect of their lives. In the initial meeting, either face-to-face or by phone, the researcher clearly explained the procedure of picture taking. The participants were asked to provide at least five photos taken over a period of five to seven days with their own mobile phones based on the research guidelines provided. They were asked to capture facts, barriers, opportunities and any interesting things related to their experience when dealing with information during their settlement process. The photovoice guidelines used simple accessible language to ensure all participants from any background could understand what to do. The participants could also provide existing photos from their phone storage as long as they were related to the study themes. In total, 258 photos were collected, which were then discussed in the follow-up interview sessions with individuals. Interviews were between 40 and 60 min in length, conducted in English, and were recorded and transcribed for analysis. The photovoice data was analysed using a participatory analysis approach, including the process of selecting, contextualizing and codifying (Wang and Burris 1997) resulting in several themes. Codifying one photo into the appropriate theme is a challenge as one photo may contain several topics worthy of discussion.

3 Findings and Discussions

3.1 Benefits of the Photovoice Approach: Underrepresented Communities and Their Information Behavior

Photovoice had advantages in reaching underrepresented communities, including migrants, marginalized social groups, children (Cox and Benson 2017) and refugees (Hicks and Lloyd 2018) related to their information behavior. For example, using photovoice, Hicks and Lloyd (2018) recently conducted a study to confirm that visual methods can be an entry point to study information behavior, focusing on information needs, literacies and the learning practices of refugee youth. The result demonstrated that visual methods can be "a useful way to mediate a more equitable and detailed exploration of information experiences" (p. 7). Another recent study discussing the effectiveness of photovoice, Shankar et al. (2018) explored embodied mobile information practices through photos. Involving nineteen smartphone users, they used 234 photo diary entries to understand how smartphones could facilitate information seeking process. They stated that mobile devices are considered as important as extensions of the mind and body embedded in "bodily rhythms and routines".

In relation to the Asian immigrants who participated in our study by using their own smartphones to capture photos, photovoice was very effective because it passed some degree of control to the participants even as it enabled the researchers to address their aims. It elicited information and data that would not be available from the sole application of either a survey or an interview. The great strength of this technique is that it empowered participants to select criteria to discuss and then allowed them to direct the interview. Photovoice prioritized the participants' concerns and enabled them to express and led the story that they would like to share. It was found that our participants felt comfortable to tell the story through photos and expressed their unmet concerns in Australia. We found that, photovoice techniques, where participants themselves take photos and then use them as a trigger of an interview, involved a sustained engagement between the researchers and participants to create a relatively natural conversation through pictures. The engagement was also shown in Gomez's

(2016) study of information behavior of undocumented Latino immigrants in the USA and Colombia using Fotohistorias which combined participatory photography and in-person interviews.

3.2 Ethical Considerations of Using Photovoice

As the research involved images, it is necessary to consider several important aspects of research ethics. Within the ethics principles dealing with vulnerable group (Hugman et al. 2011), it should be clearly stated to the participants that all photos would be treated confidentially and used only for research purposes, ensuring the participants understood when they submitted photos with people's identifiable faces. Asking permission from people before taking photos and being aware of the sign prohibiting the taking of photos were also important to note. Participants understood that all faces were blurred in the reports to respect people's privacy. An explanation on "safety first" was also crucial, including no trespassing, not going to unsafe places and not taking photos of criminal activities, sensitive, or embarrassing situations.

3.3 Overcoming Language Barriers

Undertaking an interview in a non-native language might be a challenge for some people. Translators could be employed in such situations; however, English was used as the communication language in this study considering that around 80% of the participants considered their English skills to be good or excellent. Compared to other research methods, using photovoice allowed both interviewee and interviewer to settle into a conversation, akin to a semi-directed interview, based on photos taken by the interviewee. The photos helped to stimulate their stories and made the discussion easier. Photography offers a shared platform to communicate together when English is not the first language. Photographs are a way to communicate without relying solely on words, as also in line with previous studies (Brigham et al. (2018); Hicks and Lloyd (2018)). Photovoice is a suitable method when the researcher and the participant do not share a common language (Pollak 2017).

3.4 Access to Participants' Priorities and the Inclusion of Emotion

Photovoice discloses participants' views of their personal stories and allows researchers to understand the issues around which participants feel strong emotion (Julien et al. 2013). This is enhanced when the researcher is able to establish a relaxed communication with participants. For instance, Megan, a participant from China, showed a photo of her much loved cat and talked about how she had desperately searched on the Internet about cancer in cats following the veterinarian's diagnosis. She also spoke with her friends about the treatment. She was crying when she told the story thinking about the death of her cat and expressed her feeling of loss. This gives a real insight into how information behavior and emotions were interwoven and how people prioritized situations that were meaningful to them.

For vulnerable groups like immigrants and refugees, photovoice constitutes "a way to allow participants to exercise agency over what parts of their life they choose to show and how they choose to frame their experiences" (Lambert 2014, p. 47). In a study by Brighama et al. (2018), young refugee and immigrant women's migration towards their learning experiences in Atlantic Canada was discussed by using a transnational feminist framework. Using photography over a period of two years, they focused on formal and informal learning experiences; relationships and journeys of migration, which explained how emotion was involved in the journey and integration process. Photovoice "can involve reflecting upon inner revere, or dialogue, the experience of fleeting emotions, and very visceral embodied emotions" that can be stimulated through such photo discussion (Pink et al. 2011, p. 16). A similar idea, discussed recently by Thomson (2018), is the guided tour applied as one research technique. While photovoice uses photos to stimulate discussions, the guided tour relies upon "the tangible parts of a physical setting as entry points for exploring the different dimension of a given phenomenon" (p. 516).

3.5   The Need for Interpretation

Photovoice involves interpretive touches and requires carefully and sympathetically listening to participants' perspectives and understanding the context of their images. "A key issue is how far participants are involved in offering interpretations of the images they create" (Cox and Benson 2017, p. 14). This means that the process of analysis relied on participants' interpretations of the discussed photos, without eliminating the essence of the original story. Immigrants' everyday lives are complex, as are their perspectives, and the researcher needs to embrace the narratives of the participants into the findings. For example, our participant Franklin showed a photo of his graduation. What he wanted to express was not his delightful accomplishment of a degree, but his hope for securing a job. He spoke of the anxiety he felt in finding a good job to support his family. We note that photovoice enables researchers to see a phenomenon from the participants' point of view, addressing their assessment of their needs through photos, affirming the creativity of underexplored community groups, and supporting the sampling from different social and behavioral settings (Wang and Burris 1997).

4   Conclusion

As part of the visual method, photovoice becomes a means to study information behavior. The results show how photos could provide insights into participants' perspectives and facilitate an analytic discussion about their life experiences. Photovoice is considered to be a useful method for studying vulnerable or disadvantaged populations, such as immigrants, particularly when there are language barriers between the researcher and the participants. The technique can enable the exploration of ideas, thoughts and emotions that cannot be easily gained from traditional methods. This permits the development of a more nuanced picture of the experience of immigrants. Associated ethical concerns should also be noted.

References

Brigham, S.M., Abidi, C.B., Zhang, Z.: What participatory photography can tell us about immigrant and refugee women's learning in Atlantic Canada. Int. J. Lifelong Educ. **37**(2), 234–254 (2018)

Cox, A., Benson, M.: Visual methods and quality in information behaviour research: the cases of photovoice and mental mapping. Inf. Res. **22**(2), paper 749 (2017). http://InformationR.net/ir/22-2/paper749.html. Accessed 6 Sept 2018

Creswell, J.W.: Research Design: Qualitative, Quantitative, and Mixed Methods Approaches. Sage Publications, Thousand Oaks (2009)

Given, L.M., Opryshko, A., Julien, H., Smith, J.: Photovoice: a participatory method for information science. Proc. Am. Soc. Inf. Sci. Technol. **48**(1), 1–3 (2011)

Gomez, R.: Vulnerability and information practices among (undocumented) Latino migrants. Electron. J. Inf. Syst. Developing Countries **75**(1), 1–43 (2016)

Hartel, J., Thomson, L.: Visual approaches and photography for the study of immediate information space. J. Assoc. Inf. Sci. Technol. **62**(11), 2214–2224 (2011)

Hicks, A., Lloyd, A.: Seeing information: visual methods as entry points to information practices. J. Librarianship Inf. Sci. **50**, 229–238 (2018). Special Issue: i3 Conference 2017

Hugman, R., Pittaway, E., Bartolomei, L.: When 'Do No Harm' is not enough: the ethics of research with refugees and other vulnerable groups. Br. J. Soc. Work **41**(7), 1271–1287 (2011)

Julien, H., Given, L.M., Opryshko, A.: Photovoice: a promising method for studies of individuals' information practices. Libr. Inf. Sci. Res. **35**(4), 257–263 (2013)

Khoir, S., Du, J.T., Koronios, A.: Everyday information behaviour of Asian immigrants in South Australia: a mixed-methods exploration. Inf. Res. **20**(3), paper 687 (2015). http://InformationR.net/ir/20-3/paper687.html. Accessed 03 Dec 2018

Lambert, M.W.: Old roots: place-making and hybrid landscapes of refugee urban farmers. Unpublished PhD. Utah State University, Utah (2014)

Pink, S., Hogan, S., Bird, J.: Intersections and inroads: art therapy's contribution to visual methods. Int. J. Art Ther. Inscape **16**(1), 14–19 (2011)

Pollak, A.: Visual research in LIS: complementary and alternative methods. Libr. Inf. Sci. Res. **39**(2), 98–106 (2017)

Prosser, J., Loxley, A.: Introducing visual methods (National Centre for Research Methods Review Paper) (2008). http://eprints.ncrm.ac.uk/420/1/MethodsReviewPaperNCRM-010.pdf. Accessed 03 Dec 2018

Thomson, L.: The guided tour: a research technique for the study of situated, embodied information. Libr. Trends **66**(4), 511–534 (2018)

Shankar, S., O'Brien, H.L., Absar, R.: Rhythms of everyday life in mobile information seeking: reflections on a photo-diary study. Library Trends **66**(4), 535–567 (2018)

South Australia: 2016 Census. http://www.abs.gov.au/AUSSTATS/abs@.nsf/mediareleasesby ReleaseDate/F32A4739E3C23C74CA258148000BCDD0?OpenDocument. Accessed 05 Sept 2018

Wang, C., Burris, M.A.: Empowerment through photo novella: portraits of participation. Health Educ. Q. **21**(2), 171–186 (1994)

Wang, C., Burris, M.A.: Photovoice: concept, methodology, and use for participatory needs assessment. Health Educ. Behav. **24**(3), 369–387 (1997)

Proposing "Mobile, Finance, and Information" Toolkit for Financial Inclusion of the Poor in Developing Countries

Devendra Potnis[1](✉) 📵 and Bhakti Gala[2]

[1] University of Tennessee at Knoxville, Knoxville, TN 37996, USA
dpotnis@utk.edu
[2] Central University of Gujarat, Gandhinagar 382030, Gujarat, India

Abstract. Since 2015, the Government of India has initiated and championed the effort for transforming the country with over 400 million unbanked adults into a cashless economy so that a majority of financial transactions can be carried over mobile devices, the most widely used information and communication technology in the country. However, over 200 million adults earning less than $2 a day have no or little mobile, financial, or information literacy. This short paper reports a newly proposed interdisciplinary, six-step toolkit operationalized using a survey questionnaire, focus group prompts, and hands-on training for developing mobile, financial, and information literacy among the poor in developing countries like India. Implications for public libraries, governments, and the poor in developing countries and beyond are discussed at the end.

Keywords: Financial inclusion · Cashless economy · Poor · Mobile literacy · Financial literacy · Information literacy · India

1 Introduction

1.1 Challenges to Becoming Cashless Economy: Mobile, Financial, and Information Illiteracy

Access to finance is a prerequisite to graduate out of poverty [1]. However, as of 2015, over 2 billion adults, who did not have access to banks, were mainly from developing countries. For instance, India had 400 million unbanked adults, one of the highest percentages of financially excluded citizens in any country in the world. Hence, in 2015, the government of India launched the most ambitious financial inclusion program in the world to provide affordable financial services to the unbanked poor, with support from State Bank of India (SBI), the largest lending institution in the country, Bill and Melinda Gates Foundation, and several international financial consulting firms [2]. As a result, over 111 million unbanked poor opened bank accounts for the first time in their lives. However, access does not guarantee appropriate usage of financial services; "use of financial services" is an important factor affecting one's ability to achieve the goal of financial inclusion [3]. A majority of Indians who have access to finance do not seem to be using it optimally. For instance, in January 2016, SBI reported one of the highest credit-default rates ever since its inception in 1955 [4].

© Springer Nature Switzerland AG 2019
N. G. Taylor et al. (Eds.): iConference 2019, LNCS 11420, pp. 228–235, 2019.
https://doi.org/10.1007/978-3-030-15742-5_22

Financial information illiteracy, i.e. the inability of an individual to understand how money works or how financial service providers (FSPs) manage money [5], is prevalent in developing countries [6, 7], and is one of the main reasons for the inability of the poor to use financial services responsibly [8]. Financial information illiteracy is one of the key barriers to one's ability to succeed financially [9], since it could lower the confidence of even those who have access to finance and make them uncomfortable to use any services offered by formal FSPs like banks and credit unions [10]. It can compel such individuals to borrow from unregulated moneylenders and pawnshops that often charge usurious rates of 10 to 15 percent per month, which translates to more than 120 to 180 percent per year [11, 12].

On November 8, 2016, the government demonetized the entire country overnight, leaving millions of citizens with no or little cash. Since then as part of the Digital India mission, the government has been promoting the use of mobile apps for carrying out financial transactions, which requires the user to: (a) be literate, (b) own and operate a mobile phone [13], and (c) understand and be comfortable with the financial terms and jargons used by the banking industry [14, 15]. However, around 200 million Indians, who earn less than $2 a day, have low or no information, mobile, or financial literacy [11].

Financial literacy programs in developing countries increase financial knowledge and information-seeking behavior of borrowers, thereby controlling their over-indebtedness [12]. However, existing financial information literacy programs in India do not reach, and hence, cannot serve over 200 million illiterate and semi-literate borrowers who earn less $2 a day, since these programs: (a) are run mainly through websites that are not accessible or useful to a large majority of population whose native language is not English or is illiterate, (b) require potential beneficiaries to be affiliates of institutions like banks, schools, colleges, and local government agencies [16], and (c) do not involve, and hence, do not leverage the resources of pre-established network of public libraries in rural and urban India. Financial sector regulators like the Reserve Bank of India (RBI) and Securities and Exchange Board of India have launched "Project Financial Literacy" whereby financial education is disseminated to the target audience with the help of banks, local government machinery, schools and colleges through presentations, pamphlets, brochures, films comics, and also through RBI's website [17].

1.2 Proposed Solution: Developing Mobile, Financial, and Information Literacy

In 2017, we developed a toolkit to educate the poor so that they can use mobile phones for carrying out financial transactions. This toolkit is based on a combination of (a) 2015 Toolkit for measuring financial literacy developed and used by the Organisation for Economic Cooperation and Development [5], (b) Reference and User Service Association's Guidelines and Best Practices for financial literacy education in libraries [18], (c) information literacy standards by the Association of College and Research Libraries [19], and (d) information literacy frameworks like the Seven Pillars of information literacy and I-LEARN model [20]. In 2018, we customized the toolkit by testing it with over 150 patrons earning less than $2 a day at 10 public libraries in rural and urban Gujarat, India. We considered socioeconomic opportunities, pre-existing operational network of FSPs, government regulations, and types of financial activities borrowers engage with for contextualizing our toolkit to local conditions in India.

This short paper presents the details of our original toolkit which can be customized for building mobile, financial, and information literacy among the poor in any developing country in the world.

2 Related Work

Existing theoretical frameworks and models on financial information literacy are mainly based on or related to information literacy of students in the developed world [21]. Significantly distinct contextual factors and socioeconomic conditions in the developing world warrant for literacy programs catering to the financial information needs of individuals in the developing world. Moreover, individuals in different life stages have different financial information needs [2]. Hence, it is necessary to develop a range of financial information literacy programs specifically tailored to the needs and abilities of diverse groups of library patrons (e.g., youth, seniors, unemployed, low-income families, small business owners, etc.) [22, 23].

3 Toolkit for Building Mobile, Financial, and Information Literacy Among the Poor

We developed a survey questionnaire, focus group prompts, and hands-on training exercises in Gujarati, the native language of our study participants, for operationalizing and testing our toolkit. We helped illiterate study participants take the survey. Our interactive sessions with the poor involved several hands-on activities to reinforce the key message in the following six steps of our toolkit.

3.1 Identify

Using our toolkit, the poor can identify and determine the nature and extent of the financial information needed. They can also assess their current financial knowledge and identify gaps. Sample questions in our toolkit are: List your top-3 financial needs, Can you define the following financial concepts: collateral, interest rates, and demonetization? What is the difference between simple interest rate and compound interest rate? What is the difference between savings account and checking account? Our toolkit also makes sure that study participants learn that: new financial information is constantly being produced and that there is always more to learn; financial information literacy involves developing a learning habit so new financial information is being actively sought all the time; ideas and opportunities are created by investigating/seeking financial information; types of financial information, characteristics of the different types of financial information source available to them and how they may be affected by the format (digital, print); and various issues of accessibility, and finally, various services that are available to help and how to access them.

3.2   Plan and Gather

The toolkit trains the poor to locate and access needed financial information effectively and efficiently. They learn to construct strategies for locating financial information. Sample relevant questions from our toolkit are: Do you know how public libraries provide access to various types of financial information? Have you ever used mobile phones or computers to collect (search, seek, or receive) financial information? What are the pros and cons of seeking and searching for financial information from formal vs. informal sources? We also explain the difference between formal sources such as banks, cooperative banks, credit unions, public libraries, books, news articles, etc. and informal sources like family, friends, local moneylenders, colleagues at work, etc.

With the help of our survey questionnaire, focus group prompts, and hands-on exercises, study participants understand: a range of searching techniques available for finding financial information, the differences between search tools, recognizing their advantages and limitations, why complex search strategies can make a difference to the breadth and depth of financial information found, the need to develop approaches to searching so that new tools are sought for each new question (not relying always on the most familiar resources), the need to revise keywords and adapt search strategies according to the resources available and/or results found, how financial information and data is organized, digitally and in print sources, how libraries provide access to resources, how digital technologies are providing collaborative tools to create and share financial information, the issues involved in collecting new financial information, the need to keep up to date with new financial information, the difference between free and paid-for resources, the risks involved in operating in a virtual world, and the importance of appraising and evaluating search results.

3.3   Evaluate

Using our toolkit, the poor can compare and evaluate financial information and its sources critically, and incorporate selected financial information into their knowledgebase and value system. Toolkit includes the following questions: Are you aware of any of the following digital payment methods: banking cards, USSD, AESP, UPI, mobile wallets, micro ATMs, mobile banking, Internet banking, point-of-sale, and banks pre-paid cards? [24] Report the most valuable aspect or characteristic of financial information for you (with the following choices: reliability, validity, accuracy, authority, timeliness, point of view or bias, and other: _). Hands-on-training demonstrates calculations including but not limited to: the interest they would end up paying if they borrow INR 5,000 for a year with 10% interest rate, and the rate of inflation by comparing prices of sugar, cooking oil, rice, and diesel, among other commodities, in 2001 and 2011.

Our survey questionnaire, focus group prompts, and hands-on exercises cover the following topics: the financial information and data landscape of their local context, issues of quality, accuracy, relevance, bias, reputation and credibility relating to financial information and sources, how financial information is evaluated and published, to help inform personal evaluation process, and the importance of consistency in data collection.

3.4   Manage

With the help of our toolkit, the poor, individually or as a member of a group, can organize and communicate financial information to accomplish a specific purpose like financial planning. Sample questions in our toolkit include: what key steps do you plan to take or have you already taken to secure your future financially? Are you aware of any mutual funds, stocks, bonds, fixed deposits, etc.? What factors could possibly affect your financial planning for the future? Our survey questionnaire, focus group prompts, and hands-on exercises make the poor understand: the need to keep systematic records, the role of professionals such as data managers and librarians, who can advise, assist and support with all aspects of information management, that different forms of writing/presentation style can be used to present information to different communities, that data can be presented in different ways, and that individuals can take an active part in the creation of information through traditional publishing and digital technologies.

3.5   Use

The toolkit educates the poor for understanding the economic, legal, and social issues surrounding the use of financial information professionally, ethically, and legally. Sample survey questions include: What are some of the ethical and legal challenges (e.g., your privacy, security of your financial data, etc.) to deal with financial information? [25] Can you recollect three recent instances of using financial information sought, searched, or received from any of your formal or informal sources? How was the process of using financial information in those three instances? What are some of the key lessons of using financial information? Hands-on training focused on: connecting to Wi-Fi, searching information on the Internet over mobile phones, security options available on the study participants' mobile phones, and using BHIM, a mobile app developed by the Government of India for mobile payments. Our toolkit makes sure that the poor understand: their responsibility to be honest in all aspects of financial information handling and dissemination (e.g., copyright, plagiarism and intellectual property issues), the importance of storing and sharing financial information and data ethically, and the need to adopt appropriate methods for handling financial information.

3.6   Reflect and Learn

Using this toolkit, the poor can reflect on the process of using financial information and learn from their experience for future instances of using similar knowledge to make financial decisions. Sample questions are: Can you share any of your mistakes while seeking, searching, storing, managing, processing, or using financial information in the past? What advice would you offer to others for using financial information carefully or not committing the same mistake you did? Our toolkit makes sure that study participants understand: the significance of reflecting on the process of planning, accessing, gathering, managing, evaluating, and using financial information, and the importance of leaning and applying knowledge for making financial decisions.

4 Implications

Due to lack of innovation and resources, public libraries in a majority of developing countries are in the state of despair. A drive to becoming a cashless society presents a timely opportunity for these knowledge hubs to be more relevant. Public libraries can serve the financial information needs of their communities without a sales pitch or a hidden agenda [26] by educating citizens to use their finances smartly [27]. The UNESCO Public Library Manifesto (2016) advocates that a public library should facilitate the development of information and computer literacy skills [28]. Our toolkit offers a novel opportunity for over 200K public libraries in developing countries to play a key role in building financial information skills among millions of poor. Using our survey questionnaire, focus group prompts, and hands-on training, public librarians can make patrons more confident and independent for carrying out financial transactions. Public libraries could demonstrate their value in implementing financial inclusion undertaken by governments in developing countries. The pre-existing network of public libraries could serve as a key partner for governments with minimal investment. People of all ages across the world need help managing money, and with uncertainty about jobs, paying for credit and debt issues, and complex decisions about investing, public librarians in the US are taking a leadership role in financial education [29]. Our toolkit could also guide public libraries in the US to develop customized financial information literacy programs for targeting local communities. Librarians could learn how to develop appropriate content, use our toolkit, and deliver services to diverse patron populations. Our toolkit could inform ongoing efforts like the ALA/FINRA Smart investing@your library program and the ALA/Federal Reserve Money Smart Week@Your Library program to boost financial information literacy in the US.

5 Conclusion

The interdisciplinary toolkit presents a timely learning and partnership opportunity for thousands of public libraries, governments, and millions of poor across the world. Our survey questionnaire, focus group prompts, and hands-on-training exercises effectively operationalize the toolkit for librarians and the poor to develop mobile, financial, and information literacy, for using mobile phones to carry out financial transactions.

Acknowledgement. We are thankful to OCLC/ALISE LIS Research Grant Program for funding this project.

References

1. Honohan, P.: Household financial assets in the process of development. The World Bank. Policy Research Working Paper 3965 (2006)
2. Consultative Group to Assist the Poor: Can India achieve universal digital financial inclusion? (2015). http://www.cgap.org/blog/can-india-achieve-universal-digital-financial-inclusion

3. Mohan, L., Potnis, D., Mattoo, N.: A pan-India footprint of microfinance borrowers from an exploratory survey: impact of over-indebtedness on financial inclusion of the poor. Enterp. Dev. Microfinance J. **24**(1), 55–71 (2013)
4. Antony, A.: State bank of India default swaps jumps to highest since 2014. Bloomberg, http://www.bloomberg.com/news/articles/2016-02-10/default-risk-at-state-bank-of-india-surges-on-bad-debt-concerns. Accessed 4 Dec 2018
5. Organisation for Economic Co-operation and Development (OECD): OECD/INFE Toolkit for measuring financial literacy and financial inclusion, Paris, France (2015). https://www.oecd.org/daf/fin/financial-education/2015_OECD_INFE_Toolkit_Measuring_Financial_Literacy.pdf. Accessed 4 Dec 2018
6. Amari, M.: Financial literacy and economics education among young adults: an observation from Tunisia. J. Bus. Financ. Librariansh. **20**(3), 209–219 (2015)
7. Potnis, D., Demissie, D.: Barriers to socio-economic opportunities in Africa: an eGovernment perspective. In: iConference 2009 Proceedings. University of North Carolina-Chapel Hill, NC (2009)
8. Mohan, L., Potnis, D.: Mobile banking for the unbanked poor without mobile phones: comparing three innovative mobile banking services in India. In: Proceedings of the 48th Hawaii International Conference on System Sciences, Kauai, HI, pp. 2168–2176 (2015)
9. Bisht, S., Mishra, V.: ICT-driven financial inclusion initiatives for urban poor in a developing economy: Implications for public policy. Behav. Inf. Technol. **35**(10), 817–832 (2016)
10. Hermes, N., Lensink, R.: Microfinance: It's outreach, impact, and sustainability. World Dev. **39**(6), 875–881 (2011)
11. Rosenberg, R., Gonzalez, A., Narain, S.: The new moneylenders: are the poor being exploited by high microcredit interest rates? (CGAP Occasional Paper No. 15). World Bank, Washington, D.C. http://documents.worldbank.org/curated/en/321891468337256746/The-new-moneylenders-are-the-poor-being-exploited-by-high-microcredit-interest-rates. Accessed 4 Dec 2018
12. Mohan, L., Potnis, D., Alter, S.: Information systems to support "Door-step Banking": enabling scalability of microfinance to serve more of the poor at the bottom of the pyramid. Commun. Assoc. Inf. Syst. **33**(1), 423–442 (2013)
13. Potnis, D.: Cell-phone-enabled empowerment of women earning less than $1 per day. IEEE Technol. Soc. **30**(2), 39–45 (2011)
14. Potnis, D.: Inequalities creating economic barriers to owning mobile phones in India: factors responsible for the gender digital divide. Inf. Dev. **32**(5), 1332–1342 (2016)
15. Gibson, J., McKenzie, D., Zia, B.: The impact of financial literacy training for migrants. World Bank Econ. Rev. **28**(1), 130–161 (2014)
16. Raina, N.: Financial literacy and credit counselling a demand-side solution to financial inclusion. J. Commer. Manag. Thought **5**(4), 659–675 (2014)
17. Kaur, M., Arora, A., Vohra, T.: Financial literacy among university students: a study of Guru Nanak Dev university. Asia-Pacific Manag. Res. Innov. **11**(2), 143–152 (2015)
18. Keller, K., LeBeau, C., Malafi, E., Spackman, A.: Meeting the need for library-based financial literacy education. Ref. User Serv. Q. **54**(3), 47–51 (2015)
19. Association of College and Research Libraries: Information literacy competency standards for higher education. http://www.ala.org/Template.cfm?Section=Home&template=/ContentManagement/ContentDisplay.cfm&ContentID=33553. Accessed 4 Dec 2018
20. SCONUL: The SCONUL seven pillars of information literacy: A research lens for higher education, Society of College, National and University Libraries. http://www.sconul.ac.uk/sites/default/files/documents/researchlens.pdf. Accessed 4 Dec 2018

21. Faulkner, A.: A systematic review of financial literacy as a termed concept: more questions than answers. J. Bus. Financ. Librariansh. **20**(1/2), 7–26 (2015)
22. Špiranec, S., Zorica, M., Simončić, G.: Libraries and financial literacy: perspectives from emerging markets. J. Bus. Financ. Librariansh. **17**(3), 262–278 (2012)
23. Potnis, D.: Culture's consequences: economic barriers to owning mobile phones experienced by women in India. Telemat. Inform. **33**(2), 356–369 (2016)
24. Potnis, D., Regenstreif-Harms, R., Cortez, E.: Identifying key steps for developing mobile applications & mobile websites for libraries. Inf. Technol. Libr. **35**(3), 40–58 (2016)
25. Potnis, D.: Mobile technologies & socio-economic opportunities for disadvantaged women: a study of information behavior in a developing nation context. ERIC (2010). http://www.eric.ed.gov/ERICWebPortal/recordDetail?accno=ED520178. Accessed 4 Dec 2018
26. Bell, L., Peters, T., Monsour, M., Pope, K.: Financial information literacy services at your library. Searcher **17**(6), 18–53 (2009)
27. Smith, A., Eschenfelder, K.: Public libraries in an age of financial complexity: toward enhancing community financial literacy. Libr. Q. **83**(4), 299–320 (2013)
28. UNESCO: UNESCO Public Library Manifesto, 15 August 2016. http://www.unesco.org/webworld/libraries/manifestos/libraman.html. Accessed 4 Dec 2018
29. Monsour, M.: Libraries innovate with new financial education programs. Pub. Libr. **51**(2), 36–43 (2012)

Documenting the Undocumented: Privacy and Security Guidelines for Humanitarian Work with Irregular Migrants

Sara Vannini[1], Ricardo Gomez[2], and Bryce Clayton Newell[3(✉)]

[1] Department of Communication, University of Washington, Seattle, USA
vanninis@uw.edu
[2] Information School, University of Washington, Seattle, USA
rgomez@uw.edu
[3] School of Information Science, University of Kentucky, Lexington, USA
brycenewell@uky.edu

Abstract. Humanitarian organizations frequently do not fully address the implications of collecting, storing, and using data about vulnerable populations. We propose a conceptual framework for Humanitarian Information Activities (HIA), especially in the context of undocumented migration. We examine this framework in the light of both a survey of the literature and a pilot study that examines HIA activities in three distinct contexts: (1) higher education institutions that provide support to undocumented students, (2) non-profit organizations that provide legal support to undocumented immigrants, and (3) humanitarian organizations assisting undocumented migrants near the US-Mexico border. We discuss both technological and human risks in HIA, the limitations of privacy self-management, and the need for clear privacy-related guidelines for HIA. We conclude suggesting guidelines to strengthen the privacy protection offered to vulnerable populations by humanitarian organizations in the context of irregular migration.

Keywords: Privacy · Data justice · Humanitarian Information Activities · Migration

1 Introduction

Migration and privacy crises are central topics of public discourse today, but they are only recently starting to be addressed together [1]. The growing and continuing displacement and transnational migration of millions of people around the world has been met with increased surveillance and "datafication of migration" by a variety of actors [2, 3]. Because migrants, humanitarian organizations, and governments are increasingly using digital technologies to facilitate, support, or regulate migration, migrants are increasingly leaving "digital traces of their migration" [3, 4]. Governmental institutions and humanitarian organizations are utilizing a variety of information and communication technologies (ICTs) as part of migration-related operations without any widely accepted approach for ensuring that human rights are respected throughout these information-rich activities [5].

© Springer Nature Switzerland AG 2019
N. G. Taylor et al. (Eds.): iConference 2019, LNCS 11420, pp. 236–244, 2019.
https://doi.org/10.1007/978-3-030-15742-5_23

In the context of humanitarian organizations, all "activities and programs which may include the collection, storage, processing, analysis, further use, transmission, and public release of data and other forms of information by humanitarian actors and/or affected communities" are defined by Greenwood et al. [5, p. 5] as Humanitarian Information Activities (HIA). Although humanitarian organizations often focus on helping migrants during times of personal crisis, they frequently overlook the additional vulnerabilities and unintended risks that the careless collection, storage, and use of personal information about migrants can cause. This can happen at the macro level, due to the general datafication of migration, or at the micro level (for example, during intake interviews at migrant shelters or legal-aid centers). In the humanitarian sector, these HIA-related activities are often pursued as forms of surveillance as care [6, pp. 33–34], [7].

ICTs can help organizations make their work more efficient and effective, and they can help the populations they serve by providing them access to relevant information and services. However, the use of ICTs also involves data- and privacy-related risks, as electronic data can be subjected to security breakages, leaks, hacks, inadvertent disclosure, and disclosure through legal processes (e.g., subpoenas, court orders). In certain cases, the inadvertent or malicious exposure of personal data can significantly exacerbate the risks for particularly vulnerable populations. In the case of undocumented migrants, disclosure of sensitive information and documents may expose them to detention, deportation, and other forms of physical and psychological violence. Nevertheless, the efforts organizations are making to protect the personal information of the individuals they serve, and the remaining risks related to their HIA have not been widely investigated in academic research.

The recommendations we propose echo the approach of the European Union's General Data Protection Regulation (GDPR), which now imposes significant legal obligations on humanitarian organizations to comply with strict data protection rules [7, 8].

The remainder of the paper is organized as follows: first, we briefly review related work in scholarly literature on humanitarian action related to migration and HIA. Second, we present the methodology for our work. Third, we discuss the review of the literature in contrast to the interviews. Finally, we conclude with a proposed framework and recommendations to strengthen the privacy protections in HIA-related work by humanitarian organizations serving undocumented migrants and other vulnerable populations.

2 HIA-Related Risks and Humanitarian Intervention

Humanitarian organizations provide humanitarian assistance for populations that are particularly vulnerable and deprived of their human rights. This includes humanitarian organizations that work with undocumented migrants in the US. When migrants arrive in the US fleeing from violence, climate change-related disasters, or lack of opportunities in their home countries, they frequently cross the border without authorization. They are labeled as "illegal aliens" and, as undocumented people in the country, they have almost no legal path to legalize their situation: they have limited rights, limited possibilities to appeal when abused, and limited legal access to basic societal services, such as education, healthcare, and the formal job market [9–11]. They are mostly doomed to live abjected lives [9] and in a "state of exception" [12].

For humanitarian organizations working with undocumented immigrants, coordinating humanitarian relief presents many challenges, many of which are rooted in lack of funding, conflicting organizational goals, professional and organizational status hierarchies, and the tendency of individual organizations to maximize their own autonomy [13]. They frequently do not prioritize the protection of information and privacy rights of the populations they serve. Greenwood et al. [5] point to a disconnect between theory and practice to effectively alleviate humanitarian organizations' HIA-related risks in an exhaustive and coordinated manner, showing how HIA conducted through the use of ICTs may cause harm and violate the basic human rights of the vulnerable populations the organizations are assisting. These issues tend to exacerbate the vulnerability of undocumented migrants, whose status already places them at risk.

There is a striking lack of generally accepted protocols and measures in place to ensure the privacy and protection of vulnerable people within the humanitarian space: for example, while the Signal Code promulgated by the Harvard Humanitarian Initiative offers "guidance on articulating the human rights relating to information and data" [5, p. 9], specifically addressing HIA, the commonly used Core Humanitarian Standard on Quality and Accountability [14] does not address privacy protections or on the implications of privacy disclosures as part of its standards. Furthermore, both frameworks are addressed to organizations working with populations affected by short-term crises but fail to include the specific challenges of dealing with people such as undocumented migrants or refugees, whose crises are usually more long-term.

3 Methodology

In the fall of 2017, we conducted a small set of interviews (n = 9) with staff and volunteers of humanitarian organizations working with undocumented migrants in the US, in order to assess their awareness and practices regarding the protection of information and privacy of the people they serve. We interviewed five staff members in different roles from four different advocacy groups, and four from two higher education institutions on the US West Coast. Interviewees included executive directors, coordinators, legal advisors and Information Technology department directors. We identified three emerging themes in the literature review, and used these to code and analyze the interviews using a double content analysis process: a first bottom-up phase aimed to identify thematic areas and recurrent topics with the help of qualitative analysis software Dedoose; and a second phase including a top-down approach, moving from the first thematic areas identified to a structure reflecting the three themes emerging from the literature review. Finally, we collected admissions and enrollment forms, flyers, web sites, videos, and online forms, and observed social media pages with the aim to better understand the practices of the organizations involved.

This is an exploratory study of a novel topic. The sample size is small, so it is not necessarily representative of all HIA practices, but it offers valuable insight for future work in this area. We report the results of the interviews using aggregate organizational personas, to protect our interviewees' privacy and the organizations' operations. Thus, "University of Nepantla" will represent the persona for the for the two higher education institutions, and "La Resaca" the aggregate organizational persona for the four interviewed advocacy groups.

4   HIA in Theory: A Review of the Literature on HIA

Our review of the literature identified three key trends related to HIA-related risks and different levels of awareness and security practices connected to them. First, risks are related to both *technology* (inadequate or low-quality security systems, poor routine maintenance practices, loose internal controls, and an underutilization of necessary protection tools and services) and *human behavior* (improper training amongst organizations, poor onboarding and offboarding practices, limited knowledge resources available to the organization, and even poorly engaged staff). Second, there is a *lack of clear guidelines* (reflecting a corresponding need to implement them) on how to deal with data and information. Finally, organizations need to develop strategies that go *beyond the logic of privacy self-management*. The following sections discuss these three trends in relation to related work in the specialized literature.

4.1   HIA-Related Risks Involve Both Technology and People

One of the primary issues that organizations engaging with technology must deal with is data security. The risk of data breakages, hacks, and leaks are a reality not only in the corporate and governmental worlds. In the wake of cybercrime attacks, cyber-warfare, and with more (and more sophisticated) interception and surveillance technology available to governments, the United Nations Office for the Coordination of Humanitarian Affairs (OCHA) has been vocal about concerns for humanitarian organizations' data systems and online activity [15]. Often, the inability of humanitarian organizations to introduce proper safeguards is tied to limited resources, and this is particularly true for smaller humanitarian organizations operating only at a local level. The costs of complex security technologies and properly trained personnel are often difficult for these organizations to afford or justify. Risks to the information privacy of vulnerable populations can also be increased by human factors (e.g., negligently handling information, whether willfully or not). Internal controls and plans to improve workers' knowledge and best practices are necessary but often missing [16].

4.2   Clear Guidelines for HIA Are Needed, Especially in the Context of Migration

Greenwood et al. [5, p. 61] state that there are "gaps in international humanitarian and human rights law and standards around humanitarian information activities." Based on the idea that information is a basic "humanitarian need," they advocate for the adoption of "minimum ethical and technical standards for HIA, grounded in an accepted foundation of human rights standards and international law" [5, p. 5]. They identify five rights of all people related to HIA based on three criteria: (i) they fit in with existing declarations, laws or conventions relevant to human rights; (ii) they apply to all people independently of technology, and (iii) they reinforce and translate existing rights into the specific context of HIA. These five rights are: *Right to Information*, *Right to Protection* from threats and harms, *Right to Privacy and Security*, *Right to Data Agency*, and *Right to Redress and Rectification* [5, p. 13]. Each one of these rights also applies to the protection of migrants, and especially the most vulnerable (asylum seekers, refugees, or irregular and undocumented migrants).

Current approaches to data protection within HIA are insufficient, as no comprehensive doctrine guiding the execution of HIA in accordance with ethical codes of conduct, rules, laws, or policies exists [17, 18], nor are accountability measures and auditing entities in place—even the European Union's pioneering protection of "data subjects" under the General Data Protection Regulation (GDPR) [19, Para. 4] suffers from limitations in this regard (e.g., its jurisdiction is limited to EU member states).

4.3 Privacy Self-management Is Not Enough

Privacy self-management rests on the idea that individuals need to control access to, as well as the use and retention of, their personal data through choosing to consent or not to privacy-related terms, conditions, and agreements. Privacy self-management promotes a notion of an informed user being able to make decisions about giving or withholding consent to the collection, use, and disclosure of personal data, including short and long-term consequences of such consent, in their best self-interest [20].

Although privacy self-management might resonate with the idea of empowering people to make their own choices, scholars recognize that its use is problematic and has been pushed "beyond its limits" [20, p. 1903]. Solove [20] identifies a number of cognitive and structural problems that fault privacy self-management, which prevent people's ability to truly weigh the costs and benefits of consenting.

5 HIA in Practice: Interviews with Staff and Volunteers

In this section, we present the results of interviews in the form of narratives of organizational personas, which aggregate the findings and protect the identity of the informants.

5.1 HIA-Related Risks Involve Both Technology and People

University of Nepantla: The "University of Nepantla" prohibits ICE from entering campus to conduct immigration raids or locate undocumented students. Sensitive personal information at the university is stored on a secure multi-authentication system server which gives many students peace of mind. A closer audit of the security and authentication of the information systems in use, and of the staff training for awareness and compliance with privacy and security protocols, though, could help strengthen the HIA-related practices of the university. The institution leverages technology to safeguard undocumented students who attend widely photographed events (where the risk that photos might be published and tagged on social media is heightened). They have a low-tech method of helping students to avoid cameras if they want, consisting of providing large wearable stickers as a signal that they wish to not be photographed. This system is not infallible, and a coordinator makes sure to check photos that are posted online.

La Resaca: Organizers at the non-profit organization "La Resaca" regret that they don't have enough funding to implement highly secure information systems. "La Resaca" is a small organization and cannot afford to have as much internal staffing dedicated exclusively to creating, securing, and maintaining their servers as some larger organizations. Thus, they rely primarily on volunteer labor, free online services and document management systems, and basic (if any) encryption protections. Third-party services often manage and store their databases to guarantee the data is secured. Third-party organizations are also responsible for addressing any security problems that arise. However, the privacy policies of these organizations are mostly not questioned by "La Resaca." "La Resaca" has considered moving their sensitive data to overseas servers, where information would be stored beyond the jurisdiction of the US government, and to formulate other strategies for improving data security.

"La Resaca" generally uses both paper and electronic methods to collect and store data. This is usually determined by client preferences, the affordability of technologies available to them, and staff expertise. Information that requires high levels of accuracy, such as anything related to people's legal status, is usually duplicated in both electronic and paper files. The organization normally decides to convert the paper documents into electronic form only when they are sure that they will continue working with a person. Otherwise, the initial information is collected only on paper and then shredded. The organization is reluctant to choose one way of storing data over the other.

5.2 Clear Guidelines for HIA Are Needed, Especially in the Context of Migration

Protections at University of Nepantla: At the "University of Nepantla," staff members are aware of the possibility of unwilling disclosure of sensitive information, either because of failure of technologies used within the organization or because of human errors and obliviousness in evaluating information disclosure. Obliviousness, in some cases, includes misunderstanding the privacy laws (e.g., FERPA) to which institutions are required to adhere. Only higher-ranking staff members, in fact, do receive training on FERPA and in privacy and security. According to our data, staff members who did not receive any training usually err on the side of caution and mention letting the students themselves be the ones who actively protect their own security. Also, members of the staff usually rely on previous personal knowledge and self-training to compensate for the lack of formal on-the-job data protection training. Similarly, no structured training is set up when dealing with student volunteers that help manage services.

Protections at La Resaca: Legal standards affect the work of non-profits like "La Resaca." However, non-profits normally do not have concrete sets of privacy standards or provide privacy-related training to their employees and volunteers. Staff members usually provide answers to questions that arise organically in their work, based on the unique needs of their clients. Occasionally, they might invite speakers to present about specific privacy issues that arise in their work.

5.3 Privacy Self-management Is Not Enough

Most of the organizations in our study discussed giving the undocumented individuals the agency to decide regarding their own privacy. Supporting entities and departments at the "**University of Nepantla**" mostly leave it up to the students themselves to disclose their undocumented status, except when it comes to matters of tuition and financial aid. In very few cases, Facebook groups hosted by the institution are closed to outsiders, and access is restricted to verified students that participate in in-person activities; the group moderator emphasizes the importance of privacy settings and behaviors, but ultimately, each student manages their own online presence, privacy settings and self-disclosure.

However, staff at all the organizations we spoke with declared that it is a priority for them to respond to any privacy concerns their clients had by explaining the way they do address privacy issues. For example, at the "University of Nepantla," staff explain the security protocols that are in place and the institutional obligations to each student individually. "**La Resaca**" works in a similar fashion. Lawyers and staff members dedicate time to their clients to make sure they understand what they are agreeing to, as well as the measures they can take if their confidentiality is not respected.

6 Discussion and Recommendations

Humanitarian organizations may not be doing enough to protect the information privacy of vulnerable populations in the context of irregular migration, and they may lack solid, agreed-upon best practices to draw from. Humanitarian organizations frequently fail to address both the technical and human-factor risks presented by even the most basic information systems they use to collect, process, and store information about vulnerable populations. They employ no clear and commonly accepted guidelines for protection of information of vulnerable populations. This might have several possible different consequences for how data will be handled in the case of requests from external entities, which include the disclosure of sensitive information inadvertently by untrained staff members and volunteers. Furthermore, there are no entities in charge of promoting and holding organizations accountable for their information practices, especially in the context of irregular transnational migration. Well-known guidelines for HIA-related accountability [5, 14] were not widely known within or adopted by the organizations we studied. Even though these guidelines fail to explicitly address information privacy and data security, they do provide standards for HIA which organizations did not, however, adopt.

Based on this analysis, we suggest the **HIA Privacy Guidelines** (summarized in Table 1, below) to strengthen the privacy protection by humanitarian organizations working in the context of irregular migration. These guidelines invite humanitarian organizations to collect as little personal information as possible to conduct their work, to better protect such information from technical and human risks of disclosure, to train their staff and volunteers in secure data collection and management, to work with other organizations that share in these basic privacy principles for HIA, and to make sure they provide their services even to those individuals that might decide to opt-out from complying and sharing information about themselves, either digitally or at all. These recommendations also clearly outline possible areas for future collaboration between humanitarian organizations, academic researchers, and technologists. Future work needs to test and refine these proposed guidelines.

Table 1. Privacy Guidelines for Humanitarian Information Activities (HIA)

HIA Privacy Guidelines
Guidelines to strengthen privacy protections in the context of irregular migration.
PRUDENCE
Collect as little information as possible
PROTECTION
Secure the information you do need to collect and store
TRAINING
Make sure volunteers and staff are aware and trained on privacy protection; help your users be more privacy aware
SHARE ALIKE
Work with collaborators and partners who share your concern
NON-DISCRIMINATION
Offer services to all, including those who do not want to share their personal information

The mass forced migration of people around the world has become a particularly difficult challenge of our time. Due to the significant risks potentially imposed on these vulnerable populations through the collection, analysis, and dissemination of personal (or personally-identifiable) information, humanitarian organizations must take responsibility for the implications of the data they collect about their intended beneficiaries. Otherwise, the best intentions of humanitarian organizations may well exacerbate the vulnerability of the very populations they intend to serve. Information is like toothpaste: once it is out of the tube, it is almost impossible to get it back in.

References

1. Maitland, C., Braman, S., Jaeger, P.T.: Digital Lifeline?: ICTs for Refugees and Displaced Persons. MIT Press, Cambridge (2018)
2. Broeders, D., Dijstelbloem, H.: The datafication of mobility and migration management: the mediating state and its consequences. In: van der Ploeg, I., Pridmore, J. (eds.) Digitizing Identities: Doing Identity in a Networked World, pp. 242–260. Routledge, London (2016)
3. Garelli, G., Tazzioli, M.: Migrant Digitalities and the Politics of Dispersal: An Introduction, Border Criminologies Blog, Oxford Law Faculty, 22 May 2018
4. Broeders, D.: Breaking Down Anonymity: Digital Surveillance of Irregular Migrants in Germany and the Netherlands. Amsterdam University Press, Amsterdam (2009)

5. Greenwood, F., Howarth, C., Escudero Pool, D., Raymond, N.A., Scarnecchia, D.P.: The Signal Code: A Human Rights Approach to Information During Crisis. Harvard, MA (2017)
6. Newell, B.C., Gomez, R., Guajardo, V.E.: Information seeking, technology use, and vulnerability among migrants at the United States-Mexico border. Inform. Soc. **32**(3), 176–191 (2016)
7. rbharani: The GDPR is a unique opportunity to get humanitarian data protection right. The Digital Responder, 30 December 2017
8. Pfeifle, S.: Doing data protection well in humanitarian efforts. The International Association of Privacy Professionals: the privacy advisor, 25 October 2017
9. Gonzales, R.G., Chavez, L.R.: 'Awakening to a Nightmare': abjectivity and illegality in the lives of undocumented 1.5-generation latino immigrants in the United States. Curr. Anthropol. **53**(3), 255–281 (2012)
10. Miller, S.A.D.: Faith based organizations and international responses to forced migration. In: The Changing World Religion Map, pp. 3115–3133. Springer, Dordrecht, (2015)
11. Noll, G.: Why human rights fail to protect undocumented migrants. Eur. J. Migr. Law **12**, 241–272 (2010)
12. Agamben, G.: Homo Sacer: Sovereign Power and Bare Life, 1st edn. Stanford University Press, Standford (1998)
13. Saab, D.J., et al.: Building global bridges: coordination bodies for improved information sharing among humanitarian relief agencies. In: Proceedings of the 5th International ISCRAM Conference, Washington, DC, USA (2008)
14. CHS Alliance, Groupe URD, and The Sphere Project: Core Humanitarian Standard: Core Humanitarian Standard on Quality and Accountability (2014)
15. Gilman, D., Baker, L.: Humanitarianism in the age of cyber-warfare: towards the principled and secure use of information in humanitarian emergencies. United Nations Office for the Coordination of Humanitarian Affairs, OCHA Policy Development and Studies Branch, 011 (2014)
16. Kohnke, A., Shoemaker, D., Sigler, K.E.: The Complete Guide to Cybersecurity Risks and Controls. CRC Press, Boca Raton (2016)
17. Raymond, N., Al Achkar, Z., Verhulst, S., Berens, J., Barajas, L.: Building data responsibility into humanitarian action. OCHA - United Nations Office for the Coordination of Humanitarian Affairs, 18 (2016)
18. Raymond, N.A., Card, B., al Achkar, Z.: What is 'Humanitarian Communication'? towards standard definitions and protections for the humanitarian use of ICTs. European Interagency Security Forum (EISF) (2015)
19. GDPR, Regulation (EU) 2016/679 of the European Parliament and of the Council of 27 April 2016 on the protection of natural persons with regard to the processing of personal data and on the free movement of such data, and repealing Directive 95/46/EC (General Data Protection Regulation), vol. L119 (2016)
20. Solove, D.J.: Introduction: privacy self-management and the consent dilemma. Harvard Law Rev. **126**(7), 1880–1903 (2013)

Supporting Communities Through Public Libraries and Infrastructure

The Role of Community Data in Helping Public Libraries Reach and Serve Underserved Communities

Kathleen Campana[1]([⊠]) (iD), J. Elizabeth Mills[2] (iD),
and Michelle H. Martin[2] (iD)

[1] Kent State University, Kent, OH 44240, USA
kcampan2@kent.edu
[2] University of Washington, Seattle, WA 98195, USA
{jemillsl,mhmarti}@uw.edu

Abstract. Public libraries have recognized that children and families in underserved communities, who often need their services the most, are not coming into the library due to a variety of barriers. To reach and serve these children and families, libraries have been taking their programs and services out into community locations to meet families where they are. To do this effectively libraries need to collect data on these community groups to better understand their needs. Project LOCAL, an IMLS-funded grant that explored how libraries are going out into their communities to reach and serve families in underserved communities, found that libraries are collecting community data from a variety of sources to understand the needs of their communities. Furthermore, the libraries are using this community need data in the planning and development of their programs and services offered to these families.

Keywords: Community data · Public libraries · Needs analysis ·
Underserved communities · Children and families

1 Introduction

Every day public libraries engage with children and families in their communities through various free in-library programs and services that support learning for children and families. Research has demonstrated that storytimes in particular provide a strong foundation in early learning through an intentional focus on early literacy skills in the development and delivery of the program [1, 2]. Furthermore, storytimes are sites of an array of early learning domains such as STEM, social-emotional and others, and the actors and participants in these programs embody important roles in facilitating the learning process for children [3]. The public library has also recently formally recognized its role in promoting family engagement around literacy and learning through programs and services designed for the whole family, which offer spaces for adults and children to learn and interact together [4]. Because of this family engagement and learning support, the public library is considered an important resource for supporting families in underserved communities [5]. However, there is a concern that public

© Springer Nature Switzerland AG 2019
N. G. Taylor et al. (Eds.): iConference 2019, LNCS 11420, pp. 247–253, 2019.
https://doi.org/10.1007/978-3-030-15742-5_24

libraries may not be reaching these families, who likely need the support most of all [5, 6], because the families are not coming into the library due to a variety of barriers. In fact, one study found that though public library attendance is at 66% among children with high socioeconomic status, it is only at 36% among those with the lowest socioeconomic status [7]. When families cannot or do not come into the library to take advantage of programs and services, they miss important, free resources that could help them support their children's learning and development.

While a lack of research exists that reveals the extent to which libraries "reach out to and engage members of vulnerable populations" [8, p. 316], anecdotal evidence indicated that some public libraries have found ways to transform their approach by offering programs outside of their walls to engage families in underserved communities where they are and support their children's learning and development. However, to engage these families effectively, libraries must gain a better understanding of their needs and the communities in which they exist [9]. Doing needs assessments and collecting community data is one way to gain an understanding of community needs, especially with underserved communities. There is also a lack of research, though, that reveals how, if at all, libraries are endeavoring to understand the needs of their communities.

Regardless of the lack of research, the public library field appears to have recognized the importance of interacting with and listening to their communities in order to better understand their needs and aspirations [10, 11]. Furthermore, they have acknowledged the importance of collecting community data, with ALA webinars and conference programs being offered on the topic [12, 13]. However, there remains a lack of understanding as to whether libraries are actually collecting data on their communities and how they might be doing so. And if they are collecting community data, where are they collecting it from and how might they be using the data to inform their outreach program development?

2 Methodology

To better understand how libraries are transforming their role in reaching and serving families in underserved communities, Project LOCAL[1]—an Institute of Museum and Library Services-funded grant—was designed to explore and understand how libraries are going outside of their walls into community locations to serve children and families in underserved communities. Because it is important for a library to understand a community's needs when serving them [9], as a part of Project LOCAL, researchers explored how libraries are understanding the needs of the children and families in underserved communities and how libraries are using that information to develop their programs and services for these communities.

This exploration of how libraries are working to understand the needs of children and families in underserved communities was guided by the following research questions:

---

[1] Library Outreach as a Community Anchor in Learning.

1. How, if at all, are libraries gathering data on the needs of children and families in underserved communities?
2. What, if any, common sources are libraries using for data on the needs of children and families in underserved communities?
3. How, if at all, are libraries using this data in the development of their programs and services?

To address these questions and others, the study utilized a triangulation of data collection methods—focus groups, interviews, and a national survey—with the broader goal of understanding how public libraries are going outside of their walls to offer programs to families in underserved communities. In order to be inclusive of the diversity in all communities, we asked the participating libraries to identify underserved groups they are targeting with their programs and services, rather than imposing our own definition of underserved communities.

Because libraries in the United States can differ greatly in types of communities and resources as well as geography, researchers placed an emphasis on recruiting from, and representing, a wide variety of types of libraries and communities, including small and rural. As a result, the participants included 157 library staff from small, medium and large public libraries in urban, suburban and rural areas. More specifically, the focus groups and interviews included 37 library staff and administrators from 17 states, and the survey included 120 respondents from 19 states.

The qualitative data from the focus groups were coded using iterative cycles of individual coding and group discussion between the researchers to arrive at the final set of thematic codes [14]. The thematic codes were then applied to the focus group data and the interview data. The data from the focus groups and interviews, along with the thematic code set, were used to inform the development of the survey and to populate the multiple-choice options. Because of this alignment, the data from the focus groups, interviews, and surveys were able to be analyzed together using frequency counts.

The data from the three methods were combined and analyzed in different ways to answer the three research questions. The focus groups, interviews, and survey were used to answer research question one. The focus groups and interviews were used to answer research question two and the survey was used to answer research question three. The data for research question one and two were analyzed at the response-level because across all three methods, participants were able to indicate multiple methods and sources that they might be using to gather community data. For research question three, the data was analyzed at the respondent level.

3 Research Results

In response to the broader goal of the study, which was to understand how libraries are going outside of their walls into community locations to serve children and families in underserved communities, the data revealed that libraries are offering a wide variety of programs and services out in community locations to reach and serve these families. As a part of this outreach work, the data revealed that libraries are collecting a wide variety of community data to understand the needs of these children and families.

In answer to research question one, the data from focus groups, interviews, and surveys revealed that a large majority of the participants are using a variety of methods, often in combination, to collect data and understand the needs of their underserved communities (Fig. 1). Only one respondent indicated that they were not doing anything to determine need at this time. The most widely used method, which surfaced in 43% of the responses, was conversing with both individual community members and community organizations. Pulling community data from existing data sources was the second most popular method, indicated in 28% of the responses. The other more common responses included examining their existing programs for indicators of need, and doing surveys, focus groups, and community tours.

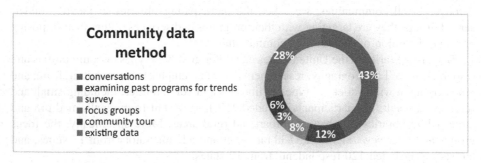

Fig. 1. Methods for collecting community data on needs of underserved communities

The focus groups and interviews also revealed that libraries are gathering data from a variety of sources (Fig. 2), thus answering research question two. Community sources were the most commonly used, with library staff going to individual community members, community partners, community organizations, and community leaders for information on the needs of children and families in underserved communities. Existing data sources were another common category, including the census; school data (free/reduced lunch numbers and standardized test scores, for example); and community data sets.

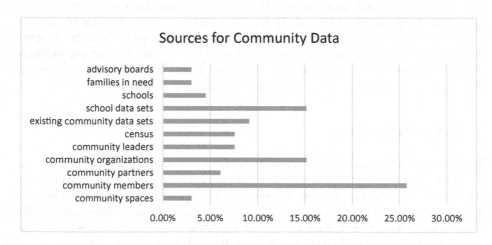

Fig. 2. Sources for community data on needs of underserved communities

Because the focus groups and interviews revealed that libraries are making significant efforts to understand the needs of underserved families, we included a question in the survey to answer research question three and uncover whether or not librarians are incorporating this data into program and service development. We distinguished between intentional and unintentional use of community data to inform programs and services because research has revealed that intentionality is important for developing effective programs and services [2]. The survey data revealed that 76% of respondents are using the community data in an intentional manner, as opposed to the 24% of the respondents who were using it in an unintentional manner or not at all. However, of the 76% of respondents who were using the data in an intentional manner, only 35% were using it consistently. The remaining 41% were only using it occasionally (Fig. 3).

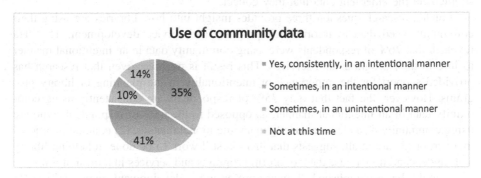

Fig. 3. Use of the community data in program and service development and delivery

4 Discussion

The findings presented here demonstrate that public libraries are responding to the directive issued by Hicken [9] and working to understand the needs of the communities they are serving through collecting community data. How they are doing this can be better understood by examining the findings under each research question.

The findings under research question one provide insight into the variety of methods that libraries are using to collect community data. The different types of data collection methods fall into two broad categories: existing data collection and emergent data collection. Existing data collection refers to libraries relying on data that is already available from sources such as the census and schools. Emergent data collection refers to collecting new data. Libraries are using emergent data collection more often, mainly due to the conversations method of collecting community data. While conversations can be a valid, rich source of community data, libraries could benefit from collecting community data in more efficient, targeted, and sustainable ways. Because the more structured data collection methods of surveys and focus groups only accounted for 11% of the responses, a need may exist for professional development opportunities focused on how to collect community data using more structured, sustainable data collection methods such as surveys, interviews, and focus groups. In addition, MLIS curricula could play a role in emphasizing data collection methods and preparing new librarians to use them for gathering community data.

The findings under research question two provide insight into the sources that libraries are using to gather data on the needs of children and families in underserved communities. A majority of these sources are community-based, which is fitting, given that the community will have the best understanding of their own needs, and reflects the centrality of community voices in the production of programs and services intended for the community. In addition, the significant use of community-based sources fits with the large amount of emergent data collection methods that libraries are using, such as conversations, surveys, and focus groups. The remaining sources to which libraries are turning for information on the needs of the families fall into the existing data category, such as the census and school data, which may serve as a starting point, and supplement the emergent data that they collect.

Finally, research question three provides insight into how libraries are using their community need data to inform their program and service development. The data revealed that 76% of respondents were using community data in an intentional manner to inform their programs and services. This result is positive given that research has provided support for the importance of intentionality in the planning of library programs. However, the fact that only 35% of respondents are consistently using community data in an intentional manner, as opposed to the 65% of respondents who are using community data (1) occasionally in an intentional manner, (2) in an unintentional manner, or (3) not at all, suggests that there is still work to be done in helping library staff understand how to use data to inform programs and services in a meaningful way. This could be accomplished through professional development opportunities for librarians that focus on the design of data-driven, need-based programs and services, or through more targeted methods of data collection that would allow librarians to interact with members of the community in a more purposeful manner and understand what might meet their needs.

5 Conclusion

This study provides insight into how libraries are collecting community data to better understand the needs of children and families in underserved communities so that they can design and develop meaningful, supportive programs and services that encourage learning and development in these communities. The fact that many libraries are collecting and incorporating community data into their programs and services demonstrates that libraries are seeking to make data-driven decisions in the work that they do. A stronger understanding of what data a library needs for their work, the best sources to locate that data, and how to then translate that data into program and service development will only benefit the libraries in their role as community anchors in learning. Basing their programming and service decisions on community need data will help libraries to offer programs and services for their community members in a more targeted and effective manner. Project LOCAL's findings provide the first step in understanding how research can inform practice and offer insights into developing more effective practice.

References

1. Campana, K., et al.: Early literacy in library storytimes: a study of measures of effectiveness. Libr. Q. **86**(4), 369–388 (2016)
2. Mills, J.E., et al.: Early literacy in library storytimes, Part 2: a quasi-experimental study and intervention with children's storytime providers. Libr. Q. **88**(2), 160 (2018)
3. Campana, K.: The multimodal power of storytime: Exploring an information environment for young children (Order No. 10825573). Available from ProQuest Dissertations & Theses A&I; ProQuest Dissertations & Theses Global (2018)
4. Lopez, M.E., Caspe, M., McWilliams, L.: Public Libraries: A Vital Space for Family Engagement. Harvard Family Research Project, Cambridge (2016). http://www.hfrp.org/librarycta
5. Neuman, S.B., Celano, D.C.: Worlds apart: one city, two libraries, and ten years of watching inequality grow. Am. Educ. **36**(3), 13–23 (2012)
6. Prendergast, T.: Beyond storytime: children's librarians collaborating in communities. Child. Libr. **9**(1), 20–40 (2011)
7. Howard, M.L.: Growing young minds: How museums and libraries create lifelong learners. Institute of Museum and Library Services (2013). https://www.imls.gov/assets/1/AssetManager/GrowingYoungMinds.pdf
8. Moxley, D.P., Abbas, J.M.: Envisioning libraries as collaborative community anchors for social service provision to vulnerable populations. Practice **28**(5), 311–330 (2016)
9. Hicken, M.: 'To each according to his needs': public libraries and socially excluded people. Health Inform. Libr. J. **21**, 45–53 (2004)
10. Scott, R.: The role of public libraries in community building. Public Libr. Q. **30**, 191–227 (2011)
11. Williment, K.: It Takes a Community to Build a Library. Public Libraries Online (2013). http://publiclibrariesonline.org/2013/04/it-takes-a-community-to-build-a-library/. Accessed 12 Dec 2018
12. Infopeople. (n.d.). Data Informed Public Libraries. https://infopeople.org/content/data-informed-public-libraries. Accessed 12 Dec 2018
13. Public Library Association: Using Data to Understand Your Community & Measure Impact (2017). http://www.ala.org/pla/education/onlinelearning/webinars/ondemand/projectoutcomeripl. Accessed 12 Dec 2018
14. Harry, B., Sturges, K.M., Klingner, J.K.: Mapping the process: an exemplar of process and challenge in grounded theory analysis. Educ. Res. **34**(2), 3–13 (2005)

Intentionality, Interactivity, and Community

A Conceptual Framework for Professional Development in Children's Librarianship

J. Elizabeth Mills[1](✉) and Kathleen Campana[2](✉)

[1] University of Washington, Seattle, WA 98195, USA
jemillsl@uw.edu
[2] Kent State University, Kent, OH 44240, USA
kcampan2@kent.edu

Abstract. Public libraries are increasingly being recognized as community anchors, sites of crucial and significant informal learning for children and families. Within children's services, early literacy storytimes are perceived as a mainstay of public library programming. That said, there is increasing pressure on both formal and informal prekindergarten learning environments to significantly improve the literacy skills in young children. Moreover, there is an expansion of library programs being designed to incorporate early literacy research. It is important for storytime providers to have a conceptual understanding of the purpose for the work they do. And yet they often lack a sufficient understanding of how to support learning for young children. Project VIEWS2, through its quasi-experimental intervention, provided a research-based framework—intentionality, interactivity, and community–that can support the work that storytime providers do to support children and families through early learning-rich storytime programs in the public library. Follow-up interviews and a survey of VIEWS2 participant storytime providers demonstrates the impact of this framework in the field, through discussion of intentional and interactive practice and the effects of community on sustaining and growing the work storytime providers do to serve their communities.

Keywords: Early learning · Librarianship · Conceptual framework · Storytimes

1 Introduction

Public libraries are increasingly being recognized as community anchors, sites of crucial and significant informal learning for children and families. According to a 2013 Pew Research Center (PRC) report, 95% of Americans ages 16 and older participating in the survey strongly agree or somewhat agree that public libraries are important because they promote literacy and the love of reading [1]. The PRC also reported 97% of the parents/primary caregivers value the importance of library services and programs for children and teens [2]. Of the 3.57 million programs provided by public libraries across the country as reported in the *2010 Public Libraries in the United States Survey*,

N. G. Taylor et al. (Eds.): iConference 2019, LNCS 11420, pp. 254–264, 2019.
https://doi.org/10.1007/978-3-030-15742-5_25

61.5% were designed for children [3]. Within children's services, early literacy storytimes are perceived as a mainstay of public library programming [4].

That said, there is increasing pressure on both formal and informal prekindergarten learning environments to significantly improve the literacy skills in young children [5]. Moreover, there is an expansion of library programs being designed to incorporate early literacy research. Capps [6] provides an overview of how public libraries are (1) supporting early literacy programs; (2) creating partnerships with early literacy organizations; (3) allocating resources for early literacy facilities, personnel, professional development, and materials; (4) conducting early literacy outreach and training for schools, families, and child caregivers; and (5) receiving grant money to support and research these early literacy initiatives. Storytime providers across the country work with families and children to encourage engagement in local early literacy environments—where print is explored and stories are celebrated. These experiences likely set the stage for children to demonstrate and practice their emerging early literacy skills [7–9].

In addition, libraries have recognized the importance of supporting parents and caregivers as their child's first and most important teacher. They have worked to do this through initiatives such as Every Child Ready to Read (ECRR) where children's librarians share and model ways for parents and caregivers to support their young child's early literacy skills [10]. Storytime providers[1] have also been using their storytimes to encourage and support both children's early literacy skills and parents' and caregivers' early literacy knowledge. In fact, McKenzie and Stooke [11] found that there was a general understanding among participants that "literacy work" is the work of storytime and that all participants played important roles in the "production of storytime." Author [12] built on this research by finding that each type of storytime participant plays a variety of roles, with the storytime provider facilitating and serving as the base for all of them.

Because this research is emerging, the field now no longer needs to rely on a colloquial understanding that these programs are valuable without precise knowledge of what early learning skills are being practiced. Moreover, there can and should be an increased emphasis not just on the emergent learning skills themselves but also on how these skills are incorporated into storytimes with young children and modeled to parents and caregivers. According to Rankin, it is "important for professionals who work with young children to have a theoretical underpinning and build their knowledge on a critical understanding of how children perceive the world" [13, p. 6].

While some of the studies that have emerged have found that storytimes are including and supporting a variety of early literacy and early learning skills for young children, it is difficult to determine what types of early literacy and early learning skills are incorporated in storytimes on an everyday basis because providers don't typically use a standard curriculum. In fact, storytime providers are often expected to create weekly programs from scratch that encourage and support a variety of early learning skills while engaging children and their caregivers in a fun, play-based manner.

---

[1] The authors have chosen to refer to staff who provide storytimes as storytime providers, to include those who may or may not have an MLIS and therefore may or may not be classified as librarians.

Authors et al. [14] proposed the idea that storytime providers are actually engaging in design work as they plan their programs by moving through an iterative cycle of planning, delivery, and reflection.

However, storytime providers often lack prior training in how to support learning for young children other than a brief introduction to early literacy, so they may feel unequipped to design programs that encourage learning for young children and their parents/caregivers. In addition, the all-too-common lack of time and staffing can contribute to situations where storytime providers may not be given the adequate resources that are needed to design these programs [15]. Given these challenges, storytime providers need research-based theories and frameworks to guide the design and production of storytimes to efficiently and effectively provide a rich, play-based, early learning environment for the children and families who attend.

2 Background on Project VIEWS2

One framework that has emerged from research and been used in practice is the VIEWS2 framework, which highlights the principles of intentionality, interactivity, and community. This framework emerged from Project VIEWS2 (Valuable Initiatives in Early Learning That Work Successfully), a four-year, quasi-experimental study of 40 libraries across Washington state that examined the early literacy impact of public library storytimes, designed in response to the need to investigate and test new ways to measure the effectiveness of public library early literacy programs for children from birth to kindergarten.[2] VIEWS2 yielded quantitative profiles of children's behavior and early literacy content of public library storytimes. The findings suggest children not only engage in a wide range of early literacy activities, but that these activities are correlated to the early literacy input of storytime providers [16]. Furthermore, the study found that a purposeful focus on early literacy principles by storytime providers in the planning and delivery of public library storytimes makes a difference in storytime programs and in children's early literacy behaviors [17]. These findings also not only further legitimize and influence practice but also provide a research-based framework that can be used in the instruction of future storytime providers as well as in everyday practice to serve children and their families through the design and production of meaningful, informed programs that emphasize learning.[3]

As part of this quasi-experimental study, researchers designed an intervention that focused on the tenets of intentionality, interactivity, and community as the basis for learning and professional development. This intervention was delivered first to the experimental group participants and later to the control group participants.

The goals of the intervention were:

- To train storytime providers to use research tools as planning tools and thereby be more *intentional* with early literacy content in their planning.

---

[2] This research was supported in part by the Institute of Museum and Library Service (IMLS).

[3] Two published papers provide in-depth details about the baseline and quasi-experimental studies that make up VIEWS2 (Campana et al., 2016 and Mills et al., 2018).

- Researchers introduced early literacy skills, including phonological awareness and alphabetic knowledge, in the delivery of storytimes, in order to provide a good foundation for storytime providers.
- To encourage *interactivity* in storytime providers' storytime delivery to facilitate learning opportunities for the children.
  - Researchers introduced various vehicles for incorporating EL skills, including *interactivity* and writing. Dialogic reading [18, 19] was highlighted in order to begin to shift storytime practice away from performance and more toward interactive dialogue.
- To create a *community* of practice to build on existing expertise through collaboration.
  - Researchers emphasized the importance of professional-development principles, including *community* building, professional expertise, and self-assessment.

3 Building Blocks of a Conceptual Framework

In the VIEWS2 study, the researchers implemented the principles of intentionality, interactivity, and community in very particular ways to guide the framing of the content and delivery of the intervention.

- Intentionality served as the WHAT—the purpose of the intervention itself, bringing an understanding of and attention to the importance of early literacy in storytime programs for young children.
- Interactivity served as the HOW—the way in which storytime providers delivered the early literacy content, through dialogic practices and scaffolding.
- Lastly, community served as the common thread woven throughout all aspects of the intervention, creating a shared environment in which the participants learned both from the researchers and from each other. Figure 1 offers a visual representation of how these pieces interacted throughout the intervention.

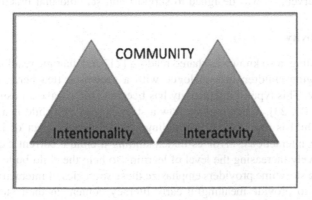

Fig. 1. Model for conceptual framework

These three building blocks compose the VIEWS2 conceptual framework, which supports the design and production of early learning programs in libraries. Each building block has a foundation in the education field and have been established through a variety of research studies performed in more formal educational settings, offering the VIEWS2 researchers an opportunity to explore this framework in the informal learning setting of a public library.

3.1 Intentionality

Intentionality is defined in the early education field as "acting with specific outcomes or goals in mind for children's development and learning. Teachers must have a repertoire of instructional strategies and know when to use a given strategy to accommodate the different ways that individual children learn and the specific content they are learning" [20]. For storytime providers, who do not necessarily operate with a set curriculum, intentionality involves being mindful and deliberate in selecting and inserting early literacy content into their storytime planning. They draw on their implicit knowledge of the developmental abilities and capabilities of the children in their communities. When storytime providers incorporate early literacy indicators into their planning process, they have program outcomes in mind, enabling them to be intentional with their storytime design and can result in an increase in the amount of early literacy indicators present in the storytime program.

In the VIEWS2 intervention, researchers provided a background on early literacy, defining terms and providing insight into child development. Researchers wanted to be sure that the storytime providers started from the same place in terms of familiarity with early literacy terminology and concepts, as the literature had showed a variance in terms of likely prior exposure to these topics in graduate library programs. Additionally, researchers introduced the research tools as planning tools. Participants were encouraged to select one to two indicators to incorporate into their storytime planning and delivery–to guide their book, song, and activity selections, and then try out delivering an early literacy-focused storytime and see what they noticed in the children who attended that storytime. This kind of intentionality takes preparation and practice and so the intervention was designed to support and scaffold that practice.

3.2 Interactivity

Interactive reading, also known as shared reading [21] and dialogic reading [18, 19, 22], involves engaging children in a dialogue with a grown-up (teacher, parent) about a particular story. This type of interactivity has been shown to have a positive impact on oral language [21, 23], indicating that how a story is read to a child is as important as how often a child is read to [4]. Scaffolding, an additional aspect of interactivity in shared-reading interactions, involves understanding a child's current capabilities, and then progressively increasing the level of learning to help the child build a certain skill [24–26]. When storytime providers emphasize these strategies of interactivity, they may be better able to provide meaningful early literacy content in their storytimes in an engaging, child-focused way that allows the child to interact with the early literacy content, thereby making a difference for the children who attend.

In the VIEWS2 intervention, researchers discussed interactivity with the storytime providers, highlighting dialogic reading and scaffolding as vehicles for transforming storytimes from performative to interactive in nature. In the second and third webinars, especially, researchers encouraged participants to ask questions and pause so that children can try and respond; to extend what children say to encourage them to think more deeply about the books and activities they're participating in; and to carefully build onto what the children have already learned to help them master a new concept or skill, all within the creative, playful, and informal environment of public library storytimes.

3.3 Community

Communities of practice have become important for many fields in helping practitioners to acquire knowledge and grow and evolve their practice. Communities of practice have been defined in many ways, but all of the definitions include similar aspects which can be brought together to form the following definition: a group or network of people who share a concern, interest, or mutual engagement and work together to build and extend shared understandings and knowledge [27–29]. Give the significance of the social aspects of learning [26, 30], the opportunities to interact with peers around shared topics can be important for helping individuals to learn and grow. Communities of practice have been used in both the education and the library field to successfully support learning and knowledge building for the individuals involved [31–33]. However, many storytime providers do not have regular opportunities to interact with peers around their practice due to reduced funding, limited staffing, and the geographic distribution of libraries.

In the VIEWS2 intervention, researchers worked to establish a community of learners in an online space. In addition to offering tech support, researchers and storytime providers shared introductions and learned a little about everyone's work and background. This was done to build community and trust among storytime providers and between storytime providers and researchers. Between each webinar, storytime providers used independent discovery times to experiment and practice using the VIEWS2 tools in their storytime planning. Storytime tips and ideas were also sent by email to the storytime providers to provide additional support for creativity. Then in the webinars, the storytime providers shared how the process went for them and discussed any successes and challenges along the way. In this way, the storytime providers were encouraged to build a community of practice to gain feedback and ideas for assimilating early literacy into their storytime content. Researchers incorporated discussion topics that covered challenges and successes in the work of planning and delivery early literacy-focused storytimes, in an effort to further elicit community feedback and support among the participants. Developing a community of practice was a central component of the planning and delivery of the intervention with the intent of supporting the storytime providers through the intervention process, especially across great geographical distances and across target age-groups of storytimes.

As the intervention implemented these three building blocks, researchers wanted to develop them into a conceptual framework to enable storytime providers to understand how these pieces fit together and to demonstrate how they can inform practice in storytimes and other programs for children.

4   A Framework in the Field

4.1   Intervention Follow-up

Following the intervention, researchers disseminated a survey and conducted interviews with the experimental group participants to gain personal insight into their experience with the intervention and understand the longer-term impact of the intervention as well as the building blocks of intentionality, interactivity, and community on their practice [34, 35]. Several key themes emerged from this research.

First, even after a period of time, the participants overall still felt that the intervention had improved their storytimes, helping them to incorporate more early literacy and interactive moments and to be more intentional with their planning. They felt that the intervention helped them to feel more positive and excited about their job. According to one participant, "*The most significant change has been the mindfulness I have in storytimes. I'm very aware and mindful of the opportunity to make storytimes a very rich experience for parents and, in my case, babies. I am mindful of all the different ways I can enrich storytime, whether it's introducing new toys or tips for parents on things that they can do.*" Another participant commented, "*I have definitely made a more conscious effort to make sure that I'm always adding early literacy stuff in general.*" Still another participant shared that she was empowered by seeing the children respond to the early literacy content, "*I've just seen such a huge connection [between the kids and the early literacy skills], and I felt so empowered because research tells us that building these early learning skills is a really important thing to do.*"

Second, engaging in the peer interactions reinforced storytime providers' current storytime activities and helped them to expand upon those activities and try out new ones. Several participants mentioned that their storytimes were more interactive and incorporated more dialogic reading. One shared, "*I've been asking more questions of the kids, inviting them to take part in the book.*" Another commented that she felt, "*a lot more comfortable just taking time to talk with kids about what's happening in the story or even, if it's a story about spots and stripes, asking who has spots on and who has stripes and taking 5 min to talk with kids about spots and stripes.*"

Third, participants indicated they benefited from hearing what other storytime providers were doing, sharing that the intervention left them feeling more excited about their job and empowered to take the lead in early learning advocacy. One participant felt that participating in the intervention helped to re-energize her practice, that it was like "*having a constant reminder that we're not just time fillers, that storytimes are important and everything we do in storytime has a purpose.*" Other participants shared that the intervention had a positive impact on advocacy for storytimes, "*It's helped me be a stronger advocate for outreach storytimes and Head Start storytimes. It's helped me be able to better articulate why those things are important to our administration.*" And, "*I think it's a great thing to know that what we do is helpful and worthwhile and that if we can add a few more little things, it will make it that much better, and hopefully, help us to take a stronger lead in early learning advocacy.*" They continued to emphasize the community aspect of the intervention, sharing that they felt less isolated and more connected to other storytime providers around the state after the intervention.

5   Storytime Assessment

During the dissemination of the study findings, researchers learned of the emergence of the phenomenon of storytime assessment in Washington state. Researchers conducted interviews with 35 providers and managers at public libraries across the state to understand what was taking place in terms of storytime assessment. Those findings were published in a white paper [15]. Figure 2 displays the research-based model developed from the study findings [14, 35].

Fig. 2. Self-reflection and peer mentoring working together.

The study found that assessment can play a part in the iterative process of creating a storytime, influencing planning, delivery, and reflection on the program. Self-reflection was one of the most common approaches to assessment among the interviewees, and it often took place in informal ways. For instance, storytime providers would reflect on their programs during room cleanup or while preparing for the following week. Peer mentoring is a second common form of assessment for participants, also taking place informally in many cases. Sometimes it's a conversation with a colleague following the program, sometimes it's asking a colleague to sit in and observe and then sharing feedback afterwards. Peer mentoring and self-reflection offer accessible, meaningful opportunities for assessment of storytimes that support the work storytime providers do and that enable them to advocate for the impact of that work. When storytime providers take the time to reflect on their programs, they can be intentional about their planning and they can look for ways to be interactive in the delivery of their programs. When they work with their peers, they're building a community that can help them be better at what they do. Thus, the principles of interactivity, intentionality, and community fit into the work around assessment as well.

6 Implications and Conclusion

The VIEWS2 framework—intentionality, interactivity, and community—has positive implications for practitioners and researchers alike. The findings from the VIEWS2 study demonstrate that the building blocks of this framework can have an impact on practice for storytime providers. The experimental storytime providers reported increased intentionality in planning the early literacy content of the storytimes as a result of the intervention, a qualitative finding that was supported by the quantitative, statistically significant difference in the pre/post comparison of the early literacy content observed in their storytimes as part of the quasi-experimental study. The principle of interactivity was reinforced through the storytime providers' survey and interview responses where they commented on their increased level of and comfort with interactive content. The last of the three principles, community of practice, was supported through the survey and interview responses of the experimental storytime providers that emphasized their experience with the benefits of being able to share and receive ideas, resources, and feedback with peers doing similar work, as well as the findings from the interviews regarding assessment strategies. This framework also provides researchers with an opportunity to apply these principles to other kinds of programs offered not only in libraries but also in other informal learning environments, such as museums and zoos, to understand how programs are designed and produced for children to support their learning and development.

In fact, this research-based framework was immediately translated into practice at the national level in the form of a professional development orientation called Supercharged Storytimes, created by OCLC in 2016. Building on the findings from the VIEWS2 study as well as the building blocks of this framework, OCLC developed online communities of practice that were rolled out to six states, initially, and then in phase two was rolled out nationwide. To complement and extend these online communities of practice at the state level, Washington State Library developed face-to-face workshops offered around the state that built on the VIEWS2 intervention. In addition, some library systems in Washington have begun their own grassroots communities of practice to provide networks for storytime providers to get the support and professional development they need. To supplement all the ways in which this research is transitioning back into practice, the researchers published an early literacy planning guide based on the VIEWS2 research that can be used by a single practitioner to develop more effective early literacy storytimes or can be used to support the communities of practice and face-to-face workshops [35].

There are several opportunities for future research in this area, including examining how this framework might be extended beyond early literacy, into STEM and social emotional development, among others. Additionally, it is worth exploring the impact this framework might have on emergent communities of practice in this and other professional fields. This framework offers pedagogical implications as well, and the researchers have already begun to teach this work in MLIS courses in a limited fashion.

As stated earlier, storytime providers need research-based theories and frameworks to guide the design and production of storytimes to help storytime providers efficiently and effectively provide a rich, play-based, early learning environment for the children and families who attend. The VIEWS2 framework, with its building blocks of intentionality, interactivity, and community, offers practitioners practical, actionable approaches to designing and delivering meaningful learning programs and environments that help support families as they nurture their child's learning trajectory. When storytime providers are intentional about incorporating early literacy indicators into their planning, when they are interactive in how they deliver storytimes, and when they rely on their community of practice for support and professional growth, they can be confident in the positive impact they are making on the lives of the families and children who come to their storytimes. Moreover, they can advocate for the learning and development that is taking place in their programs, as libraries continue to be seen as crucial sites of early learning for families and young children in the community.

References

1. Zickuhr, K., Rainie, L., Purcell, K., Duggan, M.: How Americans value public libraries in their communities. Pew Research Center (2013). http://libraries.pewinternet.org/files/legacy-pdf/PIP_Libraries%20in%20communities.pdf. Accessed
2. Miller, C., Zickuhr, K., Rainie, L., Purcell, K.: Parents, children, libraries, and reading. Pew Research Center (2013). http://libraries.pewinternet.org/files/legacy-pdf/PIP_Library_Services_Parents_PDF.pdf. Accessed
3. Swan, D.W., et al.: Public Libraries Survey: Fiscal Year 2010 (IMLS-2013–PLS-01). Institute of Museum and Library Services. Washington, DC (2013). https://imls.gov/sites/default/files/publications/documents/pls2010.pdf. Accessed
4. Ghoting, S., Martin-Diaz, P.: Early Literacy Storytimes @ Your Library: Partnering with Caregivers with Success. ALA Editions, Chicago (2006)
5. Cunningham, A.E., Perry, K.E., Stanovich, K.E., Stanovich, P.J.: Disciplinary knowledge of K-3 teachers and their knowledge calibration in the domain of early literacy. Ann. Dyslexia 54(1), 139–167 (2004)
6. Capps, J.: EL-Capstone scale development: An emergent literacy concept inventory, ProQuest Dissertations and Theses (2011)
7. Campana, K., Dresang, E.: Bridging the early literacy gulf. In: Proceedings of the 74th Annual Meeting of the American Society for Information Science and Technology, 7th electronic edn., 10 p. (2011)
8. Neuman, S.B., Celano, D.: Access to print in low-income and middle-income communities: an ecological study of four neighborhoods. Reading Res. Q. 36(1), 8–26 (2001)
9. McKechnie, L.: Observations of babies and toddlers in library settings. Libr Trends 55(1), 190–201 (2006)
10. Meyers, E., Henderson, H.: Overview of Every Child Ready to Read @ your library (2004). http://www.everychildreadytoread.org/projecthistory%09/overview-every-child-ready-read-your-library%C2%AE-1st-edition. Accessed
11. McKenzie, P.J., Stooke, R.K.: Producing storytime: a collectivist analysis of work in a complex communicative space. Libr. Q. 77(1), 3–20 (2007)
12. Campana, K.: The multimodal power of storytime: exploring an information environment for young children. ProQuest Dissertations and Theses (2018)
13. Rankin, C.: Library services for the early years: Policy, practice, and the politics of the age. Libr. Trends 65(1), 5–18 (2016)

14. Mills, J.E., Campana, K., Clarke, R.I.: Learning by design: creating knowledge through storytime production. In: Proceedings of the 79th Annual Meeting of the American Society for Information Science and Technology, vol. 53(1), pp. 1–6 (2016)
15. Mills, J.E., et al.: Impact, advocacy, and professional development: an exploration of storytime assessment in Washington state. White paper (2015). views2.ischool.uw.edu
16. Campana, K., et al.: Early literacy in library storytimes: a study of measures of effectiveness. Libr. Q. **86**(4), 369–388 (2016)
17. Mills, J.E., et al.: Early literacy in library storytimes part 2: a quasi-experimental study and intervention with children's storytime providers. Libr. Q. **88**(2), 160–176 (2018)
18. Arnold, D., Lonigan, C., Whitehurst, G., Epstein, J., Levin, J.R.: Accelerating language development through picture book reading: replication and extension to a videotape training format. J. Educ. Psychol. **86**(2), 235–243 (1994)
19. Zevenbergen, A.A., Whitehurst, G.J.: Dialogic reading: a shared picture book reading intervention for preschoolers. In: van Kleeck, A., Stahl, S.A., Bauer, E.B. (eds.) On Reading Books to Children: Parents and Teachers, pp. 177–200. Erlbaum, Mahwah (2003)
20. Epstein, A.S.: The Intentional Teacher: Choosing the Best Strategies for Young Children's Learning. National Association for the Education of Young Children, Washington, DC (2007)
21. Lonigan, C.J., Whitehurst, G.J.: Relative efficacy of parent and teacher involvement in a shared reading intervention for pre-school children from low income backgrounds. Early Child. Res. Q. **13**(2), 263–290 (1998)
22. Albright, M., Delecki, K., Hinkle, S.: The evolution of early literacy: a history of best practices in storytimes. Child. Libr. **7**(1), 13–18 (2009)
23. Mol, S.E., Bus, A.G., de Jong, M.T.: Interactive book reading in early education: a tool to stimulate print knowledge as well as oral language. Rev. Educ. Res. **79**(2), 979–1007 (2009)
24. National Association for the Education of Young Children: Developmentally appropriate practice in early childhood programs serving children from birth to age 8 (2008). http://www.naeyc.org/files/naeyc/file/positions/PSDAP.pdf. Accessed
25. Berk, L.E., Winsler, A.: Scaffolding Children's Learning: Vygotsky and Early Childhood Education. National Association for the Education of Young Children, Washington, D.C. (1995)
26. Vygotsky, L.S.: The Collected Works of L. S. Vygotsky: Problems of General Psychology Including the Volume Thinking and Speech. (N. Minick, Trans.). Plenum, New York (1987)
27. Wenger, E., McDermott, R., Snyder, W.M.: Cultivating Communities of Practice: A Guide to Managing Knowledge. Harvard Business School Press, Boston (2002)
28. Hara, N.: Communities of Practice: Fostering Peer-to-Peer Learning and Informal Knowledge Sharing in the Work Place. Springer, Heidelberg (2009)
29. Wenger, E.: Communities of Practice: Learning, Meaning, and Identity. Cambridge University Press, Cambridge (1998)
30. Brown, J.S., Collins, A., Duguid, P.: Situated cognition and the culture of learning. Educ. Res. **18**(1), 32–42 (1989)
31. Yukawa, J.: Communities of practice for blended learning: toward an integrated model for LIS education. J. Educ. Libr. Inform. Sci. **51**(2), 54–75 (2010)
32. Nadelson, L.S.: The influence and outcomes of a STEM education research faculty community of practice. J. STEM Educ. **17**(1), 44–51 (2016)
33. Warner, C.K., Hallman, H.L.: A communities of practice approach to field experiences in teacher education. Brock Educ. J. Educ. Res. Pract. **26**(2), 16–33 (2017)
34. Campana, K.: Connecting collections and cultures by creating a community of children's librarians around early literacy storytimes. In: Proceedings of the 77th Annual Meeting of the American Society for Information Science and Technology, vol. 51(1), pp. 1–4 (2014)
35. Campana, K., Mills, J.E., Ghoting, S.N.: Supercharged Storytimes: An Early Literacy Planning and Assessment Guide. ALA Editions, Chicago (2016)

Rural Broadband and Advanced Manufacturing: Research Implications for Information Studies

Sang Hoo Oh[(✉)] and Marcia A. Mardis

Florida State University, Tallahassee, FL 32306-2100, USA
sol7c@my.fsu.edu

Abstract. Advanced manufacturing (AM) is a vital driver of the U.S. economy. AM is also crucial in building U.S. competitiveness by strengthening the scientific and engineering enterprise and providing transformative science and technology solutions. AM anchors rural economies across the country and is especially important to rural America, where it accounts for a larger share of employment and earnings than in urban areas. Broadband Internet connectivity is essential affordance of the "smart" AM production technologies key to U.S. leadership because they enable manufacturers to precisely customize products and supply for increasingly segmented markets. However, our review of policy and research suggests that little is known about the extent to which the U.S. broadband environment can support and enable AM, especially in the prime rural locations. In this paper, we will explore rural communities' AM readiness. Specifically, we synthesize research and policy documents relating to the centrality of broadband Internet to AM; the state of broadband in rural communities; and the potential for AM transform rural communities. We conclude with promising directions for information science researchers to further investigate the relationship between broadband and the potential for AM to benefit rural communities' economic potential.

Keywords: Advanced manufacturing (AM) · Broadband · Rural communities

1 Introduction

According to the National Science and Technology Council (2013), advanced manufacturing (AM) is a key driver of the U.S. economy because it will produce high-income jobs and generate technological innovation. Furthermore, AM is crucial in building U.S. competitiveness by strengthening the scientific and engineering enterprise and providing transformative science and technology solutions (National Science and Technology Council 2013). Traditional manufacturing is the process of converting raw materials into a finished ready-to-sell product through the use of manual and/or mechanized transformational techniques. The end goal of traditional manufacturing is to add value to achieve the objective. Advanced manufacturing, on the other hand, typically involves manufacturing processes in specific industries such as aerospace, medical, pharmaceutical, etc., while using advanced techniques and equipment for production and logistics. A fundamental goal of advanced manufacturing is to produce

© Springer Nature Switzerland AG 2019
N. G. Taylor et al. (Eds.): iConference 2019, LNCS 11420, pp. 265–273, 2019.
https://doi.org/10.1007/978-3-030-15742-5_26

products in the least amount of time while minimizing wasted materials and time (Bonvillan and Singer 2017). In AM, high speed, uninterrupted broadband Internet connectivity is an essential affordance for technologies such as 3D printing (Petrick and Prindible 2014); for this reason, broadband is a crucial enabler to successful U.S. competition reliant upon "smart" production to customize products and supplies for increasingly segmented markets (Bonvillan and Singer 2017).

The manufacturing sector anchors rural economies across the country and is especially important to rural America, where it accounts for a larger share of employment and earnings than in urban areas (National Science and Technology Council [NSTC] 2018). Changes in manufacturing disproportionately affect rural communities. Over 70% of all manufacturing-dependent counties are non-metro (rural) and contain nearly a quarter of the United States' rural population (USDA 2017). Although the earnings gap between urban and rural manufacturers is large, median earnings for manufacturing is still the second largest in rural counties (USDA 2017). However, our review of policy and research suggests that little is known about the extent to which the broadband environment in the United States can support and enable AM in rural areas. In this paper, we explore rural communities' AM readiness. Specifically, we will examine the extent to which rural communities can provide broadband engage in AM's economic and social benefits. We will conclude with promising directions for research.

2   Rural Communities and Advanced Manufacturing

A robust American manufacturing base remains vital to maintaining America's economic strength and national security in the 21st century (Yudken et al. 2017). In line with this trend, the National Science and Technology Council (2013) identified AM as a critical driver for long-term economic prosperity and growth for the U.S. economy in regional, state, and local economies, especially in rural communities.

A recent survey of rural manufacturers revealed that the more rural the manufacturer, the more likely cost reduction and employee recruitment were challenges coupled with fewer growth opportunities and financing. The quality of specific nearby services and providers–broadband was chief among them –has disproportionately impacted rural manufacturers (Thomas and Campbell 2018). Although rural manufacturers are different demographically, face different challenges, and have different needs, they delivered the same level of economic impacts and even higher amounts of additional investment. This positive effect is likely due to rural manufacturers being slightly larger on average compared to urban manufacturers (Thomas and Campbell 2018).

The federal government supports programs that are specifically tailored to increase the strength and resilience of the manufacturing sector in rural regions. USDA programs provide a comprehensive support system for rural prosperity, including many programs that are also important to AM, such as STEM education, workforce development, rural infrastructure, and grants and loans for businesses and research organizations involved in rural development (National Science and Technology Council 2018). USDA provides many programs that support AM and features expanding rural AM capacity as a plank of its strategic plan (National Science and Technology Council

2018). For example, the Rural Business-Cooperative Service, a U.S. Department Agriculture program, provides technical assistance and financial support for rural manufacturers developing innovative value-added agricultural products for broader markets. Also, the USDA recently signed a Memorandum of Understanding (MoU) with Small Business Administration to advance federal support on providing timely access to capital and other forms of business assistance. This MoU aims to improve capital access to rural areas, increase the benefits of the Tax Cuts and Job Act of 2017, and improve technical assistance and infrastructure (National Science and Technology Council 2018). These programs operated by the U.S. Department of Agriculture are critical for supporting manufacturers in rural communities and expected to help strengthen AM in rural areas.

Currently, there is the national call for states to undertake bold initiatives in a revitalization of the manufacturing sector (FloridaMakes 2016). For example, the State of Florida is seizing upon current opportunities from global economic trends, re-shoring, and a desire for technological advancements to encourage AM companies to locate in rural communities (FloridaMakes 2016). Especially in rural Florida, competitiveness and sustainability of the manufacturing sector are essential to ensure job growth and economic prosperity. As there is renewed national interest in manufacturing research and education, AM is creating an opportunity for the state to undertake bold initiatives in a revitalization of the manufacturing sector. The most significant innovation is expected to be coming from AM's diverse and growing range of technologies (e.g., nanotechnologies, robotics, sensors) because they generate higher productivity, require more highly skilled workers who are paid higher wages than other manufacturing sectors (FloridaMakes 2016).

Moreover, the Advanced Manufacturing Institute at Kansas State University College of Engineering has been helping university faculty to connect with manufacturing industry that is in rural parts of the state. Along with their university faculty, they also have engineers and technologists that are devoted to this task. The Advanced Manufacturing Institute also has been seeking ways to help its rural industry partners connect to resources and expertise and things that they do not typically have access to because of their location; industries such as wood pellet manufacturing (Kansas State University 2018).

3 Broadband and Rural Communities

3.1 Rural Broadband Challenges

Having access to the broadband Internet has become indispensable for the development of communities in the 21st century, especially in rural areas. With broadband Internet, rural communities can benefit in many ways, including attracting new businesses, enabling access to telemedicine and low-cost online education, searching for jobs online and having access to more government information through E-government. Consequently, both the federal and local governments are working together to increase broadband adoption in rural areas. To expand broadband infrastructure, more than $260 billion has been invested by both public and private sector since 2009 (Council of

Economic Advisers 2016). Former President Obama also promised that the U.S. government would make fast and reliable broadband available to more Americans at the lowest possible cost. Initiatives like ConnectED and ConnectHome were designed to expand broadband access to more schools, libraries, and families across the United States (Council of Economic Advisers 2016).

However, even with a constant effort to improve rural broadband access through various initiatives and programs by the government, many rural Americans still lag behind urban counterparts in broadband access. According to the Federal Communications Commission (FCC), the current standard for broadband service is at least 25 megabits per second downloading and three megabits per second uploading. This standard is considered adequate to stream video and participates in other high-traffic online activities (Strover 2018). The *2018 Broadband Progress Report* stated that 31% of rural Americans still lacked access to broadband service that met the FCC standard, as compared to only 2.1% of Americans who lived in urban areas (FCC 2018). These statistics show that the digital divide between urban and rural remains significant and difficult to dispel. A main reason why rural areas are falling behind urban areas is the high costs of deployment. Internet providers must expect a high rate of adoption before they invest and for that reason, they focus their investments in urban areas where there are high-income consumers and high residential densities that maximize profits. Subsequently, both wired and wireless connections in rural areas are still comparatively worse than in cities. Overall, rural Americans have low-quality Internet service but pay higher prices when they are earning less than Urban residents (Strover 2018).

Wireless technologies, including satellite, radio links, and mobile data are ways to increase the coverage area and adoption rate in rural America (Strover 2018). Unfortunately, these technologies are not a complete solution either because their connections are still not reliable in rural areas and they are limited to consumer level applications like email, web browsing, and low-level data exchanges. These connection types are vulnerable to weather fluctuations and often require people to be within the coverage area of service towers. As many rural areas still lack access to broadband, the role of community anchor institutions such as public libraries is becoming more critical. Many people in rural areas who cannot afford broadband use free Internet connections offered by local public libraries (Strover et al. 2017). These connections, though limited, have become alternatives for many rural community residents who do not have access to broadband Internet service. In this way, broadband is important to rural AM on two levels: (1) at the industrial level, reliable connectivity is important for myriad production processes; (2) at the human level, broadband attracts and supports a skilled workforce that can collaborate, manage logistics, and engage in ongoing training (Raveyre 2011).

3.2   Federal Policy Efforts

The Trump administration has been addressing the importance of expanding broadband infrastructure and service to rural America ever since it came into power. As part of President Trump's promise to rebuild rural America, the Department of Agriculture announced that it would invest more than $200 million to help bring broadband to rural communities (White House 2018). Moreover, on January 8, 2018, President Trump signed two rural broadband executive orders that will reduce bureaucratic barriers preventing new broadband infrastructure from being built. The first executive order gives private companies access to infrastructure on government-owned land such as radio towers. The second executive order is about a plan to reduce the unnecessary government paperwork to get permission to build broadband infrastructure in rural areas (White House 2018). The Trump administration expects that these efforts will streamline broadband in rural America.

Nevertheless, many rural broadband advocates remain skeptical of President Trump's policy because it appears to be insufficient to solve the real problem for broadband in rural areas (Levin 2018; Reardon 2018). In previous studies, researchers have identified the high cost of deployment as the main reason why broadband adoption is low in rural America. Installing fiber across miles of remote countryside costs a lot of money for telecom companies, and there is no sufficient way to make profits from it. President Trump's two rural broadband executive orders and USDA's $200 million investment are insufficient to solve this problem. The Trump administration would need to provide real solutions, like giving grants or infrastructure budget to expand broadband service in rural areas (Levin 2018).

4 Rural Broadband's Importance to Advanced Manufacturing

Digitalization has been transforming manufacturing globally in the 21st century. The digitalization of manufacturing is changing how products are designed, fabricated, used, operated and serviced. In the same way, broadband is transforming the operations, processes, and energy footprint of factories and supply chains (Ezell 2018). The application of information technology (IT) to every facet of manufacturing in industries as diverse plastics, wood pellets, and biomedical allows many entrepreneurs and creative service industries to view the low land costs in rural communities as viable company sites (Conley and Whitacre 2016). Broadband affords rural manufacturers the ability to implement innovative processes, enable flexible workforce and training solutions, and manage complicated supply and delivery chains (Raveyre 2011).

The advent and maturation of many technologies are driving AM. These technologies include: cloud computing; the Internet of Things (IoT); advanced sensor technologies; 3D printing; industrial robotics; data analytics; machine learning; and wireless connectivity that better enables machine-to-machine (M2M) communications (National Academies of Sciences Engineering & Medicine [NASEM] 2017). For these technologies, the combination of sensors and software into the Internet of Things is critical. In the AM context, "IoT refers to the use of sensors in production equipment (e.g., robots, stampers, actuators, 3D printers, computer numerical control [CNC] machines), and the products they make (such as jet engines, gas turbines, radiological equipment, or vehicles) to enable a real-time flow of information about the operational status and condition of the equipment or product" (Ezell 2018, p. 2). With these functions and capabilities, IoT will help manufacturing enterprises with real-time intelligence about their production processes and bestow them with the information needed to make better operational and production decisions. Eventually, it will lead to the overall improvement of operating efficiency in manufacturing execution systems, warehouse management and control systems, and transportation management systems deployed in shop floors and warehouses (Ezell 2018; Kim and Orazem 2017).

Factories must have reliable broadband connectivity to make this happen, especially in rural areas near metropolitan communities (Mack 2014). Broadband connectivity is key to the success of most successful rural industries (Atasoy 2013; Kuttner 2012; Raveyre 2011). IoT sensors need to interact and communicate with each other so that they can create the information streams upon on which AM techniques rely. For this reason, the Internet connection that IoT relies on needs to be stable and fast, which is why broadband connectivity is crucial and why concerns about the White House commitment to direct investments in community and commercial infrastructure that supports rural economies, including broadband high-speed Internet connectivity are so significant.

5 Areas for Further Research

The relationship between broadband availability and the potential for AM to transform rural communities offers several opportunities for information science researchers. Promising exploration areas and initial lines of inquiry foreshadowed by our synthesis include:

1. What sorts of needs assessments to rural community and AM industry leaders require to make informed decisions about the suitability between rural locations and AM production needs (Conley and Whitacre 2016; NSTC 2013, 2018)?
2. In rural communities that have successfully attracted AM companies, how did Internet connectivity play into the companies' decisions to locate in the community? How has the presence of the advanced manufacturer affected broadband availability for citizens and other businesses? In what different ways has AM changed the community (Conley and Whitacre 2016; Raveyre 2011)?
3. What sorts of competencies are required for AM workers to maintain Internet-enabled production (Mardis and Jones (accepted); Mardis et al. 2018; Oh et al. 2019)? To what extent are AM technician training programs in rural communities imparting the necessary skills (Jones et al. (accepted); Mardis et al. 2018)?
4. Rural communities in other countries, such as China, Germany (Renden Schneir and Xiaong 2016), and Scotland (Townsend, Wallace, & Fairhurst, 2015), have successfully addressed broadband Internet connectivity. To what extent has a relatively stable and established Internet infrastructure worked to attract AM employers to these rural communities?
5. Are there differences between the types of rural communities that have the potential to benefit from AM? For example, do rural, remote communities stand to help in the same ways and to the same extent that rural communities adjacent to metropolitan areas (Raveyre 2011; USDA 2017)?

6   Conclusion

In this paper, we provided a synthesis of research and policy relating to the centrality of broadband Internet to AM; the state of broadband in rural communities; and the potential for AM to transform rural communities. Taken together, the studies we reviewed suggested that while rural communities could significantly benefit from the influx of highly technical innovative industries, whether these communities can provide the critical affordance of broadband, is unclear. The better we understand rural communities and the industries they rely on, the more we can do to support those industries. However, library and information studies (LIS) researchers have a heritage of broadband research, and we offered several promising directions for further investigation into the relationship between broadband and AM in rural communities.

References

Atasoy, H.: The effects of broadband Internet expansion on labor market outcomes. ILR Rev. **66**(2), 315–345 (2013)

Bonvillan, W.B., Singer, P.L.: Advanced Manufacturing: The New American Innovation Policies. The MIT Press, Cambridge (2017)

Conley, K.L., Whitacre, B.E.: Does broadband matter for rural entrepreneurs and creative class employees? Rev. Reg. Stud. **46**(2), 171–190 (2016)

Council of Economic Advisers. The digital divide and economic benefits of broadband access (Issue brief). Council of Economic Advisers, Washington, DC (2016). https://www.benton.org/headlines/digital-divide-and-economic-benefits-broadband-access

Ezell, S.: Why manufacturing digitalization matters and how countries are supporting it. Information Technology and Innovation Group, Washington, DC (2018). http://www2.itif.org/2018-manufacturing-digitalization.pdf. Accessed 13 Dec 2018

Federal Communications Commission [FCC]. 2018 Broadband deployment report (2018). https://docs.fcc.gov/public/attachments/FCC-18-10A1.pdf. Accessed 13 Dec 2018

FloridaMakes: Rural area manufacturing study: an assessment of manufacturing in Florida's rural areas and the opportunities for growth and expansion (2016). https://www.floridamakes.com/core/fileparse.php/140/urlt/Rural-Manufacturing-Study-v4.pdf. Accessed 13 Dec 2018

Jones, F.R., Pahuja, D., Mardis, M.A.: Are we teaching what they want? A comparative study of what AM employers want versus what AM frameworks require. Paper to be presented at 2019 American society of engineering educators (ASEE) annual conference & exposition, Tampa, FL (accepted)

Kansas State University: Advanced Manufacturing Institute (2018). https://www.k-state.edu/ami/. Accessed 13 Dec 2018

Kim, Y., Orazem, P.F.: Broadband internet and new firm location decisions in rural areas. Am. J. Agric. Econ. **99**(1), 285–302 (2017). https://doi.org/10.1093/ajae/aaw082

Kuttner, H.: Broadband for rural America: economic impacts and economic opportunities (2012). http://www.hudson.org/content/researchattachments/attachment/1072/ruraltelecom-kuttner-1012.pdf. Accessed 13 Dec 2018

Levin, B.: Trump infrastructure plan not likely to impact rural broadband (2018). https://www.brookings.edu/blog/the-avenue/2018/02/02/trump-infrastructure-plan-not-likely-to-impact-rural-broadband/. Accessed 13 Dec 2018

Mack, E.A.: Broadband and knowledge intensive firm clusters: essential link or auxiliary connection? Papers Reg. Sci. **93**(1), 3–29 (2014). https://doi.org/10.1111/j.1435-5957.2012. 00461.x

Mardis, M.A., Jones, F.R.: Developing an AM body of knowledge: a comprehensive tool to align curricula with industry needs. Paper to be presented at 2019 American society of engineering educators (ASEE) annual conference & exposition, Tampa, FL (accepted)

Mardis, M.A., Jones, F.R., Bouvin, D.: Advancing technician education through evidence-based decision-making. Paper presented at the 25th annual NSF advanced technician education (ATE) principal investigators conference, Washington, DC (2018)

Mardis, M.A., Jones, F.R., McClure, C.R.: Assessing IT educational pathways that support rural broadband: strategies for aligning IT curricula, policy, and employer needs. Community Coll. Res. Pract. (2018). https://doi.org/10.1080/10668926.2018.1521756

National Academies of Sciences Engineering & Medicine [NASEM]: Securing advanced manufacturing in the United States: the role of manufacturing USA. In: Proceedings of a Workshop. The National Academies Press, Washington, DC (2017)

National Science and Technology Council [NSTC]. Advanced manufacturing: A snapshot of priority technology areas across the federal government (2013). https://www.whitehouse.gov/ sites/whitehouse.gov/files/images/Blog/NSTC%20SAM%20technology%20areas%20snap shot.pdf. Accessed 13 Dec 2018

National Science and Technology Council [NSTC]: Strategy for American leadership in advanced manufacturing (report) (2018). https://www.whitehouse.gov/wp-content/uploads/ 2018/10/Advanced-Manufacturing-Strategic-Plan-2018.pdf. Accessed 13 Dec 2018

Oh, S.H., Mardis, M.A., Jones, F.R.: Analyzing and comparing three competency models of manufacturing. Paper to be presented at 2019 American society of engineering educators (ASEE) annual conference & exposition, Tampa, FL (2019)

Petrick, I.J., Prindible, M.: Broadband technology in manufacturing. TrendScape Innovation Group, Hillsboro (2014). https://www.pamade.org/wp-content/uploads/2013/01/Broadband-IRC-FINAL-Report.pdf. Accessed 13 Dec 2018

Raveyre, M.: A new form of small industrial business in rural area: to exceeding the local roots? In: Torre, A., Traversac, J.B. (eds.) Territorial Governance. Physica-Verlag HD (2011)

Reardon, M.: Trump infrastructure plan leaves out rural broadband funding (2018). https://www. cnet.com/news/trump-infrastructure-plan-leaves-out-rural-broadband-funding/. Accessed 13 Dec 2018

Rendon Schneir, J., Xiong, Y.: A cost study of fixed broadband access networks for rural areas. Telecommun. Policy **40**, 755–773 (2016). https://doi.org/10.1016/j.telpol.2016.04.002

Strover, S., Whitacre, B., Rhinesmith, C., Schrubbe, A.: Libraries, the national digital platform, and inclusion. Paper presented at TPRC 45 (2017). https://ssrn.com/abstract=2940027. Accessed 13 Dec 2018

Strover, S.: Reaching rural America with broadband internet service (2018). http:// theconversation.com/reaching-rural-america-with-broadband-internet-service-82488. Accessed 13 Dec 2018

Thomas, N., Campbell, S.: The geography of manufacturing: the case of MEP and rural manufacturers (2018). https://www.nist.gov/blogs/manufacturing-innovation-blog/geography-manufacturing-case-mep-and-rural-manufacturers. Accessed 13 Dec 2018

Townsend, L., Wallace, C., Fairhurst, G.: Stuck out here: the critical role of broadband for remote rural places. Scott. Geogr. J. **131**(3/4), 171–180 (2015). https://doi.org/10.1080/14702541. 2014.978807

United States Department of Agriculture [USDA]: Rural America at a glance 2016. Economic Information Bulletin 162 (2017). https://www.ers.usda.gov/webdocs/publications/80894/eib-162.pdf. Accessed 13 Dec 2018

White House: President Donald J. Trump is working to rebuild rural America (2018). https:// www.whitehouse.gov/briefings-statements/president-donald-j-trump-working-rebuild-rural-america/. Accessed 13 Dec 2018

Yudken, J.S., Croft, T., Stettner, A.: Revitalizing America's manufacturing communities. The Century Foundation, New York (2017). https://tcf.org/content/report/revitalizing-americas-manufacturing-communities/. Accessed 13 Dec 2018

Participatory Development of an Open Source Broadband Measurement Platform for Public Libraries

Colin Rhinesmith[1]([✉])(iD), Chris Ritzo[2], Georgia Bullen[2],
James Werle[3], and Alyson Gamble[1](iD)

[1] Simmons University, 300 The Fenway, Boston, MA 02115, USA
crhinesmith@simmons.edu
[2] Open Technology Institute, New America, 740 15th Street, N.W., Suite 900,
Washington, DC 20005, USA
[3] Internet2, 100 Phoenix Drive, Suite 111, Ann Arbor, MI 48108, USA

Abstract. Public libraries need access to reliable, automated, and longitudinal data on the speed and quality of service of their broadband Internet connections. Having such data at a local, granular level is essential for libraries to understand how their broadband infrastructure can meet their communities' digital demands, as well as inform local, state, and national broadband planning efforts in the U.S. This paper contributes a participatory research methodology and an information system design proposal to investigate how public libraries can utilize broadband measurement tools to achieve these goals. The purpose of the research is to assist public libraries in gaining a better understanding of the relationship between their network infrastructure and digital services. The paper concludes with a brief discussion of the expected findings from our project, which builds upon existing research that examined how broadband measurement tools can be utilized in public schools.

Keywords: Public libraries · Broadband · Measurement · Open source · Information systems

1 Introduction

Public libraries across the U.S. face growing demand for broadband access (wireless and wired), broadband-enabled devices (laptops and tablets), and broadband services (library databases) within their buildings. In order to support their communities' thirst for such digital content, public libraries need access to automated, reliable, and longitudinal data about the speed and quality of service (QoS) of their broadband Internet connections. These data can assist public library administrators and staff who are planning for and responding to the digital demands of their patrons, as well as help inform local, state, and national broadband planning efforts. However, there is currently no coordinated effort to develop and sustain a nationwide broadband measurement platform using open source principles for U.S. public libraries.

© Springer Nature Switzerland AG 2019
N. G. Taylor et al. (Eds.): iConference 2019, LNCS 11420, pp. 274–279, 2019.
https://doi.org/10.1007/978-3-030-15742-5_27

This paper builds on the recommendations from LIS scholars [1] to propose a participatory research methodology and an information system design proposal to support broadband measurement in public libraries across the U.S. The project is part of a two-year Institute of Museum and Library Services grant (award # LG-71-18-0110-18). The paper begins with a review of the existing research that informed the development of our project, before presenting the research question that responds to a gap in the literature. We then present the research methodology that we are using to co-design, implement, and evaluate our open source broadband measurement platform in our first year with ten public libraries across the U.S. The paper concludes with a brief discussion of our expected results based on the findings from an earlier study of broadband measurement in Alexandria, Virginia public schools.

2 Related Work

For over a decade, broadband scholars and policy experts in the U.S. have argued that as broadband infrastructure continues to support a range of applications and services the problems of broadband measurement become even more complex and difficult [2]. Having access to data on broadband speeds and QoS at a local, granular level is essential to examine the relationship between public library infrastructure and services, as well as local, state, and national broadband planning efforts. In addition, having access to reliable indicators is key to understanding challenges related to broadband access, adoption, and use [2, 3]. Others have argued that having more precise data on QoS issues is critical to understanding factors shaping the national digital divide [4].

Since 1994, the studies "Public Libraries and the Internet" and "Public Library Funding and Technology Access," and later the "Digital Inclusion Survey," have tracked the growth of Internet connectivity in U.S. public libraries and have been used to frame public library Internet policies at the federal level. The authors of these important studies have successfully accomplished this task over time by providing useful data on Internet connectivity and technology services in public libraries and have provided summary national-level estimates of Internet connectivity in U.S. public libraries [1, 5, 6]. These foundational studies have not only helped to identify the ongoing broadband challenges and needs of the public library community nationwide, but also the increasing digital expectations of public library patrons. In sum, this research helped paint a picture of the national capacity of library broadband infrastructure to support emerging digital library services. However, there are currently no large scale efforts to collect automated, longitudinal measurement data on broadband speeds and QoS issues at a local, granular level inside public libraries over time. This includes times when buildings are closed, yet their wireless connectivity remains available.

3 Research Design

Our project seeks to fill a gap in the scholarship by addressing some of the challenges that findings from these previous studies have identified. This includes gathering data to respond to our core research question: *"How can public libraries utilize broadband measurement tools and training materials to develop a better understanding of the relationship between library network infrastructure and digital services?"*

In order to respond to this question, our project team is currently co-designing a broadband measurement platform and training manual with a research panel of ten public libraries across the U.S. using techniques and tests from the open source Internet measurement community while utilizing participatory design principles [7]. Our team will co-design, implement, and evaluate a broadband measurement and analysis system with the research participants to provide additional libraries with a means of gathering automated measurements of their institutions' broadband connection speed and QoS.

Our team is collaborating with the research panel to gather quantitative and qualitative data. The quantitative data will be collected primarily through the broadband measurement devices after they have been implemented in each of the partnering public libraries in 2019. The researchers will gather initial qualitative data during our participatory design workshop in fall 2018. The additional qualitative data will include interviews with the library staff, library directors, and network administrators, who will help us design the broadband measurement platform and assist in recruiting the library patron focus groups, which will take place in at least half of the partnering libraries. We also plan to gather quantitative data from a survey distributed to the fifty to sixty libraries that we will partner with to scale the pilot during the project's second year.

Quantitative data gathered through the broadband measurement platform will be analyzed through data analysis tools for time-series data, such as Prometheus and Grafana, using statistical analysis tools such as RStudio, and through custom designed visualizations based on input from the research panel. The research team will also have the ability to export data for statistical analysis into an outside software platform, such as SPSS. The interview and focus group recordings from the participatory design workshop and the fieldwork visits with the libraries during the first year of the project will be transcribed and uploaded as files into the cloud-based software Dedoose for qualitative analysis. The researchers will use this software platform to code the data and develop themes for our final reporting. The goal for our analysis is to use our theoretical framework drawing from literature in library and information science (LIS) and science and technology studies (STS) to guide how we look at both the quantitative and qualitative data, including being able to "triangulate" [8] multiple perspectives from library staff, network administrators, and patrons.

4 System Design

The broadband measurement system for our project has built upon the Open Technology Institute's previous research in Alexandria, Virginia city public schools, where connection speeds and latency of classroom connections were measured using the Network Diagnostic Tool provided by Measurement Lab (M-Lab) [9]. Measurements were run automatically over the course of two months from small computers, which were placed in up to three classrooms per school. By conducting periodic automated measurement tests on a randomized basis and from different vantage points within the school network, researchers were able to look at broadband connection quality trends over time, for example during peak and non-peak periods. The system used for measurement in Alexandria was an early prototype and was an opportunity to uncover the challenges of automated measurement within highly managed networks. In this current project, the measurement system will be refined and expanded based on the needs expressed by the library community.

The measurement system is envisioned to consist of three main components:

1. One or more small computers, connected to the library's network, will be configured to run a range of Internet measurement tests. Placement of these computers will measure Internet connections from different locations within each library's network, which will provide a diversity of measurements that align with the access provided to the library facility as a whole, to patrons on public access computers or using WiFi, and to staff using wired or wireless connections.
2. A cloud-based service where test data collected by the small computers will be sent, analyzed, and visualized for research staff and library partners. This service will provide library partners and research staff access to the collected data, as well as provide a visualization and analysis of the data collected.
3. A second cloud-based service used to administer, provision, and update all of the measurement computers to be used on the project. This will allow easy setup of new devices and a means to access and troubleshoot them remotely during the course of the first and second stages of this research pilot.

The prototype version of the system described above has been developed in previous research [9] and will be used as a demonstration tool with an initial stakeholder engagement group of administrative, librarian, and technology staff from our research panel of ten U.S. public libraries. This group attended our in-person participatory design workshop, where the project team worked to identify both the technical specifications for the pilot measurement system, as well as some of the initial content to be included in the broadband measurement platform training manual, which will also build on Internet2's current IMLS-funded technical broadband assessment toolkit [10]. At the conclusion of the participatory design workshop, our goal was to have identified the following: the specific network measurement tests that will be available in the measurement system; the types of additional data that would be helpful to collect from existing library IT systems; and a sense of how visualizations of this data might be displayed in order to provide meaningful and actionable analysis.

During the implementation phase of our project, our team will use the data gathered from our participatory design workshop to further inform our baseline measurement system. Our team is also considering additional techniques, which now exist to measure both speed and QoS characteristics of library broadband networks. Smaller networked computers the size of a pack of cards running open-source broadband measurement tests, such as Network Diagnostic Tool and Speedtest.net, will be are installed on at the library network, measuring broadband speeds and QoS (i.e., latency and jitter), as well as identifying the broadband service provider. During this implementation phase, our project team will continue to gather feedback from our public library partners through an ongoing user-centered design process to ensure that our system best addresses their broadband measurement needs.

5 Expected Results

Data gathered during our participatory design workshop and subsequent fieldwork visits during the first two phases of the project in the first year of the grant will provide the information needed to finalize the broadband measurement platform. These data will also inform the development of the training manual, which will be used to scale the project to fifty to sixty public libraries in rural, suburban, and urban libraries across the U.S during the second year of the project. Ultimately, the project team will develop an open-source and replicable broadband measurement platform, which includes a testing platform, device management, and data visualization system outlined above.

Findings from the data collection and analysis will be used to create the project's three deliverables: (1) an open-source and replicable broadband measurement platform; (2) a broadband measurement platform training manual for public librarians; and (3) a final report on the project. The research should appeal to academics, practitioners, and policymakers interested in having data that can be used to develop a more integrated, equitable, and dynamic set of interconnected infrastructures for delivering digital library services. The research will benefit the intended audience by helping public libraries and their communities better understand the relationship between networked infrastructure and services, as well as helping libraries develop the capabilities needed to work toward setting service quality benchmarks. These issues and considerations have been recommended by scholars as key areas for future research in U.S. public libraries [1]. The research findings will assist public librarians as their institutions continue to evolve in providing a robust broadband foundation for the NDP.

6 Conclusion

In this paper, we presented a participatory research methodology and an information system design proposal for the design, development, and implementation of an open-source broadband measurement platform for public libraries in the U.S. context. We presented related work in the field from scholars who recommended that additional research is needed to understand how public libraries can utilize broadband measurement tools to develop a better understanding of the relationship between network infrastructure and digital services. The paper concluded with some of the expected results from our research, which we hope will assist public library administrators, IT network staff, as well as policymakers at the local, state, and federal levels in understanding how broadband measurement can be used to address the digital demands of public library users across the U.S.

References

1. Bertot, J.C., Jaeger, P.T., Wahl, E.E., Sigler, K.I.: Public libraries and the Internet: an evolutionary perspective. Libr. Technol. Rep. **6**, 7–18 (2011)
2. Flamm, K., Friedlander, A., Horrigan, J., Lehr, W.: Measuring broadband: improving communications policymaking through better data collection. Pew Internet and American Life Project, Washington, DC (2007). http://people.csail.mit.edu/wlehr/Lehr-Papers_files/PIP_Measuring%20Broadband.pdf
3. Bertot, J.C., McClure, C.R.: Assessing sufficiency and quality of bandwidth for public libraries. Inf. Technol. Libr. **26**(1), 14–22 (2007)
4. Prieger, J.E., Hu, W.: The broadband digital divide and the nexus of race, competition, and quality. Inf. Econ. Policy **20**, 150–167 (2008)
5. Bertot, J.C., Real, B., Lee, J., McDermott, A.J., Jaeger, P.T.: 2014 digital inclusion survey: Survey findings and results. Information Policy and Access Center, College Park (2015). http://digitalinclusion.umd.edu/sites/default/files/uploads/2014DigitalInclusionSurveyFinalRelease.pdf
6. Mandel, L.H., Bishop, B.W., McClure, C.R., Bertot, J.C., Jaeger, P.T.: Broadband for public libraries: importance, issues, and research needs. Gov. Inf. Q. **27**, 280–291 (2010)
7. Schuler, D., Namioka, A.: Participatory Design: Principles and Practices. Lawrence Erlbaum Associates, Inc., Hillsdale (1993)
8. Stake, R.: The Art of Case Study Research. SAGE Publications, Thousand Oaks (1995)
9. Ritzo, C.: Measuring Broadband in Schools: A Technical Case Study on Applied Internet Measurement in PreK-12 Schools. New America Foundation Open Technology Institute, Washington, D.C. (2017)
10. Spellman, S., Werle, J., Block, C.: Toward gigabit libraries. D-Lib Magaz. **23**(5/6) (2017). http://www.dlib.org/dlib/may17/spellman/05spellman.html

Information Behaviors in Academic Environments

Sexual Information Behavior of Filipino University Students

Dan Anthony D. Dorado$^{(\boxtimes)}$, Kathleen Lourdes B. Obille$^{(\boxtimes)}$,
Rhianne Patricia P. Garcia$^{(\boxtimes)}$, and Benedict Salazar Olgado$^{(\boxtimes)}$

School of Library and Information Studies, University of the Philippines,
Quezon City, Philippines
{dan, kate, b.olgado}@slis.upd.edu.ph,
rhiannepgarcia@gmail.com

Abstract. Having a better knowledge of sexual health could lead to having improved programs and projects in educating people who are sexually active, those who are curious about their sexuality, and those who are planning to engage in the sexual experience. Additionally, by learning more about sexual health and having an idea on what it is, it would help in letting people understand the concepts of sexuality, sexual relationships, and its role in creating better and efficient prevention programs for sexually transmitted infections (STIs) or sexually trans-mitted diseases (STDs), teen pregnancy issues, and other concerns regarding sexual health.

This study aimed to find out the following: the sexual health information needs and seeking behavior of undergraduate students; as well as if user context played a vital role in affecting their sexual health information needs and/or seeking behavior. Through the use of an online survey among undergraduate students of the University of the Philippines Diliman, the study was able to present the sexual health information needs and sexual health information seeking behavior of the undergraduate students. It has also determined that various characteristics of undergraduate students have an association on whether they would seek sexual health information or not.

Keywords: Sexual health · Sexual health information needs ·
Sexual health information seeking behavior · User context · Young adults

1 Sex and the Filipino Youth

The Philippines is mainly composed of Catholics as according to World Population Review where 81% of Filipinos are Roman Catholics [1]. This religion is known for its stand regarding sex, that this should only be done by married couples "to further participate in God's ongoing creation" thereby rendering sex outside of marriage and sex for pleasure as wrong and sinful [2]. However, as a largely Catholic Country, there is still a high incidence of teenage pregnancies. In a 2016 report by Herrin [3], there is an increase in teen age (15–19 year) pregnancy from 2003 to 2010. In 2017, the report by the Philippine Statistics Authority shows that about 7% of women ages 15–19 are pregnant, and 64.2% of those are not using any contraceptive method [4]. Aside from

© Springer Nature Switzerland AG 2019
N. G. Taylor et al. (Eds.): iConference 2019, LNCS 11420, pp. 283–289, 2019.
https://doi.org/10.1007/978-3-030-15742-5_28

teen age pregnancy, there is also a high incidence of sexually transmitted diseases which may mean that the youth do not have sufficient information in relation to sexual acts and sexual behaviors.

Reproductive health education was mandated for inclusion in the K+12 Program by the RH Bill or the Republic Act 10934 *An Act Providing for a National Policy on Responsible Parenthood and Reproductive Health*. However, there are still questions on the effectiveness of instruction across grade levels.[1] With the many criticisms by parents and the church, Mateo [5] reports how DepEd intends to teach sex education. The topics do not center on the act but focus more on the "science of reproduction, physical care, hygiene, correct norms of interpersonal relations to avoid pre-marital sex and teen-age pregnancy" (para. 6). This argues against claims that propagating sex education in the schools increases the tendency of the youth to engage in sex.

Given that reproductive health education is incorporated in the K+12 program, this should translate to a more informed population with wiser decision making. But given that this is not yet the case at this point, the study sought to determine the patterns of information behavior among university students in the Philippines. It gathered data on the reasons for seeking sexual health information, preferences of information sources, relationships among the variables on information needs, information seeking, sexual activities, and health scare/situations.

1.1 Information Seeking and Sex

Several studies, internationally, have been made in relation to behaviors of the youth in relation to sex and these show factors such as information, communication, and motivation as affecting sexual behaviors. There is a multitude of information sources online, and this is the most accessible source of information. However, the credibility of sources is also an issue. Several studies have noted that the internet is the main source of information among the youth [6–9]. Other sources of information include, peers, sexual partners, parents, and non-internet reliable sources such as books and references available in the library. The reasons for seeking information [6, 8] include information on pregnancy, STI scare, and contraceptive options. While the internet is a top source of information, it appears that social media is not a popular source of information on sex [10]. Reasons include credibility and accuracy.

1.2 Sources of Sexual Health Information

Based on different studies, there have been multiple kinds of information sources that can be used when seeking information about sexual health. These sources can be categorized into two: formal and informal sources [15]. Formal sources are sources that can be surely considered as credible and reliable information. This type of sources can usually be seen in libraries and health clinics. Examples of these are flyers and leaflets from health clinics, treatment from health professionals and various textbooks and

---

[1] There are grade level or age level appropriate topics to ensure that the students as early as Grade 1 are "protected from sexual exploitation".

materials from libraries [12, 15]. While informal sources can be less credible compared to formal sources. Some examples are from pornography, articles from the internet, advice from parents, peers, guardians, and the like [6, 11–15]. This study was also able to categorize the sources, formal and informal, which would help young adults distinguish which are better, if not the best, sources for their sexual health information needs.

2 Methodology

2.1 Population and Sample

The population of the study is identified as undergraduate students from the University of the Philippines Diliman between 16–24 years old.[2] The researchers were able to survey 206 students resulting in to a margin of error of ±7 with a 95% confidence level. Respondents were asked to define their sex, gender, and sexual orientation to take in to consideration any significant differences among identified sexual groups.

2.2 Research Instrument

An online survey was used to gather data for this study and be able to answer what are the sexual health information needs and seeking behavior of young adults and how could user context possibly affect their sexual health information needs and seeking behavior. The questions for the survey was based and patterned on the study of Charest et al. [11]. The survey of this study was able to enumerate the variables in the questions regarding gender, sexual orientation, and sexual activity since these factors could have a huge impact on the sexual health information needs and seeking behavior of young adults as well as determining the possible sexual health information sources [12–15] that can be used by young adults. A systematic-purposive sampling method was used to ensure that respondents will fit the criteria set. The research instrument was disseminated through different social networking groups recognized by the university as student organizations.

2.3 Analysis of Data

Chi-squared test for independence was used to determine if the variables in this study could influence each other or affect one another. This statistical test was used to see if there were any relationships present between the demographics, such as the sex, gender, sexual orientation, and sexual activity, and the sexual health information needs, sexual health information seeking behavior, and sexual health information sources of the respondents of this study.

---

[2] Young adults are defined as someone who is in his or her late teenage years or early twenties [16]. The age range mentioned is the operational definition used for this study.

3 Findings

The following are the principle findings of this study:

- Almost all respondents have sought information about sexual health. Most have answered that they sought sexual health information because they were curious.
- Internet was the number one source of sexual health information regardless of gender or sexual orientation.
- It was determined that the respondents were most likely to seek sexual health information after a particular situation they have encountered (pregnancy scares, STD or STI scares, used contraceptives, gotten or gotten someone else pregnant, and acquired STD/STI or HIV).
- The results of the survey also showed how the respondents verified if the sources they used when seeking sexual health information were credible. Checking the credentials of the website/s, author/s, and the like, was the top answer.
- By combining different variables in contingency tables and computing the chi-square test for dependency with a 5% level of significance, we were able to identify certain associations in information seeking behavior and sexual activity. Listed below are the variables that scored a p-value of less than 0.05 thus rejecting the null hypothesis that these paired variables are statistically independent of each other:
  - The respondents' sexual orientation and sexual health information needs. Respondents who characterized themselves as homosexuals have shown a higher frequency of sexual activities leading to a higher aptitude in seeking sexual information needs.
  - Their sexual activities and sexual health information needs.
  - Their sex and their likeliness of seeking sexual health information before or after getting pregnant or getting someone else pregnant.
  - Their gender and their likeliness of seeking sexual health information before or after getting pregnant or getting someone else pregnant.
  - The students' responses if they had a pregnancy scare and their likeliness of seeking sexual health information before or after getting a pregnancy scare.
  - Their responses if they had a STD or STI scare and their likeliness of seeking sexual health information before or after getting a STD or STI scare.
  - Their sex and their likeliness of seeking sexual health information from pamphlets or brochures.
  - Their sex and their likeliness of seeking sexual health information from meetings, classes, lectures, seminars, or presentations. Females have a higher tendency to seek sexual health information.
  - Their sex and their likeliness of seeking sexual health information from textbooks
  - Their sexual orientation and their likeliness of seeking sexual health information from sexual partner/s.
  - The respondents' sexual activity and their likeliness of seeking sexual health information from sexual partner/s.

- Their sexual activity and their likeliness of seeking sexual health information from the internet.
- The number of sexual partners of the respondents and their likeliness of seeking sexual health information from sexual partner/s.
- Responses of students if they had a pregnancy scare and their likeliness of seeking sexual health information from sexual partner/s.
- Their responses if they had a pregnancy scare and their likeliness of seeking sexual health information from the internet.
- Their responses if they had a pregnancy scare and their likeliness of seeking sexual health information from newspaper articles.
- Their responses if they had a STD or STI scare and their likeliness of seeking sexual health information from the internet.
- Their responses if they acquired a STD or STI and their likeliness of seeking sexual health information from posters, signs, or billboards.
- The sexual health information needs of the respondents and their likeliness of seeking sexual health information from sexual partner/s.

4 Discussion

As far as the respondents are concerned, sexual health information was sought because of various needs. These needs were: for health awareness, for curiosity about sexual health, for safety or protection regarding sexual health, pregnancy and pregnancy scares, and STDs or STIs and STD/s or STI/s scares. Their seeking behavior depended on what their sexual health information needs were. Undergraduate students who had pregnancy scares or gotten or gotten someone pregnant would seek topics related to this. While those who had an STD/s or STI/s scare or acquired an STD/s or STI/s would search about this topic. Additionally, those who have not engaged in any sexual activity, do not consider themselves sexually active and had zero sexual partners have sought sexual health information mainly because of curiosity, health awareness, and for their safety or protection. They do not seek information regarding pregnancy scares, STD or STI scares, and the like.

Just like the studies in the United States [6, 11, 13] United Kingdom [15], and in three Caribbean countries [14], the internet is the primary source that students and young adults use when seeking information about health and sexual health. Most of the respondents used the internet as their sources, but there are changes that can be observed because of the gender and sexual orientation of the respondents. It was then established that there were some relationships present with user context and the sexual health information needs, sexual health information seeking behavior, and sexual health information sources of the respondents. This was proven by using the chi-squared test of independence among the variables presented in the study. Finally, it was noticed that students relied more on informal sources rather than formal sources.

5   Conclusion

Majority of the respondents have the capability to seek sexual information needs on their own, but red flags were seen on how they seek this information because there were respondents that would likely seek sexual health information sources after having sexual encounters, STD/STI scare, etc. Also they rely on informal sources rather than formal sources. First is the fact that they seek sexual information after a sexual incident has happened (pregnancy scare, STD/HIV scare, etc.). This behavior is problematic because this makes the abundance of sexual health information moot in terms of preventing said sexual incident. Second is the finding that the internet is the most preferred source of sexual information need. Even though the respondents can evaluate information sources, the primary consideration was still the anonymity the internet provides and its convenience.

Not only that, based on the results, it is inevitable that young adults will seek information about sexual health whether they are experienced or not. As stated previously, they rely more on informal sources rather than formal sources. They should be taught how to depend more on formal sources in order to avoid unwanted pregnancies, STDs, STIs, and the like.

These findings have the potential to further push the call of implementing a comprehensive sexual education in the Philippines. If the government fails to address this issue and this behavior of young adults in the Philippines continues, the rising trend of teen-age frequency and the proliferation of sexually transmitted will continue.

References

1. Philippines Population 2018. http://worldpopulationreview.com/countries/philippines-population/. Accessed 6 Sept 2018
2. About Catholics. The Role of Sexual Intercourse. http://www.aboutcatholics.com/be-liefs/the-role-of-sexual-intercourse/last. Accessed 6 Sept 2018
3. Herrin, A.: Education, Earnings, and Effects of Teenage Pregnancy in the Philippines
4. Philippine Statistics Authority: Philippines National Demographic and Health Survey 2017: Key Indicators. Quezon City, Philippines, and Rockville, Maryland (2018)
5. Mateo, J.: DepEd Integrates RH Education in K+12 Program, The Philippine Star. https://www.philstar.com/headlines/2016/08/26/1617352/deped-integrates-rh-education-k-12-program. Accessed 6 Sept 2018
6. Buhi, E.R., Daley, E.M., Fuhrmann, H.J., Smith, S.A.: An observational study on how young people search for online sexual information. J. Am. Coll. Health **58**(2), 101–111 (2009)
7. Gumban, G., Martos, R.J., Rico, K.W.M., Bernarte, R.P., Tuason, I.C.: Let's talk about sex: parental communication and sexual behavior or male Filipino youth. Asia Pac. J. Multi. Res. **4**(2), 130–139 (2016)
8. Gonzalez-Ortega, E., Vicario-Molina, I., Martinez, J.L., Orgaz, B.: The internet as a source of sexual information in a sample of Spanish adolescents: associations with sexual behavior. Sex. Res. Soc. Policy **12**, 290–300 (2015)
9. Keilty, P., Seeking sex: embodiment and electronic culture. Doctoral Dissertation from the University of California School of Information (2011)

10. Rodriguez, J.L., Chaco, J., Contreras, C., Ramgoolam, D.: Exploring the role of social media in the information seeking behavior of millennials in search of safe sex and sexual health information. Poster Presented During the 2017 iConference. http://hdl.han-dle.net/2142/96724. Accessed 6 Sept 2018
11. Charest, M., Kleinplatz, P.J., Lund, J.I.: Sexual health information disparities between heterosexual and LGBTQ + young adults: implications for sexual health. Can. J. Hum. Sex. **25**(2), 74–85 (2016)
12. Kane, R., Macdowall, W., Wellings, K.: Providing information for young people in sexual health clinics: getting it right. J. Fam. Plann. Reprod. Health Care **29**(3), 141–145 (2003)
13. Rosengard, C., et al.: Family sources of sexual health information, primary messages, and sexual behavior at-risk, urban adolescents. Am. J. Health Educ. **43**(2), 83–92 (2012)
14. White, L.A.: HIV-related information seeking among Residential University students in three Caribbean countries (2009)
15. Whitfield, C., Jomeen, J., Gardiner, E.: Sexual health information seeking: a survey of adolescent practices. J. Clin. Nurs. **22**(23/24), 3259–3269 (2013)
16. Young adult [Def. 1]. https://dictionary.cambridge.org/us/dictionary/english/young-adult/. Accessed 6 Dec 2018

From Gridiron Gang to Game Plan: Impact of ICTs on Student Athlete Information Seeking Practices, Routines, and Long-Term Goals

Vincent Grimaldi[1], Jasmine Sullivan[2], Josue Figueroa[3], and Bryan Dosono[4(✉)]

[1] Suffolk University, Boston, MA, USA
vgrimaldi@su.suffolk.edu
[2] University of Maryland, College Park, MD, USA
jsulliv4@umd.edu
[3] Clemson University, Clemson, SC, USA
josuef@g.clemson.edu
[4] Syracuse University, Syracuse, NY, USA
bdosono@syr.edu

Abstract. Our qualitative study explores the lives of college student athletes and their use of information and communication technologies (ICTs) as they plan their transition from student life to life after graduation. While ICTs such as social media, smartphones, and the internet are becoming more ubiquitous on college campuses and embedded within daily routines, student athletes contend with finding the appropriate information at the right time to navigate through critical life choices. In a thematic analysis of 15 interviews with U.S. student athletes, we uncover factors that affect ICT use in both their athletic and academic environments. We discuss ICTs as transition mediaries and present implications for college athletics programs to improve the holistic student athlete experience and the transition beyond college.

Keywords: Student athletes · ICTs · Social media · Fitness · Activity trackers · Transitions

1 Introduction

According to a 2018 report compiled by the National Collegiate Athletic Association [1], approximately 480,000 college students compete annually on an athletic scholarship. Within that pool, just 1.6% of U.S. college football[1] players and 1.2% of men's basketball players end up making it "pro," that is, playing in the major leagues as a professional. As universities have an obligation to address the needs of all their student athletes, college athletics programs are missing

---

[1] In this study, all references to football are attributed to American football, also known as gridiron football.

© Springer Nature Switzerland AG 2019
N. G. Taylor et al. (Eds.): iConference 2019, LNCS 11420, pp. 290–301, 2019.
https://doi.org/10.1007/978-3-030-15742-5_29

opportunities to position ICTs to meet the complex goals their players have as both students and as athletes. In this study, we explore factors that contribute to the ICT use of student athletes both in and out of the athletic arena and provide implications for how ICTs can improve their transition beyond college.

2 Background

Previous scholarship in the athletic domain of ICTs use has taken a systems-driven approach to improve motion capture sensor technologies [2], animating athletic behaviors via control algorithms [3], and developing interfaces for augmented cooperative play [4]. We contrast our investigative approach through a human-centered lens, reviewing prior empirical work that analyzed behavioral aspects underlying ICT use across relevant athletic domains. Here we summarize prior work [5] that examines how student athletes use ICTs for tracking performance, seeking social support, and navigating life choices.

2.1 ICTs for Tracking Performance

Mueller et al. looked at how audio communication facilitates a deep sense of presence among runners who run together in real-time but at different locations [6]. In their qualitative interview study of runners (n = 17) who tested a headset and a wireless heart rate monitor, they found that the creation of a social experience augmented the physical activity at hand.

Puussaar et al. deployed a visual tool for social sensemaking of personal tracker data to understand how social context contributes to sensemaking [7]. In their sample of participants who met weekly across a 12-week focus group (n = 20), they found that users tend to share their fitness data on platforms that alleviate privacy concerns and promote contextual value when displayed competitively.

Ellis et al. interviewed seven former student athletes to generate insights for designing a wristband and web application that set up challenges among former team players [8]. In a design evaluation of former student athlete users (n = 2), they observed how facets of camaraderie and competition developed over years of athletic training were sustained through their product, easing opportunities for post-athletic transitions.

2.2 ICTs for Seeking Social Support

Stoldt surveyed members of the College Sports Information Directors of America (n = 519) and found that social media significantly impacted how athletics programs communicated with external publics by increasing organizational transparency [9]. Sanderson conducted a thematic analysis of athletic handbooks from NCAA Division I member institutions (n = 159) to understand how student athletes are getting informed on social media use [10]. He found that ambiguous language in social media policies of athletic departments sends conflicting messages to student athletes. For instance, while student athletes are restricted from posting pictures of participation in illegal activities, they could interpret such statements to assume that such engagement is acceptable as long as they "do not get caught" and create a public relations debacle for the institution. Additionally, Sanderson thematically analyzed comments (n = 514) from a blog owned by a contentious Boston Red Sox pitcher and discovered social support manifesting in ways that allow for athletes to preserve their reputation amid controversy while maintaining their support from fans [11].

McAdow et al. [12] outlined challenges associated with social media platforms in conjunction with the athlete's natural need to express themselves. The authors illustrated through a content analysis of 44 written social media policies that while the majority of college athletics programs in 2014 have social media accounts on Twitter, Facebook and Instagram, policies were ambiguous to interpretation and heavily focused on social media restrictions. Results from interviewed communications professionals (n = 6) revealed that students are aware of the imposed social media restrictions and do not feel the risks associated with social media outweigh its perceived benefits. In addition, student athletes generally had no knowledge of any monitoring techniques regarding their personal social media use. As social media policies are not reflective of actual social media education, a lack of social media training among student athletes may restrict how athletes elect to express themselves online.

2.3 ICTs for Navigating Life Choices

Both the National Basketball Association and the National Football League require a player to be out of high school for a specified amount of time before becoming eligible to play a sport professionally [13]. This time period often forces high school athletes to decide to go to college until they are eligible to declare for a professional career in their respective sport. Wong's legal analysis on providing guidance to student athletes in a regulatory environment claims that information could be made more accessible to student athletes and their families to shape crucial life choices, such as choosing to continue with higher education, finding an agent, maneuvering through healthcare options, or playing in the professional leagues [14].

Becker examined effective coaching mechanisms and their impact on athletes [15]. She interviewed both NCAA and professional athletes and condensed aspects of effective coaching into 6 factors: coach attributes, environment, relationships, the system, coaching actions, and influences. A number of participants reported that they have a strong lifelong relationship with their coaches who became mentors, teachers, and important figures in participants lives. Coaching serves a plethora of roles beyond the field, which illustrates the importance of extraordinary coaching and navigating life development.

2.4   Research Questions

In response to a dearth of literature that reports on ICT use among student athletes, we ask the following:

- **RQ1.** How do ICTs enable information seeking practices of student athletes?
- **RQ2.** What routines manifest among student athletes and their ICT use?
- **RQ3.** How are student athletes using ICTs to plan their long-term goals?

3   Methods

3.1   Participant Recruitment

From October 2017 to April 2018, we conducted semi-structured interviews with undergraduate student athletes across three U.S. research institutions. We employed multiple recruitment strategies in parallel: (1) outreach to communications staff of athletic departments, (2) solicitation of interview participation via social media, (3) distribution of promotional materials around college campuses, and (4) snowball sampling for additional participants after each interview. We situate the research context for this study to athletics in the U.S.

Table 1. Summary of participant demographics.

ID	Sex	Race	Age	Major	Sport
P1	Male	Black	19	Information Science	Football
P2	Male	Black	21	Biological Sciences	Football
P3	Male	White	18	Marketing	Baseball
P4	Male	Black	20	Education	Football
P5	Male	White	20	Psychology	Football
P6	Female	Black	19	Psychology	Track and Field
P7	Male	White	20	Economics	Cross Country
P8	Female	Black	18	Kinesiology	Lacrosse
P9	Female	White	18	Kinesiology	Lacrosse
P10	Female	White	18	Criminology	Lacrosse
P11	Male	White	21	Communications	Basketball
P12	Female	White	20	Finance	Basketball
P13	Female	White	20	Finance	Basketball
P14	Male	White	20	Human Resource Management	Football
P15	Male	White	20	Entrepreneurship	Hockey

3.2   Participant Demographics

As illustrated in Table 1, ten participants identified as white and five (33%) identified as black. Six identified as cis female (40%) and nine identified as cis male (60%). Among seven different sports represented, football was most commonly played within in the dataset (33%). Participants varied in scholarly interests, as there were 12 different academic majors reported in the sample.

3.3   Interviews

Semi-structured interviews allow for a predetermined set of open questions informed by the research goals of the study with the opportunity for the interviewer to probe particular themes or responses further [16]. Participants were asked about their athletic motivation (group affiliation, team interactions), academic motivation (educational preparation, goal setting), external support systems (financial sponsors, peer socialization), and their outlook on professional development opportunities beyond college. We analyzed our qualitative data inductively and grouped recurring themes from the interviews. All interviews were audio recorded and transcribed, and lasted approximately 30 min on average in duration. An Institutional Review Board approved the study.

4   Results

Here we present our results in the order of our research questions. Per RQ1, ICTs such as activity trackers, scheduling software, and online tutoring portals enabled student athletes to solidify healthy habits and make data-informed decisions. Per RQ2, the use of virtual reality, film reviews, and kinetic measuring systems are embedded in the routines of student athletes as a means for monitoring growth. Per RQ3, student athletes use ICTs for personal brand management, health monitoring, and career development to map out their long-term goals.

4.1   Information Seeking Practices of Student Athletes

Activity Trackers Add More Value to Workouts. Nine out of 15 participants (P1, P2, P5, P6, P7, P8, P9, P10, P12) reported using activity trackers in various capacities to track their athletic performance. For example, P5 reported using Strava, a GPS-based running tracker, to record all of his runs: *"With Strava, it is cool to be able to track the stuff about running like speed, pace, and time. My other teammates do the same so we can all compare the results. It's cool to be able to share and encourage each other to do better."* (P5)

While the types and brands of trackers varied across participants, the ability to reflect upon performance data over time gives student athletes the ability to track their progress, allowing them to make marginal adjustments to their fitness routines and see how those changes affect outcomes in the playing field.

Information Access Increases Scholarly Productivity. Five participants (P1, P3, P9, P10, P11) expressed how they relied on ICTs to access information quickly for mapping out their schedules over analog methods. P12, a female finance major who plays basketball, reported: *"Using Google Drive, I have a centralized location where I can keep everything. In high school, I lost papers and stuff all the time so that didn't help me any. So I like having everything centralized where you just go online and see everything."* (P12)

In contrast, P13, a female finance major who plays basketball, reported her willingness to stay up-to-date with her academics while on the road, as long as the information is readily available and easy to access. *"I personally like to use technology during classes to take notes and occasionally record lectures that I know are going to be important at a later time. Generally, I think a lot of people are just used to using computers and stuff to keep up in class. When the team is on the road, we can read PowerPoints that we've missed, as long as they are posted online for us."* (P13)

Student athletes stay abreast of their individual coursework and their team competition through ICTs that sync their academic and athletic schedules.

Instruction Persists Beyond the Classroom. According to 8 participants, (P1, P2, P3, P8, P9, P10, P11, P14) time management was a recurring challenge due to their busy training schedules. Student athletes often travel to distant playing fields and are thus unable to contact their professors in person when they are away for a game. Thus, they often resort to online tutoring methods. P15, a male entrepreneurship major who plays hockey, identified using his university's CLAS (Center for Learning and Academic Success) online tutoring portal to develop a close relationship with his professors.

In addition, P15 also mentions that he can access this live, free tutoring from anywhere in the world while online, which he attributed as a resource that helped him stay on top of his coursework even during the peak of his busy hockey season. *"Well, I do tend to be in contact with my professors a lot because hockey takes up a lot of time. So instead of going to see them in person, I will either email them or get tutoring from CLAS online. CLAS online has been a great addition because we can get access to tutors without being on campus, so that's a plus."* (P15)

Athletes spend time traveling on the road during their season times, and they use ICTs as tools to help them stay up-to-date on academic information, minimizing the impact travel takes away from their coursework.

4.2 ICTs and Routines of Student Athletes

Virtual Reality Augments Muscle Memory. Two participants (P2, P4) who both play football reported that their team regularly uses virtual reality (VR) to simulate what they expect to see from their future opponents, allowing them to forecast and prepare for specific scenarios before they occur in real time. By running through VR-assisted simulations, athletes develop a sense of muscle memory and can premeditate appropriate responses for a multitude of different situations.

P2, a male biology major who plays football, reported his personal experience with VR and how he used VR in an athletic setting. *"Virtual reality is primarily for quarterbacks, but it helps every position. It really prepares you for the game especially for people like me who don't get as many reps as some people. If I was a starter I wouldn't have to necessarily use virtual reality as much."* (P2)

VR techniques that simulate an on-field presence can help student athletes learn a complex set of plays more quickly in preparation for real-life competition.

Film Reviews Enable Tactical Iteration. Three participants (P9, P13, P15) used iMovie and Viddy to replay their recent game day footage before the next competition to study both their wins and areas identified for improvement. Film applications allow student athletes to manipulate the speed and frame of their game footage, which improves how they can observe and learn from each play.

P13 expressed how film technology helps her improve her athletic ability by communicating winning strategies with her team: *"Film and communication are the big two in this case. We are expected to watch film, of course. Even outside of film sessions, good players use film even by themselves to gain an advantage. Communication, I only say because our coach is always preaching communication. She probably says it like 100 times a day, at least."* (P13)

Film applications on mobile devices are becoming an increasingly common ICT on the field, which also enables student athletes to film each other as they work towards perfecting their athletic plays.

Universities Invest in Quantified Athletes. P6, a female studying psychology who runs track and field, reported using a kinetic measuring system called GymAware, which helps athletes measure metrics such as the velocity and power of their workouts. P6 also reported having access to a hamstring machine which could measure which of her legs was generating more output, allowing her to focus on training the weaker of the two. *"In the weight room, we use something called GymAware and a 10–80. GymAware measures how fast you power clean or squat. 10–80 puts resistance on you, and we go over many hurdles with that. We also use a hamstring machine, it does all those calculations and sees which hamstring is stronger, which hamstring is weaker, how much actual strength is in this hamstring."* (P6)

P7, a male economics major who runs cross country, reported using an ICT called the BodPod. Athletes could use this device to accurately measure and record their body fat percentage over a period of time. For athletes that participate in contact sports, the BodPod could also measure lean muscle mass and overall muscle density to gain insight into how they will stack up against their competition. *"BodPod, we do that semi-regularly so you can see what's working well for us and when we're in our peak fitness, because we want to extend that if it's working well for us."* (P7)

When athletic programs fund ICTs that can measure the output of full-body exercises with extreme precision, student athletes may take full advantage of such ICTs if they feel the granular data can be harnessed for a competitive advantage.

4.3   ICTs for Long-Term Goals

Digital Footprints Magnify Athletic Exposure. Participants were keenly aware of the public nature of social media, and some have shared how they used ICTs to build their personal brand. P15, a male hockey player, reflects on his experiences using Hudl, an online film software, to compile athletic clips of himself in order to use in promotion for future exposure by professional athletic recruiters. *"Well for hockey, we watch a lot of film. I think that is mostly because there is a lot of film available. We use a website called Hudl to watch film as a team. We can save our individual highlights as well for promotional purposes."* (P15)

Participants conveyed their interests in being discovered by professional agents who were scouting for athletic talent online.

Activity Trackers Perceived as Beneficial for Monitoring Health over the Long Run. Five participants (P1, P5, P6, P12, P15) indicated a positive outlook on being able to track fitness data to improve and maintain their health. P12, a white female finance major who plays basketball, describes the impact of monitoring health and fitness levels: *"I actually recently got an activity tracker... I am big into personal fitness so being able to track my steps and my calories is a cool addition to what I was already doing in terms of managing my body."* (P12)

Athletes may benefit from the accuracy of these wearable technologies as they are in a position to use this data to make changes to their daily routine in an effort to achieve increased performance.

ICTs Map Out Professional Development Objectives. Seven participants (P1, P2, P3, P4, P5, P13, P15) described the benefits of using ICTs to analyze collected data to push them forward to develop themselves professionally. For instance, P2 communicates how he uses ICTs in a multitude of ways in preparation for medical school: *"Excel is a big thing. A huge thing. That's actually how I chart my medical school shadowing hours through Excel. It calculates a lot of things and of course Microsoft words for basically every assignment that I have to do individually."* (P2)

P5, a male psychology major who plays football, describes how he utilizes ICTs over an extended period of his undergraduate coursework to chart out his academic milestones and connect with professionals who can support his academic journey. *"We use a system called Connect to do our homework assignments on the computer. My math homework is all online with computer tools to teach me about what I don't get. Also, my tutor sometimes FaceTimes me if I'm away and I'm confused about an assignment. All the time."* (P5)

Online platforms like Connect ensure student athletes have the technology available to succeed, should they opt to use it, so that they do not compromise their long-term professional goals in pursuit of their short-term athletic priorities.

5   Discussion

5.1   ICTs as Transition Mediaries: Getting Their Head in (and Out Of) the Game

Here we discuss how ICTs shape the ongoing development process of student athletes as they explore career options beyond professional play, and we advance the concept of "ICTs as transition mediaries" in the context of their post-graduate planning.

Research has shown that infomediaries, or brokers of public access to ICTs, play a critical role in connecting people to resources. Ramírez and colleagues argue that users in developing countries like Bangladesh and Chile face overwhelming life barriers in the absence of infomediaries [17]. In their research on veteran re-integration, Semaan and colleagues found that an essential factor in successful transition depends on access to a close family member or friend who acts as a transition mediary—a spouse or parent who helps bridge civilian and military contexts [18]. They found that ICTs functioned as mediaries that took on an authoritative role with the veterans, assuming the role of a commanding officer in the military, and providing them with structure as they developed executive functioning skills. Facing an entirely different set of challenges (cf. [17,18]), college athletes who have not formulated a plan after college may experience a unique set of transition issues when they enter the workforce [14].

We observe how ICTs are being used as an integral part of a student athlete's daily routine, both on and off the field, as a means for seeking social support and making life choices. For instance, ICTs as transition mediaries often connected student athletes with their peers and helped reinforce collectivist norms of camaraderie, cooperation, and group achievement. Additionally, ICTs as transition mediaries allow student athletes to make the most out of the gaps within their schedules by connecting them to academic resources even while on the road. Moreover, ICTs as transition mediaries gave way for student athletes to take it upon themselves to learn about online resources that were available to them to support their transition beyond college.

Student athletes may have less time to devote to preparing for the transition out of college and into the job market in comparison to their non-athlete counterparts, and thus have much to gain by employing ICTs as transition mediaries for mapping out critical life choices.

5.2 Implications for College Athletics Programs: Inform, Include, Inspire

In reviewing our data, we provide the following recommendations toward college athletics programs to consider for improving the holistic student athlete experience and the inevitable transitions that await beyond college.

Inform University Career Service Departments to Develop Accessible Job Readiness Materials that Guide the Transition for Life After College to Student Athletes Who Opt Not to Pursue Professional Play. A prominent theme across all 15 interviews revolved around the guilt felt by athletes from spending significantly more time on athletics than academics. Participants shared a range of goals that included becoming accountants, doctors, lawyers, and attending graduate school. Such goals require acute attention to detail from both an academic planning and career planning perspective. Universities should own the opportunity to weave more tightly cross-campus partnerships that serve the needs of student athletes and their aspirational career goals.

Include ICT Productivity Training as Supplementary Curriculum to Athletic Programs. Incorporating the proper technology into the daily routine of a student athlete may pay dividends towards their well-being down the road. Participants reported spending anywhere between 5–8 h more per week on their athletic commitments than the NCAA actually permits. Such anecdotal evidence further advances the notion that if universities chose to include more productivity-focused ICTs into the daily routine of student athletes, they could enable them to make more out of the limited time that they have. Just as top programs invest in quantified tracking technology to improve on-field performance, the same initiatives can be taken to enable student athletes to make the most of the resources around them.

Inspire Student Athletes to Pursue Academic Majors that Align with Career Goals Beyond College. Although student athlete participants in the study who identified from a low socio-economic background reported being more likely to want to attend graduate programs, a subset of those participants expressed uncertainty about whether or not they were competent to pursue a science, technology, engineering, or mathematics (STEM) program. Athletic programs should partner more closely with academic counselors to inspire a pipeline of mentorship for connecting exemplary alumni or senior student athletes with younger student athletes.

6 Conclusion

Our qualitative study contributes a deeper understanding of how ICTs are used within the daily lives of student athletes. First, we examine how ICTs expand their ability to seek information, as activity trackers add more value to workouts, information access increases productivity, and instruction persists beyond the classroom. Second, we uncover routines of ICT use among student athletes, as virtual reality augments muscle memory, film reviews enable tactical iteration, and universities invest in quantified athletes. Third, we unpack the role of ICTs and their influence on long-term goals, as digital footprints magnify athletic exposure, activity trackers monitor health over the long run, and ICTs map out professional development objectives. We build the concept of ICTs as transition mediaries to describe how student athletes navigate through career decisions that affect their post-college lifestyles and discuss implications for college athletics programs to improve the overall experience of their student athletes.

Acknowledgments. We thank our colleagues Kayla Booth, Anthony Pinter, Rachel Simons, and Mike Depew of the iSchool Inclusion Institute for their feedback of earlier drafts of this work. This research is funded in part by the Andrew Mellon Foundation.

References

1. National Collegiate Athletic Association: Estimated probability of competing in professional athletics (2018)
2. Carrington, P., Chang, K., Mentis, H., Hurst, A.: But, I don't take steps: examining the inaccessibility of fitness trackers for wheelchair athletes. In: Proceedings of the 17th International ACM SIGACCESS Conference on Computers & Accessibility, pp. 193–201 (2015). https://doi.org/10.1145/2700648.2809845
3. Hodgins, J.K., Wooten, W.L., Brogan, D.C., O'Brien, J.F.: Animating human athletics. In: Proceedings of the 22nd Annual Conference on Computer Graphics and Interactive Techniques, pp. 71–78 (1995). https://doi.org/10.1145/218380.218414
4. Oakes, K., Siek, K.A., MacLeod, H.: MuscleMemory: identifying the scope of wearable technology in high intensity exercise communities. In: Proceedings of the 9th International Conference on Pervasive Computing Technologies for Healthcare, pp. 193–200 (2015). https://doi.org/10.4108/icst.pervasivehealth.2015.259162
5. Figueroa, J., Grimaldi, V., Sullivan, J., Dosono, B.: Finding a future beyond the field: exploring ICT-mediated practices of student athletes. In: iConference 2018 Proceedings (2018). http://hdl.handle.net/2142/100251
6. Mueller, F., Vetere, F., Gibbs, M.R., Edge, D., Agamanolis, S., Sheridan, J.G.: Jogging over a distance between Europe and Australia. In: Proceedings of the 23rd Annual ACM Symposium on User Interface Software and Technology, pp. 189–198. (2010). https://doi.org/10.1145/1866029.1866062
7. Puussaar, A., Clear, A.K., Wright, P.: Enhancing personal informatics through social sensemaking. In: Proceedings of the 2017 CHI Conference on Human Factors in Computing Systems, pp. 6936–6942. ACM (2017). https://doi.org/10.1145/3025453.3025804
8. Ellis, D., Kennedy, T., Pasupuleti, V., Williams, A., Ye, Y.: Strive: student-athletes transitioning with camaraderie and competition. In: CHI '13 Extended Abstracts on Human Factors in Computing Systems, pp. 2585–2590. ACM (2013). https://doi.org/10.1145/2468356.2468834
9. Stoldt, G.C.: The impact of social media on college athletics communications. Sports Public Relations 2 (2012)

10. Sanderson, J.: To tweet or not to tweet: exploring division I athletic departments' social-media policies. Int. J. Sport Commun. **4**(4), 492–513 (2011). https://doi.org/10.1123/ijsc.4.4.492

11. Sanderson, J.: "The nation stands behind you": mobilizing social support on 38pitches.com. Commun. Q. **58**, 188–206 (2010). https://doi.org/10.1080/01463371003717884

12. McAdow, B., Jung, J.H., Lambiase, J., Bright, L.: Penalties off the field: exploring social media policies for student athletes at universities. J. Soc. Media Soc. **6**(2), 368–405 (2017)

13. Salgado, R.: A fiduciary duty to teach those who don't want to learn: the potentially dangerous oxymoron of college sports. Seton Hall J. Sports Ent. L. **17**, 135 (2007)

14. Wong, G.M., Zola, W., Deubert, C.: Going pro in sports: providing guidance to student-athletes in a complicated legal & regulatory environment. Cardozo Arts Ent. LJ. **28**, 553 (2010)

15. Becker, A.J.: It's not what they do, it's how they do it: Athlete experiences of great coaching. Int. J. Sports Sci. Coaching **4**(1), 93–119 (2009). https://doi.org/10.1260/1747-9541.4.1.93

16. Morse, J.M.: The implications of interview type and structure in mixed-method designs. Gubrium J.F., 193–204 (2012). https://doi.org/10.4135/9781452218403.n13

17. Ramírez, R., Parthasarathy, B., Gordon, A.: Infomediaries: brokers of public access. TASCHA (2014). http://hdl.handle.net/1773/25301

18. Semaan, B.C., Britton, L.M., Dosono, B.: Transition resilience with ICTs: 'Identity awareness' in veteran re-integration. In: Proceedings of the 2016 CHI Conference on Human Factors in Computing Systems, pp. 2882–2894. ACM (2016). https://doi.org/10.1145/2858036.2858109

Mobile News Processing: University Students' Reactions to Inclusion/Exclusion-Related News

Kyong Eun Oh and Rong Tang[⊠]

Simmons University, Boston, MA 02115, USA
{kyongeun.oh, rong.tang}@simmons.edu

Abstract. This paper presents the results of a diary study involving 49 university students reporting how they consume and react to news via their mobile phones. In their diary entries, participants used 23 pairs of semantic differential scales to express their reactions. Out of 265 political and society news items submitted, 68 were inclusion/exclusion-related news. The most frequent categories of inclusion/exclusion news were related to "ethnicity/race," "gender/ sexual orientation," and "religion," and these three groups of news items counted for over 85% of all inclusion/exclusion related news that were submitted. Significant differences were found in participants' choices of semantic adjectives between inclusion news and exclusion news, as well as between inclusion/exclusion news and general news. Findings provide an insightful understanding of the interests, value judgment, and emotional attachments of university students in the US to inclusion/exclusion and to general news.

Keywords: Mobile news · Inclusion · Exclusion · Reaction differences · Information behavior

1 Introduction

The development of mobile technology has transformed the media ecology and the ways that members of the general public consume their daily news. As pointed out by Li [1], "the media landscape is changing rapidly due to mobile phones working as a functional channel to deliver news information" (p. 298). According to recent reports, almost half (45%) of U.S. adults access news via mobile devices [2] and nearly 80% of the top news websites receive more traffic to their sites via mobile devices than desktop computers [3]. Reports showed that younger generations in the U.S. rely heavily on their smartphones as their main source of obtaining, consuming, and sharing news [4]. Furthermore, scholars observed that smartphones have enabled a new era of news consumption featuring participatory, interactive, and socially driven activities [5–7]. Not only have mobile devices provided their users a means to keep abreast of current political events and happenings, but the general public has also been empowered to exchange information in a real-time manner and share opinions and reactions about certain societal dynamics and political activities through private direct messages or publically viewable comments.

© Springer Nature Switzerland AG 2019
N. G. Taylor et al. (Eds.): iConference 2019, LNCS 11420, pp. 302–311, 2019.
https://doi.org/10.1007/978-3-030-15742-5_30

In library and information science research, diversity as a concept and an empirical construct has evolved from focusing on listing specific dimensions such as race, ethnicity, gender, disability, and sexual orientation to "a more holistic approach by emphasizing inclusiveness and not marginalizing groups" [8, p. 78]. As indicated by Hastings, "inclusion is the act of creating environments in which any individual or group can feel welcomed, respected, supported and valued" [9, p. 134]. In a review of diversity-related LIS dissertations completed over the span of a decade (2000–2009), Subramaniam and her colleagues discovered that while the interests of dissertation authors were in meeting the information needs of diverse populations, they tended to use the traditional definitions of diversity by focusing primarily on "ethnicity, gender, race, and age" [10, p. 372]. In addition, there was "a disconnect between diversity research that is being done in the LIS generally and diversity-related dissertations completed in LIS schools" [10, p. 371]. While the number of diversity-related dissertations had increased in recent years, "diversity-related scholarly research in the field is surprisingly limited" [10, p. 371].

Based on the content of the diversity-related dissertation research, Subramaniam et al. developed 10 dimensions of diversity as follows: (1) age or age group(s); (2) disability or accessibility issues; (3) discrimination and/or related issues; (4) diversity and/or multiculturalism; (5) ethnicity, place of origin, and/or ethnic groups; (6) gender; (7) language and/or related issues; (8) migration status; (9) race; and (10) sexual orientation. Among these dimensions, ethnicity, place of origin, and/or ethnic groups; diversity and/or multiculturalism; gender; race; and age/age group comprise 80.47% of the all diversity-related elements [10, p. 368].

In the United States' current political and social environment, a growing number of news stories about diversity and inclusion issues are published daily. However, although there is a rich body of research about mobile news information behavior, few studies have focused on the consumption of diversity and inclusion news. In this paper, inclusion/exclusion news refers to news stories that are related to the inclusion or exclusion of a specific gender, race, ethnicity, and/or class. In particular, inclusion news (IN henceforth) is about accepting and respecting diversities, while exclusion news (EN henceforth) is about discriminating against or harassing specific groups of people. General political and society news (GN henceforth) refers to news that is not related to diversity or inclusion issues.

In the areas of media and communication research, a number of studies have investigated the impact of news media on people's perceptions of diversity issues. For instance, Schemer [11] examined the effect of news media on stereotypic attitudes toward immigrants in a political campaign, and found that exposure to news stories that include both positive and negative portrayals of immigrants influenced stereotypic attitudes of the public toward immigrants. Meanwhile, Dixon [12] reported that exposure to network news was negatively associated with stereotypical perceptions of African Americans. Furthermore, Benesch [13] examined the gender gap in political news consumption and concluded that there were larger gender differences among working people with children.

At the other end of the spectrum, several studies examined news reporters' views on covering diversity news. In a large-scale study involving interviews with over 610 reporters, editors, and news directors of U.S. media, Uriarte and Valgeirsson found that over 60% of the interviewees did not have a clear notion of what "diversity in relation to journalism" means. The remaining respondents provided their definitions of "diversity," which included "news coverage reflects population demographics," "news coverage includes underrepresented views," and "news coverage includes the potential impact of events on relevant underrepresented groups" [14, p. 403].

In this study, we employed a diary research method that in part required participants to express their evaluative assessment and emotional reactions to a given news story through using 23 pairs bipolar Semantic Differential Scales (SDSs). SDS is an instrument widely used to measure the meaning of people's attitudes towards objects, products, and events. The most well-known SDS method was developed by Osgood, Suci, and Tannebaum [15]. Using Osgood et al. method, Scott [16] asked 92 engineers in his study to rate nine concepts related to morale at work using semantic differential scales. With the "Me at Work" concept, the author identified eight factors, which included General Affective Tone, General Vigor, and General Emotionality. In another study, Katzer [17] identified three factors based on participants' ratings of Syracuse University Psychological Abstract Retrieval Services searches: evaluative specific, desirability, and enormity, plus a "not assigned" category.

Among the studies using semantic differential scales, there has been a consistent affective factor. For their study involving undergraduate students completing a questionnaire of their health-related behaviors, Ajzen and Timko [18] uncovered two factors: "evaluative" and "enjoyment." Authors indicated that the second factor "is more emotional in tone ... because it reflects largely the pleasures or displeasures associated with performing generally recommended health practices" (p. 265). Meanwhile, a research study by Khan [19] engaged university students using 31 pairs of semantic differential scales to evaluate their experiences with their mobile devices. Khan discovered that the resulting "semantic differential chart ... represents the customer aesthetics, expectations, emotion and identity" (p. 149). The "emotion" factor also emerged through a series of studies by Takahashi and his colleagues [20, 21], in which participants were asked to evaluate their impressions of five different agents in their social interactions. The results of authors' Principal Component Analysis revealed three factors: emotion, intelligence, and an unlabeled third factor.

In this research study, we examine how university students consume and react to inclusion/exclusion-related political and society news, as evidenced through self-reporting their everyday mobile news consumption in the format of a diary.

2 Research Questions

The present study addresses following research questions:

RQ1. What types of inclusion/exclusion news were consumed by the study participants and subsequently submitted by them for this study?

RQ2. Are there any significant gender differences in terms of the number of inclusion/exclusion-related news (IENs henceforth) and GNs submitted and the types of adjectives selected for political and society news?

RQ3.   To what extent do participants' reactions to inclusion news differ from their reactions to exclusion news?

RQ4.   To what extent do participants' reactions to inclusion/exclusion news differ from their reactions to general political and society news?

3   Methods

Between July and October 2016, a diary study was conducted for which 51 university students in the U.S. submitted diary entries of news stories that they processed via their mobile phones in a three-week period. The researchers specifically focused on mobile news processing since mobile phones are heavily used in processing news especially among young generations in the U.S. [4]. The researchers also used a mobile app-based diary template to collect data so that participants could submit their diary entries right after processing the news in the same platform. A total of 524 news items were submitted. Participants were asked to express their evaluative thoughts and affective feelings about each news story that they submitted using adjective labels. To indicate their reactions, participants used semantic differential scales of 23 bipolar pairs of adjectives (e.g., valuable–worthless, beautiful–ugly, strong–weak). These 23 pairs (see Table 1) were selected based on an integration of scales used in existing semantic differential literature as reviewed in Sect. 1 of this paper as well as terms that we deemed to be effective to evaluate news stories. We felt that semantic differential scales were both familiar and easy to understand by participants of different backgrounds. A combination of multiple adjective pairs enables a vivid, accurate, and comprehensive capture of participants' evaluative judgment and emotional reactions to a news story.

Table 1. Bipolar adjective pairs (semantic scales) used in this study

Evaluative Pairs	How would you evaluate this news story?
Deep — Shallow; Valuable — Worthless; Heavy — Light; Clear — Hazy; Sharp — Dull; Honest — Dishonest; Fresh — Stale; Fair — Unfair; Wide — Narrow; Beneficial — Harmful; Beautiful — Ugly; Good — Bad	
Affective Pairs	Describe your emotional reaction to this news story by choosing one term that best represents your reaction from the following binary scales:
Strong — Weak; Calm — Agitated; Pleasant — Unpleasant; Happy — Sad; Ferocious — Peaceful; Relaxed — Tense; Nice — Awful; Bright — Dark; Rough — Smooth; Comfortable — Uncomfortable; Pleasurable — Painful	

This paper reports the results pertaining only to political and society news items submitted by participants. Both authors were involved in coding the types of news based on the headline and the lead paragraph of the news story. When the content could not be discerned based on the headline and lead paragraph alone, the full-text of the news stories was accessed and read; authors then coded the news type based on the full story. Of the 265 political and society news stories submitted, 68 were coded as IENs. There were a total of 197 general political and society news (GNs). In reference to Submanriam et al. [10] categories, we coded IENs by categories of "gender/sexual orientation," "ethnicity/race," "religion," "abortion," "class," "age," and "disabilities." In addition, all IEN items were coded into categories of "positive" (equivalent to INs), "negative" (equivalent to ENs), or "neutral" based on whether the news story was about supporting or disputing inclusion or simply value neutral. Among the 68 IENs, 28 (41.2%) were IN, 35 (51.5%) were EN, and 5 (7.4%) were neutral.

4   Results

Among the 49 participants who submitted political and society news, 14 were male and 35 were female. In terms of age group, 9 participants were under 20, 31 were between ages 20 and 24, 3 were between 25 and 29, and 6 were 30 years old or older. In the case of ethnicity, one participant was Native American, 14 were Asian, 4 were African American, 7 were Hispanic, and 23 were Caucasian. These participants on average had used mobile phones for 4.68 years, ranging from as short as a year to as long as 11 years.

Participants were from 21 different higher education institutions in 12 U.S. states, including Drexel University, Emerson College, Georgia Institute of Technology, Harvard University, Penn State University, Portland State University, University of Washington, University of Nebraska—Lincoln, Simmons College, Rutgers, University of California Santa Cruz, William James College, MIT, and more. Over 73% were undergraduates and close to 27% were graduate students. More than 81% were U.S. students and 18.37% were international students. In terms of students' fields of study, social sciences were the most frequent domain (38.78%), sciences the second (30.61%), followed by arts and humanities fields (20.41%). Over 8% of the participants specialized in engineering, and the remaining 2% participants had not yet declared their majors at the time of the study.

4.1   Types of IENs Submitted

Among the 68 IENs, the most frequently submitted type was "ethnicity/race" ($n = 24$, 35.3%), followed by "gender/sexual orientation" ($n = 20$, 29.4%), "religion" ($n = 14$, 20.6%), "age" ($n = 3$, 4.4%), "abortion" ($n = 3$, 4.4%), "class" ($n = 2$, 2.9%), and "disability" ($n = 2$, 2.9%). Table 2 provides the detail of each category of IENs, including a news story headline as an example for each particular category of IENs coded. Note that while race, gender, and age comprised of approximately 70% of the IENs in this study, which is less than the over 80% in Submanriam et al. [10] results, religion counted for over 20% in this study. Religion was neither listed among the top ten or mentioned much in Submanriam et al. [10] data. Of course, one should not equate the frequency counts of these two studies as the nature of Submanriam et al. study is different from the present study. While this study investigated the types of diversity news submitted and evaluated, Submanriam and her coauthors [10] examined LIS dissertations addressing diversity topics. IENs that were categorized as

Table 2. Types and frequencies of inclusion and exclusion news submitted by participants.

Types	# (%)	INs or ENs (#)	Example
Ethnicity/Race	24 (35.3%)	Positive (9) Neutral (2) Negative (12.5)	U.S. Rep. Steve King preaches literal white supremacy on national television
Gender/Sexual Orientation	20 (29.4%)	Positive (10) Neutral (1) Negative (8.5)	Fox News Allegedly Paid $3.15 million settlement to woman claiming Roger Ailes sexually harassed her
Religion	14 (20.6%)	Positive (5) Neutral (0) Negative (9)	#CanYouHearUsNow: Muslim women call out Donald Trump over Khan remarks
Abortion	3 (4.4%)	Positive (1) Neutral (1) Negative (1)	No, Donald Trump, abortions do not happen at 9 months pregnant
Age	3 (4.4%)	Positive (1) Neutral (0) Negative (2)	Abused 4 year old child tells police her name is idiot
Disability	2 (2.9%)	Positive (1) Neutral (0) Negative (1)	Japan massacre brings disabled care into public view
Class	2 (2.9%)	Positive (1) Neutral (1) Negative (0)	The White House was, in fact, built by slaves

"ethnicity/race," "gender/sexual orientation," and "religion" counted for over 85% of all the IENs submitted by participants of this study.

4.2 Gender Differences

Because more than 2/3rd of the participants were female, it is important to explore whether there are gender differences in participants' mobile news processing behavior. There is no statistically significant gender difference in terms of the number of IENs and GNs submitted (χ^2 (1, $N = 49$) = 3.59, $p = .058$). However, with regard to the adjectives selected to evaluate and express their emotional reactions to the political and society news, female participants appeared to be more critical in several aspects than male participants. Specifically, significantly higher proportion of female participants marked their news as "dark," (χ^2 (1, $N = 265$) = 4.02, $p = .045$) "sad", (χ^2 (1, $N = 265$) = 4.37, $p = .037$) "weak," (χ^2 (1, $N = 265$) = 5.57, $p = .018$) and "unfair" (χ^2 (1, $N = 265$) = 6.03, $p = .014$). The only significant difference where male participants were more negative than female participants was in the pair of "Fresh/Stale." A significantly higher proportion of male participants than female participants marked their news as "stale" (χ^2 (1, $N = 265$) = 5.27, $p = .022$).

4.3 Differences Between Reactions to INs and to ENs

A series of chi-square tests were conducted to examine whether there are different reactions to INs and to ENs. For 12 pairs of semantic scales, significantly more positive reactions were expressed for INs, whereas significantly more negative reactions were tagged for ENs. Statistically significant results include "Wide/Narrow" (χ^2 (2, $N = 68$) = 7.10, $p = .029$), "Beautiful/Ugly" (χ^2 (2, $N = 68$) = 16.53, $p = .000$), "Good/Bad" (χ^2 (2, $N = 68$) = 13.65, $p = .001$), "Calm/Agitated" (χ^2 (2, $N = 68$) = 13.35, $p = .001$), "Pleasant/Unpleasant" (χ^2 (2, $N = 68$) = 11.59, $p = .003$), "Happy/Sad" (χ^2 (2, $N = 68$) = 11.59, $p = .003$), "Relaxed/Tense" (χ^2 (2, $N = 68$) = 8.55, $p = .014$), "Nice/Awful" (χ^2 (2, $N = 68$) = 16.78, $p = .000$), "Bright/Dark" (χ^2 (2, $N = 68$) = 9.06, $p = .011$), "Smooth/Rough" (χ^2 (2, $N = 68$) = 13.35, $p = .001$), "Comfortable/Uncomfortable" (χ^2 (2, $N = 68$) = 8.80, $p = .012$), and "Pleasurable/Painful" (χ^2 (2, $N = 68$) = 8.86, $p = .012$). Significantly more INs were labeled as "Wide," "Beautiful," "Good," "Calm," "Pleasant," "Happy," "Relaxed," "Nice," "Bright," "Smooth," "Comfortable," "Pleasurable," and significantly more ENs were marked with the counterparts of previously mentioned adjectives.

4.4 Differences Between Reactions to IENs and to GNs

For general political or society news, participants expressed their emotional reactions to various news stories they submitted. For instance, upon reading the news entitled "Top DNC Officials Leave After Email Hacking Scandal," with the lead paragraph as "The Democratic National Committee's chief executive, communications director, and chief financial officer are stepping down after thousands of emails were leaked ahead of the party convention last month," P16 commented "I had mixed emotions with the news article. I thought that it was interesting and good that they had decided to leave after the scandal. However, at certain points, I felt that annoyed too because of the lack of honesty that those officials exhibited." For RQ4, we examined whether there were statistical significances between the adjectives used for IENs and GNs.

Among the 23 pairs, seven sets of semantic scales showed significant differences. Statistically significant differences were found between IENs and GNs in participants' reactions to news items as "sharp" or "dull" (χ^2 (1, $N = 265$) = 6.76, $p = .009$), "fresh" or "stale" (χ^2 (1, $N = 265$) = 6.01, $p = .014$), "deep" or "shallow" (χ^2 (1, $N = 265$) = 8.99, $p = .003$), "valuable" or "worthless" (χ^2 (1, $N = 265$) = 6.38, $p = .012$), "clear" or "hazy" (χ^2 (1, $N = 265$) = 4.39, $p = .036$), "strong" or "weak" (χ^2 (1, $N = 265$) = 4.44, $p = .035$) and "honest" or "dishonest" (χ^2 (1, $N = 265$) = 6.39, $p = .011$). Participants perceived that there were significantly more IENs that were "sharp", "fresh", "deep", "valuable", "clear", "strong", or "honest" than GNs.

Figure 1 shows the contrasts—statistically significant differences—both between INs and ENs (upper two pie slices) and between IENs and GNs (lower two pie slices).

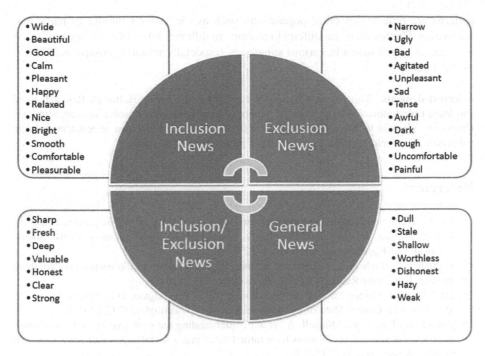

Fig. 1. Participant's reactions to INs vs. ENs, and IENs vs. GNs.

5 Conclusion

As an empirical study examining participants' reactions to INs and ENs as well as to IENs and GNs, our findings help to establish a fundamental understanding of the interests, value judgments, and emotional attachments of university students in the U.S. to these types of news. It is quite revealing that the student participants in this study were overall in favor of news that is supportive of inclusion, whereas they expressed negative reactions to the exclusion news. They labeled significantly higher proportions of ENs as "narrow," "ugly," "bad," "agitated," "unpleasant," "sad," "tense," "awful," "dark," "rough," "uncomfortable," and "painful." Meanwhile, in comparison to GNs, participants marked more IENs to be "honest," "deep," "sharp," "fresh," "strong," "clear," and "valuable." The key finding of the study confirms that university students in the U.S. have a keen sense of social justice and political issues. Their evaluative and affective reactions demonstrated their support for inclusion efforts and disagreement with exclusion or political unfairness. As an exploratory study, there are limitations associated with the research, including the unbalanced gender makeup of the participants, and the fact that participants were university students. Future research on people's reaction to inclusion/exclusion news should focus on obtaining a larger sample of news stories on this topic where meaningful comparisons can be made. It would also be useful to expand the study population beyond university students and see whether such patterns are reflected in other populations such as the general public. In particular, comparing whether there are different reactions to different types of inclusion/exclusion news among participants in various subgroups (especially minority groups) will reveal useful findings.

Acknowledgments. This research study was funded by The Emily Hollowell Research Fund and Mara Dole Innovation Fund from the School of Library and Information Science, Simmons University. We wish to thank Alison Fisher for her assistance in participant recruitment and data collection. We would also like to thank all the participants of the study.

References

1. Li, X.: Technology facility and news affinity: predictors of using mobile phones as a news device. In: Xu, X. (ed.) Interdisciplinary Mobile Media and Communications: Social, Political, and Economic Implications, pp. 278–304 (2014)
2. Barthel, M., Mitchell, A.: Americans' attitudes about the news media deeply divided along partisan lines. Pew Research Center, Washington, D.C. (2017)
3. Pew Research Center: State of the news media 2015. Washington, D.C. (2015)
4. Pew Research Center: State of the news media 2016. Washington, D.C. (2016)
5. Purcell, K., Rainie, L., Mitchell, A., et al.: Understanding the participatory news consumer: how internet and cell phone users have turned news into a social experience. Pew Research Center, Washington, D.C. (2010)
6. O'Brien, H., Freund, L., Westman, S.: What motivates the online news browser? News item selection in a social information seeking scenario. Inf. Res. **19**(3) (2017). http://www.informationr.net/ir/19-3/paper634.html#.V8ssaFQrKM8
7. Struckmann, S., Karnowski, V.: News consumption in a changing media ecology: an MESM study on mobile news. Telematics Inform. **33**(2), 309–319 (2016)
8. Sung, H., Parboteeah, P.: Diversity-related research reported in high-impact library and information science journal literature: a content analysis. Libr. Inf. Sci. Res. **39**(2), 77–84 (2017)
9. Hastings, S.: If diversity is a natural state, why don't our libraries mirror the populations they serve? Libr. Q. **85**, 133–138 (2015)
10. Subramaniam, M., Rodriguez-Mori, H., Jaeger, P., Hill, R.: The implications of a decade of diversity-related doctoral dissertations (2000–2009) in LIS: supporting inclusive library practices. Libr. Q. **82**(3), 361–377 (2012)
11. Schemer, C.: The influence of news media on stereotypic attitudes toward immigrants in a political campaign. J. Commun. **62**, 739–757 (2012)
12. Dixon, T.: Network news and racial beliefs: exploring the connection between national television news exposure and stereotypical perceptions of African Americans. J. Commun. **58**, 321–337 (2008)
13. Benesch, C.: An empirical analysis of the gender gap in news consumption. J. Media Econ. **25**, 147–167 (2012)
14. Uriarte, C., Valgeirsson, G.: Institutional disconnects as obstacles to diversity in journalism in the United States. Journalism Pract. **9**(3), 399–417 (2015)
15. Osgood, C., Suci, G., Tannenbaum, P.: The Measurement of Meaning. University of Illinois Press, Urbana (1957)
16. Scott Jr., W.: The development of semantic differential scales as measures of "morale". Pers. Psychol. **20**(2), 179–198 (1967)

17. Katzer, J.: The development of a semantic differential to assess users' attitudes towards an on-line interactive reference retrieval system. J. Am. Soc. Inf. Sci. **23**(2), 122–128 (1972)
18. Ajzen, I., Timko, C.: Correspondence between health attitudes and behavior. Basic Appl. Soc. Psychol. **7**(4), 259–276 (1986)
19. Khan, K.: User experience in mobile phones by using semantic differential methodology. In: Proceedings of the European Conference on Information Systems Management and Evaluation, Cork, Ireland, pp. 143–150 (2012)
20. Takahashi, H., Terada, K., Morita, T., et al.: Different impressions of other agents obtained through social interaction uniquely modulate dorsal and ventral pathway activities in the social human brain. Cortex **58**, 289–300 (2014)
21. Takahashi, H., Ban, M., Asada, M.: Semantic differential scale method can reveal multi-dimensional aspects of mind perception. Front. Psychol. **7**(1717), 1–5 (2016)

Data-Driven Storytelling and Modeling

Engaging the Community Through Places: An User Study of People's Festival Stories

Xiying Wang(✉)⬡, Tiffany Knearem, Han Jun Yoon, Hedgie Jo,
Jackeline Lee, Junwoo Seo, and John M. Carroll⬡

Pennsylvania State University, State College, PA 16801, USA
{xiyingwang,tak54,hvy5070,hyc5135,jcl5470,
jzs5882,jmcarroll}@psu.edu

Abstract. Peoples lived experiences, stories, and memories about local places endow meaning to a community, which can play an important role in community engagement. We investigated the meaning of place through the lens of peoples memories of a local arts festival. We first designed, developed, and deployed a web application to collect peoples festival stories. We then developed our interview study based on 28 stories collected through the web app in order to generate rich conversations with 18 festival attendees. Our study identifies three parallel meanings that a place can hold based on the following types of festival attendees: *experience seekers*, *nostalgia travelers*, and *familiar explorers*. We further discuss how information technology can facilitate community engagement based on those parallel meanings of place.

Keywords: Local festival · Place · Community engagement

1 Introduction and Related Work

Oldenburg [15] described the *'third place'* as shared public places (e.g., restaurants, sidewalks) where community members can meet, gather and socialize, which we refer to as *place* in this paper. The meaning of a place is deeper than just where it is located. People's *'felt experience'* [13] of a place, as in what people feel, express, and encounter, gives the meaning to that place [2]. For example, a newcomer may have a special feeling toward the first restaurant he or she dines at in town. A friendly smile from the staff member, food prepared by a local chef, and even the stranger in the corner may all become considered as the meaning of the restaurant to the newcomer. A local resident may remember the restaurant differently – perhaps as a causal after-work place to meet his or her colleagues. Different people have different experiences and feelings about the same place. Gradually, their collective stories and memories define what the place is [4]. When people share their personal stories about a place, they are collectively attaching their personal identities and constructing the meaning of that place.

© Springer Nature Switzerland AG 2019
N. G. Taylor et al. (Eds.): iConference 2019, LNCS 11420, pp. 315–326, 2019.
https://doi.org/10.1007/978-3-030-15742-5_31

Encouraging people to share their stories and memories attached to places can have many benefits. On one hand, this practice can facilitate the building of common ground among community members, thus increasing peoples emotional bonds with a place [12]. In this way, place attachment leads to people's appreciation of the place [1]. On the other hand, the practice can strengthen peoples sense of belonging in their local community [9,11,14], which links to engagement with the community [5,16] and the development of a sense of community [14]. People are willing to take actions on behalf of a place when they feel emotionally connected to that place [11,17]. For example, by sharing lived stories of a place, people are motivated to act on community issues [4,8,9]. Facilitating people in constructing the meaning of a place through their own experiences helps to engage them in neighborhood planning and development [12]. In contrast, if peoples feelings and expectations of a place are not well addressed, it can create a sense of alienation [10]. For example, newcomers and temporary residents may be less attached to a community, compared to permanent residents [18]. This may be due to the lack of emotional attachments to the community [11]. Thus, acknowledging and understanding the lived experiences of various types of community members becomes important because it strengthens the sense of community and reduces feelings of alienation.

As an important aspect of a thriving modern community, local festivals can turn an ordinary place into a nuanced and temporary experience while promoting the value of place [19]. For example, a food festival transfers ordinary neighborhood streets into ephemeral environments, where people can interact with vendors, socialize with friends, and learn about different foods. In this case, those streets become more than just normal sidewalks lined with trees and buildings. Instead, they are transformed into a temporary, dynamic environment for people to taste, learn, and socialize. Local festivals also have a positive impact on people [19]. For example, attendees, vendors, performers and others who attend a festival may foster useful relationship in business, strengthen their emotional ties to the place, or facilitate the development of social capital [19]. Although the festival environment is ephemeral, the social connections and emotional bonds continue to last for a long time [19]. In this sense, local festivals play an important role in engaging people in social activities and developing place attachments.

Although temporary, vibrant festivals are an important factor in establishing the meaning of a place. However, we are unclear what meaning a local festival can endow to a community and how to leverage that meaning to engage people in community participation. Understanding how people participate in, remember, and experience a local festival can provide us with greater insights.

In this study, we propose to understand peoples stories of a local arts festival and identify motivation strategies for community engagement from those stories. Specifically, we look into the following research questions: (1) What stories do people share about their experience attending a local festival, and (2) How can information technology support community engagement based on people's festival stories.

Our contributions to community research and information technology include: (1) an in-depth understanding of people's festival participation, (2) identifying the meaning of place based on the above participation, and (3) design implications for information technology to engage people in community activities, tailored to people's meaning of place. In the reminder of the paper, we use *story* or *stories* represent people's memories, moments, experiences, and activities.

Local Arts Festival. The local arts festival[1] we selected takes place annually in the summer. This arts festival is the biggest recurring event in central Pennsylvania of the United States. It is a four-day event, which brings in both local and nationally known artists to showcase and sell their artwork. Every year, the festival attracts thousands of attendees, including locals or and people who live in other places. Some people have attended the festival many times, while others are newcomers. It is a suitable event to collect stories from people of various backgrounds to understand their engagement based on those stories.

2 Methodology

To investigate the proposed research questions, we first built and deployed a web application as a research tool to collect people's festival stories. Second, we invited 18 participants to our interview study to discuss their festival stories in depth. We detail the purpose, procedure, participants, and analysis of each method in the following sections.

2.1 Method I: Memofest for a Preliminary Understanding of Festival Memories

As our first stage, we designed, developed, and deployed a research tool called Memofest (see Fig. 1) to collect people's stories to get a preliminary understanding of their lived experiences at the festival and identify possible meanings that the festival could hold based on the stories they submitted. Memofest is a mobile friendly web application built with HTML/CSS, Javascript, and a secure database service, which can be accessed from any smartphone or personal computer. Due to privacy concerns, we did not utilize existing social media tools such as Facebook to collect people's stories.

The web application has two main features. One is a function that enables people to write their stories (see Fig. 1). After a story is submitted, the system will send an email containing coupons for discounted food and drink as a reward to the user. We partnered with four restaurants to get those discounts. An user could apply the discounts from the time when the festival started until one week after the festival ended. The other is the "featured stories" function (also see Fig. 1), where Memofest randomly selects and displays three user inputs from the database. The purpose of this feature is to facilitate the usage of Memofest

---

[1] Central Pennsylvania Festival of the Arts: https://arts-festival.com/.

by providing sample stories. When we first deployed this system, we seeded this function with three fictional memories as a starting point. Those fictional memories were created based on 82 real memories of the past festival attendees, which we collected via an oral survey during a past event. Due to privacy concerns, we avoided using people's original quotes. Instead, we elaborated on those stories based on the shared patterns we observed from those memories, e.g., a common activity in the event.

To promote the use of Memofest, we distributed flyers in various downtown businesses near where the festival took place. We also shared Memofest on social media (e.g., Facebook, Twitter) and with various local community groups.

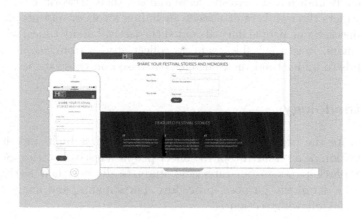

Fig. 1. Responsive Memofest web application

Stories Collected from Memofest. Due to unexpected circumstances (e.g., negotiating discounts with restaurants), we had to delay the planned deployment date for Memofest, which was initially targeted at two weeks before the festival began. In the end, we deployed it two days before the festival began and deactivated it one week after the festival ended. We decided to deactivate Memofest one week after the festival because we wanted to capture people's episodic memories, rather than their reflections on the event. Another reason involved our agreement with the partner restaurants on discounts being valid for only one week after the festival ended.

During the Memofest deployment period (12 days), we collected a total of 28 stories related to the festival. Four researchers analyzed the stories and identified four common themes using an affinity diagram (see the analysis in Table 1). The four themes indicate that people focus on and remember different aspects of their participation in the festival. Among the 28 stories, the majority (15 out of 28) were about engagement in various festival activities, four described peoples excitement from purchasing or discovering interesting artworks, seven focused on interactions with friends, and the final two were related to changes about places in the town.

Table 1. Four themes from Memofest stories

Themes	Definition	Relevant sample stories
Activities	Refers to the stories that people wrote about their engagement in festival activities, such as enjoying the musical performance	*"I loved the music and performance that made the people stand up and dance! Lots of interesting creation and also good food!"*
Arts	Refers to the stories that people wrote about the artwork they purchased or remembered seeing at the festival	*"We were walking along Main Street (pseudonym) and saw some wooden train toys. They were very intricate and a sign showed that they were made without stains or paints on the wood. This was just one of many interesting artworks that we observed at the 2018 Arts Festival"*
Social time	Describes the social experience during the festival, such as enjoying the company of friends	*"My friends and I were playing with water at the festival. It was perfect for the hot summer"*
Reminiscent	Describes changes that took place in the town itself since the last visit	*"Love the drinks there and also great to see the original and very first bubble tea shop come back in town for business!!"*

In this step, we focused on collecting people's stories and developing a preliminary understanding of those stories. Based on the themes from the Memofest stories, we further developed our interview protocol to make it more relevant to the festival attendees for the purpose of generating rich interview conversations. We did not collect the demographics of those who contributed to Memofest in this step.

2.2   Method II: Interviews to Investigate Peoples Festival Stories

After the festival ended and we deactivated Memofest, we conducted semi-structured interviews with 18 participants. The purpose was to investigate people's festival experiences in depth, identify the meaning of the festival based on stories, and cultivate motivation strategies for community engagement. We were able to generate richer conversations and probe our interviewees on the four themes we drew from our analysis of the Memofest stories. For example, we asked about how they planned their attendance, what they did at the festival, and how they felt about the local festival based on the four themes. Each interview lasted from 30 min to an hour in a private and quiet location, e.g., a private room in an office building.

Recruitment. To recruit interviewees, we used snowball sampling and also invited Memofest users who submitted their stories. Based on peoples responses and time availability, we selected 18 participants that met the following criteria: (1) must be at least 18 years old, (2) attended the 2018 arts festival, and (3) were willing to participate in the user study. Among the 18 participants, 15 participants used Memofest and three did not.

Participants. Our participants aged from 21 to 40 years old. Of the participants, eight were Americans. The rest were from Asian countries, with four Koreans, two Chinese, two Indians, and two Iranians. More than half of the participants were male (10 out of 18) and eight were female. The majority of them (12 out of 18) were temporary residents of the town, e.g., students at the local university, four were permanent residents in the town, and three travelled back to the town to attend the festival.

Analysis. Four researchers transcribed and coded the interviews using the constant comparative analysis [7]. We started with coding the first five interviews collectively. Then we synthesized and elaborated each others' codes to generate a new list of codes with a consistent format, e.g., "engagement: artists: learn about art history". Second, we used the new list to re-code the first five interviews and continued to code the rest of the interviews, adding new codes when necessary. We then grouped codes into themes. For example, "engagement: spontaneous" and "engagement: artistic experience" are two sub categories under "experience seekers", while "engagement: reunion" and "engagement: reminiscent" belong to the theme "nostalgia travelers".

3 Parallel Festival Attendees

All of our interviewees mentioned that the local festival lit up their summer or made the town come to life. Based on the participant's Memofest stories and interviews, we identified three types of attendees who experienced the festival simultaneously but in different ways, which we call *parallel experiences.* The types of attendees are: *experience seekers, nostalgia travelers,* and *familiar explorers.*

3.1 Experience Seekers

For some interviewees (12 out of 18), they explored the arts festival without creating a plan for how they wanted to spend their time beforehand. Their visit to the festival was often spontaneous and occurred in a social context. For example, some interviewees were engaging in other activities, e.g., watching sport games with friends near the festival. Then they decided to explore the event on the spot. We call this type of festival attendee *experience seekers.*

All experience seekers were newcomers or temporary residents in town. They considered the quality time they spent with friends as the experience that made the festival special.

> *"Being there with my friends that made the festival really memorable."*
> (P10, female, experience seeker)

In particular, experience seekers were more drawn into experiencing artistic activities with friends. One of their highlights was using chalks to draw on the street with the artists. Sometimes, they were invited to become part of the chalk art. For example, P9 described her favorite moment when she and her friends became part of the art.

> *"My favorite moment was somebody drew on these big colorful wings, like bird wings, on the street. They were meant so you could lay down on the street, and they would look like you had like these huge glamorous wings...my friends and I...we all took turns laying down on the street and had our own little photo shoot."* (P9, female, experience seeker)

Another highlight of experience seekers was walking through the water installation which sprayed mist. They found that installation fun in various ways. For P10, being inside the installation cooled him down. P1 and her friends walked through it with ice cream at their hands. According to P5, the installation was the *the fun part* of the festival. This was her second time attending and she was looking for the water installation on purpose.

In addition, experience seekers also found themselves stopped to enjoy the festival live music when they walked pass it. Specifically, P2 recalled his favorite moment was dancing with his friends next to that live performance.

> *"We danced to the jazz music...she (refers to P2s friend) had water bottles in her bag and we were dancing in the heat and she was pouring water over us and on herself."* (P2, male, experience seeker)

After exploring the festival, experience seekers often continued to spend time with friends in other activities throughout the day, such as attending parties in the neighborhood and watching movies at the theater. To them, the local festival not only turned the ordinary town into a vibrant place, but more importantly, it served as an social hub that bonded friends together.

3.2 Nostalgia Travelers

For some interviewees (P6, P13, and P14), they treated the festival as dedicated vacation time. They lived out of town, planned their trip in advance, and traveled to the festival to reunite with their friends. We call this type of festival participants *nostalgia travelers*.

All nostalgia travelers were alumni of the university in town. During the interviews, they often referred the festival as the perfect *place* to catch up with friends' lives. For example, P6 and P14 valued reconnecting with friends.

> *"It brings everybody back...we hadn't seen each other in a while. And it was a good time to come to (the festival) to do it."* (P6, male, nostalgia traveler)

> *"It gives me a chance to reconnect with my friends."* (P14, female, nostalgia traveler)

In particular, P13 came to the festival every year for his friends' reunion. He and his friends treated the festival as a recurring venue to enjoy the company of each other.

"I come to the arts fest every year because it's just kind of a staple for me and my friends." (P13, male, nostalgia traveler)

Nostalgia travelers also liked to revisit different places in town where memories lingered on. They often took breaks in different places to reminisce the past during the festival. For example, P6 and his friends went back to the same ice cream shop every day during the festival and talked about their campus memories.

"I got some ice cream from the Creamery. I have a lot of good memories about that place and the campus. So I went there with my friends every day." (P6, male, nostalgia traveler)

To nostalgia travelers, the town festival was an ephemeral experience that gave them the opportunity to talk about the past with friends and revisit meaningful places. Some of them even visited the festival regularly for that purpose.

3.3 Familiar Explorers

For other interviewees (P3, P4, P12, and P15), they visited the festival annually and engaged in conversations with people (e.g. artists, vendors, and local people). They participated in the festival to explore something new about art or the local community. We call this type of attendees *familiar explorers*.

Familiar explorers were permanent residents of the town. They could easily spot familiar artists or similar activities from previous events. Keen on gaining an understanding of the artwork rather than passively browsing, they often took the initiative to talk to the artists in the festival.

"I saw some local artists and their works. I went to talk to them and let them share their experiences when they made their drawings and handcrafts." (P15, female, familiar explorer)

In particular, P4, who grew up in the town, told us that he talked to more than 20 artists. Learning stories from those artists was new and interesting for him.

"I talked with him on how he got his photographs and he had a pretty interesting story about it...I thought that was pretty interesting, definitely something that I did not learn in the past festivals." (P4, male, familiar explorer)

Besides learning from the artists, familiar explorers also found themselves socializing with other festival attendees. For example, P3 shared a story about socializing with local residents who lived on one of the streets where the event took place.

"I got to know the people who lived on those really affluent houses...it was different people I hadn't met before." (P3, female, familiar explorer)

Based on our interviews, familiar explorers often engaged in conversations with others in the festival. They got excited when learning about artworks or people's lived experiences from this recurring event. To them, the festival was a place for them to absorb novel stories about art and the local community.

4   Engaging Community Through Places

The meaning of a place, endowed by people's experiences and memories, plays an important role in community engagement [8,12,19]. In this study, we investigate the meaning of a place through the lens of festival stories. We identified the rich meaning that an arts festival can hold based on the three types of festival attendees, *experience seekers*, *nostalgia travelers*, and *familiar explorers*. More than celebrating the arts, it is also a *place* for experiencing engaging and artistic activities, reminiscing, and learning. We further propose that information technology can be more successful in engaging people in community events by promoting the meaning of a place based on different types of participation.

For experience seekers, the ability to experience activities with friends is the key to their engagement. We propose that information technology suggests suitable places for social gathering in the vicinity of community events and highlights event activities that support social experiences. Carroll et al. [4] suggested that making newcomers and temporary residents aware of available activities increases their emotional bonds to the community. Our study further suggests that highlighting places for social gathering and identifying event activities that are good for social experience can be successful in encouraging community participation. As experience seekers like to spontaneously explore an event after gathering with friends, information technology can suggest suitable places for a friends' gathering closed to that event to increase the chance of their event participation. Take the arts festival as an example, a system can motivate participation by sending its users the following message *"it's beautiful outside, take a break and hang out with your friends at the Creamery?"*. Information technology can also prioritize the type of event activities in which is good for friends to participate.

For nostalgia travelers, the festival is a dedicated time for a friends' reunion and exploring familiar places where memories are held. We propose that information technology supports reminiscing activities. Han et al. [9] found out that enabling people to collectively create a place's meaning facilitates the development of place attachment. Our study further suggests that facilitating people in collaboratively reminiscing about a place engages them in community events. For example, information technology can keep track of a group of friends' stories attached to a place. When they come back to the place, technology can show those stories to them, inspiring discussions of the past. Information technology can also allow people to subscribe to places that are meaningful to them. When people are back to the town, technology can display those memory spots on a map to support their reminiscing practice.

For familiar explorers, the festival turns the ordinary neighborhood into a learning event. They are curious about peoples stories and they often seek out something new to learn. We suggest that information technology can archive past stories of a recurring community event and show those stories to familiar explorers to facilitate their social interactions in the current event. Specifically, the system only keep tracks, archives and shows the stories of those with whom the familiar explorers interact. Taking the arts festival for example, information technology can keep track of artists and their art stories with whom the familiar explorers have interacted. Then it highlights first-time artists that may be of interest as well as new artworks of returning artists. Showing family explorers the newly participated artists can add to their curiosity of knowing their stories, while highlighting the new art pieces and archiving the past stories of recurring artists may facilitate new conversation topics between familiar explorers and those artists.

We also recognize the three types of festival attendees can be interchangeable. Experience seekers may become familiar explorers or nostalgia travelers. Such change may alter their participation patterns in the community. As information technology supports people's community participation through stories, it also needs to adjust the motivation strategies over time, highlighting the meaning of the place that a person endows at the current moment.

5   Conclusion and Future Work

Our study shows ways to motivate community engagement based on peoples festival stories. For newcomers and temporary residents, a festival is a hub of social experiences. Promoting the festival activities and facilitating interaction between friends can motivate community participation. For alumni, a festival is the place for reminiscing. Supporting their memory-seeking experiences engages them in community events. Finally, for permanent residents, a festival is a place where they can learn peoples stories. Facilitating their learning about others can successfully motivate their engagement. As our next step, we aim to re-deploy Memofest as a tool to collect peoples stories about additional festivals, continue to explore peoples stories and identify new meanings of place. In addition, we plan to implement the suggested design strategies in Memofest and evaluate the influence of those strategies on community engagement with actual festival attendees.

Acknowledgements. We thank all the participants who shared their festival experiences with us. We also thank all the anonymous reviewers for their insightful feedback and suggestions.

References

1. Brown, B.B., Perkins, D.D., Brown, G.: Place attachment in a revitalizing neighborhood: individual and block levels of analysis. J. Environ. Psychol. **23**, 259–271 (2003). https://doi.org/10.1016/S0272-4944(02)00117-2
2. Carroll, J.M.: The Internet of Places. In: Soro, A., Brereton, M., Roe, P. (eds.) Social Internet of Things. IT, pp. 23–32. Springer, Cham (2019). https://doi.org/10.1007/978-3-319-94659-7_2
3. Carroll, J.M., Homan, B., Han, K., Rosson, M.B.: Reviving community networks: hyperlocality and suprathresholding in Web 2.0 designs. In: Pervasive and Ubiquitous Computing, vol. 19, pp. 477–491. https://doi.org/10.1007/s00779-014-0831-y
4. Carroll, J.M., Shih, P., Kropczynski, J., Cai, G., Rosson, M.B.: The Internet of Places at community-scale: design scenarios for hyperlocal neighborhood. In: Konomi, S., Roussos, G. (eds.) Enriching Urban Spaces with Ambient Computing, the Internet of Things, and Smart City Design, Chap. 1. IGI Global (2017)
5. Cuba, L., Hummon, D.M.: A place called home: identification with dwelling, community and region. Sociol. Q. **34**, 111–131 (1993). https://doi.org/10.1111/j.1533-8525.1993.tb00133.x
6. Freidus, N., Hlubinka, M.: Digital storytelling for reflective practice in communities of learners. SIGGROUP Bull. **23**, 24–26 (2002). https://doi.org/10.1145/962185.962195
7. Glaser, B., Strauss, A.: The Discovery of Grounded Theory: Strategies for Qualitative Research. Routledge, New York (2017)
8. Han, K., Wirth, R., Hanrahan, B.V., Chen, J., Lee, S., Carroll, J.M.: Being connected to the local community through a festival mobile application. In: Proceedings of iConference 2016 (2016). https://doi.org/10.9776/16215
9. Han, K., Shih, C.P., Rosson, M.B., Carroll, M.C.: Enhancing community awareness of and participation in local heritage with a mobile application. In: Proceedings of the 17th ACM Conference on Computer Supported Cooperative Work & Social Computing (CSCW 2014), pp. 1144–1155. ACM, New York (2014). https://doi.org/10.1145/2531602.2531640
10. Hummon, D.M.: Community attachment. Local sentiment and sense of place. In: Altman, I., Low, S.M. (eds.) Place Attachment, pp. 253–277. Plenum Press, New York and London (1992)
11. Lewicka, M.: Place attachment: how far have we come in the last 40 years? J. Environ. Psychol. **31**, 207–230 (2011). https://doi.org/10.1016/j.jenvp.2010.10.001
12. Manzo, L.C., Perkins, D.D.: Finding common ground: the importance of place attachment to community participation and planning. J. Plann. Lit. **20**, 335–350 (2006). https://doi.org/10.1177/0885412205286160
13. MaCarthy, J., Wright, P.: Technology as Experience. The MIT Press, Cambridge (2007)
14. McMillan, W.D., Charvis, M.D.: Sense of community: a definition and theory. J. Commun. Psychol. **14**, 6–23 (1986). https://doi.org/10.1002/1520-6629(198601)14
15. Oldenburg, R.: The Great Good Place: Cafes, Coffee Shops, Bookstores, Bars, Hair Salons, and Other Hangouts at the Heart of a Community. Marlowe & Company, New York (1989)
16. Perkins, D.D., Brown, B.B., Taylor, R.B.: The ecology of empowerment: predicting participation in community organizations. J. Soc. Issues **52**, 85–110 (1992). https://doi.org/10.1111/j.1540-4560.1996.tb01363.x

17. Pretty, G.H., Chipuer, H.M., Bramston, P.: Sense of place amongst adolescents and adults in two rural Australian towns: the discriminating features of place attachment, sense of community and place dependence in relation to place identity. J. Environ. Psychol. **23**, 273–287 (2003). https://doi.org/10.1016/S0272-4944(02)00079-8
18. Stedman, R.C.: Understanding place attachment among second home owners. Am. Behav. Sci. **50**, 187–205 (2006). https://doi.org/10.1177/0002764206290633
19. Waterman, S.: Carnivals for elites? The cultural politics of arts festivals. Progr. Hum. Geogr. **1**, 54–74 (1998)

Understanding Partitioning and Sequence in Data-Driven Storytelling

Zhenpeng Zhao[1]([✉]), Rachael Marr[2], Jason Shaffer[3], and Niklas Elmqvist[1]

[1] University of Maryland, College Park, USA
{zhaoz,elm}@umd.edu
[2] Cisco Systems, Inc., San Jose, USA
rachael.marr@gmail.com
[3] U.S. Naval Academy, Annapolis, USA
tshaffer@usna.edu

Abstract. The comic strip narrative style is an effective method for data-driven storytelling. However, surely it is not enough to just add some speech bubbles and clipart to your PowerPoint slideshow to turn it into a data comic? In this paper, we investigate aspects of *partitioning* and *sequence* as fundamental mechanisms for comic strip narration: chunking complex visuals into manageable pieces, and organizing them into a meaningful order, respectively. We do this by presenting results from a qualitative study designed to elicit differences in participant behavior when solving questions using a complex infographic compared to when the same visuals are organized into a data comic.

Keywords: Narrative visualization · Comics · Sequential art · Data comics

Fig. 1. Partitioning and sequence used as a method for organizing a complex visualization into the comic-strip narration style proposed by Segel and Heer [27].

© Springer Nature Switzerland AG 2019
N. G. Taylor et al. (Eds.): iConference 2019, LNCS 11420, pp. 327–338, 2019.
https://doi.org/10.1007/978-3-030-15742-5_32

1   Introduction

For many people, comics—stories told using a juxtaposition of illustrations, text, and visual annotations [6] that is also known as *sequential art* [24] or *sequential images* [7]—draw their eyes and compel them to follow the sequence of frames on the page with an almost eerie power. These are the same people who, whenever they encounter the ubiquitous comic strip taped to an office door, feel the urge— often after a furtive glance around to ensure no one's watching—to stop and read the strip, chuckle softly to themselves, and then continue about their day. Part of the reason why comics have such compelling, even spellbinding, qualities is surely the combination of characters, visual effects, and drawing styles that provide a welcoming and familiar sense to the reader [5]. However, another reason is that comics organize and present plots, even complex ones, into mostly-linear sequences of frames that not only advance the story, but also guide and pull the reader into the narrative [24]. This mechanism is obviously not restricted to children's stories, superheroes, and funnies, so comics have also been harnessed for more "serious" applications, including statistics [15], physics [14], and even the study of comics itself [24]. In fact, Segel and Heer [27] listed "comic strip" as one of the seven genres of narrative visualization, and several recent papers have since advanced the notion of "data comics" to convey data using the visual language of sequential art [2,3,13,33]. But why do data-driven comics work?

In this paper, we attempt to answer this question. While visual elements such as characters, visual language, and comic-style rendering no doubt contribute, and in fact may even strengthen the appeal and engagement of the data comic, their impact for a data-driven comic is likely secondary and cosmetic. Many data comics do not even use characters, visual effects, or freehand drawing to be effective [2,3]. Based on the literature [24,25], we instead focus on the use of the two primary storytelling mechanisms used in comic strip narration: (1) *partitioning*, or the organization of a complex story (i.e, dataset) into individual frames, and (2) *sequence*, or the ordering of frames into a narrative (Fig. 1).

To achieve this, we conduct a qualitative study investigating the impact of partitioning and sequence by comparing comprehension and experience for a complex infographic and a comic representing the same data. Our results underline the importance of the partitioning and sequence mechanisms in making even complex and large-scale datasets understandable to a lay audience.

2   Related Work

Using comics for data-driven storytelling lies at the intersection of visual communication, storytelling, and sequential art. Below we review relevant prior art.

2.1   Visual Communication and Visualization

Visualization is a particular form of visual language traditionally used for solitary sensemaking. The notion of communication-minded visualization (CMV) [29] builds on ideas from visual communication by noting that visualization can often be used for more than just individual insights. Several examples of CMV systems exist, including Themail [30], the Baby Name Explorer [32], and Isis [26].

2.2   Visual Storytelling

Already in 2001, Gershon and Page [13] suggested using storytelling in visualization to improve its use for visual communication. Despite this, it is only
recently that data-driven storytelling was fully embraced by the visualization
community, with a survey by Segel and Heer in 2010 [27], and successful workshops at the annual conference in 2010 and 2011 [9,10]. Hullman and Diakopoulos followed this up by studying how framing, context, and design impact the
rhetoric of a narrative [16]. Since then, several practical methods and techniques
have been proposed, including using sketching for narration [23], story points
in Tableau [22], and automatic spatialization for visual exploration [19]. Most
recently, Hullman et al. [17] studied sequence in narrative visualization, propos-
ing a graph-driven approach for transitioning between views to minimize load
on the viewer.

2.3   Comics for Visualization

Recent efforts have tried to harness comics for visualization. Jin and Szekely [20,
21] proposed a visual query environment that uses a comic-strip metaphor for
presenting temporal patterns. However, their system solely uses comic strips for
layout, and does not leverage the full potential of comics for communication.

The most recent and most relevant work in this vein is Graph Comics [2],
which are data-driven comics used for telling stories about dynamic networks.
More recently, Bach et al. [3] presented the generalized notion of data comics,
but does not evaluate its partitioning and sequencing mechanisms. Knowledge
can be maintained with proper temporal logic and intervals [1]. Interactive tools
is able to validate the ranks and intervals of sequenced data [31].

3   Design Space: Data Comics

Data comics is a visual storytelling method based on sequential images consisting of data-driven visual representations. The motivation is to build engaging
narratives about data through the familiar visual language of comics. Here we
synthesize existing work on data comics, including in particular Bach et al. [3].

- **Basic Model:** We define a *comic* as a sequence of *panels* organized into one-
  dimensional *tiers* (or strips) and separated by *gutters*, or spacing, between
  the panels [12,24]. The panels in a tier are organized to be read from left to
  right to form a narrative (at least in Western cultures). Tiers can in turn be
  organized into *pages*, where each tier becomes a row separated by a vertical
  gutter, and several pages can be linked together into a *book* (or comic book).
- **Panel Content:** Unlike a normal comic, most panels in a data comic consist of visualizations that convey information using graphical means.[1] These

---

[1] For engagement and effect, a few panels may consist solely of artistic content, but
this puts corresponding artistic burden on the designer.

could be simple and familiar statistical graphics such as barcharts, time-series charts, and piecharts, or more advanced visualizations such as treemaps [28], node-link diagrams, or even parallel coordinate plots [18], all depending on the visualization literacy of the intended audience.

- **Characters, Annotation, and Effects:** A data comic would not be a comic if it did not also leverage comic elements:
  - **Comic-style rendering:** To emphasize the comic medium, content can be drawn using non-photorealistic rendering (e.g. [8]).
  - **Characters:** Characters may drive narrative even in a data-driven story.
  - **Comic elements:** Access to common elements used in comics, such as motion lines, highlights, or onomatopoeia (words that mimic sounds).
  - **Captions, speech, thoughts:** Visuals are often scaffolded by text in captions as well as speech and thought balloons [12, 24].
- **Layout Management:** The layout of a data comic—the organization of panels into tiers and pages—is an important consideration in creating a narrative. To facilitate easily constructing a narrative, the model should allow a designer to control layout.
- **Viewing:** Finally, after a data comic has been created, its purpose is to be viewed by its intended audience to convey its designer's story (and message). Just like a traditional comic, the default view for a data comic is to view an entire page, with all of the panels visible. Since screens are different from the written page, however, it also makes sense to support a single-panel navigation mode, where the viewer can sequentially navigate backwards and forwards in the comic. This is not unlike slideshows in PowerPoint.

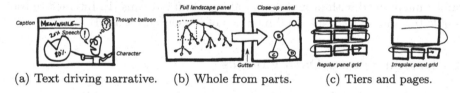

(a) Text driving narrative.   (b) Whole from parts.   (c) Tiers and pages.

Fig. 2. (a) The use of text to drive narrative. (b) Encapsulation yield closure as the viewer connects them and sees the whole. (c) Panels organized into tiers.

4   Telling Stories Using Data Comics

Creating a data comic requires some knowledge of the narrative style of comics as well as the use of text in driving the story. Here we draw on the general literature of comics to operationalize these concepts for data comics [11, 24].

4.1   Comics Narration

While comics narration is generally linear, the medium by necessity cannot present the continuous narrative used in digital video or film. Instead, comics narration depends on *encapsulation*, the focus on particular moments in the possible narrative arc to be represented in individual panels. The edges of the panels represent the limits of representation within this smaller bit of the page layout, but each panel also contributes to the larger unit, leading to an interpretive experience that is both linear and holistic since each panel is interpreted individually but also as part of the larger page. The gutters, while delineating the limits of each panel, also indicate the necessity for the reader to engage in *closure* in order to generate a more coherent narrative (Fig. 2b).

While traditional comic creators typically work in a constructivist fashion, building scenes and sequences from the bottom up, a data comic may conceptually be designed in more of a top-down fashion: starting with the data and its manifestations. However, the mechanism of *partitioning* the subject matter into a hierarchy, the lowest tier of which is the panel, is the same across both applications of the comic medium. In other words, partitioning is concerned with the subdivision of story (or data) into comprehensive units, which continues until each unit is small enough that it can be conveyed in a single panel.

The creator then decides on a partitioning *sequence*—essentially, a hierarchy traversal—to generate the order of panels. The sequence of syntagmatically related panels can follow a number of patterns. It may be temporal, following the same event as it unfolds in time. It may be spatial or spatial/temporal, moving between a number of locations at a given moment or during a specified time, or else presenting a series of localized micro-events happening within a larger framework (akin to a series of reaction shots to the same event used in film). Panels could also relate conceptually, presenting a series of related abstractions and calling upon the reader to form associations between them.

4.2 Panel Content and Size

The comic panel is among the most fungible methods of representation, capable of presenting visual data ranging from a full landscape or urban horizon to a mid-range "street scene" shot to a close-up portrait shot or even the so-called extreme close-up of a particular detail. While layout possibilities are nearly limitless, most Western comics follow some variation of a grid pattern in which rows are read left to right while proceeding from the top to the bottom of the page.

The combination of larger and smaller panels can be used to convey a large quantity of visual information in a large panel while highlighting particular elements in smaller panels. For example, this could be done by presenting a landscape or a cutaway view of a house in a larger panel, and then presenting close-ups of visual elements in smaller panels collected near the larger panel (Fig. 3).

4.3 Textual Narration

Comics panels may feature dialogue or textual narration, or these elements may be omitted, a stylistic choice embedded in the form's eighteenth-century origins. The satirical engravings of the British artist William Hogarth generally omitted dialogue, whereas politics cartoons dating from the eighteenth and nineteenth centuries often featured multiple characters speaking (to all appearances simultaneously) in a one-panel image. Narration and dialogue are typically omitted for action sequences, focusing the reader's attention on the implied movement of the characters or objects in the panels. Dialogue is generally placed in speech balloons that are superimposed on the image. Narrative captions can be placed in a box and delivered in the first, second, or third person (Fig. 2a).

Fig. 3. Data comic of the U.S. baby boom of the 1960s created from public source material using our data comics authoring tool.

5 Implementing Data Comics

We have implemented a data comics authoring tool as a web application.[2] It is a hybrid application consisting of both client-side and server-side components. Client-side components are built using JQuery for DOM manipulation and D3 [4] for visualization. The content is stored on the server-side backend, implemented as a simple Python server communicating using JSON-RPC.

6 Study: Partitioning and Sequence in Storytelling

Our working hypothesis in this paper is that data comics provide a more effective way of telling stories than a single visualization. To empirically explore the virtues of this premise, we conducted a qualitative user study comparing multi-panel data comics with a single infographic-style visualization for the same data. Here we describe the methods and results from this evaluation.

---

[2] Please see https://streamable.com/pw7xi for a video showcasing our tool. Note that this URL is anonymized, so does not break the confidentiality of the reviews.

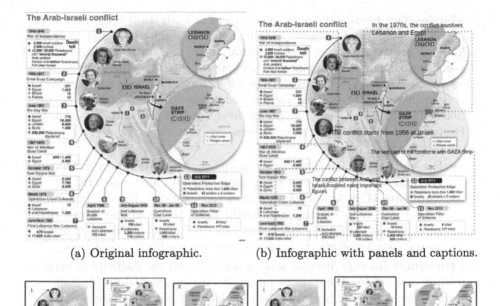

(a) Original infographic.

(b) Infographic with panels and captions.

(c) Partition with panels, no captions.

(d) Partition with panels and captions.

Fig. 4. (a) Original infographic. (b) Adding red dotted boxes to highlight panel locations. (c) The infographic is partitioned into panels. (d) The infographic is partitioned into panels and captions are added to structure the narrative. (Color figure online)

- **Participants:** We recruited 12 paid participants (9 male, 3 female); all self-selected from the student population, aged between 20 and 31 years, with normal or corrected-to-normal vision, and proficient computer users.
- **Apparatus:** We conducted the experiment on a laptop computer equipped with a 15-in. 1280×800 LCD screen, a standard keyboard, and a three-button mouse. Both interface conditions were maximized to fill the screen.
- **Task and Datasets:** Each trial consisted of the participant using four types of data stories to answer questions: a single infographic versus a data comic, with and without captions for the different parts. Each story consisted of five or six panels to maintain the simplicity while providing sufficient information for the story. Each story had an associated list of 7 to 9 questions designed to make the participant focus on details of the visualization. The stories included the Beer Origin Map (S_1), the Arab-Israeli Conflict (S_2), Smart Phishing Attacks (S_3), and World Wealthy People Distribution (S_4).

- **Metrics:** Our focus with the evaluation was to both study quantitative metrics, such as time and accuracy, as well as to collect subjective and qualitative feedback on the difference between data stories of data comics and original visualization. For this reason, we developed a questionnaire polling participants on their subjective experience of a story. This was administered to participants directly after each story, and consisted of 1–5 Likert-scale questions on engagement, speed, space efficiency, ease of use, and enjoyability.
- **Factors:** We included three factors in the experiment (all within-participants):
  - **Presentation (P):** This factor modeled the presentation technique P given for solving questions: infographic (IG) or data comic (DC).
  - **Captions (C):** Access to partitions and captions. For the infographic, having access to the captions would show the bounding boxes of the partitions as well as the associated caption for each partition (Fig. 4).
  - **Story (S):** Modeling the impact of specific stories S on outcome.
- **Procedure:** An experimental session started with the participant arriving, reading and signing the consent form, and being assigned an identifier and story order. The administrator then explained the general goals and task. Each trial started with the administrator demonstrating how to read a data comic. The participant was then given four small examples (not the above stories), two with original visualizations (w/wt highlight of panel locations) and two with data comic (w/wt captions), and was allowed to ask questions about the examples and task during this time. When the participant finished training, they were given four stories, one at a time, opened in the appropriate tool and a paper sheet with questions. Participants saw each story once in sequence $(S_1, \ldots, S_4)$, with within-participant factors P and C chosen to counterbalance learning effects. They were given up to 10 min to answer the questions, and were encouraged to use all of the time. After answering, the participant was given the subjective questionnaire polling their experience in the trial. This was repeated for all four stories—one with the infographic, one with the infographic with captions, one with panels without captions, and one with panels with captions. A full session lasted approximately 50 min, including training and questionnaires.

6.1   Quantitative Results

Figure 5 depicts boxplots of the subjective ratings for the four types of tasks: (a) infographic, (b) infographic with highlights of panel focus locations and captions, (c) data comic without captions, and (d) data comic with captions. The ratings are for following effects on a 5-point Likert scale: engagement, speed, space-efficiency, ease of use, and enjoyability (Q1 through Q5). We analyzed the 5-point Likert scale of subjective ratings for effects of the technique P (infographic vs. data comic) and captions C (no captions vs. with captions), and found that the engagement (Q1), speed (Q2) efficiency (Q3), and enjoyability

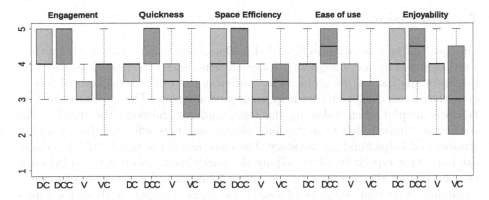

Fig. 5. Comparison between single infographic (V), infographic with caption (VC), data comic panels without captions (DC) and data comic panels with captions (DCC) of subjective ratings (Likert 1–5 scale). (Color figure online)

(Q4) were significantly different between the four techniques (Friedman tests, $p < .05$), but enjoyability (Q5) had no significant difference (Friedman tests, $p = .12$). We also found no significant effect of story S on any of the metrics.

6.2 Qualitative Feedback

Inviting Reading: Nine participants noted that the comic layout helped them view the materials as a whole story without explicit instruction.

Easy to Follow: Reading a complex infographic can be challenging. Partitioning the visualization into panels can help the reader follow the sequence of panels and captions to generate a thread. One participant mentioned that the Arab-Israeli conflict infographic is overwhelming at first glance, but that the first data comic panel is a great summary with supplementary information partitioned to other panels. Another participant noted that the data comic allows for skipping panels when reading while still following the big picture of the story.

Facilitating Focus: The data comic panels are organized in a sequence following a narrative. The audiences' attention is directed by the panel, so that the important information is contained in certain panels. One participant mentioned that "I was able to easily find the panels with information I wanted". Another participant mentioned that having captions and panels is like having labels for the whole visualization.

Facilitating Memory: In our study, one participant mentioned that "Panels view pushed me to structure my story during the study". Five participants noted that reading the data comic panels helped them remember the information when answering questions.

7 Discussion

Our qualitative evaluation indicated that data comics, especially with captions were significantly more engaging, space-efficient, faster and easier to use than original visualization/infograhic. The feedbacks from the participants also indicate that panels of partitions help focus and memory. The captions are particularly helpful when following the story and remembering the details. The participants mostly felt that the data comic was more effective that it invites reading and helps build up the story. The sequence of the panels in data comics are important especially when helping the participants recall detailed information on one of the panels with the help of captions. The overall sequence is more important than sequence of a small range, i.e. two panels about the topics parallel to each other can be changed without harming the whole storyline.

We explicitly chose not to measure time or correctness. There is likely little difference between data comics versus single visualization/infographic, and this perception was also confirmed by participants in our experiment. Rather, the strength of data comics comes from its approachable, compelling, and intuitive format. This is further validated by Lee et al. [23], who only collected subjective ratings from participants in their SketchStory evaluation.

Our work in this paper has several limitations. First of all, much of our argumentation of using sequential art for data is based on two assumptions: that the audience has (a) prior experience, and (b) a favorable opinion about comics. With no prior experience, much of the benefit of an established common ground in the visual language of comics is lost. Furthermore, given the sometimes questionable respectability of comics [12,24], its use as a communication medium may be problematic. For example, it can be argued that a data comic may not be the best vehicle for presentations in very formal settings, such as a boardroom meeting. Similarly, the intrinsically light-hearted nature of comics may be inappropriate for sensitive or difficult topics, such as natural disasters, emergency situations, and other types of crises or stories on the loss of lives or livelihoods.

8 Conclusion and Future Work

We have given a background on storytelling using data comics that is grounded in research on sequential art. We have built a data comic authoring system to investigate this topic. We presented a qualitative study designed to elicit differences in participant behavior when solving questions using a complex infographic compared to when the same visuals are organized into a data comic. The results show that the sequences of partitions help focusing and memory.

Our future work will be continuing exploring narrative visualization using sequential art. For example, there may be situations when it is appropriate to combine dynamic visualizations with a static comic. Furthermore, we also want to incorporate more collaborative features into the system.

References

1. Allen, J.F.: Maintaining knowledge about temporal intervals. Commun. ACM **26**(11), 832–843 (1983)
2. Bach, B., Kerracher, N., Hall, K.W., Carpendale, S., Kennedy, J., Riche, N.H.: Telling stories about dynamic networks with Graph Comics. In: Proceedings of the ACM Conference on Human Factors in Computing Systems, pp. 3670–3682 (2016). https://doi.org/10.1145/2858036.2858387
3. Bach, B., Riche, N.H., Carpendale, S., Pfister, H.: The emerging genre of data comics. IEEE Comput. Graph. Appl. **37**(3), 6–13 (2017). https://doi.org/10.1109/MCG.2017.33
4. Bostock, M., Ogievetsky, V., Heer, J.: D3: data-driven documents. IEEE Trans. Vis. Comput. Graph. **17**(12), 2301–2309 (2011)
5. Christiansen, H.C.: Comics and film: a narrative perspective. In: Magnussen, A., Christiansen, H.C. (eds.) Comics & Culture: Analytical and Theoretical Approaches to Comics, pp. 107–122. Museum Tusculanum Press, University of Copenhagen (2000)
6. Cohn, N.: Beyond speech balloons and thought bubbles: the integration of text and image. Semiotica **197**, 35–63 (2013). https://doi.org/10.1515/sem-2013-0079
7. Cohn, N.: The Visual Language of Comics: Introduction to the Structure and Cognition of Sequential Images. Bloomsbury, London (2014)
8. Collomosse, J.P., Rowntree, D., Hall, P.M.: Rendering cartoon-style motion cues in post-production video. Graph. Models **67**(6), 549–564 (2005). https://doi.org/10.1016/j.gmod.2004.12.002
9. Diakopoulos, N., DiMicco, J., Hullman, J., Karahalios, K., Perer, A.: Telling stories with data: the next chapter—a VisWeek 2011 workshop (2011)
10. DiMicco, J., McKeon, M., Karahalios, K.: Telling stories with data—a VisWeek 2010 workshop (2010)
11. Duncan, R., Smith, M.J.: The Power of Comics: History, Form, and Culture. Continuum, New York (2009)
12. Eisner, W.: Graphic Storytelling and Visual Narrative. W. W. Norton & Company, New York (2008)
13. Gershon, N.D., Page, W.: What storytelling can do for information visualization. Commun. ACM **44**(8), 31–37 (2001). https://doi.org/10.1145/381641.381653
14. Gonick, L., Huffman, A.: The Cartoon Guide to Physics. HarperPerennial, New York (1990)
15. Gonick, L., Smith, W.: The Cartoon Guide to Statistics. HarperCollins, New York (1993)
16. Hullman, J., Diakopoulos, N.: Visualization rhetoric: framing effects in narrative visualization. IEEE Trans. Vis. Comput. Graph. **17**(12), 2231–2240 (2011). https://doi.org/10.1109/TVCG.2011.255
17. Hullman, J., Drucker, S.M., Riche, N.H., Lee, B., Fisher, D., Adar, E.: A deeper understanding of sequence in narrative visualization. IEEE Trans. Vis. Comput. Graph. **19**(12), 2406–2415 (2013). https://doi.org/10.1109/TVCG.2013.119
18. Inselberg, A.: The plane with parallel coordinates. Vis. Comput. **1**(2), 69–91 (1985). https://doi.org/10.1007/BF01898350
19. Javed, W., Elmqvist, N.: ExPlates: spatializing interactive analysis to scaffold visual exploration. Comput. Graph. Forum **32**(3pt4), 441–450 (2013). https://doi.org/10.1111/cgf.12131

20. Jin, J., Szekely, P.A.: QueryMarvel: a visual query language for temporal patterns using comic strips. In: Proceedings of the IEEE Conference on Visual Languages and Human-Centered Computing, pp. 207–214 (2009). https://doi.org/10.1109/VLHCC.2009.5295262

21. Jin, J., Szekely, P.A.: Interactive querying of temporal data using a comic strip metaphor. In: Proceedings of the IEEE Symposium on Visual Analytics Science and Technology, pp. 163–170 (2010). https://doi.org/10.1109/VAST.2010.5652890

22. Kosara, R.: Story points in Tableau Software. Keynote at Tableau Customer Conference, September 2013

23. Lee, B., Kazi, R.H., Smith, G.: SketchStory: telling more engaging stories with data through freeform sketching. IEEE Trans. Vis. Comput. Graph. 19(12), 2416–2425 (2013). https://doi.org/10.1109/TVCG.2013.191

24. McCloud, S.: Understanding Comics: The Invisible Art. William Morrow Paperbacks (1994)

25. McCloud, S.: Comics: a medium in transition. Comput. Graph. Forum 30(3), xiii (2011)

26. Phan, D., Paepcke, A., Winograd, T.: Progressive multiples for communication-minded visualization. In: Proceedings of Graphics Interface, pp. 225–232 (2007). https://doi.org/10.1145/1268517.1268554

27. Segel, E., Heer, J.: Narrative visualization: telling stories with data. IEEE Trans. Vis. Comput. Graph. 16(6), 1139–1148 (2010). https://doi.org/10.1109/TVCG.2010.179

28. Shneiderman, B.: Tree visualization with tree-maps: a 2-D space-filling approach. ACM Trans. Graph. 11(1), 92–99 (1992). https://doi.org/10.1145/102377.115768

29. Viégas, F., Wattenberg, M.: Communication-minded visualization: a call to action. IBM Syst. J. 45(4), 801–812 (2006). https://doi.org/10.1147/sj.454.0801

30. Viégas, F.B., Golder, S., Donath, J.: Visualizing email content: portraying relationships from conversational histories. In: Proceedings of the ACM Conference on Human Factors in Computing Systems, pp. 979–988 (2006). https://doi.org/10.1145/1124772.1124919

31. Wang, T.D., Plaisant, C., Quinn, A.J., Stanchak, R., Murphy, S., Shneiderman, B.: Aligning temporal data by sentinel events: discovering patterns in electronic health records. In: Proceedings of the SIGCHI Conference on Human Factors in Computing Systems, pp. 457–466. ACM, New York (2008)

32. Wattenberg, M.: Baby names, visualization, and social data analysis. In: Proceedings of the IEEE Symposium on Information Visualization, pp. 1–7 (2005). https://doi.org/10.1109/INFVIS.2005.1532122

33. Zhao, Z., Marr, R., Elmqvist, N.: Data comics: Sequential art for data-driven storytelling. Technical report HCIL-2015-15, Human-Computer Interaction Laboratory (2015)

Modeling Adoption Behavior for Innovation Diffusion

Enguo Zhou[1], Daifeng Li[1(✉)], Andrew Madden[1], Yongsheng Chen[1], Ying Ding[2], Qi Kang[1], and Huanning Su[1]

[1] School of Information Management, Sun Yat-Sen University, Guangzhou, China
zhouenguo@126.com, lidaifeng@mail.sysu.edu.cn
[2] School of Informatics and Computing, Indiana University, Bloomington, USA

Abstract. In the current AI era, an increasing number of new technologies have been developed which promote disruptive innovation, making analysis of diffusion of innovation ever more important. Where previous studies have mainly focused on the direct influence of new technology adoption behaviors, this article proposes a new model (Adoption Behavior-based Graphical Model (ABGM)) which incorporates the effect of influencing factors (i.e., homophily and heterophily) on users' behavior regarding the adoption of new AI technologies. This model simulates the process of innovation diffusion and connects the diffusion patterns in a unified framework. We evaluate the proposed model on a large-scale AI publication dataset from 2006 to 2015. Results show that ABGM outperforms start-of-the-art baselines and also demonstrates that the probability of individual users adopting an innovation is significantly influenced by the diffusion process through the correlation network.

Keywords: Innovation diffusion · Adoption behavior · Homophily · Heterophily

1 Introduction

Diffusion is the process by which an innovation is communicated through certain channels over time among members of a social system [10]. The adoption and dissemination of new theories, technologies and algorithms is very important for accelerating innovation. In the era of AI, the deep integration of AI frontier technologies requires the rapid diffusion of innovations within and between both academic and commercial research organizations. With the success of online social networking sites (such as Twitter and Facebook), substantial efforts focusing on the properties of social network structures have been devoted to understanding the diffusion process, providing useful insights [4,9,15,16]. However, most of this research [2,3,5,8,14] is based on the assumption that all innovations are independent of each other. This is convenient, but unfortunately, impractical in the real world. It is only recently though, that researchers have started to shed light on the relationships between the diffusing innovations [7,11,12,18].

© Springer Nature Switzerland AG 2019
N. G. Taylor et al. (Eds.): iConference 2019, LNCS 11420, pp. 339–349, 2019.
https://doi.org/10.1007/978-3-030-15742-5_33

The process of diffusion is complex and there is are several potentially unknown factors which can affect decisions to adopt innovations. Research on this matter is far from conclusive and new ideas are needed to provide more insightful exploration. Previous work has focused mainly on an author's historical behavior and interactions with social network neighbors. In this work, we investigate the diffusion of innovations through the defined correlation networks between adoption behaviors. The contribution of this paper is threefold:

1. We define two types of correlation between users' adoption behaviors and use them to generate a correlation network. The correlations can improve understanding of innovation diffusion at a micro-level.
2. We investigate the diffusion process from the perspective of adoption behavior and propose an Adoption Behavior-based Graphical Model (ABGM) which combines correlations between adoption behaviors, to observe the dynamic process of diffusion.
3. The experiment on a large-scale publication dataset illustrates, at a micro level, the process by which innovations diffuse, and demonstrates that correlations between adoption behaviors can affect the adoption of innovations.

2   Literature Review

Traditional innovation diffusion researches mainly focus on detecting diffusion patterns based on classic diffusion models [6,17] while seldom considering the influence of user and innovation interactions towards the process of diffusion.

Myers et al. [7] was the first research to investigate the connections between the innovations that are diffused. In their illuminating research, a statistical model called IMM is proposed to learn the competition and collaboration interactions among the latent topics for contagions. Experiment result had found that competition relationship can suppress the diffusion of innovation while collaboration promote the diffusion. Rong et al. [11] construct an innovation networks by taking the computer algorithms as node and relationship between algorithms (competition/collaboration) as edge. The predictive power of innovation network on large-scale dataset shows that the features extracted from innovation networks do provide potential information for diffusion process.

Recent research (e.g., [18]) has started to integrate all three kinds of interaction (user-user, user-innovation, innovation-innovation) into a coherent model called IAD. Experimental results on large-scale Weibo datasets have found that the influences exerted on different groups of user are similar to the spread of contagious diseases. However, IAD was based on the assumptions that users belonging to same group have totally the same preference, which is coarse-grained in modeling diffusion process since everyone likes to be different.

Different with previous studies, we use homophily and heterophily to describe the correlations among different adoption behaviors, and use a graph model to model the diffusion process through the correlation network. The research provides a novel perspective to study how correlation network influences innovation diffusion.

3   Problem Definition

Our problem starts with an innovation diffusion network $G = <V, E>$, where V represents the set of nodes, and E represents the set of edges. Each node in V is represented as $v = <u, a, t>$, which means that user u adopts an innovation a at time t. The edge e_{ij} between v_i and v_j is used to measure the correlation between two nodes. In our research, we mainly define two types of correlations.

Definition 1. *(Homophily) Assume we have $v_1 = <u_1, a_1, t_1>$ and $v_2 = <u_2, a_2, t_2>$, and that u_2 cites u_1's work on innovation a_1 at t_1, and adopts u_2's own innovation a_2 at t_2. The adopted innovations a_1 and a_2 are based on different mechanism or theory, but have similar usage or function. For example, SVM and GBDT can be both applied in the mission of multi-classification regression and ranking, but SVM is based on kernel function, while GBDT is based on decision tree and boosting. The correlation between v_1 and v_2 is called homophily.*

Definition 2. *(Heterophily) Assume we have $v_1 = <u_1, a_1, t_1>$ and $v_2 = <u_2, a_2, t_2>$, and that u_2 cites u_1's work on innovation a_1 at t_1, and adopts u_2's own innovation a_2 at t_2. The adopted innovations a_1 and a_2 can interact, resulting in improvements despite the fact that they are based on different mechanisms or theories. For example, combining a random walk with word2vec can generalize a new algorithm. The kind of correlation that occurs between v_1 and v_2 is called heterophily.*

Based on the above definition, we can derive our objective function as $f(u, a, t + \Delta t | G_t, G_{t+\Delta t})$, which means, given the innovation diffusion network G at time t and $t + \Delta t$, whether a user u will adopt an innovation a at time $t + \Delta t$?

4   Model Descriptions

4.1   Framework of ABGM

Figure 1 is a graphical representation of Adoption Behavior based Graph model (ABGM). It consists of three networks: a social network, an innovation network and a correlation network. The social network illustrates the relationship between users based on the citations in their publications, while the innovation network represents the competitive and collaborative relationship between innovations [11]. We define adoption behavior as being when a user selects a computer algorithm as an innovation, thus the correlation network describes the mutual influence of the adoption behaviors on all users.

- User u_3 adopts an innovation a_1 (Deep Learning) in innovation network.
- User u_3 cites u_4's work.
- User u_4 adopts an innovation a_5 (Gradient) to describe his own work.
- A correlation type Heter is selected to describe the behavioral influences affecting u_3 and u_4 in the correlation network.

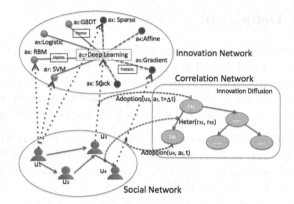

Fig. 1. Graphical representation of ABGM

ABGM consists of two main models, which model the adoption behavior and correlation between two behaviors. Assume that we have obtained a total of I behaviors $\{y_1, y_2, \cdots, y_I\}$, where each y_i is generated by (u_m, a_n, t). Adoption behavior is modeled in formula 1:

$$
\begin{aligned}
adopt(y_i, x_i(u_m, a_n, t)) &= \frac{1}{Z_\alpha} exp\{\alpha \cdot x_i(u_m, a_n, t)\} \\
&= \frac{1}{Z_\alpha} exp\{\sum_{k \in K} \alpha_k \cdot x_{ik}\}
\end{aligned}
\tag{1}
$$

$x_i(u_m, a_n, t)$ represents the K features extracted for adoption behavior, where user u_m adopts innovation a_n at time t. $y \in \{0, 1\}$ where 1 indicates adoption of an innovation, and 0 the otherwise. α is the weight parameter of x_i and x_{ik} is the kth attribute of x_i. Modeling of the correlation can be seen in formulas 2 and 3 as follows:

$$
hom(y_i, ne(y_i)|t, t + \triangle t) = \frac{1}{Z_\beta} exp\{\sum_{y_j \in ne(y_i)} \beta^T I^{hom}(y_i, y_j)\}
\tag{2}
$$

$$
heter(y_i, ne(y_i)|t, t + \triangle t) = \frac{1}{Z_\gamma} exp\{\sum_{y_j \in ne(y_i)} \gamma^T I^{heter}(y_i, y_j)\}
\tag{3}
$$

where hom represents homophily and heter is heterophily. $ne(y_i)$ represents the neighbors, who have correlation with y_i. I^{hom} and I^{heter} are indicator functions which illustrate whether conditions of homophily or heterophily correlation exist between two behaviors. $\{\alpha, \beta, \gamma\}$ are parameters for model estimation. $t, t + \triangle t$ indicates the time period in which the correlation occurs.

4.2   Model Learning

Let $\theta = \{\alpha, \beta, \gamma\}$ and normalization factor $Z = Z_\alpha Z_\beta Z_\gamma$. The joint distribution can be written as:

$$
P(Y_{t+\triangle t}|G_t, G_{t+\triangle t}) = \frac{1}{Z} \prod_i exp\{\theta^T M(y_i)\} = \frac{1}{Z} exp\{\theta^T M\}
\tag{4}
$$

where $M(y_i) = (x_i(u_m, a_n, t), \sum_{y_j} I^{hom}(y_i, y_j)^T, \sum_{y_j} I^{heter}(y_i, y_j)^T)^T$ and $M = \sum_i M(y_i)$.

In ABGM, we denote the set of all known labels as Y^L, Y is the estimated probability distribution of Y^L. In order to calculate the normalization factor Z, we need to sum up the likelihood of possible states for all nodes and the logarithm likelihood objective function is defined as:

$$\mathcal{O}(\theta) = logP(Y^L|G_t, G_{t+\triangle t}) = log \sum_{Y|Y^L} \frac{1}{Z} exp\{\theta^T M\}$$

$$= log \sum_{Y|Y^L} exp\{\theta^T M\} - log \sum_Y exp\{\theta^T M\} \qquad (5)$$

The gradient of $\mathcal{O}(\theta)$ can be derived as:

$$\frac{\partial \mathcal{O}}{\partial \theta} = \frac{\sum_{Y|Y^L} exp\{\theta^T M\} \cdot M}{\sum_{Y|Y^L} exp\{\theta^T M\}} - \frac{\sum_Y exp\{\theta^T M\} \cdot M}{\sum_Y exp\{\theta^T M\}} \qquad (6)$$

We propose a forward-backward propagation algorithm to simulate diffusion through the correlation network. The basic principles of the propagation algorithm can be seen in Fig. 2.

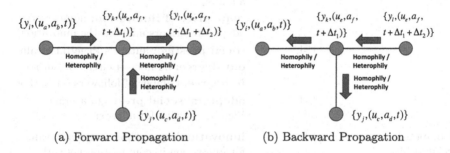

(a) Forward Propagation   (b) Backward Propagation

Fig. 2. Process of propagation algorithm

In order to estimate the probability ($\theta^T M$) of each node (whether or not an innovation is adopted), forward propagation uses the updated parameters from the last iteration to recalculate the probability of each node in the correlation network, from root nodes to leaf nodes, while backward propagation adjusts all the probabilities from leaf nodes to root nodes. The process of parameter learning is summarized in Fig. 3.

4.3   Feature Design

In Table 1, the basic feature set is based mainly on previous studies [11,12], which consist largely of three sub feature sets: Social Network, Competition network and Collaboration network. For each sub feature set, the features are

```
Input: learning rate η

Output: learned parameters θ
    1: Initialize θ with random values
    2: repeat
    3.      Calculate θᵀM for all nodes in the graph using forward backward propagation
    4:      Calculate the ∂(O(θ))/∂(θ) using formula (6)

    5:      Update θ with learning rate η
                          θ_new = θ_old − η∇_θ
    6: Until Convergence
```

Fig. 3. Learning process of ABGM

Table 1. Descriptions of features extracted for each adoption behavior. U-U: user interactions, U-I: user innovation interactions, I-I: innovation interactions.

Category	Interaction	Feature: Description
Social network related ($\mathbb{S}$)	U-I	**author's activeness:** number of innovations adopted **popularity of innovation:** number of adopters (authors adopted the innovation)
	U-U	**social prestige:** author's PageRank value **out-degree:** number of citers for author **in-degree:** number of followers for author
	U-I	**adopters' social prestige:** average PageRank value for adopters
Competition network related ($\mathbf{\Phi}$)	I-I	**innovation's prestige:** PageRank value for innovation in competition network
	U-I	**author's innovation prestige:** average PageRank value for innovations adopted **infecter:** number of its neighbors adopted by current author in competition network **inferters' prestige:** average PageRank value for innovation's neighbor adopted
Collaboration network related ($\mathbf{\Omega}$)	I-I	**innovation's prestige:** PageRank value for innovation in collaboration network
	U-I	**author's innovation prestige:** average PageRank value for innovations adopted **infecter:** number of its neighbors adopted by the author in collaboration network **infecters' prestige:** average PageRank value for innovation's neighbor adopted

mainly designed around the three dimensions, User-User, User-Innovation and Innovation-Innovation. Unlike earlier studies, we incorporate innovation diffusion factors (homophily and heterophily) into existing feature sets. The factors measure how influence diffuses through the correlation network of adoption behaviors.

5 Experimental Results

5.1 Dataset Preparation

There are many platforms providing datasets of academic social networks, such as AMiner [13]. In this work, we constructed a large-scale citation network by collecting academic publications relating to artificial intelligence, published between 2006 and 2015. We began with a search of the Library of Congress using variants of "Artificial Intelligence", e.g., "Artificial thinking". Sub-fields of AI were also included, such as "Adaptive control systems"; and related terms such as "Neurocomputers". Later, given the importance of conference proceedings in Computer Science, top conferences in Artificial Intelligence were also included. Finally, we got 484,328 academic papers written by 740,312 authors with a total of 10,660,838 citation relationships.

The construction of innovation networks conforms to Rong's work [11], which maps computer algorithms as nodes, and competition/collaboration relationships as edges. In practice, we limited our scope of algorithms to the area of Artificial Intelligence and manually removed false cases. Finally, 92 mainstream algorithms, mainly from statistical models and probabilistic models, were extracted; and we got 632 competition and collaboration edges. Another thing worth mentioning is that social networks as well as innovation networks, are dynamic in our settings. For each year, from 2006 to 2015, we take a snapshot of both the social and innovation networks, and the training set is organized as follows: given a start year t, and an end year $t + \Delta t$, all new adoption behaviors between start year t and end year $t + \Delta t$, are taken as positive cases. An equal amount of negative cases for each author appearing in the starting year are randomly generated in order to ensure fairness.

5.2 Performance Evaluation

We used two-fold cross validation for the task of predicting adoption behavior and evaluated our proposed approach in terms of F1-score, accuracy, precision and recall. We first compared our approach with two traditional baseline methods: Logistic Regression (LR) and Support Vector Machines (SVM), both of which use the static attributes of adoption behaviors as input features to conduct the prediction task. In addition, we found that the prediction of adoption can be transformed into a link prediction task, whose mainstream idea is based on topological structure. In particular, we use the popular Adamic/Adar [1] as the baseline method, which only uses topological information.

Table 2. Experiment result on three time periods

Dataset	Model	Accuracy	Precision	Recall	Fl-score
Short (2012–2013)	LR	79.27%	**88.83%**	66.95%	76.33%
	SVM	79.47%	86.42%	69.92%	77.30%
	Adamic/Adar	78.95%	82.57%	77.01%	79.69%
	ABGM	**87.37%**	81.82%	**96.10%**	**88.38%**
Middle (2007–2010)	LR	70.09%	**79.69%**	53.88%	64.27%
	SVM	74.44%	78.19%	67.72%	72.57%
	Adamic/Adar	72.85%	55.71%	84.78%	67.23%
	ABGM	**81.75%**	75.81%	**93.26%**	**83.64%**
Long (2006–2015)	LR	70.48%	77.21%	58.17%	66.32%
	SVM	69.42%	76.22%	56.93%	65.01%
	Adamic/Adar	72.02%	68.93%	73.47%	71.13%
	ABGM	**80.94%**	**78.29%**	**85.61%**	**81.79%**

In order to illustrate the authority of ABGM, we conducted the task of predicting adoption behavior over three periods with different time spans. The results are shown in Table 2. In all time periods, the ABGM outperformed the three baseline methods with a huge margin. In the period from 2007 to 2010 (Middle), ABGM achieved 16.41% improvement compared with Adamic/Adar and 11.07% improvement compared with SVM in terms of F1-score. The highest F1-score, 88.38%, was achieved by ABGM from 2012 to 2013 (Short). In the period 2006 to 2015 (Long), the ABGM outperformed LR by 15.47% and SVM by 16.78%.

5.3   Contribution of Correlation Network

The contributions of correlations defined in our model are analyzed by combining correlations with attributes. Figure 4 shows the result of combining different correlations and attributes, where AB, AB-Hom, AB-Heter stand for static features only homophily and heterophily correlations.

In all cases the correlations were helpful in predicting adoption behavior and the contributions of only considering homophily (AB-Hom) or heterophily (AB-Heter) are roughly the same despite variation in numbers. For example, in the period from 2006 to 2015 (Long), each correlation contributes about 6.6% improvement compared with AB. ABGM considers both homophily and heterophily, and compared with AB, it can make 9.19% improvement from 72.60% to 81.79% in terms of F1-score (Absolute improvement), which indicates there exists differences between two correlations. In short, the results of this quantitative experiment indicate that the two kinds of correlation between adoption behaviors are useful predictors.

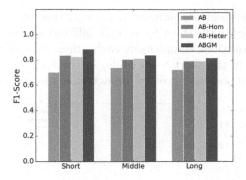

Fig. 4. Correlation contribution analysis

6 Contribution Discussion

In a correlation network, homophily and heterophily are connected to two adoption behaviors. The situations associated with these behaviors can be distinguished by decisions relating to their adoption. In particular, we define the following three adoption cases: 0-0, 0-1, 1-1, which means that homophily and heterophily are connected with different adoption decisions. Figure 5 shows the results of a quantitative analysis of the contributions of homophily. In all cases, homophily of adoption behaviors is a more powerful predictor than heterophily. This finding indicates that innovations with similar usage or function tend to be easier to adapt.

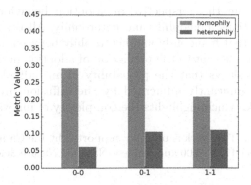

Fig. 5. Contribution of homophily and heterophily in three cases

Another thing worth mentioning is the dynamic change of heterophily and homophily. In order to investigate this, we took 2006 as the starting year, and calculated the importance of all correlations across different time spans (from 2 to 9 years). Detailed changes in homophily and heterophily are shown in Fig. 6. It is clear that the dynamic changes in homophily and heterophily differed markedly.

Where homophily has a greater impact over longer time spans, heterophily tends to be more influential in the short term. The different mechanisms may indicate, that where the innovations complement each other, they can increase the likelihood of adoption in the short term while, in the long-term, innovations with similar usage or function have greater impact on adoption decisions.

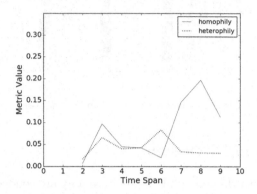

Fig. 6. Dynamic change of homophily and heterophily

7   Conclusions and Future Work

Models are representations of how we believe the world works. The diffusion of innovations is complex, and despite the substantial efforts of previous researchers, existing models do not fully capture the complexity and dynamic nature of the processes associated with diffusion. In this work, we modeled the diffusion process from the perspective of adoption behavior, and tentatively defined two correlations: homophily and heterophily. All the above experimental results indicate that homophily and heterophily between adoption behaviors provide information relevant to the prediction of adoption decisions. The experimental result also shows that the probability of an individual user adopting an innovation is significantly influenced by the diffusion process through the correlation network, which highlights the complexity of innovation diffusion.

Acknowledgments. This work is partially supported by the Chinese National Social Science Major Project 17ZDA200 and Chinese National Nature Science Youth Project 61702564.

References

1. Adamic, L.A., Adar, E.: Friends and neighbors on the web. Soc. Networks **25**(3), 211–230 (2003)
2. Cohen, E., Delling, D., Pajor, T., Werneck, R.F.: Sketch-based influence maximization and computation: scaling up with guarantees, pp. 629–638 (2014)
3. Hethcote, H.W.: The mathematics of infectious diseases. Siam Rev. **42**(4), 599–653 (2000)

4. Hong, L., Dan, O., Davison, B.D.: Predicting popular messages in Twitter. In: International Conference on World Wide Web, WWW 2011, Hyderabad, India, 28 March–April, pp. 57–58 (2011)
5. Kempe, D., Kleinberg, J., Tardos, É.: Maximizing the spread of influence through a social network. Progressive Research, pp. 137–146 (2010)
6. Min, C., Ding, Y., Li, J., Bu, Y., Pei, L., Sun, J.: Innovation or imitation: the diffusion of citations. J. Assoc. Inform. Sci. Technol. **69**(10), 1271–1282 (2018)
7. Myers, S.A., Leskovec, J.: Clash of the contagions: cooperation and competition in information diffusion. In: IEEE International Conference on Data Mining, pp. 539–548 (2012)
8. Newman, M.E.J.: The structure and function of complex networks. Siam Rev. **45**(2), 167–256 (2003)
9. Petrovic, S., Osborne, M., Lavrenko, V.: Rt to win! predicting message propagation in twitter. Dentistry Today **19**(11) (2011)
10. Rogers, E.M.: Diffusion of Innovations. Free Press, New York (2003)
11. Rong, X., Mei, Q.: Diffusion of innovations revisited: from social network to innovation network, pp. 499–508 (2013)
12. Su, Y., Zhang, X., Yu, P.S., Hua, W., Zhou, X., Fang, B.: Understanding information diffusion under interactions. In: International Joint Conference on Artificial Intelligence, pp. 3875–3881 (2016)
13. Tang, J., Zhang, J., Yao, L., Li, J., Zhang, L., Su, Z.: Arnetminer: extraction and mining of academic social networks. In: ACM SIGKDD International Conference on Knowledge Discovery and Data Mining, pp. 990–998 (2008)
14. Xiong, F., Liu, Y., Zhang, Z.J., Zhu, J., Zhang, Y.: An information diffusion model based on retweeting mechanism for online social media. Phys. Lett. A **376**(30–31), 2103–2108 (2012)
15. Yang, Y., et al.: Rain: social role-aware information diffusion (2014)
16. Yang, Z., et al.: Understanding retweeting behaviors in social networks. In: ACM International Conference on Information and Knowledge Management, pp. 1633–1636 (2010)
17. Zhai, Y., Ding, Y., Wang, F.: Measuring the diffusion of an innovation: a citation analysis. J. Assoc. Inform. Sci. Technol. **69**(3) (2017)
18. Zhang, X., Su, Y., Qu, S., Xie, S., Fang, B., Yu, P.: IAD: interaction-aware diffusion framework in social networks. IEEE Trans. Knowl. Data Eng. **PP**(99), 1 (2017)

Online Activism

Crowdsourcing Change: A Novel Vantage Point for Investigating Online Petitioning Platforms

Shipi Dhanorkar[(✉)] [iD] and Mary Beth Rosson [iD]

College of Information Sciences and Technology, Pennsylvania State University,
University Park, PA 16802, USA
{shipi,mrosson}@psu.edu

Abstract. The internet connects people who are spatially and temporally separated. One result is new modes of reaching out to, organizing and mobilizing people, including online activism. Internet platforms can be used to mobilize people around specific concerns, short-circuiting structures such as organizational hierarchies or elected officials. These online processes allow consumers and concerned citizens to voice their opinions, often to businesses, other times to civic groups or other authorities. Not surprisingly, this opportunity has encouraged a steady rise in specialized platforms dedicated to online petitioning; eg., Change.org, Care2 Petitions, MoveOn.org, etc. These platforms are open to everyone; any individual or group who is affected by a problem or disappointed with the status quo, can raise awareness for or against corporate or government policies. Such platforms can empower ordinary citizens to bring about social change, by leveraging support from the masses. In this sense, the platforms allow citizens to "crowdsource change". In this paper, we offer a comparative analysis of the affordances of four online petitioning platforms, and use this analysis to propose ideas for design enhancements to online petitioning platforms.

Keywords: Online petitioning platforms · Crowdsourcing · Design

1 Introduction

The internet is powerful. It provides us with otherwise unimaginable possibilities to communicate and connect. In today's society, the power of the internet is being harnessed to create technologies that serve as medium for creating online communities. The internet's fast speed, combined with its capability to reduce geographic and social distances is conducive for online activism, allowing interested parties to engage, organize and mobilize supporters for particular social causes in the internet world.

Popular social media websites such as Facebook and Twitter, along with specialized sites such as Change.org, MoveOn.org, and The Petition Site, have leveraged this opportunity to provide online platforms for creating social movements. But while many researchers have investigated the efficacy and impacts of online marketplaces such as Amazon.com, eBay, Craigslist, Groupon and others, there has been only limited examination of online platforms for social change. Platforms for social change are distinctive in that they seek to engage people and their empathy towards causes, not

N. G. Taylor et al. (Eds.): iConference 2019, LNCS 11420, pp. 353–364, 2019.
https://doi.org/10.1007/978-3-030-15742-5_34

objects or services. This is crucial to 21st century policy-making, as recent events (e.g., Brexit, Arab Spring) have highlighted the immensely important role of the internet and socially connected communities in shaping revolutions. In the coming years, online petitioning platforms can be expected to play a crucial role in governance and social change.

Given the increasing importance of online petitioning platforms and their potential for 'crowdsourcing change', it is crucial to examine these platforms in more detail and understand their common and unique features. In this paper, we therefore study four popular online petitioning platforms. Techniques for leveraging the knowledge of the 'crowd' have become mainstream in several domains including user studies [1], collaborative work [2, 3], and coordinating humanitarian efforts [4–6]. In this paper, we examine online petitioning platforms under the lens of crowdsourcing, arguing that these platforms can be seen as a specialized case of crowdsourced systems designed specifically to promote social change.

2　Related Work

In the following sections, we review studies of activism, with a specific focus on social movements, online activism, and crowdsourcing. These provide a context for the development of our proposition.

2.1　Social Movements

Social movements offer a way for like-minded people to express their frustrations, grievances, and suggestions regarding a shared cause. These movements arise due to people's concerns either about the status quo or as resistance to an imminent change. Social movements have been studied in history, sociology, and political science for many years [7–10]. This prior work has demonstrated that collective action can successfully drive organizational and institutional change [11–13]. More recently, organizational scholars [14] have presented diffusion effects of collective action, wherein changes in business practice are seen not only in target organizations but also in non-target organizations. Broadly, this research investigated how social activist tactics might produce cascading effects on the responsiveness of business organizations. It also highlighted two primary types of social activist tactics, namely disruption-based (e.g. strikes, sit-ins, boycotts) and evidence-based (providing more information that add to credibility), and compared the diffusion effects of these two tactics. The research was focused on adoption of supplier sanctions for the apparel brand "Russell", based on worker-rights violations at its manufacturing plants in Honduras. Subsequently the researchers found that the influence an individual or entity has on an organization is mediated by their relationship with the organization [15].

2.2　Online Activism

Technology and specifically the internet, has important implications for creating and organizing social movements [16, 17]. The internet has become a general-purpose platform for human expression and has significantly reduced the costs of communication for people with similar interests and passions. In his book, *'Here Comes Everybody'*, Shirky [16] argues that the internet is significantly affecting the ease and speed with which groups of people organize. He discusses different levels of organizing – sharing, collaborating and collective action. Social movements and activism cannot be isolated from the effects of globalization, technology and the rapid evolution of communication networks. In their edited book [18], *'Cyberactivism: Online Activism in Theory and Practice'*, the authors elaborate a similar set of points about the role of new technology platforms in political activism.

Recent studies in communication and Human Computer Interaction (HCI) have tried to explain the societal impacts of technology for online activism. One study demonstrated that participation in online activism can also have positive spillover effects on human behavior. Lee and Hsieh [19] present the results of an online experiment to show that signing online petitions affects subsequent civic action (contrary to the beliefs of critics) and the general notion of 'slacktivism' [20, 21]. Using donation to a charity as a surrogate for measuring civic action, they demonstrate that individuals are more likely to make donations if they have earlier signed petitions for a cause.

A number of studies investigate popular social media platforms like Facebook, YouTube and Twitter [22–26] and the opportunities they present for online activism. In one investigation, Halpern and Gibbs [27] examined the role of social media, specifically YouTube and Facebook, as a catalyst for online deliberation, which can be an important element of online activism. They found that the type and structure of the social platform can determine the nature and content of online deliberation. While social media platforms offer some features for garnering and demonstrating support for a cause, they are not primarily designed as platforms for organizing and mobilizing groups for social activism. This gap in our understanding calls for a deeper examination of online activism platforms, and how they may be used to drive social change.

2.3 Crowdsourcing

The past decade has seen a surge in web-based technologies with wide-ranging goals and purposes. Scholars offer an HCI framework [28] for classifying web-based systems as (a) crowdsourcing, (b) human computation, (c) social computing and (d) data mining. They draw parallels and distinctions between these classification buckets using definitions and examples. The first three categories fall within the umbrella term 'collective intelligence'. With respect to crowdsourcing, they note that the collective intelligence stems from harnessing a decentralized public to complete a task, which is known as crowdsourcing [29].

The term crowdsourcing captures the phenomenon of broadcasting a problem to large heterogeneous group of people and getting it done at relatively minimal cost. Over the years, with the advent of popular platforms such as Amazon Mechanical Turk and TaskRabbit, crowdsourcing has evolved to become a quick and low-cost way to collect vast volumes of data. Some scholars have proposed formal definitions for crowdsourcing [30, 31]. For example, in Doan et al. [31], the authors identify four key challenges that crowdsourcing systems face: (1) recruiting contributors, (2) their tasks, (3) combining their contributions, and (4) managing abuse. It is important to examine how platforms that crowdsource support for social change can address these challenges. In our paper, we discuss online petitioning platforms using the lens of crowdsourcing systems while attempting to address the above mentioned challenges.

3 Methodology

We used a purposive sampling approach, also known as selective or subjective sampling. In this approach, the researcher relies on judgment to choose specific cases as a part of the study [32]. In our case, we adopted a 'heterogeneous' purposive sampling approach where the intention is to select a sufficiently diverse range of cases that are relevant to the phenomenon being examined. Through this approach, we attempt to shine as much light as possible into the diverse array of online petitioning systems.

We chose four petitioning platforms that showed substantial diversity along the four task dimensions and their features: Change.org, Care2 petitions, MovenOn.org and We, the people. Change.org, was launched in 2011 and had about 200 million users in November 2017 [33]. According to its impact statistics, Change.org initiated petitions have led to more than 31,000 victories in about 196 countries on a wide variety of categories. Similarly, Care2 Petitions characterize themselves as 'social network for good' with 40 million members around the world [34]. It supports petitions on issues including animal welfare, human rights, education. MoveOn.org was launched in 1998 and has continued to mobilize people by combining digital innovation, data analytics and grassroots participation focused on civic and political action [35]. We, the people, on the other hand is a government platform that started under the Obama administration in 2011 [36]. It was initiated as a way for citizens to communicate with the White House. Figure 1 provides a snapshot of the main page for these platforms.

We compared the features of these four platforms to other crowdsourcing systems, with the goal of generating unique insights for managing online petitioning platforms. Using literature and concepts from the crowdsourcing literature, we propose various improvements to the design of online petitioning platforms.

Fig. 1. Screenshots of homepages of the four online petitioning platforms reviewed – Change.org (top left), Care2 Petitions (top right), Moveon.org (bottom left) and We, the People (bottom right).

4   Results and Design Implications

We conducted a comparative analysis of four online petitioning platforms based on four dimensions. Within each dimension, different features were examined. Table 1 provides a comparison of four online petitioning platforms Change.org, Care2 Petitions, We, the People and Moveon.Org along these dimensions: (i) starting petitions, (ii) updating petitions, (iii) signing petitions and (iv) petition analysis. We chose these dimensions because they reflect the range of interactions (or use cases) that users could engage in with the respective interfaces. We see that there is a sufficiently diverse range represented in the four petitioning platforms in the way petitions get started, setting signature goals, adding audio and video components, expected responses from decision makers and support for petition analysis. This comparative analysis generated a broader understanding of similarities and differences between platform.

Table 1. Comparative analysis of four online petitioning platforms

Features	Change.org	Care2 Petitions	We, the People	Moveon.Org
Signature threshold (start petition)	System Auto - 100, No subsequent edit possible	System Auto - 1000	100,000 Signatures in 30 days to get a response from government	No specifics provided
Categorize petition (start petition)	Yes	No	No	No
Signature goal (update petition)	No	Yes	No	No
Adding a Coleader (update petition)	No	No	N/A	Yes
Delete signatures from petition (update petition)	No	Yes	No	No
Expect response from decision makers (update petition)	No support from platform	No support from platform	Yes, after petition receives 100,000 signatures Within 30 days (response within 60 days)	No support from platform
Photo (update petition)	Yes optional	Yes optional	No	No
Video (update petition)	Yes optional	Yes optional	No	No
Auto-signing by petition starters (sign petition)	No	Yes	Yes	Yes

(*continued*)

Table 1. (*continued*)

Features	Change.org	Care2 Petitions	We, the People	Moveon.Org
Signature stats and trend lines (petition analysis)	No	Yes	No	Yes, signers by source + petition views
Email signatories (petition analysis)	No	Yes	N/A	Yes
Download signatures (petition analysis)	Yes	Yes	No	Yes
Download comments (petition analysis)	Yes	No	No	Yes

In online petitioning platforms, the computation required from crowd workers is minimal – just the click of a 'sign' button. Yet, several design aspects of the online petitioning platform are crucial for determining whether a petition succeeds or fails, because these features affect how the petition is submitted, reviewed, supported and promoted. If we consider the broad range of crowd sourced work, online petitioning platforms would lie on one end of spectrum (Fig. 2). Because there is scant work on defining the appropriate design features for online petitioning platforms, we adapt different design models from crowdsourcing/crowdfunding platforms to online petitioning platforms. These considerations are presented below under four main themes that are crucial to the effective functioning of online petitioning systems of the future.

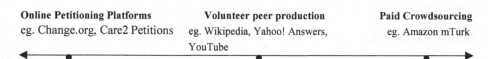

Online Petitioning Platforms
eg. Change.org, Care2 Petitions

Volunteer peer production
eg. Wikipedia, Yahoo! Answers, YouTube

Paid Crowdsourcing
eg. Amazon mTurk

Fig. 2. Spectrum of crowdsourcing systems with respect to the amount of computation by workers.

4.1   Offering Motivations to Participate

Crowdsourcing systems are essentially labor markets [37], with requesters (employers) and workers (employees) who carry out Human Intelligence Tasks (HITs). The market uses the 'crowd' to participate in HITs by providing suitable incentives such as payments on completion of HITs. Other scholars have shown that participation rates increase logarithmically as rewards are increased [38]. The perspectives presented in the crowdsourcing systems literature lead us naturally to the question as to how we can structure incentives in online petitioning platforms so as to increase participation?

Like crowdsourcing systems, online petitioning platforms can be thought of as having requesters (petition starters) and workers (petitioning signers). But because online petitioning platforms primarily target on demonstrating support in the form of signatures, the typical HIT incentive mechanisms used in crowdsourcing platforms might not transfer readily. There are also moral and ethical questions related to adding monetary rewards to showing support via signatures.

Currently, platforms acquire a simple signature, which merely is a foot-in-the door [39]. While this signature is a marker and symbol of support, it reflects only limited user motivation. From our task/feature analysis, currently there seemed to be no design affordances that emphasize the role of user motivations and incentives in online petitioning platforms. For the specific task of signing petitions, users merely have the option of including their personal details along with their signatures. Borrowing from crowdsourcing literature, we suggest that designers should explore non-monetary incentives such as points, badges and leaderboards [40, 41]. which have been shown to increase performance in crowdsourcing systems.

One way to introduce rewards into online petitioning platforms is to reinforce the signer's relationship with the website and the specific cause. This relationship could be made salient by employing a point/ranking system that encourages meaningful user participation and support for petitions. Such a point system would incentivize people to sign only those petitions that they truly support. It would eliminate fallacious signatures and ensure good-faith and conscientious support on petitions. One metric for building such a point system would be to combine number of petitions signed, type of support demonstrated and referral-based [42] incentives.

A second possible design approach to motivate signers in active participation is to offer ways to show different levels of support and investment in the petition cause. For example, online petitioning platforms could introduce levels of support for signers to choose from – (a) sign, (b) sign & pass, (c) sign & contribute, (d) sign & volunteer time. A signer offering a higher support would receive more points. There are two advantages to this approach. First, target organizations (e.g., governments, corporations) will see such public engagement as a stronger sign of an impending crisis or change and as a result, they would be motivated to act swiftly. Secondly, such an approach would create an incentive system for users that is based on healthy competition and active participation that goes beyond a mere 'click-of-the-button'.

4.2 Reputation Building for Petition Starters

The user motivation and incentive mechanism approach described earlier was aimed at petition signers. Another important feature is the reputation of petitioners (i.e. requesters) in a crowdsourced change environment. Scholars have studied incentive protocols that rely on reputation mechanisms in crowdsourcing websites [43]. Online petitioning platforms may suffer from 'gaming the system' phenomenon where petitioners create spurious petitions and are still able to attract signatures. However, such malicious behavior could be kept in check using a reputation system that honors petitioner credibility.

One means to introduce such a system is to use up-voting/down-voting techniques [44] to filter legitimate from spurious petitions. The phenomenon of fake petitions could also be somewhat controlled if there is a way to validate legitimate petitioners and signatures. A word of caution with this methodology is that up-voting could be used to advance causes that align with individual personalities and at the same time undermining other causes by down-voting related petitions.

Another deliberate option to capitalize on petition starters reputation at stake is to facilitate screening of petition starters (and signers). For example, Downs et al. [45] study the effect of a screening task in an Amazon Mechanical Turk (mTurk) HIT to filter out those workers who participate just for quick cash, instead of conscientiously. From the feature review that we conducted earlier, we didn't find any such affordances-absolutely any individual/organization can initiate petitions. There are no minimum requirements for starting a petition. A reputation system could also be designed with petition signers in mind. For example, the history of signers could serve as a valid check for ensuring that spurious/dubious petitions do not get fake signatures. Together, these design affordances could signal the legitimacy and trustworthiness of a petition. A careful and deliberate design combining one or more of the aforementioned mechanisms would safeguard online petitioning platforms from malicious behavior and ensure that no individual/organization takes undue advantage of such internet mediated activism.

4.3   Critical Mass for Collective Action

Threshold theories have been widely used in sociology to understand collective action. [46, 47]. These theories examine the participation of individuals to achieve a common goal. Crowdfunding platforms such as Kickstarter [48] have utilized these mechanisms so that a project is funded only if the amount of money specified in the goal is raised. Researchers have extended these mechanisms in new effort mobilization platforms which require person-hour & timeslot commitments for tasks like event organization [49]. These extensions are called activation-thresholds, which are in a sense critical mass required for the cause to be activated (organized).

One affordance that online petitioning platforms can offer is to indicate a threshold for support, which when attained will lead to the petition being noticed by and responded to decision-makers in target organizations. One of the online petitioning platform analyzed above, We the People by the White House relies on such functionality. The petitioner can expect an official response from the target officials within sixty days if the petition signatures reach a threshold of 100,000 within 30 days of the petition start date (Table 1). Because We the People is a petitioning system created by the government, it unintentionally puts the power in the target organization instead of the petitioner. However, a similar design feature in an independent online petitioning platform, will be valuable for users (petition signers and decision makers) grasp the expected commitment and the petition scope. Moreover, it also increases the decision-makers' accountability towards the petition.

A more nuanced addition to this design could be to ascribe different thresholds to different geographic regions. For example, some petitions with a national or international scope would require support that is geographically spread out while some petitions that have a smaller scope, say a small community, would need to meet threshold requirements for that locality. This design of threshold breakdowns could potentially provide important information piece for decision makers in target organizations.

4.4 Message Framing

At the core of online activism through online petitioning is being able to garner as much support as possible for the cause. This involves influencing peoples' perception, beliefs and attitudes. There have been several studies in psychology, communication, marketing and human computer interaction that utilize message framing, priming and persuasion to affect people's decision making [50–54]. However, these concepts are not well applied in the current designs of online petitioning platforms.

Currently, online petitioning platforms use a one-size-fits-all approach. All platform visitors (i.e. potential signers/users) view the same petition title, text, photo, video and metadata. While this is good for uniformity, this approach probably misses out on pockets of a population for whom the petition might not be appealing enough. This, in turn, could diminish the number of signatures that the petition receives.

One attraction of petitioning online is that the appeal need not be restricted to a small geographical area. Petition supporters could be and in fact are spread out geographically. A cause that receives traction in one region or community may not connect with people in other regions. Thus, an additional design feature in online petitioning platforms could be to enable targeted messaging that appeals to wider group of people in favor of the raised issue in the petition. For example, some petitions (Dakota access pipeline) are localized in nature but are of national importance, potentially due to their broader appeal to American values. However, a petition message targeted specifically to communities in Dakota might be more effective in gathering signatures (therefore support). This same petition could be customized and tailored to appeal to individuals in a totally different geographical location, say California. This would ensure that people, who are not directly faced with the specific problem, may still experience an emotional connection with the issue through the petition. These approaches would enable petitioners to achieve greater success in delivering their message to key recipients, which may in turn influence policy-making.

5 Conclusion

In this paper, we have synthesized current literature on social movements, online activism, and crowdsourcing. We have shed light on online petitioning platforms through the lens of crowdsourcing systems. Online petitioning platforms are designed to engage online communities to bring about crowdsourced social change. In light of the recent political (e.g., Brexit) and social (e.g., Arab Spring) events that were triggered by such online activism, we expect that online petitioning platforms will play a crucial role in shaping social change in the coming future.

We examined popular online petitioning platforms based on four key tasks and selected four platforms based on heterogeneous purposive sampling. After examining these platforms, we have proposed design considerations that allow balancing 'openness' and 'quality' of online petitions. In particular, these four design considerations relate to: offering motivations to participate, reputation building for petition starters, achieving critical mass for collective action, and message framing. Improvements along these four design dimensions are crucial for online petitioning platforms to catalyze lasting social change.

Although we have followed a systematic approach to select four petitioning platforms, our sampling was purposive and leaves out other platforms such as Gopetition.com and Act.Ly, which have also been successful in supporting social causes. Future research in this domain could focus on a broader array of online platforms. A natural extension to this research is conducting user studies to better understand their needs based on interviews and large scale data collection. There is an opportunity here to improve design of online petitioning platforms and enable positive social change.

References

1. Kittur, A., Chi, E.H., Suh, B.: Crowdsourcing user studies with mechanical turk. In: Proceedings of the SIGCHI Conference on Human Factors in Computing Systems, pp. 453–456. ACM, April 2008
2. Kittur, A., Kraut, R.E.: Harnessing the wisdom of crowds in Wikipedia: quality through coordination. In: Proceedings of the 2008 ACM Conference on Computer Supported Cooperative Work, pp. 37–46. ACM, November 2008
3. Ransbotham, S., Kane, G.C.: Membership turnover and collaboration success in online communities: explaining rises and falls from grace in Wikipedia. MIS Q-Manag. Inf. Syst. **35**(3), 613 (2011)
4. Palen, L., Vieweg, S.: The emergence of online widescale interaction in unexpected events: assistance, alliance & retreat. In: Proceedings of the 2008 ACM Conference on Computer Supported Cooperative Work, pp. 117–126. ACM, November 2008
5. Starbird, K., Muzny, G., Palen, L.: Learning from the crowd: collaborative filtering techniques for identifying on-the-ground Twitterers during mass disruptions. In: Proceedings of 9th International Conference on Information Systems for Crisis Response and Management, ISCRAM, April 2012
6. Tapia, A.H., Moore, K.A., Johnson, N.J.: Beyond the trustworthy tweet: a deeper understanding of microblogged data use by disaster response and humanitarian relief organizations. In: Proceedings of the 10th International ISCRAM Conference, pp. 770–778. Baden-Baden, May 2013
7. McCarthy, J.D., Zald, M.N.: Resource mobilization and social movements: a partial theory. Am. J. Sociol. **82**, 1212–1241 (1977)
8. Klandermans, B., Oegema, D.: Potentials, networks, motivations, and barriers: Steps towards participation in social movements. Am. Sociol. Rev. **52**, 519–531 (1987)
9. Tarrow, S.: Power in Movement: Social Movements and Contentious Politics. Cambridge University Press, Cambridge (1998)
10. Benford, R.D., Snow, D.A.: Framing processes and social movements: an overview and assessment. Annu. Rev. Sociol. **26**, 611–639 (2000)
11. Zald, M.N., Berger, M.A.: Social movements in organizations: Coup d'etat, insurgency, and mass movements. Am. J. Sociol. **83**, 823–861 (1978)

12. Bartley, T.: Certifying forests and factories: states, social movements, and the rise of private regulation in the apparel and forest products fields. Polit. Soc. **31**(3), 433–464 (2003)
13. Soule, S.A.: Contention and Corporate Social Responsibility. Cambridge University Press, New York (2009)
14. Briscoe, F., Gupta, A., Anner, M.S.: Social activism and practice diffusion how activist tactics affect non-targeted organizations. Adm. Sci. Q. **60**, 300–332 (2015). 0001839215579235
15. Briscoe, F., Gupta, A.: Social activism in and around organizations. Acad. Manag. Ann. 1–57 (2016)
16. Shirky, C.: Here Comes Everybody: The Power of Organizing Without Organizations. Penguin, New York (2008)
17. Earl, J., Kimport, K.: Digitally Enabled Social Change: Activism in the Internet Age. MIT Press, Cambridge (2011)
18. McCaughey, M., Ayers, M.D.: Cyberactivism: Online Activism in Theory and Practice. Routledge, New York (2003)
19. Lee, Y.H., Hsieh, G.: Does slacktivism hurt activism? The effects of moral balancing and consistency in online activism. In: Proceedings of the SIGCHI Conference on Human Factors in Computing Systems, pp. 811–820. ACM, April 2013
20. Gladwell, M.: Small change: why the revolution will not be tweeted. New Yorker **4**(2010), 42–49 (2010)
21. Morozov, E.: The brave new world of slacktivism. Foreign Policy **19**(05) (2009a)
22. Segerberg, A., Bennett, W.L.: Social media and the organization of collective action: using twitter to explore the ecologies of two climate change protests. Commun. Rev. **14**(3), 197–215 (2011)
23. Gerbaudo, P.: Tweets and the Streets: Social Media and Contemporary Activism. Pluto Press, London (2012)
24. Lim, M.: Clicks, cabs, and coffee houses: social media and oppositional movements in Egypt, 2004–2011. J. Commun. **62**(2), 231–248 (2012)
25. Tufekci, Z., Wilson, C.: Social media and the decision to participate in political protest: observations from Tahrir Square. J. Commun. **62**(2), 363–379 (2012)
26. Obar, J.A., Zube, P., Lampe, C.: Advocacy 2.0: an analysis of how advocacy groups in the United States perceive and use social media as tools for facilitating civic engagement and collective action. J. Inf. Policy **2**, 1–25 (2012)
27. Halpern, D., Gibbs, J.: Social media as a catalyst for online deliberation? Exploring the affordances of Facebook and YouTube for political expression. Comput. Hum. Behav. **29**(3), 1159–1168 (2013)
28. Quinn, A.J., Bederson, B.B.: Human computation: a survey and taxonomy of a growing field. In: Proceedings of the SIGCHI Conference on Human Factors in Computing Systems, pp. 1403–1412. ACM, May 2011
29. Howe, J.: The rise of crowdsourcing. Wired Mag. **14**(6), 1–4 (2006)
30. Estellés-Arolas, E., González-Ladrón-De-Guevara, F.: Towards an integrated crowdsourcing definition. J. Inf. Sci. **38**(2), 189–200 (2012)
31. Doan, A., Ramakrishnan, R., Halevy, A.Y.: Crowdsourcing systems on the world-wide web. Commun. ACM **54**(4), 86–96 (2011)
32. Ritchie, J., Lewis, J., Nicholls, C.M., Ormston, R. (eds.): Qualitative Research Practice: A Guide for Social Science Students and Researchers. Sage, Thousand Oaks (2013)
33. Change.org. https://www.change.org/impact. Accessed 27 Nov 2018
34. Care2. https://www.care2.com/. Accessed 27 Nov 2018
35. MoveOn.org. https://front.moveon.org/. Accessed 27 Nov 2018
36. We, the People. https://petitions.whitehouse.gov/. Accessed 27 Nov 2018

37. Horton, J.J., Chilton, L.B.: The labor economics of paid crowdsourcing. In: Proceedings of the 11th ACM Conference on Electronic Commerce, pp. 209–218. ACM, June 2010

38. DiPalantino, D., Vojnovic, M.: Crowdsourcing and all-pay auctions. In: Proceedings of the 10th ACM Conference on Electronic Commerce, pp. 119–128. ACM, July 2009

39. Freedman, J.L., Fraser, S.C.: Compliance without pressure: the foot-in-the-door technique. J. Pers. Soc. Psychol. **4**(2), 195 (1966)

40. Morschheuser, B., Hamari, J., Koivisto, J.: Gamification in crowdsourcing: a review. In: 2016 49th Hawaii International Conference on System Sciences (HICSS), pp. 4375–4384. IEEE, January 2016

41. Massung, E., Coyle, D., Cater, K.F., Jay, M., Preist, C.: Using crowdsourcing to support pro-environmental community activism. In: Proceedings of the SIGCHI Conference on Human Factors in Computing Systems, pp. 371–380. ACM, April 2013

42. Naroditskiy, V., Stein, S., Tonin, M., Tran-Thanh, L., Vlassopoulos, M., Jennings, N.R.: Referral incentives in crowdfunding. In: Second AAAI Conference on Human Computation and Crowdsourcing, September 2014

43. Archak, N.: Money, glory and cheap talk: analyzing strategic behavior of contestants in simultaneous crowdsourcing contests on TopCoder. com. In: Proceedings of the 19th international conference on World wide web, pp. 21–30. ACM, April 2010

44. Park, H., Widom, J.: Crowdfill: a system for collecting structured data from the crowd. In: Proceedings of the 23rd International Conference on World Wide Web, pp. 87–90. ACM, April 2014

45. Downs, J.S., Holbrook, M. B., Sheng, S., Cranor, L.F.: Are your participants gaming the system?: screening mechanical turk workers. In: Proceedings of the SIGCHI Conference on Human Factors in Computing Systems, pp. 2399–2402. ACM, April 2010

46. Granovetter, M.: Threshold models of collective behavior. Am. J. Sociol. **83**, 1420–1443 (1978)

47. Marwell, G., Oliver, P.: The Critical Mass in Collective Action. Cambridge University Press, Cambridge (1993)

48. Kickstarter. https://www.kickstarter.com/. Accessed 5 Sept 2018

49. Cheng, J., Bernstein, M.: Catalyst: triggering collective action with thresholds. In: Proceedings of the 17th ACM Conference on Computer Supported Cooperative Work & Social Computing, pp. 1211–1221. ACM, February 2014

50. Levin, I.P., Schnittjer, S.K., Thee, S.L.: Information framing effects in social and personal decisions. J. Exp. Soc. Psychol. **24**(6), 520–529 (1988)

51. Maheswaran, D., Meyers-Levy, J.: The influence of message framing and issue involvement. J. Mark. Res. **27**, 361–367 (1990)

52. Das, E., Kerkhof, P., Kuiper, J.: Improving the effectiveness of fundraising messages: the impact of charity goal attainment, message framing, and evidence on persuasion. J. Appl. Commun. Res. **36**(2), 161–175 (2008)

53. Hartmann, J., De Angeli, A., Sutcliffe, A.: Framing the user experience: information biases on website quality judgement. In: Proceedings of the Sigchi Conference on Human Factors in Computing Systems, pp. 855–864. ACM, April 2008

54. Byrnes, N.: Persuasive technologies surround us, and they're growing smarter. How do these technologies work? and why? In: Technology and Persuasion. MIT Technology Review, March 2015

Putting the "Move" in Social Movements: Assessing the Role of Kama Muta in Online Activism

Jennifer Pierre[✉]

University of California, Los Angeles, Los Angeles, CA 90095, USA
jp639@g.ucla.edu

Abstract. Today the structure of social media movements online is moving beyond just a means for communication and into space for growing the movement, developing a brand, and solidifying the network for group action. Thus individual posts on personal profiles and group and event pages are an increasingly important element of participation. Emotions may drive these posts, as well as the responses to them. This study seeks to enter into conversation with previous works in the areas of communication, information studies, sociology, and anthropology that investigate the intersection of social media and activism. However, this study takes a novel approach through the particular focus on individual emotional elements of social media posting, sharing, commenting, and other forms of engagement. Through qualitative and quantitative content analysis of five major activist Facebook groups, this study will examine the prevalence of content expressing or intending to evoke kama muta.

Keywords: Social movements · Social media · Kama muta · Activism

1 Introduction

Growing a movement, cultivating a brand, and motivating collective action all entail a crucial but often fickle element: emotion. How do social media evoke the emotion(s) that make social movements *move*? Today the structure of social media movements online is moving beyond just a means for communication and more into space for growing the movement, developing a brand, and solidifying the network for group action. Thus individual posts on personal profiles and group and event pages are becoming an increasingly important element of participation. Emotions may drive these posts, as well as the responses to them.

The connection between social movements and emotion is long-standing, with many studies in sociology and psychology supporting the significance of emotions in social movements [12, 15, 34]. Research from the last two decades especially has aimed to reverse the previous conceptions of emotions as generally irrational, and thus detrimental to the coherent progression and success of social movements and associated organizations. Research that broadens this discussion to consider specific aspects of emotion in online social movements is still sparse. This study contributes to previous research by continuing to move beyond the perception of emotions as irrational in

© Springer Nature Switzerland AG 2019
N. G. Taylor et al. (Eds.): iConference 2019, LNCS 11420, pp. 365–376, 2019.
https://doi.org/10.1007/978-3-030-15742-5_35

relation to social movements, and further fills a gap in work that intersects emotion and online activism by focusing on specific emotional components that motivate and facilitate personal involvement in digital activism. Specifically, this study will explore the role of kama muta in motivating personal posts and broader social participation in activist activity on social media.

Kama muta has been identified as a key part of social movements [10]. Described most simply as being "moved" or "touched", kama muta results from the sudden intensification of a communal sharing relationship, and can be experienced or observed in a variety of settings [28, 29]. Fiske et al. find that the emotion is often present among those listening to a rousing speech, experiencing a particularly patriotic moment, or undergoing a communal trauma. All three of these elements are often felt at various points of activist engagement. Moreover, the activities of community organizing and participating in social movements arguably require communal identity and empathy to succeed in garnering necessary momentum and public investment. This suggests that kama muta may play an important role in this setting.

Activist social media use has been an area of interest to communication and information scholars increasingly over the last decade. Some researchers in these fields have provided historical overviews of the changing nature of social movements with the integration of digital media and technology into their planning and development [19]. Others have used case studies, ethnographies, and other methods to reveal challenges, constraints, and affordances of social media use as part of revolutions like the Arab Spring and Occupy movements [30, 31]. Still others have investigated the role of social media in facilitating new sources of activism and/or the transformation of non-activists to activists [22, 32, 33, 37], along with other related concerns [1, 3, 14, 16, 40].

Much of this work takes a social informatics approach, focusing on the ways in which social media disrupts the current infrastructure of social movements and activism through the creation and facilitation of new forms of network building, communication, community expansion, leadership and authority, and community action. This important body of work sets the grounding for delving deeper into discussions of the intersection of social media and activism. However, the structural focus of much of this research and the framing of social media practices and social movements on the scale of a group unit of analysis in some ways impedes examination of individualized components of participation and facilitation in and of social movements. One such aspect is the broad area of emotion, and the role that emotion plays particularly in the impetus for action among individuals engaged in activism.

This study enters into conversation with previous works in the areas of communication, information studies, sociology, and anthropology that investigate the intersection of social media and activism. But, as noted in the introduction, this study takes a novel approach through the particular focus on individual emotional elements of social media posting, sharing, commenting, and other forms of engagement. In this way this research works to further combine the work on emotion, social movements, and online affordances through addressing their intersection. The significance of this work and line of inquiry is its potential application to the design and understanding of online social movements. Understanding the potential emotional motivations of online activists and the tactics employed by social movement organizations to accommodate them can enable better member engagement, with further implications for the design of social media platforms and features that may aid their success. Through quantitative and qualitative content analysis of five major activist Facebook groups, this study examines the prevalence of content expressing or intending to evoke kama muta.

2 Literature Review

This brief literature review conceptualizes and reviews previous work around key concepts of interest to this study: social media and kama muta.

2.1 Conceptualizing Social Media

One consistent definition of social media is difficult considering the rapidly changing nature of its moving parts, but marketing scholars Kaplan & Haenlein offer a broad but applicable definition of social media as "a group of Internet-based applications that build on the ideological and technological foundations of Web 2.0, and that allow the creation and exchange of User Generated Content" (p. 61) [17]. Such foundations include public accessibility, creativity, and creation outside of professional routines. They established this definition at the moment of the initial peak in Facebook's popularity, which tailored the definition as applicable to the increasingly new understanding of social networking sites moving beyond the previous age of Myspace and microblogging. Murthy highlights the continued expansion and broadening of the term, offering a definition of social media as referring to "the many relatively inexpensive and widely accessible electronic tools that enable anyone to publish and access information, collaborate on a common effort, or build relationships," which also coincides with the aims of social movements (pp. 7–8) [25]. Social media consists of social networking sites, broadly defined as web-based applications where users construct public personal profiles and make and list connections with other users [5]. Each of these definitions will be acknowledged for understanding how social media platforms function within the setting of activist use. For the purposes of this study, the expansive list of potential social media platforms will be acknowledged, but the main focus will be on Facebook, as it is the most popularly used social networking site among adults and offers the richest platform for engagement [19].

2.2 Social Media as a Tool for Activism

A growing literature across a number of interdisciplinary fields examines the potential for social media networks to act as spaces for activist expression. Gibson describes incidents where individuals who do not have a direct experiential connection to specific impacts or effects of an event still care deeply about the issue enough to be expressive about them on social media [11]. Srinivasan, and Srinivasan & Fish examine the important but complex role that media and communication technologies can play in activist communities, exposing the need for social media tools for the creation of strong ties in some cases [30, 32, 33]. They pose this as a departure from many previous assumptions about the use of social media for political action, via criticisms such as slacktivism. Such criticisms often claim that online activism leads to slacktivism due to the assumed weak ties that the online medium perpetuates. Srinivasan and Fishs' findings of strong and meaningful relationships being built using online platforms like Twitter and Facebook and the use of these sites for integral online and offline rallies and organizational tactics help combat this previous narrative.

2.3 Social Media and Positive Affect

Though less established in terms of volume of literature and theoretical backing, scholars in the fields of human-computer interaction, computer-mediated communication, social informatics, and social psychology have examined whether the sources of social support include general Internet activity, and in particular participation in social media and online communities. After analyzing the results of face-to-face structured questionnaire interviews, Leung & Lee found positive correlations between sociability-based Internet activities and various dimensions of social support, which they break down into emotional and informational support, affection, and positive social interaction [20]. These findings could potentially extend similarly to connect Internet activity to perceived kama muta, which is where this study seeks to contribute. More recently, information science literature has found positive psychological outcomes from social media use [6, 7, 18, 35, 38, 39]. Some studies have identified number of friends as a primary source of social support [4, 26] and have further identified seeking social support as a main reason for online social networking [27]. This study seeks to join this body of work through a specific examination of kama muta as one part of positive affect and emotion often associated with social media use.

2.4 Conceptualizing Kama Muta

This area of inquiry is likely one of the sparsest of the concepts described, and as a growing sub-area of research it places this pilot study in a position of potential significant contribution. As noted in the introduction, kama muta "occurs when there is a rapid emergence, renewal, restoration, or intensification of a communal sharing relationship" (p. 88) [10]. The communal sharing (CS) relationship referred to in this definition describes a situation where two or more people interact in relation to something that they share in common, which makes them "socially equivalent" [8, 9]. It is further explained as feelings of love, solidarity, and identity with a group of people perceived to be "of one's kind" [10]. Thus, indicators of a CS relationship may lead to indications of kama muta, which will play a role in the categories and strategies for observation in this study. Fiske et al. additionally offer a number of physical indicators of kama muta in particular, including warm feelings in the chest, moist eyes, a choked up feeling, goose bumps, and exclamations like *aww*.

Though these types of reactions cannot be physically viewed via observation of Facebook posts, this study will rely on descriptions of these types of reactions, as well as indicators that the post may be designed to elicit such reactions or already did on the part of the poster. These indicators of kama muta expression and CS expression are used to formulate and inform the categories of observation and data collection.

3   Research Questions

This study's primary research question examines the role of kama muta in influencing content posted on activist groups on social media.

RQ1: Does kama muta influence the content that activists share on social media?

Sub-question 1: If so, to what extent does kama muta such content?

Sub-question 2: How prevalent are posts that relate in some way to kama muta?

A central hypothesis motivating this study is that much of the content posted on activist oriented social media group pages will in some way relate to kama muta.

4   Method

This study employs methods of qualitative and quantitative content analysis of social media site postings on five Facebook pages. This method was selected as the most appropriate match for the exploratory and descriptive aims of the research questions [2, 23, 36], within the constraints of the time frame and scope of the pilot study. The analysis occurred over the course of six weeks in spring 2017. Facebook was the selected social media platform as it offers the most dynamic data in terms of design features, posts, and space for interaction as compared to other popular sites [19].

4.1   Data Collection and Analysis

Non-random purposive sampling was used to select five groups for analysis: March and Rally Los Angeles, March for Science, Women's March, Sacred Stone Camp, and ACLU. These pages vary substantially in their goals and primary content, which ideally provides variance in the demographics of posters and participants. Approximately 15 posts from each group page from the four months preceding the start of data collection were semi-randomly conveniently sampled and examined, with a focus on both the content of the original post and the associated comments and activity. This number was selected to set a reasonable scope for the current stage of the project, with plans to increase the number of posts in future follow-up studies. 15 posts per page also provided sufficient variety within the selected time frame.

A visual example of the posts is shown in Fig. 1. A systematic process for collecting relevant information about the post and its relation to elements of kama muta is shown in Table 1. It includes information used for documenting each post including, page, poster, number of likes, relation to kama muta, and descriptions of kama muta relation. Table 2 provides a deeper description of the pages analyzed. Besides descriptive statistical analysis, qualitative analysis was employed for each post to inductively reveal emergent themes using line-by-line analysis and logic diagramming techniques [23]. The conceptualization of kama muta played a large role in this analysis process, where kama muta is operationalized through its defined elements [10]. The elements were used to identify presence of kama muta in various posts, which enabled identification of broader themes related to kama muta-motivated posts and online social engagement.

Fig. 1. Visual example of social media posts analyzed

Table 1. Chart of descriptive categories for Facebook post observation

Category	Description of category
Page	Name of Facebook page of group
Poster	Name of original content poster
Type of post	Primary medium: Link, Audio, Video, Other
Content of post	Copy of text caption and/or description of audio/visual material
Number of likes, comments and shares	Includes likes and other Facebook "reactions"
Related to kama muta	Yes or No
Description of kama muta (or non-kama muta) elements	Justification of previous question, assessment of kama muta presence based on elements of kama muta described in literature and full definition by Fiske et al.
Sharing or inducing kama muta	Expression of personal kama muta, intent to elicit kama muta from group, or both
Description of comments	Qualitative description of comments and themes

Table 2. Description of observation sites (Facebook pages)

March and Rally Los Angeles: The March and Rally page represents the political organization March and Rally LA, which dedicated to "empowering The People" Total page likes: 19,623

March for Science: The March for Science group is a private Facebook group associated with the official March for Science Facebook page that "fosters civil discussion, shares ideas and personal stories, and calls each other to action(s)" Total group members: 840,095

Women's March: The Women's March page represents the Women's March on Washington, a global organization dedicated to standing in solidarity "with partners, and children for the protection of rights, safety, heath, and families" Total page likes: 11,969 likes, 12,478 follows

Sacred Stone Camp: The Sacred Stone camp page is the official page of the camp located in North Dakota fighting against the implementation and expansion of the Dakota Access Pipeline. Total page likes: 423,050

ACLU: The ACLU Nationwide page disseminates information from the American Civil Liberties Union (ACLU). Total page likes: 2,116,881

5 Results

5.1 Overall Descriptive Summary

In total, 75 posts were observed and analyzed. 58.7% of the posts (n = 44) related to kama muta, while the other 41.3% (n = 31) did not. As described in the methods section, this categorization was determined based on the characteristics of kama muta described in relevant literature. Thus, posts that were categorized as related to kama muta were in some way related to potential rapid acceleration of a communal sharing relationship. This often occurred through expressions of empathy, community, collective trauma, love, strength, and/or similar factors noted in posts and comments. 2.7% of the posts (n = 2) were aimed at solely sharing an experience of kama muta, 28% of the posts (n = 21) were aimed at inducing kama muta, and another 28% of posts aimed for both of these intentions. This category was determined based on the presentation and framing of the content provided in each post, i.e. a first, second, or third person tone, and the ways in which viewers were addressed and included in the posts. Examples included sharing of personal stories related to an activist organization's main issue using personal framing, an activist organization calling others to stand in solidarity with a subgroup using impersonal language directed toward the public, and particular hashtag use. 16% of the posts (n = 12) were image and text based, 5.3% (n = 4) were video and text based, 10.7% (n = 8) were solely text based, 6.7% (n = 5) were solely image based, 12% (n = 9) were link based, and 5.3% (n = 4) were solely video based. The highest percentage of posts were link and text based, 44% (n = 33).

5.2 Likes/Reactions, Comments, and Shares

The posts with the five highest numbers of likes/reactions received 32k, 28k, 27k, 26k, and 9.1k reactions respectively. All of these were ACLU posts, and three out of the five (60%) were kama muta related posts. A clear limitation of this portion of analysis is that the ACLU has a much larger number of page likes than the other four pages, which likely influenced their receipt of the highest number of like/reactions within the study sample. To help offset this issue, data on the posts with the highest number of likes/reactions, comments, and shares on each of the other pages observed were also collected. On the March for Science page, the top posts within the sample received 2.8k reactions, 247 comments, and 1.7k shares. The Women's March top posts received 1.3k likes, 99 comments, and 458 shares. The March and Rally page posts received up to 155 likes, 8 comments, and 1 share. The Sacred Stone page posts received a max of 6.7k likes, 49 comments, and 50 shares, and lastly the ACLU page top posts received 32k likes, 756 comments, and 4,280 shares. From the total sample, 60% (n = 3) of the five most liked posts and five most shared posts on each page were kama muta related, and 60% of the five posts with the most comments were not.

5.3 Mediums

Of the total most liked posts from each page, four were link and text based, and one was image and text based. From the total posts with the highest number of comments from each page, three were link and text based, one was video and text based, and one was image and text based. Out of the five most shared posts across the five pages, four were link and text based, and one was image and text based. 62.5% (n = 5) of all video posts were kama muta related, 50% (n = 4) of all text based posts were kama muta related, 45.2% (n = 19) of all link based posts were kama muta related, and 94.1% (n = 16) of all image posts were kama muta related.

5.4   Key Themes

Besides the quantitative and descriptive empirical elements around engagement, there were also several qualitative themes observed in kama muta and non kama muta related posts. These themes were primarily revealed through the language in and responses to posts, which required detailed note taking and line-by-line coding and analysis. The main themes noted were reference to communal identity and community, solidarity, injustice, collective struggle, trauma and bravery, and hashtag use. Out of the total 44 kama muta related posts, 59% (n = 26) of posts explicitly or implicitly referenced the importance of community and contributing to a communal identity even with individual experiences. For example, in one Women's March post the organization emphasizes the cohesive nature of individual contribution and communal collaboration: "Women's March Global supports our global sisters and sisters in the USA in their grassroots organizing of events that promote our key values of equality, diversity and inclusion, with a cross-cutting focus on climate...To highlight March 8, known around the world as International Women's Day, Women's March Global will be celebrating a week of action from March 6th–11th by supporting the events and activities of our local coalitions around the world. We honor the autonomy of our global sisters in organizing their own events and initiatives... Please share your ideas with the community in response to this message..." This post also demonstrates the promotion of solidarity, which was expressed as a theme in 38.6% (n = 17) of posts.

Another post from the March for Science relays both themes of solidarity and community: "Embracing the diversity of our experiences and perspectives is actually critical to a strong pro-science message. The march itself should reflect that. We really do need large numbers of energetic people showing up to visibly and passionately demonstrate to elected leaders and the public that SCIENCE MATTERS!...What is important is that as individuals we honor what truly motivates us most to be there and speak up on that day. Individually we should reflect our passion in our messages (signs, who we march with, and what we chant). If everyone tries to demonstrate in the same way, it will be flat because of the lack of diversity. Bring your individual passion and let it shine brightly. Seek to entertain and inspire each other as well as getting our message across. The really important thing is that you come and bring your motivation with you...See you on Earth Day!" The concept of motivation is one that ties into many references to all of the major themes found throughout the sample. The posters and post viewers see motivation as key factor in promoting community, fighting injustice, overcoming trauma and collective struggle, and displaying bravery.

38.6% (n = 26) and 18.1% (n = 16) of kama muta related posts referenced ideas of injustice, collective struggle, and trauma or bravery, respectively. The trauma referenced in posts was often one overcome by a strong figure in the cause, or a communal trauma that activist organizers are aiming to motivate group members to fight with bravery. One post on the Sacred Stone page of a video depicting the recent forced evacuation of the water protector camps paired with the caption "Every act of colonial racism is a stepping stone for our movement #nodapl," well demonstrates a combination of these three elements, referencing colonial racism as a collective struggle and source of injustice and trauma, and their movement being fueled by that trauma as an example of overcoming it with bravery. Several ACLU posts similarly reflected the themes of injustice and bravery in particular through links to articles around anti-LGBTQ bills and the Muslim ban including captions such as, "Does the First Amendment give the right to discriminate?" Many of the comments on the Sacred Stone posts in particular respond to these themes through relaying personal motivations to join the cause, anger over the injustice displayed, and solidarity with the group through mirrored use of the #nodapl hashtag. Hashtag use, which was observed in 18.1% (n = 8) of kama muta related posts, was also used across pages by organizations and posters in comments and posts. Examples include #NoDapl on the Sacred Stone Camp page, #StandforLove on the Women's March page, and #WhyIMarch and #ScienceMatters in the March for Science group page.

The majority of the non kama muta related posts were more directly informational posts without emotional appeal or emotional language, or were designed to evoke specific emotions other than kama muta such as anger or fear. From the total number of non-kama muta posts, 45.2% (n = 14) of posts were strictly informational, and 41.9% (n = 13) were written and phrased to evoke anger or fear. Examples of posts in these categories included posts that linked to events without descriptions, asked for or provided logistical information, or linked to articles describing injustices without motivational captions or calls to action attached.

6   Limitations, Discussion and Conclusion

A key limitation of the study is the discrepancy of number of likes between the pages. For future work, a sample with closer total page likes or number of members will be selected to provide more meaningful and comparable descriptive statistics. However, within this pilot study this limitation is somewhat offset by the analysis of page-specific activity, which assesses likes and comments relative to the broader number of likes and members on that page. Additionally, the qualitative theme analysis helps bring a broader perspective to strengthen the statistical description. A second major limitation of the study was the inability to directly interact with the posters and organization members and leaders to gain their perspective. Data collected from a survey or interview of this group would greatly enhance the findings and arguments made using the strictly observational data included here. A survey and interview protocol have been designed for a next iteration of this study. Deeper analysis of the significance of various media categories of posts is also a rich area for future extensions of this work. Despite these limitations, this study represents an important first stage of inquiry in this area to set the stage for future more detailed and larger scale projects.

Regarding the summary findings from the sample of posts analyzed for this study, kama muta appears to have at least some role in the production of Facebook posts within activist groups. In terms of prevalence, over half of the 75 total posts observed related in some way to kama muta. Within that group of kama muta related posts, content that was aiming to induce and induce/share kama muta each comprised 28% of the total, suggesting that inducing kama muta may play a significant role in the Facebook post planning process on activist pages. The content itself is often kama muta inducing, but the framing and language in conjunction with the content reveals that activist groups may be aware of the power that inducing kama muta could have on moving social movement members into direct action and engagement.

The finding that more than half of the most engaged with posts for each page in the categories of likes and shares were kama muta related is also a significant preliminary observation. This finding builds on the intuitive assumption that kama muta inducing content would be more widely shared and liked. The opposite statistic observed for the posts with most comments might relate to the controversy around the anger and fear inducing posts. Comment sections generally comprised of a mix of movement supporters and non-supporters, and more controversial posts often evoked fear and anger rather than kama muta, which also fueled extensive commentary.

The themes of communal identity and community, solidarity, injustice, collective struggle, trauma and bravery, and hashtag use are most significant in their contribution to the understanding of kama muta in this setting as well as understanding of organizational language use and framing in activist communities. These themes could serve as potential coding categories for future expansions of this work across a wider number of pages, and could contribute to more detailed characteristics of what kama muta entails when connected to activism. Additionally, these themes could be useful in analyzing how information is presented and received among activist networks online. These themes represent a fruitful area for combining research inquiries in social psychology and information studies to engage with the observations presented here. Overall, this pilot study represents an exciting early step into investigating the significance of kama muta and emotionality more generally in the daily online interactions of activist communities. In intersecting the areas of online activism, emotions, social movements, this study contributes to a burgeoning scholarly conversation that poses implications for design and behavioral considerations for social movement organizations and social media users invested in the success of various social movements. It seems that kama muta may indeed be a key ingredient that helps movements move.

References

1. Anderson, B., Tracey, K.: Digital living the impact (or otherwise) of the internet on everyday life. Am. Behav. Sci. **45**(3), 456–475 (2001). https://doi.org/10.1177/00027640121957295
2. Babbie, E.: The Basics of Social Research. Cengage Learning, Belmont (2013)
3. Bier, M., Gallo, M., Nucklos, E., Sherblom, S., Pennick, M.: Personal empowerment in the study of home internet use by low-income families. J. Res. Comput. Educ. **30**(2), 107–121 (1997). https://doi.org/10.1080/08886504.1997.10782218
4. Boyd, D.: Friends, Friendsters, and MySpace Top 8: Writing Community into Being on Social Network Sites. MIT Press, Cambridge (2006)

5. Boyd, D.M., Ellison, N.B.: Social network sites: definition, history, and scholarship. J. Comput.-Mediat. Commun. **13**(1), 210–230 (2007). https://doi.org/10.1111/j.1083-6101.2007. 00393.x
6. Burke, M., Marlow, C., Lento, T.: Social network activity and social well-being. In: Proceedings of the SIGCHI Conference on Human Factors in Computing Systems, pp. 1909–1912. ACM, New York (2010). https://doi.org/10.1145/1753326.1753613
7. Ellison, N.B., Steinfield, C., Lampe, C.: The benefits of facebook "friends:" social capital and college students' use of online social network sites. J. Comput.-Mediat. Commun. **12**(4), 1143–1168 (2007). https://doi.org/10.1111/j.1083-6101.2007.00367.x
8. Fiske, Alan P.: Four modes of constituting relationships: consubstantial assimilation; space, magnitude, time and force; concrete procedures; abstract symbolism. In: Haslam, N. (ed.) Relational Models Theory: A Contemporary Overview, pp. 61–146. Erlbaum, Mahwah (2004)
9. Fiske, A.P.: Structures of Social Life: The Four Elementary Forms of Human Relations. Free Press (Macmillan), New York (1991)
10. Fiske, A.P., Seibt, B., Schubert, T.: The sudden devotion emotion: Kama muta and the cultural practices whose function is to evoke it. Emot. Rev. (2017). 1754073917723167
11. Gibson, M.: YouTube and bereavement vlogging: emotional exchange between strangers. J. Sociol. **52**(4), 631–645 (2016)
12. Goodwin, J., Jasper, J.M., Polletta, F. (eds.): Passionate Politics: Emotions and Social Movements. University of Chicago Press, New York (2009)
13. Greenwood, S., Perrin, R., Duggan, M.: Social Media Update 2016. http://www.pewinternet. org/2016/11/11/social-media-update-2016/. Accessed 11 Nov 2016
14. Henderson, C.: How the internet is changing our lives. Futurist **35**(4), 38 (2001)
15. Jasper, J.M.: Emotions and social movements: twenty years of theory and research. Ann. Rev. Sociol. **37**, 285–303 (2011)
16. Jenkins, H.: Convergence Culture: Where Old and New Media Collide. NYU Press, New York (2006)
17. Kaplan, A.M., Haenlein, M.: Users of the world, unite! The challenges and opportunities of Social Media. Bus. Horiz. **53**(1), 59–68 (2010). https://doi.org/10.1016/j.bushor.2009. 09.003
18. Kim, K.-S., Yoo-Lee, E., Joanna Sin, S.-C.: Social media as information source: undergraduates' use and evaluation behavior. Proc. Am. Soc. Inf. Sci. Technol. **48**(1), 1–3 (2011). https:// doi.org/10.1002/meet.2011.14504801283
19. Lenhart, A., Duggan, M., Perrin, A., Stepler, R., Rainie, H., Parker, K.: Teens, Social Media & Technology Overview (2015)
20. Leung, L., Lee, P.S.N.: Multiple determinants of life quality: the roles of Internet activities, use of new media, social support, and leisure activities. Telematics Inf. **22**(3), 161–180 (2005). https://doi.org/10.1016/j.tele.2004.04.003
21. Lievrouw, L.: Alternative and Activist New Media, 1st edn. Polity, Cambridge (2011)
22. Lim, J.S., Golan, G.J.: Social media activism in response to the influence of political parody videos on youtube. Commun. Res. **38**(5), 710–727 (2011). https://doi.org/10.1177/ 0093650211405649
23. Lofland, J., Lofland, L.: Analyzing Social Settings: A Guide to Qualitative Observation and Analysis. Wadsworth, Belmont (1995)
24. Mikkelson, D.: Rescuing Hug. http://www.snopes.com/glurge/healinghug.asp. Accessed 28 Jan 2019
25. Murthy, D.: Twitter: Social Communication in the Twitter Age. Wiley, Chichester (2013)

26. Oh, H.J., Ozkaya, E., LaRose, R.: How does online social networking enhance life satisfaction? The relationships among online supportive interaction, affect, perceived social support, sense of community, and life satisfaction. Comput. Hum. Behav. **30**, 69–78 (2014). https://doi.org/10.1016/j.chb.2013.07.053

27. Park, N., Kee, K.F., Valenzuela, S.: Being Immersed in social networking environment: facebook groups, uses and gratifications, and social outcomes. CyberPsychol. Behav. **12**(6), 729–733 (2009). https://doi.org/10.1089/cpb.2009.0003

28. Schubert, T.W., Zickfeld, J.H., Seibt, B., Fiske, A.P.: Moment-to-moment changes in feeling moved match changes in closeness, tears, goosebumps, and warmth: time series analyses. Cogn. Emot. 1–11 (2016) https://doi.org/10.1080/02699931.2016.1268998

29. Seibt, B., Schubert, T., Zickfeld, J., Fiske, A.: Kama Muta: A social emotion emerging from the sudden intensification of a communal sharing relation. In: ISRE: Bi-Annual Conference of the International Society for Research on Emotion, Geneva (2015). http://www.isre2015.org/sites/default/files/Seibt2.pdf

30. Srinivasan, R.: Bridges between cultural and digital worlds in revolutionary Egypt. Inf. Soc. **29**(1), 49–60 (2013). https://doi.org/10.1080/01972243.2012.739594

31. Srinivasan, R.: Taking power through technology in the Arab Spring - Al Jazeera English. http://www.aljazeera.com/indepth/opinion/2012/09/2012919115344299848.html. Accessed 8 Apr 2016

32. Srinivasan, R., Fish, A.: Internet authorship: social and political implications within Kyrgyzstan. J. Comput.-Mediat. Commun. **14**(3), 559–580 (2009). https://doi.org/10.1111/j.1083-6101.2009.01453.x

33. Srinivasan, R., Fish, A.: Revolutionary tactics, media ecologies, and repressive states. Publ. Cult. **3 65**, 505–510 (2006). https://doi.org/10.1215/08992363-1336381

34. Srivastava, S.: Tears, fears and careers: anti-racism and emotion in social movement organizations. Can. J. Sociol./Cahiers canadiens de sociologie **31**, 55–90 (2006)

35. Steinfield, C., Ellison, N.B., Lampe, C.: Social capital, self-esteem, and use of online social network sites: a longitudinal analysis. J. Appl. Dev. Psychol. **29**(6), 434–445 (2008). https://doi.org/10.1016/j.appdev.2008.07.002

36. Strauss, A., Corbin, J.: Basics of Qualitative Research: Grounded Theory Procedures and Techniques, 2edn. SAGE Publications, Inc., Thousand Oaks (1990)

37. Thorson, K., et al.: Youtube, twitter and the occupy movement. Inf. Commun. Soc. **16**(3), 421–451 (2013). https://doi.org/10.1080/1369118X.2012.756051

38. Valenzuela, S., Park, N., Kee, K.F.: Is there social capital in a social network site?: Facebook use and college students' life satisfaction, trust, and participation1. J. Comput.-Mediat. Commun. **14**(4), 875–901 (2009). https://doi.org/10.1111/j.1083-6101.2009.01474.x

39. Valkenburg, P.M., Peter, J.: Adolescents' Identity experiments on the internet consequences for social competence and self-concept unity. Commun. Res. **35**(2), 208–231 (2008). https://doi.org/10.1177/0093650207313164

40. Wang, T.: Talking to Strangers: Chinese Youth and Social Media (Ph.D.). University of California, San Diego, United States – California (2013). http://search.proquest.com/docview/1490797166/abstract/C7FC68567BE34522PQ/1

Information Bridges: Understanding the Informational Role of Network Brokerages in Polarised Online Discourses

Pu Yan[✉]

University of Oxford, Oxford, Oxfordshire, UK
pu.yan@oii.ox.ac.uk

Abstract. Social networking and micro-blogging sites such as Twitter and Weibo have provided new platforms of public discussions for Internet users. As the number of online social movements has increased in recent years, the Chinese government has adopted new media and has strategically confronted online social movements with orchestrated campaigns, which lead to a dichotomy between the Chinese government and civil society. Using a network analysis perspective, this research aims at studying the polarization of Chinese online political discourse, by examining who are playing the key roles in bridging different voices and exchanging various viewpoints in an online debate. I collected data from a conversation network in a massive online protest on Weibo, visualised the polarization between the Chinese government and civil society, and analysed the typological differences between the two groups. This research demonstrated the structural role of brokers in information diffusion within conversation network by using Susceptible-Infected (SI) simulation, showing that brokerage plays a key role in bridging the polarized online opinions and facilitating information diffusion. Taking a social network analysis perspective, this research re-examined Chinese contentious social movement under its political regime and can shed lights onto the understanding of the structural and informational roles of network brokerages for the deliberative democracy.

Keywords: Information diffusion · Social media · China ·
Social network analysis

1 Introduction

1.1 Polarization of Public Discourses on Chinese Social Media

Since 1980s, China has impressed the world with its economic growth. Behind China's rapid development are a series of acute social problems: widening gap between the rich and the poor, decelerated social mobility, clashes between political power and individual freedom. These problems have resulted in an "imbalance" or "instability" in modern Chinese society (Sun 2006).

Political dissidents and social activists joined together to protest against social inequality and authoritarian regime, drawing attentions from the general public. Meanwhile, Chinese government continues to maintain the dominance of mainstream

© Springer Nature Switzerland AG 2019
N. G. Taylor et al. (Eds.): iConference 2019, LNCS 11420, pp. 377–388, 2019.
https://doi.org/10.1007/978-3-030-15742-5_36

ideology by controlling state-owned traditional media. Chinese president Xi Jinping has initiated a new media propaganda plans last year (Xinhua News Agency 2014). Under such background, conflicts in opinions aroused and grew between civil society and government, especially in topics where state's benefits and individual rights collide.

Government and civil society also compete against each other on the Internet to influence public opinion. On one hand, online activists are empowered by new media to openly express their political claims to a wider audience; on the other hand, Chinese officials and state-run media also co-evolve with online activism, through adopting new media strategy in publicizing mainstream values and ideology. Yang (2014) summarized this process as a "mutual adaptation" between authorities and citizen activists.

1.2 Dongguan Incident: An Example of Chinese Polarized Public Space

This conflict was reflected in one of the online massive movement in Feb 2014, when Chinese state-owned media China Central Television (CCTV) reported a police action aiming at arresting street prostitutes that took place in Dongguan, Guangzhou province. Similar police actions have been reported before, but this time, the action has unexpectedly triggered massive vocal protest on Weibo. During a two-week period, many online opinion leaders expressed their discontent for the authority's arbitrary arrest of individuals and violation of basic human rights. They support prostitutes in Dongguan by posting and circulating pictures of lighted white candles, as well as posting slogans such as "Be strong, Dongguan" or "We support you, Dongguan". These posts spread virally on Weibo, forming a large-scale campaign against the police. State authority and official media quickly reacted with online editorials and comments to criticize this protest. Government suppressed the movement by deleting most popular posts and shutting down several active accounts. Nevertheless, this protest had already evolved into a massive social movement and evoked a nation-wide online debate, which was referred to as "Dongguan Incident" by the media.

Dongguan Incident exemplifies how social media are both a blessing and a bane for Chinese civil movement: it can become a platform where online social movement participants self-organized; but it can also be a powerful tool for government repressions. For researchers, the study of Chinese online social movements now evolves understanding of both the activist community and the authority.

This research takes a network perspective to investigate dynamic relationship between Chinese government and its civil society. By visualizing and analysing the conversation network in Dongguan Incident, I will show the typological characteristics of the two discourses. I am also interested in studying the users who participate in both discourses, re-tweeting from both government and from civil society. When reading tweets from the Dongguan Incident, there exists a group of social media users who engage in the conversation networks with both sides, civil society and the government, and thus playing the roles of facilitating the flow of information and communication in the online movement. In this research, I define this group of users as "brokers" for their role in bridging different sides of online discourses. By using simulations model, I will explore the structural role of brokers in a polarized conversation network for connecting partitions and for enabling information exchange. This research aims at answering the following two questions:

RQ1. What are the structural differences between Chinese online activists and government communities? Do they have different structural characteristics? What are the likely consequences of these typological features?

RQ2. Are there any brokers between the two discourse networks? If there are, how important brokers are for connecting the network? How important they are for the dispersal of information in an online debate?

2 Literature Review

2.1 Polarization on Cyber-Sphere

China is not the only country where political attitudes divide. Many researches on democratic political systems show that online opinions polarize into separate groups on the Internet. Adamic and Glance (2005) studied the discussion network of liberal and conservative blogs and found that the two political camps were divided. More dense links appeared within conservative blog community. Ackland (2005) captured similar structural difference in his empirical study on political blogs.

In recent years, micro-blogging sites have enjoyed increasing popularity on the Internet (Boyd and Ellison 2010; Kwak et al. 2010). The rise of such applications and services brings about a transformation from provider-to-audience mode of communication to a "mass self-communication" (Castells 2013). Internet users increasingly "live" with the Internet and contribute user-generated data on the platform. And yet, researches still find empirical evidence of polarization on micro-blogging sites. Conover et al. (2011) mapped the re-tweet network on Twitter during 2010 U.S. midterm elections and found that this network exhibits a segregated partisan structure. Recent studies on social media networks indicate that online divisions of opinions could be influenced by organised retweets from trolling accounts (Stewart et al. 2018) or by highlight active and politicised "hijacker" users (Hadgu et al. 2013).

China, unlike other counties with multi-party systems, is led by the single-party state. Without opposition party in electoral system, the leadership of Chinese Communist Party and its government are unrestricted by formally organized political groups. However, even without formal organizations, Chinese vigorous civil society has still emerged as an oppositional force to the authority, especially on the Internet, where the power of party-state is frequently challenged by collective protests.

Polarization on Chinese social media has not yet been fully researched quantitatively; several scholars have contributed quantitative descriptions of this phenomenon. He (2009) coined the term "dual discourses" to describe the dispute between netizens and official media. Civil society and governments also have different levels of power in shaping online public opinions. Nip and Fu (2016) found that ordinary citizens on Sina Weibo are often the initiators of discourses on corruption cases, but their role in setting agenda are less prominent than official news organisations.

In Dongguan Incident, online discourses indicate a divided feature, in which civil society deconstruct the party-state by using semiotics, humours and criticisms. Despite the qualitative researches and theories on the divergence of political opinions on Chinese micro-blogging sites, very few researchers analysed the informational role of network brokerages from a graph-theoretic perspective, not to mention comparing Chinese political polarization with that of Western countries.

2.2   Brokerage and Structural Holes

In regard to connecting the partitions and enabling interactions between sub-communities, network theorists have highlighted the significance of brokerage for a network. Brokerage was first studied by Burt in the field of organizational sociology (Burt 1992, 2005). In Burt's arguments, he proposed two forms of social capital in a network: structural holes and network closure. The former constitutes interconnections between communities, while the latter entails densely linked and homogeneous network structure (Coleman 1988).

Structural holes bridge two or even more groups in a network and play an intermediate role in gatekeeping the information flow. They are beneficial to a social system in three ways: first, Granovetter (1973; 1983) theory on the strength of weak tie indicated that without weak tie, information could hardly spread out of cliques. For that reason, brokers are bridges between fragmented groups, which tie up various factions. Second, network that is rich in Structural holes, as believed by Burt (2001), is more efficient in information diffusion since brokerages have ensured various information sources are not isolated. New information and knowledge can therefore be able to spread across the whole network. Based on the two macro-level benefits, it might also be advantageous for individuals to play the role as brokers, providing them with access to different communities and exposure to various values. All the functions of brokerages/structural holes suggest that this network feature might have further implications in political and social systems.

2.3   Deliberative Democracy

Will polarization on social media lead to social segregation between different groups? Researches hold different views on this question. One array of scholars argues that homophiles and close-knit cliques result in exclusive interest communities where members are only exposed to arguments they agree with, creating more extreme opinions (Sustein 2009). Chinese researchers also found that Internet discussion groups reject different-minded participants on issues such as Maoism (political thought of Mao Zedong), Western democracy system, and Confucianism (Le and Yang 2010).

Another group of researchers believes that polarizations will not necessarily lead to an overall cleavage in society. They emphasize the potential of social media in bringing diversity to the online discourses and in enabling exchange of information. Their argument is based on the underlying requirement of deliberative democracy: to achieve consensus and design better political policy through adequate discussion of disputed topics (Mouffe 1999). Several empirical researches reveal that individuals facing with divergence of opinions do not necessarily block undesirable information (Garrett 2009).

In fact, the openness of micro-blogging applications allows users to follow members of the opposite camp, increasing broader public participations in political debate (Brundidge 2010; Munson and Resnick 2011; Bruns and Liang 2012).

Scholarly works of polarization and deliberative democracy disagree on an essential question: whether or not information exchange is possible in the polarized social system? This question reminds us to empirically examine the structural role of brokers in a social network, assessing their potential in bridging diversified communities and in facilitating the flow of information and exchange of values.

3 Data and Method

3.1 Data Collection

The author collected network data of this political discourse network from Sina Weibo, querying from its official API. 10 samples were selected as seeds tweet, 5 from the government/media account (See Table 1) and the other 5 from intellectual/online activists (See Table 2).

Table 1. Samples of civil society

No.	User name	Followers no.	Identity	Re-tweeted times
1	S	45531	Intellectual	2159
2	L	60850	Intellectual	2311
3	G	1063145	Online opinion leader	1028
4	J	4273973	Online opinion leader	8477
5	I	158313	NGO official account	10295

Table 2. Samples of official account

No.	User name	Followers no.	Identity	Re-tweeted times
1	CCTV	1846156	Central Media	4595
2	People's Daily	20233427	Central Media	5221
3	Dongguan Government	2417090	Local Gov.	1032
4	Ministry of Public Security	7493191	Central Gov.	2265
5	Nanfang Dushi Newspaper	6114862	Local Media	8250

To protect the identity of civil activists in my research, their user names are anonymized, I kept information of who they represent, to give a context background of my samples. Government and official media samples are public and professional information sources and thus user names are kept for this group. For ethical concerns, visualization of polarization hided user names since many of the users are personal accounts and the topic itself is relatively sensitive under Chinese context. In this research, I will be focusing on the structural features of polarization and brokerage rather than its content. I then used the 10 samples to snowball the conversation network in Dongguan Incident. Each user in the conversation network has re-tweeted at least one posts from either side in the debate: government or civil society.

Using this sampling technique, I constructed a directed and weighted graph with 16,239 nodes and 45,633 links. Direction of the link indicates the source/target in a re-tweet action. Each node was denoted with what side it belongs to. After visualizing the conversation network using Gephi, I found from the denotation label overlaps that there are 123 vertexes that have re-tweeted posts from both sides, linking together the government and civil society in the network.

Table 3 presents the statistical information of Dongguan Incident conversation network. I compare the statistic with that of Adamic and Glance's famous blog-sphere study on US political polarization. As shown in Table 3, conversation network in Dongguan Incident has lower average degree and maximum in-degree compared with US blog network. This is due to my sampling process of network data: Dongguan network is constructed on a snowballing re-tweet network which follows the circulation of seed samples, while Adamic and Glance's network was built on reference and citation relations, which are more reciprocal than tweet/re-tweet relations in one incident. Table 4 also suggests that Dongguan network has less circulational triads but more hierarchical triads, indicating a lack of reciprocity between nodes in this network.

Table 3. Statistics for Dongguan network and US blog network

	Dongguan Incident	US blog
Number of nodes	16239	1222
Number of links	16761	19024
Average degree	1.032	15.548
Maximum in-degree	10	337
Maximum out-degree	1643	256
Modularity (resolution: 1.0)	0.913	0.427

Table 4. Triads types and numbers in Dongguan network and US blog network

Triads type	Dongguan Incident	US blog
003	359381671	189244040
030C	2	481
030T	76	49068
021D	6247769	166717

3.2   Analysing and Modelling

Polarization. *Visualization.* I used Gephi (Version 0.8.2) to visualize the conversation network, using the denotation of which side the node follows. The visualization can demonstrate the polarization of Chinese official discourse and civil society discourse.

Partition. Although the sampling process led to the formation of 10 densely connected conversation networks, I still conducted community detection on both government and civil society to find smaller communities within each discourse network. In this research, I applied modularity to classify vertexes into subgroups. Modularity score (Q) measures the strength of community partition of a network into subgroups (Newman and Girvan 2004).

Brokerage. *Betweenness Centrality.* Graphic demonstration of polarization cannot clearly identify all brokers who bridge the two voices. I then highlighted the structural role of brokers (earlier defined as individuals who re-tweet at least once from both sides of the discourse) in Dongguan conversation network by comparing statistically the betweenness centrality (Freeman 1977) of brokers and other nodes.

K-core. To show the typological importance of brokers for the network, I assessed the role of broker for cohesion of network using k-core, by generating several sub-graphs of Dongguan network in which every node had degree of at least k.

Modelling. This research also uses Susceptible-Infected (SI) model to compare information diffusion rate when different percentage of brokers exists in the network. SI model, previously used in studies of network typology and social contagion process (Onnela et al. 2007; Karsai et al. 2011), simulates how information is transmitted between vertexes through their connections with adjacent nodes. In my research, I applied the model in different experiments where the network has different proportions of brokers in its structure. I then compared the spreading rate of information (or "virus" in SI model) to explain the change of information diffusion efficiency due to effects of brokerages. To eliminate the possible effects of taking off nodes on the robustness of network, I also designed a comparison experiment in which same number of randomly chosen nodes (can be non-brokers or brokers) is deleted from the network.

4 Results

4.1 Polarization

Visualization of the conversation network is presented in Fig. 1(A). Noticing the distinct clustering of two attitudes. Red (left) nodes represent government accounts and users who re-tweeted their posts; Blue (right) nodes represent online activists accounts and users who re-tweeted their posts. While sub-communities within the civil society discourse network compromise of a higher number of influential social media accounts such as intellectuals, lawyers and independent media, nodes that have high degree scores in the civil society discourse network retweet less frequently from each other. As a comparison, sub-communities within the government discourse network consists of social media accounts of both national and official authorises, government discourse network are more internally connected since central nodes tweet more frequently from each other. The two networks represent two communities of online users; each belongs to one side of the online discourses in Dongguan Incident. To explore the structural differences of government and civil society conversation network, we use structural statistics to compare in-group cohesion of the two networks. As indicates in Table 5, government network has higher density and higher average degree than civil society. In

Table 5. Statistics for government network and civil society network

	Government network	Civil society network
Number of nodes	8106	8182
Number of links	8219	7543
Average degree	1.014	0.922
Density	0.000125	0.000112

a communication network, this means that government accounts and its followers have more interactions in the discourses than civil society.

4.2   Typological Role of Brokerages

I defined brokers in this conversation network as users who simultaneously re-tweet from both sides of opinions. I use k-core to generate cohesive subgroups of whole network, in order to explore the role of brokers for cohesion of the network. Results indicate that in more cohesive sub-graphs, brokers constitute higher percentage among visible nodes (See Fig. 1), playing an important role in the inner core of the network.

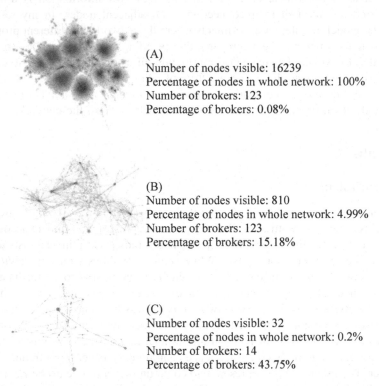

(A)
Number of nodes visible: 16239
Percentage of nodes in whole network: 100%
Number of brokers: 123
Percentage of brokers: 0.08%

(B)
Number of nodes visible: 810
Percentage of nodes in whole network: 4.99%
Number of brokers: 123
Percentage of brokers: 15.18%

(C)
Number of nodes visible: 32
Percentage of nodes in whole network: 0.2%
Number of brokers: 14
Percentage of brokers: 43.75%

Fig. 1. Conversation network of Dongguan Incident. Red represents government network and blues represent civil society. (A) Whole network with all edges is shown; (B) 2-core sub-graph of whole network, nodes in this graph are connected to at least 2 other nodes; (C) 3-core sub-graph of whole network, nodes in this graph are connected to at least 3 other nodes. (Color figure online)

Besides, looking at the betweenness centrality, broker nodes have higher values than other nodes in this discourse network. Betweenness centrality measures how likely a node locates on the shortest path between any pairs of nodes in the given network. High betweenness centrality of broker nodes (46.38) than normal nodes (3.26), therefore, suggests the potential of brokers to connect this conversation network and more importantly, to bridge between disparate and rival political opinions.

4.3 Brokerage and Information Diffusion

Previous section analysed typological characteristics of broker nodes in Dongguan conversation network. For a re-tweet network in this study, enabling sharing and diffusing information are the aim and also the consequence of re-tweet behaviours. From the network structure analysis, structural feature of broker nodes is demonstrated. Whereas using SI models could enable a simulation of information diffusion process, allowing experiments with network structures with different proportions of brokerage.

The experiments I designed in this research aim at figuring out the importance of brokers for spreading information across different subgroups and throughout the whole network. All variables are controlled except for how many brokerages exist in the network. There are 4 experiments in total, each conducted in the conversation network in which broker percentage equals to: 0, 33.33% (1/3), 66.67% (2/3), 1. In simulations where only a certain percentage of brokers are left in the network (33.33% or 66.6%), I randomly selected the brokers[1] from all the 123 broker nodes.

Figure 2 demonstrates the different diffusion rates in networks with different percentage of brokers. T-half is the threshold when half of all nodes are "infected" or received the information. The result shows that brokerages are essential for information diffusion in a network. When there are no brokerages, messages take longer time to spread across the community and can hardly spread to all the nodes within 100-time steps. In contrast, information diffuses fastest when a network has all the 123 brokers, reaching 50% of diffusion rate within 29-time steps. To reach the same diffusion rate, network with one third or two thirds of brokers take approximately 53-time steps. The role of brokers in accelerating diffusion of information in the discourse network is very important.

Deleting any 123 nodes from the network might also affect the information diffusion rate, to exclude that variable, I simulated the diffusion in a control experiment in which random 123 nodes (can be non-brokers or brokers) were deleted. The result (dash line in orange) shows that removing random nodes from the network will not significantly influence information diffusion as it does in the case where only brokers are removed. It is therefore possible to conclude that the decreased diffusion rate after taking off broker nodes is due to the structural importance of brokerages in accelerating exchange of information.

---

[1] With RANDBETWEEN function in Excel.

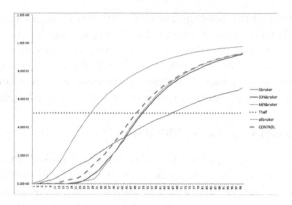

Fig. 2. Information diffusion rate in networks with different percentage of brokers

5   Discussion

Social media has empowered Chinese political activists in many ways: as the broad-casting channel and mobilising tool (Bond et al. 2012), as public discussion platform (Rainie et al. 2012), or as a knowledge base (Huang and Sun 2014). Chinese authority has increasingly suppressed the rise of online activism on the Internet and in offline politics (King et al. 2013). Dongguan incident exemplified the confrontation between government and opposition forces. In lack of legitimate and justified reasons, police action was regarded as an arbitrary abuse of power on social minority groups, leading to collective protest against authority on Weibo. Developing from a local event to a national debate, Dongguan Incident has offered another case to study Chinese online political discourses. This research shows that in Dongguan Incident, officials and civil society were not only disputed but formed two communities with different typological features. Notably, government discourse network shows more intense in-group con-nections, creating an official camp that is more coherent than online activists. In contrast, civil society is in lack of sufficient coordination and corporation both online and offline. Chinese polarisation is between a bureaucratic but well-organised gov-ernment and a vibrant but segmented civil society. However, although Chinese online discourses show a dichotomy between authority and public, these two polarities are connected and bridged through brokerages, providing channels for exchange of opinions. Exposure to diversified views is both essential for avoiding polarisation and fundamental to deliberative democracy. This research suggests the role of brokerages is crucial for connecting political communities and vital in accelerating information diffusion.

This research points out future opportunities for exploring online social movement with new perspectives. By using typological features and SI simulations, this research shows the significant role of brokers as bridges between cliques/subgroups, and in promoting the spread of information. In this research, I showed that the dynamic relation between Chinese civil society and authority by pointing out that brokers can have an influence on the information diffusion within a polarised conversation network. The debate between scholars on whether or not polarization leads to social segregation, in this case, could be answered from this study of brokerage: more efficient diffusion and exchange of opinions, ideas and values depend on the bridging role of structural holds, those who follow and spread information from diversified sources, regardless of their personal preferences. Arguably there are several limitations of this study. While selecting sample posts from both government and civil society to ensure manual check of the content and annotation of nodes, this sampling process also brings about problems in other issues: for example, the polarisation displayed in Fig. 1 is straightforward because I used the annotated information to colour each node. In the large-scale discussion, does the same recognisable polarisation still exist? Will there be third or fourth dominant voices? To answer these questions, a small sample of posts is inadequate, what might be required is a randomly chosen, large-scale data of the conversation network (re-tweet or mention network). While this research examines the structural roles of brokers in online discourse network, future studies using natural language processing approach on the content of discourses could help understand the mechanisms of network brokerages in facilitating exchange of diverse information and viewpoints.

References

Ackland, R.: Mapping the US political blogosphere: are conservative bloggers more prominent? In: BlogTalk Downunder 2005 Conference, Sydney (2005)

Adamic, L.A., Glance, N.: The political blogosphere and the 2004 US election: divided they blog. In: Proceedings of the 3rd International Workshop on Link Discovery, pp. 36–43. ACM, New York, August 2005

Bond, R.M., et al.: A 61-million-person experiment in social influence and political mobilization. Nature **489**(7415), 295–298 (2012)

Boyd, D., Ellison, N.: Social network sites: definition, history, and scholarship. IEEE Eng. Manag. Rev. **3**(38), 16–31 (2010)

Brundidge, J.: Encountering "difference" in the contemporary public sphere: the contribution of the Internet to the heterogeneity of political discussion networks. J. Commun. **60**(4), 680–700 (2010)

Bruns, A., Liang, Y.: Tools and methods for capturing Twitter data during natural disasters. First Monday **17**(4) (2012). https://firstmonday.org/article/view/3937/3193

Burt, R.S.: Structural Holes. The Social Structure of Competition. Harvard University Press, Cambridge (1992)

Burt, R.: Structural holes versus network closure as social capital. In: Lin, N., Cook, K., Burt, R. (eds.) Social Capital : Theory and Research (Sociology and Economics), pp. 31–56. Aldine de Gruyter, New York (2001)

Burt, R.S.: Brokerage and Closure. An Introduction to Social Capital. Oxford University Press, Oxford (2005)

Castells, M.: Communication Power. Oxford University Press, Oxford (2013)

Coleman, J.S.: Social capital in the creation of human capital. Am. J. Sociol. **94**, 95–120 (1988)

Conover, M., Ratkiewicz, J., Francisco, M., Gonçalves, B., Menczer, F., Flammini, A.: Political polarization on twitter. In ICWSM, July 2011

Freeman, L.C.: A set of measures of centrality based on betweenness. Sociometry **40**(1), 35–41 (1977)

Garrett, R.K.: Echo chambers online? Politically motivated selective exposure among Internet news users. J. Comput. Mediated Commun. **14**(2), 265–285 (2009)

Granovetter, M.S.: The strength of weak ties. Am. J. Sociol. **78**(6), 1360–1380 (1973)

Granovetter, M.: The strength of weak ties: a network theory revisited. Sociol. Theory **1**, 201–233 (1983)

Hadgu, A.T., Kiran, G., Ingmar, W.: Political hashtag hijacking in the US. In: Proceedings of the 22nd International Conference on World Wide Web, pp. 55–56 (2013)

He, Z.: Political communication in dual discourse universes. In: Willnat, L., Aw, A. (eds.) Political Communication in Asia, pp. 43–71. Routledge, London (2009)

Huang, R., Sun, X.: Weibo network, information diffusion and implications for collective action in China. Inf. Commun. Soc. **17**(1), 86–104 (2014)

Karsai, M., et al.: Small but slow world: How network topology and burstiness slow down spreading. Phys. Rev. E Stat. Nonlinear Soft Matter Phys. **83**, 025102 (2011)

King, G., Pan, J., Roberts, M.E.: How censorship in China allows government criticism but silences collective expression. Am. Polit. Sci. Rev. **107**(2), 326–343 (2013)

Kwak, H., Lee, C., Park, H., Moon, S.: What is Twitter, a social network or a news media? In: Proceedings of the 19th International Conference on World Wide Web, pp. 591–600. ACM (2010)

Le, Y., Yang, B.: Exploring online polarization phenomenon: content analysis of four major Chinese BBS forums. Youth Stud. **2010**(2), 1–12 (2010)

Mouffe, C.: Deliberative democracy or agonistic pluralism? Soc. Res. **66**(3), 745–758 (1999)

Munson, S.A., Resnick, P.: The prevalence of political discourse in non-political blogs. In: Fifth International AAAI Conference on Weblogs and Social Media, July 2011

Newman, M.E., Girvan, M.: Finding and evaluating community structure in networks. Phys. Rev. E Stat. Nonlinear Soft Matter Phys. **69**, 026113 (2004)

Nip, J.Y., Fu, K.W.: Challenging official propaganda? Public opinion leaders on sina weibo. China Q. **225**, 122–144 (2016)

Onnela, J.P., et al.: Structure and tie strengths in mobile communication networks. Proc. Natl. Acad. Sci. **104**(18), 7332–7336 (2007)

Rainie, L., Smith, A., Schlozman, K.L., Brady, H., Verba, S.: Social media and political engagement. Pew Internet & American Life Project (2012). http://www.pewinternet.org/2012/10/19/social-media-and-political-engagement/

Stewart, L.G., Arif, A., Starbird, K.: Examining trolls and polarization with a retweet network. In: MIS2: Misinformation and Misbehavior Mining on the Web, WSDM (2018)

Sun, L.: Gaming: Conflict and Harmony of Interest in the Fractured Society. Social Sciences Academic Press, Beijing (2006)

Sunstein, C.R.: Republic.com 2.0. Princeton University Press, Oxford (2009)

Xinhua News Agency: Integrating traditional mainstream media with new media technology, August 2014. http://news.xinhuanet.com/politics/2014-08/20/c_1112160707.htm

Yang, G.: Internet activism & the party-state in China. Daedalus **143**(2), 110–123 (2014)

Digital Libraries, Curation and Preservation

Prevalence and Use of the Term "Business Model" in the Digital Cultural Heritage Institution Professional Literature

Kristin R. Eschenfelder[1(✉)] and Kalpana Shankar[2]

[1] Information School, University of Wisconsin-Madison, Madison, USA
eschenfelder@wisc.edu
[2] College of Information and Communications Studies,
University College Dublin, Dublin, Ireland

Abstract. We investigate how the term "business model" was used in the digital cultural heritage literature from 2000 to 2015 through content analysis. We found that discussion of business models is not prevalent and there is no observable growth trend. Analysis of how authors represented business models showed predominately positive uses of the concept but include discussion of tension between the concept of business model and traditional cultural heritage field values. We found that non- element representations of business models were most common.

Keywords: Business model · Digital cultural heritage · Sustainability

1 Introduction

Increased costs and flat or declining resources have pressured digital cultural heritage (DCH) projects to evolve their business models to ensure ongoing operations. This pressure is reflected in international calls for development of new DCH business models [7, 10, 13, 18]. As part of a larger study of how DCH organizations have changed their business models over time, we sought to understand how DCH professionals represent the concept of a business model. This paper analyses how the DCH community discourse about business models from the period of 2000 to 2015 via content analysis of the professional literature. We define a business model as a "description of the value a company offers to …customers and of the architecture of the firm and its network of partners for creating, marketing and delivering this value and relationship capital, to generate profitable and sustainable revenue streams" [20, p. 17–18]. The research questions for this paper stemmed from a separate analysis of DCH articles about sustainability issues, where we found a subset of documents using the term business models in unexpected ways [8].

In this follow-up, we sought to understand the prevalence of the term business model in the DCH professional literature, and whether DCH authors presented the term business models in a positive or negative context. The concept of a business model could help DCH communicate about how to organize resources, activities and collections to generate value and cultivate revenue. On the other hand, DCH authors might

© Springer Nature Switzerland AG 2019
N. G. Taylor et al. (Eds.): iConference 2019, LNCS 11420, pp. 391–398, 2019.
https://doi.org/10.1007/978-3-030-15742-5_37

critique use of the term because of deeply-held beliefs about cultural heritage as a public good [2]. Discussing business models might imply acceptance of the proposition that DCH ought to prioritize business values over traditional values. We also wanted to know if most DCH authors referred to business models in a vague sense, or if they referred to specific parts of a business model or cited a framework from the literature [e.g., 29]. To do so, we borrowed the distinction between element representations, which communicate a business model as consisting of specific parts or relationships, and non-element representations, that use the term to refer to a general idea of what an organization does in the world without getting into details [20]. DCH discourse that includes element representations might suggest a higher level of knowledge of, or engagement with the idea of business models.

2 Methodology

Our data consist of articles from the DCH professional discourse from 2000 to 2015 published in journals indexed by the following three databases: Library Information Science Full Text, LISTA and LISA We started with eleven articles from the prior inquiry on sustainability that we had already identified as addressing business models [8]. We supplemented this with a new database search using the same databases and time period. Because we wanted to capture articles where authors chose to use the term business model in a prominent way, we searched in title or abstract. An initial search of titles brought too few results, but inclusion of the term in the abstract brought 53 unique initial results. We used the query string "business model in abstract AND digital in abstract AND (library or archive or repository)." We reviewed each abstract for applicability and removed articles that addressed business models of non-DCH projects, future services, and general library/vendor relationships. Because we were interested in business models to relation to organization and projects as opposed to a field, we excluded theoretical or field-level trends that did not refer to specific projects or organizations (real or imaginary). For example we saw several discussions of scholarly publishing that stayed at a theoretical level and did not describe actual or fictional projects. Eleven relevant documents remained, which when combined with our initial 11 documents, made a total of 22 documents for our analysis.

Our analysis of these 22 articles combined basic description with inductive thematic analysis. To identify trends, we tracked publication date of our articles. To understand how DCH professionals use the term business model, we employed inductive analysis to develop themes. The thematic analysis also addresses if authors used the term in a positive and negative manner. To analyze whether each representation employed "element" or "non-element" representations we noted if they described any specific sub elements, parts or relationships through a close read of texts.

3 Findings and Analysis

3.1 Prevalence of Business Model Concept in the DCH Literature

Documents employing the term business models are not highly prevalent in the DCH literature. The maximum number of articles per year was 3, but some years saw no articles published. The mean number of articles per year was 1.4. The temporal data in Fig. 1 show no clear trend. Comparable analysis of the business literature found 50–200 articles per year in the early 2000s, and an upward trend in the late 2000's [6, 26]. The business field is larger, so the higher number of articles is not surprising; but, the lack of a parallel upward trend in the DCH literature is noteworthy.

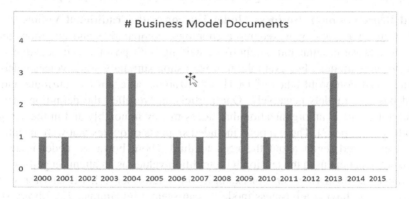

Fig. 1. Number of business model documents per year in the DCHI literature

3.2 Thematic Analysis of Business Model Representation

We had expected that some DCH authors might use the term business model negatively because of perceived conflicts with the traditional cultural heritage values of stewardship, access, and education [2]. We did not find any articles that were entirely critical of the concept of business models or their applicability do DCH. But we did find completely positive examples, and we found mixed positive/negative representations. In the positive representation, authors talked about business models are tools to achieve other positive outcomes. In one mixed theme DCH authors described the tensions between the concept of business model and traditional field values, and in the second mixed theme, some authors presented a wish for broadly applicable DCH business model solutions while others warned of the lack of universal solutions.

Positive Representation: Business Models Are Useful Tools
Positive representations of business models dominated and many authors wrote about business models as useful tools that DCH organizations should use to solve problems or survive. For example one author urges organizations to "join the [business model] innovation spiral" in order to "find new ways to survive in this competitive environment" [9: p. 163]. Authors presented the idea of business models as: a solution to funding projects while providing free or low cost access [21], necessary foundations for

cooperative arrangements [21], a solution to the problem of ensuring continuity once short-term money runs out [24], and a tool that one uses to obtain financial independence. For example an author urges the "development of sustainable business models to reduce the dependence on support from initial funders" [23, p. 569].

A variation of the useful tools theme emphasized the necessity of having a business model for other various positive outcomes. For example, authors represented business models as an antecedent to sustainability: "the formal business plan required by many funders should not be regarded as one more bureaucratic hurdle, but the passport to a successful, sustainable digital library" [11, p. 394]. Another represented business models as necessary to win favor with government funders: "business models... are important" and that presenting the institution as effective and sustainable "are part of the ongoing debate" with "the e-government funding authority" [14, p. 185].

Mixed Representation: Business Model Tension with Traditional Values

There were two types of mixed representations: comparative and attention getting. Some articles were comparative reports containing both positive and negative voices about business models. For example, in a workshop summary some voices celebrated the traditional non-profit ethos of DCH organizations as a positive attribute and presented business models negatively. One participant "recalled the definition of a successful non-profit as an organization that 'loses money honorably and in the service of high ideals'" [5: p. 13]. These reports included snippets of quotes that were negative, or at least expressed regret about the need to think about business model issues. The second set of papers used the tension with tradition values as an attention getting device in an otherwise positive paper. For example, one author began her discussion with the admission that "having a business model... can seem a bit strange. The library should not earn money on the services they offer should they?" but then went on to discuss them in positive terms [12: p. 81]. Similarly, another author began with the admission that "nonprofit cultural organizations... are not naturally inclined toward business modeling" to introduce a section on business models [19: p. 156]. In another example, authors acknowledges that some "models may be inconsistent with an institution's public and cultural goals" [9: p. 160] and urge that "business model innovation... should not oppose the organizations' social and cultural priorities" [9: p. 163].

Mixed Representation: Idealized Solutions vs Ongoing Chore

Another theme we found in our articles that we count as a mixed positive/negative representation included authors expressing desire for a set of business model materials that would reliably assist DCH organizations and other authors advising that no easy solutions exist. In the first set of articles authors yearned for development of a set of new business models that they could count on to solve problems. For example, a participant expressed frustration about not knowing which business model was the correct model "Despite a great deal of experimentation, no one is certain which [business] models work" [25]. This implies that a subset of business models exist that will work for all DCH and we just have to identify them. Another example asked for development of "cross community business models" again suggesting a subset of models exist that will work for most DCH [5, p. 20]. In the companion theme, authors warned that simple business model solutions that will work for all DCH do not exist. For example some authors warned that "one size does not fit all" [5, p. 15]. Another reminded readers that business models "may vary from institutions to institution" [15, p. 90]. Authors also warned of the temporal specificity of business model, "Changes in the environment require the business model to adapt over time" [19, p. 160]. In another example, one wrote "business models for library services are constantly being renegotiated, and are constantly changing. This is a challenge..." [12, p. 180]. These authors put limits on the positive nature of business models.

3.3   Element vs Non Element Representations

We distinguished between documents that employed element and non-element representations of business models [20]. More use of element representations might suggest a higher level of knowledge of, or engagement with the idea of business models. Use of an element representation was complicated by the fact that during most of our period of analysis, no agreed upon set of business model elements existed to which our authors could have referred. The term business model lacked any strict definition, although people likely shared a general rough conceptual idea [6, 17, 20, 26]. Given this we employed a liberal approach: To count as an element representation in our analysis, an author had to represent a business model as composed of two or more elements of any type.

Six of our 22 DCHI documents employed element representations. For example, in one document asked participants were asked to "outline the elements of their business models" and the most holistic included discussion of the elements of revenue, pricing models, governance, relationships, and changes in user segments [5]. A second example represented business models in terms of the elements of (1) income, (2) other means of support, and (3) reputation [25]. Another discussed business models as consisting of two elements: organizational structure and revenue models but then defined organizational structure as including elements of (1) workflows, (2) partnerships, (3) staff skills, and (4) value propositions [9, p. 160]. Analysis was complicated by authors discussing elements without formally identifying them as part of their business model. For example, one report asked respondents to describe their business models in terms of the elements of (1) customer segments, (2) revenue streams, and (3) key partnerships. It later discussed value propositions, cost structures and costs for key activities, but did not list these as elements of the business model [10].

Only two documents employed published models with explicit sets of elements. Both of these examples are from later years (2011, 2012) in our sample. Both draw on earlier versions of business model frameworks which later appeared in the popular literature and on public-oriented "how to" web sites. For example, [1] was published in 2011 and drew on the Business Model Canvas which was published in a popular book in 2013 [4]. A second example, [19] published in 2012 drew on the STOF model which later became adapted into a web portal as part of EU funded project in 2014 [3].

Having identified the elements described, we compared them to the nine elements of the Business Model Canvas. The most common elements were income, customers and partnerships, but arguably all our articles indirectly address distribution channels because they written by DCH organizations coming to terms with digital delivery of cultural materials. Least discussed elements included value proposition, cost structures, key resources, and key activities.

The majority of our documents (n = 16) employed non-element representations of business models. In these documents, authors used the term business model to refer to a vague general idea of "what an organization does in the world" without naming two or more specific elements as being part of a business model. Complicating our methodology, in many cases the documents did talk about elements even though authors did not identify them as being elements of a business model. This suggests authors have some innate knowledge about subtopics relevant to business models even if they are not familiar with more formal representations. The same elements remained common: pricing, revenue, relationships/partnerships and challenges with digital delivery. For example, one author talked about a new differentiated pricing model [21] while others discussed new revenue sources [14, 22], or about relationships, differences in pricing, and revenue [24].

4 Conclusion

We found that business models are not prevalent in the DCH literature, and we found no trend suggesting growth in attention to this topic, despite the appearance of more user-friendly frameworks after 2010 [3, 4]. Our thematic analysis shows that authors use the term in positively to argue for a link between business models and other positive outcomes. They use it in a mixed way to discuss tensions with traditional field values and to express a desire for easily adoptable solutions to complex challenges facing the field. We found most documents employed non-element representations of business models although some of those documents indirectly discussed elements. The smaller number of component representations of business models suggests that knowledge about business models has been low and authors likely lacked a strong shared understanding of formal business model frameworks and the typical components.

The results of this paper are limited due to our reliance on indexed articles. Future studies could include other forms of discourse. Further, we limited our analysis to documents whose authors included the term business model in their document abstract. Other search strategies would add to our results. Further, searches for terms referring to specific components (e.g. "cost structures" or a synonym) will yield additional articles representing a separate, but related, line of professional discourse.

The topic of business models continues to be of increasing importance to repositories and funders, as evidenced by recent reports on the topic [27, 28]. Our analysis suggests the DCH writing about business models as frameworks consisting of various components remains rare. We believe that greater education about business models employing recent user friendly frameworks [3, 4], and DCH-customized materials [10, 16], could aid DCH organizations in thinking about how to manage organizational change. We hope our analysis contributes to more nuanced discussion on business models for digital cultural heritage organizations.

References[1]

1. Arnoldus, M., Keller, P., Verwayen, H., de Niet, M., Streefkerk, M.: Banking on heritage business. Informatie Prof. **10**, 40–47 (2011)
2. Brown, W.: Undoing the Demos: Neoliberalism's Stealth Revolution. MIT Press, Cambridge (2015)
3. Business Makeover STOF Business Model. Envision. https://www.businessmakeover. eu/platform/envision/tool-detailed-view?id=f6a1edce7ea84edex-515e165ex1581e85462 dx20a5. Accessed 17 July 2018
4. Osterwalder, A., Pigneur, Y., Clark, T.: Business Model Generation: A Handbook for Visionaries, Game Changers, and Challengers. Wiley, Hoboken (2013). See also https:// strategyzer.com/
5. Council on Library and Information Resources: Building and Sustaining Digital Collections: Models for Libraries and Museums. CLIR, Washington DC (2001)
6. DaSilva, C.M., Trkman, P.: Business model: what it is and what it is not. Long Range Plan. **47**(6), 379–389 (2014)
7. Members of the RDA/WDS Publishing Data Cost Recovery for Data Centres IG: Income Streams for Data Repositories (2016). https://doi.org/10.5281/zenodo.46693
8. Eschenfelder, K.R., Shankar, K., Williams, R., Langham, A., Zhang, M., Salo, D.: A nine dimensional framework for digital cultural heritage organizational sustainability: a content analysis of the LIS literature (2000–2015). Online Inf. Rev. (in press). https://doi.org/10. 1108/OIR-11-2017-0318
9. Evens, T., Hauttekeete, L.: Challenges of digital preservation for cultural heritage institutions. J. Librarianship Inf. Sci. **43**(3), 157–165 (2011)
10. Charles Beagrie Ltd. and CESSDA: Cost Benefit Advocacy Toolkit (2017). http://dx.doi. org/10.18448/16.0001
11. Hamilton, V.: Sustainability for digital libraries. Libr. Rev. **53**, 392 (2004)
12. Hansen, J.H.: How to make digital objects available to library users in a sustainable way. Microform Digitization Rev. **41**(3/4), 180–185 (2012)
13. Horizon 2020 Advisory Group. Horizon 2020 Expert Advisory Group European Research Infrastructures Including e-Infrastructures. European Commission, Brussels (2015)
14. Abdul Karim, H.S.B.H.A.: Digital transformation of libraries in Brunei Darussalam: addressing the sustainability issues of VILIS Brunei. Program Electron. Libr. Inf. Syst. **38**, 184 (2004)
15. Knight, S.: Early learnings from the National Library of New Zealand's National Digital Heritage Archive project. Program **44**(2), 85–97 (2010)
16. DEN Foundation/Knowledgeland. Business Model Innovation: Cultural Heritage. Knowledgeland, The Hague (2010)
17. Morris, M., Schindehutte, M., Allen, J.: The entrepreneur's business model: toward a unified perspective. J. Bus. Res. **58**(6), 726–735 (2005)
18. OECD. Business Models For Sustainable Research Data Repositories: OECD Science, Technology and Innovation Policy Paper. Brussels (2017)
19. Ongena, G., Huizer, E., Van de Wijngaert, L.: Threats and opportunities for new audiovisual cultural heritage archive services: the Dutch case. Telematics Inform. **29**(2), 156–165 (2012)
20. Osterwalder, A., Pigneur, Y., Tucci, C.L.: Clarifying business models: origins, present, and future of the concept. Commun. Assoc. Inf. Syst. **15**(9) (2005). https://doi.org/10.17705/ 1cais.01601

---

[1] References [1, 5, 9, 11, 12, 14, 15, 19, 21–25] are from analysis corpus.

21. Peters, D.: Giving form to the future of preservation: a trusted digital repository. S. A. Archives J. **43**, 89 (2003)
22. Royan, B.: The art of partnership: a Scottish case study. Art Libr. J. **28**(3), 15–21 (2003)
23. Tait, E., MacLeod, M., Beel, D., Wallace, C., Mellish, C., Taylor, S.: Linking to the past: an analysis of community digital heritage initiatives. Aslib Proc. New Inf. Perspect. **65**(6), 564–580 (2013)
24. Young, G.: UK research libraries collaborate to digitise a million pages of 19th century political and social pamphlets. ALISS Q. **4**(3), 28–31 (2009)
25. Zorich, D.M.: A survey of digital cultural heritage initiatives and their sustainability concerns. In: A Survey of Digital Cultural Heritage Initiatives and Their Sustainability Concerns (2003)
26. Zott, C., Amit, R., Massa, L.: The business model: recent developments and future research. J. Manage. **37**(4), 1019–1042 (2011)
27. Kitchin, R., Collins, S., Frost, D.: Funding models for open access digital data repositories. Online Inf. Rev. **39**(5), 664–681 (2015)
28. OECD. Business Models for Sustainable Research Data Repositories, OECD Science, Technology and Industry Policy Papers, No. 47, OECD Publishing, Pari (2017). https://doi.org/10.1787/302b12bb-en
29. Osterwalder, A., Pigneur, Y.: Business Model Generation: A Handbook for Visionaries, Game Changers, and Challengers. Wiley, Hoboken (2010)

Additional articles from analysis corpus, not included above:

Cousins, J. The European Library - pushing the boundaries of usability. The Electronic Library 24(4), 434–444 (2006)

Fricker, D. The National Archives of Australia's Business Model. Archifacts, 25–35 (2013)

Gatenby, P. Digital archiving: developing policy and best practice guidelines at the National Library of Australia. ICSTI Forum (33) (2000)

LeFurgy, W. G. NDIIPP Partner Perspectives on Economic Sustainability. Library Trends 57(3), 413–426 (2009).

Markscheffel, B., Fischer, D., & Stelzer, D. Classification of Digital Libraries - An e-Business Model-Based Approach. Journal of Digital Information Management 6(1), 71–80 (2008)

McCargar, V. Digital Repositories. Charleston Advisor 10(2), 48–49 (2008)

Menabney, N. Irish Studies online: a digital library of core resources on for Irish Studies. ALISS Quarterly 3(1), 7–11 (2007).

Morgan, P. DSpace@Cambridge: a digital institutional repository for the University of Cambridge. Assignation 21(3), 23–26 (2004)

Velarde, D. Illusion and Achievement in Open-Access Digitization. Feliciter 59(3), 37–39 (2013).

Understanding Change in a Dynamic Complex Digital Object: Reading Categories of Change Out of Patch Notes Documents

Ayse Gursoy[1](✉), Karen M. Wickett[2], and Melanie Feinberg[3]

[1] School of Information, University of Texas at Austin, Austin, TX, USA
agursoy@utexas.edu
[2] School of Information Sciences, University of Illinois,
Champaign-Urbana, IL, USA
[3] School of Information and Library Science,
University of North Carolina at Chapel Hill, Chapel Hill, NC, USA

Abstract. Digital games are complex digital objects that straddle the line between leisure and work, and offer a unique source for contextualizing the role of change in engaging with digital objects. Understanding how complex digital objects evolve over time and how such objects are framed as changing objects allows us to develop a more nuanced model for how different kinds of changes function in the lives of complex digital objects. This paper analyzes several years of patch notes for the digital game *League of Legends* through the methodology of reading to construct categories of kinds of changes and interpret the different roles of those categories. We propose a taxonomy of changes to a key part of the game ecosystem and describe how the categories in this taxonomy limn a perspective on dynamic, complex digital objects that can lead to more nuanced and robust preservation efforts.

Keywords: Digital preservation · Digital games · Complex digital objects

1 Introduction

Change presents a challenge for digital preservation artifacts, especially complex digital objects made up of multiple different digital parts [1]. Each part must be taken on its own terms, which means addressing component parts with sometimes different preservation strategies. In addition, different components may be changed at different times, as in the case of a faculty directory website that retains the same digital photographs but updates the text every year and the formatting every five years. Progressive changes that ostensibly improve the object and destructive changes that make the object difficult to access both make preservation difficult. These are not the only kinds of changes to digital objects, however, and it is vital to unpack the different functions of changes to complex digital objects. Some changes tinker, some changes flipflop, and some changes improve. Understanding how complex digital objects evolve over time, as well as how such objects are framed as changing objects allows us to develop a more nuanced model for how different kinds of changes function in the lives of complex digital objects.

© Springer Nature Switzerland AG 2019
N. G. Taylor et al. (Eds.): iConference 2019, LNCS 11420, pp. 399–410, 2019.
https://doi.org/10.1007/978-3-030-15742-5_38

In this paper, we focus on a specific digital game's software as a complex system similar to the complex software systems in scholarly or scientific software. We use the case of *League of Legends* (2009-present) as a rich case of a dynamic complex digital object that offers different kinds of change. In particular, we examine the various roles of incremental changes to the code in the form of patches, and build categories of kinds of changes by using the methodology of reading to analyze over two hundred patch notes documents spanning nearly a decade.

League of Legends is a multiplayer game where the core activity has two teams of five players compete with one another for resources in order to control territory. Players can interact with their allies, opponents, and neutral characters. Direct combat is a key part of the game where players fight each other, relying on abilities, items, and levels to gain an advantage over their opponents. Certain characters, items, and playstyles are strong to some and weak to others. The developers encourage a shifting dance of advantage over the years that ostensibly moves towards a perfectly even state; this dance and the idealized state are both known as "balance." In order to accommodate the state of the game at a given moment and to compensate for imbalance, players build consensus over the best ways to play *League of Legends* at a specific point in time. This consensus is known as "the meta[game]," and is a key part of the work that players do as they engage with a dynamic, living game.

Though the multiplayer competition is the central activity of the game, playing the game involves a set of related activities such as maintaining an updated version of the software, engaging in private or group chats, and unlocking access to game content through the store. In order to enter a game, the player must open the game client, ensure that the client is up-to-date, enter a queue to be matched with fellow players, and finally select their configuration before the match begins. Only at that point does the software that is associated with "playing *League of Legends*" appear on screen.

The developers of *League of Legends* release documents describing the changes made for the audience of regular players. These documents, known as patch notes, have evolved from simple lists of changes to structured documents including descriptions of changes and justifications for why changes are made. Through a process of close, distant, and medium reading, we develop categories of different kinds of changes in order to explore the various roles that change plays in the complex ecosystem of the game. The richness of variety in kinds of changes documented in the digital game *League of Legends* is particularly compelling for information professionals to study. Understanding how different categories of change function in the complex system of *League of Legends* can help professionals build more robust systems for supporting version documentation and help researchers develop nuanced models of the role of change in complex digital objects.

This paper draws from a larger project on the role of change in complex digital objects. Here, we focus specifically on understanding the different kinds of changes that are documented during the active development of *League of Legends* and the different functions of such changes to the game over time.

2 Background

In the following section, we first lay out perspectives in game studies to orient this project, and then describe the research setting of *League of Legends*. Game studies scholars have traditionally considered patches as developer- or player-created edits to a final released version of a software object, but some have attended to new modes of game creation where regular patching is considered a part of active development. *League of Legends* offers a rich case of a complex code environment that receives active, incremental patches for a sustained period of time and documents these patches through distributed "patch notes."

2.1 Patches

The idea of a patch in software development suggests a small, limited fix to a bug in code. For a long time, patches in games had a similar function of unintentional additions to the already-distributed version of a software object [2–4]. The resources required to maintain and distribute multiple regular patches for a game were infeasible for the modes of distribution commonly used in game publication. Within game studies, recent scholars have attended to new modes of game development and play that incorporate regular patches such as free-to-play games and esports [5, 6]. Few scholars, however, have attended to the dynamic nature of these objects except to attempt to fix a specific patch or version as the object of study—the dynamic nature is then a challenge to research rather than a productive source [7, 8]. There is room to explore different overlapping functions of change for these dynamic complex digital objects, such as change for novelty, change for improvement, and change to correct an error. In this paper, we use patch notes documents to explore what kinds of changes are made to a game, *League of Legends*, and thus to conceptualize what different functions of change might be.

2.2 Research Setting

League of Legends relies on 3 major pieces of software that run on player machines: the patcher client, the game client, and the game executable. When a player decides to play the game, she opens the game client which will check with central servers to see if any updates are required. If an update to the client is required, the game client will close at this point and notify the player that she must update before continuing. The patcher client only manages upgrades to the game client and executable. The majority of updates as of April 2017 are now handled in the new game client with no separate patcher client visible to the player [9]. Once the player has updated her game files as required by the central servers, she can continue to the game client, which facilitates playing individual matches. The game client manages paraludic elements like match-making. Figure 1a depicts the game client from 2018 in the middle of a game queue. The player is expected to have the client running in the background as she plays her matches. Once the player finalizes matchmaking, the game client launches an instance of the game executable. The game executable runs the actual matches by sending and receiving information about the game state to and from the central servers that facilitate the matches. This information gets converted via the game engine and interface to the actual events happening on screen in front of the player. Figure 1b depicts a moment in a multiplayer match. The game presents a great deal of information to the player through various interface elements and cosmetic elements such as colors, effects, and sounds. The player's actions are similarly converted to data sent to the central server. The game's various pieces of software and hardware must coordinate with one another and with a variety of hardware and software configurations that players may have access to.

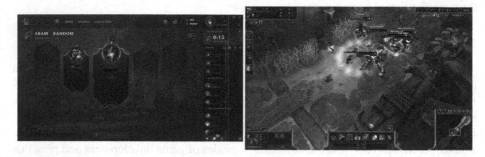

Fig. 1. a (left). Lobby and queue formation in game client in 2018 **b.** 2015 multiplayer match depicting interface elements and game events. The two teams are indicated by red and blue interface elements. (Images supplied by author.) (Color figure online)

3   Methods

The patch notes documents are a rich and unique genre form that have developed through years of use. In dynamic digital games, patch notes documents are often critical pieces of the paratextual ecosystem supporting play [8, 10, 11]. In the case of *League of Legends*, the patch notes documents have evolved from forum posts simply listing individual changes to extensive structured documents with justifications and implications in addition to descriptions of changes. Reading patch notes documents for a significant portion of the life of the game (2009–2017) allows us to identify categories of changes and to reveal the language used to describe those categories.

Reading is a method that originated in literary studies and is used to understand blocks of text on scales ranging from individual words to many pages. While the individual techniques used in our reading such as annotation, discussion of themes, and tracing of patterns may resemble techniques in interpretive or critical social science methods, the methodology of reading supports a contextual, perspectival approach to understanding the impact of words. Reading is specifically oriented to language use on different scales of analysis, which is ideal for our corpus of 222 patch notes documents spanning almost a decade, with 750–15000 words each. A single reader read all of the patch notes documents, using NVivo's coding and memoing tools to make notes on the documents as part of a close reading process. Then, all three authors discussed these annotations in order to develop analyses of language use describing changes in the patch notes documents. We use this process of attention on different scales to develop themes and relationships between themes that emerge from texts in order to produce a taxonomy of kinds of change described in the patch notes.

4 Findings

4.1 Basic Categories of Changes

The patch notes documents describe many different changes. There are changes to different parts of the complex system described above in Sect. 2.2, as well as different kinds of changes. The most common and most prominent changes are adjustments to in-game elements such as character abilities or items, either to values or to functionality. The patch notes documents also describe varied changes such as redesigning the interface, implementing new infrastructure to improve graphical performance, and introducing behavioral feedback to ensure that players act appropriately. Our use of reading as a methodology allows us to explore how these different categories of change are constituted through the evolving patch notes documents, which foreground change as a significant part of the game over time.

The language of these patch notes documents informs our typology of the different kinds of change in *League of Legends*. The patch notes documents are communication between the developers and the players, and thus are key records not only of the different categories of changes, but of the evolution of those categories and their framing. We discuss the framing in more detail in the following section. Not all kinds of changes apply to all parts of the complex game system. In this paper, we focus specifically on the categories of changes to the game executable.

First, we lay out the different software targets of change, and then we describe the typology of kinds of changes to the game executable (Fig. 2).

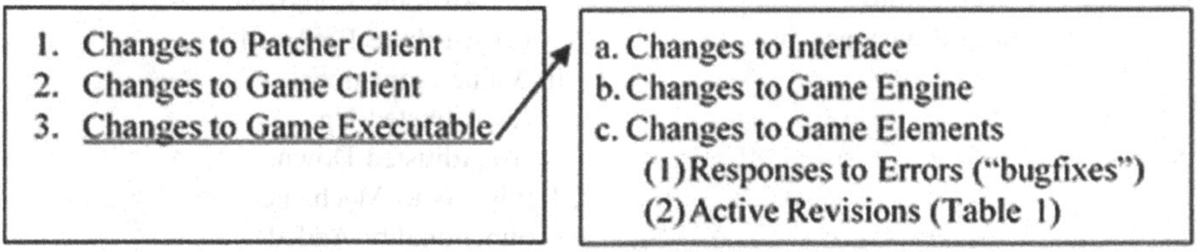

1. Changes to Patcher Client   a. Changes to Interface
2. Changes to Game Client   b. Changes to Game Engine
3. <u>Changes to Game Executable</u>   c. Changes to Game Elements
                                       (1) Responses to Errors ("bugfixes")
                                       (2) Active Revisions (Table 1)

Fig. 2. Software targets of changes to *League of Legends*.

Changes documented in the patch notes documents have one of three software targets: the patcher client, the game client ("League Client" or "PVP.net"), and the game executable. Changes to the patcher client prior to its retirement in April 2017 typically involved performance upgrades or improvements to the patch downloading process. Changes to the game client typically involve either player interaction elements such as friends lists or match queues, or interface elements such as display of information or activity flows. Both categories tend to be described as improvements or upgrades. Changes to the game executable are more nuanced in their framing, and typically involve the kinds of "tinkering" changes to game elements that are designed to maintain a shifting "game balance" [12]. These changes include character attribute adjustments and redesigns of character abilities, and will be discussed in more detail below.

This paper hones in on changes in category 3.c, Changes to Game Elements, within the game executable. Game elements can include such aspects as Player Characters, Items, Non-Player Characters, Structures and Terrain, Map Design, or Game Flow and Experience. This category forms the bulk of changes recorded in patch notes documents, as well as the primary focus of player discussions on online forums such as the official *League of Legends* Discussion Boards and the semi-official *League of Legends* subreddit.

Even within this scoped category, there is a great deal of variety in kinds of changes. At this juncture, we propose a typology of categories of changes to game elements described in patch notes documents. We consider changes that are described as responses to errors as "bugfixes" in a separate category. The other primary category describes active or intentional revisions, including cosmetic revisions and functional revisions to game elements. In this taxonomy, we defer to the language used in patch notes documents to inform our category names.

In the following subsection, we explore how the categories are framed in the evolving documentary genre form of the patch notes documents (Table 1).

Table 1. Detailed taxonomy of changes to game elements

1. Cosmetic revisions	2. Functional revisions
a. Visual Revisions	a. Changes to Multiple Elements ("rework")
1. Particles	b. Changes to Individual Elements
2. Appearances	1. Revisions to Attributes
i. Textures	i. Attribute Changes
ii. 3-D Models and Rigging	(a) Attribute Added
3. Animations	(b) Attribute Removed
b. Audio Revisions	(c) Attribute Replaced
	ii. Value Adjustment
	(a) Adjusted Up
	(b) Adjusted Down
	2. Revisions to Mechanics
	i. Functionality Added
	ii. Functionality Removed
	iii. Functionality Replaced

4.2   Framing Categories of Change in Patch Notes Documents

Responses to Errors ("Bugfixes"). Bugfixes refers to changes made in response to a known bug, error, or issue. Some examples of changes that are bugfixes include:

☐ "Fixed a Bug where chain missiles would end after hitting a dead target." (Document 10)

☐ "Fixed a bug where Let's Bounce! was applying a 0.25 Ability Power ratio on every bounce rather than 0.4 on the first bounce, halved on subsequent bounces" (Document 112)

Bugs, and by extension bugfixes, are cases where the designers of the game failed to anticipate how the code would create a certain undesired outcome. Bugfixes, however, often bring those game elements back in line with what they were intended to be, and thus do not have the same exploratory intent of other game element changes.

Cosmetic Revisions. Cosmetic changes include changes to things like appearances, animations, particles, or audio effects. The developers often bundle cosmetic changes into a complete "art or visual update" or into part of a "VGU (Visual and Gameplay Update)."

Cosmetic changes make the game feel more coherent and responsive; often, animation or particle changes are framed as increasing the amount of information available to the player about the game state. For example, in the 1.0.0.109 patch notes document, the writers note that "Counter Strike now shows a brighter particle when Jax has recently dodged an attack and Counter Strike is ready" (Document 34). While this is a cosmetic change, it clearly has an impact on how the game may be played. Cosmetic changes also reveal that the game is an imperfect representation of ideal design forms. For example, the patch notes document for v7.9 describes an update to a character's voice over: "Maokai's VO has been updated to match his lore. He's a mad tree, not a sad tree" (Document 206).

Cosmetic revisions to game elements impact how the game is played as well as less ludic aspects of design such as world-building or immersion. The words "updated" and "improved" appear in patch notes documents to describe how cosmetic changes fit a narrative of constant progress. Thus, cosmetic revisions are not presented as experimental changes the way that functional revisions may be, but as intentional improvements.

Functional Revisions. Functional revisions scope the main kinds of experimental changes to game elements. These changes are often justified as responding to current play, filling a design gap, or taking time to experiment. Unlike cosmetic changes and bugfixes, functional revisions are not necessarily presented as concrete improvements, but simply as actions that shake up the current state of *League of Legends* and provide opportunities for players to engage with the game in new ways. In this subsection, we describe reworks, attribute revisions, and action revisions.

Changes to Multiple Elements ("Reworks"). When a few functional revisions are made to the same game element (character, ability, or item), they are often described collectively as a "remake" or a "rework." These terms, used throughout the patch notes documents, indicate a new version of the game element that is designed to interact more productively with other game elements. The idea of a rework is a rather interesting concept and one that potentially drives engagement with the game over time. Instead of replacing characters or items with new, different characters or items that better fill a design gap, the developers edit existing characters or items in order to ensure that they are still relevant in the current state of the game.

Revisions to Attributes. Attributes form the backbone of interactions in *League of Legends*. Each game element has a set of attributes with specific values that define how that element works. Several examples of attribute changes follow, with the attributes in question underlined by the authors for ease of identification:

☐ "Bandage Toss <u>Mana Cost</u> reduced to 90/100/110/120/130 from 130 at all ranks" (Document 61).

☐ "No longer grants +30 <u>Armor</u>" and "Now grants +10% <u>Cooldown Reduction</u>" (Document 114).

Value adjustments to attributes, shown in the first example above, include changes described as "increased," "reduced," "changed," "modified," or "adjusted," as well as changes described with the structural forms "now…instead of," or "⇒." Value adjustments are often summarized with words like "buffed," "nerfed," "lowered," or "raised" when the patch notes writers justify the changes or describe their goals for changes. Value adjustments are the most common and most basic kinds of changes to game elements, often contextualized as solving a balance problem or exploring design possibilities. Value adjustments are described as "minor changes" or as "balance changes" interchangeably in the patch notes documents.

Attributes may also be replaced, added, or removed, as in the second example above (Document 114). The language used for attribute changes is similar to the language used for value adjustments, with two notable differences. First, attribute changes use "changed" more often than adjustments do. Second, attribute changes are described similarly to revisions to mechanics in using the words "now" and "no longer" to describe added and removed attribute interactions.

Revisions to Mechanics. Revisions to mechanics are changes to how game elements work. They are often described by noting what the ability, character, or item does now, sometimes in contrast to what it did before. Mechanical changes do not simply add or remove attributes or modify values, but change how different game elements work and interact. Some examples of mechanical changes follow:

☐ "Now increases the magic damage Ahri deals to the target by 20% for 6 s" (Document 105)

☐ "removed WARD KILLERS: Azir's Soldiers can no longer attack wards or trinkets." (Document 196)

Changes to mechanics, along with changes to attributes, comprise the set of active revisions to the game that are intended not to march along a narrative of continual progress but to tinker with the complex system of the game as it exists at a point in time. These kinds of changes contribute to the continued maintenance of the unstable equilibrium of game balance, constantly revising the way the game works in order to produce new kinds of interactions and modes of play. While these kinds of changes are particularly salient in this example of a digital game, such changes may occur in all kinds of dynamic complex digital objects and are thus worth considering as significant features of these objects in their own right.

5   Discussion

5.1   A Constantly-Shifting Artifact

Understanding the different kinds of changes in the patch notes documents paints a picture of gameplay as an intricate network of objects, attributes, values, and relationships, where gaining fluency in the possible interactions of this network is how players gain skill. The goal of the designers of this network is not to create a single optimal network, but to shift the network around into semi-stable configurations that always seem fair and engaging for the players. This idea is known as "balance" and treated in the patch notes with respect [12]. In fact, sometimes patch notes describe the game-element changes contained within as "balance changes" or "balance updates"; for example, document 114 is identified as "V3.5 (Balance update)" which complements the earlier document 115, "V.3.5," by making adjustments and slight functionality changes to a few characters and items. The idea of balance drives the intentional changes to game elements explored above and the continuous evolution of balance is part of what players engage with meaningfully as part of play.

The goal of balance motivates revisions to *League of Legends* that are not explicitly improvements but rather experimental, or tinkering, changes. Such a motivation is rarely explored in existing research on versions of complex digital objects, which instead focus on how new versions improve or complicate the object over time. Change here is a critical part of the game's development as well as the game's demands of its players. In order to maintain one's identity as a player, one must stay informed about changes and integrate awareness of tinkering revisions into their development of skills. Thus, *League of Legends* presents a rich environment for studying the role of various kinds of changes in how typical players develop an engagement with complex digital objects over time.

5.2   Preservation Implications

Taking a more nuanced view of the role of change is not only significant for understanding games as artifacts, but for preservation as well. Digital preservation practice relies on specific models of digital artifacts. A popular model describes complex digital objects as bundles of significant properties, where the key features of the artifact are defined and maintained through transformative preservation acts like emulation or migration [1]. For instance, a significant property of the Google.com homepage is a centered search box that takes user input. In this mode of thinking about digital artifacts, the artifact must be fixed and the significant properties defined by the preservationist. Scholars such as Dappert and Farquhar [13] or Hedstrom et al. [14] further emphasize the role of user and stakeholder communities in defining significant properties. In the *League of Legends* patch notes documents, designers describe changes to the look and feel of the game and provide context for players to understand changes to a living game, two critical aspects identified in [14] as important to users of preserved objects. Thus, the research presented here is one step towards a "new model in which stakeholders state requirements expressing significance" [13, p. 298].

The complication with significant properties is in the assumption that the set of significant properties for a given complex digital object, when fixed, defines the artifact. Becker argues against such assumptions, offering instead that we consider significant properties as a set of requirements necessary for the design and maintenance of a system that continually reproduces the performance of what we think of as a digital object [15]. Becker's explicit acknowledgment of the possibility for changes that preserve the meaning of digital objects suggests that already-dynamic digital objects like *League of Legends* do not present as much of a challenge to digital preservation as we might think. Instead, what is necessary for successful digital preservation is to develop nuanced ways of talking about how digital objects perform semiotic effects. We offer this typology of changes in *League of Legends* to provide one such vocabulary based on existing communication about digital objects. Dynamic complex digital objects like *League of Legends* demonstrate not only that significant properties may evolve over the functional lives of these objects, but that change itself may be a property worth retaining as significant. The emphasis given to the patch notes documents indicates that the regular patches to *League of Legends* are offered to players as a form of meaningful engagement with the game over time. What, then, do we do with the productive framework of significant properties, that seeks to maintain one version of an artifact through transformative acts of preservation?

By developing an understanding of the different functions of change in complex digital objects like digital games, information professionals can build more robust frameworks for preserving these objects in ways that respect their various parts. For example, attending to the various reworks in *League of Legends* might help identify key versions of the game to keep as before and after snapshots in order to document a specific change. The Preserving Virtual Worlds project final report exhorts preservationists to attend to unconventional ways of documenting the rich experiences in digital games, and we extend that by pointing to change as a key feature of such experiences [16]. Thus, foregrounding a history of functional revisions to one game element might mean interviewing players who have long-term experience with the game element in question.

Digital objects are at their heart interactive, and preserving them means preserving this interactive quality. In order to preserve a complex digital object that is dynamic, and which has dynamism as a key quality, information professionals must tackle the question, "what does change do in this system?" As we have demonstrated in this paper, there are multiple overlapping answers to this question—change may improve, change may fix an error, change may lead to unintended consequences, and change may offer hooks for developing player skill—and only by attending to the question can we develop more nuanced and robust ways of preserving dynamic complex digital artifacts.

6   Conclusion

The case of *League of Legends* demonstrates that change can have different functions when considered in a dynamic complex digital object. In this paper, we focus on changes to game elements in the game executable and map out the various categories of changes described in over two hundred patch notes documents. We propose a set of kinds of changes including responses to errors, cosmetic revisions, and functional revisions. Within the taxonomy described in Sect. 4.1, we further break down specific sub-categories of changes and unpack how the framing of such changes in patch notes documents reflects an attention to the different functions of change circulating within this dynamic complex digital object. For example, responses to errors described as "bugfixes" reflect an orientation towards bringing the software object in line with the original intent of the developers and accommodating unexpected software interactions. On the other hand, functional revisions to attributes or mechanics reflect an orientation towards adjusting the playing field in order to encourage diversity of play. This latter set of categories, often described in the patch notes as balance changes, foregrounds how change does not need to solve a defined problem or introduce unexpected problems in order to have a meaningful role in the identity of dynamic complex digital objects. The various categories of change, and their attendant functions, described in the patch notes for *League of Legends* offer a more nuanced perspective on change and can help information professionals conceptualize how different kinds of change may require different preservation considerations.

References

1. Hedstrom, M., Lee, C.A.: Significant properties of digital objects: definitions, applications, implications. In: Proceedings of the DLM-Forum, pp. 218–227, Barcelona (2002)
2. Swalwell, M.: Towards the preservation of local computer game software challenges, strategies, reflections. Convergence **15**(3), 263–279 (2009)
3. McDonough, J., Kirschenbaum, M., Reside, D., Fraistat, N., Jerz, D.: Twisty little passages almost all alike: applying the FRBR model to a classic computer game. Digital Humanit. Q. **4**(2), 1869–1883 (2010)
4. Newman, J.: Ports and patches: digital games as unstable objects. Convergence **18**(2), 135–142 (2012)
5. Taylor, T.L.: Raising the Stakes: E-Sports and the Professionalization of Computer Gaming. MIT Press, Cambridge (2012)
6. Witkowski, E.: On the digital playing field: how we "do sport" with networked computer games. Games Cult. **7**(5), 349–374 (2012)
7. Nardi, B.A.: My Life as a Night Elf Priest: An Anthropological Account of World of Warcraft. University of Michigan Press, Ann Arbor (2010)
8. Paul, C.A.: Process, paratexts, and texts: rhetorical analysis and virtual worlds. J. Virtual Worlds Res. **3**(1), 8 (2010)
9. Legacy Client Now Retired. https://na.leagueoflegends.com/en/news/game-updates/features/legacy-client-now-retired. Accessed 30 Sept 2018
10. Švelch, J.: Resisting patches and errata: motivations and tactics. In: Proceedings of the First International Joint Conference of DiGRA and FDG. DiGRA and FDG, Dundee (2016)
11. McDaniel, R., Daer, A.: Developer discourse: exploring technical communication practices within video game development. Tech. Commun. Q. **25**(3), 155–166 (2016)
12. Sirlin, D.: Game balance. In: Lowood, H., Guins, R. (eds.) Debugging Game History: A Critical Lexicon, pp. 169–175. MIT Press, Cambridge (2016)

13. Dappert, A., Farquhar, A.: Significance is in the eye of the stakeholder. In: Agosti, M., Borbinha, J., Kapidakis, S., Papatheodorou, C., Tsakonas, G. (eds.) ECDL 2009. LNCS, vol. 5714, pp. 297–308. Springer, Heidelberg (2009). https://doi.org/10.1007/978-3-642-04346-8_29
14. Hedstrom, M., Lee, C.A., Olson, J.S., Lampe, C.A.: "The old version flickers more": digital preservation from the user's perspective. Am. Archivist **69**, 159–187 (2006)
15. Becker, C.: Metaphors we work by: reframing digital objects, significant properties, and the design of digital preservation systems. Archivaria **85**, 6–36 (2018)
16. McDonough, J.P., et al.: Preserving Virtual Worlds Final Report (2010)

Save Point/s: Competing Values and Practices in the Field of Video Game Preservation

Benedict Salazar Olgado[1,2]([⊠]) [iD]

[1] University of California, Irvine, Irvine, CA 92697, USA
bolgado@uci.edu
[2] University of the Philippines, Metro Manila 1100, Philippines
b.olgado@slis.upd.edu.ph

Abstract. This paper presents a Bourdieuvian way of understanding video game preservation as a nascent field with its discourse and praxis shaped by ontological differences and conflicting power structures. This is illustrated through a spectrum of valuation that treats video games as material artifacts on one end and embraces its ephemerality on the other. Video game preservation literature and initiatives are likely to lean towards one of these extremes which focuses either on ensuring the playability of games or documenting of gameplay and its expressions. These competing values and practices can be seen further by classifying and mapping out participants, illustrating power relations. There are points of overlap and tensions between industry players, cultural institutions, and fans given their respective conflicting nature, intent, and mechanisms when it comes to video game preservation. The shape and sustainability of this emerging field and frontier, the paper posits in the end, depend on how these tensions are addressed, hopefully towards inclusion and collaboration.

Keywords: Video game · Preservation · Pierre Bourdieu · Field · Habitus · Practice

1 Introduction

For decades, video games have had an impact on how people play, express, learn, and connect with each other. Given its breadth as an industry and its permeating presence [1], video games continue to reflect, question, document, and shape society, technology, and culture. But despite its growth and ubiquity, scholar and archivist James Newman, declares that "videogames are disappearing" [21].

Research and literature during the last decade [4, 12, 14, 15, 17, 28] echo his call pointing out the medium's inherent and planned obsolescence together with the volatility of its market and sociocultural environment as mechanisms of deterioration and loss. In response, such scholarly works accompany nascent video game preservation projects and initiatives by cultural institutions, industry players, and fans [11, 18, 19, 28, 29]. Though forms of video game preservation existed well before, it is only recently that an emergent field of scholarship and praxis has begun to take shape.

This paper highlights and presents a way of looking at video game preservation as a field with competing values and practices that ground and surround its structure,

© Springer Nature Switzerland AG 2019
N. G. Taylor et al. (Eds.): iConference 2019, LNCS 11420, pp. 411–418, 2019.
https://doi.org/10.1007/978-3-030-15742-5_39

functions, and interactions. The frameworks presented in this study are proposed to be used in future research to critically look at the intersecting work of scholars and practitioners of video game preservation as a whole. This is to account for underlying theoretical and pragmatic tensions towards building a more inclusive and sustainable field.

2   The 'Field' of Video Game Preservation

Pierre Bourdieu refers to a field [6] as a social system wherein multiple agencies and structures exist, interact, and struggle with each other as to shape the rules and activities within. Individuals and institutions participating in a field come with their respective habitus [7] of histories, dispositions, and expectations. Their habitus together with their capital [8] – from material to symbolic – and their engagements with every other agent in the field shape, limit, and produce their practices [9] that compete for legitimization and control.

Video game preservation as a field can be seen and critiqued through this Bourdieuvian theoretical lenses. That is to take a look at the various stakeholders, multiple contexts, differing valuations, and conflicting actions that populate the field. Gracy [13] applied this in her foundational work on film preservation showing that it is "neither a universally defined term, a standardized practice, nor a value-neutral pursuit [5]. " The premise of the frameworks put forth by this paper resonates with Gracy's findings, while being specific to the intricacies of the video game preservation field.

This field is inhabited by both those who think about video game preservation and those who work on it, functions that are not necessarily mutually exclusive.

2.1   Video Game Preservation Studies

In 2008, Gooding and Terras [12] noted the dearth of literature on video game preservation. As librarians and LIS scholars, they pointed out that though there are a number of works in video game studies covering the history of gaming, none of them gave a critical scrutiny to the idea of preserving that of which they study. Barwick et al. [4] expanded this criticism pointing out that video games barely, if at all, received attention in preservation literature as well.

A decade since, video game preservation as an area of inquiry has garnered the interest not only of scholars of video games and LIS – with their respective subfields and related disciplines – but also those of museology, media archeology, and computer science to name a few. Olle Sköld has done a systematic literature review [24] of these. This present paper applies Bourdieuvian theoretical lenses to Skold's precodified analyses in looking at the politics and embedded valuations of this emerging field of study being occupied by related and often conflicting disciplinal paradigms.

2.2   Video Game Preservation Initiatives

This paper also looks at video game preservation initiatives and the stakeholders behind them. There is no central directory that lists such initiatives but scholars throughout the years [3, 4, 28] have attempted to survey and account for them. The closest to an exhaustive list is a loose uncredited document available online [18] that upon checking contains outdated information. This reflects the seeming shapelessness of the field which this paper attempts to draw.

To this end, the frameworks proposed by this study broadly classifies initiatives based on the nature and context of the agencies who carry them out. These are cultural institutions, industry players, and fans. The goal is not to address the absence of a database accounting for these classifications, but rather to illustrate the power relations and capital structures between them.

The paper utilizes the aforementioned literature and through Bourdieuvian lenses develops the (1) spectrum of valuation and (2) frontier of power as frameworks to illustrate and understand the field of video game preservation.

3 Spectrum of Valuation

Video game preservation questions the very ontology of the video game [14]. What is it precisely that we pertain to when we speak of a video game? What are its significant properties that determine what ought to be preserved? While this has been an on-going discussion in video game studies, framing such conversations through the lenses of archival practice and thought may prove to be beneficial.

The framework below illustrates a spectrum of valuation based on two ontological ends that form specific practices articulated and seen in the field. These ontologies are rooted from participants' respective habitus accounting for the different definitions of video game preservation. Along this spectrum, video game preservation thought and praxis can be located (Fig. 1).

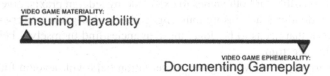

Fig. 1. Video game preservation's spectrum of valuation

3.1 Materiality: Playability

One end puts premium on ensuring the playability of games which are treated both as artifacts of materiality and interactivity. "How do we make sure that these games can be played way into the future?" is the main preoccupation. A particular focus is given to the traditional notions of conservation and with it questions of authenticity, intent, and fixity in maintaining or recreating games in playable forms.

Research by Guttenbrunner, Becker and Rauber [15], and Takhteyev [26], occupy this space as they measure, identify, and push the limits of the technicalities involved in preserving the playability of video games. This position can be seen in initiatives such as retro gaming collections, emulation projects, software preservation, retrocomputing, and platform conservation.

3.2   Ephemerality: Gameplay

On the other end, there are scholars like Newman [21] who calls that we "embrace the extinction of game in playable forms and with it shift the core objective of video game preservation instead to capturing of games in and at play." Vowell [27] echoes this, as he points out the over-emphasis on the game, while Swalwell [25] calls to move on from the "original experience." Anable [2] pushes these ideas further by musing about the creation of archives centering on affect. Documenting gameplay focuses then on what Sköld [24] calls the "expanded notion" of video games which includes its culture, community activity, and acts of play.

This includes, but is not limited to, making and archiving Twitch and LetsPlay videos, collecting commercial paraphernalia and published documentation, and accounting for expressions of fandom such as online threads and unofficial walkthroughs.

3.3   Ontological Politics

These ontologies are made by a multiplicity of participants who come to the field from different and at times conflicting perspectives and positions. Neither side discredits the importance of the other, but the difference lies in emphasis. This ontological politics shape the values of their arguments and practices.

While it is possible for both values to exist side-by-side, in praxis, given the limited resources of individuals and institutions engaged in video game preservation and the amount of work that needs to be done, these agencies find themselves being pulled to one end of this spectrum.

Which ontology in the video game preservation field will develop further? Which one will weaken? Will alternative ontologies arise outside of the spectrum? Ontological politics [23] captures this process in nascent fields eventually taking a more definite shape. These tensions open up the field of video game preservation – and video games themselves – to examination, experimentation, and creation.

4   Frontier of Power

In mapping out the various participants involved in video game preservation, power relations in the field are illustrated. The authority to legitimize and consecrate, following Bourdieu, is being fought as initiatives by and values of cultural institutions, the industry, and the fans overlap. This is illustrated as follows (Fig. 2).

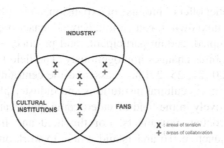

Fig. 2. Video game preservation's frontier of power

4.1 Areas of Tension

The current state of affairs is, of course, not as equally co-determinate as illustrated given emergences, tensions, and displacements in the field. Some game publishers who are starting to see new market opportunities are cracking down on fan-based ROM repositories declaring them as illegal. This is seen in the case of EmuParadise which after 18 years has closed down folding to the legal pressures of the industry [22].

The commercial asset valuation of the industry can also go against the cultural heritage valuation of cultural institutions. The Museum of Play for example continually negotiates with development companies to secure internal materials such as concept art, interface flowcharts, and texture models which companies are generally wary of releasing to the public [11].

With the rise of these institutional video game archives, the preservation space of amateur-fan-archivists is also being threatened by "professional archivists," on the grounds of legitimacy and sustainability [10, 16]. Displaced, some of the fans who were once at the center of the field, are now in the dark web underbelly or have been completely wiped out.

4.2 Shape of the Field

Given these tensions, the predominant shape of video game preservation field has yet to take form. Multiplicity in an emerging field generally leads to initial clashes as a central status quo attempts to rise. Who will occupy that center and what values will dominate will depend on these social dimensions. These points of tension though, are also points of possible collaboration. In identifying these tensions both in practice and their underlying values, the possibility of addressing them as to work on and through these overlaps is more likely to happen.

4.3 Frontier Movements

The relations between these participants are not precise and oppositional, but rather they are characterized by multidirectional movements, arduous exchanges, and continuous conflicts and collaborations. The power and capital structures, together with the habitus driven ontological politics at play, conceive the field into what Papadopoulos [23] calls a 'frontier.' While a frontier offers a promise of expansion, and with it perceived liberation from limits and/or the unknown, it can simultaneously enact oppression. As territories and structures are occupied, certain participants and practices can be appropriated or even displaced. The habitus changes homogenously. The field takes shape.

Scholars [10, 16, 20, 21, 25, 29] have asserted the centrality and value of fans in video game preservation. As cultural institutions and industry players find cultural and material capital respectively in the field of video game preservation, it is imperative to be vigilant of such frontier movements. For the field and frontier of video game preservation is at this juncture. To understand it, and to work on it, is to see it through such frameworks of valuation and power.

5   Inclusive and Sustainable Field

While broadly construed as to illustrate frameworks of this study, participants are not homogenous and contains cross-sections. Fandom for example is its own field with its own conflicting structures, politics, and practices within. These invariably impact the field of video game preservation which they concurrently occupy. Mechanisms of gender and class in fandom, for instance, invariably impact what gets preserved and who gets to access them. The same extends to cultural institutions and their curatorial stances, to industry players and their corporate values.

Looking at both scholars and practitioners of video game preservation, it is predominantly white, primarily male, and concentrated outside the global south. Other established cultural institutions like museums and archives are finally grappling with such issues of diversity when it comes to the people who work in them, the materials they keep, the approaches they apply, and the people they provide access to. From the preservation of indie games to the documentation of #GamerGate, video game preservation, emerging as it is, can and should aspire to shape an inclusive field with these in mind early on.

Inclusivity within and between the participants of the field is key in securing its sustainability. By maximizing overlaps as points for collaboration and productive tension, participants can work towards developing a shared field-specific habitus while still upholding diverse practices across various contexts of structure and capital. Future studies grounded in the theoretical foundation and framework presented in this work will employ archival ethnography [13] to be able to account for these. Forming the next generation of video game archivists as a community with articulated shared values and philosophies is key. Similar to how other fields of preservation painstakingly formed theirs, the field of video game preservation will depend on all of these.

References

1. Video Game Industry Statistics, Trends, and Data. https://www.wepc.com/news/video-game-statistics/. Accessed 9 Aug 2018
2. Anable, A.: Playing with Feelings: Video Games and Affect. University of Minnesota Press, Minneapolis (2018)

3. Bachell, A., Barr, M.: Video game preservation in the UK: independent games developers' records management practices. Int. J. Digital Curation 9(2), 139–170 (2014)
4. Barwick, J., Dearnley, J., Muir, A.: Playing games with cultural heritage: a comparative case study analysis of the current status of digital game preservation. Games Cult. 6(4), 373–390 (2010)
5. Becker, S.: Review: film preservation: competing definitions of value, use, and practice. Mov. Image 8(1), 52–54 (2008)
6. Bourdieu, P.: The Field of Cultural Production: Essays on Art and Literature. Columbia University Press, New York (1993)
7. Bourdieu, P.: Distinction: A Social Critique of the Judgement of Taste. Routledge, London (1984)
8. Bourdieu, P.: The forms of capital. In: Richardson, J.G. (ed.) Handbook of Theory and Research for the Sociology of Capital, pp. 241–258. Greenwood Press, New York (1986)
9. Bourdieu, P.: The Logic of Practice. Stanford University Press, Stanford (1990)
10. deWinter, J., Kocurek, C.: Repacking my library. In: Swalwell, M. (ed.) Fans and Videogames: Histories, Fandom, and Archives, pp. 166–179. Routledge, New York (2017)
11. Dyson, J.: Collecting, preserving, and interpreting the history of electronic games. Am. J. Play 10(1), 1–19 (2017)
12. Gooding, P., Terras, M.: Grand theft archive: a quantitative analysis of the state of computer game preservation. Int. J. Digital Curation 3(2), 19–41 (2008)
13. Gracy, K.: Film Preservation: Competing Definitions of Value, Use, and Practice. American Library Association, Chicago (2007)
14. Guins, R.: Gamer After: A Cultural Study of Video Game Afterlife. MIT Press, Cambridge (2014)
15. Guttenbrunner, M., Becker, C., Rauber, A.: Keeping the game alive: evaluating strategies for the preservation of console video games. Int. J. Digital Curation 5, 64–90 (2010)
16. Kraus, K., Donahue, R.: Do you want to save your progress? The role of professional and player communities in preserving virtual worlds. Digital Humanit. Q. 6 (2012)
17. Lowood, H. (ed.): Before It's Too Late: A Digital Game Preservation White Paper. American Journal of Play, vol. 2, no. 2, pp. 139–166 (2009)
18. List of videogame and game-related archives and preservation projects. https://deserthat. com/downloads/ArchivesandPreservationProjects.doc. Accessed 9 Nov 2018
19. Mcdonough, J, et al.: Preserving Virtual Worlds final report. University of Illinois IDEALS Repository (2010)
20. Navarro-Remesal, V.: Museum of failure: fans as curators of 'bad', unreleased, and 'flopped' videogames. In: Swalwell, M. (ed.) Fans and Videogames: Histories, Fandom, and Archives, pp. 128–145. Routledge, New York (2017)
21. Newman, J.: Best Before: Videogames, Supersession and Obsolescence. Routledge, New York (2012)
22. Onanuga, T.: All that's wrong with Nintendo's heavy-handed ROM crackdown. In: Wired. https://www.wired.co.uk/article/nintendo-roms-emulator-loveroms-loveretro-lawsuit. Accessed 9 Sept 2018
23. Papadopoulos, D.: Experimental Practice: Technoscience, Alterontologies, and More-Than-Social Movements. Duke University Press, Durham (2018)
24. Sköld, O.: Understanding the 'expanded notion' of videogames as archival objects: a review of priorities, methods, and conceptions. J. Assoc. Inf. Sci. Technol. 69(1), 134–145 (2018)
25. Swalwell, M.: Moving on from the original experience: philosophies of preservation and display in game history. In: Swalwell, M. (ed.) Fans and Videogames: Histories, Fandom, and Archives, pp. 213–233. Routledge, New York (2017)

26. Takhteyev, Y.: Retrocomputing as preservation and remix. Library Hi Tech. **31**, 355–370 (2013)
27. Vowell, Z.: What constitutes history? In: Lowood, H. (ed.): Before It's Too Late: A Digital Game Preservation White Paper (2009). American Journal of Play, vol. 2, no. 2, pp. 139–166
28. Winget, M.A., Murray, C.: Collecting and preserving videogames and their related materials: a review of current practice, game-related archives and research projects. In: Proceedings of the American Society for Information Science and Technology, pp. 1–9. Wiley, Hoboken (2008)
29. Winget, M.A.: Collecting the artifacts of participation: videogame players, fan-boys, and individual models of collection. In: Winget, M.A., Aspray, W. (eds.) Digital Media: Technological and Social Challenges of the Interactive World, pp. 27–72. Scarecrow Press, Plymouth (2011)

Characterizing Same Work Relationships in Large-Scale Digital Libraries

Peter Organisciak(✉)(iD), Summer Shetenhelm,
Danielle Francisco Albuquerque Vasques, and Krystyna Matusiak

University of Denver, 1999 E Evans Ave, Denver, CO, USA
`peter.organisciak@du.edu`

Abstract. As digital libraries grow, they are prompting new consideration into same-work relationships. They provide unique opportunities for resource discovery, but their scale and aggregated models lead to challenges presented by duplicates and variants. Addressing this problem is complicated by metadata inconsistencies as well as structural/content differences. Following from work in algorithmically identifying duplicate works in the HathiTrust Digital Library, we present some cases that complicate our existing language for work entity relationships. These serve to contextualize the complexities of same-work alignment in digital libraries, ground future discussion around content similarity, and inform methods to better identify duplicates in large-scale digital libraries.

Keywords: Digital libraries · Entity alignment · Text mining · Text duplication

1 Introduction

As the next generation of digital libraries (DLs) has grown to massive scales by aggregating materials from multiple collections, they are prompting new consideration into same-work relationships. This new environment of large-scale DLs provides unique opportunities for resource discovery but also poses challenges in distinguishing between duplicates and finding the most representative edition. Reconciling duplicate volumes from multiple sources is important for practical information organization and retrieval. It also allows for better downstream uses of digitized print collections, such as improving the quality of metadata, reconciling better OCR text quality, and effectively utilizing text mining for higher-level concepts and trends. However, determining the relationships between DL volumes is complicated by metadata inconsistencies as well as structural/content differences, such as variant editions, anthologies, derivatives, and aggregated works. Following from ongoing work in content-based alignment of digital works, this paper characterizes the scope of the issue.

We present a set of cases that complicate our existing language for work entity relationships. These three cases serve to demonstrate the complexities of same work alignment in massive DLs and ground the discussion around various levels of content similarity. These case studies are derived from a manual review of algorithmically matched duplicate works. Our content-based algorithm was intentionally preliminary, and our expectation was that the evaluation of its results would surface areas where

© Springer Nature Switzerland AG 2019
N. G. Taylor et al. (Eds.): iConference 2019, LNCS 11420, pp. 419–425, 2019.
https://doi.org/10.1007/978-3-030-15742-5_40

content-based analysis is challenged. Instead, the results often reveal metadata failures, where inconsistencies in practice or the standards themselves are insufficient for ascertaining relationships between items contributed from multiple libraries.

Large-scale DLs like the 16.7 million work HathiTrust Digital Library present great potential value in their scale and coverage but are also quite complex. They carry the inconsistencies in bibliographic data from the print environment but add another layer of complexity by presenting users with multiple digitized versions of the same edition. The versions may differ in the symbolic representation because of the quality of OCR and scanning technology. What criteria could end-users apply to distinguish between different versions?

The remainder of the paper introduces early work in algorithmically identifying duplicate works in the HathiTrust Digital Library at various levels of granularity, from variant existing versions of content (same work, different expression) to variant presentations of the same content (same expression, different manifestation) to simply different copies from the same print run (same manifestation, different item). We introduce issues related to this task through demonstrative cases. Same-work relationships are a pertinent issue in large-scale DLs, and these case studies provide a language for better exploring that issue.

2   Background

Why should we identify same-work relationships? Library practice has traditionally focused on preserving duplicate relationship information only at the level of the artifact; e.g. same OCLC or ISBN number. To understand the need for identifying more nuanced same-work relationships, it is important to understand the context of recent large-scale DLs.

Recent projects have grown digital collections in consortial fashion. Europeana and the Digital Public Library of America aggregate cultural heritage metadata from institutions throughout Europe and the United States, and Internet Archive and Google Books have scanned holdings from libraries around the world. One of the largest DL projects is the HathiTrust Digital Library, a collection of 16.7 million scanned volumes [1]. The HathiTrust aggregates metadata and full-text materials not only from multiple libraries, but from multiple digitization initiatives.

Large DLs present a great deal of value in information science and other fields, due to their broad coverage, accessibility, and malleable digital representations. However, they also hold many duplicates and variants, and identifying them is difficult due to metadata inconsistencies and differing representations of the work. Identifying same-work duplicate relationships may (a) improve access and retrieval, (b) assist with the normalization of metadata, (c) improve OCR capabilities, and (d) better discover trends about history and culture via text mining and topic modelling.

For traditional access and retrieval, a massive searchable DL makes it easier to connect information-seeking users to the published record. However, culturally prominent – and well-represented – works may overwhelm search results. As such, a retrieval system knowing exact or near-duplicate works could fold same results and provide room for other results. As per Xu and Smith, "…removing duplicates improves efficiency and user satisfaction," [2]. Such information can also aid people seeking to compare multiple versions of a work, perhaps contrasting forewords to a novel or evaluating translations of a foreign book.

For cataloguing practice, identifying matching works allows metadata to be compared and normalized. Inconsistencies as fundamental as title differences become apparent when matching works in large-scale DLs. More complete metadata can be created by aligning complementary records [3], like the date of first publication [4]. Identifying duplicates can address coverage and text quality issues as well. Our ongoing work seeks to overcome issues of poor OCR text by determining the 'cleanest' copy of multiple options. Alternately, Xu and Smith propose 'consensus decoding' of aligned documents for improved OCR [2]. Another area of improved access may be in completing incomplete multi-volume sets; e.g. if a scanning project at one library missed two volumes of a set, they may be found elsewhere in the collection.

The most revolutionary potential presented by large-scale DLs is in text mining the collection, to learn more about aggregate trends in history, language, and culture. However, redundancy confounds any language model's efficacy, and removing it is in the interest of many text mining uses. A model that tries to learn from words in a collection like the HathiTrust's will be have a skewed view of reality from repeating texts [5]. Removing duplicates helps mitigate the potential for skewed results that do not accurately reflect the reality of a certain topic or time period.

A note about language: we uses materials from the HathiTrust, and adopt their term *volume* to refer to a scanned copy of a single physical library item. In discussing various levels of similarity, we adopt the FRBR class 1 entities. Here, *work* refers to an abstract concept that denotes intellectual content of a distinct creation; e.g. *Hamlet* as concept. Works are realized through *expressions*, the "distinct combination of signs conveying intellectual or artistic content" [6], such as various versions of Hamlet. Expressions are embodied by *manifestations*, e.g. a physical or e- book. An individual copy of a manifestation – i.e. the specific bound set of pages for a book – is an *item*.

3 Related Work

Much of the literature regarding using the FRBR model leverages catalog records rather than content. Bennett, Lavoie and O'Neill used FRBR to examine how works were shown in WorldCat [7], finding in their sample of 996 works that 20% contained more than one manifestation, and only 1% had eight or more. More recently, the Global Library Manifestation Identifier (GLIMIR) project clusters WorldCat records into work-clusters using a heuristic-based metadata matching approach [8]. Our exploration of work relationships uses content rather than metadata, allowing us to consider duplicates with divergent metadata as well as works that exist in varying forms.

A survey on translating FRBR to practice found a desire for verification of the model with real data applied in different communities. Participants also expressed a desire for "…tools that facilitate the FRBRization processes,", albeit with appropriately broad testing and research. Our ongoing work pursues both of these goals.

FRBR and its related standards are being consolidated through the IFLA Library Reference Model (LRM) [6]. LRM maintains the FRBR entities and refines them further by defining attributes and relationships. In recognition of end-users' needs and tasks, LRM introduces a new attribute of a work – representative expression [6, p. 41]. This attribute can be particularly useful in the large-scale DL environment where users are faced with duplicates, multiple editions, and aggregated expressions. It is essential for users to distinguish between editions and to identify that a certain group of editions relates to the same work. In some cases, users may want to identify and select an expression that is the most representative of a work. LRM still has a focus on forms and relationships established in the print environment but states that extension can be developed for DL needs. It suggests a *digital item* entity as an intermediary between the *manifestation* and *item* entities [6].

4 Approach

This work uses a sample of 102k literature books from the HathiTrust Digital Library [9], all of which are in the public domain and easily accessible for manual review. From the sample, we subsampled 20 'target' volumes, asked a basic algorithm to rank other volumes in the set by their similarity to the target volume, and then manually reviewed the top results to determine their relationship to the target. The purpose was in uncovering quirks and complexities that a mature algorithm needs to account for.

The basic algorithm used word frequencies from the HathiTrust Research Center's Extracted Features Dataset [10], term weighted with TF-IDF and modelled using Latent Semantic Analysis (LSA) [11]. LSA has the effect of reducing the term count representation of a text to a smaller set of dimensions, each signaling a latent set of co-occurrence patterns. It has the effect of smoothing between trivial differences in word usage (e.g. 'car' and 'automobile' may be represented together), allowing better comparisons between texts than by directly comparing words. Pairwise comparisons of texts' LSA representations were performed with cosine similarity.

The evaluation surfaced many areas of complexity for thinking through the conceptual boundaries and technical complexities of same work relationships. In this paper, we do not report on the entire evaluation; rather, we aim to tell the story of three cases that provide a face to some of the issues we see.

5 Case Studies

Nested Whole/Part Work-to-Work Relationships. A difficulty in considering manifestations of a work is when they do not neatly align with the physical or organizational form; e.g. a work that manifests across a set of physical volumes. FRBR and LRM allow for these types of whole/part relationships, where a work may exist as a subset of another work.

Such whole/part relationships can nest, as in *The Works of Charles Dickens* (1897). Our evaluation's target text was volume 31 of 36 for this work (*w1*), which was entirely comprised of *Christmas Stories* (*w1.1*). This is a typical whole/part work-to-work relationship; however, *w1.1* itself is comprised of 21 smaller stories across two volumes (15 in v.1, or v.31 of the greater work, and 6 in v.2/v.32). That means that a story like *A Message from the Sea* may be published on its own, but also exists as part of *Christmas Stories*, which may be published alone or as part of an even larger "*Works of*" work. Our basic algorithm found instances of each circumstance.

LRM affords consideration into aggregate manifestations, which may allow for better classification of these relationships in the future. However, this particular example was complicated in further ways that do not appear in the current HathiTrust metadata. *w1.1* in this version of *w1* is a facsimile of an earlier manifestation, represented in a special kind of manifestation-to-manifestation relationship. The algorithm found numerous exact duplicates, with the same appearance but different titles, years, control numbers, and volume numbering. These cataloguing quirks may be understandable given the hodgepodge nature of *w1* - the title page of our target volume says "Vol. XXXI" followed shortly by "Vol. I".

Identical Manifestations with Differing Catalogue Metadata, Control Numbers. Why not match same-work relationships by metadata, particularly by title and author? Currently, HathiTrust identifies duplicate manifestations in their holdings by grouping items by OCLC or institutional control numbers [12]. This metadata-based approach is also used by OCLC for their FRBR work matching algorithm, and later the GLIMIR project to allow fuzzier matching. It is effective but not complete, due to inconsistencies in practice and record completeness. A telling example was observed with *Writings of Samuel Richardson, vol. 19* (1902, *w1*), which includes *vol. 6* of the book *The History of Sir Charles Grandison (w1.1)*. The matching algorithm surfaced four volumes which manual review confirmed were identical, manifestations. However, between the four matches and the target text, there were four different titles, five different OCLC control numbers, and even variation in the volume numbering. Once the metadata was classified as *w1.1*, the other four times it was classified as *w1*, though with inconsistent titles.

HathiTrust Digital Library volumes are linked by the catalogue records from the contributing institution, and records are grouped together in the interface using OCLC numbers, roughly intended to keep identical manifestations together. Considering the coverage of catalogue records for our five identical volumes, only two records have complete coverage of their multi-volume set: *Writings of Samuel Richardson* (OCLC:12097044) and *The history of Sir Charles Grandison, Bart* (OCLC:6359966). *The novels of Samuel Richardson* (OCLC:3451879), *The novels* (OCLC:68137659), and *Writings of Samuel Richardson* (No OCLC) are incomplete.

Between just these five HathiTrust records, there are 126 scans of physically bound books, but limited ability to infer their relationships - perhaps guessable through title heuristics but otherwise requiring manual or automated content review.

Same Works with Itinerant Expressions. One complicated history seen in our evaluation was *The Life and Adventures of Robinson Crusoe*, by Daniel Defoe. This book has many small variants, non-canonical tweaks, and additions by publishers. It shows the breadth of how expressions may deviate beyond more common instances like editions, translations, and abridgements. This work was frequently adjusted by publishers who saw the story as more interesting to new readers than the style that Defoe wrote it in [13]. Consider these three observed variants on the opening line:

- About the year 1632, I was born in the ancient city of York, of respectable parents.
- I was born at York, in the year 1632, of a reputable family.
- I was born in the year 1632, in the city of York, of a good family, though not of that country, my father being a foreigner of Bremen, who settled first at Hull.

There are 1198 English-language manifestations of the first book listed in one bibliography [13], ranging in date from 1719 to 1979. After the first edition was published, publishers found "means to increase the size and price of Robinson Crusoe," [13] including adding images, new introductions, biographies, and information about Alexander Selkirk, a Scottish sailor who spent four years alone on Juan Fernandez Island. Abridgment was common practice for broadening the audience in *Robinson Crusoe*'s time, such as removing mention of cannibals or "leaving out the dull parts" [13, 14]. The copyright frequently changed hands, further exasperating the issue.

A case such as *Robinson Crusoe* illustrates some of the hurdles that content-based methods for identifying same-work relationships must overcome: an evolving and branching text. It also challenges assessment of representative expressions in LRM.

6 Conclusion

The scale and biases introduced by multi-institutional aggregations in large-scale DLs have prompted new consideration of same-work relationships, not only at the traditionally considered level of exact duplicates (i.e. same manifestation) but in tracking a work across different iterations or configurations. This type of alignment can improve traditional access and retrieval, as well as providing important evidence for improving metadata, correcting OCR, and mining history and culture in aggregate.

Conceptual models provide a language for thinking through these types of relationships, but the reality is complicated, as this paper shows through a selection of lucid examples. In future work, we are developing content-based methods to match relationships in large DLs, informed by the complex real relationships described in this paper. Where duplicates are usually identified by metadata, as with the HathiTrust [12], we aim to create a more thorough inventory of same-work relationships.

Same-work relationships are not exclusively useful to DLs. As cataloguing standards transition to FRBR-based Resource Description and Access (RDA), there is now the ability to encode higher-level relationships between works and expressions. Leveraging these new fields is difficult due to the effort required in identifying duplicate relationships, punctuated by the complexities discussed in this paper. As we produce data on the massive HathiTrust collection, it will be possible to align with other collections, aiding other libraries in meeting modern cataloguing standards.

Acknowledgements. This project is supported by IMLS grant #LG-86-18-0061-18.

References

1. "About". HathiTrust digital library. https://www.hathitrust.org/about. Accessed 6 Sept 2018
2. Xu, S., Smith, D.: Retrieving and combining repeated passages to improve OCR. In: Proceedings of the 17th ACM/IEEE Joint Conference on Digital Libraries, pp. 269–272. IEEE Press (2017)
3. Hillmann, D.I., Dushay, N., Phipps, J.: Improving metadata quality: augmentation and recombination (2004). http://hdl.handle.net/1813/7897
4. Bamman, D., Carney M., Gillick, J., Hennesy, C., Sridhar, V.: Estimating the date of first publication in a large-scale digital library. In: Proceedings of the 17th ACM/IEEE Joint Conference on Digital Libraries (JCDL 2017), pp. 149–158. IEEE Press, Piscataway (2017)
5. Schofield, A., Thompson, L., Mimno, D.: Quantifying the effects of text duplication on semantic models. In: Proceedings of the 2017 Conference on Empirical Methods in Natural Language Processing, pp. 2737–2747 (2017)
6. Riva, P., Le Boeuf, P., Žumer, M.: IFLA library reference model. International Federation of Library Associations (IFLA) (2017). https://www.ifla.org/files/assets/cataloguing/frbr-lrm/ifla-lrm-august-2017_rev201712.pdf
7. Bennett, R., Lavoie, B.F., O'Neill, E.T.: The concept of a work in WorldCat: an application of FRBR. Libr. Collect. Acquisitions Tech. Serv. **27**(1), 45–59 (2003). https://doi.org/10.1080/14649055.2003.10765895
8. Thornburg, G.: A candid look at collected works: challenges of clustering aggregates in GLIMIR and FRBR. Inf. Technol. Libr. **33**(3), 53–64 (2014). https://doi.org/10.6017/ital.v33i3.5377
9. Underwood, T., et al.: Word frequencies in English-Language Literature, 1700–1922 (0.2) [Dataset]. HathiTrust Research Center (2015). http://dx.doi.org/10.13012/J8JW8BSJ
10. Organisciak, P., Capitanu, B., Underwood, T., Downie, J.S.: Access to billions of pages for large-scale text analysis. In: iConference 2017 Proceedings, vol. 2, pp. 66–76 (2017). https://doi.org/10.9776/17014
11. Deerwester, S., Dumais, S.T., Furnas, G.W., Landauer, T.K., Harshman, R.: Indexing by latent semantic analysis. J. Am. Soc. Inform. Sci. **41**(6), 391–407 (1990)
12. HathiTrust Collection Committee. Discussion document: recommendations for handling duplicates in HathiTrust (2012). https://www.hathitrust.org/documents/hathitrust-collections-duplicates-report-201204.pdf
13. Lovett, R.W., Lovett, C.C.: Robinson Crusoe: a bibliographical checklist of English language editions (1719–1979) (No. 30). Greenwood Pub Group (1991)
14. Howell, J.: Eighteenth-century abridgements of Robinson Crusoe. Library **15**(3), 292–343 (2014). https://doi.org/10.1093/library/15.3.292

Social-Media Text Mining and Sentiment Analysis

Analyzing Sentiment and Themes in Fitness Influencers' Twitter Dialogue

Brooke Auxier[1]([✉]) [iD], Cody Buntain[2] [iD], and Jennifer Golbeck[1] [iD]

[1] University of Maryland, College Park, MD 20742, USA
bauxier@umd.edu
[2] SMaPP Lab, New York University, New York, USA

Abstract. Social media allows anyone to distribute content and build an audience. Natural language processing, sentiment analysis, and psycholinguistic text analysis have proven to be powerful tools for characterizing and classifying social media text. Furthermore, the combination of text and sentiment analysis have allowed researchers to identify influencers both by their structural roles and the content they produce. In this paper, we investigate fitness-oriented social media influencers. This research aims to understand how fitness influencers (N = 92) on Twitter speak to their audiences through thematic and sentiment analysis of their tweets (N = 273,868). Findings suggest sentiment and topics discussed vary between male and female health and fitness influencers on the platform. The analysis also determined no sentiment differences between self-identified fitness trainers/coaches and influencers who do not identify as such. The results have implications for personalization and recommendation algorithms that operate in this space.

Keywords: Social media · Sentiment analysis · Twitter · Fitness influencers

1 Introduction

The affordances of social media platforms allow ordinary individuals to share their experiences, expertise and content with a wide audience. Many of these individuals have become brand ambassadors for specific products or have branded themselves as experts in specific domains. There are several social media influencers in the health and fitness industry, and these influencers are active across social platforms like Twitter, Facebook, YouTube, and Instagram, just to name a few. In the health and fitness space, many fitness professionals (e.g. trainers, instructors, coaches) who are active on social media sites use the platforms to educate others about exercise science and nutrition, and motivate audiences to live healthier lifestyles. Many of these individuals brand themselves as experts in the industry by selling workout and nutrition plans, posting instructional videos and building a community around their programming. Others in this space align themselves with bigger brands in the industry (e.g. Nike, lululemon, Athleta) to serve as more traditional brand ambassadors. In this role, they promote the brand's image along with more tangible items like workout gear and programming. Some influencers mix these two models.

© Springer Nature Switzerland AG 2019
N. G. Taylor et al. (Eds.): iConference 2019, LNCS 11420, pp. 429–435, 2019.
https://doi.org/10.1007/978-3-030-15742-5_41

This research aims to understand how fitness influencers on Twitter speak to their audiences through thematic analysis and the use of natural language processing for topic and sentiment analysis. Understanding how influencers engage in this space is beneficial not only for marketers looking to connect with influencers, but it also benefits budding influencers in the health and fitness space. This work also has possible implications for program designers who may want to better understand the types of language used by popular fitness influencers to build products (e.g. a workout or health-related app) aimed at helping consumers reach their health and fitness goals.

Understanding the sentiment of the language used on social media is important in this industry. Past studies have shown the connection between language processing and motor activity—and research from [1] suggests that action verbs used in affirmative sentences triggered an automatic and significant response, measured by grip force, whereas there was no significant response observed in reaction to action words used in negative contexts. Other research focused on fitness centers found that when people perceived the space as caring and task-oriented, they had more positive experiences [2]. The importance of language use and audience perception of fitness experts may translate to online spaces where influencers are promoting health and fitness initiatives.

These findings from past studies are important, since obesity, poor diet, and lack of exercise are major health risks facing the United States today [3]. At the same time, the population is increasingly turning to online social platforms for advice and information across numerous aspects of their lives, such as fashion, news, and fitness [4]. The confluence of obesity-related health issues and influence of online celebrities and may yield new opportunities for social good if an influential online personality can motivate his or her followers to adopt a healthier lifestyle. These findings could also be utilized in the development of interactive fitness personas on mobile applications, websites and smart technology workout equipment that could impact public perceptions of exercise. Understanding how influential fitness-related personalities engage with their audience is a first step towards these goal.

2   Related Work

To establish themselves on social media, influencers engage in self-branding, which involves the development of a distinctive public image for the purposes of commercial or cultural gain [5]. To succeed in the crowded social media environment, they must also use the affordances of social media platforms to build an audience (e.g. gain followers).

Though some influencers focus on building their own personal brands from the bottom-up, other influencers are closely connected to a specific already-existing (e.g. Tiffany Haddish and Groupon) brand. In both cases, the goal is often to make oneself synonymous with that brand [5]. In these business partnerships, social media influencers (or SMIs) are expected to promote (e.g. via post, tweet, blog) the brands and products they represent. In social media spaces, these are known as sponsored posts, branded content or advertisements.

However, problems, specifically related to authenticity arise when these relationships form. Work by [6] suggests that followers of SMIs value the authentic and noncommercial nature of these individuals. But of course, SMIs gain both financial and social capital when these partnerships form, so these relationships are sought after. When SMIs post content promoting a product, they often include signals of authenticity [6]: (1) showing intrinsic satisfaction in producing and sharing the posts (e.g. using exclamation points, emoji, capital words); (2) sharing emotions triggered (e.g. using verbs and nouns expressing positive emotion and enthusiasm); (3) showing a fit between oneself and the product or brand represented (e.g. incorporates elements related to interests and personal taste); (4) offering fact-based opinions about the product or service (e.g. offering objective information about the brand). When the authenticity of the personal brand gets threatened, SMIs attempt to manage that erosion [6] through passion (e.g. choosing brands that align with personal image, allow for creativity and self-expression and guarantee a mutually beneficial relationship) and transparency (e.g. disclosing partnerships, offering objective evaluations of products and services). If SMIs are successful at partnering with brands, remaining authentic and building audiences, they have the potential to play a key role on behalf of brands.

Social media influencers are important in the marketing and public relations space because of their unique ability to persuade audiences [7]. Some work suggests that these social media personalities are indeed influential, even when examined next to more traditionally-influential individuals, like CEOs. In a study [7] that examined participant ($N = 32$) perceptions of influencers based off of fact sheets, a photos and a video, the researchers found that SMIs were perceived as smart, ambitious, productive, poised, power-oriented, candid and dependable—the same attributes assigned to CEOs in a similar study [8]. The characteristics ranked as least related to SMIs were self-pitying, indecisive, easily frustrated, self-defeating and lacking meaning in life. These findings suggest that SMI are indeed highly regarded by individuals and are perceived as having similar attributes as CEOs, who are seen as having credibility and influence.

Social media influencers are core players in the marketing and branding of many health- and fitness-related programs, products and initiatives, which makes this examination of their language and use of Twitter an strong addition to the literature in this space.

RQ1: What major content themes appear in the Twitter accounts of fitness influencers?

RQ2: What kind of language (positive, negative, neutral) do fitness influencers use in online spaces? Does sentiment vary between male and female account-holders, and between types of influencers (e.g. trainers and coaches, general fitness accounts)?

3 Methods

To build a list of social media influencers in the online health and fitness industry, we started with a list of top 10 fitness influencers from [9]. To get more influencers to analyze, we used Twitter's search function and used keywords "fitness," "fitness coach," "fit," "health & fitness," "fitness expert," "workout," "yoga," "running," "strength training," "personal trainer," "weight loss," "fitness instructor," "fitness influencer," "fitness pro" to find accounts associated with these keywords. We limited our sample to individual influencers (as opposed to brands) who have over 10K followers. After all 92 influencers were gathered, their profiles were analyzed in order to determine their self-identifying gender. There are several studies that examine how males and females use language differently [10, 11], which is why it was explored among this sample. Their self-identifying role in the fitness community (e.g. coach, trainer, nutritionist) was also determined. Then, the content of their tweets (N = 273,868) was analyzed to establish some "themes" common across the accounts (e.g. motivational, informational, promotional, self-disclosure, etc.).

Six content themes were identified via grounded theory-based inductive analysis and are defined as follows:

- *Motivational:* Inspirational quotes, supportive messages.
- *Informational:* Instructional workout videos; information about exercise science and/or nutrition.
- *Promotional:* Promoting programs, plans, classes; product and brand endorsements; linking to personal website; promoting television appearances or features on other Twitter accounts.
- *Self-disclosure:* Talking about personal life including family and travel.
- *Physique photos:* Images of account holder's progress and/or physique.
- *Sports-related content:* Information and links to sports-related content (e.g. golf, boxing, UFC, MMA).

These content themes were established by examining the Twitter profiles of the influencers, along with the text in their tweets. These themes capture the general "feel" of each account and describe the main category of content featured on each account. They serve to place accounts into generalized themes, though these themes do not explore sentiment of language. Each account was labeled with at least one content theme, though some accounts were labeled with up to three themes.

In addition to exploring content themes, sentiment of tweet text was explored. Extracting sentiment, or positive-versus-negative attitude, from text is a common text mining task, but this task can be heavily influenced by the context in which the text appears. For instance, journalistic style one may find in newspapers or movie reviews (where much of the sentiment analysis training data was originally sourced) differs widely from the highly colloquial and abbreviated text one may find in length-constrained social media platforms like Twitter.

To account for these differences, we use the VADER sentiment analysis package, as it is designed for social media data and integrates emoticons into its sentiment scoring [12]. VADER returns several sentiment scores for positive, negative, neutral, and compound sentiment, where compound sentiment is a weighted average of the positive, negative, and neutral scores and is in the range $[-1, +1]$, where -1 represents the most negative and $+1$ the most positive sentiment. We applied several text analysis techniques to extract insights about the content and tone of the influencers' tweets.

The psycholinguistic text analysis tool LIWC [13] was used to analyze the types of words used in the tweet text itself, which goes far beyond the generalized analysis captured in the content themes established earlier. We used the following categories that we identified as fitness-related:

- "sexual" - related to sexuality (e.g. "butt", "hugs", "sexy")
- "health" - related to health and illness (e.g. "digest", "sick", "heal")
- "body" - related to the body (e.g. "abs", "naked", "foot")
- "ingest" - related to ingesting (e.g. "meal", "starving", "water")
- "work" - related to personal concerns of work (e.g. "fired", "overtime", "vita")
- "achieve" - related to achievement as a core drive and need (e.g. "master", "best", "quit").

4 Findings

In analyzing accounts for content theme, we found that the majority of accounts were promotional in nature (58 accounts were labeled with this theme). The next most common themes among the accounts were informational (35) and motivational (32). The other themes appeared with lower prominence: self-disclosure (24), sports-related (15) and physique photos (10).

Sentiment of tweet text was also explored. Results from a one-sided t-test suggest that while there is no statistically significant difference in the negative sentiment used in tweets between male and female influencers, female influencers' tweets ($M = 0.17$, $SD = 0.06$) contain more positive sentiment than male influencers' tweets ($M = 0.14$, $SD = 0.05$); $t(90) = 2.4$, $p < 0.01$. Our data also suggests that there is no statistical significance in the amount of positive or negative sentiment used between those who self-identify as being a fitness "trainer" or "coach" compared to general fitness accounts or influencers who identify closely with one type of exercise like yoga, Pilates or running.

In addition to sentiment, we explored several variables we identified as being related to the health and fitness industry in LIWC (e.g. "sexual," "health," "body," "ingest," "work," "achieve") and explored the differences in discourse between accounts.

When exploring variance between influencer attributes and the discourse used, there was no statistically significant difference between influencers self-identifying as fitness "trainers" or "coaches" and other account types. Differences do exist, however, between male and female influencers. Between male and female-held accounts, there was a statistically significant difference in the use of words related to "sexual, "work" and "achieve." When examining the variable "sexual," female influencers ($M = 0.54$, $SD = 0.33$) used related words more often than male influencers ($M = 0.28$, $SD = 0.18$); $t(86) = 4.54$, $p < 0.01$. Concerning the term "work," male influencers ($M = 1.78$, $SD = 0.68$) were more likely to use related terms than female influencers ($M = 1.41$, $SD = 0.49$); $t(63) = -2.86$, p < 0.001. Male influencers ($M = 2.55$, $SD = 1.03$) were also more likely to use terms related to "achievement" than female influencers ($M = 2.04$, $SD = 0.78$); $t(65) = -2.57$, $p = 0.01$.

5 Discussion

This analysis suggests that there is no one-size-fits all when it comes to successfully influencing audiences on Twitter regarding health and fitness. Our findings suggest that female influencers use more words associated with sexual, like "butt", "hugs", and "sexy." Female influencers also employ more positive sentiment then their male influencer counterparts. Male influencers, however, use more words associated with personal concerns of work and achievement as a core need. These findings fall seemingly in-line with normative gender expectations in Western culture. Our findings also suggest that there is no difference in the use of positive or negative sentiment between those who identify themselves as fitness trainers or coaches and those who do not identify themselves as such. One might assume that the trainers and coaches may tap into their role as a strict, disciplinary leader, rather than a comforting and uplifting one, but this doesn't appear to be the case. Perhaps the use of neutral language helps these online trainers and coaches, who often sell, or simply offer, fitness and/or nutrition programs to their online audiences, appeal to a larger and wider audience online.

6 Limitations and Future Work

This work is not without its limitations. Our set of fitness influencers was limited to 92 and could be expanded to include more influencers. We started with a batch of 100, but 8 were removed for a lack of focus on fitness and health content, or were removed from analysis because the account had been suspended or deleted. Additionally, in order to identify the gender of the account-holder, we simply looked at the account photo and used other photos and tweet content to assign gender to each account, which is a limitation of the classification. Ideally, we would have been able to ask account-holders about the gender they identify with. In regard to sampling, we also recognize that health and fitness influencers engage on other platforms aside from Twitter, so future research could be expanded to include other platforms, or look at cross-platform behavior.

However, this work is potentially useful to scientists, researchers and practitioners in multiple industries. The findings from this Twitter sentiment analysis could help computer scientists create classification systems or algorithms that would detect fitness influencers on the platform, especially those who identify as coaches and trainers. Such a classification system could be used to aggregate top fitness coaches on Twitter, which could be used to feed a recommender system or similar automated entity. This research could also be built upon by researchers who are hoping to better understand how central social media users deploy language on social media, and Twitter specifically. This method could be applied to influencers or central nodes in a variety of industries, across social media platforms. These findings could also have implications for budding fitness influencers looking to gain social capital in the industry. This information could also be potentially helpful to designers of online fitness programs and applications, who may be particularly mindful of the language and sentiment used to motivate consumers to attain health and fitness goals.

References

1. Aravena, P., et al.: Grip force reveals the context sensitivity of language-induced motor activity during "action words" processing: evidence from sentential negation. Plos One **7**(12), e50287 (2012)
2. Brown, T., Fry, M.: Helping members commit to exercise: specific strategies to impact the climate at fitness centers. J. Sport Psychol. Action **2**(2), 70–80 (2011)
3. Center for Disease Control: "At a glance 2016: Nutrition, physical activity, and obesity" [Report]. Centers for Disease Control and Prevention National Center for Chronic Disease Prevention and Health Promotion (2016)
4. Smith, A., Anderson, M.: Social media use in 2018. Pew Research Center. http://www.pewinternet.org/2018/03/01/social-media-use-in-2018/
5. Khamis, S., Ang, L., Welling, R.: Mastering the brand: how an 'ordinary' cook achieved extraordinary cook book success. TEXT J. Writ. Writ. Courses **24**, 1–8 (2013)
6. Audrezet, A., De Kerviler, G., Moulard, J.G.: Authenticity under threat: when social media influencers need to go beyond self-presentation. J. Bus. Res. (2018). https://doi.org/10.1016/j.jbusres.2018.07.008
7. Freberg, K., Graham, K., McGaughey, K., Freberg, L.: Who are the social media influencers? A study of public perceptions of personality. Public Relat. Rev. **37**(1), 90–92 (2011). https://doi.org/10.1016/j.pubrev.2010.11.001
8. Freberg, K., Graham, K., McGaughey, K., Freberg, L.: Leaders or snakes in suits: public perceptions of today's CEO. In: Poster Presented at 22nd Annual Convention of the Association for Psychological Science, Boston, MA (2010)
9. n/a, Top influencers fitness, Forbes. https://www.forbes.com/top-influencers/fitness/#287f77df690e. Accessed 5 Aug 2018
10. Newman, M.L., Groom, C.J., Handelman, L.D., Pennebaker, J.W.: Gender differences in language use: an analysis of 14,000 text samples. Discourse Process. **45**, 211–236 (2008)
11. Schwartz, H.A., et al.: Personality, gender, and age in the language of social media: the open-vocabulary approach. Plos One **8**, e73791 (2013)
12. Hutto, C.J., Gilbert, E.: Vader: a parsimonious rule-based model for sentiment analysis of social media text. In: Eighth International AAAI Conference on Weblogs and Social Media, pp. 216–225 (2014)
13. Tausczik, Y.R., Pennebaker, J.W.: The psychological meaning of words: LIWC and computerized text analysis methods. J. Lang. Soc. Psychol. **29**(1), 24–54 (2010)

Spatiotemporal Analysis on Sentiments and Retweet Patterns of Tweets for Disasters

Sijing Chen⦿, Jin Mao⁽⊠⁾⦿, and Gang Li

Wuhan University, Wuhan 430071, Hubei, China
{csjl6912,maojin,ligang}@whu.edu.cn

Abstract. Twitter provides an important channel for public to share feelings, attitudes and concerns about disasters. In this study, we aim to explore how spatiotemporal factors affect people's sentiment in disaster situations and how the area type, time stage and sentiment of the tweets affect the extent and speed of tweets' diffusion. After analyzing 531,912 geo-tagged tweets about Hurricane Harvey, we found that on-site tweets are more positive than off-site tweets across the time; neutral tweets spread broader and faster than tweets with sentiment propensity; on-site tweets and tweets posted at early stages tend to be more popular. These findings could enable authorities and response organizations to better comprehend people's feelings and behaviors in social media and their changes over time and space. In future, we will analyze the influence of the interactions among sentiment, location and time to retweet patterns.

Keywords: Disaster · Sentiment analysis · Retweet pattern

1 Introduction

Social media (e.g., Twitter) has become an important alternative information channel to traditional media during emergencies and disasters [1, 2]. Individuals and communities have used social media for many purposes from updating situation to expressing financial or emotional support [2]. The Federal Emergency Management Agency (FEMA) in United States has regarded social media as an indispensable tool for emergency management [3]. Sentiment analysis of disaster-related posts in social media provides a semantic abstract of situation awareness, which could help better understand the dynamics of disasters, including users' feelings, attitudes and concerns. Although there have been several studies on sentiment analysis of disaster-related posts, how sentiment expressions about disasters vary from spatial areas and time still needs more explorations.

Retweet is the core mechanism for information diffusion in Twitter [4]. Previous studies have shown that various factors could affect retweet patterns. For example, Suh et al. [5] found that content factors like the inclusion of hashtags or URLs has positive influences on retweet frequencies. Users who act as amplifiers or information starters are likely to acquire more retweets [6]. Additionally, Zhang et al. [7] found that the degree of activity and the popularity of the author shorten the response time, and so does the involvement of emotional expressions. Neppalli et al. [8] reveals that tweets with low divergence of sentiment are prone to be retweeted during the hurricane.

© Springer Nature Switzerland AG 2019
N. G. Taylor et al. (Eds.): iConference 2019, LNCS 11420, pp. 436–443, 2019.
https://doi.org/10.1007/978-3-030-15742-5_42

However, the relationship between sentiment polarity and retweet patterns and how they change over time and space has not been explored.

In this study, we focus on analyzing the sentiment property of tweets and its influence to retweet pattern in a spatiotemporal manner. A case about Hurricane Harvey on Twitter was investigated. The findings of this study would enable authorities and response organizations to better comprehend people's feelings and behaviors and then develop local region insights of decision making at disaster management.

2 Methods

2.1 Dataset

The Hurricane Harvey Twitter Dataset [9] provided by University of North Texas Libraries was used in the study. The dataset contains 7,041,866 tweets captured between Aug. 18, 2017 and Sept. 22, 2017. Tweets in English were selected in this study, accounting for 93.9% of the dataset.

2.2 Data Processing

Hyperlinks and symbols, such as "RT@xxx", "@xxx", "#xxx", were removed from the text of all tweets. The string pattern of "RT@xxx" in twitter messages was applied to identify retweet relationships. All the uppercase letters were converted into lowercase characters. Plural words were converted to singular words. NLTK 3.2.5 was adopted to perform the preprocessing.

2.3 Location Classification

Raw data was filtered to include only those messages with location information. Since only a minority (about 1.25%) of tweets in the dataset are geo-tagged by Twitter, we attempt to extract additional information from self-reported data in users' personal profiles, assuming that the self-reported location reflects the geographic area he or she belongs to or cares about [10]. We did not use the location-specific text within twitter messages to avoid ambiguity of dealing with the context of such in-text location mentions [10]. An additional 39% of tweets were assigned with location information, resulting in circa 2,697,000 geo-tagged tweets.

We further classified geographic regions into two categories, disaster-affected areas and disaster-unaffected areas. Reports of Disaster Declaration about Hurricane Harvey issued by FEMA [11, 12] were referred to for defining the affected areas. Users who produced at least one geo-tagged tweet within the defined affected areas and whose self-report location refers to these areas were designated as on-site users. A user's self-report location may contain several addresses, for example, "Houston, TX/Edloe Island, SL". To avoid such conflicts when classifying users, we assumed that once a user's self-report location contains an address in the affected areas, the user should be classified as an on-site user. All tweets in the dataset produced by on-site users, including those non-geocoded tweets, were categorized into on-site tweets. The users that were not affected were designated as off-site users and their tweets were classified into off-site tweets. The location classification methodology was tested on 52,649 tweets geo-tagged by Twitter and obtained an accuracy of 94.66%.

2.4 Time Slicing

To disclose the spatiotemporal characteristics on the sentiment of the tweets, we divided the time span of the dataset into four stages, including before-disaster (Aug 18–25), during-disaster (Aug 26–Sept 1), short-after-disaster (Sept 2–8), and long-after-disaster (Sept 9–22). The period division was based on the knowledge of socio-behavioral phenomena with respect to different phases of disaster events [13, 14].

2.5 Sentiment Classification

For sentiment analysis, retweets were firstly filtered and only original tweets (about 531,912) were analyzed in that retweets are not recognized as reflecting personal opinions [15]. The SentiStrength algorithm [16] was used for the sentiment analysis in this study. Designed for short informal text with emoticon, abbreviations and slang, this algorithm has been tested on Twitter texts, showing better performance than a few baselines [17]. We used the SentiStrength tool [18] to classify the sentiment polarities of the original tweets and assign them with sentiment scores within the range [−4, 4]. A score of 4 indicates the highest positive sentiment, −4 the lowest negative sentiment and 0 the neutral sentiment.

3 Results

3.1 Sentiment Polarities in the Affected vs. Unaffected Areas Across the Four Stages

The result of sentiment labeling for the tweets of the affected and unaffected areas across the four stages is shown in Fig. 1. For both affected and unaffected areas, it's observed that neutral tweets accounts for the most, and positive tweets are more than negative tweets in all the stages of the disaster. Compared with unaffected areas, affected areas have more positive tweets and less negative tweets in terms of percentages. From the lens of time, we found that the number of positive tweets reached the highest shortly after the disaster in affected areas, while the number of negative tweets reached the peak during the disaster in unaffected areas.

We conducted a two-way ANOVA, with the sentiment score as the dependent variable. Significant main effects of both area type and time stage on sentiment ($p < 0.001$) were observed. The interaction effect on sentiment is also significant ($p < 0.001$). Figure 2 shows that the average sentiment score of on-site tweets is higher than that of off-site tweets across the time. In affected area, the average sentiment score of short-after-disaster tweets is the highest. While in unaffected area, the average sentiment score of during-disaster tweets is the lowest.

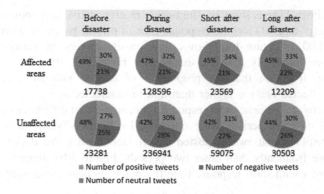

Fig. 1. The distribution of tweets with different sentiment polarities

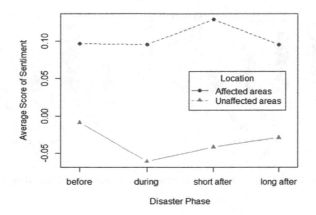

Fig. 2. Average scores of the sentiment

3.2 Retweet Patterns Influenced by Sentiment, Location and Time

We measured retweet patterns by the two aspects of frequency and speed. Retweet frequency refers to the quantity of retweets a tweet triggers. Retweet speed is measured by the response time between the original tweet and the first retweet [19]. We thus investigated on how retweet patterns are influenced by the sentiment of tweets, different areas and the four stages of the hurricane.

Kruskal-Wallis tests suggest significant difference among sentiment polarities with respect to both retweet frequency ($p < 0.001$) and response time ($p < 0.001$). Figure 3 (a) details the difference. It shows that there is a larger proportion of neutral tweets than that of negative tweets at each level of retweet frequencies, and negative tweets are more than positive tweets at the middle level and low levels of retweeting frequencies (RT <= 2000). Interestingly, positive tweets have the highest proportion at the level of high retweeting (RT > 2000). Figure 3(b) presents that, tweets with short response time (t <= 1 h) are more than expected to have neutral and negative sentiment and less than expected to have positive sentiment.

Mann-Whitney U tests show on-site tweets receive statistically more retweets than off-site tweets (p < 0.001) and the response time of on-site tweets is short than off-site tweets (p < 0.001). Figure 4(a) shows that on-site tweets in general have been retweeted more frequently than off-site tweets. From Fig. 4(b), the distribution of response time, it's seen that the proportion of tweets with short response time (t <= 1 h) in affected areas is higher than that in unaffected areas.

For both retweet frequency and response time, significant differences among tweets posted during different periods were observed by Kruskal-Wallis tests (p < 0.001). Figure 5(a) displays that tweets posted before and during the disaster have been retweeted more frequently than other two periods. Figure 5(b) suggests that the proportion of tweets with short response time (t <= 1 h) is decreasing over time.

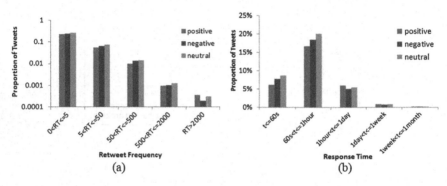

Fig. 3. The distribution of retweet frequency and retweet speed across type of polarity

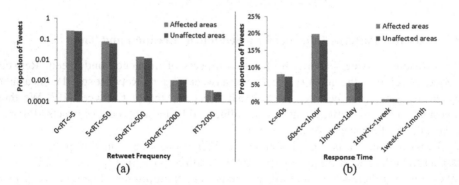

Fig. 4. The distribution of retweet frequency and retweet speed across type of location

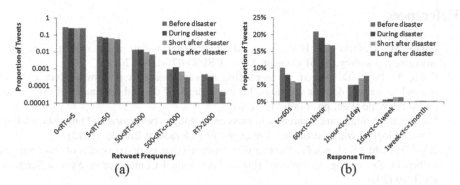

Fig. 5. The distribution of retweet frequency and retweet speed across type of period

4 Discussion and Conclusion

This paper presents exploratory results on how area type and time stage could affect people's sentiment expressed in disaster-related tweets and how area type, time stage and sentiment polarity could affect retweet patterns. The results suggested that on-site tweets are more positive than off-site tweets across the time, which could be explained by people's positive attempt to self-calm and raise confidence about their coping with the threat [20]. By analyzing the relationship between disaster-related tweets' sentiment and their redistribution, we found that tweets with neutral polarity spread significantly broader and faster than tweets with negative polarity, and negative tweets spread slightly broader and faster than positive tweets. This finding is different from previous research [21], which might due to the difference in types of data. Our work focused on disasters, whereas the dataset used by Stieglitz et al. [21] was about political elections. By comparing the retweet patterns of on-site tweets and off-site tweets, we found that on-site tweets spread faster and broader than off-site tweets, which consists with previous studies [22]. By comparing the retweet pattern across time stage, we found that tweets posted before and during the disaster have been retweeted more frequently and quickly than tweets after the disaster. The result indicates that the diffusion of information declines over time [23].

This exploratory study provides some initial insight into the relationship between sentiment and information diffusion, and may have implications for authorities and response organizations to better comprehend people's feelings and behaviors in social media and their changes over time and space. In future, we will analyze the influence of the interactions among sentiment, location and time to retweet patterns, which would give us a more holistic view about retweet patterns under disaster situations.

Acknowledgements. The paper is supported by the National Natural Science Foundation of China (No. 71790612, No. 71804135 and No. 71603189).

References

1. Imran, M., Castillo, C., Diaz, F., et al.: Processing social media messages in mass emergency: a survey. ACM Comput. Surv. (CSUR) **47**(4), 67 (2015)
2. Cobo, A., Parra, D., Navón, J.: Identifying relevant messages in a twitter-based citizen channel for natural disaster situations. In: Proceedings of the 24th International Conference on World Wide Web, pp. 1189–1194 (2015)
3. Vieweg, S.E.: Situational awareness in mass emergency: a behavioral and linguistic analysis of microblogged communications. University of Colorado at Boulder (2012)
4. Boyd D., Golder S., Lotan G.: Tweet, tweet, retweet: conversational aspects of retweeting on twitter. In: Proceedings of the 43rd Hawaii International Conference on System Sciences, pp. 1–10 (2010)
5. Suh, B., Hong, L., Pirolli, P., Chi, E.H.: Want to be retweeted? Large scale analytics on factors impacting retweet in twitter network. In: Proceedings of IEEE Second International Conference on Social Computing, pp. 177–184 (2010)
6. Pervin, N., Takeda, H., Toriumi, F.: Factors affecting retweetability: an event-centric analysis on Twitter. In: Proceedings of Thirty Fifth International Conference on Information Systems, pp. 1–10 (2014)
7. Zhang, L., Xu, L., Zhang, W.: Social media as amplification station: factors that influence the speed of online public response to health emergencies. Asian J. Commun. **27**(3), 322–338 (2017)
8. Neppalli, V.K., Caragea, C., Squicciarini, A., et al.: Sentiment analysis during Hurricane Sandy in emergency response. Int. J. Disaster Risk Reduct. **21**, 213–222 (2017)
9. Phillips, M.E.: Hurricane Harvey Twitter Dataset. https://digital.library.unt.edu/ark:/67531/metadc993940/. Accessed 22 Nov 2017
10. Kryvasheyeu, Y., Chen, H., Moro, E., et al.: Performance of social network sensors during Hurricane Sandy. PLoS ONE **10**(2), e117288 (2015)
11. Texas Hurricane Harvey (DR-4332). https://www.fema.gov/disaster/4332. Accessed 5 Mar 2018
12. Louisiana Tropical Storm Harvey (DR-4345). https://www.fema.gov/disaster/4345. Accessed 5 Mar 2018
13. Powell, J.W.: An introduction to the natural history of disaster. University of Maryland: Disaster Research Project (1954)
14. Kogan, M., Palen, L., Anderson, K.M.: Think local, retweet global: retweeting by the geographically-vulnerable during Hurricane Sandy. In: Proceedings of the 18th ACM Conference on Computer Supported Cooperative Work and Social Computing, pp. 981–993 (2015)
15. Ozturk, N., Ayvaz, S.: Sentiment analysis on Twitter: a text mining approach to the Syrian refugee crisis. Telemat. Inform. **35**(1), 136–147 (2018)
16. Thelwall, M., Buckley, K., Paltoglou, G., et al.: Sentiment strength detection in short informal text. J. Am. Soc. Inform. Sci. Technol. **61**(12), 2544–2558 (2010)
17. Thelwall, M., Buckley, K., Paltoglou, G., et al.: Sentiment in Twitter events. J. Am. Soc. Inf. Sci. Technol. **63**(1), 163–173 (2012)
18. SentiStrength. http://sentistrength.wlv.ac.uk/. Accessed 20 Mar 2018
19. Tsugawa, S., Ohsaki, H.: Negative messages spread rapidly and widely on social media. In: Proceedings of the 2015 ACM on Conference on Online Social Networks, pp. 151–160 (2015)

20. Gaspar, R., Pedro, C., Panagiotopoulos, P., et al.: Beyond positive or negative: qualitative sentiment analysis of social media reactions to unexpected stressful events. Comput. Hum. Behav. **56**, 179–191 (2016)
21. Stieglitz, S., Dang-Xuan, L.: Emotions and information diffusion in social media—sentiment of microblogs and sharing behavior. J. Manag. Inf. Syst. **29**(4), 217–248 (2013)
22. Kryvasheyeu, Y., Chen, H., Obradovich, N., et al.: Rapid assessment of disaster damage using social media activity. Sci. Adv. **2**(3), e1500779 (2016)
23. Yoo, E., Rand, W., Eftekhar, M., et al.: Evaluating information diffusion speed and its determinants in social media networks during humanitarian crises. J. Oper. Manag. **45**, 123–133 (2016)

Impact of Reddit Discussions on Use or Abandonment of Wearables

Radhika Garg[1]([✉]) and Jenna Kim[2]

[1] School of Information Studies, Syracuse University, Syracuse, USA
rgarg01@syr.edu
[2] School of Information Sciences, University of Illinois at Urbana-Champaign,
Urbana-Champaign, USA
jkim682@illinois.edu

Abstract. Discussion platform, Reddit, is the third most visited website in the US. People can post their questions on this platform to get varying opinions from fellow users, which in turn might also influence their behavior and choices. Wearables are becoming widely adopted, yet challenges persist in their effective long term use because of technical and device related, or personal issues. Therefore, by employing sentiment analysis, this paper aims to analyze how decisions of use or abandonment of wearables are influenced by discussions on Reddit. The results are based on the analysis of 6680 posts and their associated 50,867 comments posted between December 2015 – December 2017 on the subreddit (user created groups) on android wear. Our results show that sentiment of the discussion is majorly dictated by the sentiment of the post itself, and people decide to continue using their devices when fellow Redditors offer them workarounds, or the discussion receives majority of positive or fact-driven neutral comments.

Keywords: Reddit · Sentiment analysis · (Non-)use of technology

1 Introduction

Companies nowadays often use social media as a marketing tool to engage customers and promote their products and services [6]. Users/customers also post their opinion on social media with the belief that they can influence public viewpoint and businesses. Participants in our preliminary survey-based study also pointed that social opinion influences their decision to use such devices or abandon them [5]. Therefore, this paper explores how people use social platform of Reddit to make decisions regarding continued use or abandonment of wearables such as smart watches and activity trackers.

Reddit is an online social system with attributes of a forum. It comprises of several user created and controlled subreddits, which are topical forums for content. Users of Reddit, frequently referred to as Redditors, can interact in these

---

J. Kim—All the work was done during author's affiliation with Syracuse University.

© Springer Nature Switzerland AG 2019
N. G. Taylor et al. (Eds.): iConference 2019, LNCS 11420, pp. 444–455, 2019.
https://doi.org/10.1007/978-3-030-15742-5_43

subreddits either by creating a self-post, or by commenting on the existing posts. The comments help sustain discussions on various subtopics initiated through posts. We chose to explore our research questions through discussions on subreddit of r/androidwear because (1) the user community of smart devices on r/androidwear is very active, specifically on the topic of device use and adoption due to the dwindling popularity and sales of android wear, and (2) all postings, comments, and other meta data about users and their postings are publicly available.

While researchers have explored the sentiment aspect of product reviews (e.g., [16]), social media posts (e.g., [12]), and blogs (e.g., [9]), the role of discussions' sentiments on the decision-making process of using or not-using the devices have not been studied thus far. Our work aims to fill this gap by analyzing the sentiment of 6680 posts and corresponding 50,867 comments posted from December 2015 to December 2017 on r/androidwear. We found that majority of comments to positive posts also had a positive sentiment, negative posts had more neutral comments, and neutral posts had more positive comments. Further, the final decision of the person, who started the post, regarding continued use or abandonment of the device was dictated by the sentiment that was associated with the majority of the comments in the discussion thread. For example, if a Redditor started a discussion with a negative post owing to his/her frustrations of using a devices, but then received majority of positive or neutral (fact driven) comments, he continued to use his/her device due to the advise and workarounds offered to him in the discussion. Further methodological details and results will be discussed in the sections that follow.

2   Related Work

Our work is related to two broad streams of research: Technology (non-)use and sentiment analysis of social media's content. Therefore, first, we review literature that concentrates on exploring decisions of use or abandonment of wearables. Second, we review literature on sentiment analysis of social media's content that unpacks how sentiment analysis has been used to analyze users' opinions and decisions.

2.1   Use or Non-use of Technology

Studies exploring use or non-use a technology focus on understanding the process and choices current users of any technology make to either continue using the technology or abandon it. Previous studies have employed observations, interviews, and surveys to understand the users' practices of continued use and the challenges users experience while using smart devices such as activity trackers and/or wearables [4,5,8,17]. For example, survey-based study [5] found that increased control in daily activities, and competitive edge among peers and friends led people to continue using smart devices. Another study done with 26 participants, who were given physical activity trackers for 6 weeks, found that there are gender differences in use and adoption of wearable devices [17]. 65% of the participants stopped their devices within two weeks, because they felt device was very obtrusive and it was too difficult to manage and integrate data across multiple devices. In summary, existing research focuses mostly on the technical- or device-related challenges for long-term use. However, such studies are limited in terms of number of people who can be studied, and are based mostly on self-reported data from the participants who were using the devices only for the purpose of the study. In fact, researchers (e.g., [15]) have pointed out that behavior change is not just a possible outcome of using an individual technology, but is something that is achieved by people, potentially across various technologies that they interweave.

Additionally, previous research has shown that sentiment of online discussion forums or social media can be used to understand and predict public opinion [10], including that of technology use [5]. But, how people use platforms like Reddit to discuss their technology use, and how discussions on platform influence users' decision of technology (non-)use has not been studied so far.

2.2 Sentiment Analysis of Social Media's Content

Researchers in the past have studied how sentiment of the posts, tweets, and reviews affect the discussion, retweets, and emotional state or opinions of the participants. For example, [18] found that emotionally charged Twitter messages tend to be retweeted more often and more quickly compared to neutral ones. Another study on emotional contagion in social media highlighted the presence of a linear relationship between the average emotional valence of the stimuli users are exposed to, and that of the responses they produce [3]. A study on online health support groups, found that negative messages attracted a larger number of comments to reinforce positivity [19]. Finally, [16] concluded that consumer reviews with neutral polarity in the text are perceived to be more helpful. However, influence of posts' and comments' sentiment on the discussion that occurs on Reddit has not been yet investigated.

Therefore, motivated by these open issues our work is driven by two Research Questions (RQ). **RQ1:** Does the sentiment of posts influence the sentiment of following discussion? **RQ2:** What is the role of sentiment in influencing the decision of use or non-use of new technologies?

3   Sentiment Analysis

There are large number of models that have utilized machine learning to perform sentiment analysis across different domains such as product reviews, online health support, and twitter discussions. However, as users might use different words to express sentiment in different domains, sentiment analysis models developed for one domain can not necessarily be used for other domains [13]. Therefore, the following sections describe the method and results of supervised sentiment analysis model that we developed for the context of discussions on Reddit.

3.1   Dataset

r/androidwear gained popularity in December 2015 and has currently 44,866 Redditors or subscribers. We obtained comments and posts from December 2015 to December 2017 in r/androidwear from a public Reddit comment dataset [1] that also contains meta information such as ID of the author, date of comment, position in discussion thread. The information was retrieved using SQL commands on Google BigQuery[1], which is Google's low cost enterprise data warehouse.

We first retrieved all the posts (13,037) and the comments in response to each post between December 2015 and December 2017. Thereafter, we observed that there were few posts in the corpus that were related to troubleshooting steps or updates that Android released during that time period. In other words in this subreddit people not only share their opinion regarding android wear but also use this platform for troubleshooting any technical difficulties they face while using their devices.

Few examples of such posts are: "The preview of my watch, a Moto 360 V1 Silver, has disappeared from the blue space of the app..Any thoughts?", "good news for the Chinese Android wear users, soon they will have access to Google service, like play store..", and "I was wondering if you guys get perfect smooth scrolling through the menus or do you get a few jitters while doing it with the Huawei Watch?" Therefore such posts were removed from the corpus before conducting sentiment analysis. In the end approximately half of the posts (6680), with an average sentence per post of 8.01, contained opinions.

These 6680 posts and all the their corresponding 50,867 comments (average sentence per comment 2.86) were included in the analysis. Our final dataset included contribution from 27,136 Redditors. We preprocessed the screened data using NLTK library [2] as follows:

- Unwanted hyperlinks and html tags embedded in the comments were removed
- Unwanted characters, punctuations, numbers, e.g., 8n9lnxr, zw1, -, comma (,), and others were cleaned.
- Text was converted to lowercase and stemming was done to reduce words to their stem.
- Stop words were removed, excluding negation words such as not, never, or no.

3.2   Training Dataset

Our sentiment analysis model uses a supervised machine learning algorithm. Therefore, the first step involved creating manually labeled data. To this end, random 1026 posts and their corresponding comments were chosen from our dataset. To classify the training data set, first, both authors individually labelled each message into positive, negative, or neutral class. Then the authors worked together discussing and assigning final label (or class) to each message (posts and comments), with a Cohen's Kappa of 0.90.

---

[1] https://cloud.google.com/bigquery/.

3.3 Sentiment Analysis Model

After labelling the training data, features were extracted from these posts and comments. Extracted features included n-grams (unigram, bigram, and trigram), tf-idf weights, and unigrams with negation tagging. For negation we followed the approach proposed in [11], which considers bigrams (and n-grams in general) to be an orthogonal way to incorporate context. Therefore we did not add negation tags to bigrams and trigrams, and only unigrams were included with negation tagging. [11] also suggested that a product review might begin with an overall sentiment statement, proceed with details about the product, and conclude by summarizing the author's views. Therefore, position of the word in comments were treated as an additional feature. Furthermore, for treating number of positive and negative words in a comment or post as a feature, we used domain specific positive and negative word lists [7, 14] to count the words belonging to each category.

Using these features and our training dataset, we trained four different classifiers: Support Vector Machine, Logistic Regression, Random Forest, Multinomial Naive Bayes. The best accuracy (accuracy: 79.6%, F1-measure: 0.78) was achieved using logistic regression classifier. In order to avoid overfitting we employed 10-fold cross validation. Hence, this reported accuracy is the average accuracy of the model across all the 10-folds.

4 Results of Sentiment Analysis of Discussion on r/androidwear

The ability to automatically identify sentiment of messages allowed us to study the interrelations between sentiment of the posts/comments and sentiment fluctuations in discussion threads. Following sections illustrate our findings.

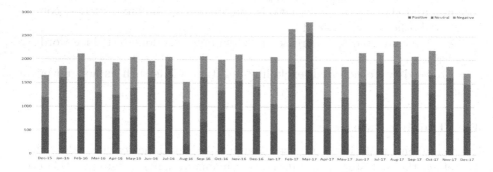

Fig. 1. Sentiment distribution of comments over time

4.1 Sentiment Distribution for Discussions

Based on the sentiment label assigned by our model, 20478 positive (40.13%), 12218 negative (24.47%), and 18171 neutral (35.39%) comments were posted

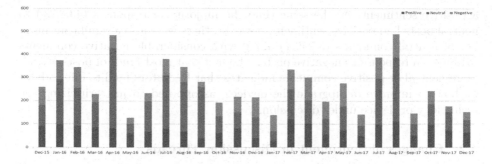

Fig. 2. Sentiment distribution of posts over time

over the period of our data collection. The distribution of comments' sentiment over time can be seen in Fig. 1. In general, majority of the comments posted in this subreddit were positive. In fact, majority of comments posted in months with highest number of comments also had positive tone. For example, 63.84% of comments made in March, 2017 (month with highest number of comments) were positive. Similar pattern in comments' sentiment exists in months of February and August, 2017 that had next highest number of total comments. Qualitative analysis of these comments revealed that excitement due to the release of new android wear (e.g., LG Watch Sport/Style (Feb, 2017), Q Venture (Aug, 2017)) in the market led to a peak in neutral or positive discussions. Even though, this euphoria did not necessarily increase the number of posts, it triggered long discussions amongst Redditors regarding their opinion about the newly released products in the market. The distribution of posts' sentiment over time can be seen in Fig. 2.

Table 1. Sentiment distribution of posts and comments

Posts Count per Sentiment	Comment Count per Sentiment
Positive, 1889 (28.27%)	Positive 8128 (51.40%)
	Negative, 3405 (21.53%)
	Neutral, 4278 (27.05%)
Neutral, 3187 (47.67%)	Positive, 8084 (43.25%)
	Negative, 3598 (19.25%)
	Neutral, 7008 (37.49%)
Negative, 1604 (24.01%)	Positive, 4266 (26.06%)
	Negative, 5215 (31.86%)
	Neutral, 6885 (42.06%)

Furthermore, in terms of Redditors response to posts, the sentiment of the post indeed influenced the sentiment of the discussion that follows (cf. Table 1, RQ1). The majority of the comments (51.40%) in response to positive posts had a positive sentiment. At the same time the majority of responses (43.25%) to neutral posts had positive sentiment; however, there were also a significant number of neutral comments (37.49%) along with considerable negative comments (31.86%) in response to negative posts. The fact that most kinds of posts attract more neutral or positive comments indicates that Redditors tend to offer advice on how to improve or upgrade the devices, as opposed to just criticizing the technology or device under discussion.

4.2   Changes of Sentiment in Discussion Threads

As noted in the research questions, we are particularly interested in (1) identifying distinct sentiment patterns in comments within a discussion thread, and (2) to assess how such patterns impact the decision of (non-)use. To this end, Figs. 3, 4, and 5 illustrate the two most commonly occurring patterns of sentiment changes in posts with positive, neutral, and negative sentiments respectively. For each sentiment pattern, posts with longest discussion (highest number of comments) were chosen for demonstrative purposes in these figures.

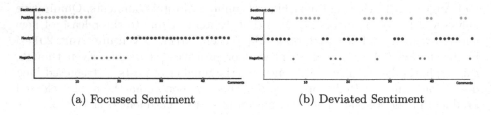

(a) Focussed Sentiment   (b) Deviated Sentiment

Fig. 3. Patterns of discussion sentiment on positive post

Figure 3a presents a pattern of stable positive responses in response to a positive post, followed by a complete shift to a number of negative responses, and then discussion ending with neutral comments. Discussion in almost 44% of positive posts had such focussed sentiment pattern. Our qualitative investigation of such threads highlighted that Redditors try to help the fellow member (who started the discussion) to make an informed decision of either continuing to use the device (with the help of workarounds to their device issues through positive or neutral comments) or abandoning the device (due to lack of functionality or other issues in the device through negative comments).

For example, a Redditor posted: *I'm thoroughly enjoying my Moto360, except now when I say "OK google, play blah," it tries to find music on my phone that is potentially not even there. How do I fix this? I might have to stop using the device because of this.* Even though some people shared their frustrations of going through the same issue by posting comments such as *this is exactly what irritates me, my usage is going down because of that,* other Redditors through neutral and positive comments such as *I ended up disabling the Music app and that seems to have done the trick* or *Try to get app picker that will help, this is an amazing device I would not give up for that reason* offered workarounds that helped in continued use of the device.

In comparison, the continuous change of sentiment (illustrated in Fig. 3b), which was seen in 32% positive posts indicated contentious discussion between Redditors due to their different experiences of using such devices or awareness of the device's capabilities under discussion.

For example, in response to post: *I was using my Gear live for a LONG time. I loved it, especially the screen, thinking back, though, the watch broke 4 times, the charging cradle, the strap, and the contacts for charging on the back corroded away. Well, Best Buy has ASUS Zenwatch 2 on sale, this watch has the thing I wanted most: A square, AMOLED screen. It is phenomenal. However I need you opinion on the reliability problems before I get converted,* people commented with neutral comments that did not necessary answer the question posed but gave some factual information such as *It has a thinner, proper strap mounting claws, and a slightly curved screen vertically, which makes the light reflect off of it in a way that you might appreciate.* People also commented positively by giving their opinion on the issue under discussion *I recently got a Zenwatch 2, its my 2nd smartwatch and I think its a keeper, so reliable lasts for 3 days without charging again.* However, presence of argumentative negative comments such as *I don't believe people are not writing correct things about the watch, its so misleading. People like you are false sales men of such watches. It has been an utter disappointment. Watch sucks when I'm trying to show someone the watch and it doesn't work. It's even more frustrating when I'm taking 10x's the amount of time to look at a notification on the watch when I could have done it faster with the phone* made such threads end abruptly without offering any substantial help to the Redditor who initiated the thread.

Discussion on neutral posts was always driven by facts-based comments. Most of the neutral posts (∼40%) had relatively stable neutral discussion as illustrated in Fig. 4a. This pattern of neutral discussion emerged specifically in response to posts that were explicitly seeking experience-based opinions on device use from fellow Redditors. Our investigation further revealed that such neutral comments motivated the person, who started the thread, to adopt a new device by providing him device alternatives that existed in the market.

For example, in response to the post: *I've been debating this with myself for weeks and I'm stuck between the Urbane 2 and the Huawei watch. Huawei has pretty solid battery life, good performance, and it looks nice. But every time I see a pic from an angle it looks really thick and makes me question whether I'd want it on my wrist all the time. I was pretty sure I was going to get the Huawei watch until I saw Urbane 2 demo a few days ago. So which of these would you guys get? Does anyone have any personal experience with them that should tip my decision one way or another?,* majority of people responded with fact-driven positive comments similar to: *Looks wise Huawei with black metal band is gorgeous. I'm not familiar enough with the urbane 2, but its uglier than the apple watch, and limited app wise. Personally got Huawei for very cheap, and planning to wait for the next Gen and get that as that is going to be brilliant,* or neutral comments such as *It doesn't look bad when on the wrist though. At least not in my opinion. I've only had it for a day so I haven't gotten a feel of the battery life yet. It was syncing music which killed the first 25% quickly. It's got the largest battery, and with the cellular not being used it should not have any more energy usage than anything else. But you may want to wait a few more days if you want a good review of the battery life.* These reviews helped the person to make the decisions in favor of Huawei Watch and was even satisfied with his choice based on his first few days of use.

The second most prevalent pattern, observed in ∼32% of neutral posts, was of deviated sentiment. Figure 4b illustrates this phenomenon with respect to one of the post - *Just curious what people think now that smartwatches have been around for a little while. Do you think you get a lot of value out of owning a smartwatch? Does it make your life easier? Or is it just an extra device to charge and an extra screen to distract you? Should I get one?* - that had highest number of comments. People responded with positive comments like *It is a life savior. You will have never to take out your phone outside your pocket in meetings*, negative comments like *the battery life is annoying so doesnt help at all,* or neutral comments such as *I just wish you could pair to multiple Bluetooth devices, so I could use my watch to control my Bluetooth headphones, and still answer calls.*

Analysis of several of such posts revealed that instead of being contentious, discussion with deviated sentiment in response to a neutral post validated the presence(absence) of the device-issue through negative(positive) comments. People also provided rationale for abandonment or continued use of the device through interleaved fact-driven neutral comments in the discussion.

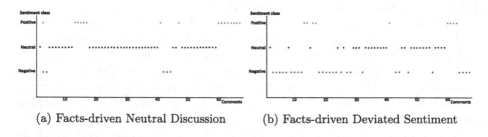

(a) Facts-driven Neutral Discussion   (b) Facts-driven Deviated Sentiment

Fig. 4. Patterns of discussion sentiment on neutral post

Negative posts specifically represented the struggles of the users with their devices, which in turn led to change in usage pattern. Our further investigation of responses to negative posts revealed two patterns (cf. Fig. 5a and b).

Majority of the people responded negatively by sharing a similar negative experience with the device in about 21% of negative posts. These comments reconfirmed problems with the devices, and towards the end of the discussion people started talking about either upgrading to a new device or stopping their use of the device altogether. For example, Redditor who posted: *Very frustrated with my watch at the moment. I feel with every update, the platform degrades more and more and I keep wondering if it's just me*, after reading several comments of following order: *I am totally with you. Seriously hoping that this gets fixed because my watch went from amazing to frustratingly useless in such a short time*, responded by saying: *I think it is better to save time and energy in bearing such issues and stop wearing the watch alltogether.*

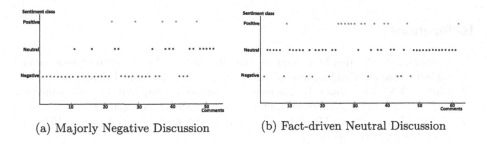

(a) Majorly Negative Discussion   (b) Fact-driven Neutral Discussion

Fig. 5. Patterns of discussion sentiment on negative posts

Redditors responded neutrally (sometimes even positively) using facts, workarounds, and other forms of informational support to around 18% of negative posts. These comments, are often longer (average length of 48 words), and they helped people know other people's opinion, troubleshoot the problems they had, and continue using their devices. For example in response to the post: *Strongly considering ditching Android wear. The watch can become incredibly slow even when connected to my phone. I'll say "ok Google show me my agenda" and the watch fails to respond. When it works, is wonderful. When it doesn't work, it is frustrating to no end*, other Redditors responded with: *I have the original LG G Watch and I have no issues like this at all. The watch is 99% working. I will say when something isn't working, there is always a reason (e.g., no data for voice recognition). So try checking your updates and connectivity.*

It is important to note, 61% of remaining negative posts did not seem to follow any specific sentiment pattern, particularly no common pattern of sentiment existed in more than 3% of those remaining posts.

5 Discussion and Conclusion

In this study we utilized sentiment analysis to understand how discussions on social media influence user-decisions of using or abandoning relatively newer devices such as wearables. The analysis was based on 6680 posts and their corresponding 50,867 comments posted between December 2015–2017 on the r/androidwear, a dedicated subreddit for discussions regarding Android Wear on Reddit. Our findings suggest that majority of the comments posted in response to positive and neutral posts are positive in sentiment. Furthermore, even though a lot of discussion with a negative sentiment materializes in response to negative posts, such posts also see fact-driven neutral discussions. The study also revealed connection between sentiment of discussion on the posts and its influence on the user's decision of using or abandoning devices. In general, discussions on Reddit prove to be of high assistance for the people to make such decisions, except for rare cases when discussions become contentious due to comments with negative sentiment. Future work may aim to investigate if similar patterns exist on other subreddits of the platform and their influence on user-decisions.

References

1. Baumgartner, J.: Reddit Comment Dataset. https://bigquery.cloud.google.com/table/fh-bigquery:reddit_comments.2015_05?pli=10. Accessed 1 Sept 2018
2. Bird, S., Klein, E., Loper, E.: Natural language processing with Python: analyzing text with the natural language toolkit. O'Reilly Media, Inc. (2009)
3. Ferrara, E., Yang, Z.: Measuring emotional contagion in social media. PloS one 10(11), e0142390 (2015)
4. Fritz, T., Huang, E.M., Murphy, G.C., Zimmermann, T.: Persuasive technology in the real world: a study of long-term use of activity sensing devices for fitness. In: Proceedings of the SIGCHI Conference on Human Factors in Computing Systems, pp. 487–496, April 2014
5. Information Removed to Ensure Anonymity (2018)
6. Hays, S., Page, S.J., Buhalis, D.: Social media as a destination marketing tool: its use by national tourism organisations. Curr. Issues Tourism 16(3), 211–239 (2013)
7. Hu, M., Liu, B.: Mining and summarizing customer reviews. In: Proceedings of the 10th ACM SIGKDD International Conference on Knowledge Discovery and Data Mining, pp. 168–177, August 2004
8. Lazar, A., Koehler, C., Tanenbaum, J., Nguyen, D.H.: Why we use and abandon smart devices. In: Proceedings of the 2015 ACM International Joint Conference on Pervasive and Ubiquitous Computing, pp. 635–646, September 2015
9. Melville, P., Gryc, W., Lawrence, R.D.: Sentiment analysis of blogs by combining lexical knowledge with text classification. In: Proceedings of the 15th ACM SIGKDD International Conference on Knowledge Discovery and Data Mining, pp. 1275–1284, June 2009
10. Mukherjee, A., Liu, B.: Mining contentions from discussions and debates. In: Proceedings of the 18th ACM SIGKDD International Conference on Knowledge Discovery and Data Mining, pp. 841–849, August 2012
11. Pang, B., Lee, L., Vaithyanathan, S.: Thumbs up? sentiment classification using machine learning techniques. In: Proceedings of the ACL-02 Conference on Empirical Methods in Natural Language Processing, vol. 10, pp. 79–86. Association for Computational Linguistics, July 2002
12. Pak, A., Paroubek, P.: Twitter as a corpus for sentiment analysis and opinion mining. In: LREc, vol, 10(2010), May 2010
13. Pan, S.J., Ni, X., Sun, J.T., Yang, Q., Chen, Z.: Cross-domain sentiment classification via spectral feature alignment. In: ACM Proceedings of the 19th International Conference on World Wide Web, pp. 751–760 (2010)
14. Qiu, B., et al.: Get online support, feel better- sentiment analysis and dynamics in an online cancer survivor community. In: Privacy, Security, Risk and Trust (PASSAT) and 2011 IEEE Third International Conference on Social Computing (SocialCom), pp. 274–281, October 2011

15. Rooksby, J., Rost, M., Morrison, A., Chalmers, M.C.: Personal tracking as lived informatics. In: Proceedings of the 32nd annual ACM Conference on Human Factors in Computing Systems, pp. 1163–1172, April 2014
16. Salehan, M., Kim, D.J.: Predicting the performance of online consumer reviews: a sentiment mining approach to big data analytics. Decis. Support Syst. **81**, 30–40 (2016)
17. Shih, P.C., Han, K., Poole, E.S., Rosson, M.B., Carroll, J.M.: Use and adoption challenges of wearable activity trackers. In: iConference 2015 Proceedings (2015)
18. Stieglitz, S., Dang-Xuan, L.: Emotions and information diffusion in social media-sentiment of microblogs and sharing behavior. J. Manag. Inf. Syst. **29**(4), 217–248 (2013)
19. Zheng, K., Li, A., Farzan, R.: Exploration of online health support groups through the lens of sentiment analysis. In: Chowdhury, G., McLeod, J., Gillet, V., Willett, P. (eds.) iConference 2018. LNCS, vol. 10766, pp. 145–151. Springer, Cham (2018). https://doi.org/10.1007/978-3-319-78105-1_19

Political Popularity Analysis
in Social Media

Amir Karami$^{(\boxtimes)}$ (iD) and Aida Elkouri

University of South Carolina, Columbia, SC 29208, USA
karami@sc.edu, aelkouri@email.sc.edu

Abstract. Popularity is a critical success factor for a politician and
her/his party to win in elections and implement their plans. Finding
the reasons behind the popularity can provide a stable political movement. This research attempts to measure popularity in Twitter using
a mixed method. In recent years, Twitter data has provided an excellent opportunity for exploring public opinions by analyzing a large number of tweets. This study has collected and examined 4.5 million tweets
related to a US politician, Senator Bernie Sanders. This study investigated eight economic reasons behind the senator's popularity in Twitter.
This research has benefits for politicians, informatics experts, and policymakers to explore public opinion. The collected data will also be available
for further investigation.

Keywords: Opinion mining · Popularity analysis · Text mining ·
Social media

1 Introduction

Social media play an important role in politics and people show their political
Internet activity by posting and sharing their opinions [37]. This communication
technology has been bringing more citizens into the political process and has
provided a personal accessible level through the posted political information
[33]. For example, the percentage of US adults got news from social media has
increased from 49% in the 2012 US election to 62% in the 2016 US election [14].
Considering the impact of social media on their public's impression, politicians
have utilized this new communication technology [17].

Twitter with 80 million US users has been considered as one of the top social
media platforms. For instance, former president of Chile has asked the members
of his cabinet to use Twitter [53] and Hillary Clinton has officially announced
her campaign in Twitter [60]. More than 80 million US Twitter users is a great
motivation for local and regional campaigns to analyze tweets [52]. Most politicians have a Twitter account and many have a social media team to manage
their Twitter account. For example, Barack Obama had a team with 100 staff
to work on his social media such as Twitter during his campaign [16]. Besides,

© Springer Nature Switzerland AG 2019
N. G. Taylor et al. (Eds.): iConference 2019, LNCS 11420, pp. 456–465, 2019.
https://doi.org/10.1007/978-3-030-15742-5_44

there is a new trend that politicians such as Donald Trump have started writing their tweets themselves to have more exciting and informal communications [43].

Public opinion poll is an essential tool in politics. To collect data measuring public opinion, traditional opinion polls use different methods such as face-to-face interview, and phone interview [9]. However, the conventional approaches are labor-intensive and time-consuming. Social media with millions of users and messages per day is a big focus group to mine public opinion [51]. Among social media, Twitter with millions of tweets per day has provided a cost-effective data access platform for collecting millions of tweets containing feelings and opinions to facilitate social media research [48]. Twitter data has been used in different political applications election analysis [20] and non-political applications such as business [15], libraries [8,21], social bot analysis [32], and health like analyzing diabetes, diet, obesity [22,49], exercise [50], LGBT health [28,62]. However, this data has not been considered for popularity analysis.

The popularity of a politician is an critical success factor for the politician and her/his party to win in elections and implement their plans. Finding the reasons behind the popularity can provide a stable political movement. This research investigates Twitter data using computational methods to understand the most important reasons behind a politician's reputation. For our case study, we selected a popular US politician, Bernie Sanders [54]. He received the highest amount of small donations from American people in the 2016 US presidential primary election and his campaign has raised more money than Donald Trump's campaign [55]. Although our approach can detect different reasons behind a politician's popularity, we focus on economic issues, as it was the most important issue for the 2016 US voters [40].

2 Related Work

The fast growth of Twitter and its large-scale public available have drawn the attention of researchers for political applications of Twitter data in three directions: (1) social movement analysis, (2) election prediction, and (3) election analysis. Two examples of the first direction are exploring the role of social media in organizing protesters [1,5,56] and studying the behavior of protesters in social media and its effect on social movements [58,59]. The second direction has adopted quantitative methods to determine the popularity of candidates [6,12,57] and find the most popular candidate and predict the elections [2,47]. The third research category attempts to investigate an election at a macro level such as studying the social media strategy [34] or analyzing economic factors [20].

Although previous studies have provided valuable insights into political processes, there is a need to find the essential reasons behind a politician's popularity. This paper addresses this gap by applying a mixed method on millions of tweets.

3   Methodology and Results

This research proposes a popularity analysis framework with four steps using two text mining techniques including sentiment analysis and topic modeling along with qualitative coding.

3.1   Data Collection

We used Twitter4j, a Twitter Java API (Application Programming Interfaces), to collect data using four queries: "@berniesanders," "bernie AND sanders", "sanders", and "#sanders". The tweets were collected from January 1, 2016 to July 31, 2016. The collected data will be publicly available in the first author's websites[1].

3.2   Sentiment Analysis

We used Linguistic Inquiry and Word Count (LIWC) tool [39] having good sensitivity value, specificity value, and English proficiency measure [13, 29–31] for sentiment analysis. Using LIWC, we found 2.1 million positive, 1.7 million negative, and 700,000 neutral tweets. Fig. 1 shows two positive tweets discussing free education and minimum wage. To maintain user privacy, we have lightly edited the represented tweets in this paper to avoid detection.

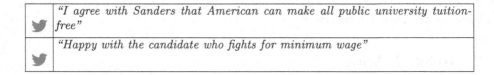

	"I agree with Sanders that American can make all public university tuition-free"
	"Happy with the candidate who fights for minimum wage"

Fig. 1. A sample of positive tweets

3.3   Semantic Analysis

The third part of our analysis detects main topics discussed by Twitter users during a time frame. Our approach is based on the assumption that people show their support with positive feelings in their tweets. Analyzing a large number of documents like the tweets in our dataset needs computational methods for processing high dimensional data [19, 23, 27]. This step applies a topic model to find discussed topics in the detected positive tweets. Latent Dirichlet allocation (LDA) is the most popular and effective general probabilistic topic model to group related words in a corpus [24–26, 35].

LDA assumes that each tweet in a corpus contains a mixture of topics and each topic is a distribution of the corpus's words [4, 18]. For example, this model assigns "gene," "dna," and "genetic" to a topic with Genetics theme (Fig. 2).

---

[1] https://github.com/amir-karami/Sanders-Tweets-Data.

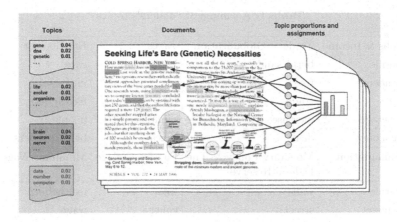

Fig. 2. An example fo LDA [3]

After removing the duplicate tweets, retweets, and the tweets containing a URL to retrieve pure personal opinion, we found 307,237 positive tweets. We applied a Java implementation of LDA, Mallet [36], with its default settings and stopwords list to disclose the topics of the 307,237 positive tweets. Using log-likelihood estimation method to identify the optimum number of topics [61], 175 topics were selected as the optimum number of topics.

3.4 Topic Analysis

The popularity analysis approach of this research is based on detecting essential reasons. According to the surveys of Gallup and Pew Research Center, the economy was the most critical issue not only in the 2016 election but also in the 2004, 2008, and 2012 US elections [7, 40, 44, 45]. In the 2016 US election, Economic was considered in ten dimensions: Jobs & Income, Trade & Globalization, Taxes, Entitlement, National Debt, Immigration, Infrastructure, Monetary Policy & The Federal Reserve, Pay for College, and Minimum Wage. Then we started to the qualitative analysis to identified economic-related topics and labeled them. The authors separately removed nonrelevant topics, either because they were not economic-related topics such as climate change and minorities rights or they were not understandable. By reviewing the top related words such the ones in Table 1, we agreed upon assigning single or multiple label(s) based on the ten economic dimensions for each of the relevant topics. For example, we assigned "Minimum Wage" label to a topic containing "Minimum Wage" label to a topic containing *"feelthebern"*, *"wage"*, *"support"*, *"minimum"*, and *"workers"*.

We also explored the distribution of labels to determine the importance of topics for supporters. Table 2 shows that the total weight of the top three reasons, 71%, was more than the total weight of the rest of the reasons, 29%. Pay for college, jobs & income, and entitlement were the top three reasons behind Sanders's popularity. This result confirms the result of a survey plan [42].

Table 1. A sample of Sanders's topics

Jobs & Income	Trade & Globalization	Taxes	Entitlement
bernie	berniesanders	berniesanders	care
sanders	free	tax	universal
job	trade	back	feelthebern
leverage	increase	millions	people
economy	deals	taxes	berniesanders
Immigration	Monetary Policy & The Federal Reserve	Pay for College	Minimum Wage
bernie	wall	free	feelthebern
sanders	street	college	wage
reform	berniesanders	berniesanders	supports
immigration	money	tuition	minimum
good	arguing	public	workers

Table 2. Distribution of economic positive topics

Economic issue	Distribution (%)	Rank
College	28.8%	1
Jobs & Income	22.1%	2
Entitlement	20.3%	3
Trade & Globalization	8.4%	4
Minimum Wage	6.8%	5
Monetary Policy & The Federal Reserve	6.8%	5
Taxes	5.1%	7
Immigration	1.7%	8
Infrastructure	0%	NA
National Debt	0%	NA

The second reason behind the popularity was a plan to raise a national minimum wage. This plan is also in line with traditional surveys [10,11]. Although jobs & income and the minimum wage were considered as independent issues, we found an overlap between these two issues. In this case, if we assume that these two reasons represent a single cause, the importance of the combination of these two reasons, 28.9%, is similar to the importance of the pay for college reason, 28.8%. The next reason was entitlement including healthcare and social security that were also in favor of US majority [38,46]. Considering the next reason, traditional polls have shown that most Americans were not in favor of the 2016 trade policies and had supported renegotiating major trades [41]. We found that taxes and immigration were the least important reasons for Sander's popularity. This study did not find topics covering national debt and infrastructure issues.

4   Discussion

This study applied a mixed method for popularity analysis in social media. There are some key finding informed by this research. First, users don't assign the same weight for all the economic issues. Further, two issues were not among the leading economic concerns of users. Second, college tuition, jobs, and income were the main concerns in the 2016 US election. Third, findings show that the potential of this paper for large-scale social media studies. Fourth, the proposed method can be used with traditional surveys to provide a comprehensive perspective for political events. Fifth, we think that this study has other applications such as analyzing and tracking positive and negative comments for business purposes like the stock market. Finally, the flexibility of the mixed method can help to utilize other computational and qualitative methods.

5   Conclusion

This study seeks to the analysis of the economic reasons behind the public's positive feeling. To address the research question, we used a mixed method to develop a popularity analysis approach considering ten economic dimensions. We applied our approach to a massive number of tweets mentioned a popular US politician in 2016 and 2017 to understand the reasons for his popularity. This paper can help politicians, public opinion analysts, knowledge discovery experts, and social scientists to understand people's opinions better.

This study has two limitations. First, the data was collected from one single social media source. Collecting data from other social media such as Facebook can represent more population and opinions. Second, while we considered English tweets, the location of the users was not considered in this analysis. To address these limitations, we will collect data from other social media platforms and consider location of users in our future research.

Acknowledgements. This research is supported in part by the South Carolina Alliance for Minority Participation and the Science Undergraduate Research Fellowships and Exploration Scholars Program programs at the University of South Carolina. All opinions, findings, conclusions and recommendations in this paper are those of the authors and do not necessarily reflect the views of the funding agency.

References

1. Bellin, E.: Reconsidering the robustness of authoritarianism in the middle east: lessons from the arab spring. Comp. Politics **44**(2), 127–149 (2012)
2. Bermingham, A., Smeaton, A.F.: On using twitter to monitor political sentiment and predict election results. In: Sentiment Analysis where AI meets Psychology (SAAIP), p. 2 (2011)
3. Blei, D.M.: Probabilistic topic models. Commun. ACM **55**(4), 77–84 (2012)
4. Blei, D.M., Ng, A.Y., Jordan, M.I.: Latent dirichlet allocation. J. Mach. Learn. Res. **3**, 993–1022 (2003)
5. Bonilla, Y., Rosa, J.: # Ferguson: digital protest, hashtag ethnography, and the racial politics of social media in the united states. Am. Ethnol. **42**(1), 4–17 (2015)
6. Boutet, A., Kim, H., Yoneki, E.: What's in your tweets? I know who you supported in the UK 2010 general election. In: The International AAAI Conference on Weblogs and Social Media (ICWSM) (2012)
7. Carroll, J.: Economy, Terrorism Top Issues in 2004 Election Vote (2003). http://www.gallup.com/poll/9337/economy-terrorism-top-issues-2004-election-vote.aspx
8. Collins, M., Karami, A.: Social media analysis for organizations: Us northeastern public and state libraries case study. In: Proceedings of the Southern Association for Information Systems (2018)
9. Cowling, D.: How political polling shapes public opinion (2015). http://www.bbc.com/news/uk-31504146
10. Desilver, D.: 5 Facts About the Minimum Wage. Pew Research Center (2016). http://www.pewresearch.org/fact-tank/2017/01/04/5-facts-about-the-minimum-wage/
11. Edwards-Levy, A.: Raising the Minimum Wage Is A Really, Really Popular Idea. The Huffington Post (2017). http://www.huffingtonpost.com/entry/minimum-wage-poll_us_570ead92e4b08a2d32b8e671
12. Gaurav, M., Srivastava, A., Kumar, A., Miller, S.: Leveraging candidate popularity on twitter to predict election outcome. In: Proceedings of the 7th Workshop on Social Network Mining and Analysis, p. 7. ACM (2013)
13. Golder, S.A., Macy, M.W.: Diurnal and seasonal mood vary with work, sleep, and daylength across diverse cultures. Science **333**(6051), 1878–1881 (2011)
14. Gottfried, J., Shearer, E.: News Use Across Social Media Platforms 2016 (2016). http://www.journalism.org/2016/05/26/news-use-across-social-media-platforms-2016/
15. He, X., Karami, A., Deng, C.: Examining the effects of online social relations on product ratings and adoption: evidence from an online social networking and rating site. Int. J. Web Based Communit. **13**(3), 344–363 (2017)
16. Hong, S.: Who benefits from twitter? Social media and political competition in the us house of representatives. Gov. Inf. Q. **30**(4), 464–472 (2013)
17. Hong, S., Nadler, D.: Which candidates do the public discuss online in an election campaign? The use of social media by 2012 presidential candidates and its impact on candidate salience. Gov. Inf. Q. **29**(4), 455–461 (2012)
18. Karami, A.: Fuzzy topic modeling for medical corpora. University of Maryland, Baltimore County (2015)
19. Karami, A.: Taming wild high dimensional text data with a fuzzy lash. In: IEEE International Conference on Data Mining Workshops (ICDMW), pp. 518–522. IEEE (2017)

20. Karami, A., Bennett, L.S., He, X.: Mining public opinion about economic issues: twitter and the us presidential election. Int. J. Strateg. Decis. Sci. (IJSDS) **9**(1), 18–28 (2018)
21. Karami, A., Collins, M.: What do the us west coast public libraries post on twitter? Proc. Assoc. Inf. Sci. Technol. **55**(1), 216–225 (2018)
22. Karami, A., Dahl, A.A., Turner-McGrievy, G., Kharrazi, H., Shaw, G.: Characterizing diabetes, diet, exercise, and obesity comments on twitter. Int. J. Inf. Manag. **38**(1), 1–6 (2018)
23. Karami, A., Gangopadhyay, A.: Fftm: a fuzzy feature transformation method for medical documents. Proc. BioNLP **2014**, 128–133 (2014)
24. Karami, A., Gangopadhyay, A., Zhou, B., Karrazi, H.: Flatm: a fuzzy logic approach topic model for medical documents. In: Fuzzy Information Processing Society (NAFIPS) held jointly with 2015 5th World Conference on Soft Computing (WConSC), 2015 Annual Conference of the North American, pp. 1–6. IEEE (2015)
25. Karami, A., Gangopadhyay, A., Zhou, B., Kharrazi, H.: A fuzzy approach model for uncovering hidden latent semantic structure in medical text collections. In: iConference 2015 Proceedings (2015)
26. Karami, A., Gangopadhyay, A., Zhou, B., Kharrazi, H.: Fuzzy approach topic discovery in health and medical corpora. Int. J. Fuzzy Syst. **20**(4), 1334–1345 (2018)
27. Karami, A., Pendergraft, N.M.: Computational analysis of insurance complaints: GEICO case study. In: International Conference on Social Computing, Behavioral-Cultural Modeling, & Prediction and Behavior Representation in Modeling and Simulation (2018)
28. Karami, A., Webb, F., Kitzie, V.L.: Characterizing transgender health issues in twitter. Proc. Assoc. Inf. Sci. Technol. **55**(1), 207–215 (2018)
29. Karami, A., Zhou, B.: Online review spam detection by new linguistic features. In: iConference 2015 Proceedings (2015)
30. Karami, A., Zhou, L.: Exploiting latent content based features for the detection of static sms spams. Proc. Am. Soc. Inf. Sci. Technol. **51**(1), 1–4 (2014)
31. Karami, A., Zhou, L.: Improving static sms spam detection by using new content-based features. In: The 20th Americas Conference on Information Systems (AMCIS) (2014)
32. Kitzie, V.L., Mohammadi, E., Karami, A.: "Life never matters in the democrats mind": examining strategies of retweeted social bots during a mass shooting event. Proc. Assoc. Inf. Sci. Technol. **55**(1), 254–263 (2018)
33. Kushin, M.J., Yamamoto, M.: Did social media really matter? College students' use of online media and political decision making in the 2008 election. Mass Commun. Soc. **13**(5), 608–630 (2010)
34. LaMarre, H.L., Suzuki-Lambrecht, Y.: Tweeting democracy? Examining twitter as an online public relations strategy for congressional campaigns. Public Relat. Rev. **39**(4), 360–368 (2013)
35. Lu, Y., Mei, Q., Zhai, C.: Investigating task performance of probabilistic topic models: an empirical study of PLSA and LDA. Inf. Retr. **14**(2), 178–203 (2011)
36. McCallum, A.K.: MALLET: A Machine Learning for Language Toolkit (2002). http://mallet.cs.umass.edu/topics.php
37. Najafabadi, M.M., Domanski, R.J.: Hacktivism and distributed hashtag spoiling on twitter: tales of the# irantalks. First Monday **23**(4) (2018)
38. Newport, F.: Majority in US Support Idea of Fed-funded Healthcare System. Gallup (2016). http://www.gallup.com/poll/191504/majority-support-idea-fed-funded-healthcare-system.aspx

39. Pennebaker, J.W., Boyd, R.L., Jordan, K., Blackburn, K.: The Development and Psychometric Properties of LIWC2015. UT Faculty/Researcher Works (2015)
40. Pew Research Center: Top Voting Issues in 2016 Election (2016). http://www.people-press.org/2016/07/07/4-top-voting-issues-in-2016-election/
41. Polling Report: International trade/global economy. NBC News/Wall Street J. (2016). http://www.pollingreport.com/trade.htm
42. Pounds, S.: Is College Worth It? Americans See it as a Good Investment, Bankrate Survey Finds. Bankrate (2016). http://www.bankrate.com/finance/consumer-index/money-pulse-0816.aspx
43. Rumer, A.: President Trump's Twitter Habit is Leading other Politicians to Pick Up Their Smartphones. Time (2017). http://time.com/4822054/donald-trump-twitter-social-media-politicians/
44. Saad, L.: Iraq and the Economy Are Top Issues to Voters (2008). http://www.gallup.com/poll/104320/iraq-economy-top-issues-voters.aspx
45. Saad, L.: Economy Is Dominant Issue for Americans as Election Nears (2012). http://www.gallup.com/poll/158267/economy-dominant-issue-americans-election-nears.aspx
46. Sander Website: Broad public support for bernies plan to expand social security. NBC News/Wall Street J. (2015). https://berniesanders.com/broad-public-support-for-bernies-plan-to-expand-social-security/
47. Sang, E.T.K., Bos, J.: Predicting the 2011 dutch senate election results with twitter. In: Proceedings of the Workshop on Semantic Analysis in Social Media, pp. 53–60. Association for Computational Linguistics (2012)
48. Sewell, R.R.: Who is following us? Data mining a library's twitter followers. Libr. Hi Tech. **31**(1), 160–170 (2013)
49. Shaw Jr., G., Karami, A.: Computational content analysis of negative tweets for obesity, diet, diabetes, and exercise. Proc. Assoc. Inf. Sci. Technol. **54**(1), 357–365 (2017)
50. Shaw Jr., G., Karami, A.: An exploratory study of (#)exercise in the twittersphere. In: iConference 2019 Proceedings (2019)
51. Smit, K.: Marketing: 96 Amazing Social Media Statistics and Facts (2016). https://www.brandwatch.com/2016/03/96-amazing-social-media-statistics-and-facts-for-2016
52. Stein, J.: Why Snapchat's Snappy. Time (2017)
53. The Economist: Politics and Twitter: Sweet to Tweet (2010). http://www.economist.com/node/16056612
54. The Huffington Post Pollster: Bernie Sanders Favorable Rating (2017). http://elections.huffingtonpost.com/pollster/bernie-sanders-favorable-rating
55. Thomas, Z.: US Election 2016: Who's Funding Trump, Sanders and the Rest? (2016). http://www.bbc.com/news/election-us-2016-35713168
56. Tufekci, Z., Wilson, C.: Social media and the decision to participate in political protest: observations from tahrir square. J. Commun. **62**(2), 363–379 (2012)
57. Tumasjan, A., Sprenger, T.O., Sandner, P.G., Welpe, I.M.: Predicting elections with twitter: what 140 characters reveal about political sentiment. In: ICWSM 2010 (2010)
58. Valenzuela, S.: Unpacking the use of social media for protest behavior: the roles of information, opinion expression, and activism. Am. Behav. Sci. **57**(7), 920–942 (2013)
59. Valenzuela, S., Arriagada, A., Scherman, A.: The social media basis of youth protest behavior: the case of chile. J. Commun. **62**(2), 299–314 (2012)

60. Velencia, J.: Hillary Clinton's 2016 Announcement Caused Twitter To Freak Out (2015). http://www.huffingtonpost.com/2015/04/13/hillary-clinton-announcement-on-social-media_n_7057020.html
61. Wallach, H.M., Murray, I., Salakhutdinov, R., Mimno, D.: Evaluation methods for topic models. In: Proceedings of the 26th Annual International Conference on Machine Learning, pp. 1105–1112. ACM (2009)
62. Webb, F., Karami, A., Kitzie, V.: Characterizing diseases and disorders in gay users' tweets. In: Proceedings of the Southern Association for Information Systems (2018)

Data and Information in the Public Sphere

"Just My Intuition": Awareness of Versus Acting on Political News Misinformation

Yong Ming Kow[1(✉)], Yubo Kou[2], Xitong Zhu[1], and Wang Hin Sy[1]

[1] School of Creative Media, City University of Hong Kong,
18 Tat Hong Ave, Kowloon Tong, Hong Kong SAR
yongmkow@cityu.edu.hk
[2] College of Communication and Information, Florida State University,
142 Collegiate Loop, Tallahassee, FL 32306, USA

Abstract. Citizens are becoming increasingly aware of the prevalence of misinformation, disinformation, and rumors, especially on political topics. But currently, the literature lacks clarity on how citizens are dealing with this issue. And information science and HCI researchers propose design solutions such as *diverse information platforms* assuming that citizens - with more information at hand - will be able to rationalize political misinformation on their own. In this paper, we conducted semi-structured interviews with 21 Hong Kong residents. Our findings point out that while most of our participants were aware of misinformation, they mostly did not act on them. This suggests that while it is important for designers to further develop information rich news representations, researchers also need to develop alternative solutions such as news literacy education as long term remedies.

Keywords: Political news · Hong Kong · Misinformation · Social media

1 Introduction

Political news misinformation is a topic of increasing academic and societal concern, especially after recent political events (e.g., the US presidential election and Brexit), which were laden with "fake news" accusations, but also increased citizens' awareness of the reality of misinformation, disinformation, and rumors in various forms of media [4, 5].

Currently, it lacks clarity on how citizens are dealing with this issue. On the one hand, researchers of Internet use and political polarization argue that citizens commonly only seek to read news which aligns with their own political stance [7, 8, 16], and that social media companies and news agencies are merely aggravating this bias by only showing to users news which align with their beliefs [12, 18, 20]. On the other hand, empirical evidences in the literature demonstrate that some citizens are not naïve but are capable of taking advantage of multiple social media platforms to reach diverse information and audiences [18, 20, 21].

Building on this notion that citizens are rationale news readers, information science and HCI researchers propose design solutions of *diverse information platforms*, which provide additional information such as alternative news headlines and news propagation pattern to citizens as their browse the Internet for news information [17, 20].

© Springer Nature Switzerland AG 2019
N. G. Taylor et al. (Eds.): iConference 2019, LNCS 11420, pp. 469–480, 2019.
https://doi.org/10.1007/978-3-030-15742-5_45

To some extent, these designs assume that by providing citizens with more information, they will be able to rationalize political misinformation on their own [17]. To date, there are few studies which examine whether citizens' day-to-day news reading practices took diverse information sources into consideration.

In this study, we performed task-based information search and in-depth interviews with 21 Hong Kong residents. Our findings suggest that most citizens reading practices are nuanced: despite claiming that they are aware of misinformation, they seldom take further action to develop impartial views of political events. We conclude by suggesting that HCI designers need to go beyond providing diverse information and also consider longer term solutions in resolving issues of misinformation.

2   Misinformation and Diverse Information Platforms as a Solution

In recent years, more researchers are raising concerns about biased and partial news reporting creating a more attitudinally polarized society [1]. Information and HCI researchers have found evidence of such biases forming in news sites, Facebook, Twitter, and blogging networks [8, 12, 18, 20].

In information science and HCI, researchers had leveraged this understanding of biased technology representation and human rationality to develop diverse information platforms. For example, Semaan et al. [20], proposed an web platform called "Poli," to display diverse political news information – collected across different social media and representing different political ideologies. Likewise, Metaxas et al. [17] developed a complex graphical representation to visualize the propagation of news information on Twitter. Even mainstream media, such as Google News, have been redesigned to arrange alternate views of the same news story side by side, in an attempt to provide a more balanced coverage of news stories.

But this solution—that of providing diverse information to citizens—assumes that citizens are rationale actors, that is, if they have complete information, they would have been able to develop unbiased political views. Apart from not having clear evidence that diverse information platforms are effective in reducing misinformation, by relying on a design-only solution, researchers may have given technologies too much credit for being able to resolve social problem directly – an assumption too familiar in technology-determinism [23].

In fact, to Habermas, the reading of political news is by itself a socially-constructed and highly cultural process. In his theory of communicative action, Habermas [14] points out that in the normal writing of a statement, what makes the statement compelling is that it is framed in a way that justifies its correctness. Such justifications, or what Habermas called *validity claims*, ground these statements using incontestable moral, ethical, or aesthetic arguments (e.g., "equality," or "democracy" are terms often seen in political news) in order for statements to appear rational and objective [14]. Allen [2], from the perspective of *intertextuality*, further argues that news organizations had in fact, by leveraging such socially constructed claims, propagated "their own political and social agendas... [by employing] processes of framing, editing, and other reproduction of images and speech which the viewer, possessing only what is presented, cannot challenge. A constructed news report thus comes to substitute for any real experience of the event. The 'simulacrum,' the copy, comes to replace the 'real.'" Thus, the notions by Habermas and Allen indicate the presence of nuances and messiness in political news reading.

Given the conceptual gap between the assumption of citizens' willingness to read diverse news information and Habermas' thesis, few studies have examined how citizens' read news and whether they actively seek more information to rationalize misinformation. And how likely are they to use diverse information in their news reading?

3   Method

Between February 2017 and April 2017, we conducted semi-structured interviews with 21 Hong Kong residents. We recruited these residents through the snowball sampling method, starting with friends and relatives of two of our research team members. The 21 interviewees included 12 males and nine females. The age of these interviewees ranged from 20 to 62, with an average age of 29.8. Nine of these interviewees were students, 11 were working adults, and one was a retiree. Nine of these interviewees were born in Hong Kong, with the rest born in other regions in China. Of the 12 interviewees who were born outside of Hong Kong, they had resided in Hong Kong between 6 months and 20 years, with an average residency period of 5.9 years, and five had lived in Hong Kong for less than one year. Our interviewees did not receive remuneration for their participation in this study.

Each of our semi-structured interviews consisted two parts: task-based information search, and in-depth interview.

3.1   Part I: Searching for Political News Information Regarding Recent Events

In the first part, our interviewees were given three independent tasks, one at a time, to look up news information regarding a recent political issue and tell us what they concluded from their searches. We introduced each task to our participants. The first task concerned a controversial incident in which two newly elected localist and pro-independence legislators refused to swear allegiance to and insulted the People's Republic of China during their oath-taking ceremony. The second task concerned a collaboration between Hong Kong and Shenzhen (a Chinese city at the border of Hong Kong) to develop a natural reserve into a technology hub. The third task concerned the recent election of Hong Kong's chief executive among three candidates. We had chosen these three tasks out of seven based on their recency and diversity in terms of Hong Kong political news coverage.

The interviewees were advised to use any electronic devices they liked (e.g., laptop, mobile phone, tablet, etc.), and all of them chose to use only one device. In Table 1, we show a list of participants whom we interviewed, along with the device they chose to use. Thirteen interviewees chose to use their mobile phones. Three chose to use a tablet. Three interviewees (S2, S9, and S13) who had access to a laptop or desktop during the interviews chose to use these devices. While the choice to use a laptop or desktop during the search tasks may have allowed them to type and read faster, participants using their own mobile devices had the advantage of having access to familiar apps, search history, and remembered password features. These familiar operations helped expose their routine practices more easily. This part of the interview took between 15 to 25 min.

Table 1. List of participants and themes mentioned during each interview

| | | | | | Misinformation strategies mentioned by participant during interview | | | | |
| | | | | | Awareness of Misinformation | Seeking Out Diverse Information | Self-perceived Rationality | Looking for Condensed Information | Identifying "Authoritative" Sources |
Participant	Gender	Occupation	Age	Computing device chosen to perform tasks					
S1	Male	Working adult	60	None			x		
S2	Male	Student	25	Desktop or laptop	x		x	x	
S3	Male	Working adult	25	Mobile phone/ tablet	x	x	x	x	
S4	Female	Student	21	Mobile phone/ tablet	x	x	x		
S5	Male	Student	25	Mobile phone/ tablet	x	x	x		x
S6	Male	Working adult	24	Mobile phone/ tablet	x		x	x	
S7	Female	Working adult	23	Mobile phone/ tablet	x		x	x	x
S8	Female	Working adult	28	Mobile phone/ tablet	x	x	x	x	
S9	Male	Working adult	25	Desktop or laptop	x		x		x
S10	Female	Working adult	20	Mobile phone/ tablet	x			x	x
S11	Female	Retiree	62	None			x		x
S12	Male	Working adult	60	Mobile phone/ tablet	x		x	x	
S13	Male	Student	23	Desktop or laptop	x	x	x	x	x
S14	Female	Student	23	Mobile phone/ tablet	x		x	x	x
S15	Female	Student	26	Mobile phone/ tablet	x		x		
S16	Female	Student	24	Mobile phone/ tablet			x	x	x
S17	Female	Student	23	Mobile phone/ tablet	x	x	x		x
S18	Male	Working adult	25	Mobile phone/ tablet		x	x		x
S19	Male	Working adult	27	Mobile phone/ tablet	x	x	x	x	
S20	Male	Student	23	Mobile phone/ tablet			x	x	x
S21	Male	Working adult	28	Mobile phone/ tablet	x		x	x	

3.2   Part II: Validating Information

The first part of the interviews gave us a good understanding of each interviewee's search routine and preferred sources of news information. In the second part of the interviews, we leveraged this understanding to ask each of them to tell us how they recognized problematic information in a piece of news. This part of the interview lasted about 30 min.

Data Analysis

We conducted an iterative and inductive analysis of our field notes and interview transcripts using grounded theory coding and memoing [9]. Through this iterative process, we developed codes based on our analysis at the end of each interview in order to identify conceptual themes within our data corpus. We started coding from our first interview, and we continued this iterative process until the interviews were completed. Over time, the number of codes which we generated was gradually reduced under axial coding, until the themes which we will present in the next section emerged.

4   Findings

In our analysis, we found that most citizens were aware of existence of misinformation, but few took measures to identify them. When asked, most of them discussed their daily news reading routines and reasons for not actively seeking diverse information, which we discuss in the following sections.

4.1   Most Citizens Are Aware of Misinformation, But Only a Few Sought Out Diverse Information

Our analysis revealed that most of our participants were aware of the existence and prevalence of misinformation. For example, S19 (27 M) told us that:

> Nowadays, many platforms only show you information which you like, and thus we only get to see one side of the story. This is worrisome as we will not get to understand [perspectives] which you dislike or do not understand. We need to get to know more friends with different perspectives.

Likewise, other participants such as S9 (25 M) told us, "Different media have their own strengths."

But our participants' in their daily practices tended to focus only on a small subset of media. S3, who routinely read Facebook and HK01 [a Hong Kong Chinese online news organization] told us:

> Firstly, I will check Facebook. While at Facebook I will also type *cpjobs* [a job agency in Hong Kong which also posts career articles] and then HK01.

Importantly, participants like S3 told us that they are aware of misinformation, but in their routine, they had continued to read news from only a small set of information sources. They may, only if they feel necessary, to examine alternate news information, but this is performed only occasionally (16 out of 21). As S10 (20F) explained:

> If I am really interested and want to know the entire thing, I would look at the reports by TVB [the largest Hong Kong television broadcaster today, established in 1967], then newspapers—look for the context through wiki, or other sites. If I am really, really interested, I would look at the comments made by people involved and imagine what if I were there, how would I react to the event?

When these participants cross-compared news sources, these acts were mostly triggered by rare instances of suspicion of information biases or incorrectness.

Fewer participants mentioned that they would routinely cross-compare news information to improve their political understanding (8 out of 21) (see also [20]). While S17 had her own daily news reading routine, she subsequently mentioned in the interview that when she had time, she would conduct a deeper search on her own. She had read news in such a way that she would intentionally seek contradictory information reported by various information sources. An example that she gave us came from the Lok Ma Chau Loop project she had just looked into. She said:

> I want to see how the different sides, the left and the right, write about this. Actually they can be very different. For instance, Apple Daily started off with a quote by Mo Man Tsing, who criticized the government for not explaining to the public and went on to collaborate privately with Shen Zhen [China] [10]. But you can also see that Wenweipo [文汇报] started off by saying that Hong Kong should take advantage of the [Lok Ma Chau] Loop and the area between Guangdong and Hong Kong. You can see there is a lot of bias here.

But our participants who reportedly cross-compared and sought out news information regularly, and from multiple perspectives, remained a minority. Most of them were only aware of misinformation, but otherwise would not change their news reading practices without strong reasons to do so. In the following, we describe three reasons the interviewees had not routinely cross-compared news information.

4.2   Self-perceived Rationality in News Reading

When we asked our participants how they could validate information, all of them expressed with ease and self-confidence. They put much trust in their own knowledge, ability, and experience, using terms such as "logic," "intuition," "intelligence," and "common knowledge;" for example:

S2, 25 M: "Intuition. Just my intuition."
S7, 23F: "From the information and thoughts I had accumulated in the past."
S19, 27 M: "I use logic to judge a piece of news."

They held their own judgment in high regard, while believing that misinformation only affected the *other* citizens. Among our participants, S13 (23 M), expressed this perspective:

> When [fake news] are released, actually to most rational people, including those who have been educated, and have real world experiences, I do not see as a particularly big problem. But to those who are extremely narrow-minded, they may feel sufficient about what they already knew. There is nothing that can be done as I can't control these people. But to someone who is well-learned, to someone with a basic cultural background, they can selectively watch news instead of believing everything.

In our interviews, only a few participants, such as S18 (25 M), experienced a realization that there are news which may be true yet beyond his own ability to understand. He said:

When I first arrived [in Hong Kong from mainland China], I had not been exposed to outside voices ("声音") and opinions, and there was only one kind of voice [in the media]. My mind could only see things from that one voice; and I naturally followed [news] only from this perspective. This is especially true for normal people, they will be completely led by this voice, and follow the majority. I was terrified at the beginning and weird out - that both sides [Hong Kong and mainland China] said things in two completely different ways. But I gradually understood that every opinion exists for its own reasons.

Participants like S18 told us how difficult it was, while reading news published in Hong Kong, to ignore their own opinion and logic encultured while growing up in mainland China. He loved the communist party, and before living in Hong Kong, felt that the Hong Kong protestors were troublemakers. But now, he tried not to make judgement at face value of each piece of news.

Despite this, we heard more instances of our participants claiming that they had sufficient "logic," or other abilities, to judge and validate information. But this willingness to make quick judgment on news may also be related to their general lack of engagement in political events.

4.3   Preferring Condensed Information

Participants talked about how they needed to balance between their work and life routines in the midst of keeping up with daily news.

Our participants suggested that inconvenience was an important reason for their reluctance to search for more information—they suggested they had simply watched and read whatever was available during the appropriate time. For example, S17 (23F) told us that she had routinely caught up with news information only when she was alone during her daily commutes, and while watching TV with family members. In Hong Kong, the subway train is the most common form of transportation for citizens. And Hong Kong has a reliable and comprehensive mobile Internet coverage. Thus S17 could, during her daily train rides and alone, use her mobile phone to catch up with news information posted on Facebook. At home, another news reading opportunity presented itself when S17 would watch TVB on the television as a family activity.

Other participants, such as S6 (24 M), told us that their friends tended not to talk about political issues, which was why S6 said he had not paid too much attention to this information:

I seldom discuss politics with my colleagues... I usually talk about where to buy clothes and shoes... Where you can buy them and where you can buy them cheap. It is like this once you leave school and [start] working [in the industry].

When citizens rely on condensed news information in their day-to-day news reading, they tend to stay with a small number of trusted news sources, even though this practice carries danger of not understanding political events fully.

4.4   Falling Back on News "Authorities"

We asked our participants what types of news sources may be considered more trustworthy.

Some participants, such as S10 (20F) trusted news organizations that are "large" and well known. She said:

> Actually, I trust public media, for instance, newspapers, magazines, and those that are bigger and more authoritative. For example, organizations with a long history such as TVB, *Sing Tao* [a major Hong Kong Chinese newspaper established since 1938], and *Ming Pao* [a major Hong Kong Chinese newspaper established since 1959]. Those are relatively more objective media. I feel that an individual's opinion can be used as a reference but such information on social media may not be trustworthy.

S10 represents a group of participants who did not trust citizens' comments on social media, and found organizational news more trustworthy. S11 (62F) said, "When people from the government come out and say something, I trust them." S5 (25 M) said he considered "official news (官方的)" more trustworthy, and when we discussed the term "official" further, he defined it as "sanctioned by [and agreed among] news organizations."

Even for participants such as S17, who often used online news platforms such as Facebook, there was a notion of "authoritative" news sources. She told us,

> This is because if [a media outlet] has plenty of legitimacy, it should be widely mentioned and discussed. But I have never heard of this name before. I feel I read plenty of news and if not even I have heard of it, I feel it lacks in legitimacy.

For S17, an "authoritative" news organization need not be old, but has to be popular among Hong Kong people.

Therefore, our participants favored news "authorities" which have a historic presence in Hong Kong, or are popular among Hong Kong people. What is important, however, is that our participants' notions of "authoritative" news sources help justify their selection and maintenance of a limited number of information sources.

5   Discussion

In the interviews, the mentioning of "intuition" in news reading echoes Habermas' notion of *validity claims*, which is counter-productive to intent of diverse information platforms for citizens to cross-compare news information. Thus, design solutions which rest on presumption of citizens' rationality in news reading may need to re-examine the perceived effectiveness of such designs.

While our participants were aware of misinformation, they expressed an array of reasons for not seeking wider spectrum of news information on a regular basis. These reason may have reinforced our participants' daily visits only to familiar news platforms, and thus constructed the "echo chamber" in which citizens mainly sought information which aligned with their own views [7, 8, 16].

5.1   Aware of Misinformation (But Not Really): News Reading in Everyday Life

Our participants developed news reading practices out of their everyday life experiences and habits that were deeply situated. They assessed the trade-off between their own time and effort and their interest in a news topic. This resonates with the premise of the theory of seeking information in everyday life—namely, that people's information-seeking goals and methods are conditioned by a wide array of factors such as habits, culture, and norms [19]. Most of these citizens were aware of misinformation - but only in a rhetorical sense. For example, in actual search tasks, all of our participants reported high confidence in determining the trustworthiness of the news reports on their own.

In their daily reading, most of our participants had seen news reading as a filler task to be fitted into gaps within their routines. This exemplified the extent a citizen's social environment mediated their news reading practices. The findings suggest that news reading activities are often woven into gaps of time within and between work and social activities, for example, the gap of personal time available during commute (S17), and which extends existing social discourses with friends and family members (S6 and S17). Thus, a majority of them chose to only use condensed news digests which took fewer efforts to read and agreeable to most citizens. Some of them obtained these condensed forms of news from what they perceived as "authoritative" sources of information. This largely aligns with previous studies, which found that social media posts made by organizations are seen to be more trustworthy [3, 5]. Also, social media posts which have already been shared by a large crowd of people are seemingly more trustworthy [5]. For example, S11's trust in the government kept her away from reading alternative opinions [22]. But by limiting the number of additional perspectives they could have read, our participants left behind information "blind spot" which they were not immediately aware of.

Taken together, our findings painted a picture of citizens' widespread awareness of misinformation, but also its seemingly secondary importance in their everyday life. Rather than being informative, news may be by themselves media to extend our social discourses among friends and family members – that is – to reinforce our moral values, social norms, and *validity claims* [13]. Participants such as S18 told us how difficult it was to read news outside of familiar validity claims (what other participants referred to as "logic" and "educated" views), a realization he had attained only after moving from mainland China to live in Hong Kong.

One limitation of this study is that our participants, being Hong Kong residents, may conduct news reading differently from citizens in other parts of the world (e.g., the US). But what makes Hong Kong, even as a Chinese city, similar to places like the US, is its status as a Special Administrative Region, that has allowed it to keep an international border with mainland China, and still possesses freedom of speech and press similar to many democratic countries. For this reason, at the time of our study, Hong Kong's political news fields had been as contested and diverse as some of these countries.

5.2   Alternative Long-Term Solution

If any, our findings painted a bleak picture of limited impact of designing diverse information platforms, and suggested also paying attention to alternate and longer-term solutions.

For citizens disinterested in political new accuracy, their statements such as "*If* I am really interested…" are a concern to us. In light of this evidence, simply feeding these citizens with diverse information may not be enough. Rather, designers may need to intervene by curating news and removing those which sway too far from truths. But even this raises the issue of how we could avoid news curators' biases so that the curated corpus represents a "balanced" perspective - which further challenges us to consider the curators' computing methods and their political consequences.

Another solution comes in a form of news literacies perspective suggesting educating citizens to develop critical news reading practices, such as actively synthesizing news information to comprehend the bigger picture [22]. From this perspective, citizens need to establish the purview that every news agency can be biased by writing up news stories [6]. Thereafter, these citizens need to acquire knowledge of news production processes, as well as the social constructedness of political frames in each news source to perceive the reality of the story [6, 22].

In sum, our findings suggest that providing citizens with more information is likely not enough, but the proliferation of engaged and participative citizens who actively construct realistic scenes of news production may be needed before we can resolve issues of misinformation in our society.

6   Conclusion

There is an increasingly urgent need to identify solutions to assist citizens in identifying political misinformation. In this study, we conducted semi-structured interviews with 21 Hong Kong residents to determine if – in their day-to-day news reading practices – having diverse news information may aid them in this activity. Through grounded theory coding, we identified that while most of our participants were aware of existence of news misinformation, they seldom act on them. Through the concept of validity claims suggested by Habermas [13], we suggest that news reading may be by itself a socially constructed and cultural activity, and most citizens are unlikely to analyze news corpus in a rationale manner. While design solutions which provide diverse news information remained useful, we propose further developing alternate and longer term solutions such as educating news literacy to citizens.

Acknowledgement. This research is supported by City University of Hong Kong research grant #7005175.

References

1. Abramowitz, A.I., Saunders, K.L.: Is polarization a myth? J. Politics **70**(2), 542–555 (2008). https://doi.org/10.1017/S0022381608080493
2. Allen, G.: Intertextuality. Routledge, Abingdon-on-Thames (2000). https://doi.org/10.4324/9780203131039
3. Andrews, C.A., Fichet, E.S., Ding, Y., Spiro, E.S., Starbird, K.: Keeping up with the tweet-dashians: the impact of "official" accounts on online rumoring. In: Proceedings of the 19th ACM Conference on Computer-Supported Cooperative Work & Social Computing - CSCW 2016, pp. 451–464 (2016). https://doi.org/10.1145/2818048.2819986
4. Arif, A., et al.: A closer look at the self-correcting crowd. In: Proceedings of the 2017 ACM Conference on Computer Supported Cooperative Work and Social Computing - CSCW 2017, pp. 155–168 (2017). https://doi.org/10.1145/2998181.2998294
5. Arif, A., et al.: How information snowballs: exploring the role of exposure in online rumor propagation. In: Proceedings of the 19th ACM Conference on Computer-Supported Cooperative Work & Social Computing - CSCW 2016, pp. 465–476 (2016). https://doi.org/10.1145/2818048.2819964
6. Ashley, S., Maksl, A., Craft, S.: Developing a news media literacy scale. Journal. Mass Commun. Educ. **68**(1), 7–21 (2013). https://doi.org/10.1177/1077695812469802
7. Colleoni, E., Rozza, A., Arvidsson, A.: Echo chamber or public sphere? Predicting political orientation and measuring political homophily in twitter using big data. J. Commun. **64** (2005), 317–332 (2014). https://doi.org/10.1111/jcom.12084
8. Conover, M., Ratkiewicz, J., Francisco, M.: Political polarization on twitter. Icwsm **133**(26), 89–96 (2011). https://doi.org/10.1021/ja202932e
9. Corbin, J., Strauss, A.: Basics of Qualitative Research: Techniques and Procedures for Developing Grounded Theory. SAGE Publications, Thousand Oaks (2007)
10. Apple Daily.: Lok Ma Chau Loop Project Refuses to Set Local Employment Ratio. Apple Daily (2017). hkm.appledaily.com/detail.php?guid=56392321&category_guid=6996647&category=instant&issue=20170306
11. Finlayson, G.: Habermas: a very short introduction. OXFORD University Press (2005). 125, 125: 156
12. Grevet, C., Terveen, L.G., Gilbert, E.: Managing political differences in social media. In: Proceedings of the 17th ACM Conference on Computer supported cooperative work & social computing - CSCW 2014, pp. 1400–1408 (2014). https://doi.org/10.1145/2531602.2531676
13. Habermas, J.: The theory of communicative action. Book 1, 1: v (1984). https://doi.org/10.1086/228287
14. Habermas, J.J.: The Structural Transformation of the Public Sphere: An Inquiry into a Category of Bourgeois Society. MIT Press, Cambridge (1991). https://doi.org/10.2307/2072652
15. Kou, Y., Kow, Y.M., Gui, X., Cheng, W.: One social movement, two social media sites: a comparative study of public discourses. **26**(4–6), 807–836 (2017). https://doi.org/10.1007/s10606-017-9284-y
16. Lawrence, E., Sides, J., Farrell, H.: Self-segregation or deliberation? Blog readership, participation, and polarization in American politics. Perspect. Politics **8**(01), 141 (2010). https://doi.org/10.1017/S1537592709992714

17. Metaxas, P.T., Finn, S., Mustafaraj, E.: Using twittertrails.com to investigate rumor propagation. In: Proceedings of the 18th ACM Conference Companion on Computer Supported Cooperative Work & Social Computing – CSCW 2015 Companion, pp. 69–72 (2015). https://doi.org/10.1145/2685553.2702691
18. Munson, S.A., Resnick, P.: Presenting diverse political opinions: how and how much. In: Conference Companion on Human Factors in Computing Systems 2010, pp. 1457–1466 (2010). https://doi.org/10.1145/1753326.1753543
19. Savolainen, R.: Everyday life information seeking: approaching information seeking in the context of "way of life". Libr. Inf. Sci. Res. 17(3), 259–294 (1995). https://doi.org/10.1016/0740-8188(95)90048-9
20. Semaan, B., Faucett, H., Robertson, S.P., Maruyama, M., Douglas, S.: Designing political deliberation environments to support interactions in the public sphere. In: Proceedings of the 33rd Annual ACM Conference on Human Factors in Computing Systems - CHI 2015, pp. 3167–3176 (2015). https://doi.org/10.1145/2702123.2702403
21. Stromer-Galley, J.: diversity of political conversation on the internet: users' perspectives. J. Comput.-Mediat. Commun. 8 (2003). https://doi.org/10.1111/j.1083-6101.2003.tb00215.x
22. Toepfl, F.: Four facets of critical news literacy in a non-democratic regime: how young Russians navigate their news. Eur. J. Commun. 29(1), 68–82 (2014). https://doi.org/10.1177/0267323113511183
23. Wyatt, S.: Technological determinism is dead. Long Live Technol. Determ. Technol. 10(1), 165–180 (2008). https://doi.org/10.1111/j.1467-8691.1996.tb00237.x

Public Private Partnerships in Data Services: Learning from Genealogy

Kalpana Shankar[1]([⊠]) (iD), Kristin R. Eschenfelder[2] (iD),
Laurie Buchholz[2], and Christine Cullen[1] (iD)

[1] School of Information and Communication Studies,
University College Dublin, Dublin, Ireland
{kalpana.shankar,christine.cullen}@ucd.ie
[2] The Information School, University of Wisconsin-Madison,
Madison, WI 53706, USA
{eschenfelder,lbuchholz2}@wisc.edu

Abstract. As one strategy for expanding access to archival data, libraries and data archives are increasingly entering into Public-Private Partnerships (PPP) with commercial entities. In exchange for access to publicly held sources of information of interest to genealogists, commercial companies are providing financial resources for digitization and access. This paper reviews recent literature on these public-private partnerships, considers challenges and long-term implications of these relationships in data services by reviewing issues experienced in the including tensions with institutional missions, access differentiation, exclusivity agreements and nondisclosure agreements and marginalization of services financed by public data.

Keywords: Public-private partnerships · Genealogy · Data access

1 Introduction

In recent years there has been a steady increase in the provision, and demand for, online access to archival material, particularly genealogical material held in national and local archives. Many existing archives and libraries have sought to fill this need through the digitization of the collections they hold but this process is costly and time consuming [1]. To continue to meet demand and ongoing storage and digital curation costs, libraries are now facing the problem of how to sustain these services. Often collections were digitized as one-off projects to commemorate an event or were expansion of an existing one, setup with no long-term funding models but have become essential to their own institutions, researchers, as well as others. In an effort to secure the future and further expansion of these services they must look at long-term, sustainable ways in which to secure their position. The need for sustainability is expressed by Eschenfelder and Shankar [2] when they write:

> "Although there has been significant research into the preservation of the data themselves, there has been less attention paid to the sustainability of the institutions that curate the data. For data to remain accessible over time, the data repository organization and its services... must themselves be sustainable."

© Springer Nature Switzerland AG 2019
N. G. Taylor et al. (Eds.): iConference 2019, LNCS 11420, pp. 481–487, 2019.
https://doi.org/10.1007/978-3-030-15742-5_46

This case illustrates one potential role for Public-Private Partnerships (PPPs) in the data economy, but they have also have been put forward as one of several possible solutions to the question of sustainability for data archives and repositories. Overall, the literature views, and discusses, the need for partnership and collaboration in a very positive light, giving recommendations on how to approach and negotiate with partners but there is little or no, analysis of *specific* cases in the sphere of libraries and archives [3–5].

In this paper, we review the PPP literature in one arena where there has been the most significant growth: genealogical data. The expansion of digital research tools has sparked immense growth in this field, making genealogy "the second most popular hobby in the U.S. after gardening, … and the second most visited category of websites, after pornography" [6]. A report commissioned by Europeana found that interest in genealogy research doubled between 2008–2013 and was expected to double again by 2015 [7]. By 2018, an editor for Forbes estimates that online genealogy research will be a three billion dollar business [8]. This increased demand has led to a race for market share in the provision of digital genealogical materials. We do not claim that genealogical data is particularly illustrative of PPP in general but instead focus on them as they are the one of the useful PPP relationships when examined through the lens of a strategy for longevity.

2 The Landscape of Genealogical Data

2.1 Background

Over the past several years, four websites have emerged as leaders in the field of online genealogy research. These include Ancestry.com, FamilySearch.org, Findmypast.com, and MyHeritage.com [7, 9]. Ancestry contains by far the largest store of materials, at approximately 11 billion records, while Findmypast is the smallest of the big four with almost 3 billion records [9]. Findmypast is based in the UK and contains records from only seven countries (primarily Anglo-European), while the others each contain records from 75 or more countries [9]. While both Ancestry and FamilySearch are based in the United States, MyHeritage is an Israeli company which has the largest collection of materials about Jewish people worldwide [9]. Each of these data serviceswebsites provides access to content from FamilySearch, the genealogy website of The Church of Jesus Christ of Latter-day Saints, which is renowned for its rich cache of genealogical records. FamilySearch contains the largest collection of records from countries in central and South America, Asia and Africa—places where people generally can't afford to pay to preserve family history data or undertake genealogy research [9].

A review of the relevant literature suggests that most often, PPP are formed when private entities approach public organizations. Private partners have learned the importance of using a low-key, non-legalistic style when initiating discussions with libraries and archives. As Kriesberg [10] reports, archivists tend to reject potential private partners who approach them with lawyers and contracts before establishing a connection.

With the genealogy data business booming, an issue of supply to meet the demand for genealogical records, such as birth, death, and marriage certificates, has arisen. There is not a dearth of materials; instead, the issue is the form in which those materials exist. Countless genealogical records are not available online, but rather in paper or microfilm versions [8, 11]. Traditionally, genealogists visited publicly funded libraries and archives to consult these resources. Most publicly funded libraries and archives do not have the resources to undertake the large digitization processes necessary to make their billions of genealogical records accessible online. Ironically, libraries and archives possess the content most desired by family history researchers, yet these organizations usually don't have the resources to make that content accessible online. Public-private partnerships in genealogy have become commonplace [10].

2.2 Why PPPs?

Public-private partnerships to provide access to genealogical records and materials are generally characterized as a mutually beneficial exchange of content supplied by the public entity and resources provided by the private partner [10, 12, 13]. The private partner's resources include technology and manpower for digitization and indexing as well as hosting. In short, the libraries and archives contain the product that private companies would like to sell and family history researchers would like to acquire, but they lack the resources to make that product widely accessible [10]. As Brian Geiger, Director of the Center for Bibliographical Studies and Research at the University of California, Riverside, writes, a partnership with Ancestry.com "will double the size of the California Digital Newspaper Collection" [12]. Ancestry is an especially powerful example of a private entity's ability to bring online enormous volumes of publicly-held records that would otherwise be accessible only in archives.

3 Access and Terms of Service

3.1 Collaborations

Ancestry, FindMyPast, and MyHeritage all collaborate with several National Archives and Libraries such as the British Library, and the Irish, UK and US National Archives which hold records of births, deaths, marriages, prison records, military records and legal archives. According to their founding remit and principles this material should be accessible free of charge and as the genealogy companies are primarily subscription sites, archives must negotiate the provision of access to this content in such a way to facilitate this. The National Archives in Kew have been subject to Freedom of Information requests on the provision of access to public records, as well as the revenue earned [14, 15]. While collaborations with archives, such as that with the UK National Archives, require that access is free, in many cases researchers still need an account with the genealogy service to access the content, and a subscription to make use of other aspects of the service such as creation of a family tree, for example the Arizona State Archives collaboration with Ancestry.com [11]. For the researchers accessing this material the process by which it was made available is of no real concern and in many cases, they prefer to access it via one centralized platform [10].

All of the main companies have been involved in some kind of collaboration with publicly funded archives and non-for-profit institutions with their primary motivation being the acquisition and provision of content that will maximize commercial gain, which is at odds with the primary remit of publicly funded archives [10]. The Digital Repository of Ireland emphasizes this point when they write that "such partnerships only work where there is a clear benefit to both parties, delivering a profit to the private partner" [16]. As a result, when negotiating these PPP's, it is important to ensure that the material digitized is not only that which has a larger profit margin but also includes material that adds value to the services provided by the archives themselves. There are several cases of collaboration between publicly funded institutions that have been undertaken recently In Ireland, the UK and Europe. Recently in Ireland, the Department of Foreign Affairs & Trade and the Heritage Council founded a new volunteer-based non-profit called Ireland Reaching Out aimed at the Irish diaspora. While this aims to be an independent community-based organization but it in an attempt to be non-profit making, free service they are sponsored by a Google AdSense stream. Given that elsewhere Google is in partnership with Ancestry and others, it is only a question of how long they can remain fully independent.

3.2 Exclusivity

PPPs in the realm of digital genealogy seem to be always bilateral and non-exclusive. For instance, both Ancestry and Family Search are currently involved in bilateral partnerships with multiple organizations as well as with each other [11, 12]. In its document outlining principles for partnerships NARA [14] reserves the right to partner with multiple organizations on its digitizing projects. On its website, NARA [15] provides links to current bilateral partnerships with eight organizations, including Ancestry and FamilySearch. Each agreement focuses on a particular set of archived materials and a specific time frame.

Exclusivity in the realm of access to digitized materials is a more complicated area of negotiation. While private entities desire exclusive rights to purvey the digitized materials as a source of revenue, public entities are responsible for seeing that their users retain access tort-term, exclusive rights to provide access to the digitized materials.

NARA [14] has outlined similar principles regarding exclusive rights to digitized materials. A recent agreement between NARA and Ancestry.com specifies a five year embargo period, "within which all Digital Materials for that series or segmented portion created by Ancestry will be published exclusively by Ancestry". During that period, NARA can display sample images and provide free online access to its materials on Ancestry at NARA locations. After the five-year period, NARA will have "full and unrestricted rights" to the digitized. This is in distinct contrast to some early contracts with thirty-year terms and use restrictions which were, in effect, perpetual [5].

3.3   Nondisclosure Agreements

Nondisclosure agreements (NDAs) were common between private and public vendor partners in the early twentieth century, and they were usually entered into at the request of the private partner. As Kaufman and Ubois [5] report, "Most mass digitization partnership negotiations have started with a request from the prospective commercial partner for a confidentiality agreement—often commercial partners have asked cultural institutions to treat even the act of considering a partnership as a secret." The motives for requesting a NDA include protecting information about company practices as well as maintaining a competitive edge in subsequent negotiations with new public partners. As the U.S. state archivists discovered, refusing to sign NDAs enabled them to compare strategies and negotiate more favorable contract terms. Kriesberg [10] reports the experience of one state archivist who claims that having knowledge of Ancestry's contract terms with another state empowered her to reject that company's initial terms and reach an agreement that benefitted her organization.

As librarians and archivists have become more skilled in negotiations, NDAs in PPPs have become much less common. In fact, the Association of Research Libraries (ASL) has a strongly worded policy against non-disclosure agreements, which reads "Libraries should refrain from signing nondisclosure agreements (NDAs) as part of digitization negotiations" [17]. An explanation of the policy asserts that the libraries should maintain transparency since they are guardians of public goods. Kaufmann and Ubois [7] advocate a more nuanced perspective on NDAs, asserting that some types of agreements that prohibit discussion of "technical processes unique to a commercial partner" may be acceptable, but that public entities should always maintain their right to disclose the terms of their own agreements with their communities and users.

4   The Value of Data

Much has been written about the advantages and possibilities offered by PPPs in this period of growing demand and decreasing finances. Genealogical data is a natural source of income for archives and libraries. While few specific cases have been covered in the academic literature, the overall discussion does show that much thought and planning must go into the negotiations when drawing up PPPs. Apart from the questions of cost and revenue, which are hidden in the confidential partnerships agreements, the questions of curation (physical and digital), access and storage costs, indexing and metadata and, progressively, data justice will ensure that this is an area it will be interesting to follow over the coming years.

However, as Cifor and Lee [18] observe, neoliberal attitudes have come to dominate the privatization of personal and public data, and this discussion about PPPs among genealogy resource providers needs to be understand within that context. As librarian Jonathan Cope asserts, "Neoliberalism creates a discursive framework in which the value of information is determined by its ability to be monetized" [18, p.10]. By extension, the value of information workers is also connected primarily to their ability to generate marketable products. While this framing of archived materials as products, and of archive users as customers, is problematic, it does form the context within which the negotiations between potential collaborators in genealogy PPPs currently take place.

5   Future Work

This review is part of a larger study on the sustainability of social science data archives and the numerous ways that business models, relationships, policies, and practices that social science data archives have undertaken over the last six decades to remain open. The authors have used historical and qualitative methods to identify moves by which such archives have their institutional longevity, including partnerships with other stakeholders. In this light, we will continue to examine how PPP in data archives have developed over time, with attention to how PPP are justified, negotiated, and managed and how historical cases influence current practice.

Acknowledgements. This study was funded by the Alfred P. Sloan Foundation G-2014-14521.

References

1. Brown, C.: Digitisation projects at the University of Dundee archive services. Program **40**(2), 168–177 (2006). http://dx.doi.org.ucd.idm.oclc.org/10.1108/00330330610669280. Accessed 21 Aug 2018
2. Eschenfelder, K.R. Shankar, K.: Designing sustainable data archives: comparing sustainability frameworks. In: iConference 2016 Proceedings (2016). https://www.ideals.illinois.edu/bitstream/handle/2142/89439/Eschenfelder243.pdf?sequence=1&isAllowed=y. Accessed 12 Dec 2018
3. Erway, R.: Increasing access to special collections. LIBER Q. **21**(2), 294–307 (2012)
4. Fogg, M.: Digitization: a successful collaborative partnership between library and publisher. Insights **27**(2), 186–191 (2014)
5. Kaufman, P.B., Ubois, J.: Good terms: improving commercial-noncommercial partner-ships for mass digitization: a report prepared by intelligent television for RLG programs, OCLC Programs and Research. D-Lib Magaz. **13**, 11–12 (2007)
6. Rodriguez, G.: How genealogy became almost as popular as porn. Time.com (2014). http://time.com/133811/how-genealogy-became-almost-as-popular-as-porn/?xid=email-share. Accessed 21 Aug 2018
7. Hoitink, Y.: Investigating the genealogy services market. Report for the European Commission within the ICT Policy Support Programme. https://pro.europeana.eu/files/Euro-peana_Professional/Projects/Project_list/Europeana_Awareness/Documents/eAware-ness%20Genealogy%20Services%20Market.pdf. Accessed 21 Aug 2018
8. Anderson, A.R.: Opportunity is about to knock so get ready to open your door. Forbes. https://www.forbes.com/sites/amyanderson/2014/11/23/opportunity-is-about-to-knock-so-get-ready-to-open-your-door/#1537f470daf6. Accessed 21 Aug 2018
9. Morton, S.: Comparing Ancestry, Findmypast, FamilySearch and MyHeritage. RootsTech (2018). https://www.rootstech.org/videos/sunny-morton. Accessed 21 Aug 2018
10. Kriesberg, A.: The future of access to public records? Public–private partnerships in US state and territorial archives. Arch. Sci. **17**(1), 5–25 (2017)
11. Walker, J.: LDS FamilySearch + Ancestry.com = 1 billion new historical records online. Deseret News, http://www.deseretnews.com/article/865585877/LDS-FamilySearch–Ancest-rycom–1-billion-new-historical-records-online.html. Accessed 21 Aug 2018

12. Miller, B.: UC Riverside partner to digitize historical newspapers (2017). https://www.universityofcalifornia.edu/news/ancestrycom-uc-riverside-partner-digitize-historical-newspapers. Accessed 22 Aug 2018
13. Council of State Archivists (CoSA). Statement on digital access partnerships (2007). https://www.statearchivists.org/files/8714/4071/0112/CoSA-Stmt-DigitalAccessPartnerships.pdf. Accessed 22 Aug 2018
14. The National Archives (NARA): Information relating to legal rulings allowing the National Archives to sell access to public records (2016). http://www.nationalarchives.gov.uk/about/freedom-of-in-formation/information-requests/information-relating-to-legal-rulings-allowing-the-na-tional-archives-to-sell-access-to-public-records/. Accessed 22 Aug 2018
15. The National Archives (NARA): Revenue earned from licenses to family history companies (2017). http://www.nationalarchives.gov.uk/about/freedom-of-information/information-re-quests/revenue-earned-from-licenses-to-family-history-companies/. Accessed 22 Aug 2018
16. Kitchin, R., Collins, S., Frost, D.: Funding models of open access repositories (2015). http://dri.ie/sites/default/files/files/funding-models-open-access-repositories.pdf. Accessed 22 Aug 2018
17. Association of Research Libraries (ARL): Principles to guide vendor/publisher relations in large-scale digitization projects of special collections materials (2010). http://www.arl.org/storage/doc-uments/publications/principles_large_scale_digitization.pdf. Accessed 21 Aug 2018
18. Cifor, M., Lee, J.: Towards an archival critique: opening possibilities for addressing neoliberalism in the archival field. J. Crit. Libr. Inf. Stud. 1(1) (2017). http://libraryjuice press.com/journals/index.php/jclis/article/view/10

Connecting Users, Data and Utilization: A Demand-Side Analysis of Open Government Data

Di Wang[1,2(✉)] ⓘ, Deborah Richards[2], and Chuanfu Chen[1]

[1] Wuhan University, Wuhan 430072, Hubei, China
di.wang18@students.mq.edu.au, cfchen@whu.edu.cn
[2] Macquarie University, Sydney, NSW 2109, Australia
deborah.richards@mq.edu.au

Abstract. Open government data (OGD) could bring various aspects of benefits through transparency and access. Thus, governments have proposed policies and practices to disclose more data to the public. However, studies have shown the utilization of OGD instead of disclosure as a key problem. Although citizens are recognized as a key participant in the utilization process of OGD from demand-side, few studies have revealed the possible relationship among OGD users, their demands of data and utilization. Therefore, our study carried out a survey on a Chinese population to analyse the possible relationship between these three. Results show citizens' limited awareness of OGD and portals, and their different demands of OGD subjects due to different socio-demographic characteristics. Daily life and anticorruption were the two main types of OGD utilization by citizens. Their types of usage are affected by their education and knowledge of OGD. Different types of utilization could lead to different demands for OGD subjects. We suggest governments to improve citizens' awareness of their efforts to provide OGD, and deliver more data in the subject categories that are in greater need by citizens. Further studies need to be carried out on citizens' motivation of OGD utilization.

Keywords: Open government data · Data utilization · Data need · Data user

1 Introduction

Open government data (OGD) are government-related data [1] that are commonly treated as an intersection of open data and government data [2]. It has recently drawn lots of attention from both researchers and governments around the world, not only because citizens' rights to public access to government information serves as a fundamental tenet of democracy [3–7], but also due to the great benefits that could be derived from OGD programs [8].

The release of larger amount of government data to the public, however, does not guarantee the achievement of OGD programs in their targeted aims [1, 9] of promoting proactive citizen engagement [10]. On the contrary of the constant development on the supply-side of OGD, numerous studies have emphasized the lack of OGD use as a key problem [11–13]. In order to stimulate the utilization of OGD, researchers have tried to

© Springer Nature Switzerland AG 2019
N. G. Taylor et al. (Eds.): iConference 2019, LNCS 11420, pp. 488–500, 2019.
https://doi.org/10.1007/978-3-030-15742-5_47

understand decisive factors of OGD usage [12, 14]. Reviews have shown that these studies carried out analysis either from the aspects of data, portals, or users [15], but failed to consider the specific context of OGD utilization. Besides, "users of OGD are relatively less researched as subjects" [11] (p. 16). Thus, this leaves a gap in the literature for analyzing the links of utilization, data and users from the demand-side of OGD, which puts the user at a central position.

Investigating and understanding users' demand and motivation could be a promising approach to enhance OGD utilization, since they are consumers of utilization effects [11], including transparency [16, 17], participation in policy [18] and economic benefits [16]. In addition, because one of the aims of disclosing government data on the web is for its use, reuse, and distribution [1], a further understanding of the OGD users could promote meaningful citizen engagement [18], and improve the efficiency of utilization, as well as its positive results.

To better understand users' OGD using habits and fill the identified knowledge gaps, we proposed the core research question for this study: What is the relationship among OGD users, their demand and utilization? To answer this question, we carried out a study from the demand-side of open government data, focusing on the OGD demand and utilization of users with different characteristics.

The objective, which is also the main contribution of this paper, is twofold: First, to get a clear view of users' knowledge of OGD and OGD portals through an investigation involving data collection. Second, to analyze the possible relationship of OGD users, data, and utilization based on the investigation. We also hope to find practical suggestions for improving the utilization of OGD and citizen's engagement based on our findings of the connections identified.

The structure of the remaining paper is as follows. Section 2 presents the theoretical foundation for our design of the investigation. Section 3 explains in detail the overall investigation procedure. After presenting the analysis results in Sect. 4, Sect. 5 presents the discussion of the results with comparison to other related studies. This paper ends with our final conclusions in Sect. 6.

2 Theoretical Foundation

To form the foundation of our study, and to find literature to support the design of a survey instrument, we have drawn on prior research carried out by both scholars and organizations related to OGD users, their demand and utilization.

2.1 OGD User

In the study of OGD, users are treated as a main actor in the open data process who could directly affect the coordination of OGD utilization from the demand side [13]. Thus many studies target their participation in the OGD value extraction process [11]. It is commonly accepted by researchers to divide users into different types [19], including citizens [20, 21], business [22, 23], researchers [24, 25], developers [26] and journalists [9]. Among them, citizens are identified as a primary stakeholder who receive major beneficiaries from the utilization of OGD [21].

Researchers have noticed different OGD users show different levels of interest in OGD [24], but the relationship between users and their preferences for data is unclear [11]. Considering various types of users in OGD utilization, we proposed the first hypotheses of our study:

- H1: OGD users' characteristics have an effect on their OGD demands.

In the area of e-Government, researchers have used users' characteristic including gender, age, education and personality for explaining their usage of e-Government portals [27]. However, similar studies have not been carried out on OGD portal users. Thus, we proposed the second hypotheses of our study:

- H2: OGD users' characteristics have an effect on their utilization.

2.2 Utilization of OGD

The utilization of OGD refers to the exploitation of users for a particular purpose [11]. According to their separate aim, the usage of OGD has also been divided into different types, including innovation [23, 26], data analytics [28, 29], decision-making [30, 31], anti-corruption [32, 33], research [25, 28], etc. In marketing, consumption refers to a broad set of practices including people's utilization of services and products [34, 35], which in OGD is the usage of the data. Economists assume that people's consumption reveal their demands [34]. Applying this relation of consumption and demand to the case of OGD, we proposed our third hypotheses:

- H3: Users' OGD utilization is influenced by their data demands.

3 Research Design and Methods

The primary aim of this study is to find out the possible relationship among OGD, its users, and its utilization through an investigation of our above stated hypotheses. Previous literature and our study objectives lead to the research model shown in Fig. 1.

Because the key motivation for releasing government data to the public is reducing the asymmetry of information among citizens and governments bodies [2, 36], we chose citizens to represent OGD users, as well as to be our investigation objects for analyzing the hypotheses. Besides their vital importance as participants in OGD utilization recognized by scholars [13], using citizens as the study objects offers the advantages of wider representation of the population and range of diverse characteristics. The source of OGD is the government, thus OGD portals usually provided OGD in certain subjects [37]. By referring to OGD evaluations and existing OGD portals, we have selected 15 subjects in Fig. 1 which are commonly used [38].

Overlaps are recognized in the scope of different types of OGD utilization, since some, like innovation and decision-making, are very broad, while others, like anti-corruption, are very specific. Thus, in the research model, we only included six specific types and exclude innovation and data analysis which have too much intersection with other specific types of utilization.

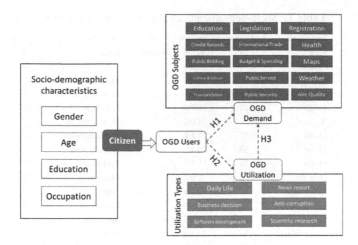

Fig. 1. Research model

A survey was designed and developed by operationalizing questions that reflect the aims and hypotheses of our study. Besides the socio-demographic characteristics, our survey contains questions covering four aspects. The first aspect includes four questions about the socio-demographic characteristics (gender, age, occupation and education) of citizens. Detailed options of each characteristics are shown later in Table 1. The second aspect is about citizens' knowledge of open government data. As pointed out above, OGD projects are carried out in order to improve the transparency of governments. But are citizens aware of the data and portals built by OGD programs? If citizens have never heard of OGD before, they would never try to make use of it. Thus, we asked four questions in the survey about whether users are aware of or have ever used OGD or OGD portals. The third aspect of the survey is about users' demand for OGD and different subject categories. A 7-point Likert scale (from "Strongly don't need" to "Strongly need") is used for exploring users' needs for open data. We asked the users to what degree they need OGD data in general and whether they need each kind of the 15 subjects in Fig. 1. We also asked users whether and to what extent they need other kinds of open government data. The last aspect of the survey is a set of multiple-choice questions to understand their utilization of OGD. We have listed 6 kinds of usage (Fig. 1) derived from the previous literature review for users to choose from. They could add additional uses beyond these six in their reply. Due to the recent efforts of the Chinese government for developing open data including establishing open data policies [39] and building local OGD portals throughout the country [40], we chose to administer the survey to a sample of the Chinese population. By using an online tool called *Sojump* which is a free website for creating and collecting online survey data, we produced our questionnaire and distributed it from August 1st to 10th 2017 through WeChat and Weibo. We recruited citizens by putting advertisements on the above two social media.

Table 1. Socio-demographic characteristics of the dataset.

Topic	Dimension	Frequency	Percent	Topic	Dimension	Frequency	Percent
Gender	Male	76	36.5%	Occupation	Student	24	11.5%
	Female	131	63.0%		Production worker	9	4.3%
	Other	1	0.5%		Marketing/salesman	18	8.7%
Age	Under 18	2	1.0%		Customer service	4	1.9%
	18–25	10	4.8%		Logistics	16	7.7%
	26–30	54	26.0%		Human resources	7	3.4%
	31–40	57	27.4%		Financial/auditor	12	5.8%
	41–50	59	28.4%		Civilian post	12	5.8%
	51–60	24	11.5%		Technician	15	7.2%
	Over 60	2	1.0%		Manager	33	15.9%
Educational qualification	Junior high	1	0.5%		Teacher	22	10.6%
	Senior high	28	13.5%		Consultant	4	1.9%
	Under graduate	110	52.9%		Specialist	9	4.3%
	Post graduate	57	27.4%		Other	23	11.1%
	Beyond post graduate	12	5.8%	Total		208	100.0%

4 Results

We received 208 valid responses. Table 1 shows the socio-demographic characteristics of the sample. Gender of respondents was reported as 63% females and 36.5% males. We got participants from different ages, and they are almost evenly distributed in the age groups 26–30, 31–40, and 41–50, which are also the main groups with a total percentage of 81.8%. The most common level of education is undergraduate, which is over 50%. Respondents covered all kinds of occupations listed in the survey, with student, manager and teacher being the three main kinds.

We have examined the reliability of the scale for users' OGD demand with Cronbach's alpha [41]. The commonly accepted range for alpha is 0.70 to 0.95 [42]. Our results show high reliability with a score of 0.923 (Table 2). We also examined the scale with Kaiser-Meyer-Olkin (KMO) measure of sampling adequacy [43]. The results showed with 0.923, which indicates the variables to be suitable for factor analysis [44]. The significance of Bartlett's test of sphericity is less than 0.05, which also indicated high validity of the variables. Thus, the measurement of citizen's OGD demand in this survey can be seen as reliable.

Table 2. Reliable and adequacy test of the dataset.

Dimension	Variable no.	Valid	%	Cronbach's alpha
OGD demand	16	208	100%	0.923
	Bartlett's test of sphericity			Kaiser-Meyer-Olkin measure of sampling adequacy
	Approx. Chi-square	df	Sig.	
	2185.744	120	0.000	0.923

Our first goal was to find out whether the participants have ever known of or used OGD before, which could give us a general view of citizen's awareness of open government data. We then carried out detailed analysis according to our three hypotheses. We compared participants' demand of different OGD subjects, and its relation to user's characteristics. We also compared participants' utilization of OGD with their characteristics as well as their knowledge about the data. Finally, we tried to analyze the possible effect of utilization on user's demand for certain kinds of open government data.

4.1 Users' Knowing of OGD

Regarding whether users have ever known of or used OGD, results show that 59.6% of the respondents have never heard of OGD before, nor do they know about the portal (72.6%). We also found that only 19.71% of the respondents have used the data or the portal before, which is less than the rate of knowing about the data (40.38%) or the portal (27.4%). Thus, we could deduce that some of them choose not to use the data or the portal even they have heard about it.

We have carried out Chi-Square tests (Table 3) of the choices of the four questions with respondents' socio-demographic characteristics including gender, age, education and occupation. Because some groups contain less than 5 members, we chose Likelihood Ratio instead of Pearson Chi-square to test their relationship. Results show that gender is related to whether people know about OGD. The rates of "ever heard of OGD" in females (53.6%) is much higher than in males (46.4%). It is also apparent that educational qualification is related with people's awareness of and usage of OGD. People with higher educational qualification are more likely to know about and use OGD. Occupation is also related to whether people know of and use OGD and portals. We noticed students, specialists and human resource workers are three kinds of occupations that are more likely to know about and use OGD and portals. Age did not significantly affect people's knowledge of OGD and portals.

Table 3. Chi-square tests of public's knowledge of OGD.

Demographic factor	Know OGD		Use OGD		Know portal		Use portal	
	L-R	P	L-R	P	L-R	P	L-R	P
Gender	6.749	0.034	2.889	0.236	1.086	0.581	0.930	0.628
Age	5.538	0.477	6.273	0.393	8.122	0.229	6.500	0.370
Educational qualification	19.209	0.001	19.505	0.001	4.124	0.389	4.505	0.342
Occupation	36.439	0.001	17.991	0.158	31.59	0.003	32.795	0.002

4.2 Users' Demand of OGD

We have asked respondents about their general demand of OGD and specific needs of 15 different subject categories, and got the results shown in Table 4. Generally, the average score for specific categories of data is higher than the general need, which may be due to citizens' not knowing what OGD really is. The largest variation of respondents' scores lie in general need. Health and education got the highest average score of demand. Education also got the smallest standard deviation, which indicates that citizens agreed most that this category was of high demand. International trade got the lowest average score. Although we asked the respondents whether they have any other categories of data need, their replies show that their needs all belong to our listed categories. Thus, we did not carry out a further analysis of these replies.

Table 4. Descriptive statistics of OGD demand.

	A	B	C	D	E	F	G	H	I	J	K	L	M	N	O	P
Min	1	1	1	1	1	1	1	1	1	1	1	1	1	1	1	1
Max	7	7	7	7	7	7	7	7	7	7	7	7	7	7	7	7
Mean	5.13	6.25	6.25	6.22	6.22	6.17	6.15	6.05	6.00	5.85	5.71	5.58	5.56	5.46	5.19	5.13
SD	1.738	1.156	1.006	1.058	1.099	1.120	1.064	1.160	1.224	1.174	1.252	1.302	1.403	1.503	1.633	1.563

A = General, B = Health, C = Education, D = Public Service, E = Public Security, F = Transportation, G = Air Quality, H = Legislation, I = Credit Records, J = Weather, K = Maps, L = Culture & Leisure, M = Budget & Spending, N = Registration, Q = Public Bidding, P = International Trade

We carried out two independent samples T-test for the correlation of gender and OGD demand. Results show no significant differences in the average and standard deviation of male and female's score for OGD demand.

We carried out one-way Anova to analyze the effect of age, education and occupation on people's OGD demand (Table 5). We found that age has a significant effect on respondent's need of registration and international trade data. People of different educational background have significant different demands for registration, budget & spending, and public bidding data. Occupation affected the demand for culture & leisure and transportation data significantly.

Table 5. One-way Anova of age, education, occupation and OGD demand.

Group by	Data type	F	P	Levene	p
Age	Registration	2.762	0.013	1.093	0.368
	International trade	2.283	0.037	1.432	0.204
Educational certification	Registration	2.552	0.040	2.499	0.061
	Budget & spending	2.472	0.046	2.156	0.094
	Public bidding	2.712	0.031	2.577	0.055
Occupation	Entertainment	1.809	0.044	1.657	0.073
	Transportation	1.852	0.038	2.221	0.010

4.3 Users' Utilization of OGD

We gave respondents seven specific choices of utilization of OGD, which are daily life, software development, scientific research, news report, business decision, anti-corruption, and other. These are the commonly accepted utilizations of OGD found in the literature [11], and have little intersect with one another. Respondents could choose as many types as they want. Results show that citizens mainly used OGD for their daily life (25.7%), followed by anti-corruption (20%). However, these two types of data involve direct utilization of OGD that does not require deeper exploration of the data or innovative uses. The least utilized data concerned software development (3.6%).

We examined the correlation of users' socio-demographic characteristics and their knowing of OGD, with their choices of utilization with Chi-square tests. We still chose Likelihood Ratio instead of Pearson Chi-Square to test the results. According to Table 6, there was high possibility that citizen's education affected their OGD utilization. Users ever knowing and using of OGD also affected their choices of utilization. For users' education background, results show that highly educated users are less likely to use OGD for daily life, but more likely for scientific research. The percentage of use of business decision and anti-corruption data are almost the same in senior high, under graduate and post graduate users. Results also show that citizens who have known and used OGD are more likely to choose scientific research and business decision as their purpose of utilization, while citizens who have not known and used OGD prefer to use OGD for daily life and news reports. The differences based on users' demographics in usage of software development and anti-corruption data is not significant.

Table 6. Chi-Square tests of OGD utilization.

Socio-demographic	Likelihood ratio			Knowing of OGD	Likelihood ratio		
	Value	df	sig.		Value	df	sig.
Gender	4.631	6	0.592	Know OGD	22.831	6	**0.001**
Age	41.784	36	0.234	Use OGD	15.615	6	**0.016**
Education	39.657	18	**0.002**	Know portal	6.761	6	0.343
Occupation	59.926	78	0.936	Use portal	9.874	6	0.130

4.4   Correlation Between OGD Utilization and Demand

To examine our third hypothesis about citizens' utilization affecting their OGD demand, we used two independent samples T-test to test the 15 subjects of OGD with the 6 different types of utilization. The results shown in Table 7 indicated that citizens who chose to use OGD in their daily life scored a much higher demand of health data than those who did not choose daily life. Citizens were also in greater need of maps data if they used OGD for their scientific research. For business decision, users show higher demand of maps, credit records, international trade, and budget & spending data from the government. For users interested in anti-corruption data, citizens reported higher needs for health, culture & leisure, legislation, weather and registration. For other subjects that are not listed in Table 7, results did not show a significant difference in the scores for demand within each type of OGD utilization.

Table 7. T-test of OGD utilization and demand subjects.

Utilization	Subject	Select		Not Select		F	P	t	df	p
		Mean	Std. D	Mean	Std. D					
Daily life	Health	6.41	1.034	5.88	1.327	4.823	0.029	−2.860	98.396	0.005
Scientific research	Maps	5.91	1.040	5.56	1.380	7.332	0.007	−2.125	205.813	0.035
Business decision	Maps	5.99	1.083	5.46	1.344	6.066	0.015	−3.151	203.190	0.002
	Credit records	5.75	1.466	5.20	1.496	14.317	0.000	−4.225	173.917	0.000
	International trade	5.63	1.314	4.68	1.638	4.568	0.034	−4.620	202.965	0.000
	Budget & spending	5.95	1.173	5.20	1.502	7.224	0.008	−4.021	201.566	0.000
Anti-corruption	Health	6.49	0.880	5.96	1.360	7.500	0.007	−3.291	157.989	0.001
	Culture & leisure	5.88	1.092	5.23	1.440	10.903	0.001	−3.597	175.248	0.000
	Legislation	6.32	0.932	5.74	1.316	8.653	0.004	−3.623	167.730	0.000
	Weather	6.10	0.986	5.55	1.305	11.003	0.001	−3.360	174.899	0.001
	Registration	5.73	1.294	5.15	1.667	7.412	0.007	−2.798	177.903	0.006

5 Discussion

The results above have tested our three hypotheses of the relation among OGD users, their demand and utilization. Our first analysis of citizen's knowing of OGD shows that currently, relatively few of them knew about or ever used OGD and OGD portals established by the government. This finding is in line with previous studies showing that a serious problem with OGD development is its usage, compared with its disclosure [9, 13, 25, 29]. Since OGD is intended to reduce the asymmetry of information among citizens and governments bodies [36, 45], it becomes a precondition for OGD utilization that citizens are conscious of the data being released by the government. Although governments have built portals to make their open data accessible for the public, it seems that their goals for promoting transparency and facilitating accountability [1] have not been achieved due to citizen's unawareness of their efforts. Therefore, it is important for governments to make effort to improve the citizens' awareness of the data that they have disclosed. Referring to Chinese OGD portals, they could stop blocking search engines [38] for collecting portal information and also put links of OGD portals on other e-government websites to increase online visibility [46].

Our results also show some citizens choose not to use OGD or portals even after they are informed about them, which is against the conclusion of [18] that citizens who already knew an OGD project are more willing to participate than those who never heard of OGD before. Thus, researchers could study about citizen's motivations of OGD utilization in future studies. If we understand about why citizens choose not to use OGD, it would help the governments to improve the OGD quality and services accordingly to promote the utilization.

Our analysis has shown citizen's preferences in different OGD subjects. The statistics have supported their greater demand for health and education data, which has the potential to make key public services more effective and inclusive [47]. However, according to Open Data Barometer's 4th report in 2017, although the rate of open datasets published by governments in health (7%) and education (8%) is not the lowest (1%) among all OGD subjects, their availability shows a significant decline. In addition, health data also shows low quality in updating and sustainable. This would affect public services for citizens as a whole. Therefore, governments should improve their data quality and open data that citizens show great need in order to reach their aim of OGD programs. For Chinese OGD portals, it would be helpful to encourage citizens to use the data if they could release more data about health and education and update the data regularly to ensure the availability of the latest version. Our results about citizens' preferences of map data for scientific research supported [47]'s view of using map data for innovation and produce significant economic value.

The correlation of citizens' OGD utilization with their demand of certain data subjects shows support for the view that different societal issues would involve different needs of different users [22]. Thus, it is possible to improve the usage of open data in future development of OGD portals by recognizing user's requirements on specific purpose or context during their visits to OGD portals or platforms [12, 20].

6 Conclusion

Open government data could bring various types of benefits [8]. Related research has highlighted the utilization of OGD rather than the disclosure as a vital issue to be addressed by OGD programs [9, 13, 25, 29]. However, there is a gap in the literature concerning the link between OGD utilization and the users [11]. The aim of disclosing government data on the web is for its use, reuse, and distribution [1]. Since citizens are recognized as a main participant in the open data process who have a direct effect on OGD utilization from the demand side [13], taking a deep look into the OGD utilization process by investigating users could, thus, help to improve OGD usage and its benefits.

In order to fill the observed knowledge gap, we carried out this study from the perspective of citizens as the OGD users to find out possible relationships between users, their OGD demands, and types of OGD utilizations. Three hypotheses were proposed about the correlations among these three. We supposed that users' characteristics would affect their OGD demands and utilization, and different types of utilization could affect users' demands for different data subjects.

We designed and carried out an online survey involving Chinese citizens to collect our data for analysis, and drew the following key conclusions:

- Few users have ever known of or used OGD or portals set by governments. Users' occupation and education have an effect on their knowledge of OGD.
- Users show different degrees of demand for different OGD subjects. Their age, occupation and education affect their preferences for certain data subjects, while gender shows no effect on their preferences.

- Citizens chose to use OGD mainly to access data concerning daily life and anti-corruption, which are in line with the main aim of OGD programs. Their types of utilization have correlation with their education and knowledge of OGD. Gender, age and occupation show no significant effect on OGD utilization.
- Different types of utilization could lead to differences in the demand for OGD subjects.

Based on the conclusions drawn from our data analysis and comparison with related studies, we recommend governments take effort to improve public awareness of OGD programs and portals. Only if citizens know about OGD, could they think about using it. Governments should also improve the quality of datasets and disclose more data in subject areas that citizens have shown greatest need and interest, such as health and education. Additionally, providing OGD according to users' specific scenario in visiting OGD portals to meet their specific data demands could be a possible way to improve OGD utilization. Since our study shows some citizens choose not to use OGD even if they are aware of its existence, researchers could carry out further study of citizens' motivation and needs concerning of OGD and OGD portals.

Our study displays both strengths and limitations. Based on data analysis, we have confirmed our hypotheses of the relationship between OGD users, their demand and utilization. Out study also clarified for our sample population of citizens' the extent of their awareness of OGD and portals. However, our methodology has some limitations. We carried out our survey on a sample of the Chinese population. Therefore, the results may not be generalizable to other populations and citizens of other countries. There are also not enough populations who have used OGD or OGD portals before in the participants of our survey, which may infect our analysis of comparison between experienced users and potential users. But this bias reflects the current OGD utilization and agrees with other studies noticing lack of use as the problem in OGD development. Future studies using data samples of other countries should be conducted to test our hypotheses and confirm conclusion for other populations. We will also carry out research for analyzing the specific reasons of citizens' choosing not to use OGD when they know their existence to help find out more specific methods to improve OGD utilization.

References

1. Attard, J., et al.: A systematic review of open government data initiatives. Gov. Inf. Q. 32(4), 399–418 (2015)
2. Ubaldi, B.: Open government data: towards empirical analysis of open government data initiatives. OECD Work. Pap. Pub. Gov. (22), p. 0_1 (2013)
3. Conradie, P., Choenni, S.: On the barriers for local government releasing open data. Gov. Inf. Q. 31, S10–S17 (2014)
4. Jaeger, P.: Deliberative democracy and the conceptual foundations of electronic government. Gov. Inf. Q. 22(4), 702–719 (2005)
5. Jaeger, P., Bertot, J.C.: Transparency and technological change: ensuring equal and sustained public access to government information. Gov. Inf. Q. 27(4), 371–376 (2010)

6. Jaeger, P., Burnett, G.: Information access and exchange among small worlds in a democratic society: the role of policy in shaping information behavior in the post-9/11 United States. Libr. Q. **75**(4), 464–495 (2005)
7. Zuiderwijk, A., Janssen, M.: Open data policies, their implementation and impact: a framework for comparison. Gov. Inf. Q. **31**(1), 17–29 (2014)
8. Janssen, M., Charalabidis, Y., Zuiderwijk, A.: Benefits, adoption barriers and myths of open data and open government. Inf. Syst. Manag. **29**(4), 258–268 (2012)
9. Heise, A., Naumann, F.: Integrating open government data with stratosphere for more transparency. Web Seman. Sci. Serv. Agents World Wide Web **14**, 45–56 (2012)
10. Kassen, M.: A promising phenomenon of open data: a case study of the Chicago open data project. Gov. Inf. Q. **30**(4), 508–513 (2013)
11. Safarov, I., Meijer, A., Grimmelikhuijsen, S.: Utilization of open government data: a systematic literature review of types, conditions, effects and users. Inf. Polity **22**, 1–24 (2017)
12. Ruijer, E., et al.: Connecting societal issues, users and data. Scenario-based design of open data platforms. Gov. Inf. Q. **34**, 470–480 (2017)
13. Zuiderwijk, A., Janssen, M.: A coordination theory perspective to improve the use of open data in policy-making. In: Wimmer, M.A., Janssen, M., Scholl, H.J. (eds.) EGOV 2013. LNCS, vol. 8074, pp. 38–49. Springer, Heidelberg (2013). https://doi.org/10.1007/978-3-642-40358-3_4
14. Wang, H.-J., Lo, J.: Adoption of open government data among government agencies. Gov. Inf. Q. **33**(1), 80–88 (2016)
15. Meijer, A., de Hoog, J., van Twist, M., van der Steen, M., Scherpenisse, J.: Understanding the dynamics of open data: from sweeping statements to complex contextual interactions. In: Gascó-Hernández, M. (ed.) Open Government. PAIT, vol. 4, pp. 101–114. Springer, New York (2014). https://doi.org/10.1007/978-1-4614-9563-5_7
16. Willinsky, J.: The unacknowledged convergence of open source, open access, and open science. First Monday **10**(8) (2005). http://firstmonday.org/issues/issue10-8/willinsky/index.html
17. Florini, A.: Making transparency work. Glob. Environ. Politics **8**(2), 14–16 (2008)
18. Wijnhoven, F., Ehrenhard, M., Kuhn, J.: Open government objectives and participation motivations. Gov. Inf. Q. **32**(1), 30–42 (2015)
19. King, W.R., He, J.: A meta-analysis of the technology acceptance model. Inf. Manag. **43**(6), 740–755 (2006)
20. Power, R., Robinson, B., Rudd, L., Reeson, A.: Scenario planning case studies using open government data. In: Denzer, R., Argent, R.M., Schimak, G., Hřebíček, J. (eds.) ISESS 2015. LNCS, vol. 448, pp. 207–216. Springer, Cham (2015). https://doi.org/10.1007/978-3-319-15994-2_20
21. Parycek, P., Hochtl, J., Ginner, M.: Open government data implementation evaluation. J. Theor. Appl. Electron. Commer. Res. **9**(2), 80–99 (2014)
22. Susha, I., Grönlund, Å., Janssen, M.: Driving factors of service innovation using open government data: an exploratory study of entrepreneurs in two countries. Inf. Polity **20**(1), 19–34 (2015)
23. Magalhaes, G., Roseira, C. Manley, L.: Business models for open government data. In: Proceedings of the 8th International Conference on Theory and Practice of Electronic Governance. ACM (2014)
24. Gonzalez-Zapata, F., Heeks, R.: The multiple meanings of open government data: understanding different stakeholders and their perspectives. Gov. Inf. Q. **32**(4), 441–452 (2015)

25. Whitmore, A.: Using open government data to predict war: a case study of data and systems challenges. Gov. Inf. Q. **31**(4), 622–630 (2014)
26. Veeckman, C., van der Graaf, S.: The city as living laboratory: empowering citizens with the citadel toolkit. Technol. Innov. Manag. Rev. **5**(3), 6–17 (2015)
27. Venkatesh, V., Sykes, T.A., Venkatraman, S.: Understanding e-Government portal use in rural India: role of demographic and personality characteristics. Inf. Syst. J. **24**(3), 249–269 (2014)
28. Kalampokis, E., Tambouris, E., Tarabanis, K.: Linked open government data analytics. In: Wimmer, Maria A., Janssen, M., Scholl, Hans J. (eds.) EGOV 2013. LNCS, vol. 8074, pp. 99–110. Springer, Heidelberg (2013). https://doi.org/10.1007/978-3-642-40358-3_9
29. Kuhn, K.: Open government data and public transportation. J. Publ. Transp. **14**(1), 5 (2011)
30. Chakraborty, A., et al.: Open data for informal settlements: toward a user' s guide for urban managers and planners. J. Urban Manag. **4**(2), 74–91 (2015)
31. Desouza, K.C., Bhagwatwar, A.: Citizen apps to solve complex urban problems. J. Urban Technol. **19**(3), 107–136 (2012)
32. Rajshree, N., Srivastava, B.: Open government data for tackling corruption-a perspective. In: Workshops at the Twenty-Sixth AAAI Conference on Artificial Intelligence (2012)
33. Leontieva, L.S., et al.: Social-communicative innovations in anti-corruption activities (regional aspect). Asian Soc. Sci. **11**(7), 387 (2015)
34. Harvey, M., et al.: Between demand and consumption: a framework for research. Centre Res. Innov. Compe. Discuss. Paper **40**, 1–77 (2001)
35. Warde, A.: Consumption and theories of practice. J. Consum. Cult. **5**(2), 131–153 (2005)
36. Murillo, M.J.: Evaluating the role of online data availability: the case of economic and institutional transparency in sixteen Latin American nations. Int. Polit. Sci. Rev. **36**(1), 42–59 (2015)
37. Bogdanović-Dinić, S., Veljković, N., Stoimenov, L.: How open are public government data? An assessment of seven open data portals. In: Rodríguez-Bolívar, M.P. (ed.) Measuring E-government Efficiency. PAIT, vol. 5, pp. 25–44. Springer, New York (2014). https://doi.org/10.1007/978-1-4614-9982-4_3
38. Wang, D., Chen, C., Richards, D.: A prioritization-based analysis of local open government data portals: A case study of Chinese province-level governments. Gov. Inf. Q. **35**(4), 644–656 (2018)
39. StateCouncil, Notice of the State Council on Issuing the Interim Measures for the Administration of Sharing of Government Information Resources, T.S. Council, Editor, Beijing (2016)
40. Huang, R., Wang, C.: An investigation into the open government data platform in china. Inf. Stud.: Theory Appl. **39**(7), 50–55 (2016)
41. Cronbach, L.J.: Coefficient alpha and the internal structure of tests. Psychometrika **16**(3), 297–334 (1951)
42. Tavakol, M., Dennick, R.: Making sense of Cronbach's alpha. Int. J. Med. Educ. **2**, 53 (2011)
43. Kaiser, H.F.: A second generation little jiffy. Psychometrika **35**(4), 401–415 (1970)
44. Dziuban, C.D., Shirkey, E.C.: When is a correlation matrix appropriate for factor analysis? Some decision rules. Psychol. Bull. **81**(6), 358 (1974)
45. Fuentes-Enriquez, R., Rojas-Romero, Y.: Developing accountability, transparency and government efficiency through mobile apps: the case of Mexico. In: Proceedings of the 7th International Conference on Theory and Practice of Electronic Governance. ACM (2013)
46. Yi, K., Jin, T.: Hyperlink analysis of the visibility of Canadian library and information science school web sites. Online Inf. Review **32**(3), 325–347 (2008)
47. OpenDataBarometer Open Data Barometer Global Report, 4th edn. (2017)

Engaging with Multi-media Content

"Looking for an Amazing Game I Can Relax and Sink Hours into...": A Study of Relevance Aspects in Video Game Discovery

Toine Bogers[1]([✉]), Maria Gäde[2], Marijn Koolen[3], Vivien Petras[2], and Mette Skov[4]

[1] Science, Policy and Information Studies,
Department of Communication and Psychology, Aalborg University Copenhagen,
Copenhagen, Denmark
toine@hum.aau.dk

[2] Berlin School of Library and Information Science, Humboldt-Universität zu Berlin,
Berlin, Germany
{maria.gaede,vivien.petras}@ibi.hu-berlin.de

[3] Royal Netherlands Academy of Arts and Sciences – Humanities Cluster,
Amsterdam, The Netherlands
marijn.koolen@di.huc.knaw.nl

[4] Department of Communication and Psychology, Aalborg University,
Aalborg, Denmark
skov@hum.aau.dk

Abstract. With the rapid growth of the video game industry over the past decade, there has been a commensurate increase in research activity focused on a variety of aspects of video games. How people discover the video games they want to play and how they articulate these information needs is still largely unknown, however. A better understanding of video game-related information needs and what makes a game relevant to a user could aid in the design of more effective, domain-specific search engines. In this paper we take a first step towards such domain-specific understanding. We present an analysis of a random sample of 521 complex game requests posted on Reddit. A coding scheme was developed that captures the 41 different aspects of relevance and information needs expressed in these requests. We find that game requests contain an average of close to 5 different relevance aspects. Several of these relevance aspects are geared specifically to video games, while others are more general.

Keywords: Query analysis · Video games · Game search · Complex search · Information need categorization · Relevance aspects

© Springer Nature Switzerland AG 2019
N. G. Taylor et al. (Eds.): iConference 2019, LNCS 11420, pp. 503–515, 2019.
https://doi.org/10.1007/978-3-030-15742-5_48

1 Introduction

Today, the global video game market is valued at 78.61 billion USD and growing with more than half a billion people worldwide playing video games for around six hours a week on average [1]. As a result, video games are a fruitful domain for research on a variety of topics, such as the benefits and hazards of playing video games [10], analysis and prediction of player behavior [12], and recommendation of games and in-game player match-ups [20]. Given the vast monetary potential of video games, we know surprisingly little about how people discover new video games to play and what makes games relevant to them. While there is work on casual leisure search in other domains—such as books [5,18], television [8], and movies [4,5]—video games search remains unexplored. Yet, understanding game discovery and the aspects used to identify relevant games is crucial for building successful search and discovery systems.

In this paper, we take a first step towards a better understanding of this scenario by collecting, annotating, and analyzing a set of real-world information needs related to video game discovery[1]. We focus on requests that elaborate a searcher's information need to a greater degree than simple Web search queries would, to get a more complete view of their relevance aspects. Relevance aspects are components of stated information needs with the intent of finding relevant results. Relevance aspects, when appropriately described as metadata or features in a search system, can guide a searcher to their stated goal. If the search system uses features different from the stated relevance aspects, a mismatch and consequent search failure occurs. This work identifies those relevance aspects, which may decide between search failure or success in video game discovery.

To achieve this, we collected over 2,000 discussion threads from Reddit subreddits dedicated to game discovery and annotated a random sample of 521 video game search requests expressed in these threads. We developed a coding scheme for capturing the variety of relevance aspects and information need types expressed in these requests. Several of these relevance aspects are geared specifically to video games, while others are more general. Through a detailed analysis of our coded requests, we find that they contain an average of almost 5 different relevance aspects, making this a truly complex search scenario. Our work could thereby contribute to future development of game search and discovery systems.

2 Related Work

There has been research focused on video games in many disciplines. Within IR and LIS, video games are mainly treated as part of everyday information seeking [19] or from an organizational and preservational perspective [17,22]. With tremendous choice and growing interest in games, the design of effective information systems for search and discovery is a crucial task. However, this requires a better understanding of games as well as information needs from diverse user

---

[1] In this paper, we focus exclusively on video games; table-top, role-playing and other game types are not considered.

groups [13,14]. Compared to other information objects like books, movies or even music, the classification and organization of games is a rather young and inter-disciplinary research field [2]. Traditional metadata schemes seem only partly suitable to describe games in their complexity due to the interactive character of games. Several researchers have made an effort to include these character-istics by defining metadata elements and a standardized vocabulary for games [14]. Video game genres have also seen considerable discussion [3,16]. Results from user appeal studies suggest that game appeal is strongly affected by com-plex narrative elements including engaging characters and gameplay mechanics as well as challenging tasks [13]. These would have to be described as (metadata) features in order to be incorporated successfully into search systems.

A large body of HCI research has examined players' interactions, motivations and experiences with games. From a complex search perspective, the experience of and motivation for playing video games is described widely as multi-faceted [7,11]. For example, [23] proposed 10 different sub-motivations for playing video games (advancement, mechanics, competition, socializing, relationship, team-work, discovery, role-playing, and customization), grouped into three overall components (achievement, social, and immersion).

Information science studies have focused mainly on user behavior and infor-mation needs within game playing contexts [6,21]. Very few studies have inves-tigated game-related information needs or seeking behavior. Accordingly, little is known about relevance aspects with respect to game search and discovery strategies. Lee et al. [15] investigated organizational principles behind the game collections of 56 users. Amongst others, participants mentioned visual metadata such as trailers or videos as well as similarity aspects as crucial information to decide, which games are relevant to them [15]. Furthermore, "price" and "plat-form" were mentioned by users as the most important metadata elements for games [14]. To the best of our knowledge, the work in this paper is the first attempt to analyze and categorize complex game requests from Internet fora.

3   Methodology

3.1   Data Collection

In order to perform a detailed analysis of the aspects that users think they need to describe when searching for video games, we collected and analyzed a rep-resentative sample of video game search requests. To collect a realistic sample of complex game requests, we turned to discussion forums, similar to earlier work on book and movie requests [5]. We identified three dedicated discussion groups for video game-related information needs on Reddit[2], a popular discus-sion and social news website. Two of these subreddits, /r/gamingsuggestions and /r/gamesuggestions contained a wide variety of requests for new games to play, while the third (/r/tipofmyjoystick), is dedicated to known-item (i.e., re-finding) requests for video games. One reason to choose Reddit is that it has dedicated

---

[2] Available at http://reddit.com, last visited September 4, 2018.

discussion groups, also known as *subreddits*, centered around different types of game-related search and discovery, which suggests that such requests are common enough to warrant a dedicated subreddit and signals a low threshold for users to post them. It is possible that Reddit users are not representative of all gamers, but we have no reason to believe their requests differ in any significant way from those of others. To collect game requests from these subreddits, we adapted an existing Reddit crawler[3] to continuously crawl all threads and comments posted to these three subreddits from June 2–22, 2018, resulting in 2,266 threads. Table 1 shows the distribution of these threads over the three subreddits, along with descriptive statistics of the different subreddits. It shows that /r/gamesuggestions is the least active subreddit with only 51 threads posted during our 20-day crawling window. The other two subreddits show considerably higher thread activity, but vary in terms of commenting activity. This suggests a fundamental difference between these types of needs and how they are resolved on Reddit; an analysis of this commenting behavior is left for future work.

3.2   Coding

Open Coding. To develop our coding scheme for relevance aspects expressed in requests for video games, we used an open coding approach. We selected a random sample of 75 threads from our Reddit crawl to serve as development set. Three of the five authors developed their own individual coding schemes on this development set. We settled on a sample size of 75 threads as other studies have shown it balances effort with recall, so that even infrequent but meaningful relevance aspects stand a chance of being identified [4,5]. For each thread, coders were shown the title and the full text of the first post.

Table 1. Overview of the 2,266 threads and comments crawled from the three subreddits. Request length is the length of the first post (in words), i.e., the original game request.

Subreddit	Threads		Comments		Request length		
	Total	Average	Total	Min	Average	Max
/r/tipofmyjoystick	1,131	4.4	4,969	1	115.5	1,137
/r/gamingsuggestions	1,084	8.2	8,925	1	80.2	1,569
/r/gamesuggestions	51	2.2	112	4	103.2	772

Axial Coding. The open coding phase resulted in three different coding schemes with a combined total of 95 different codes. Card sorting was used in the axial coding phase to produce a single, unified coding scheme to identify

---

[3] Available at https://github.com/lucas-tulio/simple-reddit-crawler, last visited September 4, 2018.

relationships between codes and re-arrange them into higher-level categories. Many codes were proposed by two or more annotators. We based the decision whether or not to merge to codes on the underlying purpose: developing systems that can help satisfy these complex game requests automatically. For example, the two different aspects 'soundtrack' (for music playing in the background) and 'sound effects' (for any kind of sound in the game) were grouped together under the aspect Sound design (hereafter stylized as such), denoting any game-related sound information. After the merging phase, related categories were grouped into top-level categories. The resulting coding scheme was then discussed by all five authors until consensus was reached. In general, all axial coding decisions were made with the aim of informing information systems that support heterogeneous real-life user requests with different strategies. Textual descriptions of the different aspects were added for each aspect along with prototypical examples to aid the final annotation process. Our final coding scheme is described in the Sect. 4.

Final Coding. For the final coding phase, every author annotated their own random sample of 140 subreddit threads. Posts from the development set were not re-used. Not every subreddit thread is necessarily a search request, so each post was first categorized as a request or not, after which only the requests were annotated. This resulted in a total of 521 annotated requests. After the first round of coding, all annotators discussed their experiences, which led to small refinements of the code labels and descriptions. Each annotator then revisited their 140 requests to adjust their annotations. To examine reliability, a total number of 80 posts overlapped between pairs of authors; agreement on these posts was calculated using Fleiss' kappa and is covered in Sect. 4.1.

4   Results

Figure 1 shows our final coding scheme, which includes seven top-level categories: five representing different categories of relevance aspects—Content, Metadata, Experience, Context, and Interactivity—and two representing aspects of the information needs—Search process and Information need. These seven main categories are further divided into 41 sub-categories. None of these categories are mutually exclusive; requests could be assigned more than one relevance or information need category, although at least one information need was assigned to each request.

The top-level category Content covers 11 sub-categories on what the game should be about. The majority of these sub-categories are domain-agnostic metadata elements such as Character, Design, Dialogue, Plot, Setting, Time, and Topic. In contrast, other sub-categories are highly domain-specific such as Cutscene(s), Sound design, World building, and Gameplay mechanics, which covers descriptions of the rules and rewards of a game and the tasks and choices provided to the player.

	Top-level aspect	Sub-aspect	Description
RELEVANCE ASPECTS · What should it be about?	Content	Characters	Games that identify specific characters, types of characters or character development
		Cutscene(s)	Games that feature a specific cutscene, intro, or loading screen
		Design	Games that feature particular graphics, art style(s), or special effects
		Dialogue	Games that feature a particular line or style of dialogue
		Gameplay mechanics	Games that feature particular gameplay mechanics or functionality
		Plot	Games with specific plot lines, narrative elements, or scripted events
		Setting	Games that take place in a specific setting, location, or near geographical landmarks
		Sound design	Games that feature particular sound effects, in-game music, or soundtrack
		Time	Games that are set in a particular time period or around a specific historical event
		Topic	Games that cover one or more specific topics
		World building	Games that feature a particular level design or quality of world building
What kind of properties should it have?	Metadata	Audience	Games that are aimed at a specific audience
		Availability	Games that are available through a particular purchasing model (e.g., shareware, Steam)
		Creator	Games from a particular developer or publisher
		Genre	Games that fall into one or more specific genres
		Language	Games written in a particular language
		Platform	Games that run on a specific platform or device
		Popularity	Games with a certain level of popularity or obscurity
		Price	Games that fall in particular price range or payment model
		Properties	Games with specific physical properties (or their packaging)
		Release date	Games that were released or played on a specific date or during a specific period
		Series	Games that are part of a particular franchise or intellectual property
		Technical specifications	Games that meet the user's requirements for the hardware and/or software it should run on
		Title	Games that have a particular title
What experience should it provide?	Experience	Mood	Games that evoke a certain mood, tone, or gaming experience
		Perspective	Games played from a particular perspective (e.g., first-person, third-person, isometric, top-down)
		Playability	Games that require a certain level of skill or hand-eye coordination
		(Re)play value	Games that offer certain levels of replay value, longevity and/or complexity
How should the user interact with it?	Interactivity	Connectivity	Games with a desired level of online connectivity
		Controls	Games that are playable with specific input devices
		Expandability	Games that are expandable through DLC, level editors, modding, or other user efforts
		Game mode	Games with particular game modes (e.g., single-player, multi-player, co-op, split-screen)
How is it used?	Context	Context	Games for playing in a specific context or for a particular purpose
INFORMATION NEED ASPECTS · What type of need is it?	Information need	Choice	Requests for help in deciding which of a set of games should be picked in a specific situation
		Discovery	Requests for games where the searcher is not aware of any games that match the search criteria
		Known-item	Requests for games already known with the purpose of re-finding them
		Similarity	Requests for games by listing other games that the requested games should (not) be similar to
How is the request expressed?	Search process	Link to external resource	Link to an external resource with helpful information to aid in the search process
		Not this one	Supporting the search process by explicitly ruling out candidate games as the right answer
		Search history	Supporting the search process by describing the previous steps taken by the user
		Situation of exposure	Supporting the re-finding process by describing where the user first encountered the game

Fig. 1. The coding scheme for video game search requests.

The top-level Metadata category includes a combination of traditional metadata, well-known from other domains of information resources, and categories specific to the game domain. The game-specific categories include Availability (requests for games available through a particular purchasing model, e.g., as a demo or shareware), Platform (requests specifying the platform or device, e.g., PS4 or PC), and Technical specifications (describing the user's requirements for the hardware or software the game should run on, e.g., specifying required disk space or processor power).

We identified four sub-categories under the top-level category Experience. The domain-agnostic Mood category describes the desired mood, tone, or gaming experience. In contrast, Playability and (Re)play value are domain-specific categories describing the skill level or coordination required to play the game, and the potential duration, longevity and/or complexity of the game respectively. Perspective includes requests for games played in a particular perspective (e.g., first-person view or top-down perspective).

The top-level category Interactivity and its four sub-categories are unique to the game domain and reflect a core characteristic of video games. The category Connectivity includes requests for either online or offline opportunities, Controls describes the input device (e.g., joystick, mouse, keyboard), Expandability includes requests that allow for game expansion through, e.g., downloadable content or bonus levels. Game mode specifies the desired gaming mode such as single-player, multi-player, cooperative, turn-based, or same-device versus multiple devices.

Finally, some users searching for games also describe the relevant Context, in which the requested games will be played or their purpose for playing them.

In addition to five top-level categories representing aspects of relevance, we also included two top-level categories representing the information need and the characteristics of the search process. We identified four different information need types: Choice, Discovery, Known-item, or Similarity. Discovery requests represent the typical scenario where users need help in finding games that match their desired search criteria. In contrast, the goal of Known-item requests is to re-find a specific video game. Choice requests are formulated by users who need help in deciding which of a small set of video games best match their stated relevance criteria, while Similarity-type needs always include at least one example of games that are (dis)similar in some respect.

Finally, several users included information to help support the Search process. For example, some users provided a Link to external resource, while others explicitly rule out candidate games by, e.g., title or genre (Not this one). Other users describe the previous steps taken in their Search history, or the Situation of exposure where the user first encountered a game (e.g., in school, watching a trailer).

4.1   Inter-annotator Agreement

In order to calculate inter-annotator agreement, we arranged for an overlap of 20 posts between successive annotators. For instance, annotators 1 and 2 overlapped on 20 posts, annotators 2 and 3 overlapped on 20 different posts, and so on. Finally, inter-annotator agreement was calculated over a total of 80 overlapping posts. We calculated Fleiss' kappa, because agreement[4] was calculated between different pairs of annotators [9]. The subreddits that these posts were crawled from focus on requests, so almost all posts contain search requests. Of the 80 double-assessed posts, annotators agreed only on one as not being a request and disagreed on two others.

For all categories, we computed agreement based only on the posts that both annotators labeled as requests. On the top-level categories, agreement is $\kappa = 0.81$ for the Content aspect, $\kappa = 0.61$ for Metadata, $\kappa = 0.45$ for Experience, $\kappa = 0.36$ for Context, $\kappa = 0.55$ for Search process and $\kappa = 0.7$ for Interactivity. Agreement on the type of information need is mostly high: $\kappa = 0.95$ for Known-item, $\kappa = 0.84$ for Discovery, $\kappa = 0.66$ Similarity and $\kappa = 0.47$ for Choice.

For the sub-categories, generally agreement is higher for common aspects than for rare aspects. Aspects that occur in more than 50% of all posts (Gameplay mechanics, Genre, Platform, Release date, Known-item and Similarity) have an agreement of $\kappa > 0.6$ and aspects that occur in 20%-50% of requests (Character, Design, Plot, Setting, Perspective, Discovery, Not this one, and Game mode) tend to have an agreement of $\kappa > 0.4$, with the exception of Setting, which has no agreement ($\kappa = -0.06$) while primary annotators coded 27% of request posts as having a Setting aspect. Some rare aspects (less than 10% of requests) with high agreement are concrete aspects like Price ($\kappa = 0.85$), Title ($\kappa = 0.71$), Link to external resource ($\kappa = 0.85$) and Situation of exposure ($\kappa = 0.71$). In general, agreement is high for high-level aspects, common aspects and concrete aspects, but drops for increasingly rare or affective aspects.

5   Analysis

5.1   Information Need Types and Search Process Aspects

Table 2 shows the frequency and co-occurrence statistics of information need types among the 521 annotated requests. The requests fall in two large groups. The first group covering about half of all requests with a re-finding intent (Known-item), which is not surprising, because 265 requests originated in the /r/tipofmyjoystick subreddit (subtitled *"What was that game called again?"*), which was created for just this type of question. The Known-item information need is a mostly independent type, but has a slight overlap of 20% with Similarity. A typical Known-item information need would be *"Childhood Mystery PC game. I distinctly remember playing a click interactive mystery game. There's a funeral of a sort of inventor/scientist/important guy going on (I couldn't get past it for some reason) the character was staying in a hotel, i believe. It was cloudy and had a sad vibe most of the time, but that was only the beginning, I think."* The other group consists of needs to discover new games, with more overlap

---

[4] Agreement scores for all aspects are available at http://toinebogers.com/?page_id=779.

between aspects. Particularly Similarity and Discovery often co-occur with each other: 68% of Discovery requests and 71% of Similarity requests co-occur with the other type. Similarity is rarely the sole information need of a request, but often co-occurs with some Content aspects, which adds a Discovery need. An example of a Similarity request which also includes a Discovery need is the following: *"Looking for a Mac/iOS/Xbox One game where I can create buildings/bases/homes etc. I love architecture and want a game where I can design buildings (besides Minecraft). I like the building mechanics of Rust and Raft, but my Macbook Air isn't powerful enough to run Rust and Raft is only available for PC."* Vice versa, a Similarity need is combined with a Discovery need based on previous gaming experiences. When a Similarity need is combined with a Known-item need, it is often to indicate what the sought-after game is similar to and to help others narrow down the direction(s) in which to search. Choice is not common, and only co-occurs with Discovery and Similarity.

Table 2. Co-occurrence statistics of information needs over 521 requests. Probabilities represent the likelihood of also observing the need marked in a column, given the need marked in a row.

		Choice	Discovery	Known-item	Similarity
	Frequency	23	234	265	224
All	521	0.04	0.45	0.51	0.43
Choice	23	1	0.52	0	0.43
Discovery	234	0.05	1	0	0.68
Known-item	265	0	0	1	0.2
Similarity	224	0.05	0.71	0.23	1

Aspects of the Search process are described in 132 out of 521 requests (25%), and is fairly common in Known-item requests (35%) and Similarity requests (24%) (mainly in combination with Known-item), but less so in Discovery (16%). It is not mentioned in Choice requests. Search history (2%) and Link to external resource (5%) are rare, but Not this one (10%) and Situation of exposure (12%) are somewhat more common. Situation of exposure is fairly common in the group of KI requests (22%), but rare in the other group of Discovery (1%) and Similarity (6%) requests as these focus on finding new games. In contrast, Not this one is somewhat common in the group of Discovery (13%) and Similarity (15%) requests, but rarer in Known-item group (8%). For KI requests, Situation of exposure might trigger memories of forum members who experienced similar exposure to quickly zoom in on candidates for re-finding requests. Not this one is less useful, as it only excludes a few of many options. For Discovery and Similarity requests, the Not this one aspect is helpful to avoid getting obvious suggestions, but they have no previous exposure to new games.

5.2   Relevance Aspects

We do not have space in this paper to report all individual numbers for the occurrence of relevance aspects in our data, but Table 3 reports the most frequent ones per category. Content and Metadata aspects are mentioned in almost all requests, whereas Context is the least frequent category. Content and Metadata aspects could be more easily described in information systems, so they might be characteristics (content or metadata details) that are not yet described or that would not be described, because they are too detailed. This is certainly true for the Gameplay mechanics aspect, which contains many fine-grained descriptions of sometimes minuscule details within the games that searchers remembered. A typical example would be *"I remember you could launch warheads that exploded, bio-heads that had a green mist, seals rode in on a boat, there was like a media tower I think that you could use to do propaganda."* Perhaps search requests like this could be solved by using sophisticated content-based information retrieval algorithms that allow for searching directly within images or videos. On average, searchers mentioned 4.6 different relevance aspects in their information need statements from 2.3 relevance aspect categories on average. In 10% of our analyzed cases, searchers mentioned relevance aspects from four or all five of the categories in our coding scheme. This shows the complexity of the search requests, which cannot be fulfilled using the simple search interfaces we are used to in Web search today.

Table 3. Frequency statistics of the five top-level relevance categories ($N = 521$), along with the most frequent aspect for each category.

Category	Frequency	%	Most frequent aspect	Frequency	%
Content	419	80.4	Gameplay mechanics	321	61.6
Metadata	436	83.7	Platform	311	59.7
Experience	187	35.9	Perspective	85	16.3
Interactivity	122	23.4	Game mode	93	17.9
Context	53	10.2	–	–	–

5.3   Relevance Aspects by Information Need Type

Tabulating relevance aspects by information need type shows some interesting differences (see Fig. 2). Relatively speaking, Known-item requests more often contain comments about Content or Metadata aspects, whereas Discovery requests mention Context, Experience and Interactivity aspects more often than other information need types do.

The subreddit /r/tipofmyjoystick, where most of the Known-item requests come from, provides a template for relevance aspects, which searchers attempt

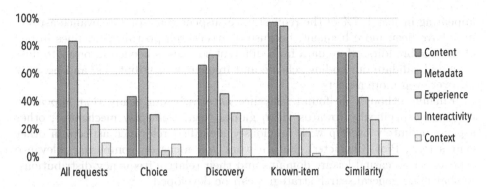

Fig. 2. Distribution of search aspect categories per information need type.

to fill in describing their request. This template[5] contains the relevance aspects Genre, Platform, and Release date (all from Metadata); Characters, Design, and Gameplay mechanics (all from Content) as well as other comments. These relevance aspects are named at least twice as often in connection with the Known-item information need type than any of the other ones. While a more precise listing of Content and Metadata aspects can be expected for a re-finding goal, we still wonder whether their disproportionately high frequency—they are by far the most frequent in our dataset—is due to the standardization effect of the template, which forced searchers to elaborate more on their searched relevance aspects than usual.

6   Discussion and Conclusions

In this study, we developed a coding scheme for complex video game discovery comprising 33 relevance aspects. When considering that the average video game request covers close to 5 different relevance aspects, it is fair to describe video game discovery as a complex search scenario.

Our results are in line with previous findings from qualitative studies [13, 14], confirming a combination of commonly-used aspects, such as Content and Metadata (especially game-specific elements, such as Platform at 69%) as well as engagement characteristics, such as Experience (32% of all requests), Interactivity (23%) and Context (10%). In addition, the present study has identified several novel relevance aspects, including Sound design, Popularity, Playability, and Expandability. Future steps include further comparison of the identified 33 relevance aspects with existing metadata elements and vocabularies for games [14] as well as, if necessary, the extension and prioritization of (metadata) features in order to be incorporated successfully into search systems. As our annotations are limited to 521 requests from three subreddits with some relevance aspects

---

[5] Available at https://www.reddit.com/r/tipofmyjoystick/comments/64i787/psa_a_gui de_to_better_results, last visited September 9, 2018.

appearing in just 1–2% of the requests, we suspect that some relevance aspects may have been more frequent, because of structured posting guidelines in one of these subreddits. More data from different sources is needed in order to fine-tune and validate our coding scheme and frequency distributions, and possibly uncover even more aspects.

Finally, although we found relevance aspects in our study that appear to be geared specifically towards video games (e.g., Gameplay mechanics), other aspects definitely overlap with previously identified relevance aspects in other genres (e.g., Plot, Character). Future work will focus on comparing relevance aspects across casual leisure domains and their relative frequency distributions, so that more general search strategies can be developed.

References

1. Video Game Industry Statistics, Trends & Data. https://www.wepc.com/news/video-game-statistics/. Accessed 4 Sept 2018
2. Aarseth, E., Smedstad, S.M., Sunnanå, L.: A multidimensional typology of games. In: Proceedings of 2003 DiGRA International Conference on Level Up (2003)
3. Apperley, T.H.: Genre and game studies: toward a critical approach to video game genres. Simul. Gaming **37**(1), 6–23 (2006)
4. Bogers, T.: Searching for movies: an exploratory analysis of movie-related information needs. In: Proceedings of iConf 2015. iDEALS (2015)
5. Bogers, T., Gäde, M., Koolen, M., Petras, V., Skov, M.: "What was this movie about this chick?": A comparative study of relevance aspects in book and movie discovery. In: Chowdhury, G., McLeod, J., Gillet, V., Willett, P. (eds.) iConference 2018. LNCS, vol. 10766, pp. 323–334. Springer, Cham (2018). https://doi.org/10.1007/978-3-319-78105-1_36
6. Bullard, J.: Playfully serious information for serious play: the integration of community values in an information resource. In: Proceedings of iConf 2013, pp. 389–397. iDEALS (2013)
7. Cairns, P., Cox, A., Nordin, A.I.: Immersion in digital games: review of gaming experience research. In: Angelides, M.C., Agius, H. (eds.) Handbook of Digital Games, pp. 337–361. John Wiley & Sons Inc., New York (2014)
8. Elsweiler, D., Mandl, S., Lunn, B.K.: Understanding casual-leisure information needs: a diary study in the context of television viewing. In: IIiX 2010, pp. 25–34 (2010)
9. Fleiss, J.L.: Measuring nominal scale agreement among many raters. Psychol. Bull. **76**(5), 378–382 (1971)
10. Gentile, D.A., Lynch, P.J., Linder, J.R., Walsh, D.A.: The effects of violent video game habits on adolescent hostility, aggressive behaviors, and school performance. J. Adolesc. **27**(1), 5–22 (2004)
11. Hochleitner, C., Hochleitner, W., Graf, C., Tscheligi, M.: A heuristic framework for evaluating user experience in games. In: Bernhaupt, R. (ed.) Game User Experience Evaluation. HIS, pp. 187–206. Springer, Cham (2015). https://doi.org/10.1007/978-3-319-15985-0_9
12. Kaytoue, M., Silva, A., Cerf, L., Meira Jr., W., Raïssi, C.: Watch me playing, i am a professional: a first study on video game live streaming. In: Proceedings of 21st WWW, pp. 1181–1188. ACM (2012)

13. Lee, J., Clarke, R., Cho, H., Windleharth, T.: Understanding appeals of video games for readers' advisory and recommendation. Ref. User Serv. Q. **57**(2), 127 (2017)
14. Lee, J.H., Clarke, R.I., Perti, A.: Empirical evaluation of metadata for video games and interactive media. JASIST **66**(12), 2609–2625 (2015)
15. Lee, J.H., Clarke, R.I., Rossi, S.: A qualitative investigation of users discovery, access, and organization of video games as information objects. J. Inf. Sci. **42**(6), 833–850 (2016)
16. Lee, J.H., Karlova, N., Clarke, R.I., Thornton, K., Perti, A.: Facet analysis of video game genres. In: Proceedingds of iConf 2014 (2014)
17. McDonough, J., Kirschenbaum, M., Reside, D., Fraistat, N., Jerz, D.: Twisty little passages almost all alike: applying the FRBR model to a classic computer game. Digit. Humanit. Q. **4**(2), 1869–1883 (2010)
18. Reuter, K.: Assessing aesthetic relevance: children's book selection in a digital library. JASIST **58**(12), 1745–1763 (2007)
19. Savolainen, R.: Everyday life information seeking: approaching information seeking in the context of 'Way of Life'. Libr. Inf. Sci. Res. **17**, 259–294 (1995)
20. Sifa, R., Bauckhage, C., Drachen, A.: Archetypal game recommender systems. In: LWA, pp. 45–56 (2014)
21. Sköld, O., Adams, S., Harviainen, J.T., Huvila, I.: Game research methods. chapter studying games from the viewpoint of information, pp. 57–73. ETC Press, Pittsburgh (2015)
22. Winget, M.A.: Videogame preservation and massively multiplayer online role-playing games: a review of the literature. JASIST **62**(10), 1869–1883 (2011)
23. Yee, N.: Motivations for play in online games. CyberPsychol. Behav. **9**(6), 772–775 (2006)

Moving Beyond Text: How Teens Evaluate Video-Based High Stakes Health Information via Social Media

Kayla M. Booth[1]([✉]) and Eileen M. Trauth[2]

[1] University of Pittsburgh, Pittsburgh, PA 15213, USA
kbooth@pitt.edu
[2] The Pennsylvania State University, University Park, PA, USA
emtrauth@gmail.com

Abstract. This paper qualitatively examines how teenagers in the US evaluate high stakes health information via social media. Through 30 semi-structured interviews with teens ages 13–18, we explore how teens interact with and make decisions about the quality of video-based exercise and nutrition content. Participants indicated that they are wary of advertisements and language that encourages extreme weight loss, yet prefer video content that is "fun" and engaging. Additionally, participants reported having explicit and implicit criteria for evaluating videos with health content that includes both graphic and content quality.

Keywords: Social media · Information behavior · Information quality · Health information

1 Introduction

The Age of Information, and Web 2.0 in particular, have unearthed a tectonic shift in how information is disseminated. Traditional "gatekeepers," such as publishing companies, editors, news organizations once developed and enforced criteria to assess what content was distributed to the masses. Now any user with an Internet connection (and the required skillset) can create and share content across audiences. While some scholars argue that this shift has enhanced the democracy of information sharing, others suggest that this places the onus of evaluation and decision-making onto users who may not have the appropriate level of training. This is particularly important given that many users make decisions based on the information they interact with online.

The exploration of how users evaluate information online, particularly via social media, has been a consistent thread of inquiry across information, computing, and related venues, including the iConference [1, 3, 4]. This inquiry is relevant across geographical regions, but is an increasingly "hot topic" in the United States regarding high-stakes contexts, such as politics and health. High-stakes information refers to content that individuals use to make decisions that can result in life-altering consequences. As the role of social media in both the 2016 Presidential Election and current

© Springer Nature Switzerland AG 2019
N. G. Taylor et al. (Eds.): iConference 2019, LNCS 11420, pp. 516–525, 2019.
https://doi.org/10.1007/978-3-030-15742-5_49

"anti-vaccination" or "vaccine safety" movements[1] demonstrate, it is more important than ever to understand how users make decisions about the quality of the information they interact with via social media.

There is a sea of extant literature that explores how users evaluate and assess the quality, trustworthiness, and credibility of information online [10–12]. While social media is increasingly a source of information, much of this literature focuses on how users interact with text. Social media, however, provides a space for users to create, share, and interact with a variety of content, including photographs, infographics, memes, videos, etc. While videos in particular make up a large portion of social media content and users are increasingly turning to video-based platforms like YouTube to learn about new topics [5], there is far less literature exploring how people make decisions specifically about video content [2].

While this line of inquiry is relevant across user demographics, this paper examines youth in particular. Youth are of particular interest given: (1) their relatively limited life experience and ranging stages of cognitive development [2], (2) their high rates of social media use in comparison to other age groups, and (3) their proclivity towards using social media to interact with high-stakes information and make decisions based on the content with which they interact [14, 15].

This paper examines young people's decision-making within a specific health-related, high-stakes context. Teenagers in the United States search for exercise and nutrition (the combination of which is often referred to as "fitness") information more than any other health-related topic and make real health-related decisions based on the information with which they interact [14, 15]. The study reported here explored how US teenagers evaluate high-stakes information in the form of videos on social media by examining the strategies young people employ to assess fitness information across social media platforms.

2 Related Work

2.1 High-Stakes Information Context: Teens, Health, and Social Media

Teens in the US engage with a myriad of health information sources, including parents, teachers, healthcare providers, and online spaces such as social media platforms [2, 14, 15]. While extant literature has largely focused on teens' online search behavior surrounding sexual health and drugs, teenagers search for exercise and nutrition information more than any other type of health information [14, 15].

While teens engage with an array of digital spaces and tools, there are a myriad of channels, accounts, and pages on social media platforms that are dedicated to fitness content. This freely available content can be instrumental for those who want to take charge of their health, but might not have physical or financial access to resources or

---

[1] While there are a myriad of names used to describe people and communities who debate the safety of vaccines (anti-vaccination, anti-vaxxers, vaccine safety advocates, etc.) [8], this example speaks to a current debate in which individuals and groups use social media platforms to exchange information and perspectives surrounding the effects of vaccines [9] (a high-stakes health topic).

healthcare providers. However, online fitness content can also be dangerous. In addition to the ability for untrained, unqualified users to share advice on how to exercise and lose weight, there are several online movements and communities that are problematic in terms of health. For example, pro-anorexia ("pro-ana") and pro-bulimia ("pro-mia") communities advocate that eating disorders are lifestyle choices rather than serious mental health conditions. These communities often post videos that they call "thinspiration" (the inspiration to be thin) [16]. Similar communities based on "fitspiration" (the inspiration to be "fit") emerged as a response to pro-ana and pro-mia movements to emphasize "fit" instead of skinny, but literature suggests that this content is just as unhealthy in terms of using video and images to glorify over-exercising, unattainable beauty standards, and unrealistic body composition [17, 18]. Extant literature suggests that because of the array of healthy and disordered fitness content on social media platforms, it is increasingly difficult for users to discern the difference between what is helpful vs. harmful [19].

The prevalence of disordered content on social media platforms is problematic for two reasons: (1) teens are at a higher risk of poor body image and the development of eating disorders [20], and (2) teens make real, offline decisions about their nutrition and exercise regimens based on the content with which they interact [14, 15]. While teens and fitness information on social media is the specific context of this specific paper, the study from which it is drawn speaks to a larger issue of how users who are at a heightened risk of developing health conditions evaluate relevant high-stakes content online.

2.2 Information Quality Framework

There are a myriad of approaches to exploring how users make decisions about online content. These approaches often examine trust, credibility, and information quality, yet there is little consensus on concrete definitions and differences between these constructs [10–12]. Scholars at the Berkman Klein Center for Internet & Society completed a cross-disciplinary literature review surrounding youth and information behavior [2]. The authors argue that while there are numerous theories, frameworks, and approaches to understanding how young people make decisions, there is a need for an approach that embodies: (1) decision-making as a holistic process of search, evaluation, and content creation rather than a single moment of use, and (2) a youth-oriented approach to understanding what young people do and value, as opposed to an adult-normative approach that seeks to determine whether or not young people are interacting with information in ways that adults require. The authors propose a youth-oriented information quality framework, which is utilized in this paper to gain insight into what teens value when interacting with fitness-related videos via social media. The research question guiding this paper is: *How do teenagers, ages 13–18 in the United States, evaluate the video-based fitness information they interact with via social media?*

3 Methods

This study is part of a larger research program guided by Gasser et al.'s (2012) framework [2], conceptualizing information quality as a holistic process that includes search, evaluation, and creation behaviors. While this holistic approach is particularly valuable when conceptualizing information behavior, this study focuses specifically on *evaluation*, considering how teens evaluate the health information they interact with via social media. It explores young people's decision making, what they value, and what they perceive to be important when making decisions about high-stakes content that is presented in the form of videos and images. This paper is informed by an interpretive epistemology, exploring the subjective realities, values, and experiences that inform information behavior. To gain insight into these realities and values, Author 1 conducted semi-structured interviews and walk-throughs with teenagers across the US.

3.1 Data Collection

Thirty teenagers (ages 13–18) were recruited to participate in semi-structured interviews and walk-throughs. Based on extant literature expressing: (1) differences in information behavior across socioeconomic status (SES), and (2) a socioeconomic health-gradient in which high-SES individuals experience greater health than low-SES individuals [21], participants were recruited from two low-SES school districts and two high-SES school districts. Participants were equally distributed across high and low-SES districts. Twenty-three participants identified as young women and seven identified as young men. Eight participants identified as Black, five as Hispanic, 17 as White, and one as Asian (see Fig. 1).

Recruitment Site	SES	US Region	Number of Participants	Gender	Race / Ethnicity
Site 1	Low-SES	Midwest	8	7 W 1 M	5 B 2 W 1 H
Site 2	Low-SES	Northeast	7	4 W 3 M	3 B 4 H
Site 3	High-SES	Northeast	9	7 W 2 M	9 W
Site 4	High-SES	Northeast	6	5 W 2 M	6 W 1 A

Fig. 1. Participant demographics

Based on the importance of parental consent and the safety of participants, participants were recruited via high school faculty and parents in local Parent Teacher Organizations (PTAs). Faculty and parents distributed flyers and scheduled the interviews. Participants were not required to have an interest in fitness; beyond the 13–18 year age range, the only participation requirement was having at least one active social media account. All interviews lasted approximately an hour and took place in school or in participants' homes. Participant (and parental, for those under the age of 18) consent was obtained prior to all interviews, and a parent or guardian was in the home for all house-based interviews. Participants were assured they could skip questions or stop the interview at any time without penalty. All interviews were audio-recorded.

As previously mentioned, this paper reports on one aspect of a larger study that explored how participants search for, evaluate, and create fitness information via social media. Interview questions were created based on Gasser et al.'s (2012) Information Quality Framework. This particular paper focuses on the section of the interviews that asked about participants' *evaluation* processes; these questions mapped directly to the four "main criteria" that Gasser et al. (2012) list in their review of extant literature surrounding youth information evaluation behaviors: (1) topicality, (2) cues and heuristics, (3) visual and interactive elements, and (4) judgement of 'objective' qualities. These questions were vetted and edited by one of the Gasser et al. (2012) authors. While asking participants about their search, evaluation, and creation behaviors, Author 1 provided each participant with an iPhone 6. Participants were encouraged to participate in "walk-throughs" in which they recalled a recent fitness-related search or went directly to a fitness-related social media account or channel they enjoy. This allowed participants to use the platforms they are familiar with to *show* and *explain* what they valued, liked, and disliked about the content with which they interact. Author 1 took screenshots of the content participants showed, as well as written notes regarding non-verbal expressions and behavior.

3.2   Data Analysis

Gasser et al. (2012) articulate four "main criteria" or sub-constructs of evaluation: (1) topicality, (2) cues and heuristics, (3) visual and interactive elements, 4) and judgements of 'objective' qualities. The authors provide a literature review for each of these sub-constructs. Using these literature reviews, Author 1 identified sub- themes (ex: for topicality, eight sub-themes were identified). Each interview question was informed by one of the sub-constructs or sub-themes. All interviews were transcribed. During the analysis of each transcript, every response was numerically coded according to which sub-construct and sub-theme they related. Not all sub- themes were present during data analysis. This paper is specifically interested in the sub-themes that were not only present, but directly related to how participants evaluate specifically *video-based* content.

4   Results

Results are organized by Gasser et al.'s evaluation sub-constructs. While all of the sub-constructs were present during data analysis, these results focus on those specifically related to teens' evaluation of video content, rather than social media content in general.

4.1   Cues and Heuristics

Gasser et al. (2012) review literature surrounding the cues and heuristics that young people observe and use to evaluate quality. In their review, "cues" are something a user observes about a *website*. In this study, however, participants reflected on cues relevant to the platform, the source (the person who is creating the video), and the video itself.

Cues: Advertisements. More than any other cue, participants indicated that the presence of advertising led them to negatively evaluate a video. The phrase that emerged across several interviews as participants explained why advertising makes them skeptical was that the information "isn't real." Participants negatively evaluated platforms with the presence of advertisements, but they also negatively evaluated "sources" or people who advertised within videos. This was particularly true for people who run YouTube channels and Instagram accounts. Daniel (13) explains,

> *"When they advertise other websites or other things at the beginning of their videos, I don't usually trust those, because, I mean, I just don't know. I just don't trust those ads...Yeah, they're advertising something, like: "Oh you should get this" or "Oh, you should try out this", then I usually don't trust it... It seems more of just a way to get publicity for something else that they need, rather than trying to help other people in that subject."*

Daniel prefers fitness content that helps people, which was echoed by several participants, especially when explaining how they evaluate YouTube vloggers or personalities. Joaquin (16) explained that his favorite "YouTuber" is a person named "Nickocado Avocado" who makes videos about nutrition. When asked why he liked this person, he explained that he felt this YouTuber genuinely "tries to help people." To many participants, this notion of helping people appears to be opposed to advertising or selling products. Joaquin explained that he can tell when people "aren't real" if they try to sell products in their YouTube videos; if a person is only posting for sponsorships, he can tell by their multiple posts about a product (or several products).

Cues: Negative, Unrealistic, or Dangerous Language. In addition to advertising, participants identified "negativity" as a sign of poor quality. Shana (18) explained that negative comments and judgmental attitudes "annoy" her. Similarly, perceived "positivity" helped participants evaluate YouTube videos favorably. For example, Ally (13) explained that she preferred to watch vloggers who are happy and motivated. Within the vein of "negativity," participants also expressed distrust of content that is either unrealistic or dangerous. Participants discussed several cues they use to identify unrealistic content. For YouTube videos, Charlotte (15) explained that she avoids videos with "obnoxious titles" that are used for "clickbait," like "get a bigger butt" or "lose 50 lb in a week." The majority of participants discussed advertisements and language as the main cues they use to evaluate quality.

4.2   Visual and Interactive Elements

During "walkthroughs," participants explained what they liked and disliked about the content they found and what was important to them.

Engagement. Several participants valued fitness content that is entertaining or fun. This is particularly true for participants who indicated that they don't love to exercise, but force themselves to do so anyway. Nicole (15) explained that she likes to find content that "make[s] exercise more fun" and looks for "fun videos." This notion of "fun" and entertaining content emerged repeatedly. When asked why YouTube was a good place to find fitness information, Ally (13) responded,

> *"Just because it's more fun to go and watch. Because I usually click on, the more lifestyle, beauty YouTubers. Because their videos are really fun and exciting to watch. And I always go on, there's this girl, I don't know her YouTube name, but she always post vlogs of her working out. And I just like going on there, because being able to watch a video of people giving you ideas and showing them make it look really fun. It's just a lot more interesting and satisfying than going on the internet, on like a doctor website, and reading a long article."*

Ally prefers these lifestyle bloggers to websites or articles because they are "exciting to watch." While many participants who watched YouTube videos followed along with workouts, she went on to explain that she prefers these types of videos instead. An important part of fitness content, particularly videos, is how "fun" and engaging they are. The more "fun" a video is, the more likely participants are to watch them instead of other types of media with similar information (especially text-based).

Graphic Quality vs. Content Quality. Participants discussed caring about the quality of videos more than still images, particularly "blurriness." Many participants echoed Jasmine's (17) sentiments, who said that the quality of a video matters and that bad quality means it's "not professional." Darnell (18) elaborated on what he expects from a video, stating that if it isn't shot with at least an HD720 camera, he won't watch it.

Participants evaluated videos based on graphic quality and blurriness, but they also value the information communicated within the videos. When asked how they know if information is "good" or "bad," some provided abstract qualifiers such as "if [the video] has facts." Others were more specific, like Angela (18) and Nina (16), who emphasized the importance of explaining how to exercise safely with "proper form." For Nina, these explanations take shape in the form of step-by- step instructions. For Jasmine (17), she positively evaluated a stretching video on YouTube because the speaker provided explicit "do's and don'ts" when explaining how to stretch the hip flexors. Renato (18) and Gina (14) echoed these sentiments, but also wanted an explanation of how an exercise works scientifically. Participants value detailed explanations, particularly when it comes to exercises, that they feel help them perform safely.

Video-Specific Criteria. Participants identified several criteria that is unique to how they evaluate videos. Before watching, participants looked at the number of subscribers the YouTube channel had (as well as who subscribes), the number of views that specific video had, and the number of "thumbs up" or "thumbs down" the video had. All of these criteria are listed right below the video on YouTube. Some participants had specific numbers in mind that clearly communicated quality. Darnell (18) explained that if a video has over 100,000 views, that means it has a good audience. Jasmine (17) selects the video in her search results that has the most views. Another element that participants look for when deciding which video to watch is the length of the video. While Charlotte (15) prefers shorter videos when choosing a workout to do, Nina (16) explains that long videos are a serious commitment in terms of time.

The criteria listed above are facets of a video that participants can evaluate before pressing "play." Once they are watching, however, there are several more elements that they consider when evaluating, many of which surround the *person* in the video.

Participants observed the featured person's: (a) appearance, (b) abilities, (c) demeanor, (d) actions, and (e) professionalism. When considering exercises, participants wanted the person leading the workout to be the same gender as them. Jasmine (17) explained that she wanted to watch girls the same age with bodies similar to hers. Similarly, Renato (18) wouldn't click on a female athlete "because females want to tone and males want to sculpt, which means they're doing different workouts." When he chose a video during his walk through, Renato remarked that the guy is "totally built," which means "whatever he's doing is working." Angela (18) felt similarly when she found a video with a woman who "looks very fit." She explained it is her goal "to look that fit." Participants wanted to watch videos where the featured person is the same gender and looks similar to their physical goals. In addition to gender and physique, participants also noticed a person's abilities, particularly when looking for how to do something sports-related. Participants like Emma (16) and Treyvon (18) wanted to see the person demonstrate what they were teaching, not just explain it. They wanted to know that they were learning from someone with expertise. In the previous section, it was discussed that participants cared about the depth and explanations the person in a video provides. For many, this served as an indicator of expertise. Participants also examined the person's demeanor as a similar indicator. Participants like Nina (16) indicated that a person's confidence will communicate whether or not they know what they're talking about.

5 Discussion

Overall, the results of this study suggest that teens have active strategies when evaluating the quality of high stakes, health-related videos on social media, although these strategies may differ significantly from those outlined in extant literature surrounding how youth evaluate text [2]. The strategies participants outline have several implications that extent far beyond fitness, but rather speak to larger themes about criteria young people value when interacting with high-stakes content via social media. Several participants reported valuing "fun" videos run by engaging "lifestyle vloggers." It may be beneficial for healthcare advocates and professionals to collaborate with these social media influencers on health campaigns and getting messages to young people, who are already tuned in and assigning these "vloggers" levels of credibility. Contrary to extant literature that suggests young people struggle to identify online advertisements, participants demonstrated an advanced understanding of how social media users and influencers use their platforms to earn money and distrust their content if they advertise too frequently. This may stem from frequent engagement with social media platforms or stricter policies enforcing the labeling of ads on platforms like Facebook and Instagram. One theme that repeatedly emerged, however, was their tendency to value numbers (number of followers, number of "likes," number of views, number of comments, etc.). This is particularly important given recent literature that outlines the effects of automated "bots" [22] that flood videos with either increased "likes" or "dislikes" and alter the numbers upon which participants made several judgements prior to even watching a video.

6 Conclusion

This paper offers three main contributions. The first is exploring teen information behavior in the context of fitness information; much of the extant literature examines how youth evaluate health information related to sex and drug use, yet nutrition and exercise are the two health-topics teens search for most often. The second is a specific focus on how users evaluate high-stakes *video* content, rather than text-based content; this is particularly valuable given the shifting landscape of social media. The third contribution is the use of a youth-oriented approach, which provides insight into teens' existing strategies and values and can help shape how we interact with and educate young ICT users. While this paper offers several contributions, it does not explore relationships between user identities and their evaluation behaviors. Further research is required to ensure that we study user behavior in ways that do not assume homogenous needs, experiences, and values.

References

1. Choi, W., Stvilia, B.: A new framework for web credibility assessment. In: iConference 2015 Proceedings (2015)
2. Gasser, U., Cortesi, S., Malik, M., Lee, A.: Youth and digital media: from credibility to information quality (2012)
3. Yang, J.Y., Rieh, S.Y.: A dyadic approach to information mediation at work: examining credibility and value perceptions (2013)
4. Starbird, K., Maddock, J., Orand, M., Achterman, P., Mason, R.M.: Rumors, false flags, and digital vigilantes: misinformation on Twitter after the 2013 Boston Marathon bombing. In: iConference 2014 Proceedings (2014)
5. Scolari, C.A., Masanet, M.J., Guerrero-Pico, M., Establés, M.J.: Transmedia literacy in the new media ecology: teens' transmedia skills and informal learning strategies. El profesional de la información (EPI) **27**(4), 801–812 (2018)
6. Mudliar, P., Raval, N.: "They are like personalized mini-Googles": seeking information on Facebook groups. In: Proceedings of the 51st Hawaii International Conference on System Sciences (2018)
7. Barkhuus, L., Bales, E., Cowan, L.: Internet ecologies of new mothers: trust, variety and strategies for managing diverse information sources. In: Proceedings of the 50th Hawaii International Conference on System Sciences (2017)
8. Koltai, K., Fleischmann, K.R.: Questioning science with science: the evolution of the vaccine safety movement. Paper presented at the 80th annual meeting of the association for information science and technology, Washington, DC (2017)
9. Wilson, K., Keelan, J.: Social media and the empowering of opponents of medical technologies: the case of anti-vaccinationism. J. Med. Internet Res. **15**(5), e103 (2013). https://doi.org/10.2196/jmir.2409
10. Metzger, M.J.: Making sense of credibility on the Web: models for evaluating online information and recommendations for future research. J. Am. Soc. Inf. Sci. **58**, 2078–2091 (2007)
11. Fogg, B.J., Tseng, H.: The elements of computer credibility. In: Proceedings of the SIGCHI Conference on Human Factors in Computing Systems (CHI 1999), pp. 80–87. ACM, New York (1999)

12. Gefen, D.: Reflections on the dimensions of trust and trustworthiness among online consumers. ACM SIGMIS Database **33**(3), 38–53 (2002)
13. Gasser, U., Cortesi, S., Malik, M., Lee, A.: Youth and digital media: from credibility to information quality. Berkman Center Research Publication No. 2012–1 (2012). http://ssrn.com/abstract=2005272
14. Wartella, E., Rideout, V., Zupancic, H., Beaudoin-Ryan, L., Lauricella, A.: Teens, technology, and health: a national survey. Center on Media and Human Development, School of Communication, Northwestern University (2015)
15. Wartella, E., Rideout, V., Montague, H., Beaudoin-Ryan, L., Lauricella, A.: Teens, health and technology: a national survey. Media Commun. **4**(3), 12 (2016)
16. Eikey, E.V., Booth, K.: Recovery and maintenance: how women with eating disorders use Instagram. In: iConference 2017, Wuhan, China, 22–25 March 2017
17. Tiggemann, M., Zaccardo, M.: Exercise to be fit, not skinny: the effect of fitspiration imagery on women's body image. Body Image **15**, 61–67 (2015). http://linkinghub.elsevier.com/retrieve/pii/S174014451150008
18. Tiggemann, M., Zaccardo, M.: Strong is the new skinny: a content analysis of #fitspiration images on Instagram. J. Health Psychol. **23**, 1003 (2016)
19. Syed-Abdul, S., et al.: Misleading health-related information promoted through video-based social media: anorexia on YouTube. J. Med. Internet Res. **15**(2), e30 (2013)
20. Carrotte, E.R., Vella, A.M., Lim, M.S.: Predictors of "liking" three types of health and fitness-related content on social media: a cross-sectional study. J. Med. Internet Res. **17**(8), e205 (2015)
21. Evans, W., Wolfe, B., Adler, N.: The SES and health gradient: a brief review of the literature. In: Biological Consequences of Socioeconomic Inequalities, p. 292 (2012)
22. Boichak, O., Jackson, S., Hemsley, J., Tanupabrungsun, S.: Automated diffusion? Bots and their influence during the 2016 U.S. Presidential Election. In: Chowdhury, G., McLeod, J., Gillet, V., Willett, P. (eds.) iConference 2018. LNCS, vol. 10766, pp. 17–26. Springer, Cham (2018). https://doi.org/10.1007/978-3-319-78105-1_3

Interacting with Personal Music Collections

Sally Jo Cunningham$^{(\boxtimes)}$ (iD)

Waikato University, Hamilton 3240, New Zealand
sallyjo@waikato.ac.nz

Abstract. Over the past three decades, everyday music listening practices have transitioned from physical music media (vinyl, CDROM) to personally held digital (MP3, MPEG) to cloud-based streaming services (Spotify, Pandora). The academic research community has surprisingly neglected the impacts of these media changes on personal attachment to music and on the concept of a personal music collection. This paper reflects on a series of studies on personal music collections/consumption in New Zealand dating back to 2002, focusing on the shifting concept of what constitutes a personal music collection and on the individual's sense of engagement with that collection.

Keywords: Personal music collections · Music services

1 Introduction

The present near-ubiquity of digital music has shifted how people access, acquire, and store music [10]; never before have people had so many ways to access such large and diverse music collections [9, 11]. The development first of portable, digital devices with large storage capacities, then the availability of mobiles with an affordable, uninterrupted connection to cloud-based and streaming services, has allowed ordinary people to integrate music into their everyday activities to a hitherto unprecedented extent [7, 8, 12]. Streaming has had a particularly profound impact on our relationship with music by turning it into a shared, communal resource [14]. In a streaming service, music and media can be viewed as a kind of 'utility'—implying free flowing access to a resource supporting other activities [15].

With these far-reaching transformations in music availability and access, our conceptualizations are also changing over what constitutes a personal music collection or 'my music' is inevitably shifting, together with the mechanisms for, and meanings that we attach to, significant music behaviours such as sharing, listening engagement, and self-representation through music (e.g., [7, 10]).

In this paper we explore the effects of these sweeping changes in music accessibility in New Zealand, by re-examining the original interview transcripts from a series of music behaviour studies conducted between 2002 and 2016 (Sect. 2). One intriguing question raised by this review is whether use of streaming services may lead to an attenuation of the definition of a personal collection.

© Springer Nature Switzerland AG 2019
N. G. Taylor et al. (Eds.): iConference 2019, LNCS 11420, pp. 526–536, 2019.
https://doi.org/10.1007/978-3-030-15742-5_50

2   Retrospective Studies

This section re-examines the interviews and observations from a series of qualitative studies of music behavior in New Zealand, to tease out shifts in the understanding of what constitutes a personal music collection and in the personal engagement with the collection afforded by the different media used at the time. Participants are referred to by the code assigned in the original investigation (e.g., P2, A, etc.).

2.1   2002–2004: Mixed Physical and Digital Collections

This section is based on a set of 34 interviews and self-interviews (auto-ethnographies) conducted between 2002 and 2004, primarily of IT students and academic staff at Waikato University (Hamilton, New Zealand), focusing on individuals' curation of their personal music collections [4, 6].

It is clear from the interviews that most participants thought of their collection in terms of the physical media owned (vinyl LPs, cassette tapes, and CDs), with CDs seeing the most use in day-to-day music listening. Vinyl LPs were owned by a minority of the participants, held mainly for sentimental purposes or as a backup for acquisitions not readily available in digital form (e.g., for [O], LPs "are seldom used, being treated as irreplaceable. Most have been recorded onto tape cassette and are normally only played to provide replacements for damaged tapes."). Cassette tapes, mainly self-created compilations or copies of CDs or LPs, continued to see use in cars (which at that time mainly supported cassette tape players rather than CDs or mp3s).

All of the participants reported that the majority of their personal collection was held on CDs, mainly legally acquired. These legal CDs often, but not always, had their files 'ripped' for ease of use, to support playing of individual songs rather than entire albums or to create personal compilations of favorite songs. The existence of these files generally was mentioned only as an afterthought in the interviews; they were seen as copies or backups of the actual collection contents, which were held on physical media. Physical CDs were also the medium of choice for transporting music from one location to another, partly for practical reasons (internet costs for file transfer were hefty at the time and slow as well, since most home connections were dial-up) and partly to show off the 'real' version of the new acquisition (e.g., O reports that, *"[when I buy a new CD] I'll rip it to my computer so I can make a copy, and then I'll take it round to friends to show it off and maybe let them touch the case."*

Illegally acquired MP3 files were generally held both on the hard drive and also stored on self-created CDs—partly as backup in case of hard drive failure (recalling that at that point large scale portable storage devices were not commonly available) but also to make the illegal CDs feel like part of the 'real' music collection. To that end, participants often downloaded cover art and printed their own inserts to store in the homemade CDs. Access to quality printers was limited, however, so these CDs were not prominently placed in the physical display. For example, S reported that, *"on the CD rack, all my original music is placed at the front, with all the copied CDs at the back. I do this because I don't want anyone to see my 'ugly' plain, copied CD covers and I place them at the very end in the hopes that any guests I entertain in my room will loose [sic] interest before they get too far along the rack."*

While a minority of the participants were content to store their physical collection haphazardly near the player (E.g., *"I don't care how it looks."* [T], the majority took pride in the organization and display of the physical media. Most used racks specifically designed for CD cases or re-purposed bookshelves for their CDs, with consideration given to both aesthetic appearance and to what the display would reveal about themselves to others. Participant C, for example, pointed out that,

> ...*CDs that I like are mostly grouped on one rack with the other, less played CDs are on the other. This is probably because I can rotate my rack in a way that "shows off" my best CDs while partially obscuring the average and embarrassing CDs. ... I feel that my character is partially judged on the contents of my collection, as I myself consider the contents of a person's music collection when evaluating what type of person they are. ...*

Particularly striking cover art or inserts could also be used as decoration, to further distinguish an individual's music tastes (*"Occasionally CD inserts with effective graphic design are used as decoration, by being U-Tacked to the wall. This ... adds an aesthetic element to my room."* [O]).

Legacy media (vinyl, cassettes) retained but usually 'archived' in drawers, closets, or, if held near the active collection, stored on or near the floor, furthest from view and from the music system (CD player or computer). Participants also kept CDs that saw little or no play, sometimes deliberately sorted into a specific space in the CD display (e.g., E had a shelf for *"CDs I never listen to"*, just above the LP storage). Often, however, these CDs simply drifted to the bottom of a CD rack or to the lowest shelves of a wall display, as more frequently played or better liked CD cases were allocated the more prominent (upper, closer to eye view) spots in the display (*"less frequently played discs (or discs the writer wishes to live in denial of owning) get slowly pushed further towards the bottom and to the back."* [A]).

Perhaps because of limitations in space (both physical and digital), the collections were all of a humanely manageable and memorable size: between approximately 30 and 200 CDs. The bulk of items in a collection were deliberately acquired, primarily through purchase, as a gift, or borrowed and copied from a friend, mainly on an album-by-album basis: collections were predominantly curated rather than accumulated. The attention required to create an attractive physical display and to directly interact with friends and family in sharing music also supported an intimate knowledge of one's own music.

Notably, none of the participants had any plans to eventually discard legacy media or CDs that they disliked, partly because of their personal investment in selecting and purchasing the legal items, in creating the bootleg CDs, and in arranging the collection display. As well, participants recognized that their collection also served as a personal history: *"The collection as a whole, that is CDs, DVDs and LPs, has been collected over a period of many years and consequently each addition has a connection to where [I] was at that stage in life and therefore signifies an emotional investment in the collection."* [A] Clearly collections represented something to their owners beyond convenient sources of music to play while studying, driving, and so forth; participant J, reflecting back on his responses and those of fellow interviewees, noted that, *"one of the more interesting issues that arose...was the level of emotional attachment that the owner has with the collection. For many people, their music collection is something very personal: it is a statement that defines part of their person."*

Despite the clear emotional attachment to physical collections, for many participants the items themselves were seeing less and less actual use in favor the 'ripped' MP3 files. Those who did listen to the physical CDs also created compilation CDs or devised clever work-arounds to simulate the playing flexibility afforded by MP3 players (for example, *"[F] owns a three disk CD player and when selecting music he chooses three CDs at a time. He then plays these three CDs on random in order to gain what is in effect a compilation of these CDs."*) Clearly MP3 players were affecting expectations as well as music behavior: S noted that,

> ... *I seem to demand the same ease of use found in my mp3 player for my regular physical music collection.* ... *I have become accustomed to the idea of a music collection and music player being only one entity, as is the case with all mp3 software; and is not the case with a CD collection and stereo.*

2.2   2006–2007: Shifting to Digital Collections

This section is based on a set of 13 interviews exploring playlist construction [4] and 16 self-interviews (auto-ethnographies) associated with a study of encounters with novel music [3], conducted in 2006 and 2007. The majority of the participants were IT tertiary students or staff at Waikato University in New Zealand.

A striking difference between the music behaviors uncovered in Sect. 3 is that we begin to see a distinction between a collection proper and music that, while in the individual's possession, is casually, temporarily listened to. The participants continued to acquire legal CDs that were the core of their collection, typically music produced by favorite artists—or a newly discovered song/album might prompt further purchases:

> *When any of my favourite bands releases a new album I will always buy the album, usually without having heard any or nearly all of the songs on the album. This has also worked in reverse. I have bought a later album by a band and been so impressed with what I have heard I will go out and buy earlier albums. Maybe around halve [sic] the CD's I own are different CD's from some of my favourite bands.* [I]

For these special artists, a collection might also be fleshed out with other distinctive physical media (e.g., *"official or non-official album[s] and many other related releases such as music video DVDs or live concert DVDs and many other related accessories"* [N]).

For less desirable artists, the decision as to whether to include a given song or album in the collection becomes multi-stage. At this point we see a striking disconnect between the source for the new acquisition itself and the source of information used to identify the prospective song or album. Typically the participants used a set of text-based sites to 'research' a potential acquisition (Google searches for information on a particular artist or song/album, an artist's website or MySpace page, music review websites, etc.) or perhaps a print magazine (*"I also sometimes go to the local bookshop and skim through any relevant magazines to find new music of my preferred genre."* [P]). Online or print reviews might be taken into account in deciding whether a song/album/artist warranted further investigation.

Once a potentially interesting album or song was identified, participants went to another online source to locate and listen to either a sample of the song (for example, a snippet on iTunes or Amazon) or perhaps a full file (on a torrenting site) to decide whether to acquire the music legally (typically as a full album) or illegally (possibly as a full album but generally on a song-by-song basis). This decision might hinge on whether the participant liked a majority of the songs on the album (and so could justify both the expense and the need to formally incorporate the album into the collection proper) or whether only one or two songs were *"euphonious"* [E]. Participants carefully noted that their engagement with illegal downloading was limited—and at this point that was likely to be true; high internet traffic charges, coupled with slow download speeds and buggy peer-to-peer filesharing software that triggered frequent restarts, made large scale downloading, even of a few albums, financially risky. Full albums, then, were generally purchased as CDs or perhaps copied from friends (seen to be a more ethical approach than downloading). Single songs were might, or might not, be retained permanently *("I might delete them [if] I do not like them after I listen to them."* [C]).

Sharing music among friends and family had at this point become much easier. Two participants regularly shared links to online songs with family and friends, using MSN Messenger, which was preferred over direct transfer because the download costs were borne by the other person. USB flash memory drives were available but pricey by student standards (a 256 MB drive might cost the equivalent of two weeks of rent); the cheaper, and much more common, option for sharing offline was to borrow or copy a CD, or to ask that a compilation CD be made of up of selected songs (possibly from the online collection as well as from physical CDs). While CDs were no longer the entirety of an individual's collection, looking through a friend's CDs could still uncover unexpected aspects of their tastes *("Sometimes, I find this exceedingly interesting and full of surprises."* [C]).

Flatmates routinely set up a LAN so that they could *"share out our music collection to others and allow others to stream the media files."* [N] Individuals did not report copying over other flatmate's songs and albums wholesale, as a single hard drive had limited free space. The local LAN gave the access but possibly at the cost of having to wade through unfamiliar music that was of limited interest (O reports, *"'pressing the 'skip to next song' button until I find something that sounds appealing. ... However, this method has a large ratio of disliked music to liked music..."*). No 'hiding' of guilty pleasures in music was reported—indeed, several participants enjoyed being able to give and receive recommendations on songs in their flat's pooled collection—but one wonders how participant O's flatmates would have reacted to his assessment of their musical tastes.

While CDs were no longer routinely created as backups to copied or downloaded music, the CD—complete with hand crafted insert—continued to be popular when giving a set of songs as a gift (sometimes still referred to as a 'mix tape', more commonly as a 'mix'). Putting together a mix was usually more complex than simply copying an existing album. The best gift mix consisted of a playlist reflecting a theme or message meaningful to the recipient, complemented by appropriate cover art and back-case notes. Creating such a gift required a comprehensive and fine-grained knowledge of the songs in one's own collection: first by identifying candidate songs fitting the overall theme, then by ordering the songs to ensure a good flow.

Since one impetus to acquire new music is tiring of current collection, it appears that the participants' collections are still of a manageable size in that the owner can remember its contents well enough to create gift mixes, recommend songs for others to copy, and. Financial constraints imposed by internet charges and the cost of large scale storage, as well as concerns about illegally acquiring music, limited any impulses towards hoarding rather than collecting. Additions were made to fill gaps in the collection (for example, to acquire the latest album by a favorite artist) or when one's music becomes overfamiliar and stale through repetition ("There are not many motivations for me to go out and find new music. This is because the size of my music collection is quite substantial and there is a long period of time between hearing the same track again." [K]).

The collections were reported to grow slowly as careful choices are made to purchase or download new additions—and the selection process itself familiarizes the owner with the music itself, its metadata, and perhaps a personal context as well (for example, that the song was recommended by a friend or was acquired on a shopping trip with family). At the same time, participants who had access to large, pooled collections (for example, from flat LANs) were experiencing the problems that emerge when exploring large, relatively unfamiliar, unstructured collections of music that were unstable over time (as flatmates moved or as LAN parties ended).

2.3   2016: Large Scale Collections and Streaming

This section re-examines results from a 2016 investigation of practices for music collection management [2], based on a set of 29 self-interviews and music management diaries created by tertiary students in New Zealand.

By 2016, both home and mobile internet traffic charges had dropped considerably: over 90% of the country had stable 3G mobile network coverage and in the cities, 4G; home broadband internet connection speed increased to an average 12 Mbps and nearly half of home plans had no data cap [16]; and mobile carriers offered plans that included unlimited access to music, video, and social media applications.

For these participants, physical music media was now almost entirely viewed as legacy music. Exceptions were minor: CDs or cassettes played in an elderly car lacking a sound system compatible with MP3 players, the very occasional LP or CD purchase for an album from a favorite artist ("... because it's nice to have something real" [P15]), or CDs given or received as gifts. Most participants never or rarely purchased CDs ("Now I will purchase a CD or vinyl if it is one of my favorite bands, ... to support the artists at the same time." [P15]). Digital files may also be seen as part of a legacy collection; many participants reported possessing outdated external hard drives, MP3 players, and other storage devices that had been loaded with thousands of downloaded or ripped MP3 files in the past but that now were rarely, if ever, accessed.

At this point, collections can include both streamed music (often over more than one service) and locally stored digital files (usually scattered across multiple devices and multiple software services):

Physically downloaded songs, I would estimate to be ~ 800, but this is something I do very rarely nowadays so this number doesn't increase anymore. Across online streaming services, I would estimate thousands of songs that I have added to my collection in some form. However, there is a large overlap in songs between my offline and online collection (i.e. if I have downloaded, I have also most likely added it on some online playlist). There is also large overlap in the playlist content between different online services. [P17]

Collections now can be unruly and amorphous, and many participants found it difficult to draw crisp boundaries defining their own holdings—and it is particularly difficult to estimate collection size. In the earliest studies a collection would be described primarily in terms of number of songs and albums. As locally stored digital collection sizes grew, descriptions shifted to number of gigabytes or perhaps a system-generated estimate of listening hours. For streaming services, participants often struggled to differentiate 'their' music from the service offerings: should they count all of their playlists (including playlists shared by friends or automatically generated by the provider) or only playlists that they themselves constructed? Only currently active playlists? How could they estimate the duplicates across playlists?

A minority of participants maintained sizeable curated MP3 collections. These required considerable effort to maintain as a collection rather than a hoard: keeping duplicates from creeping in; ensuring that all songs had accurate metadata (by, for example, matching a download's metadata to the songs Last.fm record); and checking all downloads for acceptable sound quality. Playlists were essential as scanning the entire collection for a one-off set of songs to play was now infeasible; most participants reported creating standing playlists (e.g., *'gaming playlist'* [P1], *'getting ready for the day'* [P17], *'Original Philippine Music'* [P21], *'favs'* [P10]). Curating these idiosyncratic playlists could be exceptionally time-consuming, as they had to be updated when they become over-familiar:

I am currently in the midst of redoing my playlists. This is a process where I will review each playlist, adding and deleting songs as I see fit for my current taste, for example, removing songs that I am growing tired of and adding ones I have recently found. ... I will go through my entire collection for each playlist to ensure my playlists are perfectly up to date. This process generally takes around 2 weeks as going through 6000 songs does take time. [P1]

Not surprisingly, participants who curated sizeable MP3-based collections tended to be the most passionate about their collection as such, and to consider themselves collectors rather than simply music lovers (*"My collection is my baby."* [P15]). But while working intensively with a collection can be enjoyable, it is also easy to fall hopelessly behind as procrastination sets in or other, more pressing, obligations intervene. Additionally, shifts from one platform or service to another can require extensive re-organization of the existing collection—a task so daunting that some participants abandoned their old music entirely (*"Having moved to reputable online services, I now spend minimal time organizing my collection as everything is standardized in each online service that I use (with the exception of YouTube)."* [P17]). For those participants with less interest in collecting in the first place, the level of commitment required to organize a file-based music collection was off-putting *(""I generally consider myself a busy person, and simply cannot be bothered managing a collection. When I want to hear music, I just want to hear, and don't want to have to muck around with managing music."* [P28]).

Small wonder, then, that streaming services were embraced by over half (15 of 28) of the participants as their primary mechanism for accessing music. Streaming services were affordable, if one chose a mobile plan that did not include music and YouTube in the data cap, allowing easy access to one's entire collection without having to manually transfer files between the primary storage device and a mobile. Sticking to a single streaming service meant that all accessible music included full and consistent metadata, together with tools to automatically or semi-automatically group and organize songs in standard ways (e.g., tracks into an album, albums by artist).

Streaming services also enabled new sharing mechanisms: the ability to easily share self-constructed playlists and to allow friends to view current listening activities. These functions were valued as an effective way to add variety to one's own listening, as friends knew each other's tastes and could 'mine' like-minded music lovers' activities for potentially interesting new music. For participant P2, this strategy was so effective that she no longer needed to construct her own playlists *("I barely keep private playlists anymore, and instead listen to playlists set by others. I easily get bored hearing the same songs again and change what I am listening to quite regularly.")*. At the same time, for a minority this style of sharing could be problematic. Participant P23 recognized that his listening habits included, *"... music I would never share with other people. This is any piece of music that I feel other people would judge me by. It could be a tune that I know few other people would appreciate and might be considered strange or pathetic."* Further, the structure and contents of a personally curated playlist might give an uncomfortable amount of insight into the creator's life *("I believe that by looking through my current playlist. You'll be able to tell what type of emotion I'm feeling and/or want to feel."* [P29]).

The streaming services provided affordable, even by student standards, access to a vast body of music (at the time, over 30 million songs). Coupled with automatically created, individualized playlists and recommendation services, participants could vastly expand their listening repertoire with very little effort (e.g., using *"...curated playlists, which are an excellent way to easily find new music, and enjoy all music based on a particular genre. I find it is the best option for expanding my listening tastes, with very little hassle or research."* [P2]).

Unfortunately, this unprecedented access to new music could also be a double-edged sword. Participant P2 goes on to explain that, *"Spotify has changed the way I listen to music. When previously I would stick to the music I had always listened to due to the high level of work required to source new music that I like, I now enjoy large varieties of music and get bored quickly of the same music over and over."* For P1, this novelty-seeking had reached its natural limit: *"I have found recently that I have run out of music to look for, as it seems ... there [are] not being songs released as fast as I can listen to and manage."*

The presence of album cover art has again become important to a minority of participants. For both streaming an MP3 file collections, the presence of full metadata for each item, including cover art, is now the hallmark of a *"tidy... neatly organised and well presented collection"* [P2]. Cover art also serves a practical purpose for both by effectively supporting browsing across large collections (*"album art, which makes it easier to sort through music visually"* [P24])—though as collections grow larger, it becomes more difficult to associate cover art with particular songs/albums/artists. Video associated with songs, when streaming from YouTube, is less useful in curation and is more of a novelty collection accessory (*"However, after viewing this a few times, I tend to just listen to the recording."* [P3]).

3 Discussion

These snapshots of music activities across 15 years in New Zealand illustrate how changes in music media both drive, and are driven by, an individual's music behaviors in the context of their daily lives. Perhaps the most striking change is the vastly increased ease of access to both music and to music information (metadata, reviews, discographies, etc.). In the initial periods (Sects. 2.1 and 2.2) participants found it difficult to discover new music and relied on a number of time-intensive strategies (asking friends, perusing others' CD collections, visiting music stores, reading reviews both in print and online, etc.); once identified, another resource was consulted to actually obtain the music (a shop, borrowing a CD from a friend, finding and downloading a file online), and then yet another step was required to add the music to the collection proper (possibly including locating and adding metadata). First cloud-based and then streaming services brought 'researching', acquisition, and playing together. Curating a collection can now be as effortful, or as effortless, as the individual desires: one can build an extensive, carefully tailored collection manually or allow a service to customize one's music playlists automatically.

For music aficionados, it can be unsettling that the musically uninformed or uninterested can so readily access personalized music that is then essentially used as a background score to their lives, the individual songs interchangeable (e.g., *"songs that I use to listen to when I study... Those kinds of songs are usually just background noise that isn't too distracting, and I'm not bothered when I can't find THAT exact song later, as I just grab a new public playlist"* [P15]. One such music enthusiast, P2, argued that,

> *One issue with Spotify is that everything is there at the user's fingertips, they are in a sense overwhelmed with choice, and take for granted the fact that they do not really need to 'collect' music anymore, as there will always be something else out there they may enjoy just as much. Spotify really discourages collecting of music, and does away with a user's emotional attachment to music.*

Another possibility is that rather than discouraging collecting by people already so inclined, these new streaming services allow native non-collectors an unprecedented access to personally enjoyable music in their everyday activities—access at a level previously only achievable by dedicated music lovers with the time to build expertise and create their personal music resources. Essentially, these streaming services may do away with the need for 'emotional attachment' and, indeed, music expertise in order to achieve a high degree of interaction with music.

4 Conclusions

This paper paints a broad picture of the changes in everyday music activities and in personal relationships with music brought about by digital music media. Clearly there have been radical changes since 2000 in how people interact with, and the personal meanings that they assign to, 'their' music. At present, music software has focused on increasing availability and access to music, together with interfaces designed to require little effort in selecting songs to listen to. Streaming services in particular are effective in providing continuous access to music tailored to an individual's tastes, with minimal input: recommender functions eliminate the need to search or browse to find new songs or artists; entire ready-made playlists can be selected if the user lacks the time or inclination to create one; and playlists are fine-tuned automatically as the listener indicates which songs are liked/disliked. The reduction of effort can, however, also reduce the individual's sense of attachment to the music that they listen to, to the extent that some participants in the most recent study found it difficult to define what constitutes 'their' music—even though they listened to music daily.

The move to digital formats has nearly eliminated the physical, tactile, and visual aspects of engaging with a personal music collection, further diminishing the experience of collecting and curating one's own music. The accompanying demise of music stores makes it difficult to share the experience of interacting with a large music collection—current online music stores don't support the casual, collaborative music interactions formerly possible when friends and families could wander into a music shop to while away time browsing CD or vinyl racks together [1, 5]. It remains to be seen whether new music software functionality can be developed to encourage a more active role for individuals in finding, sharing, and curating music collections—by changing the focus in software design from efficiency of interaction to enjoyable interactions.

References

1. Cunningham, S.J., Reeves, N., Britland, M.: An ethnographic study of music information seeking: implications for the design of a music digital library. In: Proceedings of the Joint Conference on Digital Libraries, Houston, pp. 5–16, May 2003
2. Cunningham, S.J., Bainbridge, D., Bainbridge, A.: Exploring personal music collection behavior. In: Choemprayong, S., Crestani, F., Cunningham, S.J. (eds.) ICADL 2017. LNCS, vol. 10647, pp. 295–306. Springer, Cham (2017). https://doi.org/10.1007/978-3-319-70232-2_25
3. Cunningham, S.J., Bainbridge, D.: Finding new music: a diary study of everyday encounters with novel songs. In: Proceedings of the International Conference on Music Information Retrieval (ISMIR 2007), Austria, October 2007
4. Cunningham, S.J., Bainbridge, D., Falconer, A.: More of an art than a science: playlist and mix construction. In: Proceedings of the International Conference on Music Information Retrieval (ISMIR 2006), Vancouver (2006)
5. Cunningham, S.J.: What people do when they look for music: implications for design of a music digital library. In: Proceedings of the International Conference on Asian Digital Libraries (ICADL 2002), Singapore, pp. 177–178, December 2002

6. Cunningham, S.J., Jones, M., Jones, S.: Organizing digital music for use: an examination of personal music collections. In: Proceedings of the International Symposium on Music Information Retrieval (ISMIR 2004), Barcelona, pp. 447–454, October 2004
7. Hagen, A.N., Lüders, M.: Social streaming? Navigating music as personal and social. Convergence 23(6), 643–659 (2017)
8. Heye, A., Lamont, A.: Mobile listening situations in everyday life: the use of MP3 players while travelling. Music Sci. 14(1), 95–120 (2010). https://doi.org/10.1177/1029864910 01400104
9. Juslin, P.N., Liljeström, S., Västfjäll, D., Barradas, G., Silva, A.: An experience sampling study of emotional reactions to music: listener, music, and situation. Emotion 8(5), 668–683 (2008)
10. Kibby, M.: Collect yourself. Inf. Commun. Soc. 12(3), 428–443 (2011). https://doi.org/10.1080/13691180802660644
11. Krause, A.E., North, A.C., Hewitt, L.Y.: Music-listening in everyday life: devices and choice. Psychol. Music 43(2), 155–170 (2015)
12. Nill, A., Geipel, A.: Sharing and owning of musical works: copyright protection from a societal perspective. J. Macromarketing 30, 33–49 (2010)
13. Sloboda, J.A., Lamont, A., Greasley, A.E.: Choosing to hear music: motivation, process, and effect. In: Hallam, S., Cross, I., Thaut, M. (eds.) The Oxford Handbook of Music Psychology, pp. 431–440. Oxford University Press, Oxford (2009)
14. Krause, A.E., North, A.C.: Music listening in everyday life: devices, selection methods, and digital technology. Psychol. Music 44(1), 129–147 (2016)
15. Morris, J.W., Powers, D.: Control, curation and musical experience in streaming music services. Creat. Ind. J. 8(2), 106–122 (2015)
16. Bridges, S.: New Zealand broadband speeds continue to surge, 16 March 2017. https://www.national.org.nz/new_zealand_broadband_speeds_continue_to_surge

Understanding Online Behaviors and Experiences

What Prompts Users to Click on News Headlines? A Clickstream Data Analysis of the Effects of News Recency and Popularity

Tingting Jiang[1,2](✉) ⓘ, Qian Guo[1] ⓘ, Yaping Xu[1] ⓘ, Yang Zhao[1] ⓘ, and Shiting Fu[1] ⓘ

[1] School of Information Management, Wuhan University, Wuhan, Hubei, China
tij@whu.edu.cn
[2] Center for Studies of Information Resources, Wuhan University, Wuhan, Hubei, China

Abstract. A new headline nowadays has to compete for readers' attention and sometimes it needs to entice readers to click and read the news article. The peripheral indicators of news headlines would provide visual suggestions for user to decide on which news to read and which to ignore. This study focused on the recency and popularity indicators of online news. For the purpose of revealing the relationships between news recency/popularity and users' clicking behavior, a 2-month server log file containing 39,990,200 clickstream records from an institutional news site was analyzed in combination with the news recency and popularity information crawled from its homepage. It was found that more recent or more popular news headlines received more clicks. The results have important implications for news providers in creating effective news headlines and in publishing and disseminating news more responsibly. The introduction of unobtrusive clickstream data to user behavior analysis is a major methodological contribution.

Keywords: News headlines · Recency · Popularity · Clickstream data

1 Introduction

In the era of print newspapers, people used to glance through a newspaper page by page and read the news articles of interest [1]. The headline was a succinct and accurate summary of the corresponding news story [2]. As more and more news is consumed online today, news reading has become increasingly rapid and shallow [3]. The major role of headlines has shifted to attracting attention [4].

In the face of a tremendous amount of information, users tend to avoid extra efforts and take advantage of peripheral indicators to make a selection. These indicators, e.g. source of information, are useful cues that help users determine information salience, especially when they are involved in casual scanning [5]. On social media, users make evaluation of information quality in virtue of bandwagon cues, i.e. the number of an individual's followers, and they are likely to imitate others' judgment and behavior [6]. With the development of Web technologies, online news sites have been enabled to

© Springer Nature Switzerland AG 2019
N. G. Taylor et al. (Eds.): iConference 2019, LNCS 11420, pp. 539–546, 2019.
https://doi.org/10.1007/978-3-030-15742-5_51

indicate past readers' interaction with the news, such as the frequency of reading and the overall rating of news story, to inform future readers. Such indicators are usually displayed around news headlines so that readers can find them easily [7].

Recency and popularity indicators are widely seen on news sites. News is time-sensitive information, and recency is a dominant criterion for judging newsworthiness in news media. A piece of news will carry more weight if it is recent [5, 8]. The popularity of a new story can be measured with the number of clicks, likes, or comments it has received. The lapse of time decreases recency while more reading increases popularity. The two indicators are essentially the variable properties of news headlines [8].

Although news sites make efforts to provide recency and popularity indicators, there still lacks empirical evidence of how users actually make use of them. As a result, this study aimed to investigate whether the indicated recency and popularity prompt users to click on news headlines. For this purpose, a 2-month server log file containing 39,990,200 clickstream records from an institutional news site was analyzed in combination with the news recency and popularity information crawled from its homepage.

2 Related Work

2.1 Recency and Popularity of Online Information

Both recency and popularity indicators have been used to attract attention and/or interaction to online news as well as other types of online information.

Recency or timeliness refers to how recent the information is. It is an important aspect of information quality and has an impact on users' assessment of the credibility of information [9]. According to a study of social news aggregators, when the credibility of the source was low, more recent news received more attention; whereas in the case of high-credibility source, more recent news had higher perceived newsworthiness [5]. Social media enable the real-time sharing of all kinds of information and cater to users' desire to be kept up-to-date. Further evidence has suggested that faster updates would lead to higher source credibility as mediated by cognitive elaboration [10]. Also for electronic word-of-mouth messages, i.e. online comments or reviews provided by customers about a product or company, their currency has been found to positively influence customers' perception of their usefulness which in turn predicts purchase intention [11].

As the overwhelming amounts of information may create cognitive overload, it is natural for individuals to follow others' choices and attitudes when evaluating the information rather than relying on their own judgement [12]. User-generated content on social media, e.g. micro-posts, will receive likes, reposts, and comments and replies which together indicate popularity. Higher popularity is often associated with greater perceived usefulness and stronger preferences and thus increases the intention of interaction and possibility of actual interaction [13, 14]. Similar results have been obtained for online shopping: the social popularity of a product, i.e. having a large number of people liking or purchasing it, would affect positively customers' trust, perception of product quality and value as well as purchase intention and behavior [15, 16].

Ksiazek and Peer [17] measured the popularity of online news videos in terms of the numbers of views, favorited, and ratings and found that more popular videos would attract more comments while less popular ones more replies to comments.

2.2 Clickstream Data Analysis

Clickstream data is a typical type of trace data generated on Web servers when users visit websites or APPs for their own purposes. It captures all the clicks or page requests made by users in sequence from entering to leaving a site. Each clickstream record basically informs us which user performs which type of action on which page at what time. Clickstream data analysis now can be found in user behavior research in many contexts, such as social media, social commerce, online courses, information portals, and so on [18]. A general framework for analyzing clickstream data has taken shape which consists of three levels, i.e. footprint, movement, and pathway. When a user visits a site, each click causes a movement, the changing of location from one page to another, and leaves a footprint, a mark showing the user's presence on a page. The click series during that visit, i.e. chaining all the movements in a chorological order, engenders a pathway, indicating the process in which the user interacts with the site. This framework has been successfully applied in the studies of users' information seeking behavior in social library systems [19, 20] and academic library OPAC systems [21].

3 Data Collection and Preparation

This study introduced clickstream data analysis to the investigation of real-world users' news reading behavior. A server log file was obtained from an institutional news site that affiliates to the official site of a renowned Chinese university. It contains a total of 39,990,200 clickstream records generated between March 1st, 2017 and April 30th, 2017. The six basic fields in the log are *User-IP* (client IP address, e.g. "202.114.65.***"), *Date* (date on which request is made, e.g. "28/Mar/2017"), *Time* (time when request is made, e.g. "08:00:10"), *Method* (type of client to server request, e.g. "GET"), *URL* (URL of the resource requested, e.g. "/info/1002/40929.htm"), and *Status* (HTTP status code returned by server, e.g. "200").

The log was cleaned to eliminate corrupted and redundant records in the first place. Corrupted records were errors produced when the server performed logging incorrectly and were easily recognizable for not fitting the patterns of the normal data in the same field. Redundant records were those irrelevant to the objective of this study, including unsuccessful requests, data submission requests, and requests for pictures, styles, scripts, and other resources.

The next step was to define sessions. Each session is composed of all the records deriving from one visit to the site, and a user may have more than one session for visiting the site multiple times during the two months. So different users were identified with their IP addresses (*User-IP* field); for the same user, if the time interval between any two records exceeded 30 min, they would be divided into different sessions. Given that some visits recorded in the log file might be attributed to search engine spiders, a cut-off of 101 records was adopted to determine non-human sessions: if a session contained 101 or more records, it was assumed to represent a non-human visit and thus excluded. As a result, approximately 10% (N = 3,987,030) of the records remained which involved 839,685 sessions.

4 Data Analysis and Results

The institutional news site allows users to find news in multiple ways. With an explicit need or interest, users would perform keyword searching or browse through particular categories (e.g. *Academic News* and *Alumni News*). However, news reading has become a daily monitoring activity to many people [22]. It is common for users to start from the homepage where hundreds of selected news headlines were displayed to see what was happening to the university. Their undirected scanning on the homepage was more likely to be affected by the peripheral indicators. Therefore, this study analyzed the clickstream data mainly at the movement level with a focus on the movements from the homepage to news article pages. The type of a page was identified with a specific string in its URL.

During the two-month time period, a Web crawler tool was meanwhile employed to scrape the homepage of the news site once a day at 23:00, for the purpose of capturing its daily update of news headlines, including the changes of the recency and popularity indicators which refer to the date of publishing and the number of reads respectively. The crawled data could be linked to the clickstream data as each news headline points to a news article which has a distinct URL identifiable in the log file. Specifically, the crawled data provided information about a headline's recency and popularity, while the clickstream data how many clicks it attracted.

4.1 Headlines with Recency and Popularity Indicators on the Homepage

The homepage of the institutional news site demonstrates a traditional layout with a navigation bar on the top and news headlines enclosed into 18 blocks below it. These blocks correspond to different news categories. Only two of the blocks have recency and/or popularity indicators appended to each news headline. The *Important News* (news events happening to the university) block displays both indicators, whereas the *Media News* (news about the university published on mainstream media) block only the former.

Both blocks are updated every day. Newly published headlines will be inserted to the top and gradually edge out older ones on the bottom from the blocks. There was an overlap between the headlines on different days. Even if a headline stayed in these blocks for days, its recency would decrease and popularity might increase. Therefore, this study treated every headline on a single day as a distinct headline.

As extracted from the crawled data, all the distinct headlines that ever appeared in both blocks during the two months added up to 888, with 488 in *Important News* and 400 in *Media News* respectively. According to the movement level analysis based on the clickstream data, the headlines on the homepage attracted 98,016 clicks in total. About one third of the clicks (N = 33,919, 34.61%) were contributed by the headlines in the above two blocks. This is reasonable given that they are placed in the most conspicuous positions on the homepage.

4.2 Relationships Between News Recency/Popularity and Users' Clicking Behavior

The news published on the institutional news site became obsolete at a much slower rate than general online news for confined to the university. The oldest important news or media news that users might see on the homepage could be traced back to more than 2 months ago (probably due to the winter vacation during which news was published infrequently). This study defined two different levels of news recency for the convenience of analysis: high (published within 1 week, including 7 days) and low (published more than 7 days ago). High-recency headlines were in the majority (N = 698) while low-recency ones much less frequently seen (N = 190).

As mentioned above, the popularity indicator is only available to important news. The numbers of reads varied from news to news, ranging from hundreds to thousands. They averaged around 1,000 which was used as the boundary to distinguish two groups of headlines of different popularity: high (read more than 1,000 times) and low (read 0-1,000 times). There were almost twice as many low-popularity headlines (N = 312) as high-popularity ones (N = 176).

The Mann-Whitney U test was conducted to examine the relationships between news recency/popularity and users' clicking behavior. As can be found in Table 1, significant results were obtained for both recency (Z = −15.366, p < .05) and popularity (Z = −17.889, p < .05). To be more specific, users were more likely to click on high-recency headlines than on low-recency ones (mean rank: high 513.50 > low 191.00), and high-popularity headlines attracted more clicks than low-popularity ones (mean rank: high 396.50 > low 158.76) (Table 2).

Table 1. Results of the Mann-Whitney U test for recency and popularity

	Recency	Popularity
Mann-Whitney U	18,145	704.000
Z	−15.366	−17.889
Asymp. Sig. (2-tailed)	.000	.000

Table 2. Mann-Whitney U test statistics for recency and popularity

	Groups	N	Mean rank	Sum of ranks
Recency	High	698	513.50	358,426.00
	Low	190	191.00	36,290.00
	Total	888		
Popularity	High	176	396.50	69,784.00
	Low	312	158.76	49,532.00
	Total	488		

5 Discussion and Conclusions

Reading news online has become an integral part of modern life. The ever-increasing amount of available news and the fragmentation of users' time engender a great challenge to news providers. A news headline must compete for users' attention and be attractive enough to induce clicks. Attaching peripheral indicators to headlines is one way toward this end. This study shed light on the effects of news recency and popularity on users' clicking behavior. It was found through a clickstream data analysis that the presence of both indicators had an impact on the selection of news headlines. The higher the recency or popularity, the more the clicks a headline would attract. The significance of this study not only consists in its implications for news providers in creating effective news headlines and in publishing and disseminating news more responsibly, but also the introduction of clickstream data that is unobtrusive and more reliable in reflecting real behavior.

5.1 Implications for News Providers

The peripheral indicators are important visual cues that indicate news salience. They help users make quick judgments about the headlines before exploring their semantic content. This study echoed previous studies in terms of the findings that more recent or more popular news headlines received more clicks. Recency has been a major factor affecting the perceived value of information, especially news [5]. A low frequency of updating may decrease users' trust in information [10]. The pursuit of popular information has its psychological root. The "bandwagon effect" suggests that individuals tend to believe the information when many other people also believe it [6].

Nevertheless, the researchers have a concern about the potential risks of misusing users' preferences for recent and popular news. On the one hand, news providers nowadays strive to win attention by updating the news almost every minute, and some even make use of computer-written news articles to do so [23]. Valuable news may be mixed with reproduced stories, clickbaits, and advertisements, etc. It is undesirable for users to be addicted to or waste time on such "news" despite its high recency. On the other hand, following popular behavior may save people's efforts to make their own judgement, but it may also lock them in information cocoons [24]. If popular news contains bias, the negative effects of the bias can be strengthened as the news gets more popular. This is detrimental to the diversification of opinions, knowledge, and interests.

5.2 The Advantages of Unobtrusive Data

Most existing studies depended on self-report methods and experiments to investigate users' information behavior. They are typical obtrusive methods of data collection [25, 26]. The participants of surveys or interviews may not provide authentic, accurate, and complete information for various reasons. The problem of reactiveness is even more obvious in experiments. The researchers may introduce consciously or unconsciously their own bias to the experiment design, and the participants may behave not as usual due to the pressure of being observed, artificial tasks, and the environment.

This study introduced two types of unobtrusive data, i.e. the clickstream data from the Web server and the data crawled from the homepage. The collecting of both types of data did not intervene the occurrence of users' clicking behavior. Therefore, the clickstream data analysis was able to provide the most reliable information about the clicks each headline received. Another advantage of the unobtrusive method is that it could achieve considerably larger data size, which made it easier to detect trends. It will be very difficult for obtrusive methods to record such a huge volume of clicks. With the rise of big data, the field of information behavior should consider making use of a wide variety of trace data generated as a result of users' interaction with the Internet. However, the generalizability of the findings of this study could be enhanced if clickstream data were collected from mainstream news sites. It should also be mentioned that clickstream data analysis only reveals users' behavioral patterns without considering what shapes their behavior.

5.3 Future Research

The current study focused on the recency and popularity indicators which were in essence external to the news headlines. When it comes to the internal elements of the headlines, their influences on users' attention and behavior should be even stronger. The researchers plan to extract more information from the crawled data, such as the text lengths of the headlines, and the use of numbers and punctuation marks in the headlines. It is interesting to explore whether differences in these characteristic dimensions will arouse differences in clicks. It is also desirable to increase the size of the clickstream data in order to enhance the validity of the analysis of user behavior. In addition, traditional obtrusive methods, e.g. surveys and interviews, will be introduced to complement the clickstream data analysis for the purpose of revealing users' motivations.

Acknowledgement. This research has been made possible through the financial support of the National Natural Science Foundation of China under Grants No. 71774125 and No. 71420107026.

References

1. Holmqvist, K., Holsanova, J., Barthelson, M., et al.: Reading or scanning? a study of newspaper and net paper reading. In: Hyona, J.R., Deubel, H. (eds.) The Mind's Eye: Cognitive and Applied Aspects of Eye Movement Research, pp. 657–670. Elsevier, Oxford (2003)
2. Dor, D.: On newspaper headlines as relevance optimizers. J. Pragmat. **35**(5), 695–721 (2003)
3. Kruikemeier, S., Lecheler, S., Ming, M.B.: Learning from news on different media platforms: an eye-tracking experiment. Polit. Commun. **35**(1), 75–96 (2017)
4. Kuiken, J., Schuth, A., Spitters, M., et al.: Effective headlines of newspaper articles in a digital environment. Digit. Journalism **5**, 1300–1314 (2017)
5. Xu, Q.: Social recommendation, source credibility and recency: effects of news cues in a social bookmarking website. Journalism Mass Commun. Q. **90**(4), 757–775 (2013)
6. Lee, J.Y., Sundar, S.S.: To tweet or to retweet? that is the question for health professionals on Twitter. Health Commun. **28**(5), 509–524 (2013)

7. Knoblochwesterwick, S., Sharma, N., Hansen, D.L., et al.: Impact of popularity indications on readers' selective exposure to online news. J. Broadcast. Electron. Media **49**(3), 296–313 (2005)
8. Sundar, S.S., Knobloch-Westerwick, S., Hastall, M.R.: News cues: information scent and cognitive heuristics. J. Assoc. Inf. Sci. Technol. **58**(3), 366–378 (2007)
9. Metzger, M.J.: Making sense of credibility on the Web: models for evaluating online information and recommendations for future research. J. Assoc. Inf. Sci. Technol. **58**(13), 2078–2091 (2007)
10. Westerman, D., Spence, P.R., Heide, B.V.D.: Social media as information source: recency of updates and credibility of information. J. Comput. Mediated Commun. **19**(2), 171–183 (2014)
11. Cheung, R.: The influence of electronic word-of-mouth on information adoption in online customer communities. Global Econ. Rev. **43**(1), 42–57 (2014)
12. Wang, S.M., Lin, C.C.: The effect of social influence on the bloggers' usage intention. Online Inf. Rev. **35**(1), 50–65 (2011)
13. Chang, Y.T., Yu, H., Lu, H.P.: Persuasive messages, popularity cohesion, and message diffusion in social media marketing. J. Bus. Res. **68**(4), 777–782 (2015)
14. Chin, C.Y., Lu, H.P., Wu, C.M.: Facebook users' motivation for clicking the "like" button. Soc. Behav. Pers. Int. J. **43**(4), 579–592 (2015)
15. Yi, C., Jiang, Z., Zhou, M.: The effects of social popularity and deal scarcity at different stages of online shopping. In: Thirty Fifth International Conference on Information Systems, pp. 1–16. AIS eLibrary, Auckland (2014)
16. Mou, J., Shin, D.: Effects of social popularity and time scarcity on online consumer behavior regarding smart healthcare products: an eye-tracking approach. Comput. Hum. Behav. **78**, 74–89 (2017)
17. Ksiazek, T.B., Peer, L., Lessard, K.: User engagement with online news: Conceptualizing interactivity and exploring the relationship between online news videos and user comments. New Media Soc. **18**(3), 261–270 (2016)
18. Jiang, T., Xu, Y.P., Guo, Q.: Review of clickstream data analysis and visualization studies. J. China Soc. Sci. Tech. Inf. **37**(4), 436–450 (2018)
19. Jiang, T.: Characterizing and evaluating users' information seeking behavior in social tagging systems. Dissertation (2010)
20. Jiang, T.: A clickstream data analysis of users' information seeking modes in social tagging systems. In: iConference 2014 Proceedings, Berlin, pp. 314–329 (2014)
21. Jiang, T., Chi, Y., Gao, H.Q: A clickstream data analysis of Chinese academic library OPAC users' information behavior. Libr. Inf. Sci. Res. **39**(3), 213–223 (2017)
22. Boczkowski, P., Mitchelstein, E., Matassi, M.: Incidental news: how young people consume news on social media. In: Hawaii International Conference on System Sciences, Hawaii (2017)
23. van der Kaa, H.A.J., Krahmer, E.J.: Journalist versus news consumer: the perceived credibility of machine written news. In: The Computation and Journalism Symposium, New York (2014)
24. Zuiderveen Borgesius, F.J., Trilling, D., Moeller, J., Bodó, B., De Vreese, C.H., Helberger, N.: Should we worry about filter bubbles? Internet Policy Rev. **5**(1), 1–16 (2016)
25. Jiang, T., Zhang, C., Li, Z., et al.: Information encountering on social Q&A sites: a diary study of the process. In: International Conference on Information. Sheffield, UK (2018)
26. Makri, S., Bhuiya, J., Carthy, J., et al.: Observing serendipity in digital information environments. In: Proceedings of the 78th ASIS&T Annual Meeting, St. Louis, MO, USA (2015)

How Users Gaze and Experience on Digital Humanities Platform?: A Model of Usability Evaluation

Dan Wu[(✉)] and Shuang Xu

School of Information Management, Wuhan University, Wuhan, Hubei, China
woodan@whu.edu.cn

Abstract. Digital humanities platform has been developing rapidly. Using eye-tracking in usability evaluation can make a difference in user experience. In this paper we propose a gaze-experience model for usability evaluation on digital humanities platform, and select the "Digital Dunhuang" platform as the case study. A user experiment was carried out to verify the application value of the model through a large amount of eye-tracking and user experience data collection and analysis. We found that the features of eye-tracking (such as fixation and saccade) and those of user experience (such as satisfaction, efficiency and effectiveness) had correlations. Implications were also put forward to improve the usability of digital humanities platform and can be extended to similar platforms.

Keywords: Usability evaluation · Evaluation model · Eye-tracking · User experience · Digital humanities

1 Introduction

With the deepening of digital technology in humanities computing, the display and research methods of humanities research have begun to use various digital tools [1]. They have vastly extended access and provided researchers with new opportunities [2]. With the rapid development of Internet and information digitization, especially in websites, user experience and user-centered design are spreading fast. Usability has become a must-have feature for website development and operation, and the usability evaluation based on user experience has become an essential element [3].

Eye-tracking, as a research method for usability evaluation, trace a viewer's eye movements while viewing on-screen information [4]. It will not only analyze users' cognition, but also organize users' gaze data, and excavate users' habits, behavior characteristics and areas of interest (AOI), which relates closely to user experience, emotion and attitude using a particular product, system or service. The digital humanities platform mainly include some library, museum, archive or art exhibition websites, with high interaction and many images, videos and multimedia. Taking Digital Dunhuang and Palace Museum website as examples, pages browsing and the featured panoramic roaming system (PRS) are widely used. Eye tracking can reflect users' attention and browsing behaviors. Therefore, the usability evaluation of digital

© Springer Nature Switzerland AG 2019
N. G. Taylor et al. (Eds.): iConference 2019, LNCS 11420, pp. 547–553, 2019.
https://doi.org/10.1007/978-3-030-15742-5_52

humanities platform based on eye-tracking provides a new perspective, which gets more direct feedback on user's visual experience.

The purpose of this paper is to combine users' gaze features with experience features to build an evaluation model to test the usability of digital humanities platform and find their relationships. The specific research questions are as follows:

RQ1: What are the features of users' gaze and experience to evaluate the usability of digital humanities platform?
RQ2: What are the relationships of users' gaze and experience features for usability evaluation of digital humanities platform?

2   Usability Evaluation Model of Digital Humanities Platform

In this study, we borrowed usability evaluation from previous studies and built a set of gaze and experience metrics with mapping to each other for the evaluation of digital humanities platform. And the eye-tracking features were mainly selected as fixation, saccade and their derived metrics. Based on its characteristics, digital humanities platform had three main functions [5]: freely browsing, visual search and interactive function, corresponding to the user experience metrics according to basic usability elements. Then we created a mapping between them shown in Table 1:

Table 1. The mapping of gaze and experience metrics.

Task category	Gaze metric	Interpretation	Experience metric
Freely browsing	Fixation number [6]	The number of fixation in an area of interest	Satisfaction
	Average fixation duration	Average fixation duration of every gaze point in an area of interest	
	Total fixation duration	Total fixation duration of every gaze point in an area of interest	
Visual search	Saccade number [7]	The number of saccade in an area of interest	Satisfaction
	Average saccade distance	Average value of every saccade distance in an area of interest	
	Total saccade distance	Total value of every saccade distance in an area of interest	
	Ratio of fixation number	The proportion of fixation number in AOI1 to AOI2	Efficiency
Interactive function [8]	Ratio of fixation duration	The proportion of fixation duration in AOI1 to AOI2	Effectiveness [10]
	Time interval between first gaze and click [9]	The difference value of first view time and click time to an element	

The hypotheses in the model were: (1) the fixation-related metrics were positively correlated with the degree of interest in each area when browsing freely; (2) the saccade-related metrics were negatively related to the satisfaction of the user when performing visual search, and the fixation number ratio was related to the efficiency which refers to task completion time; (3) the ratio of fixation duration and time interval between first gaze and click were related to the task completion rate, and they could reflect the effectiveness.

3 Experiment Design

3.1 Platform, Participant and Task

The experiment was to use the above model to evaluate a digital humanities platform.

The "Digital Dunhuang" (https://www.e-dunhuang.com) is a brilliant digital humanities project in China. It is pursuing overall digitization, including collection, processing and storage of the Dunhuang Grottoes and related cultural relics by using advanced science and technology. Taking it as a case study helps it make efforts for the permanent preservation and sustainable use of Dunhuang's cultural heritage.

40 participants were recruited, with 20 males and 20 females. They were from 32 majors in 19 schools, distributed evenly from freshman to graduate students. We gave some labor fee for the participants to ensure the quality. The experiment included preparation, training, testing and survey which lasted about 40 min in all.

The experiment was intended to design a complete task that run through all the functions and related pages of the "Digital Dunhuang". The three sub-tasks were:

(1) Freely browse task: Freely browse the home page for 30 s and sort the 8 AOIs for personal interest, then submit a report of 100 words.
(2) Visual search task: Search "Mogao Grottoes Cave 194" and observe the result pages, then try to find a key word and submit the questionnaire.
(3) Interactive task: Try to find the function entry and count the cave number which is in accordance with the requirements, then submit the questionnaire.

3.2 Data Collection and Cleaning

There were two main methods in data collection. One was the eye-tracking data recorded by Tobii Studio. In our lab we used Tobii Pro X3-120 working under Windows 8 (x64) which had a 120 Hz sampling frequency. And the other was the questionnaire that was an improved scale based on the System Usability Scale (SUS), which was widely regarded as the classical usability scale standard by John Brooke [11]. Each task had a task-corresponding questionnaire.

In order to eliminate the interference and ensure the quality of data, we selected 31 subjects whose gaze sampling rate reached 85% and above for analysis. The task completion rate in each task was 100%, 90.32% and 77.42%.

4 Result Analysis and Discussion

4.1 The Correlations of Eye-Tracking and User Experience Features

Result of Freely Browsing

We divided the homepage into 8 AOIs: background, text description, classic cave, classic mural, search bar, navigation bar, platform introduction, website logo.

In the task-corresponding questionnaire, the participants were asked to sort the 8 AOIs according to the degree of interest. The most interesting area was recorded as 8 points, and the least as 1 point. Based on this, a percentage histogram showing the user's interest in each AOI of the home page was constructed, as shown in Fig. 1.

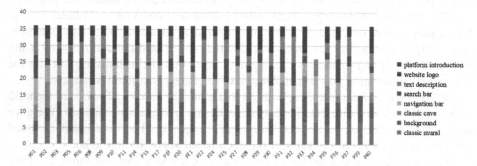

Fig. 1. Percentage stacking histogram of interest degree. (Color figure online)

From the Fig. 1, we could see that: (1) blue and orange columns appeared in each participant at long length, which meant the background and the classical cave got the highest points of the questionnaire, and were considered to be areas with higher interest by users. (2) The appearance of brown and dark blue columns was unstable, and the length was short at the same time, indicating that the users were not interested in the platform introduction and the website logo, the missing colors revealed that some users even ignored them in the homepage.

Table 2. Correlation analysis on freely browsing.

Mean value	Fixation number	Average fixation duration	Total fixation duration	Satisfaction-Sort points
Website logo	1	16875	16875	3.065
Navigation bar	3.75	30258.718	101519.938	4.323
Background	51.161	24137.214	1271250.581	6.194
Search bar	0	0	0	3.968
Text description	8.583	21470.576	198662.583	4.129
Classic cave	46.324	26930.658	1491945.706	5.613

(continued)

Table 2. (*continued*)

Mean value	Fixation number	Average fixation duration	Total fixation duration	Satisfaction-Sort points
Classic mural	26.242	29650.746	1010160.97	4.806
Platform introduction	8.412	25321.909	228065.353	1.742
r	0.778*	0.205	0.756*	
P-	0.023	0.627	0.030	

The Pearson Correlation Analysis was used to measure the linear correlation between numerical variables in Table 2, with the ranking scores of 8 AOIs according to the questionnaire. A strongly positive correlation between the user's interest and the fixation number (r = 0.778*) indicated the more users have interest in an AOI, the more fixation number is, and the total fixation duration as well (r = 0.756*). However, the linear correlation between the user's interest and the average fixation number (r = 0.025) indicated a weak and no significant correlation between them.

Table 3. Correlation analysis on visual search.

	Saccade number	Average saccade distance	Total saccade distance	Ratio of fixation number	Satisfaction-SUS score	Efficiency-task completion time
Mean	508.489	41.031	19385.691	0.063	74.286	6542.645
r	−0.688**	0.343	−0.622**	0.487**		
P-	0.000	0.074	0.000	0.005		

Result of Visual Search

From the Table 3 above, a strong correlation (r = −0.688**) indicated user's satisfaction negatively affects saccade number. The same was true when analyzing with total saccade distance (r = −0.622**). And there was with no significant correlation with the average saccade distance (r = 0.343). A positive correlation (r = 0.487**) between ratio of fixation number and efficiency was also found, which revealed the higher proportion of fixation number in a target AOI might be a symbol of high efficiency with short task completion time.

Result of Interactive Function

From the Table 4 above, we can see that the ratio of fixation duration was positively correlated to the effectiveness (r = 0.468**). However, time interval between first gaze and click were negatively related to it (r = −0.476**). It showed that the higher effectiveness was associated with bigger ratio of fixation duration and shorter time interval between first gaze and click. Task 3 had the lowest rate among three tasks. We knew it in later interviews that participants found it hard to find required function in task 3, because the entrance was single and hidden, users must click one specific button to enter, which made them confused, and delaying the click or making time interval longer, decreasing the ratio of fixation duration as well.

Table 4. Correlation analysis on interactive function.

	Ratio of fixation duration	Time interval between first gaze and click	Effectiveness-task completion rate
Mean	0.074	218102.5294	77.419%
r	0.468**	−0.475**	
P-	0.008	0.007	

4.2   The Adjusted Model

From the verification in the previous section, we got the adjusted model for usability evaluation as shown in Fig. 2 and we figured out the relations as follows:

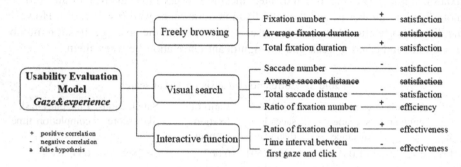

Fig. 2. The adjusted model for usability evaluation.

Positive Correlation: The more fixation number and total fixation duration are, the higher the users' interest in the AOI have, signifying more attention is fixed here; two of ratios stand for the efficiency and effectiveness of using the platform.

Negative Correlation: Few saccade number, small total saccade distance and short time interval signify that, users spend few visual searches and easy to find the target, the platform structure and layout is to users' great satisfaction with high effectiveness.

No Correlation: The satisfaction of the user has no significant effect on the average fixation duration and average saccade distance.

5   Implication and Conclusion

From the analysis, we can get implications for digital humanities platform: (1) The interface design should be optimized, including the aesthetic design and the layout [12]. More key elements should be concentrated on specific areas to increase fixation number and total fixation duration. (2) It should make organization structure reasonable, allowing users to access information quickly by replacing passive and static services with active and dynamic services. (3) It needs to enhance the interactive function, reduce time interval between first gaze and click on functional area. Also, this model can be extended to other similar platform or domains properly.

In the research, by evaluating the usability of Digital Dunhuang, we found the correlation between gaze and user experience by identifying their features and built a model for the usability evaluation of digital humanities platform.

At present, there are few researches on eye-tracking in panoramic roaming system (PRS). Related research of usability evaluation on PRS can be studied in the future.

Acknowledgement. This work was supported by the project "Research on Mobile Visual Search and Its Application in Intelligent Public Cultural Service" of School of Information Management, Wuhan University.

References

1. Hockey, S.: The history of humanities computing. In: Schreibman, S., Siemens, R., Unsworth, J. (eds.) A Companion to Digital Humanities. Blackwell Publishing Ltd., Oxford (2007)
2. Brennan, C.: Digital humanities, digital methods, digital history, and digital outputs: history writing and the digital revolution. Hist. Compass **10**(16), 8–9 (2018)
3. Soussan, D., Marisa, S., Tom, T.: Efficiency trust and visual appeal: usability testing through eye tracking. In: Proceedings of the 43rd Hawaii International Conference on System Sciences, pp. 1–10 (2010)
4. Han-Chin, L., Meng-Lung, L., Hsueh-Hua, C.: Using eye-tracking technology to investigate the redundant effect of multimedia web pages on viewers' cognitive processes. Comput. Hum. Behav. **27**(6), 2410–2417 (2011)
5. Garrett, J.: The Elements of User Experience: User-Centred Design for the Web. New Riders, New York (2003)
6. Lorigo, L., Haridasan, M., Brynjarsdóttir, H., et al.: Eye tracking and online search: lessons learned and challenges ahead. J. Am. Soc. Inform. Sci. Technol. **59**(7), 1041–1052 (2008)
7. Edelman, J., Goldberg, M.: Saccade-related activity in the primate superior colliculus depends on the presence of local landmarks at the saccade endpoint. J. Neurophysiol. **90**(3), 1728–1736 (2003)
8. Preece, J., Sharp, H., Rogers, Y.: Interaction Design: Beyond Human-Computer Interaction, 4th edn. Wiley, Chichester (2015)
9. Byrne, M.D., Anderson, et al.: Eye tracking the visual search of click-down menus. In: Proceedings of the SIGCHI Conference on Human Factors in Computing Systems, pp. 402–409. ACM, PA (1999)
10. Nielsen, J.: Usability Engineering. Elsevier, Amsterdam (1993)
11. Jordan, P.W., Thomas, B., Weerdmeester, B.A., et al.: Usability Evaluation in Industry. Taylor and Francis, London (1996)
12. Thuering, M., Mahlke, S.: Usability, aesthetics and emotions in human–technology interaction. Int. J. Psychol. **42**(4), 253–264 (2007)

Effects of the User-Need State for Online Shopping: Analyzing Search Patterns

Hsin-Kai Yu and I-Chin Wu[✉]

School of Learning Informatics, Graduate Institute of Library and Information Studies, National Taiwan Normal University, Taipei, Taiwan
icwu@ntnu.edu.tw

Abstract. With the fast growth of e-commerce and the emerging trend of "New Retail"—that is, online and offline integration—the important research issues are how to know the best ways to collect and analyze users' search behaviors online for a streamlined shopping process. Accordingly, we proposed a search pattern analytical method to analyze users' search behavior in the entire shopping process on the target website from the perspective of the users' need states. We have focused on the recommendation functions (RFs) and the search functions on Taobao.com to evaluate the effectiveness of each RF to support the online shopping process in different user-need states, namely in a goal-oriented or an exploratory-based approach to online shopping. We first adopted zero-order state transition matrices and then used lag sequential analysis (LSA) to derive the significant repeating search patterns. The results show that the goal-oriented shoppers tend to search directly, whereas exploratory shoppers tend to explore the categories of products as their initial RFs. In addition, goal-oriented users have much more simple search paths compared to the exploratory-based users when engaged in online shopping. Furthermore, based on the results of the LSA, there are two typical search patterns for goal-oriented users and no search pattern for the exploratory ones. Interestingly, the results reveal that exploratory-based users are easily stimulated by context even if they have moved to specific stores. The aim of this research is to summarize users' search paths and patterns with different need states to help the e-store design the website.

Keywords: Lag sequential analysis · Need state · Recommendation function · Search patterns

1 Introduction

According to statistics published by eMarketer (2018), worldwide retail e-commerce sales surged from 1,336 billion USD in 2014 to 2,842 billion USD in 2015 and are expected to reach 4,878 billion USD in 2021 [1]. With the flourishing growth in e-commerce and the emerging trend of what Jack Ma referred to as "New Retail," the current research needs include how to collect and analyze users' online search behaviors in order to help online stores to refine their websites, how to optimize shopping experiences, and then how to set marketing strategies. Wolfinbarger and Gilly [2] have pointed out that one of the key factors influencing consumers' optimal purchasing decisions in the e-commerce (EC) environment is whether they pay attention to

© Springer Nature Switzerland AG 2019
N. G. Taylor et al. (Eds.): iConference 2019, LNCS 11420, pp. 554–561, 2019.
https://doi.org/10.1007/978-3-030-15742-5_53

the availability of information. In order to motivate consumers' willingness to conduct on-line shopping, the recommendation functions and the related recommendation mechanism are widely adopted on contemporary EC websites to boost website conversion rates and promote the electronic trade of goods [3, 4]. Furthermore, users' shopping motivation, preferences, and need states may influence their choice of recommendation functions (RFs), the shopping process and even final decision-making results [5–8].

Accordingly, we proposed a search pattern analytical method to analyze how RFs on Taobao.com support the user's entire shopping process on the website from the perspective of user-need states. We conducted a preliminary small study by inviting 12 users to participate in our evaluation by executing simulated shopping tasks to observe how different RFs help different types of users do on-line shopping. We further aimed to evaluate two types of users who have different need states: a goal-oriented user group and an exploratory-based user group. The goal-oriented search users are very focused on finding specific products, whereas the exploratory-based search users tend to take some time to do information gathering and may include stimulus-driven users [5, 9]. Technically, we first adopted zero-order state transition matrices (ZOSTs) to calculate the frequency (probabilities) of using each RF and then employed lag sequential analysis (LSA) to derive the significant repeating patterns [10–12]. The aim of this research was to summarize the users' searching or browsing patterns based on LSAs with different demand situations on the website.

2 Research Objectives and the Research Process

2.1 The Research Objectives

In this research, we designed two types of user-need states—goal-oriented shopping and exploratory-based shopping—to understand how users adopt RFs to analyze their search behavior in the entire shopping process. We wanted to clarify the difference between the concepts of the users' preferences and their need states. Users' preferences refers to users' long-term tastes and preferences, especially for products or services with which they have prior experience, whereas the users' need states or demand situations refers to current or situational needs [8]. We wanted to know if the goal-oriented user group would use stored search patterns and then have much more simple search paths compared to the exploratory-based users [9]. We also further examined if the exploratory-based group would be unconsciously stimulated by context to do online browsing and shopping [5, 9]. Furthermore, we adopted a sequence-based method to investigate how two types of RFs—personalized and non-personalized functions—support users' online shopping with different states of need. Accordingly, our research objectives were to understand the effects of the two types of RFs to help users who are goal-oriented shoppers or exploratory-based shoppers. We believed that the urgency of the users' shopping demand situation would lead to different interaction sequences between each RF on the website. Thus, we could discover how the effects of each RF support users with different need states.

2.2   The Evaluation Process and the Tasks

Herein, we briefly explain each phase of the research process.

- **Specifying the RFs on the website:** The RFs and the snapshots of Taobao.com website are illustrated in Fig. 1. We have identified important RFs in the target website and then encoded them. We mainly classified them into personalized and non-personalized functions, which helped us analyze how users adopt different types of RF to do online shopping. Table 1 shows the codes for each RF with associated explanations.

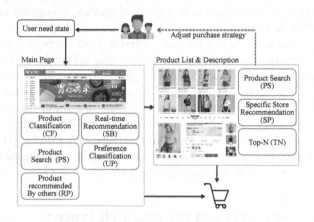

Fig. 1. RF functions and the snapshots on Taobao.com website

Table 1. The codes for each RFs with associated explanations

Types	RF (Code)	Definition
Non-personalization	Product Classification (CF)	Denotes the categories of products
	Product Search (PS)	Enter keywords to find out the products
	Preference Classification (UP)	Recommend products based on the characteristics of the products the most users have purchased
Personalization	Real-time Recommendation (SB)	Recommend products a user might like based on the user's browsing behavior and shopping history
	Product Recommended by Others (RP)	Recommend products that may interest a user based on users who have similar product preferences
	Top-N (TN)	Show the best sellers of each store based on the user's keywords
	Specific Store Recommendation (SP)	Recommend products from specific stores based on the user's browsing behavior and shopping history

- **Evaluation process:** In this phase, we recruited participants by purposive sampling based on our task design. Herein, we preliminary invited 12 users to participate in our evaluation by conducting simulated shopping tasks. The participants were undergraduate students between 22 and 27 years old, with an equal distribution of men and women. Most of them have Taobao accounts and all of them shop online at least once a month. Accordingly, they have similar shopping experience on the target website. Then, we designed simulated on-line shopping task based on the concepts of the experimental components for the evaluation of interactive information retrieval systems [13, 14]. It is to be noted that we use Morae software to record the participants' search and online shopping behaviors. Table 2 shows the details of the two types of tasks.

Table 2. Task design

Task Types	Descriptions
Goal-oriented	**Task:** Your best friend's birthday is coming. You are planning to buy a present for her/him Requirement: ✓ She/he wants to buy some new clothes for the coming winter ✓ She/he is into fashion with an interest in Western style clothes ✓ You plan to buy a totally new outfit for her/him
Exploratory-based	**Task:** For some reason, you are planning to buy products for yourself or your friend There is no requirement. It can be based on you or your friend's preferences to buy the gift

Notes:
✓ You can add the product to or delete it from the shopping cart at any time.
✓ No time limit and the shopping budget is based on your monthly shopping expenses.

- **Online shopping behavior analysis:** After the evaluation process, we adopted ZOSTs to calculate the frequency of using each RF for having search paths between RFs. Furthermore, we used LSA to derive the significant repeating patterns from search paths [10–12]. The results can help explain how the two types of user groups adopt RFs during the entire shopping process.

3 Preliminary Findings and Discussions

3.1 ZOST Analysis Results

Figures 2 and 3 shows the ZOSTs of the two groups of the users. The search paths are directional arrows among RFs.

Observation 1: Figures 2 and 3 show that the exploratory-based group has many more search paths—namely 16 distinct paths in total—compared to the goal-oriented group, which has 10 distinct paths in total. The exploratory shoppers have more

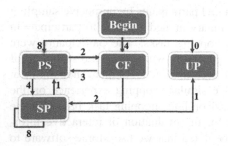

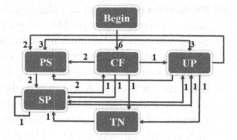

Fig. 2. ZOSTs of the goal-oriented group   **Fig. 3.** ZOSTs of exploratory-based group

complicated shopping behaviors, namely diversities of search paths in the website, compared to those who have a specific goal. It may indicate that the exploratory-based group are easy to be unconsciously stimulated by the context to do online shopping [5, 9]. It is reasonable that users without a specific goal will explore the website to find the products that may interest them.

Observation 2: We further checked the frequencies of search paths between RFs. For the goal-oriented group, 67% of users (n = 8) started with Product Search (PS), which indicates that users with a specific goal preferred to use keywords to find products. On the other hand, six users (50%) of the exploratory-based group started with Product Classification (CF), while three each (25% + 25%) of the exploratory users started with PS and Preference Classification (UP), respectively. It seems the users without specific goals for shopping have more diverse behaviors for finding products.

Observation 3: For the goal-oriented user group, there were six paths going to the SP function. The results show that this group of users generally go to a specific online store instead of staying in the category-based pages on the website. The search behaviors are the same as the user group of directed buying proposed by Moe [5]. This indicates that the goal-oriented user group have stored search patterns (routines) and then have much more simple search patterns compared to the exploratory-based user group for performing online shopping [9]. We would confirm this finding in the next section.

3.2   Significant Repeating Pattern Analysis Results

We used LSA to identify significant repeat search patterns from the search path between RFs, according to Bakeman and Gottman [10]. Tables 3 and 4 show the full set of transition probabilities between the different RFs which can be viewed as a matrix.

Observation 1 (goal-oriented task): Table 3 shows the matrix for the goal-oriented shopping group. It shows that SP → SP (Specific Store Recommendation → Specific Store Recommendation) has the highest probability value. It reveals that the users prefer to check product-level pages, which aligns with the search finding of Moe (2003). Furthermore, if we check the significance of the search paths between each RF

Table 3. Transitional probabilities for goal-oriented user group

RFs	CF	PS	SP	UP
CF	0	0.143	0.095	0
PS	0.095	0	0.190	0
SP	0	0.048	**0.381**	0.048
UP	0		0	0

Table 4. Transitional probabilities for exploratory-based user group

RFs	CF	PS	SP	TN	UP
CF	0.063	**0.125**	0.063	0.063	0.063
PS	0	0	**0.125**	0	0
SP	0.063	0	0.063	0	0.063
TN	0	0	0.063	0	0
UP	0	0.063	0	0	0

based on a computation of z-values and Yule's Q—that is, z > 1.96 and Q > 0.30—the CF → PS and PS → CF are significant search patterns. We can confirm that the two bidirectional search patterns are significant repeating patterns for the goal-oriented task, as shown in Rules (1) and (2). That is, there is a loop between the search function (PS) and categories of products for the user group (CF).

$$\text{CF (Product Classification)} \rightarrow \text{PS (Product Search)} \{z = 2.672,\ Q = 0.915\} \quad (1)$$

$$\text{PS (Product Search)} \rightarrow \text{CF (Product Classification)} \{z = 2.351,\ Q = 1.000\} \quad (2)$$

Observation 2 (exploratory-based task): Table 4 also shows that CF → PS and PS → SP have the highest probability value. However, we cannot find any significant repeat-search pattern for this group of users. Furthermore, the results show that there are several paths from one of the RFs to get to a specific store (SP). They reveal that the search paths of exploratory-based users are quite diverse; thus, there is no stored search pattern for them. In addition, they may adopt either non-personalized or personalized RFs during the shopping process.

Observation 3 (types of RFs): For the goal-oriented ones, the results show that the RFs in the significant repeat-search patterns belong to the non-personalized RFs. This suggests that the group of users prefers not to adopt personalized RFs to find products.

4   Conclusion

We proposed a search pattern analytical method to analyze the user's search behavior in the entire shopping process in a famous C2C e-store website from the perspective of the users' need states. The aim of this research is to summarize the users' search paths and patterns with different need states. Interestingly, the two types of users have much different search paths initially to find the products they desire to buy, and they also have significantly different search patterns in the end. The results show that goal-oriented shoppers prefer to search for a product directly in the initial entry to the website and will go to the product- or store-level pages. We suggest that the sellers of the website should select precise keywords to help buyers find specific products and avoid including too many advertisements that can disturb them. On the contrary, the results reveal that exploratory-based users have complicated search paths and are easily stimulated by context even if they have moved to specific stores. We suggest that sellers design and adopt different types of RFs to help buyers explore their websites. We will enlarge the scale of the evaluation to confirm our assumptions and conduct post-questionnaire with interview to provide implications in detail in future work. We sought to provide a reference for designing RFs for an e-commerce website and deciding the timing to launch advertisements to attract different kinds of users with different demand situations.

Acknowledgments. This research was financially supported by the Ministry of Education (MOE) of Taiwan under Grant MOST 105-2410-H-003-153-MY3 & the Institute for Research Excellence in Learning Sciences of National Taiwan Normal University (NTNU) from The Featured Areas Research Center Program within the framework of the Higher Education Sprout Project by the MOE in Taiwan are gratefully acknowledged.

References

1. eMarketer: Number of digital buyers worldwide from 2014 to 2021 (in billions). https://www.statista.com/statistics/251666/number-of-digital-buyers-worldwide/. Accessed 6 Sept 2018
2. Wolfinbarger, M., Gilly, M.C.: Shopping online for freedom, control, and fun. Calif. Manage. Rev. **43**(2), 34–55 (2001)
3. Li, Y.M., Wu, C.T., Lai, C.Y.: A social recommender mechanism for e-commerce: combining similarity, trust, and relationship. Decis. Support Syst. **55**(3), 740–752 (2013)
4. Schafer, J.B., Konstan, J.A., Riedl, J.: E-commerce recommendation applications. Data Min. Knowl. Disc. **5**(1–2), 115–153 (2001)
5. Moe, W.W.: Buying, searching, or browsing: differentiating between online shoppers using in-store navigational clickstream. J. Consum. Psychol. **13**(1–2), 29–39 (2003)
6. Rohm, A.J., Swaminathan. V.: A typology of online shoppers based on shopping motivations. J. Bus. Res. **57**(7), 748–757 (2004)
7. Kau, A.K., Yingchan, E.T., Ghose, S.: Typology of online shoppers. J. Consum. Mark. **20**(2), 139–156 (2003)

8. Zhang, W., Wang, J., Xu, S.: The probing of e-commerce user need states by page cluster analysis-An empirical study on women's clothes from Taobao.com. New Technol. Libr. Inf. Serv. **31**(3), 67–74 (2015)
9. Janiszewski, C.: The influence of display characteristics on visual exploratory search behavior. J. Consum. Res. **25**(3), 290–301 (1998)
10. Bakeman, R., Gottman, J.M.: Observing Interaction: An Introduction to Sequential Analysis. Cambridge University Press, New York (1999)
11. Sackett, G.P.: The lag sequential analysis of contingency and cyclicity in behavioral interaction research. In: Osofsky, J.D. (ed.) Handbook of Infant Development, pp. 623–649. Wiley, New York (1979)
12. Wildemuth, B.M.: The effects of domain knowledge on search tactic formulation. J. Am. Soc. Inform. Sci. Technol. **55**(3), 246–258 (2004)
13. Borlund, P.: Experimental components for the evaluation of interactive information retrieval systems. J. Documentation **56**(1), 71–90 (2000)
14. Borlund. P.: The IIR evaluation model: A framework for evaluation of interactive information retrieval systems. Inf. Res. **8**(3) (2003). http://informationr.net/ir/8-3/paper152.html. Accessed 06 Sept 2018

Algorithms at Work

Context-Aware Coproduction: Implications for Recommendation Algorithms

Jiawei Chen[1]([✉]), Afsaneh Doryab[2], Benjamin V. Hanrahan[1],
Alaaeddine Yousfi[3], Jordan Beck[1], Xiying Wang[4], Victoria Bellotti[5],
Anind K. Dey[6], and John M. Carroll[1]

[1] The Pennsylvania State University, University Park, PA, USA
{jzc245,bvh10,jeb560,jmcarroll}@psu.edu
[2] Carnegie Mellon University HCI Institute, Pittsburgh, PA, USA
adoryab@cs.cmu.edu
[3] Hasso Plattner Institute, University of Potsdam, Potsdam, Germany
alaaeddine.yousfi@hpi.de
[4] WorkSpan, Foster City, CA, USA
xiying@workspan.com
[5] Lyft, San Francisco, CA, USA
bellotti@lyft.com
[6] University of Washington, Seattle, WA, USA
anind@uw.edu

Abstract. Coproduction is an important form of service exchange in local community where members perform and receive services among each other on non-profit basis. Local coproduction systems enhance community connections and re-energize neighborhoods but face difficulties matching relevant and convenient transaction opportunities. Context-aware recommendations can provide promising solutions, but are so far limited to matching spatio-temporal and static user contexts. By analyzing data from a transportation-share app during a 3-week study with 23 participants, we extend the design scope for context-aware recommendation algorithms to include important community-based parameters such as sense of community. We find that inter- and intra-relationships between spatio-temporal and community-based social contexts significantly impact users' motivation to request or provide service. The results provide novel insights for designing context-aware recommendation algorithms for community coproduction services.

Keywords: Context-awareness · Community · Coproduction

1 Introduction

Coproduction is an important form of community service exchanges where people help one another based on generalized reciprocity and for the good of the neighborhood [7,10]. Information infrastructures, such as *Kassi* [24] and *Nextdoor*

© Springer Nature Switzerland AG 2019
N. G. Taylor et al. (Eds.): iConference 2019, LNCS 11420, pp. 565–577, 2019.
https://doi.org/10.1007/978-3-030-15742-5_54

[25], facilitate community coproduction exchanges. One of the most successful community exchange systems is timebanking [8], where local community members perform services for each other by spending or earning labor time. These community coproduction services foster reciprocal respect and trust, strengthen social bonds and enhance social capital within the neighborhood [9].

Despite the benefits, many opportunities for coproduction are missed as members are not aware of them [27] or fail to find and respond to them timely [30]. In response to these challenges, Jung *et al.* [23] introduced an algorithm to match transaction partners in terms of similarity of interests and complementarity of abilities and needs. An evaluation of the algorithm with volunteer timebankers demonstrated that it can help people identify transaction partners more effectively. However, Jung's algorithm only considers static user context of user profile and transaction history. In an *in situ* study, Doryab *et al.* [15] further found that matching spatio-temporal context and predictive modeling are promising in enhancing service recommendations, and that people are more willing to accept service requests that are convenient for them to perform, especially in terms of time and location. The recommendation algorithm, however, only includes location, time and static user preferences (*e.g.*, gender). So far, contextual factors on the community level, and the combinatory impact of different context have been little considered when designing recommendation algorithms for coproduction community services.

In this paper, we extend the design scope of context-aware recommendation algorithms to include community-based social parameters such as sense of community. With an iOS transportation-share app as technology probe, we analyze the role of various contexts and highlight inter- and intra-relations between spatiotemporal and non-spatiotemporal parameters through correlation graphs. Our analysis provides useful novel insights for context-aware recommendations in coproduction community services: (1) people's generosity and willingness to help others in their community has the potential to make them more willing to get out of their existing social circle and taking opportunities for more transaction interactions; (2) by considering community-based social parameters together with spatio-temporal context, we can look for alternative factors for recommendation when one or more of the user's priory context category is missing.

2   Related Work

2.1   Coproduction Community Services

Coproduction was first coined by Nobel Prize winner Elinor Ostrom in the 1970's to explain the case that the police should interact and collaborate with local residents to coproduce community safety. Edgar Cahn later extends the core value of coproduction to local community exchanges [8]: in timebanking, for example, every community member, regardless of financial status, gender or age, is encouraged to participate in social activities, help others, and receive help from the neighborhood [9]. As information platforms facilitate these service transactions within the social network, coproduction exchanges foster group identity and solidarity among community members over time [26].

Prior studies have illustrated the potential of novel information technologies in supporting coproduction community services. Smartphone timebank app brings benefits of transaction time reduction and real-time coordination [21]. In a recent survey study of nation-wide timebankers, Yuan *et al.* [31] also suggest that higher usability of mobile apps leads to more active transactions. It calls for the need to study more advanced intelligent technologies, which have seen numerous applications in commercialized area, for community coproduction scenarios.

2.2   Context-Aware Recommendations

Context-aware systems discover and react to user activities and environment changes [14,29]. Context denotes any information about interactions between a user and an application, ranging from time, location, to users' interest or status of surrounding devices [16]. Context-awareness has various applications [3], *e.g.* shopping guide [6], location-based services [5] and Internet-of-Things [28].

In recent years, context-awareness has drawn special attention from recommendation systems [1]. Incorporating contextual information into the recommendation process allows recommendations adapt to dynamic user needs and requirements. Such properties make context-awareness especially promising to the application of service exchanges. Opportunities for service exchanges are context-sensitive: service providers and recipients need timely coordination to be present at the same time and place to perform the service transaction [9]; the skills and availability of providers should also be matched with the needs of service recipients [23]. However, so far contextual parameters at the community level have not been considered for context-aware coproduction services.

2.3   Transportion-Share

Transportation-share is an important category of coproduction community services. In a study of timebanks at three large U. S. cities, transportation was the second largest category of timebank services [30]. Transportation-share, esp. ride-sharing [19] can also reduce traffic, pollution, and energy usage [12].

Transport-share is a typical example of context-sensitive community services. Rides or delivery requests are usually time and location sensitive, and rely highly on the availability and travel patterns of potential service providers. Prior research has mostly focused on algorithmic optimizations of grouping travelers with similar itineraries and time schedules [2,13]. Nevertheless, there is more to understand about users of context-aware transport-share, especially from the perspective of coproduction community services. This motivates our study design through a technology probe described in the following section.

Fig. 1. User interfaces of the technology probe

3 Study Design and Procedures

We conducted the study in the local community of the researchers, a small university town in the Northeastern US with students, faculties, and other local residents. As different populations have their own daily itineraries, we targeted college students as participants to ensure they would share a proportion of their context. Eligible students owned an iPhone 5S or above with a data plan. We advertised the study on the university's research website and in classrooms. We recruited 32 students and 9 dropped out because of vacation plans. The remaining 23 (13 female, age ($\bar{x} = 21.57$, $\sigma = 1.51$)) participants all lived off-campus and 15 of them drove their own cars as the main transportation method.

The study consisted of three steps: a two-week travel pattern tracking, a three-week use of technology probe application, and a post-study survey. We describe details of each step in the following.

At the beginning of the study, we sent participants an email with instructions to download and configure Aware app [17], which they kept running on their smartphones for 2 weeks. The Aware app tracked GPS traces on users' smartphones, which we used to extract their daily travel patterns for context-aware matching. More specifically, we sampled location data every 3 min to trade off between battery uses and up-to-date information, and sent the data to our back-end server. In line with [15], we developed 2 algorithms to model the temporal daily patterns of users' significant locations. Our significant location algorithm creates time slots every 2 h and then within each slot clusters the location traces. Our travel route algorithm creates temporal frequent-route trees for each user from those clusters. To match a potential rider and driver, we used the frequent-route trees to rank their distance in terms of location and time.

After 2 weeks of travel pattern tracking, we emailed the participants with instructions to download and use an iOS mobile app to request rides

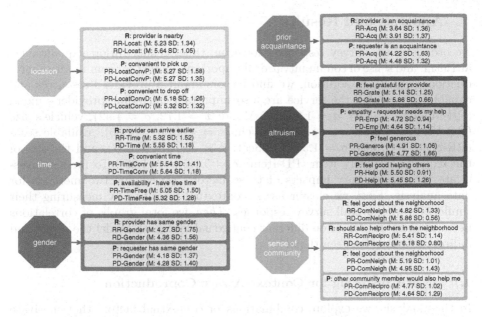

Fig. 2. Importance of different context according to participants' ratings (1 = least important; 7 = most important). RR: context for ride requesters; RD: context for delivery requesters; PR: context for ride providers; PD: context for delivery providers.

or deliveries. Upon requesting a service, the app shows a list of users to fulfill these requests recommended based on user profiles, current location, and predicted future travel routes (Fig. 1). Participants were asked to post 3 requests about rides or deliveries whenever they felt such needs. Participants posted 77 requests in total - 43 for rides and 34 for delivery. We presented this app as a technology probe [22] in order to collect information about how users interact with the novel technology, context-aware transport-sharing, in natural settings. Therefore, we did not require participants to carry out any services, but focused on people's attitudes towards various contextual factors when interacting with the app. This study design allows us to tackle the challenges of adoption and critical mass issues [20], while stay focus on the main research questions.

After using the app for 3 weeks, we emailed out a post-study survey to ask participants about the impacts of different contexts when requesting and offering a ride or delivery. In addition to location, time, gender preferences, prior acquaintance and altruism factors as previously studied [15], we also investigated community-based parameters by adapting measures from the sense of community index [11] (see Fig. 2 for specified items). We received 22 survey responses. Participants recruited from classroom announcement received 2% extra credit from their instructors, while other participants received $20 cash.

4   Analysis and Results

According to the survey responses, location, time, gender, prior acquaintance, altruism, and sense of community are all important context for community coproductions (Fig. 2). In addition, we find factors about a provider's resources and capabilities to fulfill the service are also important, including provider's mood (PR-Mood: $\bar{x} = 4.68$, $\sigma = 1.29$; PD-Mood: $\bar{x} = 4.72$, $\sigma = 1.42$), vehicle's size (RR-Veh: $\bar{x} = 4.14$, $\sigma = 1.55$; RD-Veh: $\bar{x} = 4.05$, $\sigma = 1.36$), available seats (RR-Seat: $\bar{x} = 3.64$, $\sigma = 1.36$; RD-Seat: $\bar{x} = 3.91$, $\sigma = 1.37$), and the size of the requested delivery item (PD-Item: $\bar{x} = 5.18$, $\sigma = 1.29$). To further investigate the combinatory impacts of these factors, we employ two methods for data analysis. *First*, we cluster users' contextual priorities by measuring their similarities with overall survey responses. *Then*, we form graphs of correlations between users' responses on different contextual factors to model the direct and indirect relations between them.

4.1   User-Clustering for Context-Aware Coproduction

In this analysis, we explore combinations of contextual factors that motivate participation in coproductions for different users. In other words, we seek to identify contextual priorities among users that affect their decisions in requesting or offering a ride/delivery. For each participant, we calculate the average response to questions in each of the 6 context categories: *location, time, gender, altruism, prior acquaintance* and *sense of community*. We then calculate the ratio of these average responses to the average of max response scores of that category. We set the threshold as the minimum ratio score among the maximum ratio scores for all participants, *i.e.*, each participant will have at least one favored context category, and this helps us to identify user clusters based on their combined contextual preferences (Table 1). For example, P7, P11, P15 tend to enter a transportation-share encouraged by any of the 6 categories of context, while P2, P4 and P5 would do so even without knowing the transaction partner before.

All participants in our study are influenced by more than 2 categories of context. This indicates that *context-aware recommendation algorithm should take into account a combination of contextual parameters for matching, when the situation in the user's most favored context category is missing*. To further explore this implication, we calculate the ranking of context priorities for each participant (Table 2). Comparing Table 1 with Table 2, we see that people's preference profiles are more diversified in terms of ranking of context priorities. We find that spatio-temporal convenience appears as the most important context for 11 out of the 22 participants. However, there are also 6 participants who put altruism and sense of community as the most important context for entering a coproduction service. The implication of this type of user modeling for recommendation algorithm is that *in situation when the dominant category is missing or unfavored, the algorithm can look into parameters in the second or third dominant category for matching*. In the following sections, we will support this implication through analysis of inter and intra-category relations between contextual parameters.

Table 1. Combination of context favored by different participants. L: location; T: time; G: gender; A: altruism; P: prior acquaintance; C: sense of community.

Context combination	Participants
LTGAPC	P7, P11, P15
LTGAC	P2, P4, P5
LTA	P1
LTAPC	P3, P10, P12, P22
LTAC	P8, P9, P17, P19–P21
LTPC	P13
LTC	P18
TC	P6
GC	P14
AC	P16

Table 2. Ranking of context priorities by different participants. L: location; T: time; G: gender; A: altruism; P: prior acquaintance; C: sense of community. Context on the left of the combinatory string has higher priority.

	Context ranking		Context ranking
P1	ALT	P12	TLCAP
P2	ACGLT	P13	LTPC
P3	CALTP	P14	GC
P4	GTLAC	P15	PTGCLA
P5	GTLAC	P16	CA
P6	TC	P17	TALC
P7	TCAGLP	P18	CTL
P8	TLAC	P19	CTLA
P9	TLCA	P20	TACL
P10	LPTAC	P21	TALC
P11	GLTPAC	P22	LTCAP

4.2 Modeling Behavior Proxies for Context-Aware Recommendation

Design of context-aware recommendation algorithms for community coproductions requires understanding behavior-proxies towards each type of activity herein transportation-share. By behavior-proxy, we mean the tendency of a certain behavior in different contextual situations, *e.g.*, accepting a ride request from a stranger nearby vs. rejecting a request from a friend in a further location. To gain this understanding, we first calculate pairwise correlations between all survey responses where participants retrospectively reflected on their choices and actions during the study. We then construct behavior-proxy graphs where the nodes are contextual parameters and edges are correlations between those parameters acquired from participants' ratings. We construct these graphs for all 4 user scenarios: RR (request for ride), RD (request for delivery), PR (provide ride service), PD (provide delivery). The graphs are made using Gephi software [4] with Fruchterman Reingold layout [18]. We use green edges for positive and red for negative correlation. Edges are weighted by the correlation coefficient, and thicker lines indicate stronger correlations between the contextual parameters.

Direct Behavior-Proxies. Understanding direct behavior-proxies allows us to investigate how one contextual factor impacts people's decision to enter a coproduction activity given other contexts. To gain such understanding, we extract ego-networks of specific parameters from the full behavior-proxy graphs. We identify contextual relationships both within and across different categories.

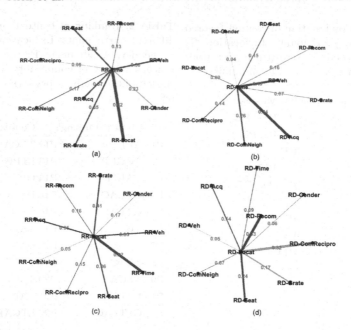

Fig. 3. Behavior-proxy of spatio-temporal context for service requesters. (a) temporal context for ride requesters; (b) temporal context for delivery requesters; (c) spatial context for ride requesters; (d) spatial context for delivery requesters. (Color figure online)

Spatio-temporal context is a direct indication of *convenience*, and significantly impact people's decision to offer community service [15]. Our graph (Fig. 3) shows heavy weight between the time and location parameters, indicating them as significant inter-related factors to consider when matching a requester and provider in a transportation-share service. However, such strong association does not appear for delivery requesters. An implication of this is that a good delivery provider can be either a temporal match or a spatial match if not both.

From Fig. 3, we also see that for delivery requesters, the feeling of gratefulness towards providers and willingness to reciprocate other community members would remedy conditions when the provider is not nearby. Part of the reason for this is that compared to ride services, delivery services are more flexible in terms of spatiotemporal factors. Therefore, even if a potential provider is not close at the moment, people may still want to send a request and appreciate the help.

Previous study has identified the importance of empathy in accepting service requests [15]. Our analysis shows in more detail how empathy would impact people's behavior given other context. The behavior-proxies of empathy (Fig. 4) indicate that ride providers would accept a request when they feel that the requester needs their help, although the requester is not a prior acquaintance as they prefer. This shows that people's generosity and willingness to help others may encourage them to get out of their existing social circle for transaction opportunities. Interestingly, such strong relation was not observed in delivery services, partly because deliveries involve fewer person-to-person interactions.

Indirect Behavior-Proxies. In addition to direct pairwise relations, our proxy graph provides the behavior paths between different contextual parameters (the nodes) that indicate indirect relationships between those parameters and their corresponding weight. Analysis of these indirect relations enables us to look into *alternative factors for recommendation when one or more of the user's priory context category is missing.* We extract the indirect paths from pairs of two context from the full behavior-proxy graph. We threshold the edges with correlations greater than 0.3, and only extract 1-hop paths to show the factors of stronger influence. In the situation when either context is missing, we find that other context can serve as alternative factors for context-aware recommendations. The following examples describe this observation in different scenarios.

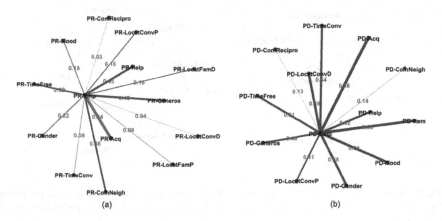

(a)   (b)

Fig. 4. Behavior-proxy of empathy for: (a) ride providers; (b) delivery providers. (Color figure online)

1. In Fig. 5, we show the indirect behavior-proxy paths between convenient pick-up location and gender preference for service providers. In case the requester is not of the same gender as preferred, the provider would still likely accept the request if it is spatiotemporally convenient, if the requester is a prior acquaintance, or if the provider feels generous and wants to help. On the other hand, however, when the pick-up location is not convenient, it is still important that some other spatiotemporal and reciprocal context are present to make a provider more willing to accept the request.
2. In Fig. 6, we show the indirect behavior-proxy paths between convenient pick-up location and preference of prior acquaintance for service providers. In case the requester is not a prior acquaintance, the provider is still likely to accept

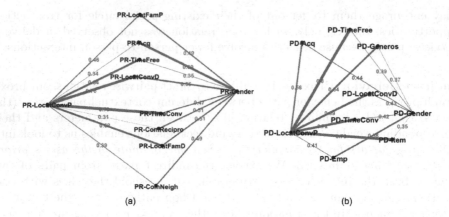

Fig. 5. Indirect behavior-proxy between convenient pick up location and gender preference for: (a) ride providers; (b) delivery providers. (Color figure online)

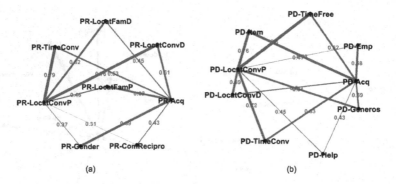

Fig. 6. Indirect behavior-proxy between convenient pick up location and preference of prior acquaintance for providers: (a) ride providers; (b) delivery providers. (Color figure online)

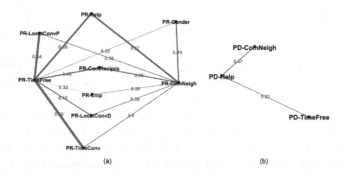

Fig. 7. Indirect behavior-proxy between spatio-temporal context (having free time at the moment) and community context (doing good for neighborhood) for: (a) ride providers; (b) delivery providers. (Color figure online)

the request if the drop-off location is convenient or if it is at a convenient time. If the provider is familiar with the pick-up or drop-off location, or if the requester matches the gender preference, the ride provider would also be likely to accept the request. Similarly, a delivery provider would be likely to accept a request from a stranger if it is convenient in terms of other spatiotemporal factors or if the item is convenient to carry. It also makes the delivery providers more likely to accept a request when they feel the requester needs help or they feel generous and wants to help others.

3. In Fig. 7, we show another example for spatiotemporal context (having free time at the moment) and community social context (doing good for neighborhood). This example illustrate that when a user bears a strong feeling of doing good for the neighborhood, even if he or she does not have free time at the moment, the user will choose to accept a request as he or she has strong altruistic motivation and feels good helping others. Convenient spatio-temporal factors would also help, but altruism stands out as the strongest remedy in this situation.

5   Conclusion and Future Work

In this study, we probe people's attitudes towards different contexts and study their combinatory impacts on community coproductions through the case of transportation-share. We focus on two types of transportation-share services - ride-sharing and deliveries - and analyze different contextual behaviors among users towards those two services in a local college community. We suggest that by considering community-based social parameters together with spatio-temporal context, context-aware recommendations can look for alternative factors when one or more of the user's priory context category is missing.

Since we used the same recommendation algorithm and data collection app in [15], we skipped the analysis of accuracy for location and arrival-time predictions which was adequately evaluated in prior work. Instead, we focused on extending our understanding of the role of different context categories and their combined effect on recommendation to inform the next version of context-aware recommendation algorithms. This analysis also motivates and directs our next step towards the implementation of our context-aware recommendation algorithm and integrating it into a deployed community service application.

References

1. Adomavicius, G., Tuzhilin, A.: Context-aware recommender systems. In: Ricci, F., Rokach, L., Shapira, B. (eds.) Recommender Systems Handbook, pp. 191–226. Springer, Boston, MA (2015). https://doi.org/10.1007/978-1-4899-7637-6_6
2. Agatz, N., Erera, A., Savelsbergh, M., Wang, X.: Optimization for dynamic ride-sharing: a review. Eur. J. Oper. Res. **223**(2), 295–303 (2012)
3. Baldauf, M., Dustdar, S., Rosenberg, F.: A survey on context-aware systems. Int. J. Ad Hoc Ubiquit. Comput. **2**(4), 263–277 (2007)

4. Bastian, M., Heymann, S., Jacomy, M., et al.: Gephi: an open source software for exploring and manipulating networks. ICWSM **8**, 361–362 (2009)
5. Biancalana, C., Flamini, A., Gasparetti, F., Micarelli, A., Millevolte, S., Sansonetti, G.: Enhancing traditional local search recommendations with context-awareness. In: Konstan, J.A., Conejo, R., Marzo, J.L., Oliver, N. (eds.) UMAP 2011. LNCS, vol. 6787, pp. 335–340. Springer, Heidelberg (2011). https://doi.org/10.1007/978-3-642-22362-4_29
6. Black, D., Clemmensen, N.J., Skov, M.B.: Pervasive computing in the supermarket: designing a context-aware shopping trolley. In: Social and Organizational Impacts of Emerging Mobile Devices: Evaluating Use, pp. 172–185. IGI Global (2012)
7. Cahn, E.: Co-production 2.0: retrofitting human service programs to tap the renewable energy of community. Community Currency Mag., 36–39 (2010)
8. Cahn, E.S.: No More Throw-Away People: The Co-production Imperative. Edgar Cahn (2000)
9. Carroll, J.M.: Co-production scenarios for mobile time banking. In: Dittrich, Y., Burnett, M., Mørch, A., Redmiles, D. (eds.) IS-EUD 2013. LNCS, vol. 7897, pp. 137–152. Springer, Heidelberg (2013). https://doi.org/10.1007/978-3-642-38706-7_11
10. Carroll, J.M., Chen, J., Yuan, C.W.T., Hanrahan, B.V.: In search of coproduction: smart services as reciprocal activities. Computer **49**(7), 26–32 (2016)
11. Chavis, D.M., Lee, K.S., Acosta, J.D.: The sense of community (SCI) revised: the reliability and validity of the SCI-2. In: 2nd International Community Psychology Conference, Lisboa, Portugal (2008)
12. Cici, B., Markopoulou, A., Frias-Martinez, E., Laoutaris, N.: Assessing the potential of ride-sharing using mobile and social data: a tale of four cities. In: Proceedings of the 2014 ACM International Joint Conference on Pervasive and Ubiquitous Computing, pp. 201–211. ACM (2014)
13. Cici, B., Markopoulou, A., Laoutaris, N.: SORS: a scalable online ridesharing system. In: Proceedings of the 9th ACM SIGSPATIAL International Workshop on Computational Transportation Science, pp. 13–18. ACM (2016)
14. Dey, A.K., Abowd, G.D., Salber, D.: A conceptual framework and a toolkit for supporting the rapid prototyping of context-aware applications. Hum.-Comput. Interact. **16**(2), 97–166 (2001)
15. Doryab, A., Bellotti, V., Yousfi, A., Wu, S., Carroll, J.M., Dey, A.K.: If it's convenient: leveraging context in peer-to-peer variable service transaction recommendations. Proc. ACM Interact. Mob. Wearable Ubiquit. Technol. **1**(3), 48 (2017)
16. Feng, L., Apers, P.M.G., Jonker, W.: Towards context-aware data management for ambient intelligence. In: Galindo, F., Takizawa, M., Traunmüller, R. (eds.) DEXA 2004. LNCS, vol. 3180, pp. 422–431. Springer, Heidelberg (2004). https://doi.org/10.1007/978-3-540-30075-5_41
17. Ferreira, D., Kostakos, V., Dey, A.K.: AWARE: mobile context instrumentation framework. Front. ICT **2**, 6 (2015)
18. Fruchterman, T.M., Reingold, E.M.: Graph drawing by force-directed placement. Softw. Pract. Experience **21**(11), 1129–1164 (1991)
19. Furuhata, M., Dessouky, M., Ordóñez, F., Brunet, M.E., Wang, X., Koenig, S.: Ridesharing: the state-of-the-art and future directions. Transp. Res. Part B Methodol. **57**, 28–46 (2013)
20. Grudin, J.: Groupware and social dynamics: eight challenges for developers. Commun. ACM **37**(1), 92–105 (1994)

21. Han, K., Shih, P.C., Bellotti, V., Carroll, J.M.: It's time there was an app for that too: a usability study of mobile timebanking. Int. J. Mob. Hum. Comput. Interact. (IJMHCI) **7**(2), 1–22 (2015)
22. Hutchinson, H., et al.: Technology probes: inspiring design for and with families. In: Proceedings of the SIGCHI Conference on Human Factors in Computing Systems, pp. 17–24. ACM (2003)
23. Jung, H., et al.: 'MASTerful' matchmaking in service transactions: inferred abilities, needs and interests versus activity histories. In: Proceedings of the 2016 CHI Conference on Human Factors in Computing Systems, pp. 1644–1655. ACM (2016)
24. Lampinen, A., Lehtinen, V., Cheshire, C., Suhonen, E.: Indebtedness and reciprocity in local online exchange. In: Proceedings of the 2013 Conference on Computer Supported Cooperative Work, pp. 661–672. ACM (2013)
25. Masden, C.A., Grevet, C., Grinter, R.E., Gilbert, E., Edwards, W.K.: Tensions in scaling-up community social media: a multi-neighborhood study of nextdoor. In: Proceedings of the 32nd Annual ACM Conference on Human Factors in Computing Systems, pp. 3239–3248. ACM (2014)
26. Molm, L.D., Collett, J.L., Schaefer, D.R.: Building solidarity through generalized exchange: a theory of reciprocity. Am. J. Soc. **113**(1), 205–242 (2007)
27. Ozanne, L.K.: Learning to exchange time: benefits and obstacles to time banking (2010)
28. Perera, C., Zaslavsky, A., Christen, P., Georgakopoulos, D.: Context aware computing for the internet of things: a survey. IEEE Commun. Surv. Tutorials **16**(1), 414–454 (2014)
29. Schilit, B., Adams, N., Want, R.: Context-aware computing applications. In: First Workshop on Mobile Computing Systems and Applications, WMCSA 1994, pp. 85–90. IEEE (1994)
30. Shih, P.C., Bellotti, V., Han, K., Carroll, J.M.: Unequal time for unequal value: implications of differing motivations for participation in timebanking. In: Proceedings of the 33rd Annual ACM Conference on Human Factors in Computing Systems, pp. 1075–1084. ACM (2015)
31. Yuan, C.W.T., Hanrahan, B.V., Carroll, J.M.: Is there social capital in service exchange tools? Investigating timebanking use and social capital development. Comput. Hum. Behav. **81**, 274–281 (2018)

Algorithmic Management and Algorithmic Competencies: Understanding and Appropriating Algorithms in Gig Work

Mohammad Hossein Jarrahi[1](✉) and Will Sutherland[2]

[1] University of North Carolina at Chapel Hill, Chapel Hill, NC 27599, USA
jarrahi@unc.edu
[2] University of Washington, Seattle, WA 98195, USA
willsk88@uw.edu

Abstract. Data-driven algorithms now enable digital labor platforms to automatically manage transactions between thousands of gig workers and service recipients. Recent research on algorithmic management outlines information asymmetries, which make it difficult for gig workers to gain control over their work due a lack of understanding how algorithms on digital labor platforms make important decisions such as assigning work and evaluating workers. By building on an empirical study of Upwork users, we make it clear that users are not passive recipients of algorithmic management. We explain how workers make sense of different automated features of the Upwork platform, developing a literacy for understanding and working with algorithms. We also highlight the ways through which workers may use this knowledge of algorithms to work around or manipulate them to retain some professional autonomy while working through the platform.

Keywords: Algorithmic management · Algorithmic competency · Gig work · Online freelancing

1 Introduction

The "datafication" of many organizational processes and activities has paved the way for algorithms to aggregate and analyze data, and thereby contribute to the processes of management and decision-making [1]. Algorithms are now beyond simple data-processing code, as they prescribe protocols for work in different organizational contexts [2, 3]. Due to their analytical capacities, algorithms and smart agents are replacing some of the tasks that were seen as the responsibility of middle managers [4, 5]. For example, sensor data and algorithmic processing can provide more accurate predictions about the arrival or departure of flights or recommendations about high performing stocks [6].

With the increasing reliance on algorithms in various contexts of decision-making, researchers have begun to voice concerns over the opaque nature of algorithms and "blind' dependence on the algorithmic approach [7]. Given the automated quality of the algorithm, it is easy for one to develop a kind of "complacency", or overreliance on smart systems to make autonomous decisions [8]. To work effectively with algorithms,

© Springer Nature Switzerland AG 2019
N. G. Taylor et al. (Eds.): iConference 2019, LNCS 11420, pp. 578–589, 2019.
https://doi.org/10.1007/978-3-030-15742-5_55

the human decision-maker (at all levels) still needs to retain an understanding of algorithms and the process through which they transform data into decisions, recommendations etc. [1, 9].

1.1 Algorithmic Management in the Gig Economy

Algorithmic management has emerged in digital labor platforms as a method of organizing and coordinating extremely large groups of workers and clients in an automated way [4, 10, 11]. By reducing the hiring and transacting processes programmatically, the platform can facilitate a large number of short term, and often on-demand projects [12]. The digital platform then is an organizing model which produces flexibility through a process of scaling and automation [10, 13].

The work of coordinating and organizing workers at scale was traditionally the work of middle managers and human foremen [5], but the algorithm-based platform gains some efficiency by offloading this work to information-based decision systems [14]. This means that many of the tasks which were the responsibility of that class of managers are now carried out by automated systems, including matching workers and service recipients, assigning tasks, evaluating gig workers' performance (through summary statistics of ratings and comments), providing information to transacting parties, and even implementing human resource management decisions [15]. The goals of this process, scaling and automation, require the minimization of human intervention, such that transactions can be carried out quickly and efficiently [4].

A consequence of this transition is that much of the process of management and decision-making is subducted into opaque algorithmic processes [16, 17]. The exact process by which an algorithm produces decisions may be convoluted and inaccessible to the common worker [2, 18]. For this reason, the decision produced by an algorithmic system can seem impenetrable, erratic, and unpredictable, and workers can become frustrated with the inscrutability of this decision-making system [15, 16].

As such, monitoring and attempting to grasp the functions of various algorithms has become an important component of gig work [19–21]. Digital platforms, which have become some of the primary facilities for the gig economy [11], operate largely on programmatic processes, and are characteristically convoluted, presenting a complex working environment for the gig worker [17, 22, 23]. However, gig workers are creative in investigating these algorithmic systems, and such investigations serve as a foundation for gaming the system, working around constraints, and generally mobilizing the algorithmic platform for the benefit of the worker's autonomy [15, 20].

It is in fact critical not to overlook the agency of workers in adapting and leveraging algorithmic working environments. Our objective in this paper is therefore to observe the moments of agency in which workers develop a functional understanding of an algorithm, or knowledge of how to use or subvert that algorithm. The platform Upwork serves as a good context for this particular line of investigation because it supports a variety of skilled knowledge work, which is hard to deskill or decompose [14, 24]. The coordinating core of the Upwork platform is a suite of algorithms which match workers with clients, support transactions, and police user behavior. However, the nature of this work makes it difficult to measure, verify, and decompose algorithmically.

To unpack the value of Upwork as a research context briefly, it is helpful to look at the kind of work that is done on the platform. To date, research on algorithmic management has primarily focused on the microwork or ridesharing contexts of gig work [e.g., 2, 15, 16, 19, 22, 23]. Online freelancing—as a more knowledge intensive form of gig work—presents different work dynamics [25], and therefore workers' engagement with algorithmic management can be different. Online freelancing typically requires specialized skills, and personal professional development. For example, on online freelancing platforms such as Upwork or Fiverr, gig workers are presented with opportunities to customize a profile, take proficiency tests and promote themselves as knowledge experts in different domains [26]. Evaluation of workers performance is also more dynamic and qualitative, and projects often involve close communication between the freelancer and their clients.

We therefore chose Upwork (as the largest online freelancing platform) with the premise that this environment gives workers more room to maneuver in the face of algorithmic constraints, or leverage them to their own benefit [27]. This makes it a valuable space in which to broaden our understanding of how workers have reacted and adapted to the inscrutability of the gig platforms as a working environment. To support this contribution, we build on an empirical study of gig workers on Upwork and their encounters with algorithms that manage their work. More specifically, this study examines how Upworkers generate an understanding of algorithms, and use this understanding to leverage algorithms to their professional advantage on the online freelance marketplace provided by Upwork.

2 Methods

Our findings are based on 33 interviews with Upwork workers, and 26 policy statements and help documents collected from Upwork's website, as well as 98 threads collected from Upwork related online forums. The study is designed to first give the researchers an understanding of the Upwork community and its context through the forum and Upwork page data, and second to use that data to guide a more directed investigation through interviews. The forum and help page data allowed the researchers to become familiar with the services and policies operating on the Upwork platform, and acquire a broad overview of common strategies, problems, interests, and complaints of the Upwork user community surrounding those services and policies. The researchers were able to move back and forth between the two sources, discovering worker concerns or strategies in relation to Upwork's algorithms in the forum data, and then comparing those accounts with official accounts in the help documentation. The forum data and help documentation was then used to inform a more directed investigation through interviews.

Forum data was collected from two separate forums, the "Community Discussions" section of Upwork's website, and from a subforum known as r/Upwork on the forum site Reddit. The Upwork forum was selected because it was moderated by Upwork directly, and was a place where workers could interact with Upwork representatives, while the Reddit forum was chosen because it is not associated with Upwork (and it is semi-anonymous), and therefore allows users a little more openness in discussing things which contravene Upwork policy. The subreddit r/upwork was also chosen because it has a large, active community. The authors scanned the forums and collected posts that had at least one response, and which had some relevance to the Upwork platform itself, rather than focusing solely on the worker's trade. Posts were collected and analyzed iteratively, until new posts were no longer introducing new concepts. Help documentation was collected from different sections of upwork.com, including help pages and policy statements from a section devoted to technical support, and articles and recommendations from the "hiring headquarters". All the documents in the forum data and help documentation ranged between 2015 and 2018.

Interview participants were selected for diversity in the kind of work that they do. They were identified on Upwork itself, through social media platforms such as Reddit, Quora, and Twitter, and through professional websites maintained by the workers themselves. Of the 33 participants recruited this way, 20 had only used the platform as freelancers, and 13 had experience using the platform as both a client and as a free-lancer. Their ages ranged from 20 to 58, and there was a high variation in profession (e.g., UX design, copywriting, industrial design, voice acting, legal writing, and animation). In order to surface latent understandings workers had about algorithms as tools and as a managerial structure, we focused on breakdowns and solutions to breakdowns in the worker's experiences with the platform and its algorithms.

More specifically, the interview protocol included questions inquiring about:

(1) The general experience of the workers with the Upwork platform.
(2) How they use the platform to find work.
(3) What they know about the underlying algorithms, and how they function.
(4) How they perceive the job recommender algorithm.
(5) How they understand the rating and evaluation algorithms.
(6) How they seek information about the ways the platform actually works.
(7) How they deal with algorithmic control.

All interviews were conducted through video conferencing software, and they on average lasted one hour in length.

Data collection and analysis proceeded concurrently, allowing us to iteratively identify and refine themes iteratively, as per Maxwell [28]. Data analysis involved two major steps, and was inductive, following iterative protocols like those of grounded theory building [29]. First, the initial analysis involved subjecting the interview transcripts and forum data to interpretation using open coding [30], which resulted in common themes. Common themes were elicited based on problems or solutions in the worker's experiences with the gig algorithms that directly influenced their work. These themes were refined after the earliest interviews, and refined again after the continuous conversation between the researchers. These themes helped us identify relevant statements in the interviews and enabled us to compare them through meaning condensation. Specifically, we identified moments/statements where the worker shows some cognizance of the algorithm's process, or takes action to mobilize or adapt the algorithm towards their own ends.

3 Findings

Management of large groups of highly independent, highly skilled gig workers on Upwork is achieved through a variety of algorithms. The proceduralization of evaluation and decision-making processes in the form of a constellation of algorithms is a significant aspect of Upwork managerial function. However, users may experience these algorithms differently; that is, for some, algorithms and their role in organizing gig work is visible. For instance, workers involved in niche areas paid less attention towards algorithms since the platform worked relatively well for them and they were operating in an area with low labor supply. Likewise, more established gig workers in our dataset were not as cognizant of algorithms and their impact on their work, since the algorithm tended to reinforce their positions (e.g., by listing them higher in searches).

This noted, accounts provided in interviews and the dominant sentiments on the online forums portrayed a rather different picture about users' interactions with algorithmic management: many gig workers keep themselves informed of Upwork algorithms and their functioning. In the remainder of this article, we outline three related activities that enable users to raise their understanding of algorithms, and to engage more effectively with algorithmic management.

3.1 Sensemaking

While the platform is easy to join and easy to use initially, it is in fact a large and complex collection of services, often coordinated automatically. Many workers put in a significant amount of time and effort developing a more sophisticated understanding of Upwork's various ratings, timeframes, policies, and procedures. For instance, workers monitor the functioning of the platform's rating and score-calculating algorithms very closely as they are critical to a worker's ability to find work and charge higher rates. Participant 3 discovered that clients could leave hidden feedback after he had a bad interaction with a client and noticed that his job success score dropped afterwards: "They told me they were not going to leave me a review as long as I didn't leave them one, so I held up my end of the bargain. A few days after the contract ended, I noticed my job success score went down from 99 to 93%." Upwork does mention the fact that clients can leave "private" ratings in a help page, but much of the workers' understanding of features like this and more importantly, their impact on ratings comes from close personal observation.

Workers also attempt to get a better understanding of algorithms by approaching them from the client side of the platform. This involves making a client account in order to see what information is presented about a worker, the order in which worker bids are displayed, the prominence of certain ratings or badges, and other functions of the platform's algorithms. For example, even though Participant 3 never posted a job as a client, he used a client account to ascertain how the results of technical competency tests he had taken changed his position in search results. He found that he was the highest rated gig workers residing in the US in that technical area and consequently used that as a promotional element in the proposals he sent to clients through Upwork.

Sensemaking is not necessarily a personal activity. Workers may use social channels such as online forums to share knowledge about underlying algorithms or collectively bring together different pieces of experiences and generate a more comprehensive understanding about algorithms. The forums were a resource for people seeking advice about how to deal with difficult clients or how to interpret certain Upwork policies. It also makes it easy to maintain a detailed perspective of many features and policies, which make up the platform. Participant 26 stated that the forums were good for "keeping on top of the platform changes, so specifically like this is the new thing and the terms of service you have to look out for, or like this change is going to affect top rated freelancers because they're doing this, and they kind of summarize and do all of this for me, so I don't have to dig through the documentation every time they change it." Some workers also learn directly from other, more experienced workers. Participants 15 and 17 both took classes from an experienced Upwork freelancer, which provided concrete strategies for promoting oneself on the platform. For instance, it was from this class that Participant 15 learned that most of the jobs on Upwork are hidden, and can only be acquired on invitation from the clients, not by applying through the bidding system.

3.2 Circumventing

Understanding the algorithms and algorithmic management through sensemaking is in itself useful; this understanding provides workers with more confidence and sense of control [10]. However, as algorithms impose some constraints on the worker, gig workers may seek ways to avoid algorithmic processes, or to substitute them with outside tools. Upwork's work diary, for instance, which tracks user activity for hourly contracts by taking intermittent screenshots and recording the number of clicks, introduces a variety of challenges for workers. Some workers are not comfortable with the surveillance it requires, and for others it becomes problematic because it does not fit into the tasks and workflows of different jobs (e.g., art and design). Participant 1 worked largely on a tablet, which would not run the tracking application. She also spent time walking when she was thinking about a particularly difficult design problem. The time tracker would not capture this kind of work, and would make it look as if she was not working at all. She, and many others, therefore avoided the time tracking system by arranging fixed price contracts, which do not require the use of the work diary and tracking system. Avoiding certain aspects of the platform in this way is a required skill for workers, as the platform presents a large number of resources, many of which may serve as a means of control or surveillance, or may not fit into a worker's own professional habits and processes.

Similarly, the contracting system, with its automated escrow and invoicing features, is also avoided by some workers due to its transaction fee (Upwork's commission). In these situations, the worker is leveraging the matching capabilities, profile system, and bidding system of the platform, but actively avoiding the security provided by the contracting system. Workers find circumventing this part of the platform risky, so they often create a careful process to move transactions off the programmatically-driven contracting system (on Upwork) into a trust-based transaction through Paypal or another payment platform. Participant 6 described the need to build rapport with the client before taking payment processing off-platform: "Well after the first time they actually see that I'm not a freak and I do a good job and will do the work that's when I'll usually ask." In this sense, circumvention is not just ignoring or avoiding some component of the platform, but actively extending contracts on the platform into external, third-party applications.

The challenge of using Upwork's algorithmic resources then becomes an issue of leveraging those resources selectively, and sometimes integrating outside tools to fill in the gaps. External communication tools were specifically leveraged by Upworkers. Upwork reinforces the use of its communication channels, particularly its messaging application, which allows automatic recording and monitoring of conversations. The algorithm reacts to the use of terms such as skype or phone when typed into the chat box. However, workers often go around this communication channel and employ other communication and information sharing tools. For example, they may switch to email once a project is arranged, or join the project management tools of their clients. Participant 15 uses the Upwork messenger in addition to other communication and cloud services to coordinate and communication with clients. Like several other participants, he shares large work deliverables (e.g. images) via Dropbox and shares his writing with clients via Dropbox Paper (a collaborative document-editing service), but leaves traces of these as completed milestones in the Upwork messenger so that Upwork has a record of transactions (as evidence just in case of a disputes with a client).

3.3 Manipulating Algorithms

By providing different inputs to the platform's various data collection processes, workers can alter, observe and improve its output, manipulating various platform algorithms. This allows workers to make better use of some parts of the system. One of the well-known inefficiencies in the Upwork platform is the inaccuracy of its job recommendations. Participant 9 described how inaccurate these ratings could be: "a lot of jobs I was kind of just throwing my hands in the air and saying this is an entirely different branch from what I am doing, why are you suggesting this? Like they're looking for a special effects artist in this 3D thing and…I'm a 3D character artist and animator." However, Participants 6 and 15 both learned that they could 'save' searches with the Upwork platform. Through experimentation with the platform, they discovered these saved searches would be used by Upwork's recommender system to improve the recommendations it made to them. This is a lesser known feature amongst the other workers we interviewed, and many, like Participant 9 complained about the inaccuracy of the platform's recommendations.

Even without understanding the intricacies of an algorithm's rules, workers are able to manipulate their results simply by changing the data that goes into it. For instance, Participant 29 described how he helped a subcontractor improve his hourly rate by altering the hours they reported to the platform: "he did like 4 h for me but he wanted to do it as 1 h of work on Upwork at four times the rate so it looks like he's getting a much higher payment." Having a higher rate recorded on the subcontractor's profile would help him get a higher rate on future projects. In a similar way, Participant 21 would close and reopen contracts in order to acquire more ratings: "every time you spend over \$5 on the platform you can basically close a contract and get a rating." Working long-term projects means receiving fewer total ratings, which makes it more difficult to maintain a solid job success score because a single bad rating has more influence. This strategy is an effective way for Participant 21 to bolster his overall base of good ratings, thereby generating more professional stability on the platform.

By understanding how certain components of the platform work, workers can improve their functionality, or even make alternative uses of a certain feature. Some participants were able to do this with Upwork's large collection of proficiency tests (e.g., knowledge of English grammar or user experience design). While some participants perceived these tests as useful, most did not think they were accurate reflections of their skills and therefore did not take them, partially because they did not think that clients looked at them. Those participants who also worked as clients largely confirmed this. However, Participant 15 found that taking the skills tests provided by Upwork made him more prominent in search results for terms related to his skill. In this way, he was able to make use of the tests not to better present his skills on his profile, but to appear more competitive to the search algorithm.

4 Discussion

Algorithms undergirding important functions such as reputation and search systems serve as key resources in managing digital platforms and mediating the transaction of services, but they also act as a means of coordinating and controlling workers. Therefore, algorithmic management may diminish workers sense of autonomy by impeding their ability to navigate and control important aspects of their work due to the complex and opaque nature of the algorithms themselves.

However, research findings presented here make it clear that workers are not passive recipients of algorithmic management and control. They develop what we call *algorithmic competencies* to deal with and appropriate algorithmic management exercised by the platform. Sensemaking activities allow users to create a working understanding about algorithms and how they may affect their work. Gig workers use sensemaking strategies to open the black box of algorithms used by digital platforms, or at least gain enough familiarity with the platform's functions to effectively work with and around them.

Building on this learning process, workers may decide to circumvent or manipulate the algorithms to their advantage. They may go around the constraints posed by the algorithm by pulling together other resources and technologies, or may use their knowledge of algorithms to manipulate them for desired outcomes. As such, the platform's algorithms, which can be understood as an automated manifestation of the interests of the platform organizer (here Upwork Global Inc.) are not deterministic rules [2]. Rather, workers appropriate and extend the digital platform's system of programmatic processes as part of an information infrastructure [14].

It is clear then that the relationships established between gig workers and algorithms are mutually constitutive. As shown in Fig. 1, algorithms shape workers and clients interactions on the platform, but are simultaneously shaped by worker activities. In this process, workers develop and draw on their algorithmic competency, which we define as a form of "data infrastructure literacy" [23] or "infrastructural competency" [31] needed to effectively interact with algorithms. Algorithmic competency refers to workers' understanding of algorithms that assign and assess work conducted on gig platforms, and learning how to work with and around those algorithms. Our data suggests algorithmic competency here is comprised of three key practices of sense-making, circumventing and manipulating algorithms.

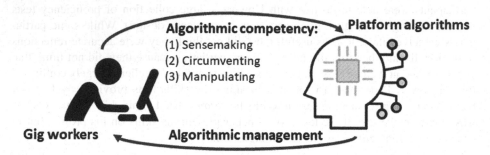

Fig. 1. The mutual shaping of gig workers and platform algorithms.

A consequence of this agency is that the platform's algorithms are embedded in the professional and personal contexts of the platform's population of users. Algorithmic management is therefore a sociotechnical process that emerges as the result of continuous interactions between platform algorithms and users. It is not only the algorithms that shape the work practices of the gig worker; how workers encounter algorithms also shape algorithmic outcomes and decision-making. For example, previous research indicates social biases against certain races or genders (in rating and reviews done by the user) can be easily fed back into the recommendation and search algorithms [15]. Therefore, these interactions can be understood as example of "heteromated systems" whereby both algorithms and humans are reconfigured [16].

5   Conclusion

Many gig workers are considered independent, contingent workers, but what may make them distinct from other traditional independent workers is their usage of digital labor platforms, which are a cornerstone of the gig economy [32, 33]. A defining characteristic of digital labor platforms is their reliance on algorithms that perform many management functions previously conducted by human managers in traditional work organizations. Algorithmic management therefore has an important bearing on the overall experience of gig workers. The lack of clarity and transparency are often intentional elements of algorithmic management, since the platform organizers do not wish the workers to game the system [15, 17, 34]. Nevertheless, previous research indicates transparency about algorithmic decisions provides users with a higher level of trust, resulting in more effective cooperation with smart technologies [35, 36].

Our findings suggest that the inner workings of many algorithms on Upwork are not completely clear to the gig workers, and this information asymmetry may hinder the workers' ability to gain control over their work. The ability to understand and make use of algorithms has therefore become a core competency of workers attempting to retain autonomy in the dynamic and uncertain working conditions that have emerged in the gig economy.

Online labor platforms extend the reach of online freelancers by providing a marketplace to land new projects [24], but the global scale of this platform often results in fierce competition with people all over the world. Algorithmic competency can therefore also be seen as a source of personal competitive advantage in this global marketplace, whereby gig workers can distinguish themselves from thousands of online workers competing for the same type of projects/gigs. In addition to other key competencies such as social or knowledge skills (to keep up with the different and changing knowledge domains) that support all forms of independent, self-employed work [33], gig workers need to understand how to interact effectively with platform algorithms that assign and evaluate work.

References

1. Newell, S., Marabelli, M.: Strategic opportunities (and challenges) of algorithmic decision-making: A call for action on the long-term societal effects of 'datification'. J. Strateg. Inf. Syst. **24**, 3–14 (2015)
2. Wagenknecht, S., Lee, M., Lustig, C., O'Neill, J., Zade, H.: Algorithms at work: empirical diversity, analytic vocabularies, design implications. In: Proceedings of the 19th ACM Conference on Computer Supported Cooperative Work and Social Computing Companion, pp. 536–543. ACM (2016)
3. Schildt, H.: Big data and organizational design–the brave new world of algorithmic management and computer augmented transparency. Innovation **19**, 23–30 (2017)
4. Möhlmann, M., Zalmanson, L.: Hands on the wheel: navigating algorithmic management and Uber drivers' autonomy. In: Proceedings of the International Conference on Information Systems (ICIS 2017), Seoul, South Korea, 10–13 December (2017)
5. Howcroft, D., Bergvall-Kåreborn, B.: A typology of crowdwork platforms. Work Employ. Soc. **29**(6): 969–988 (2018). 0950017018760136
6. McAfee, A., Brynjolfsson, E.: Big data: the management revolution. Harv. Bus. Rev. **90**, 60–66, 68, 128 (2012)
7. Galliers, R.D., Newell, S., Shanks, G., Topi, H.: Datification and its human, organizational and societal effects: the strategic opportunities and challenges of algorithmic decision-making. J. Strateg. Inf. Syst. **26**, 185–190 (2017)
8. Cegarra, J., Hoc, J.M.: The role of algorithm and result comprehensibility of automated scheduling on complacency. Hum. Factors Ergon. Manuf. Serv. Ind. **18**, 603–620 (2008)
9. Ananny, M., Crawford, K.: Seeing without knowing: limitations of the transparency ideal and its application to algorithmic accountability. New Media Soc. **20**, 973–989 (2018)
10. Sutherland, W., Jarrahi, M.H.: The sharing economy and digital platforms: a review and research agenda. Int. J. Inf. Manage. **43**, 328–341 (2018)
11. Newlands, G., Lutz, C., Fieseler, C.: Algorithmic management in the sharing economy. Acad. Manage. Glob. Proc. **2018**, 130 (2018)

12. Wood, A.J., Graham, M., Lehdonvirta, V., Hjorth, I.: Good gig, bad gig: autonomy and algorithmic control in the global gig economy. Work Employ. Soc. **5**(1), 1–16 (2018)
13. Newlands, G., Lutz, C., Fieseler, C.: Collective action and provider classification in the sharing economy. New Technology, Work and Employment (2018)
14. Alkhatib, A., Bernstein, M.S., Levi, M.: Examining crowd work and gig work through the historical lens of piecework. In: Proceedings of the 2017 CHI Conference on Human Factors in Computing Systems, pp. 4599–4616. ACM (2017)
15. Lee, M.K., Kusbit, D., Metsky, E., Dabbish, L.: Working with machines: the impact of algorithmic and data-driven management on human workers. In: Proceedings of the 33rd Annual ACM Conference on Human Factors in Computing Systems, pp. 1603–1612. ACM (2015)
16. Rosenblat, A., Stark, L.: Algorithmic labor and information asymmetries: a case study of Uber's drivers. Int. J. Commun. **10**, 3758–3784 (2016)
17. Jhaver, S., Karpfen, Y., Antin, J.: Algorithmic anxiety and coping strategies of Airbnb hosts. In: Proceedings of the 2018 CHI Conference on Human Factors in Computing Systems, p. 421. ACM (Year)
18. Kumar, N., Jafarinaimi, N., Bin Morshed, M.: Uber in Bangladesh: The Tangled Web of mobility and justice. Proc. ACM Hum. Comput. Inter. **2**, 98 (2018)
19. Raval, N., Dourish, P.: Standing out from the crowd: emotional labor, body labor, and temporal labor in ridesharing. In: Proceedings of the 19th ACM Conference on Computer-Supported Cooperative Work & Social Computing, pp. 97–107. ACM (2016)
20. Martin, D., O'Neill, J., Gupta, N., Hanrahan, B.V.: Turking in a global labour market. Comput. Support. Coop. Work **25**, 39–77 (2016)
21. Lampinen, A., Lutz, C., Newlands, G., Light, A., Immorlica, N.: Power struggles in the digital economy: platforms, workers, and markets. In: Companion of the 2018 ACM Conference on Computer Supported Cooperative Work and Social Computing, pp. 417–423. ACM (2018)
22. Ma, N.F., Yuan, C.W., Ghafurian, M., Hanrahan, B.V.: Using stakeholder theory to examine drivers' stake in uber. In: Proceedings of the 2018 CHI Conference on Human Factors in Computing Systems, p. 83. ACM (2018)
23. Shapiro, A.: Between autonomy and control: strategies of arbitrage in the "on-demand" economy. New Media Soc. **20**, 2954–2971 (2018)
24. Popiel, P.: "Boundaryless" in the creative economy: assessing freelancing on Upwork. Crit. Stud. Media Commun. **34**, 220–233 (2017)
25. Shafiei Gol, E., Stein, M.-K., Avital, M.: Why take the risk? motivations of highly skilled workers to participate in crowdworking platforms. In: ICIS 2018. Association for Information Systems (2018)
26. Green, D.D., Walker, C., Alabulththim, A., Smith, D., Phillips, M.: Fueling the gig economy: a case study evaluation of Upwork.com. Manage. Econ. Res. J. **4**, 104–112 (2018)
27. Kalleberg, A.L., Dunn, M.: Good jobs, bad jobs in the Gig Economy. Perspectives on Work, vol. 20 (2016)
28. Maxwell, J.A.: Qualitative Research Design: An Interactive Approach. Sage Publications, USA (2012)
29. Strauss, A., Corbin, J.M.: Basics of Qualitative Research: Grounded Theory Procedures and Techniques. Sage Publications Inc., Thousand Oaks (1990)
30. Glaser, B.G.: Advances in the Methodology of Grounded Theory: Theoretical Sensitivity. Sociology Press, Mill Valley (1978)
31. Sawyer, S., Erickson, I., Jarrahi, M.H., Thomson, L.: Infrastructural competence. In: Ribes, D., Vertesi, J., Jackson, S.J. (eds.) Digital STS Handbook. Princeton University Princeton, NJ (2018) (in Press)

32. Sutherland, W., Jarrahi, M.H.: The gig economy and information infrastructure: the case of the digital nomad community. In: Proceedings of the ACM on Human-Computer Interaction, vol. 1 (2017)
33. Barley, S.R., Bechky, B.A., Milliken, F.J.: The changing nature of work: careers, identities, and work lives in the 21st Century. Acad. Manage. Discoveries 3, 111–115 (2017)
34. Eslami, M., Vaccaro, K., Karahalios, K., Hamilton, K.: "Be careful; things can be worse than they appear": understanding biased algorithms and users' behavior around them in rating platforms. In: ICWSM, pp. 62–71 (2017)
35. Hannák, A., Wagner, C., Garcia, D., Mislove, A., Strohmaier, M., Wilson, C.: Bias in online freelance marketplaces: evidence from TaskRabbit and Fiverr. In: CSCW, pp. 1914–1933 (2017)
36. Lee, M.K.: Understanding perception of algorithmic decisions: fairness, trust, and emotion in response to algorithmic management. Big Data Soc. 5 (2018). http://doi.org/10.1177/2053951718756684

Agency Laundering and Algorithmic Decision Systems

Alan Rubel[1](✉), Adam Pham[1], and Clinton Castro[2]

[1] University of Wisconsin-Madison, Madison, USA
arubel@wisc.edu
[2] Florida International University, Miami, USA

Abstract. This paper has two aims. The first is to explain a type of wrong that arises when agents obscure responsibility for their actions. Call it "agency laundering." The second is to use the concept of agency laundering to understand the underlying moral issues in a number of recent cases involving algorithmic decision systems.

Keywords: Algorithms · Big data · Information ethics · Agency · Agency laundering

1 Introduction

There is a growing literature on ethics in big data, social media, and algorithmic decision-making. Much of this literature examines how such socio-technical systems cause harms [1, 2], reflect and engender discrimination [3–7], and lack transparency [8]. Some commentators link wrongs in such systems to failures of respect for agency and autonomy [9].

This paper departs from the literature in a key way. Whereas most scholarship focuses on individuals and groups who are subject to information systems (as sources of data, subjects of algorithmic decision-systems, users of social media, etc.), this paper considers the agency of those who *deploy* information technologies (as collectors of big data, users of algorithmic decision-systems, developers of social media sites, and so on).

We begin with a mundane example that allows us to articulate our conception of agency laundering and explain why agency laundering is a moral wrong. We then turn to a case study to further specify our conception. In late 2017, the news organization ProPublica discovered that Facebook's system for tracking user interest and selling advertisements based on those interests allowed people to purchase ads targeting users expressing anti-Semitic views. We argue that Facebook's response to the discovery obscures its responsibility for misuse of its platform, and that it serves as a paradigm case of agency laundering. Next, we apply our conception to the use of algorithms in criminal sentencing [10]. Our paper concludes by distinguishing agency laundering from other critiques of information technology, including "masking" and the so-called "responsibility gap."

© Springer Nature Switzerland AG 2019
N. G. Taylor et al. (Eds.): iConference 2019, LNCS 11420, pp. 590–598, 2019.
https://doi.org/10.1007/978-3-030-15742-5_56

2 Agency Laundering

The key claim in this paper is the following: Using algorithms to make decisions can allow a person or persons to distance themselves from morally suspect actions by attributing the decision to the algorithm. Put slightly differently, invoking the complexity or automated nature of an algorithm to explain why the suspect action occurred allows a party to imply that the action is unintended and something for which they are not responsible.

Call it "agency laundering."

We are using 'laundering' in the sense it is used in money laundering [12]. In order to hide cash from authorities (because it is the result of illegal activities, because one wishes to evade taxes, or because one wishes to avoid attention generally), one can mix it with money from legitimate (or more savory) sources to that the tainted cash appears legitimate. So, e.g., one might mix cash from an illegal source into the revenue of a cash-reliant enterprise. The illegal cash is hidden by some similar phenomenon.

Consider the following example. Suppose that a department chair (insert your favorite discipline) has control (via rules of governance) over curriculum. She, and a number of colleagues, think that subfield Z is unimportant and would like to get rid of it. The chair could simply stop offering the courses, stop assigning instructors to related areas, and alter degree requirements that do not include subfield Z. But because at least some people in the department value subfield Z, the chair may wish not to act so boldly. Instead, she assigns curriculum decisions to a committee composed only of people hostile to subfield Z. In that case, the chair might respond to complaints about eliminating field Z courses on the grounds that "it was the committee's recommendation," though of course the chair justifiably believed all along that the committee would recommend eliminating subfield Z courses. The chair's actions ensure the result that she wants, but by deferring to a committee the chair launders her agency. She obscures her role in the decision. She wanted to eliminate field Z courses; she had the power to do so; but she also justifiably believed the committee would recommend eliminating subfield Z. Hence, the committee's work appears to be the relevant power, even when it remains the chair.

What's morally important about Chair? First is that the chair had de jure and de facto power to make a decision about curriculum. That is to say that the chair had legitimate institutional authority over curriculum decisions, and from the internal perspective of the university she would have been within her rights to do so (de jure). It is also to say that, had the chair unilaterally decided to change the curriculum, that change would have occurred (de facto). Second, she delegated the decision to a separate body. In so doing, she implied that the body was neutral, would weigh evidence fairly, and could realistically act in a way that the chair didn't anticipate. But that's false. The chair justifiably believed that the committee would act just as the chair would act. The chair obscures the fact that she orchestrated the action by ascribing responsibility for the action to the committee. And, hence, the chair's actions are laundered. Note that the committee may bear responsibility, too (there is plenty to pass around). But whatever agency they exercise is evident.

Note the importance of both de jure and de facto authority. A different case, similar to Chair (call it "Associate Chair") is that the department chair is a bit clueless. The chair's canny associate knows that the chair would just as soon let subfield Z wither, but has no such plans. And the associate chair knows that he could just push the chair to eliminate subfield Z. But the associate chair instead gets the chair to form a committee and fill it with people the associate chair reasonably believes are (but chair doesn't) Z-eliminationists. The associate chair has de facto, but not de jure authority. And it does not seem that the associate chair has laundered his agency. He has connived, and he has used the chair's gullibility to achieve an aim. But that is just acting manipulatively and surreptitiously. Laundering involves acting openly in some way, but making those actions appear proper.

That's the idea. Here's a definition:

An agent (a) launders her agency where:

1. a has de facto and de jure authority (power) with respect to Φ-ing (where to Φ is an action), AND
2. a gives b (some process, person, or entity) de facto practical authority with respect to Φ-ing, AND
3. a ascribes (implicitly or explicitly) morally relevant qualities to b's conclusions (relevance, neutrality, reliability), AND
4. in so-doing, a obscures her de facto and de jure responsibility for Φ-ing.

Now, what is the moral problem with agency laundering? The first question is whether there is any moral concern with agency laundering that goes beyond the action from which a launderer distances herself. Clearly there is. In Chair, there is an open question as to whether it is morally justifiable to eliminate subfield Z. Suppose that subfield Z is not particularly valuable, and getting rid of it would be beneficial to the department's students, to the university, and to the broader community. It would still seem that obscuring one's responsibility for eliminating Z is wrong. This leads to the second question: what makes the laundering wrong? Our view is that other moral agents—in Chair it is other stakeholders in whether a department covers subfield Z—have a claim to make sense of important facets of their lives. That includes understanding how changes to those facets of their came about. Respecting others as agents demands providing them with sufficient information to understand their world, and obscuring responsibility for key actions affecting that world are a failure of respect [13].

3   Facebook and Anti-semitic Advertising

Using this understanding of agency laundering, consider a couple of examples. The first involves Facebook's automated system for sorting users by interest and affiliation in order to sell advertising. In 2017, a study by a team at ProPublica revealed that by using categories generated on the Facebook platform, advertisers could purchase ads targeting users who had identified with anti-Semitism [14] The team sought to purchase an ad, and used Facebook's targeting system to locate a category called "Jew hater," which had over 2200 members. That means that 2200 Facebook users had chosen to include "Jew hater" in their user profile. That is too small a number for effective advertising. Hence, Facebook informed the ProPublica team that they needed more categories to get a big-enough audience. It suggested "Second Amendment" as an additional category, possibly because of some overlap in category interests. ProPublica used Facebook's automated suggestion system to find and choose to target other anti-Semitic categories. Facebook approved ProPublica's ad, with only minor suggested changes. The summary of one of the targeted ad purchases is shown in Fig. 1. Note that the categories used appear to have been generated algorithmically, based on what users had entered into their profiles.

This type of problem crops up in other ways on Facebook. For one, ProPublica has also shown that in addition to targeting people by affiliation, advertisers can exclude by racial and ethnic categories. So, for example advertisers may choose to target users in certain geographic areas and income brackets, but exclude from advertising to people who exhibit various "ethnic affinities." Those affinities are generated algorithmically, based on content users had liked or viewed. In some cases it is not the category targeted by advertising that creates a problem, but the purpose of the ad. For example, targeting an ad by age makes sense in some contexts (life insurance, toys), but is discriminatory in others (job recruitment).

When ProPublica revealed the anti-Semitic categories and other news outlets reported similarly odious categories [22], Facebook responded by explaining that algorithms had created the categories based on user responses to target fields (i.e., answers to questions about education and hobbies). It also pledged to address the issue, possibly algorithmically. But Facebook was loath to admit its own agency. Chief

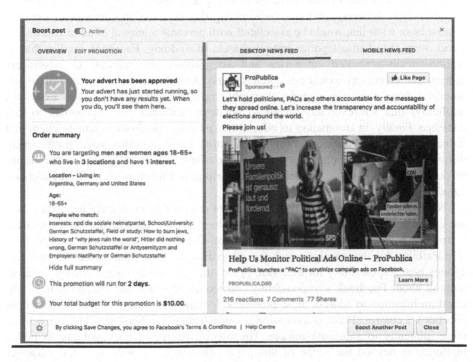

Fig. 1. Buying targeted ads based on algorithmically-generated and -suggested categories. (Source: ProPublica)

Operating Officer Sheryl Sandberg claimed in a public response that "[w]e never intended or anticipated this functionality being used this way" [15]. That is no doubt true, though Facebook both wishes to sell advertising and employ as little labor as possible to monitor how that advertising functions.

Consider it as a case of agency laundering. An agent (Facebook) launders its agency where:

1. Facebook has de facto and de jure authority (power) with respect to targeted advertising on its platform, AND
2. Facebook gives its algorithmic advertising process de facto authority with respect to targeted advertising, AND
3. Facebook ascribes (implicitly or explicitly) morally relevant qualities to its algorithmic advertising process conclusions (relevance, appropriateness), AND
4. In so-doing, Facebook obscures its de facto and de jure responsibility for advertising.

Each of these conditions appears to obtain. Certainly Facebook has de facto and de jure authority over targeted advertising on its platform. By taking a "hands off" approach and letting users generate profile information, letting an algorithm pick out characteristics from user profiles, and letting advertisers peruse those categories (and letting an algorithm suggest compatible categories to build better ad target groups), Facebook gave an algorithmic process de facto authority over what ads appear on Facebook's platform.

Facebook's business model includes allowing advertisers to target groups of people narrowly and effectively, and it includes doing this in a way that minimizes the substantial labor costs that would be associated with personal approval of ad targets and/or direct oversight of ad categories and purchases. In so doing, Facebook implies that its algorithmically-generated categories and suggestions are relevant to advertisers (otherwise, advertisers would not purchase ads). And the fact that one can place ads based on those categories without oversight implies that Facebook believes (at least implicitly) that whatever ads served to whatever audience are appropriate to that audience. Finally, in automating its advertising process, Facebook is able to claim that it "never intended or anticipated this functionality being used this way." It effectively distances itself from the fact that a system for which it is morally responsible allows noxious or illegal advertising. Hence, the algorithm is a mechanism by with Facebook launders its agency.

Now, one might argue that Facebook is not responsible or that the algorithm does not in fact launder their responsibility, as they have accepted responsibility. Certainly it is true that users populating categories with anti-Semitic and other racist answers bear responsibility for those actions, and any advertising targeting ads based on such categories bear responsibility for that. But, again, that others have acted wrongly tells us nothing about Facebook's responsibility. Moreover, the fact that Facebook has indicated an intention to address these problems demonstrates that it is a problem within Facebook's control. There is a question about whether Facebook should have worked more diligently to anticipate misuse. The precise degree of responsibility to police platforms is beyond the scope of this paper. However, we will note that whatever responsibility that is, Facebook's reliance on algorithms to do work and to explain its failures is (on the conception outlined here) an instance of agency laundering.

4   Laundering in Criminal Sentencing (COMPAS and *Wisconsin v. Loomis*)

Eric Loomis pleaded guilty to crimes related to a drive-by shooting. The trial judge ordered a presentence investigation report ("PSI"), using a proprietary risk assessment tool called COMPAS that was developed by Northpointe, Inc.[1] COMPAS incorporates a wide range of data about individuals charged with crimes (family, educational, work, substance abuse history; prior criminal activity; responses to a questionnaire; impressions of members of the criminal justice system) and uses an algorithm to create a risk profile. The COMPAS report indicated that Loomis had a high risk of recidivism and violent recidivism. COMPAS is not designed for determining offender sentences, and Northpointe specifically warns against using it in sentencing decisions. Regardless, the trial judge referenced the COMPAS report and PSI in his decision to sentence Loomis in the maximum range.

The *Loomis* case has received substantial attention since it was decided, and much of the literature is critical of the use of tools like COMPAS. Indeed, we have been critical of the *Loomis* decision elsewhere. However, the Wisconsin Supreme Court's decision in *Loomis* is an example in which use of a proprietary algorithm does not involve laundering. This is important in demonstrating that the conception offered here is not so broad as to be meaningless.

Recall our conception of laundering. A trial court launders its agency where:

1. The trial court has de facto and de jure authority (power) with respect to sentencing, AND
2. The trial court gives COMPAS (some process, person, or entity) de facto practical authority with respect to sentencing, AND
3. The trial court ascribes (implicitly or explicitly) morally relevant qualities to COMPAS's conclusions (relevance, neutrality, reliability), AND
4. in so-doing, the trial court obscures her de facto and de jure responsibility regarding sentencing.

The trial court certainly has de facto and de jure authority with respect to sentencing in cases like *Loomis*. There is some question, though, as to whether the trial court gave COMPAS de facto authority with respect to sentencing in Loomis. The judge did indeed reference the COMPAS risk scores and it plausibly had an effect on sentencing, but he also explained the relevance of the read-in charges and Loomis's history under supervision. Let's interpret this as giving some degree of de facto practical authority to COMPAS with respect to sentencing.

The third condition is also arguable. The use of COMPAS does implicitly ascribe some morally relevant qualities to COMPAS. It certainly implies usefulness and reliability, and it plausibly implies neutrality.

The interesting thing from the standpoint of agency laundering in the Wisconsin supreme court's decision, however, is condition four. The supreme court emphasizes

---

[1] COMPAS stands for "Correctional Offender Management Profiling for Alternative Sanctions." Northpointe is now a part of Equivant, Inc.

the importance of supporting any use of COMPAS scores with other, independent factors and that the scores not be the sole determinant in sentencing and supervision. It writes:

> We determine that because the circuit court explained that its consideration of the COMPAS risk scores was supported by other independent factors, its use was not determinative in deciding whether Loomis could be supervised safely and effectively in the community. Therefore, the circuit court did not erroneously exercise its discretion. [10, p. 9]

Moreover, the court imposed a number of conditions for using COMPAS scores at all in sentencing. These include requiring that courts must weigh all relevant factors in order to sentence an individual defendant [10, p. 74], prohibiting use of scores to determine whether to incarcerate a person or not, the length and severity of sentence, and as aggravating or mitigating factors in sentencing. [10, pp. 88–98]. And the court required that any PSI that uses a COMPAS report carry a number of warnings about the limitations of such reports.

The supreme court's understanding of the trial court's use of COMPAS (limited, and incorporating other factors) and its imposition of limits on use of similar algorithms addresses condition four. That is, under the supreme court's understanding, sentencing decisions are wholly the trial court's responsibility. Relying completely on the COMPAS algorithm is prohibited and (hence) cannot be a way for the trial court to distance itself from responsibility.

In sum, then, while relying on COMPAS could in principle be a way for actors in the criminal justice system to launder their agency, the *Loomis* decision appears to tailored precisely to avoid that. *Loomis*, then, appears to be a good test case for our conception of agency laundering.

5   Conclusion

Our goals in this paper were to, first, explain a type of wrong that arises when agents obscure responsibility for their actions. We have outlined this type of wrong and called it "agency laundering." Second, we used the concept to understand underlying moral issues in recent cases: Facebook's automated advertising platform and use of risk assessment tools (e.g., COMPAS) in criminal sentencing. Each of these involves use of an algorithmic decision system to do important work. We have argued that using such a system launders agency the Facebook case but not in the COMPAS case. But there are aspects of agency laundering that warrant further exploration.

First is to distinguish agency laundering from superficially similar concepts. For example, Barocas and Selbst [4] describe "masking," or the intentional use of algorithmic systems to obfuscate discrimination. Laundering could accompany (or follow) masking, but a key component of laundering is that the person with authority ascribes morally relevant qualities to the algorithm. Masking does not require this. Mattias [21] discusses the idea of a responsibility gap, which refers to the inadequacy of traditional ascription of responsibility in the context of automated computational artifacts. The belief in a responsibility gap may enable agency laundering, but agency laundering entails that some agent actually has responsibility.

Next, it will be important to more fully articulate the moral wrong in agency laundering. In Sect. 2 we offer an autonomy-based concern about agency laundering. However, there may well be other concerns. For example, there may be practical concerns about understanding legal liability or about being able to assert meaningful control over algorithmic systems. Further, there are open questions about precisely when agency laundering is morally problematic. In Sect. 2 we explained that the wrong of laundering need not depend on the underlying action being wrong. But there are no doubt other factors relevant in determining when agency laundering is justifiable (if it is). Nonetheless, our project so far can help explain at least some morally problematic aspects of algorithmic information systems.

References

1. Eubanks, V.: Automating Inequality: How High-Tech Tools Profile, Police, and Punish the Poor. St. Martin's Press, New York (2018)
2. O'Neil, C.: Weapons of Math Destruction: How Big Data Increases Inequality and Threatens Democracy. Crown, New York (2016)
3. Noble, S.: Algorithms of Oppression: How Search Engines Reinforce Racism. NYU Press, New York (2018)
4. Barocas, S., Selbst, A.: Big data's disparate impact. SSRN Scholarly Paper. Social Science Research Network, Rochester (2016). https://papers.ssrn.com/abstract=2477899
5. Angwin, J., Larson, J.: Machine Bias. ProPublica, 23 May 2016. https://www.propublica.org/article/machine-bias-risk-assessments-in-criminal-sentencing
6. Sweeney, L.: Discrimination in online ad delivery. ArXiv:1301.6822 [Cs], 28 January 2013. http://arxiv.org/abs/1301.6822
7. Citron, D.: Technological due process. Washington Univ. Law Rev. **85**, 1249–1314 (2008)
8. Pasquale, F.: The Black Box Society: The Secret Algorithms That Control Money and Information. Harvard University Press, Cambridge (2016)
9. Mittelstadt, B., Allo, P., Taddeo, M., Wachter, S., Floridi, L.: The ethics of algorithms: mapping the debate. Big Data Soc. **3**(2), 2053951716679679. https://doi.org/10.1177/2053951716679679
10. Wisconsin v. Loomis. 2016 WI 68, 881 N.W.2d 749, 757, 760–64, cert. denied, 582 U.S. _ (U.S. June 26, 2017) (No. 16-6387) (2017)
11. Houston Federation of Teachers, Local 2415 v. Houston Independent School District. 251 F. Supp.3d 1168 (S.D. Tex. 2017)
12. U.S. Code § 1956 - Laundering of monetary instruments
13. Hill, T.: Autonomy and benevolent lies. J. Value Inq. **18**(4), 251–267 (1984). https://doi.org/10.1007/BF00144766
14. Angwin, J., Varner, M.: Facebook enabled advertisers to reach 'Jew Haters.' Text/html, 14 September 2017. https://www.propublica.org/article/facebook-enabled-advertisers-to-reach-jew-haters
15. Sanberg, S.: Facebook post, 20 September 2017. https://www.facebook.com/sheryl/posts/10159255449515177. Accessed 30 Dec 2017
16. Wagner v. Haslam, 112 F. Supp. 3d 673 (M.D. Tenn. 2015)
17. Walsh, E., Dotter, D.: Longitudinal analysis of the effectiveness of DCPS teachers. Mathematica Policy Research Reports. Mathematica Policy Research. https://ideas.repec.org/p/mpr/mprres/65770df94dde4573b331ce1cb33a9e07.html. Accessed 21 Apr 21 2018

18. Isenberg, E., Hock, H.: Measuring School and Teacher Value Added in DC, 2011–2012 School Year. Mathematica Policy Research, Inc., 31 August 2012. https://eric.ed.gov/?id=ED565712
19. American Statistical Association: ASA statement on using value added models for educational assessment, Alexandria, VA (2014)
20. http://static.battelleforkids.org/documents/HISD/EVAAS-Value-Added-FAQs-Final-2015-02-02.pdf
21. Matthias, A.: The responsibility gap: ascribing responsibility for the actions of learning automata. Ethics Inf. Technol. **6**(3), 175–183 (2004). https://doi.org/10.1007/s10676-004-3422-1
22. Oremus, W., Carey, B.: Facebook's offensive ad targeting options go far beyond 'Jew Haters.' Slate, 14 September 2017. http://www.slate.com/blogs/future_tense/2017/09/14/facebook_let_advertisers_target_jew_haters_it_doesn_t_end_there.html

Innovation and Professionalization in Technology Communities

Whether the Evolution of iSchool Revolves Around "Information, Technology and People"?

Yao Cai[ID], Peng Wu[✉][ID], and Peng Zhu[ID]

Nanjing University of Science and Technology, Nanjing, China
{caiyao,wupeng,pzhu}@njust.edu.cn

Abstract. As the research topics and specialties of the Information Schools (iSchool) have always been evolving, the new trends in research are emerging constantly. Whether the evolution of iSchool is still pursuing its vision and focusing on specific tracks of the information, technology and people deserves to be investigated. In this paper, the literatures published on 86 Information Science and Library Science journals, included in the Social Sciences Citation Index database of Web of Science between 2006 and 2015 are selected as the dataset. A co-word analysis is conducted to study the research topics of iSchool first. Then, combined with temporal and longitudinal information from literatures, under the help of Citespace, we identify the evolution of each topic. Based on the knowledge evolution, we reveal that the information is the primary line of all topics in the studied period. Technology helps create innovative information systems and designs information solutions to promote the evolution of iSchool, and the evolution of iSchool aims to maximize the potential of humans. In such a comprehensive way of exploring iSchool, a clear identity about iSchool vision is not only can be made, an effective research framework and a reliable reference for real-time tracking research is also provided.

Keywords: iSchool vision · Knowledge evolution · Co-word analysis

1 Introduction

Since the establishment of Information [7] or Interdisciplinary [18] schools (iSchool), the iSchool's vision is to seek to maximize the visibility and influence of its member schools, and their interdisciplinary approaches to harnessing the power of information and technology, and maximizing the potential of humans.

ISchool recognize that achieving it's vision is beyond the purview of one single discipline, and requires interdisciplinary work [7]. Thus, the knowledge domain of iSchool has been the subject of numerous studies in the past that aims primarily to uncover its interdisciplinary character. Such as [5,13,21,25,41,50] etc., they all showed that the iSchool research domains cover information, technology and people. Thus, it is revealed that the iSchool still pursue its vision.

© Springer Nature Switzerland AG 2019
N. G. Taylor et al. (Eds.): iConference 2019, LNCS 11420, pp. 601–613, 2019.
https://doi.org/10.1007/978-3-030-15742-5_57

However, the vision of iSchool detected in terms of knowledge domain is real but subtle. As the research topics and specialties of the iSchool have always been evolving, the new trends in research are emerging constantly. Whether the evolution of iSchool always revolves around its vision is still deserving investigation.

In this paper, a co-word analysis combined with temporal and longitudinal literature information is conducted to analyze the research topics and their evolution of iSchool. Research topics can provide a general picture of interdisciplinary work of iSchool. And based on the evolution of each topic, we aim to answer the questions:

1. Whether the information is the primary line of all topics in iSchool?
2. Whether the technology helps create innovative information systems and designs information solutions to make the information better utilized?
3. Whether the evolution of iSchool aims to empower people in all kinds of fields to create, find, store, manipulate and share information?

2   Methodology

In this study, the co-word analysis, with the help of Citespace, is conducted to reveal the research topics and evolution of iSchool. Co-word analysis is a method of content analysis with the main purpose of identifying the research focus, knowledge structure and relevance of a keyword in a field [12]. The literatures published on 86 Information Science and Library Science journals, included in the Social Sciences Citation Index database of Web of Science between 2006 and 2015 are selected as the dataset. All these journals represent the cognitive outputs of the entire Library and Information Science (LIS) field. In this paper, all research and review articles (16,732 in total) are extracted. Afterwards, the co-word network is constructed by using keywords contained in those papers.

The analysis tool "Citespace" is used to produce and analyze co-occurrence networks of keywords. It incorporates a good visualization technique, making the visualization of temporal patterns in a knowledge domain and the identification of evolution of a knowledge domain easier [6,16,20].

Ten years (2006–2015) are divided into five consecutive periods of two years each. Each research topic is displayed horizontally alone timelines. In timeline visualization, primary keywords are displayed every two years to represent the research hotspot. This will help us to analyze the evolution of research topics. The Fig. 1 show more details about the research.

3   Results

This section describes the research results. The first part reveals the research topics of iSchool. The second part tracks the evolution of each research topic during different time periods.

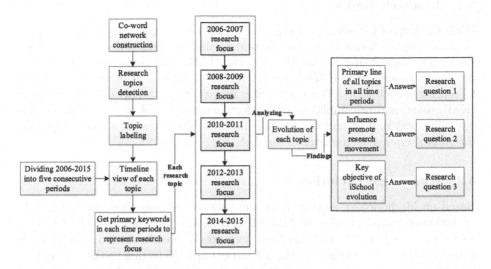

Fig. 1. Research workflow. The first three steps aim to identify the research topics of iSchool. Through the following three steps, the research focus over five time intervals can be obtained. Which will benefit to construct the evolution of research topics. Then, making an in-depth analysis of the topic evolution, three main findings will be revealed to answer research questions.

Fig. 2. Co-word network. Each node represents one keyword or keyword plus. The size of each node is proportional to the co-occurrence frequencies of the corresponding keywords. Nodes are linked with co-occurrence relation between them. Colors indicate the temporal orders of keywords: oldest in blue, and newest in orange. (Color figure online)

3.1   Research Topics

With the help of Citespace, a merged network including 540 keywords and 2531 co-word edges is formed (see Fig. 2), and finally, nine research topics are identified. The algorithms log-likelihood ratio (LLR) and term frequency-inverse document frequency (TF-IDF) are combined to choose appropriate keywords to represent each topic. The results are: library, trust, knowledge management (KM), social network, bibliometrics, information retrieval, information technology (IT), text mining and information literacy. These research topics represent the interdisciplinary character of iSchool.

3.2   Knowledge Evolution

Based on Methodology section, from the timeline visualization, we can get the evolution of research topics. In Tables 1, 2, 3, 4, 5, 6, 7, 8 and 9, the first column shows the time interval. And this paper extracts keywords which are displayed in timeline view and lists them in the second column. Referring to the papers contain those keywords at corresponding time interval, we can obtain the research focus and present them in third column. In this way, different research focus form the evolution of topics. The knowledge evolution of each topic are as follows:

Library. The library provides information services aimed at fulfilling learning and academic research for students and faculty members. In the age of rapidly growing Internet technology, the library has been brought to the new dimension of modern digital world. Studying the new types of libraries has attracted widespread attention. Table 1 describes in detail the research focus over five time intervals.

Table 1. Knowledge evolution of library topic.

Time period	Keywords	Research focus
2006–2007	Academic library, digital library	Research content changing from academic library to digital library [37]
2008–2009	Digital library	Digital library system evaluation and updating [49]
2010–2011	User study	Updating digital library systems to meet users needs [45]
2012–2013	Inter-library loan, resource sharing	Research on online inter-library loan, and promotion of resource sharing among libraries [10,23]
2014–2015	Mobile communication system	Examination of Web 2.0 technology usage in mobile libraries [35]

Trust. The trading behavior of enterprise has been changing from offline to online under the development of Internet. Trust has been found to be a significant adoption facilitator to decide whether the transformation of this service mode is successful or not. The increased application scale and changeable transaction systems all brings about the forward to study the trust mechanism of users' adoption of new business service mode. Table 2 describes in detail the research focus over five time intervals.

Table 2. Knowledge evolution of trust topic.

Time period	Keywords	Research focus
2006–2007	E-commerce, theory of planned behavior	Examine the role of trust in e-commerce success [9]
2008–2009	E-government	Examine the role of trust in e-government success [40]
2010–2011	Virtual community	Examining trust in virtual community [8]
2012–2013	Social-commerce	The effect of trust in social network commerce [17]
2014–2015	Mobile banking	Examining consumer trust in mobile services [11]

KM. KM is the process of creating, sharing, using and managing many spheres of knowledge. Knowledge has become a dominant source of comparative advantage in various organizations. Research scope of KM is expanding and its research depth is strengthening constantly. Whether KM in individuals, business or virtual communities is studied, the ultimate goal is to make knowledge better used, shared, transferred, and created. Table 3 describes in detail the research focus (the research focus between 2012–2013 and 2014–2015 are similar, thus, we combine these two periods).

Table 3. Knowledge evolution of KM topic.

Time period	Keywords	Research focus
2006–2007	Organization	Exploring the KM systems in organizations [48]
2008–2009	Personal KM	Introducing Personal KM [31]
2010–2011	Culture, knowledge sharing, knowledge transfer	The influence of culture on KM and knowledge sharing [19]
2012–2015	Social network, knowledge creation	Knowledge creation and sharing in online communities [14, 30]

Social Network. Social network, the graph of relationships and interactions within a group of individuals, plays a fundamental role as a medium for the spread of information, idea, and influence among its members. The popularity of mobile devices makes a more convenient way to build and participates in social network sites. The social network can provide a set of methods as well as a variety of theories for analyzing the structure of whole social entities and revealing the patterns observed in these structures. Table 4 shows in detail the research focus (the research focus of the last three time intervals are similar, thus, we combine these three periods).

Table 4. Knowledge evolution of social network topic.

Time period	Keywords	Research focus
2006–2007	Co-authorship	Co-authorship network analysis [51]
2008–2009	Social network visualization	Visualization facilitates social network analysis [29]
2010–2015	Web 2.0, social media, Facebook, privacy	Privacy issues and political information in social network sites [42]

Bibliometrics. Bibliometrics is the statistical analysis of written publications, such as books or articles. And it has been widely taught in LIS. Under the influence of IT, great changes have taken place in bibliometrics, particularly in measuring methods, studying objects, research content and application. Table 5 shows in detail the research focus (2008 to 2011 sharing the similar research focus).

Table 5. Knowledge evolution of bibliometrics topic.

Time period	Keywords	Research focus
2006–2007	Impact factor, citation, public productivity	Providing a 'picture' of the output of scientific publications [2]
2008–2011	Webometrics, H-index	Studying the structure of the World Wide Web and usage patterns [34]
2012–2013	Informatrics	Researching on the quantitative aspects of information in any form [24]
2014–2015	Altmetrics	Tracking impact of scientific outputs by exploring the shares, likes, reviews, discussions, tweets of scientific publications and sources in social media [3]

Information Retrieval. Information retrieval is the act of storing, searching, and retrieving information that matches a users' request. With the explosion of digital media that is available on the Internet, it is important to find and present desired information on users' computer techniques quickly and accurately. Much effort has been made to improve accuracy of results and enhance satisfaction of users. Table 6 shows in detail the research focus (2008–2011 sharing the similar research focus, 2012–2015 sharing the similar research focus).

Table 6. Knowledge evolution of information retrieval topic.

Time period	Keywords	Research focus
2006–2007	Search engine	Improving search engine effectiveness [28]
2008–2011	Tagging, image retrieval	Improving the retrieval effect by using tagging [26], dealing with formats other than plain text, especially multimedia retrieval [15]
2012–2015	Cross-lingual	Investigating the ability to find information in one or more different languages [32]

IT. IT has made rapid advances in the last 100 years and is part of the process of information systems implementation. It aims at storing, studying, retrieving, transmitting and manipulating data and information in the context of a business. The surprising growth of the Internet, coupled with the rapid development of web technique results in more and more emergence of IT implementation. Table 7 shows in detail the research focus (the research focus of last two time interval is similar, thus, we combine these two periods).

Table 7. Knowledge evolution of IT topic.

Time period	Keywords	Research focus
2006–2007	Organization, information system	Factors affecting the implementation of IT in organization [36]
2008–2009	E-government, library	Implementation of IT in government and library [43]
2010–2011	Green IT	An increased environmental awareness has caused greater interest in green IT [4]
2012–2015	Health organization, public sector	Application of IT to health organization and public sector [38]

Text Mining. Text mining is defined as the process of deriving high quality information from text. With the huge amount of information available online, extracting information from text and transforming it into future use has become a popular research topic. Table 8 shows in detail the research focus (the research focus of 2006–2009 and 2012–2015 are similar respectively, thus, we combine these periods).

Table 8. Knowledge evolution of text mining topic.

Time period	Keywords	Research focus
2006–2009	Clustering, information retrieval natural language processing	Managing documents into categories [39], using text mining in information retrieval [1]
2010–2011	User generated content, sentiment analysis	Analyzing the sentiments of users generated content in social media [44]
2012–2015	Electronic health records, distributed data mining	Using text mining in health sector, studying the different physically distributed data [52]

Information Literacy. Information literacy is defined as 'the ability to know when there is a need for information, to be able to identify, locate, evaluate, and effectively use that information for the issue or problem at hand. Information literacy is increasingly important in the contemporary environment of rapid technological change and proliferate information resources. Much effort has been made to improve students' information literacy skills. Table 9 lists the research focus (five time intervals sharing the similar research focus).

Table 9. Knowledge evolution of information literacy topic.

Time period	Keywords	Research focus
2006–2015	Library	The role of the library in delivering information literacy skills [22]
	Framework, student	Studying the information literacy among different occupations [27]
	E-learning, higher-education assessment	Developing lifelong learners is central mission of higher education institutions, improving and accessing information literacy [33, 46]

4 Findings

Based on the research topics and their evolution identified in the 'Results' section, we can highlight three major findings.

4.1   Information Is the Primary Line of iSchool

The results, as reported in Sect. 3.2, reveal that the research focus varied among different research topics and the research focus of a topic has been changing continuously throughout the years. However, the line connecting all research topics is 'information'.

The "library" is a collection source of information and aims to provide information in a better way. "Trust" is helping users to receive information better that comes from various online and mobile systems. Knowledge is a kind of information, and "KM" is the process of creating, sharing, using, managing many spheres of knowledge. "Social network" refers mainly to the communication of information online. "Bibliometrics" and its offshoots mainly aim to use mathematical and statistical methods to analyze and measure information in any form. "Information retrieval" is an activity referring to obtain information. "IT" is the use of computers to store, retrieve, transmit and manipulate information, making the information processing more efficient. "Text mining" is mainly used to extract information from text, and transformed information into future use. "Information literacy" is a kind of ability to know when there is a need for information.

The first finding is in line with [7, 47] point of view which referred to the study of information as the core mission of iSchool. This finding answers the first question, that the "information" connects all topics together and is the primary line of iSchool.

4.2   Technology Promotes the Evolution of iSchool

The results session indicate that the evolution of iSchool has a close relationship with the technology.

The research focus of library changed from academic library to digital library and later, to mobile library. Trust mechanism has been used in electronic organizations, then virtual community and mobile banking. The research content under the KM topic changed from personal, enterprise to online communities. The research scope of social network is constantly expanding from co-authorship's network to social media's network. Firstly, the research focus of bibliometrics is to analyze and measure the output of scientific publications. Then, it gives birth to many offshoots, for example webometrics, to measure the number and types of hyperlinks of website. With the digital media available on the web, the research scope of information retrieval expanding to multimedia retrieval. IT has expanded its application to a wider field, and has been used in all organizations. Text mining is to study virtual communities' user-generated content. As more data was produced from many different physically distributed locations, distributed data mining became a hot topic. The changeable of information storage and proliferate information resources make the information literacy become more and more important.

All those research topics continually develop along with the development of technology. This finding answers the second question, that technology helps create innovative information systems and designs information solution to promote the iSchool evolution and utilize the information better.

4.3   The Key Objective of iSchool Is to Empower People

An in-depth analysis of evolution of each research topic helps us to conclude that the "people" is the ultimate goal of the iSchool. Such as, the advent of mobile library aims to provide a convenient way for users to approach library services. The research on trust mechanism aims to promote the adoption of technology for users. Managing knowledge hopes to help people use, transfer and share knowledge better. The purpose of information retrieval is to find desired information quickly and accurately to improve user's satisfaction. The application of IT in various organizations can help people process information and make decisions. Text mining aims to derive high quality information, and transform it into a kind of knowledge that can meet people's needs. Studying information literacy is to help people effectively identify and evaluate information, etc.

The development of Internet and communication technologies changed users' information behavior and information needs. Which promote the research focus of nine research topics evolving steadily to create innovative systems to make user's needs met and better service provided. This finding answer third questions, that iSchool aim to empower people in all kinds of fields to create, find, store, manipulate and share information in useful forms.

5   Discussion and Conclusion

By adding temporal and longitudinal information to the co-word networks, this study makes an in-depth analysis about the iSchool vision. And the results show that the knowledge domains of iSchool include: library, trust, KM, social network, bibliometrics, information retrieval, IT, text mining and information literacy. The current iSchool is a mixture of traditional LIS and new phenomena and technologies. The evolution of iSchool always revolves around its vision. Which is attached to the development of technology. ISchool research content has always been related to information and its ultimate goal is to provide a better service to users.

There are two contributions of this study. First, this paper goes beyond traditional co-word analysis and employs Citespace to identify and visualize the research topics and evolution of iSchool. The results not only do an effort to understand iSchool current research landscape and shape its strategies directions and goals, but also offers researchers, in particular research students and "newcomers" to the field, a more comprehensive picture of its overall intellectual development.

Second, this research offer dynamic evolution of research topics, which allow researchers have a clear idea of the origin of the iSchool theme, their evolution over time. This analysis could be of interest to identify the trend in research of iSchool field of knowledge, as well as to examine the specialization of certain research topic.

In such a comprehensive way of exploring iSchool, a clear identity about iSchool vision is not only can be made, an effective research framework and a reliable reference for real-time tracking research is also provided. However, focusing on LIS papers may miss some relevant iSchool papers. To further complete and follow-up the research performed in the proposed work, future studies may consider investigating other datasets, such as Ph.D. dissertations, to further explain iSchool evolution and its vision.

Acknowledgements. This work was supported in part by the National Natural Science Foundation of China under contract No. 71774084, 71471089, 71503124, 71503126, 71874082, the National Social Science Fund of China under contract No. 15BTQ063, 17ZDA291; Jiangsu "Qinlan" project [2016] 15, Postgraduate Research & Practice Innovation Program of Jiangsu Province [grant number: KYCX18_0488].

References

1. Arazy, O., Woo, C.: Enhancing information retrieval through statistical natural language processign: a study of collocation indexing. MIS Q. **31**(3), 525–546 (2007)
2. Biswas, B.C., Roy, A., Sen, B.: Economic botany: a bibliometric study. Malays. J. Libr. Inf. Sci. **12**(1), 23–33 (2017)
3. Bornmann, L.: Validity of altmetrics data for measuring societal impact: a study using data from altmetric and F1000prime. J. Inf. **8**(4), 935–950 (2014)
4. Bose, R., Luo, X.: Integrative framework for assessing firms' potential to undertake green it initiatives via virtualization-a theoretical perspective. J. Strateg. Inf. Syst. **20**(1), 38–54 (2011)
5. Chang, Y.W., Huang, M.H., Lin, C.W.: Evolution of research subjects in library and information science based on keyword, bibliographical coupling, and co-citation analyses. Scientometrics **105**(3), 2071–2087 (2015)
6. Chen, C., Ibekwe-SanJuan, F., Hou, J.: The structure and dynamics of cocitation clusters: a multiple-perspective cocitation analysis. J. Am. Soc. Inf. Sci. Technol. **61**(7), 1386–1409 (2010)
7. Dillon, A.: What it means to be an iSchool. J. Educ. Libr. Inf. Sci. **53**(4), 267–273 (2012)
8. Dimoka, A.: What does the brain tell us about trust and distrust? Evidence from a functional neuroimaging study. MIS Q. **34**(2), 373–396 (2010)
9. Flavián, C., Guinalíu, M., Gurrea, R.: The role played by perceived usability, satisfaction and consumer trust on website loyalty. Inf. Manag. **43**(1), 1–14 (2006)
10. Goldner, M., Birch, K.: Resource sharing in a cloud computing age. Interlending Doc. Supply **40**(1), 4–11 (2012)
11. Hanafizadeh, P., Behboudi, M., Koshksaray, A.A., Tabar, M.J.S.: Mobile-banking adoption by Iranian bank clients. Telematics Inform. **31**(1), 62–78 (2014)
12. He, Q.: Knowledge discovery through co-word analysis. Libr. Trends **48**(1), 133–159 (1999)
13. Hu, C.P., Hu, J.M., Deng, S.L., Liu, Y.: A co-word analysis of library and information science in China. Scientometrics **97**(2), 369–382 (2013)
14. Iskoujina, Z., Roberts, J.: Knowledge sharing in open source software communities: motivations and management. J. Knowl. Manag. **19**(4), 791–813 (2015)
15. Jansen, B.J.: Searching for digital images on the web. J. Doc. **64**(1), 81–101 (2008)

16. Kim, M.C., Chen, C.: A scientometric review of emerging trends and new developments in recommendation systems. Scientometrics **104**(1), 239–263 (2015)
17. Kim, S., Park, H.: Effects of various characteristics of social commerce (s-commerce) on consumers' trust and trust performance. Int. J. Inf. Manag. **33**(2), 318–332 (2013)
18. King, J.L.: Identity in the I-school movement. Bull. Am. Soc. Inf. Sci. Technol. **32**(4), 13–15 (2006)
19. Levy, M., Hadar, I., Greenspan, S., Hadar, E.: Uncovering cultural perceptions and barriers during knowledge audit. J. Knowl. Manag. **14**(1), 114–127 (2010)
20. Liu, P., Wu, Q., Mu, X., Yu, K., Guo, Y.: Detecting the intellectual structure of library and information science based on formal concept analysis. Scientometrics **104**(3), 737–762 (2015)
21. Ma, R., Dai, Q., Ni, C., Li, X.: An author co-citation analysis of information science in china with chinese google scholar search engine, 2004–2006. Scientometrics **81**(1), 33–46 (2009)
22. Maitaouthong, T., Tuamsuk, K., Tachamanee, Y.: The roles of university libraries in supporting the integration of information literacy in the course instruction. Malays. J. Libr. Inf. Sci. **17**(1), 51–64 (2012)
23. Mangiaracina, S., Tugnoli, A.: NILDE reloaded: a new system open to international interlibrary loan. Interlending Doc. Supply **40**(2), 88–92 (2012)
24. Milojević, S., Leydesdorff, L.: Information metrics (iMetrics): a research specialty with a socio-cognitive identity? Scientometrics **95**(1), 141–157 (2013)
25. Milojević, S., Sugimoto, C.R., Yan, E., Ding, Y.: The cognitive structure of library and information science: analysis of article title words. J. Am. Soc. Inf. Sci. Technol. **62**(10), 1933–1953 (2011)
26. Morrison, P.J.: Tagging and searching: search retrieval effectiveness of folksonomies on the world wide web. Inf. Process. Manag. **44**(4), 1562–1579 (2008)
27. Mutula, S.M.: Challenges of information illiterate first-year entrants for the University of Botswana. Inf. Dev. **26**(1), 79–86 (2010)
28. Nuray, R., Can, F.: Automatic ranking of information retrieval systems using data fusion. Inf. Process. Manag. **42**(3), 595–614 (2006)
29. Ortega, J.L., Aguillo, I.F.: Mapping world-class universities on the web. Inf. Process. Manag. **45**(2), 272–279 (2009)
30. Pan, Y., Xu, Y.C., Wang, X., Zhang, C., Ling, H., Lin, J.: Integrating social networking support for dyadic knowledge exchange: a study in a virtual community of practice. Inf. Manag. **52**(1), 61–70 (2015)
31. Pauleen, D.: Personal knowledge management: putting the "person" back into the knowledge equation. Online Inf. Rev. **33**(2), 221–224 (2009)
32. Petrelli, D., Clough, P.: Analysing user's queries for cross-language image retrieval from digital library collections. Electron. Libr. **30**(2), 197–219 (2012)
33. Pinto, M.: Cyberabstracts: a portal on the subject of abstracting designed to improve information literacy skills. J. Inf. Sci. **34**(5), 667–679 (2008)
34. Prathap, G.: Going much beyond the durfee square: enhancing the hT index. Scientometrics **84**(1), 149–152 (2010)
35. Pu, Y.H., Chiu, P.S., Chen, T.S., Huang, Y.M.: The design and implementation of a mobile library APP system. Libr. Hi Tech **33**(1), 15–31 (2015)
36. Rivard, S., Raymond, L., Verreault, D.: Resource-based view and competitive strategy: an integrated model of the contribution of information technology to firm performance. J. Strateg. Inf. Syst. **15**(1), 29–50 (2006)
37. Rosenberg, D.: Towards the digital library in Africa. Electron. Libr. **24**(3), 289–293 (2006)

38. Sandeep, M., Ravishankar, M.: The continuity of underperforming ICT projects in the public sector. Inf. Manag. **51**(6), 700–711 (2014)
39. Shahnaz, F., Berry, M.W., Pauca, V.P., Plemmons, R.J.: Document clustering using nonnegative matrix factorization. Inf. Process. Manag. **42**(2), 373–386 (2006)
40. Teo, T.S., Srivastava, S.C., Jiang, L.: Trust and electronic government success: an empirical study. J. Manag. Inf. Syst. **25**(3), 99–132 (2008)
41. Tuomaala, O., Järvelin, K., Vakkari, P.: Evolution of library and information science, 1965–2005: content analysis of journal articles. J. Assoc. Inf. Sci. Technol. **65**(7), 1446–1462 (2014)
42. Vallor, S.: Social networking technology and the virtues. Ethics Inf. Technol. **12**(2), 157–170 (2010)
43. Van Dijk, J.A., Peters, O., Ebbers, W.: Explaining the acceptance and use of government internet services: a multivariate analysis of 2006 survey data in the Netherlands. Gov. Inf. Q. **25**(3), 379–399 (2008)
44. Vechtomova, O.: Facet-based opinion retrieval from blogs. Inf. Process. Manag. **46**(1), 71–88 (2010)
45. Wade Bishop, B., Mandel, L.H.: Utilizing geographic information systems (GIS) in library research. Libr. Hi Tech **28**(4), 536–547 (2010)
46. Walsh, A.: Information literacy assessment: where do we start? J. Librarianship Inf. Sci. **41**(1), 19–28 (2009)
47. Wu, D., He, D., Jiang, J., Dong, W., Vo, K.T.: The state of iSchools: an analysis of academic research and graduate education. J. Inf. Sci. **38**(1), 15–36 (2012)
48. Wu, J.H., Wang, Y.M.: Measuring KMS success: a respecification of the DeLone and McLean's model. Inf. Manag. **43**(6), 728–739 (2006)
49. Xie, H.I.: Users' evaluation of digital libraries (DLs): their uses, their criteria, and their assessment. Inf. Process. Manag. **44**(3), 1346–1373 (2008)
50. Yang, S., Han, R., Wolfram, D., Zhao, Y.: Visualizing the intellectual structure of information science (2006–2015): introducing author keyword coupling analysis. J. Inf. **10**(1), 132–150 (2016)
51. Yin, L.C., Kretschmer, H., Hanneman, R.A., Liu, Z.Y.: Connection and stratification in research collaboration: an analysis of the COLLNET network. Inf. Process. Manag. **42**(6), 1599–1613 (2006)
52. Zeng, L., et al.: Distributed data mining: a survey. Inf. Technol. Manag. **13**(4), 403–409 (2012)

The Innovation Ecology: Collaborative Information, Community Support, and Policy in a Creative Technology Community

Guo Freeman[1]([⊠]), Jeffrey Bardzell[2], Shaowen Bardzell[2],
and Nathan J. McNeese[1]

[1] Clemson University, Clemson, SC 29634, USA
guof@clemson.edu
[2] Indiana University, Bloomington, IN 47405, USA

Abstract. In this paper, we explore a network of distributed individuals' collective efforts to establish an innovation ecology allowing them to engage in bottom up creative technological practices in today's information society. Specifically, we present an empirical study of the technological practices in an emerging creative technology community – independent [indie] game developers in the United States. Based on indie game developers' own accounts, we identified four themes that constitute an innovation ecology from the bottom up, including problem solving; collaborative information seeking, sharing, and reproducing; community support; and policy and politics. We argue that these findings inform our understanding of bottom up technological innovation and shed light on the design of sociotechnical systems to mediate and support such innovation beyond the gaming context.

Keywords: Bottom-up innovation · Collaborative information exchange · Informal learning · Online communities · Indie game development

1 Introduction

Innovation turns knowledge and ideas into value [1]. We are now witnessing an era when social computing and collaborative technologies have fundamentally changed the Web "from a comprehensive information repository to a set of collective projects, a worldwide community of communities" [2]. This change has led to the emergence of a bottom-up user-centric innovation model (i.e., users of products and services are increasingly able to innovate for themselves) [3, 4]. In this new model, innovation is initiated and driven by end users rather than introduced top-down by large firms, corporations, and enterprises such as technology giants [5]. From Wikipedia, digital volunteerism, open source software development, citizen science, to crowdsourcing platforms such as Amazon Mechanical Turk, a body of information science and social computing research (e.g., [6, 7, 9–11]) has tackled important problems on innovation in an information society, including how social computing tools and platforms support the collaborative construction of knowledge (e.g., [12, 14]) and team coordination within online creative communities (e.g., [7]). Yet, how exactly technological innovation can happen from bottom up and what mechanisms support its operation remain understudied.

© Springer Nature Switzerland AG 2019
N. G. Taylor et al. (Eds.): iConference 2019, LNCS 11420, pp. 614–624, 2019.
https://doi.org/10.1007/978-3-030-15742-5_58

In this paper, we explore a network of distributed individuals' collective efforts to establish an innovation ecology allowing them to engage in creative technological practices from the bottom up. We understand innovation ecology as an important concept in social informatics. It refers to the sociotechnical infrastructure of interrelated institutions, regulations, technologies, and resources that can enable, encourage, foster, and catalyze the generation of ideas and creation of value out of them [1, 13]; it also involves core social informatics themes such as social contexts and work processes, sociotechnical networks, and public access to information [8]. Specifically, we present an empirical study of the technological practices in an emerging creative technology community – independent [indie] game developers in the United States. A common understanding of indie games is that they are games made by amateurs who are not professional game developers. We choose this community as an exemplar to explore bottom up innovation ecology because indie games are often praised as a "moral, artistic high-ground" for their new forms of gameplay, innovative design, engaging experiences, and nostalgic properties [15]. What makes indie game developers' creative practices possible, and how their practices inform our design and development of sociotechnical systems for end-user driven innovation and content creation beyond the gaming context deserves research attention not only from game researchers but from information scientists and social computing scholars concerned with social creativity and bottom-up innovation.

2 Background: Indie Game Development and Innovation in Social Computing

A body of research in information science and social computing has sought to design and implement systems and applications that mediate and support social creativity and collective innovation. A common design principle is to facilitate the presentation, spread, and use of information within groups. For example, Gregg [16] proposed that such systems and applications should be data centric, which not only enable data collection and sharing among users but also support user-generated/modified data.

Other researchers noted that improving online users' awareness of collaboration and co-presence can help design, develop, and evaluate interactive systems for group creativity. For example, Geyer et al. [17] designed a digital team collaborative space (i.e., TeamSpace) to integrate both synchronous and asynchronous team interactions into a task-oriented environment. Similarly, Gutwin et al. [18] suggested that information required for group awareness included "knowledge about who is on the project, where in the code they are working, what they are doing, and what their plans are."

However, new bottom-up models of innovation and participatory culture have raised new and important questions about how to better support innovation and emerging creative technology communities' information needs [5, 19]. One example is the indie game development community. Indie games are broadly defined as games that are consciously created within alternative production and distribution structures compared to mainstream game companies [15]. Tools such as easy-to-use free game engines (e.g., Unity and Unreal), comprehensive online coding libraries (e.g., Unity Scripting Reference) and Assets Stores (e.g., Unity Assets Store), unlimited online and offline community support (e.g., Unity online live training, Unity online forums, offline social gatherings of indie game development Meetup groups), and direct developer-to-consumer digital distribution platforms (e.g., App Store) have also contributed to game development no longer being a closed and secretive tech industry.

In general, the indie game development community in the United States has become a novel technology community, who endeavors to collectively innovate cutting-edge graphic and interactive technologies, explore new forms of gameplay, create inspiring and refreshing human experiences, and promote open development process. These new phenomena raise a number of interesting research questions, including how indie game developers can innovate and how their practices inform the design and development of sociotechnical systems that mediate and support bottom-up innovation. This paper endeavors to explore these questions.

3   Methodology

To collect data, we joined six Facebook Groups for indie game developers and indie game development. We then posted a message on these groups to recruit indie game developers who were willing to be interviewed as voluntary participants. All developers who responded to our requests and agreed to participate were inter-viewed. As a result, 12 semi-structured in-depth interviews were conducted via text/audio Skype chat based on participants' preferences from December 2017 to February 2018. In each interview, 15 predefined open-ended questions were asked and the average length of interviews was 80 min. All 12 participants are Americans. Six are female (50%) and 3 are non-Caucasian (25%). The average age of the participants was 31 years old (min. = 25, max. = 51) and average years of experience in indie game development were 8.5 years (min. = 2 years, max. = 17 years). Five of them (42%) developed indie games full time as freelancers or working in small studios (two to three people) while seven (58%) as part time or a hobby.

We then used an empirical, in-depth qualitative analysis of the collected data with a focus on indie game developers' innovative practices. We first closely read through the collected data to acquire a sense of the whole picture as regards developers' technological practices. We then collectively identified thematic topics and common features in the data for further analysis and carefully examined and reviewed the thematic topics and developed sub-themes. Finally, we collaborated in an iterative coding process to discuss, combine, and refine themes to generate a rich description synthesizing how and why indie game developers can innovate from the bottom up.

4   Findings

Digital game production was considered a professional technological practice for profit. Everyday users had little role beyond purchasing and accepting produced games as commodities. Yet, the increasing growth of indie game development seems to signify a cultural shift in how people perceive games and the gaming industry, as one participant reported, *"You get to be on the cutting edge of technology or see really cool things or be a part of the really cool thing before the public goes crazy over it. This is the reason why so many have gone indie"* (P4, female, 33, African American). Many participants, who were not professional game developers, acknowledged that innovative games might originate from individual creativity and passion. However, they explained that (1) *problem solving*; (2) *collaborative information seeking, sharing, and reproducing*; (3) *community support*; and (4) *broader politics and social* policies constituted an innovation ecology – through which they engaged in a bottom-up movement to turn their creativity into IT products (e.g., digital games) and reshape the ways that games were designed, created, and shared. In this section, we explain each of the four themes using quotes from indie developers' own accounts.

4.1 Innovation Emerges in Problem Solving

Many participants highlighted that actively identifying problems and seeking solutions was the first step to transform creative ideas to innovative products. For many of them, the willingness and persistence to encounter various problems in a tech field that they were not professionally trained for was essential for any creative endeavors. One participant summarized, *"The best thing about making indie games is that we become better problem solvers. Most of us had no experience in game development before. This means we usually seek solutions that are 'outside of the box.' That's the start point for any innovation in this field."* (P6, female, 29, Asian) Some others also related problem solving to the fact that gaming as a rapid changing industry: *"I love learning how to use software to a tee. However recently the game development tools have been updating so quickly it's hard to keep up. Most of the time when that happens I have to look at it to see if it's worth upgrading and risking re-doing certain pieces. I have to solve so many problems but I feel I get better every time after I solve some problems."* (P5, male, 27, white)

However, many others described that problem solving was not merely limited in the technical aspect of game making (e.g., programming and using game engines) but also about design, aesthetic, and teamwork – all of which made game development a challenging practice but opened new and emerging opportunities for experimentation and innovation. One participant revealed,

Game development is fraught with challenges. If you're a one-man-band, you have to become knowledgeable in many areas. Programming and logical thought, design and aesthetic sense, sound design–the whole kit. Aside from the technical difficulties, there's also the social aspect of making games. Having team members or even just interested bystanders helps a lot with motivation and training and growth. Making indie games is not just about making software but about imagination, creativity, collaboration, management, marketing, fundraising... etc. You are solving all kinds of problems – tech, social, political, financial. That's why indies grow up so fast and can keep making cool things. (P7, male, 25, white)

For indie game developers, solving problems across various domains often inspired them to innovate. Their problem solving practices not only helped them prepare and sharpen necessary technical skills to develop games but also encouraged them to "think outside the box," leading to creative approaches and strategies beyond the gaming area.

4.2   Innovation Centers on Collaborative Information Seeking, Sharing, and Reproducing

Many participants regarded collaborative information seeking, sharing, and producing as the core mechanisms through which they not only solved problems but also pursued new and innovative solutions in their game development process. Participants shared how they benefited from information and resources shared by others and also contributed to creating, updating, and spreading useful information to benefit other indie game developers:

Sometimes I am the one asking questions and some other times I am the one who provides answers of my own from experience. I especially like to interact with other users on forums for specific tool kits or plugins. I think those information are very valuable for both experienced and new developers. (P6, female, 29, Asian)

Open forums where users can share experiences, experiments, code, and open source tools are the reason why many indie developers and some studios like ours can survive and make new things. Since we are so small, many of our technologies were developed by a third party of some sort, like on Unity's asset store or snippets of code shared by users on GitHub. I think the community as a whole across many platforms is what makes endeavors like ours possible and we are happy to provide what resources we can for the community as well. (P10, male, 27, African American)

These two quotes highlight the importance of voluntary and free information exchange for bottom up technological innovation- innovation is initiated and driven by individual indie game developers or small studios rather than massive game companies. Comparing to companies who enjoy abundant information and cutting edge tools, indie developers often have limited access to resources, money, platforms, and tools. How to provide them with necessary resources at low or no cost became a crucial component in the innovation ecology. The indie gaming context represents a subculture within a broader tech culture: everyone is benefited from free knowledge and information in the innovation ecology; everyone is also producing, sharing, and spreading free knowledge and information to promote more innovation.

However, some participants pointed out the challenges of such a subculture:

I think in general, mid level information is very hard to find. There is so many tutorials on how to get started in a project. And there are forums about super technical programming stuff, but there is a big gap between those two things. [...] you have to reinvent that information yourself. (P8, male, 30, white)

The availability of information and being able to find what you need quickly and efficiently is important. A lot of time is wasted in searching for information and finding up-to-date requirements, specs, techniques, etc. Unity has great support, but finding practical examples on places like YouTube can be frustrating. You get the theory from the documents, but watching someone do it makes it that much easier. YouTube can do that, but there is so much bad information to sift through on YouTube, it eats valuable time. (P9, male, 51, white)

According to these developers, they learnt most from step by step tutorials that were appropriate to their skill level and visual/video information such as YouTube videos. Yet two large issues persist: limited resources for intermediate level difficulty, and abundant low quality or irrelevant information. The indie culture of volunteerism and free labor thus becomes a double-edged sword. On the one hand, it makes essential experiences and knowledge for game development available to everyday users, turning game development into a bottom up innovation movement. On the other hand, all indie developers are encouraged to contribute to a central "knowledge/skill repository" but no mechanism has been established to evaluate those shared information, making their quality and relevance questionable.

4.3   Community Support Sustains Innovation

Problem solving and information exchange may build the foundation for an innovation ecology in indie game development. Yet it is community support that retains indie developers and sustains their efforts to innovate. One participant described, *"Community is so important. Without it, I probably already quitted long time ago. People help each other out, share what they have found or what worked for them. No matter whether you work alone or with others on a project, you need those people to point you to the right direction, and as a member of any community, it's one's responsibility to reciprocate these help and contribute to the community"* (P9, male, 51, white).

Other participants added that the support they received from the indie community was not limited to technical assistance but also for social and emotional purposes, because creating games could be both physically and emotionally challenging:

Absolutely, there are many supportive communities online for game development that I take part in. Some of them are more about mentoring people who are just learning game design and some are very much about social support. Doing something creative is not just about you but also people supporting you, since this can be very stressful. (P1, female, 33, white)

Typically you're scattered across the country, if not the world. There has to be passion, and agency. [...] you need a well functioning and coordinated team. And it can be tough emotionally and physically. You need friends. You need this community. (P11, male, 32, white)

Regardless of working alone or as a distributed team, indie developers seemed to value and appreciate all types of help they received from the indie community – ideas, knowledge, teammates, friends, or just someone they could talk to. For them, bottom-up innovation was a long and emotionally exhausting journey where personal persistence was not enough. To continue this journey, they needed confidence, encouragement, bravery, endurance, and sympathy, which they gained from other fellow indie developers and the broader indie community. One participant (P7, male, 25, white) summarized how the community supported his growth both as a developer and as a human being: *"Game developers are generally very nice and socially progressive people. People learn from each other and push each other to new heights and encourage each other. I have made good friends in the community and found role models to learn from, engaged with artists' new growth of the medium, and even developed part of my own personal identity from it."*

4.4   Policy and Politics Facilitate (or Hinder) Innovation

A few participants stressed how policy and politics in the broader social context affected how they innovated. They especially highlighted the role of the nation's economic development policies in facilitating or hindering technological innovation:

When I was in college, I knew that the "tech growth Ohio" program helped fund our school's small game conventions as part of the STEM education program and helped link various tech businesses together. (P6, female, 29, Asian)

I know of one indie studio that has thrived because of government grants for their work in ecological storytelling. And I know of one studio that flopped after becoming complacent with major funding from the state (as an economic investment), which drew a lot of ire from people. Government involvement can be both an asset and a liability. There's a history of misunderstanding by Congress of the video game industry (See: Mortal Kombat in the 90s) and some knee-jerk legislation, but we do have people more familiar with the medium coming into office and doing positive things. (P7, male, 25, white)

In these quotes, developers were well aware that the upper level national development and economic policies could affect how people created and innovated in the indie community. Their technological practices were not conducted in a vacuum. Rather, what they could innovate and how they innovated was intertwined with policymakers' attitudes towards technology. As they described, the current emphasis on STEM and technology-driven U.S. economy fostered a supportive environment for their technological practices. Though not being widely recognized, indie gaming has been playing an important role in enhancing STEM education and game-based learning (e.g., educational games). Innovation in indie gaming also contributes to the growing technological power (e.g., in terms of creative design, improved user experience, novel interaction mode, and upgraded visual effects). Yet they were anxious that high level policy makers might hinder their innovation due to misunderstandings or unfamiliarity with gaming and game development. In particular, some participants pointed out how the current tax law and political atmosphere might undermine indie game development as a creative technology industry:

I think national laws certainly play a role., particularly in how teams can raise money. And tax law is certainly hard on indies. We spent a big chunk of our budget just to hire decent accountants to track our expenses and make sure we were prepared for taxes. (P11, male, 32, white)

The xenophobic policies that have become prominent in the last few years have made it very difficult for people I know from other countries to live and work in the US. They just want to come here and make games, but current politics has become a huge hurdle there. They're often waiting for months to years just hoping their name comes up in a lottery. (P10, male, 27, African American)

P11 was worried that the current tax policy was not friendly to the indie community (or technological startups in general), which made game development – an already technologically and psychologically challenging creative practice – more financially challenging. This may discourage people to continue their efforts or even enter this field. P10 further pointed to the risk of losing workforce and diversity in indie game development due to the ambiguous political atmosphere. According to him, if people did not feel safe, welcomed, or comfortable in a society, they simply would not participate in innovative activities despite of how much they loved doing so.

5 Discussion

Using indie gaming as a context, in this paper we have identified four themes emerging in indie game developers' accounts that constituted an innovation ecology from bottom up. Though innovation often originates in personal creativity and ideas, how it can be materialized and generate values depends on a sophisticated sociotechnical infrastructure. This infrastructure involves: (1) innovators' active problems seeking and solving that transform creativity to feasible ideas; (2) collaborative information seeking, sharing, and reproducing that enable innovators to turn feasible ideas to innovative products; (3) consistent community support that encourages innovators to continue their efforts and catalyze their creation; and (4) policies and politics that foster a supportive social environment and public perception for technological innovation. In this section, we discuss how these four themes informed our understanding of bottom-up technological innovation and the design of sociotechnical systems that mediate and support such innovation.

Above all, a user-centric bottom up innovation mode is distinctive from other types of innovation; it is driven by everyday users with various backgrounds, knowledge bases, and motivations. In addition, it is often built on users' personal and subjective experiences and it suffers from limited information and resources but provides an alternative way of creating and producing technology. Finally, it requires tremendous social support due to its technological, emotional, and financial challenges. All of these features raise important questions about how to (re)design sociotechnical systems to support this new and emerging form of technological innovation. Our research confirms previous findings regarding the presentation, spread, and use of information as a key design principle to facilitate collaborative innovation [16]. Yet our focus on bottom-up innovation also points to some aspects of technological innovation that may have been overlooked in other studies. We suggest that a sociotechnical system that supports innovation from bottom up involve design features to facilitate informal learning, effective searching and filtering information, social and emotional support, and an awareness of policies and politics.

Informal Learning. People who participate in bottom-up innovation are often non-stereotypical technology workforce; they may be new to a given tech area (e.g., game development) and have little or no experience of designing and creating technology. Yet they are passionate about turning their creativity into technological products. During this process, mechanisms of informal learning make their innovative practices possible. Rather than taking classes in a formal learning environment, they learn by doing (e.g., making their own games), by trial and error, by acquiring and verifying useful information online (e.g., forum posts and YouTube videos), and by peer assistance (e.g., questions and answers). Therefore, designing and developing systems that better support and evaluate informal learning in STEM become crucial to foster an innovation ecology from bottom up. For example, our participants complained that the available learning materials were either too easy or too challenging but they had no control over what was shared and published. A system that facilitates nominating tutorials for topics of various levels of difficulty and supports crowdsourcing feedback for user created content/products would improve bottom up innovator's learning experiences.

Effective Searching and Filtering Information. Our findings point to the risk of wasting innovators' time on low quality or irrelevant information online. Most innovators dedicate their personal spare time to innovating. Therefore, they regard wasting time on unnecessary information search and verification as one of the most significant challenges in their innovation process. For example, many innovators depend on YouTube and its commenting feature to decide whether a tutorial video is relevant to their practices or not. Yet YouTube as a general video viewing site has little quality control on its content's technical matter, which hinders rather than benefits their innovation. Therefore, in addition to information presentation as suggested in previous studies [16], a system that affords sharing and verifying accurate information on specific technical topics and offers effective searching and filtering mechanisms for such information (e.g., searching keywords in scripts of videos) would be central to support technological innovator's efforts.

Social and Emotional Support. Our findings also highlight that bottom-up innovation is a highly challenging practice both technologically and socially, as many indie developers are not tech savvy and may not financially benefit from their practices for a long time. We found that regardless of working alone or as a team, innovators highly appreciate the social and emotional support that they receive from the community. Such support may not directly help them solve a technical or management problem but lead to a friendly and encouraging social atmosphere for bottom-up innovation as a long-term endeavor. In this sense, design features that facilitate social and emotional support from the community should be encouraged to be implemented so as to better support technological innovation. Such features may include gifting and donating, dedicated online social space (e.g., a sub-forum) for anonymously sharing sensitive personal concerns and seeking advice, and value-sensitive designs that encourage and reinforce particular community norms and ethics [22] (e.g., protection of personal privacy and effective reporting and reaction mechanism to tackle harassment).

Awareness of Policy and Political Concerns. The idea of policy preceding and prefiguring design and practice [20, 21] in social computing is not new: As Jackson et al. [20] discussed, policy, as a third factor, can determine the "shape, meaning, and trajectory of shifting computational forms" together with design and practice. Our data have shown that indie developers perceived their technological practices as driven and influenced by a series of national policies – for example, the current focus on STEM education and technology-driven economy. They also believed that how appropriately indie game development fit into these national priorities significantly affected the quality and the public perception of their products. In addition, they acknowledged that politics (e.g., immigration) played a role in encouraging or discouraging the growth and diversity of a technology workforce. Taken together, there seems to be a demand for an increasing awareness of the broader sociopolitical context surrounding innovation.

Building an ecology for bottom-up innovation does not only include designing and creating sociotechnical systems for collective informal learning, information exchange and filtering, and social/emotional support but also requires a better understanding of the intertwining relationships among design, policy, and technology.

6 Conclusions

Using indie gaming as a context, we have explored the innovation ecology that makes bottom-up innovation possible in today's information society. We have identified four themes that constitute an innovation ecology from bottom up, including problem solving; collaborative information seeking, sharing, and reproducing; community support; and policy and politics. We argue that these findings inform our understanding of bottom up technological innovation and shed light on the design of sociotechnical systems that mediate and support such innovation beyond the gaming context.

We offer three interrelated contributions to information science and social computing. First, we emphasize the new information needs and requirements from innovators who are non-stereotypical technology users, which presents empirical evidence on how technological innovation can happen from the bottom-up in today's information society. Second, we extend previous studies on designing sociotechnical systems for distributed innovation by highlighting the importance of supporting informal learning, effective searching and filtering information, social and emotional support, and awareness of policy and political concerns. Finally, we point to how national policies and politics on STEM education, economic development, and technology workforce significantly affect the motivations, trajectories, and public perceptions of bottom up innovation. As innovation is seen as a key economic driver, our findings concerning the mechanics by which innovative ecologies operate can inform policy makers' effective decision-making.

Acknowledgements. We thank our participants and the anonymous reviewers. This work was supported in part by the National Science Foundation under award 1513604 and 1849718, the University of Cincinnati Office of Research, and Clemson University School of Computing.

References

1. Dvir, R., Pasher, E.: Innovation engines for knowledge cities: an innovation ecology perspective. J. Knowl. Manage. **8**(5), 16–27 (2004)
2. Carroll, J.M.: Beyond being social: prospects for transformative social computing. Commun. Assoc. Inform. Syst. **27**(1), 641–650 (2010)
3. Von Hippel, E.: Democratizing innovation: the evolving phenomenon of user innovation. Int. J. Innov. Sci. **1**(1), 29–40 (2009)
4. Ahonen, M., Antikainen, M., Mäkipää, M.: Supporting collective creativity within open innovation. In: European Academy of Management (EURAM) Conference Paris, pp. 1–18 (2007)

5. Freeman, G., Bardzell, S., Bardzell, J.: Bottom-up imaginaries: the cultural-technical practice of inventing regional advantage through IT R&D. In: Proceedings of the 2018 ACM Conference on Human Factors in Computing Systems (CHI 2018), paper 325, pp. 1–11. ACM, New York (2018)
6. Kittur, A., Chi, E.H., Suh, B.: Crowdsourcing user studies with mechanical turk. In: Proceedings of the SIGCHI Conference on Human Factors in Computing Systems, pp. 453–456. ACM (2008)
7. Kittur, A., Lee, B., Kraut, R.E.: Coordination in collective intelligence: the role of team structure and task interdependence. In: Proceedings of the SIGCHI Conference on Human Factors in Computing Systems, pp. 1495–1504. ACM (2009)
8. Kling, R.: Learning about information technologies and social change: the contribution of social informatics. Inform. Soc. 16(3), 217–232 (2000)
9. Rotman, D., et al.: Dynamic changes in motivation in collaborative citizen-science projects. In: Proceedings of the ACM 2012 Conference on Computer Supported Cooperative Work, pp. 217–226. ACM (2012)
10. Starbird, K.: Delivering patients to sacré coeur: collective intelligence in digital volunteer communities. In: Proceedings of the SIGCHI Conference on Human Factors in Computing Systems, pp. 801–810. ACM (2013)
11. Yamauchi, Y., Yokozawa, M., Shinohara, T., Ishida, T.: Collaboration with lean media: how open-source software succeeds. In: Proceedings of the 2000 ACM Conference on Computer Supported Cooperative Work, pp. 329–338. ACM (2000)
12. Kim, S., Mankoff, J., Paulos, E.: Sensr: evaluating a flexible framework for authoring mobile data-collection tools for citizen Science. In: Proceedings of the 2013 Conference on Computer Supported Cooperative Work, pp. 1453–1462. ACM (2013)
13. Wulf, W.A.: Changes in innovation ecology. Science 316(5829), 1253 (2007)
14. Li, Z., Shen, H., Grant, J.E.: Collective intelligence in the online social network of Yahoo! answers and its implications. In: Proceedings of the 21st ACM International Conference on Information and Knowledge Management, pp. 455–464. ACM (2012)
15. Lipkin, N.: Examining Indie's Independence: the meaning of "Indie" games, the politics of production, and mainstream cooptation. Loading 7(11), 8–24 (2013)
16. Gregg, D.G.: Designing for collective intelligence. Commun. ACM 53(4), 134–138 (2010)
17. Geyer, W., Richter, H., Fuchs, L., Frauenhofer, T., Daijavad, S., Poltrock, S.: A team collaboration space supporting capture and access of virtual meetings. In: Proceedings of the 2001 International ACM SIGGROUP Conference on Supporting Group Work, pp. 188–196. ACM (2001)
18. Gutwin, C., Penner, R., Schneider, K.: Group awareness in distributed software development. In: Proceedings of the 2004 ACM Conference on Computer Supported Cooperative Work, pp. 72–81. ACM (2004)
19. Freeman, G., Bardzell, J., Bardzell, S.: Aspirational design and messy democracy: partisanship, policy, and hope in an Asian city. In: Proceedings of the 20th ACM Conference on Computer Supported Cooperative Work and Social Computing (CSCW 2017), pp. 404–416. ACM, New York (2017)
20. Jackson, S. J., Gillespie, T., Payette, S.: The policy knot: re-integrating policy, practice and design in CSCW studies of social computing. In: Proceedings of the 17th ACM Conference on Computer Supported Cooperative Work & Social Computing (CSCW 2014), pp. 588–602. ACM, New York (2014)
21. Light, A.: Troubling futures: can participatory design research provide a generative anthropology for the 21st century? Interact. Des. Archit. 26, 81–94 (2015)
22. Shilton, K.: Values levers: building ethics into design. Sci. Technol. Human Values 38(3), 374–397 (2013)

Professional Identity and Information Use: On Becoming a Machine Learning Developer

Christine T. Wolf[✉]

IBM Research, Almaden, San Jose, CA, USA
ctwolf@us.ibm.com

Abstract. Recently, information behavior (IB) research has drawn attention to the broader life of information, noting its role in discursive practices around social and organizational identity. We explore information's role in occupational and professional identity and identification. How information use figures into the ways that individuals become interested in certain professions (and the barriers to entry they experience) can be helpful in developing policy interventions to foster occupational diversity and inclusion, a particular concern in science, technology, engineering, and math (STEM) fields. This paper reports on a qualitative interview study of machine learning (ML) developers, examining their accounts of how they became interested in the ML field, the barriers they experienced when entering the field, and their patterns of information use in these processes. We discuss the implications of our findings, which reveal information use as an organizing principle that simultaneously defines and continually binds a professional community of practice together.

Keywords: Information behavior · Information use · Professional identity · Occupational choice · STEM careers · Machine learning

1 Introduction

Information use has been a growing topic of interest to information behavior (IB) researchers, with recent work drawing attention to the social uses of information. This work notes how, alongside its functional or practical utility, information is also a resource in discursive practices [18] and in particular discursive practices around identity making [21, 22], which comprise the social processes through which people develop "contextually appropriate answers to the question '*Who am I?*'" [1: 327]. Wolf [21] examined information use and identity processes beyond the individual, demonstrating information's role in maintaining and renewing organizational identity and image. This paper engages with identity processes at another scale – at the professional or occupational level – and asks questions of the role of information use in such arenas. Socialization and identity processes figure central in the subjective experience of and commitment to work [e.g., 1–5] and can be instructive in understanding how individuals become interested in and pursue different professions, as well as their ongoing social processes which shape their affiliation and sense of belonging within a chosen field. A focus on professional identity adds both a temporal component to analyses of social identity making and an implicit focus on change [1: 351] – it asks not only: "*who*

© Springer Nature Switzerland AG 2019
N. G. Taylor et al. (Eds.): iConference 2019, LNCS 11420, pp. 625–636, 2019.
https://doi.org/10.1007/978-3-030-15742-5_59

am I?" But also: *"who am I going to be?"* Understanding more about the relationship between information use and professional identity processes can help to inform policy interventions to foster occupational diversity and inclusion, a particular concern in science, technology, engineering, and math (STEM) fields. By drawing on a qualitative interview study with machine learning (ML) developers, this paper examines the relationship between information use and professional identity, in particular how individuals become interested in a professional domain and the barriers to entry they face, and how they address those barriers.

2   Related Work: Information Use and Identity Making

Information use is a relatively understudied aspect of IB [5], though recent work has drawn attention to its role in social and discursive processes [18, 21, 22]. This work has looked at the ways in which information serves as a resource in everyday social practice, for example, in constructing authority in everyday talk [18]. Recent work has expanded on this to conceptualize the role of information use in social processes around identity – how people go about answering the question *"Who am I?"* [21, 22]. For example, Wolf and Veinot [22] examined the topic of information use among people with chronic illness and laid out ways in which biomedical information was a resource not only in individuals' managing their health conditions (what we might characterize as information's "functional" or "instrumental" use), but also in creating a "valued self" that enabled a sense of personal expertise and know-how. These uses were particularly reparative for individuals dealing with negative social emotions around their chronic conditions like shame and stigma. Subsequent work built on these insights by examining information use in organizational identity processes [21]. That paper looked at a strategic decision within an organization and how workers made sense of and evaluated it; assessing the strategic decision and even questioning it, workers' IB practices enabled both the maintenance and renewal of organizational identity and cohesion in the process [21]. In this paper, we build on this work by examining the role of information use in identity processes at another scale – where [22] examined identity at the individual level, and [21] examined identity at the organizational level, we turn our attention to the professional or occupational level. Socialization and identity processes figure centrally in the subjective experience of and commitment to work, with one's professional occupation serving as a key symbol of belonging and affiliation both internally within specific organizations but also importantly across one's biography and career [e.g., 1–5]. This temporal aspect adds a new foci to questions of social information use by turning our attention to the role of IB in constituting not only professional senses of self but also possibility – *"Who am I?"* becomes also: *"who am I going to be?"* – particularly instructive in investigating how individuals become interested in a particular professional field and the barriers to entry they experience.

Our investigation is motivated by the theory of occupational choice from the sociology of work which conceptualizes career choice as an ongoing, interactional process punctuated by key events in the pre-professional and early professional period of one's life [7, 8]. The relationship between career choice and social identity has been a growing topic of interest in a number of fields; in line with sociological perspectives on labor [3, 20], recent economic perspectives on career choice have drawn attention to the role of social identity (rather than purely pecuniary factors) in individuals' career choices [9]. While we know that information seeking features prominently in adolescents' exploration of career choice [12, 13], we know little about the relationship between IB, career choice, and identity/identification. This motivates our research questions which ask: *what is the role of information use in professional identity processes? How do individuals become interested in a professional domain and how do they address barriers to entry they face?*

3 Study Details

This paper reports on a qualitative interview study of ML developers. The interview study was exploratory in nature, investigating the everyday work practices of ML developers, understanding the range and variety of artifacts used in these practices, and ways to better support ML work practices. The study was also interested more broadly in how participants became interested in ML and what challenges or barriers they encountered in becoming familiar with ML. The author conducted interviews with eleven (11) participants during August 2018 who were employees of a research and development (R&D) lab of a large, global technology corporation and were recruited through word-of-mouth and snowball sampling at the lab. The interviews were semi-structured and typically lasted one hour, were audio recorded and transcribed verbatim. Participant details are provided below in Table 1.

Table 1. Participant details

Pseudonym (gender, length of ML experience)	Recent projects
Andie (female, 4 years)	Health/Medical; Operations Management
Benjamin (male, 6 years)	User Behavior; Social Network Analysis
Chester (male, 3 years)	Sales; Operations Management
Dinesh (male, 5 years)	Natural Language Processing (NLP)
Emil (male, 3 years)	Computer Vision; Image Processing
Frank (male, 4 years)	Computational Biology; NLP
Georgie (female, 9 years)	Systems Monitoring
Hiroshi (male, 2 years)	Predictive Modeling
Imelda (female, 5 years)	Biometric Data; Image Processing
Jonathan (male, 6 years)	NLP; Semantic Modeling
Kai (male, 11 years)	User Behavior; NLP

Given our research question on the role of information use, career choice, and professional identity, analysis used inductive, thematic analysis techniques [4] and focused on participants' response to two open-ended protocol questions: "how did you get interested in machine learning?" and "what did you find challenging about getting started in machine learning?".

4 Findings

4.1 Origin Stories – Getting Interested in Machine Learning

When asked how they got interested in ML, several participants talked about popular press events which reported fantastical results from new ML algorithms: *"Actually, it started from the ImageNet,"* Dinesh said, talking about the annual image processing competition. *"About five or six years ago, there were very astonishing results, and everyone was like 'Wow! Those are really astonishing results' Now, maybe those kinds of breakthroughs seem more common. But back then, it was really something special."* Popular press coverage like this is consequential because it creates awareness of ML progress outside the specific technical community. As we see in Dinesh's account "everyone" was talking about the breakthrough, meaning it had mass, societal appeal, creating awareness and inciting interest of those beyond technical domain experts.

Chester talked about coverage of another famous ML breakthrough, Alpha Go. *"I heard about Alpha Go when I was a sophomore in college, or maybe freshman,"* he explained, *"And that was really a wow moment for me! Because I was more into mathematics and mathematical finance at that time, but Alpha Go was amazing you know!"* He went on to explain that Alpha Go didn't use any human knowledge, instead learning the game strategy *"from scratch."* Continuing, he said: *"For me, Alpha Go was all about how you find some strategy, to process the data in a way computers can process and learn from the data."* Reflecting on the impact of the Alpha Go coverage, he said: *"Actually that was what really got my interest in the topic, that was the switching point in my interests from mathematical stuff to more computer science and machine learning stuff."* Here in Chester's account, we can see how professional identity figures closely with his use of popular press coverage. In looking back on the Alpha Go coverage, it represented a shift in his own interests, from mathematical finance towards ML. While he still deals with finance questions, his work now takes a different approach – he went on to explain how he might still be working in the same domain but now takes a more ML-first approach. *"In ML, it's all about the data, finding some strategy to process and analyze the data,"* he explained, *"it's very different than mathematical finance."* In this account, we can see how the Alpha Go coverage was a turning point for Chester – while still working on questions around finance, he now identifies with a ML orientation (data first) rather than a mathematical finance orientation as he did before the coverage.

In addition to these widespread, public breakthroughs, shifting norms within the Computer Science (CS) field mean that students are often encouraged to learn ML skills; here, the implication being that contemporary computer scientists must be familiar with ML techniques. *"I was getting my Masters in Computer Science and I got interested in ML because it was a core technology they strongly suggested we become familiar with,"* Hiroshi said. Similarly, Andie was also working on a Masters in Computer Science, and wanted to gain experience in one of her department's research labs. *"I was interested in getting research experience, because that's kinda the whole point of getting the Masters,"* Andie said, *"and most of the labs were doing something related to ML. So that's how I first got involved in it."* For others, their interest in ML surfaced through their engagements in specific domains. *"The problems that were coming up in my field of computational biology, they seemed to be well-suited for ML techniques,"* Frank explained. Georgie described a similar shift in the field of systems monitoring and engineering, where, like many domains, the increasing Big Data deluge required new techniques to manage data and put data-driven insights to use: *"there's just so much more data now, to do really cutting-edge stuff in systems requires ML now."*

What is interesting in these examples is how different sources of information – popular press coverage of famous breakthroughs, shifting norms within the CS field, or challenging new problems within other professional domains like biology or systems engineering – invite individuals to re-consider their own interests but also their technical work and its professional mandate. While Chester is still fundamentally dealing with the same domain problems (finance) he adopts an "ML perspective" where the issues are first and foremost tackled as data problems; similarly, those who are encouraged to become familiar with ML during their CS degrees are signaled that professional norms demand that familiarity. But in domain-driven forays into ML, like we see with Frank and Georgie, we can see that ML remains a flexible set of techniques and approaches that enable them to bring innovation and ingenuity to their "home" domains. While all participants in our study identified as a "machine learning developer" (this was the study's recruitment criteria) that identity is flexible in that it allows for different orientations among individuals. Being a "machine learning developer" means different things to our participants – for Chester, it means taking a data-first approach; for Hiroshi and Andie, it's part of being a modern, contemporary computer scientist; for Frank and Georgie, it means bringing innovation to their home disciplines of biology and systems engineering. Whereas traditionally we see the boundaries amongst technical and scientific disciplines carefully policed to maintain professional authority [6], ML is flexible in that it is both a set of computational techniques (that can be used in a variety of domains) and a data-driven orientation towards problems (a self-stance that individuals can take on). With our focus on information use and professional identity, we can see how the array of information sources allow for flexible uses – rather than a boxed-in, rigid definition of what it means to be a "machine learning developer," these different sources of information (popular press coverage, professional advice at universities, shifting norms within domains) offer a variety of avenues and spaces for individuals to "fit" within the ML community.

4.2 Getting Used to the Day-to-Day Work of Machine Learning

All participants discussed difficulties they experienced getting acclimated to the actual work of machine learning, often talking about a gap between "theory and practice." As Benjamin put it: *"The actual barrier to getting started for me was the difference between the theory and practice."* He described reading ML papers which typically introduce new algorithms or report novel results, *"but in many articles they don't say how to preprocess data or how would you actually realize the end result, you know, how they cleaned the data, how they tuned the parameters, how they decided on the modeling, and so on."* That's where you really spend the bulk of your time, he explained. *"All those decisions, those are key parts of ML work,"* he said, *"and the hardest to get started with."* Here we see a new source of information in the ML developer's journey, scholarly publications about ML. All participants talked about reading new papers and staying up on recent developments and trends – but they also talked about how such papers only tell part of the story.

Often the focus on technical ML papers is on presenting novel techniques and algorithms; the datasets paradoxically become "invisible" to the paper's main contributions. There are standard, publicly available datasets that are used frequently in such publications, so many times issues around data never come up in the papers because of the standardized datasets. This can make it difficult to then apply the paper's algorithms into real-world settings, which have messy data. *"Dealing with your data, that's everything,"* Imelda said, *"I think it's like the most important part in my opinion, of the whole process. Dealing with your data and making the data consumable and making it full, complete, you know dealing with problems, with entity resolution problems and stuff like that."* Processing data involves a lot of iterative trial-and-error, which is often intricately tied to the specific domain problem or task at hand, she explained: *"When you have your data, you have to ask yourself, is this a good candidate dataset? Will it highlight the thing I'm trying to talk about or not? It can take a long time."* Jonathan similarly emphasized the data work involved in ML practice: *"I feel like I spend so much time working on really data-dependent problems, fixing my datasets to be just right,"* he said, *"of course I didn't realize that when I started (laughs) that's like the whole thing, data is pretty much **the thing** (emphasizes) that you do in machine learning."*

There was a sense among the participants that the only way to really learn what makes a "good dataset" is through experience – working on different projects, being attentive, and learning as you go. *"The key to being successful is all about thinking through the problems or questions you want to work on,"* Kai explained, *"one that fits appropriately with your data."* He reflected on the recent explosion of interest in ML: *"there's a lot interest in ML today, but I always stress that yes, it's a hot topic, but it's like any other technical sub-field,"* he explained, *"it's got to make sense for what you are trying to do."* His common advice to newcomers is to be patient and think through: *"...it isn't a cure-all, it's not right for every problem you are trying to work on."*

Talking of barriers to entry in the machine learning field, Andie reflected: *"I've found that a lot of people feel like they need to be **really** (emphasizes) into like the math and understand the theory and that's usually pretty off-putting if people feel they don't have the right background for it."* She continued: *"I've found that people who are interested are like 'If I can't, I'm not some sort of mathematician, I don't know all this theory and background knowledge. I'll never know what's really going on here so I'm just going to use some off-the-shelf algorithms and see what I get,' which can be its own problem."* Andie stressed that one doesn't need to be a mathematician to work in ML, but neither can one just dabble – using "off the shelf" algorithms without care can be harmful.

What we see in these accounts is that there is a difference between doing ML and doing ML *well* – the latter requiring iterative, reflective practice that involves both being engrossed in one's data and the application domain it represents and matching it appropriate with computational, algorithmic techniques that fit well to the task at hand. When we approach these insights from the vantage of IB and in particular information use and professional identity, we can see how the emergent professional norms around doing "good ML" involve a careful integration of formal information (ML "on the books") and the informal expertise and know-how that comes from experience (ML "in practice"). The everyday work of good ML practice, then, means that the technical approaches, the algorithms and techniques gleaned from scholarly ML papers, must be woven together with reflective, data-dependent experimentation, the thoughtful know-how gleaned through careful experience, to create a hybrid, theory-informed, yet data-driven professional practice.

4.3   Multi-modal, Multi-scalar Social Support – Machine Learning's Communities of Practice

Given the distance between ML in papers and ML in practice, how do developers go about gaining the hybrid knowledge that weaves together formal and informal information? How do you know if you've appropriately fit an ML technique to the problem at hand? Participants talked of numerous sources of information that helped them not only when they first started working with ML, but also continued to be an invaluable resource as they encountered new issues or questions in their everyday work practice.

Other people – colleagues also working with ML – were central here, which can be conceptualized as a community of practice [15, 19]. Those participants who first become familiar with ML during their undergraduate coursework talked about inter-actions with their classmates: *"Talking to people, of course, is really helpful to figuring out problems. For classes, obviously talking to other people in the class,"* Emil explained, *"because we're all working on the same assignments so it's easy to talk about issues that came up."* In the context of his work at the R&D lab, Emil, like many participants, talked of working through questions with project teammates or other co-workers. *"If I run into a problem now, I usually will ask people around the lab,"* Georgie said. Turning to colleagues was echoed in all of interviews. *"I'll ask different people in my group here at the lab,"* Benjamin explained, *"and if I'm still stuck, I have a pretty good network of colleagues working on similar topics at other places. So I can always ask around."* A few participants even mentioned individuals who had a repu-tation around the lab as being particularly knowledgeable – or particularly deft at finding answers in secondary sources like documentation or online forums – *"Have you talked to Frank?,"* Emil asked during his interview, *"he's great, he really knows a lot about ML. I ask him stuff all the time."* Kai even joked about being known as an "old timer" at the lab, meaning colleagues often stopped by his office with questions. He also talked about enjoying summers because it was "intern season" and provided lots of opportunities for him to help more novice developers hone their ML knowledge.

Another source of information participants talked often of were online platforms like StackOverflow: *"With StackOverflow, sometimes I have a question and I can get the answer, you know, in five minutes,"* Hiroshi said, *"It's pretty incredible!"* Partici-pants talked of asking their own questions on these platforms, but were often able to find previously-asked questions as well, as Jonathan shared:

> The ML Facebook Group, it's very, very active. Sometimes I can just search and get the answer immediately…But sometimes it's people, you know, following up on the question, maybe I had a more general question and then other people were adding other questions in the replies, more complicated points and nuances… It's really, really useful, you can learn a lot that way.

So while the information gleaned from online platforms can be interactional (directly asking one's questions), it can also be observational (watching others discuss and debate). Both serve as a precious resource in everyday ML practice that not only provides instrumental information (useful in writing code), but also paints the portrait of a community tied together through information sharing and collective problem solving.

Emil shared a story during his interview about when he was getting onboarded at the lab and picking up his teammates code. He tried to execute the code on his machine, but kept getting errors returned which puzzled both him and his teammate. *"We were both using Keras (a common, open source AI framework), so we were both like what is going on?,"* he explained. Perplexed, Emil spent some time searching online forums but couldn't find anything particularly useful. *"Keras is known for not having the best documentation,"* he explained, *"but usually I can find relevant discussions online."* Discouraged from the lack of insight online, Emil felt stuck and shared his frustration with others who shared his workspace. *"That's when I was just talking about it in our room, asking if anybody else had this problem when they started,"* Emil said. He continued:

> It was kinda funny (laughs) after all those issues and trying everything I could think of, trying for several days, [Frank] was like 'Oh yeah, what version of Keras are you using? The most recent release caused a lot of portability issues.' And just like that, we figured it out.

Like all kinds of software development, ML takes place in collaborative working arrangements – a developer does not work alone, but instead works with others. While this may seem like an unremarkable finding, when we read these practices in relation to the paper's other findings (Sect. 4.1 on getting interested in ML and then Sect. 4.2 on learning the difference between ML on the books and ML in practice) we are able to see how membership in the ML professional community is an ongoing, iterative and information-rich process. When we consider Emil's example, together with the other examples of social information support, we are able to see how machine learning developers' everyday work takes place within a community of practice [15, 19]. But this community operates at multiple scales – in small groups of classmates working on shared assignments, in teammates and coworkers across the lab working on unique though related problems, and also in online interactions at a global scale via platforms like StackOverflow or Facebook Groups. In each, we can see an expression of what it means to be a ML developer – rather than merely a set of technical skills or lines of code, ML practice is defined by the ongoing, ingenuous, and relentless problem-solving, that occurs together with colleagues and takes place through a myriad of information-rich encounters.

5   Discussion and Conclusions

In this paper, we set out to explore the relationship between information use and professional identity. In doing so we built on prior work that has demonstrated the role of information use in individual- [22] and organizational-level identity processes [21]. What has our attention to information use and identity at another scale – that of professions – shown us? One's professional occupation serves as a key symbol offering a sense of belonging and affiliation across one's biography and career. By turning our attention to the role of IB in constituting not only professional senses of self but also possibility – "*Who am I?*" becomes also: "*who am I going to be?*".

Through interviews with ML developers we examined how participants first became interested in the ML field. From popular press media coverage of famous ML breakthroughs, to professional career advice given during CS programs, to domain-driven problems that needed innovative techniques, we see the different types of information pique individuals' interest in ML. In these processes, the notions of what it means to be a ML developer surfaces as a flexible construct, allowing for individuals to creatively take a data-centric approach to solving emergent domain problems, rather than a rigid set of skills or tasks they will perform. Getting familiar with the nitty-gritty details of day-to-day ML practice, though, can be difficult for newcomers as the gap between "ML on the books" and "ML in practice" is vast – while formal resources like scholarly publications establish the state-of-the-art algorithmic techniques in the field, they fail to set out the messy, complex forms of data work that comprise the bulk of everyday ML practice. A central part of the enculturation journey for ML newcomers, then, becomes learning to navigate the gap between formal ML information like scholarly publications and the informal know-how that comes from everyday experimentation and improvisation on "real world" projects. Understanding the difference between the two becomes a key part of becoming an ML developer – but while these two are distinct, they inseparably together comprise the knowledge world and information ecosystem of the contemporary ML community. Navigating this hybrid knowledge world becomes as much a defining characteristic of ML practice as writing code and processing datasets.

In the ongoing patterns of information seeking and use that ML developers engage in to address questions, problems, dilemmas, and uncertainties that continually arise in their everyday ML practice, we can see how a multi-scalar community of practice emerges as participants described a number of examples where they turned to their colleagues, other ML practitioners – whether in person or online, or even both simultaneously. In these examples, we see professional information behavior that we are familiar with – ML, like all forms of software development (and other knowledge work too), takes place with and through information-rich interactions with colleagues. But when we consider these practices from the vantage of information use and professional identity, together with our other findings, we see a portrait begin to emerge that paints information use as a central process through which "good" ML practice is accomplished. There is not an expectation that an ML developer's sense of professional identity relies on having all the answers or rigidly applying algorithmic techniques to datasets; instead, what we see in our participants' accounts is the stressing that being a ML developer requires reflexivity, careful experimentation, and a data-centric stance that is open and honest about the limitations of one's dataset and the problems it can answer. What's more, in these accounts of information seeking and use, we can also see an affective dimension to these practices – an impulse to seek out answers, a curiosity to learn more, a willingness to share problems with colleagues – information use, here, emerges as an integral part of the professional ML practice. Where [22] demonstrated that information use can be reparative for those dealing with negative social emotions and [21] examined how information use can renew debate and workers' affiliation within an organization, we show that information use is equally important at the professional level, acting as a centrifugal force that simultaneously defines and binds a professional community of practice together.

In addition to expanding our scholarly knowledge of the relations between information use and identity-making processes, this paper also offers insights relevant for educational and policy practice. Diversity, and in particular issues of fairness, accountability, and transparency (FAT), have been a growing topic of concern in ML communities. Often tackled as technical problems under the moniker "FAT/ML,"[1] such work draws attention to the risks of bias and discrimination in various applications of ML techniques. Alternatively, this paper highlights the work of ML developers – as an intellectually diverse community of practice. There have been significant efforts in recent years to increase interest and participation in STEM fields, but such efforts typically focus on coding, math, and other "hard" skills as the key criteria for membership. An attention to – and even emphasis of – the role of information behavior in STEM practice can help people imagine themselves in such fields. You don't have to be a *mathematician or theory person*," as Andie puts it, which frequently scares off people who don't identify with those roles (or causes them to disengage with the reflexive practice central to good ML practice, as Andie cautioned with the "off the shelf" practice). Instead, when ML is framed not just as theory, coding, and math, and instead as a technical craft – one that takes place within a vibrant community of practice where information seeking, ingenuity, and an openness and willingness to learn are prized – suddenly these are skills and traits that many can identify with. A concept from the sociology of work reverberates here – that of *invisible work* [17], which is typically associated with labor practices that are commonly rendered invisible in certain regimes of value and remuneration (e.g., in cases of domestic or emotional labor). Efforts to make work practices visible – in all the varied, mundane, and often hidden spheres they arise – is political for exactly these reasons. By drawing attention to specific work practices, their value becomes a topic of concern and even contention. Similarly, here, we have the opportunity to contribute to dialogues about STEM participation and inclusion. By making the role of information use visible, prominent, central – by stressing its constitutive role in defining and binding technical communities like we see here in the case of ML – we are able to open up STEM discourses. Doing so not only demonstrates the ongoing relevance of library and information science in these domains, it also argues for the carving out of spaces within professional fields that allow for outsiders' imagination to flourish, allowing for the possibility that they might come to imagine themselves not only joining the field, but also imagining a career where they are capable of making meaningful contributions – a career where they are capable of thriving.

Acknowledgements. Thank you to study participants; to project collaborators Nathalie Baracaldo Angel and Bryant Chen; and to Roderic Crooks for comments on earlier drafts. All opinions are my own and do not reflect any institutional endorsement.

---

[1] https://fatconference.org; http://www.fatml.org.

References

1. Ashforth, B.E., et al.: Identification in organizations: an examination of four fundamental questions. J. Manag. **34**(3), 325–374 (2008). https://doi.org/10.1177/0149206308316059
2. Ashforth, B.E., Mael, F.: Social identity theory and the organization. Acad. Manag. Rev. **14**(1), 20–39 (1989). https://doi.org/10.5465/amr.1989.4278999
3. Bourdieu, P.: Distinction: A Social Critique of the Judgement of Taste. Harvard University Press, Cambridge (1984)
4. Braun, V., Clarke, V.: Using thematic analysis in psychology. Qual. Res. Psychol. **3**(2), 77–101 (2006). https://doi.org/10.1191/1478088706qp063oa
5. Case, D.O., O'Connor, L.G.: What's the use? Measuring the frequency of studies of information outcomes. J. Assoc. Inf. Sci. Technol. **67**(3), 649–661 (2016). https://doi.org/10.1002/asi.23411
6. Gieryn, T.F.: Boundary-work and the demarcation of science from non-science: strains and interests in professional ideologies of scientists. Am. Sociol. Rev. **48**(6), 781–795 (1983). https://doi.org/10.1002/asi.23411
7. Ginzberg, E.: Toward a theory of occupational choice. Occup. Vocat. Guidance J. **30**(7), 491–494 (1952). https://doi.org/10.1002/j.2164-5892.1952.tb02708.x
8. Ginzberg, E.: Toward a theory of occupational choice: a restatement. Vocat. Guidance Q. **20**(3), 2–9 (1972)
9. Humlum, M.K., et al.: An economic analysis of identity and career choice. Econ. Inq. **50**(1), 39 (2012)
10. Ibarra, H.: Provisional selves: experimenting with image and identity in professional adaptation. Adm. Sci. Q. **44**(4), 764–791 (1999). https://doi.org/10.2307/2667055
11. Ibarra, H., Barbulescu, R.: Identity as narrative: prevalence, effectiveness, and consequences of narrative identity work in macro work role transitions. Acad. Manag. Rev. **35**(1), 135–154 (2010). https://doi.org/10.5465/amr.35.1.zok135
12. Julien, H.: Adolescent career decision making and the potential role of the public library. Publ. Libr. **37**(6), 376–381 (1998)
13. Julien, H.E.: Barriers to adolescents' information seeking for career decision making. J. Am. Soc. Inf. Sci. **50**(1), 38–48 (1999). https://doi.org/10.1002/(SICI)1097-4571(1999)50:1<38:AID-ASI6>3.0.CO;2-G
14. Kreiner, G.E., et al.: Where is the "Me" among the "We"? Identity work and the search for optimal balance. Acad. Manag. J. **49**(5), 1031–1057 (2006). https://doi.org/10.5465/amj.2006.22798186
15. Lave, J., Wenger, E.: Situated Learning: Legitimate Peripheral Participation. Cambridge University Press, Cambridge (1991)
16. Reid, A., et al.: Identity and engagement for professional formation. Stud. High. Educ. **33**(6), 729–742 (2008). https://doi.org/10.1080/03075070802457108
17. Star, S.L., Strauss, A.: Layers of silence, arenas of voice: the ecology of visible and invisible work. Comput. Support. Coop. Work (CSCW) **8**(1), 9–30 (1999). https://doi.org/10.1023/A:1008651105359
18. Tuominen, K., Savolainen, R.: A social constructionist approach to the study of information use as discursive action. In: Proceedings of an International Conference on Information Seeking in Context, London, UK, pp. 81–96 (1997)
19. Wenger, E.: Communities of Practice: Learning, Meaning, and Identity. Cambridge University Press, New York (1999)
20. Willis, P., Aronowitz, S.: Learning to Labor: How Working Class Kids Get Working Class Jobs. Columbia University Press, New York (1981)

21. Wolf, C.T.: Reckoning with: information use and engaging with strategic decisions in high tech work. In: Chowdhury, G., McLeod, J., Gillet, V., Willett, P. (eds.) iConference 2018. LNCS, vol. 10766, pp. 550–559. Springer, Cham (2018). https://doi.org/10.1007/978-3-319-78105-1_61

22. Wolf, C.T., Veinot, T.C.: Struggling for space and finding my place: an interactionist perspective on everyday use of biomedical information. J. Assoc. Inf. Sci. Technol. **66**(2), 282–296 (2015). https://doi.org/10.1002/asi.23178

Information Behaviors on Twitter

Categorization and Comparison of Influential Twitter Users and Sources Referenced in Tweets for Two Health-Related Topics

Aseel Addawood[1,2(✉)], Priyanka Balakumar[1], and Jana Diesner[1]

[1] University of Illinois at Urbana-Champaign, Champaign, IL, USA
{aaddaw2, pb3, jdiesner}@illinois.edu
[2] Al Imam Mohammad Ibn Saud Islamic University, Riyadh, Saudi Arabia

Abstract. The internet's evolution has had a profound influence on how people acquire medical information. The innovation of web 2.0 has been regarded as the primary motivating factor for people who want to access health-related education. In this work, we identify the URL categories that Twitter users incorporate into their messages when engaging in two selected health-related topics (MMR vaccines and healthy diets). Moreover, we identify the categories of influential message authors who engage in these two topics. Finally, we explore the relationship between different user categories and their patterns of URL sharing. Our results show that when it comes to influential users sharing fake news, users discussing vaccine-related topics were more than twice as likely to share a fake news URLs than those discussing healthy diets.

Keywords: Social media · Influential users · Health issues

1 Introduction

A recent study has shown that 59% of Twitter users in 2016 got their news from social media platforms [1]. However, as an information source, social media presents some drawbacks. These drawbacks include the spread of false information, rumors, and fake news. Fake news refers to false information or propaganda published under the appearance of being authentic information. Despite these drawbacks, social media users utilize these platforms to discuss personal issues, including health issues [2]. The Pew Research Center showed that one in three adults in the United States goes online to identify a diagnosis or to learn more about a health complaint [3]. Previous research has also stated that many patients seek and follow advice from medical websites rather than visiting doctors due to the amount of health information available online [4].

However, online health information has an important drawback. Verifying the credibility of these online information has become challenging, as previous studies of the quality of online healthcare information have found that these information are not always reliable [5]. Previous research has found that the reliability of information is a concern for those who use social media to access and communicate health information [6, 7]. Many people make health decisions based on inaccurate or misleading medical advice found online and specifically on social media, which can affect their health negatively [8, 9].

© Springer Nature Switzerland AG 2019
N. G. Taylor et al. (Eds.): iConference 2019, LNCS 11420, pp. 639–646, 2019.
https://doi.org/10.1007/978-3-030-15742-5_60

This information may have a significant effect on people's health-related behaviors and decisions [10]. So, there is a need for better mechanisms to identify and extract credible and accurate health information from vast, noisy social media data.

One of the well-studied approaches to identifying credible social media messages online is examining the different factors available in the social media environment itself. For example, several studies have shown that incorporating URLs into social media texts is considered to be one of the main features of credibility [11, 12]. Researchers have shown that people who see an article from a trusted sharer, even when it is written by an unknown media source, have more trust in the information than people who see the same article from a reputable media source shared by a non-trusted person [13]. These factors could serve as cues for a credibility system that can automatically detect and flag low-quality information on social media, as the availability of such systems to assess, whether automatically or semi-automatically, the credibility of health-related information in social media is limited [14].

We focus our analysis on tweets collected for two selected health-related topics (MMR vaccines and healthy diets). First, we analyze only the URLs shared in the tweets in our dataset. Second, we identify and categorize influential Twitter users into several categories at the *individual* and *organizational* levels. We then examine the distribution of these types across the two selected health-related topics. Finally, we analyze the relationship between different user categories and their patterns of URL sharing.

This study aims to (a) develop a classification schema for influential user types who tweet health-related issues, (b) reveal URL sharing patterns for URLs belonging to various categories, (c) find the relationship between URL sharing and influential user types, (d) apply these analyses across two selected health-related topics (MMR vaccines and healthy diets). Studying who participates in online health-related discussions can help us to better understand why misinformation appears on social media and who is responsible for the dissemination of misinformation. Our work can contribute to (1) raising public awareness about online health misinformation, (2) supporting educators, librarians, and health information specialists in promoting healthy digital literacy practices, and (3) developing technologies for assisting social media users in vetting, verifying, fact-checking, filtering, and flagging dubious information.

2 Related Work

One of the main challenges of using social media for health is the information credibility [15]. One line of work from the recent burst of studies on information credibility on Twitter focuses on identifying sets of features that are indicative of credibility [11, 16, 17]. One of these features is the presence of links in the tweet text. Castillo, Mendoza and Poblete [11] used a complex set of features found in tweets, re-tweets, the text of the posts, references to external sources, and users to predict the credibility of tweeted information. Their results showed that among other features, having a URL in the tweet tends to indicate that a tweet is credible. Gupta and Kumaraguru [18] analyzed tweets posted during the terrorist bomb blasts in Mumbai and proposed a credibility analysis approach enhanced with event graph-based optimization. They found that nearly half of the tweets about that event were spam. This may indicate that in similar situations, users might not check the credibility of tweets. Morris, Counts, Roseway, Hoff and Schwarz [19] conducted a survey to study users' perceptions of information credibility by asking participants to identify the indicators of credibility on Twitter. They discovered that users have poor judgement about the truth of information on Twitter based on content alone, and that they are influenced by other heuristics such as user name and user image when making their assessments. Their results showed that URLs or locations in tweet metadata were perceived as enhancing tweet credibility. In this paper, we extend this body of research by building an evidence lexicon to categorize different types of information sources referenced in tweets concerning two health-related issues.

Table 1. Search query and number of tweets per topic

Topic	Twitter query	# Tweets
MMR vaccine	("vaccinations" OR "vaccines" OR "vaccine" OR "measles-mumps-rubella" OR "MMR" OR "mmr") AND ("autism" OR "autistic disorder")	109,694
Healthy diet	("nutrient" OR "nutrition" OR "clean diet" OR "diet") AND ("public health" OR "health" OR "wellness" OR "healthy lifestyle" OR "wellbeing")	36,709

3 Data

The dataset for this study was collected using Crimson Hexagon[1], and is composed of a sample of tweets posted between 1 January 2016 and 28 November 2016. One prominent public health issue that has been debated widely concerns a possible relationship between MMR vaccinations and autism. One of the least debated health topics is the benefits gained from keeping a healthy diet. The two topics have been chosen as they represent different ends of the health debatable spectrum. Table 1 shows the search query terms used and the number of tweets per topic. As with any study that involves social media data, we were aware that we may be missing data. For examples, if a user tweets about MMR vaccines without using one of the specified keywords, our data would not include this tweet. Issues around data retrieval have potential to lead to a biased sample, however we have sourced a large enough dataset to avoid extreme bias.

4 Method

First, URLs were pulled straight from user tweets and were classified based on a mutually exclusive domain lexicon[2] created to classify expanded domains into 12 different categories: *News, Videos, Fake News, Social Media, Blog, Commercial, Government, Scientific, Educational institutions, Health Magazines, National or state*

---

[1] https://www.crimsonhexagon.com/.
[2] The lexicons are shared in this GitHub repository: https://bit.ly/2EiT6l5.

professional medical societies and associations, Health Insurance. Our lexicon is constructed by assimilating publicly available categorizations of web domains into the aforementioned categories [20]. To identify influential users, we used the pre-defined Klout Score obtained from Crimson Hexagon through Klout API, which is a measure of a user's overall influence, it was shown previously as a valid measure of influence [21]. Based on the Klout Score, the top 25th percentile of users were considered to be influential [22]. Within the top 25th percentile, 150 tweets were randomly chosen for each health topic. Finally, a codebook was developed by incorporating past research on classifying social media users [23]. This codebook was used to categorize influential users into two main categories: individuals and organizations, as well as several sub-categories (as seen in Fig. 2 below). Using the codebook, two coders were trained to review and assign each of the Twitter profiles to one of the categories identified above. The types of users were determined through each user's personal user profile, most commonly through the information found in the user's bio. The coders agreed on 252 out of 300 profiles (Cohen's Kappa coefficient 81.5%).

5 Results

5.1 URL Analysis

In the dataset, there were a total of 97,694 URLs shared by users within their tweets. Out of all the URLs, 78.7% of the URLs appeared in tweets related to the topic of diet and 21.3% in tweets discussing vaccines. Figure 1 shows the distribution of the different types of information sources used in both vaccines and diet tweets. Our results showed that Twitter is among the most cited source type for tweets on both topics, which may be due to the nature of Twitter as a community where people refer to and cite each other by replying to each other's messages and quoting each other's tweets. As shown in Fig. 1, many tweets about diet use URLs linking to news websites and articles (65.5% of all news URLs). This may be because Twitter users do not have space to include their full opinions, so they refer to an article to strengthen their arguments. We find that the number of references to fake news is considerably higher for the vaccine issue than for diet. Posts discussing vaccine-related topics were more than twice as likely to reference fake news URLs compared to those discussing diet. This suggests that since topics such as MMR vaccines do not have a basis of truth that everybody can agree on, misleading information such as fake news, click-bait, and satire are shared widely in the context of controversies; or that topics such as MMR vaccines may trigger a higher perceived need of backing up one's point of view with external information, evidence, or endorsement. On the other hand, tweets discussing the topic of diet were about twice as likely to reference commercial URLs than tweets discussing vaccines.

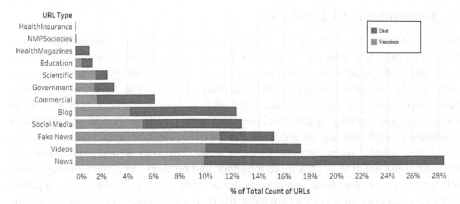

Fig. 1. Information source usage between health topics

5.2 Influential User Analysis

For both topics, our results suggest that individuals tend to engage with health issues more than organizations (64.7% compared to 35.3%). Within the entire dataset, lay people were the most common type of individuals (36.6%), and healthcare companies were the most common type of organization (39.6%). For accounts tweeting on the topic of healthy diet, 62% were organizational. Figure 2a shows the breakdown of user types for the topic of MMR vaccines, 90.7% of influential user accounts were individuals (39.3% lay people, 29% health activists). Although *organizational* profiles were not as engaged in this topic, non-profits made up 34% of all *organizational* user types. In contrast to those findings, the breakdown of user types for the diet topic (Fig. 2b) shows that 28% - the largest group of *organizational* users - were health-care companies. This may imply that these companies disseminate more information about the topic of nutrition and diet than individuals do. Among *individual* users, bloggers were the most common type (9.42%).

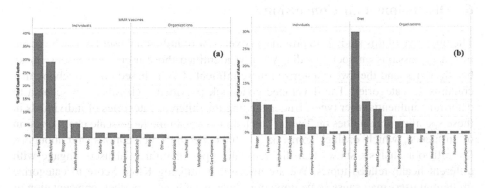

Fig. 2. (a) Breakdown of user dimensions within the topic of MMR vaccines. (b) Breakdown of user dimensions within the topic of healthy diet.

5.3   Relationship of URL and User

The focus of this study are the types of URLs that influential users' post in their tweets, and whether there is a difference in the URL types used by the different influential users versus other influential users. Our results show that certain URL types are more commonly used by one influential user group than others. For example, 96.7% of blog URLs shared come from *individual* user accounts such as bloggers and lay persons. Even though blogs are regularly updated websites that are typically written in an informal or conversational style and are not guaranteed to provide scientific or factual information, *individual* influential users continue to share blogs. This may indicate that influential *individual* users are able to gain more influence and be more persuasive through these URL types. On the other hand, *organizational* accounts such as health-care companies (18.9%) and media profiles (13%) are more likely to share sources containing scientific information than health professionals. This suggests that *individual* users gain influence through personal connections, while *organizational* accounts gain influence when presenting factual, scientific, or published information. The top *individual* user categories when it came to the use of URLs in tweets were Bloggers (7.9%), Health Activists (10.1%), Health Professionals (7.7%), and Lay Persons (18.6%). Within these individuals, lay people shared video URLs More often than any other type of *individual* user accounts. Surprisingly, the most common URL shared by health professionals were social media links (56%). Health professionals can be commonly perceived as sharing credible information; however, our results suggest that this may not always be the case. In addition, health professionals share scientific URLs just as frequently as health activists and less often than lay people. Based on our results, the occupation of the influential user does not play an important role in the credibility of the information being shared. This might offer a possible explanation as to be why the most influential *individual* user accounts for both topics consist of a large portion of lay people. Overall, influence is not obtained through the sharing of scientific or factual evidence, as our results show that health information disseminated by influential users are questionable. Rather, influence can be just as effectively gained through personal connections not necessarily based on a user's occupation or an account's status.

6   Discussions and Conclusion

The objective of this study is to provide an overview of influential user types who guide health discussions on social media. We first identified those users who discuss these health issues, and then we categorized these influential users based on a codebook that contains 12 categories. The developed codebook provided a classification schema to determine influential user types. Understanding the different categories of individuals in these specific communities on Twitter can help to explain the large-scale chain reaction of influence, which enables someone to shape people's perceptions and thoughts. Overall, our analysis shows that different sub-types of influential users engage with different health-related topics. We are aware that utilizing Klout Score to categorize influential users may cause some limitations because it is not a perfect representation of user influence due to its focus on interaction quantity over quality. Understanding influential users within specific health domains reveals the most effective ways to diffuse public health information. Health-companies can use this information to most efficiently advertise their products, while health public policy makers can find the right users to raise awareness about specific health issues. Our results are limited by issues with sampling from social media, e.g., bot activities.

References

1. Shearer, E., Gottfried, J.: News use across social media platforms 2017. Pew Research Center (2017)
2. Miller, L.M.S., Bell, R.A.: Online health information seeking: the influence of age, information trustworthiness, and search challenges. J. Aging Health **24**(3), 525–541 (2012)
3. Fox, S., Duggan, M.: Health online 2013 (2013). http://www.pewinternet.org/2013/01/15/health-online-2013/
4. Gualtieri, L.N.: The doctor as the second opinion and the internet as the first. In: Proceedings of the CHI'09 Extended Abstracts on Human Factors in Computing Systems. ACM (2009)
5. Morahan-Martin, J., Anderson, C.D.: Information and misinformation online: recommendations for facilitating accurate mental health information retrieval and evaluation. CyberPsychol. Behav. **3**(5), 731–746 (2000)
6. Antheunis, M.L., Tates, K., Nieboer, T.E.: Patients' and health professionals' use of social media in health care: motives, barriers and expectations. Patient Educ. Couns. **92**(3), 426–431 (2013)
7. Moorhead, S.A., Hazlett, D.E., Harrison, L., Carroll, J.K., Irwin, A., Hoving, C.: A new dimension of health care: systematic review of the uses, benefits, and limitations of social media for health communication. J. Med. Internet Res. **15**(4), e85 (2013)
8. Freeman, K.S., Spyridakis, J.H.: An examination of factors that affect the credibility of online health information. Tech. Commun. **51**(2), 239–263 (2004)
9. Eysenbach, G.: Credibility of health information and digital media: new perspectives and implications for youth. In: Digital Media, Youth, and Credibility, pp. 123–154 (2008)
10. Kitchens, B., Harle, C.A., Li, S.: Quality of health-related online search results. Decis. Support Syst. **57**, 57454–57462 (2014)
11. Castillo, C., Mendoza, M., Poblete, B.: Information credibility on Twitter. In: Proceedings of the 20th International Conference on World Wide Web. ACM (2011)
12. Kinsella, S., Wang, M., Breslin, John G., Hayes, C.: Improving categorisation in social media using hyperlinks to structured data sources. In: Antoniou, G., et al. (eds.) ESWC 2011. LNCS, vol. 6644, pp. 390–404. Springer, Heidelberg (2011). https://doi.org/10.1007/978-3-642-21064-8_27
13. The Media Insight Project. 'Who shared it?' How Americans decide what news to trust on social media, 12 June 2017. http://mediainsight.org/Pages/%27Who-Shared-It%27-How-Americans-Decide-What-News-to-Trust-on-Social-Media.aspx
14. Viviani, M., Pasi, G.: Credibility in social media: opinions, news, and health information—a survey. Wiley Interdisc. Rev. Data Mining Knowl. Discov. **7**(5), e1209 (2013)
15. Munson, S.A., Cavusoglu, H., Frisch, L., Fels, S.: Sociotechnical challenges and progress in using social media for health. J. Med. Internet Res. **15**(10), e226 (2013)
16. Gupta, A., Kumaraguru, P.: Credibility ranking of tweets during high impact events. In: Proceedings of the 1st Workshop on Privacy and Security in Online Social Media. ACM (2012)

17. Mendoza, M., Poblete, B., Castillo, C.: Twitter under crisis: can we trust what we RT? In: Proceedings of the First Workshop on Social Media Analytics. ACM (2010)
18. Gupta, A., Kumaraguru, P.: Twitter explodes with activity in mumbai blasts! A lifeline or an unmonitored daemon in the lurking? Technical report, IIITD-TR-2011-005, Delhi (2011)
19. Morris, M.R., Counts, S., Roseway, A., Hoff, A., Schwarz, J.: Tweeting is believing? Understanding microblog credibility perceptions. In: Proceedings of the ACM 2012 Conference on Computer Supported Cooperative Work. ACM (2012)
20. Addawood, A., Rezapour, R., Mishra, S., Schneider, J., Diesner, J.: Developing an information source lexicon (2017)
21. Rao, A., Spasojevic, N., Li, Z., DSouza, T.: Klout score: measuring influence across multiple social networks. In: 2015 IEEE International Conference on Proceedings of the Big Data (Big Data). IEEE (2015)
22. Krauss, M.J., et al.: Hookah-related Twitter chatter: a content analysis. Preventing chronic Dis. **12**, E121 (2015)
23. Liu, Y.: Mining social media to understand consumers' health concerns and the public's opinion on controversial health topics (2016)

Twitter Activity at Recent LIS Academic Conferences

Dan Albertson[✉]

University at Buffalo, The State University of New York, Buffalo, USA
dalbert@buffalo.edu

Abstract. The present paper reports on different Twitter activities throughout several library and information science (LIS) focused research conferences which took place over the summer of 2018. Current findings show levels of activity and engagement, both overall and at different time-points throughout the conferences. The study provides descriptive findings about Twitter use and ways in which researchers can analyze social media activities as measures of scholarly communication at academic conferences. Opportunities remain for future in-depth studies of social media and its broader implications for scholarly communications from academic conferences.

Keywords: Twitter · Social media · Scholarly communication · Academic conferences

1 Introduction and Background

Social media has been the subject of many different studies on scholarly communication. Previous studies have examined and reported on social media as a type of technology, as a data or information source, ethical and/or policy considerations, its users and uses, and of course its role and impact on alternative metrics (i.e. "altmetrics") [1, 2].

Academic conferences together with social media have also been the subject of recent of research [3]. Microblogging sites, particularly Twitter, are used as channels of (almost) real-time discussions and deliberations taking place at academic conferences. Many conferences these days delegate a standardized hashtag so that posts (e.g. Tweets) can be aggregated into conversations centered around the conference and its content and activities. These online conversations are forms of scholarly communication, and prior research on social media use during academic conferences has been examined across diverse domains and disciplines, such as education, cardiology, urology, and others [4–7]. The unique role that social media plays in academic conferences makes for an important context for better understanding the communications of scholars.

© Springer Nature Switzerland AG 2019
N. G. Taylor et al. (Eds.): iConference 2019, LNCS 11420, pp. 647–653, 2019.
https://doi.org/10.1007/978-3-030-15742-5_61

2 Research Objectives

The primary research objective of the present study is to report on social media use and activity from recent LIS research-oriented conferences. Secondly, the present study also provides a set of descriptive measures for analyzing social media activity at future academic conferences as part of broader more in-depth studies.

Academic conferences are meaningful venues, many times with highly-regarded reputations for disseminating quality research. Many conferences publish full-length research papers, comparable with that of articles of high-ranking journals, with quick turn-around. Beyond the official published proceedings, there are other forms of scholarly discourse happening onsite, which – traditionally – could only be captured and engaged in by attendees [2]. Since its adoption into academic conferences, social media has been used to disseminate content to both conference participants and followers online, and to facilitate conversations. As a result, social media use throughout academic conferences warrants further research.

Twitter is the social media tool used for the present study. Twitter is widely used by conference attendees and other participants for posting (Tweeting) about what's happening onsite at academic conferences (e.g. talks) or different perspectives thereof. Like other forms of social media, Twitter makes use of hashtags, allowing users to aggregate and follow conversations around specific topics, events, or other keyword.

3 Data Collection

Tweets (and corresponding metadata) from different academic conferences, including those occurring before, during, and after the conferences, were collected. Three LIS academic conferences, each held in the summer of 2018, were included in the study. These conferences were *The ACM/IEEE Joint Conference on Digital Libraries* (JCDL), *The Annual Conference of the Canadian Association for Information Science* (CAIS), and *Libraries in the Digital Age* (LIDA). The conferences ranged from small meetings (e.g. CAIS was under 40 participants) to medium-sized conferences (i.e. LIDA was reported at 165 registered attendees and JCDL was not reported). Twitter data were combined across these different conferences in accordance with the central goal of the study: to get an understanding of the Twitter activity occurring at LIS academic conferences. Here, findings can depict scholarly communication centered around a particular type of event, within a highly condensed timeframe. Aggregating data across multiple conferences is appropriate as the data (i.e. Twitter actions of users) are standard and the conferences themselves are fairly consistent in terms of their structures. It is important to note that larger conferences can be analyzed separately in future studies as the measures and indicators used here were shown to be useful and reliable.

Data from Twitter conversations from these particular conferences were collected and analyzed. Twitter4J API was used to build the application for collecting Twitter data based on the conference hashtag (e.g. "#JCDL18"). These Twitter data were analyzed in ways to achieve the research objectives provided above.

4   Analysis

Data elements within Tweets were used to form different variables for analysis. Definitions of the primary variables as examined in the study include:

- *Original Tweet:* Non-Retweet (RT), an original post/Tweet by a user.
- *Retweet (RT):* A RT of a Tweet, identified as "true" within the RT data element.
- *Original Tweet and Retweet (combined):* Sum of Tweet and RT counts.
- *Like:* A count of Likes of Original Tweets.
- *Secondary Action:* Sum of Likes and RT counts.
- *Tweet Retweeted:* A count of Original Tweets that were Retweeted.
- *Overall Actions:* Sum of Original Tweets, RTs, and Like counts.
- *Unique Users:* A distinct user (ID), whether of Original Tweets or RTs (users of Likes are not accessible through the Twitter4J API).

Analysis of these variables included counts overall, by comparison across different time-points or days within the conference (from pre- to post-conference), and according to the number of unique users participating in the Twitter conversations. Results were also examined by percentage of overall observed Twitter actions.

5   Results

Twitter data from all three academic conferences were included in the analysis. Overall counts are first presented in Figs. 1 and 2. In sum, 5,504 actions of users were collected and analyzed, and 364 unique users were identified in the data. The overall counts are broken down into specific types of Twitter actions and users.

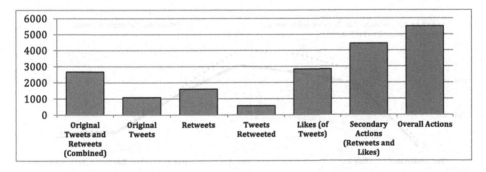

Fig. 1. Counts for different types of Twitter actions.

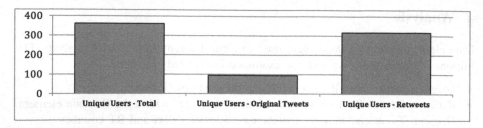

Fig. 2. User counts, both overall and for different Twitter actions.

Next, these variables were analyzed across different time-points within the conferences, spanning from pre- to post-conference; see Figs. 3 and 4.

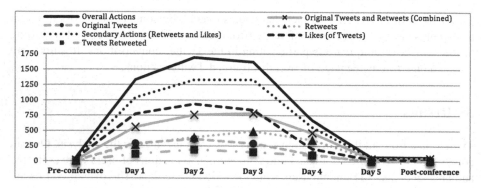

Fig. 3. Counts of different Twitter actions by day of conference.

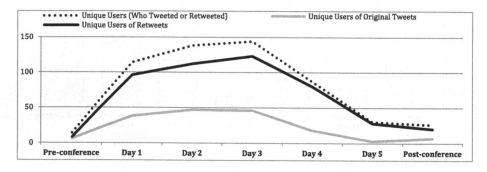

Fig. 4. User counts by day of conference.

Figure 5 presents the ratio of these particular variables (i.e. types of Twitter actions) according to the number of unique users. Figure 6 shows the same analysis, yet at different time-points of the conferences. These findings provide the average number of actions as performed for each user contributing to the Twitter conversations, both overall and by day.

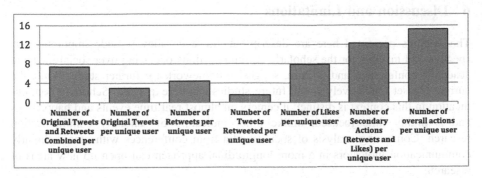

Fig. 5. Average Twitter actions per unique user.

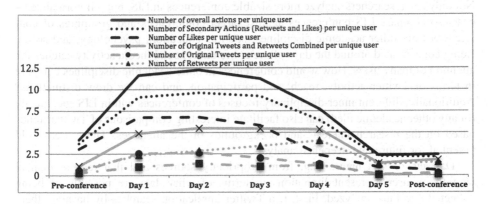

Fig. 6. Average Twitter actions per unique user by day of conference.

Finally, Fig. 7 shows the percentage for each type of action proportionally to the overall number of actions both in total and at different time-points of the conferences.

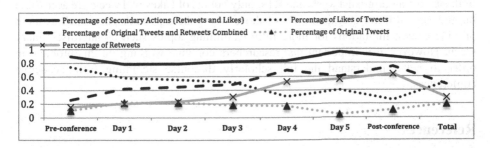

Fig. 7. The percentage for by each type of Twitter action including by day and overall.

6 Discussion and Limitations

The findings presented here are descriptive, however, they provide important per-spective and insights for the scholarly communications occurring over social media at academic conferences and, in turn, suggest a framework for further study. While the current dataset is relatively small, future studies can be expanded. Scholarly commu-nication in this context is distinct; it centers on almost real-time events and happenings and is highly time focused, unlike other indicators of scholarly communication research. Combining analysis of social media from conferences with other scholarly communication indicators in a more longitudinal approach can open up new areas of research.

Another research area moving forward is how can social media data from academic conferences be an indicator of the reach of the conference and perhaps the larger field? Not only can researchers analyze more sizable conferences in LIS, but – if normalized – can also compare LIS conferences against larger conferences and groupings of con-ferences from other academic disciplines, such as education, psychology, and so on. Being concentrated around the days of the conference, social media activity catches the attention of many users. How would conferences in other academic disciplines compare in terms of Twitter activity, reach, and participation, and can we draw distinctions? Additionally, different inner-disciplinary focuses of conferences within LIS specifically (or any other academic filed) can also facilitate interesting comparisons of Twitter trends based on the research interests and backgrounds of the attendees. These areas hold potential for future and deepened analysis.

Datasets of this nature (e.g. from proprietary sources and that require manual tagging by users) present limitations in terms of what data are possible of being collected and thus analyzed. First, if a Twitter application searches by hashtag, there may be original Tweets or RTs from conference attendees and/or other participants in the conversations that may be missed if not manually included. Secondly, the Twit-ter4J API and other Twitter APIs limit the number of Tweets and the metadata that can be downloaded via the applications. For example, Tweet downloads are capped both in 15 min intervals (max of 100 per) and are only accessible through applications within a seven-day window. Additionally, while applications can retrieve user IDs and handles of those posting original Tweets and RTs, only counts of Likes of Tweets are accessible through the API, not usernames/IDs of those who Like a post. Aspects such as these provide certain limitations for more fully examining topics such as interdisciplinary reach. However, it is important that researchers continue working on this problem in order to better understand the full scholarly discourse stemming from academic conferences.

References

1. Sugimoto, C.R., Work, S., Larivière, V., Haustein, S.: Scholarly use of social media and altmetrics: a review of the literature. J. Assoc. Inf. Sci. Technol. **68**(9), 2037–2062 (2017)
2. Orizaola, G., Valdés, A.E.: Free the tweet at scientific conferences. Science **350**(6257), 170–171 (2015)

3. Reinhardt, W., Ebner, M., Günter, B., Costa, C.: How people are using Twitter during conferences. In: Hornung-Prähauser, V., Luckmann, M. (eds.) Creativity and Innovation Competencies on the Web, Proceeding of 5. EduMedia Conference, pp. 145–156 (2009)
4. Chung, A., Woo, H.: Twitter in surgical conferences. ANZ J. Surg. **86**(4), 224–227 (2016)
5. Ferguson, C., Inglis, S.C., Newton, P.J., Cripps, P.J., Macdonald, P.S., Davidson, P.M.: Social media: a tool to spread information: a case study analysis of twitter conversation at the Cardiac Society of Australia & New Zealand 61st annual scientific meeting 2013. Collegian **21**(2), 89–93 (2014)
6. Holmberg, K., Thelwall, M.: Disciplinary differences in Twitter scholarly communication. Scientometrics **101**(2), 1027–1042 (2014)
7. Kimmons, R., Veletsianos, G.: Education scholars' evolving uses of twitter as a conference backchannel and social commentary platform. Br. J. Educ. Technol. **47**(3), 445–464 (2016)

Understanding Online Trust and Information Behavior Using Demographics and Human Values

Nitin Verma[(✉)], Kenneth R. Fleischmann, and Kolina S. Koltai

School of Information, The University of Texas at Austin, Austin, TX, USA
{nitin.verma,koltai}@utexas.edu,
kfleisch@ischool.utexas.edu

Abstract. In the aftermath of the 2016 U.S. Presidential Election, the role of social media in influencing the dissemination of information is a timely and critical issue. To understand how social media-based information, misinformation, and disinformation work in practice, it is critical to identify factors that can predict social media users' online information behavior. To this end, we designed an experiment to study the influence of the independent variables, demographics, and human values, on the dependent variables, social media users' observed trust behavior, self-reported trust behavior, and information behavior. We report the statistically significant results of these comparisons; for example, we found that liberals were more likely to trust mainstream media ($p < 0.05$) and scientific journals ($p < 0.05$) and to state that the content of the linked pages influenced their trust ($p < 0.01$) than moderates; for values, we found that participants who more highly valued security were more likely to trust mainstream media articles ($p < 0.05$), to notice the presence or absence of hyperlinks, and to click on fake news articles ($p < 0.05$). Ultimately, both demographics and values can be used to predict online trust and information behavior; while demographics are commonly captured or predicted in online marketing, values represent a much less tapped opportunity to predict social media users' online trust and information behavior.

Keywords: Online trust · Demographics · Human values · Information behavior

1 Introduction

What factors can be used to predict online trust and information behavior? Information shared via social media can influence decisions ranging from choosing which candidate to vote for, to which food truck serves the best breakfast tacos, to whether or not to vaccinate one's children. This paper explores the potential impact of demographics and human values on online trust and information behavior. Specifically, we look at demographic categories such as gender, age, educational attainment, political leaning, and social media use. According to Friedman, Kahn, and Borning [1], "A value refers to what a person or group of people consider important in life" (p. 2). This paper operationalizes values at the middle level of Schwartz's [2] four-level value inventory,

© Springer Nature Switzerland AG 2019
N. G. Taylor et al. (Eds.): iConference 2019, LNCS 11420, pp. 654–665, 2019.
https://doi.org/10.1007/978-3-030-15742-5_62

including the following ten values: achievement, benevolence, conformity, hedonism, power, security, self-direction, stimulation, tradition, and universalism. This paper focuses on users' clicking on hyperlinks as a specific type of information behavior.

This paper begins with a background focusing on prior research on the impact of demographics and human values on online trust and information behavior. The section after that describes how we collected and analyzed our data. The following section reports the results from the study. After that, we discuss the implications of our findings. Finally, we conclude by suggesting some future directions for research.

2 Background

The majority of Americans report getting at least some of their news on social media [3]. This is alarming due to the rise of 'fake news' stories being spread on social media platforms [4] by both social bots [5] and humans [6]. Coupled with the steady decline of trust in public trust towards mainstream media [7], understanding how people trust news sources online becomes critical. The difficulty of assessing online news sources is present across topics, including politics [4, 8], health [9], and science [10]. Since the general public and scientists' view on science topics can have great variance [11] and science-related content on social media is highly popular [12], there is a need to focus on understanding social media users' trust in science-related content online. Fleck [13] argued that scientific fact is invented and not discovered. This humanistic perspective on what we know to be scientifically true could also explain the persistence of fake news, particularly in science. However, Berghel [14] argues that the lack of emphasis on critical analysis in our educational system ill-equips the general population to make informed judgments about what to trust. This raises the question about how the public assesses trustworthiness of scientific news online, and whether demographic factors (e.g., education, age, gender) or values (e.g., what we hold to be important) influence how people trust science-related content on social media platforms.

The goal of this paper is to dig deeper into the role of demographic factors (e.g., gender, age, education attainment, political leaning, and frequency of social media use) and human values in influencing trust in different sources of online science news, including fake news, mainstream media, and scientific journals. We selected these factors as our focus due to their emergent importance in the research on trust in online news sources. This paper reports results from a larger study on factors that influence trust. A previous study on trust and social media and demographics found some significant relationships between age, gender, social media use and different concepts of trust, but they had a predominantly young participant sample and relied solely on a survey [15]. The findings of our study shed new light on these factors using an experimental design which allows us to measure trust more directly and specifically on real news items instead of concepts of trust.

There has been prior work that suggests that there is a relationship between gender and trust in online content. For example, Warner-Søderholm et al.'s [15] study on trust and social media found a significant relationship between gender and trust values: women had statistically higher scores on the trust values of "integrity" and "identification." This could lend support to an earlier study that focused on how Chinese students assessed Wikipedia pages. That study found that women relied significantly more on validity when assessing trust whereas men focused more on accuracy and stability [16]. A study focused on how journalists source and trust information found that men had higher levels of trust in online news sources compared to women [17]. However, there is work that suggests there are no differences across gender [18]. Overall, findings regarding the effect of gender on trust in online news sources seem to be inconclusive, leaving room for further research.

The trope of the young outperforming the old in new technology is present in online news media research: age is a commonly discussed demographic factor in discussing trust in online news sources. While there is often higher use of online news sources among younger adults, there has been a substantial increase in older adults using the Internet and social media [3, 19, 20]. However, research seems to be mixed in regard to trust in online content. The 2017 Gallup/Knight Foundation Survey found that younger adults were more likely to have an unfavorable opinion of online news media compared to older adults [19]. This seems to suggest that young adults would be less trusting of online news media, however, several other studies seem to contradict this. In a study focusing on journalists' trust of online content and in a study on privacy and trust on Facebook, young adults had higher trust levels in online content from social media [17, 18]. However, there are studies to suggest that trust could be low among both older and younger adults [21]. In general, findings regarding age and trust online also seem inconclusive, again demonstrating the need for further research.

Prior work on educational attainment also has had mixed results. Data from the Gallup/Knight Foundation survey supports the idea that those with higher education have higher trust in news media, other studies found that educational attainment did not impact interaction in online news [19, 22]. While these two studies are not identical to each other, there is a need to further explore the relationship between educational attainment and trust in online news sources.

Previous work indicated that political leaning certainly influences how people trust online news media. Liberals, overall, tend to have higher trust in the media, compared to conservatives [19]. Gallup's data is supported by [23] study on news sources that found that liberals trusted a larger number of news sources compared to conservatives. Pew Research Center [24] also found that this trend continued to be true with liberals having higher trust in mainstream scientific outlets compared to conservatives. While literature does tend to provide a cohesive image, it is important to explore deeper into the role of political leaning.

Previous research also argues that the more people watch TV and read newspapers, the more likely they are to trust the media [25]. This trend seems to be consistent for social media outlets. With the majority of Americans getting some news from social media, frequency of social media use emerges as an important trust factor. An important distinction in measuring social media use is the difference between online skills (e.g., how familiar people are with using social media platforms) and the frequency of use of online news media (e.g., how often do they use it). There has been previous work that suggests that those who self-report a high skill level in using social media use social media outlets more frequently than those do have lower skills [26]. In this study, self-reported online skills were the main predictor of frequency of use of online news media, more so than gender, age, or amount of time the participant had been using online news media. This finding is supported by a study that found that those who had high knowledge of social media also had higher trust in it [17]. Interestingly, another study from Israel found that those who were less experienced online became more skeptical as they were exposed to more online news sources [27]. And in a recent cross-national study involving 44 countries, researchers found that people using the Internet to find political information had lower trust in the media over those who did not use the Internet to search for political information [28]. With the rise of social media being a dominant platform to get news, there is a need for further research into this factor.

With the rise in the polarization of politics and science, human values naturally enter the conversation. Martin [29] argues that opposing sides nearly always involve values as these topics often focus on topics of human life, economics, and other passionate topics. Values often play an important role in people's behavior, attitudes, and sentiment [30] and can have a strong relationship with the development of opinions about polarizing topics [31, 32]. Price [33] argues, since it is impossible for us to be completely informed on a topic, we rely on our values, schemas, and group identifications to guide our attitudes and opinions on topics. Therefore, human values are arguably an important area to focus on to understand trust in online news media.

The goal of this study is to explore the impact of demographics and human values on online trust and information behavior. Specifically, this study sets out to answer the following three main research questions. First, do demographics and human values influence observed trust behavior? Second, do demographics and human values influence self-reported trust behavior? Third, do demographics and human values influence information behavior? We answer these questions using an experimental design that models how Twitter users review their timelines.

3 Methods

3.1 Study Design

We developed our scientific claims corpus by browsing two notorious fake news sites, InfoWars and Natural News [34]. We browsed articles in the "Science" section of Natural News and the "Science & Tech" section of InfoWars and hunted for links to open-access articles published in reputable scientific journals. For fake news articles that linked to an open-access scientific article, we then used Google News to search for open-access mainstream news articles that also discussed the same scientific claim and directly hyperlinked to the same scientific article. Our criteria for inclusion of a scientific claim were as follows: (1) the scientific article was publicly available; (2) a mainstream media news source directly linked to the scientific article; and (3) a fake media news source directly linked to the scientific article. To label the claim, the authors independently attempted to create a generic claim that corresponded with the titles and contents of all three articles, and then decided on the most neutral label. Thus, our corpus of scientific claims included a generic scientific claim, a "Scientific Journal" article from which the claim originated, a "Mainstream Media" article that covered the claim, and a "Fake News" article that provided a different perspective on the claim. It is important to note that this is an inherently biased sample of articles from InfoWars and

Natural News, as many of the articles within the sites as a whole are not based on credible information. However, despite linking back to the open-access scientific article, the fake news articles tended toward a significant degree of sensationalization, with the mainstream media articles demonstrating arguably a somewhat lesser degree of sensationalization. Thus, for example, one of the scientific articles in the corpus, from Proceedings of the National Academy of Sciences (PNAS), was entitled, "Bottlenose dolphins can use learned vocal labels to address each other," the corresponding mainstream media article from the Los Angeles Times was entitled, "Dolphins use signature whistles to call each other by 'name,'" and the corresponding fake news article from Natural News was entitled, "Animal intelligence now irrefutable: Bottlenose dolphins call each other by name." Here, the PNAS article uses the far more qualified phrase "learned vocal labels" while the article in the LA Times uses 'name' within scare quotes, and Natural News abandons the scare quotes and takes the finding to a somewhat more extreme level. Using this method, we were able to identify ten triads of mainstream media and fake news articles referencing the same scientific journal article.

Our instrument emulated Twitter's timeline interface to approximate a modern online social media-based news feed. Each "post" in the mock timeline began with one of the ten scientific claims from our corpus. Two of these posts belonged to the "No Hyperlink" condition, and thus contained only the scientific claim with no hyperlink. The other eight posts included two with the corresponding "Fake News" hyperlink, two with the "Mainstream Media" hyperlink, two with the "Scientific Journal" hyperlink, and two with a "Hidden Hyperlink" (a shortened, obscured, version of the URL ultimately leading to the scientific journal article for the claim). Thus, there were a total of five conditions: "No Hyperlink (NH)," "Fake News (FN)," "Mainstream Media (MM)," "Scientific Journal (SJ)," and "Hidden Hyperlink (HH)." Thus, each participant was presented with a timeline featuring the same 10 claims but in a randomized sequence such that each of the five hyperlink types was represented twice in a given timeline.

We packaged the mock Twitter feed into Human Intelligence Tasks, or HITs, to be completed by "workers" on Amazon's Mechanical Turk platform ("MTurk"). We chose MTurk based on a body of literature suggesting that MTurk offers higher accuracy of results, and greater demographic diversity in the participant pool than other commonly used samples such as college students or other Internet-based survey tools [35–37]. MTurk also afforded us with a pool of participants who presumably had at least basic computer literacy and were, therefore, likely to be familiar with the idea of obtaining news and other information from the Internet.

Each HIT consisted of the following: an informed consent screen; a gender-neutral version of the 21-item Portrait Values Questionnaire (PVQ) designed by Schwartz [38, 39] to measure the 10 human values as described in the Schwartz [2] Value Inventory (SVI); the mock Twitter timeline; a repeat of the same mock timeline but with a five-point Likert-type trust rating scale (ranging from "Don't Trust At All" to "Trust Completely") alongside each post; a 10-item questionnaire that presented 10 first-person assertions (eight unique assertions, one repeated assertion, and one to test workers' attentiveness to the instrument) about workers' perusal of information presented in the timeline; an open-ended question asking workers to describe how they arrived at their trust judgments; and a demographic questionnaire. In the 10-item questionnaire (see Table 1) we asked workers to indicate their level of agreement with each assertion on a five-point Likert-type scale ("Completely Disagree" to "Agree Completely") to enable them to self-report their trust behavior. In the demographic questionnaire we asked workers to self-report their age, gender ("female", "male", and "other" with an option to specify their gender identity), political leaning & affiliation, number of years spent living in the US, and how frequently they used online social media along with names of the top three social networking platforms they used most frequently.

Table 1. Questionnaire items

Serial No.	Item Prompt
1	I noticed the presence or absence of links
2	The text portion of the post influenced my trust in the post
3	Seeing a link made me want to click on it
4	The text portion of the post influenced my decision of whether or not to click the link
5	The URL of the link influenced my trust in the post
6	The URL of the link influenced my decision to click on the link
7	I carefully reviewed the linked articles
8	The content of the linked page influenced my trust in the post

We collected data in two batches by requesting a batch of 100 HITs to be completed in April 2017, and a second batch of 150 HITs six weeks later in June 2017. HITs in the second batch contained two additional, open-ended questions at the end of the HIT asking workers for feedback and suggestions for improving any future versions of the study.

3.2 Data Analysis

We used nonparametric statistical methods; specifically, Mann-Whitney U to compare two independent samples [40] and Kruskal-Wallis H test to compare more than two independent samples [41]. Our choice for using these methods was driven by the fact that they minimize the number of assumptions one has to make about a given data distribution, while not increasing the likelihood of Type I errors or decreasing the power of the analysis [42]. To further decrease the likelihood of Type I errors based on computing multiple comparisons, we used the Holm-Bonferroni method to control the family-wise error rate [43]. To derive a combined trust rating for each post type per participant, we computed the mean of the two trust ratings they gave for the two posts they saw and rated per post type.

Across both phases of data collection, we eliminated 45 responses on account of non-completion of the HIT, incorrect answer to the attentiveness item in the questionnaire, and inconsistent responses (separated by a distance of more than one on the five-point scale) to the two repeated items in the questionnaire. This resulted in a final sample of 205 participants.

To simplify the analysis of demographic factors, we redefined the categories or levels within each factor to ensure all levels had relatively comparable numbers of individuals. For gender, the two most frequent responses were male ($n = 116$) and female ($n = 88$). To ensure the reliability of our analysis we dropped the data for the only participant who chose "other" as their gender identity. We categorized age data into three age categories: 18–29 years ($n = 74$), 30–39 years ($n = 77$), and ≥ 40 years ($n = 54$). We partitioned the educational attainment data into two categories: "Less than College" (those who chose either of "High School or Less", or "Some College"; $n = 106$), and "College or Higher" (those who chose either of "College Graduate" or "Graduate Degree"; $n = 99$). For political leaning, participants reported their leaning on a five-point scale extending from "Conservative" to "Liberal". We categorized those who chose the middle value on the scale as Moderates ($n = 54$), those who chose one of the two options on the conservative side of the scale as Conservatives ($n = 51$), and the rest as Liberals ($n = 100$). Finally, for social media use frequency, we created two categories: Light users (those who selected either of "Less Than Once a Week", "Once a Week", "Multiple Times a Week", or "Once a Day"; $n = 87$), and Heavy users (those who selected "Multiple Times a Day"; $n = 114$).

4   Results

4.1   Observed Trust Behavior

Demographics. This is the one comparison that has been previously reported [44]. Among the five demographic categories that we included in the study, only political leaning and social media use frequency revealed significant correlations with trust ratings. For political leaning, Kruskal-Wallis H tests showed significant differences in average trust rating for FN ($p < 0.05$), MM ($p < 0.05$), and SJ ($p < 0.001$) posts across conservatives, moderates, and liberals. Post-hoc pairwise Mann-Whitney U tests (with Holm-Bonferroni correction) revealed that, as compared to moderates, conservatives gave significantly higher trust ratings to FN posts ($p < 0.05$), and liberals gave significantly higher trust ratings to MM and SJ posts than moderates ($p < 0.05$). Liberals also gave significantly higher trust ratings to SJ posts when compared to conservatives ($p < 0.01$). Looking at social media use frequency, Mann-Whitney U tests showed that heavy social media users gave significantly lower trust ratings to FN posts than light users ($p < 0.05$).

Values. Mann-Whitney U tests showed that people with high achievement displayed lower trust towards MM posts ($p < 0.05$) than people with low achievement. Compared to people with low universalism, those with high universalism showed higher trust in SJ posts ($p < 0.01$). Those with high security displayed higher trust for MM posts ($p < 0.05$).

4.2 Self-reported Trust Behavior

Demographics. Among all demographic factors, only political leaning appeared to have any significant relationship with responses to the questionnaire on self-reported trust behavior. A Kruskal-Wallis H test revealed that liberals, moderates, and conservatives gave significantly different responses to item 8 on the questionnaire ("The content of the linked page influenced my trust in the post."; $p < 0.01$). Post-hoc pairwise Mann-Whitney U tests (with Holm-Bonferroni correction) showed that liberals showed a significantly higher degree of agreement with the assertion in item 8 than moderates ($p < 0.01$).

Values. We found that those who had high self-direction tended to agree with item 1 ("I noticed the presence or absence of links") and item 4 ("The text portion of the post influenced my decision of whether or not to click the link"; both $p < 0.05$); and those who had high universalism tended to agree to item 1 ($p < 0.01$), item 5 ("The URL of the link influenced my trust in the post"; $p < 0.05$), and item 8 ("The content of the linked page influenced my trust in the post"; $p < 0.05$). Similarly, high security was also correlated with high agreement ($p < 0.05$) with item 1; high stimulation was correlated with high agreement to item 2 ("The text portion of the post influenced my trust in the post"; $p < 0.01$); and high benevolence was correlated with high agreement with item 7 ("I carefully reviewed the linked articles"; $p < 0.01$).

4.3 Information Behavior

Demographics. Out of gender, age, educational attainment, political leaning, and social media use frequency, only age seems to have an impact on clicking behavior. A Kruskal-Wallis H test revealed a significant relationship between clicking behavior and age category ($p < 0.01$). Mann-Whitney U tests showed that people in the ≥ 40 year age category clicked on more hyperlinks ($p < 0.01$) than those in the 18–29 year category.

Looking at the number of hyperlinks clicked per post type, Kruskal-Wallis H tests revealed a significant relationship between click count and age category for FN ($p < 0.01$), MM ($p < 0.05$), and SJ ($p < 0.01$) posts. Mann-Whitney U tests (with Holm-Bonferroni correction) showed that for FN, MM, and SJ posts the ≥ 40 years age category displayed significantly higher ($p < 0.05$) number of clicks than the 18–29 years category. For SJ posts, however, the 30–39 year category also showed significantly higher number of clicks than the 18–29 year category ($p < 0.05$).

Values. When we compared clicking behavior of the high and low value priority groups for each of the 10 values using Mann-Whitney U tests we found that only hedonism had a significant ($p < 0.001$) relationship with the total number of clicks: high hedonism was associated with a significantly lower total number of clicks than low hedonism.

Looking at the number of hyperlinks clicked per post type, we found that for HH posts high achievement is associated with a lower number of clicks ($p < 0.05$) than low achievement, and high self-direction is associated with a higher number of clicks ($p < 0.05$) than low self-direction. For FN posts, highly valuing security is associated with a higher number of clicks on FN hyperlinks ($p < 0.05$). High hedonism is associated with significantly lower number of clicks for each of FN ($p < 0.01$), MM ($p < 0.001$), and SJ ($p < 0.01$) post types.

5 Discussion

Our results suggest that the demographic categories of political leaning and social media use frequency bear potential to explain people's trust behavior in relation to science news shared via social media. What is particularly noteworthy is that the influence of political leaning in shaping observed trust behavior is matched by people's self-reported trust behavior. For instance, liberals not only gave higher trust ratings to mainstream media and scientific journal posts than moderates, but also reported a significantly higher degree of agreement with the assertion "The content of the linked page influenced my trust in the post" than moderates. The emergence of political leaning as a common thread in observed and self-reported trust behaviors is in line with the trends reported by the Gallup/Knight Foundation survey [19], and the Pew Research Center [24]. Our experiment therefore helps strengthen the case for further investigation into political leaning as a predictor or moderator of trust in online news about science.

We also observed that people's trust behavior is influenced by their values: achievement and security seem to impact trust in mainstream media reporting of science news, whereas universalism seems to be directly related to trust in scientific journals as primary sources of science news. When it comes to users' self-reporting of factors they believe influence their trust behavior, we found that people with high universalism were more likely to notice the presence of hyperlinks in social media posts, and their trust judgments were more likely to be influenced by the URL and content of the linked pages.

Our findings also shed light on the potential role values play in shaping people's interaction with hyperlinks (and potentially other features of online information interfaces) on social media posts. The observed association between values such as hedonism, achievement, self-direction, and security with the number of times people clicked on hyperlinks helps add nuance to understanding the role of values in studying information behavior in general. It further underscores the importance of considering these core human characteristics both in the study and design of information systems.

The role played by values in turn may help shed light on the underpinnings of political leaning and its influence on trust behavior. Since values help shape people's beliefs, attitudes, and sentiments [30], it is plausible that values also contribute in shaping people's political leaning.

As with all studies, there are some limitations to the experimental design here. First, the data does not allow us to objectively separate the effects of the claim and the hyperlink on trust and clicking behavior. We do have self-report data along these lines, but asking people to assess the factors that influenced their decisions is much more subjective than observing would be. Second, we do not know if participants actually reviewed the contents of linked web pages after clicking. We know which users clicked on hyperlinks, but not whether or not they actually reviewed the linked site, and which aspects of the linked site they skimmed or read. Finally, based on this data it is challenging to determine if there are any cognitive 'footprints' that characterize trust formation and clicking behavior. Such analysis would best be performed in a usability laboratory.

6 Future Research Directions

As outlined by our findings above, we feel encouraged about the potential of human values, political leaning, age, and frequency of social media use to serve as reliable predictors of people's information behavior online. The overarching question that will guide our future efforts is: how do people experience social media news feeds? Measuring their experience will enable us to understand how that experience shapes their trust judgments and information behavior vis-a-vis fake news.

One way to address the limitations described above would be to measure participants' physiological responses to stimuli typically experienced when consuming information on social media. Employing eye tracking to collect data on participants' visual fixations, saccades, and scanpaths can determine any correlations between their cognitive activity and trust judgment behavior. Fixation data would help to determine on which parts of the posts, or the timeline, participants were focusing. Saccades (the rapid movements between fixations) and scanpaths (a visual map of the fixations and saccades) allow for visualization of how participants brain scan the visual stimuli present in a (mock) social media feed as well as in actual websites. Eye trackers also record data on pupil size, which is a reasonably direct indicator of the cognitive effort exerted by the brain. In addition to eye tracking, facial recognition software can be used to record the movements of facial muscles to determine emotions displayed by participants as they interact with different stimuli.

Another refinement would be to use the Retrospective Verbal Protocol [45] to ask participants about the factors they believe influenced their trust judgments in a post-experience interview in which we will also ask them about factors that influence their trust in websites and social media posts in general.

Based on the questions raised by our current analyses, as well as the added capabilities provided by a usability lab environment, we propose the following preliminary hypotheses that could be tested in a usability lab context:

1. Long fixations on the hyperlink followed by a decision not to click on the hyperlink will be negatively associated with trust.
2. Participants who have negative facial expressions when fixating on a hyperlink, whether or not they click on the hyperlink, will have lower trust.
3. The explicit requirement to provide a trust rating will be associated with higher cognitive load than when just looking at the post.
4. Clicking on a hyperlink has a direct relationship with cognitive load (i.e., clicking is associated with high cognitive load, and not clicking is associated with low cognitive load).

References

1. Friedman, B., Kahn, P.H., Borning, A., Huldtgren, A.: Value sensitive design and information systems. In: Doorn, N., Schuurbiers, D., van de Poel, I., Gorman, Michael E. (eds.) Early engagement and new technologies: Opening up the laboratory. PET, vol. 16, pp. 55–95. Springer, Dordrecht (2013). https://doi.org/10.1007/978-94-007-7844-3_4
2. Schwartz, S.H.: Are there universal aspects in the structure and contents of human values? J. Soc. Issues **50**, 19–45 (1994)
3. Shearer, E., Gottfried, J.: News Use Across Social Media Platforms 2017 (2017). http://www.journalism.org/2017/09/07/news-use-across-social-media-platforms-2017/
4. Silverman, C.: This Analysis Shows How Viral Fake Election News Stories Outperformed Real News On Facebook. https://www.buzzfeed.com/craigsilverman/viral-fake-election-news-outperformed-real-news-on-facebook
5. Shao, C., Ciampaglia, G.L., Varol, O., Flammini, A., Menczer, F.: The spread of fake news by social bots. ArXiv170707592 Phys. (2017)
6. Vosoughi, S., Roy, D., Aral, S.: The spread of true and false news online. Science **359**, 1146–1151 (2018)
7. Smith, T.W., Son, J.: Trends in Public Attitudes About Confidence in Institutions. Chicago, NORC (2013)
8. Allcott, H., Gentzkow, M.: Social media and fake news in the 2016 election. J. Econ. Perspect. **31**, 211–235 (2017)
9. Broniatowski, D.A., et al.: Weaponized health communication: twitter bots and Russian trolls amplify the vaccine debate. Am. J. Public Health **108**(10), 1378–1384 (2018)
10. Verma, N., Fleischmann, K.R., Koltai, K.S.: Human values and trust in scientific journals, the mainstream media and fake news. Proc. Assoc. Inf. Sci. Technol. **54**, 426–435 (2017)
11. Funk, C., Rainie, L.: Public and Scientists' Views on Science and Society (2015). http://www.pewinternet.org/2015/01/29/public-and-scientists-views-on-science-and-society/
12. Hitlin, P., Olmstead, K.: The Science People See on Social Media (2018). http://www.pewinternet.org/2018/03/21/the-science-people-see-on-social-media/
13. Fleck, L.: Genesis and Development of a Scientific Fact (1935)
14. Berghel, H.: Lies, damn lies, and fake news. Computer **50**, 80–85 (2017)
15. Warner-Søderholm, G., et al.: Who trusts social media? Comput. Hum. Behav. **81**, 303–315 (2018)
16. Huang, J., Shi, S., Chen, Y., Chow, W.S.: How do students trust Wikipedia? An examination across genders. Inf. Technol. People. **29**, 750–773 (2016)
17. Heravi, B.R., Harrower, N.: Twitter journalism in Ireland: sourcing and trust in the age of social media. Inf. Commun. Soc. **19**, 1194–1213 (2016)
18. Malik, A., Hiekkanen, K., Nieminen, M.: Privacy and trust in Facebook photo sharing: age and gender differences. Program **50**, 462–480 (2016)
19. Gallup, A.: American Views: Trust, Media and Democracy. 71 (2018)
20. Anderson, M., Perrin, A.: Tech Adoption Climbs Among Older Adults (2017). http://www.pewinternet.org/2017/05/17/tech-adoption-climbs-among-older-adults/
21. Towner, T., Lego Munoz, C.: Boomers versus millennials: online media influence on media performance and candidate evaluations. Soc. Sci. **5**, 56 (2016)
22. Hoelig, S.: Social participation in online news usage in Europe and its underlying causes: individual versus structural factors. Eur. J. Commun. **31**, 393–410 (2016)
23. Mitchell, A., Gottfried, J., Kiley, J., Matsa, K.E.: Political Polarization & Media Habits (2014). http://www.journalism.org/2014/10/21/political-polarization-media-habits/

24. Funk, C., Gottfried, J., Mitchell, A.: Science News and Information Today (2017). http://www.journalism.org/2017/09/20/science-news-and-information-today/
25. Tsfati, Y., Cappella, J.N.: Do people watch what they do not trust? Exploring the association between news media skepticism and exposure. Commun. Res. **30**, 504–529 (2003)
26. Opgenhaffen, M., d'Haenens, L.: Heterogeneity within homogeneity: impact of online skills on the use of online news media and interactive news features. Communications **37**, 297–316 (2012)
27. Tsfati, Y.: Online news exposure and trust in the mainstream media: exploring possible associations. Am. Behav. Sci. **54**, 22–42 (2010)
28. Tsfati, Y., Ariely, G.: Individual and contextual correlates of trust in media across 44 countries. Commun. Res. **41**, 760–782 (2014)
29. Martin, B.: The Controversy Manual. Irene Publishing, Sparsnäs (2014)
30. Fleischmann, K.R.: Information and Human Values. Morgan & Claypool Publishers, San Rafael (2013)
31. Templeton, T.C., Fleischmann, K.R.: The relationship between human values and attitudes toward the Park51 and nuclear power controversies. Proc. Am. Soc. Inf. Sci. Technol. **48**, 1–10 (2011)
32. Koltai, K.S., Fleischmann, K.R.: Questioning science with science: the evolution of the vaccine safety movement. Proc. Assoc. Inf. Sci. Technol. **54**, 232–240 (2017)
33. Price, V.: Public Opinion. Sage, Newbury Park (1992)
34. Fake News Watch. http://fakenewswatch.com/
35. Behrend, T.S., Sharek, D.J., Meade, A.W., Wiebe, E.N.: The viability of crowdsourcing for survey research. Behav. Res. Methods **43**, 800 (2011)
36. Hauser, D.J., Schwarz, N.: Attentive turkers: MTurk participants perform better on online attention checks than do subject pool participants. Behav. Res. Methods **48**, 400–407 (2016)
37. Paolacci, G., Chandler, J.: Inside the turk: understanding mechanical turk as a participant pool. Curr. Dir. Psychol. Sci. **23**, 184–188 (2014)
38. Schwartz, S.H.: A proposal for measuring value orientations across nations. Quest. Package Eur. Soc. Surv. 259–290 (2003)
39. Schwartz, S.H.: Value orientations: measurement, antecedents and consequences across nations. In: Measuring Attitudes Cross-Nationally, pp. 169–203. SAGE Publications, Ltd, London (2007)
40. Mann, H.B., Whitney, D.R.: On a test of whether one of two random variables is stochastically larger than the other. Ann. Math. Stat. **18**(1), 50–60 (1947)
41. Kruskal, W.H., Wallis, W.A.: Use of ranks in one-criterion variance analysis. J. Am. Stat. Assoc. **47**, 583–621 (1952)
42. Gibbons, J.D., Chakraborti, S.: Comparisons of the mann-whitney, student's "t", and alternate "t" tests for means of normal distributions. J. Exp. Educ. Wash. DC Wash. **59**, 258–267 (1991)
43. Holm, S.: A simple sequentially rejective multiple test procedure. Scand. J. Stat. **6**(2), 65–70 (1979)
44. Verma, N., Fleischmann, K.R., Koltai, K.S.: Demographic factors and trust in different news sources. Proc. Assoc. Inf. Sci. Technol. **55**(1), 524–533 (2018)
45. Bojko, A.: Eye Tracking the User Experience: A Practical Guide to Research. Rosenfeld Media, New York (2013)

Data Mining and NLP

How to Make a Successful Movie: Factor Analysis from both Financial and Critical Perspectives

Zheng Gao[1](✉), Vincent Malic[1], Shutian Ma[2], and Patrick Shih[1](✉)

[1] Indiana University Bloomington, Bloomington, USA
{gao27,vmalic,patshih}@indiana.edu
[2] Nanjing University of Science and Technology, Nanjing, China
mashutian0608@hotmail.com

Abstract. Over the past twenty years, people have seen considerable growth in film industry. There are two common measurements for movie quality, financial metric of net profit and reception metric in the form of ratings assigned by moviegoers on websites. Researchers have utilized these two metrics to build models for movie success prediction separately, while few of them investigate the combination. Therefore, in this paper, we analyze movie success from perspectives of financial and critical metrics in tandem. Here, optimal success is defined as a film that is both profitable and highly acclaimed, while its worst outcome involves financial loss and critical panning at the same time. Salient features that are salient to both financial and critical outcomes are identified in an attempt to uncover what makes a "good" movie "good" and a "bad" one "bad" as well as explain common phenomenons in movie industry quantitatively.

Keywords: Movie success prediction · Social network analysis · Feature construction

1 Introduction

These days, people are deeply influenced by the film industry from both financial and cultural aspects. According to the Box Office Mojo annual report[1], 724 movies were released in 2017 and this industry generated over \$10 billion gross in the United States domestic market alone. Such statistics are just the latest indication of a consistent growth in both number of movies produced and amount of money earned over the past 20 years. With the film industry firmly positioned as a pillar of cultural production in the 21st century, the question of what makes a movie financially and critically successful is worthy of investigating.

As we can see, most researchers suppose that critical success or financial success of the movie can represent its overall success directly. However, we find

---

[1] Box office mojo annual report: http://www.boxofficemojo.com/yearly/.

© Springer Nature Switzerland AG 2019
N. G. Taylor et al. (Eds.): iConference 2019, LNCS 11420, pp. 669–678, 2019.
https://doi.org/10.1007/978-3-030-15742-5_63

that, these two kinds of successes are not correlated with each other. Ideas of investing more money to obtain better critical reception, or crafting a well-designed movie to aim for a significant profit, are not necessarily valid. By way of illustration, the 2008 crime drama *Nothing But the Truth* has an average user rating of 7.2 with 31,490 votes, putting it above the 75th percentile in terms of user reception. It made a total gross profit of $3,045 in the US, a staggering loss in light of the movie's $11,500,000 budget - essentially a complete failure in terms of ROI. The 2015 horror film *The Gallows*, on the other hand, has a user rating of 4.2 with 14,983 votes, which is below the 5th percentile. It nevertheless obtained a total gross of $22 million dollars on a budget of $100,000 - an ROI of 226.58. In light of our primary findings and existing examples, it's argued that modeling financial and critical success simultaneously is distinct from modeling them separately. Therefore, in this paper, we predict movie success from critical and financial aspects at the same time.

The Contribution of This Work is Fourfold. Firstly, a combination of return on investment and user rating is defined as a composite criteria to evaluate movie success. Secondly, an quantitative analysis is conducted on not only basic features from metadata but also complex movie features calculated synthetically to determine the role these features play in light of our new success metric. Thirdly, the identified features are utilized in machine learning models to see if they are able to predict success of a given film. Finally, this paper is able to reveal three phenomenons which also exist in real movie industry:

1. Among all the genres of movie, family dramas tend to attract audience more easily;
2. The success of a movie heavily relies on the success of its cast's past career.
3. Stable collaboration between directors and actors are more likely to achieve long term movie success especially in series movies.

2   Related Works

The motion picture industry in the United States is a big business. A report by the industry tracking firm Nash Information Services shows that ticket sales have grown steadily over the past 20 years[2]. This growth coincides with an increasing amount of data about movies, which researchers have turned to in order to find ways to discover features that characterize blockbusters or flops [17] and to examine the interplay between ratings and revenue after a movie has been released [14].

Various kinds of social media platforms are heavily involved in gross earning predictions. some researches use features generated from those online open resources to predict gross earnings. In [1], Armstrong and Yoon extracted features from IMDB and used a regression model to predict the user rating of a movie, while other works focus specifically on the effect that the "star power"

---

[2] http://www.the-numbers.com/market/.

of the leading actors and actresses has on a movie's reception and income [8]. In [12], the authors rely on Twitter buzz surrounding a film's release to predict its box office revenue. [11] also extracts data from Twitter, but measure the sentiment present in the Twitter conversation to see if such sentiment effects box office performance. In [13], the authors look at Wikipedia activity surrounding upcoming films to make similar predictions. Other large scale social medias are also discussed in [6] to explore its power to movie success.

Some researches argue that user reviews are not a helpful indicator for predicting box office revenue [5]. However, such reviews still remain a factor contributing to success [3] since many potential audience members refer to such reviews when deciding to see a film. Previous research studies explicitly show the influence that user ratings and individual reviews have on prospective audience members [19]. Existing works [15] use movie reviews on Twitter for profit prediction. Some other works such as [10] examine critical reviews from other review sites to see if such sites are predictive of revenue. Moreover, besides online review, there are other ways to spread movie information such as news and word of mouth, etc. Those methods are also used for movie profit prediction [20] to see how much effect rating can influence movie profit. While earlier research dealt with primary features extracted from movie datasets or social medias, another research focuses on generating novel features from existing ones to improve prediction performance [18]. Lash and Zhao [9] obtain new gains in predicting movie ROI by systematically categorizing the types of features available for analysis and recombining them in novel ways.

3 Experiment

3.1 Dataset

Our data consists of data from IMDB on movies produced before October 2016. As the movie industry boosts in recent 20 years based on motion picture yearly report, movies released domestically within this period are the valid examples to use for exploring the reason. After keeping movies released in past 20 years with abundant meta information, 6,981 movies remain.

The average IMDB user rating is used as a metric for critical performance and represent financial performance through Return on Investment, which is defined as:

$$ROI = \frac{gross - budget}{budget} \tag{1}$$

A movie that makes a large gross profit is not necessarily a "profitable" movie. A general rule of thumb for qualifying a movie as a "financial success" is to compare its gross revenue to twice its reported budget - in other words, an ROI of at least 1. A movie "doubly" is successful if it performs well both financial and critically while deem it a "total" failure if it loses money and is panned. Therefore a label of "success" is assigned to a movie that attains ROI bigger than 1 and its average user rating is above the global user rating average, and a label of "failure" means a movie's ROI is less than 0 and user rating is below the global average. Under this schema, 2,076 movies qualify as successes and 1,960 are failures.

3.2 Feature Calculation

To incorporate elements of the movie's plot into our model, Latent Direchlet Allocation [4] is utilized to create a topic model of movie plot summaries, which can generate a series of ranked topics associated with a list of ranked words in each topic to quantitatively represent movie plots in a latent vector space. [7] uses Gibbs sampling method on LDA to choose 15 optimized topics as the best representations for movie plots. We manual-coded the interpretation of the 15 topics based on the top ranked words, which are 'world war', 'misfortune', 'youths in trouble', 'crime drama', 'family', 'place stories', 'love and marriage', 'school life', 'survival', 'sex and relationships', 'marriage and family', 'making it in society', 'show business', 'political intrigue', 'high life drama'.

In addition to basic features belonging intrinsically to the movie itself, it is necessary to explore whether career performance of actors and directors as well as their collaborations affect movie success. Hence, actor and director data are aggregated for a given movie into a set of composite features. For example, the historical performance of actors in a film is calculated by finding the average user rating of all previous films for every actor in the current film, and then averaging those results to create the feature *average_ActorRating_average*. In the end Each movie is represented as a set of 24 features in three categories. Details are shown in Table 1.

3.3 Main Approach

Feature Correlation Detection. Our analysis first find and examine correlations in the obtained data. First, as all advanced features are synthetic, there is the potential that the synthetic features contain too high a degree of overlapping information. Second, it also offers a logical way to filter out some features containing duplicated information. Pairwise Pearson Correlation [2] is applied to detect correlation between all factor pairs. In this paper, if a pair of features meet both two criteria: (1) the correlation score between them is above 0.5 with a significant p value below 0.1; (2) their correlation similarity difference with the rest of features are all smaller than 0.1, one of the features will be removed.

Latent Feature Exploration. After feature construction and processing, two concerns still remain. First, as most of the features are high number of synthetic features may introduce a large amount of noise that any potential model may overfit on. Second, we also want to explore the possibility that the features we have arrived at are instead representations of latent variables which themselves are more influential in predicting movie success. Therefore, Principle Component Analysis (PCA) [16] is applied to convert a set of observations of possibly correlated variables into a set of linearly uncorrelated variables. In the end, a

Table 1. Feature description

Feature name			Abbr.	Feature description
Basic features	Content based	genre	genre	movie genres (24 types)
		MPPA rating	rating	MPPA ratings (23 types)
	Time based	released year	year	the released year
		released season	season	the released season
		week day	day	the released week day
Advanced features	Actor based	average_ActorTenure	aAT	the average years of the actors career length
		total_ActorTenure	tAT	the total years of the actors career length
		total_ActorGross_total	tAGt	sum of all actors' career movie gross
		total_ActorGross_average	tAGa	sum of all actors' average movie gross
		average_ActorGross_average	aAGa	average of all actors' average movie gross
		total_ActorProfit_total	tAPt	sum of all actors' career movie profit
		total_ActorProfit_average	tAPa	sum of all actors' average movie profit
		average_ActorProfit_average	aAPa	average of all actors' average movie profit
		top_ActorProfit_average	tpAPa	the largest average value among all actors' average movie profit
		top_ActorProfit_top	tpAPt	the largest value of all actors' most profitable movie
		average_ActorRating_average	aARa	average of all actors' average movie rating
	Dirctor based	average_DirectorRating_average	aDRa	average of all directors' average movie rating
		total_DirectorGross_total	tDGt	sum of all directors' career movie gross
		total_DirectorGross_average	tDGa	sum of all directors' average movie gross
		average_DirectorGross_average	aDGa	average of all directors' average movie gross
	Collaboration based	actorDirectorCollab_frequency	aDCf	the number of times the actors collaborated with the directors before
		actorDirectorCollab_rating	aDCr	the average rating of all the movies that the actors and directors collaborated before
		actorDirectorCollab_profit	aDCp	the average net profit of all the movies that the actors and directors collaborated before
Topic modeling feature			topic	movie plot distribution on 15 topics

denser, lower-dimensional representation of the data is obtained which reveals latent relationships among features and reduces computation workload. Usually, components with eigenvalue above 1 contain noticeable feature information.

Prediction Model. Support Vector Machines (SVM) is one of the most widely used classification methods which uses a kernel function to separate instances into different categories with good performance. In this paper, a Support Vector Machine with a linear kernel is trained to predict the outcome variable of financial and critical success. To evaluate model performance, 10-fold cross validation is leveraged to ensure the weight accuracy of each feature.

4   Results

4.1   Correlation Analysis

Correlation between advanced features as well as ROI and rating is presented as a heatmap in Fig. 1[3]. Red and blue indicate positive and negative correlation, respectively, while color saturation represents the magnitude of the correlation.

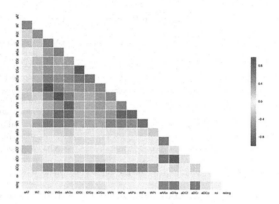

Fig. 1. Advanced features & ROI & rating correlation heat map (Color figure online)

The heatmap shows that most advanced features are not highly correlated, and ROI is not correlated with user rating. Quantitatively, from the correlation result of each feature associated with p value, there is no feature that meets the criteria to be eliminated. All features have the potential to contribute to movie success prediction.

One interesting finding is that features involving the history of gross box office for a given film tend to have a weak positive correlation among themselves and no correlation to ratings-based features. It implies a win-win collaboration between actors and directors. If their collaborations can help movies achieve more box office, they are willing to continue their relationship in future movies, which refers to common phenomenon (3) mentioned in the Introduction section. Basically for all American series movies such as *Transformers*, the directors and main actors keep same for all series as it can lead to huge box office. However not all movies in the whole series have high IMDB user rating. Another finding also implies common phenomenon (3): One of the highest correlations is between the

---

[3] Please zoom in if the font size is too small to read.

feature actorDirectorCollab_rating and average_DirectorRating_average. Both of these features are generated from the director's rating history, and the strong correlation here reflects the tendency for directors to work multiple times with a chosen set of actors if their movies achieve critical success.

4.2 Feature Impact

By applying Principle Component Analysis all the features are reduced to 5 components with an associated eigenvalue greater than 1 that are able to explain 66.62% of the variance in the success label. The amount of explained variance refers to how well the features can explain the difference between movie failure and movie success. Table 2 shows the result of PCA component matrix where larger weights implies more contribution to form the condensed component. The weighting of each feature in a particular principle component is shown only if it exceeds a threshold of 0.3.

Table 2. PCA component & SVM weight matrix

Feature		PCA components				
		PC-1	PC-2	PC-3	PC-4	PC-5
Basic features	genre (Drama)			0.9314		
	genre (Comedy)			0.5852		
	genre (Western)					0.8259
	rating (USA:TV-MA)				0.4208	
	rating (USA:PG)				0.3463	
Advanced features	tAPt	0.3262				
	aAPa	0.3905				
	tAGt	0.3794				
	tAGa	0.3344				
	tpAPt	0.3165				
	tpAPa	0.3097				
	aDCP	0.4477	0.3429			
	aDRa		0.3736			
	aARa		0.3467			
	aDGa		0.4099			
Topic modeling features	topic_5 (family)					0.5750
	topic_11 (marriage and family)					0.4356
Eigenvalue		6.7552	3.2879	2.8152	1.1912	1.0574
Explained variance		29.78%	14.49%	12.41%	5.25%	4.63%
SVM model weight		0.1704	1.2955	0.2243	−0.0262	−0.1447
Total explained variance		66.62%				

The first component PC-1 is composed of a mix of actor financial metrics and explains 29.87% of the variance in the label. PC-1 can be regarded as a composite actor feature based on a suite of financial indicators, which implies common phenomenon (2) listed previously: Actors make the most contributions for a movie success. Director features are weighted more strongly, and the analysis shows that when the actor and director financial features are aggregated, they are capable of explaining a greater proportion of movie success, which also explains common phenomenon (3): stable collaboration is important.

Actor and director critical performance, in contrast, are part of the make up of the second principle component, along with the average profit of actor-director collaboration and the average gross earnings of the director. This principle component PC-2 explains 14.49% of the variance. The top 2 main components are basically formed by advanced features, which means there are existing latent factors of the actor-director relationship and the career histories of the actor and director influence movie success the most.

Component PC-3 combines and provides high weights to the comedy and drama genres, while component PC-4 accounts for the effect of certification. Those two components have really clear meanings. In component PC-3, genre "Drama" has a really high positive impact weight. That may be part of the reason why movie industry is willing to produce movies in this genre, which refers to the common phenomenon (1). Though PC-4 is clearly connected to certification, it is difficult to provide it with a consistent interpretation.

Finally, the interpretability of the retrieved principle components drops at principle component five, which explains only 4.63% of the variance. Here, we begin to see the effects of specific topics, as well as the Western genre. Two topics about families form the component PC-5, meaning that the most important movie topic to audience is "family", which also refers to common phenomenon (1).

4.3   Predictions

The original data is re-expressed in the form of the five principle components as the input to a Support Vector Machine model with a linear kernel to predict if a movie will be a success or failure in terms of financial and critical reception. Table 2 shows that for the prediction of success the SVM assigned a significantly higher weight to PC-2, once again suggesting that directors and rating history play a more significant role in the final success or failure of a given movie. In other words, actor financial performance explains the variance in success or failure, which refers to common phenomenon (2), while director and actor critical performance are more pertinent to a movie actually becoming successful. It notes that actor-director collaboration profit feature exists with a high weight in both PC-1 and PC-2, suggesting that this advanced feature is relevant to both variance in outcome and likelihood of success, which explains common phenomenon (3).

Table 3. Evaluation metrics

Accuracy	0.7915	Precision	0.7919
Recall	0.7915	F1 score	0.7914
Hamming loss	0.2084	Matthews coefficient	0.5835

The performance of the SVM model is shown in Table 3. Since we took measures to ensure that the categories were equal in number, the baseline accuracy is 50%. Our model attains an accuracy of 79.15%, indicating that the feature selection and the PCA process has successfully zeroed in on the features of movies that are pertinent to success or failure. Other than accuracy, other evaluation metrics attain satisfactory levels. Precision reflects that movie successes can be identified correctly while high recall value means most of successes are retrieved in the model. F1 score integrates both precision and recall. The Hamming loss indicates that the model can predict movie success correctly with little error. A relatively high Matthews correlation coefficient also testifies to the performance of the model. The evaluation metrics support the reliability of our prediction model and interpretation analysis.

5   Conclusion

Movie user rating and profit are two separate but related factors in judging the ultimate performance of a movie. As a result, there exists much research that focuses on one or the other, but to the best of our knowledge this is the first work that attempts to predict financial and critical success simultaneously. According our analysis, three common phenomenons for movie industry is well explained quantitatively. There are more interesting findings explored in this approach. Advanced features with actor and director information play a considerable role in a movie's success. The created composite features add to the power of the model. And movie genre and plot are another two important features for successful movie production. Movies about humanity, family and comedy are better welcomed by people. And violence, horror and cult movies are tend not to be as successful.

In future work, we hope to improve this work by incorporating social media which has proven successful in recent literature as a predictor of financial success, but not of combined critical and financial success. We also wish to examine if the factors for success differ substantially in different cultural settings by using data from the Chinese equivalent of IMDB, Douban. Given the growth and impact of the motion picture industry, our research should be useful for those who desire to invest in a movie that not only earns a decent profit, but is also has a high cultural impact.

References

1. Armstrong, N., Yoon, K.: Movie rating prediction. Technical report. Citeseer (1995)
2. Benesty, J., Chen, Y., Huang, Y., Cohen, I.: Pearson correlation coefficient. In: Noise Reduction in Speech Processing. Springer Topics in Signal Processing, vol. 2, pp. 1–4. Springer, Heidelberg (2009). https://doi.org/10.1007/978-3-642-00296-0_5
3. Berg, J., Raddick, M.J.: First you get the money, then you get the reviews, then you get the internet comments: a quantitative examination of the relationship between critics, viewers, and box office success. Q. Rev. Film Video **34**, 101–129 (2017)

4. Blei, D.M., Ng, A.Y., Jordan, M.I.: Latent Dirichlet allocation. J. Mach. Learn. Res. **3**, 993–1022 (2003)

5. Brown, A.L., Camerer, C.F., Lovallo, D.: To review or not to review? Limited strategic thinking at the movie box office. Am. Econ. J. Microecon. **4**(2), 1–26 (2012)

6. Ding, C., Cheng, H.K., Duan, Y., Jin, Y.: The power of the "like" button: the impact of social media on box office. Decis. Support Syst. **94**, 77–84 (2017)

7. Griffiths, T.: Gibbs sampling in the generative model of latent Dirichlet allocation (2002)

8. Karniouchina, E.V.: Impact of star and movie buzz on motion picture distribution and box office revenue. Int. J. Res. Mark. **28**(1), 62–74 (2011)

9. Lash, M., Fu, S., Wang, S., Zhao, K.: Early prediction of movie success — what, who, and when. In: Agarwal, N., Xu, K., Osgood, N. (eds.) SBP 2015. LNCS, vol. 9021, pp. 345–349. Springer, Cham (2015). https://doi.org/10.1007/978-3-319-16268-3_41

10. Legoux, R., Larocque, D., Laporte, S., Belmati, S., Boquet, T.: The effect of critical reviews on exhibitors' decisions: do reviews affect the survival of a movie on screen? Int. J. Res. Mark. **33**(2), 357–374 (2016)

11. Lehrer, S., Xie, T.: Box office buzz: does social media data steal the show from model uncertainty when forecasting for hollywood? Technical report, National Bureau of Economic Research (2016)

12. Liu, T., Ding, X., Chen, Y., Chen, H., Guo, M.: Predicting movie box-office revenues by exploiting large-scale social media content. Multimed. Tools Appl. **75**(3), 1509–1528 (2016)

13. Mestyán, M., Yasseri, T., Kertész, J.: Early prediction of movie box office success based on wikipedia activity big data. PloS One **8**(8), e71226 (2013)

14. Moon, S., Bergey, P.K., Iacobucci, D.: Dynamic effects among movie ratings, movie revenues, and viewer satisfaction. J. Mark. **74**(1), 108–121 (2010)

15. Oh, C., Roumani, Y., Nwankpa, J.K., Hu, H.-F.: Beyond likes and tweets: Consumer engagement behavior and movie box office in social media. Inf. Manag. (2016)

16. Pearson, K.: Liii on lines and planes of closest fit to systems of points in space. London, Edinburgh, Dublin Philos. Mag. J. Sci. **2**(11), 559–572 (1901)

17. Ravid, S.A.: J. Bus. **72**(4), 463–492 (1999)

18. Sharan, P.: Movie success predictor. Indian J. Appl. Res. **6**(6) (2016)

19. Wang, H., Guo, K.: The impact of online reviews on exhibitor behaviour: evidence from movie industry. Enterp. Inf. Syst., 1–17 (2016)

20. Zhang, F., Yang, Y.: The effect of internet word-of-mouth on experience product sales—an empirical study based on film online reviews. Int. J. Bus. Adm. **7**(2), 72 (2016)

Identifying Finding Sentences in Conclusion Subsections of Biomedical Abstracts

Yingya Li and Bei Yu[✉]

Syracuse University, Syracuse, NY 13244, USA
{yli48, byu}@syr.com

Abstract. Segmenting scientific abstracts and full-text based on their rhetorical function is an essential task in text classification. Small rhetorical segments can be useful for fine-grained literature search, summarization, and comparison. Current effort has been focusing on segmenting documents into general sections such as introduction, method, and conclusion, and much less on the roles of individual sentences within the segments. For example, not all sentences in the conclusion section are describing research findings. In this work, we developed rule-based and machine learning methods and compared their performance in identifying the finding sentences in conclusion subsections of biomedical abstracts. 1100 conclusion subsections with observational and randomized clinical trials study designs covering five common health topics were sampled from PubMed to develop and evaluate the methods. The rule-based method and the bag-of-words based machine learning method both achieved high accuracy. The better performance by the simple rule-based approach shows that although advanced machine learning approaches could capture the main patterns, human expert may still outperform on such a specialized task.

Keywords: Text classification · Rule-based approach · Machine learning · Biomedicine

1 Introduction

Categorizing sentences by their rhetorical functions is an important task in literature mining. It is particularly useful for the fields that face the challenge of overwhelming volume of publications. For example, identifying the results in empirical studies is a critical step for writing systematic reviews in Evidence-Based Medicine (EBM) [11]. It is also a step toward further analyses, such as identifying potential exaggerations in conclusions [6, 8].

To date many studies have tried to automatically segment sentences either in abstracts or full-texts into sections (e.g., [2, 7, 13, 15, 20]). Nearly all existing studies focus on the general rhetorical level of sentences in the given contexts, classifying abstracts or full text into introduction, method, result and discussion (IMRaD) format. However, simply classifying sentences into the IMRaD structure does not provide adequate granularity for retrieving key information such as study findings, because sentences in each subsection may still serve different rhetorical functions. For instance, sentences in the conclusion subsection can describe studies' findings, limitations, or

N. G. Taylor et al. (Eds.): iConference 2019, LNCS 11420, pp. 679–689, 2019.
https://doi.org/10.1007/978-3-030-15742-5_64

implications for future studies respectively. As shown in the following excerpt, the underscored sentence is the finding of the study, while the second and third sentences represent the implications for future studies.

> *The present meta-analysis suggests that insulin therapy may increase the risk of CRC*. More prospective cohort studies with longer follow-up durations are warranted to confirm this association. Furthermore, future studies should report results stratified by gender and race and should adjust the results by more confounders. (PMID 25099257)

In this work, we focus on the automatic categorization of sentences in conclusion subsections from structured biomedical abstracts. Our goal is to determine whether sentences in conclusions subsections describe study *findings*, as opposed to the *non-finding* ones that describe study implications, limitations, recommendations, and clinical trial registration information.

Rule-based and machine learning methods are the two mainly used approaches in prior sentence categorization studies. Most studies found the machine-learning approaches using features of bag-of-words, semantic relations or structural information of sentence positions work well (e.g., [2, 11, 13, 15]); however, studies also suggest that for texts with controlled vocabularies, rule-based approaches can also be effective [5, 10]. Therefore, we developed both rule-based and machine learning methods and compared their performance in identifying the *finding* sentences in conclusion sections. We used 1000 biomedical abstracts from PubMed as training and 100 abstracts for testing to validate these two methods.

2   Related Work

The task of identifying *finding* sentences in conclusion subsections of abstracts is closely related to automatic section identification and summarization for scientific articles. To realize the automatic process, many studies have aimed at developing schemas and corpora for categorization (e.g., [21, 23, 25]). For example, Teufel and Moens [24] introduced a scheme of Argumentative Zoning (AZ) which classifies sentences in scientific text into categories such as aim, background, own, contrast, and basis on their rhetorical status in scientific discourse. Their experiments suggest that the proposed AZ framework can be used to identify and summarize novel contributions and backgrounds of scientific articles. Liakata et al. [17] proposed two classification schemas to capture the hypotheses, motivations, methods, conclusions etc. based on the rhetorical nature of 265 full papers in physical chemistry and biochemistry. Guo et al. [12] compared the validity of three pre-existing categorization schemas developed from full-text articles on the abstracts of cancer risk assessments. Their results suggest the possibility of applying full-text sentence categorization schema on abstracts.

Previous studies typically modeled section identification process as text classification task, which determines a pre-defined label to each individual sentence based on their rhetorical function. In this line of method, classifiers such as Multinomial Naïve Bayes (MNB) and Support Vector Machines (SVM) are widely used (e.g., [2, 11, 12, 23]). Studies reached different conclusions regarding the performance of the classifiers. For example, Agarwal and Yu [2] trained both MNB and SVM classifiers to identify sentences of articles sampled from BioMed Central into IMRaD structures. Their results show that MNB performed better than SVM at classifying sentences using bag-of-words with enriched features of words tenses. Gabb et al. [11] compared the performance of models using Naïve Bays (NB) and SVM to automatically identify result sentences from full-text journal articles. Their experiment results indicate that though models built with NB and SVM obtain similar results, classifier trained with SVM using top-100 terms and sentence locations as features tended to have slightly higher F1 scores. In addition to modeling sentence type or section identification as text classification task, some studies modeled the structure of article sections as a sequence labeling problem. Hirohata et al. [13] used n-gram, relative sentence location, and the features from previous and proceeding sentences for text representation to classify the sections of academic abstract into objectives, methods, results, and conclusions using Conditional Random Fields (CRFs). The feature sets of ngram with surrounding sentence features trained with CRFs outperformed the model using SVM. However, these studies used different dataset to develop their methods, thus classification results may not be necessarily comparable to each other.

Other than these machine learning approaches, previous studies also applied rule-based methods to identifying sections or to similar biomedical applications. Friedman et al. [10] built a language processor which relied on semantic grammars to extract clinical information in patient documents and mapped them into controlled vocabulary terms. Chapman et al. [5] developed a simple algorithm for identifying negated sentences in discharged summaries. They implemented a sets of negation phrases with regular expression to detect a large portion of pertinent negatives in the document. Yu et al. [26] relied on a set of pattern-matching rules for mapping an abbreviation in biomedical articles into its full forms. Kilicoglu et al. [14] applied a rule-based approach to automatically recognize self-acknowledged limitations in clinical research publications. The success of these studies indicates that for text with controlled language indicators and patterns, the simple rule-based approach might be an effective one. In recent years, the lexicon-enhanced approach also shows its success in other NLP applications such as sentiment analysis [3, 16], and emotion-detection [4].

Different from previous studies of classifying scientific abstracts and full-text into the general categories, our work intends to identify sentences about study findings from the conclusion subsections in biomedical abstracts. We took advantage of the lexicon-enhanced rule-based NLP approach for sentence type recognition and compared its performance to the commonly used machine learning methods in this work.

3   Method

In this section, we first introduce the process of corpus construction for training and testing (Sect. 3.1). Then we discuss about the rule-based approach (Sect. 3.2), the machine learning classification methods (Sect. 3.3) and evaluation measures used in this study.

3.1   Corpus Construction

To the best of our knowledge, no prior corpus is available for *finding* sentence identification, we then used structured abstracts from original scientific research papers for corpus construction. We focused on the biomedical domain and chose PubMed as the source. The PubMed database has more than 27 million citations for biomedical literature from Medline, life science journals, and online books. Since different study designs may use varied language to describe their research, we applied stratified sampling approach to collect both observational and randomized clinical trials (RCTs) studies from the platform. PubMed's search interface provides one search criterion "Publication Type" that is derived from the MeSH terms for PubType in MEDLINE records (2018MeSH). We applied article's MeSH term to select the RCTs articles (MeSH Unique ID: D016449); used the searching method introduced in [1] to collect case-control, cross-sectional, retrospective, and prospective studies within observational studies; and rescanned the abstracts sections with the keywords to exclude the irrelevant ones. To account for the vocabulary variation among different health issues, we selected five common health topics – nutrition, diabetes, obesity, breast cancer, and cholesterol. The whole downloaded set contains 63498 conclusion subsections from structured abstracts in total. The XML files in PubMed contain occasional parsing errors, so sometimes the conclusion subsections may include paragraphs in the following sections. For quality control purpose, we used the Stanford CoreNLP tool [18] to split the conclusion subsections into sentences, and removed the articles with conclusions longer than four sentences. We then sampled equal number of articles with conclusion length as 1, 2, 3, or 4 sentences from the 63498 set. Our sampled corpus includes 1100 structured abstracts, within which we used 1000 as the training set and 100 as the testing set.

To construct a reliable human-annotated dataset to serve as ground truth, we annotated each sentence in the selected corpus as either *category-0 (non-finding)* or *category-1 (finding)*. Table 1 shows examples of the two sentence types. *Category-0* refers to *non-finding* sentences (as shown in Examples 1 and 2); while *category-1* refers to sentences explicitly talking about study *finding* (as shown in Examples 3 and 4). An inter-coder reliability test on a sample of 200 articles with 510 sentences from the training set showed almost perfect agreement of the schema. Specifically, two graduate students with the education background of information studies labelled the sentences extracted from the conclusion subsection of the structured abstracts. Annotators identified the sentence category based on their linguistic indicators. We applied Cohens Kappa k as the inter-coder agreement measure [9]. Kappa values of .61 or above are considered as substantial agreement and .81 or above as almost perfect agreement [19]. The overall k value was .85, indicating the annotation schema for finding sentence identification reached almost perfect inter-coder agreement (Table 2 shows the detailed inter-coder agreement). Disagreements in the annotation were later resolved by the two annotators through discussion.

Annotator 1 annotated the conclusion subsection of the rest 900 articles from both training and testing sets. The final corpus contained 2735 annotated sentences in the conclusion subsections of abstracts from 1100 articles, of which 711 sentences in the conclusion subsections belonged to *category-0*, and 2024 sentences belonged to *category-1*. Table 3 shows the number of sentences per category in the developed corpus.

Table 1. Finding and non-finding sentences from conclusion subsections.

Sentence	Annotation
Example 1: (PMID: 28640840) We propose a novel AI disease-staging system for grading diabetic retinopathy that involves a retinal area not typically visualized on fundoscopy and another AI that directly suggests treatments and determines prognoses	Category-0
Example 2: (PMID: 26504068) This approach may, however, be difficult to implement on a large scale	Category-0
Example 3: (PMID: 28953631) The results of this study showed that TPVBRA combined with bupivacaine and dexmedetomidine can enhance the duration and quality of analgesia without serious adverse events	Category-1
Example 4: (PMID: 28746662) Our current analysis does not support the existence of an association between age at first childbirth and adult-onset diabetes among postmenopausal women, which had been reported previously	Category-1

Table 2. Confusion matrix for the sentence type annotation.

Kappa = .85		A2		
		Category-0	Category-1	All
A1	Category-0	163	11	174
	Category-1	23	313	336
	All	186	324	510

Table 3. Sentence type distribution in annotated corpus.

Dataset	Category-0	Category-1	Total
Training set	659	1841	2500
Testing set	52	183	235
Total	711	2024	2735

3.2 A Rule-Based Approach for Automatic Finding Sentence Identification

We framed the automated identification process as a sentence-level text classification task, and manually identified rules indicative of sentence types. A total of 181 rules were derived from training set, of which 14 were study backgrounds, 13 were study limitations, 59 were implications, 84 were recommendations, and 11 ones were about the clinical trial registration. These rules were generated based on iterative rounds of keywords searching and pattern matching for the linguistic indicators of study backgrounds, limitations, implications, recommendations, and information of clinical trial registration. Similar as the existing rule-based approaches [2, 5], we used regular expression to identify those generated patterns in the original annotated sentences.

We looked for keywords like *"exist in literature"*, *"growing literature"*, *"literature to date"* for introduction of study backgrounds; indicators like *"limited by"*, *"limitations"* for study limitations; phrases such as *"further assessment"*, *"future studies"*, *"future research"*, *"follow-up exploration"* for the implications of current study findings for future explorations; expressions of *"clinicians should"*, *"health policy makers should"*, *"actions should focus on"* for the recommendations of practitioners and experiments alike; and words like *"trial registration"*, *"clinical trial registration"* for the information of clinical trial registration in sentences of conclusion subsections.

All identified rules were grouped into two sets. The first set included 153 short language patterns represented by regular expressions, which were short terms and keywords indicative of *non-finding* sentences (e.g., *"future research"*, *"further investigation"*, *"other studies"*, *"should confirm these findings"*). The second set contained 28 rules that captured longer language patterns describing *non-finding* sentences. For example, one rule in the second set is that if a sentence has phrases of *"is warranted"* or *"are warranted"*; and it does not have conjunctions of *"although"* or *"though"*, it is a *non-finding* sentence. We applied all rules into a rule-based classifier, detecting the category of each input sentence. If a sentence matches any of the rules in the first pattern set, it will be assigned to *category-0* as a *non-finding* sentence; else the classifier will continue to check if the sentence matches any of the other rules in the second set. If the input sentence does not match any of the identified 181 patterns in the first and second pattern sets, it will then be assigned to *category-1*; namely the sentence depicts the study findings. We used macro-averaged precision, recall and F1 scores to evaluate the performance of the proposed rule-based approach on the testing dataset.

3.3   Machine Learning Approaches for Automatic Finding Sentence Identification

We measured the performance of machine learning approaches using variations of bag-of-words representations, and the language indicators from the identified 181 rules as features. For the bag-of-words representations, we chose NB and SVM algorithms with different vectorization methods and enriched features to train the sentence type classifiers, using Scikit-learn python package [22]. NB and SVM are the most popular classification algorithms in current studies of segmenting scientific abstracts and full-text [2, 11, 12]. We used two NB algorithms – multivariate Bernoulli model and the multinomial model. The first one uses word presence and absence as feature value (BNB); while the second one uses word frequency (MNB). For SVM, we combined the SVM (Liblinear) algorithm with three different frequency measures – word presence and absence (SVM-boolean), word frequency (SVM-tf), and word frequency weighted by inverse document frequency (SVM-tfidf).

To further validate the performance of syntactic and semantic structures in classification, we extracted part-of-speech (POS) and dependency parsing from the input sentences using Stanford CoreNLP [18]. The bag-of-words machine-learning approaches then contained the following four feature vectors with different representation methods: (1) simple bag-of-words; (2) bag-of-words with POS tagging; (3) bag-of-words with enhanced dependency parsing; (4) bag-of-words enriched with both POS tagging and enhanced dependency parsing (combining features in (2) and (3) together). For example,

Original sentence: Physical activity is also associated with favorable HDL-C. *(PMID: 28167327)*

Bag-of-words: Physical, activity, is, also, associated, with, favorable, HDL-C

Bag-of-words with POS tagging: Physical-JJ, activity-NN, is-VBZ, also-RB, associated-VBN, with-IN, favorable-JJ, HDL-C-NN

Bag-of-words with enhanced dependency parsing: amod(activity-2, Physical-1) nsubjpass(associated-5, activity-2) auxpass(associated-5, is-3) advmod(associated-5, also-4) root(ROOT-0, associated-5) prep(associated-5, with-6) amod(HDL-C-8, favorable-7) pobj(with-6, HDL-C-8)

For the machine learning approach based on language indicators from the hand-crafted rules as features, the presence or absence of the identified 181 patterns in the rule-based approach was used in training the classifier. We applied the Decision Tree classifier in Scikit-learn [22] with its default parameter settings as the implementation of the Decision Tree algorithm and compared its performance to the BNB and SVM algorithms using the same representation.

Considering the size of current dataset and the imbalance distribution of *category-0* and *category-1*, we used 10 folds cross-validation for the evaluation of machine learning approaches and reported precision, recall, F1 scores of each category, in addition to the macro-averaged precision, recall, and F1 scores.

4   Result

The majority vote baseline of the test set is .78. Among the three approaches, our experiment result shows that the rule-based method achieved the best performance with an macro-averaged F1 score at .96 level on the test set (as shown in Table 4).

Table 4. Performance of the rule-based model.

Method	Sentence type	Accuracy	Precision	Recall	F1 Score
Rule-based	Category-0	.90	.92	.90	.91
	Category-1	.98	.97	.98	.98
	Macro-averaged	**.96**	**.96**	**.96**	**.96**

The machine learning models based on bag-of-words feature also achieved high performance. The best machine learning model is BNB with unigram and bigram features with a macro-averaged F1 score at .86 level, lower than the .96 by the rule-based model. Tables 5 and 6 list the feature engineering options and results. Table 5 lists the results of unigram experiments. BNB, MNB, and SVM-tfidf have very similar macro-averaged scores across the two sentence type categories, but BNB has slightly higher macro-averaged precision (.84) and recall (.85) values. Table 6 shows that adding bigram features slightly improves the performance of all models except SVM-tf and SVM-tfidf. As shown in Table 6, BNB with unigram and bigram bag-of-words representation has the highest precision (.86), recall (.87) and F1 scores (.86) among all the machine-learning methods using the same representation. It also has higher accuracy than its counterpart in the bag-of-words unigram experiment and the best performance in bag-of-words unigram representation.

Table 5. Performance of the machine learning models based on unigram features.

Method	Sentence type	Accuracy	Precision	Recall	F1 score
BNB	Category-0	.79	.76	.79	.77
	Category-1	.91	.93	.91	.92
	Macro-averaged	**.88**	**.84**	**.85**	**.85**
MNB	Category-0	.74	.79	.74	.76
	Category-1	.93	.91	.93	.92
	Macro-averaged	.88	.85	.83	.84
SVM-boolean	Category-0	.76	.73	.76	.74
	Category-1	.91	.91	.90	.91
	Macro-averaged	.86	.82	.83	.82
SVM-tf	Category-0	.75	.73	.75	.74
	Category-1	.90	.91	.90	.91
	Macro-averaged	.86	.82	.83	.82
SVM-tfidf	Category-0	.70	.82	.70	.76
	Category-1	.95	.90	.95	.92
	Macro-averaged	.88	.86	.82	.84

Adding the enriched features introduced in Sect. 3.3 did not further improve the performance of the machine learning models. Among all the models with enriched features, SVM-tfidf using unigram bag-of-words feature with dependency parsing

Table 6. Performance of the machine learning models based on unigram and bigram features.

Method	Sentence type	Accuracy	Precision	Recall	F1 score
BNB	Category-0	.82	.78	.82	.80
	Category-1	.92	.94	.92	.93
	Macro-averaged	**.89**	**.86**	**.87**	**.86**
MNB	Category-0	.75	.80	.75	.77
	Category-1	.93	.91	.93	.92
	Macro-averaged	.89	.86	.84	.85
SVM-boolean	Category-0	.75	.75	.75	.75
	Category-1	.92	.91	.91	.91
	Macro-averaged	.87	.83	.83	.83
SVM-tf	Category-0	.75	.74	.75	.74
	Category-1	.91	.91	.91	.91
	Macro-averaged	.86	.82	.83	.82
SVM-tfidf	Category-0	.72	.84	.72	.78
	Category-1	.95	.91	.95	.93
	Macro-averaged	.89	.87	.84	.85

relations had the best performance. However, it did not outperform the best machine learning model with only bag-of-words feature.

The machine learning models based on the language indicators from the hand-crafted rules did not perform the ruled-based method. Table 7 shows the model using Decision Tree has the best macro-averaged precision (.96), recall (.88) and, F1 scores (.91).

Table 7. Performance of using language indicators from hand-crafted rules as features.

Method	Sentence Type	Accuracy	Precision	Recall	F1 Score
Decision Tree	Category-0	.77	.99	.77	.87
	Category-1	.99	.92	.99	.96
	Macro-averaged	**.94**	**.96**	**.88**	**.91**
BNB	Category-0	.68	.99	.68	.81
	Category-1	.99	.90	.99	.95
	Macro-averaged	.92	.94	.84	.88
SVM	Category-0	.73	.99	.73	.84
	Category-1	.99	.91	.99	.95
	Macro-averaged	.93	.95	.86	.90

5 Discussion

In our experiment, the rule-based method and the bag-of-words based machine learning method both achieved high accuracy, suggesting that the two approaches are effective in identifying *finding* sentences in conclusion subsections of structured abstracts. The high precision, recall and F1 scores of the rule-based approach on the testing set confirm our previous assumption that the rules developed based on linguistic indicators and patterns of sentences in conclusion subsections are more effective to identify *finding* sentences extracted from structured abstracts.

In comparison, machine learning models based on bag-of-words representations and indicators in identified rules as features tend to have higher precision and recall values in classifying *category-1*, but relatively lower values in *category-0*. Feature analyses of the best machine learning method using bag-of-words representation indicate that the classifier has learned some basic sentence type indicators like *"further studies"*, *"further research"*, *"future studies"*, *"larger studies"*, *"associated with"*. However, it was not able to learn linguistic patterns capturing larger language units in *non-finding* sentence as included in the second set of identified rules.

Compared to the rule-based approach, the machine learning models based on linguistic indicators in rules as features are more sophisticated in the process of deciding sentence types. Feature ranking result of the most important features learned by the Decision Tree model shows that rules of the clinical trial registration information, and implications of future studies are the most important ones, thus the model has learned some patterns on *non-finding* sentences. However, this more complicated model did not outperform the simpler rule-based model.

Though the rule-based approach achieved satisfactory results detecting *finding* sentences, error analyses of the misclassified cases suggest room for improvement. The most common error can be attributed to the confounding keywords in finding sentences: a finding sentence can mention both study findings and the implication for future study. The keywords of future study implications will then lead to detection error. On the other hand, current rules can capture the *non-finding* sentences which contain explicit language indicators. However, for *non-finding* sentences lacking the clear cues like indications of study limitations (e.g., *"limitations", "limited by"*) or recommendations (e.g., *"these findings suggest that", "should be introduced to"*), such as *"Such information is crucial to target Web-based support systems to different patient groups"*, the rules would not be able to capture them.

6   Conclusion

In this work, we focus on detecting *finding* and *non-finding* sentences from the conclusion subsections of structured abstracts. The rule-based method and the bag-of-words based machine learning method both achieved high accuracy. The better performance by the simple rule-based approach shows that although advanced machine learning approaches could capture the main patterns, human expert may still outperform on such a specialized task. For text with controlled linguistic patterns, the rule-based one could be more suitable. Considering the errors caused by the current rules, in future work we will conduct deeper semantic analysis on the generated rules to either introduce more synonyms of identified keywords or to prevent the confounding effects of those patterns for higher precision and recall during the classification. Meanwhile, we will further explore the effectiveness of this rule-based approach for finding sentence recognition in unstructured abstracts.

Acknowledgement. We would like to thank Shiqi Qu who have contributed to the inter-coder agreement checking and corpus construction.

References

1. Search strategies: Study Type public health: Search strategies by study type. http://libguides. adelaide.edu.au/c.php?g=165091p=5799888. Accessed 2 Jan 2018
2. Agarwal, S., Yu, H.: Automatically classifying sentences in full-text biomedical articles into introduction, methods, results and discussion. Bioinformatics **25**(23), 3174–3180 (2009)
3. Asghar, M.Z., Khan, A., Ahmad, S., Qasim, M., Khan, I.A.: Lexicon-enhanced sentiment analysis framework using rule-based classification scheme. PLoS ONE **12**(2), e0171649 (2017)
4. Asghar, M.Z., Khan, A., Bibi, A., Kundi, F.M., Ahmad, H.: Sentence-level emotion detection framework using rule-based classification. Cogn. Comput. **9**(6), 868–894 (2017)
5. Chapman, W.W., Bridewell, W., Hanbury, P., Cooper, G.F., Buchanan, B.G.: A simple algorithm for identifying negated findings and diseases in discharge summaries. J. Biomed. Inform. **34**(5), 301–310 (2001)
6. Chiu, K., Grundy, Q., Bero, L.: Spin in published biomedical literature: a methodological systematic review. PLoS Biol. **15**(9), e2002173 (2017)

7. Chung, G.Y.: Sentence retrieval for abstracts of randomized controlled trials. BMC Med. Inf. Decis. Making **9**(1), 10 (2009)
8. Cofield, S.S., Corona, R.V., Allison, D.B.: Use of causal language in observational studies of obesity and nutrition. Obes. Facts **3**(6), 353–356 (2010)
9. Cohen, J.: A coefficient of agreement for nominal scales. Educ. Psychol. Measur. **20**(1), 37–46 (1960)
10. Friedman, C., Alderson, P.O., Austin, J.H., Cimino, J.J., Johnson, S.B.: A general natural-language text processor for clinical radiology. J. Am. Med. Inform. Assoc. **1**(2), 161–174 (1994)
11. Gabb, H.A., Lucic, A., Blake, C.: A method to automatically identify the results from journal articles. In: iConference 2015 Proceedings (2015)
12. Guo, Y., Korhonen, A., Liakata, M., Karolinska, I.S., Sun, L., Stenius, U.: Identifying the information structure of scientific abstracts: an investigation of three different schemes. In: Proceedings of the 2010 Workshop on Biomedical Natural Language Processing, pp. 99–107. Association for Computational Linguistics (2010)
13. Hirohata, K., Okazaki, N., Ananiadou, S., Ishizuka, M.: Identifying sections in scientific abstracts using conditional random fields. In: Proceedings of the Third International Joint Conference on Natural Language Processing: Volume-I (2008)
14. Kilicoglu, H., Rosemblat, G., Mališki, M., ter Riet, G.: Automatic recognition of self-acknowledged limitations in clinical research literature. J. Am. Med. Inform. Assoc. **25**(7), 855–861 (2018)
15. Kim, S.N., Martinez, D., Cavedon, L., Yencken, L.: Automatic classification of sentences to support evidence based medicine. BMC Bioinf. **12**, S5 (2011). BioMed Central
16. Kundi, F.M., Khan, A., Ahmad, S., Asghar, M.Z.: Lexicon-based sentiment analysis in the social web. J. Basic Appl. Sci. Res. **4**(6), 238–248 (2014)
17. Liakata, M., Teufel, S., Siddharthan, A., Batchelor, C.R., et al.: Corpora for the conceptualisation and zoning of scientific papers. In: LREC. Citeseer (2010)
18. Manning, C., Surdeanu, M., Bauer, J., Finkel, J., Bethard, S., McClosky, D.: The stanford coreNLP natural language processing toolkit. In: Proceedings of 52nd Annual Meeting of the Association for Computational Linguistics: System Demonstrations, pp. 55–60 (2014)
19. McHugh, M.L.: Interrater reliability: the kappa statistic. Biochemia medica: Biochemia medica **22**(3), 276–282 (2012)
20. McKnight, L., Srinivasan, P.: Categorization of sentence types in medical abstracts. In: AMIA Annual Symposium Proceedings, vol. 2003, p. 440. American Medical Informatics Association (2003)
21. Mizuta, Y., Korhonen, A., Mullen, T., Collier, N.: Zone analysis in biology articles as a basis for information extraction. Int. J. Med. Inf. **75**(6), 468–487 (2006)
22. Pedregosa, F., et al.: Scikit-learn: machine learning in Python. J. Mach. Learn. Res. **12**, 2825–2830 (2011)
23. Ruch, P., et al.: Using argumentation to extract key sentences from biomedical abstracts. Int. J. Med. Inf. **76**(2–3), 195–200 (2007)
24. Teufel, S., Moens, M.: Summarizing scientific articles: experiments with relevance and rhetorical status. Comput. Linguist. **28**(4), 409–445 (2002)
25. Teufel, S., Siddharthan, A., Batchelor, C.: Towards discipline-independent argumentative zoning: evidence from chemistry and computational linguistics. In: Proceedings of the 2009 Conference on Empirical Methods in Natural Language Processing, vol. 3, pp. 1493–1502. Association for Computational Linguistics (2009)
26. Yu, H., Hripcsak, G., Friedman, C.: Mapping abbreviations to full forms in biomedical articles. J. Am. Med. Inform. Assoc. **9**(3), 262–272 (2002)

Authority Claim in Rationale-Containing Online Comments

Lu Xiao[(⊠)] and Xin Huo

Syracuse University, Syracuse, NY 13210, USA
{lxiao04, xihuo}@syr.edu

Abstract. We examined whether the existence of authority claims signifies one's rationales in online communication content, potentially contributing to the research on rationale identification and rationale generation. Authority claims are statements that reveal the writer's intention to bolster the writer's credibility. In open online communications, the anonymity and the dynamic participation make it challenging to establish the credibility of their viewpoints and reasoning. Therefore, we hypothesize these online participants will tend to use authority claims to bolster their credibility when presenting their justifications. We annotated authority claims in 271 text segments that contain online users' rationales. These text segments are adapted from the open access corpora provided by Rutgers' Argument Mining group. Contrary to our hypothesis, we found that in our dataset the users scarcely attempted to bolster their credibility when presenting their reasoning to the others in these activities. We call for more investigations to explore the role of activity context affects participants' use of authority claims in their reasoning traces. We further state that the effects of communication medium on individuals' cognitive and meta-cognitive processes are important to consider in argument mining research.

Keywords: Annotation · Authority claim · Computer-mediated communication

1 Introduction

Internet users increasingly interact with others through new and advanced forms of online communication. Compared to face-to-face communications, participation in these activities is often large-scale, anonymous, asynchronous, and open to any Internet user or registered community member. In addition, users can choose when to join and when to leave the communication, and may have quite heterogeneous demographic information and varied domain expertise and professional background. Because of these characteristics, it can be challenging for individual users evaluate the others' ideas and keep track of the others' perspectives and justifications in these Online Open Participative (OOP) environments. One approach to address this challenge is to first automatically identify statements that contain one's rationales from the communication record and then present them to the participants to raise their awareness of these rationale statements. These rationale-containing statements are argumentative discourse units that include rationales and some limited context around them. Various studies are conducted to explore how to detect them automatically [15, 23]. For example, a few

© Springer Nature Switzerland AG 2019
N. G. Taylor et al. (Eds.): iConference 2019, LNCS 11420, pp. 690–696, 2019.
https://doi.org/10.1007/978-3-030-15742-5_65

studies have focused on examining discourse relations that are commonly present in rationale-containing statements [3, 10, 11, 24].

In this study, we explore the existence of authority claims in rationale-containing statements. Authority claims are statements made by a discussion participant aimed at bolstering their credibility in the discussion [2]. We speculated that people tend to make such statements when they provide their justifications in OOP environments because they have little knowledge about the others they communicate with, the participation is open with little or no background check or requirement, and there are many participants in a discussion context. In addition, OOP environments often have little or no non-verbal cue that helps them establish their credibility. If we do discover strong correlations between rationale-containing statements and authority claims, then the detection of authority claims may contribute to the detection of rationale-containing statements.

We annotated authority claims in the rationale-containing statement datasets from [21, 24]. In the following sections, we present in details our annotation process and results, and then discuss the implication of our findings and our next step.

2   Our Datasets

We leveraged the rationale-containing statements from [24]. [24] obtained five substantial data sets from Rutgers' argument mining group. Each data set consists of text segments from a blogpost at Technorati (technorati.com) between 2008–2010 and its first 100 comments. These five blogpost datasets are about different issues. Specifically, Android and iPad datasets are about the user interface and usability of the android device and iPad. Ban dataset is about the ban of sharing music on social media. Layoff is about the layoff and outsourcing in the United States. And Twitter is about the Twitter as a social media tool. Rutgers' researchers had human experts and Amazon Mechanical Turkers annotate the blogposts and the comments to identify two types of text segments: targets and call-outs. According to their annotation guidelines [21], a target is a prior action that a call-out responds to or comments on in some way. A call-out includes one or both of the following: (a) explicit stance (indication of attitude or position relative to the target), and (b) explicit rationale (argument/justification/explanation of the stance taken). With these datasets, [24] analyzed the call-outs in these datasets to identify those that contain rationales. They then annotated the discourse relations in these rationale-containing statements using rhetorical structure theory (RST) [13] and identified ten common discourse relations in the statements.

In our study, we reviewed the rationale-containing statements from [24] and filtered overlapping sentences. We then proceeded to annotate the authority claims.

3   Annotation of Authority Claims

Authority claims are statements made by a discussion participant aimed at bolstering their credibility in the discussion [2]. According to [2], a writer may use various strategies to bolster one's credibility, e.g., external credible source, common sense, and personal experiences. Our analysis examined whether the statement reveals that the writer had an intention to bolster his/her credibility in making the statement. We are interested in the writer's intention because we speculated that there would As pointed out in the Introduction section, we speculated that participants would feel a need to bolster their credibility when giving their claims and rationales in OOP environments.

We give three examples to illustrate our annotation focus. Consider this statement: *Apples are good for your health. They are extremely rich in important antioxidants, flavonoids, and dietary fiber.* The first sentence is the writer's claim. From the writer's perspective, it is relatively clear that the function of the second sentence is to provide an explanation of the claim, whereas its function to bolster the writer's credibility in making the claim is not evident. In our analysis, we did not consider this statement to contain authority claim.

Consider this second example: *I remember Apple telling people give the UI and the keyboard a month and you'll get used to it. Plus all the commercials showing the interface. So, no, you didn't just pick up the iPhone and know how to use it. It was pounded into to you.* In this statement, the last two sentences reflect the writer's claim – "*No, you didn't just pick up...It was ...*" The first two sentences provide rationales to this claim. To us, the act of adding "*I remember*" to the utterance hints the writer's intention to bolster his/her credibility. Also, by saying that "*all the commercials...*" the writer bolsters the credibility using the common sense strategy explained by [2].

The third example uses this statement: *On the other hand, from what I've seen with Android, it's not so much the differences in the UI, it's the inconsistency from one part of the UI to another. It's the classic Linux desktop problem. It's so open that everything on it has its own way of working and interacting.* To us, the key phrase for annotating the authority claim in this sentence is "*from what I've seen with Android*". The statement is still grammatically correct and the core meaning does not change. The addition of this phrase reflects the writer's intention to bolster his/her credibility by emphasizing the personal experience.

Before the annotation, we first separated sentences in the text based on the punctuation marks - sentences are separated by period, exclamatory mark, question mark, and suspension points. While the intended or actual influence of an authority claim may span multiple sentences, it is the occurrence of the bolstering intention in a sentence that is considered in our study hence our analysis was at the sentence level. The following statements are considered individual sentences according to this rule. While suspension points are often ellipses, there are cases in which users used other punctuation marks like hyphen in the last example below.

- *But once one scaled the usage up, the number of windows open to reach a specific file exploded.*
- *I took Nexus on a trial basis for a week and have decided that it's a much better fit for a peculiar audience, primarily MIT engineers.*
- *I have a macpro and a macbookpro, and on my MPB, I run Win7 as the default OS because I find it more intuitive and easy*

Our annotation process was iterative. At the beginning, the two authors met and discussed the authority claim concept and annotated a snippet of the data independently (their academic background: the first author majors in Information Science, and the second majors in Computational Linguistics program at Department of Linguistics). They then exchanged the analysis results and discussed the differences. After two rounds of this process, they finalized the criteria of an authority claim. The second author then annotated the rest of the data. Intra-coder reliability measure [20] was used to calculate the reliability of the second author's annotation work. Specifically, he annotated the data again after two weeks and we compared the two results using Krippendorff's Alpha [6]. We calculated this value using a sentence as the unit. That is, we identified total number of sentences and the total number of authority claim sentences in two annotation exercises and compared the results.

This reliability check showed good agreement between the two annotation results for all five datasets, as shown in Table 1.

Table 1. Number of rationale-containing callouts in our dataset.

Dataset name	Number of rationale-containing callouts	Number of sentences	Number of authority claims (Annotation 1)	Number of authority claims (Annotation 2)	Krippendorff's Alpha
Android	52	198	14	11	0.90
Ban	51	213	6	6	0.84
iPad	63	218	12	13	0.99
Layoffs	55	307	7	7	0.89
Twitter	50	188	4	3	0.85

In the subsequent semester, we recruited and trained a graduate student majoring in Information Management to annotate authority claims based on our coding instruction, and had her annotate the datasets again. We compared and discussed her annotation result with the second author's and achieved agreement in the end.

4   Results and Discussion

As shown in Table 1, our dataset contains 271 rationale-containing call-outs and 1,124 sentences. We only have 42 authority claim sentences which is only about 3.7% of the data. This result is contradictory to our speculation. In other words, the participants in our dataset scarcely attempted to bolster their credibility when presenting their reasoning to the others.

There are several possible explanations to this finding. First, the datasets we examined are online blogs and the comments below them, not content of online deliberations or debates. Therefore, the participants' intention may be more so of expressing their views than persuading others to agree with their views. So they were little concerned about whether the others would view them credible or not. To examine whether this explanation is valid, we are annotating online Reddit discussions to explore the existence and percentage of authority claims in their arguments. We also plan to explore other online debate dataset such as Internet Argument Corpus [22].

Second, it is possible that while the participants had the intention to persuade others they used different persuasion strategies. Commonly defined as "human communication that is designed to influence others by modifying their beliefs, values, or attitudes" ([19], p. 21), persuasion can appear in various forms in communication record through different strategies. For example, Aristotle's work focuses on the speaker's acts to make the comment persuasive and is commonly adopted by the related communities [8]. In Aristotle's view, persuasion depends on the credibility of the speaker (ethos), the emotions of the audience (pathos), as well as on the cogency of the arguments employed and their ability to show our claims to be correct (logos). Authority claims reflect the use of ethos in persuasion strategies. Therefore, it is a possibility that the participants in our datasets used other persuasion acts more than ethos. Interestingly, a recent annotation study [7] also shows that out of the three persuasion modes ethos were used least when participants offering the premise for their claims in an online persuasive forum. In that study, the authors annotated 78 discussion threads that include 278 turns of dialogues. These consist of 2,615 propositions in 2,148 total sentences. Of these sentences, 1,068 contain a premise and only 3% of these premise sentences contain ethos. We also note that [7] annotated the text at the sentence level as well.

Third, it has been shown that we behave differently in online social activities than offline social interaction [17, 18]. It is possible that the type of communication medium affects how one's credibility is established in communication or how people reason. For example, in online communications, the user's credibility or authority may be established through other information channel in the environment such as the user's profile. If this is the case, it is perhaps not sufficient in argument mining research that only depends on existing theoretical frameworks on argumentation and reasoning which are mainly based on face-to-face communication and interactions. Further investigation is needed that helps us better understand the effects of communication medium on argumentation process at individuals' cognitive and meta-cognitive level.

5   Conclusion

Internet users increasingly interact with others through these new and advanced forms of online communication. Many of these interactions involve complex processes of persuasion and influence [9, 14]. Researchers explore computational techniques to automatically identify components of participants' arguments in these activities, such as their stances [1, 16] and justifications and supporting statements [4, 12].

In this research program, we explore indicators of one's reasoning traces focusing on one's rationales. Our objective in this annotation study is to examine whether the existence of authority claims is an indicator of one's rationale places in OOP environments. Our work is preliminary both in terms of the size of the data and the communication context. We are exploring the occurrence of authority claims in larger datasets and how the online activity's context correlates with the occurrence. Interestingly, research study of scientific discourse has overlapping work with ours, e.g., the knowledge attribution and epistemic evaluation model in scientific discourse by

De Waard and Maat [5]. One of our future work is to compare the findings from social media content and scientific discourse to further explore the contextual factor on the choices of the argumentation strategies.

References

1. Bar-Haim, R., Edelstein, L., Jochim, C., Slonim, N.: Improving claim stance classification with lexical knowledge expansion and context utilization. In: Proceedings of the 4th Workshop on Argument Mining, pp. 32–38 (2017)
2. Bender, E.M., et al.: Annotating social acts: authority claims and alignment moves in Wikipedia talk pages. In: Proceedings of the Workshop on Languages in Social Media, pp. 48–57 (2011)
3. Biran, O., Rambow, O.: Identifying justifications in written dialogs. In: Proceedings of 5th IEEE International Conference on Semantic Computing, pp. 162–168 (2011)
4. Boltužić, F., Šnajder, J.: Back up your stance: recognizing arguments in online discussions. In: Proceedings of the 1st Workshop on Argumentation Mining, pp. 49–58 (2014)
5. De Waard, A., Maat, H.P.: Epistemic modality and knowledge attribution in scientific discourse: a taxonomy of types and overview of features. In: Proceedings of the Workshop on Detecting Structure in Scholarly Discourse, pp. 47–55 (2012)
6. Hayes, A.F., Krippendorff, K.: Answering the call for a standard reliability measure for coding data. Commun. Methods Measures 1(1), 77–89 (2007)
7. Hidey, C., Musi, E., Hwang, A., Muresan, S., McKeown, K.: Analyzing the semantic types of claims and premises in an online persuasive forum. In: Proceedings of the 4th Workshop on Argument Mining, pp. 11–21 (2017)
8. Kennedy, G.A.: History of Rhetoric, Volume I: The Art of Persuasion in Greece, vol. 1. Princeton University Press, Princeton (2015)
9. Khazaei, T., Xiao, L., Mercer, R.: Writing to persuade: analysis and detection of persuasive discourse. In: Proceedings of iConference. https://www.ideals.illinois.edu/handle/2142/96673. Accessed 15 Sept 2018 (2017)
10. Khazaei, T., Xiao, L., Mercer, R.: Identification and disambiguation of lexical cues of rhetorical relations across different text genres. In: Proceedings of the First Workshop on Linking Computational Models of Lexical, Sentential and Discourse-Level Semantics, pp. 54–63 (2015)
11. Khazaei, T., Xiao, L.: Corpus-based analysis of rhetorical relations: a study of lexical cues. In: Proceedings of the IEEE International Conference on Semantic Computing, pp. 417–423 (2015)
12. Koreeda, Y., Yanase, T., Yanai, K., Sato, M., Niwa, Y.: Neural attention model for classification of sentences that support promoting/suppressing relationship. In: Proceedings of the 3rd Workshop on Argument Mining, pp. 76–81 (2016)
13. Mann, W.C., Thompson, S.A.: Rhetorical structure theory: toward a functional theory of text organization. Text 8(3), 243–281 (1988)
14. Mao, W.T., Xiao, L., Mercer, R.: The use of text similarity and sentiment analysis to examine rationales in the large-scale online deliberations. In: Proceedings of 5th Workshop on Computational Approaches to Subjectivity, Sentiment & Social Media Analysis, pp. 147–153 (2014)
15. Park, J.S., Cardie, C.: Identifying appropriate support for propositions in online user comments. In: Proceedings of the Annual Meeting on Association for Computational Linguistics (ACL), p. 29 (2014). http://aclweb.org/anthology/W/W14/W14-2105.pdf

16. Rajendran, P., Bollegala, D., Parsons, S.: Contextual stance classification of opinions: a step towards enthymeme reconstruction in online reviews. In: Proceedings of the Third Workshop on Argument Mining (ArgMining2016), pp. 31–39 (2016)
17. Rouhshad, A., Wigglesworth, G., Storch, N.: The nature of negotiations in face-to-face versus computer-mediated communication in pair interactions. Lang. Teach. Res. **20**(4), 514–534 (2016)
18. Schulze, J., Schultze, M., West, S.G., Krumm, S.: The knowledge, skills, abilities, and other characteristics required for face-to-face versus computer-mediated communication: similar or distinct constructs? J. Bus. Psychol. **32**(3), 283–300 (2017)
19. Simons, H.W.: Persuasion: Understanding, Practice, and Analysis. Addison Wesley Publishing Company, Reading (1976)
20. Van den Hoonaard, W.C.: Inter-and intracoder reliability. In: The Sage Encyclopedia of Qualitative Research Methods, vol. 1, pp. 445–446 (2008)
21. Wacholder, N., Muresan, S., Ghosh, D., Aakhus, M.: Annotating multiparty discourse: challenges for agreement metrics. In: Proceedings of LAW VIII-The 8th Linguistic Annotation Workshop, pp. 120–128 (2014)
22. Walker, M.A., Tree, J.E.F., Anand, P., Abbott, R., King, J.: A corpus for research on deliberation and debate. In: Proceedings of the 8th International Conference on Language Resources and Evaluation (LREC), 21–27 May, Istanbul, Turkey, pp. 812–817 (2012)
23. Wyner, A., Schneider, J., Atkinson, K., Bench-Capon, T.: Semi-automated argumentative analysis of online product reviews. In: Proceedings of 4th International Conference on Computational Models of Argument, vol. 245, pp. 43–50 (2012)
24. Xiao, L., Conroy, N.: Discourse relations in rationale-containing text-segments. J. Am. Soc. Inform. Sci. Technol. **68**(12), 2783–2794 (2017)

Informing Technology Design Through Offline Experiences

Firefighters' Strategies for Processing Spatial Information During Emergency Rescue Searches

Julia Cope[1,6], Marco Arias[2,6], DeAndre' Williams[3,6], Cristina Bahm[4,6(✉)], and Vusumuzi Ngwazini[5,6]

[1] University of Pittsburgh, Pittsburgh, USA
[2] California State Polytechnic University, Pomona, USA
[3] Indiana University, Bloomington, USA
[4] La Roche College, Pittsburgh, USA
cristina.bahm@laroche.edu
[5] Oakwood University, Huntsville, USA
[6] iSchool Inclusion Institute, Pittsburgh, USA

Abstract. Firefighters face a unique wayfinding situation when they are in emergency situations. This study aims to examine the strategies that firefighters use when in an emergency situation to provide insights for future research. In this study, we interview 12 firefighters from three regions of the US to understand the navigation strategies they use during rescue missions.

After analyzing the results using grounded theory as a basis, we found that firefighters use various navigational strategies that serve one of four purposes, (1) to build a path, (2) to improve vision, (3) to create a cognitive map, and (4) to make directional decisions. From here, we hope to link these unique navigational purposes to actual tools that can help firefighters save lives.

Keywords: Spatial cognition · Firefighters · Human factors

1 Introduction

Indoor navigation is complicated by factors such as repetitive structure, stacked floor plans, and a lack of recognizable landmarks [4, 6, 8]. These difficulties are further complicated for firefighters during rescue searches due to the conditions under which they must navigate. Conditions such as low visibility due to dark smoke and limited movement due to heavy gear and hot gases means firefighters often crouch or crawl on the ground while searching. In many cases, firefighters do not know where survivors will be or what to expect inside the building. Additionally, the structure of the house may change due to collapses or spreading fire, potentially making past routes unnavigable.

In this paper we define navigational strategies as behavioral patterns between the subject, the environment, and any tools that decrease the cognitive load of navigation. The navigation strategies that firefighters use must help them to overcome the unique challenges they face while trying to navigate indoor spaces. The design of user-centered wayfinding tools must be informed by the interactions between the user's internal representation of space and the environment itself [3, 9]. It follows that to create personalized navigation aids for firefighters, we must first understand the current navigation strategies and tools in use by firefighters during emergency rescue searches.

This work is a continuation of the work started in [9] which pointed out the need for cognitively salient wayfinding aids for firefighters specifically. In this study, we interview 12 firefighters from three regions in the USA, in California, Pennsylvania, and Maryland, to investigate the navigational strategies they use during rescue searches. After analyzing the results using grounded theory as a basis, we found that firefighters use various navigational strategies that serve one of four purposes, (1) to build a path, (2) to improve vision, (3) to create a cognitive map, and (4) to make directional decisions. From here, we hope to link these unique navigational purposes to actual tools that can help firefighters save lives.

2 Literature Review

The broad purpose of a navigational strategy is to help the user interact with the environment in a "consistent and unambiguous way," Freksa [3]. One reason it is difficult to navigate in a complex indoor environment according to [5] is that staircases, or floor to floor transition points, are often not depicted well on wayfinding aids. Battles and Fu [1] examined a variety of wayfinding strategies that are adopted by travelers using a schematic map of a multi level building.

[2] showed how the role of background knowledge is used to evaluate indoor landmarks. This coupled with the fact that firefighters face a particular let of difficulties that call for cognitively salient wayfinding aids [9] means that it is important that we take into account what firefighters actually do in the field when they are on rescue missions and design our tools around that.

3 Methodology

This research intends to lay the groundwork for understanding the strategies and tools that firefighters currently use so that advanced technologies can be applied to specifically fit the needs of firefighters in the field. To begin examining this, we performed semi-structured interviews with 12 firefighters, asking them to verbally explain how they navigate indoor environments during rescue searches. Table 1 displays information about each participant.

After gathering basic demographic information, we asked participants about how they were trained to navigate as a firefighter and what they believed were the most effective strategies for indoor searches. We also asked firefighters what problems they encounter during indoor navigation and any potential solutions they could imagine. All interviews were recorded and later transcribed. Transcriptions were then analyzed using a thematic analysis methodology based in grounded theory. We analyzed the verbalizations of all firefighters and grouped their navigational strategies into four categories according to the purpose of the strategy.

Table 1. Demographic information for participants

Participant	Number of years active as a firefighter	Last active location
1	25	Pittsburgh, PA
2	19	Pittsburgh, PA
3	3	Lake Elsinore, CA
4	33	Kensington, MD
5	3.5	San Diego, CA
6	20	Pittsburgh, PA
7	12	Pittsburgh, PA
8	10	Kensington, MD
9	10	Wheaton, MD
10	15	Wheaton, MD
11	26	Wheaton, MD
12	16	Los Angeles, CA

4 Results and Discussion

As shown below in Fig. 1, firefighters reported using a variety of different strategies to navigate indoor spaces. Using grounded theory, we analyzed the verbalizations of all firefighters and grouped their strategies into four categories according to the purpose of the strategy in helping the firefighter achieve their goals of searching the building and exiting safely.

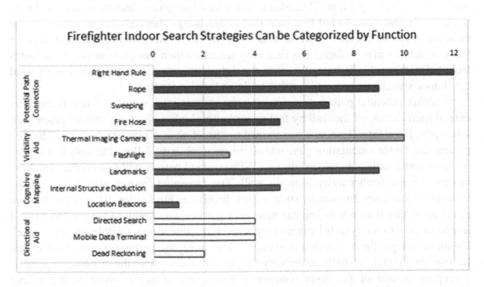

Fig. 1. Figure showing firefighters' indoor search strategies

Although from different parts of the country and with different years of service, there were clear similarities in the way that firefighters processed and used spatial information in an environment to find their way around. We were able to group these into four groups:

- Potential Path Connection Strategies as Navigational Aids
- Visibility Aids as Navigational Aids
- Cognitive Mapping Strategies as Navigational Aids
- Directional Aids as Navigational Aids

4.1 Potential Path Connection Strategies as Navigational Aids

The location and number of survivors in the building is often unknown, so firefighters must perform an extensive search of the building. This proves difficult due to low visibility and potentially changing structure of the indoor space. Firefighters use specific search patterns, which we have named potential path connection strategies, to perform an extensive search while remaining oriented and connected to a path to an exit.

An example of a potential path connection strategy is the right-hand rule, where firefighters feel their way around a room by keeping their right side along the wall to search the entire perimeter of a room, before moving on to the next room. The right-hand rule allows firefighters to perform an extensive search of the building while remaining connected to the wall. As seen in Fig. 1, all firefighters reported using the right-hand rule while navigating indoors during emergency situations. Firefighter 2 described, "In a fire we are trained to feel the wall as a left-hand or right-hand search and stick to that because if you need to get out you can turn around and follow that." Additionally, firefighter 3 mentioned that the right-hand search "allows you to do a full circle inside the house... that way you don't get lost." The idea is that when firefighters remain connected to the wall, they remain connected to a path that either brings them all the way through the building or can be traced backwards to an exit. However, this is only a potential path out since structures may collapse and fires may spread, which can prevent previous routes from being taken. Firefighters described the right-hand rule as the baseline strategy used for indoor searches, upon which other tools and strategies built.

Another potential path connection strategy is sweeping, which is when firefighters extend their search off the wall by feeling with their bodies and tools that lengthen their wingspan. Firefighter 7 says he was trained to "function as a two-person team. The first person can be the orientation guy, whose primary job is to follow the wall and search for landmarks such as windows, doors..." The second person will extend the search by sweeping areas further away from the wall. The sweeping firefighter will call out the landmarks that they encounter, such as any furniture. Firefighter 10 explained, "you never go farther than where you can hear your partner, you know, if we go into a fire, I like to be able to see you. If I can no longer see you, [due to low visibility from smoke], I want to be right there... within proximity." The sweeping partner(s) extend the search into the room while visually or verbally keeping in contact with the orientation partner. Sweeping is one of the most commonly mentioned strategies used during rescue missions and is used in conjunction with right-hand rule.

Additionally, for large area searches, firefighters extend their search by using rope. Firefighter 6 described using "a piece of rope or a piece of webbing...[to] give an anchor point if the visibility is bad." A rope can be tied off at a fixed point or held by another firefighter to allow a firefighter to extend the search farther into a large area while being anchored to a fixed position. Similarly, to a rescue rope, a fire hose can also be used as a path to an exit: firefighters can follow to hose line back outside.

4.2 Visibility Aids as Navigational Aids

One of firefighters' challenges during rescue searches is limited visibility inside the structure due to heavy smoke. Visibility aids function as navigational aids as they provide the firefighter with more spatial information than they could directly experience from the environment without the tool. Many firefighters report using a handheld thermal imaging camera which allows them to see heat signatures as seen in Fig. 2. Firefighter 3 mentions that "the thermal imaging camera is really effective...if we are inside a structure that has heavy smoke and you can't see through it, that camera allows us to see heat signatures." Firefighters additionally use flashlights which are typically attached to their jackets. The use the flashlights to see in front of them as well as to be visible to other firefighters and any survivors inside the structure.

Fig. 2. Showing the handheld thermal image scanner

4.3 Cognitive Mapping Strategies as Navigational Aids

Cognitive mapping navigational strategies help subjects create mental representations of space based on external information. Firefighters must process new spatial information quickly as their first exposure to the internal layout of a building is usually during the rescue search. An example of a cognitive mapping strategy is internal structure deduction, when an individual predicts the internal structure of an indoor space based on present features that are similar to those in previous experiences. Firefighter 4 states that, "houses are configured in such a way so that you look at a type of house and you can tell the basic layout before you even go through the front door. Cape Cod [houses] usually have a central stairwell, more modern houses have the stairwells usually to one side...in older houses, it's usually in the back." Firefighters use internal structure deduction as a mental shortcut to predict spatial information. Firefighters use the strategy to create a cognitive map to remain oriented and to make spatial decisions in their search. Also, Firefighters remember specific landmarks, notably doors and windows, as points of reference in case they must turn around and find the nearest exit. Their use of landmarks primarily seems to be an aid to recalling a short route to an escape more so than an aid to deciding which direction to go next.

4.4 Directional Aids as Navigational Aids

Directional aids help individuals decide which specific direction to go. Firefighters typically do not know the layout of the building or where survivors will be inside the building, so they are unable to find or follow specific directions to a useful location. For this reason, directional aids are some of the least commonly used search strategies by firefighters. Firefighters may follow a directed search, which is when they go directly to a room in a building if there is known to be a survivor there. Firefighter 7 described that "if somebody says, 'My kid's in there,' and they point to a window... we're going to use a ladder to get to that particular window... That method as far as targeted [or directed] search is actually very effective." Firefighters will use verbal directions if they lead directly to a known location of a survivor. However, this information is not often available, and thus extensive search strategies such as the right-hand rule are more commonly implemented.

Fewer than half of the firefighters interviewed mentioned using the mobile data terminal suggesting that it is not used as a source of information as commonly as strategies such as the right-hand rule or the thermal imaging camera. That is not to say that the firefighters we interviewed do not have access to mobile data terminals, rather it implies that this is not thought of as a "go-to" strategy for indoor searches.

5   Conclusion and Future Work

The purpose of a navigational aid is to provide a tool to interact with the environment in a "consistent and unambiguous way," Frankenstein [2]. Firefighters have unique goals and challenges while navigating indoors during high stake situations. In this research, we examine the specific strategies that firefighters currently use to understand how they process the spatial information around them. We found that firefighters around the country use similar rules that allow them to either (1) build a path (2) improve their vision (3) use cognitive strategies and (4) use directional aids. Future work should focus on incorporating the results of this study directly into the design of wayfinding aids for firefighters.

References

1. Battles, A., Fu, W.T.: Navigating indoor with maps: representations and processes. In: Proceedings of the Annual Meeting of the Cognitive Science Society, vol. 36, no. 36, January 2014
2. Frankenstein, J., Brüssow, S., Ruzzoli, F., Hölscher, C.: The language of landmarks: the role of background knowledge in indoor wayfinding. Cogn. Process. **13**(1), 165–170 (2012)
3. Freksa, C., Klippel A., Winter, S.: A cognitive perspective on spatial context in spatial cognition: specialization and integration, Volume 05491 of Dagstuhl Seminar Proceedings. Dagstuhl, Germany (2007)
4. Hirtle, S.C., Bahm, C.R.: Cognition for the navigation of complex indoor environments. In: Indoor Wayfinding and Navigation, Chicago, pp. 1–12 (2015)
5. Hölscher, C., Meilinger, T., Vrachliotis, G., Brösamle, M., Knauff, M.: Up the down staircase: wayfinding strategies in multi-level buildings. J. Environ. Psychol. **26**(4), 284–299 (2006)
6. Ohm, C., Müller, M., Ludwig, B., Bienk, S.: Where is the landmark? Eye tracking studies in large scale indoor environments (2014)
7. Richter, K.F., Dara-Abrams, D., Raubal, M.: Navigating and learning with location based services: a user-centric design. In: Gartner, G., Li, Y. (eds.) 7th International Symposium on LBS & Telecartography, Guangzhou, China, pp. 261–276 (2010)
8. Robles Bahm, C., Hirtle, S.C.: Global landmarks in a complex indoor environment. In: LIPIcs-Leibniz International Proceedings in Informatics, vol. 86. Schloss Dagstuhl-Leibniz-Zentrum fuer Informatik (2017)
9. Speckels, K., et al.: Towards the creation of cognitively salient wayfinding aids for emergency first responders. In: iConference 2018 Proceedings (2018)

"Happy Rides Are All Alike; Every Unhappy Ride Is Unhappy in Its Own Way": Passengers' Emotional Experiences While Using a Mobile Application for Ride-Sharing

Dedema and Pengyi Zhang(✉)

Department of Information Management, Peking University,
Beijing 100871, China
{dedema, pengyi}@pku.edu.cn

Abstract. Ride-sharing is a rising approach that provides more convenience and flexibility for road users. Previous research has examined the process, existing forms, and matching algorithms of real-time dynamic ride-sharing technology, but we know little about how users feel when they use a ride-sharing application. In this paper, we describe a study that investigates passengers' emotional experiences when using a ride-sharing application and examines factors related to passengers' emotional experiences. We conducted a survey with 1,129 users of a major ride-sharing app from four cities in China. Results show that: (1) passengers feel more positive emotional experiences (75%) such as "satisfaction" (47%) than negative emotions; (2) negative emotional experiences (worry, disappointment, anger) differ from each other in causal agency, emotional outlet, and action tendency; (3) context of use, interaction, and user characteristics are related to passengers' emotional experiences. The results provide some preliminary understanding of the passengers' emotional experiences, and could be helpful to improve the design of such socio-technical solutions.

Keywords: Ride-sharing · HCI · Emotional experiences · Sharing economy

1 Introduction

Road transportation is one of the major challenges in today's world. Therefore, many Web and smartphone-based solutions have emerged for promoting intelligent traffic management [1]. In particular, ride-sharing is a rising approach for reducing car usage in a city, which is arguably beneficial both to individual users, e.g. reducing gasoline expenses, and to a city as a whole [2], e.g. reducing traffic congestion and pollution [3]. Users' positive experience in using ride sharing applications (apps) is essential to their continuous usage as well as to boosting the whole ride-sharing system.

Previous research has examined the process, existing forms, and matching algorithms of dynamic ride-sharing [4]. For example, Chan and Shaheen characterize ride-sharing into three forms: "acquaintance-based", "organization-based", and "ad hoc" [5]. Models and algorithms have been developed for matching large groups of passengers to

© Springer Nature Switzerland AG 2019
N. G. Taylor et al. (Eds.): iConference 2019, LNCS 11420, pp. 706–717, 2019.
https://doi.org/10.1007/978-3-030-15742-5_67

shared vehicles in real time [6, 7]. Other research has examined social issues of smartphone-based ride-sharing technology such as safety (traveling with strangers), liability (e.g. accidents), as well as privacy [8, 9]. Prior research has paid much attention to application design and optimization rather than users' actual usage and experiences. In particular, we know little about how users feel and what factors influence their emotional experience when using a ride-sharing mobile app.

In this paper, we conducted a survey of users of a major mobile app for ride-sharing in China, aiming to understand their emotional experiences. We focused on six major types of emotions, including three positive (happiness, satisfaction, and surprise) and three negative (worry, disappointment, and anger), and explored the influences of factors including context of use, interaction, and user characteristics on these emotions. Our research questions are:

RQ1: How are passengers' emotional experiences when using a ride-sharing app?
RQ2: Are passengers' emotional experiences related to their characteristics, the contexts of use, and satisfaction of the interaction when using a ride-sharing app?

Our findings provide insights into how passengers feel when using a ride-sharing app, what causes these emotions, how they deal with the emotions, and what factors influence the emotional experiences. In the rest of the paper, we first review related literature, describe our methodology, present the findings, and conclude and discuss the future role of HCI in designing more user-friendly ride-sharing applications.

2 Literature Review

2.1 Ride-Sharing

"A growing concern about climate change and a yearning for social embeddedness by localness and communal consumption" [10] have made the "collaborative consumption"/"sharing economy" an appealing alternative for consumers [11]. Based on the idea of the "sharing economy", researchers and practitioners has proposed shared transport systems, such as bike or car sharing, taxi applications [12, 13].

Ride-sharing participants can benefit from shared travel costs, travel-time savings from high occupancy vehicle lanes, and reduced commute stress [5]. Despite its benefits, there are several barriers to increased ride-sharing use, including reluctance to sacrifice the flexibility and convenience of the private automobile [14], desire for personal space and time [15], and personal security concerns about riding with strangers.

Previous research has examined the process of ride-sharing. For example, Agatz and others divide the process of ride-sharing into steps of "request", "set location", "pick up", and "deliver" [4]. Berbeglia and others focus on pickup and delivery problems and come up with some solution strategies [16, 17]. Others focus on the algorithm for dynamic ride-sharing. For example, Alonso-Mora and others present a mathematical model for real-time high-capacity ride-sharing that can be used for multitask assignment problems [18]. Kleiner and others present an approach which is adaptive to individual preferences of the passengers [6]. To enrich data sources in matching models, Cici and others take mobile and social data into consideration for matching passengers and shared vehicles [7]. In terms of users' role in ride-sharing, Sarriera and others report that having a negative social interaction is a deterrent for passengers to use ride-sharing application [19]. However, we know little about passengers' emotional experiences during their shared rides using ride-sharing applications.

2.2 Emotional Experiences in HCI

HCI researchers have defined user experiences as composed of several elements, such as usability (effectiveness and efficiency), user interface, interaction design, emotional experiences and so on [20, 21]. Therefore, emotional experience is one important aspect of user experience.

Emotional experience appears to help users evaluate outcomes when interacting with products [22]. Positive emotions have been demonstrated to have additional beneficial effects during application usage. When using complex technology, positive emotions decrease usage anxiety [23] and contribute to the experience of usage comfort [24] and to general usability [25]. Norman proposed three levels of emotional response include the visceral-level, behavioral-level, and reflective-level [26]. In addition, context of use plays an important role in shaping the experience when users interact with technology [27]. A model of context of use lists the components of context include physical, temporal, social, and technical and information context [28].

In our study, we focus on emotional experiences as how users feel while using a mobile app for ride-sharing. To conceptualize the complexity of emotional experiences, we refer to Norman's three levels and the above context model to investigate "feeling", "behavior", "cognition", and "context of use" in our research framework.

2.3 Positive and Negative Emotions

Emotion is defined as "a complex pattern of bodily and mental changes that includes feelings, cognitive processes, and specific behavioral reactions made in response to a situation perceived as personally significant" [29]. Previous research has studied emotion from many components such as valence (positive/neutral/negative), core affect, action tendencies [30].

Prior research has found that both positive and negative emotions can be evoked depends on user's needs, use case, and interface [31]. As for action tendency, Frijda and others divide emotions to "engage" (such as interesting), "unpredictable" (such as surprise), and "withdraw" (such as sadness) [32]. In this paper, we focus on six most common emotions, and their description are shown in Table 1.

Table 1. Six most common emotions.

Type	Valence	Action tendency	Definition
Happiness	Positive	Engage	You are pleased about in something or some desirable event [33]
Satisfaction	Positive	Engage	You enjoy the recent fulfilment of a need or desire [33]
Surprise	Positive	Unpredictable	You are pleased by something that happened suddenly and unexpectedly [33]
Worry	Negative	Unpredictable	Something happened that could mean something bad will happen to you or someone else [34]
Disappointment	Negative	Withdraw	You find out that something you had hoped for has not happened [34]
Anger	Negative	Withdraw	Someone did something bad that harmed or offended you [34]

3 Methodology

3.1 Research Design

We conducted a survey aiming to learn about passengers' emotional experiences when they used a ride-sharing mobile app. Participants were asked to recall the most recently ride-sharing experience when they experienced one of the following six kinds of emotions: happiness, satisfaction, surprise, worry, disappointment, and anger, and fill an online questionnaire. We also asked users to rate the contextual factors (0–10 Likert Scale) and the satisfaction level of interaction (0 being least satisfactory, 10 being most satisfactory) with the app. The questionnaire included four parts (Table 2).

Table 2. Survey framework

Part	Item	Question
Part 1: emotional experiences	Feeling	Type of emotions
		Strength of emotions
	Cognition	Causal agency
	Behavior	Emotional outlet
		Action tendency
Part 2: context of use	Temporal	Time of use
	Physical	Vehicle comfort
		Road traffic
	Technical	Accuracy of navigation
	Task	Urgency
		Presence of other passengers

(*continued*)

Table 2. (*continued*)

Part	Item	Question
Part 3: interaction	Ordering	Wait for response
	Picking up	Go to the site
		Connect the driver
	Delivering	Pick up other passengers
		Talk and chat
	Arriving	Comment and complain
Part 4: user characteristics	Demographic	Gender
		Age
		Education
	Usage	Weekly frequency
		Weekly cost

3.2 Data Collection

Surveys were conducted on users of a major ride-sharing mobile app in four cities with populations ranging from two to four million in China. Surveys links were sent via SMS to users through the app. Participants were informed about the privacy policy and provided consent before filling out the questionnaires. We sent questionnaires to about 10,000 users and received 1,233 responses, among which 1,129 questionnaires were complete. Data was collected over three days in June, 2018. Table 3 shows the demographics of the participants.

Table 3. Participant demographics.

Characteristic	Value	Percentage	Characteristic	Value	Percentage
Gender	Male	50.3%		Middle school	2.9%
	Female	49.7%		High school	13.6%
Age	<22	10.8%	Education	Junior College	24.7%
	22-35	60.1%		College	48.8%
	35-50	25.2%		Graduate	9.9%
	>50	3.8%	Weekly expense (in CNY)	<50	38.4%
Number of use per week	0-5	55.6%		50-100	41.9%
	6-10	27.3%		100-200	13.9%
	>10	17.1%		>200	5.8%

3.3 Data Analysis

We conducted descriptive statistics of the six types of emotions. We then examined and compared the causal agencies that evoked passengers' emotions, the outlets of their emotional expressions if any, and the actions passengers took among different types of emotions. We conducted Chi-square tests to see if the differences in causal agency, emotional outlet, and action tendency are significant between positive and negative emotions. We also conducted K-Wallis tests to examine whether passengers' ratings on contextual factors and interaction satisfaction are related to the types of emotions they experience. We also tested whether emotional experiences differ across different user groups.

4 Results

4.1 Emotional Experiences

As shown in Fig. 1, passengers experience more positive emotions (75%) in ride-sharing. Nearly half of passengers feel satisfied (47%). 21% passengers feel happy, and 7% passengers feel surprised during the ride-sharing process. As to negative emotions, passengers feel more disappointed (14%) than worried (6%) and angry (5%).

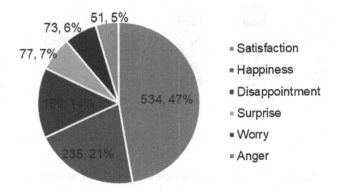

Fig. 1. Distribution of emotions.

As to strength of emotions, most passengers' emotions are moderate (47.9%) and strong (32.3%). In positive experiences, passengers' emotions are more moderate (51.2%) while in negative experiences passengers' emotions are very strong (20.5%).

Causal Agency. As to the agency that evokes passengers' emotions when using the ride-sharing app, the top three most mentioned agencies are app (45%), circumstance (such as traffic) (24%), and driver (23%). Figure 2 shows the frequency of causal agency of six types of emotions in ride-sharing experience respectively.

There is a significant difference on causal agency between six types of emotions. Happiness and satisfaction are more evoked by oneself comparing to other emotions ($\chi^2 = 67.232$, p < 0.01). Anger is more evoked by driver ($\chi^2 = 11.395$, p < 0.05), and worry is more evoked by other passengers ($\chi^2 = 33.875$, p < 0.01). Though app is the most causal agency to passengers' emotions, surprise is more evoked by app in particular ($\chi^2 = 18.449$, p < 0.01). Worry and disappointment are more evoked by circumstance ($\chi^2 = 12.142$, p < 0.05). To generalize, positive emotions are more similarly evoked by oneself and application, but negative emotions are evoked by different agency on each of them.

Emotional Outlet. As shown in Fig. 3, passengers often choose to withhold their emotions (47%), express them to someone (such as family or friends) (40%), and to the driver (19%). Chi-square test shows that there is a significant difference on emotional outlet between six types emotions. For example, passengers express more happiness, surprise, and anger to the driver in their rides ($\chi^2 = 17.793$, $p < 0.05$). Passengers express more anger to customer service comparing to other emotions ($\chi^2 = 34.005$, $p < 0.01$).

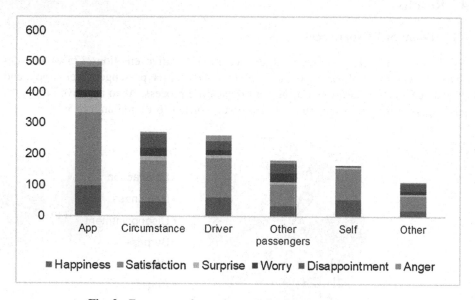

Fig. 2. Frequency of causal agency in six types of emotions.

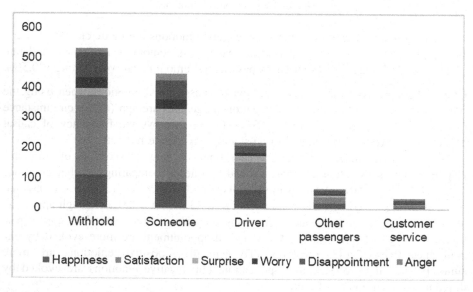

Fig. 3. Frequency of emotional outlet in six types of emotions.

Action Tendency. Comparing to passengers with negative emotions, passengers give more good ratings to drivers ($\chi^2 = 221.686$, $p < 0.01$), more good ratings to other passengers ($\chi^2 = 8.549$, $p < 0.01$), and are more likely to recommend the app ($\chi^2 = 191.015$, $p < 0.01$) to others when they experience positive emotions using ride-sharing application.

Passengers usually give more bad ratings on driver ($\chi^2 = 30.937$, p $p < 0.01$), give more bad ratings on other passengers ($\chi^2 = 13.228$, $p < 0.01$), give more bad comments on the app ($\chi^2 = 349.656$, $p < 0.01$) or stop using the app ($\chi^2 = 228.879$, $p = p < 0.01$) when they get negative emotions using ride-sharing application comparing to when getting positive emotions.

In every specific negative emotion, passengers take different actions as shown in Table 4. For example, passengers often ignore it when they are in worry ($\chi^2 = 26.014$, $p < 0.01$). Passengers give more bad ratings on driver when they get angry ($\chi^2 = 53.375$, $p < 0.01$), and stop using the app when they get disappointed and angry ($\chi^2 = 272.847$, $p < 0.01$).

Table 4. Percentages of action tendency in six types of emotions (multiple choices).

	Happiness	Satisfaction	Surprise	Worry	Disappointment	Anger
Ignoring it	17%	22%	8%	38%	19%	14%
Good ratings on driver	69%	57%	65%	12%	12%	2%
Bad ratings on driver	1%	2%	1%	8%	6%	20%
Good ratings on other passengers	7%	3%	9%	3%	0%	0%
Bad ratings on other passengers	1%	1%	0%	4%	4%	4%
Recommend the app to others	49%	48%	55%	5%	2%	2%
Bad comments on the app	3%	1%	4%	36%	50%	47%
Stop using the app	0%	1%	0%	12%	31%	43%
Other	2%	2%	0%	11%	12%	6%

4.2 Context of Use

Time of Use. When passengers use the ride-sharing app is not related to the types of emotion they experience ($\chi^2 = 24.724$, $p = 0.212$).

Presence of Other Passengers. When other passengers are present, passengers have more negative emotions ($\chi^2 = 16.153$, $p < 0.01$).

We asked participants rate the contextual factors by 0–10 Likert Scale, and Table 5 shows mean ratings of them. K-W Test suggests there is a significant difference in vehicle comfort ($\chi^2 = 139.387$, $p < 0.01$), road traffic congestion ($\chi^2 = 65.333$, $p < 0.01$), accuracy of navigation ($\chi^2 = 137.332$, $p < 0.01$), and urgency ($\chi^2 = 246.186$, $p < 0.01$) across different types of emotions.

Table 5. Mean ratings of contextual factors.

	Vehicle comfort	Road traffic	Accuracy of navigation	Urgency
Happiness	8.17	6.65	8.40	7.36
Satisfaction	7.70	6.30	8.13	6.79
Surprise	8.09	6.73	8.23	7.03
Worry	6.34	5.07	6.62	4.71
Disappointment	5.44	4.69	5.40	3.36
Anger	5.18	4.84	5.18	2.98

When passengers feel more comfortable of vehicle environment, they feel more positive emotions. Passengers also have more positive emotions with higher accuracy of navigation.

Passengers have more positive emotions with severer traffic congestion and higher urgency. It's more difficult for passengers to take taxis during traffic jam, but to use ride-sharing app a car can serve four even more passengers once. It also shorts waiting time of passengers when they are urgent.

4.3   Interaction Satisfaction

We asked participants to evaluate their satisfaction of interactions during using the ride-sharing app. K-W test was conducted and results show that there is a significant difference on evaluation score between six types of emotions. When passengers get more smoothly interaction in every step with ride-sharing app, they have more positive emotions.

As shown in Table 6, in positive emotional experiences, the means of three positive emotions are almost the same. In negative emotional experiences, the means of three emotions are significantly different. Ordering-wait for response process gets the lowest evaluation whether the emotional experiences are positive or negative, which means the difficulty of matching passengers and shared vehicles in real time. Picking up-connect the driver process gets the highest evaluation (6.84) in negative experience. Delivering-picking up other passengers gets low evaluation in negative experience (disappointment = 4.95, anger = 3.82). It's possibly because this process wastes the passengers' time and increases the concerns about riding with strangers.

Table 6. Means of the evaluation on satisfaction of interaction.

	Positive			Negative		
	Happiness	Satisfaction	Surprise	Worry	Disappoint-ment	Anger
Ordering-wait for response	7.92	7.20	7.57	5.00	3.91	3.80
Picking up-go to the site	8.55	8.42	8.65	6.63	6.10	5.51
Picking up-connect the driver	8.87	8.55	8.84	7.60	6.71	6.84
Delivering-pick up other passengers	8.44	8.01	8.21	5.56	4.95	3.82
Delivering-talk and chat	8.80	8.55	8.56	6.74	6.10	4.53
Arriving-Comment and complain	8.87	8.76	8.86	6.90	6.16	4.25

4.4 User Characteristics

Gender. Women have more negative emotions than men in ride-sharing ($\chi^2 = 5.059$, $p = 0.05$), especially women feel more worried and angry.

Age & Education. Passengers' age and education are not related with their emotional experiences.

Number of Use in a Week. Passengers who used the ride-sharing app more often have more negative emotional experiences ($\chi^2 = 13.964$, $p < 0.05$).

Weekly Expense. Passengers who spend more on ride-sharing app have more negative emotional experiences ($\chi^2 = 18.403$, $p < 0.01$).

5 Conclusion and Discussion

This paper presents results from a survey study of passengers' emotional experiences. Major conclusions are:

1. Passengers feel more positive emotions than negative emotions when using the ride-sharing mobile app. Positive and negative emotional experiences are different in causal agency, emotional outlet, and action tendency. Specifically, positive emotions are more similar whereas negative emotions are more diverse. For example, anger is more evoked by the driver and passengers express it more to customer service. Worry is more evoked by other passengers and circumstance and passengers choose to withhold it and just ignore it.
2. Context factors such as vehicle comfort, road traffic, accuracy of navigation, urgency, and presence of other passengers are related to passengers' emotional experiences. Satisfaction of interaction also is related to passengers emotional experience, when interactions with ride-sharing application are more successful, passengers' get more positive emotions [35]. Women and more frequent users tend to have more negative experiences.

The results provide some insights into how passengers feel in ride-sharing and factors influencing their experiences, and may have implications for improving user experiences in platform design by improving on factors that causes negative user experiences and focusing on factors that foster positive experience. There are some limitations of the survey research. First of all, people sometimes experience mixed emotions. Although we asked the participants to only recall experiences when a primary emotion is identifiable, some participants may have difficulty in doing so. Secondly, passengers are only part of the socio-technical system, drivers' emotional experiences are as important as passengers' and are often ignored by the platform that offers the ride-sharing services. To better understand drivers, passengers, and the platform, future research could use some qualitative methods such as in-depth interview and observation to better understand the mixed emotional experience and underlying values that drives the usage of such platforms. Out results show that passengers experience positive emotions when basic functional needs are met such as comfortable in-vehicle environment, accuracy of navigation and smooth interaction, while negative emotional experiences could be caused by more complex and nuanced factors which are likely to be culture-dependent. Mutual trust is found to be one of the most important factors in ride-sharing in western countries [36]. As ride-sharing is a social activity, it may carry potential harms and risks especially ones related to gender-based violence and sexism according to our results. What values are behind China's fast-blooming sharing economy and what are potential unsafety issues need further study in terms of other populations.

References

1. Thiagarajan, A., et al.: VTrack: accurate, energy-aware road traffic delay estimation using mobile phones. In: Proceedings of the 7th ACM Conference on Embedded Networked Sensor Systems, pp. 85–98. ACM, Berkeley (2009)
2. Amey, A.M.: Real-time ridesharing: exploring the opportunities and challenges of designing a technology-based rideshare trial for the MIT community. Massachusetts Institute of Technology (2010)
3. Triki, C., Al-Maimani, A., Akil, J.: Ridesharing in muscat: can it be a sustainable solution for the traffic congestion? Iran. J. Oper. Res. **8**, 98–109 (2017)
4. Agatz, N., Erera, A., Savelsbergh, M., Wang, X.: Optimization for dynamic ride-sharing: a review. Eur. J. Oper. Res. **223**, 295–303 (2012)
5. Chan, N.D., Shaheen, S.A.: Ridesharing in north America: past, present, and future. Transp. Rev. **32**, 93–112 (2012)
6. Kleiner, A., Ziparo, V.A.: A mechanism for dynamic ride sharing based on parallel auctions. In: International Joint Conference on Artificial Intelligence, pp. 266–272 (2011)
7. Cici, B., Markopoulou, A., Frias-Martinez, E., Laoutaris, N.: Assessing the potential of ride-sharing using mobile and social data: a tale of four cities. In: ACM International Joint Conference on Pervasive and Ubiquitous Computing, pp. 201–211 (2014)
8. Feeney, M.: Is ridesharing safe? (2015)
9. Goel, P., Kulik, L., Ramamohanarao, K.: Privacy-aware dynamic ride sharing. ACM Trans. Spat. Algorithms Syst. (TSAS) **2** (2016). 4
10. Hamari, J., Sjöklint, M., Ukkonen, A.: The sharing economy: why people participate in collaborative consumption. J. Assoc. Inf. Sci. Technol. **67**, 2047–2059 (2016)
11. Belk, R.: You are what you can access: sharing and collaborative consumption online. J. Bus. Res. **67**, 1595–1600 (2014)
12. Cohen, B.D., Kietzmann, J.: Ride on! Mobility business models for the sharing economy. Organ. Environ. **27**, 279–296 (2014)
13. Brownstone, D., Golob, T.F.: The effectiveness of ridesharing incentives: discrete-choice models of commuting in Southern California. Reg. Sci. Urban Econ. **22**, 5–24 (1992)
14. Dueker, K.J., Levin, I.P.: Carpooling: attitudes and participation (1976)
15. Bonsall, P.W., Spencer, A.H., Tang, W.-S.: What makes a car-sharer? Transportation **12**, 117–145 (1984)
16. Berbegliaaba, G.: Dynamic pickup and delivery problems. Eur. J. Oper. Res. **202**, 8–15 (2010)
17. Berbeglia, G., Cordeau, J.F., Gribkovskaia, I., Laporte, G.: Static pickup and delivery problems: a classification scheme and survey. TOP **15**, 37–40 (2007)

18. Alonso-Mora, J., Samaranayake, S., Wallar, A., Frazzoli, E., Rus, D.: On-demand high-capacity ride-sharing via dynamic trip-vehicle assignment. Proc. Natl. Acad. Sci. U.S.A. **114**, 462–467 (2017)
19. Sarriera, J.M., Álvarez, G.E., Blynn, K., Alesbury, A., Scully, T., Zhao, J.: To share or not to share: investigating the social aspects of dynamic ridesharing. Transp. Res. Rec. **2605**, 109–117 (2017)
20. Deaton, M.: The Elements of User Experience: User-Centered Design for the Web. ACM (2003)
21. Kuniavsky, M.: Smart Things: Ubiquitous Computing user Experience Design. Morgan Kaufmann Publishers Inc. (2010)
22. Forlizzi, J., Battarbee, K.: Understanding experience in interactive systems. In: Conference on Designing Interactive Systems: Processes, Practices, Methods, and Techniques, pp. 261–268 (2004)
23. Picard, R.W.: Affective Computing. MIT Press, Cambridge (1997)
24. Vink, P.: Comfort and Design: Principles and Good Practice. CRC Press, Boca Raton (2004)
25. Tractinsky, N., Katz, A.S., Ikar, D.: What is beautiful is usable. Interact. Comput. **13**, 127–145 (2000)
26. Norman, D.A.: Emotional Design: Why We Love (or Hate) Everyday Things (2004)
27. Dourish, P.: What we talk about when we talk about context. Pers. Ubiquit. Comput. **8**, 19–30 (2004)
28. Jumisko-Pyykkö, S., Vainio, T.: Framing the context of use for mobile HCI. In: J. Mob. Hum. Comput. Interact. (IJMHCI) **2**, 1–28 (2010)
29. Gerrig, R.J., Zimbardo, P.G.: Psychology and Life. Pearson, Boston (2010)
30. Frijda, N.H.: The Emotions. Cambridge University Press, Cambridge (1986)
31. Brave, S., Nass, C.: Emotion in human-computer interaction. In: Julie, A.J., Andrew, S. (eds.) The Human-Computer Interaction Handbook, pp. 81–96. L. Erlbaum Associates Inc. (2003)
32. Frijda, N.H., Kuipers, P., Ter Schure, E.: Relations among emotion, appraisal, and emotional action readiness. J. Pers. Soc. Psychol. **57**, 212 (1989)
33. Desmet, P.: Faces of product pleasure: 25 positive emotions in human-product interactions. Int. J. Des. **6**, 1–29 (2012)
34. Desmet, P.M.A., Fokkinga, S.F., Ozkaramanli, D., Yoon, J.K.: Emotion-driven product design (2016)
35. Jordan, P.W.: Human factors for pleasure in product use. Appl. Ergon. **29**, 25–33 (1998)
36. Merat, N., Madigan, R., Nordhoff, S.: Human factors, user requirements, and user acceptance of ride-sharing in automated vehicles. In: International Transport Forum Roundtable on Cooperative Mobility Systems and Automated Driving, pp. 6–7 (2016)

From Paper Forms to Electronic Flowsheets: Documenting Medical Resuscitations in a Time of Transition

Swathi Jagannath[1]([✉]), Aleksandra Sarcevic[1], and Sage Myers[2]

[1] Drexel University, Philadelphia, PA, USA
sj532@drexel.edu
[2] The Children's Hospital of Philadelphia, Philadelphia, PA, USA

Abstract. Electronic Health Records (EHRs) have a critical role in supporting continuity of patient care and effective clinical decision-making. Although EHRs are widespread today, many emergency departments (EDs) have been slow in adopting them for documenting time-critical scenarios such as resuscitations. Introduction of an electronic flowsheet for documenting medical resuscitations at our research site provided a unique opportunity for studying the nuances of the transition from paper to electronic documentation. We observed 44 medical resuscitations and conducted post-event interviews with 24 nurse documenters to examine their interactions and behaviors with the newly implemented electronic flowsheet. While our findings showed many advantages of electronic documentation, such as improved access to patient records and auto-population of flowsheet sections, we also identified several challenges associated with the flowsheet navigation, technical issues, and lack of practice and use opportunities. We observed different workarounds used by nurse documenters to overcome these challenges, including the use of paper-based mechanisms, free-text fields, and simultaneous documentation by two nurses. Based on our findings, we provide design guidelines for improving the electronic flowsheet to support its use during resuscitations.

Keywords: Electronic Health Records · Emergency medicine ·
Nursing documentation · Workarounds · Information behavior · Observations ·
Interviews

1 Introduction

Electronic Health Records (EHRs) capture critical information to support clinical decision-making, effective patient care, and coordination among care providers. Although EHRs have been implemented in various medical settings, documentation during resuscitations within emergency departments (EDs) has not been completely digitized due to the time-critical and high-stress nature of these events. Resuscitation flowsheets have a key role in facilitating communication and coordination during resuscitation events, while also contributing to continuity of care and patient safety [1]. Documentation in these dynamic environments, however, is an overwhelming task. A nurse documenter is responsible for capturing the information from multiple team

© Springer Nature Switzerland AG 2019
N. G. Taylor et al. (Eds.): iConference 2019, LNCS 11420, pp. 718–724, 2019.
https://doi.org/10.1007/978-3-030-15742-5_68

members and information sources, and producing a comprehensive record of all activities. The mental effort needed to gather patient information, record the diagnosis and treatment steps, and monitor the effects of clinical decisions is therefore high. These complexities in documentation have led some medical experts to dismiss the idea that electronic tools could ever replace paper flowsheets given the concerns about thoroughness, correctness, and timeliness of data recording [2]. For these reasons, many EDs have continued to use paper-based documentation during resuscitations.

Introduction of an electronic flowsheet associated with the EHR for documenting medical resuscitations at our research site in May 2017 provided an opportunity to study the nuances of the transition process from paper to electronic documentation in this high-risk medical setting. In this paper, we examine the nurse documenters' interactions with the newly implemented flowsheet, and discuss the advantages of electronic charting, challenges of use, and workarounds to overcome these challenges. We contribute to the existing literature by providing design recommendations for improving the use of the electronic flowsheet in dynamic medical settings.

2 Related Work

Prior HCI, CSCW, and health informatics studies have examined the implementation of electronic documentation in different medical settings, including intensive care units [3, 4], ED [5], and obstetrical units [6]. While some studies found the advantages of EHR implementation, such as the improved clinical workflow [3, 4], many studies identified misalignments between the EHR designs and clinicians' work practices [6–8]. We extend this body of work by discussing the challenges with the use of the EHR in a dynamic setting that requires the production of a complete and accurate record in real time, leading to the use of workarounds.

Specifically in resuscitation settings, some EDs have adopted electronic flowsheets despite the challenges of accurate and real-time data capture [1, 9–13]. These studies focused on different aspects of documentation, including completeness of the record [9, 10], the process of flowsheet design and implementation [1], evaluation of electronic documentation systems [11, 12], and efficiencies gained with electronic recording [13]. Most studies reported on a successful and seamless implementation of the electronic flowsheet, with only a few barriers (e.g., waiting for the appropriate technology to fit the needs of resuscitation settings) [1], finding an increase in completion rates on electronic flowsheets when compared to their paper-based predecessors. For example, Coffey et al. [10] compared the completions of electronic and paper flowsheets, focusing on 10 key fields related to patient care and safety. They found that more information was captured on the electronic versions, and key elements like vital signs, administered fluids and medications were all available in a single place in the EHR. Some studies also described different training strategies for the nurses before the EHR implementation [1, 13]. In sum, this prior research examined the effects of electronic charting and provided insights into the process of flowsheet implementation in emergency medical settings from a technological perspective. In contrast to this prior work, we examine the information behaviors of nurse documenters as they use the flowsheet to understand the documentation practices during resuscitations. In doing so, we aim to provide recommendations for improving the current EHR designs to support the work of nurse documenters in these time-critical medical settings.

3 Methods

We conducted our study in an ED of a pediatric teaching hospital in the U.S. Mid-Atlantic region serving over 90,000 patients per year, including those with time-critical, acute medical illnesses such as seizures, respiratory distress, cardiac arrest and altered mental status. Medical resuscitations take place in a dedicated room called the resuscitation bay. The room has three bed spaces, each equipped with the necessary equipment for rapid evaluation and treatment of patients. The resuscitation teams are multidisciplinary, consisting of seven to 15 members, each having a specific role and pre-determined yet flexible responsibilities. A typical resuscitation team consists of an attending physician (team leader), a fellow or a senior resident, a physician surveyor, a nurse documenter, a medication nurse, two or three bedside nurses, and a respiratory therapist. Other specialists may be called, if needed.

Our fieldwork spanned 11 months (April 2017–February 2018) and involved 616 h of in-situ observation in four- to eight-hour shifts. We observed the documentation practices by shadowing nurse documenters during resuscitation events in the resuscitation bay and in common ED areas. During observations, we took notes of nurse documenters' attitudes towards the electronic flowsheet and their information and communication behaviors. Medical resuscitations that occurred outside of researcher work shifts were observed using video review of recorded resuscitations available at the time. Videos are recorded for quality improvement and research purposes and deleted within 30 days of the event date based on the hospital's Institutional Review Board policy. The length of observed resuscitations ranged from 7 to 98 min (average = 33, SD = 23). We also conducted post-event, semi-structured interviews with the documenters, asking about nurse documenters' experience levels, their views of electronic flowsheet, including preferences, barriers, and workarounds to overcome the challenges. The interviewed nurses had, on average, four years of experience as a nurse in the emergency department. In this paper, we report the results from analyzing 14 in-situ observations and 30 video recordings of medical resuscitations, and 24 interviews. Field notes from observations and video review were transferred to an observation log, and interviews were audio-recorded and transcribed. We used thematic analysis [14] to identify various aspects of documentation on the electronic flowsheet including advantages, challenges, and the use of workarounds.

4 Results

We identified three advantages of electronic documentation during medical resuscitations. First, the documenters reported that the electronic flowsheet facilitated better patient handoff by providing *improved access to the patient record* from anywhere in the hospital, eliminating the need to carry around paper flowsheets. Second, the electronic flowsheet provided a *timeline of events* that occurred in the resuscitation bay in an overview screen, which was valuable for formulating a care plan, reviewing data, and improving handoff efficiency. On paper flowsheets, the documenters time-stamped events in different sections that were spread across the flowsheet, making it difficult to visualize a summary of events. Third, the electronic flowsheet allowed for *auto-populating* patient data from sources such as vital signs monitor, medication orders, blood gas and laboratory tests, reducing the time required to manually document these values. Even so, our results showed several challenges that the documenters faced and workarounds for overcoming those challenges, as described next.

4.1   Electronic Flowsheet Navigation

We identified three major navigational issues with the electronic flowsheet. First, the documenters reported that they spent more time locating flowsheet sections on the electronic version. They found it difficult to keep up with the information from different sources while they searched for specific sections. We observed how documenters were sometimes distracted while searching, which led to skipping information on the flowsheet. Second, unlike the paper flowsheet, the electronic version does not support at-a-glance overview for viewing multiple sections at once. It also does not allow concurrent multiple windows opened for the same patient. Because the documenters were required to complete and close the current window before moving on to the next, they found it difficult to follow and capture the reports from multiple information sources. They also spent time switching between multiple sections to communicate last entry with the team (e.g., vitals). Finally, some assessment sections contain many fields. The documenters simply skipped those sections because they could not complete them in real time. Although "Vitals" is one of the most frequently documented sections, the nurses stated that it was not easily accessible on the main screen, requiring additional time to navigate to the section and record every three minutes.

To work around these navigational issues, the documenters relied on additional mechanisms such as scrap paper, paper towel, and paper flowsheet to quickly jot down information along with timestamps. Our observations showed that 34 (out of 44, 77.27%) documenters used scrap paper with the electronic flowsheet; five (11.36%) used scrap paper only; four (9.09%) documented on the electronic flowsheet only; and one (2.27%) used a paper flowsheet with the electronic flowsheet. The documenters also extensively used the free-text field on the electronic flowsheet. To build a complete narrative of the resuscitation, they first entered the information on paper or free-text fields on the flowsheet, and then transcribed it into appropriate sections by modifying timestamps accordingly. This process of retrospective documentation is commonly known as "backcharting." For example, a documenter typed, "*22 left A.C. IV placed at this time*" in the free-text field and backcharted the size and location of the IV in the "Peripheral IV" section with the timestamp on the free-text field.

4.2   Electronic Flowsheet Auto-Population

The electronic flowsheet has an advantage of auto-populating information from several sources such as vital signs monitor and laboratory tests. Despite the advantage of auto-populating vitals, only 14 of the 24 interviewed documenters were aware of this feature. Among the 14, six documenters (42.85%) reported that the patient was not appropriately setup on the monitor to allow for data feed to other systems, either because the team did not prioritize this task or the resuscitation was short; five (35.71%) stated that they forgot how to use the feature; two (14.28%) indicated that the vitals did not auto-populate due to technical issues; and, one (7.14%) reported that they did not use the feature because they were worried about missing the data in case auto-population failed. In addition, our observations showed a significant delay (>10 min) in the auto-population of values from other sources such as blood gas tests, posing a challenge for communicating these values to the team. For these reasons, the nurses mainly relied on paper-based mechanisms to quickly note down information along with the timestamps or manually enter the values in the flowsheet sections.

4.3   Use Opportunities and Unfamiliarity with the Interface

We observed that the ordering of sections on the electronic flowsheet does not reflect the ordering on the paper flowsheet. In addition, the documenter role is not always assigned to the same nurse, leading to infrequent use of the electronic flowsheet across nurses and resulting in unfamiliarity with the interface. In 20% of the resuscitations, two nurses assumed the role of the documenters per resuscitation, where one recorded on scrap paper and the other on the electronic flowsheet. Documenters described that double documentation was helpful because they had assistance with keeping track of information when one documenter was unfamiliar with the interface.

5   Discussion and Conclusion

Technology implementation in emergency medical scenarios is a complex task, given their safety-critical and high-risk nature. In this study, we sought to understand the information behaviors of nurse documenters and their attitudes towards the use of a newly implemented electronic flowsheet during medical resuscitations. Our findings about the challenges of flowsheet use and workarounds to overcome those challenges led to four design recommendations for improving the flowsheet design.

First, our findings showed that the documenters were either not aware of the auto-population of vitals or could not recall how to use the feature. An *auto-population notification* in the corner of the screen indicating that the data is ready to be validated could encourage the documenters to use the feature, thereby greatly reducing the time spent on manually entering those sections. Second, although providing an at-a-glance view of the entire electronic flowsheet is challenging, an on-screen *timer* indicating the time elapsed since the last entry could alleviate its absence, mainly for repeatedly filled out sections (e.g., Vitals, Medications). The timer feature could reduce the docu-menter's time spent on switching sections and support their current time-keeping practices to communicate different information to the team. Third, because the documenters extensively used free-text fields on the electronic flowsheet, providing *auto-complete suggestions* similar to those found when searching online with a search engine could reduce their typing time. For example, when a documenter starts typing "Peripheral IV on...," suggestions such as "Peripheral IV on left AC" could assist the documenters to quickly complete the typing task. Also, a prompt that would allow documenters to transfer their documentation to the actual flowsheet section simultaneously as they type in the free-text fields could reduce the time spent on backcharting. For example, typing in "Peripheral IV" in the free-text field could prompt the nurse to transfer this note to the "Peripheral IV" section. Finally, our findings showed that the documenters increasingly spent time searching for different flowsheet sections. Presence of a *find bar*, with a function similar to "control + find" or "command + find" that searches through all the sections, including the collapsed ones, could allow the documenters to quickly locate the appropriate sections.

With this study, we found that electronic documentation in complex medical settings has advantages with supporting continuity of patient care. However, the issues related to flowsheet navigation, auto-population, and use and practice opportunities created barriers to achieving real-time documentation during resuscitations. Recording all activities *during* these events is critical for supporting team communication and coordination, as well as for maintaining team members' situational awareness. Our findings on technical issues of auto-population resonated with Bilyeu and Eastes [9], where they reported a decline in the completion rate of vital signs on electronic flowsheet due to similar challenges. Wurster et al. [1] also described the navigational barriers with documenting multiple flowsheet sections at once as time-consuming. Although we found that the nurses managed to work around these issues by relying on paper-based documentation mechanisms, these workarounds increased their workload because they had to transcribe (or "backchart") all the information into the flowsheet fields at a later point of time. Park et al. [8] similarly found that the flexibility provided by the electronic flowsheet to edit and save at any time contributed to piling up of incomplete patient records, which potentially required more time to complete. If the documenters missed noting down timestamps on the paper, they had to estimate the timestamps in the electronic flowsheet based on their memory, which often led to inaccuracies in patient records. In addition, the ability to modify the timestamps could potentially lead to falsifying information after a bad patient outcome [15].

Through continued research, we next aim to investigate different facets of documentation on electronic flowsheet including its impact on team communication, completion and error rates, as well as timeliness of data entry and its effects on patient outcomes. Understanding the social and organizational aspects of medical work affecting documentation practices on electronic flowsheet is also critical, because it will lead to further improvement of EHR designs.

Acknowledgments. This research has been supported by the NSF Award Number 1253285. We thank the medical staff at the hospital for their participation.

References

1. Wurster, L.A., Groner, J.I., Hoffman, J.: Electronic documentation of trauma resuscitations at a level 1 pediatric trauma center. J. Trauma Nurs. **19**(2), 76–79 (2012)
2. McGonigal, M.: Trauma flow sheets vs the electronic medical record. The Trauma Professional's Blog (2010). http://regionstraumapro.com/post/370717358. Accessed 21 June 2018
3. Berg, M.: Accumulating and coordinating: occasions for information technologies in medical work. Comput. Support. Coop. Work (CSCW) **8**(4), 373–401 (1999)
4. Reddy, M.C., Dourish, P., Pratt, W.: Coordinating Heterogeneous Work: Information and Representation in Medical Care. In: Prinz, W., Jarke, M., Rogers, Y., Schmidt, K., Wulf, V. (eds.) Proceedings of the European Conference on Computer Supported Cooperative Work (ECSCW). Springer, Dordrecht (2001). https://doi.org/10.1007/0-306-48019-0_13
5. Park, S.Y., Chen, Y.: Adaptation as design: learning from an EMR deployment study. In: Proceedings of the SIGCHI Conference on Human Factors in Computing Systems (CHI), pp. 2097–2106. ACM (2012)
6. Pine, K.H., Mazmanian, M.: Institutional logics of the EMR and the problem of 'perfect' but inaccurate accounts. In: Proceedings of the 17th ACM Conference on Computer Supported Cooperative Work & Social Computing (CSCW), pp. 283–294. ACM (2014)
7. Ash, J.S., Berg, M., Coiera, E.: Some unintended consequences of information technology in health care: the nature of patient care information system-related errors. J. Am. Med. Inform. Assoc. **11**(2), 104–112 (2004)
8. Park, S.Y., Lee, S.Y., Chen, Y.: The effects of EMR deployment on doctors' work practices: a qualitative study in the emergency department of a teaching hospital. Int. J. Med. Inform. **81**(3), 204–217 (2012)
9. Bilyeu, P., Eastes, L.E.: Use of the electronic medical record for trauma resuscitations: how does this impact documentation completeness? J. Trauma Nurs. **20**(3), 166–168 (2013)
10. Coffey, C., et al.: A comparison of paper documentation to electronic documentation for trauma resuscitations at a level I pediatric trauma center. J. Emerg. Nurs. **41**(1), 52–56 (2015)
11. McLean, L.E., Elwell, S., DePiero, A.: Assessment of the electronic medical record in documenting trauma resuscitations in the pediatric ED. Am. J. Emerg. Med. **33**(4), 589–590 (2015)
12. Eastes, L.E., Johnson, J., Harrahill, M.: Using the electronic medical record for trauma resuscitations: is it possible? J. Emerg. Nurs. **36**(4), 381–384 (2010)
13. D'Huyvetter, C., Lang, A.M., Heimer, D.M., Cogbill, T.H.: Efficiencies gained by using electronic medical record and reports in trauma documentation. J. Trauma Nurs. **21**(2), 68–71 (2014)
14. Braun, V., Clarke, V.: Using thematic analysis in psychology. Qual. Res. Psychol. **3**(2), 77–101 (2006)
15. Kenneth, T.Y., Green, R.A.: Critical aspects of emergency department documentation and communication. Emerg. Med. Clin. **27**(4), 641–654 (2009)

Digital Tools for Health Management

Do Recovery Apps Even Exist?: Why College Women with Eating Disorders Use (But Not Recommend) Diet and Fitness Apps Over Recovery Apps

Elizabeth V. Eikey$^{(\boxtimes)}$, Yunan Chen, and Kai Zheng

University of California, Irvine, USA
{eikeye,kai.zheng}@uci.edu, yunanc@ics.uci.edu

Abstract. Getting individuals to adopt condition-specific apps over general health apps remains an issue. Using eating disorders (EDs) as an example, we explored (1) if users recommend the general diet and fitness apps they repurpose for ED recovery and (2) if they use condition-specific apps intended for recovery. We used semi-structured interviews and four questionnaires to investigate use and perceptions of diet and fitness apps and recovery apps with 24 college women with self-identified and clinically-diagnosed EDs. Using inductive coding, we generated themes to address their lack of use of recovery apps. We found the majority ($n = 13$) would not recommend using general diet and fitness apps for recovery (compared to only 3 who would), yet most participants did not seek out a condition-specific app even when their objective was recovery. Four themes emerged around the non-use of recovery apps: lack of awareness, unpopularity or unfamiliarity, unwillingness, and lack of features or poor usability. In order to improve awareness as well as perceived popularity and familiarity of condition-specific apps, we suggest researchers and clinicians develop approved app lists, primary care clinicians become expert recommenders for evidence-based apps, and clinicians and educators leverage social media and college settings to reach these "hard to reach" populations.

Keywords: Eating disorder recovery app · Diet and fitness app · Mental health · mHealth · Personal informatics · Self-tracking

1 Introduction

In recent years, there has been a proliferation of condition-specific applications (apps) – especially those for mental health conditions, such as depression and anxiety [1], bipolar disorder [2], and eating disorders [3, 4]. This is no surprise given the high rates of mental illness. The Centers for Disease Control and Prevention estimate that 50% of adults in the U.S. will develop at least one mental illness during their lifetime [1]. With the advancements to and prevalence of mobile devices, condition-specific apps hold significant promise as a supplement or alternative to delivering mental health services [5, 6]. However, one major challenge is getting individuals to adopt these condition-specific

© Springer Nature Switzerland AG 2019
N. G. Taylor et al. (Eds.): iConference 2019, LNCS 11420, pp. 727–740, 2019.
https://doi.org/10.1007/978-3-030-15742-5_69

apps over more general apps. Using eating disorders (EDs) as an example, we investigate users' perceptions of using general and condition-specific apps for recovery.

We focus on college women who experience ED symptoms and investigate why recovery apps are not used when the users themselves do not recommend the diet and fitness apps they repurpose for recovery. This is an important group to study given their high rates of ED symptoms and app use. Research has found that 13.5% of undergraduate women have positive screens for EDs [7], and 40–49% of college women engage in ED behaviors at least once a week [8]. Because ED behaviors are associated with poor dietary quality [9], depression, anxiety, self-injury, and substance use [7, 10], and can lead to malnutrition, amenorrhea, organ failure, depression, suicide, and death [11], treatment is crucial. However, treatment-seeking is low [1].

Although widely available, apps intended to support ED recovery and treatment may be underused. For instance, research has shown that some individuals with EDs repurpose or "appropriate" general diet and fitness apps, such as MyFitnessPal, in an attempt to support ED recovery rather than download and use a recovery-specific app [12, 13]. This is problematic because diet and fitness apps are not made with this population in mind and thus can trigger and exacerbate ED symptoms [12, 14–18]. Additionally, researchers, clinicians, and developers are exerting much effort to design and evaluate condition-specific apps that are better suited for those with EDs. Unfortunately, this means the potential promise of these apps to help with access to care, illness management, and symptom reduction may be at least partially unfulfilled. In order to develop solutions to this issue, there is a need to understand *why* ED recovery apps are not used – particularly from a population who appropriates yet would not recommend general diet and fitness apps. This research is part of a larger study about the use and perceptions of health apps among college women with EDs.

2   Methods

2.1   Research Questions

We sought to understand users' perceptions of using general diet and fitness apps for ED recovery and their use and non-use of recovery-specific apps. Therefore, we identified two primary research questions:

> *RQ1: Do users recommend general diet and fitness apps for recovery?*
> *RQ2: Do users utilize condition-specific apps (i.e., recovery apps) when their motivation is recovery? RQ2a: If not, then why not?*

2.2   Data Collection

We used two data collection methods: surveys and semi-structured interviews. In total, four questionnaires were administered on Qualtrics: a demographic survey to obtain information about participants' age, ethnicity, ED status, and type of apps used and three well-established surveys to assess their ED symptoms (similar to [17]): the Eating

Disorder Examination Questionnaire (EDE-Q 6.0) [19], the Eating Attitudes Test (EAT-26) [20], and the Clinical Impairment Assessment (CIA 3.0) [21, 22][1].

The EDE-Q 6.0 is a self-report questionnaire that measures the frequency of key behavioral features of EDs in terms of number of episodes and in some instances number of days that the behavior occurred in the last 28 days [19]. It is comprised of four subscales that assess the severity of aspects of the psychopathology of EDs: restraint, eating concern, shape concern, and weight concern, which make up the global score [19]. A highly reliable and validated tool, the EDE-Q is the most commonly used assessment for EDs [17, 23]. While there is no single cut-point, higher scores indicate greater levels of symptomatology. Similar to the EDE-Q, the EAT-26 is a 26-item self-report questionnaire that measures symptoms and concerns characteristic of EDs using quantitative items on a 6-point scale and five yes/no behavioral questions [20]. It is particularly useful in assessing ED risk. We included this in addition to the EDE-Q because it has a cut-point. The recommended cut-off score is 19 and/or one or more of the behavioral questions; however, the EAT-26 score can be used as a continuous measure of disordered eating behaviors. Unlike the other measures, the CIA 3.0 assesses the severity of psychosocial impairment, such as general well-being, due to ED features in the last 28 days across 16 items on a 4-point scale [21, 22]. Because it captures aspects like mood, self-perception, cognitive functioning, meaningful friendships, and work performance not captured by the other measures, we chose to include it as a different indicator of ED symptoms. Higher scores indicate greater psychosocial impairment. Studies have found that a score of 16 is the best cut-point for predicting ED case status.

The semi-structured interviews sought to answer users' perceptions of diet and fitness apps and their knowledge and use of ED recovery apps. All data collection procedures took place April-November 2016. We audio recorded all interviews. All participants completed the demographic survey and interview, and 5 declined to participate in the other three surveys. At approximately 14 interviews, we saw repetitive themes in the participant responses, and they converged into the same points (i.e., data saturation) [24]. All 24 participants completed the interviews.

2.3 Data Analysis

The audio recordings consisted of 21 h and 36 min for a total of 436 transcribed pages. We used open, inductive coding to generate themes based on our research questions [25]. After becoming familiar with the data, we generated high-level themes based on our aims. For example, in order to answer RQ2, we first marked each transcript based on if they use recovery apps. Then we iteratively labeled textual data based on participants' answers, which resulted in more specific categories. These codes were then grouped and refined to determine our final categories. For the quantitative data from the

---

[1] For more details about these measures, please see [13].

questionnaires, we used Excel and SPSS. Body Mass Index (BMI) for those 20 years old and older was computed using the U.S. National Institutes of Health calculator[2]. For those under 20 years old, BMI was calculated using the Centers for Disease Control and Prevention (CDC) calculator[3] because for teens, BMI has to be interpreted relative to others of the same sex and age and thus is given as a percentile, calculated from CDC growth charts [26].

2.4 Participants

Participants were recruited using paper flyers posted throughout a large university in the Northeastern U.S. as well as digital flyers in some classrooms at the same location and compensated $25 each for approximately 1.5 h of their time. Institutional Review Board approved all study measures, and informed consent was obtained in person for all but one participant who did a phone interview. Our inclusion criteria focused on college women with disordered eating behaviors (i.e., symptoms related to anorexia and bulimia nervosa [AN, BN]) who use(d) general diet and fitness apps because AN, BN, and related disordered eating behaviors tend to affect college women [7] and diet and fitness apps users tend to be younger [27, 28]. Because many women do not see a professional for their symptoms and thus never receive a diagnosis, we recruited both participants who were self-diagnosed and clinically-diagnosed. ED behaviors in this context may or may not indicate full clinical EDs (e.g., AN or BN) or qualify to be categorized as other specified feeding and eating disorder (OSFED) or unspecified feeding and eating disorder (UFED). We emphasize women's own perspectives and experiences with EDs and the importance of studying EDs even in the absence of a clinical diagnosis. We focus on symptoms and behaviors associated with AN and BN, which could be categorized as OSFED or UFED, because a number of behaviors associated with AN and BN are related, making differentiating AN and BN difficult [11]. Table 1 shows the ranges, means, and standard deviations for each ED measurement.

Participants were ages 18 to 23 with the mean being 20.63 years. The majority of participants identified as White (non-Hispanic) ($n = 18$, 75%) with one from Israel. Three (12.5%) identified as Asian, Asian American, or Pacific Islander, 2 (8.3%) identified as multi-racial, and 1 (4.2%) identified as Native American or American Indian. All participants were current university students. Most participants had not been professionally diagnosed with an ED ($n = 17$, 70.8%), and most reported being in recovery or recovered ($n = 20$, 83.3%). Participants estimated they had an ED anywhere from 2 months to 7 years (mean = 34.93 months; $SD = 26.78$). Reported current BMI ranged from 18.7 to 32 (mean = 22.90; $SD = 3.58$).

---

[2] https://www.nhlbi.nih.gov/health/educational/lose_wt/BMI/bmicalc.htm.

[3] https://nccd.cdc.gov/dnpabmi/calculator.aspx.

Table 1. EAT-26, EDE-Q, and CIA ranges, means, and standard deviations

Measurement	Range	Mean (SD)	Interpretation
EAT-26 score	2–47	21.32 (10.63)	The mean exceeded cut-point of 19. Fifteen of 19 (78.9%) participants exceeded the cut-point. The mean score on the diet subscale was higher than the mean scores on either the bulimia and food preoccupation subscale or the oral control subscale, indicating higher levels of symptomology associated with diet, such as feeling guilt after eating, awareness of calories, etc.
Diet	2–32	14.37 (7.96)	
Oral control	0–6	2.42 (2.06)	
Bulimia & food preoccupation	0–9	4.53 (2.74)	
EDE-Q global Score	0.38–4.35	2.70 (1.04)	The global score is significantly higher than the norms reported in [29], $t(1550) = 3.5064$ $p = 0.0005$. The restraint, eating concern, shape concern, and weight concern subscales were all significantly higher than the norms, $t(1550) = 2.7932$ $p = 0.0053$, $t(1550) = 4.6036$ $p = 0.0001$, $t(1550) = 2.6623$ $p = 0.0078$, and $t(1550) = 2.9262$ $p = 0.0035$, respectively. This indicates high levels of symptomology.
Restraint	0.40–3.80	2.27 (1.13)	
Eating concern	0.20–5.00	2.05 (1.22)	
Shape concern	0.50–6.00	3.39 (1.37)	
Weight concern	0.40–5.80	3.06 (1.50)	
CIA score	3–36	14.84 (10.39)	The mean did not exceed the cut-point of 16. However, 9 of 19 (47.4%) participants reached this threshold, meaning they exhibit psychosocial impairment characteristic of EDs.

3 Findings

3.1 Diet and Fitness Apps for ED Recovery (RQ1)

In our past publications, we reported that college women often appropriate diet and fitness apps for ED recovery (see [13]). However, this publication did not report whether or not users recommend these apps. When asked if they would recommend general diet and fitness apps to be used by others with EDs, the majority of participants ($n = 13$, 59.1%) said no (7 [31.8%] said maybe and 2 [9.1%] said yes)[4]. Many felt very strongly that general diet and fitness apps were not appropriate for anyone with an ED let alone when trying to recovery from one. For example, one participant said *"I feel like, I feel like it's probably not the best app to like recover from an ED." [U07.* In response to recommending diet and fitness apps for those recovering from EDs, one participant simply said: *"No. Not at all." [U13]* Another felt so adamantly against them that she believes individuals with EDs should never use the app: *"I'd probably just ban them [someone with an ED] from the app, like completely ban them from the app. I definitely would probably take [it] away... just to prevent them entirely [from*

---

[4] 2 participants did not provide an answer for this question.

using the app]." [U06] Participants who were on the fence about recommending general diet and fitness apps believed the apps could be harmful or helpful depending on the type of ED a person has as well as their commitment and stage of recovery. Even many of those who believed the effects of general diet and fitness apps were dependent on these factors expressed concern about those with AN or individuals at risk of becoming too obsessive using these apps at any point, including recovery.

Most participants felt general diet and fitness apps trigger, fuel, or worsen ED symptoms (see [12] for more details). For instance, one participant said she would not recommend diet and fitness apps for ED recovery *"because obviously it's [the app is] just worsening it [ED] at this point."* [U02] Similarly, another participant explained that these apps can be harmful by feeding into the nature of EDs: *"I think eating disorders, it's a control mechanism. And I think the more control you have over things like that, the more you can do harm."* [U19] These general apps could have adverse consequences on users, making them unsuitable for recovery. The fact that diet and fitness apps are not recommended is unsurprising given the reported negative effects of them, such as encouraging restriction and compensatory behaviors and making users feel extreme negative emotions [12].

3.2   ED Recovery App Use (RQ2)

Although most participants would not recommend diet and fitness apps for individuals with an ED or those trying to recover from an ED, they do not turn to condition-specific apps even when their objective is recovery. Despite many of them ($n = 20$, 83.3%) reporting being in recovery and many attempting to use diet and fitness apps to help with their recovery process, most participants[5] had never used ED recovery apps. In fact, 22 (95.7%) participants had never used recovery apps, and of those, 17 (73.9%) were unaware of their existence. Although 6 (26.1%) participants were aware of ED recovery apps, only 1 (4.3%) had every used a recovery app. Some who had heard of recovery apps became aware through college courses ($n = 2$, 8.7%) and 1 (4.3%) through a nutritionist. Because the majority of participants did not use recovery apps, we focus on reported reasons why they *do not* use these ED-specific apps, including lack of awareness, unpopularity or unfamiliarity, unwillingness, and lack of features or poor usability, which is shown in Table 2.

Table 2. Reasons for not using ED recovery apps

Reason	# of Participants[a]
Lack of awareness	17
Unpopularity or unfamiliarity	4
Unwillingness	2
Lack of features or poor usability	1

[a] 1 participant mentioned more than one reason for not using recovery apps.

---

[5] 23 of 24 participants answered questions related to ED recovery apps.

Lack of Awareness. When asked if they had ever heard of or used ED recovery apps, many did not know of their existence. In these cases, participants had never been exposed to the idea of recovery apps at all. For instance, one participant replied: *"No. Do they exist?" [U07]* Some participants talked about how they never thought about searching for recovery apps. For example, one participant stated: *"Huh! No. I don't know about that [recovery apps] actually. I've never thought about looking it up. I probably should do that." [U11]* Similarly, another participant said: *"No. I didn't even know that they existed. I know about support groups. I didn't know about [recovery] apps." [U12]* This lack of awareness of ED recovery apps was prevalent and contributes to their lack of use.

Unpopularity and Unfamiliarity. Users' perceptions of recovery apps' popularity and their familiarity with them were cited as reasons not to use recovery apps. Unlike the lack of awareness theme, in these cases, participants had heard about ED recovery apps but chose not to explore them. Two participants had heard of ED recovery apps in technology courses but did not use them. Not hearing about these types of apps outside of class led to the perception that these apps are unpopular, and in some cases, although participants had heard of these apps, they lacked a sense of familiarity about what they are and what they do. For example, one participant said she assumed ED recovery apps were not commonly used, which partially explained why she did not use one herself: *"My [technology] class, I think we did go over something about apps like that. But since I never really heard of them [recovery apps], I probably assumed that they're not that popular and like don't really, I never really explored them." [U04]* She had some level of awareness of their existence but never looked into them due to perceived unpopularity. Another participant said she was not familiar with the features and functions of recovery apps, so she never bothered to use one: *"They mentioned something like them [recovery apps] in my class, but I don't really know what they look like or like kind of what they do honestly." [U05]*

Along those same lines, a couple of participants who were aware of recovery apps explained that they were not motivated to use them. For instance, one participant discussed how ED recovery apps were not at the forefront of her thoughts about apps. When asked if she ever used recovery apps, she said: *"No. I'm sure they [recovery apps] exist, I just never thought to look for one." [U10]* Another participant stated how recovery apps were not commonly discussed because of society's lack of understanding of ED recovery. She said she had not heard much about recovery-specific apps *"because people don't really think you have to recover from things like that too much." [U16]*

Unwillingness. Participants expressed an unwillingness to use ED-specific apps despite knowing about them. For example, one participant described a conversation with her nutritionist about using a recovery app but she refused: *"My nutritionist mentioned an app... mentioned getting one for people with EDs. I was like, 'Listen, [nutritionist's name], that's not gonna work. Sorry.' [laughs] I respect that they have that for people and I'm sure it works for people, but that's not gonna fly. She was like, 'Don't worry...' I mean, she's like, 'Just putting it out there, just letting you know.' I was like, 'Yeah, not gonna fly.'" [U17]* Another participant did not want to use a recovery app because it was an admittance of a very real yet undiagnosed issue: *"I* *never really explored them [recovery apps] just because I never really wanted to self-diagnose myself as having one [an ED] even though I know like I did." [U04]* This suggests that some users are not necessarily ready to commit to recovery, and therefore, they are not ready to give up general apps for condition-specific ones.

Lack of Features or Poor Usability. Of those who were aware of ED recovery apps, only 1 participant had ever used any. The recovery apps she used focused mainly on positive messages: *"I think the one [recovery app] had positive quotes all the time, which was nice, but I don't think they were super, super helpful... I didn't have it for that long. So, I don't think they were very... I don't know. It [was] more of a positive thing, so. I don't think you could track food or anything on them." [U13]* Although she thought the content of the app was appropriate, its lack of features made it unhelpful in supporting her recovery needs.

4 Discussion

Our findings show that while users repurpose diet and fitness apps for recovery, the majority would not recommend them to others with EDs. Recovery apps may be more appropriate, but users are not always aware of them.

4.1 Condition-Specific Goal Does Not Mean Condition-Specific App

Research has shown that some users with EDs initially select a diet and fitness app with weight loss or awareness in mind [12, 13]. However, when individuals' motivations change from weight loss to ED recovery, some users continue to use general diet and fitness apps rather than search for and select a condition-specific app tailored to their needs (i.e., recovery) [13]. These prior works do not explore why this happens. Thus, our findings extend this research by shedding light onto why recovery apps are not used when diet and fitness apps are not recommended.

Part of this may be explained by users' lack of awareness and the perceived popularity of apps specifically for ED recovery. Because some had not heard of these apps at all, they did not think to search for them. Even if they thought there may be ED recovery apps or had heard of condition-specific apps, some assumed these types of apps were unpopular. This lack of name recognition and popularity contributed to why some users did not search for recovery apps. Compared to diet and fitness apps, recovery apps receive much less attention and have a smaller user base. Further, there may be stigma and privacy concerns associated with using recovery apps, which may falsely reinforce a perception that they are unused and unpopular. Research has shown women with disordered eating do not want to share information associated with diet and fitness when using an app [30]. This tendency to self-conceal is common among those with EDs, and some studies have shown that self-concealment predicts psychological distress in individuals with perfectionistic tendencies [31] (common with EDs) and disordered dieting [32]. Additionally, stigma predicts attitudes toward counseling for people with disordered eating [33], so it may also affect attitudes towards non-traditional treatment, such as recovery apps.

Further, some may be in denial about their ED. Thus, users' unwillingness to use these apps may reflect this; choosing to use a recovery app requires users acknowledge their ED in a more visible way, which some may be reluctant to do. Because recovery apps are not as well-known, they are not discussed in day-to-day life like more general, popular apps such as MyFitnessPal, which may further contribute to the potential stigma of using one. There is little opportunity for recovery apps to be viewed as typical (in contrast to diet and fitness apps which are normalized) and recommended by friends, which has been shown to influence the use of health apps [34]. For the few users that had looked for apps more appropriate for ED recovery, they mentioned poor usability of these apps, which is consistent with prior analyses of some ED recovery apps [3]. This suggests that for some users, first impressions of one app may lead to a negative impression of an entire app genre.

4.2 Improving Awareness of Condition-Specific Apps

While we do not claim that apps will "solve" EDs nor should they be used in the absence of professional treatment, there is promise for apps in the mental health domain [5, 6]. Thus, investigating why these apps may not be used is important. While there may be numerous reasons (e.g., stigma) why recovery apps may not be selected, part of the issue may be cyclical: because ED recovery apps are not as popular, they are not as recommended, yet because they are not recommended, they are less popular (or at least perceived as such). The question is how do we not only improve individuals' awareness of condition-specific apps that are appropriate (usable, safe, effective), especially for less common or stigmatized health conditions, but also promote these apps so individuals become more likely to search for and use them? We offer three suggestions, including expert-approved app lists, clinician involvement, and leveraging education and other settings (e.g., social media).

One important step in increasing awareness of condition-specific apps is to involve clinicians and other experts in deciding which apps are suitable and developing ways to "get the word out" about appropriate apps. Although there is research that aims to evaluate apps on their adherence to evidence-based principles [3, 35], there is no standard list of approved apps based on condition, and app stores do not evaluate apps for content. Through cross-disciplinary panels and workshops, a collaborative discussion among researchers in fields like Information Science, Medical Informatics, Human Computer Interaction, and Psychology could yield lists of approved apps for specific conditions. This could be a first step at creating and disseminating app information that can then be used and distributed.

In addition to developing a list of appropriate apps, creating an open dialogue about condition-specific apps is essential to increasing awareness of them, which is critical because our findings suggest perceived popularity and familiarity with apps help determine whether or not they are used. As research has also shown, recommendations play a key role in users' awareness and willingness to search for and select certain apps [13, 34]. Perhaps primary care clinicians and other experts can act as advocates of certain apps and become trusted recommenders even for individuals not seeking mental health services, especially in university settings, where we know individuals are at an increased risk of developing EDs. For instance, one participant discussed how her nutritionist recommended an ED recovery app, which led her to search for and use it.

This approach can be used by other experts to help individuals learn about different tools to support their illness management. University health services, for example, could discuss or circulate approved recovery apps as part of all patients' visits (not just mental health visits). Healthcare providers could incorporate this practice when weight is measured at the beginning of appointments.

However, clinicians and other experts acting as trusted recommenders requires individuals have access to nutritionists or other healthcare professionals. How then can we bridge these pathways for those who do not seek any clinical care? We may be able to access these individuals by identifying other places and means to reach them, such as through social media and education settings. For instance, research has shown that most young adults and adolescents use social media [36, 37]. We may be able to partner with community organizations, universities, and national ED entities to have them "spread the word" about approved recovery apps via social media channels, like Twitter, Instagram, Facebook, and Snapchat, in order to increase awareness and popularity of these apps. Further, primary care clinicians may be able to reach individuals through social media and act as expert recommenders of recovery apps on these platforms. Studies have shown young people are receptive to this. In fact, in a study of adolescents and young adults with psychotic disorders and non-psychotic mood disorders, Birnbaum et al. [36] found 63.6% were willing to have clinicians approach them on social media when they were experiencing symptoms. Therefore, this could be a space where otherwise "difficult to reach" individuals could be reached and alternative or supplemental healthcare services, such as apps, could be discussed and promoted. This is promising; however, more research is needed to understand clinicians' shifting roles and workload as technology evolves.

Another hopeful avenue is education settings. Given the high rates of mental health issues among college students [38] and the fact that college may be the only time where one setting encompasses most aspects of an individual's life (e.g., career-related, social, health, and support services) in an integrated way [39], higher education settings may be ripe with opportunity to reach individuals dealing with mental health issues. It may be possible to run campaigns across campus (e.g., dining halls, gyms, classes, student resource centers, web-based resources) about evidence-based condition-specific apps, such as ED recovery apps like Recovery Record [40]. Creating an open culture around mental health could help improve the knowledge and identification of mental health issues [41] and reduce stigma [39] (which may make condition-specific app adoption more normalized), and developing intervention approaches around trusted resources, such as "approved" apps, could improve the awareness and perceived popularity and familiarity of those apps. Although interventions and campaigns may be successful in reducing stigma for mental health conditions (e.g., depression [42, 43]), more research is needed to test the effectiveness of these approaches for improving mental health app *adoption* for specific conditions.

4.3   Limitations and Future Research

It is important to note that these findings are not meant to generalize to all users, but rather provide a case in which we can look into users' perceptions of general health apps for recovery and why users may not use condition-specific (i.e., recovery-focused) apps. It is possible that there is some sampling bias as all participants were recruited from one university. These findings may not represent an exhaustive list of all reasons users do not use recovery apps. Also, this research does not evaluate the role of app stores in promoting and contributing to the popularity of certain apps through proprietary algorithms as well as possible false-ratings. Thus, more industry—academic collaboration is needed. This research does not intend to claim that all participants have clinical EDs but rather draw attention to the need to consider subclinical or underdiagnosed populations. This is important in order to improve individuals' well-being if they are not ready to or cannot access professional services or are deemed "not severe enough" to qualify for a clinical diagnosis. Participants in this study did not use recovery apps, despite them being designed specifically to aid in the recovery process. Future research should explore who *is* using these apps, how do they find out about them, and how do their outcomes compare to those who are using diet and fitness apps. Additionally, researchers should consider why users with other conditions may use general apps rather than condition-specific ones.

5 Conclusion

We examined users' perceptions of using diet and fitness apps for ED recovery and found that while they do not recommend using diet and fitness apps for recovery, they do not utilize recovery or treatment apps. Through our qualitative investigation, we provide explanations as to why these condition-specific apps may be underutilized – most notably a lack of awareness of recovery apps. This study is a promising first step and provides a foundation to begin to address this issue.

Acknowledgements. We would like to thank our participants for sharing their experiences. This work was supported by the National Center for Research Resources, the National Center for Advancing Translational Sciences, National Institutes of Health (NIH) under grant UL1 TR001414. It is solely the responsibility of the authors and does not necessarily represent the official views of the NIH.

References

1. CDC Mental Illness Surveillance Fact Sheet. Centers Dis. Control Prev. (2011). https://www.cdc.gov/mentalhealthsurveillance/fact_sheet.html
2. Nicholas, J., Larsen, M.E., Proudfoot, J., Christensen, H.: Mobile apps for bipolar disorder: a systematic review of features and content quality. J. Med. Internet Res. **17** (2015). https://doi.org/10.2196/jmir.4581
3. Juarascio, A.S., Manasse, S.M., Goldstein, S.P., Forman, E.M., Butryn, M.L.: Review of smartphone applications for the treatment of eating disorders. Eur. Eat. Disord. Rev. **23**, 1–11 (2015). https://doi.org/10.1002/erv.2327
4. Fairburn, C.G., Rothwell, E.R.: Apps and eating disorders: a systematic clinical appraisal. Int. J. Eat. Disord. **48**, 1038–1046 (2015). https://doi.org/10.1002/eat.22398

5. Bakker, D., Kazantzis, N., Rickwood, D., Rickard, N.: Mental health smartphone apps: review and evidence-based recommendations for future developments. JMIR Ment. Heal. **3**, e7 (2016). https://doi.org/10.2196/mental.4984
6. Leigh, S., Flatt, S.: App-based psychological interventions: friend or foe? Evid. Based Ment. Health **18**(4), 97–99 (2015)
7. Eisenberg, D., Nicklett, E.J., Roeder, K., Kirz, N.E.: Eating disorder symptoms among college students: prevalence, persistence, correlates, and treatment-seeking. J. Am. Coll. Heal. **59**, 700–707 (2011). https://doi.org/10.1038/nature13314.A
8. Berg, K.C., Frazier, P., Sherr, L.: Change in eating disorder attitudes and behavior in college women: prevalence and predictors. Eat. Behav. **10**, 137–142 (2009). https://doi.org/10.1016/j.eatbeh.2009.03.003
9. Woodruff, S.J., Hanning, R.M., Lambraki, I., Storey, K.E., McCargar, L.: Healthy Eating Index-C is compromised among adolescents with body weight concerns, weight loss dieting, and meal skipping. Body Image **5**, 404–408 (2008). https://doi.org/10.1016/j.bodyim.2008.04.006
10. Gillen, M.M., Markey, C.N., Markey, P.M.: An examination of dieting behaviors among adults: Links with depression. Eat. Behav. **13**, 88–93 (2012). https://doi.org/10.1016/j.eatbeh.2011.11.014
11. American Psychiatric Association: Diagnostic and Statistical Manual of Mental Disorders (DSM-5), 5th edn. American Psychiatric Publishing, Washington, D.C., London, England (2013)
12. Eikey, E.V., Reddy, M.C.: "It's Definitely Been a Journey": a qualitative study on how women with eating disorders use weight loss apps. In: ACM CHI Conference on Human Factors in Computing Systems (CHI 2017), Denver, CO, pp. 1–13. ACM (2017)
13. Eikey, E.V., Booth, K.M., Chen, Y., Zheng, K.: The use of general health apps among users with specific conditions: why college women with disordered eating adopt food diary apps. In: AMIA, San Francisco, CA (2018)
14. Levinson, C.A., Fewell, L., Brosof, L.C.: My fitness pal calorie tracker usage in the eating disorders. Eat. Behav. **27**, 14–16 (2017). https://doi.org/10.1016/j.eatbeh.2017.08.003
15. Simpson, C.C., Mazzeo, S.E.: Calorie counting and fitness tracking technology: associations with eating disorder symptomatology. Eat. Behav. **26**, 89–92 (2017). https://doi.org/10.1016/j.eatbeh.2017.02.002
16. Eikey, E.V.: Providers' perceptions of the impact of weight loss apps on users with eating disorders. In: Proceedings of the 2016 ACM SIGMIS Conference on Computers and People Research, pp. 19–20. ACM, New York (2016)
17. Tan, T., Kuek, A., Goh, S.E., Lee, E.L., Kwok, V.: Internet and smartphone application usage in eating disorders: a descriptive study in Singapore. Asian J. Psychiatr. **19**, 50–55 (2016). https://doi.org/10.1016/j.ajp.2015.11.007
18. Eikey, E.V., et al.: Desire to be underweight: an exploratory study on a weight loss app community and user perceptions of the impact on disordered eating behaviors. JMIR mHealth uHealth **5** (2017). https://doi.org/10.2196/mhealth.6683
19. Fairburn, C.G., Beglin, S.: EDE-Q. In: Cognitive Behavior Therapy and Eating Disorders, pp. 1–5. Guilford Press, New York (2008)
20. Garner, D.M., Olmsted, M.P., Bohr, Y., Garfinkel, P.E.: The eating attitudes test: psychometric features and clinical correlates. Psychol. Med. **12**, 871–878 (1982)
21. Bohn, K., Fairburn, C.G.: The clinical impairment assessment questionnaire (CIA 3.0). In: Fairburn, C.G (ed.) Cognitive Behavior Therapy and Eating Disorders. Guilford Press, New York (2008)

22. Bohn, K., Doll, H.A., Cooper, Z., O'Connor, M., Palmer, R.L., Fairburn, C.G.: The measurement of impairment due to eating disorder psychopathology. Behav. Res. Ther. **46**, 1105–1110 (2008). https://doi.org/10.1016/j.brat.2008.06.012

23. Berg, K.C., Peterson, C.B., Frazier, P., Crow, S.J.: Psychometric evaluation of the eating disorder examination and eating disorder examination-questionnaire: a systematic review of the literature. Int. J. Eat. Disord. **45**, 428–438 (2012). https://doi.org/10.1002/eat.20931

24. Marshall, M.N.: Sampling for qualitative research. Fam. Pract. **13**, 522–526 (1996)

25. Thomas, D.R.: A general inductive approach for analyzing qualitative evaluation data. Am. J. Eval. **27**, 237–246 (2006). https://doi.org/10.1177/1098214005283748

26. CDC Centers for Disease Control and Prevention About Child & Teen BMI. Heal. Weight CDC. https://www.cdc.gov/healthyweight/assessing/bmi/childrens_bmi/about_childrens_bmi.html

27. Fox, S., Duggan, M.: Mobile Health 2012. Pew Internet Am. Life Proj. 1–29 (2012). Accessed http://pewinternet.org/Reports/2012/Mobile-Health.aspx

28. Smith, A.: The Smartphone Difference. Pew Research Center, April 2015. http://www.pewinternet.org/2015/04/01/us-smartphone-use-in-2015/

29. Quick, V.M., Byrd-Bredbenner, C.: Eating disorders examination questionnaire (EDE-Q): norms for US college students. Eat. Weight Disord. **18**, 29–35 (2013). https://doi.org/10.1007/s40519-013-0015-1

30. Eikey, E.V.: Privacy and weight loss apps: a first look at how women with eating disorders use social features. In: Proceedings of the International Conference on Supporting Group Work (GROUP), pp. 413–415 (2016)

31. Kawamura, K.Y., Frost, R.O.: Self-concealment as a mediator in the relationship between perfectionism and psychological distress. Cognit. Ther. Res. **28**, 183–191 (2004). https://doi.org/10.1023/B:COTR.0000021539.48926.c1

32. Masuda, A., Latzman, R.D.: Psychological flexibility and self-concealment as predictors of disordered eating symptoms. Sch Words Georg State Univ. (2012)

33. Hackler, A.H., Vogel, D.L., Wade, N.G.: Attitudes toward seeking professional help for an eating disorder: the role of stigma and anticipated outcomes. J. Couns. Dev. **88**, 424–431 (2010). https://doi.org/10.1002/j.1556-6678.2010.tb00042.x

34. Peng, W., Kanthawala, S., Yuan, S., Hussain, S.A.: A qualitative study of user perceptions of mobile health apps. BMC Public Health **16**, 1158 (2016). https://doi.org/10.1186/s12889-016-3808-0

35. Breton, E.R., Fuemmeler, B.F., Abroms, L.C.: Weight loss-there is an app for that! But does it adhere to evidence-informed practices? Transl. Behav. Med. **1**, 523–529 (2011). https://doi.org/10.1007/s13142-011-0076-5

36. Birnbaum, M.L., Rizvi, A.F., Correll, C.U., Kane, J.M., Confino, J.: Role of social media and the Internet in pathways to care for adolescents and young adults with psychotic disorders and non-psychotic mood disorders. Early Interv. Psychiatry **11**, 290–295 (2017). https://doi.org/10.1111/eip.12237

37. Smith, A., Anderson, M.: Social media use in 2018, pp. 1–17. Pew Research Center. Accessed http://www.pewinternet.org/2018/03/01/social-media-use-in-2018/

38. Auerbach, R.P., et al.: Mental disorders among college students in the world health organization world mental health surveys. Psychol. Med. **46**, 2955–2970 (2016). https://doi.org/10.1017/S0033291716001665

39. Hunt, J., Eisenberg, D.: Mental health problems and help-seeking behavior among college students. J. Adolesc. Heal. **46**, 3–10 (2010). https://doi.org/10.1016/j.jadohealth.2009.08.008

40. Tregarthen, J.P., Lock, J., Darcy, A.M.: Development of a smartphone application for eating disorder self-monitoring. Int. J. Eat. Disord. **48**, 972–982 (2015). https://doi.org/10.1002/eat.22386

41. Jorm, A.F.: Mental health literacy; empowering the community to take action for better mental health. Am. Psychol. **67**, 231–243 (2012). https://doi.org/10.1037/a0025957
42. Hammer, J.H., Vogel, D.L.: Men's help seeking for depression: the efficacy of a male-sensitive brochure about counseling. Couns. Psychol. **38**, 296–313 (2010). https://doi.org/10.1177/0011000009351937
43. Finkelstein, J., Lapshin, O.: Reducing depression stigma using a web-based program. Int. J. Med. Inform. **76**, 726–734 (2007). https://doi.org/10.1016/j.ijmedinf.2006.07.004

Turning Points: Motivating Intergenerational Families to Engage on Sustainable Health Information Sharing

Jomara Sandbulte[1]([⊠])(iD), Jordan Beck[1]([⊠])(iD), Eun Kyoung Choe[2]([⊠])(iD), and John M. Carroll[1]([⊠])(iD)

[1] Pennsylvania State University, University Park, PA 16802, USA
{jmb89,jeb560,jmc56}@psu.edu
[2] University of Maryland, College Park, MD 20742, USA
choe@umd.edu

Abstract. Family relationships present a space for provision of support in which the members reciprocate and help one another at times of necessity. Yet, family members face obstacles in providing support to one another because they are unaware that it is needed. In this study, we investigated different motivating factors that influence family member's decision to share (or not share) health information. We conducted focus group discussions with independent living elderly parents (n = 16) and adult children (n = 21). We learned that the change of family member's sharing behaviors was often due to a disruptive moment which we refer to here as "turning point." Based on the concept of "turning points", we discuss how those moments could promote sustainable health information sharing within families and are useful tools for designing technology to support family collaboration on health.

Keywords: Health · Information sharing · Intergenerational families · Family collaboration · Family informatics

1 Introduction

In many family relationships, there is a desire to provide support and maintain contact even with variations on family backgrounds [28,29]. In the context of family relationships, specifically between elderly parents and adult children, which, following others, we refer to as *intergenerational family*, aging imposes challenges that may enhance family members' desire to support one another. As elderly parents age, many adult children want to know more about their parents' health so that they can provide necessary support. At the same time, elderly parents continue to provide parental assistance as needed, for example, with child care [29]. This reciprocity, wherein family members help each other and contribute to the whole family's common good, provides an opportunity to promote family engagement, including on health interventions. Yet, some families face obstacles in providing support to each other because members may not

© Springer Nature Switzerland AG 2019
N. G. Taylor et al. (Eds.): iConference 2019, LNCS 11420, pp. 741–753, 2019.
https://doi.org/10.1007/978-3-030-15742-5_70

share information. How can an adult child provide support if he/she is unaware that it is needed? Given that sharing information plays an important role in support provision, understanding the different factors that influence an individual's decision to share (or not share) information is essential to promote collaboration within the family, specifically on health.

In this paper, we focus on the importance of sharing health information within the family and how problematic it could be if individuals decide to *not share* health information. For the purpose of this study, we define health information sharing as: *"any information relevant to an individual's mental or physical health."* For example, family members share with one another information about social activities (e.g., card crafting or board games groups), healthy eating, or exercise and physical activity.

To investigate health information sharing routines between elderly parents and adult children, we conducted a focus group study. We learned that sharing health information is not pervasive in most routine familial conversations. In fact, we observed that families may wait until what we refer to here as a "turning point" to change their sharing behaviors. Turning Points are disruptive moments that change family members' sharing behaviors. While previous studies have considered behavior change a long-term and complex process [12,20], our work elaborates the concept of "turning point" and emphasizes it as an important insight that could provide an innovative design nuance for developing applications for families to engage collaboratively on health.

The specific contributions of our research are as follows:

1. to provide nuanced understanding of motivating factors that influence health information sharing within intergenerational families, and
2. to introduce and expand turning points as a generative tool for designers and the design of family-centered health technologies.

2   Related Work

In this section, we summarize previous research into technological support for positive health information sharing within the family. We emphasize two factors that may play a role in health information sharing within the family: the desire to maintain constant communication and awareness as well as the desire to collaborate with family members for the family's common good.

2.1   Technological Support on Family Health Information Sharing

Researchers have investigated families sharing positive (e.g., wellness [5,17,24]) and negative (e.g., disease [11,18,25]) health information. In the context of families sharing wellness-related health information, researchers have proposed technology solutions to inspire family members to share information with each other and to collaborate with one another in order to achieve positive health outcomes. For example, Katule et al. [17] developed a family health application consisting of a journal for monitoring nutrition and physical activity. Similarly, Colineau et al. [8] investigated the requirements for a collaborative family weight management site to promote lifestyle changes by engaging family members to support one another in weight management. Finally, Schaefbauer et al. [27] explored the use of a sociotechnical mobile app called Snack Buddy which aimed to encourage healthy eating behaviors and promote positive support within the family.

All in all, this body of literature contributes with valuable insights into how families share wellness-related health information and collaborate with one another to achieve positive health outcomes. Furthermore, this literature contains interesting design concepts aiming to engage families around health goals. However, designing for families regarding health goals can be challenging because designers have to take into consideration, among others factors, important design aspects that influence family support and information sharing such as how well the application fulfills the users' need and how to effectively implement a specific behavior-change technique [9,20]. Given all that, we inquire, are there other motivating factors that might be useful for the design of family-centered health technologies?

2.2 Factors that Influence Family Support

The desire to maintain constant communication and awareness of one another's lives as well as the desire to collaborate on their family's common good motivate family members' interactions with one another [28,29]. Many individuals consider family as a source of support in which the members help one another not only at times of necessity, such as during the treatment of a disease [25], but also to engage in behavioral changes for a healthy lifestyle [8]. In this study, we consider two factors that can affect family support including demographic change and geographical distance.

In the U.S., 37% of young adults provide the most help to their elderly parents aging 65 or older [7] with practical support to their parents, for example by helping with housekeeping or with social and emotional support such as making a phone call to check-in and visiting. Furthermore, 47% of those young adults are in their 40s and 50s [7], which means the majority of those young adults are either raising a young child or financially supporting a grown child (age 18 or older). Under such circumstances, examining how intergenerational family members currently communicate and collaborate on the arrangements of support giving, including health care, may provide a new perspective on sharing and collaboration among family members.

Finally, it has become increasingly typical for family members to be distributed by temporal or spatial distances due to different reasons such as work or educational opportunities, or lifestyle preferences [16,28]. Despite the distance, family members still want to stay in touch and aware of one another's current status [19,26]. In most cases, those families use technology as a way to maintain regular communication (e.g., phone calls, texting, emails [7,30]).

In this paper, we present motivating factors that affect family members' decision to share (or not share) health-related information. We also introduce and argue for turning points as an innovative approach for design that may lead to more family openness to share health information and collaborate in healthy behaviors. Our work contribution could be broadly applicable to researchers interested in how families collaborate to achieve health goals and the design of family-centered health technologies.

Furthermore, our work broadens previous studies since we focus on health information sharing between elderly parents and adult children. Previous studies have considered the family relationship between elderly parents and adult children in the context of informal care-giving [13,14] and in the context of tracking health information [3,4]. Others have proposed tools to support inter-generational relationship ties and communication between elderly and younger relatives across states/countries [2,23,26]. We, therefore, propose to complement previous research by expanding the knowledge of motivators that influence inter-generational family members' decision to share (or not share) health information.

3   Methods

Given our interest in learning about health information sharing in intergenerational families, we conducted semi-structured focus-group discussions. Although focus groups present the limitation of retrospective data due to participants reporting their own perspective on their families' practices of health information sharing, we argue that focus group is a suitable approach to understand participants' practices, motivate them to share ideas, and learn about their existing obstacles with respect to health information sharing [10,22].

3.1   Participants

In order to examine varied intergenerational families practices on health information sharing, we identified elderly parents and adult children as our target participants. We established the following inclusion criteria to evaluate participant eligibility:

- For elderly participants, individuals should be elders (55+ yrs old) living independently of their adult children.
- For adult participants, individuals should be non-student, working adults (18+ yrs old) living independently of their parents and financially self-reliant.

We used several different strategies to recruit participants. We sent emails through university listservs, distributed fliers in public spaces (e.g., public library, YMCA, local churches, university boards), and posted recruitment requests at our local university research website and on Facebook. Participants received financial compensation of $ 20 USD.

37 people participated in our study, including: 21 Adult Children (7 males and 14 females) and 16 Elderly Parents (6 males and 10 females) were recruited from a small eastern U.S. town. In the remainder of the paper, we refer to these participant groups as AC (adult children) and EP (elderly parents). The age

range of the AC was from 21–51 years old ($M = 33.14$, $SD = 7.82$). The EP ranged from 55 - 91 years old ($M = 67.75$, $SD = 22.43$; one EP participant age information is missing). The EP participants had a variety of living arrangements, including assisted living community and independent housing. None of the participants came from the same family.

3.2 Data Collection and Data Analysis

We held ten focus group sessions with 21 AC participants (2 or 3 participants per session) and three focus group sessions with 16 EP participants (2 to 5 participants per session). We had sessions for both elderly parents and adult children separately. The sessions were conducted either at a quiet room at the university lab or at a public space in the assistive care community with which we have partnership. During the discussion, the moderator asked approximately 8–12 open ended questions to guide the participants through an in-depth exploration of the topic. All focus group sessions were audio-recorded and transcribed. Each session lasted about 60 min. During each session, at least two members of our research group were present to moderate and to take notes from the discussion.

We used thematic analysis to construct "themes" within the data as proposed by Braun and Clark [6]. As we gather data from the focus group sessions, our research team met regularly to discuss the data. Each research team member independently reviewed the same transcripts and looked deeper into them for interesting findings. Then, we piece the findings together into themes. The themes include how the strength of relationships between the children and their parents influence their health information sharing, current sharing practices and ways of communication, willingness to share, issues around health information sharing, and when sharing behaviors change.

4 Findings

In this section, we describe motivating factors for health information sharing in intergenerational families. We focus this description on what we call "turning points," which are disruptive life events that can facilitate and sustain family members in soliciting and sharing health information with each other.

4.1 Factors that Influence Sharing Practices

During the discussion sessions, participants were prompted to think about their family's health sharing practices. We learned about factors that can motivate family members to share (or not share) health information including relationships, care, and health problems.

Relationships Motivate Sharing. For some participants, talking about health is part of their routine, and they feel comfortable sharing within their families. For example, participant AC-6 reported actively asking her parents about their health: *"I would just ask. I would feel comfortable asking my parents. That's the relationship I have with them, so I wouldn't feel uncomfortable asking."* *(AC-6)* Similarly, participant EP-13 characterized her relationship with her son as one where they talk about everything, including health information: *"We are more up front with each other and he'll tell me what he thinks I should do. I can be with him at any time or talk to him."* *(EP-13)* So, in these cases, health information is just another topic of discussion, which is also evident in participant AC-8's statement: *"My mom and I talk every other day, and we talk about whatever... I don't feel awkwardness if I need to ask her something especially pertaining to my health as it's related to her."* *(AC-8)* However, AC-8 also drew attention to special circumstances that could precipitate sharing health information. *"If either of us are sick, we talk about it. If we go to the doctor, we talk about it... If I have questions about anything that I'm going through, I'll ask her if she's gone through something similar. We'll discuss it openly."* *(AC-8)*

Care Motivates Sharing. In some cases, a lack of special circumstances (e.g. getting sick, going to the doctor) made participants question the need or value of sharing health information. For example, participant EP-5 said: *"As far as I know, none of our children or grandchildren or great-grandchildren have any health issues, so why?"* *(EP-5)* Some, such as participant AC-17, even characterized talking about health information with family members as a bother. *"[My mom and I don't talk about our health] because she knows I'm busy and she doesn't want to bother me."* *(AC-17)* This situation is curious because it raises the question as to whether they used to talk about it but stopped? When might talking about health *not* be a bother?

Health Problems Motivate Sharing. Some of our participants explained that they only have conversations about health if something major or unusual happens, otherwise, the conversations are focused on other, routine information. As participant EP-6 explained: *"If there's something meaningfully wrong that's dangerous and they [children] need to know about it, we would share immediately. Other than that, it's just, 'How you doing today?'"(EP-6)* An interesting insight here has to do with what counts as health information. We did not impose a definition on our interviewees. However, it is clear that, in this case, a general inquiry "how someone is doing" does not count as health information.

Health information in some cases skews in the direction of health problems, and health problems are highly motivating when it comes to sharing. For example, participant EP-2 mentioned that if a major health event happens, he would share it immediately: *"Let's say I had a heart attack, then I would want their[children] help in keeping me on a regular exercise program. Then I'd be willing to share. [Share] For prevention, I don't really care."* *(EP-2)* Similarly, participant AC-18 explained that she will share health information whenever something unusual happens: *"So anything that looks weird to me health wise, I'd [call my mom and] be like 'I think I'm dying!'"* *(AC-18)*

4.2 Turning Points

We became interested in an emergent theme in our data whereby family members seemed to describe an increase in health information sharing practices following a significant life event. Significant life events could include strokes, heart attacks, diagnosis with a chronic illness, diagnosis of a terminal illness, and so forth. They might also include things like major surgery, genetic conditions, and so forth. In discussing turning points, participants described changing patterns of health information sharing.

Participant AC-11 explained that in his family, his parents preferred to keep things private because they do not want to cause 'worriedness' within the family: *"My parents try to keep things very awkwardly private. It's not like we're not going to find out. It goes back to them not wanting us to worry about the same types of things I don't share, like, 'Hey, I have a cold.' You don't need to worry about that, right?" (AC-11)* And then, his family made an adjustment to a critical situation when his mom was diagnosed with cancer and *"...at that point, that's when things just changed."* Participant AC-11 said that he became more proactive and involved in his parents' health, and engaged in more sustained conversations about his parents' health status *"...so because of that I knew exactly when she was going to the doctor. I knew exactly when she was having appointments. I knew the results right away. I asked her, I became much more involved as far as asking about things about both of my parents' health, knowing that was going on." (AC-11)* It is interesting to notice that the adult child started soliciting more health information from both parents even though only one had been diagnosed with cancer.

In participant AC-12's case, she explained that her family engaged on occasional health conversations: *"When my parents were younger, and they're a little healthier, and small issues emerge, let them not share that. That's okay. But as they get older and things get serious I feel like now I need to just be more involved."* Her family made an adjustment to a different situation when her mom was diagnosed with breast cancer. Participant AC-12 mentioned: *"...that's when I became more proactive, and just very direct about their [parents] health issues."* According to participant AC-12, her attitude changed due to this turning point experience: *"I had to know exactly what was happening at all times. When the appointments were, and everything. I think that was really a turning point." (AC-12)* Participant AC-12 further elaborated her opinion and said: *"When you have that type of an experience, when you go through that level of health risk, where you know that there's the potential that they might not make it out of that experience, I think that that changes your understanding of why it's so important to have that information quickly, and to know as often as possible." (AC-12)*

Participant AC-9 mentioned that his family typically would not bring conversations about health up: *"It [conversation] was, 'How's it going? What's going on?' And usually there would be some political conversation or this happened in life, etc. but it was less they went to the doctor or they got some bad news. There was really no [health] discussion to that point."* However, after his father reported having a small stroke, he shifted and started to ask on a more regular basis about his father's health: *"It was one of these situations where you would talk and see how things were going, and then you'd have nice conversations. Then maybe a week later he would say something like, 'Oh, a week ago I forgot to tell you, but I woke up and I could barely talk and I was drooling.' 'You were having a mini-stroke, Dad!' Things that maybe you should have gone to a doctor a week and a half ago."* Participant AC-9 further reflected on his experience before the turning point: *"It's not like we would avoid talking about what was going on, but you never really just brought it up in casual conversation at a distance." (AC-9)*

Finally, in participant AC-10's experience, he would talk with his mother regularly and was aware of her back pain: *"I knew it was bothering her, but it was never something that was outright brought up [in conversations]."* Participant AC-10 changed when his mother needed a back surgery: *"She[mother] just had some back surgery about a year ago. If she went to the doctor or she had an appointment coming up, it would be part of the conversation." (AC-10)* After this incident, participant AC-10 explained how his family shares health information: *"I think it [health conversation] would usually come up, if it was something that was pressing. Or if she [mother] felt it was pressing, she would call me and say 'By the way my back's bothering me today'. Or, for example, if I had been sick that week. Well, of course, I'm going to say: 'Hey, I was out of work for a couple of days. I've had the flu.'" (AC-10)*

4.3   Other Motivators for Health Sharing Behaviors Change

Besides turning points, we also learned that family's health history is a motivator that influences family members' sharing routines. For example, participant AC-13 explained that her father suffered a major motorcycle accident years ago and has had several surgeries in his wrist. Due his medical history, her dad was open to share about his health: *"It was a couple days before the [new] surgery, and he was like, 'I'll be out of work for a month or two.' We're like, 'Oh, thanks for telling us.'" (AC-13)*

According to our data, major health concerns or issues are also motivators to influence health sharing within the family: *"My mom has diabetes, and has a couple other health concerns. We talk several times a week and I just ask her how she's doing and how she's feeling and usually she's pretty honest and truthful with me." (EP-14)* Likewise, in participant AC-14's case, his father has hypertension and some heart problems. Participant AC-14 mentioned: *"So I always ask him this question, like, how do you feel? Have you visited the hospital or recently like what medicines do you take now or something? He [father] will say something. So I can get an idea of what things he is doing, like how he's doing." (AC-14)*

Similarly, family genetic conditions motivate family members to share health information with each other. Participant EP-10 said that her son usually asked a lot of questions about her health and she did the same with him because *"...we've done our genetic makeup and we've discovered that we're very susceptible to blood clots." (EP-10)* Therefore, both parties exchange information back and forth.

Finally, participant EP-1 said that her family was open to discuss about health because she was diagnosed breast cancer at a very young age and so she decided to get genetic counseling together with her daughters to consider what types of medical decision they were going to take and to get information they needed to know: *"We tested for bracket one, bracket two, and two of the markers for ovarian cancer that are attached to breast cancer, and my daughters were extremely interested in that. It turned out that I was negative on all four markers, so that was kind of good news for them." (EP-1)*

5 Discussion

Our findings reveal factors that influence family member's motivation to share health information, including: relationships, care, and turning points. We found that, in many cases, turning points seemed to function as catalysts for increased health information sharing within intergenerational families.

Our findings complement existing work [5,18,24] by demonstrating the importance of sharing health information quickly/often. We argue that communicating more health information (more often) with family members is a good practice because it can in some cases be preventative. For example, a nagging cough might be a sign of a bigger problem in need of a medical expert's attention, which might only come to pass with gentle nudges from a family member to have it checked out. Things that we take for granted as unimportant or mundane health details can be problematic.

Take the mini-stroke victim. If he had told his children about his experience sooner, then he may have gotten medical attention sooner, and it is possible that further damage could have been avoided. Perhaps he thought that his drooling and slurred speech was not major, or perhaps he saw his decision not to share as an act of care in the sense that he did not want to burden his children. Our interviewees reported many different reasons as to why they did not share health information, but turning points could be seen to change these common ways of thinking about health information.

We, however, do not mean to suggest that those cases (e.g., cancer, mini-stroke) are not necessarily examples of health problems that could have been anticipated and preempted. Rather, we suggest that those cases possess crucial insights that could be applicable in others. For example, turning points disrupt the status quo of health (and health information sharing) and this is perhaps the most salient insight of our work. Furthermore, our purpose is not to undermine anyone's sense of personal privacy or to create the impression of burdening anyone. In fact, having more (and regular) access to health information in the family may increase anxiety or worry within the family [1,15]. Instead, we want to encourage more health information sharing in the hopes that potentially problematic symptoms, like a cough, might be caught before they evolve into a health problem, like pneumonia. We propose that understanding the characteristics of turning points themselves can help us motivate this kind of behavior.

Turning points disrupt daily routines. Their impact appears to be profound and lasting. Arguably, they result in re-framing the importance or value of sharing health information. Things that may have seemed insignificant, such as a cough or skin rash, may assume new significance. Thus, turning points might change the way people make sense of their daily life experiences when it comes to health, including when to share information about those experiences with family members. The question for us becomes: how can we change the way people make sense of their daily lives without experiencing a turning point? One answer to this question might be that we can create novel ways for people to make sense of their diet or daily activities. Technological solutions (e.g., mobile apps, wearable fitness trackers) could be seen as creating "turning points" at the point of adoption. These solutions are novel and exciting, and they provide users with new ways to make sense of their daily lives. However, eventually this novelty wears off [21]. Our interpretation of turning points leads to the insight that technological solutions designed to support health information sharing within the family must evolve so as to retain a sense of novelty over time.

6   Limitations and Future Work

We aimed to gather data from different intergenerational families; however, we did not have a full range of family dynamics. In future work, we are interested in talking to family members living together or low-income families. Furthermore, in our focus groups, the adult children and elderly participants came from different families, and they self-reported their perspectives on their family's sharing practices which may not represent the other members' viewpoints. We, therefore, plan in talking to members of the same family to know whether members from the same family would describe similar health information sharing patterns. Talking to multiple members of the same family might also help us triangulate health information sharing practices in ways individual family members might not. In addition, we plan to develop the concept of turning point as a generative tool for designers. We are interested in evaluating this concept with design practitioners and conducting workshops to understand how practitioners might make use of it when designing tools to promote health information sharing within the family. We believe that turning points could be an effective insight for the design of family-centered health technologies.

7   Conclusion

In this paper, we report the results of a focus group study aimed at understanding health information sharing in intergenerational families. Given our interest in facilitating more sharing between intergenerational family members, we were intrigued by changes in sharing practices that followed a significant life event, which we refer to as a turning point. Although we heard stories of health sharing from some of our interviewees, consistent, sustained sharing of health information seemed rare unless some kind of significant life event disrupted routine sharing and motivated sustainable sharing practices. We argue that turning points appear to be catalysts for sustainable sharing of health information among family members, and so they might provide useful insights for designers interested in promoting collaboration on health in a family context.

References

1. Bawden, D., Robinson, L.: The dark side of information: overload, anxiety and other paradoxes and pathologies. J. Inf. Sci. **35**(2), 180–191 (2009)
2. Bentley, F.R., Basapur, S., Chowdhury, S.K.: Promoting intergenerational communication through location-based asynchronous video communication. In: Proceedings of the 13th International Conference on Ubiquitous Computing, UbiComp 2011, pp. 31–40. ACM, New York (2011). https://doi.org/10.1145/2030112.2030117
3. Binda, J., Georgiva, E., Yang, Y., Gui, F., Beck, J., Carroll, J.M.: Phamilyhealth: a photo sharing system for intergenerational family collaboration on health. In: Proceedings of the Companion of the 2018 ACM Conference on Computer Supported Cooperative Work and Social Computing. CSCW 2018 Companion. ACM, New York (2018). https://doi.org/10.1145/3272973.3274091
4. Binda, J., Park, H., Carroll, J.M., Cope, N., Yuan, C.W.T., Choe, E.K.: Intergenerational sharing of health data among family members. In: Proceedings of the 11th EAI International Conference on Pervasive Computing Technologies for Healthcare, PervasiveHealth 2017, pp. 468–471. ACM, New York (2017). https://doi.org/10.1145/3154862.3154895
5. Binda, J., Yuan, C.W., Cope, N., Park, H., Choe, E.K., Carroll, J.M.: Supporting effective sharing of health information among intergenerational family members. In: Proceedings of the 12th EAI International Conference on Pervasive Computing Technologies for Healthcare. PervasiveHealth 2018. ACM, New York (2018). https://doi.org/10.1145/3240925.3240936
6. Braun, V., Clarke, V.: Using thematic analysis in psychology. Qual. Res. Psychol. **3**(2), 77–101 (2006)
7. Center, P.R.: Pew research center - family support in graying societies, January 2013. http://www.pewsocialtrends.org/2015/05/21/family-support-in-graying-societies/
8. Colineau, N., Paris, C., Marendy, P., Bhandari, D., Shu, Y.: Supporting family engagement in weight management. In: CHI 2009 Extended Abstracts on Human Factors in Computing Systems, CHI EA 2009, pp. 3991–3996. ACM, New York (2009). https://doi.org/10.1145/1520340.1520606
9. Consolvo, S., Klasnja, P., McDonald, D.W., Landay, J.A.: Designing for healthy lifestyles: design considerations for mobile technologies to encourage consumer health and wellness. Found. Trends Hum.-Comput. Inter. **6**(3–4), 167–315 (2014). https://doi.org/10.1561/1100000040
10. Creswell, J.W.: Qualitative Inquiry & Research Design Choosing Among Five Approaches. Thousand Oaks, CA (2007)
11. Eschler, J., et al.: Shared calendars for home health management. In: Proceedings of the 18th ACM Conference on Computer Supported Cooperative Work & #38; Social Computing, CSCW 2015, pp. 1277–1288. ACM, New York (2015). https://doi.org/10.1145/2675133.2675168
12. Glanz, K., Rimer, B.K., Viswanath, K.: Health Behavior and Health Education: Theory, Research, and Practice. John Wiley & Sons, San Francisco (2008)
13. Gutierrez, F.J., Ochoa, S.F.: It takes at least two to tango: understanding the cooperative nature of elderly caregiving in Latin America. In: Proceedings of the 2017 ACM Conference on Computer Supported Cooperative Work and Social Computing, CSCW 2017, pp. 1618–1630. ACM, New York (2017). https://doi.org/10.1145/2998181.2998314

14. Gutierrez, F.J., Ochoa, S.F., Vassileva, J.: Identifying opportunities to support family caregiving in chile. In: Proceedings of the 2016 CHI Conference Extended Abstracts on Human Factors in Computing Systems, CHI EA 2016, pp. 2112–2118. ACM, New York (2016). https://doi.org/10.1145/2851581.2892386
15. Janssen, R., de Poot, H.: Information overload: Why some people seem to suffer more than others. In: Proceedings of the 4th Nordic Conference on Human-computer Interaction: Changing Roles. pp. 397–400. NordiCHI '06, ACM, New York, NY, USA (2006). https://doi.org/10.1145/1182475.1182521
16. Judge, T.K., Neustaedter, C., Harrison, S., Blose, A.: Family portals: connecting families through a multifamily media space. In: Proceedings of the SIGCHI Conference on Human Factors in Computing Systems, CHI 2011, pp. 1205–1214. ACM, New York (2011). https://doi.org/10.1145/1978942.1979122
17. Katule, N., Rivett, U., Densmore, M.: A family health app: engaging children to manage wellness of adults. In: Proceedings of the 7th Annual Symposium on Computing for Development, ACM DEV '16, pp. 7:1–7:10. ACM, New York (2016). https://doi.org/10.1145/3001913.3001920
18. Kaziunas, E., Ackerman, M.S., Lindtner, S., Lee, J.M.: Caring through data: attending to the social and emotional experiences of health datafication. In: Proceedings of the 2017 ACM Conference on Computer Supported Cooperative Work and Social Computing, CSCW 2017, pp. 2260–2272. ACM, New York (2017). https://doi.org/10.1145/2998181.2998303
19. Kim, H., Monk, A.: Emotions experienced by families living at a distance. In: CHI 2010 Extended Abstracts on Human Factors in Computing Systems, CHI EA 2010, pp. 2923–2926. ACM, New York (2010). https://doi.org/10.1145/1753846.1753886
20. Klasnja, P., Consolvo, S., Pratt, W.: How to evaluate technologies for health behavior change in HCI research. In: Proceedings of the SIGCHI Conference on Human Factors in Computing Systems, CHI 2011, pp. 3063–3072. ACM, New York (2011). https://doi.org/10.1145/1978942.1979396
21. Kocielnik, R., Hsieh, G.: Send me a different message: utilizing cognitive space to create engaging message triggers. In: Proceedings of the 2017 ACM Conference on Computer Supported Cooperative Work and Social Computing, CSCW 2017, pp. 2193–2207. ACM, New York (2017). https://doi.org/10.1145/2998181.2998324
22. Krueger, R.A., Casey, M.A.: Focus Groups: A Practical Guide for Applied Research. Sage Publications, Thousand Oaks (2014)
23. Muñoz, D., Cornejo, R., Gutierrez, F.J., Favela, J., Ochoa, S.F., Tentori, M.: A social cloud-based tool to deal with time and media mismatch of intergenerational family communication. Future Gener. Comput. Syst. **53**, 140–151 (2015)
24. Pan, R., Forghani, A., Neustaedter, C., Strauss, N., Guindon, A.: The family board: an information sharing system for family members. In: Proceedings of the 18th ACM Conference Companion on Computer Supported Cooperative Work & #38; Social Computing, CSCW 2015 Companion, pp. 207–210. ACM, New York (2015). https://doi.org/10.1145/2685553.2699008
25. Pang, C.E., Neustaedter, C., Riecke, B.E., Oduor, E., Hillman, S.: Technology preferences and routines for sharing health information during the treatment of a chronic illness. In: Proceedings of the SIGCHI Conference on Human Factors in Computing Systems, CHI 2013, pp. 1759–1768. ACM, New York (2013). https://doi.org/doi.org/10.1145/2470654.2466232

26. Santana, P.C., Rodríguez, M.D., González, V.M., Castro, L.A., Andrade, A.G.: Supporting emotional ties among mexican elders and their families living abroad. In: CHI 2005 Extended Abstracts on Human Factors in Computing Systems, CHI EA 2005, pp. 2099–2103. ACM, New York (2005). https://doi.org/10.1145/1056808.1057107

27. Schaefbauer, C.L., Khan, D.U., Le, A., Sczechowski, G., Siek, K.A.: Snack buddy: supporting healthy snacking in low socioeconomic status families. In: Proceedings of the 18th ACM Conference on Computer Supported Cooperative Work & #38; Social Computing, CSCW 2015, pp. 1045–1057. ACM, New York (2015). https://doi.org/10.1145/2675133.2675180

28. Stuifbergen, M.C., Van Delden, J.J., Dykstra, P.A.: The implications of today's family structures for support giving to older parents. Ageing Soc. **28**(3), 413–434 (2008)

29. Sun, R.: Intergenerational age gaps and a family member's well-being: a family systems approach. J. Intergenerational Relat. **14**(4), 320–337 (2016)

30. Tee, K., Brush, A.B., Inkpen, K.M.: Exploring communication and sharing between extended families. Int. J. Hum.-Comput. Stud. **67**(2), 128–138 (2009)

"It Only Tells Me How I Slept, Not How to Fix It": Exploring Sleep Behaviors and Opportunities for Sleep Technology

Shikun Zhang[1]([⊠]) [iD], Florian Schaub[2] [iD], Yuanyuan Feng[1] [iD],
and Norman Sadeh[1] [iD]

[1] Carnegie Mellon University, Pittsburgh, PA 15213, USA
{shikunz,yuanyua2,sadeh}@cs.cmu.edu
[2] University of Michigan, Ann Arbor, MI 48109, USA
fschaub@umich.edu

Abstract. We present an online survey study examining people's sleep behaviors as well as their strategies and tools to improve sleep health. Findings show that certain demographic features and sleep behaviors may impact sleep quality, and that current sleep technology is not as effective in promoting sleep health as expected. We discuss the importance of understanding sleep behaviors, design insights for future sleep technology, and the value of a holistic approach to sleep technology design.

Keywords: Sleep technology · Sleep behavior ·
Human-computer interaction · Health informatics ·
Personal informatics

1 Introduction

Sleep plays a vital role in a person's health and well-being, yet according to the U.S. Centers for Disease Control and Prevention (CDC), one third of U.S. adults regularly sleep fewer than the recommended 7 h per day [11]. To improve people's sleep health, researchers in health and information sciences have explored sleep technology, broadly defined in this paper as a class of information and computing technologies designed to help people sleep better through a range of approaches including monitoring, measurements, and interventions.

Many of today's commercial mobile and wearable devices enable users to track their nightly sleep length [13,40] and sleep quality [31] with considerable accuracy [42]. These devices include wrist-worn activity trackers (e.g. Fitbit), smartwatches (e.g. Apple Watch), and smartphones that work with various sleep tracking apps (e.g. Sleep Cycle [35], Sleep Time [3]). Existing human-computer interaction (HCI) and health informatics (HI) research regarding sleep

This work was supported in part by the National Science Foundation (SBE1330596) and the Defense Advanced Research Projects Agency (FA87501520277) of the U.S. Federal Government.

© Springer Nature Switzerland AG 2019
N. G. Taylor et al. (Eds.): iConference 2019, LNCS 11420, pp. 754–766, 2019.
https://doi.org/10.1007/978-3-030-15742-5_71

technology has largely focused on effective sleep data measurements and visualization [13,15,16,23,31,40]. Some research initially explored interventions to improve people's sleep [4,30], but existing sleep technology still faces numerous challenges to effectively promote sleep health [27,28,38].

Admittedly, it is impossible to design effective sleep technology without a comprehensive understanding of people's sleep-related behaviors. This research contributes new knowledge to HCI and HI by surveying people's sleep behaviors in relation to their sleep quality, as well as a wide range of strategies and tools they use to improve sleep health. Our findings elicit research and design opportunities for sleep technology, namely, exploring a wider range of sleep behavior factors, providing actionable interventions and personalized sleep support, and advocating a holistic approach for sleep technology design.

2   Related Work

2.1   Sleep Quality Assessment

The gold standard of clinical sleep quality assessment is the collection of detailed physiological data through polysomnography [39], but polysomnography is not only expensive but also requires participants to wear multiple obtrusive sensors. The wrist-worn clinical alternative, actigraphy, is still too expensive for consumers [7]. Most of today's commercial sleep tracking devices largely rely on computer algorithms to estimate sleep quality, the accuracy of which is affected by the type and quality of embedded sensors. One validation study showed that wrist-worn Fitbit devices had significantly lower accuracy compared to actigrahy and polysomnography [33]. Furthermore, it is difficult to perform external and ecological validation of commercial devices' data accuracy [6], raising concerns about using them as tools for clinical intervention.

Besides quantitative sleep monitoring, standard self-report measurements developed by clinicians, such as the Pittsburgh Sleep Quality Index (PSQI) [10] and the Epworth Sleepiness Scale [22], are valid methods to assess sleep quality. The PSQI is a clinically-validated self-report sleep quality metric widely used in medical sleep research [5,9,24,29]. The PSQI consists of 19 questions that elicit sleep behavior and experience in the past month. The PSQI score ranges from 0–21, with low values indicating better sleep quality. PSQI scores above 5 indicate poor sleep [10]. Since this research aims to explore sleep behaviors of the general public (not only sleep technology users), we use the PSQI in our survey as a comparable sleep metric to perform quantitative analysis.

2.2   Sleep Hygiene and Sleep Behavior

Sleep hygiene is "a variety of different practices and habits that are necessary to have good nighttime sleep quality and full daytime alertness" [34], which is also commonly used by clinicians as an important component of insomnia treatment [41]. The sleep medicine community has developed different sets of sleep hygiene rules and recommendations [2,18,21,41], covering a range of adjustable behaviors, environmental conditions, and other sleep-related factors that could promote sleep health. For example, the National Sleep Foundation's sleep hygiene recommendations [34] include limiting daytime naps, avoiding stimulants close to bedtime, obtaining adequate physical exercise and so on.

However, there is limited data on how people adhere to sleep hygiene recommendations and the effectiveness of each individual recommendation [41]. It is time to examine a broader concept, **sleep behavior**, an umbrella term we use in this paper to describe a wide range of personal practices and daily activities that could impact a person's sleep health. We specifically address two components of sleep behavior, people's sleep hygiene practices and their pre-sleep behaviors.

2.3 Sleep Technology

HCI and HI research related to sleep technology has largely focused on improving sleep tracking and sleep data visualization with sensor-based smartphones and wearables. Choe et al. [14] first explored opportunities for sleep tracking technology, which lead to systems like Lullaby [23] and SleepTight [15]. Toss'N'Turn [31] and Sensible Sleep [16] proposed new methods to track sleep data with higher accuracy. As sleeping tracking is considered part of personal informatics [26], researchers have tried to incorporate persuasive technology commonly used in personal informatics systems [1,19] into sleep tracking. ShutEye reminds users of sleep hygiene through smartphone wallpapers [4], and SleepCoacher combines sleep tracking with personalized advice from sleep clinicians [30].

However, more recent studies with users of commercial sleep technology revealed considerable challenges and barriers [25,27,28,38]. Liu et al.'s [28] online forum content analysis showed that sleep technology users had difficulty in interpreting and manipulating their own data. Liang and Ploderer [27] identified three user barriers of not knowing what is healthy sleep, how to figure out reasons for poor sleep, and how to act. Ravichandran [38] discovered that the feedback provided by sleep technology did not match evidence-based methods to promote sleep health. Against the backdrop of these challenges and barriers, we take a broader perspective to examine a wide range of strategies and tools people use to improve sleep health, including all behavioral, procedural, or technological approaches to improve sleep health, which is not limited to sleep technology.

3   Study Design and Methods

3.1   Research Questions

This research aims to answer two research questions (RQs):

RQ1: How well do people sleep in relation to their sleep behaviors? This research question explores behavioral predictors for sleep quality. Among a wide range of sleep behaviors that may affect sleep health, we specifically focus on people's sleep hygiene practices and pre-sleep activities.

RQ2: What are people's experiences with strategies and tools to improve sleep health? This research question investigates the types of strategies and tools being used and people's perceived effectiveness of them. Note that sleep technology is a subset of these strategies and tools.

3.2 Questionnaire Design and Recruitment

Our survey questionnaire included three parts: (1) Background questions to collect some demographic features of participants; (2) Questions to address RQ2, which focused on participants' sleep in the past month using the 19-item PSQI [10] to measure participants' sleep quality, and additional close-ended and open-ended questions on a range of activities that could impact their sleep quality; (3) Questions to address RQ2, which included both close-ended and open-ended questions on strategies and tools participants used to improve sleep health and the perceived effectiveness of them.

We used a convenience sample by recruiting participants via Amazon Mechanical Turk (MTurk). A recent sleep research paper showed that participants recruited from online platforms (e.g. MTurk) and from a college campus reported similar PSQI score distributions [8], so MTurk could be a reasonably general participant pool for sleep research despite certain unavoidable biases. To be eligible, participants must be at least 18 years old and live in the United States. Participants each received 50 U.S. cents upon completion of the survey.

3.3 Data Analysis Methods

Qualitative Data Analysis. We analyzed participants' textual responses to the open-ended questions using iterative thematic analysis [20]. For each question, two of the authors first coded all responses independently and then merged their codes to create an initial codebook. Next, they discussed coded data to reconcile conflicts in their coding schemes, generated a finalized codebook, and then consistently re-coded the responses. The research team then conducted iterative affinity diagramming [37] to identify high-level themes derived from the coded data. Note that the affinity diagramming results on pre-sleep activities are used as independent variables for our quantitative analysis.

Quantitative Data Analysis. We used descriptive statistics to report quantitative data collected through close-ended questions, such as PSQI scores and Likert-type scale ratings. To answer RQ1, we ran regression analysis using a mixed linear model in the Python module StatsModels [36] to identify potential predictors for sleep quality. We used PSQI scores as the dependent variable and tested various independent variables, including 5 demographic features (age, gender, education level, occupation, work schedule), 9 sleep hygiene practices summarized from related work [2,34,41], and 12 categories of pre-sleep activities from the qualitative data analysis. To investigate RQ2, we ran additional between-groups t-tests using PSQI scores as the dependent variable to validate participants' perceived effectiveness.

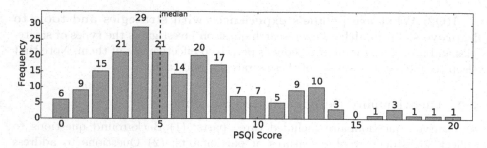

Fig. 1. Distribution of participants' PSQI scores. PSQI > 5 indicate poor sleep quality.

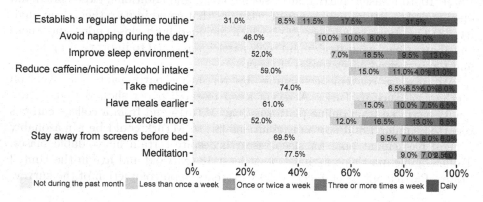

Fig. 2. Participants' (N = 200) adherence to recommended sleep hygiene practices.

4   Results

We received 200 survey responses. Of the participants 53.5% were female. The median age was 33 (range: 18–70). Almost all participants (99%) had graduated from high school, with 49% of them having a Bachelor's degree.

4.1   RQ1: Sleep Quality in Relation to Sleep Behaviors

Sleep Quality. We computed participants' PSQI scores and the distribution is shown in Fig. 1. The sample mean is 6.375 ($SD = 4.1$, Median = 5), meaning near half of the participants reported poor sleep quality (PSQI > 5). This PSQI score distribution also resembles that reported in a clinical research study from a community sample [9], indicating our MTurk sample is reasonably valid.

Sleep Behaviors. We focused on two aspects of sleep behaviors: sleep hygiene practices and pre-sleep activities. For **sleep hygiene practices**, we asked participants how often they adhere to 9 sleep hygiene practices recommended by clinicians. Figure 2 shows the results. Overall, participants' adherence to these practices was low. Only the two most popular practices ("establish a regular

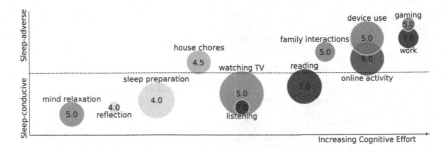

Fig. 3. Affinity diagram of 12 categories of pre-sleep activities.

bedtime routine" and "avoiding napping during the day") had over 50% of participants reporting different levels of adherence during the past month being surveyed. For **pre-sleep activities**, we asked participants what they do during the 30 min before going to bed with the purpose to explore potential behavioral factors that affect sleep quality. Participants reported 1.98 pre-sleep activities on average (max = 7) based on our qualitative analysis.

The affinity diagramming process surfaced 12 categories of pre-sleep activities. In Fig. 3, the categories are arranged from sleep conducive to sleep-adverse vertically and by the increasing degree of cognitive effort horizontally. For each category, the circle size represents the frequency of pre-sleep activities reported. For example, *watching TV* was the most dominant activity (41.5%). The number inside each circle and the color of the circle represent the average PSQI score of participants who reported pre-sleep activities of the category. The diagram shows that *house chores*, *sleep preparation*, and *reflection* were associated with better sleep quality (average PSQI < 5), while *work*, reading, and listening to music, radio, or podcasts were associated with poorer sleep quality (average PSQI > 5). It is worth noting that almost a quarter of participants reported using mobile devices during the 30 min before bedtime, which suggests an opportunity for mobile-based interventions to improve sleep health.

Predictors for Sleep Quality. Our regression analysis revealed a few predictors ($p < 0.05$) for sleep quality. None of the 12 pre-sleep activities are predictors for PSQI scores. Among 9 recommended sleep hygiene practices, only "take medicine" is a predictor for high PSQI scores. Interestingly, a few demographic features turned out to be statistically significant. Age is a predictor of higher PSQI scores, showing a gradual decrease (coefficiency = .102) in sleep quality as people age, but being "retired" in occupation indicates a significant improvement in sleep quality (coefficiency = −5.706). Furthermore, having a rotating shift in work schedule is a significant predictor of high PSQI scores, which is consistent with prior studies showing that shift workers have poor sleep quality [32]. Overall, most of the sleep behavior factors that we tested did not significantly impact participants' PSQI scores. This could mean the sleep behavior factors tested were not comprehensive enough or the sample size was too small.

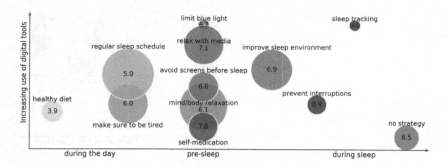

Fig. 4. Affinity diagram of 12 useful strategies and tools to improve sleep health.

4.2   RQ2: Experiences with Strategies and Tools for Sleep Health

Useful Strategies and Tools. We asked participants to describe the most useful strategies and tools they have used to improve their sleep. Participants reported 1.57 strategies and tools on average and we identified 12 major categories through affinity diagramming. As show in Fig. 4, categories are arranged by two dimensions indicated in the diagram. The circle size represents the frequency of that category, where the top two strategies and tools are mind and/or body relaxation (25%) and maintaining a regular sleep schedule (22%). The number inside each circle and the color of the circle represent the average PSQI score of participants who reported each category. Interestingly, those who reported using sleep tracking technology had highest PSQI scores among 12 categories.

Most of these useful strategies and tools are in accordance with general sleep hygiene recommendations [2,34] with a few exceptions. It is recommended one should avoid screens before sleep, which is opposed to those participants who reported relaxing with media. Additionally, no participants mentioned "ensure adequate exposure to natural light" [34] as a strategy. It is possible participants did not explicitly associated environmental factors such as sunlight exposure during the day with sleep quality.

Experiences with Useful Strategies and Tools. We asked participants to rate the effectiveness of the strategies and tools they described on a 7-point scale (1 = very ineffective, 4 = neutral, 7 = very effective) and explain their ratings. 174 participants ($M = 6.01$, $SD = 3.90$) rated the effectiveness of their strategies and tools positively (rating = ≥ 5), while 26 ($M = 8.85$, $SD = 4.45$) rated their strategies and tools neutral or ineffective (rating ≤ 4). The PSQI scores are significantly lower in the first group (t-test: $t(198) = 3.38$, $p \leq .01$, $r = .68$), possibly because people with poor sleep quality tend to regard their current strategies and tools as ineffective.

Among participants who reported relaxing with media against the sleep hygiene recommendations, a t-test showed no significant difference in PSQI scores between participants who positively rated the effectiveness of the strategy (rating ≥ 5, $M = 7.29$, $SD = 4.36$) with the rest of the group ($M = 6.21$, $SD = 4.01$),

Table 1. Participants' (N = 38) sleep technology use and perceived effectiveness

Sleep technology	N	Ratings mean	Ratings median	Ratings STD
Wrist-wore sleep tracker	17	2.82	3.0	1.5
Sleep-tracking alarm apps	8	3.75	3.5	0.83
Calming sounds/noise apps	4	5.25	5.5	0.83
Sleep-tracking apps	3	3.0	3.0	0.82
Blue light filter	3	2.67	3.0	1.25
Phone	2	4.0	4.0	1.0
Hypnosis apps	1	4.0	4.0	0.0

despite the first group's slightly higher average PSQI score. This indicates avoiding screens may not be a clearcut sleep hygiene practice for everyone.

Noticeably, among participants who positively rated the effectiveness of their strategies and tools, we found that many of their pre-sleep activities departed from the strategies and tools they deem useful. For example, 80% of those who considered avoiding screens before sleep useful reported using electronic devices before sleep. Only 20% of the those who described mind/body relaxation as the best strategy actually mentioned that as a pre-sleep activity. The most consistent strategy was relaxing with media, for which 72.7% also reported reading, watching TV or listening to various media before sleep.

Sleep Technology Use and Perceived Effectiveness. Since this research aims to explore opportunities for sleep technology, we asked sleep technology users in our sample to rate the effectiveness of such sleep technology using the same 7-point scale and explain their ratings. 38 (19%) participants reported having used some types of sleep technology. Participants ($M = 31.2$, $SD = 7.11$) who reported having used sleep technology were significantly younger (t-test: $t(198) = 3.01$, $p < .01$, $r = .62$) and female dominated (χ^2-test: $\chi^2(1, N = 200) = 5.16$; $p = .02$, $r = .37$) than the rest of our sample ($M = 37.3$, $SD = 11.9$). A t-test shows no significant difference in PSQI between participants who reported having used sleep technology and those who did not, suggesting that sleep technology use does not necessarily improve sleep quality. Table 1 shows the 7 types of sleep technology participants reported and their effectiveness ratings. Surprisingly, a wrist-worn sleep tracker is the most common sleep technology, yet it has the second lowest effectiveness ratings. We further present qualitative results to explain the rationale for participants' effectiveness ratings below.

Calming sounds or noise apps has the highest effectiveness rating. One participant pointed out: *"I think it blocks out the silence and other noises in the house that disturb me. It makes a consistent sound I can fall asleep, too."* Participants who positively rated the effectiveness of their sleep technology also provided other reasons, including *"increases sleep awareness," "helps fall asleep,"* and *"helps waking up."* On the other hand, despite the increasing popularity of sleep tracking devices, wrist-worn sleep trackers, sleep-tracking alarms, and sleep-tracking apps all received low ratings on effectiveness. The top reasons participants gave for rating these technologies as ineffective are *"information only, no advice"* and *"inaccurate tracking."* One participant further noted about a wrist-worn sleep tracker: *"It only tells me how I slept, not how to fix it."*

5   Discussion and Implications for Sleep Technology

5.1   Understanding Sleep Behavior Is Key

Though our regression analysis identified few sleep behavior factors that strongly impact PSQI scores, our qualitative data analysis revealed that certain pre-sleep activities and useful strategies and tools are associated with sleep quality. These initial results call for future research to **examine a wider range of sleep behavior factors and develop a deeper understanding of how these factors influence sleep health**. For example, we could extend the time range (30 min in this study) for pre-sleep activities to explore more behavioral factors. Also, we found participants' pre-sleep activities often depart from the useful strategies and tools they reported, indicating opportunities for targeted sleep interventions through persuasive technology [17]. Furthermore, the significant demographic features, including work schedule and retirement, urge us to consider people's relevant activities during the day as sleep behavior factors. Only by understanding how sleep behavior factors impact sleep health can we develop effective sleep technology that could steer people away from sleep-adverse habits and promote sleep-conducive behaviors – at night or even during the day (e.g. monitoring and cautioning about caffeine and alcohol intake).

5.2   Actionable Interventions and Personalized Sleep Support

The findings on perceived effectiveness of sleep technology indicate that sleep tracking technology increases users' awareness of their sleep behaviors but does not help them form actions to improve sleep health, which resonates with recent sleep technology [27,38] and personal informatics [1,19] research that emphasize interventions for behavior change. Future sleep technology should not only focus on accurately tracking sleep-related data, but also **help users understand issues in their sleep behaviors and provide actionable interventions to improve their sleep health**. The various sleep behaviors and useful strategies and tools reported by participants call for **personalized sleep support**. Personalization is not a new concept in personal informatics, but current sleep technology often takes the easy path: ShutEye [4] uses general sleep hygiene recommendations; SleepTight [15] uses self-reflection as personalization. Leveraging data collected by various personal informatics devices and self-reporting measures can help us understand how certain sleep hygiene recommendations could affect different individuals in order to tune and refine intervention designs. Specifically, we should make sure that **sleep support recommendations are truly actionable**. For example, even though shift schedule often leads to poor sleep quality, maintaining regular bedtime is not a feasible recommendation for shift workers. In this case, advanced machine learning models trained by various personal and contextual factors could help generate smarter sleep support recommendations for each individual user.

5.3   A Holistic Approach to Sleep Technology Design

The sleep technology use ratio (19%) in our sample is similar to the ratio (18%) Choe et al. observed in 2010 [14], despite the recent rapid growth of commercial devices with sleep tracking functions. As an implication, researchers should not only examine **current users** of sleep technology and their needs but also investigate how sleep technology could be designed to support **current non-users** to increase adoption. For example, sleep technology users are significantly younger than non-users in our sample, which suggests future design space for sleep technology to better support the needs of the elderly population.

Another contribution of this research is the identification of 12 categories of strategies and tools considered useful by participants. Since sleep technology is a subset of the full range of strategies and tools being examined, this research generates more comprehensive insights than existing work only focusing on sleep technology users [27,28,38]. Many participants still largely rely on traditional strategies and tools to improve sleep health, such as following sleep hygiene practices or developing their own bedtime routines. This finding underscores the importance to **integrate sleep technology into existing strategies and tools proven to be useful for current non-users**. Future sleep technology should provide novel solutions to enhance existing useful strategies and tools, for example, integrating calming sounds/noise apps into smart home devices such as Amazon Echo to promote sleep health.

6   Conclusion

We conducted an online survey with 200 participants exploring their sleep behaviors to shed light on future sleep technology. We found that certain demographic features (e.g. age, occupation, schedule) and sleep behavior factors (e.g. medication) may impact sleep quality, and that current sleep technology is not very effective in promoting sleep health. We discussed the importance of further investigation into sleep behaviors, the design opportunities for actionable interventions and personalized sleep support, as well as the value of a holistic approach to sleep technology design.

As most studies, this research has some limitations. Supplementing self-reported PSQI scores with other quantitative measurements for sleep quality could shed some additional light on how well people sleep. As has been reported by other researchers [12], there are some limitations to relying solely on data collected via MTurk, including unavoidable sampling biases. Third, we acknowledge that a larger dataset would likely help in building a more robust regression model. Despite these limitations, we were able to shed light on people's sleep-related behaviors and opportunities for new, more effective sleep technology.

References

1. Adams, A.T., Costa, J., Jung, M.F., Choudhury, T.: Mindless computing: designing technologies to subtly influence behavior. In: Proceedings of the 2015 ACM International Joint Conference on Pervasive and Ubiquitous Computing, UbiComp 2015, pp. 719–730. ACM, New York (2015). https://doi.org/10.1145/2750858.2805843
2. American Sleep Disorders Association: Diagnostic Classification Steering Committee: The International Classification of Sleep Disorders: Diagnostic and Coding Manual. American Sleep Disorders Association (1990)
3. Azumio Inc: Sleep time smart alarm clock (2016). http://www.azumio.com/s/sleeptime/index.html. Accessed 14 Dec 2018
4. Bauer, J.S., et al.: Shuteye: encouraging awareness of healthy sleep recommendations with a mobile, peripheral display. In: Proceedings of the SIGCHI Conference on Human Factors in Computing Systems, CHI 2012, pp. 1401–1410. ACM, New York (2012). https://doi.org/10.1145/2207676.2208600
5. Beaudreau, S.A., et al.: Validation of the Pittsburgh Sleep Quality Index and the Epworth Sleepiness Scale in older black and white women. Sleep Med. 13(1), 36–42 (2012). https://doi.org/10.1016/j.sleep.2011.04.005
6. Bianchi, M.T.: Sleep devices: wearables and nearables, informational and interventional, consumer and clinical. Metab. Clin. Exp. 84, 99–108 (2018). https://doi.org/10.1016/j.metabol.2017.10.008
7. BMedical Pty Ltd.: Actigraphy (2018). https://bmedical.com.au/product-category/fatigue-stress-sleep-related-devices/actigraphy/. Accessed 14 Dec 2018
8. Briones, E.M., Benham, G.: An examination of the equivalency of self-report measures obtained from crowdsourced versus undergraduate student samples. Behav. Res. Methods 1–15 (2016). https://doi.org/10.3758/s13428-016-0710-8
9. Buysse, D.J., et al.: Relationships between the Pittsburgh Sleep Quality Index (PSQI), Epworth Sleepiness Scale (ESS), and clinical/polysomnographic measures in a community sample. J. Clin. Sleep Med. 4(6), 563–571 (2008). http://www.ncbi.nlm.nih.gov/pmc/articles/PMC2603534/
10. Buysse, D.J., Reynolds III, C.F., Monk, T.H., Berman, S.R., Kupfer, D.J.: The Pittsburgh Sleep Quality Index: a new instrument for psychiatric practice and research. Psychiatry Res. 28(2), 193–213 (1989). https://doi.org/10.1016/0165-1781(89)90047-4
11. Centers for Diseases and Prevention: 1 in 3 adults don't get enough sleep (2016). http://www.cdc.gov/media/releases/2016/p0215-enough-sleep.html. Accessed 14 Dec 2018
12. Chandler, J., Shapiro, D.: Conducting clinical research using crowdsourced convenience samples. Ann. Rev. Clin. Psychol. 12, 53–81 (2016)
13. Chen, Z., et al.: Unobtrusive sleep monitoring using smartphones. In: 2013 7th International Conference on Pervasive Computing Technologies for Healthcare and Workshops, pp. 145–152, May 2013
14. Choe, E.K., Consolvo, S., Watson, N.F., Kientz, J.A.: Opportunities for computing technologies to support healthy sleep behaviors. In: Proceedings of the SIGCHI Conference on Human Factors in Computing Systems, CHI 2011, pp. 3053–3062. ACM, New York (2011). https://doi.org/10.1145/1978942.1979395
15. Choe, E.K., Lee, B., Kay, M., Pratt, W., Kientz, J.A.: Sleeptight: low-burden, self-monitoring technology for capturing and reflecting on sleep behaviors. In: Proceedings of the 2015 ACM International Joint Conference on Pervasive and Ubiquitous Computing, UbiComp 2015, pp. 121–132. ACM, New York (2015). https://doi.org/10.1145/2750858.2804266

16. Cuttone, A., Bækgaard, P., Sekara, V., Jonsson, H., Larsen, J.E., Lehmann, S.: Sensiblesleep: a Bayesian model for learning sleep patterns from smartphone events. PLoS ONE **12**(1), e0169901 (2017). https://doi.org/10.1371/journal.pone.0169901

17. Fogg, B.J.: Persuasive technology: using computers to change what we think and do. Ubiquity (December 2002). https://doi.org/10.1145/764008.763957

18. Friedman, L., et al.: An actigraphic comparison of sleep restriction and sleep hygiene treatments for insomnia in older adults. J. Geriatr. Psychiatry Neurol. **13**(1), 17–27 (2000)

19. Gouveia, R., Karapanos, E., Hassenzahl, M.: Activity tracking in vivo. In: Proceedings of the 2018 CHI Conference on Human Factors in Computing Systems, CHI 2018, pp. 362:1–362:13. ACM, New York (2018). https://doi.org/10.1145/3173574.3173936

20. Guest, G., MacQueen, K.M., Namey, E.E.: Applied Thematic Analysis. Sage Publications (2011). https://doi.org/10.4135/9781483384436

21. Hauri, P.J.: Sleep hygiene, relaxation therapy, and cognitive interventions. In: Hauri, P.J. (ed.) Case Studies in Insomnia. CIPS, pp. 65–84. Springer, Boston (1991). https://doi.org/10.1007/978-1-4757-9586-8_5

22. Johns, M.W.: A new method for measuring daytime sleepiness: the Epworth Sleepiness Scale. Sleep **14**(06), 540–545 (1991). http://www.ncbi.nlm.nih.gov/pubmed/1798888

23. Kay, M., et al.: Lullaby: a capture & access system for understanding the sleep environment. In: Proceedings of the 2012 ACM Conference on Ubiquitous Computing, UbiComp 2012, pp. 226–234. ACM, New York (2012). https://doi.org/10.1145/2370216.2370253

24. Knuston, K.L., Rathouz, P.J., Yan, L.L., Liu, K., Lauderdale, D.S.: Stability of the pittsburgh sleep quality index and the epworth sleepiness questionnaires over 1 year in early middle-aged adults: the cardia study. Sleep **29**(11), 1503–1506 (2006). http://www.ncbi.nlm.nih.gov/pubmed/17162998

25. Ko, P.R.T., Kientz, J.A., Choe, E.K., Kay, M., Landis, C.A., Watson, N.F.: Consumer sleep technologies: a review of the landscape. J. Clin. Sleep Med. **11**(12), 1455–1461 (2015). https://doi.org/10.5664/jcsm.5288

26. Li, I., Dey, A., Forlizzi, J.: A stage-based model of personal informatics systems. In: Proceedings of the SIGCHI Conference on Human Factors in Computing Systems, CHI 2010, pp. 557–566. ACM, New York (2010). https://doi.org/10.1145/1753326.1753409

27. Liang, Z., Ploderer, B.: Sleep tracking in the real world: a qualitative study into barriers for improving sleep. In: Proceedings of the 28th Australian Conference on Computer-Human Interaction, OzCHI 2016, pp. 537–541. ACM, New York (2016). https://doi.org/10.1145/3010915.3010988

28. Liu, W., Ploderer, B., Hoang, T.: In bed with technology: challenges and opportunities for sleep tracking. In: Proceedings of the Annual Meeting of the Australian Special Interest Group for Computer Human Interaction, OzCHI 2015, pp. 142–151. ACM, New York (2015). https://doi.org/10.1145/2838739.2838742

29. Lund, H.G., Reider, B.D., Whiting, A.B., Prichard, J.R.: Sleep patterns and predictors of disturbed sleep in a large population of college students. J. Adolesc. Health **46**(2), 124–132 (2010). https://doi.org/10.1016/j.jadohealth.2009.06.016

30. Metaxa-Kakavouli, D.: SleepCoacher: combining computational and clinician-generated sleep recommendations. B.s. thesis, Brown University (2015)

31. Min, J.K., Doryab, A., Wiese, J., Amini, S., Zimmerman, J., Hong, J.I.: Toss 'n' turn: smartphone as sleep and sleep quality detector. In: Proceedings of the SIGCHI Conference on Human Factors in Computing Systems, CHI 2014, pp. 477–486. ACM, New York (2014). https://doi.org/10.1145/2556288.2557220

32. Monk, T.H., et al.: Shiftworkers report worse sleep than day workers, even in retirement. J. Sleep Res. **22**(2), 201–208 (2013). https://doi.org/10.1111/jsr.12003

33. Montgomery-Downs, H.E., Insana, S.P., Bond, J.A.: Movement toward a novel activity monitoring device. Sleep Breath. **16**(3), 913–917 (2012)

34. National Sleep Foundation: Sleep hygiene (2016). https://sleepfoundation.org/ask-the-expert/sleep-hygiene. Accessed 14 Dec 2018

35. Northcube AB: Sleep cycle alarm clock (2016). https://www.sleepcycle.com/. Accessed 14 Dec 2018

36. Perktold, J., Seabold, S., Taylor, J.: Statsmodels, statistics in python (2009). https://www.statsmodels.org/dev/generated/statsmodels.regression.mixed_linear_model.MixedLM.html. Accessed 10 Sept 2018

37. Plain, C.: Build an affinity for k-j method. Qual. Prog. **40**(3), 88 (2007)

38. Ravichandran, R., Sien, S.W., Patel, S.N., Kientz, J.A., Pina, L.R.: Making sense of sleep sensors: how sleep sensing technologies support and undermine sleep health. In: Proceedings of the 2017 CHI Conference on Human Factors in Computing Systems, CHI 2017, pp. 6864–6875. ACM, New York (2017). https://doi.org/10.1145/3025453.3025557

39. Shepard, J.W., et al.: History of the development of sleep medicine in the United States. J. Clin. Sleep Med. **1**(01), 61–82 (2005). http://www.ncbi.nlm.nih.gov/pmc/articles/PMC2413168/

40. Shirazi, A.S., et al.: Already up? Using mobile phones to track & share sleep behavior. Int. J. Hum. Comput. Stud. **71**(9), 878–888 (2013). https://doi.org/10.1016/j.ijhcs.2013.03.001

41. Stepanski, E.J., Wyatt, J.K.: Use of sleep hygiene in the treatment of insomnia. Sleep Med. Rev. **7**(3), 215–225 (2003). https://doi.org/10.1053/smrv.2001.0246

42. de Zambotti, M., Claudatos, S., Inkelis, S., Colrain, I.M., Baker, F.C.: Evaluation of a consumer fitness-tracking device to assess sleep in adults. Chronobiol. Int. **32**(7), 1024–1028 (2015). https://doi.org/10.3109/07420528.2015.1054395

Environmental and Visual Literacy

Creen: A Carbon Footprint Calculator Designed for Calculation in Context

Jacob Abbott$^{(\boxtimes)}$, Gege Gao, and Patrick Shih

Indiana University, Bloomington, USA
{jaeabbot,gegegao,patshih}@indiana.edu

Abstract. Concerns regarding the environment and the impact humans constantly have on the environment has been a growing concern for decades, but there is still a substantial lack of environmental literacy and action among most of the population in what they can do to reduce the damage they may be indirectly causing. Given that many people express an interest in helping the environment, this paper presents a prototype of a carbon footprint calculator which interprets a carbon footprint estimate into a form that can be more accessible to people so that they may be empowered to make more informed decisions with greater awareness of their own impact.

Keywords: Human-computer interaction · Sustainability · Internet of Things

1 Introduction

Many people express their environmental impact as being important, yet there is a significant gap in the understanding of carbon output, carbon footprints, and their calculation [4,10,20]. The measurement of carbon output in pounds, kilograms, or tons is difficult for people to conceptualize as a gas by volume is not something readily accessible for many [1,21]. It is often hard for users to evaluate their energy consumption and to further take actions on saving energy. This study aims at resolving these issues through effective design with feedback which incorporates a metric to display carbon output in relation to the number of trees required to offset the CO_2 footprint and integrating Internet of Things (IoT) devices to improve measurements while limiting the need for user input.

To identify core challenges experienced by users in attempting to understand their environmental impact regarding carbon footprints, we conducted personal interviews and an online survey. Based on collected feedback, we developed a prototype Carbon Footprint Calculator app that asked a minimized number of questions in order to reduce the burden of usage and create a system with understandable feedback to enhance user awareness of their carbon footprint.

N. G. Taylor et al. (Eds.): iConference 2019, LNCS 11420, pp. 769–776, 2019.
https://doi.org/10.1007/978-3-030-15742-5_72

2   Related Work

Interest in greenhouse gas emissions and carbon footprints has been on the rise and continues to be a topic of discussion across many fields of science, yet standards for measuring and reporting carbon footprints are still developing. Pandey et al. reviewed numerous carbon footprint calculators that exist online or through consultants and found very few reported the same results even when given identical inputs [14]. Goodier discussed the calculation of carbon footprints on larger scales for companies, cities, and even countries and reported measurements in tons of carbon dioxide [8] while Weidema et al. suggested alternatives for presenting carbon footprint measurements [23].

As concerns grow regarding methods to reduce carbon footprints and environmental impact, insights from previous eco-design literature influence new attempts at communicating the knowledge of carbon footprint impact. In an attempt to understand the motivation of people's environmental behaviors, psychologists proposed several different models revealing human behavior. In the pro-environmental context, we focus mostly on norm-activation and rational-choice models. Norm-activation models prescribe that people's social behaviors are mainly subject to moral or personal norms [2,7,16,18], while the premise of rational-choice models is that environmentally conscious behaviours are aggregated from individual preferences which seek to minimize cost and maximize benefits [2,7,16]. As environmental behaviours usually impact a community base, in which personal behaviors can affect others as well as future generations, Schwartz's model [18] suggests that people's environmental behaviors will be improved when they are aware of the negative consequences they have on others. The "self-centered" rational choice models suggest that people would improve their environmental behaviours to improve personal benefits.

These models serve as the fundamental frameworks helping people understand human behaviors towards the environment. Yet to incorporate these models into products and interventions through integration of motivational techniques is an essential task for a designer. Previous work [7,16,19] has found comparative feedback an efficient way to motivate people's behaviors. Comparative feedback, with certain kinds of comparisons, used in persuasive applications promote behaviour change in areas such as energy conservation [6,13,16]. This comparative feedback includes self-comparison and social comparison. Self-comparison, refers to comparing one's current performance to past performance, whereas social comparison refers to comparing one's performance to that of others. However, these comparisons usually prove too complex for users to perceive the impact of their energy consumption on the environment [17].

Researchers [9,15–17] utilized eco-visualization to reveal energy consumption. Pierce et al. defines eco-visualization as *"any kind of interactive device targeted at revealing energy use in order to promote sustainable behaviours or foster positive attitudes towards sustainable practice"* [17]. Consumption data is often visualized as descriptive graphs [15,24] or metaphors [3,11,16], while some designers apply critical design to eco-visualization by utilizing different levels of artifacts and animations to increase people's environmental awareness [17].

The review of previous research has shown the potential of utilizing comparative feedback and eco-visualization to encourage pro-environmental behaviours. However, these have not been well applied to carbon footprint calculation. Furthermore, as IoT devices become popular among users, it is meaningful to work on designs that connect IoT devices with sustainable behaviors, which serves as the main motivation of this study. This paper addresses how eco-visualized comparative feedback could be designed to calculate carbon footprints. In particular, our work aims at providing design implications on eco-visualized comparative feedback through mobile and IoT devices.

3   Methodology

Informal semi-structured interviews were conducted with different groups to gauge their behaviors, insights, and ideas regarding the use of technology, environmental conservation concepts, and their intersection. Our participants included a PhD Student in environmental science, an owner of a construction company, attendees of a meeting by a student sustainability committee, and a group of four undergraduates. Through the interviews we gained insights regarding recycling practices, resource conservation habits, technology use, transportation methods, and levels of environmental literacy and understanding.

We additionally conducted an online survey generated from previous findings [1,4,10,20,21] and our interview results. The survey link was posted to social media and sent in email for participants to submit responses. Of the 31 total respondents (20 males, 10 females, 1 other), approximately 84% were between 18 and 34 years of age. Although the distribution is not representative of the United States at large, it is still a fairly diverse population for an initial investigation. Participants were asked questions regarding environmentally conscious shopping habits, recycling, transportation, attitude towards environmental concerns, and use and perception of Internet of Things (IoT) devices.

4   Preliminary Findings

Based off the information gleamed from previous work [5,7,12,16,17,22] and our user study, we concluded the main findings below to help create our initial design. From our interviews and questionnaires, most participants expressed their demands on measuring resource consumption and the effect it had on the environment. They also stated that measurements should be given in understandable formats. For example, the standard reported measurement of carbon output is in tons of CO_2, which is not clear for users. Therefore, the calculation should utilize understandable metaphors such as the number of trees needed to process the amount of carbon output. Participants expressed their concerns about manually inputting data. Since the footprint calculation requires many variables, users normally need to input all data manually, and have to re-enter data each time. Moreover, certain variables such as energy consumption are not easy to collect, which increases the difficulty of calculating their carbon footprint.

Based on user needs, our carbon footprint calculator is designed as a mobile app for users to calculate their carbon footprint based on their general energy consumption. In order to automatically acquire energy usage through smart devices, the app needed access to APIs of smart home devices (e.g., Nest, Wemo). Participants showed their willingness to connect indoor smart devices for energy consumption calculation to automate portions of measuring consumption.

Fig. 1. Initial prototype design of calculator questionnaire.

Fig. 2. Initial prototype design of calculation results.

Nationwide energy usage estimates are stored in the back-end to enable usage comparison between personal and national averages. Finally, personal information (e.g., number of cars, bikes, etc.) will be collected and logged with account information for carbon footprint calculations to protect privacy. Energy usage data will be stored in the app to calculate the carbon footprint automatically.

To get users familiar with our app immediately, the application would provide users a guide to learn about the app (e.g. how to adjust the settings, how to setup the connection between smart devices and the app). Considering a potentially broad user group, the guidance should be simple and easy to understand. Moreover, the app is designed with incremental information requests since requesting large amounts of data during initial use may overwhelm users. Therefore, the app initially requests a minimal amount of information from users to give an estimate of the user's carbon footprint, then incrementally asks for further information to refine and give more accurate estimates over time.

5   Design Process

5.1   Initial Prototype Design and User Study

Based on the findings above, we made our initial design using paper prototyping (see Figs. 1 and 2 for examples). The paper prototypes include several potential main interfaces such as calculation questionnaire, the calculation results and analysis, and the smart home devices connection and input.

To evaluate our prototype idea and gather further user insights and feedback, we conducted think-aloud walkthroughs with 8 participants. We presented our paper prototypes to each participant, and asked them to verbalize their thoughts and feelings while interacting with the prototypes. Insightful user feedback was collected, specifically, many users showed interest in how their energy consumption and carbon footprint compared to the national average, which supports the idea of comparative feedback we discussed previously. To incorporate these features, we reworked our design and developed a demo app for further study.

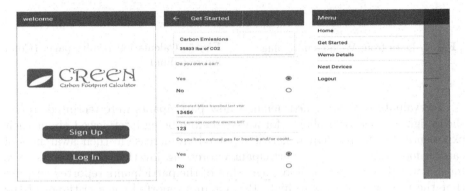

Fig. 3. Main interfaces of Creen (left to right): login, information collection, and menu.

5.2 Advanced Design Demo and Field Pilot

Based on the results of our study, we revised our prototypes and implemented a low-fi functional demo. In our design (see Fig. 3), users need to provide the basic information about their energy consumption. All the information we gathered was based on carbon footprint calculation equations [1]. The app automatically stores information and recalls it for users to edit or update on subsequent uses.

Figure 5 shows the final calculation page. By applying the comparative eco-visualization, the personal carbon footprint result is presented along with the average carbon footprint in the United States. In order to improve user's awareness of their environmental impact, each result comes with a value in pounds and the number of trees needed to process that value. Less than average results are shown in green and results higher than average are shown in red. The salient colors aim to strengthen the feedback comparison. The results show a distribution of energy consumption for categories based on U.S. averages. We compare electricity usage with average consumption in the U.S. and an energy efficient home generated by a local electrical provider, and illustrate it according to monthly usage. We provided users the detailed energy consumption breakdowns using their smart home devices as seen in Fig. 4. Once users chose the tab for smart devices, they saw a detailed consumption page detailing how much energy was consumed in real time and a distribution for different appliances.

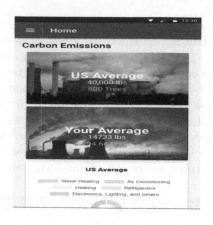

Fig. 4. Data from Wemo smart plug.

Fig. 5. Calculation results page. (Color figure online)

To evaluate the redesigned demo, 8 new participants were recruited to test the design on their own phones for a week before being interviewed about their experience. Of the participants, 75% reported an increase in their awareness of carbon footprints, with one participant expressing joy that their results were much lower than the national average. Half of the participants reported surprise that the U.S. average was so high. Participants reported some critiques of the application, such as some measurements being difficult to estimate (e.g. number of therms of gas used). Suggestions of a specific breakdown for the total carbon footprint and not just energy usage were received by half of the participants.

6   Conclusion and Future Work

As global warming contributes to environmental impacts, people continue to take interest by seeking actions to take on their own. Carbon footprints as a measure of carbon output, is growing as a personal impact factor for people. Current carbon footprint calculation requires complex user inputs and present results in a complicated and non-user-friendly manner. Therefore, the goal of this research was to create an application that assists in not only measuring carbon footprints, but to also convey that measurement in an accessible and easy to understand manner while reducing the potential for incorrect estimates of resource usage. Through interviews, literature reviews, think-alouds, and iterative design, we created a mobile carbon footprint calculator that utilizes user input and real time data from IoT devices to measure energy consumption and report a personalized carbon footprint. In future work, we will conduct larger field deployment studies with our functional prototype to explore how user input and calculation results affect user behavior, increase automated calculation of measurements through IoT devices and mobile phones, and gain more insights to refine our design.

Acknowledgements. We thank all our participants and Dr. Jean Camp for her invaluable insights.

References

1. Energy awareness quiz (2012). https://energy.gov/eere/education/downloads/energy-awareness-quiz
2. Bamberg, S., Möser, G.: Twenty years after hines, hungerford, and tomera: a new meta-analysis of psycho-social determinants of pro-environmental behaviour. J. Environ. Psychol. **27**(1), 14–25 (2007)
3. Carroll, J.M., Mack, R.L., Kellogg, W.A.: Interface metaphors and user interface design. In: Handbook of Human-Computer Interaction, pp. 67–85. Elsevier (1988)
4. Coyle, K.: Environmental literacy in America: what ten years of NEETF/ROPER research and related studies say about environmental literacy in the US. National Environmental Education & Training Foundation (2005)
5. Diekmann, A., Preisendörfer, P.: Environmental behavior: discrepancies between aspirations and reality. Rationality Soc. **10**(1), 79–102 (1998)
6. Foster, D., Lawson, S., Blythe, M., Cairns, P.: Wattsup? Motivating reductions in domestic energy consumption using social networks. In: Proceedings of the 6th Nordic Conference on Human-Computer Interaction: Extending Boundaries, pp. 178–187. ACM (2010)
7. Froehlich, J., Findlater, L., Landay, J.: The design of eco-feedback technology. In: Proceedings of the SIGCHI Conference on Human Factors in Computing Systems, pp. 1999–2008. ACM (2010)
8. Goodier, C.I.: Carbon Footprint Calculator. SAGE Publications, London (2011)
9. Holmes, T.G.: Eco-visualization: combining art and technology to reduce energy consumption. In: Proceedings of the 6th ACM SIGCHI Conference on Creativity & Cognition, pp. 153–162. ACM (2007)
10. Krause, D.: Environmental consciousness: an empirical study. Environ. Behav. **25**(1), 126–142 (1993)
11. Krippendorff, K.: The Semantic Turn: A New Foundation for Design. CRC Press, Boca Raton (2005)
12. Levine, D.S., Strube, M.J.: Environmental attitudes, knowledge, intentions and behaviors among college students. J. Soc. Psychol. **152**(3), 308–326 (2012)
13. Mankoff, J., et al.: Stepgreen.org: increasing energy saving behaviors via social networks. In: ICWSM (2010)
14. Pandey, D., Agrawal, M., Pandey, J.S.: Carbon footprint: current methods of estimation. Environ. Monit. Assess. **178**(1–4), 135–160 (2011)
15. Petersen, D., Steele, J., Wilkerson, J.: WattBot: a residential electricity monitoring and feedback system. In: CHI'09 Extended Abstracts on Human Factors in Computing Systems, pp. 2847–2852. ACM (2009)
16. Petkov, P., Köbler, F., Foth, M., Krcmar, H.: Motivating domestic energy conservation through comparative, community-based feedback in mobile and social media. In: Proceedings of the 5th International Conference on Communities and Technologies, pp. 21–30. ACM (2011)
17. Pierce, J., Odom, W., Blevis, E.: Energy aware dwelling: a critical survey of interaction design for eco-visualizations. In: Proceedings of the 20th Australasian Conference on Computer-Human Interaction: Designing for Habitus and Habitat, pp. 1–8. ACM (2008)

18. Schwartz, S.H.: Normative influences on altruism. In: Advances in Experimental Social Psychology, vol. 10, pp. 221–279. Elsevier (1977)
19. Siero, F.W., Bakker, A.B., Dekker, G.B., Van Den Burg, M.T.: Changing organizational energy consumption behaviour through comparative feedback. J. Environ. Psychol. **16**(3), 235–246 (1996)
20. Synodinos, N.E.: Environmental attitudes and knowledge: a comparison of marketing and business students with other groups. J. Bus. Res. **20**(2), 161–170 (1990)
21. Vandyke, C.: An environmental footprint quiz for WPI students. Ph.D. thesis, Worcester Polytechnic Institute (2009)
22. Vicente-Molina, M.A., Fernández-Sáinz, A., Izagirre-Olaizola, J.: Environmental knowledge and other variables affecting pro-environmental behaviour: comparison of university students from emerging and advanced countries. J. Cleaner Prod. **61**, 130–138 (2013)
23. Weidema, B.P., Thrane, M., Christensen, P., Schmidt, J., Løkke, S.: Carbon footprint: a catalyst for life cycle assessment? J. Ind. Ecol. **12**(1), 3–6 (2008)
24. Wood, G., Newborough, M.: Dynamic energy-consumption indicators for domestic appliances: environment, behaviour and design. Energy Build. **35**(8), 821–841 (2003)

Environmental Monitoring of Archival Collections: An Exploratory Study of Professionals' Data Monitoring Dashboard Needs and Related Challenges

Monica Maceli(✉), Elena Villaespesa, and Sarah Ann Adams

Pratt Institute School of Information, 144 W. 14th Street, 6th Floor,
New York, NY 10011, USA
{mmaceli, evillaes}@pratt.edu,
s.ann.adams5761@gmail.com

Abstract. This work explores the data dashboard monitoring needs and challenges encountered by archives professionals engaged in environmental monitoring, such as collection of temperature and humidity data, across a variety of cultural heritage domains. The results of a practitioner focus group and data dashboard feature ideation session are presented. Findings suggest that practitioners' environmental monitoring struggles include a variety of factors ranging from little budget or staff buy-in, to struggles with environmental monitoring device features, data collection, and interpretation. Suggested revisions to popular data dashboard tools in use included integrating multiple sensors' data into a single, remotely-accessible real-time control interface. Participants' required features in a data dashboard included: charts, export options, value ranges and exceeded alerts, web and mobile access, real-time data, and a date range selector. An initial data dashboard mockup based on the expressed end user needs and challenges is presented.

Keywords: Archives · Environmental monitoring · Data dashboard ·
End users

1 Introduction

In the cultural heritage domain, archivists and other professionals seek to effectively preserve archives and collections consisting of a variety of types of materials, through monitoring and controlling of environmental conditions. A great deal of existing literature guides professionals in assessing the conditions that materials are being subjected to, and advocates for the use of environmental data (most commonly - temperature and humidity, but also light exposure and air quality) in identifying and correcting poor conditions [1, 2]. Building design and HVACs (heating, ventilation and air conditioning) systems can be constructed and configured to achieve the desired environmental conditions, but best practices advise archivists to operate independent devices that can monitor the actual conditions achieved and any problem areas [3, 4].

© Springer Nature Switzerland AG 2019
N. G. Taylor et al. (Eds.): iConference 2019, LNCS 11420, pp. 777–784, 2019.
https://doi.org/10.1007/978-3-030-15742-5_73

Digital environmental monitoring devices and data dashboard interfaces are increasingly being deployed to verify that HVAC readings are accurate [3] and are produced by companies such as the Image Permanence Institute (who provide the popular eClimateNotebook® data dashboard tool), OnSet, Vaisala, and Dickson. Such devices and services take a variety of forms, from non-networked stand-alone data-loggers to more complex wireless systems [5], and are available at a variety of price points. In contrast to the available commercial devices, research work has explored new approaches to wireless sensor networks designed to overcome limitations in building layout and manage technical tradeoffs, while ensuring high accuracy and ease-of-use [6–9]. Studies largely focused on temperature and humidity, often in the micro-climates that may develop around artworks, with some addressing light, such as Zhang and Ye [7], particularly in the museums context. Most solutions were designed for indoor environments, though some designed for outdoor context include both light and rain sensors [10]. Notably, much of this research emphasizes remote monitoring and utilizing common protocols and techniques borrowed from the Internet-of-things and open source hardware realms [9, 11]. Many of the products at the lower end of the commercial offerings lack such features entirely. Dashboards are a common visualization tool for monitoring a set of indicators in a single screen and highlight those that require immediate attention [12]. Using dashboards brings efficiencies in the data collection and reporting process due to automation and low staff training needs [13, 14]. In the preservation area, the eClimateNotebook tool, developed by the Image Permanence Institute, generates an overview report to monitor environmental data uploaded after collection [15].

Though there is a great deal of research and practical focus on what the desired conditions should be, what tools to employ to monitor such systems, and general best practices, less work directly seeks to understand the end users of such systems, their data dashboard needs, and their challenges encountered in environmental monitoring. Some of the existing research on novel wireless monitoring systems conducted small-scale user tests on the prototype device, such as the Peralta et al. 2013 study of a monitoring mobile application [16], motivating small iterative design improvements. Few recent works explored end user requirements in greater depth from the beginning of the design process and outside of the context of an already-developed system.

To close this gap in research, this exploratory study seeks to understand: (1) *what are the data monitoring dashboard needs of archives professionals engaged in environmental monitoring?* and (2) *what challenges do they encounter in their monitoring activities?* This paper reports on the findings of a practitioner focus group, comprised of professionals from a variety of types of cultural heritage domains, all engaged in environmental monitoring work. The data are analyzed using qualitative methods, and a proposed solution of integrating multiple sensors' data into a single, remotely-accessible data dashboard control interface is developed.

2   Research Methods

A focus group of participants involved in environmental monitoring, within cultural heritage organizations, was conducted in August 2018. A total of 4 participants were recruited from listservs relevant to archival practices in the New York City area. The focus group consisted of the following activities: (1) a series of initial questions drawn from related literature, (2) a dot voting activity, and (3) a data dashboard sketching exercise, all described in more detail below. All activities were guided by the researchers (authors one and two), with a graduate assistant taking notes, audio-recording the discussion, and photographing the designs created. Participants were asked to read and sign a consent form, introduce themselves, then respond to an initial series of questions aimed at understanding: what environmental data is tracked and how, who accesses the data within the organization and to what ends, as well as any challenges they had encountered in these activities.

Next, the participants of the focus group were asked to do a dot voting exercise based on a predefined list of data and dashboard features. The goal of the exercise was to get a full list of features prioritized by the potential future users. The exercise was undertaken in two rounds. During the first round, participants were provided with five green dots to mark the "must have" features; the second-round dots had a different color (yellow) to select an additional five "nice to have" features. The list of desired features was created based on common dashboard features as well as specific data points and functionalities identified in the literature review and existing reporting tools in the market. The list included a total of sixteen potential features and provided a space for participants to add other requirements.

Finally, participants carried out a drawing activity in groups of two, where the task was to sketch in a poster size sheet the visual look of the dashboard. The drawings were presented by each group and a discussion about the results followed. The goal of this task was to understand the key components of the visual elements required for the user interface as well as a confirmation of what the most valuable features would be.

The final anonymized session transcript was analyzed using inductive qualitative analysis to code the transcript, in pursuit of identifying themes and concepts of interest to the stated research question - namely the users' data dashboard needs and challenges in environmental monitoring. A final coding scheme was then developed and the findings were integrated into a preliminary data dashboard mockup by the researchers.

3   Results and Discussion

During the initial background questions, participants described their environmental monitoring work in a variety of cultural heritage organizations, including: one participant from an art gallery, two from museums, and one from an archive. All participants were engaged in some level of environmental monitoring activities, ranging from just beginning to monitor conditions with generic consumer devices, to operating dozens of commercial environmental monitoring devices. Participants reported using or having used devices and web-based data dashboards from a variety of popular manufacturers in this area, including dataloggers from the Image Permanence Institute and

OnSet. All participants reported similar needs in assessing and reporting environmental monitoring data. Participants' organizational data is used on an ongoing basis to monitor different metrics, primarily about temperature and relative humidity, but some of the organizations were also collecting data about air quality, light exposure, and water presence. The data are used to detect any critical situation that needs be addressed quickly and also gradually improve the collection environmental conditions. Reports based on this data are distributed to managers and partners to advocate for better conditions for the collection objects. For those organizations with current or upcoming construction work, data is also used for building planning, as well as fundraising and artwork loan requests.

Many challenges were reported by participants in conducting environmental monitoring activities within their organizations (summarized in Table 1, below). Difficulties were experienced in a wide range of environmental monitoring activities, including: lack of resources ("*I don't have a line item for my department, so I just have to wait until grant money comes in or write a special request.*" [P1]), interpersonal ("*There has been a lot of resistance from other staff members about keeping doors closed, about keeping the temperature ranger where we want it*" [P3]), and, for those organizations that could afford environmental monitoring devices, technical issues with the devices themselves. One participant noted difficulty in interpreting the data provided:

> "*I'm still learning how to use the Onset data logging reporting. It gave me this really complicated graph, and I just couldn't zoom in or understand the data on the granular level in the way I was hoping to... I wanted to know, "What time was this happening? What's going on?" Was it because the door's opening a bunch during the day? Or is the humidity bumping up in the middle of the night, and why?*" [P3]

Table 1. Participants' environmental monitoring challenges, ordered by frequency of mention

Technical & sociotechnical	Difficulty monitoring conditions of remote locations (3)
	Unaware of technical possibilities, e.g. monitoring air quality (2)
	Device alerts (audible) useless in remote/unstaffed locations (1)
	Intimidated by novel technology (1)
	Sensors failing over time (1)
Resources	Lack of environmental monitoring budget (3)
	Lack of time to learn a new device (2)
	Lone advocate for monitoring activities (2)
	Excessive staff time consumed by data gathering (1)
Physical Space	Difficulty placing and securing sensors in ideal locations (3)
	Dealing with changing physical conditions, e.g. construction (1)
	Obscuring devices too large or prominent for public spaces (1)
Data Context	Difficulty understanding fluctuation of conditions (2)
	Difficulty assessing value of existing monitoring systems (1)
	Difficulty interpreting device data (1)
Communication	Need for executive summaries for stakeholders (2)
	Difficulty explaining complex preservation concepts (1)
Organizational	Staff resistance to environmental monitoring policies (2)
	Balancing professional guidelines vs sustainability practices (1)

Other participants reported that the perceived difficulty of operating the devices, and lacking the time to dedicate to learning a new system, were also barriers to use.

To explore the feature needs of practitioners in environmental monitoring, the results of the dot voting activity and dashboard drawing exercise were analyzed. First, the results of the dot voting activity are shown in Fig. 1 (below) with green bars denoting required features and yellow bars identifying nice-to-have features. The most popular features, required by half or more of participants, included: charts, export options, value ranges and exceeded alerts, web and mobile access, real-time data, and a date range selector.

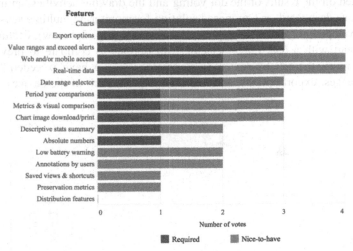

Fig. 1. Focus group participants required and nice-to-have features for a data dashboard (n = 4) (Color figure online)

In terms of the features needed and how those are presented visually, clear priorities emerged in the dashboard drawing exercise, which were aligned well with the findings from the previous dot voting exercise. Participants' drawings emphasized the need to monitor trends and detect areas of improvement, with charts prominently featured in all the sketches. Related to the chart other features were considered key: a date range selector and the ability to compare metrics with previous year or periods. In the list of highly desired features in the list, participants also highlighted export options as a PDF or the raw data as a CSV file to distribute the reports or carry out further data analysis.

One of the main purposes of environmental control is to quickly detect anomalies to avoid any risks of damage in the collection objects. This brings a major requirement of the reporting tool, the possibility to receive alerts and notifications when the data goes outside the established normal parameters. This was mentioned by all the participants, and is nicely summarized in this comment:

> "*It would be beneficial to have an alert system or even something that would just make it easier so that I wouldn't have to think about getting up and going and collecting the data*" [P1].

This need brings another essential requirement mentioned by all participants as either a required or nice-to-have feature: remote access via mobile and/or web. There were several comments about this necessity to access the data on real time due to the daily tasks of the participants at work which involve moving in the storage areas or working remotely from the different locations of the organization: "*I am not frequently at a desk over the course of a day...a way to access that information when I'm moving around in the warehouse is really helpful*" [P3].

Based on the results of the dot voting and the drawing activities, an initial mockup of the data dashboard, as a proposed solution for monitoring multiple sensors remotely, was developed to capture the expressed user needs (Fig. 2, below). Features include: a main chart with a date range selector with options to compare to previous periods, filters to view the data by device, an alerts area if values have exceeded the predefined value ranges, export options, and real-time data for each of the devices.

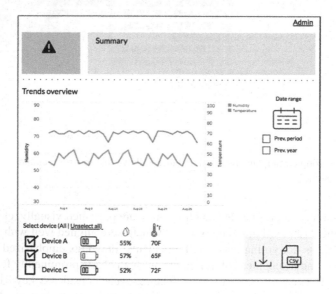

Fig. 2. Data dashboard mockup of web-based desktop

Though many of the features suggested by participants were well-supported by existing systems, such as charts and remote access, the focus group elicited additional requirements. Participants emphasized their need to constantly be advocating for greater budget, seeking buy-in from other staff, and regularly needing to produce executive summaries for various stakeholders. This deeper organizational context is difficult to observe from a hardware-focused user study, as was typically the user-centered emphasis of prior work. To address these problems, the mockup (Fig. 2, above) included an admin view and a read-only view, as well as a summary of findings, to assist in creating an executive report for other stakeholders.

4 Conclusion

This research study details the findings of a focus group of archival practitioners involved in environmental monitoring work, exploring their data dashboard needs and challenges in monitoring activities. Technical and resources-related challenges dominated, that have not been the focus of existing research literature. An initial mockup of a data dashboard supporting these unmet needs was developed; future work will explore integrating this work into environmental monitoring systems and practice.

References

1. Harvey, R., Mahard, M.R.: The Preservation Management Handbook: A 21st-Century Guide for Libraries, Archives and Museums. Rowman & Littlefield, Lanham (2014)
2. Temperature, relative humidity, light, and air quality: Basic guidelines for preservation. https://www.nedcc.org/free-resources/preservation-leaflets/2.-the-environment/2.1-temperature,-relative-humidity,-light,-and-air-quality-basic-guidelines-for-preservation
3. Wilsted, T.P.: Planning New and Remodeled Archival Facilities. Society of American Archivists, Chicago (2007)
4. Pacifico, M.E., Wilsted, T.P. (eds.): Archival and Special Collections Facilities: Guidelines for Archivists, Librarians, Architects, and Engineers. Society of American Archivists, Chicago (2009)
5. Morris, P.: Achieving a preservation environment with data logging technology and microclimates. Coll. Undergrad. Libr. **16**(1), 83–104 (2009). https://doi.org/10.1080/10691310902754247
6. Bacci, M., Cucci, C., Mencaglia, A.A., Mignani, A.G.: Innovative sensors for environmental monitoring in museums. Sensors **8**(3), 1984–2005 (2008). https://doi.org/10.3390/s8031984
7. Zhang, Y., Ye, W.: Design and placement of light monitoring system in museums based on wireless sensor networks. In: Proceedings of 2011 International Symposium on Advanced Control of Industrial Processes (ADCONIP), Piscataway, N.J., pp. 512–517. IEEE (2011)
8. D'Amato, F., Gamba, P., Goldoni, E.: Monitoring heritage buildings and artworks with wireless sensor networks. In: Proceedings of 2012 IEEE Workshop on Environmental Energy and Structural Monitoring Systems (EESMS), Perugia, Italy, pp. 1–6. IEEE (2012)
9. Londero, P., Fairbanks-Harris, T., Whitmore, P.M.: An open-source, internet-of-things approach for remote sensing in museums. J. Am. Inst. Conserv. **55**(3), 1–10 (2016). https://doi.org/10.1080/01971360.2016.1217671
10. Mecocci, A., Abrardo, A.: Monitoring architectural heritage by wireless sensors networks: San Gimignano—a case study. Sensors **14**(1), 770–778 (2014). https://doi.org/10.3390/s140100770
11. Mesas-Carrascosa, F.J., Santano, D.V., Meroño de Larriva, J.E., Cordero, R.O., Fernández, R.E.H., García-Ferrer, A.: Monitoring heritage buildings with open source hardware sensors: a case study of the Mosque-Cathedral of Córdoba. Sensors **16**(10) (2016). https://doi.org/10.3390/s16101620

12. Few, S.: Information Dashboard Design: The Effective Visual Communication of Data. O'Reilly, Sebastopol (2006)
13. Eckerson, W.W.: Performance Dashboards: Measuring, Monitoring, and Managing Your Business. Wiley, Hoboken (2011)
14. Chen, C.Y., Rasmussen, N.H., Bansal, M.: Business Dashboards: A Visual Catalog for Design and Deployment. Wiley, Hoboken (2013)
15. About eClimate Notebook. https://www.eclimatenotebook.com/about.php
16. Peralta, L.M.R., Abreu, A.M.M., Brito, L.M.P.L.: Environmental monitoring based on wireless sensor network via mobile phone. In: Proceedings of 7th International Conference on Sensor Technologies and Applications, Wilmington, D.E., pp. 25–31. IARIA (2013)

Exploring and Visualizing Household Electricity Consumption Patterns in Singapore: A Geospatial Analytics Approach

Yong Ying Joanne Tan[✉] and Tin Seong Kam

Singapore Management University,
80 Stamford Road, Singapore 178902, Singapore
yy.tan.2017@mitb.smu.edu.sg, tskam@smu.edu.sg

Abstract. Despite being a small country-state, electricity consumption in Singapore is said to be non-homogeneous, as exploratory data analysis showed that the distributions of electricity consumption differ across and within administrative boundaries and dwelling types. Local indicators of spatial association (LISA) were calculated for public housing postal codes using June 2016 data to discover local clusters of households based on electricity consumption patterns. A detailed walkthrough of the analytical process is outlined to describe the R packages and framework used in the R environment. The LISA results are visualized on three levels: country level, regional level and planning subzone level. At all levels we observe that households do cluster together based on their electricity consumption. By faceting the visualizations by dwelling type, electricity consumption of planning subzones can be said to fall under one of these three profiles: low-consumption subzone, high-consumption subzone and mixed-consumption subzone. These categories describe how consumption differs across different dwelling types in the same postal code (HDB block). LISA visualizations can guide electricity retailers to make informed business decisions, such as the geographical zones to enter, and the variety and pricing of plans to offer to consumers.

Keywords: Electricity consumption · Exploratory spatial data analysis · Spatial autocorrelation

1 Introduction

Currently, electricity consumption in Singapore is closely monitored by the Energy Market Authority (EMA) and reported on annually through the Singapore Energy Statistics publication [1]. Despite being a small country-state, there are observed differences in electricity consumption across geographical areas and dwelling types (1-room and 2-room flats, 3-room flats, 4-room flats, 5-room and executive flats) which could be attributed to demographic factors such as household size, household income or proportion of economically active population in the region.

© Springer Nature Switzerland AG 2019
N. G. Taylor et al. (Eds.): iConference 2019, LNCS 11420, pp. 785–796, 2019.
https://doi.org/10.1007/978-3-030-15742-5_74

Looking at the average monthly household electricity consumption by dwelling type in Table 3.4 of Singapore Energy Statistics report, it is obvious that households in bigger dwelling types have higher consumption [1]. However, it becomes difficult to compare across planning zones in a tabular format in Table 3.5 [1]. Thus, the author downloaded the data to perform an exploratory data analysis to discover if electricity usage is indeed heterogeneous across dwelling types or geographical areas.

Figure 1 shows the distribution of consumption by postal codes in each planning area, faceted by dwelling type and sorted by median consumption. The results are consistent with those reported by EMA in that bigger dwelling types correspond to higher electricity usage. We also see that consumptions are different across planning areas of each dwelling type, proving that electricity usage is heterogeneous across both dwelling types and geographical areas. On top of that, we see that within each planning area, distributions are wide and most of them have outliers, which debunks generalizations that electricity usage is homogeneous within an administrative area.

Motivated by the differences observed at multiple facets: across dwelling types, across planning areas and within planning areas, this study will explore the application of local indicators of spatial association (LISA) on electricity consumption data in Singapore to answer two questions: where are the outliers located at? And do households of high electricity usage cluster together spatially, or are they randomly distributed throughout Singapore? As we have the advantage of possessing highly disaggregated data at the postal code level, we will explore spatial autocorrelation on point features, which is different from most LISA applications that explore spatial autocorrelation on polygon features.

In this paper, we will use data provided by EMA [2] in the month of June 2016 to analyze spatial autocorrelation of electricity consumption among Singapore's public housing postal codes using the local Moran's I statistic. Then, we will interpret the statistic into four quadrants and map the results on three levels. The maps are faceted

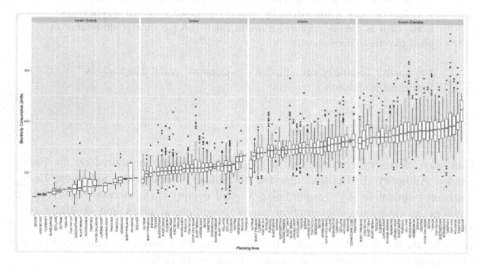

Fig. 1. Boxplots of electricity consumption by planning area, faceted by dwelling type and sorted by median electricity consumption.

by dwelling type, so that we can identify local clusters of electricity consumption patterns and observe how the clusters are similar or dissimilar across dwelling types in the same administrative area. In the end, we come up with three hypotheses for future work.

2 Literature Review

2.1 Analysis and Modeling of Energy Consumption Outside Singapore

Urquizo, Calderon and James analyzed spatial patterns of Annual Energy Consumption Intensity (AECI) in South Heaton, Westgate and Castle districts using hotspot maps [3]. They investigated Houses in Multiple Occupation (HMOs) which serve low income people, students and migrants who do not have much money to spend on accommodation. As HMOs are rented on a room-by-room basis, typical measures of density such as 'population density' or 'dwelling density' may not be suitable for modeling energy consumption in these dwellings. Thus, 'space per person' is proposed as a new measure, which is defined as "the dwelling size of a habitable unit divided by household size".

Urquizo also developed a framework to estimate energy consumption in sub-city areas on three levels: district level, neighborhood level and a retrofitted model from single dwellings to community level [4]. The study found that national or regional indices often do not capture important factors in modeling energy consumption that exist at the local area level. For example, the neighborhood model had over- or underestimated energy consumption in all the three districts studied, because the assumptions made for each district/neighborhood were unable to account for its heterogeneity in building types, resident background and energy systems. Therefore, the paper concluded that local area characteristics should be included in energy modeling to produce more robust estimates that can influence policy decisions more effectively.

Yang et al. used a city-wide household survey to collect and map data on carbon emissions in Shanghai [5]. It also found that carbon emissions are not homogeneous throughout Shanghai, as the spatial pattern of carbon emissions by households can be described as donut-shaped: low in the urban center, high in suburban areas, and low again in rural areas. Factors that were found to influence household emissions include car ownership, type/size/age of dwelling and household income, all of which cannot be easily described or detected at the highly aggregated level.

2.2 Analysis and Modeling of Energy Consumption in Singapore

There are also some studies done on electricity consumption in Singapore. Agarwal, Satyanarain, Sing, and Vollmer [6] investigated how construction activities led to an increase in electricity consumption as residents sought to reduce the impact of noise pollution by closing their windows and using air conditioners. They found that electricity consumption does not rebound back to pre-construction levels after the construction works were completed, which could be a significant finding for stakeholders interested in reducing energy consumption in Singapore.

Loi and Ng [7] found that residential users in Singapore are more sensitive to price decreases than price increases of electricity, which implies it may be difficult to induce energy conservation via increasing electricity prices. Other motivators, such as education or the creation of green champions in communities, should be used to promote energy conservation instead.

Luo and Ukil simulated electrical load profiles of dwelling types in Singapore based on a probabilistic model of when an electrical appliance will be activated and the average time of appliance usage daily, before the load profiles were successfully verified against measurements of actual electricity consumption at campus housings in National Technological University [8]. Their work successfully established a bottom-up approach of simulating households' electricity consumption based on one household or one electric appliance, which could be helpful for future studies on the smart grid.

3 Methodology

3.1 Local Indicators of Spatial Association (LISA)

Local indicators of spatial association were introduced by Anselin in 1995 [9] to identify local spatial clusters which may not be picked up by global indicators or uncover local spatial trends that are opposite of global spatial patterns. The null hypothesis assumes that there is no autocorrelation between attribute values in neighboring features, while the alternative hypothesis states that the neighboring features are spatially autocorrelated and therefore said to be spatially clustered. A positive statistic value denotes that the neighboring features are similar, while a negative statistic denotes dissimilarity.

Taking the 2016 data on electricity consumption from Energy Market Authority, a Local Moran's I statistic is calculated for each postal code each month using Eq. (1). x_i refers to the electricity consumption of postal code i expressed in kilowatt hour (kWh), $w_{i,j}$ refers to the spatial weight between postal codes i and j, $\bar{X}$ refers to the national average electricity consumption and n refers to the total number of target postal codes included for comparison with the origin postal code. Since a rule of thumb is to have at least 30 features in each calculation to achieve reliable results [10], $n = 30$ in this research.

$$I_i = \frac{x_i - \bar{X}}{S_i^2} \sum_{j=1, j \neq i}^{n} w_{i,j} \left(x_j - \bar{X} \right) \tag{1}$$

Based on the point pattern distribution of the raw dataset, we ran 1000 Monte Carlo simulations under the assumption that there is no spatial pattern in electricity consumption of households. After getting a Local Moran's I statistic for each postal code, its statistic is interpreted by calculating which of the five categories it falls into based on their electricity consumption figures relative to Singapore's average value, statistic value and P-value:

1. Insignificant: Even though I have a local Moran's I statistic, it is not statistically significant at the p-value of 0.1.
2. Low-low: If my electricity consumption is lower than the national average and my neighbors' consumptions are as low or lower, I am a low-low point.
3. Low-high: If my electricity consumption is lower than the national average but my neighbors' consumptions are relatively higher than me, I am a low outlier among high points.
4. High-low: If my electricity consumption is higher than the national average but my neighbors' consumptions are not as high as me, I am a high outlier among low points.
5. High-high: If my electricity consumption is higher than national average and my neighbor's consumptions are as high/higher than me, I am a high-high point.

3.2 Implementing LISA Analysis in R Environment

R-Markdown. The R Markdown framework was chosen to document the analytical process and methods. It is a tool for good coding practices as the R-Markdown document is easily distributed, reproducible and comes with a well-rounded syntax for documentation [11]. It also enables users to write code in chunks, which is excellent for debugging and ensuring readability. The R Markdown document makes it easy for the author to edit only the relevant parameters to generate new output on an ad-hob basis without having to redo the entire code chunk.

LISA Methods in R. The LISA analysis is powered by the 'spdep' package which provides methods for analyzing spatial dependence [12]. Firstly, for each postal code in the dataset, a list of 30 nearest neighbors is generated using the '*knearneigh*' and '*knn2b*' functions. Then, distances were calculated between the origin point and the 30 neighbors using '*nbdists*', before inverse distance weights are supplied to the neighbors using '*nb2listw*'. Finally, the local Moran's I statistic for each postal code is calculated using the '*localmoran*' function, before its quadrant is calculated based on its local Moran's I statistic and electricity consumption figures relative to its neighbors and to Singapore.

LISA Visualizations. Finally, the interpreted LISA results are plotted on faceted visualizations of maps using the 'tmap' package [13]. Methods for generating visualizations in 'tmap' follow the same grammar as 'ggplot2', meaning a base 'tmap' object is first defined using '*tm_shape(<spatial object>)*' before multiple methods are "added" on top of the base object to fine-tune the aesthetics such as color, transparency and shapes. This feature makes it much more desirable to plot maps using 'tmap' rather than base R functions which produce plots that look less refined and are difficult for the researcher to modify when one wants to try adding or removing elements from the visualization.

4 Findings and Discussion

4.1 Overview of Clusters in Singapore

Figure 2 shows a plot of postal codes color-coded by their respective quadrants in June 2016. The plot is faceted by Dwelling Type to show differences in distributions across different types of housing. 1-room/2-room flats do not show obvious clusters in the plot due to the low number of postal codes (Table 1). Across all dwelling types, clear hot clusters and cold clusters can be observed in different parts of Singapore, which implies that households of similar consumption patterns indeed cluster together geographically. The East region has many clusters of households with high electricity usage, while the West region has many clusters of households with low electricity usage.

Fig. 2. Postal codes in Singapore, color-coded by their respective quadrants in June 2016. Plot is faceted by dwelling type. (Color figure online)

Table 1. Number and proportion of units for each dwelling type

	1-room/2-room	3-room	4-room	5-room/Executive flats
Insignificant	97 (0.78%)	1646 (13.30%)	3603 (29.12%)	3395 (27.44%)
Low-low	0 (0%)	14 (0.11%)	75 (0.61%)	97 (0.78%)
Low-high	11 (0.09%)	168 (1.36%)	789 (6.38%)	675 (5.46%)
High-low	2 (0.02%)	14 (0.11%)	45 (0.36%)	49 (0.40%)
High-high	10 (0.08%)	173 (1.40%)	801 (6.47%)	708 (5.72%)
Total	**120 (0.97%)**	**2015 (16.29%)**	**5313 (42.94%)**	**4924 (39.80%)**

4.2 Overview of Clusters at Planning Area Level

When we zoom down into the planning area level, we see two scenarios. The first scenario is when the HDB blocks exhibit similar consumption patterns across dwelling types, such as that observed in the North-East region (Fig. 3). There is a cluster of households (denoted with a solid outline circle) that exhibit high consumption patterns throughout, while there is another cluster of households (denoted with a dashed outline circle) that exhibit low consumption patterns throughout.

The second scenario is when the HDB blocks exhibit different consumption patterns across dwelling types, such as that observed in the North region (Fig. 4). In many subzones in this region, there are clusters of HDB blocks that exhibit low consumption among 4-room households but high consumption among 5-room households. We drilled down further into several planning subzones within these regions to further investigate differences across dwelling types.

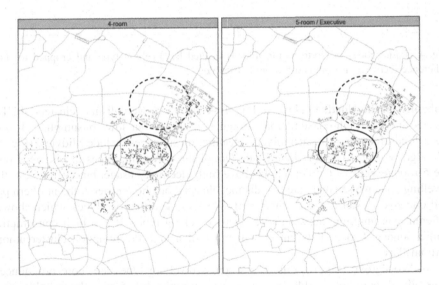

Fig. 3. Postal codes in North-East region. Plot is faceted by dwelling type and cropped to show differences between 4-room and 5-room households.

4.3 Overview of Clusters at Planning Subzone Level

Planning subzones are the lowest level of administrative boundaries in Singapore. Generally at the subzone level, three types of phenomenon can be observed:

1. Low consumption subzone: Households across all dwelling types in this subzone are low-low points.
2. High consumption subzone: Households across all dwelling types in this subzone are high-high points.
3. Mixed-consumption subzone: Households in this subzone exhibit different consumption habits at different dwelling types (for example 3-room households may be low-consumption households, while 4-room households may be high-consumption households in the same subzone).

Fig. 4. Postal codes in North region. Plot is faceted by dwelling type and cropped to show differences between 4-room and 5-room households.

Subzones in the North Region. In Fig. 4 we saw there were distinct clusters of HDB blocks that had high-consumption 5-room households but low-consumption 4-room households. Examples of such mixed-consumption subzones include Midview (Fig. 5), Woodgrove (Fig. 6) and Yishun South. Out of three dwelling types in Midview, only the 5-room/executive flat households have high electricity usage, but even within this dwelling type, we see there are two distinct clusters: one hot cluster at the northern part and one cold cluster at the southern part. We also identified one block which showed different consumption characteristics across dwelling types: it is a high consumption outlier among 4-room flats but is a member of a high consumption cluster among 5-room flats.

In Woodgrove (Fig. 6), differences across dwelling types are more pronounced: generally, 4-room households are of low consumption while 5-room households are of high consumption. Even among 4-room households, consumption patterns are not homogeneous: there is a cluster of low outliers among high consumption households, while there is another cluster of low consumption household.

Subzones in the North-East Region. In the North-East region, there are few mixed-consumption subzones, and most subzones are either purely high-consumption or low-consumption. Examples of high-consumption subzones are Hougang West (Fig. 7), Hougang East and Trafalgar, while examples of low-consumption subzones are Anchorvale (Fig. 8) and Matilda.

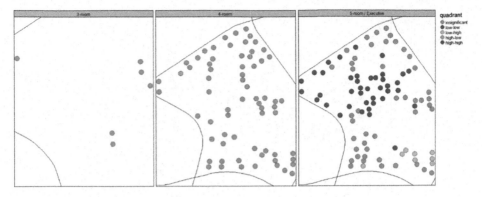

Fig. 5. Midview planning subzone located in the North region.

Fig. 6. Woodgrove planning subzone located in the North region.

Fig. 7. Hougang West Planning Subzone located in the North-East region.

Fig. 8. Anchorvale planning subzone located in the North-East region.

4.4   Overall Discussion of Results

These results highlight the value of analyzing spatial data at lower levels of visualization, and more importantly the value of increasingly disaggregated data. In Sect. 4.1, the country overview only enables us to make general conclusions on the regional level. As we go deeper, we start to reveal differences within one area that could not be observed in the macro level: electricity consumption is not necessarily homogeneous within each dwelling type or administrative area. In fact, differences have been identified at every level of visualization, which prompts us to reflect that any generalizations, forecasting models or time-series predictions that do not account for spatial information will probably not perform well, and we should rethink what other disaggregated factors could influence electricity consumption habits.

4.5   Relevance to Singapore Electricity Market

Our work will be increasingly relevant to electricity retailers in Singapore as the country is moving towards the concept of an "Open Electricity Market" (OEM). Previously, there were no "electricity retailers" in Singapore's electricity industry structure, and non-contestable consumers (households and small businesses) could only purchase electricity from SP Group at a regulated tariff. Starting 1 April 2018, consumers in selected zones of Singapore could choose to purchase electricity from one of the 13 retailers with a price plan [14]. Since the OEM is launched by geographical zones progressively, retailers can choose the zones they want to enter and the plans to offer in each zone. However, only three types of plans exist as of December 2018: (i) a fixed rate per kWh; (ii) a fixed percentage discount off the SP Group tariff; and (iii) a higher fixed rate during peak hours and a lower fixed rate during off-peak hours to appeal to the "night owls" (refer to [15] for current list of retailers and plans). No retailers had offered plans to differentiate between high- or low-usage consumers. Here, our visualizations can help retailers to: (i) decide on the zones to enter and (ii) identify the different consumer groups by usage levels in each zone, thereby enable them to devise and offer a wider range of plans to cater to their different demands and improve market strategy.

5 Conclusion

First, the paper established that electricity usage patterns are not homogeneous throughout Singapore. Then, the LISA statistic is calculated for each postal code and interpreted as one of the four quadrants (low-low, low-high, high-low, high-high), before the postal codes are color-coded and plotted on faceted map visualizations to uncover similarities and differences in electricity usage among households across geographical boundaries and dwelling types. Visualizations reveal that consumption levels are not homogeneous both within and across geographical boundaries and dwelling types, thus we should consider testing the influence of more disaggregated factors on electricity consumption and see if they may explain the differences better than aggregated factors. Electricity retailers in Singapore can leverage on these visualizations to guide their business decisions on the zones to enter, and the variety and pricing of plans to offer.

References

1. Singapore Energy Statistics. https://www.ema.gov.sg/cmsmedia/Publications_and_Statistics/Publications/ses/2017/downloads/SES2017_Chapter_1_to_9.pdf
2. EMA: Statistics. https://www.ema.gov.sg/statistics.aspx
3. Urquizo, J., Calderon, C., James, P.: A spatial perspective of the domestic energy consumption intensity patterns in sub-city areas. A case study from the United Kingdom. In: 2016 IEEE Ecuador Technical Chapters Meeting (ETCM), pp. 1–7. IEEE Press, New York (2016). https://doi.org/10.1109/etcm.2016.7750848
4. Urquizo, J.: A spatial model for domestic end-use energy diagnostic and support of energy efficiency policy to reduce fuel poverty in UK (2015). http://proceedings.esri.com/library/userconf/proc15/papers/606_395.pdf
5. Yang, S., Wang, C., Lo, K., Wang, M., Liu, L.: Quantifying and mapping spatial variability of Shanghai household carbon footprints. Front. Energy 9(1), 115–124 (2015). https://doi.org/10.1007/s11708-015-0348-8
6. Agarwal, S., Satyanarim, R., Sing, T.F., Vollmer, D.: Effects of construction activities on residential electricity consumption: evidence from Singapore's public housing estates. Energy Econ. 55, 101–111 (2016). https://doi.org/10.1016/j.eneco.2016.01.010
7. Loi, T.S.A., Ng, J.L.: Analysing households' responsiveness towards socio-economic determinants of residential electricity consumption in Singapore. Energy Policy 112, 415–426 (2018). https://doi.org/10.1016/j.enpol.2017.09.052
8. Luo, C., Ukil, A.: Modeling and validation of electrical load profiling in residential buildings in singapore. IEEE Trans. Power Syst. 30(5), 2800–2809 (2015). https://doi.org/10.1109/tpwrs.2014.2367509
9. Anselin, L.: Local indicators of spatial association—LISA. Geogr. Anal. 27(2), 93–115 (1995). https://doi.org/10.1111/j.1538-4632.1995.tb00338.x
10. How Cluster and Outlier Analysis (Anselin Local Moran's I) works. http://pro.arcgis.com/en/pro-app/tool-reference/spatial-statistics/h-how-cluster-and-outlier-analysis-anselin-local-m.htm
11. R Markdown Cheat Sheet. https://www.rstudio.com/wp-content/uploads/2015/02/rmarkdown-cheatsheet.pdf
12. CRAN – Package spdep. https://cran.r-project.org/package=spdep

13. CRAN – Package tmap. https://cran.r-project.org/web/packages/tmap/index.html
14. EMA: Overview of Electricity Market. https://www.ema.gov.sg/electricity_market_overvi
    ew.aspx
15. List of Retailers. https://www.openelectricitymarket.sg/residential/list-of-retailers

Addressing Social Problems in iSchools Research

Unmapped Privacy Expectations in China: Discussions Based on the Proposed Social Credit System

Yuanye Ma[(✉)]

University of North Carolina at Chapel Hill, Chapel Hill, NC 27599-3360, USA
yuanyel@live.unc.edu

Abstract. Privacy has become a global topic of concern. Meanwhile, it is a concept that is deeply rooted in local cultures. This paper is conceptual exploration of privacy in China, it proposes that privacy is a concept yet to be fully mapped out in Chinese culture. Specifically, this paper uses the proposed Social Credit System in China as an example of discussion, for this example not only helps with capturing the urgency and significance of the topic, but also is particularly provocative in revealing the scope of privacy as a cultural concept. This paper begins with a brief introduction to the proposed Social Credit System; then, it discusses what might constitute a cultural perspective to understand privacy, and cautions the complexity of comparing privacy across cultures. This paper could serve as a meaningful reflection for both countries who are concerned with privacy issues in face of large scale application of big data analytics, and for privacy scholars in cross-culture contexts.

Keywords: Privacy · Social Credit System · China

1 Introduction

How is privacy understood in Chinese culture? Is the conception of privacy different in Chinese culture than in other cultures? With these questions in mind, this paper proposes to study privacy as a cultural concept, and suggests using the proposed Social Credit System in China as a real world example to frame the discussion. As a conceptual exploration, this paper builds on existing research of privacy with a cultural perspective, and aims to illustrate not only how privacy might be understood differently in Chinese culture but also what privacy might be constituted of as a cultural concept. This paper contributes to existing research by suggesting a more unified perspective to understand privacy. Past studies typically only consider privacy from one aspect, while in order to understand a complex phenomenon as the proposed Social Credit System, a more expansive cultural perspective is needed to better demonstrate the complex nature of privacy, and to capture the nature of privacy in the real world environment. This paper contributes to existing privacy research by drawing attention to the understanding of privacy in Chinese culture; by constructing a cultural perspective to study privacy, this paper reveals the complex nature of privacy under the influence of cultural norms, human behaviors, and mechanisms; lastly, by adopting a cultural perspective to study

© Springer Nature Switzerland AG 2019
N. G. Taylor et al. (Eds.): iConference 2019, LNCS 11420, pp. 799–805, 2019.
https://doi.org/10.1007/978-3-030-15742-5_75

privacy it could help avoid potential misunderstandings when researching privacy in cross-culture contexts.

In early 2014, the State Council of China announced the Chinese government's plan to launch a mandatory Social Credit System by 2020. The proposed Social Credit System will give each citizen a credit score taking into consideration various factors including one's purchase history, political leanings, and social interactions [1]. Like other credit rating systems, this Social Credit System relies on huge amounts of personal data (from governmental organizations, industry associations and commercial organizations) being integrated into one national level system, and the algorithms and criteria running the system remain unknown to the public [2]. However, important observations can be made based on some of the pilot projects run by the eight companies appointed by the government.

Ant Financial as one of the eight companies who had launched its credit rating service *Sesame Credit* via Alipay (Alibaba's mobile wallet offer). Sesame Credit rates each individual user from 350 to 950 points using five dimensions of data. Since March 2017, people with a Sesame Score above 650 points can enjoy certain benefits (for example, being waived from paying a fee for using the bike sharing service); it seems that people with low Sesame Scores are not being "punished" yet, except for not being able to enjoy the convenience mentioned. How Sesame Credit makes use of data inside of Alibaba and data from other commercial partners and government organizations remains unclear to the public [3].

Considering the wide use of Alipay as well as its rapid expanding business in China, this app and its development in the credit scoring arena could have a powerful influence on Chinese people's lives and in particular on how people think of and expect privacy. In fact, digital companies like Alibaba might already have made more impact on Chinese people's understandings and behaviors of privacy than has government and regulation. For instance, Ant Financial in early 2018 was widely criticized by its users in China for making it default to opt-in for its social credit scoring service when a user tried to generate a report that summarizes one's total 2017 transaction [4]. Chinese users' criticisms toward Ant Financial is not only an outstanding example of how user interactions with Alipay (or similar super apps like WeChat) have shaped and will keep on shaping user expectation and behavior of privacy, it is also a great illustration of how privacy has grown into this complex phenomenon where its multiplicity consists of digital technology, user behavior, and cultural norm, each stands as an indispensable aspect to understand privacy in the current Chinese culture.

2   Related Work

Existing research on conceptualizing privacy from a cultural perspective produces conflicting results. The culture dimension model of Hofstede [5–7] identified Chinese culture as collectivist (compared to individualist) with a higher level of power distance, and it is less open to uncertainty, especially when compared to American culture [8]. Using Hofstede's culture dimensions model, [9] suggests that people in individualistic countries (who value their individual rights and privacy) are more reluctant to accept data collection, while people in collectivistic societies might find it acceptable to disclose personal information. This observation runs in opposition with what [10] found with social network users, whereas people in more collectivist-oriented countries reported it was more important for them to avoid privacy risks than people from individualist cultures, as people who are more collectivist-oriented place higher importance on social gratifications. In other words, people in collectivist cultures could be more cautious with privacy than people from individualistic cultures. Therefore, it could be misleading or at least too simplified to conceive of people in individualistic cultures as more strict with personal data disclosure than people in collectivist cultures.

In addition to figuring out the general tendency a culture might render in terms of personal information disclosure, the real difference in how individualist and collectivist cultures treat personal information might exist in a more specific context, for instance, the type of information involved. For example, Americans are more open about sexual matters than Chinese, whereas Chinese people are more open about financial matters (such as income, etc.) [11]. These inconsistencies in privacy prediction using the culture dimension model could be resolved if the cultural perspective can be expanded to include not just social norms but also human behavior.

Various studies have attempted to understand privacy from the human behavior perspective. Privacy calculus suggests that privacy at the individual level involves making trade-offs between perceived benefits and perceived privacy risks [12–14]; decisions about whether to disclose information or not, are viewed as a product of a rational, independent assessment of perceived risks and benefits [15]. However, inconsistency occurs between people's stated privacy concerns and their actual behaviors, which is known as the "privacy paradox" as a result of bounded rationality [16, 17]. Furthermore, both behavior and belief of privacy are under the influence of "nudging", which describes how designs can act as soft paternalism to support privacy decision-making by providing a "choice architecture" (p. 6) that shapes people's behavior in predictable ways [18].

Nudging mechanisms have been used to guide users on a social networking site [19], but what makes the expanded perspective potentially more powerful is that it could help understand the complexity when privacy behavior comes into play with traditional cultural norms. [20] found that perceived usefulness is more important in Western cultures while perceived ease of use is more important in Eastern cultures when people are making trade-off decisions about disclosing personal information in exchange for certain benefits.

Taking human behavior into constructing the cultural perspective of understanding privacy helps explain the inconsistency from only conceiving social norms as culture. When a more expansive cultural perspective is used, a complete picture of privacy can be captured, which is crucial as we will see in the following discussion of privacy in the context of the proposed Social Credit System in China.

3 Discussion

The Social Credit Score System has been introduced to the Chinese people as something that can promote trust [21], with the potential implication that personal information can become a sacrifice when necessary. This notion of sacrificing personal information for greater trust in society will be accepted if the "public" benefit is considered as something other than or superior to individual benefit. Then privacy regulation in China will continue on its way to being subordinated to the public interest (p. 1021) as observed by [22].

However, two opposing views are found when trying to establish the conceptualization of privacy as a cultural concept within the broader Chinese culture. [23] observed that in much of China's history, the idea of "public" has received much more "salience" (p. 1012) than "private". As a result "the needs and goals of the individual must be subordinated to those of the group" (pp. 154–155). [23]'s opinion differs from that of [24] and [25] who stated clearly it is not the case at least in early Confucian tradition of China that the individuals have to subordinate to the group. How these fundamental social values will be further conceptualized will have a significant impact on the conception of privacy and the Social Credit Score.

Secondly, recognizing that the foundational aspects of privacy within Chinese culture is yet to be established, one should be careful to not stop at any conclusions when comparing the concept of privacy in China to those in Western cultures. In particular, statements saying privacy as a concept was imported to Chinese culture, or the concept of privacy might not have existed at all in traditional Chinese culture [26], should be re-examined. For example, [22] suggested that the English word "privacy" and its Mandarin Chinese language translation might not be a simple equation. Whenever a comparison is attempted across cultures, it is important to be mindful of potential cultural connotations, and also be aware that the concept of privacy has been and is still undergoing evolution. The concept of privacy in the U.S. has gone through significant evolution in the past hundred years since [27] Warren and Brandeis (1890) defined privacy as the "right to be let alone"; similarly, privacy in China has also been going through evolution to the point of it being manifested as users criticisms towards Alipay's default setting in early 2018, and there is no reason such evolution shall stop there.

In addition to recognizing the social norm and human behavior aspects of privacy, the third aspect to a complete understanding of privacy as a cultural concept is the specific tools and mechanisms of privacy. [28] argued that privacy is "an interpersonal process" that can be achieved via four different "privacy mechanisms" among which one is "culture"; the "culture" here refers more to the social and cultural norm aspect, and the actual privacy process is dialectic which requires further negotiations as [29] hypothesized. [30] recognized that different societies have various mechanisms for privacy regulation, "some do not rely as heavily on environmental mechanisms as other cultures, but use nonverbal, verbal, or other means. (p. 100)" In a sense, it is these privacy mechanisms that materialize what privacy could be in actual life. As long as the specific mechanisms used for privacy are not properly recognized, privacy remains elusive, or invisible.

"Some cultures may appear to have little privacy, this is probably due to a traditional view of privacy as solely a physical-environment process and not as a complex behavioral system which draws on many levels of functioning" (p. 42) [29].

Both the privacy calculus theory and nudging can be useful frameworks to understand the Social Credit Score in China as a complex behavioral system. For example, the criticism towards the Alipay app is a great example showing how people are already balancing the potential benefit and risk of personal information disclosure.

In addition, despite Alipay's poor privacy setting, it is important to recognize that the app functions as a mechanism through which people could manage their privacy, and the specific designs of the app will act two ways to both afford and bound privacy behavior at the same time.

4 Conclusion

This paper argues that privacy is a cultural concept whose meaning in Chinese culture is yet to be fully explored. In addition, using a cultural perspective can not only better illustrate the meaning of privacy, but also better reveal the practical implications of privacy in real world examples like in the proposed Social Credit System. Using an expanded cultural perspective is necessary for future privacy research, because to study privacy as a complex cultural and social phenomenon means to understand it from multiple perspectives, including cultural norms, human behaviors, and specific mechanisms.

The Chinese language name of the Social Credit, *Zhengxin,* is from the ancient Chinese narrative history, the *Zuo Zhuan*; with its rich cultural connotations in mind, it is hard to say how the English word "credit" corresponds exactly to *Zhengxin*, just like it would be too simple to equate the English word privacy with its Chinese language translation *Yinsi*. In contrast with the critiquing tones many western media adopt when reporting China's Social Credit System, criticism is less seen among Chinese media, however it is hard to tell how many in China actually believe that the proposed system can indeed promote trust in the society. Some believe that compared to the U.S., where individualism reigns and privacy is protected, China lacks such notions in both a legal and largely societal sense [31]. However, as the discussions in this paper have been trying to demonstrate, the concept of privacy is yet to be fully mapped out in Chinese culture, so any conclusions drawn from comparing privacy in China to other cultures shall be subject to careful examination.

This paper as a conceptual exploration can help open up new research areas for future privacy work, as discussions in this paper on the Social Credit System is not limited to China, but can be meaningful reflections for other countries of the world who are also concerned with privacy issues in the face of large scale use of big data analytics. Lastly, privacy research in cross-cultural environments can benefit from keeping an open mind and using a more expansive cultural perspective to re-examine an old concept like privacy.

References

1. Shankar, A.: What's your citizen 'trust score'? China moves to rate its 1.3 billion citizens. USA Today. https://www.usatoday.com/story/news/world/2017/11/10/whats-your-citizen-trust-score-china-moves-rate-its-1-3-billion-citizens/851365001/. Accessed 9 Dec 2017
2. Meissner, M.: China's Social Credit System: A big-data enabled approach to market regulation with broad implications for doing business in China, Mirjam Meissner, Mercator Institute for China Studies (MERICS). https://www.merics.org/fileadmin/user_upload/downloads/China-Monitor/merics_ChinaMonitor_39_englisch_Web.pdf. Accessed 9 Dec 2017

3. Botsman, R.: Big data meets Big Brother as China moves to rate its citizens. Wired. http://www.wired.co.uk/article/chinese-government-social-credit-score-privacy-invasion. Accessed 6 Dec 2017
4. Soo, Z.: Ant Financial apologises for opting in users for credit scoring system. http://www.scmp.com/tech/china-tech/article/2126772/chinas-ant-financial-apologises-over-alipay-user-data-gaffe. Accessed 9 Apr 2018
5. Hofstede, G.: Culture's Consequences: International Differences in Work-Related Values. Sage, Beverly Hills (1980)
6. Hofstede, G.: Cultures and Organizations: Software of the Mind. McGraw-Hill, London (1991)
7. Hofstede, G.: Culture's Consequences: Comparing Values, Behaviors, Institutions, and Organizations Across Nations, 2nd edn. Sage, Thousand Oaks (2001). Google
8. Li, Y., Xiong, Y.: The difference between Chinese and American culture and advice for cross-cultural management-based on Hofstede's four cultural dimensions. Paper presented at the 2012 International Conference on Information Management, Innovation Management and Industrial Engineering, vol. 1, pp. 374–377 (2012). https://doi.org/10.1109/iciii.2012.6339678
9. Li, Y., Kobsa, A., Knijnenburg, B.P., Nguyen, M.-H.C.: Cross-cultural privacy prediction. Proc. Priv. Enhanc. Technol. **2**, 113–132 (2017). https://doi.org/10.1515/popets-2017-0019
10. Trepte, S., Reinecke, L., Ellison, N.B., Quiring, O., Yao, M.Z., Ziegele, M.: A cross-cultural perspective on the privacy calculus. Soc. Media + Soc. **3**(1) (2017). https://doi.org/10.1177/2056305116688035
11. Acquisti, A., Brandimarte, L., Loewenstein, G.: Privacy and human behavior in the age of information. Science **347**(6221), 509–514 (2015). https://doi.org/10.1126/science.aaa1465
12. Laufer, R.S., Wolfe, M.: Privacy as a concept and a social issue: a multidimensional development theory. J. Soc. Issues **33**(3), 23–42 (1977)
13. Wilson, D., Valacich, J.: Unpacking the privacy paradox: irrational decision-making within the privacy calculus. In: Proceedings of the 33rd International Conference on Information Systems, Orlando (2012)
14. Smith, H.J., Dinev, T., Xu, H.: Information privacy research: an interdisciplinary review. MIS Q. **35**(4), 989–1016 (2011)
15. Culnan, M.J., Armstrong, P.K.: Information privacy concerns, procedural fairness, and impersonal trust: an empirical investigation. Organ. Sci. **10**(1), 104–115 (1999)
16. Koumakhov, R.: Conventions in Herbert Simon's theory of bounded rationality. J. Econ. Psychol. **30**(3), 293–306 (2009). https://doi.org/10.1016/j.joep.2009.03.001
17. Barnes, S.B.: A privacy paradox: social networking in the United States. First Monday **11**(9) (2016)
18. Thaler, R.H., Sunstein, C.R.: Nudge: Improving Decisions about Health, Wealth, and Happiness. Yale University Press, New Haven (2008)
19. Wang, Y., Leon, P.G., Scott, K., Chen, X., Acquisti, A., Cranor, L.F.: Privacy nudges for social media: An exploratory facebook study. Paper presented at the Proceedings of the 22nd International Conference on World Wide Web, pp. 763–770 (2013)
20. Zhang, L., Zhu, J., Liu, Q.: A meta-analysis of mobile commerce adoption and the moderating effect of culture. Comput. Hum. Behav. **28**(5), 1902–1911 (2012). https://doi.org/10.1016/j.chb.2012.05.008
21. Mistreanu, S.: China is implementing a massive plan to rank its citizens, and many of them want in. https://foreignpolicy.com/2018/04/03/life-inside-chinas-social-credit-laboratory/. Accessed 3 Apr 2018, 9 Dec 2017
22. Farrall, K.N.: Global privacy in flux: illuminating privacy across cultures in China and the U.S. Int. J. Commun. **2**, 38 (2008)

23. Guo, R.X.: An Introduction to the Chinese Economy: The Driving Forces Behind Modern Day China. Wiley Asia, Singapore (2010)
24. Shun, K.-L.: Conception of the person in early confucian thought. In: Shun, K.-L., Wong, D.B. (eds.) Confucian Ethics: A Comparative Study of Self, Autonomy, and Community, pp. 183–199. Cambridge University Press, Cambridge (2004)
25. Ames, R., Wimal, D., Kasulis, T.P.: Self as Person in Asian Theory and Practice. State University of New York Press, Albany (1994)
26. Wang, H.: The conceptual basis of privacy standards in China and its implications for China's privacy law. Front. Law China, Beijing 7(1), 134–160 (2012). https://doi.org/10.3868/s050-001-012-0007-4
27. Warren, S.D., Brandeis, L.D.: The right to privacy. Harvard Law Rev. 4(5), 193–220 (1890). https://doi.org/10.2307/1321160
28. Altman, I.: The Environment and Social Behavior: Privacy, Personal Space, Territory, Crowding, 1st Irvington edn. Irving Publishers, New York (1981)
29. Altman, I.: Privacy regulation: culturally universal or culturally specific? J. Soc. Issues 33(3), 66–84 (1977)
30. Altman, I., Chemers, M.M.: Culture and Environment. Brooks/Cole Pub. Co., Monterey (1980)
31. Winslow, J.: Chapman expert explains the rise of social credit scores in China. TCA Regional News (2016)

'Berrypicking' in the Formation of Ideas About Problem Drinking Amongst Users of Alcohol Online Support Groups

Sally Sanger$^{(\boxtimes)}$ ⓘ, Peter A. Bath ⓘ, and Jo Bates ⓘ

University of Sheffield, Sheffield, UK
Ssanger1@sheffield.ac.uk

Abstract. Beliefs held by individuals about the illnesses or problems that affect them have been shown to impact upon the health and other outcomes that they achieve. Online support groups (OSGs) are one source of information used by those with health problems which may influence or determine what they think about their particular issue and how to resolve it. Problem drinking remains a major source of significant costs to society. This article explores whether the discussion forums of alcohol OSGs that do not follow the 12-step philosophy of Alcoholics Anonymous influence the formation of these beliefs, reporting on the outcome of thematic analysis of interviews with 25 users from five groups. It argues that Bates' 'Berrypicking' model of information searching is helpful in illuminating group members' information seeking activities. It looks at the four key aspects of berrypicking identified by Bates – the nature of the search query, the information 'domains' drawn on, the information retrieved and the search techniques used. The study finds that users are typically berrypickers, selecting information from different sources and forming their own interpretations.

Keywords: Berrypicking · Information seeking · Online support groups · Alcohol

1 Introduction

The beliefs/views that an individual holds about an illness or problem affecting them have been shown to have an important impact on how they deal with the issue, and consequently on its outcomes in terms of health, social welfare or other factors [1–4]. It is therefore important to understand more about how these ideas develop and which sources are influential in this regard. In the case of problem drinking, an issue with many serious costs for society, families and individuals, there are many differing beliefs about what an alcohol problem is and how to deal with it. There is no universally accepted explanation and the choice of interpretation is not automatic (options available include that it is a brain disease, a learnt habit, a moral 'failing' or personality flaw). Differing sources, including support groups, an important source of help for problem drinkers, espouse differing approaches. Exploring how lay ideas are constructed could help to illuminate what matters for creating a good match between users and these groups, an area where the evidence is mixed [5, 6].

© Springer Nature Switzerland AG 2019
N. G. Taylor et al. (Eds.): iConference 2019, LNCS 11420, pp. 806–816, 2019.
https://doi.org/10.1007/978-3-030-15742-5_76

The internet provides access to several different types of online communities which provide people with information (e.g., wikis, social question and answer sites). Many are now turning to online support groups (OSGs) for information as well as support in dealing with a very wide range of health problems e.g., diabetes, cancers, stroke, heart disease. Since the 1990s there has been an increase in the number of alcohol online support groups (AOSGs) which can be especially useful for people who want more anonymity than a face-to-face group offers, those with problems accessing face-to-face groups or who simply prefer online interaction. This paper explores whether and how these groups impact on the beliefs about problem drinking held by their users. It focuses on the under-researched area [7] of groups that do not follow 12-step programs for recovery. The 12-steps were developed in the 1930s by Alcoholics Anonymous (AA) the most well-known and widespread support group for problem drinkers. They set out how to recover from problem drinking and have been adopted by many other addictions and by many treatment programs [8]. The paper explores the general development of users' perceptions of problem drinking overall in terms of the 'berrypicking' model of information searching proposed by Bates [9]. It will show that this is a helpful model to describe the information search processes occurring in AOSGs, which may also apply to online support groups for other addictions and/or other health conditions. (Please note: this study uses the term problem drinking to include all drinking that is deemed problematic and makes no distinction between this and alcoholism, seeing these as on a continuum in line with DSM-5's definition of Alcohol Use Disorder [10].)

2   Literature Review

Information seeking, or the "strategies a person devises in order to find information" (Ford [11], p. 14) is an important facet of information behaviour. One model of information searching within this area is Bates' berrypicking model. This arose from work on human information searching which showed that the common 'one stop model' of searching did not reflect the reality of what happens in real life. Bates distinguished berrypicking from the linear 'one stop' searching model in four ways:

1. Queries change and evolve during the course of the search, and do not remain static from start to finish
2. The domain searched may change, with individuals using multiple sources of different kinds
3. The query is not satisfied by one ('best match') set of references, but "by a series of selections of individual references and bits of information at each stage of the ever-modifying search" ([9], p. 410)
4. A range of search techniques are used, not just formal subject searching

Bates' work has been drawn upon by many researchers in the field of information searching including Lueg and Bidwell [12] in their writing on information behaviour and 'wayfinding', and Kumpulainen [13] on information trail modelling.

A wide range of health-related support groups are available in face-to-face and online format, with different health areas attracting different levels of research interest (breast cancer, for example, has enjoyed considerable research attention). These groups frequently include discussion forums amongst their other functions. Within these, people can ask questions, read others' stories and exchange information, especially that borne out of the personal experience of someone else who has the problem and therefore understands it from the inside. Information behaviours in these virtual communities have been studied from differing perspectives, for example, as small worlds exhibiting normative behaviour [14] or as sites of the co-creation of distributed knowledge [15], which are outside the scope of this paper.

In terms of alcohol support groups, AA in its face-to-face form, has received much research attention including on how it impacts on users' ideas of problem drinking. For example, Cain [16, 17], Lave and Wenger [18] and Swora [19] amongst others have examined how AA transmits its beliefs through story-telling, radically altering users' ideas about the issue. There has been less attention paid to online AA and other 12-step groups, and less still on non-12-step groups, as recently noted by Zemore [7], despite the fact that the latter are helpful alternatives to the AA approach. They expand the choices available to users who might not otherwise receive support. Research on information behaviors in AOSGs includes analysis of topics discussed online [20, 21] and analysis of the types of information, e.g., advice, referral, shared in different online formats including the discussion forums of support groups [22]. Humphreys and Kaskutas, explored the idea that "As members become committed to mutual help organizations, many of them absorb some or all of the organizations' core beliefs" ([23], p. 231) and that these can act as what Antze called a "cognitive antidote" to the person's problems, helping them feel better by altering their interpretation of problem drinking and therefore their beliefs about themselves and their problem. Antze even stated that 'peer therapy groups' (he counted AA in this number) were "especially well adapted" ([24] p. 326), to changing members' views in line with their beliefs.

Humphreys and Kaskutas [23] compared the world views transmitted by two 12-step groups and Women For Sobriety, which has a very different approach to problem drinking, finding some support for the cognitive antidote theory, although they make the important point that not all members want to change world view, accessing the group primarily for its social aspects. To date, no research appears to have been carried out that aims to understand information seeking in AOSGs through the lens of Bates' berrypicking model: our research seeks to address this gap in the literature.

3   Methods

Five non-12-step AOSGs (Groups A–E) which varied in size, location and beliefs about problem drinking and how to treat it, were recruited from a list of groups developed by the researcher from extensive Google, Bing and Yahoo searches. All met the criteria that they were aimed at adults with alcohol problems, in English, included discussion forums and did not follow the 12-step approach. Groups were recruited via contact with their owners or administrators who gave consent and assisted in alerting their members to the study. Users then self-selected, contacting the researcher by email. Semi-structured interviews were held with 25 such users: these were predominantly female, middle aged, white and highly educated. The interviews were conducted by phone or via skype apart from one held in person and one undertaken via email at the user's request. Interviews were held between October 2017 and February 2018, and lasted between 60 and 114 min. Data was coded in NVivo 11 using a mixture of data driven codes and a priori ones derived from the literature and the previous arm of the study, in which forum messages from three AOSGs had been analysed. Themes were then developed using Braun and Clarke's approach to thematic analysis [25]. The following account of the findings is structured in line with the four aspects of berrypicking noted above. Ethical approval was obtained from the University of Sheffield prior to data collection. Users gave informed consent prior to the interviews and all names were anonymised.

4 Findings

4.1 The Query

In berrypicking the nature of the query does not remain static. As Bates suggested:

> "In real-life searches in manual sources, end users may begin with just one feature of a broader topic, or just one relevant reference, and move through a variety of sources. Each new piece of information they encounter gives them new ideas and directions to follow and, consequently, a new conception of the query...the query itself (as well as the search terms used) is continually shifting, in part or whole." ([9], p. 410)

Initially, the AOSG users began their journeys with the groups in one of three ways. They may have started by searching for information and help around the topic of 'How do I deal with my drinking?' Anna (Group A), for example, googled 'alcohol help', Marianne (Group C) googled 'alternative treatments', and Robert (Group E) 'alcohol recovery forums'. Bethany (Group B) googled for ways to taper and Joe (Group D) for online programs that were not AA. Secondly, they may have been referred to the group, although not necessarily at their request: Joanne (Group E), for example, was referred by her hospital nurse. Thirdly, they may have heard of the group serendipitously, via other media or when searching for something unrelated. For example, Jackie read about Group D in a popular magazine, Dawn (Group D) found it mentioned in something unrelated that she was looking at online, Alan (Group B) heard about his group on the radio and Cara (Group E) found hers via a newspaper article. The path from reference to group might be straightforward or circuitous: Julie (Group C), for instance, googled an alternative therapy and accidentally found a DVD about a particular treatment for problem drinking. She then found a website about the treatment and from this linked to Group C whose forums she uses. Users may immediately access their group on hearing of it or put the information aside and come back to it later (e.g., Megan & Cara of Group E). Whilst some might have previous good experience of online support groups, which would incline them to look at AOSGs (e.g., Dawn and Jackie of Group D), most did not have this.

Users were attracted to their group for a variety of reasons, for example, functionality (Jackie, Group D), getting responses to their initial post quickly (Anna, Group A), the compassion and support available (Christine, Group D). General group approaches, if not specific ideas, were important to many, particularly whether or not they followed the AA/12-step approach: Joe and Cathy (Group C), Anna (Group A), Bethany (Group B),

Jackie (Group D), Isabelle and many others from Group E all mentioned this. Others were drawn to a group because of the particular treatment it endorsed (particularly members of Group C which exists to promote and assist with use of a specific treatment, e.g., Marianne, Ben, Julie) or because the group was supportive of the general approach they wanted to take e.g., moderate drinking (e.g., Dawn, Group D). Alan does not mention being drawn to Group B because of its support for moderate drinking, but does say that he is now backing away from it as it clashes with his current approach:

> "I found that moderation is not a solution for me, and that reading stories and helping people maintain moderation made me think that I could or should do moderation as well and I simply don't have that willpower and can't....So I've backed away from the site because of that."

A common reason for attraction was encountering other people like themselves for the first time. They could identify with existing members, see their own story in those told, and therefore felt less isolated and unique. The group helped them to realize that drink problems are common and there is a way out of them: members from all five groups emphasized the importance of this. The following was typical:

> "I think the first thing that drew me in were the personal stories...and realizing how stark they were and how much they had mirrored some of my own experience and some family experiences" (Tina, Group E)

The general query 'How do I deal with my drinking?' 'evolved' as Bates described it, as members' experience and use of the forums progress. A common pattern was increased specificity as the person moved on to questions about how to deal with practical, difficult situations that arise on the journey, such as how to cope with holidays such as Christmas (Grace, Group E), dealing with an upcoming event where they will be encouraged to drink (Isabelle and Theresa, Group E, Anna Group A), and how to cope with specific activities like attending a concert sober for the first time (Cara, Group E). Over the longer term there was typically a move from seeking information to giving it, as information needs were satisfied and helping others became more important:

> "And so now I have this pay-it-forward mentality that because those people posted for me and I was able to read about their successes, now it's time for me to post about my past and my successes and maybe it'll find somebody else that's struggling and, and they can be encouraged by what has happened to me." (Ben, Group C)

The understanding of what it is to be a problem drinker also evolved over time from a negative to a positive image:

> "[it] helps you to just feel sort of normal and quite proud of what you're doing [stopping drinking]. Instead of like, the skulking weirdo with the drink problem" (Isabelle, Group E)

4.2   The Information 'Domain'

Bates stated that a berrypicker typically: "searches in a much wider variety of sources" ([9], p. 414) than traditional searchers. Individuals were likely to arrive at their group with some existing ideas about problem drinking received from multiple sources of very different types over their lifetime, including individuals (e.g. family members, peer group members), the cultural attitudes of the society they grew up in or had lived in, previous reading about drinking, treatment services or groups attended and media such as cinema and TV.

"a big misconception right now is that one needs to be drunk to have fun. Media and real-life role models portray this every day. If a person grows up learning this as a fact of life, even experiencing it themself, it will be very difficult to un-learn it." (Joe, Group D)

In the online groups themselves there were different information areas that they could access: for example, information pages presenting the official ideas of the site owners/administrators; forums, chat rooms or blogs carrying those expressed by members themselves. The information pages were typically used more at the start of members' time on the forums: Christine, for example, "squirrell[ed] away everything" when new to Group D, including the information pages.

Ideas expressed on the information pages were not necessarily endorsed by the members (for example, few participants from Group A seemed to adopt its stated belief that Cognitive Behavioral Therapy is the way to treat problem drinking). Equally members' beliefs did not necessarily correspond with each other, exposing the user to different perspectives. This was seen as an advantage:

"I think that is one of the real strengths of [Group A] that you can have a whole range of opinions, and a whole range of approaches" (Anna)

Most users also found and pursued references on the site which led them out to information elsewhere, for example in articles, books (known in at least one group as 'Quit Lit') and less frequently other formats such as film or YouTube videos.

In summary, the information 'domain' for people interested in problem drinking was very wide ranging, including information provided by administrators and owners on the site, the ideas expressed by different members in the forums and other interactive parts of the site, traditional types of information resources such as articles and books, and non-traditional media. People were likely to acquire information before they arrived at the site, whilst they were on it, and when they moved away from the site to other sources.

4.3 Selecting Information

Bates described the selection of information as not the production of one set of resources from a perfected search query, but as:

"A bit-at-a-time retrieval.... called berry-picking. This term is used by analogy to picking huckleberries or blueberries in the forest. The berries are scattered on the bushes; they do not come in bunches" [9, p. 410].

Most of the interviewees described acquiring their ideas in a way that fits Bates' model well. The following was very typical of what interviewees reported:

"Yeah, it really [was] a mix of multiple sources and information for me to change the way that I think about alcohol. [As well as experience within the family] it was a mix of educational sources from the people that I met and, and my intensive outpatient program from rehab, from AA sources, from reading books, from *Rational Recovery*, I read that book, you know reading the AA literature and books and getting educated on the forums....I've learned a ton" (Alan, Group B)

Some of these resources influenced Alan before he accessed the group (e.g., his family, the rehabilitation program attended), but he also learned from Group B and from AA which he was attending at the same time. The philosophy of AA is very clear and well established, set out in 'Alcoholics Anonymous', commonly known as the Big Book of AA, focusing around the 12-step program for recovery, service and attendance at meetings. Its attitude to problem drinking, i.e., that it requires absolute abstinence, conflicts directly with the approach of Group B, which favors the individual making their own choice of abstinence, reduced or moderate drinking, and provides information and advice about the latter. This appeared to occur frequently, for example, Erin accessed groups with differing beliefs (AA and Group E) and Robert spent over a year in a forum where he did not agree with the approach, only leaving it due to harassment from some other members. The conflict of approaches on its own did not appear to cause them problems, they selected or 'berrypicked' the parts that they liked:

> "There were always people who you were like-minded with, and I could always take the attitude of, you know I'll hang onto that and forget about the rest." (Robert, Group E)

This was reiterated frequently, for example:

> "I take a bit of everything" (Bethany, Group B)

> "you just choose what you listen to" (Julie, Group C)

> "I took in all the information…I immersed myself in it, but then what I'd do is I sieved it…and I hold on to what connects to my reality, and so what I came up with is just my reality…I get all the information but then I make up my own mind." (Theresa, Group E)

This approach to difference was used within the group as well. Isabelle described disagreement in the forums and added:

> "I think pretty much everybody does accept that it's all a very, very personal journey. And what might be 100% true for one person won't be at all true for another person. So you kind of just read everything and then pick out what speaks to you really" (Isabelle, Group E)

To extend the berrypicking metaphor, this presents a picture of individuals drawing not just on separate blueberry bushes, but on a variety of different types of berries and merging them into their own unique interpretation, which is self-developed rather than following a set recipe.

4.4   Search Techniques

Bates stated that effective berrypickers will use many different search techniques in order to find what they need. They may use different techniques at the same time or they may move from one strategy to another over time. The group users demonstrated a number of different ways of searching for information. For example, they asked specific questions and received answers, requested feedback on plans or ideas, followed up a wide range of references, and/or sometimes engaged in debate, and discussed or argued with each other, working their ideas out through this. They browsed the site for interesting topics (e.g., Julie, Group C Christine Group D, Alan Group B, Robert, Group E), looked for recent posts (e.g., Joe Group C, Ariana Group E), for replies to their own posts (e.g., Julie Group C) and/or they habitually used one or more specific threads or areas of the site, always checking this when they went online (e.g., Anna Group A, Cathy Group C, Bethany and Alan Group B, Theresa, Grace, and Isabelle Group E). They also searched by types of material, for example, seeking out stories and anecdotes from people's experiences (e.g., Julie Group C, Yvonne and Ariana Group E). Frequently, they searched for people rather than topics or types of threads. This might be newcomers in order to help them (e.g., Anna, Group A) or people who were at the same stage as them and with whom they could exchange ideas and support:

> "you're looking to identify with somebody, so I suppose you trawl through looking for the people who are like you" (Erin, Group E)

> "I also bookmark people that I like, their writing style that are at the same stage as me. So there'll be other people that, you know, stopped about the same time, so we're going through the same sort of things." (Megan, Group E)

They may look for users who write well, for thought leaders or role models to learn from (e.g., Julie Group C; Robert, Megan and Isabelle Group E).

5 Discussion

Problem drinking remains a major issue with high costs to society, families and individuals, including in terms of economic cost, crime, domestic violence, lost work productivity and family breakdown [26]. AOSGs provide support and information for problem drinkers, offering easier access for many than face-to-face groups. Limited research has been undertaken into the information seeking behavior of AOSG users, particularly as regards non-12-step groups. This article has explored the role of these groups in the process of developing beliefs about problem drinking, using the lens of Bates' berrypicking model of information seeking. There does not appear to be any existing research into these groups using Bates' model, which this article shows to be helpful and appropriate for understanding the information seeking processes at work.

The findings show that users' interviewed for this study followed a process closer to the berrypicking model than the traditional linear model of one query resulting in one perfected set of references. In line with Bates' model, users queries changed with their time on the forums, they used different information 'domains' and a variety of information seeking techniques. Most significantly they did not find conflicting ideas disturbing and were not necessarily discouraged from using the forums even if the majority view was at odds with their own ideas. Instead they berrypicked: taking what resonated as true to them and leaving what did not. The exception to this is that the overall approach of the group was important to the majority, specifically that it either followed a different approach to AA (which they rejected), or supported the general direction in which they wanted to go, e.g., moderate drinking rather than abstinence. This work contributes to the existing literature, [e.g., 5, 6], about the need to match individuals and treatment approaches taking account of users' beliefs. It showed that overall approach was important here, influencing choice of a group, but at a high level: 12-step or non-12-step. Within those two envelopes individuals formed their own more detailed beliefs, berrypicking from a variety of sources. Further research is needed to determine whether these finding extend to other groups.

Antze's argument that online support groups have ideologies which they teach their members to endorse and adopt wholesale does not appear to be supported in relation to non-12-step groups. He stated that:

> "Each [self-help group] claims a certain wisdom concerning the problem it treats. Each has a specialized system of teachings that members venerate as the secret of recovery....as far as members themselves are concerned, a group's teachings are its very essence" ([24], p. 324)

Whilst the groups studied here did hold ideas as to how a person might understand problem drinking and recover from it, Antze's view is not supported. Members are not obliged to follow the beliefs set out in the site's information pages, nor are they required to agree with each other. This allows a context in which berrypicking can take place. The findings instead support Finfgeld's work on Moderation Management, a non-12-step AOSG:

> "Although MM offers guidelines for changing problem drinking habits, it is important to emphasize that the listserv members in this study did not limit themselves to this approach. Instead, they exposed themselves to a variety of therapeutic philosophies and paradigms and chose what appeared to work best for them." ([27], p. 37)

The present study extends this finding to other non-12-step AOSGs, as well as analyzing the information seeking practices by which it is enacted, which has not been researched before.

5.1 Limitations of the Study

The sample studied was self-selected and its demographics indicated that almost all interviewees had high levels of education, continuing their education post school. It is possible that this cohort has more confidence in selecting and assessing information and therefore felt more at ease with rejecting group beliefs that did not appear true to them. However, high levels of education amongst study participants have been noted in several studies of users of non-12-step alcohol support groups, e.g., [7, 28]. It is possible that the interviewees studied here are in fact representative of active users of these groups.

6 Conclusion

This paper has shown that the process of developing beliefs/ideas about problem drinking using the discussion forums of AOSGs can be seen as a berrypicking one, whereby the query changes over time and multiple sources and search techniques are used to develop ideas. The interviewees who participated in this study largely self-defined their beliefs, taking what resonated with them from different sources and forming their own understanding of problem drinking.

References

1. Leventhal, H., Nerenz, D.R., Steele, D.J.: Illness representations and coping with health threats. In: Baum, A., Taylor, S.E., Singer, J.E. (eds.) Handbook of Psychology and Health. Social Psychological Aspects of Health, vol. IV, pp. 219–252. Lawrence Erlbaum Associates, New Jersey (1984)
2. Leventhal, H., Diefenbach, M., Leventhal, E.A.: Illness cognition: using common sense to understand treatment adherence and affect cognition interactions. Cogn. Therapy Res. **16**(2), 143–163 (1992)
3. Hagger, M.S., Orbell, S.: A meta-analytic review of the common-sense model of illness representations. Psychol. Health **18**(2), 141–184 (2003)
4. Petrie, K.J., Jago, L.A., Devcich, D.A.: The role of illness perceptions in patients with medical conditions. Curr. Opin. Psychiatry **20**, 163–167 (2007)
5. Glaser, F.B., et al.: Comments on project MATCH: matching alcohol treatments to client heterogeneity. Addiction **94**(1), 31–69 (1999). Society for the Study of Addiction to Alcohol and Other Drugs
6. Atkins, R.G., Hawdon, J.E.: Religiosity and participation in mutual-aid support groups for addiction. J. Subst. Abuse Treat. **33**(3), 321–331 (2007)
7. Zemore, S.E., Kaskutas, L.A., Mericle, A., Hemberg, J.: Comparison of 12-step groups to mutual help alternatives for AUD in a large, national study: differences in membership characteristics and group participation, cohesion, and satisfaction. J. Subst. Abuse Treat. **73**, 16–26 (2017)
8. Alcoholics Anonymous: The twelve steps of AA. https://www.alcoholics-anonymous.org.uk/about-aa/the-12-steps-of-aa. Downloaded 3 Dec 2018
9. Bates, M.J.: The design of browsing and berrypicking techniques for the online search interface. Online Rev. **13**(5), 407–424 (1989)
10. American Psychiatric Association: Diagnostic and Statistical Manual of Mental Disorders (DSM–5), 5th edn. American Psychiatric Association, Arlington, USA (2013)
11. Ford, N.: Introduction to Information Behaviour. Facet Publishing, London (2015)
12. Lueg, C.P., Bidwell, N.J.: Berrypicking in the real world: a wayfinding perspective on information behavior research. Proc. Am. Soc. Inf. Sci. Technol. **42**(1) (2005). https://doi.org/10.1002/meet.14504201241
13. Kumpulainen, S.: Trails across the heterogeneous information environment: manual integration patterns of search systems in molecular medicine. J. Doc. **70**(5), 856–877 (2014)
14. Burnett, G., Besant, M., Chatman, E.A.: Small worlds: normative behavior in virtual communities and feminist bookselling. J. Am. Soc. Inf. Sci. Technol. **52**(7), 536–547 (2001)
15. Kazmer, M.M., et al.: Distributed knowledge in an online patient support community: authority and discovery. J. Assoc. Inf. Sci. Technol. **65**(7), 1319–1334 (2014)
16. Cain, C.: Personal stories in alcoholics anonymous. In: Holland, D., Lachicotte Jr., W., Skinner, D., Cain, C. (eds.) Identity and Agency in Cultural Worlds, pp. 66–97. Harvard University Press, Massachusetts (1998)
17. Cain, C.: Personal stories: identity acquisition and self-understanding in alcoholics anonymous. Ethos **19**(2), 210–253 (1991)
18. Lave, J., Wenger, E.: Situated Learning: Legitimate Peripheral Participation. Cambridge University Press, Cambridge (1991)
19. Swora, M.G.: Commemoration and the healing of memories in alcoholics anonymous. Ethos **29**(1), 58–77 (2001)

20. Coulson, N.S.: Sharing, supporting and sobriety: a qualitative analysis of messages posted to alcohol-related online discussion forums in the United Kingdom. J. Subst. Use **19**(1–2), 176–180 (2014)

21. Cunningham, J.A.: Comparison of two internet-based interventions for problem drinkers: randomized controlled trial. J. Med. Internet Res. **14**(4), e107 (2012)

22. Chuang, K., Yang, C.C.: Informational support exchanges using different computer mediated communication formats in a social media alcoholism community. J. Assoc. Inf. Sci. Technol. **65**(1), 37–52 (2014)

23. Humphreys, K., Kaskutas, L.A.: World views of alcoholics anonymous, women for sobriety, and adult children of Alcoholics/Al-Anon mutual help groups. Addict. Res. **3**(3), 231–243 (1995)

24. Antze, P.: The role of ideologies in peer psychotherapy organizations: some theoretical considerations and three case studies. J. Appl. Behav. Sci. **12**(3), 323–346 (1976)

25. Braun, V., Clarke, V.: Using thematic analysis in psychology. Qual. Res. Psychol. **3**(2), 77–101 (2006)

26. Public Health England: Alcohol: applying All Our Health. https://www.gov.uk/government/publications/alcohol-applying-all-our-health/alcohol-applying-all-our-health, Updated 7 February 2018. Accessed 7 Sep 2018

27. Finfgeld, D.: Resolving alcohol problems using an online self-help approach: moderation management. J. Psychosoc. Nurs. Mental Health Serv. **38**(2), 32–38 (2000)

28. Sinclair, J.M.A., Chambers, S.E., Manson, C.C.: Internet support for dealing with problematic alcohol use: a survey of the Soberistas online community. Alcohol Alcohol. **52**(2), 220–226 (2016)

Australian Library Job Advertisements: Seeking Inclusion and Diversity

Kim M. Thompson[1,2](✉) ⓘ, Rebecca Muir[2] ⓘ, and Asim Qayyum[2] ⓘ

[1] University of South Carolina, Columbia, SC 29208, USA
KimThompson@sc.edu
[2] Charles Sturt University, Wagga Wagga, NSW 2678, Australia

Abstract. A growing body of literature is drawing our attention to diversity in librarianship, arguing for improved inclusion through better recruitment, retention, and career advancement of minority professionals. While much of the discussion about diversity in libraries is taking place in United States, this article attempts to extend the discussion, bringing attention to diversity and inclusion in Australian librarianship through analysis of Australian library job ads. This article uses content analysis of 96 Australian job ads posted from 22 January to 3 February 2018 in key Australian library job search engines. The analysis focuses on how diversity is reflected in these ads, with a content analysis of wording focused on inviting diversity in terms of ability/disability, ethnicity and language, and gender and sexuality.

Keywords: Social inclusion · Workplace disability · Library hiring · Diversity

1 Introduction

Australia's population is incredibly diverse. During 2016–2017, a total of 137,750 people from over 190 different countries became Australian citizens. More than 300 languages are spoken in Australian homes, and more than 100 religions are represented nationwide [1]. In the 2015 Census one in five Australians (18.3%) reported having a disability, and almost 650,000 Australians (2.8% of the population) identified as being Aboriginal or Torres Strait Islander. Yet as Australia becomes increasingly diverse, there is little or no publicly available data about diversity in Library and Information Science (LIS) education or in the Australian library workforce. Are library staff presenting a face that reflects the diversity we serve? We simply do not have the data. However, by examining library job advertisements, we can explore whether libraries and archives are recruiting for the diversity in their community.

Traditionally, Australian definitions of diversity have focused on race/ethnicity, gender, and physical ability/disability. Australia's Equal Employment Opportunity Act (EEO) of 1987, the Fair Work Act of 2009, and the Australian Human Rights Commission, along with other laws and government agencies, provide clear guidelines of what steps can be taken to ensure equitable hiring practices to prevent discrimination in recruitment. While it is not legally mandated to include EEO or other statements for fair recruitment, it is not uncommon for LIS job advertisements (particularly government-funded) to include EEO wording. This study examines whether and how these job

N. G. Taylor et al. (Eds.): iConference 2019, LNCS 11420, pp. 817–825, 2019.
https://doi.org/10.1007/978-3-030-15742-5_77

advertisements meet the IFLA/UNESCO Multicultural Library Manifesto core principle of "employing staff to reflect the diversity of the community, who are trained to work with and serve diverse communities" [2]. We approached this study with the research questions: In what way is diversity reflected in Australian LIS job advertisements? Is there any wording that might discourage applicants from minority or underrepresented groups? Is there explicit or implicit openness in terms of ability/disability, ethnicity and language, and gender and sexuality?

2 Literature Review

We are not the first to explore diversity in the field of LIS. For example, during the 1980s Grover [3], Randall [4], and the American Library Association [5] researched issues related to minority recruitment and library services to minority groups. In the 1990s researchers such as McCook and Lippincott [6] found that while there were some gains in minority graduates from LIS fields during the 1980s and 1990s, and while the growth rate was encouraging, "it still reflects a small percentage of the total graduates for those years." Recent United States studies [7–9] have reflected on inclusive recruitment practices in various contexts, particularly around student recruitment, job placement and retention, and inclusion in the workplace, as well as how effectively LIS education programs are preparing students for a diverse workplace [10]. Jaeger and Franklin [11] argue that diversity needs to begin with the hiring of more diverse faculties. This idea that a more diverse faculty will attract more diverse students (who then become a more diverse workforce) parallels the social and psychology research that describes how we, as social beings, look for connections with others who are similar to ourselves [12]. In locations such as libraries, mosques, the gym, and so forth, we find access to others with similar beliefs (e.g., religious beliefs), values (e.g., fitness values), and needs (e.g., economic need). Seeing others who physically look similar to us can also impact our levels of social inclusion; for example, in a recent study in the United States, researchers found that Black school children who had at least one Black teacher in their time in primary school were 30% less likely to drop out than the students who had never had a teacher of their same race [13]. Seeing "ourselves" in the social world around us helps us construct a sense of self by offering social comparison, feedback, and identity [14, 15, 17]. Sharing values leads to trust [17], which then leads to cooperation, and provides the basis of successful social relations [18, 19].

Research has shown that the language of job ads (as with any advertising and marketing) can be exclusive and discriminatory, discouraging minority populations from even applying [e.g., 20, 21], or it can be inclusive and welcoming to diverse applicants [e.g., 22]. In previous LIS job ad studies by North American [23–26] and Australian [27, 28] researchers, job ad content analyses have resulted in lists of attributes and skills employers are recruiting for. Many of these of attributes (e.g., foreign language skills, good communication) lend themselves to more inclusive and diverse workplaces and a wider range of inclusive services in and of themselves. However, this pilot study aims to take a different approach, looking at the wording in job ads themselves to explore how the wording represents, or does not represent, the inclusivity in the profession that we desire to have in the field.

3 Methodology

Job ads were collected over a fortnight (22 January to 3 February 2018). We chose this period as it is the time of year when Australian school and academic libraries are preparing to hire for the start of the academic year (February and March); public, government, and special libraries are likely to hire year-round. Job ads were collected only if they were posted between these specific dates. Three Australian job sites were searched: Australian Library and Information Association (ALIA) Jobs (https://www.alia.org.au/jobs), SEEK (https://www.seek.com.au/), and Adzuna (https://www.adzuna.com.au/). These three databases cover national job listings and either specialize in library jobs (ALIA), or are searchable for library job posts (SEEK and Adzuna). All relevant job ads posted in the ALIA database were collected during the noted time period, whereas on the SEEK and Adzuna sites, the search terms used were "librarian," and "library" with the filter "any classification." The keyword "libraries" retrieved the same results, so was not used after the first day of collection. We tried the keyword "librar*" to cover words like librarian(s), libraries, library, etc. but this search returned non-library focused, ambiguous results, or no results at all, and so was not used. ALIA and SEEK sites search jobs in Australia by default, so no location filter was used. For Adzuna, we used the keyword "Australia" to filter results.

The collected job listings were collated and skimmed to ensure the ad included potential involvement with patrons or the public, as we were interested in the diverse "face" of librarianship. Casual, part-time, and full-time position ads were collected, and duplicate listings removed. In total, 96 job listings were retained for content analysis for this project. While a small number in comparison with United States job ads, these 96 ads are well representative of the eight Australian states and territories, and the overall smaller Australian population. For example, while there were an estimated 9,057 public libraries in the United States in 2016 and 3,094 academic libraries [29], in 2015 there were only 1,631 public libraries [30] and a total of 39 university libraries [31] in Australia.

We used a combination of quantitative and qualitative content analysis techniques to analyze our data. According to Pickard, a diverse nature of analysis can happen where the researcher may (1) let the concepts emerge from the content in a qualitative sense, or (2) look at the frequency counts of key occurrences in the data for a more quantitative approach, or (3) use a mix of both quantitative and qualitative elements [32]. The mixed approach was used in this project. The identification and highlighting of key terms and phrases (diverse/diversity, disabled/disability/ability/accommodation, Indigenous/Aboriginal/Torres Strait Islander descent, ethnic/ethnicity, language, women, gender, inclusive/inclusion, etc.) in the dataset was done independently by the three primary researchers and a Graduate Assistant. Following this initial review, we compared our findings to maintain consistency, then sorted and compiled them into a single repository. The review of previous literature was also used to identify meaningful themes. Finally, key terms or themes were identified, discussed, and agreed upon by the team members in joint meetings. Keywords were analyzed in context of the text where they appeared, to preserve the connection with the originating data. We also coded the data in terms of whether the job ad included specific wording about diversity (e.g., disability, ethnicity, gender), or whether there was generic wording about hiring and supporting diversity in staffing (e.g., "…is an equal opportunity employer and encourages applications from all sectors of the community").

The research team analyzed the job listings and created categories based on definitions of diversity from the literature related to disability, gender, sexuality, ethnicity, and language diversity, and mapped these categories into a smaller set of key themes as connections were discovered. Race, a common discussion point in U.S. diversity studies, was considered in our analyses, but we found it was not as relevant to Australian demographic discussions, as the Australian Bureau of Statistics uses the term "ethnicity" rather than "race" to distinguish between Australians of different cultural, ethnic, and racial backgrounds [33]. We use this race-inclusive definition to discuss ethnicity in our Findings and Analyses.

4   Findings and Analyses

Each of the eight states and territories of Australia posted at least one job ad during the time period of our data collection (see Table 1). New South Wales–the Australian state with the largest population–had the most jobs posted, with Victoria and Queensland coming second and third. Parliament, national government institutions, and the National Library of Australia are based in the Australian Capital Territory, and so this territory has a higher number of LIS jobs for its size. The dataset includes job ads posted for academic libraries, school libraries, public libraries, state libraries, the National Library, government records and libraries, law libraries, and other special libraries.

Table 1. Job postings by state and territory.

State or territory	Total population in 2017 [34]	Percentage of total Australian population	Number of job ads in dataset (n = 96)	Percentage of total job ads in dataset (n = 96)
New South Wales	7,915,100	32%	32	33%
Victoria	6,385,800	26%	27	28%
Queensland	4,965,000	20%	14	14%
Western Australia	2,584,800	10%	7	7%
South Australia	1,728,100	7%	6	6%
Tasmania	524,700	2%	2	2%
Australian Capital Territory	415,900	2%	7	7%
Northern Territory	246,700	1%	1	1%

23 of the 96 job ads described the employer as being dedicated to diversity. 17 described the community they serve as "diverse" or "vibrant." Seven connected a statement of the diversity of their community to a statement of the diversity in their workplace, such as "providing an inclusive workplace that respects the values of a diverse workplace," and/or "encouraging a diverse workforce that is reflective of the community." These diversity statements could potentially be interpreted as including the flexibility to support diversity, such as to provide disability accommodation in the workplace; however, this was not clearly specified in the individual job ads. We considered exploring how diversity was reflected in terms of whether the positions were "entry" or "upper level" jobs, but we found there was no consistency in the level of detail of the job posting to be able to know how senior or entry-level the position was.

The job ads varied greatly. Some were very brief and provided only cursory information about the position and the attributes and skills required or desired in an applicant. Other positions were very detailed, listing duties, qualifications and experience needed, and additional experience, skills, and/or attributes that were desirable in an applicant. This included wording such as "strong communication skills," "experience in document delivery," or "a health science degree required." Some of the ads included the overall values of the hiring institution, such as "We value: respect for people; integrity and excellent performance; professional, quality service; and open, accountable communication." As has been noted in previous studies of Australian LIS job ads, this wide variety of detail is not new [27, 28]. We will discuss our findings in terms of the diversity areas of ability/disability, ethnicity and language, and gender and sexuality.

4.1 Ability/Disability

Seven of the job ads specifically named disability as one of the values of diversity and inclusion of the institution; however, only four of the 96 job ads stated that their organization was committed to providing support to apply or interview for the position, such as an additional assessment activity for the vacancy where the applicant met the minimum requirements for the job and declared they had a disability. It is notable that of these four ads, three were for government library services (state or national).

Three ads in our dataset specified that a medical assessment may, or would, be required prior to employment. One ad specified that this examination would be required of shortlisted candidates; the remaining two ads did not outline when the assessment would be required, aside from pre-employment. One of the three ads stated that drug and alcohol testing would be conducted as part of the medical assessment, although it was not clear why this was a component of the hiring process, and no other job ads from this state contained this wording. One ad noted that the medical assessment would be used in order to determine the applicant's fitness to carry out duties, yet none of the skills and attributes listed as required for the position related to medical fitness or a specific physical ability (i.e., leadership, the ability to work in a busy organization, strong previous experience, communication and problem solving skills, and research skills). The criteria all related to the applicant demonstrating sufficient experience and skills to complete the role successfully, rather than related to medical fitness or ability.

4.2 Ethnicity and Language

Indigenous Australians (nearly 3% of the nation's population) are a group of great importance. In 2008 the Australian government set targets aimed at eliminating the significant gaps in education and employment between Indigenous and non-Indigenous Australians, with targeted recruitment of Aboriginal and Torres Strait Islander people outlined by the Australian Human Rights Commission in 2015 as one measure to help bridge some of these gaps [35]. We would expect to see specific wording inviting people of Indigenous descent to apply for library jobs, particularly in the Northern Territory, where 25.5% of the population identify as Aboriginal and Torres Strait Islander [36]. 17 of the total 96 job ads contained specific invitations for applicants of Aboriginal or Torres Strait Islander or Indigenous descent, with all job ads from South Australia (SA) and the Northern Territory (NT) specifically inviting applicants from the Aboriginal and Torres Strait Islander people.

As in many parts of the world, new overseas migration has increased in Australia in recent years. During 2016–2017 there was an annual gain of 262,500 persons, a 27.3% increase on 2015–2016 [37]. Wording such as "At ____, we embrace difference in… ethnicity, race, cultural background…" was found in 18 of the 96 job ads collected. Four of these ads specifically invited speakers of non-English languages to apply.

4.3 Gender and Sexuality

Eight of the job advertisements specified that women were encouraged to apply (NSW, VIC, SA), with four of these ads inviting women to apply for positions with management and supervisory responsibilities. Two (NSW) job ads invited LGBTIQ+ applicants, although neither of these were for management or supervisory roles. As Australian Government labor statistics note that 88.7% of Australian librarians are women [38], we also looked for gendered wording that might either specifically invite or exclude men from applying, aside from the specific EEO wording inviting applications from women. No such wording was found in any of the collected job advertisements.

5 Conclusion

This pilot study provides a review of how diversity is currently invited in library job ads in Australia through an analysis of wording that invites a diverse workforce. With a prediction that 2,600 new library jobs are expected to be created each year for the next five years in Australia, now is an excellent time to start building the diversity we hope to see in the future [38]. That the majority of the job ads were relatively neutral and not overtly discriminatory was encouraging, as was the finding that some libraries are taking the next step and providing inclusive wording specifically inviting minority applicants. Our findings also show that there is definitely room for improvement.

Acknowledgement. We gratefully acknowledge the graduate assistance during the coding and analysis segment of this study provided by University of South Carolina doctoral student Doug Tuers.

References

1. Australian Bureau of Statistics: 2016 Census: Multicultural. http://www.abs.gov.au/ausstats/abs@.nsf/lookup/Media%20Release3. Accessed 14 Dec 2018
2. IFLA/UNESCO Multicultural Library Manifesto. https://www.ifla.org/node/8976. Accessed 14 Dec 2018
3. Grover, M.L.: Library school recruitment of Spanish-speaking Americans: Problems and prospects. Catholic Libr. World **55**, 163–168 (1983)
4. Randall, A.K.: Minority recruitment in librarianship. In: Moen, W.E., Heim, K.M. (eds.) Librarians for the New Millennium, pp. 11–25. American Library Association, Office for Library Personnel Resources, Chicago (1988)
5. American Library Association: Equity at issue: Library services to the nation's major minority groups. American Library Association, Chicago (1985)
6. McCook, K., Lippincott, K.: Planning for a Diverse Workforce in Library and Information Science Professions. University of South Florida, Tampa (1997)
7. Dewey, B., Keally, J.: Recruiting for diversity: Strategies for twenty-first century research librarianship. Libr. Hi-Tech **26**(4), 622–629 (2008). https://trace.tennessee.edu/cgi/viewcontent.cgi?article=1000&context=utk_libpub. Accessed 14 Dec 2018
8. Switzer, A.T.: Redefining diversity: Creating an inclusive academic library through diversity initiatives. Coll. Undergraduate Libr. **15**(3), 280–300 (2008). https://doi.org/10.1080/10691310802258182. Accessed 14 Dec 2018
9. Morales, M., Knowles, E.M., Bourg, C.: Diversity, social justice, and the future of libraries. Portal Libr. Acad. 14(3), 439–451 (2014). https://muse.jhu.edu/article/549202/pdf. Accessed 14 Dec 2018
10. Al-Qallaf, C.L., Mika, J.J.: The role of multiculturalism and diversity in library and information science: LIS education and the job market. Libri **63**, 1–20 (2013)
11. Jaeger, P.T., Franklin, R.E.: The virtuous cycle: Increasing diversity in LIS faculties to create more inclusive library services and outreach. Educ. Libr. **30**(1), 20–26 (2007). http://educationlibraries.mcgill.ca/article/download/233/233. Accessed 14 Dec 2018
12. Bahns, A.J., Crandall, C.S., Gillath, O., Preacher, K.J.: Similarity in relationships as niche construction. J. Pers. Soc. Psychol. **112**(2), 329–355 (2017)
13. Gershenson, S., Hart, C.M.D., Lindsay, C.A., Papageorge, N.: The long-run impacts of same-race teachers. IZA Discussion Paper No. 10630 (2017)
14. Campbell, W.K., Sedikides, C., Reeder, G.D., Elliot, A.J.: Among friends? An examination of friendship and the self-serving bias. Br. J. Soc. Psychol. **29**, 229–239 (2000). https://doi.org/10.1348/014466600164444
15. Fehr, B.: Friendship formation and development. In: Reis, H.T., Sprecher, S.K. (eds.) Encyclopedia of Human Relationships. Sage Publications, Thousand Oaks (2009)
16. Hogg, M.A., Hains, S.C.: Friendship and group identification: A new look at the role of cohesiveness in groupthink Eur. J. Soc. Psychol. **28**, 323–341 (1998). https://doi.org/10.1002/(SICI)1099-0992(199805/06)28:3<323::AID-EJSP854>3.0.CO;2-Y
17. Goldbeck, J.: Trust and nuanced profile similarity in online social networks. ACM Trans. Web 3(4), 12–42 (2009)

18. Green, M.C., Brock, T.C.: Trust, mood, and outcomes of friendship determine preferences for real versus erstaz social capital. Polit. Psychol. **19**, 527–544 (1998)
19. Rotter, J.B.: Generalized expectancies for interpersonal trust. Am. Psychol. **26**(5), 443–452 (1971)
20. Kuhn, P., Shen, K. Gender discrimination in job ads. Q. J. Econ. **128**(1), 287–336 (2012). https://academic.oup.com/qje/article/128/1/287/1839620. Accessed 14 Dec 2018
21. Avery, D.R.: Reactions to diversity in recruitment advertising–are differences black and white? J. Appl. Psychol. **88**(4), 672 (2003)
22. Stevens, F.G., Plaut, V.C., Sanchez-Burks, J.: Unlocking the benefits of diversity. J. Appl. Behav. Sci. **44**(1), 116–133 (2008). https://journals.sagepub.com/doi/pdf/10.1177/0021886308314460. Accessed 14 Dec 2018
23. Reser, D.W., Schuneman, A.P.: The academic library job market: A content analysis comparing public and technical services. Coll. Res. Libr. **53**(1), 49–59 (1992)
24. Choi, Y., Rasmussen, E.: What qualifications and skills are important for digital librarian positions in academic libraries? A job advertisement analysis. J. Acad. Librarianship **35**(5), 457–467 (2009)
25. Kim, K., Sin, S.: Recruiting and retaining students of color in LIS programs: Perspectives of library and information professionals. J. Educ. Libr. Inf. Sci. **47**(2), 81–95 (2006). https://doi.org/10.2307/40324324
26. Reeves, R.K., Hahn, T.B.: Job advertisements for recent graduates: Advising, curriculum, and job-seeking implications. J. Educ. Libr. Inf. Sci. **51**, 103–119 (2010)
27. Clyde, L.A.: An instructional role for librarians: An overview and content analysis of job advertisements. Aust. Acad. Res. Libr. **33**(3), 150–166 (2002)
28. Kennan, M.A., Cole, F., Willard, P., Wilson, C., Marion, L.: Changing workplace demands: What job ads tell us. Aslib Proc. **58**(3), 179–196 (2006). https://doi.org/10.1108/00012530610677228
29. American Library Association. Library statistics and figures: Number of public libraries in the United States over time (2016). http://libguides.ala.org/librarystatistics/numberoflibrariesovertime. Accessed 14 Dec 2018
30. Australian Library and Information Association. Public libraries (2018). https://www.alia.org.au/node/184/public-libraries. Accessed 14 Dec 2018
31. Australian Library and Information Association. University and research libraries. https://www.alia.org.au/which-sector-are-you-interested/university-and-research-libraries. Accessed 14 Dec 2018
32. Pickard, A.J.: Research Methods in Information. Facet, London (2017)
33. Australian Bureau of Statistics. 1249.0 - Australian Standard Classification of Cultural and Ethnic Groups (ASCCEG) (2016). http://www.abs.gov.au/ausstats/abs@.nsf/mf/1249.0. Accessed 14 Dec 2018
34. Australian Demographic Statistics, December 2017 http://www.abs.gov.au/AUSSTATS/abs@.nsf/mf/3101.0. Accessed 14 Dec 2018
35. Australian Human Rights Commission. Targeted recruitment of Aboriginal and Torres Strait Islander people (2015). https://www.humanrights.gov.au/sites/default/files/document/publication/AHRC_Targeted_recruitment_ATSI_people_guideline2015.pdf. Accessed 14 Dec 2018
36. Australian Bureau of Statistics. Media release: 2016 Census shows growing Aboriginal and Torres Strait Islander population. http://www.abs.gov.au/ausstats/abs@.nsf/mediareleasesbyReleaseDate/02D50FAA9987D6B7CA25814800087E03. Accessed 14 Dec 2018

37. Australian Bureau of Statistics. Migration, Australia, 2016-17. http://www.abs.gov.au/ausstats/abs@.nsf/0/66CDB63F615CF0A2CA257C4400190026?Opendocument. Accessed 14 Dec 2018
38. Australian Government. Job outlook: Librarians (2018). https://joboutlook.gov.au/Occupation.aspx?search=&code=2246. Accessed 15 Dec 2018

Author Index